Student Guide to Technology

For *Progress in Mathematics* Grades 1–2

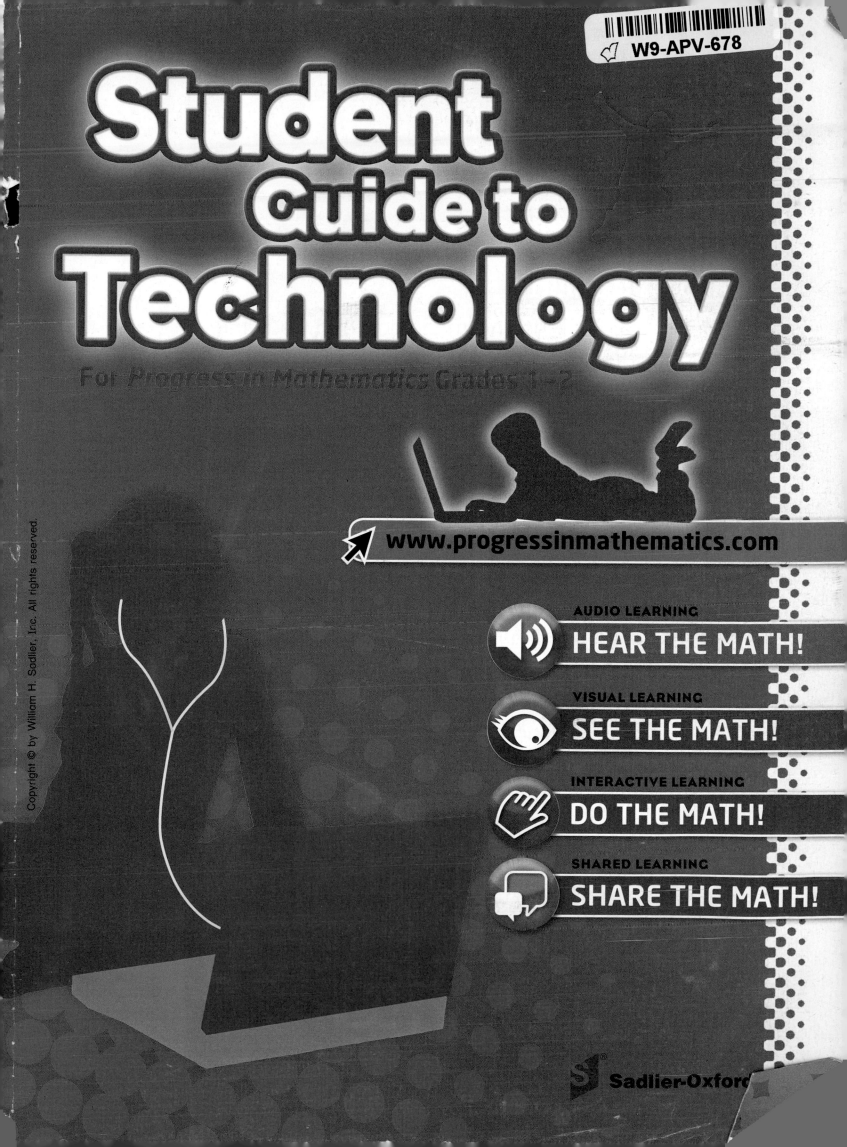

www.progressinmathematics.com

AUDIO LEARNING
HEAR THE MATH!

VISUAL LEARNING
SEE THE MATH!

INTERACTIVE LEARNING
DO THE MATH!

SHARED LEARNING
SHARE THE MATH!

Copyright © by William H. Sadlier, Inc. All rights reserved.

Sadlier-Oxford

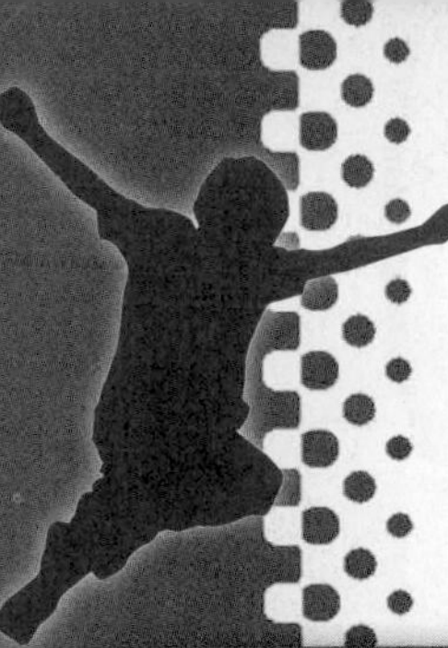

Introduction

Go to www.progressinmathematics.com

Click on your grade.

You will see this list of technology resources.

Technology Resources:

www.progressinmathematics.com

AUDIO GLOSSARY

From A to Z Find the meanings and hear the pronunciations of math words and phrases.

ALTERNATIVE TEACHING MODELS

Tutorials Watch and listen to these animated math lessons.

VIRTUAL MANIPULATIVES

Manipulatives Practice and model math concepts with virtual manipulatives.

PRACTICE

Problem of the Day Tackle a new problem every day!

Skills Update Review your skills with Lesson and Practice pages.

Math Minutes Race against the clock with timed activities!

Practice Activities Practice makes perfect with these fun activities!

Vocabulary Activities Review your math vocabulary while playing Hangman or Word Scramble.

ENRICHMENT

Activities Challenge yourself with these interactive activities.

MATH ALIVE AT HOME

Take-Home Activities Share your math experience at home!

AUDIO LEARNING

Hear the Math!

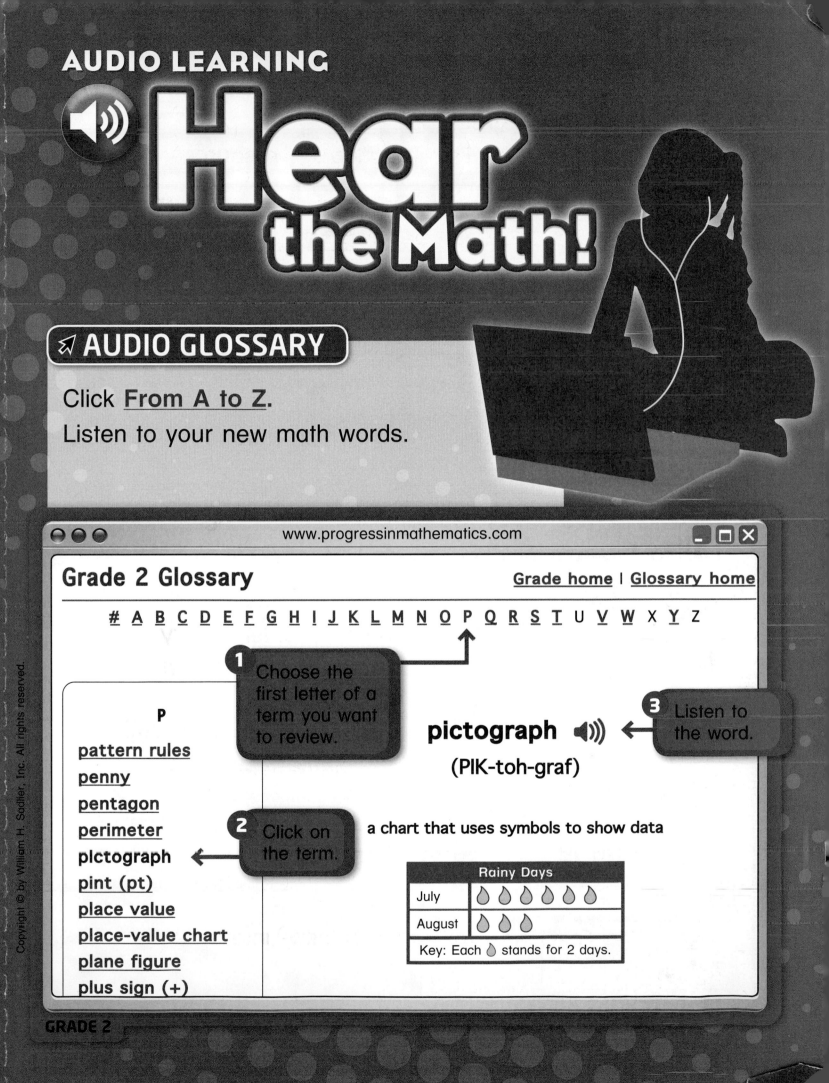

AUDIO GLOSSARY

Click From A to Z.

Listen to your new math words.

www.progressinmathematics.com

Grade 2 Glossary

Grade home | Glossary home

A B C D E F G H I J K L M N O P Q R S T U V W X Y Z

1 Choose the first letter of a term you want to review.

P

pattern rules
penny
pentagon
perimeter
pictograph
pint (pt)
place value
place-value chart
plane figure
plus sign (+)

2 Click on the term.

pictograph

(PIK-toh-graf)

3 Listen to the word.

a chart that uses symbols to show data

Rainy Days	
July	💧💧💧💧💧💧
August	💧💧💧
Key: Each 💧 stands for 2 days.	

Copyright © by William H. Sadlier, Inc. All rights reserved.

INTERACTIVE *Whiteboard* COMPATIBLE

VISUAL LEARNING

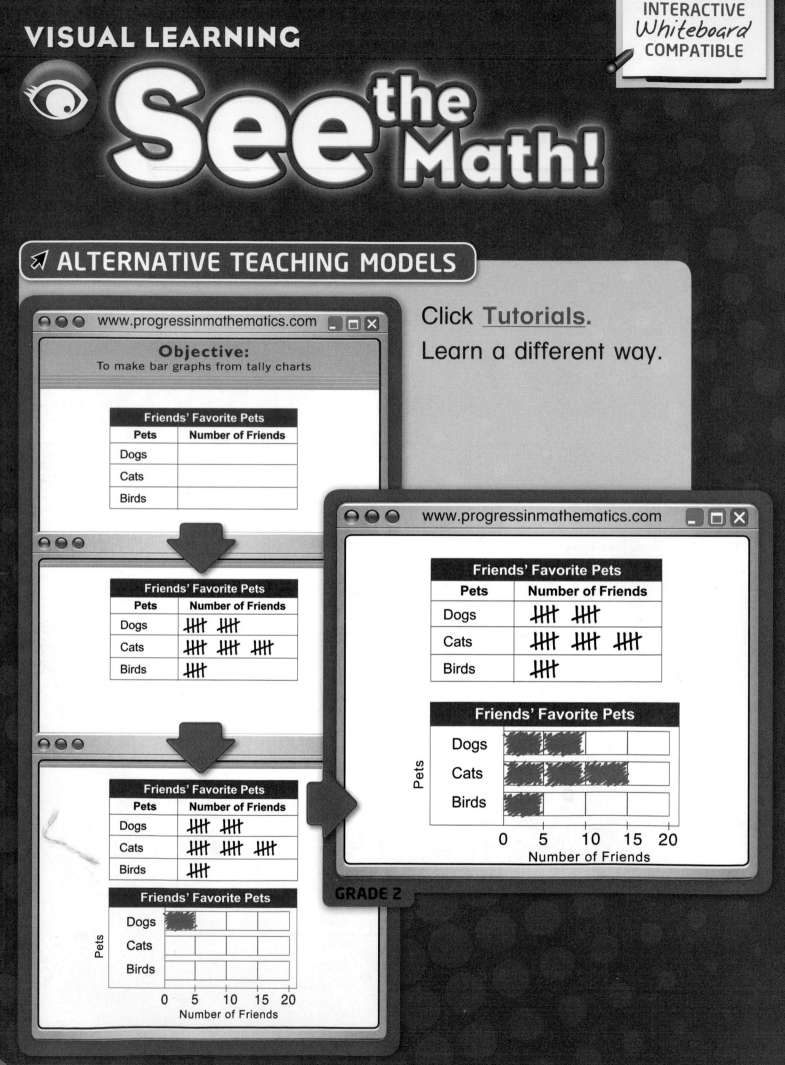

ALTERNATIVE TEACHING MODELS

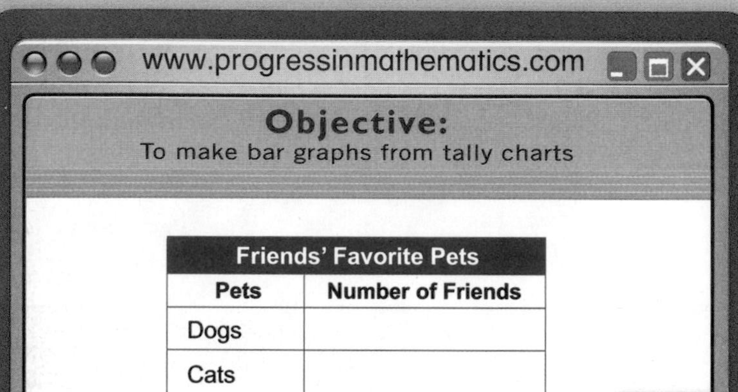

Friends' Favorite Pets	
Pets	Number of Friends
Dogs	
Cats	
Birds	

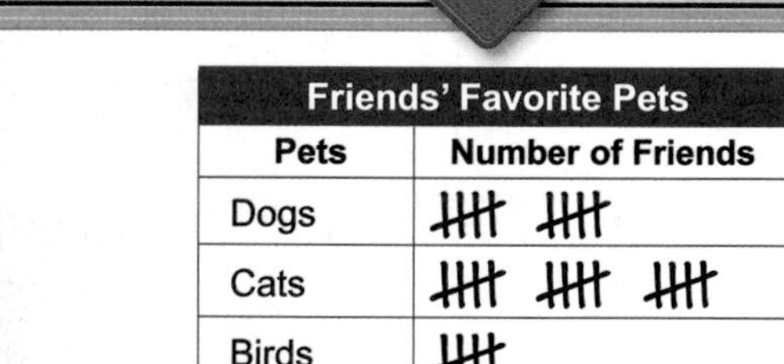

Friends' Favorite Pets	
Pets	Number of Friends
Dogs	𝍸 𝍸
Cats	𝍸 𝍸 𝍸
Birds	𝍸

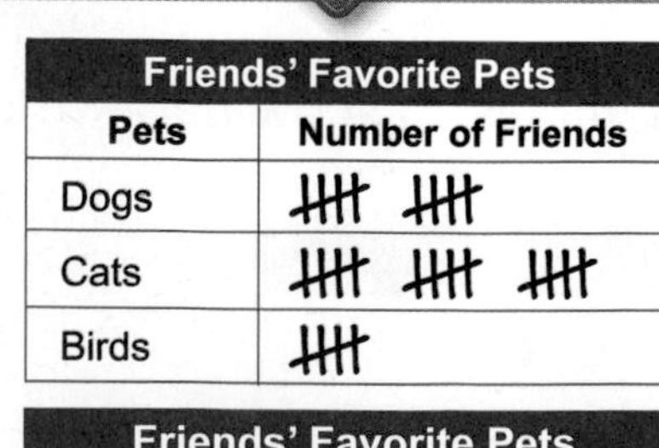

Friends' Favorite Pets	
Pets	Number of Friends
Dogs	𝍸 𝍸
Cats	𝍸 𝍸 𝍸
Birds	𝍸

Click Tutorials.

Learn a different way.

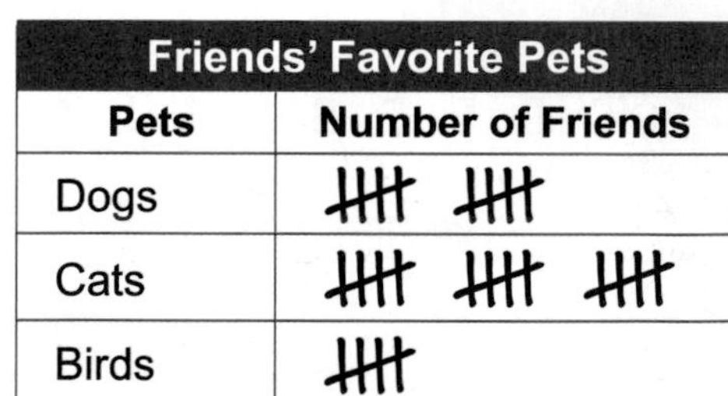

Friends' Favorite Pets	
Pets	Number of Friends
Dogs	𝍸 𝍸
Cats	𝍸 𝍸 𝍸
Birds	𝍸

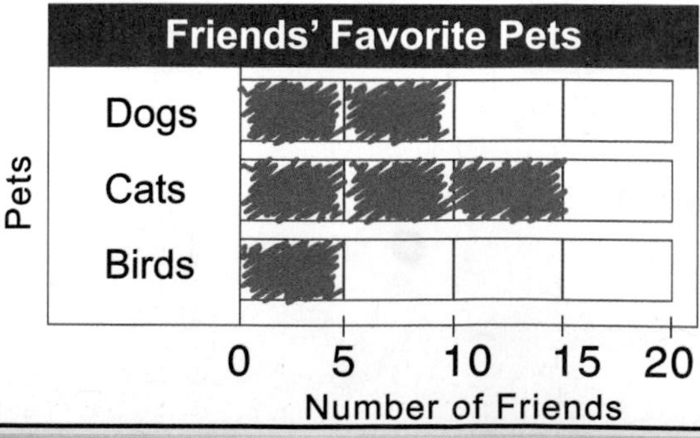

GRADE 2

VIRTUAL MANIPULATIVES

Click **Manipulatives.**

Use models to learn math.

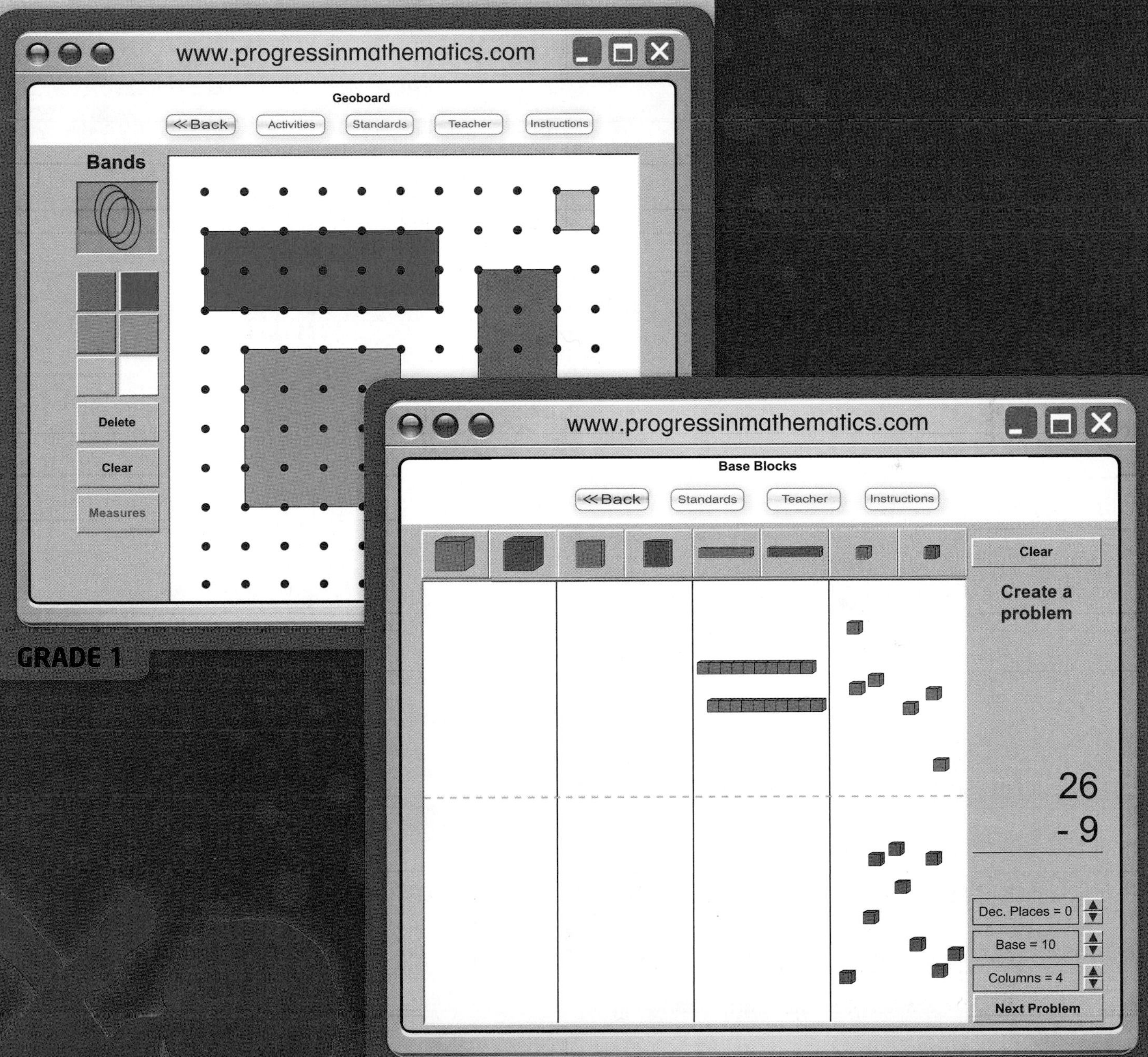

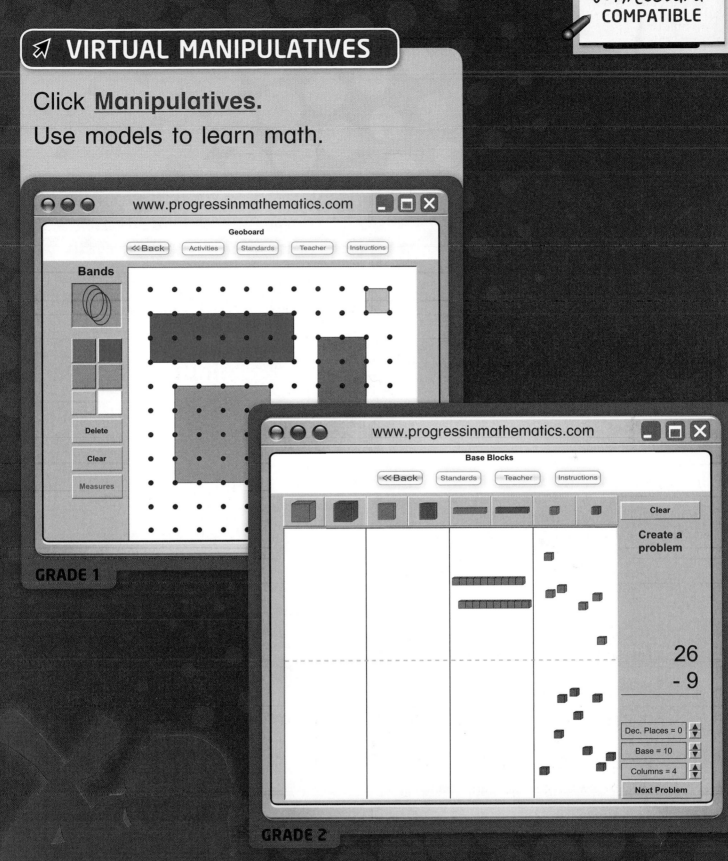

Copyright © by William H. Sadlier, Inc. All rights reserved.

INTERACTIVE LEARNING

Do the Math!

PRACTICE

Click **Practice Activities**.
Practice what you learn!

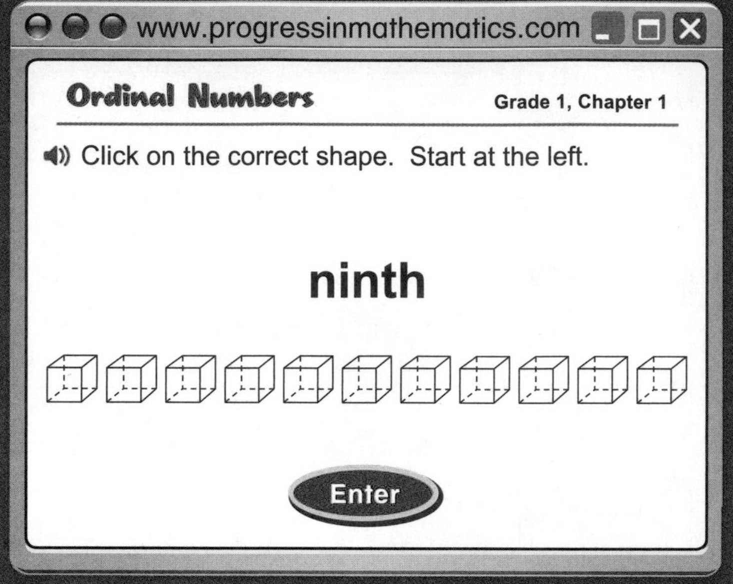

Click **Math Minutes**.
Challenge yourself to compute faster.

Click **Vocabulary Activities**.
Practice using your new math words.

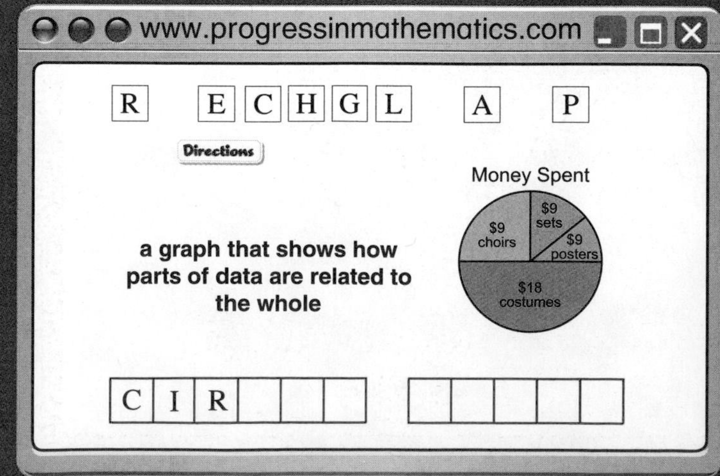

INTERACTIVE *Whiteboard* COMPATIBLE

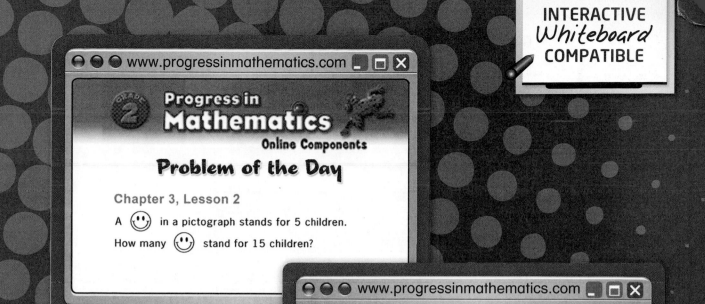

www.progressinmathematics.com

Progress in Mathematics

Online Components

Problem of the Day

Chapter 3, Lesson 2

A ☺ in a pictograph stands for 5 children.

How many ☺ stand for 15 children?

GRADE 1

Click and print **Problem of the Day.***

Sharpen your problem-solving skills.

www.progressinmathematics.com
Skills Update
Practice online resource
Name
Next To, In Front, Far, Near
Look at the picture to answer each question.
Circle Yes or No.

GRADE 2

Click and print **Skills Update*** lessons and practice.

Review math skills and concepts.

ENRICHMENT

Click **Activities.**

Challenge yourself!

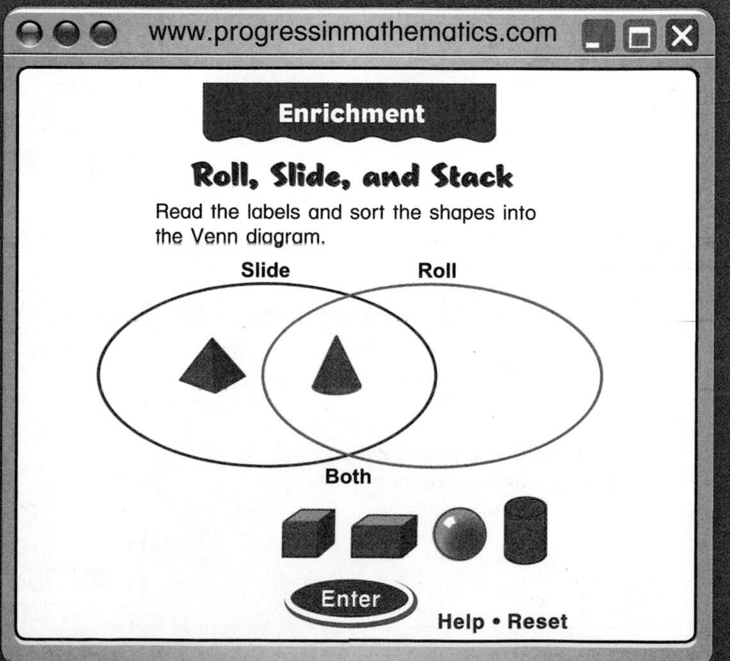

GRADE 2

*Whiteboard projectable only.

Copyright © by William H. Sadlier, Inc. All rights reserved.

SHARED LEARNING

Share the Math!

MATH ALIVE AT HOME

Click **Take-Home Activities** for family letters.
Share what you learn!

They are available in both English and Spanish.

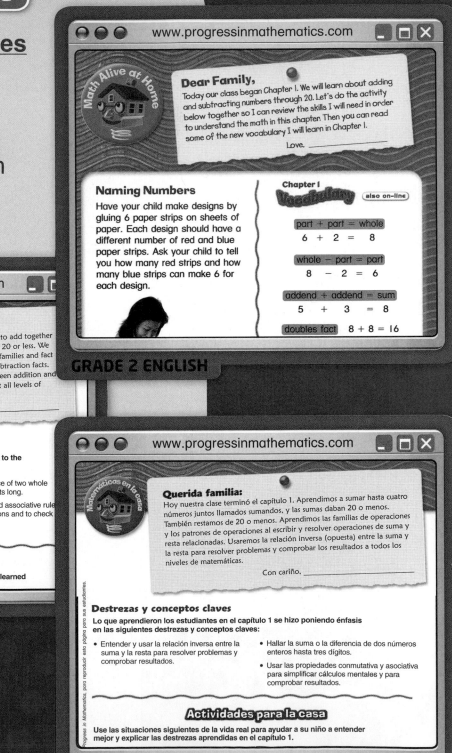

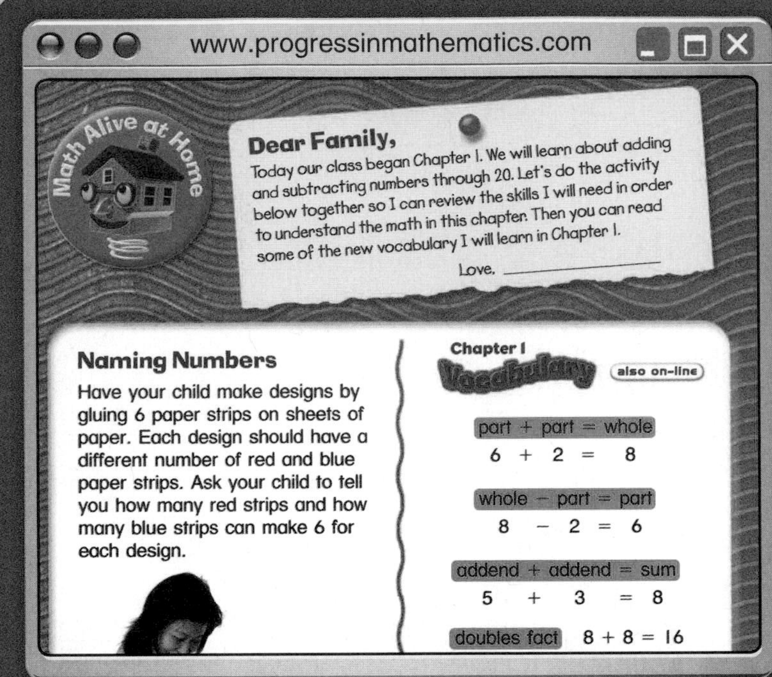
www.progressinmathematics.com

Math Alive at Home

Dear Family,
Today our class began Chapter 1. We will learn about adding and subtracting numbers through 20. Let's do the activity below together so I can review the skills I will need in order to understand the math in this chapter. Then you can read some of the new vocabulary I will learn in Chapter 1.

Love, __________

Naming Numbers
Have your child make designs by gluing 6 paper strips on sheets of paper. Each design should have a different number of red and blue paper strips. Ask your child to tell you how many red strips and how many blue strips can make 6 for each design.

Chapter 1 Vocabulary (also on-line)

part + part = whole
6 + 2 = 8

whole − part = part
8 − 2 = 6

addend + addend = sum
5 + 3 = 8

doubles fact 8 + 8 = 16

GRADE 2 ENGLISH

www.progressinmathematics.com

Dear Family,
Today our class completed Chapter 1. We learned how to add together as many as four numbers, called addends, with sums of 20 or less. We also subtracted from 20 or less. We learned about fact families and fact patterns by writing and solving related addition and subtraction facts. We will use the inverse, or opposite, relationship between addition and subtraction to solve problems and to check solutions at all levels of mathematics.

Love, __________

Key Skills and Concepts
Students' learning in Chapter 1 was guided by giving particular emphasis to the following key skills and concepts:

- Understand and use the inverse relationship between addition and subtraction to solve problems and check solutions.
- Find the sum or difference of two whole numbers up to three digits long.
- Use the commutative and associative rule simplify mental calculations and to check results.

At Home Activities
Use these real-life situations to help your child maintain and explain skills learned in Chapter 1.

quantities granted to users of Progress in Mathematics.

GRADE 2 ENGLISH

www.progressinmathematics.com

Matemáticas en la casa

Querida familia:
Hoy nuestra clase terminó el capítulo 1. Aprendimos a sumar hasta cuatro números juntos llamados sumandos, y las sumas daban 20 o menos. También restamos de 20 o menos. Aprendimos las familias de operaciones y los patrones de operaciones al escribir y resolver operaciones de suma y resta relacionadas. Usaremos la relación inversa (opuesta) entre la suma y la resta para resolver problemas y comprobar los resultados a todos los niveles de matemáticas.

Con cariño, __________

Destrezas y conceptos claves
Lo que aprendieron los estudiantes en el capítulo 1 se hizo poniendo énfasis en las siguientes destrezas y conceptos claves:

- Entender y usar la relación inversa entre la suma y la resta para resolver problemas y comprobar resultados.
- Hallar la suma o la diferencia de dos números enteros hasta tres dígitos.
- Usar las propiedades conmutativa y asociativa para simplificar cálculos mentales y para comprobar resultados.

Actividades para la casa
Use las situaciones siguientes de la vida real para ayudar a su niño a entender mejor y explicar las destrezas aprendidas en el capítulo 1.

Progress in Mathematics, para reproducir esta página para sus estudiantes.

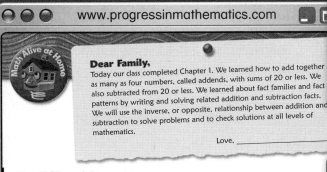

GRADE 2 SPANISH

SADLIER-OXFORD

Progress in Mathematics

Authors

Catherine D. LeTourneau

Alfred S. Posamentier

with

Elinor R. Ford

Program Consultants

Madelaine Gallin
Former Math Coordinator
Community School District #6
New York, NY

Lucy Lugones
Math Coordinator
St. Luke's School
Whitestone, NY

Tim Mason
District Math Resource Teacher
Palm Beach County School District
West Palm Beach, FL

Sadlier-Oxford
A Division of William H. Sadlier, Inc.
www.sadlier-oxford.com

The publisher gratefully acknowledges Rose Anita McDonnell (1905–2003) and her colleagues for the important role they played in the development of *Progress in Mathematics* for more than sixty years.

Field Test Participants

The authors and editors wish to thank the following Grade 1 teachers and administrators, who participated in the Field Test of *Progress in Mathematics*, for their valuable comments and suggestions.

Barbara Reiter
Principal
Whitestone, NY

Kathy Fabregas
Grade 1 Teacher
Whitestone, NY

Lorraine Radice
Grade 1 Teacher
Whitestone, NY

Dr. James Godlewski
Principal
Larksville, PA

Valerie Packer
Grade 1 Teacher
Larksville, PA

Mary Ann Wassel
Grade 1 Teacher
Larksville, PA

Kevin Smith
Principal
Bronx, NY

Iraida Fernandez
Grade 1 Teacher
Bronx, NY

Ruth DeJimenez
Grade 1 Teacher
Bronx, NY

Sr. Mary Joanne Deegan, R.S.M.
Principal
Hicksville, NY

Sr. Mary Beth Faber, R.S.M.
Grade 1 Teacher
Hicksville, NY

Marion Vassallo
Grade 1 Teacher
Hicksville, NY

Reviewers

The publisher wishes to thank the following teachers and administrators, who read portions of the series prior to publication, for their valuable contributions.

Shannon Barry-Hale
Grade 1 Teacher
Las Vegas, NV

Marie Bicsak
Math Coordinator
Mount Clemens, MI

Lisa Buechel
Grade 1 Teacher
Dallas, TX

Sheri Cahoon
Grade 1 Teacher
Las Vegas, NV

Diane Clarke
Grade 1 Teacher
North Arlington, NJ

Judith A. Devine
Educational Consultant
Springfield, PA

Sue DiGeronimo
Grade 1 Teacher
Independence, OH

Nichole Fischer
Grade 2 Teacher
Las Vegas, NV

Stephanie D. Garland
Educational Consultant
St. Louis, MO

Maria Giordano
Grade 1 Teacher
Eastchester, NY

Dr. Anthony Gnanarajah
Associate Superintendent,
Archdiocese of Seattle
Seattle, WA

Daphne Griffin
Grade K Teacher
Ponchatoula, LA

Kathie Hughes
K–6 Math Tutor
Bartlett, TN

Kathy Kaiser
Grade K Teacher
Orlando, FL

Carla Lambousy
Grade 1 Teacher
Crowley, LA

Myra Laux
Grade 1 Teacher
Metairie, LA

Diana Maresch
Grade 2 Teacher
Pittsburgh, PA

Dr. Karen Matthews
Assistant Superintendent,
Archdiocese of Seattle
Seattle, WA

Jennifer Morse
Grade K Teacher
Chelsea, MA

Maureen Roitman
Grade 1 Teacher
Pawtucket, RI

Delores A. Schmid
Teacher Consultant
Wilmington, NC

Kevin Smith
Principal
Bronx, NY

Shane Steltenpohl
Grade 1 Teacher
Nekoosa, WI

Sally Todd
Associate Superintendent,
Diocese of Orange
Orange, CA

Kimberley Warren
Grade 2 Teacher
Las Vegas, NV

Sr. Agnes White
Grade 1 Teacher
Rockaway Park, NY

Jeanne Wilkens
Grade 1 Teacher
Cincinnati, OH

Andrew Woods
Principal
New York, NY

Copyright © 2009 by William H. Sadlier, Inc. All rights reserved.
This publication, or any part thereof, may not be reproduced in any form, or by any means, including electronic, photographic, or mechanical, or by any sound recording system, or by any device for storage and retrieval of information, without the written permission of the publisher. Address inquiries to Permissions Department, William H. Sadlier, Inc., 9 Pine Street, New York, NY 10005-4700.
S® is a registered trademark of William H. Sadlier, Inc.

Printed in the United States of America
ISBN: 978-0-8215-3602-5
10 11 12 13 RRDW 16 15 14 13

Welcome to Math!

Dear Second Grader,

Do you know why math is important? Well, we all use math everyday. We use it when we:

- cook
- build something
- read a clock
- shop
- and so much more!

Throughout this book are special signs and symbols. When you see them, be sure to stop and look. Here are some of the signs and symbols you will see:

Let's Learn! ·······► This is where a lesson begins!

Listen ·······► Listen as your teacher reads a story, poem, or important directions.

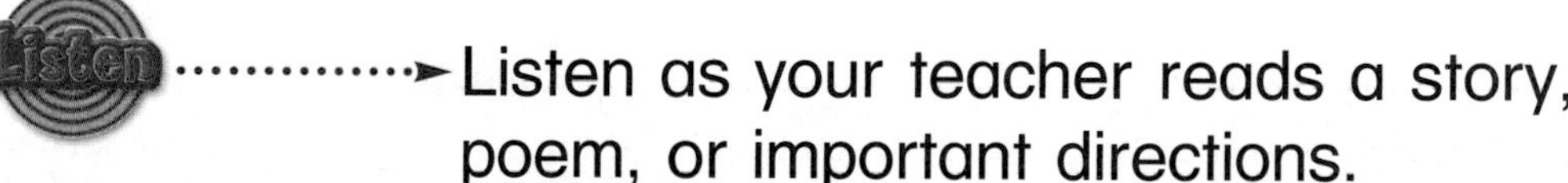

Math Words ·······► Look at these words. They are new math vocabulary words.

Talk It Over ·······► This is a question or topic for you to talk about with your classmates.

Math Journal ·······► Get ready to use your Math Journal!

Write About It ·······► This is a question or topic for you to write about in your Math Journal.

We wrote this book just for you!

The Authors

Hi. We are your new math friends. When you see us, pay attention. We have a lot to say!

Copyright © by William H. Sadlier, Inc. All rights reserved.

Dear Family

Progress in Mathematics, now in its sixth decade of user-proven success, was written by experienced teacher-authors. It integrates a traditional course of study and today's academic standards with the most up-to-date methods of teaching.

By the end of Grade 2 children should be able to identify any three-digit number, know that each digit in a three-digit number has a definite value, and understand the meaning of regrouping in addition and subtraction.

Ongoing teacher-family-student interaction is vital to your child's achievement in any academic endeavor.

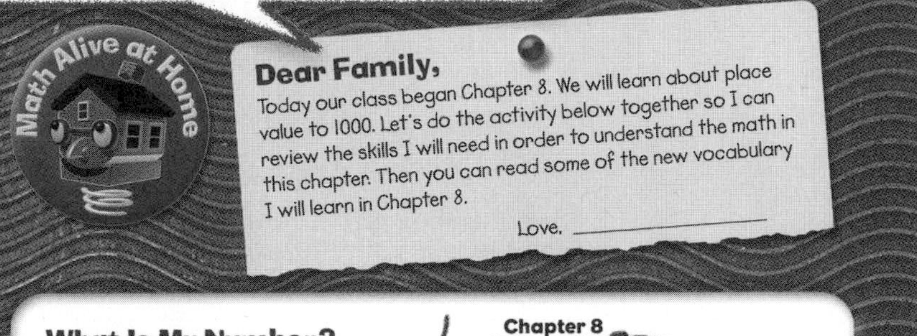

Dear Family,

Today our class began Chapter 8. We will learn about place value to 1000. Let's do the activity below together so I can review the skills I will need in order to understand the math in this chapter. Then you can read some of the new vocabulary I will learn in Chapter 8.

Love, ____________

What Is My Number?

Draw the ten rods and ones units shown below. Ask your child to write how many tens and ones and the number shown by the models drawn. Continue the activity by drawing different numbers of ten rods and ones units, then having your child write the number. Do this for several numbers to 99. You might also ask her/him to order the numbers from greatest to least or from least to greatest.

By doing fun-filled activities with you, your child will learn to value math and become a confident problem solver.

Chapter 8

Vocabulary also on-line

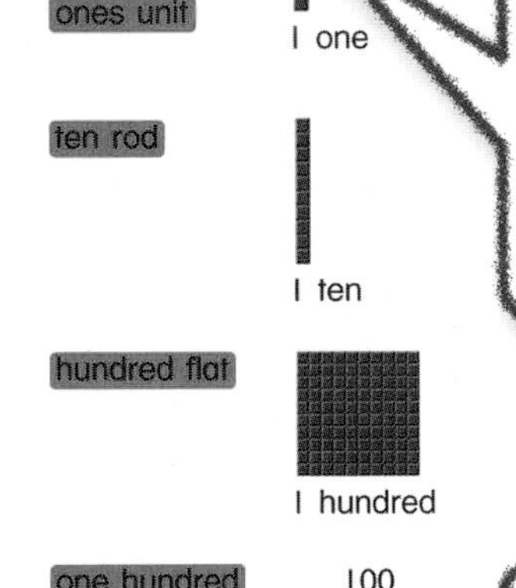

ones unit — 1 one

ten rod — 1 ten

hundred flat — 1 hundred

one hundred — 100

3-digit number — 423

place-value chart

hundreds	tens	ones
4		3

It is important for your child to learn these words, as understanding them will allow your child to achieve success in mathematics.

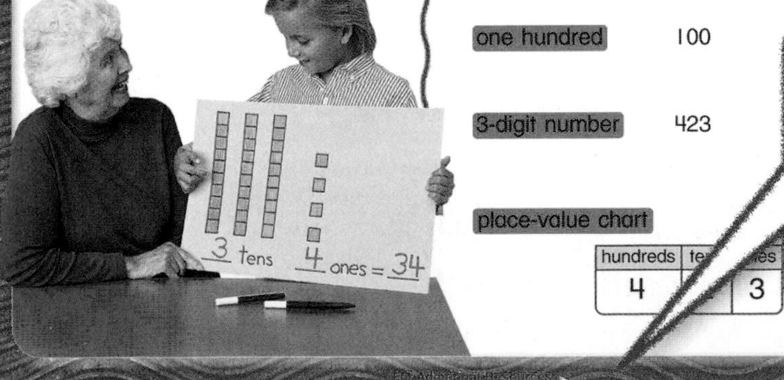

Incorporating on-line activities allows your child to practice math concepts and skills while having fun learning mathematics.

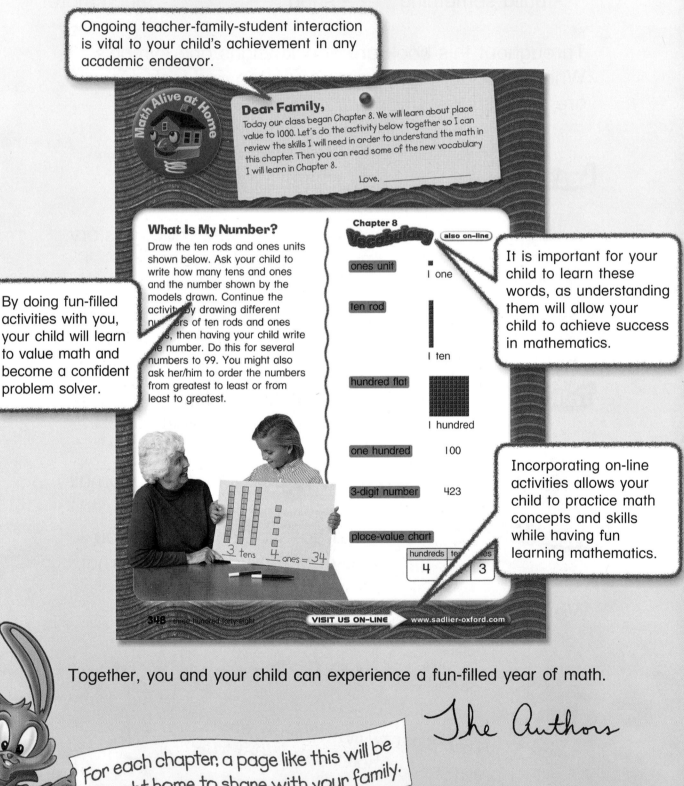

348 three hundred forty-eight

VISIT US ON-LINE www.sadlier-oxford.com

Together, you and your child can experience a fun-filled year of math.

The Authors

For each chapter, a page like this will be brought home to share with your family.

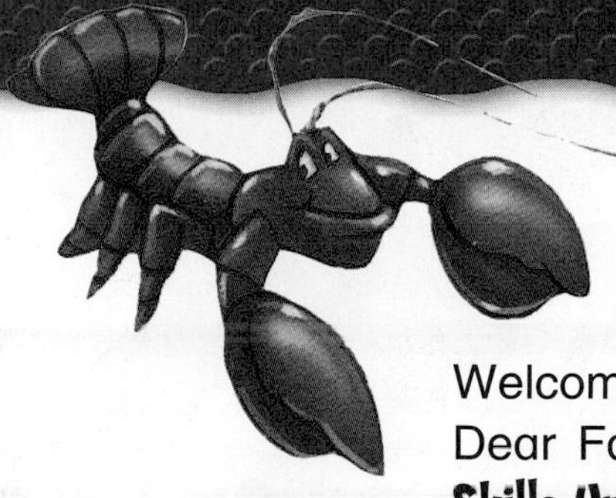

Contents

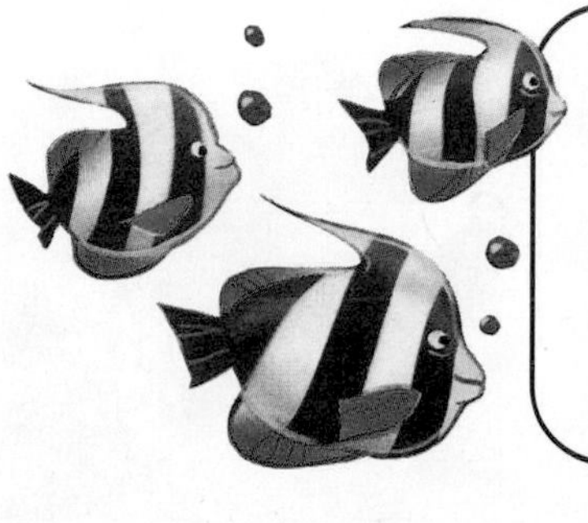

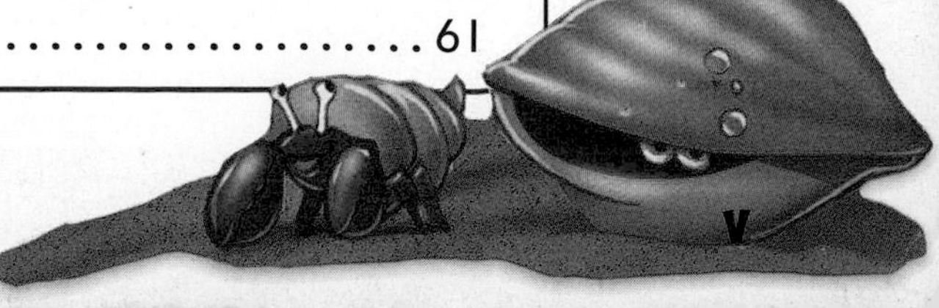

★ Denotes use of manipulatives. 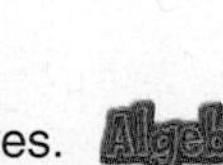  Lesson promotes algebraic reasoning.

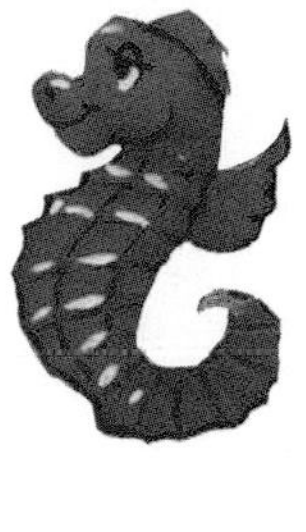

Copyright © by William H. Sadlier, Inc. All rights reserved.

Chapter 2

Place Value to 100

Theme: Rainforest

* Denotes use of manipulatives. Algebra Lesson promotes algebraic reasoning.

Data and Graphs: Using Operations

Theme: Friends

Copyright © by William H. Sadlier, Inc. All rights reserved.

Addition: Two-Digit Numbers

Theme: Places to Go and Things to Do

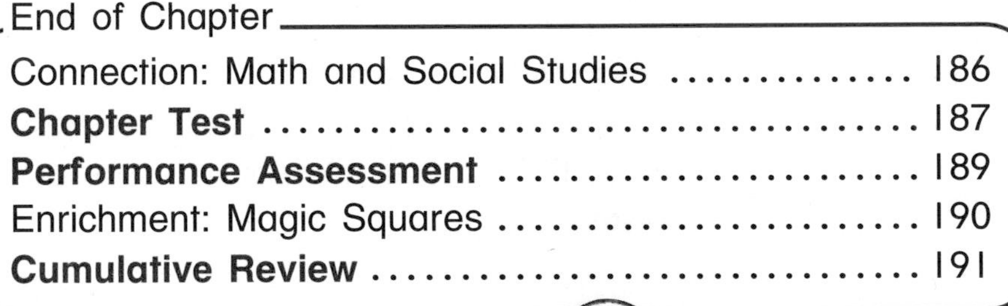

End of Chapter

* Denotes use of manipulatives. Algebra Lesson promotes algebraic reasoning.

Subtraction: Two-Digit Numbers

Theme: Arts and Crafts

Copyright © by William H. Sadlier, Inc. All rights reserved.

*Denotes use of manipulatives. Algebra Lesson promotes algebraic reasoning.

Geometry

Theme: Shapes Around Us

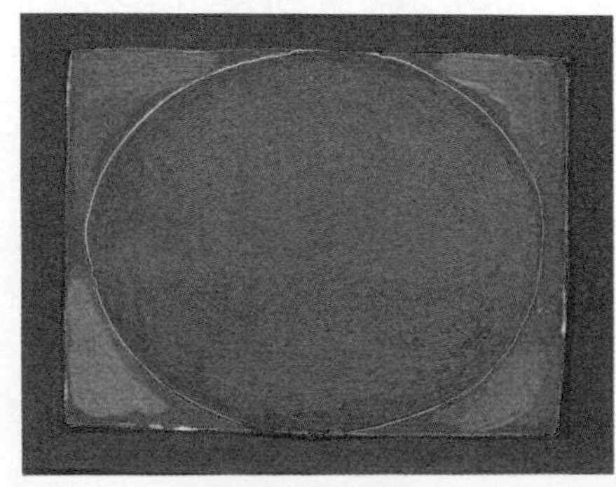

* Denotes use of manipulatives. Algebra Lesson promotes algebraic reasoning.

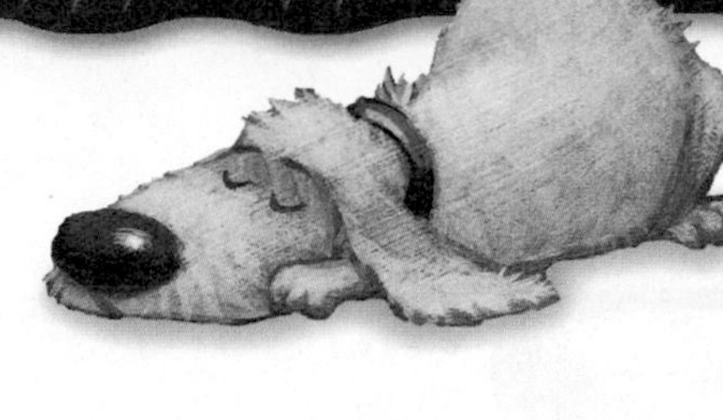

Money and Time

Theme: Time Travel

Copyright © by William H. Sadlier, Inc. All rights reserved.

* Denotes use of manipulatives. Algebra Lesson promotes algebraic reasoning.

CHAPTER 8 Place Value to 1000

Theme: Inventions and Discoveries

* Denotes use of manipulatives.
Algebra Lesson promotes algebraic reasoning.

Addition and Subtraction: Three-Digit Numbers

Theme: Sports

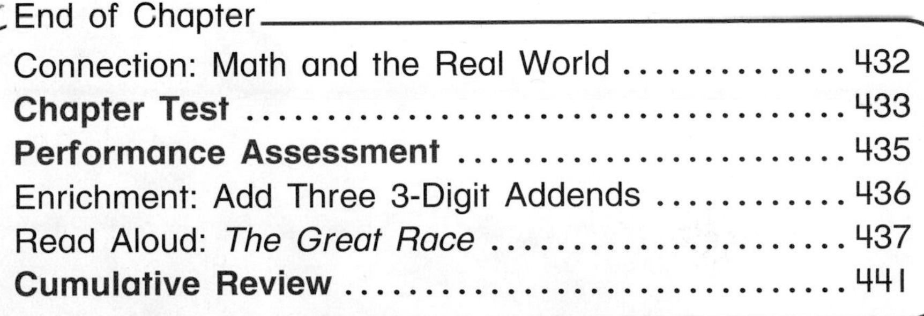

End of Chapter

Copyright © by William H. Sadlier, Inc. All rights reserved.

★ Denotes use of manipulatives.

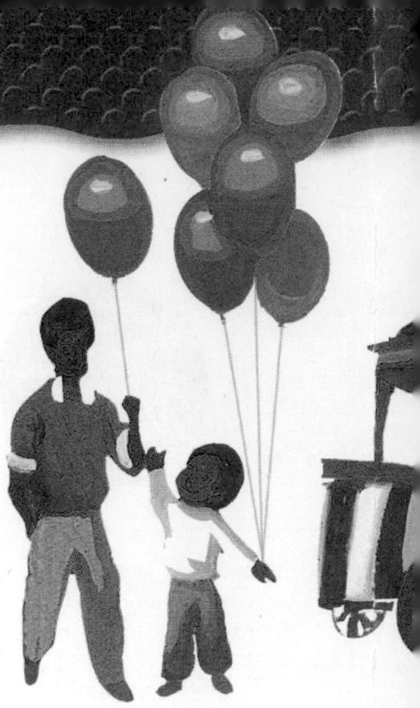

Fractions and Probability

Chapter 10

Theme: Party and Games

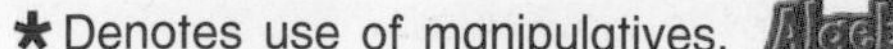

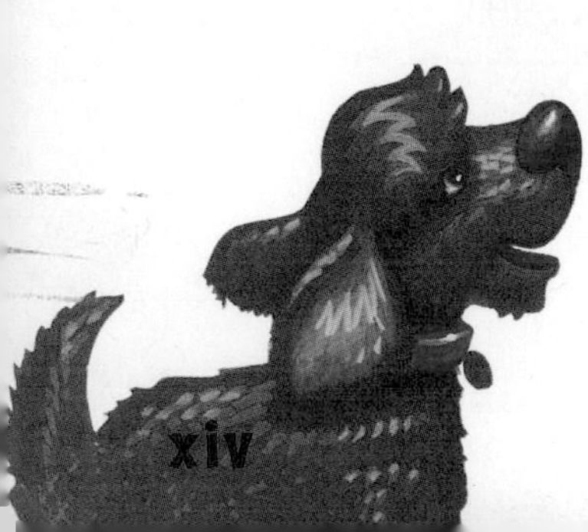

* Denotes use of manipulatives. Algebra Lesson promotes algebraic reasoning.

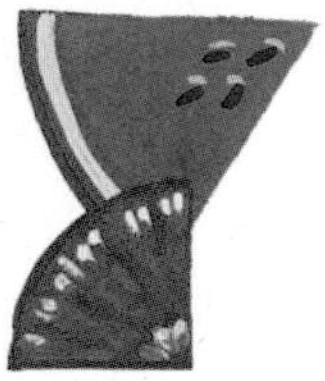

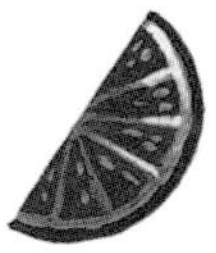

CHAPTER 11

Measurement

Theme: School

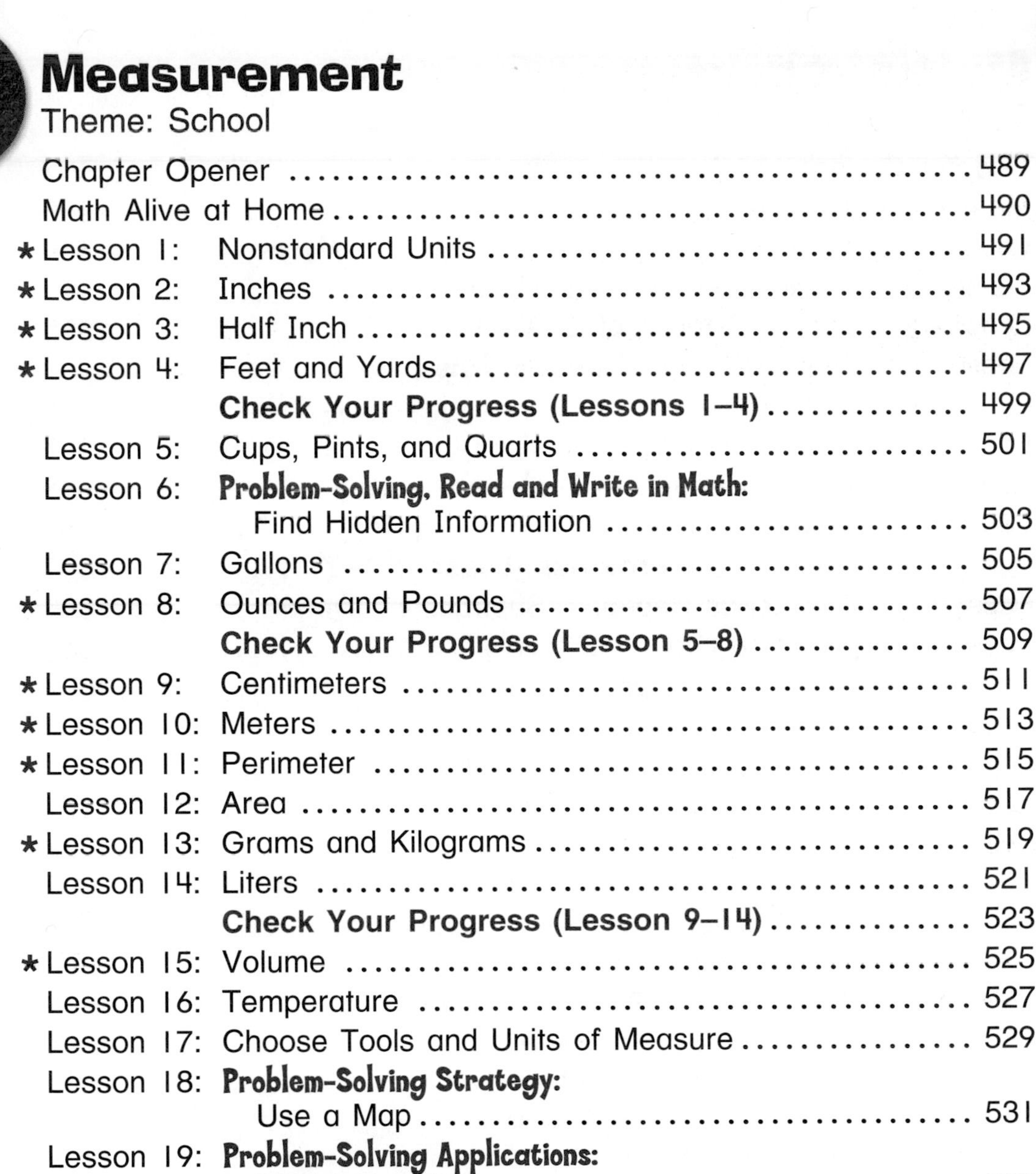

Copyright © by William H. Sadlier, Inc. All rights reserved.

* Denotes use of manipulatives.

Chapter 12 Multiplication and Division

Theme: Collections

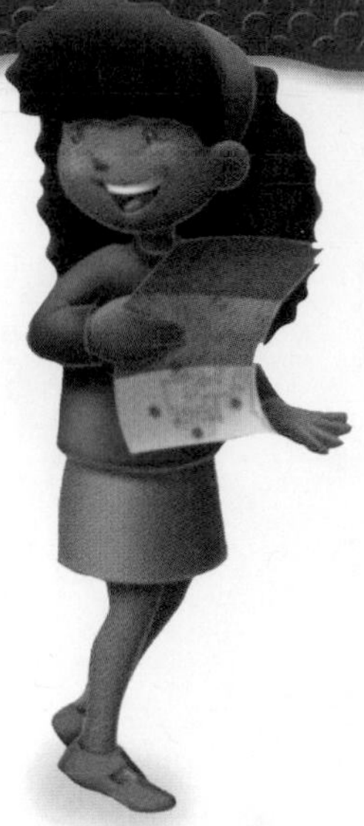

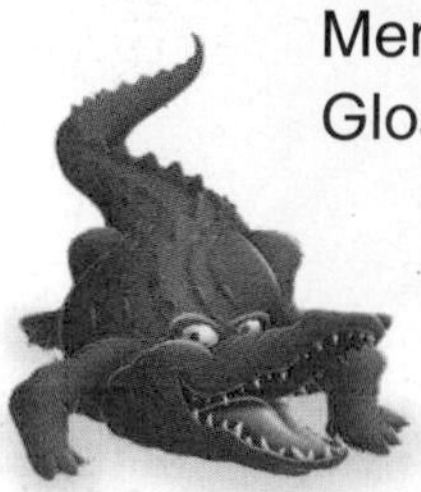

* Denotes use of manipulatives.  Lesson promotes algebraic reasoning.

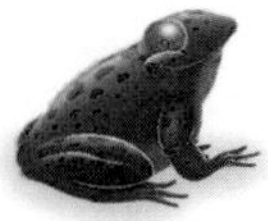

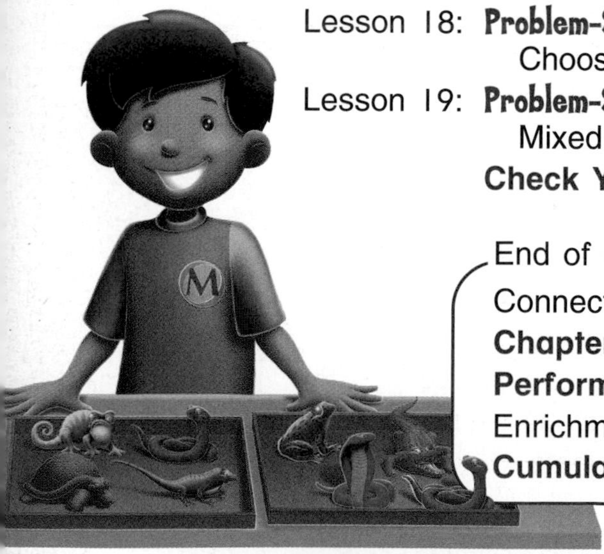

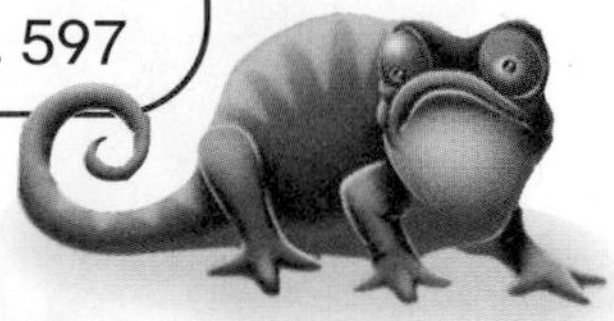

Skills Update

A Review of Mathematical Skills from Grade 1

Contents

Copyright © by William H. Sadlier, Inc. All rights reserved.

______________________ can add to 10.

$$\begin{array}{r} 4 \\ +\ 3 \\ \hline 7 \end{array}$$

$$\begin{array}{r} 6 \\ +\ 4 \\ \hline 10 \end{array}$$

4 + 3 = 7

6 + 4 = 10

Add.

1. $\begin{array}{r} 7 \\ +2 \\ \hline 9 \end{array}$	2. $\begin{array}{r} 3 \\ +3 \\ \hline \end{array}$	3. $\begin{array}{r} 5 \\ +1 \\ \hline \end{array}$	4. $\begin{array}{r} 8 \\ +2 \\ \hline \end{array}$	5. $\begin{array}{r} 6 \\ +3 \\ \hline \end{array}$
6. $\begin{array}{r} 2 \\ +6 \\ \hline \end{array}$	7. $\begin{array}{r} 1 \\ +9 \\ \hline \end{array}$	8. $\begin{array}{r} 0 \\ +3 \\ \hline \end{array}$	9. $\begin{array}{r} 4 \\ +2 \\ \hline \end{array}$	10. $\begin{array}{r} 6 \\ +1 \\ \hline \end{array}$
11. $\begin{array}{r} 8 \\ +1 \\ \hline \end{array}$	12. $\begin{array}{r} 4 \\ +4 \\ \hline \end{array}$	13. $\begin{array}{r} 6 \\ +0 \\ \hline \end{array}$	14. $\begin{array}{r} 5 \\ +4 \\ \hline \end{array}$	15. $\begin{array}{r} 3 \\ +4 \\ \hline \end{array}$

16. 7 + 1 = ___	17. 9 + 0 = ___	18. 5 + 5 = ___
19. 3 + 5 = ___	20. 2 + 8 = ___	21. 1 + 4 = ___
22. 1 + 8 = ___	23. 3 + 7 = ___	24. 4 + 5 = ___
25. 9 + 1 = ___	26. 7 + 0 = ___	27. 3 + 6 = ___

____________________ can subtract facts to 10.

$$\begin{array}{r} 10 \\ -\ 4 \\ \hline 6 \end{array}$$

10 − 4 = 6

$$\begin{array}{r} 8 \\ -\ 1 \\ \hline 7 \end{array}$$

8 − 1 = 7

Subtract.

1. $\begin{array}{r} 9 \\ -\ 4 \\ \hline 5 \end{array}$	2. $\begin{array}{r} 9 \\ -\ 8 \\ \hline \end{array}$	3. $\begin{array}{r} 7 \\ -\ 5 \\ \hline \end{array}$	4. $\begin{array}{r} 8 \\ -\ 3 \\ \hline \end{array}$	5. $\begin{array}{r} 9 \\ -\ 9 \\ \hline \end{array}$
6. $\begin{array}{r} 8 \\ -\ 4 \\ \hline \end{array}$	7. $\begin{array}{r} 10 \\ -\ 8 \\ \hline \end{array}$	8. $\begin{array}{r} 7 \\ -\ 3 \\ \hline \end{array}$	9. $\begin{array}{r} 8 \\ -\ 6 \\ \hline \end{array}$	10. $\begin{array}{r} 10 \\ -\ 7 \\ \hline \end{array}$
11. $\begin{array}{r} 9 \\ -\ 3 \\ \hline \end{array}$	12. $\begin{array}{r} 4 \\ -\ 3 \\ \hline \end{array}$	13. $\begin{array}{r} 7 \\ -\ 6 \\ \hline \end{array}$	14. $\begin{array}{r} 10 \\ -\ 9 \\ \hline \end{array}$	15. $\begin{array}{r} 6 \\ -\ 4 \\ \hline \end{array}$

16. 7 − 7 = ___	17. 3 − 2 = ___	18. 10 − 6 = ___
19. 6 − 5 = ___	20. 10 − 2 = ___	21. 9 − 5 = ___
22. 9 − 1 = ___	23. 6 − 3 = ___	24. 7 − 2 = ___
25. 6 − 6 = ___	26. 8 − 7 = ___	27. 10 − 5 = ___

Copyright © by William H. Sadlier, Inc. All rights reserved.

______________________________ knows number words to twenty.

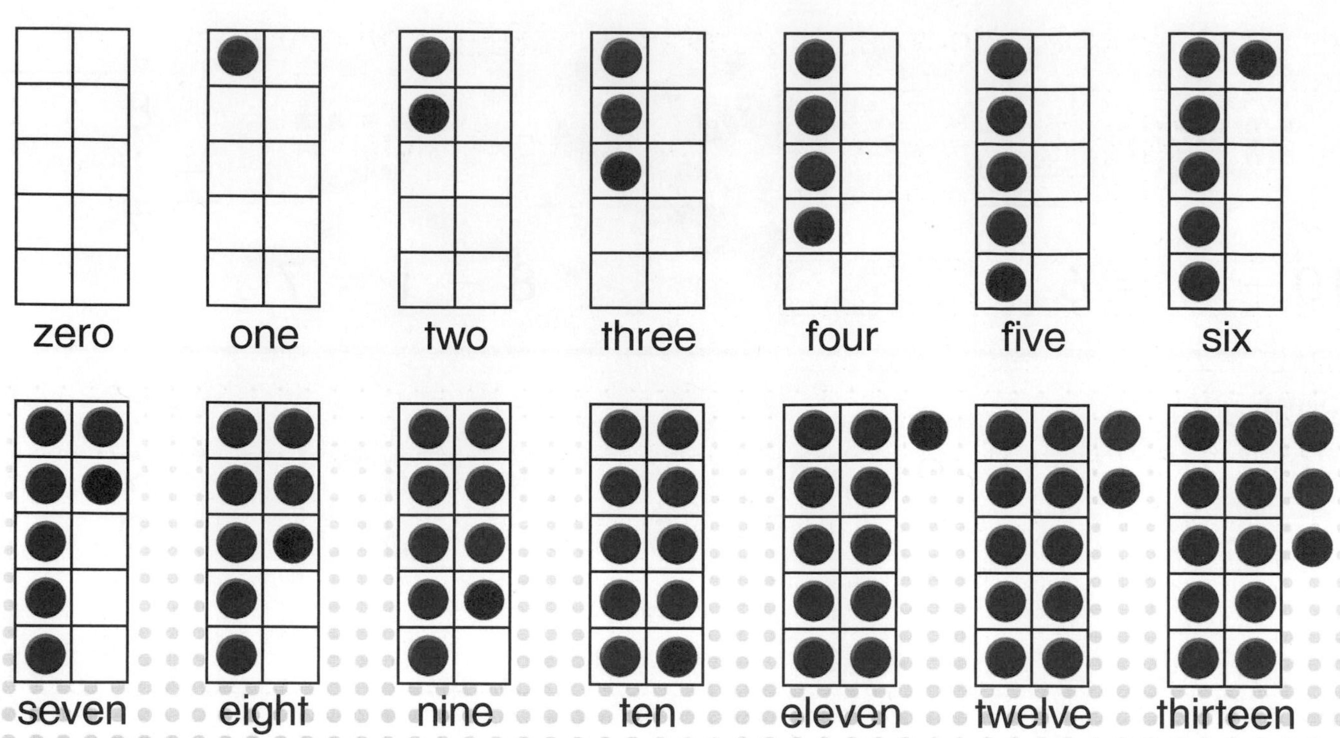

Color and count the counters. Circle the number word.

1.

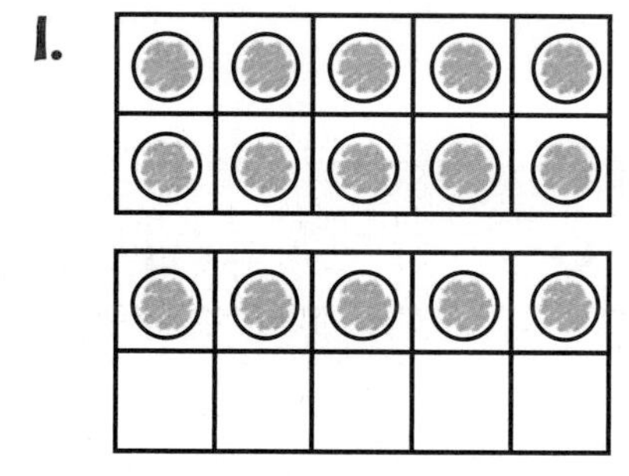

fourteen

fifteen

2.

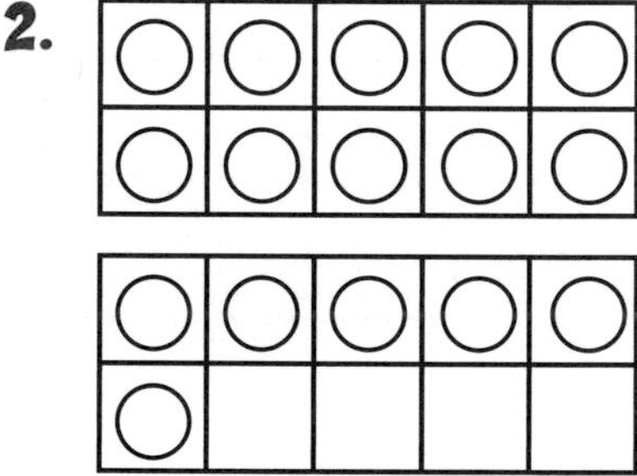

sixteen

seventeen

3.

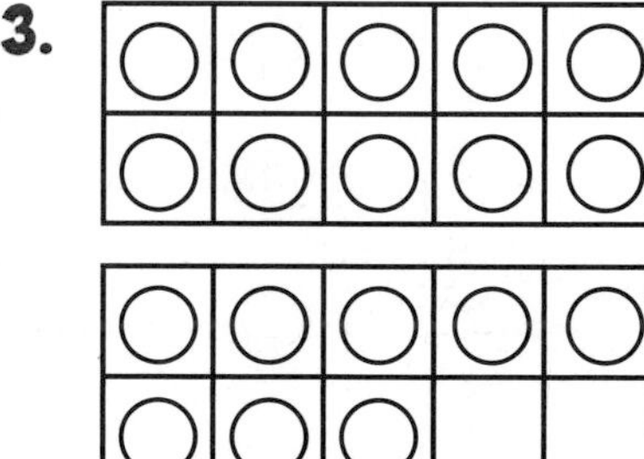

eighteen

nineteen

4.

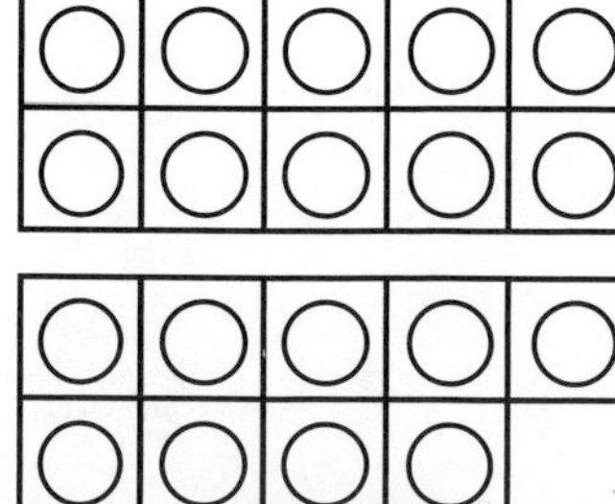

nineteen

seventeen

5. Two groups of 10 are twenty. Show how to model twenty.

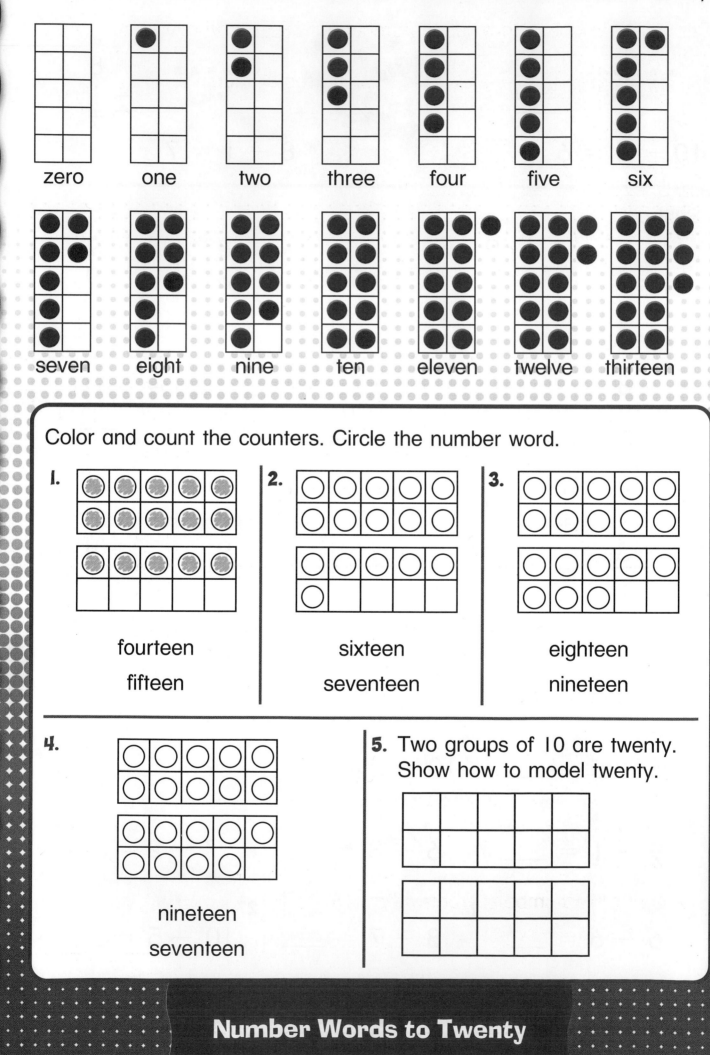

REVIEW OF GRADE 1 SKILLS

_________________________ can compare numbers.

Compare 19 to 16. Show each number with ▦ and counters.

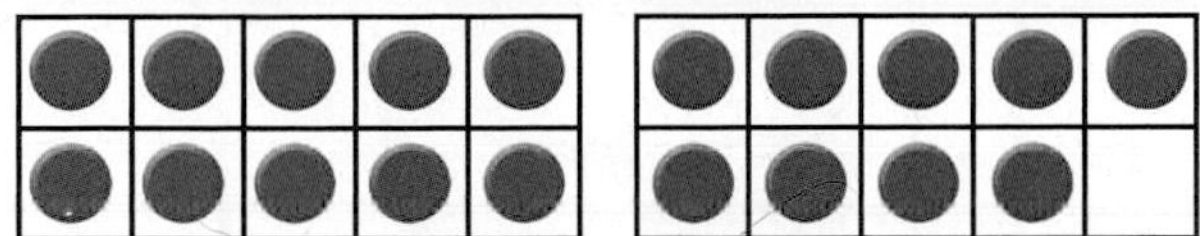

19 is greater than 16.

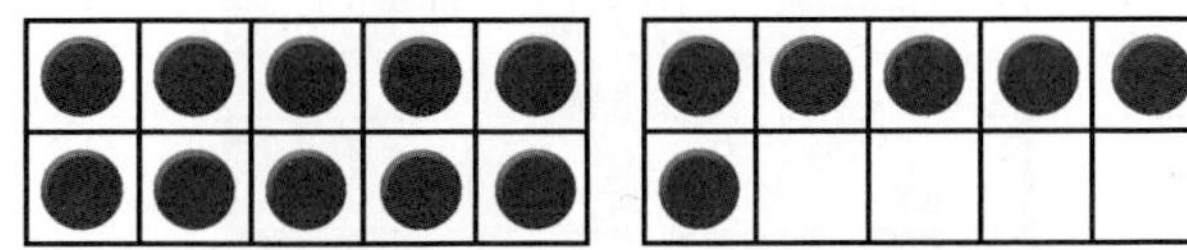

16 is less than 19.

Use a ▦. Circle the number that is greater.

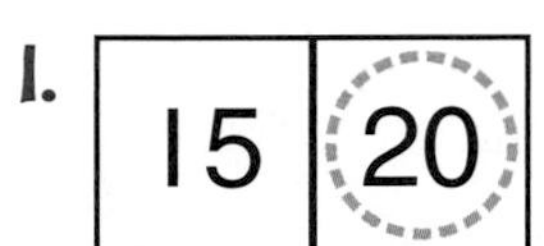

1.	15	20	2.	6	4	3.	19	7	4.	9	13
5.	3	7	6.	6	16	7.	14	7	8.	20	10

Use a ▦. Circle the number that is less.

9.	6	2	10.	11	7	11.	8	9	12.	3	6
13.	20	2	14.	19	15	15.	4	8	16.	18	13

17. Write two numbers greater than 10.

_____ _____

18. Write two numbers less than 10.

_____ _____

19. Write two numbers greater than 15.

_____ _____

Copyright © by William H. Sadlier, Inc. All rights reserved.

_______________________________ can tally.

This tally chart shows how many bags of leaves the Clean Team filled each day.

Sunday	Monday	Tuesday	Wednesday	Thursday	Friday	Saturday
III	~~IIII~~	~~IIII~~ IIII	~~IIII~~ ~~IIII~~ II	~~IIII~~ ~~IIII~~ ~~IIII~~	~~IIII~~ I	

1. How many bags were filled on Tuesday? _____ bags

2. How many bags were filled on Wednesday? _____ bags

3. On which day were the most bags filled? _______________

4. On which day were the least number of bags filled? _______________

5. On Monday and Tuesday, how many bags in all were filled? _____ bags

6. On Saturday the team plans to fill 13 bags. Show the tally for 13 bags. _______________

7. How many more bags will be filled on Saturday than on Monday? _____ more

_________________________________ can add tens.

3 ones + 5 ones = 8 ones

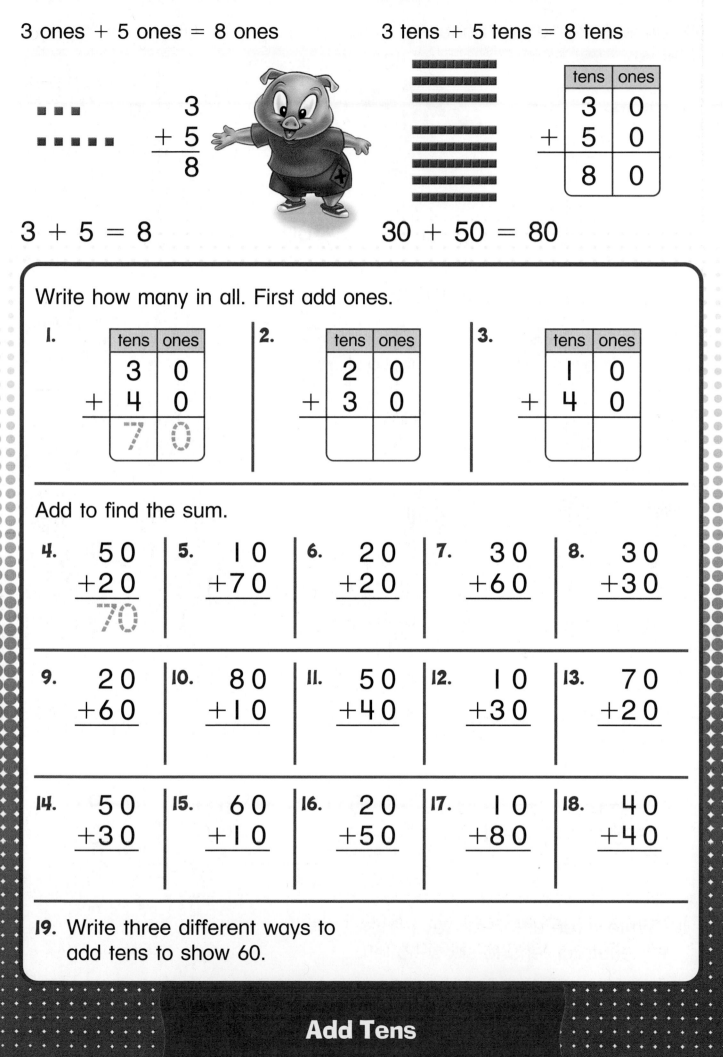

$$\begin{array}{r} 3 \\ +\ 5 \\ \hline 8 \end{array}$$

3 + 5 = 8

3 tens + 5 tens = 8 tens

	tens	ones
	3	0
+	5	0
	8	0

30 + 50 = 80

Write how many in all. First add ones.

1.

	tens	ones
	3	0
+	4	0
	7	0

2.

	tens	ones
	2	0
+	3	0

3.

	tens	ones
	1	0
+	4	0

Add to find the sum.

4. $\begin{array}{r} 50 \\ +20 \\ \hline 70 \end{array}$ **5.** $\begin{array}{r} 10 \\ +70 \\ \hline \end{array}$ **6.** $\begin{array}{r} 20 \\ +20 \\ \hline \end{array}$ **7.** $\begin{array}{r} 30 \\ +60 \\ \hline \end{array}$ **8.** $\begin{array}{r} 30 \\ +30 \\ \hline \end{array}$

9. $\begin{array}{r} 20 \\ +60 \\ \hline \end{array}$ **10.** $\begin{array}{r} 80 \\ +10 \\ \hline \end{array}$ **11.** $\begin{array}{r} 50 \\ +40 \\ \hline \end{array}$ **12.** $\begin{array}{r} 10 \\ +30 \\ \hline \end{array}$ **13.** $\begin{array}{r} 70 \\ +20 \\ \hline \end{array}$

14. $\begin{array}{r} 50 \\ +30 \\ \hline \end{array}$ **15.** $\begin{array}{r} 60 \\ +10 \\ \hline \end{array}$ **16.** $\begin{array}{r} 20 \\ +50 \\ \hline \end{array}$ **17.** $\begin{array}{r} 10 \\ +80 \\ \hline \end{array}$ **18.** $\begin{array}{r} 40 \\ +40 \\ \hline \end{array}$

19. Write three different ways to add tens to show 60.

Copyright © by William H. Sadlier, Inc. All rights reserved.

_______________ can subtract tens.

6 ones − 2 ones = 4 ones

6 tens − 2 tens = 4 tens

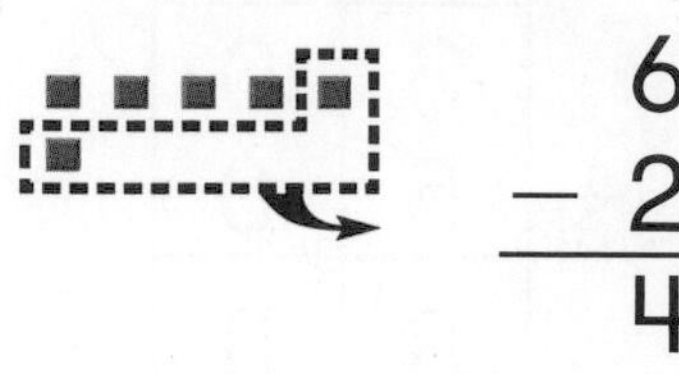

$$\begin{array}{r} 6 \\ -\ 2 \\ \hline 4 \end{array}$$

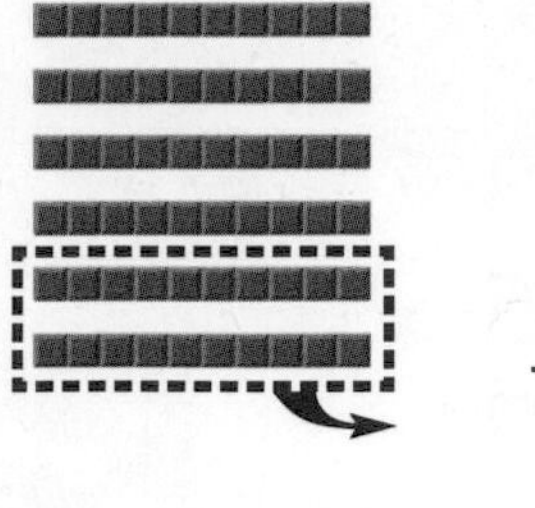

	tens	ones
	6	0
−	2	0
	4	0

6 − 2 = 4

60 − 20 = 40

Write how many are left. First subtract ones.

1.

	tens	ones
	9	0
−	6	0
	3	0

2.

	tens	ones
	8	0
−	2	0

3.

	tens	ones
	7	0
−	4	0

Subtract to find the difference.

4. $\begin{array}{r} 60 \\ -40 \\ \hline 20 \end{array}$ **5.** $\begin{array}{r} 60 \\ -10 \\ \hline \end{array}$ **6.** $\begin{array}{r} 70 \\ -60 \\ \hline \end{array}$ **7.** $\begin{array}{r} 40 \\ -20 \\ \hline \end{array}$ **8.** $\begin{array}{r} 90 \\ -10 \\ \hline \end{array}$

9. $\begin{array}{r} 20 \\ -10 \\ \hline \end{array}$ **10.** $\begin{array}{r} 30 \\ -20 \\ \hline \end{array}$ **11.** $\begin{array}{r} 90 \\ -70 \\ \hline \end{array}$ **12.** $\begin{array}{r} 60 \\ -30 \\ \hline \end{array}$ **13.** $\begin{array}{r} 80 \\ -70 \\ \hline \end{array}$

14. $\begin{array}{r} 80 \\ -80 \\ \hline \end{array}$ **15.** $\begin{array}{r} 10 \\ -10 \\ \hline \end{array}$ **16.** $\begin{array}{r} 50 \\ -30 \\ \hline \end{array}$ **17.** $\begin{array}{r} 50 \\ -40 \\ \hline \end{array}$ **18.** $\begin{array}{r} 90 \\ -80 \\ \hline \end{array}$

19. Write three different ways to subtract tens to show 40 left.

_______________ can identify plane figures.

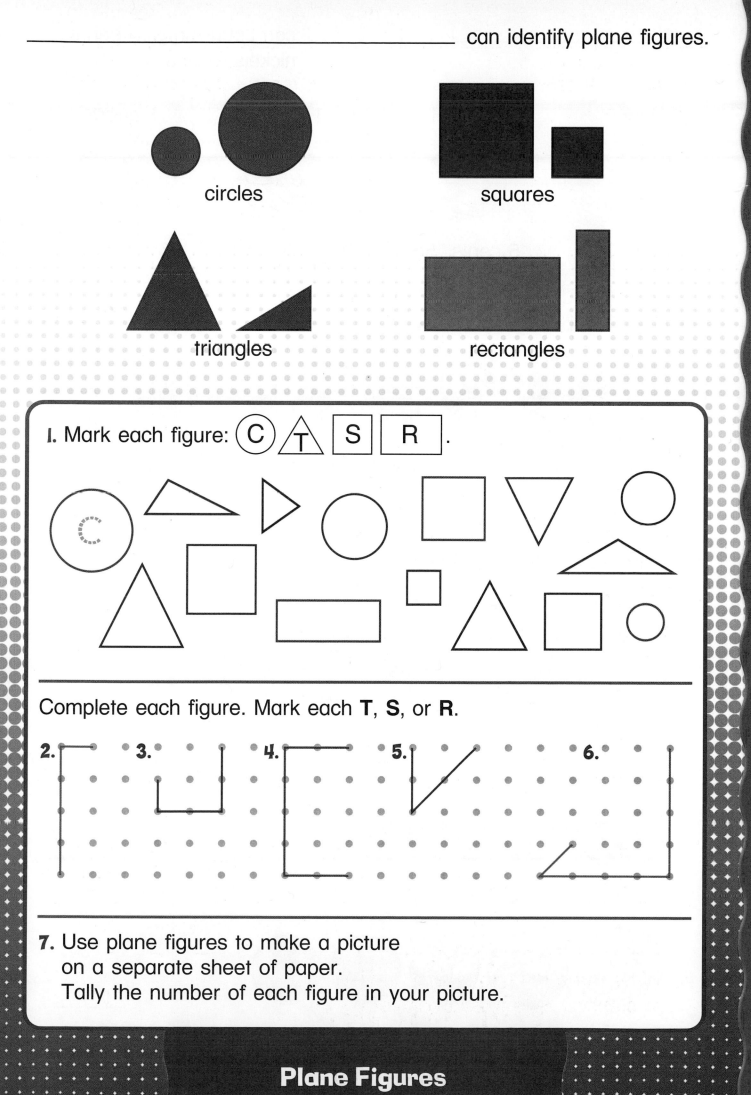

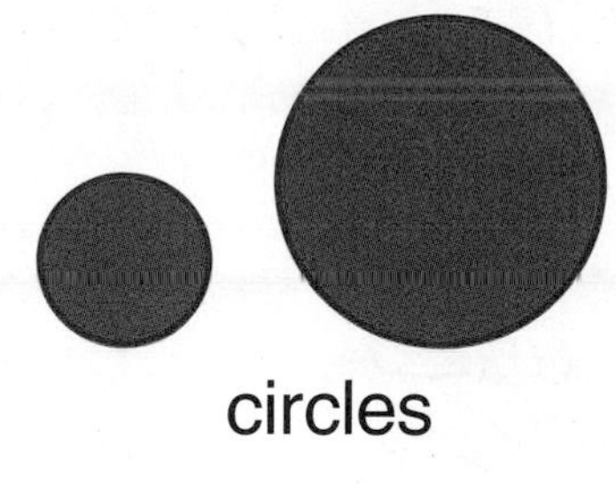
circles

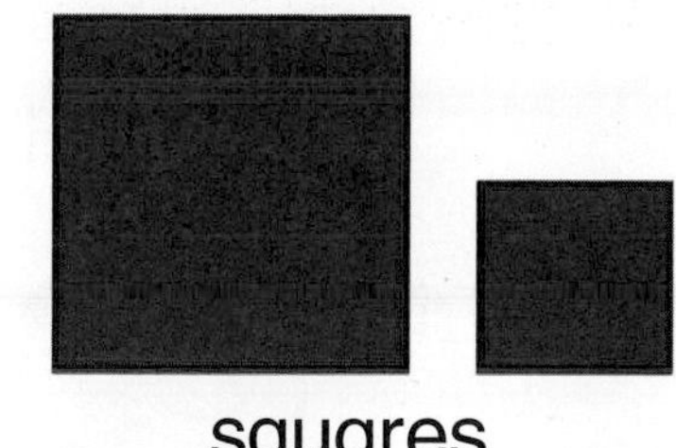
squares

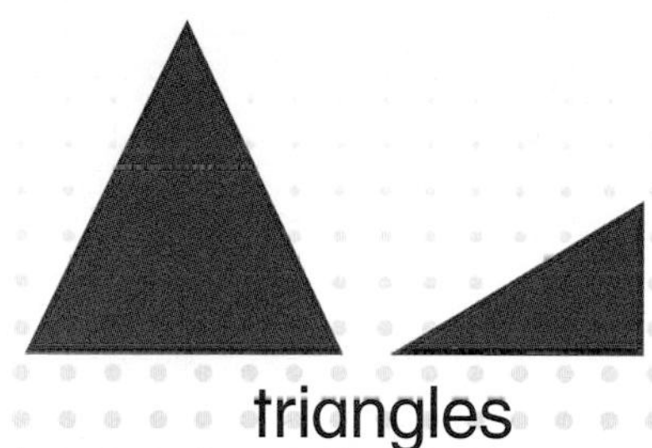
triangles

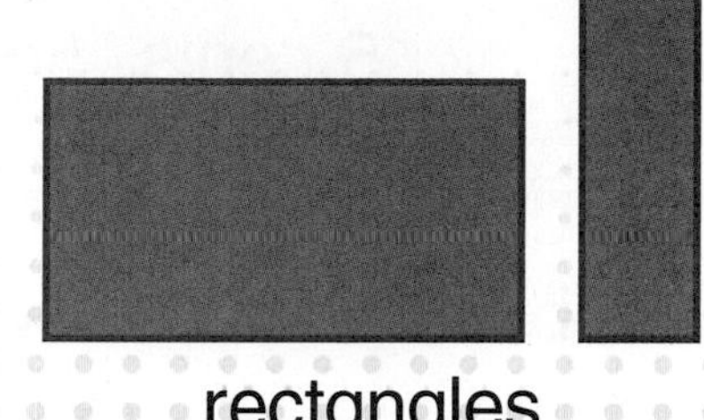
rectangles

1. Mark each figure: (C) (T) [S] [R].

Complete each figure. Mark each **T**, **S**, or **R**.

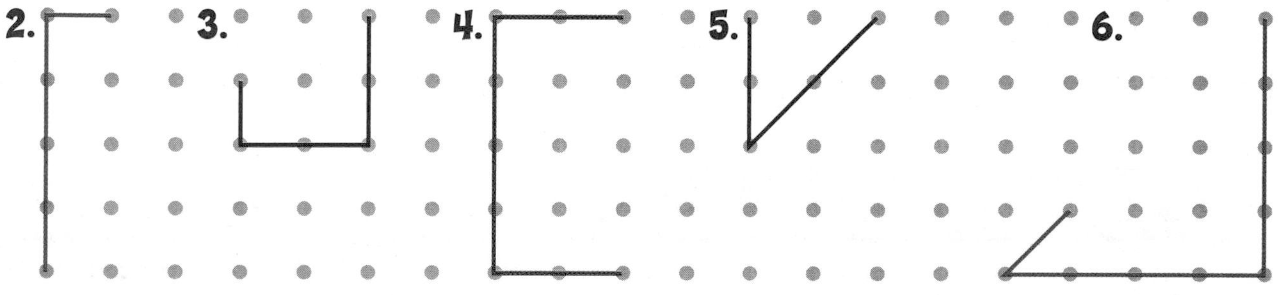

7. Use plane figures to make a picture on a separate sheet of paper. Tally the number of each figure in your picture.

REVIEW OF GRADE 1 SKILLS

Copyright © by William H. Sadlier, Inc. All rights reserved.

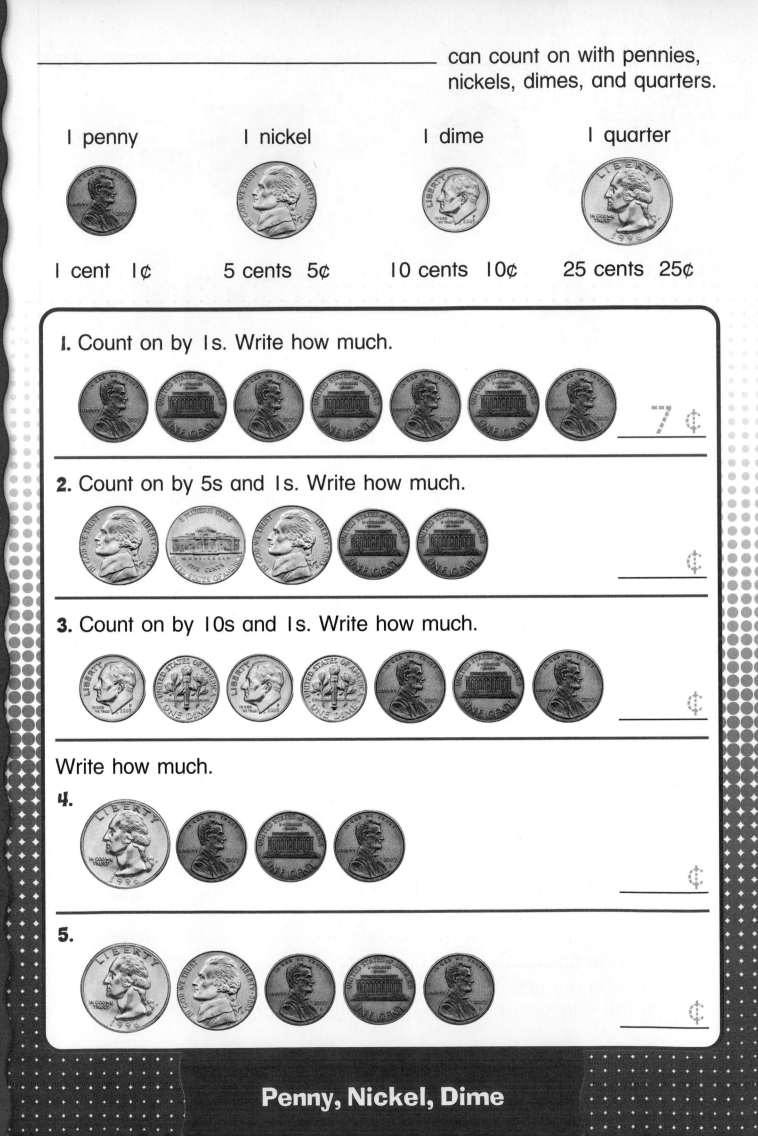

_____________________ can count on with pennies, nickels, dimes, and quarters.

I penny	I nickel	I dime	I quarter

I cent I¢	5 cents 5¢	10 cents 10¢	25 cents 25¢

1. Count on by 1s. Write how much.

7 ¢

2. Count on by 5s and 1s. Write how much.

_____ ¢

3. Count on by 10s and 1s. Write how much.

_____ ¢

Write how much.

4.

_____ ¢

5.

REVIEW OF GRADE I SKILLS

______________________________ can tell time.

I can name the hour.

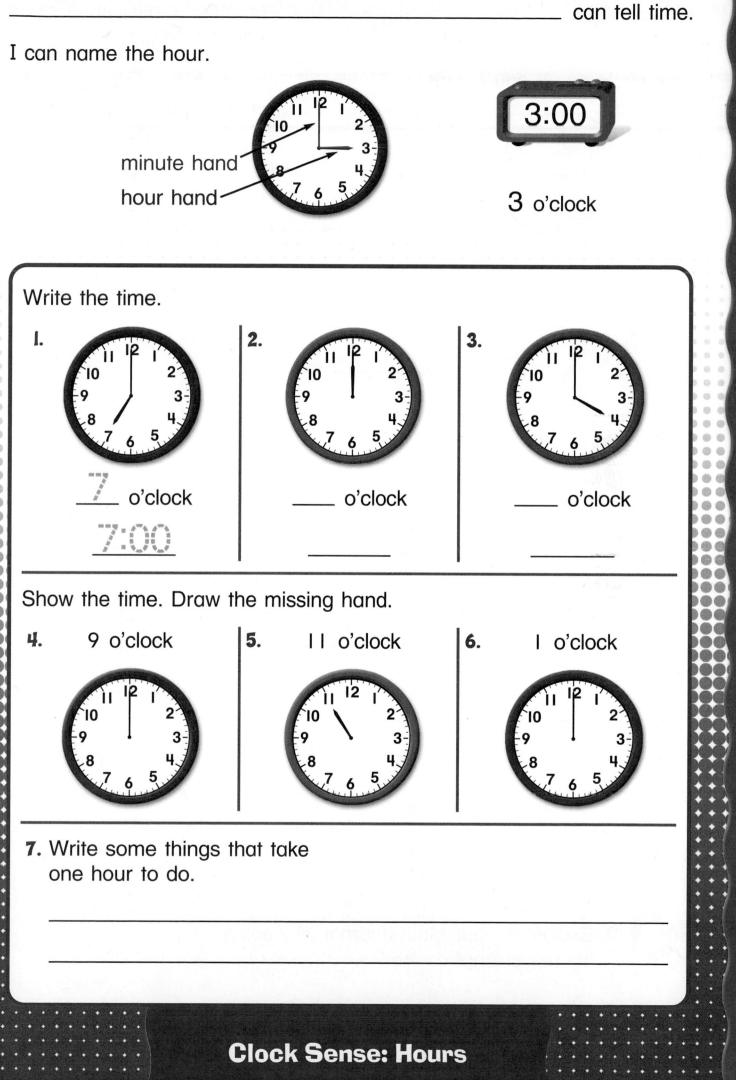

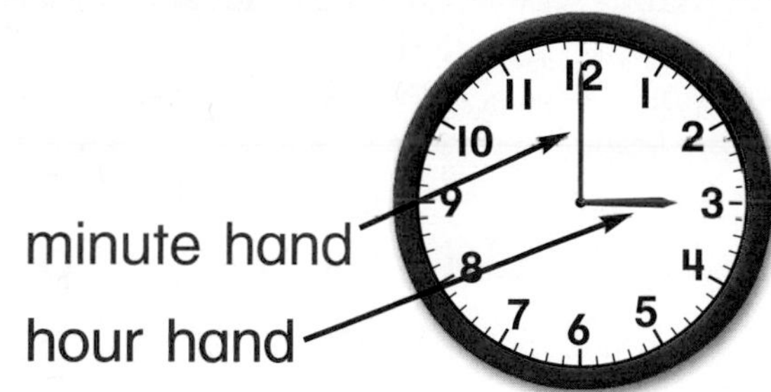

3:00

3 o'clock

Write the time.

1.

7 o'clock

7:00

2.

____ o'clock

______

3.

____ o'clock

______

Show the time. Draw the missing hand.

4. 9 o'clock

5. 11 o'clock

6. 1 o'clock

7. Write some things that take one hour to do.

____

____

Copyright © by William H. Sadlier, Inc. All rights reserved.

_______________________ can identify equal parts of a whole.

This circle has 5 equal parts.

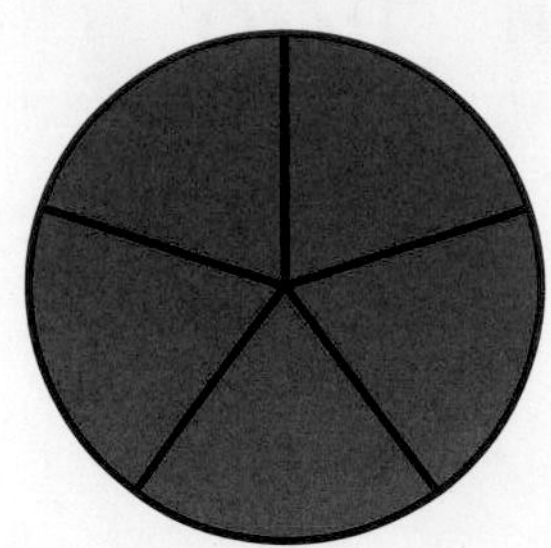

Color Code
purple
for 2 equal parts
blue
for 3 equal parts
green
for 4 equal parts
red
for 5 equal parts

Color each figure with equal parts. Use the color code above.

1. 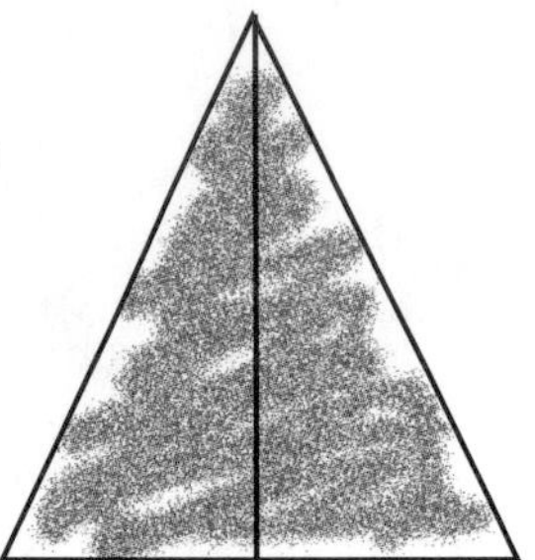

2. 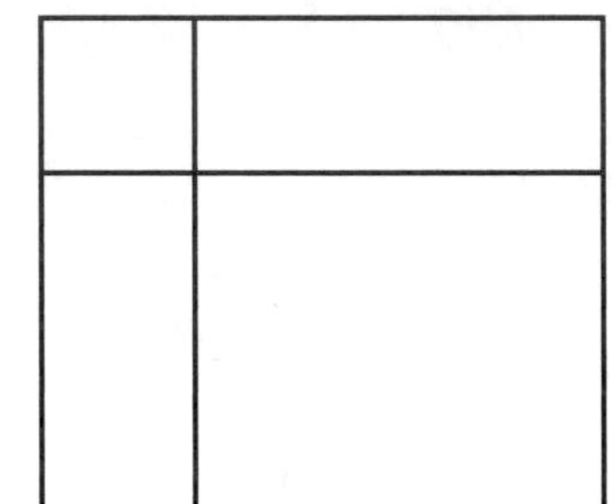

3. 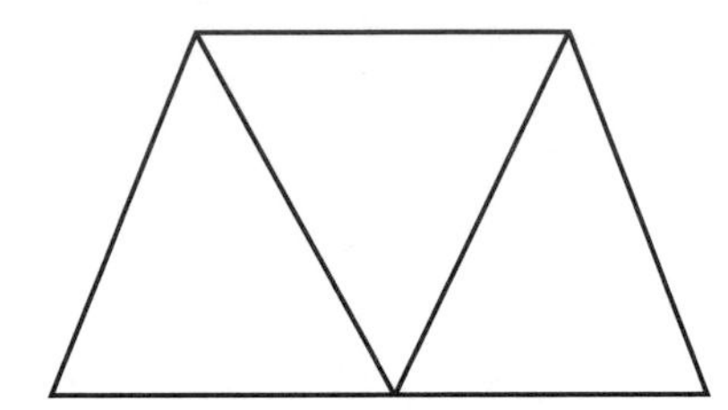

4. 

5. 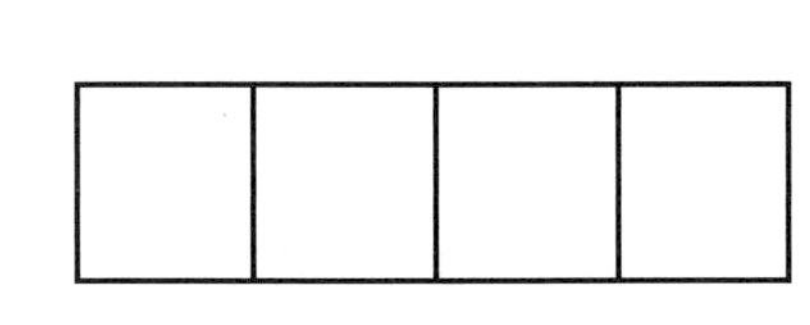

6. 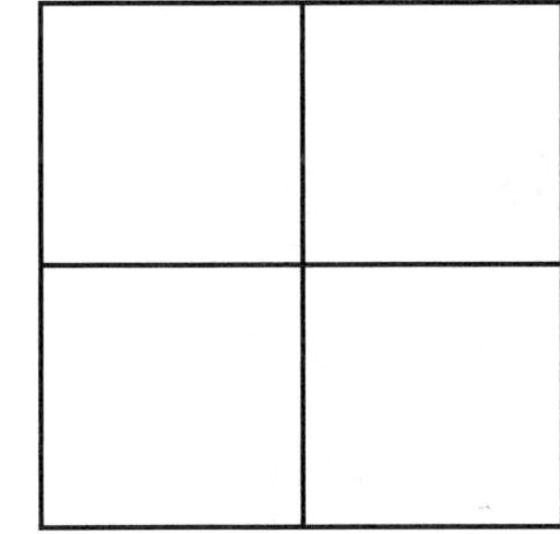

7. 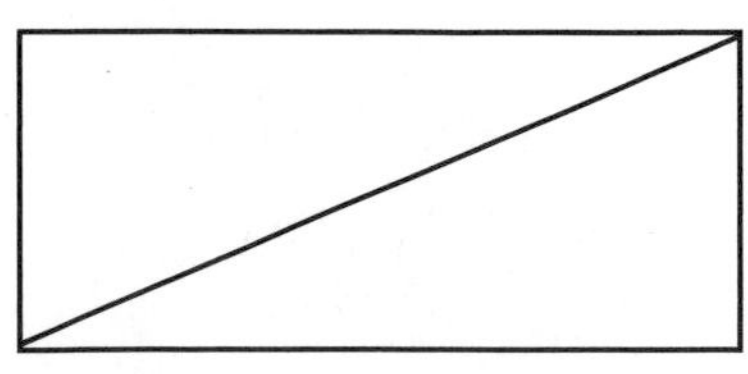

8. 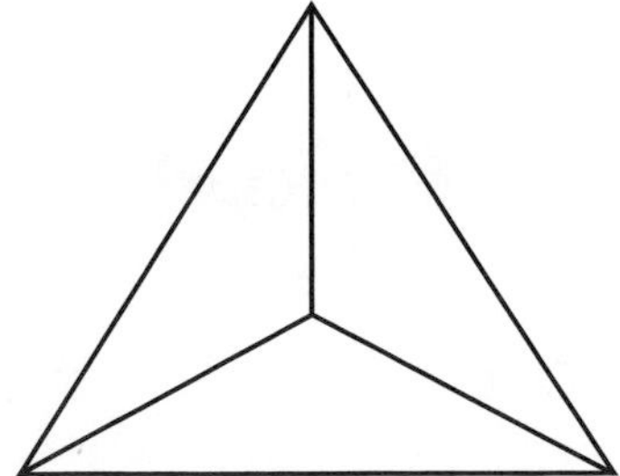

9. 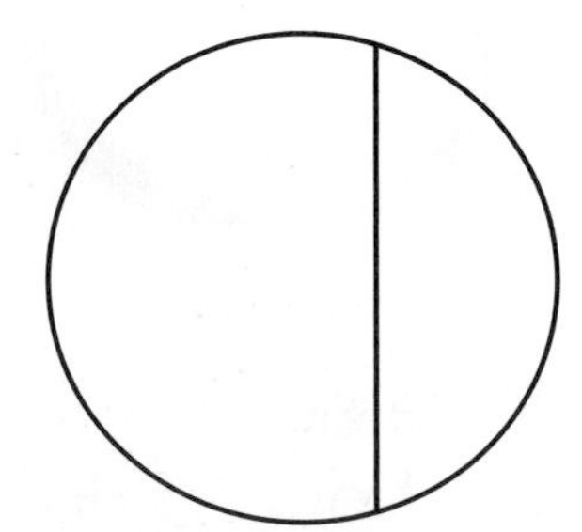

10. Explain in your Math Journal why some figures are not colored.

____________________ can measure length.

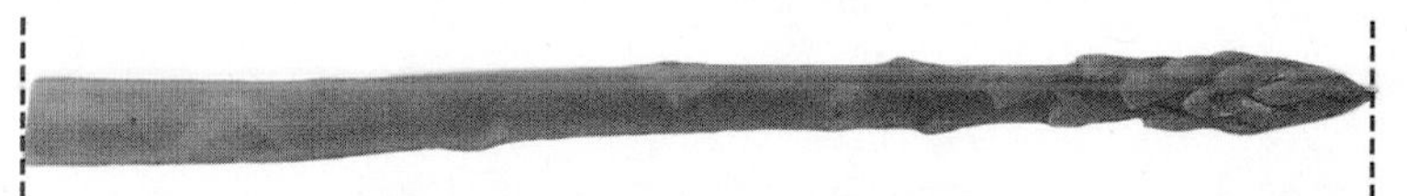

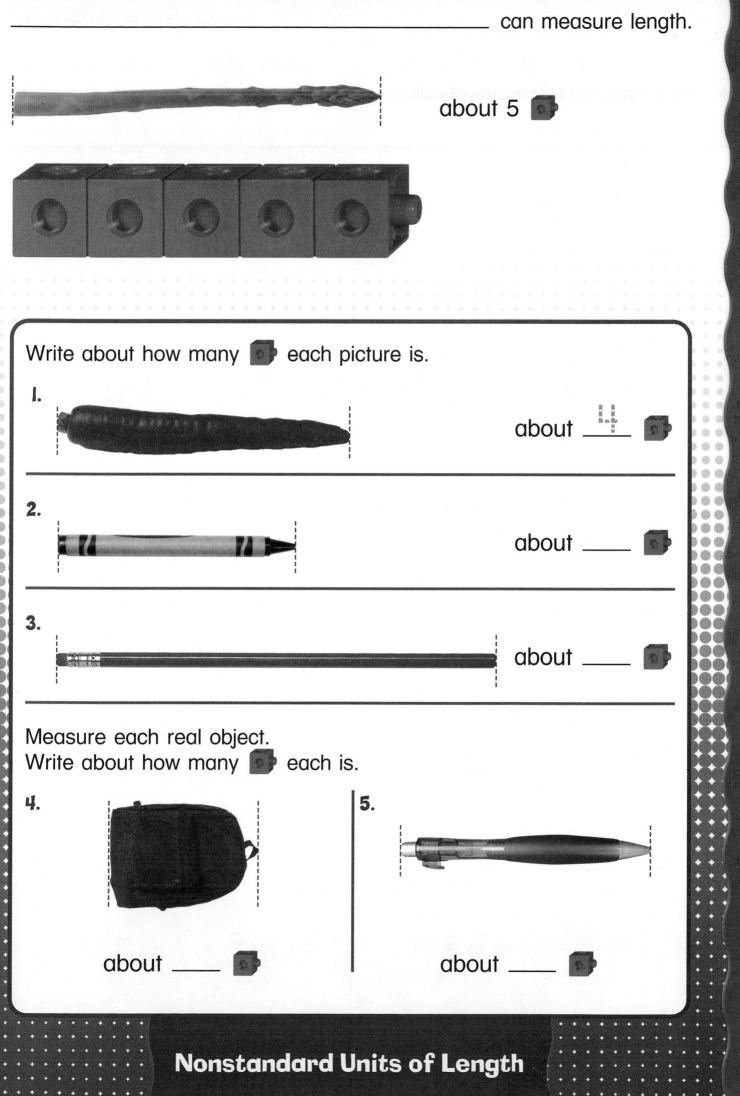

about 5

Write about how many each picture is.

1\. 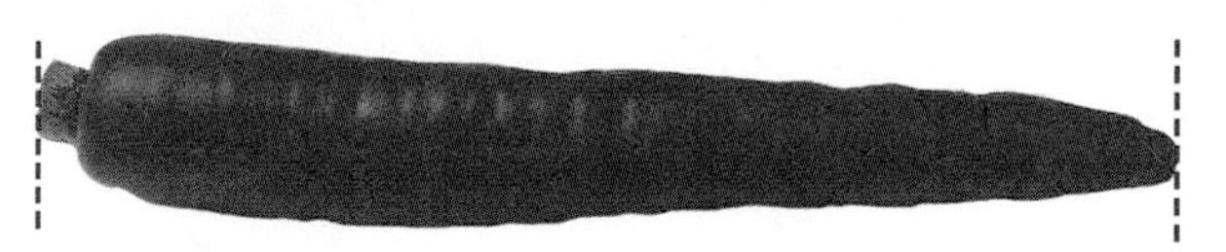 about 

2\. 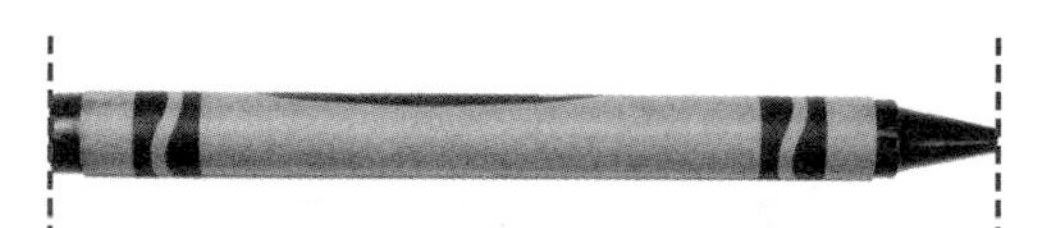 about ____

3\.  about ____

Measure each real object.
Write about how many  each is.

4\. 

about ____ 

5\. 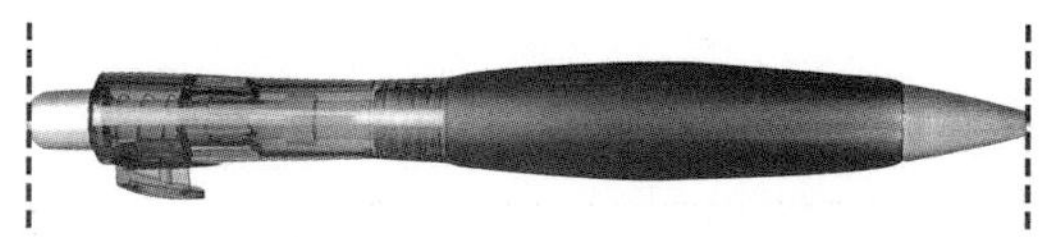

about ____ 

REVIEW OF GRADE 1 SKILLS

Copyright © by William H. Sadlier, Inc. All rights reserved.

______________________ can identify equal groups.

Each bag has 5 marbles.
These groups are equal.

These groups of marbles are not equal.

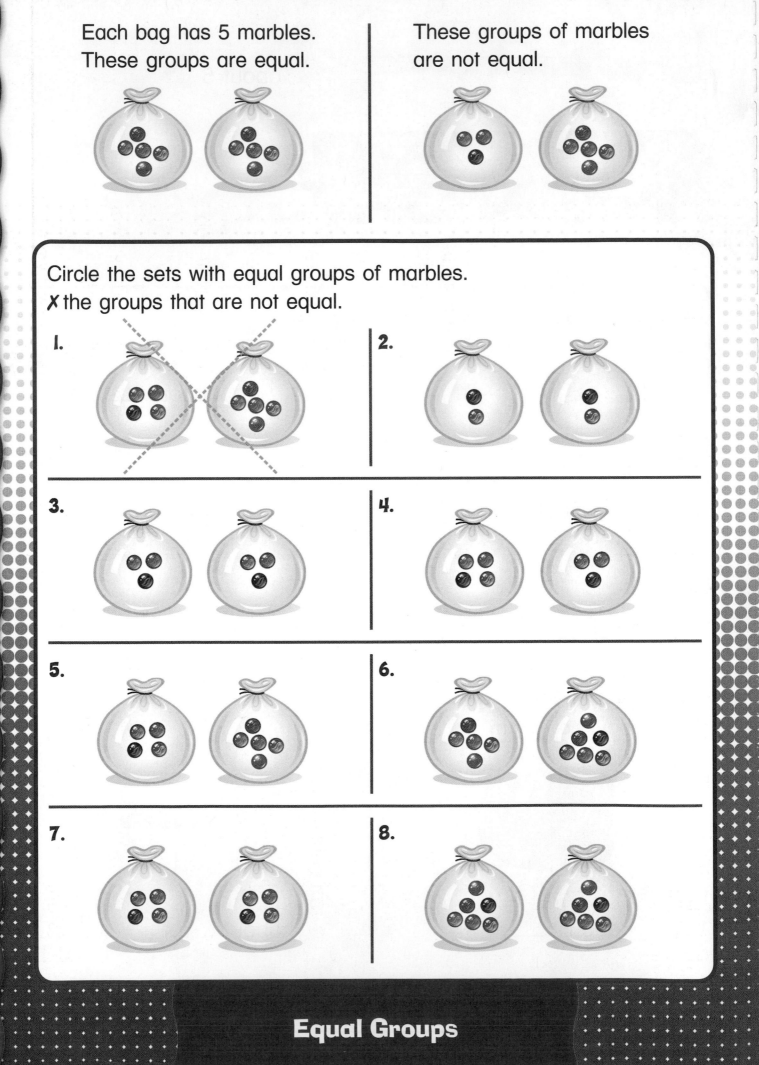

Circle the sets with equal groups of marbles.
✗ the groups that are not equal.

1.

2.

3.

4.

5.

6.

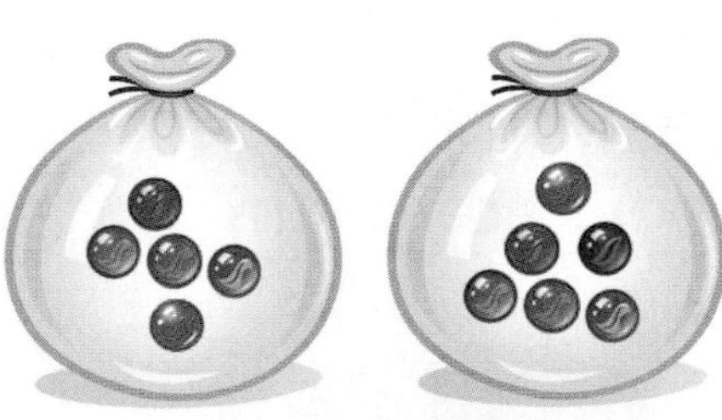

7.

8.

Use this strategy:
Write a number
sentence.

Read Sam found 6 rocks on Monday.
He found 3 rocks today.
How many rocks did Sam find in all?

Plan Write the number of rocks found each day.
Write a number sentence to find how many in all.

Write 6 + 3 = 9

Sam found 9 rocks in all.

Check Use ▪ to act it out.

fold

Copyright © by William H. Sadlier, Inc. All rights reserved.

Introduction to

Problem Solving

This magazine belongs to

____

To be a super
problem solver,
use these steps.

Read Read the problem.
Study the facts.
Know what the question asks.

Plan What will you do to solve the problem?

Write Work your plan.
Write your answer.
Make sure to label your answer.

Check Does your answer make sense?
Work the problem a different way.
Did you get the same answer?

Here are some problem-solving strategies.

Act It Out

Draw a Picture

Use a Pattern

Choose the Operation

Logical Reasoning

Make a Table

Use a Graph

Use a Map

Use More Than One Step

Guess and Test

Make an Organized List

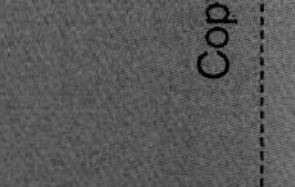

Copyright © by William H. Sadlier, Inc. All rights reserved.

Use this strategy: Logical Reasoning.

Read In a race the  finished before the 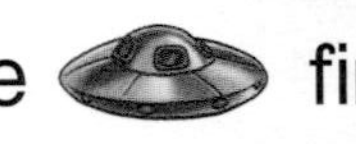. The 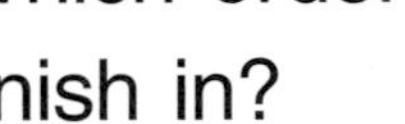 finished first. Which order did the finish in?

Plan Draw each on a separate index card. Move the cards around to solve the problem.

Write The order is

   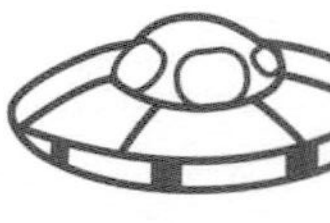

1st 2nd 3rd

Check Act it out with your classmates.

CHAPTER 1

Addition and Subtraction Facts

Listen

Listen to your teacher read the poem.

Are there fewer butterfly fish than angelfish—or more?

Copyright © by William H. Sadlier, Inc. All rights reserved.

Dear Family,

Today our class began Chapter 1. We will learn about adding and subtracting numbers through 20. Let's do the activity below together so I can review the skills I will need in order to understand the math in this chapter. Then you can read some of the new vocabulary I will learn in Chapter 1.

Love, ______________

Naming Numbers

Have your child make designs by gluing 6 paper strips on sheets of paper. Each design should have a different number of red and blue paper strips. Ask your child to tell you how many red strips and how many blue strips can make 6 for each design.

Chapter 1 Vocabulary

also on-line

part + part = whole
6 + 2 = 8

whole − part = part
8 − 2 = 6

addend + addend = sum
5 + 3 = 8

doubles fact 8 + 8 = 16

doubles + 1 8 + 9 = 17

doubles − 1 8 + 7 = 15

related addition facts

6 + 8 = 14 8 + 6 = 14

related subtraction facts

17 − 9 = 8 17 − 8 = 9

fact family

$$\begin{array}{r} 5 \\ +8 \\ \hline 13 \end{array} \quad \begin{array}{r} 8 \\ +5 \\ \hline 13 \end{array} \quad \begin{array}{r} 13 \\ -5 \\ \hline 8 \end{array} \quad \begin{array}{r} 13 \\ -8 \\ \hline 5 \end{array}$$

For Additional Resources VISIT US ON-LINE www.sadlier-oxford.com

Name ____________________

Addition Concepts

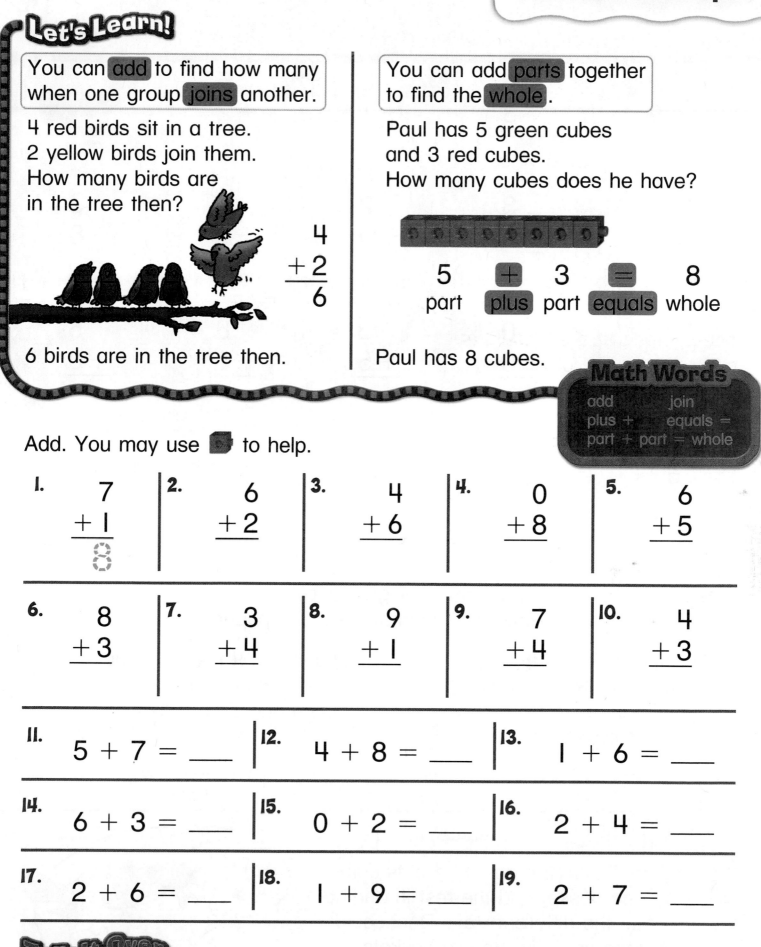

Let's Learn!

You can **add** to find how many when one group **joins** another.

4 red birds sit in a tree.
2 yellow birds join them.
How many birds are in the tree then?

$$\begin{array}{r} 4 \\ +2 \\ \hline 6 \end{array}$$

6 birds are in the tree then.

You can add **parts** together to find the **whole**.

Paul has 5 green cubes and 3 red cubes.
How many cubes does he have?

5	+	3	=	8
part	plus	part	equals	whole

Paul has 8 cubes.

Math Words

add — join
plus + — equals =
part + part = whole

Add. You may use cubes to help.

1. $\begin{array}{r} 7 \\ +1 \\ \hline 8 \end{array}$
2. $\begin{array}{r} 6 \\ +2 \\ \hline \end{array}$
3. $\begin{array}{r} 4 \\ +6 \\ \hline \end{array}$
4. $\begin{array}{r} 0 \\ +8 \\ \hline \end{array}$
5. $\begin{array}{r} 6 \\ +5 \\ \hline \end{array}$
6. $\begin{array}{r} 8 \\ +3 \\ \hline \end{array}$
7. $\begin{array}{r} 3 \\ +4 \\ \hline \end{array}$
8. $\begin{array}{r} 9 \\ +1 \\ \hline \end{array}$
9. $\begin{array}{r} 7 \\ +4 \\ \hline \end{array}$
10. $\begin{array}{r} 4 \\ +3 \\ \hline \end{array}$

11. 5 + 7 = ___
12. 4 + 8 = ___
13. 1 + 6 = ___
14. 6 + 3 = ___
15. 0 + 2 = ___
16. 2 + 4 = ___
17. 2 + 6 = ___
18. 1 + 9 = ___
19. 2 + 7 = ___

20. Name the parts and the whole in 5 + 4 = 9.

Copyright © by William H. Sadlier, Inc. All rights reserved.

Practice

Add.

21. 2 + 9 = 11	22. 5 + 3	23. 0 + 1	24. 5 + 2	
25. 7 + 5	26. 3 + 6	27. 2 + 0	28. 4 + 7	29. 3 + 8
30. 2 + 5	31. 0 + 0	32. 3 + 5	33. 8 + 1	34. 5 + 0

35. 6 + 4 = ___	36. 0 + 7 = ___	37. 3 + 1 = ___
38. 3 + 0 = ___	39. 3 + 9 = ___	40. 5 + 6 = ___

Solve. Use a problem-solving strategy.
Show your work on a separate sheet of paper.

41. 8 cats sit near a tree. 4 more cats come to sit. How many cats sit near the tree then?

___ cats

42. Leon has 4 fish. Terri has 5 fish. How many fish do Leon and Terri have?

___ fish

CHALLENGE

MATH JOURNAL

43. Dani finds 12 crabs. She puts some in one basket and the rest in another. Write the different ways Dani could put the crabs in the two baskets.

Math Alive at Home Ask your child to choose 2 numbers from 0 through 6 and then to add them. Have your child repeat this several times with other numbers.

Name ______________________________

Find Extra Information

• You can reread a problem to see which information you need and which information you do not need. The information you do not need is called **extra information**.

Listen
Eric sees 3 owls at the nature center. Then he sees 6 hawks. He stays for 2 hours. How many birds does Eric see?

1. Reread the problem. Draw a line under the question you need to answer.

2. How many owls does Eric see? Use a blue crayon to circle the part of the problem that tells how many. ____ owls

3. How many hawks does Eric see? Use a red crayon to circle the part of the problem that tells how many. ____ hawks

4. Cross out the extra information.

5. Now add to solve the problem.

____ + ____ = ____

Eric sees ____ birds.

Copyright © by William H. Sadlier, Inc. All rights reserved.

Practice

Find Extra Information

Listen
Sara takes care of animals at the animal shelter. She walks 5 dogs. She also feeds 7 cats. 6 of the cats are kittens. How many animals does Sara take care of?

6. Reread the problem. Draw a line under the question you need to answer.

7. How many dogs does Sara walk? Use a blue crayon to circle the part of the problem that tells how many. ____ dogs

8. How many cats does Sara feed? Use a red crayon to circle the part of the problem that tells how many. ____ cats

9. Cross out the extra information.

10. Now add to solve the problem. ____ + ____ = ____

Sara takes care of ____ animals.

Math Alive at Home Today your child used Find Extra Information to work through math problems.

Name ________________________________

Related Addition Facts

You can add in any **order**.

These facts use the same numbers.

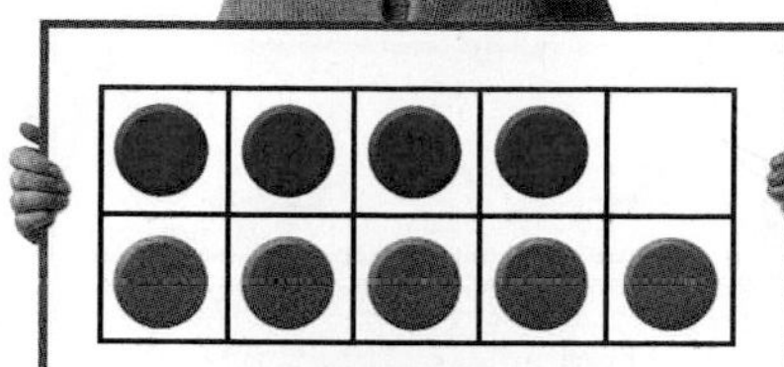

$$\begin{array}{r} 4 \\ +5 \\ \hline 9 \end{array} \qquad \begin{array}{r} 5 \\ +4 \\ \hline 9 \end{array}$$

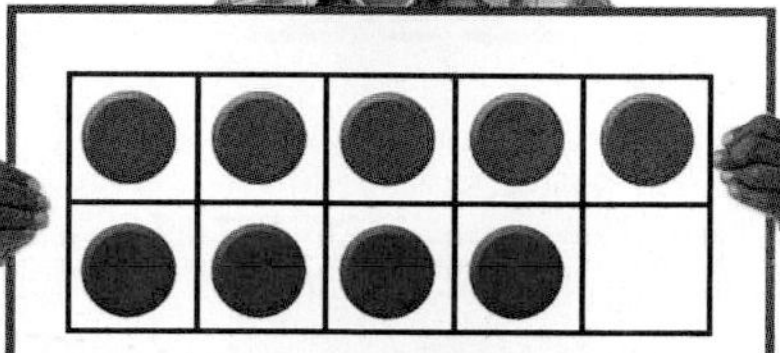

These are **related addition facts**.

Math Words
related addition facts
order

Find the sum. Write the related addition fact.

1. $\begin{array}{r} 0 \\ +9 \\ \hline 9 \end{array}$ $\begin{array}{r} 9 \\ +0 \\ \hline 9 \end{array}$	**2.** $\begin{array}{r} 5 \\ +6 \\ \hline \end{array}$ $\begin{array}{r} \square \\ +\square \\ \hline \end{array}$	**3.** $\begin{array}{r} 7 \\ +2 \\ \hline \end{array}$ $\begin{array}{r} \square \\ +\square \\ \hline \end{array}$
4. $\begin{array}{r} 8 \\ +1 \\ \hline \end{array}$ $\begin{array}{r} \square \\ +\square \\ \hline \end{array}$	**5.** $\begin{array}{r} 9 \\ +3 \\ \hline \end{array}$ $\begin{array}{r} \square \\ +\square \\ \hline \end{array}$	**6.** $\begin{array}{r} 1 \\ +9 \\ \hline \end{array}$ $\begin{array}{r} \square \\ +\square \\ \hline \end{array}$
7. 5 + 0 = ___ ___ + ___ = ___	**8.** 2 + 8 = ___ ___ + ___ = ___	**9.** 4 + 7 = ___ ___ + ___ = ___
10. 5 + 3 = ___ ___ + ___ = ___	**11.** 2 + 6 = ___ ___ + ___ = ___	**12.** 5 + 7 = ___ ___ + ___ = ___

13. Explain why 4 + 5 = 5 + 4.

Copyright © by William H. Sadlier, Inc. All rights reserved.

Practice

Find the sum. Write the related addition fact.

14. 6 + 0 = 6
0 + 6 = 6

15. 8 + 4 = ___
___ + ___ = ___

16. 3 + 6 = ___
___ + ___ = ___

17. 2 + 9 = ___
___ + ___ = ___

18. 7 + 2 = ___
___ + ___ = ___

19. $\begin{array}{r} 5 \\ +4 \\ \hline \end{array}$ $\begin{array}{r} \square \\ +\square \\ \hline \end{array}$

20. $\begin{array}{r} 7 \\ +5 \\ \hline \end{array}$ $\begin{array}{r} \square \\ +\square \\ \hline \end{array}$

21. $\begin{array}{r} 3 \\ +8 \\ \hline \end{array}$ $\begin{array}{r} \square \\ +\square \\ \hline \end{array}$

Solve. Use a problem-solving strategy.
Show your work on a separate sheet of paper.

22. Kay finds 4 clams and 2 shells at the beach. Then she finds 6 more clams. How many clams does she find?

___ clams

23. Jerry sees 6 ants march up an anthill. Then he sees 4 more ants. How many ants does he see?

___ ants

24. Write the addition fact shown on the number line.
Then write the related addition fact.

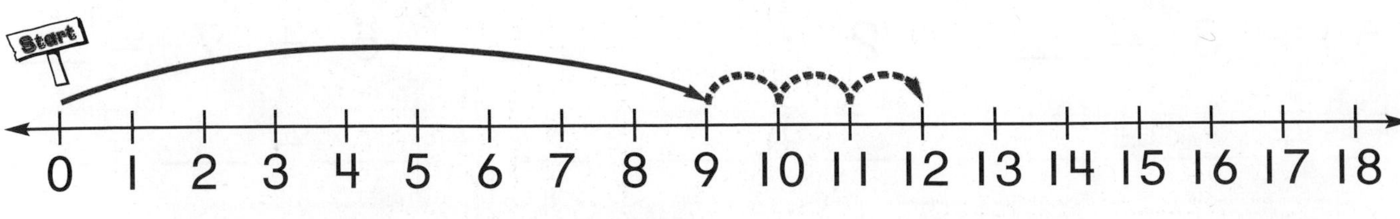

9 + ___ = ___ ___ + ___ = ___

Math Alive at Home Choose several addition facts from this lesson and ask your child to name the related addition fact.

Name ______________________

Let's Learn!

Numbers you add are called **addends**.

$3 + 5 = ?$

When one addend is 1, 2, or 3, start with the greater addend. **Count on** to find the sum.

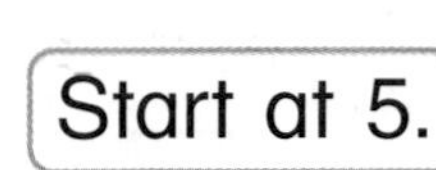

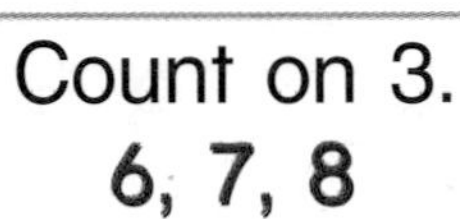

3	addend
+ 5	addend
8	**sum**

0 1 2 3 4 5 6 7 8 9 10 11 12

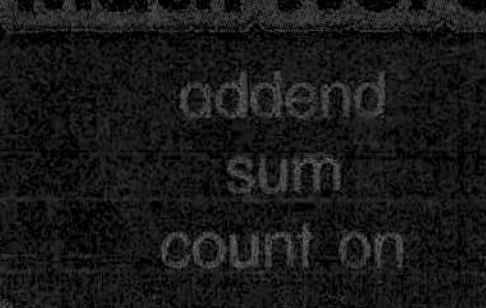

Circle the greater addend. Find it on the number line. Then count on to find the sum.

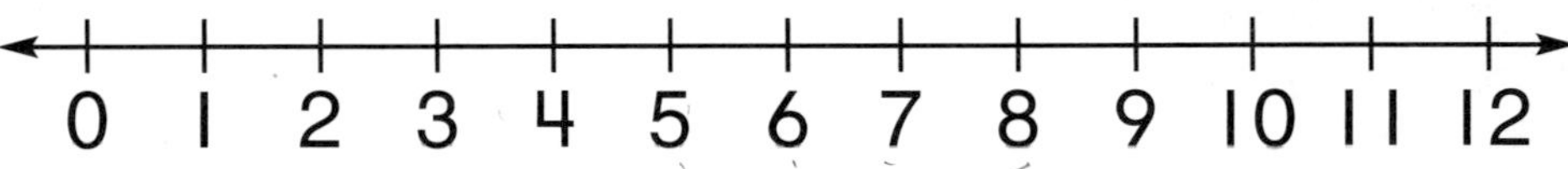

0 1 2 3 4 5 6 7 8 9 10 11 12

1. $7 + 1 =$ 8
2. $3 + 2 =$ 5
3. $2 + 8 =$ 10
4. $5 + 3 =$ 8
5. $1 + 4 =$ 5
6. $3 + 6 =$ 9
7. $5 + 1$ = 6
8. $7 + 2$ = 9
9. $1 + 9$ = 10
10. $2 + 6$ = 8
11. $3 + 7$ = 10
12. $9 + 3$ = 12
13. $2 + 4$ = 6
14. $1 + 5$ = 6
15. $9 + 2$ = 11
16. $4 + 3$ = 7

17. Explain how you can find the sum of $2 + 7$ on a number line.

Copyright © by William H. Sadlier, Inc. All rights reserved.

Practice

Count on to add 1, 2, or 3.

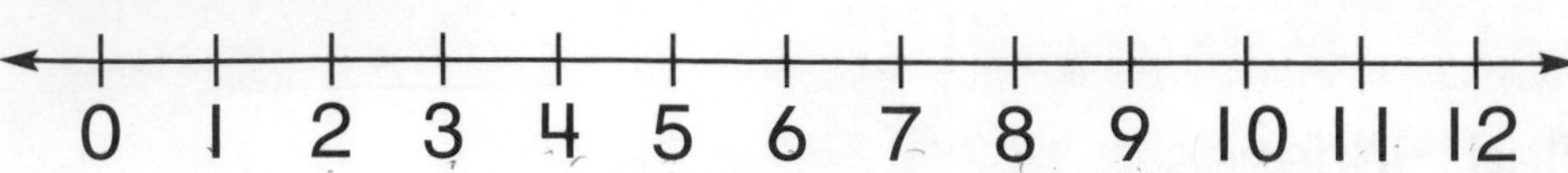

Find the sum. You can use a number line.

18. 1 + 8 = ___	**19.** 8 + 3 = ___	**20.** 6 + 1 = ___
21. 5 + 2 = ___	**22.** 3 + 5 = ___	**23.** 6 + 2 = ___
24. 2 + 8 = ___	**25.** 4 + 2 = ___	**26.** 9 + 1 = ___

27. 3 + 1	**28.** 7 + 3	**29.** 1 + 7	**30.** 2 + 9	**31.** 2 + 7
32. 6 + 3	**33.** 2 + 3	**34.** 1 + 2	**35.** 3 + 9	**36.** 3 + 8

Solve. Use a problem-solving strategy.
Show your work on a separate sheet of paper.

37. 4 turtles and 3 fish swim in the pond. 1 more turtle comes to swim. How many turtles swim then?

___ turtles

38. A frog jumps from a log. Then the frog jumps 6 more times. How many times does the frog jump?

___ times

CRITICAL THINKING

39. There are 9 dogs in the park. Some of them are light. Some are dark. Write the different ways to show how many light dogs and dark dogs could be in the park.

Math Alive at Home Have your child count on to add 5 + 1, 9 + 2, and 7 + 3. (6, 11, 10)

Extend Facts to 20

Name ________________________________

Let's Learn!

Addition sentences use the symbols + and =.

This is an addition sentence.

10 + 8 = 18

These are related addition sentences.

10 + 9 = 19
9 + 10 = 19

Math Words
addition sentence

Find the sum.

1. $\begin{array}{r} 8 \\ +5 \\ \hline 13 \end{array}$

2. $\begin{array}{r} 7 \\ +7 \\ \hline \end{array}$

3. $\begin{array}{r} 8 \\ +9 \\ \hline \end{array}$

4. $\begin{array}{r} 6 \\ +7 \\ \hline \end{array}$

5. $\begin{array}{r} 9 \\ +5 \\ \hline \end{array}$

6. $\begin{array}{r} 7 \\ +9 \\ \hline \end{array}$

7. $\begin{array}{r} 9 \\ +4 \\ \hline \end{array}$

8. $\begin{array}{r} 7 \\ +6 \\ \hline \end{array}$

9. $\begin{array}{r} 7 \\ +8 \\ \hline \end{array}$

10. $\begin{array}{r} 8 \\ +6 \\ \hline \end{array}$

11. 6 + 8 = ___
12. 8 + 7 = ___
13. 9 + 10 = ___
14. 9 + 8 = ___
15. 4 + 9 = ___
16. 10 + 10 = ___

Talk It Over

17. How are 6 + 8 = 14 and $\begin{array}{r} 6 \\ +8 \\ \hline 14 \end{array}$ alike?
How are they different?

Copyright © by William H. Sadlier, Inc. All rights reserved.

Practice

The addends are the numbers in the first column and first row. The sums are inside the addition table.

18. Write the missing sums.

+	0	1	2	3	4	5	6	7	8	9	10
0	0	1	2	3	4	5	6	7	8	9	10
1	1	2	3								
2		3		5	6		8				
3	3		5		7						
4				7						13	
5		6			9						
6	6		8								
7				10							
8		9								17	
9											
10											

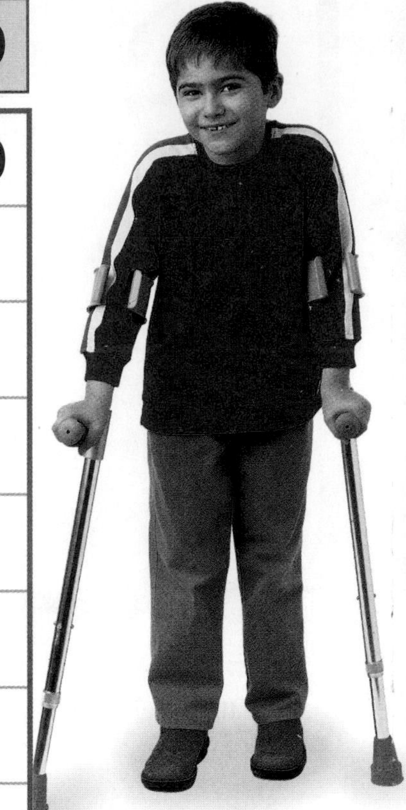

TEST PREPARATION

Fill in the circle under the correct answer.

19. Matt looked at puppies for 10 minutes and at kittens for 9 minutes. How many minutes did Matt look at the animals?

14 ○ 　16 ○　17 ○ 　19 ○

Math Alive at Home Ask your child to choose 2 numbers from 5 through 10 and then to add them. Have your child repeat this activity several times with other numbers from 5 through 10.

Check Your Progress
Lessons 1-5

Name ______________________

TEST PREPARATION

Listen to your teacher read the directions.
Fill in the circle under the correct answer.

1. $3 + 4$

2 ○ 6 ○ 7 ○ 4 ○

2. $8 + 3 = ?$

3 ○ 11 ○ 12 ○ 8 ○

3. $10 + 9$

10 ○ 18 ○ 9 ○ 19 ○

4. $8 + 9 = 17$

$7 + 9 = 16$ ○ $9 + 8 = 17$ ○

$10 + 9 = 19$ ○ $10 + 10 = 20$ ○

5. $2 + 9$

10 ○ 12 ○ 11 ○ 13 ○

6. $7 + 5$

12 ○ 6 ○ 13 ○ 7 ○

7. $0 + 5 = ?$

0 ○ 5 ○ 15 ○ 4 ○

8. $8 + 4$

12 ○ 6 ○ 14 ○ 7 ○

9. $6 + 3 = 9$

$3 + 6 = 9$ ○ $6 + 6 = 12$ ○

$6 + 5 = 11$ ○ $3 + 3 = 6$ ○

10. $8 + 7$

13 ○ 14 ○ 16 ○ 15 ○

Copyright © by William H. Sadlier, Inc. All rights reserved.

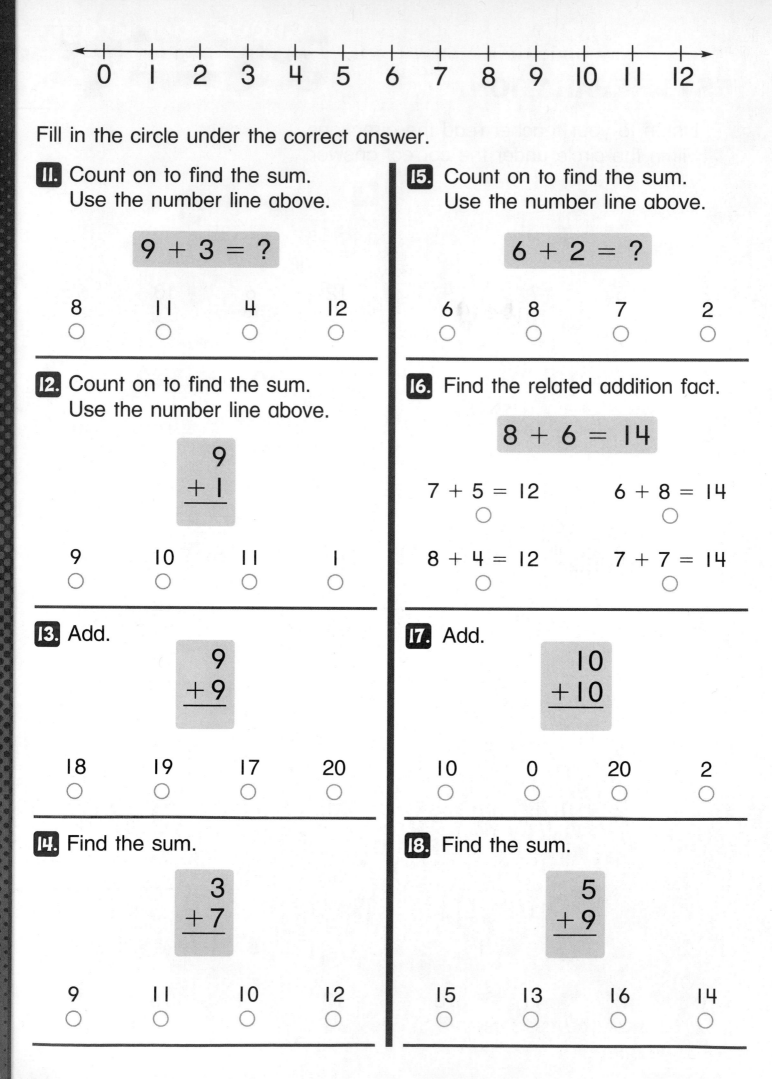

0 1 2 3 4 5 6 7 8 9 10 11 12

Fill in the circle under the correct answer.

11. Count on to find the sum.
Use the number line above.

$9 + 3 = ?$

8 ○ 11 ○ 4 ○ 12 ○

12. Count on to find the sum.
Use the number line above.

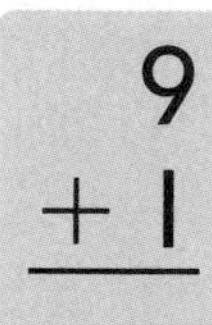

9 ○ 10 ○ 11 ○ 1 ○

13. Add.

$$\begin{array}{r} 9 \\ +9 \\ \hline \end{array}$$

18 ○ 19 ○ 17 ○ 20 ○

14. Find the sum.

$$\begin{array}{r} 3 \\ +7 \\ \hline \end{array}$$

9 ○ 11 ○ 10 ○ 12 ○

15. Count on to find the sum.
Use the number line above.

$6 + 2 = ?$

6 ○ 8 ○ 7 ○ 2 ○

16. Find the related addition fact.

$8 + 6 = 14$

$7 + 5 = 12$ ○ $6 + 8 = 14$ ○

$8 + 4 = 12$ ○ $7 + 7 = 14$ ○

17. Add.

$$\begin{array}{r} 10 \\ +10 \\ \hline \end{array}$$

10 ○ 0 ○ 20 ○ 2 ○

18. Find the sum.

$$\begin{array}{r} 5 \\ +9 \\ \hline \end{array}$$

15 ○ 13 ○ 16 ○ 14 ○

Name ______________________________

Make 10 to Add

Let's Learn!

8 + 7 = ?

When one addend is 8 or 9, you can add by **making 10**. Break apart 7 to make 10.

8 + 7 = ?

8 + 2 + 5 = ?

10 + 5 = 15

So 8 + 7 = 15.

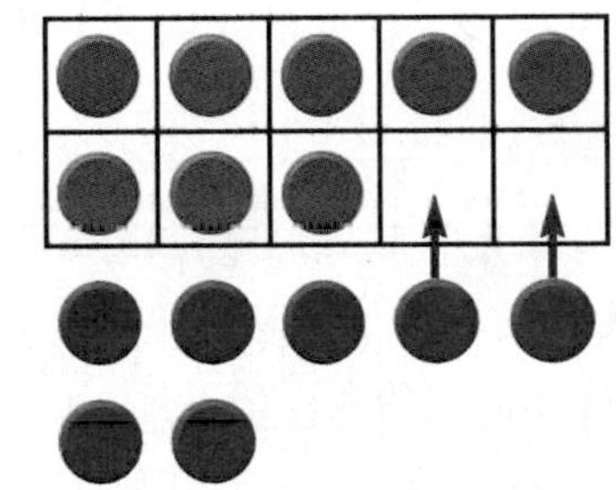

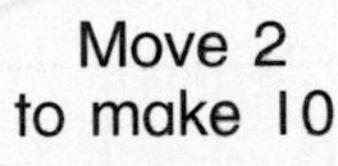

Move 2 to make 10.

$$\begin{array}{r} 8 \\ +7 \\ \hline 15 \end{array}$$

Math Words

make 10

Add by making 10.
Draw ● and ● to help.

1. 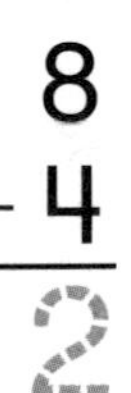

$$\begin{array}{r} 8 \\ +4 \\ \hline 12 \end{array}$$

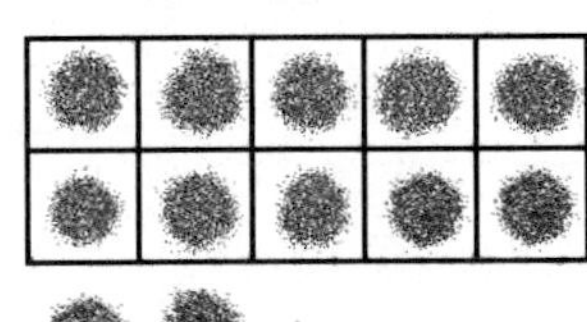

2.

$$\begin{array}{r} 9 \\ +9 \\ \hline \end{array}$$

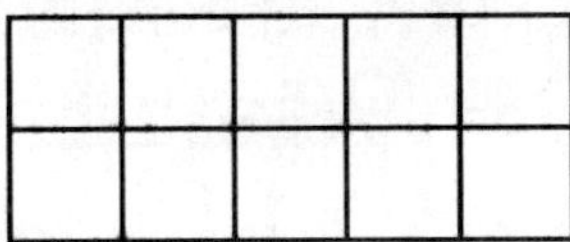

3.

$$\begin{array}{r} 9 \\ +3 \\ \hline \end{array}$$

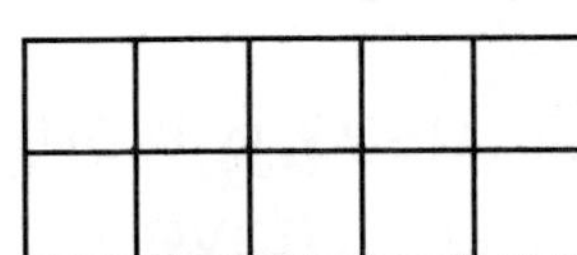

4.

$$\begin{array}{r} 8 \\ +5 \\ \hline \end{array}$$

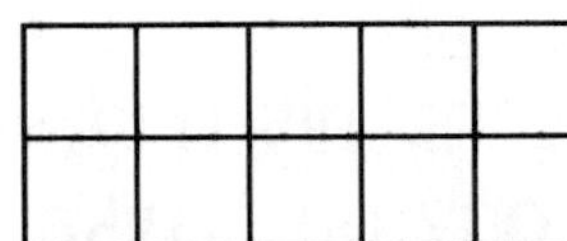

5. 9 + 5 = ____

6. 9 + 4 = ____

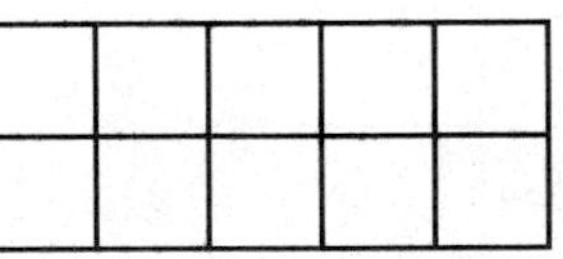

7. 8 + 8 = ____

8. 9 + 8 = ____

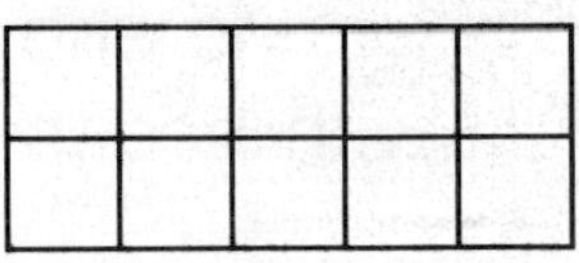

Talk It Over

9. Explain how you used a ten-frame to help find the sum of 9 + 8.

Copyright © by William H. Sadlier, Inc. All rights reserved.

Practice

Find the sum. Use a ten-frame to help.

10. $\begin{array}{r} 8 \\ +5 \\ \hline 13 \end{array}$

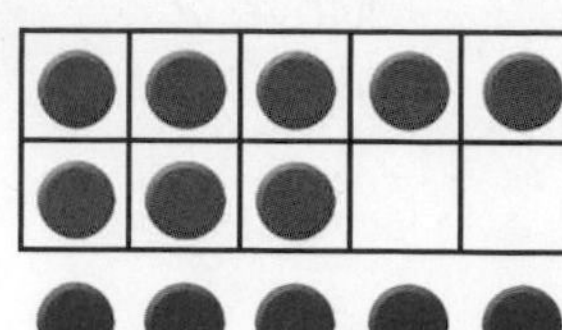

11. $\begin{array}{r} 6 \\ +9 \\ \hline \end{array}$

12. $\begin{array}{r} 9 \\ +7 \\ \hline \end{array}$

13. $\begin{array}{r} 8 \\ +6 \\ \hline \end{array}$

14. $\begin{array}{r} 9 \\ +6 \\ \hline \end{array}$

15. $\begin{array}{r} 8 \\ +7 \\ \hline \end{array}$

16. $\begin{array}{r} 5 \\ +8 \\ \hline \end{array}$

17. $\begin{array}{r} 5 \\ +9 \\ \hline \end{array}$

18. $\begin{array}{r} 7 \\ +8 \\ \hline \end{array}$

19. $\begin{array}{r} 8 \\ +9 \\ \hline \end{array}$

20. $\begin{array}{r} 4 \\ +8 \\ \hline \end{array}$

21. $\begin{array}{r} 3 \\ +8 \\ \hline \end{array}$

22. $4 + 9 =$ ___

23. $9 + 8 =$ ___

24. $3 + 9 =$ ___

Solve. Use a problem-solving strategy.
Show your work on a separate sheet of paper.

25. Max and his dad see 7 deer one day on a hike. They see 9 deer the next day. How many deer do they see?

___ deer

26. Linda uses 6 worms to fish in the lake. Steve uses 8 worms. They catch 4 fish. How many worms do they use?

___ worms

CHALLENGE

27. Donna shows 10¢ nine different ways with heads and tails. Finish her table.

heads	9¢	8¢							
tails	1¢	2¢							

Math Alive at Home Have your child use objects to show and explain how to make 10 when adding 8 + 7.

Name ______________________________

Algebra

Doubles Facts

Let's Learn!

Lee puts 3 stickers on the left page of her sticker book. She puts 3 stickers on the right page. How many stickers does she put in her book?

When both addends are the same number, the fact is called a **doubles fact**.

$3 + 3 = 6$

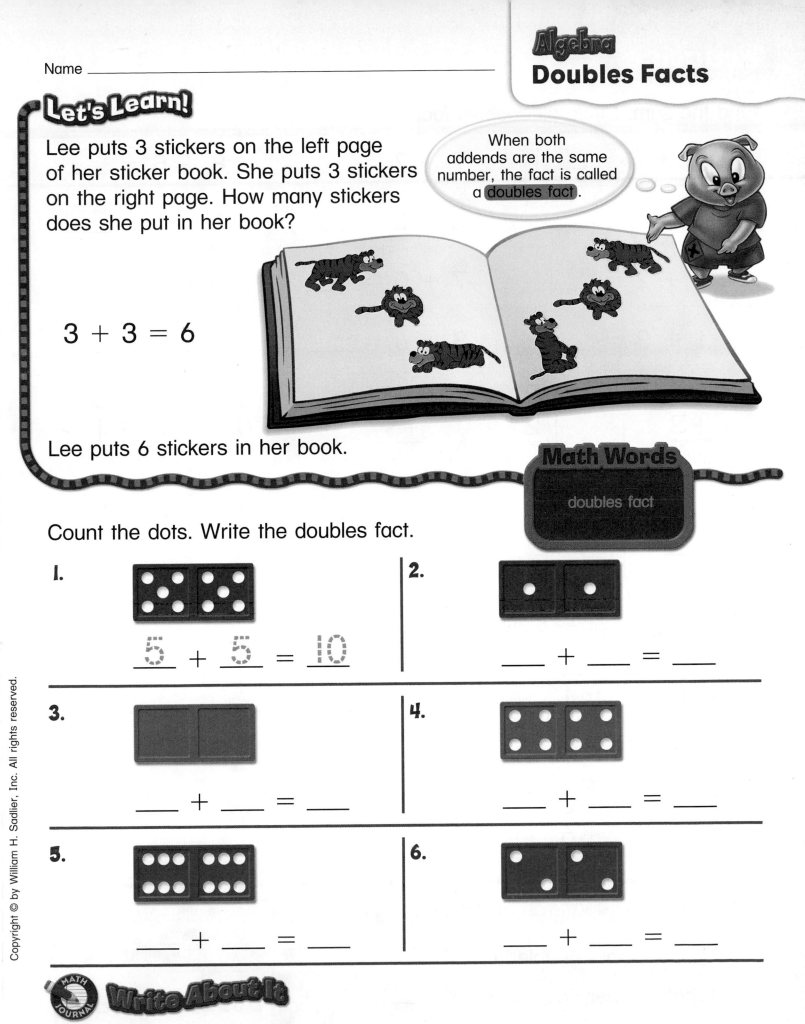

Lee puts 6 stickers in her book.

Math Words
doubles fact

Count the dots. Write the doubles fact.

1. 

5 + 5 = 10

2. 

___ + ___ = ___

3. 

___ + ___ = ___

4. 

___ + ___ = ___

5. 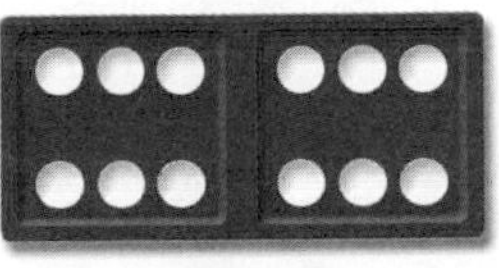

___ + ___ = ___

6. 

___ + ___ = ___

7. Write a doubles fact that is not on this page. Explain why it is a doubles fact.

Copyright © by William H. Sadlier, Inc. All rights reserved.

Practice

Find the sum. Circle all doubles facts.

8. 3 + 3 = 6 | 9. 7 + 7 = ___ | 10. 8 + 5 = ___

11. 9 + 9 = ___ | 12. 6 + 8 = ___ | 13. 1 + 1 = ___

14. 7 + 2 = ___ | 15. 7 + 0 = ___ | 16. 5 + 5 = ___

17. 1 + 3 = ___ | 18. 3 + 6 = ___ | 19. 6 + 6 = ___

20. $5 + 3$ | 21. $2 + 2$ | 22. $7 + 9$ | 23. $0 + 0$ | 24. $6 + 1$

25. $10 + 10$ | 26. $5 + 4$ | 27. $8 + 8$ | 28. $9 + 4$ | 29. $4 + 4$

Complete the doubles pattern.

30. $0 + 0$ $1 + 1$ $2 + 2$ ☐ + ☐   ☐ + ☐   ☐ + ☐

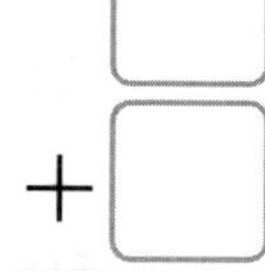

31. $5 + 5$ $6 + 6$ $7 + 7$ ☐ + ☐   ☐ + ☐   ☐ + ☐

CRITICAL THINKING 

32. What number doubled is 16? ___

33. What number doubled is 10? ___

34. What number doubled is 14? ___

Math Alive at Home Ask your child to use objects to show a doubles fact. Then have your child tell you the sum of the addends.

Name ____

Doubles +1, Doubles −1

Let's Learn!

You can use doubles facts to help find other sums.

Doubles	Doubles +1	Doubles −1
6 + 6 = 12	6 + 7 = ?	6 + 5 = ?
	Think 6 + 6 = 12. Since 7 is one more than 6, 6 + 7 is one more than 6 + 6.	**Think** 6 + 6 = 12. Since 5 is one less than 6, 6 + 5 is one less than 6 + 6.
	6 + 7 = 13	6 + 5 = 11

Math Words
doubles +1
doubles −1
one more one less

Complete the facts.

	Doubles	Doubles +1	Doubles −1
1.	3 + 3 = 6	3 + 4 = ___	3 + 2 = ___
2.	9 + ___ = ___	9 + ___ = ___	9 + ___ = ___
3.	5 + ___ = ___	5 + ___ = ___	5 + ___ = ___
4.	2 + ___ = ___	2 + ___ = ___	2 + ___ = ___
5.	7 + ___ = ___	7 + ___ = ___	7 + ___ = ___
6.	4 + ___ = ___	4 + ___ = ___	4 + ___ = ___

Talk It Over

7. How does knowing 9 + 9 = 18 help you add 9 + 8?

Copyright © by William H. Sadlier, Inc. All rights reserved.

Practice

Remember, you can use a doubles fact to help you.

Find the sum.

8. $4 + 5 =$ 9	9. $1 + 1 =$ ___	10. $8 + 8 =$ ___
11. $6 + 6 =$ ___	12. $6 + 7 =$ ___	13. $9 + 9 =$ ___
14. $7 + 8 =$ ___	15. $2 + 2 =$ ___	16. $7 + 7 =$ ___
17. $5 + 6 =$ ___	18. $1 + 2 =$ ___	19. $0 + 0 =$ ___
20. $0 + 1 =$ ___	21. $3 + 2 =$ ___	22. $8 + 9 =$ ___
23. $4 + 4 =$ ___	24. $1 + 0 =$ ___	25. $3 + 4 =$ ___

Write the answer.

26. Double 1. Write 1 more. 3	27. Double 4. Write 1 less. 7
28. Double 7. Write 1 less. ___	29. Double 9. Write 1 more. ___
30. Double 0. Write 1 more. ___	31. Double 6. Write 1 less. ___
32. Double 4. Write 1 more. ___	33. Double 8. Write 1 less. ___

CRITICAL THINKING

34. Henry saw 4 camels.
Fran saw 4 more than Henry.
José saw 1 more than Fran.

How many camels did Fran see? Fran saw ___ camels.

How many camels did José see? José saw ___ camels.

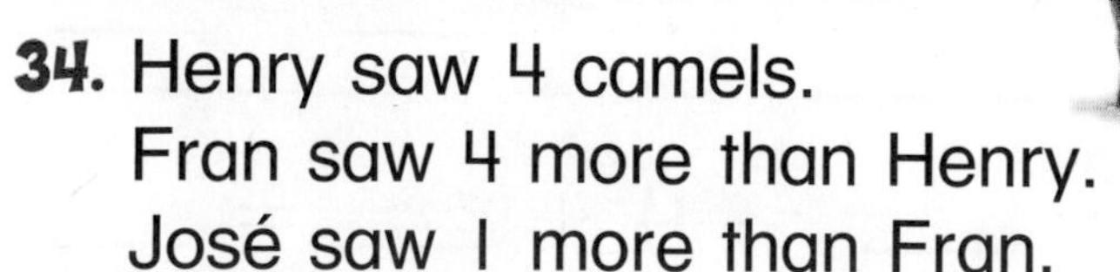

Math Alive at Home Ask your child to name the doubles fact that helps him/her find the sum of 6 + 7. (6 + 6)

Name ______________________

Algebra

Three Addends

Let's Learn!

You can group addends in different ways.

Add only two numbers at a time.

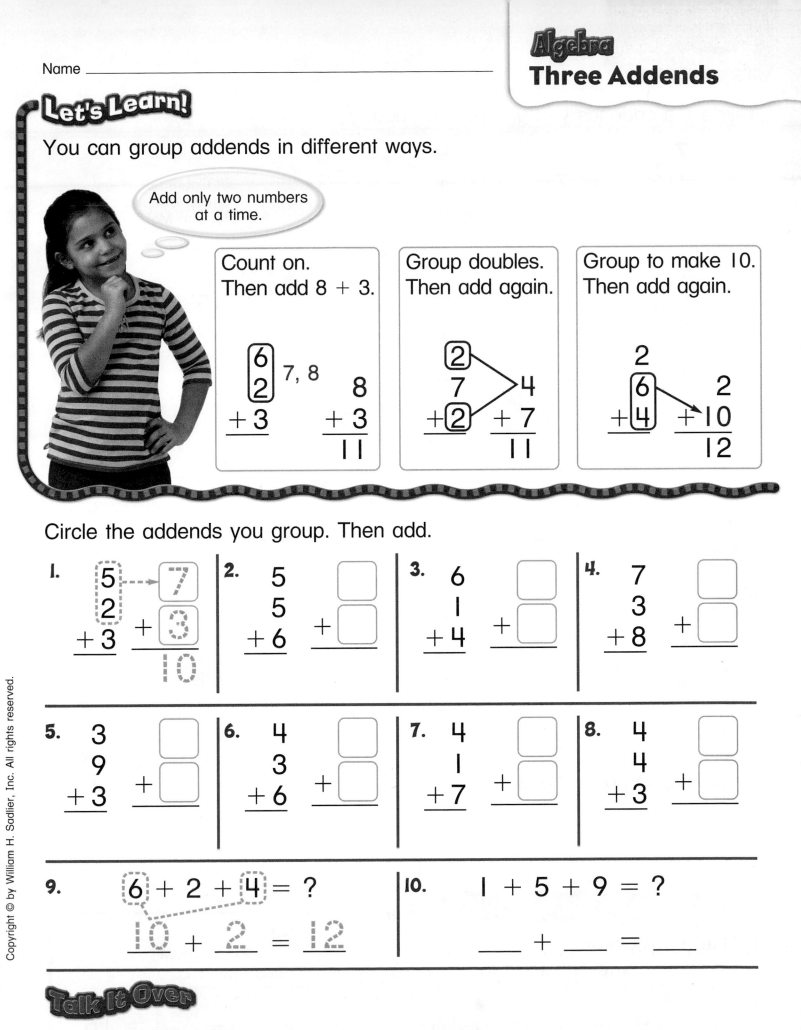

Count on. Then add 8 + 3.	Group doubles. Then add again.	Group to make 10. Then add again.
[6] [2] 7, 8 + 3 → 8 + 3 = 11	[2] 7 + [2] → 4 + 7 = 11	2 [6] + [4] → 2 + 10 = 12

Circle the addends you group. Then add.

1. 5 + 2 + 3 → 7 + 3 = 10
2. 5 + 5 + 6 → ☐ + ☐
3. 6 + 1 + 4 → ☐ + ☐
4. 7 + 3 + 8 → ☐ + ☐
5. 3 + 9 + 3 → ☐ + ☐
6. 4 + 3 + 6 → ☐ + ☐
7. 4 + 1 + 7 → ☐ + ☐
8. 4 + 4 + 3 → ☐ + ☐
9. 6 + 2 + 4 = ?

   10 + 2 = 12
10. 1 + 5 + 9 = ?

   ___ + ___ = ___

Talk It Over

11. Name all the different ways you can group the addends to add 2 + 2 + 8.

Copyright © by William H. Sadlier, Inc. All rights reserved.

Practice

Circle the addends you group. Then add.

12.	13.	14.	15.
7	4	9	6
1	7	1	3
+ 9	+ 4	+ 5	+ 3
17			

16.	17.	18.	19.	20.	21.
9	4	2	4	5	3
0	6	7	6	2	3
+ 1	+ 5	+ 1	+ 6	+ 4	+ 4

22. 1 + 8 + 2 = ___

23. 1 + 8 + 5 = ___

24. 2 + 6 + 8 = ___

25. 4 + 2 + 4 = ___

Solve. Use a problem-solving strategy.

26. Joe buys 2 red bugs and 1 bee. How much does he spend?

___¢ + ___¢ + ___¢ = ___¢

27. Susan buys 2 bees and 1 fish. How much does she spend?

___¢ + ___¢ + ___¢ = ___¢

CALCULATOR ACTIVITY

Use a calculator.
Show two different ways to make 16.

Hint Each addend must be less than 10.

28. ☐ + ☐ + ☐ = 16

29. ☐ + ☐ + ☐ = 16

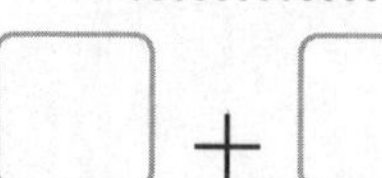

Math Alive at Home Ask your child to explain how he/she grouped the addends to solve exercises 12–25.

Name ______________________

Four Addends

Let's Learn!

Ways to Add Numbers
Count On
Group Doubles
Group to Make 10

You can use more than one way to add.
Add only two numbers at a time.

$$3 + 3 + 8 + 2 = ?$$

Group Doubles	Group to Make 10	Add
$\boxed{3}$		
$\boxed{3}$ →	6	
8	$\boxed{8}$	6
+ 2	+ $\boxed{2}$ →	+ 10
		16

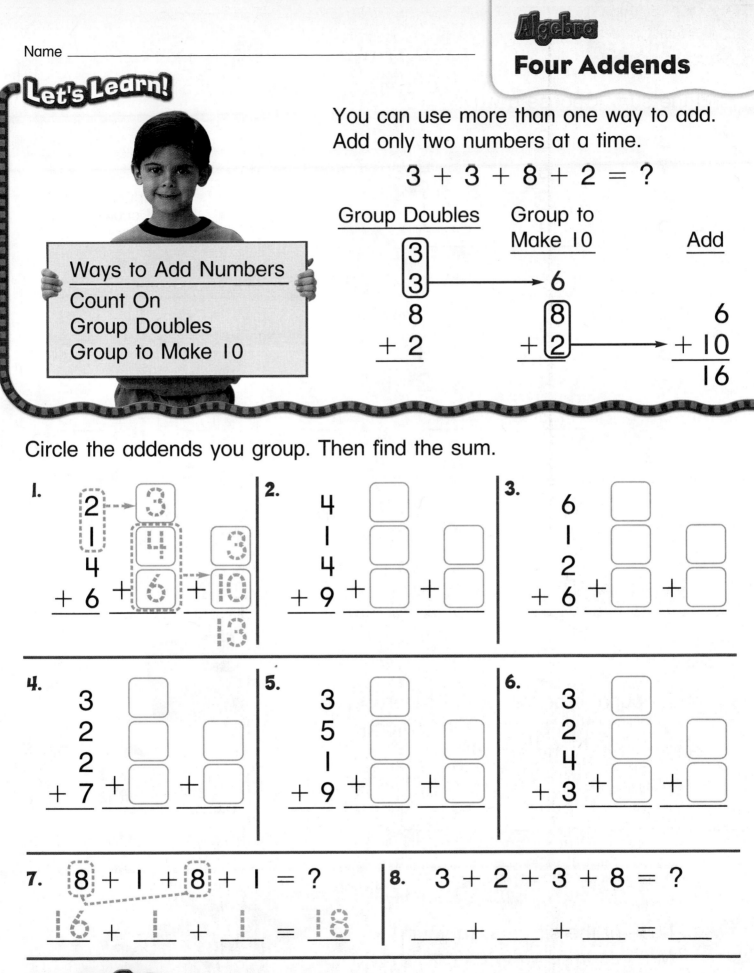

Circle the addends you group. Then find the sum.

1. 2 + 1 + 4 + 6: (2 + 1) → 3; 3 + 4 + 6: (4 + 6) → 10; 3 + 10 = 13

2. 4 + 1 + 4 + 9 = ☐ + ☐ + ☐ = ☐ + ☐ = ___

3. 6 + 1 + 2 + 6 = ☐ + ☐ + ☐ = ☐ + ☐ = ___

4. 3 + 2 + 2 + 7 = ☐ + ☐ + ☐ = ☐ + ☐ = ___

5. 3 + 5 + 1 + 9 = ☐ + ☐ + ☐ = ☐ + ☐ = ___

6. 3 + 2 + 4 + 3 = ☐ + ☐ + ☐ = ☐ + ☐ = ___

7. 8 + 1 + 8 + 1 = ?
16 + 1 + 1 = 18

8. 3 + 2 + 3 + 8 = ?
___ + ___ + ___ = ___

Talk It Over

9. Does the sum change if you use different ways to add? Explain.

Copyright © by William H. Sadlier, Inc. All rights reserved.

Practice

Find the sum. Choose a way.

10.
$$\begin{array}{r} 3 \\ 7 \\ 1 \\ +\ 2 \\ \hline \end{array}$$

11.
$$\begin{array}{r} 2 \\ 6 \\ 2 \\ +\ 4 \\ \hline \end{array}$$

12.
$$\begin{array}{r} 3 \\ 4 \\ 1 \\ +\ 6 \\ \hline \end{array}$$

13.
$$\begin{array}{r} 8 \\ 1 \\ 1 \\ +\ 2 \\ \hline \end{array}$$

14.
$$\begin{array}{r} 5 \\ 3 \\ 5 \\ +\ 3 \\ \hline \end{array}$$

15.
$$\begin{array}{r} 4 \\ 3 \\ 4 \\ +\ 2 \\ \hline \end{array}$$

16.
$$\begin{array}{r} 1 \\ 4 \\ 2 \\ +\ 5 \\ \hline \end{array}$$

17.
$$\begin{array}{r} 8 \\ 2 \\ 3 \\ +\ 3 \\ \hline \end{array}$$

18.
$$\begin{array}{r} 3 \\ 1 \\ 4 \\ +\ 7 \\ \hline \end{array}$$

19.
$$\begin{array}{r} 4 \\ 3 \\ 2 \\ +\ 5 \\ \hline \end{array}$$

20. $1 + 1 + 3 + 7 =$ ___

21. $4 + 1 + 2 + 8 =$ ___

22. $3 + 3 + 3 + 8 =$ ___

23. $3 + 4 + 2 + 7 =$ ___

Solve. Use a problem-solving strategy.

24. Nick bought a pencil for 8¢, an eraser for 2¢, and two stickers for 3¢ each. How much did he spend?

___¢ + ___¢ + ___¢ + ___¢ = ___¢

CRITICAL THINKING

25. Look at the stickers. In your Math Journal, write an addition problem with 4 addends. Solve it.

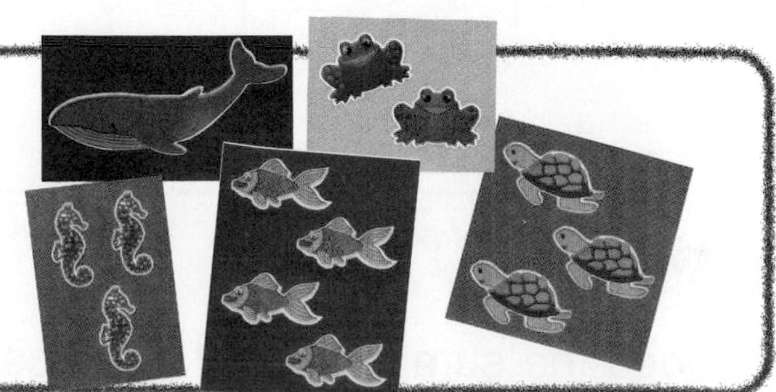

Math Alive at Home Have your child find the sum of 6+4+4+3 by making 10 or adding doubles first. (Add 6+4 to make 10 first or add 4+4 to group doubles.)

Name ______________________________

TEST PREPARATION

Listen to your teacher read the directions.
Fill in the circle under the correct answer.

1.

$$\begin{array}{r} 5 \\ +8 \\ \hline \end{array}$$

8 ○ 12 ○ 5 ○ 13 ○

2.

$3 + 3 = 6$ ○ $4 + 4 = 8$ ○

$6 + 0 = 6$ ○ $6 + 6 = 12$ ○

3.

$7 + 8 = ?$

14 ○ 15 ○ 16 ○ 17 ○

4.

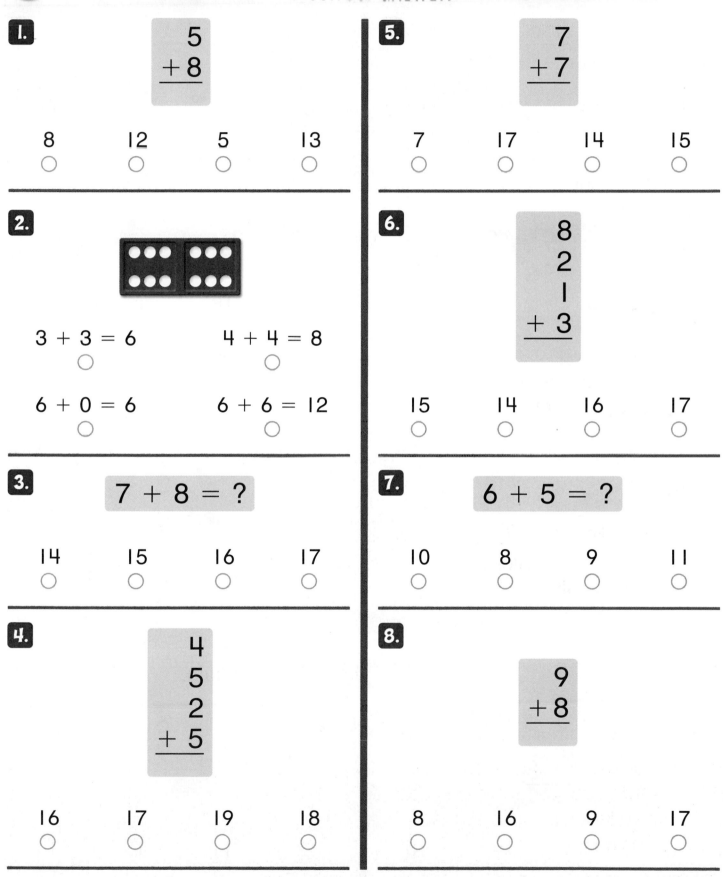

$$\begin{array}{r} 4 \\ 5 \\ 2 \\ +5 \\ \hline \end{array}$$

16 ○ 17 ○ 19 ○ 18 ○

5.

$$\begin{array}{r} 7 \\ +7 \\ \hline \end{array}$$

7 ○ 17 ○ 14 ○ 15 ○

6.

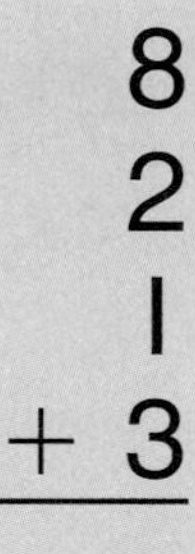

$$\begin{array}{r} 8 \\ 2 \\ 1 \\ +3 \\ \hline \end{array}$$

15 ○ 14 ○ 16 ○ 17 ○

7.

$6 + 5 = ?$

10 ○ 8 ○ 9 ○ 11 ○

8.

$$\begin{array}{r} 9 \\ +8 \\ \hline \end{array}$$

8 ○ 16 ○ 9 ○ 17 ○

Copyright © by William H. Sadlier, Inc. All rights reserved.

Fill in the circle under the correct answer.

9. Find the sum.

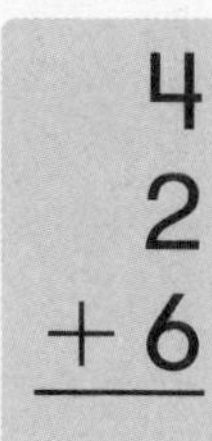

$$\begin{array}{r} 4 \\ 2 \\ +6 \\ \hline \end{array}$$

13 ○ 14 ○ 15 ○ 12 ○

10. Find the sum.

$7 + 9 = ?$

16 ○ 18 ○ 15 ○ 17 ○

11. Fill in the circle under the doubles fact.

$9 + 9 = 18$ ○ $8 + 9 = 17$ ○

$4 + 3 = 7$ ○ $5 + 7 = 12$ ○

12. Add.

$$\begin{array}{r} 4 \\ 5 \\ +6 \\ \hline \end{array}$$

16 ○ 15 ○ 14 ○ 10 ○

13. Add.

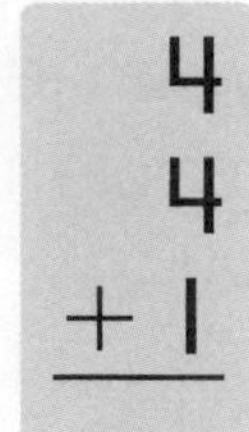

$$\begin{array}{r} 4 \\ 4 \\ +1 \\ \hline \end{array}$$

8 ○ 10 ○ 9 ○ 11 ○

14. Add.

$2 + 8 + 8 + 1 = ?$

19 ○ 18 ○ 17 ○ 16 ○

15. Find the sum.

$$\begin{array}{r} 2 \\ 3 \\ 2 \\ +3 \\ \hline \end{array}$$

8 ○ 5 ○ 10 ○ 9 ○

16. Find the sum.

$$\begin{array}{r} 6 \\ +7 \\ \hline \end{array}$$

12 ○ 11 ○ 13 ○ 14 ○

Name ______________________________

Subtraction Concepts

Let's Learn!

When you **take away** some from a group, you can **subtract** to find how many are left.

6 birds are in a tree.
Then 2 fly away.
How many birds are left?

$$\begin{array}{r} 6 \\ -\,2 \\ \hline 4 \end{array}$$

4 birds are left.

You can subtract to find one part of a whole.

Joan has 8 cubes. 3 are red.
The rest are blue.
How many are blue?

8 − 3 = 5
whole **minus** part equals part

5 cubes are blue.

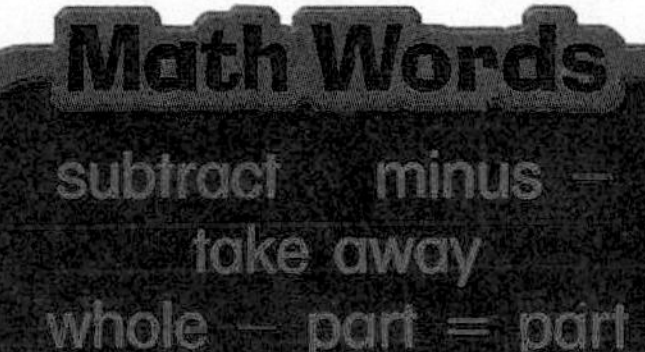

Subtract. You may use ▪ to help.

1. 8 − 4 = 4	2. 9 − 5 = ___	3. 10 − 3 = ___
4. 6 − 2 = ___	5. 11 − 3 = ___	6. 3 − 0 = ___
7. 8 − 6 = ___	8. 7 − 3 = ___	9. 12 − 6 = ___
10. 9 − 8 = ___	11. 6 − 0 = ___	12. 10 − 4 = ___
13. 12 − 8 = ___	14. 7 − 6 = ___	15. 6 − 5 = ___

16. $\begin{array}{r} 9 \\ -\,0 \\ \hline \end{array}$ 17. $\begin{array}{r} 12 \\ -\,5 \\ \hline \end{array}$ 18. $\begin{array}{r} 4 \\ -\,3 \\ \hline \end{array}$ 19. $\begin{array}{r} 1 \\ -\,0 \\ \hline \end{array}$ 20. $\begin{array}{r} 10 \\ -\,7 \\ \hline \end{array}$

21. Name the parts and the whole in 9 − 4 = 5.

Copyright © by William H. Sadlier, Inc. All rights reserved.

Practice

Subtract.

22. $10 - 8 =$ 2

23. $8 - 1 =$ ___

24. $6 - 4 =$ ___

25. $7 - 4 =$ ___

26. $4 - 4 =$ ___

27. $11 - 2 =$ ___

28. $6 - 3 =$ ___

29. $7 - 5 =$ ___

30. $5 - 4 =$ ___

31. $\begin{array}{r} 2 \\ -\,2 \\ \hline \end{array}$

32. $\begin{array}{r} 8 \\ -\,7 \\ \hline \end{array}$

33. $\begin{array}{r} 9 \\ -\,6 \\ \hline \end{array}$

34. $\begin{array}{r} 8 \\ -\,0 \\ \hline \end{array}$

35. $\begin{array}{r} 4 \\ -\,1 \\ \hline \end{array}$

Find the missing part.

To find the missing part, subtract.

36. whole: 8; part: 5; part: ?

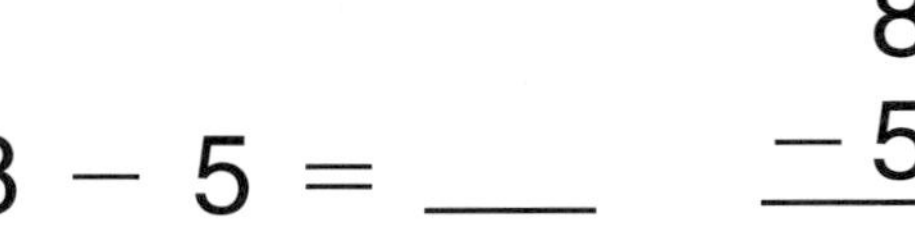

$8 - 5 =$ ___

$\begin{array}{r} 8 \\ -\,5 \\ \hline \end{array}$

37. whole: 12; part: 3; part: ?

$12 - 3 =$ ___

$\begin{array}{r} 12 \\ -\,3 \\ \hline \end{array}$

MENTAL MATH

Subtract.

38. $\begin{array}{r} 4 \\ -\,0 \\ \hline \end{array}$

39. $\begin{array}{r} 7 \\ -\,0 \\ \hline \end{array}$

40. $\begin{array}{r} 5 \\ -\,0 \\ \hline \end{array}$

41. $\begin{array}{r} 2 \\ -\,0 \\ \hline \end{array}$

42. $\begin{array}{r} 12 \\ -\,0 \\ \hline \end{array}$

MATH JOURNAL: In your Math Journal, tell what you notice about subtracting zero from a number.

Math Alive at Home Have your child model subtraction. Ask your child to take away part of 9 objects and tell you what part of the whole is left.

Name ______________________________

Count Back to Subtract

Let's Learn!

Kim has 11 fish in all.
She gives 3 to Mike.
How many fish does Kim have left?

$11 - 3 = ?$

To subtract 1, 2, or 3, **count back** from the number in all.

Start at 11.
Count back 3.
10, 9, 8

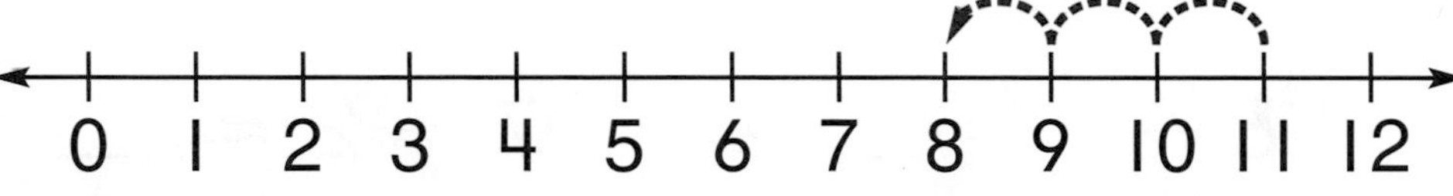

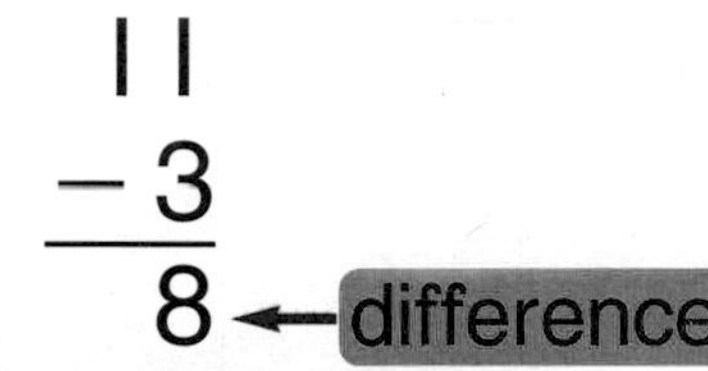

Kim has 8 fish left.

Math Words
count back
difference

Count back from the number in all to find the difference.

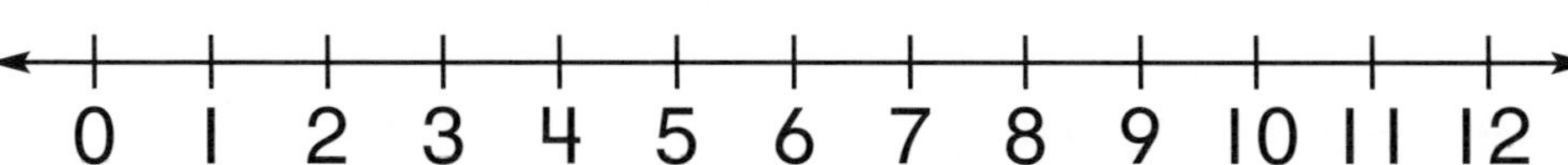

1. $7 - 3 =$ 4
2. $10 - 2 =$ ___
3. $12 - 3 =$ ___
4. $5 - 3 =$ ___
5. $4 - 1 =$ ___
6. $8 - 2 =$ ___
7. $9 - 3$
8. $7 - 2$
9. $8 - 3$
10. $6 - 2$
11. $3 - 1$
12. $4 - 2$
13. $1 - 1$
14. $11 - 2$
15. $9 - 2$
16. $10 - 3$

17. When you count back to subtract, is the last number you say the part taken away or the difference?

Copyright © by William H. Sadlier, Inc. All rights reserved.

Practice

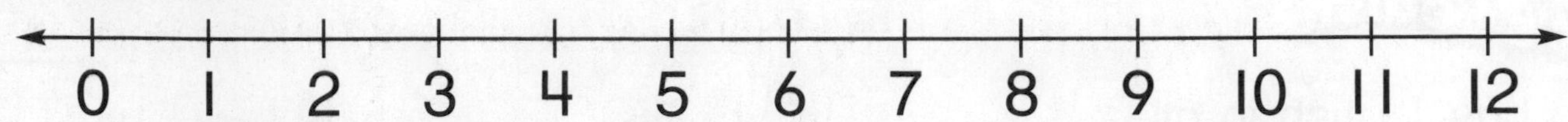

Find the difference. You can use a ←+++++→.

18. 4 − 2 = 2 | 19. 10 − 3 = ___ | 20. 8 − 3 = ___

21. 3 − 1 = ___ | 22. 6 − 2 = ___ | 23. 7 − 1 = ___

24. 9 − 2 = ___ | 25. 11 − 3 = ___ | 26. 9 − 1 = ___

27. 9 − 3 = ___ | 28. 6 − 1 = ___ | 29. 7 − 2 = ___

30. $\begin{array}{r} 10 \\ -2 \\ \hline \end{array}$ | 31. $\begin{array}{r} 8 \\ -2 \\ \hline \end{array}$ | 32. $\begin{array}{r} 7 \\ -3 \\ \hline \end{array}$ | 33. $\begin{array}{r} 4 \\ -1 \\ \hline \end{array}$ | 34. $\begin{array}{r} 10 \\ -1 \\ \hline \end{array}$

Solve. Use a problem-solving strategy.
Show your work on a separate sheet of paper.

35. 11 sheep are in the barn. 5 are eating. Then 2 run out to the field. How many sheep are still in the barn?

___ sheep

36. Nina has 10 butterfly stickers. 1 butterfly is red and the rest are blue. How many butterflies are blue?

___ butterflies

CHALLENGE

Subtract across and down to complete each table.

37.

12	8	4
6	2	
6		

38.

10	5	
4	1	

39.

11	9	
7	5	

Math Alive at Home Ask your child to use the number line at the top of this page to count back and subtract 5 - 1, 9 - 2, and 7 - 3. (4, 7, 4)

Name ______________________________

Algebra

Related Subtraction Facts

Let's Learn!

These are **related subtraction facts**.

The numbers are the same in each fact.

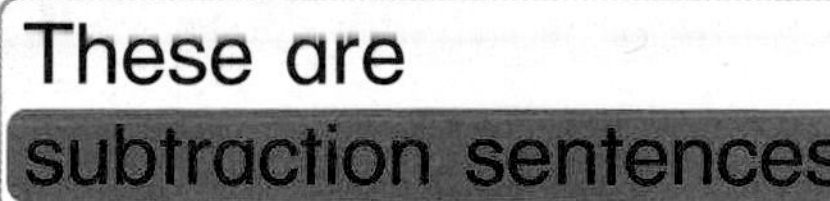
These are **subtraction sentences**.

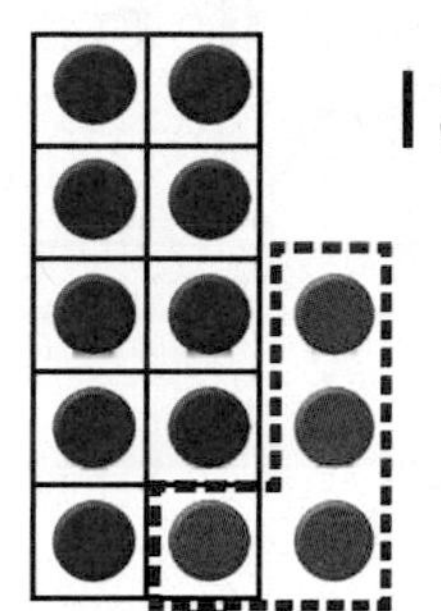
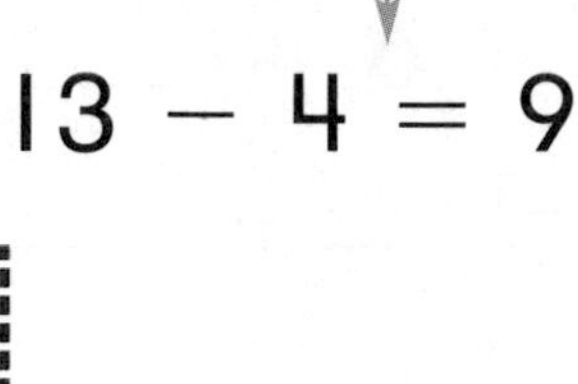

13 − 4 = 9

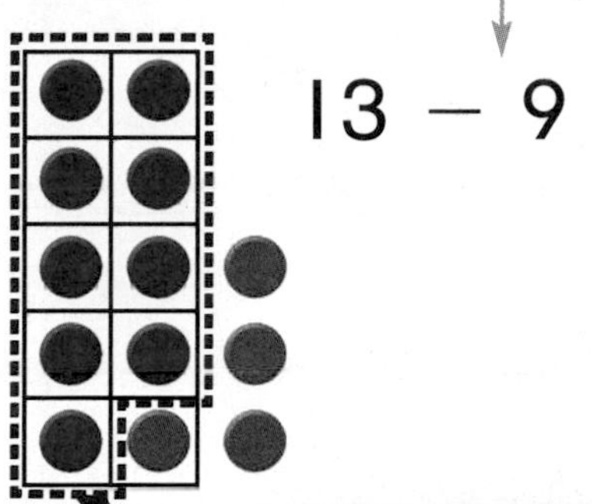

13 − 9 = 4

Math Words

related subtraction facts
subtraction sentence

Subtract. Write the related subtraction fact.

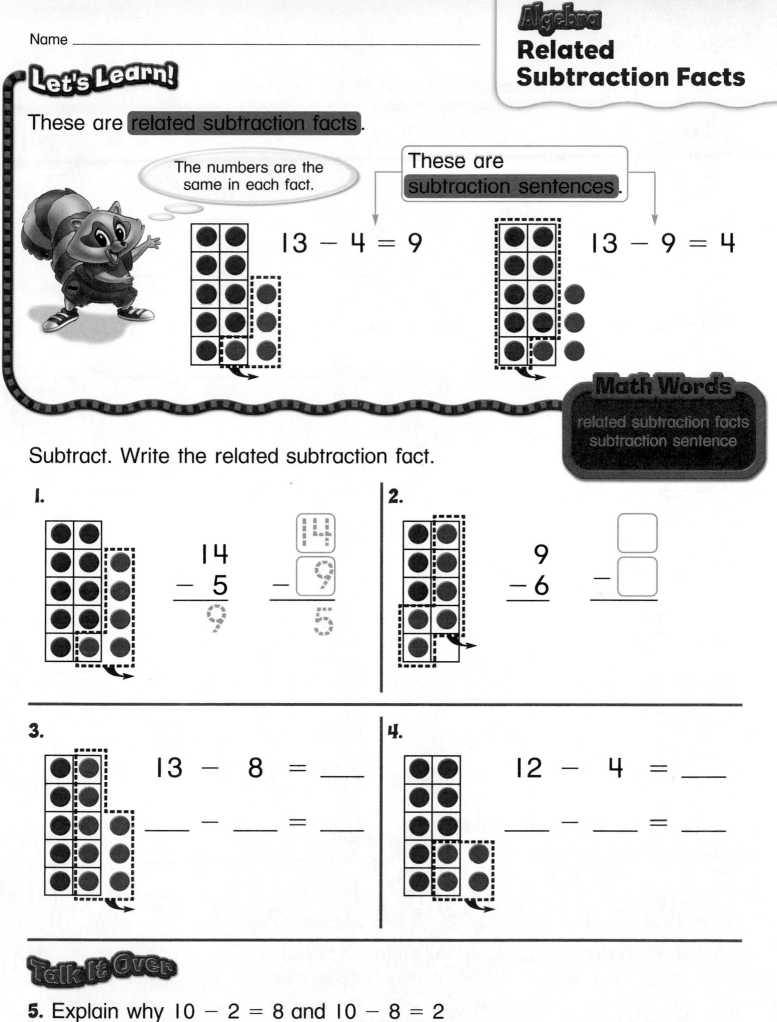

1.

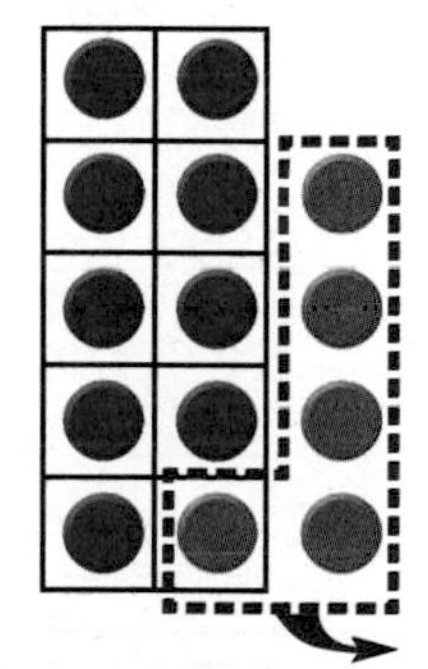

$$\begin{array}{r} 14 \\ -\ 5 \\ \hline 9 \end{array} \qquad \begin{array}{r} 14 \\ -\ 9 \\ \hline 5 \end{array}$$

2.

$$\begin{array}{r} 9 \\ -\ 6 \\ \hline \end{array} \qquad \begin{array}{r} \square \\ -\ \square \\ \hline \end{array}$$

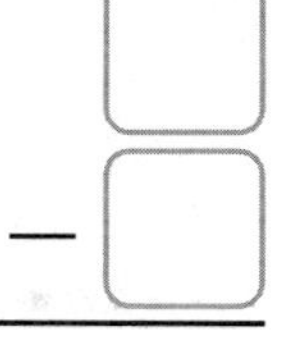

3.

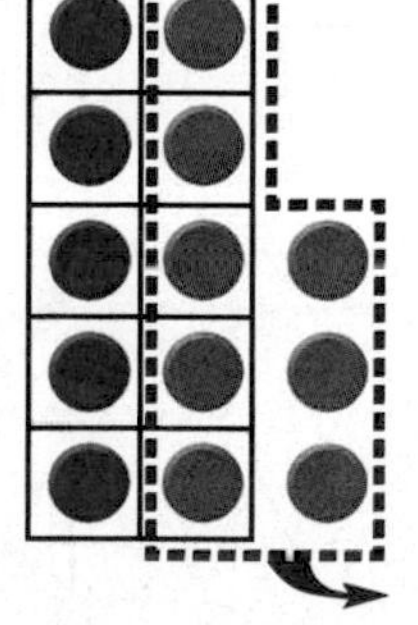
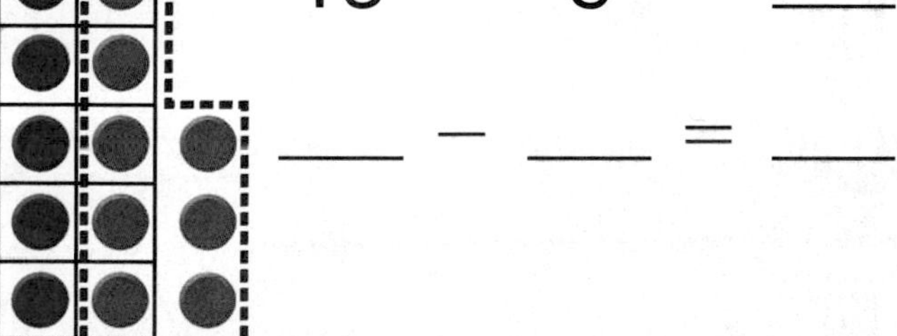

13 − 8 = ____

____ − ____ = ____

4.

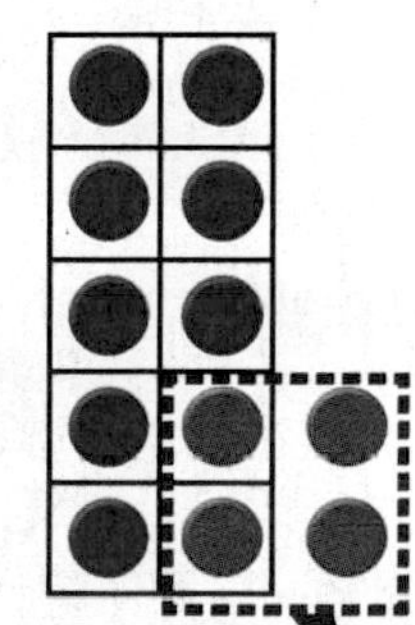

12 − 4 = ____

____ − ____ = ____

Talk It Over

5. Explain why 10 − 2 = 8 and 10 − 8 = 2 are related facts.

Copyright © by William H. Sadlier, Inc. All rights reserved.

Practice

Subtract. Write the related subtraction fact.

6. 10 − 4 = 6
   10 − 6 = 4

7. 9 − 4 = ___
   ___ − ___ = ___

8. 10 − 9 = ___
   ___ − ___ = ___

9. 8 − 5 = ___
   ___ − ___ = ___

10. 11 − 6 = ___
   ___ − ___ = ___

11. 9 − 7 = ___
   ___ − ___ = ___

12. 8 − 2 = ___
   ___ − ___ = ___

13. 11 − 9 = ___
   ___ − ___ = ___

14. 17 − 8 = ___
   ___ − ___ = ___

15. $\begin{array}{r} 13 \\ -\ 7 \\ \hline 6 \end{array}$ $\begin{array}{r} \boxed{13} \\ -\ \boxed{6} \\ \hline 7 \end{array}$

16. $\begin{array}{r} 14 \\ -\ 8 \\ \hline \end{array}$ $\begin{array}{r} \square \\ -\ \square \\ \hline \end{array}$

17. $\begin{array}{r} 11 \\ -\ 7 \\ \hline \end{array}$ $\begin{array}{r} \square \\ -\ \square \\ \hline \end{array}$

18. $\begin{array}{r} 15 \\ -\ 9 \\ \hline \end{array}$ $\begin{array}{r} \square \\ -\ \square \\ \hline \end{array}$

19. $\begin{array}{r} 10 \\ -\ 7 \\ \hline \end{array}$ $\begin{array}{r} \square \\ -\ \square \\ \hline \end{array}$

20. $\begin{array}{r} 16 \\ -\ 9 \\ \hline \end{array}$ $\begin{array}{r} \square \\ -\ \square \\ \hline \end{array}$

21. $\begin{array}{r} 7 \\ -\ 5 \\ \hline \end{array}$ $\begin{array}{r} \square \\ -\ \square \\ \hline \end{array}$

22. $\begin{array}{r} 13 \\ -\ 4 \\ \hline \end{array}$ $\begin{array}{r} \square \\ -\ \square \\ \hline \end{array}$

23. $\begin{array}{r} 11 \\ -\ 8 \\ \hline \end{array}$ $\begin{array}{r} \square \\ -\ \square \\ \hline \end{array}$

CRITICAL THINKING

24. Look at the pattern.

15 − 6 = 9   14 − 6 = 8   13 − 6 = 7

Write the next 3 facts in the pattern.

___ − ___ = ___   ___ − ___ = ___   ___ − ___ = ___

Math Alive at Home Ask your child to tell you the related subtraction facts for 14 − 8 = 6, 13 − 6 = 7, and 11 − 4 = 7. (14 − 6 = 8, 13 − 7 = 6, 11 − 7 = 4)

Name ______________________________

Algebra

Relate Addition and Subtraction

Let's Learn!

On Monday Bob had 14¢ in his bank.
He took 5¢ out. On Friday Bob put back 5¢.

These number sentences show what Bob did.

14¢ − 5¢ = 9¢
9¢ + 5¢ = 14¢

These are **related addition and subtraction facts**.
They use the same numbers.

The number taken away
and the number joined
are the same.

Math Words
related addition and subtraction facts

Read the story. Write two number sentences to show what happens.

1. 9 birds sit in a tree. 4 birds join them. Then the 4 birds leave.

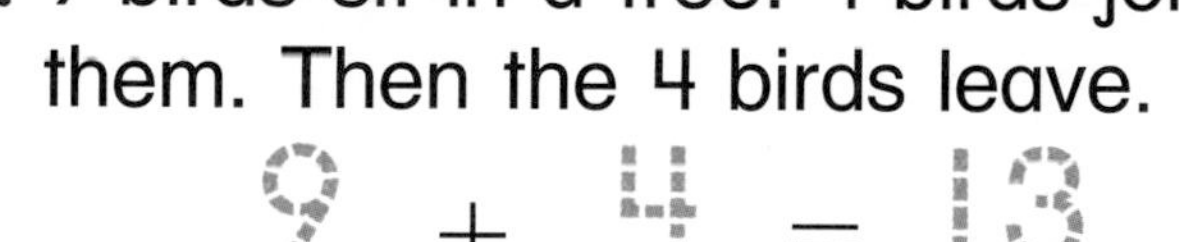

9 + 4 = 13
13 − 4 = 9

2. 14 lions are at a water hole. 6 leave. Then 6 other lions come.

___ − ___ = ___
___ + ___ = ___

3. Jay has 15 jungle animal stickers. He gives 7 to Laura. Then he buys 7 new stickers.

___ − ___ = ___
___ + ___ = ___

4. 8 elephants stand in a clearing. 4 more elephants come. Then 4 walk away.

___ + ___ = ___
___ − ___ = ___

5. 7 owls are flying. 5 owls join them. Then 5 owls land on a tree.

___ + ___ = ___
___ − ___ = ___

6. Pat sees 10 toads. 2 toads hop away. Then he sees 2 more toads.

___ − ___ = ___
___ + ___ = ___

Write About It

7. Explain how you find the related subtraction fact for 8 + 3 = 11. Write the fact.

Copyright © by William H. Sadlier, Inc. All rights reserved.

Practice

Read the story.
Write two number sentences to show what happens.

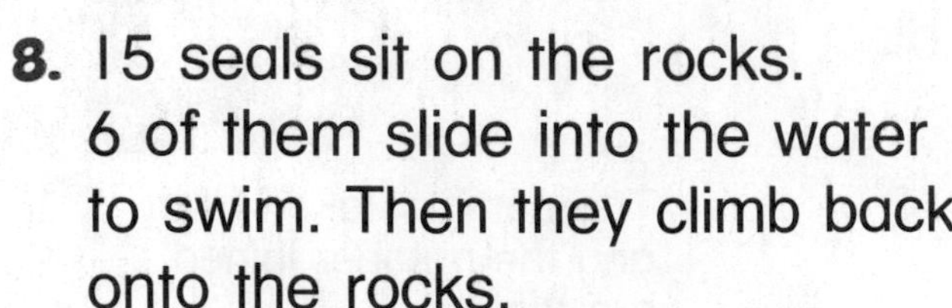

8. 15 seals sit on the rocks. 6 of them slide into the water to swim. Then they climb back onto the rocks.

15 − 6 = 9

9 + 6 = 15

9. Jamie finds 7 starfish on the beach. Then she finds 3 more. She gives 3 to her little brother.

___ + ___ = ___

___ − ___ = ___

10. People see 11 dolphins swim near their boat. 2 swim away to the other side. Then they swim back again.

___ − ___ = ___

___ + ___ = ___

11. 12 seagulls fly over the boat. 3 dive into the water to catch fish. Then the 3 seagulls join the others flying over the boat.

___ − ___ = ___

___ + ___ = ___

12. Ray buys 6 cards that show pictures of whales. Then he buys 3 cards that show sharks. He mails the shark cards to 3 friends.

___ + ___ = ___

___ − ___ = ___

13. Ray's dad buys 9 whale T-shirts. He also buys 8 dolphin shirts. He gives the dolphin shirts to Sheila's mom for her family.

___ + ___ = ___

___ − ___ = ___

CHALLENGE

14. Color related addition and subtraction facts the same color.

seven plus seven

sixteen minus eight

eight plus nine

fourteen minus seven

seventeen minus nine

eight plus eight

Math Alive at Home Ask your child to name the related subtraction facts for 9 + 8 = 17, 8 + 7 = 15, and 5 + 6 = 11. (17 − 8 = 9, 15 − 7 = 8, 11 − 6 = 5)

Name ______________________________

Use Addition to Check

Let's Learn!

11 rabbits are in a field. 4 are white. The rest are brown. How many rabbits are brown?

$11 - 4 = ?$

$11 - 4 = 7$

7 rabbits are brown.

You can use the related addition fact to check the subtraction.

$7 + 4 = 11$

The answer checks.

Subtract. Check by adding.

1. $17 - 8 = 9$; $9 + 8 = 17$
2. $15 - 9$; $\square + \square$
3. $12 - 4$; $\square + \square$
4. $13 - 6$; $\square + \square$
5. $12 - 9$; $\square + \square$
6. $14 - 9$; $\square + \square$
7. $11 - 5$; $\square + \square$
8. $14 - 8$; $\square + \square$
9. $16 - 7$; $\square + \square$
10. $12 - 7 = 5$
    $5 + 7 = 12$
11. $13 - 5 =$ ___
    ___ + ___ = ___
12. $15 - 8 =$ ___
    ___ + ___ = ___

Talk It Over

13. Explain why the related addition fact helps you checks your subtraction.

Copyright © by William H. Sadlier, Inc. All rights reserved.

Practice

Subtract. Check by adding.

14. 13 − 8 = 5
5 + 8 = 13

15. 16 − 9 = ___
___ + ___ = ___

16. 14 − 5 = ___
___ + ___ = ___

17. 15 − 7 = ___
___ + ___ = ___

18. 17 − 9 = ___
___ + ___ = ___

19. 13 − 7 = ___
___ + ___ = ___

20. 10 − 6 = ___ ; ☐ + ☐ = ___

21. 18 − 9 = ___ ; ☐ + ☐ = ___

22. 15 − 6 = ___ ; ☐ + ☐ = ___

Solve. Use a problem-solving strategy.
Show your work on a separate sheet of paper.

23. Rita draws 13 spiders and 4 ants. She shows 9 spiders on webs. How many spiders are not on webs?

___ spiders

24. Daryl draws 14 bears. He makes 7 of them black. The rest are brown. How many brown bears does Daryl draw?

___ brown bears

CHALLENGE

Would you add or subtract to make each sentence true? Write + or −.

25. 10 + 2 = 9 ◯ 3
___ = ___

26. 17 − 8 = 6 ◯ 3
___ = ___

27. 3 + 4 = 15 ◯ 8
___ = ___

28. 11 − 3 = 2 ◯ 6
___ = ___

Math Alive at Home Ask your child to use objects to first model 16 − 9 and to then check the results by adding. (7, 7 + 9 = 16)

Name ______________________________

TEST PREPARATION

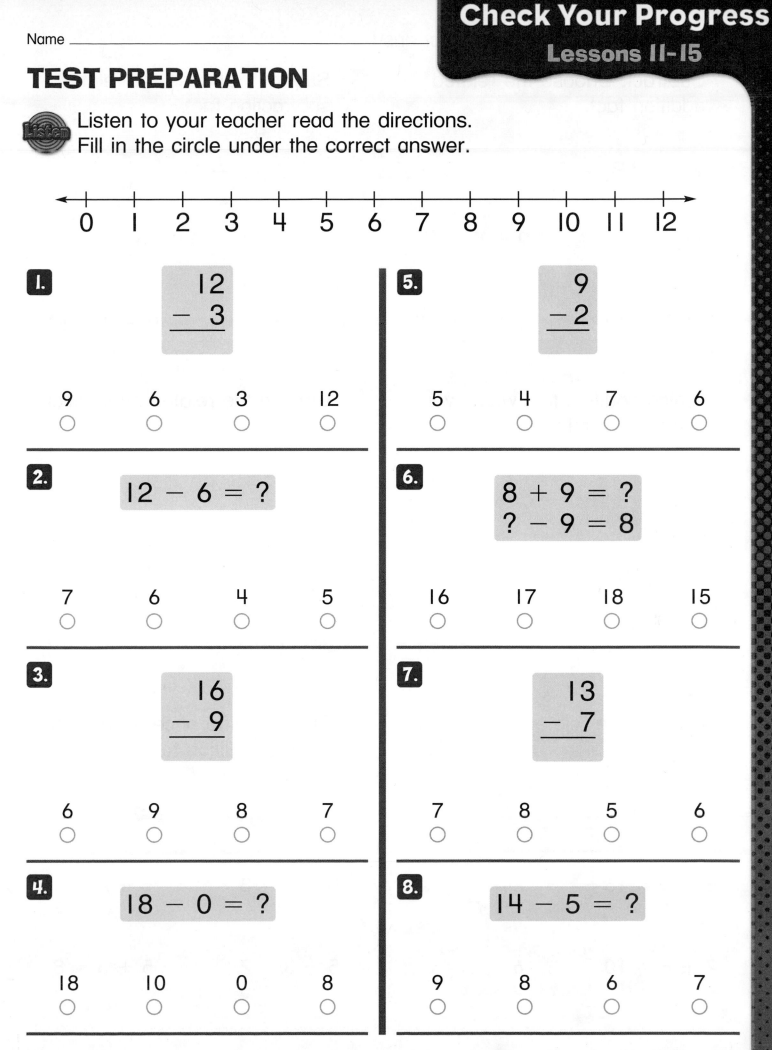

Listen to your teacher read the directions.
Fill in the circle under the correct answer.

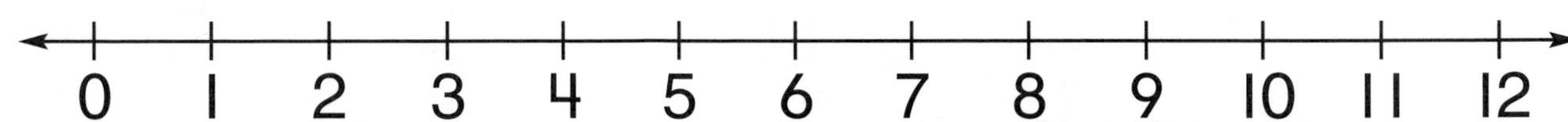

1.

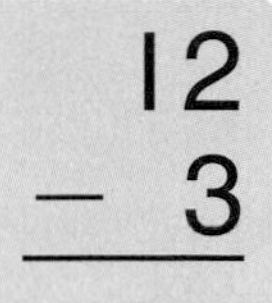

9 ○ 6 ○ 3 ○ 12 ○

2. $12 - 6 = ?$

7 ○ 6 ○ 4 ○ 5 ○

3.

$$\begin{array}{r} 16 \\ -\ 9 \\ \hline \end{array}$$

6 ○ 9 ○ 8 ○ 7 ○

4. $18 - 0 = ?$

18 ○ 10 ○ 0 ○ 8 ○

5.

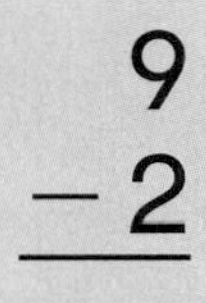

5 ○ 4 ○ 7 ○ 6 ○

6. $8 + 9 = ?$
$? - 9 = 8$

16 ○ 17 ○ 18 ○ 15 ○

7.

$$\begin{array}{r} 13 \\ -\ 7 \\ \hline \end{array}$$

7 ○ 8 ○ 5 ○ 6 ○

8. $14 - 5 = ?$

9 ○ 8 ○ 6 ○ 7 ○

Copyright © by William H. Sadlier, Inc. All rights reserved.

Fill in the circle under the correct answer.

9. Subtract. Choose the related addition fact.

$13 - 5 = ?$

- ○ $8 + 5 = 13$
- ○ $9 + 5 = 14$
- ○ $7 + 5 = 12$
- ○ $6 + 5 = 11$

10. Which addition fact would you use to check $11 - 7 = 4$?

- ○ $4 + 3 = 7$
- ○ $4 + 7 = 11$
- ○ $8 + 3 = 11$
- ○ $7 + 3 = 10$

11. Choose the related addition fact.

$10 - 8 = 2$

- ○ $8 + 8 = 16$
- ○ $2 + 6 = 8$
- ○ $2 + 8 = 10$
- ○ $6 + 2 = 8$

12. Subtract. Choose the related subtraction fact.

$15 - 7 = ?$

- ○ $8 - 7 = 1$
- ○ $15 - 8 = 7$
- ○ $8 + 7 = 15$
- ○ $9 + 8 = 17$

13. Choose the related subtraction fact.

$5 + 7 = 12$

- ○ $12 - 9 = 3$
- ○ $7 - 5 = 2$
- ○ $12 - 7 = 5$
- ○ $7 + 5 = 12$

14. Find the difference. Choose the related addition fact.

$8 - 3 = ?$

- ○ $5 - 2 = 3$
- ○ $6 + 2 = 8$
- ○ $5 - 3 = 2$
- ○ $5 + 3 = 8$

Name ______________________________

Count Up to Subtract

You can subtract to find how many more or how many fewer.

Count up from the lesser number to the greater number to find the difference.

Jim rides his bike 14 blocks. Darla rides 9 blocks. How many more blocks does Jim ride than Darla?

14 − 9 = ?

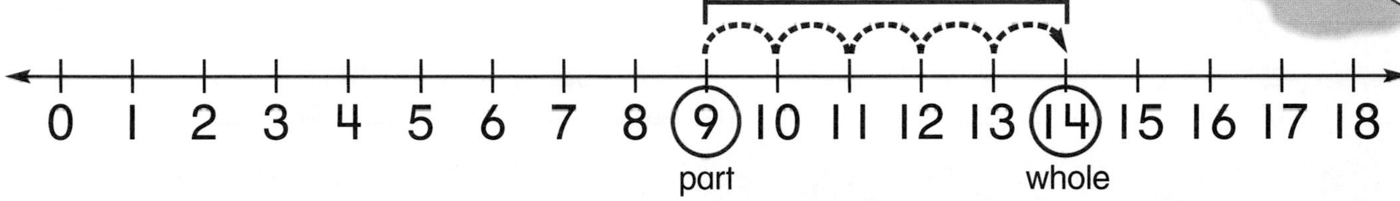

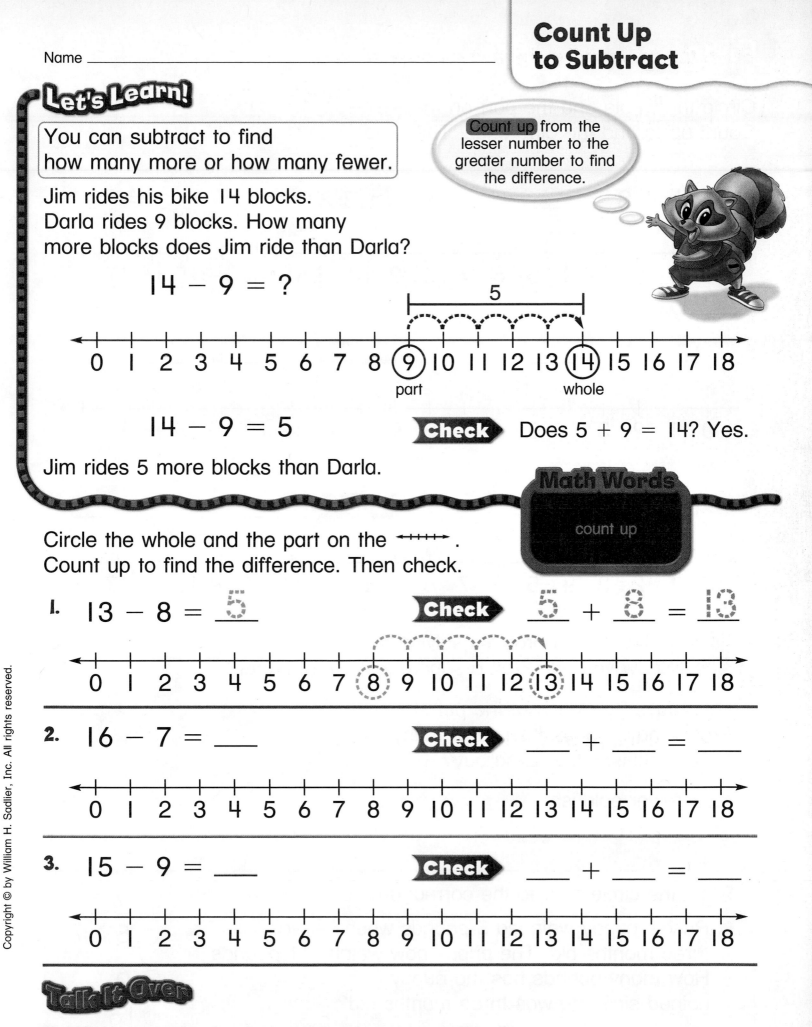

14 − 9 = 5

Check Does 5 + 9 = 14? Yes.

Jim rides 5 more blocks than Darla.

Math Words
count up

Circle the whole and the part on the number line. Count up to find the difference. Then check.

1. 13 − 8 = 5 **Check** 5 + 8 = 13

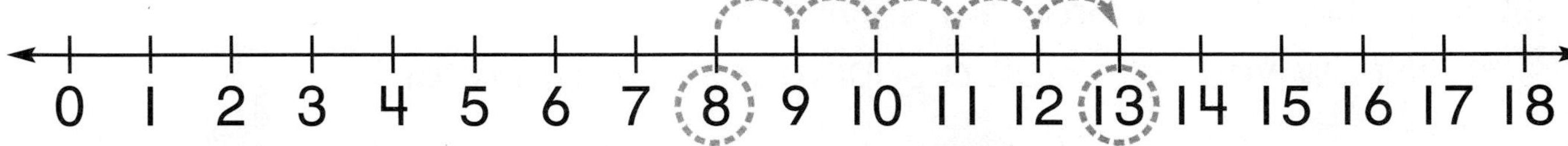

2. 16 − 7 = ___ **Check** ___ + ___ = ___

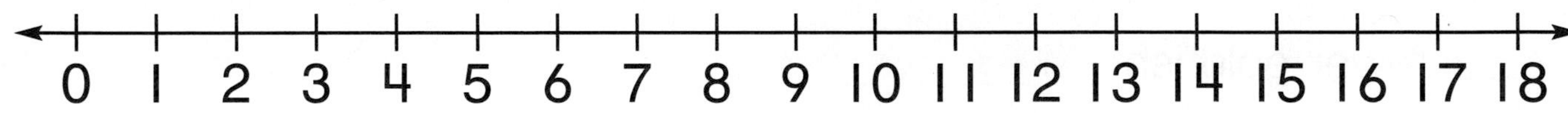

3. 15 − 9 = ___ **Check** ___ + ___ = ___

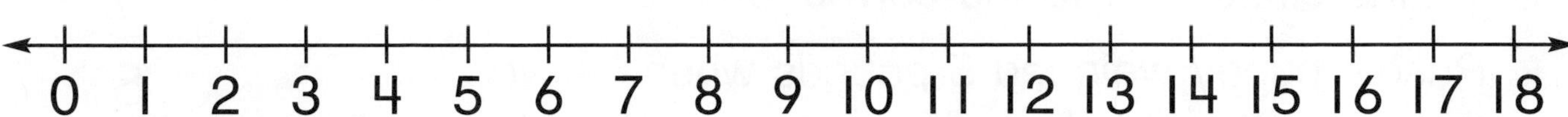

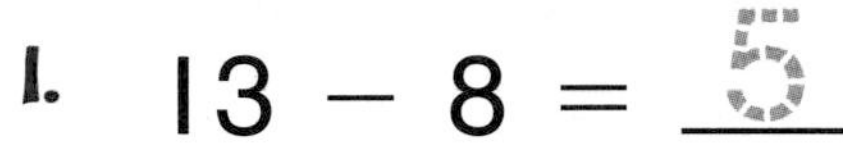

4. When you count up to subtract on a number line, what does the number of hops stand for?

Copyright © by William H. Sadlier, Inc. All rights reserved.

Practice

Circle the whole and the part on the ←+++++→ .
Count up to find the difference. Then check.

5. 14 − 8 = 6 **Check** 6 + 8 = 14

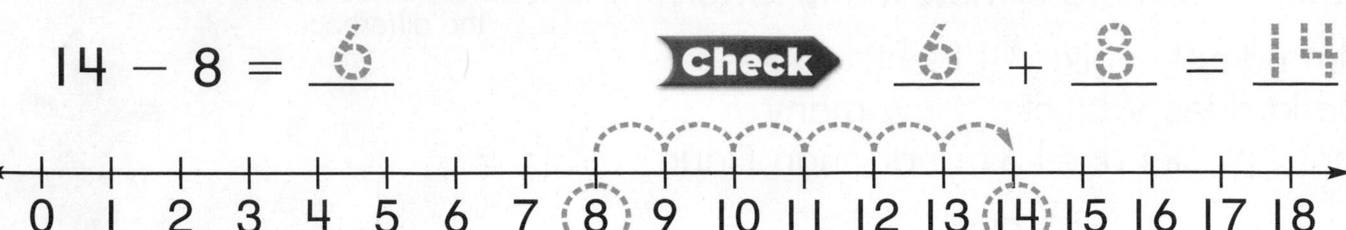

6. 13 − 7 = ___ **Check** ___ + ___ = ___

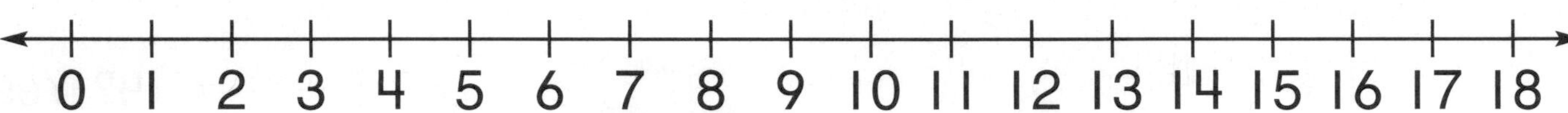

7. 15 − 8 = ___ **Check** ___ + ___ = ___

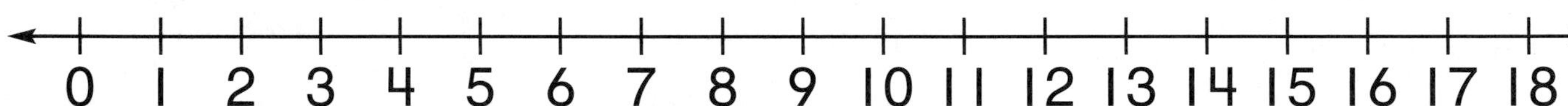

Solve. Use a problem-solving strategy.
Show your work on a separate sheet of paper.

8. Elisa buys 8 goldfish at the pet store. Franks buys 15 goldfish. How many fewer goldfish does Elisa buy?

___ fewer goldfish

TEST PREPARATION

Fill in the circle next to the correct answer.

9. Rosa's puppy weighed 5 pounds when he was three months old. The puppy now weighs 11 pounds. How many pounds has the puppy gained since he was three months old?

- ○ 8
- ○ 5
- ○ 6
- ○ 16

Math Alive at Home Ask your child to make up a subtraction story and to solve it by counting up.

Name ______________________________

Fact Families

Let's Learn!

A fact family is the set of all related facts for a given group of numbers.

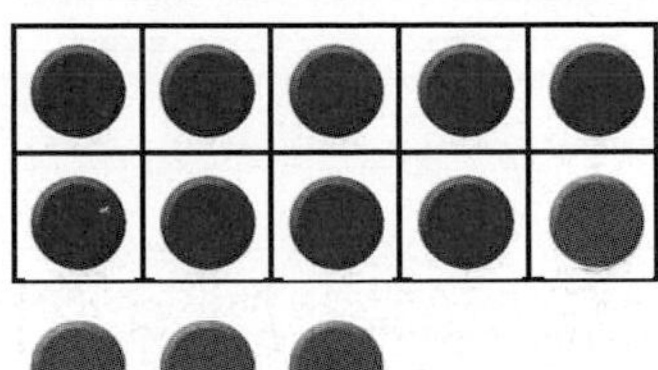

Here is the fact family for 4, 9, and 13.

$$\begin{array}{r} 9 \\ +4 \\ \hline 13 \end{array} \quad \begin{array}{r} 13 \\ -4 \\ \hline 9 \end{array} \quad \begin{array}{r} 4 \\ +9 \\ \hline 13 \end{array} \quad \begin{array}{r} 13 \\ -9 \\ \hline 4 \end{array}$$

Math Words

fact family

Complete each fact family.

1.

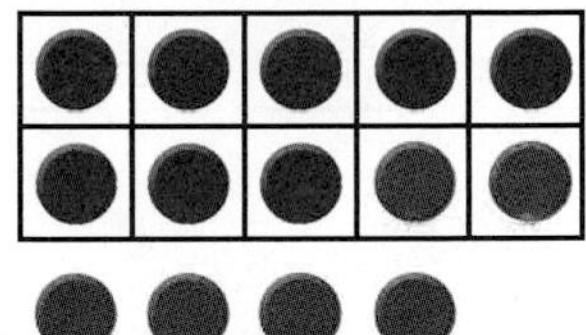

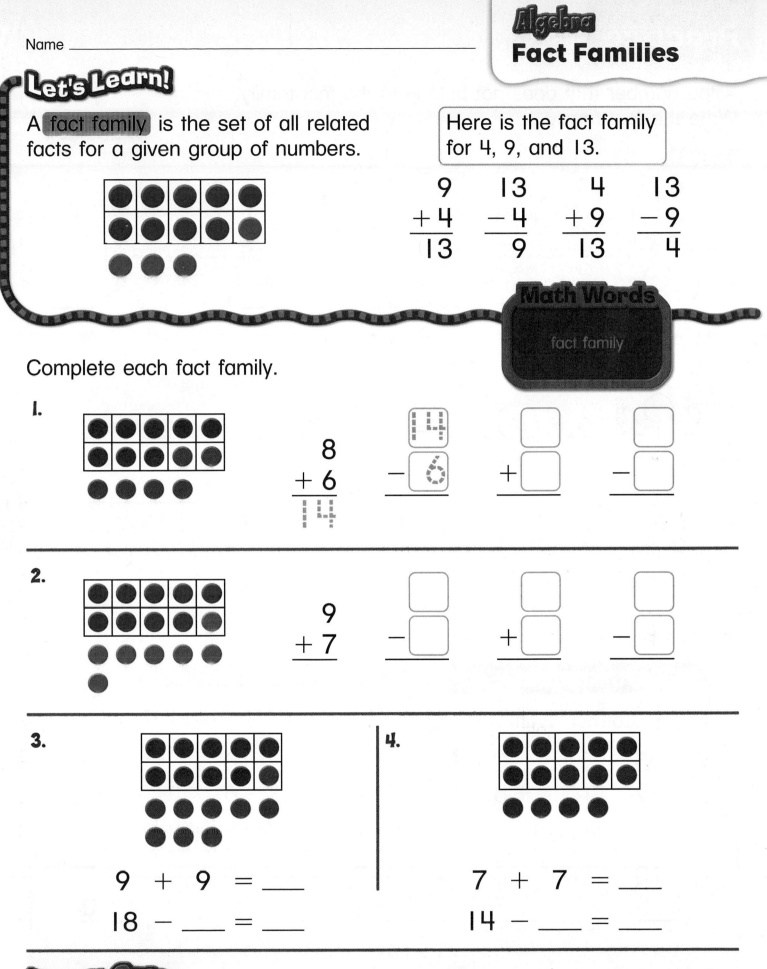

$$\begin{array}{r} 8 \\ +6 \\ \hline 14 \end{array}$$

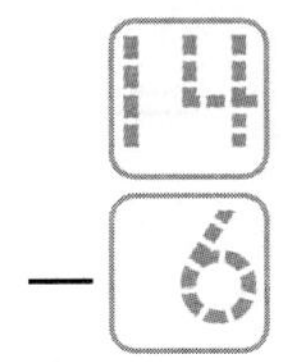

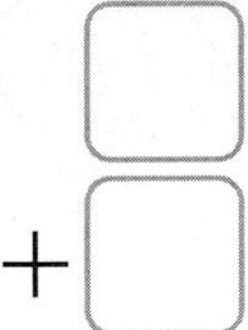

$\begin{array}{r} \square \\ -\square \\ \hline \end{array}$

2.

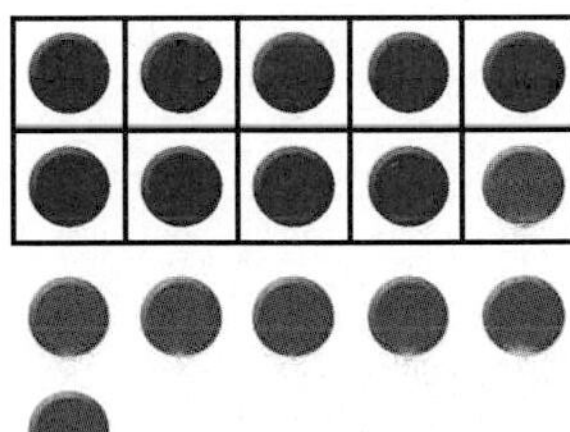

$$\begin{array}{r} 9 \\ +7 \\ \hline \end{array}$$

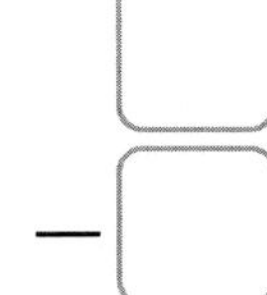

$\begin{array}{r} \square \\ +\square \\ \hline \end{array}$ $\begin{array}{r} \square \\ -\square \\ \hline \end{array}$

3.

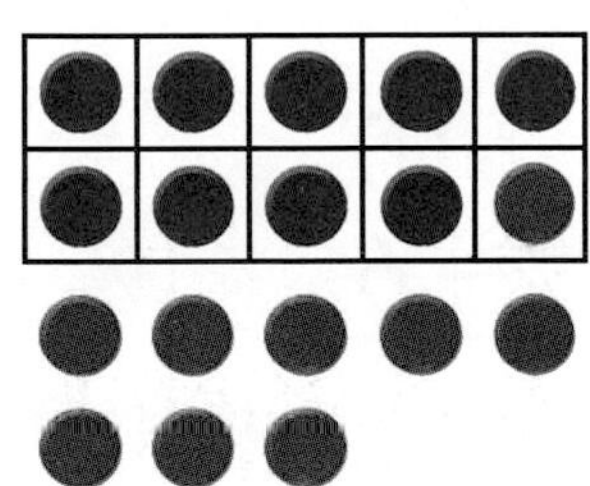

9 + 9 = ___

18 − ___ = ___

4.

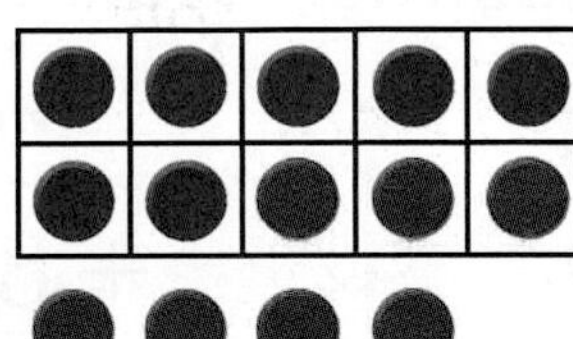

7 + 7 = ___

14 − ___ = ___

5. Does a doubles fact family have four facts? Explain your reasoning.

Copyright © by William H. Sadlier, Inc. All rights reserved.

Practice

✘ the number that does not belong to the fact family.
Write the fact family.

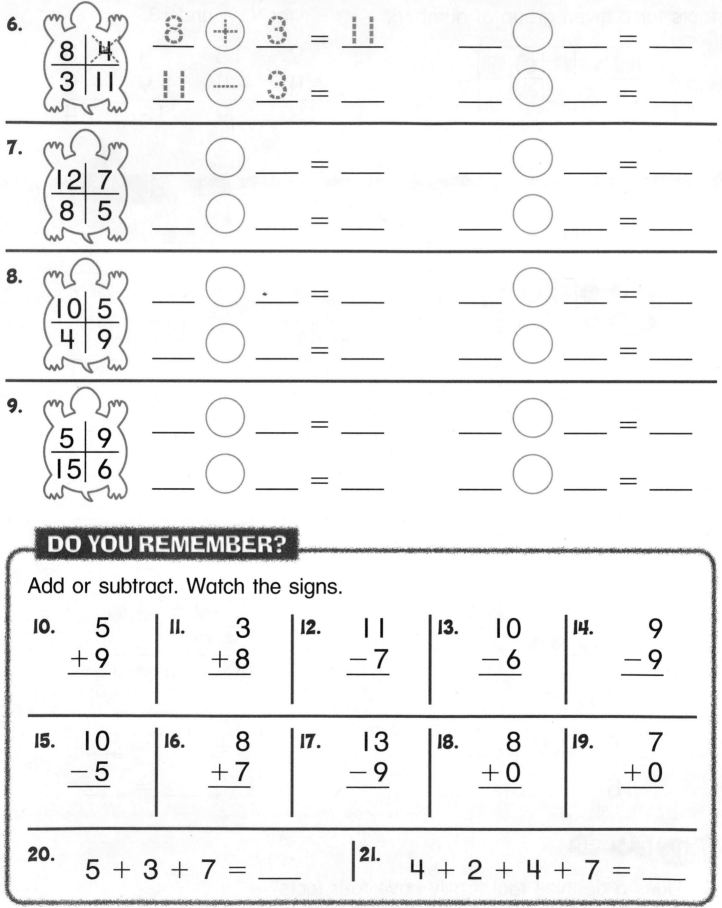

6. | 8 | 4 | / | 3 | 11 |

8 + 3 = 11 ___ ◯ ___ = ___

11 − 3 = ___ ___ ◯ ___ = ___

7. | 12 | 7 | / | 8 | 5 |

___ ◯ ___ = ___ ___ ◯ ___ = ___

___ ◯ ___ = ___ ___ ◯ ___ = ___

8. | 10 | 5 | / | 4 | 9 |

___ ◯ ___ = ___ ___ ◯ ___ = ___

___ ◯ ___ = ___ ___ ◯ ___ = ___

9. | 5 | 9 | / | 15 | 6 |

___ ◯ ___ = ___ ___ ◯ ___ = ___

___ ◯ ___ = ___ ___ ◯ ___ = ___

DO YOU REMEMBER?

Add or subtract. Watch the signs.

10. $5 + 9$
11. $3 + 8$
12. $11 - 7$
13. $10 - 6$
14. $9 - 9$
15. $10 - 5$
16. $8 + 7$
17. $13 - 9$
18. $8 + 0$
19. $7 + 0$

20. 5 + 3 + 7 = ___

21. 4 + 2 + 4 + 7 = ___

Math Alive at Home Ask your child to write the fact families for 7, 9, 16 (7+9=16, 9+7=16, 16−7=9, 16−9=7) and 8, 16 (8+8=16, 16−8=8).

Name ______________________________

Algebra
Missing Addends

Tara wants to put 12 animal patches on her backpack. She has 9. How many more patches does she need?

Count up or use a subtraction fact to find a **missing addend**.

$9 + \boxed{?} = 12$

Count up from 9.		Use a subtraction fact.
10, 11, 12	or	$12 - 9 = 3$
$9 + \boxed{3} = 12$		So $9 + \boxed{3} = 12$.

Tara needs 3 more patches.

Math Words
missing addend

Choose a way. Find the missing addend.

1. $8 + \boxed{2} = 10$
   9, 10
2. $5 + \boxed{7} = 12$
   $12 - 5 = 7$
3. $7 + \boxed{} = 8$
4. $9 + \boxed{} = 11$
5. $6 + \boxed{} = 15$
6. $8 + \boxed{} = 15$
7. $\begin{array}{r} 5 \\ + \boxed{3} \\ \hline 8 \end{array}$
   6, 7, 8
8. $\begin{array}{r} 9 \\ + \boxed{} \\ \hline 14 \end{array}$
9. $\begin{array}{r} 4 \\ + \boxed{} \\ \hline 13 \end{array}$

10. How does knowing the related subtraction fact help you find a missing addend?

Copyright © by William H. Sadlier, Inc. All rights reserved.

Practice

Find the missing addend.

11. $6 + \boxed{4} = 10$

12. $7 + \square = 9$

13. $5 + \square = 13$

14. $9 + \square = 18$

15. $7 + \square = 10$

16. $6 + \square = 14$

17. $6 + \square = 12$

18. $6 + \square = 11$

19. $7 + \square = 15$

20. $\square + 8 = 11$

21. $\square + 6 = 13$

22. $\square + 8 = 17$

Solve. Use a problem-solving strategy.
Show your work on a separate sheet of paper.

23. Cheryl needs 16 swan stickers to make a border for a box. She has 9 swan stickers. How many more does she need?

____ more stickers

24. Robert wants to paint 15 shells as gifts. He finds 6 shells today. How many more does he need to find?

____ more shells

CRITICAL THINKING

Find the missing number in each number sentence.

25. $17 = 9 + \square$

26. $16 - \square = 7$

27. $13 = 7 + \square$

28. $12 - \square = 9$

Math Alive at Home Show your child 12 pennies. Ask him/her to turn away as you hide some pennies under a cup. Then ask your child how many pennies are hidden under the cup.

Name ____________________

Algebra

Fact Patterns

Let's Learn!

Look at the parts of each number sentence to name the **pattern rule**.

9 + 4 = 13

8 + 5 = 13

7 + 6 = 13

Pattern Rule:
The first addends decrease by 1.
The second addends increase by 1.
The sums are 13.

6 + 7 = 13 is the next addition sentence in the pattern.

Math Words
pattern rule

Look for a pattern. Complete the pattern.

1.
0 + 3 = 3
0 + 4 = 4
0 + 5 = 5
0 + 6 = 6

2.
5 − 5 = ___
6 − 6 = ___
7 − 7 = ___
___ − ___ = ___

3.
9 + 3 = ___
8 + 4 = ___
7 + 5 = ___
___ + ___ = ___

4.
2 − 0 = ___
3 − 0 = ___
4 − 0 = ___
___ − ___ = ___

5.
2 + 9 = ___
3 + 8 = ___
4 + 7 = ___
___ + ___ = ___

6.
10 − 5 = ___
9 − 4 = ___
8 − 3 = ___
___ − ___ = ___

Talk It Over

7. Choose a pattern above. Explain the pattern rule.

Copyright © by William H. Sadlier, Inc. All rights reserved.

Practice

Look for a pattern.
Write the missing numbers.

8.
18 − 9 = 9
17 − 8 = 9
16 − 7 = 9
15 − 6 = 9

9.
11 − 8 = ___
12 − 7 = ___
13 − 6 = ___
___ − ___ = ___

10.
7 + 4 = ___
6 + 5 = ___
5 + 6 = ___
___ + ___ = ___

11.

1	2	3	4	☐	☐
+6	+5	+4	+3	+☐	+☐

12.

9	10	11	12	☐	☐
−2	−3	−4	−5	−☐	−☐

13.

5	6	7	8	☐	☐
+9	+8	+7	+6	+☐	+☐

TEST PREPARATION

Fill in the circle under the correct answer.

14. 6 + 4 = ☐

12 ○ 11 ○ 10 ○ 9 ○

15. 13 − 4 = ☐

10 ○ 9 ○ 8 ○ 7 ○

Math Alive at Home Ask your child to make up one addition and one subtraction pattern similar to those above.

Name ____________________

Problem Solving
Strategy

Choose the Operation

Read There are 9 dogs on a hill.
There are 7 dogs on another hill.
How many dogs are there in all?

Plan Decide whether to add or subtract.

To find how many in all, add or subtract.

Write a number sentence.

Write 9 + 7 = 16

There are 16 dogs in all.

Check Draw a picture to find how many in all.

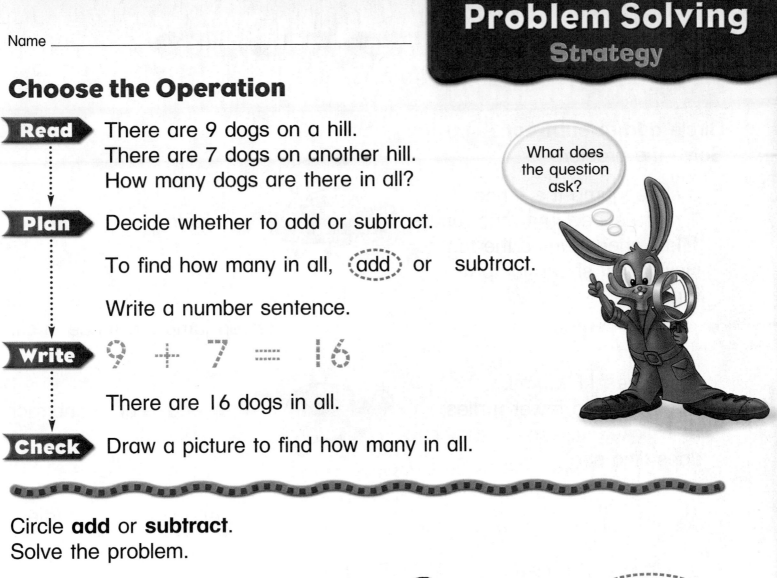

What does the question ask?

Circle **add** or **subtract**.
Solve the problem.

1. Jamal has 10 cats.
He gives 4 cats away.
How many cats are left?

add or subtract

10 − 4 = 6

There are 6 cats left.

2. 8 frogs are in the pond.
5 more frogs jump into the pond. How many frogs are in the pond altogether?

add or subtract

There are ____ frogs altogether.

3. There are 12 crabs on the sand.
Then 7 crawl away. How many crabs are left?

add or subtract

There are ____ crabs left.

Copyright © by William H. Sadlier, Inc. All rights reserved.

Practice

Read → Plan → Write → Check

Choose the Operation

Circle **add** or **subtract**.
Solve the problem.

4. 3 sheep jump the fence.
7 more sheep jump the fence.
1 last sheep jumps the fence.
How many sheep jump the fence in all?

add or subtract

____ sheep jump the fence in all.

5. Jake sees 11 turtles.
Ana sees two fewer turtles than Jake. How many turtles does Ana see?

add or subtract

Ana sees ____ turtles.

6. 5 owls are in a tree.
The number of owls doubles.
How many owls are in the tree then?

add or subtract

____ owls are in the tree then.

7. 9 ducks are in a pond.
Then three fly away.
How many ducks are left?

add or subtract

____ ducks are left.

8. Write one addition problem and one subtraction problem in your Math Journal. Solve them.

Math Alive at Home Ask your child to explain how he/she decided whether to add or subtract to solve some of the problems in this lesson.

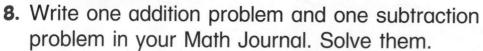

Name ______________________

Read Plan Write Check

Mixed Strategies

Use a strategy you have learned.

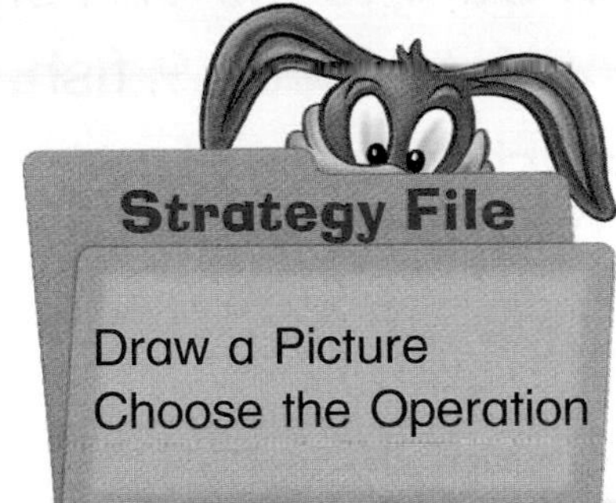

1. There are 10 horses.
   4 of them are running.
   The rest are eating.
   How many horses are eating?

   ____ horses are eating.

2. Nadia sees 6 big pigs.
   She sees 6 small pigs.
   How many pigs does she see altogether?

   Nadia sees ____ pigs altogether.

3. 9 birds are in the yard.
   2 birds fly away.
   How many birds are left?

   ____ birds are left.

4. Carlos sees 7 cows.
   Gail sees 11 cows.
   How many fewer cows does Carlos see?

   Carlos sees ____ fewer cows.

5. Jack finds 9 eggs in nests.
   He finds 3 in each nest.
   How many nests does he find?

   Jack finds ____ nests.

Copyright © by William H. Sadlier, Inc. All rights reserved.

Practice

Read Plan Write Check

Use a strategy you have learned.

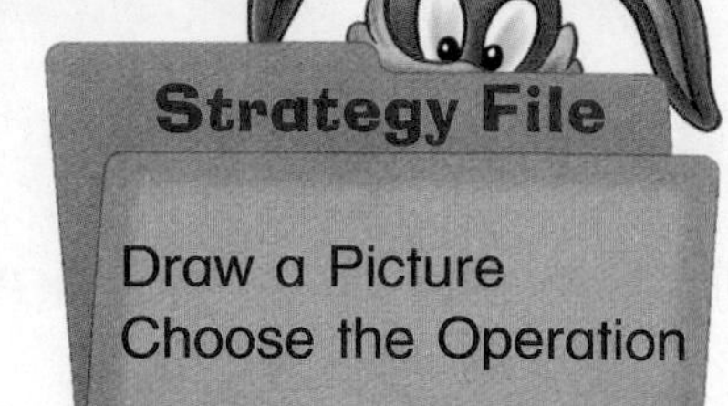

6. Sam feeds 12 fish.
   Kate feeds 9 fish.
   How many fewer fish does Kate feed?

   Kate feeds ____ fewer fish.

---

7. Mark has 11 shark pictures.
   He gives away 6 of them.
   How many pictures does Mark have left?

   Mark has ____ pictures left.

---

8. Animal erasers cost 1 penny.
   Lucy buys 5 tiger erasers, 5 lion erasers, and 1 fish eraser.
   How much does she spend?

   Lucy spends ____¢.

---

9. Dale is in line at the zoo.
   6 children are in front of him.
   2 children are behind him.
   How many children are in line?

   ____ children are in line.

---

10. Jan draws 10 lizards.
    She gives away 5 of the drawings.
    How many does she have left?

    Jan has ____ drawings left.

Math Alive at Home Ask your child to tell you how he/she solved some of the problems in this lesson.

Name ______________________________

Check Your Progress
Lessons 16-21

TEST PREPARATION

Listen to your teacher read the directions.
Fill in the circle under the correct answer.

1. $16 - 8 = ?$

10 ○ 8 ○ 11 ○ 9 ○

2. $5 + ? = 7$

2 ○ 3 ○ 7 ○ 5 ○

3. $\begin{array}{r} 9 \\ +\ 6 \\ \hline \end{array}$ $\begin{array}{r} 6 \\ +\ 9 \\ \hline \end{array}$ $\begin{array}{r} 15 \\ -\ 6 \\ \hline \end{array}$

$\begin{array}{r} 9 \\ -3 \\ \hline 6 \end{array}$ ○ $\begin{array}{r} 6 \\ -3 \\ \hline 3 \end{array}$ ○ $\begin{array}{r} 15 \\ -9 \\ \hline 6 \end{array}$ ○

4.

$7 + ? = 16$
$16 - ? = 7$
$? + 7 = 16$
$16 - 7 = ?$

10 ○ 9 ○ 8 ○ 7 ○

5. $13 - 7 = ?$

7 ○ 6 ○ 5 ○ 8 ○

6. $9 + ? = 14$

6 ○ 2 ○ 5 ○ 7 ○

7.

$5 + 0 = 5$
$6 + 0 = 6$
$7 + 0 = 7$

$8 + 0 = 8$ ○ $0 + 8 = 8$ ○

$0 + 7 = 7$ ○ $6 + 0 = 6$ ○

8. 8, 9, 17

$8 + 9 = 17$
$17 - 9 = 8$
$9 + 8 = 17$
$17 - 8 = 9$
○

$8 + 9 = 17$
$9 + 8 = 17$
$9 + 9 = 18$
$9 - 8 = 1$
○

$8 + 8 = 16$
$7 + 7 = 14$
$9 + 9 = 18$
○

$8 + 9 = 17$
$9 + 8 = 17$
$17 - 0 = 17$
○

Copyright © by William H. Sadlier, Inc. All rights reserved.

Connection
Math and History

Name ________________

This table shows Roman numerals from 1 through 20.

I	II	III	IV	V
VI	VII	VIII	IX	X
XI	XII	XIII	XIV	XV
XVI	XVII	XVIII	XIX	XX

Key: I = 1 V = 5 X = 10

Did You Know?

The ancient Romans used addition and subtraction to count.

I **in front of** a letter means subtract 1.

IV 5 − 1 = 4

I **after** a letter means add 1.

VI 5 + 1 = 6

Look at the Roman numerals in red in the table. Notice that I is subtracted to make each numeral.

Use the table and the key.
Write the Roman numeral for each number.

1. 2 ______ 2. 7 ______ 3. 12 ______
4. 3 ______ 5. 8 ______ 6. 13 ______
7. 4 ______ 8. 9 ______ 9. 14 ______
10. 5 ______ 11. 10 ______ 12. 15 ______

Solve. Rewrite each addition sentence using Roman numerals.

13. 6 + 2 = ___ ________________
14. 5 + 3 = ___ ________________
15. 10 + 9 = ___ ________________
16. 10 + 10 = ___ ________________

You can put this in your Math Portfolio.

Name ______________________

Chapter 1 Test

1. Write the answer.

Double 8. Add 1. ____

2. Fill in the blank.

If ____ is added to 7, the answer will be 16.

3. Write the fact family for 7, 14.

4. Complete the fact family.

$9 + 2 = 11$
$11 - 2 = 9$
$2 + 9 = 11$

____

5. Write the number sentence that is most likely to come next in the pattern.

$7 + 5 = 12$
$6 + 6 = 12$
$5 + 7 = 12$

____

6. Write the number sentence that is most likely to come next in the pattern.

$16 - 9 = 7$
$15 - 8 = 7$
$14 - 7 = 7$

____

7. Find the missing part.
Write the subtraction sentence.

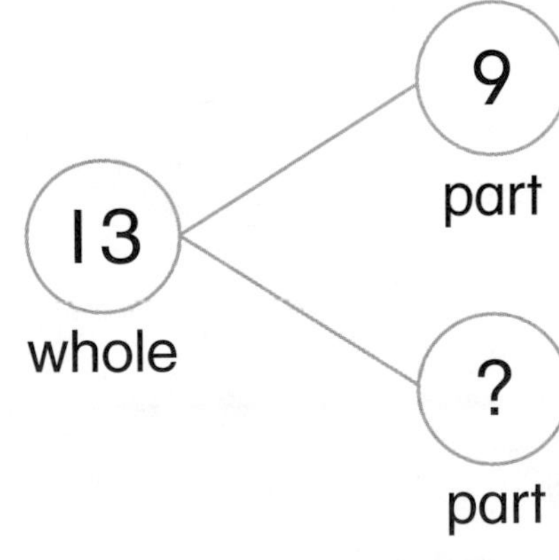

____

8. Add by making 10.

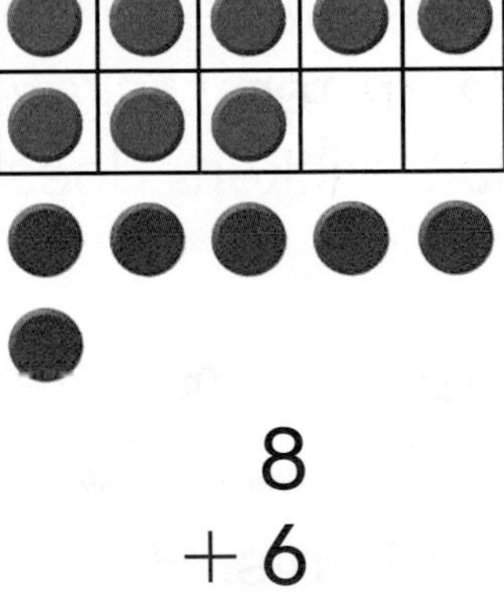

$$\begin{array}{r} 8 \\ +\,6 \\ \hline \end{array}$$

9. Add.

$5 + 5 =$ ____

10. Subtract.

$12 - 3 =$ ____

Copyright © by William H. Sadlier, Inc. All rights reserved.

Add or subtract.

11. $\begin{array}{r} 7 \\ -0 \\ \hline \end{array}$

12. $\begin{array}{r} 3 \\ +9 \\ \hline \end{array}$

13. $\begin{array}{r} 15 \\ -6 \\ \hline \end{array}$

14. $\begin{array}{r} 8 \\ +8 \\ \hline \end{array}$

15. $\begin{array}{r} 14 \\ -9 \\ \hline \end{array}$

Circle the addends you group. Then find the sum.

16. $\begin{array}{r} 7 \\ 2 \\ 6 \\ +2 \\ \hline \end{array}$

17. $\begin{array}{r} 3 \\ 5 \\ 8 \\ +2 \\ \hline \end{array}$

Solve. Use a problem-solving strategy.

18. The second-grade classes have ant farms. Mr. Rather's class has 10 ants. Mrs. Lee's class has 10 ants. How many ants do both classes have altogether?

Both classes have ____ ants altogether.

19. Vicki has 17 red stickers and 9 blue stickers. How many more red stickers than blue stickers does she have?

Vicki has ____ more red stickers.

20. Mac has 4 cats. He also has 4 fish and 1 dog. How many pets does Mac have?

Mac has ____ pets.

Name ______________________

1. Use the number line.
Show how to add 1, 2, or 3 to 8.

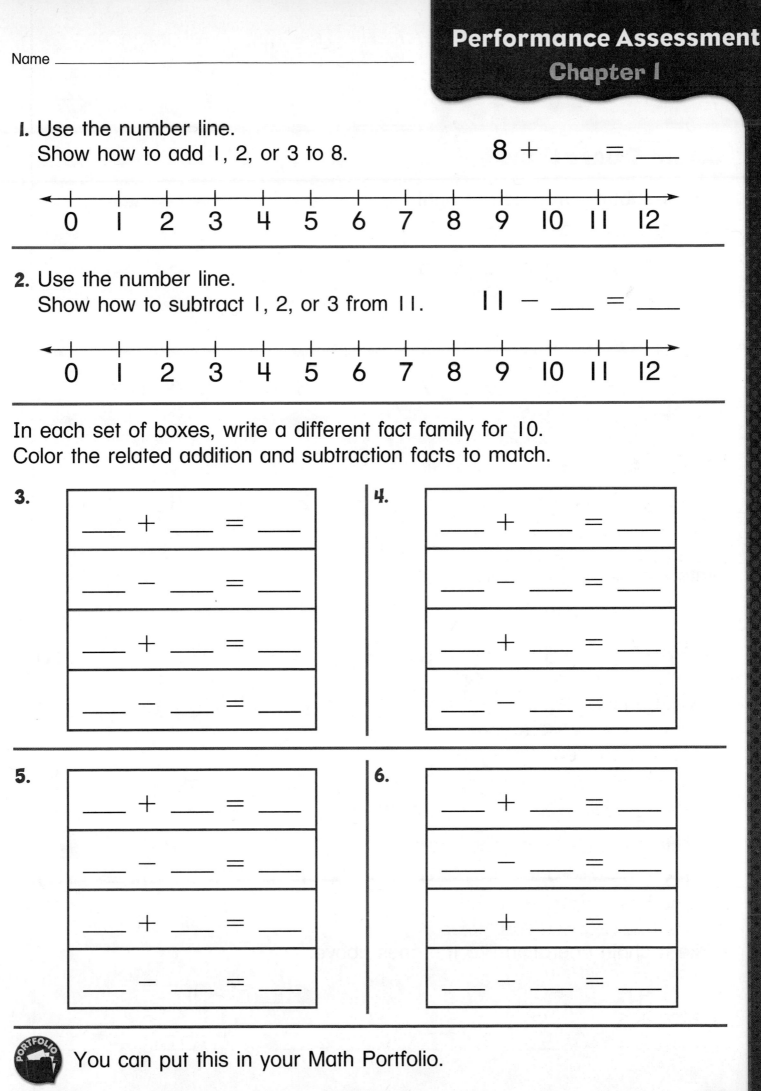

8 + ___ = ___

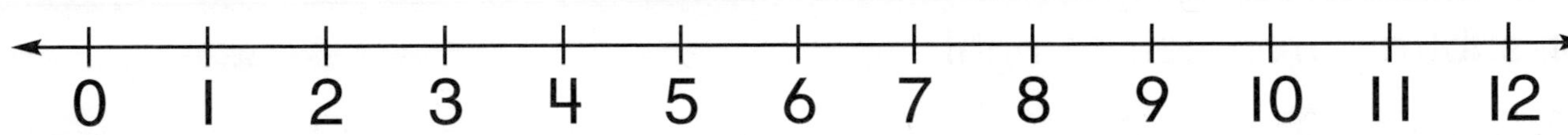

2. Use the number line.
Show how to subtract 1, 2, or 3 from 11.

11 − ___ = ___

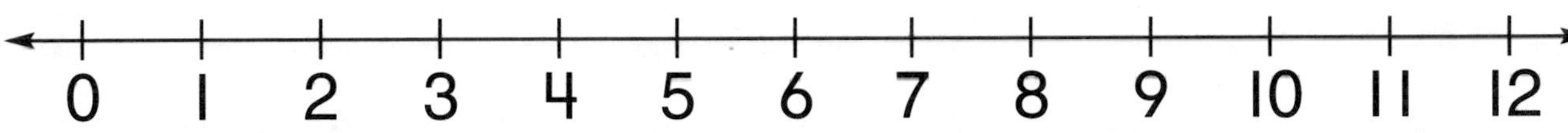

In each set of boxes, write a different fact family for 10.
Color the related addition and subtraction facts to match.

3.

___ + ___ = ___
___ − ___ = ___
___ + ___ = ___
___ − ___ = ___

4.

___ + ___ = ___
___ − ___ = ___
___ + ___ = ___
___ − ___ = ___

5.

___ + ___ = ___
___ − ___ = ___
___ + ___ = ___
___ − ___ = ___

6.

___ + ___ = ___
___ − ___ = ___
___ + ___ = ___
___ − ___ = ___

You can put this in your Math Portfolio.

Copyright © by William H. Sadlier, Inc. All rights reserved.

Algebra

Enrichment

Name ______________________________

Chain Operations

Add or subtract from left to right.

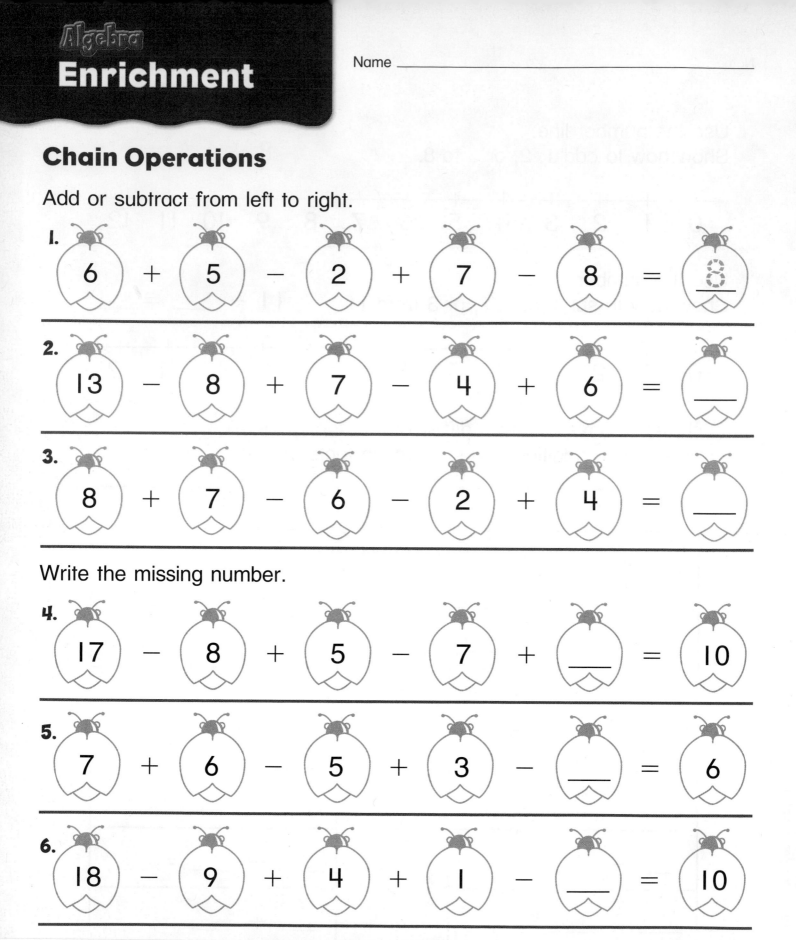

1. 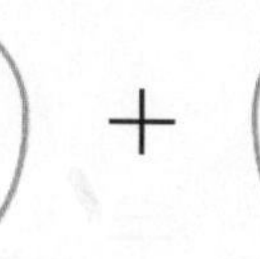 6 + 5 − 2 + 7 − 8 = 8 

2.  13 − 8 + 7 − 4  + 6 = ____

3.  8 + 7 − 6 − 2 + 4 = ____

Write the missing number.

4.  17 − 8 + 5 − 7 + ____ = 10

5.  7 + 6 − 5 + 3 − ____ = 6

6.  18 − 9 + 4 + 1 − ____ = 10

Write a chain operation like the ones above.

7.  ____ −  ____ + ____ − ____ + ____ = ____

The Watering Hole

Read ALOUD

Would you like to go to the grasslands?
Is animal-watching your goal?
Then the place you should visit
is a watering hole.

Look! 4 thirsty zebras stop by for a drink.
Who might stop by next?
Who do you think?

Copyright © by William H. Sadlier, Inc. All rights reserved.

Next 3 thirsty giraffes stop by to fill up.
Now how many animals are there?
Can you add them up?

4 + 3 = ___

Along comes 1 lion.
That's right, just one.

So now there's a sum of 7 + 1.

$7 + 1 = \_\_\_$

Copyright © by William H. Sadlier, Inc. All rights reserved.

The other animals run off.
They don't want to stay.

So now how many are left
if you take 7 away?

$8 - 7 = \_\_\_$

Name ______________________________

TEST PREPARATION

Listen to your teacher read the directions.
Fill in the circle under the correct answer.

1.

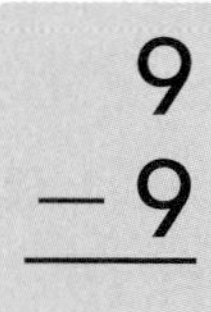

$$\begin{array}{r} 9 \\ -9 \\ \hline \end{array}$$

9 ○ 18 ○ 0 ○ 99 ○

2. 8 + 3 = 11
11 − 3 = 8

9 + 3 = 12
12 − 3 = 9
○

3 + 8 = 11
11 − 8 = 3
○

8 + 3 = 11
11 − 3 = 8
○

11 − 8 = 3
11 − 7 = 4
○

3. 6 + 9 = ?

16 ○ 3 ○ 15 ○ 14 ○

4. Nan has 10 goldfish and 10 blue fish. How many fish does she have?

20 ○ 100 ○ 10 ○ 0 ○

5. 9 + 10 = 19

10 + 9 = 19 ○
19 − 10 = 9 ○
9 + 9 = 18 ○
19 − 9 = 10 ○

6.

$$\begin{array}{r} 14 \\ -\ 5 \\ \hline 9 \end{array} \quad \begin{array}{r} 14 \\ -\ 6 \\ \hline 8 \end{array} \quad \begin{array}{r} 14 \\ -\ 7 \\ \hline 7 \end{array}$$

$$\begin{array}{r} 14 \\ -\ 4 \\ \hline 10 \end{array} \quad \begin{array}{r} 15 \\ -\ 8 \\ \hline 7 \end{array} \quad \begin{array}{r} 16 \\ -\ 7 \\ \hline 9 \end{array} \quad \begin{array}{r} 14 \\ -\ 8 \\ \hline 6 \end{array}$$

○ ○ ○ ○

7. ? + 9 = 13

4 ○ 9 ○ 5 ○ 6 ○

8. Zak has 10 mice. He feeds 8 of them. How many does he have left to feed?

18 ○ 2 ○ 4 ○ 8 ○

Copyright © by William H. Sadlier, Inc. All rights reserved.

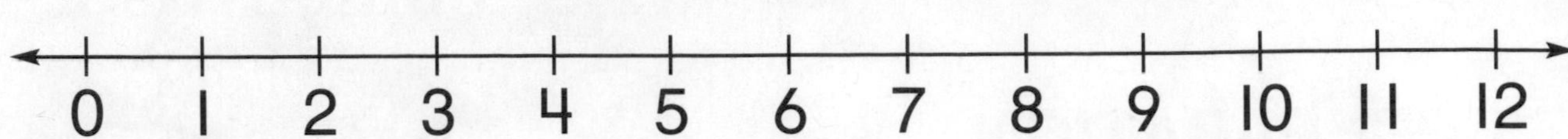

Fill in the circle under the correct answer.

9. The bunny starts at 8. He hops 3 times. Where is he now?

8 ○ 11 ○

10 ○ 3 ○

10. 5 + 9 = ?

14 ○ 15 ○ 59 ○ 4 ○

11. Choose the related subtraction fact.

12 − 5 = 7

7 − 2 = 5 ○ 7 + 5 = 12 ○

12 − 7 = 5 ○ 5 + 7 = 12 ○

12. John sees 4 bugs. Cole sees 1 more bug than John. How many bugs does Cole see?

4 ○ 3 ○ 6 ○ 5 ○

13. Gray catches 7 fish. Lisa catches 2 fish. How many fish do they catch in all?

7 ○ 5 ○ 9 ○ 14 ○

14. 7 + 7 = ?

13 ○ 12 ○ 15 ○ 14 ○

15. Choose the related addition fact.

6 + 7 = 13

6 + 1 = 7 ○ 7 + 6 = 13 ○

13 − 7 = 6 ○ 13 − 6 = 7 ○

16. There are 13 birds in a tree. 4 fly away. How many birds are left?

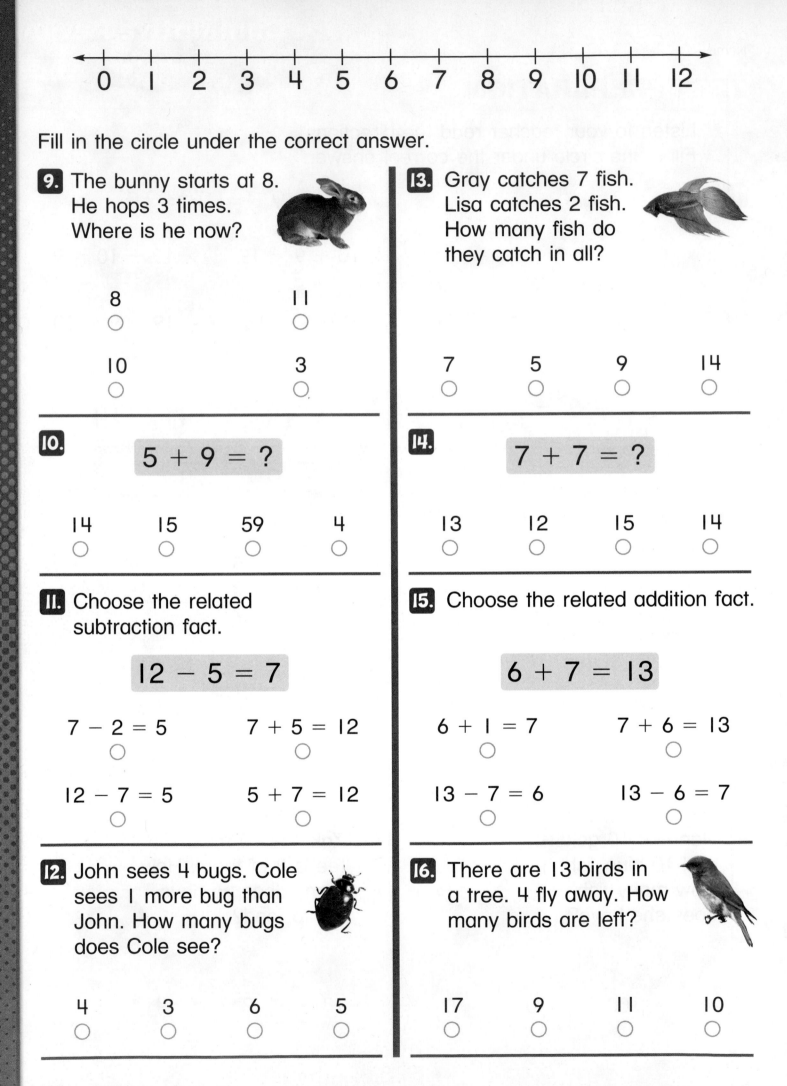

17 ○ 9 ○ 11 ○ 10 ○

Place Value to 100

CHAPTER 2

Listen Listen to your teacher read the poem.

What groups of ten do you see in the rainforest?

Dear Family,

Today our class began Chapter 2. We will learn about place value to 100. Let's do the activity below together so I can review the skills I will need in order to understand the math in this chapter. Then you can read some of the new vocabulary I will learn in Chapter 2.

Love, ____________________

10 Plus

Make a group of 10 objects, such as beans or small pieces of pasta or paper. Count how many with your child.

Then show other groups of from 1 to 9 objects and have your child add each group, one object at a time, to the group of 10 to find how many in all.

Chapter 2 Vocabulary

also on-line

ones unit ▪

ten rod ▬▬▬▬▬▬▬▬▬▬

place-value chart

tens	ones

expanded form $40 + 6 \longrightarrow 46$

value 3 tens 1 one = 31

6 is less than 7 — $6 < 7$

7 is greater than 6 — $7 > 6$

7 is equal to 7 — $7 = 7$

4, 5, 6

4 is just before 5

6 is just after 5

5 is between 4 and 6

even numbers 2, 4, 6, 8, 10

odd numbers 1, 3, 5, 7, 9

count by 3s 3, 6, 9, 12

count by 4s 4, 8, 12

For Additional Resources: VISIT US ON-LINE www.sadlier-oxford.com

Name ____________________

Tens and Ones

HANDS-ON LESSON

Let's Learn!

How many **tens** and **ones** are in 36 ones?

I make groups of 10 to find how many tens and ones.

10 ones = 1 ten

36 ones = 3 tens 6 ones

36

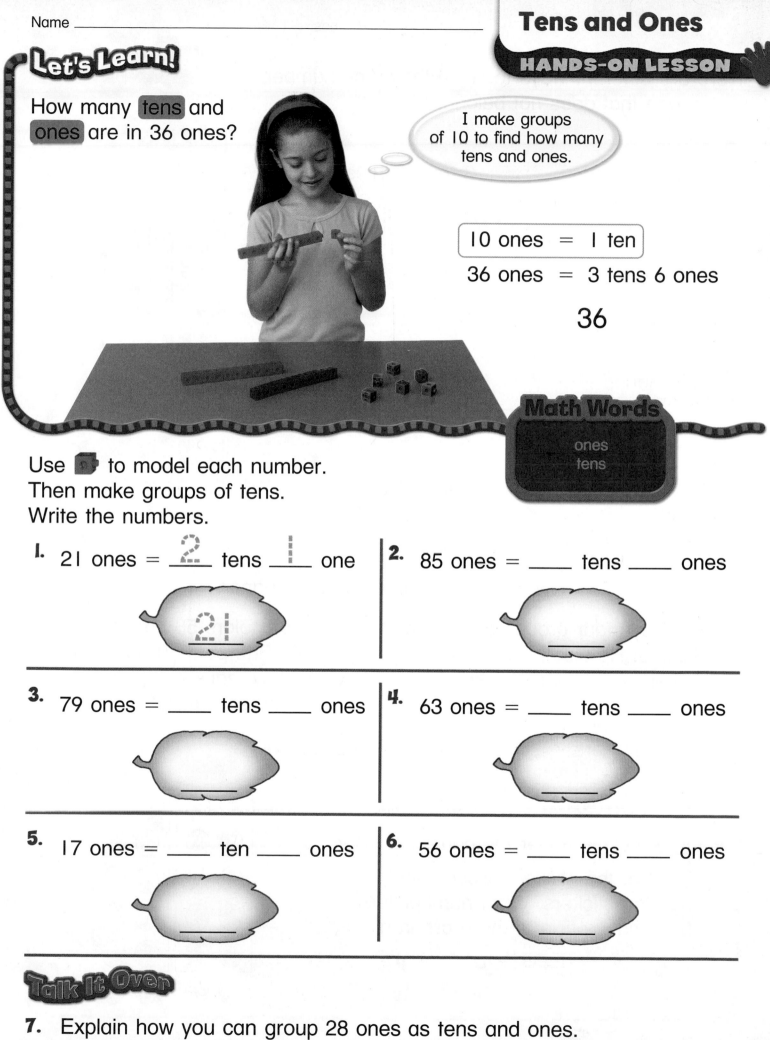

Math Words
ones
tens

Use [cube] to model each number.
Then make groups of tens.
Write the numbers.

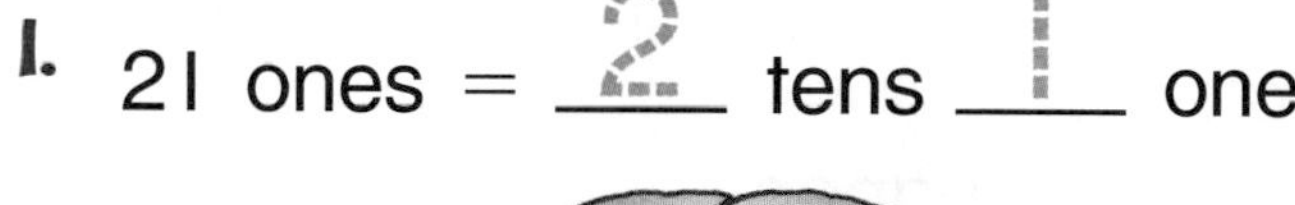

1. 21 ones = 2 tens 1 one

21

2. 85 ones = ____ tens ____ ones

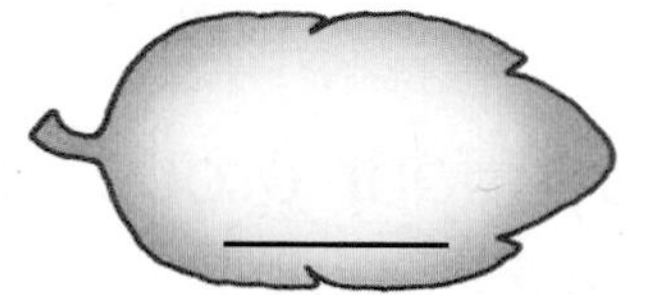

3. 79 ones = ____ tens ____ ones

4. 63 ones = ____ tens ____ ones

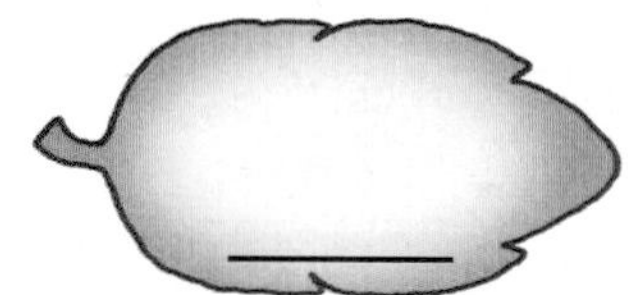

5. 17 ones = ____ ten ____ ones

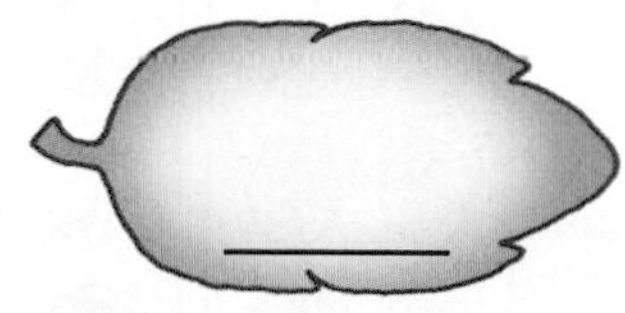

6. 56 ones = ____ tens ____ ones

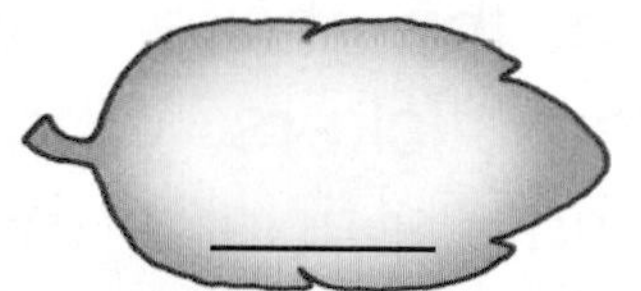

Talk It Over

7. Explain how you can group 28 ones as tens and ones.

Copyright © by William H. Sadlier, Inc. All rights reserved.

Practice

Here are different ways to show the same number.
✘ the one that does not belong.

8. 32 ones | 3 tens 2 ones

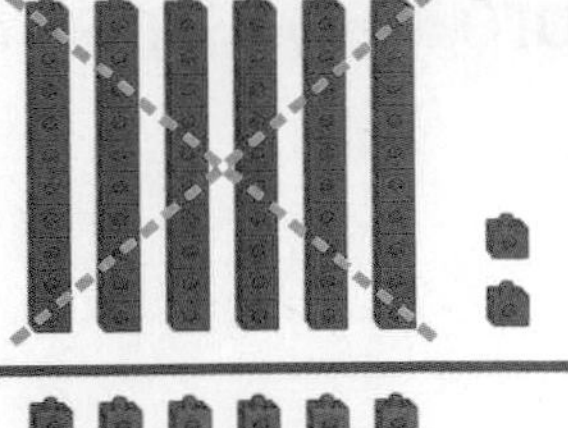

9. 64 ones | 6 tens 6 ones

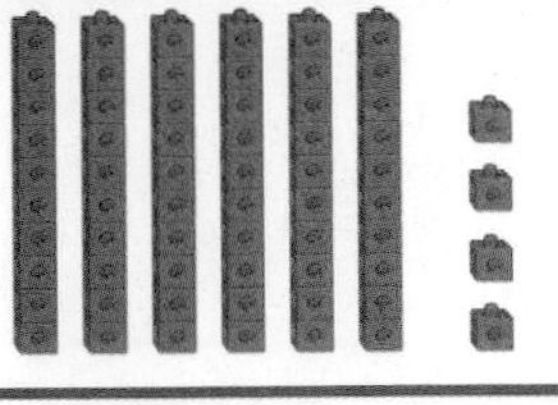

10. 59 ones | 9 tens 5 ones

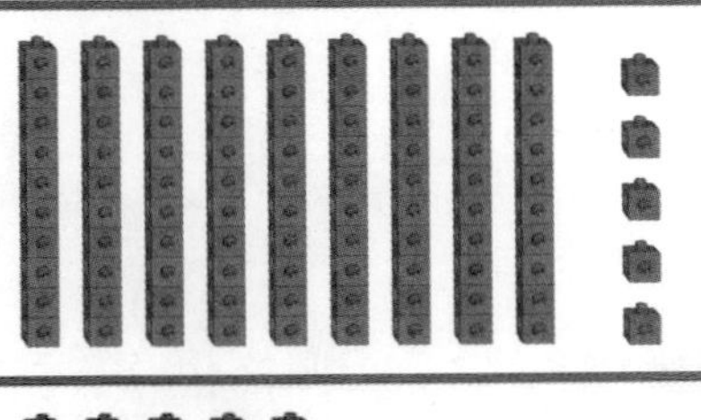

11. 40 ones | 4 tens 0 ones

Solve. Use a problem-solving strategy.
Show your work on a separate sheet of paper.

12. Raz buys four groups of 10 bird stickers. He also buys 2 snake stickers. How many stickers does he buy in all?

_____ stickers

13. Theresa colors 58 paper leaves. She puts 10 on each vine. How many complete vines can she make?

_____ vines

TEST PREPARATION

Fill in the circle under the correct answer.

14. Look at the stickers. Each sheet has ten stickers. What number tells how many stickers there are in all?

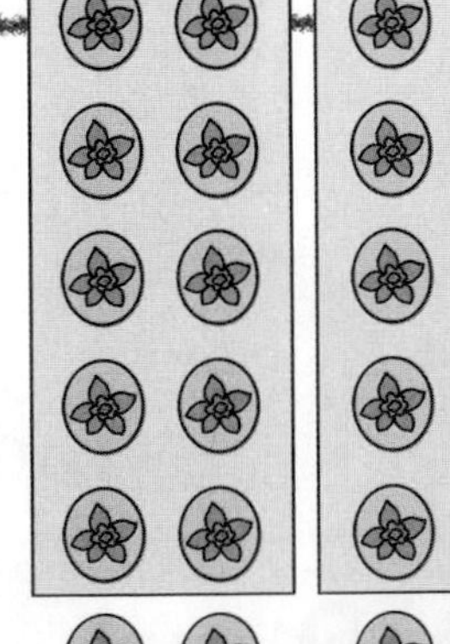

6	14	24	34
○	○	○	○

Math Alive at Home Give your child 32 objects, such as beans. Ask her/him to make groups of 10 and to tell how many tens and ones are in 32.

Name ______________________________

Place Value

Let's Learn!

Tim models 4 tens 2 ones with **ten rods** and ones units.
What **2-digit number** does Tim model?

Place-Value Chart

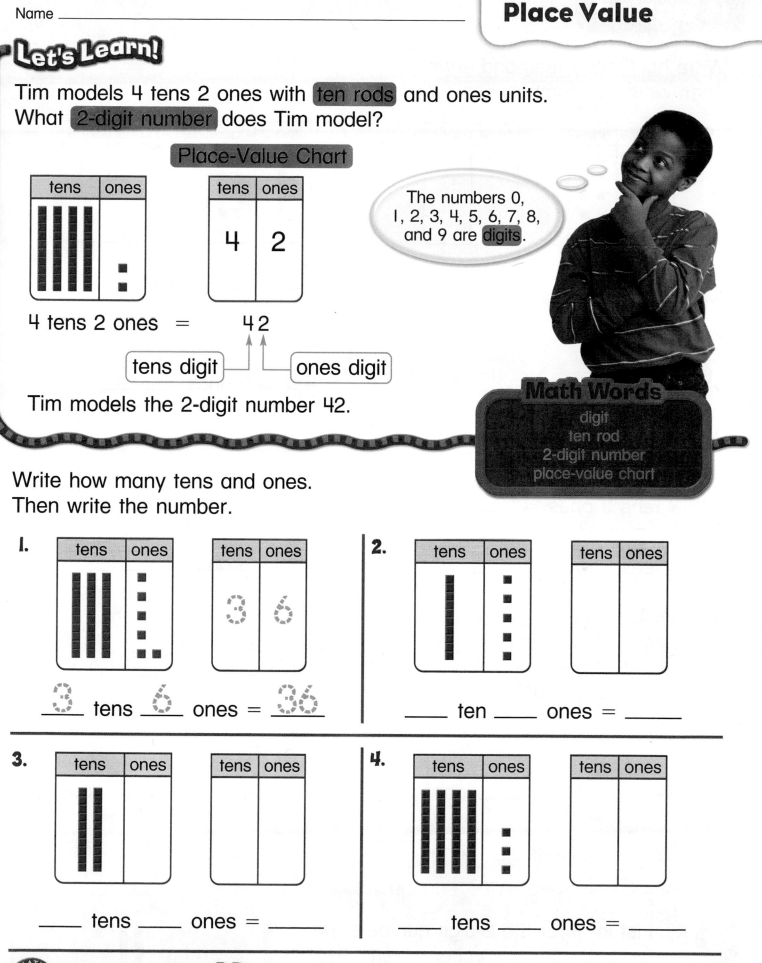

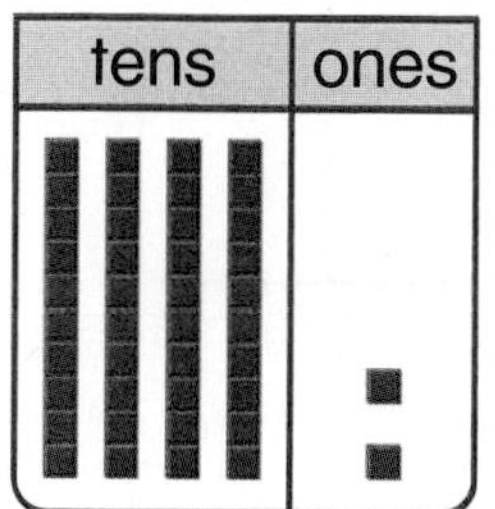

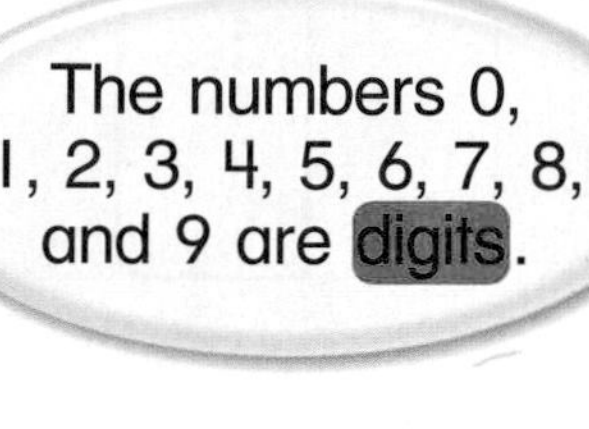

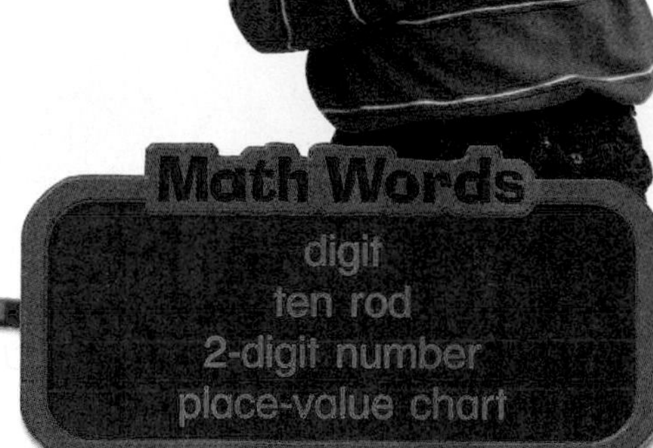

The numbers 0, 1, 2, 3, 4, 5, 6, 7, 8, and 9 are digits.

4 tens 2 ones = 42

tens digit ↑ ↑ ones digit

Tim models the 2-digit number 42.

Math Words
digit
ten rod
2-digit number
place-value chart

Write how many tens and ones.
Then write the number.

1.

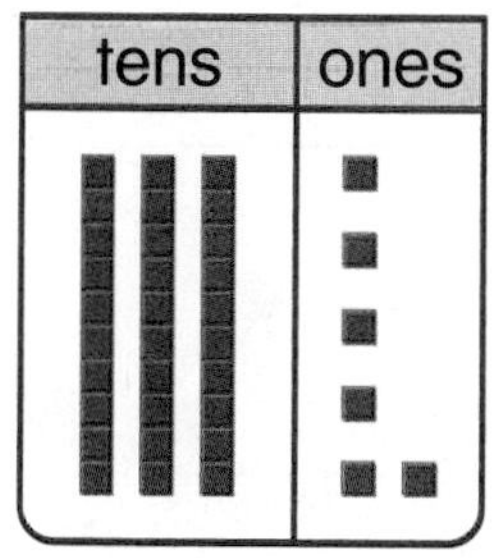

tens	ones
3	6

3 tens 6 ones = 36

2.

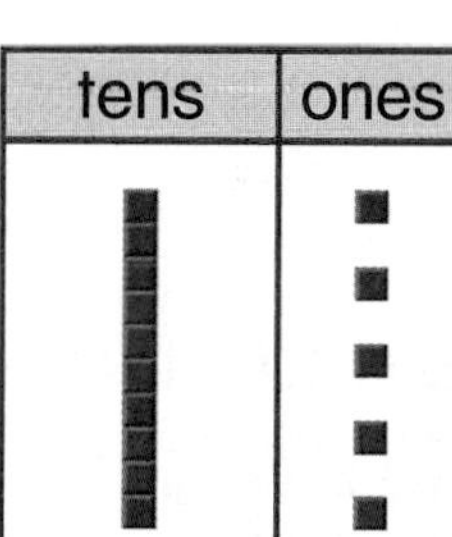

tens	ones

____ ten ____ ones = ____

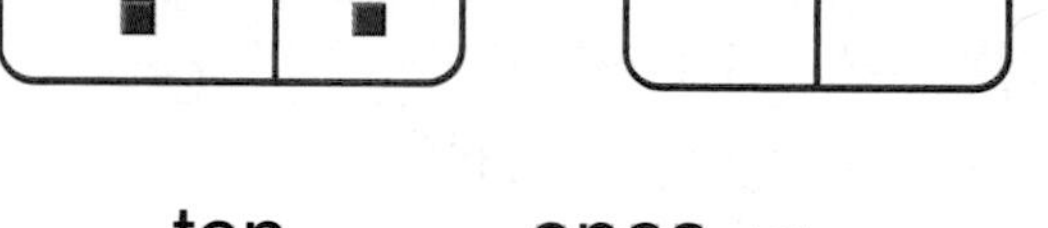

3.

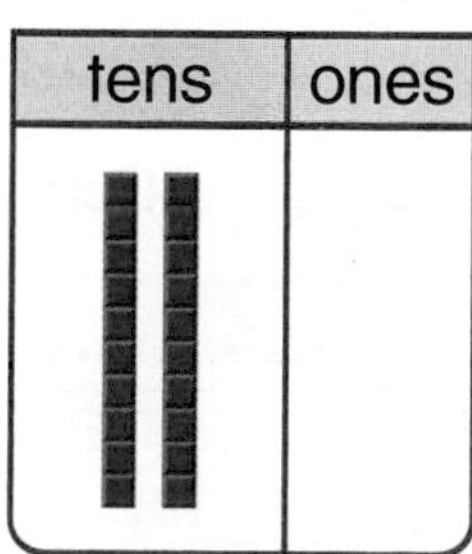

tens	ones

____ tens ____ ones = ____

4.

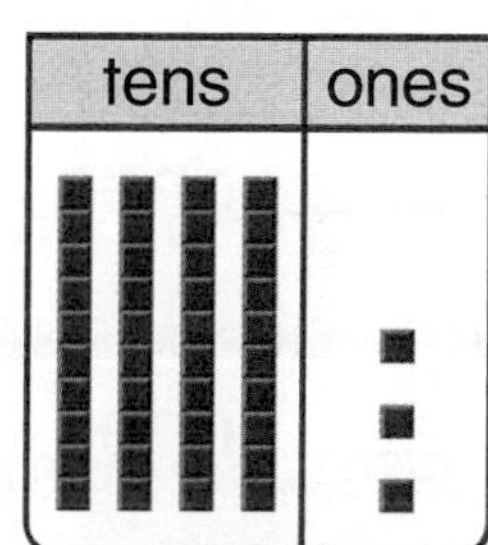

tens	ones

____ tens ____ ones = ____

5. How are 46 and 64 alike? How are they different?

Copyright © by William H. Sadlier, Inc. All rights reserved.

Practice

Write how many tens and ones.
Then write the number.

6.

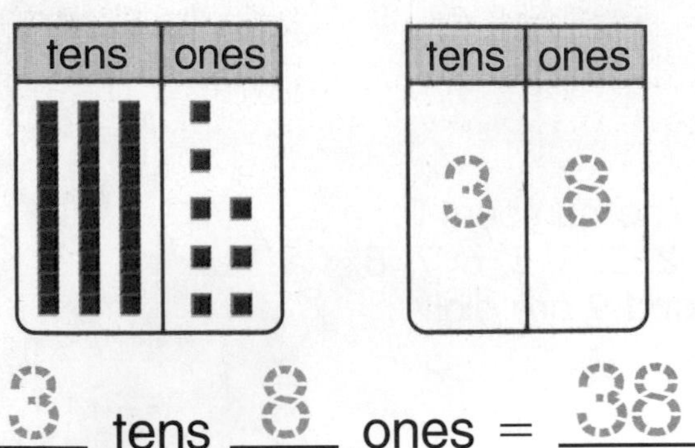

3 tens 8 ones = 38

7.

tens	ones

tens	ones

____ ten ____ ones = ____

Write the number.

8. 5 tens 2 ones = ____

9. 4 tens 5 ones = ____

10. 7 tens 0 ones = ____

11. 8 tens 9 ones = ____

12. 9 tens 3 ones = ____

13. 6 tens 1 one = ____

14. 8 tens 4 ones = ____

15. 2 tens 6 ones = ____

Write how many tens and ones.

16. 18 = ____ ten ____ ones

17. 24 = ____ tens ____ ones

18. 67 = ____ tens ____ ones

19. 73 = ____ tens ____ ones

20. 59 = ____ tens ____ ones

21. 96 = ____ tens ____ ones

22. 32 = ____ tens ____ ones

23. 41 = ____ tens ____ one

CRITICAL THINKING

MATH JOURNAL

24. List in order the 2-digit numbers that have the same number of tens and ones. Describe the pattern you see.

= 11 = 22

Math Alive at Home Ask your child to draw or model a number that has 4 tens 6 ones.

Name ______________________________

Number Words Twenty to Forty-Nine

Let's Learn!

Here are some **number words**.

20 twenty	30 thirty	40 forty
21 twenty-one	31 thirty-one	41 forty-one
22 twenty-two	32 thirty-two	42 forty-two
23 twenty-three	33 thirty-three	43 forty-three
24 twenty-four	34 thirty-four	
25 twenty-five	35 thirty-five	
26 twenty-six		
27 twenty-seven		
28 twenty-eight		
29 twenty-nine		

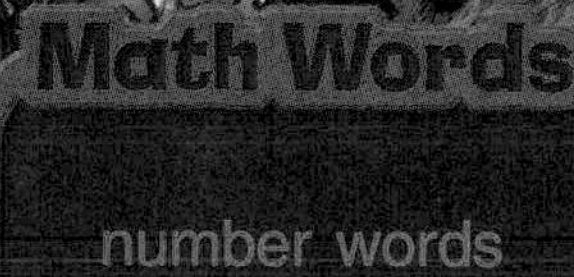
Use a - to write
number words ending in
one through nine.

Math Words
number words

Write the number for each number word.

1. forty-five 45	2. twenty-four ____	3. thirty-nine ____
4. twenty-six ____	5. forty-four ____	6. twenty ____
7. thirty-seven ____	8. twenty-three ____	9. forty-eight ____
10. twenty-one ____	11. thirty ____	12. thirty-five ____

Talk It Over

13. How does knowing the number words one through nine help you with other number words?

Copyright © by William H. Sadlier, Inc. All rights reserved.

Practice

Write the number word.

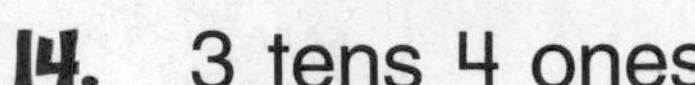

14. 3 tens 4 ones

thirty-four

15. 2 tens 8 ones ____________

16. 2 tens 9 ones ____________

17. 2 tens 2 ones ____________

18. 2 tens 5 ones ____________

19. 4 tens 0 ones ____________

20. 3 tens 1 one ____________

21. 4 tens 3 ones ____________

22. 4 tens 7 ones ____________

23. 3 tens 3 ones ____________

24. 4 tens 6 ones ____________

Draw lines to connect three ways to write the same number.

25. 2 tens 5 ones	forty-one	38
26. 4 tens 9 ones	thirty-eight	25
27. 3 tens 8 ones	twenty-five	49
28. 4 tens 1 one	forty-nine	41

CRITICAL THINKING

29. Jill draws 36 ones.
Tom draws 3 tens and then 6 more tens.
Mary draws 3 ☐☐☐☐☐☐☐☐☐☐ and 6 ☐.
Who does not draw thirty-six?

____________ does not draw thirty-six.

Math Alive at Home Ask your child to name a number between 20 and 50, and then to write that number word.

Name ______________________________

Number Words Fifty to Ninety-Nine

Let's Learn!

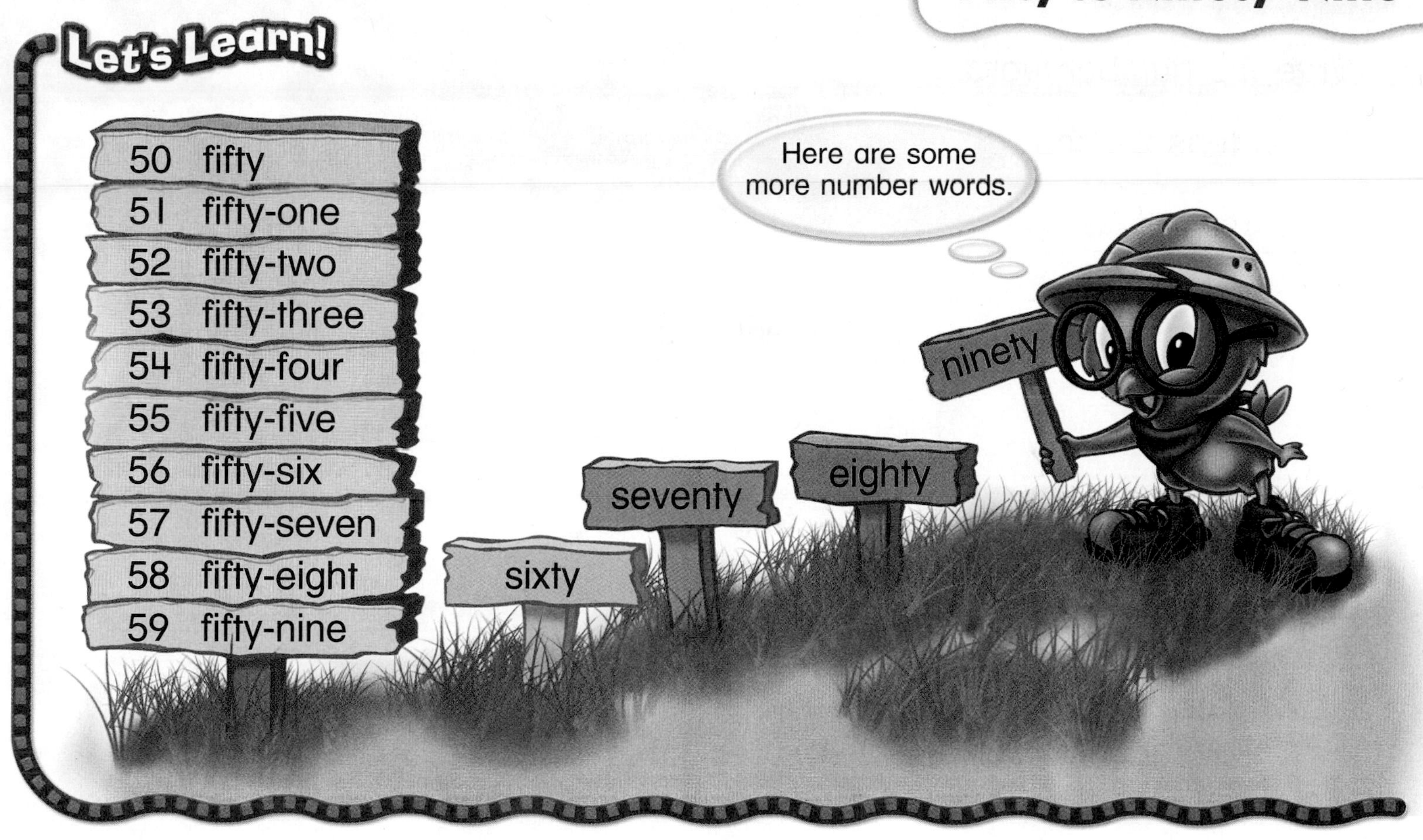

Write the number for each number word.

1. sixty-five 65	**2.** ninety-three _____	**3.** eighty-two _____
4. fifty-nine _____	**5.** seventy-one _____	**6.** ninety _____
7. eighty-six _____	**8.** sixty-four _____	**9.** fifty-eight _____
10. ninety-nine _____	**11.** eighty _____	**12.** seventy-three _____

Math Journal — Write About It

13. Explain why in the number words fifty through fifty-nine the first part of the number words stays the same.

Copyright © by William H. Sadlier, Inc. All rights reserved.

Practice

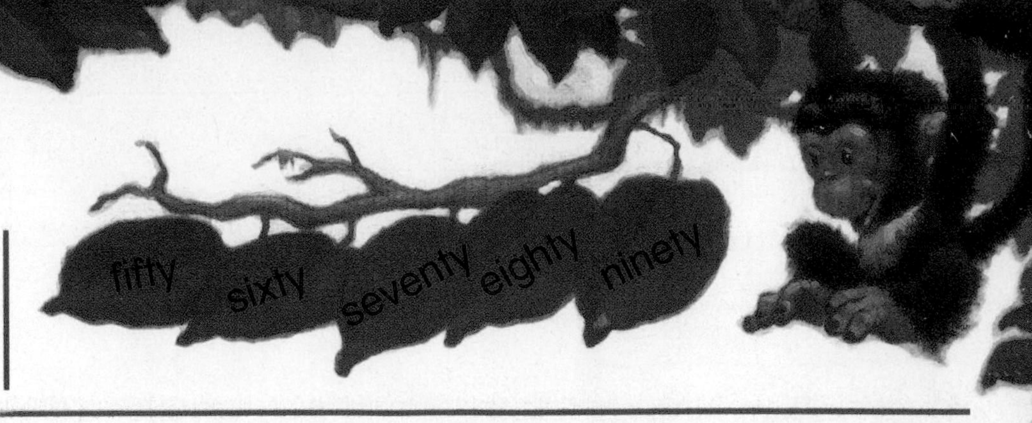

Write the number word.

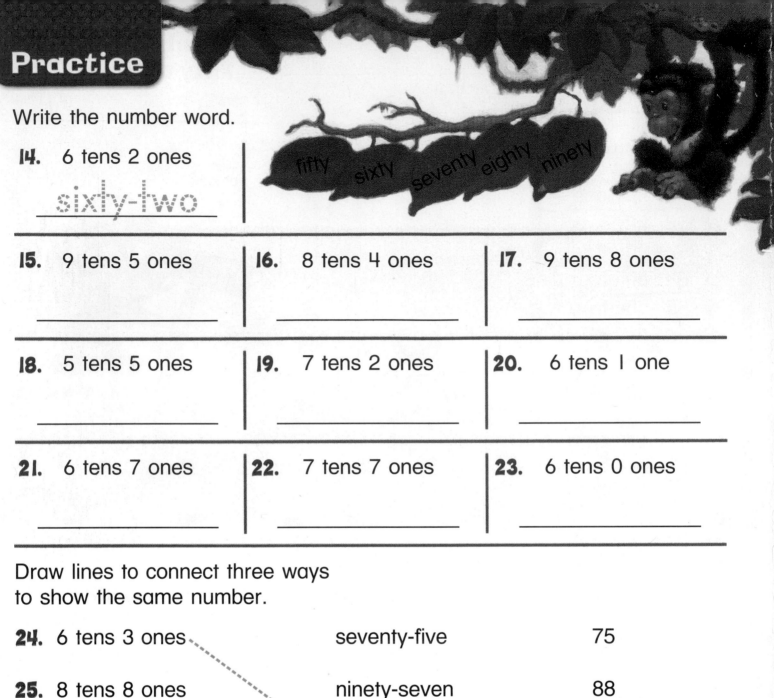

14. 6 tens 2 ones

sixty-two

15. 9 tens 5 ones ________

16. 8 tens 4 ones ________

17. 9 tens 8 ones ________

18. 5 tens 5 ones ________

19. 7 tens 2 ones ________

20. 6 tens 1 one ________

21. 6 tens 7 ones ________

22. 7 tens 7 ones ________

23. 6 tens 0 ones ________

Draw lines to connect three ways to show the same number.

24. 6 tens 3 ones	seventy-five	75
25. 8 tens 8 ones	ninety-seven	88
26. 5 tens 4 ones	sixty-three	54
27. 9 tens 7 ones	fifty-four	97
28. 7 tens 5 ones	eighty-eight	63

CALCULATOR ACTIVITY

Use a calculator.

29. Count by 1s from 90 to 100.

How many numbers did you count? ____

Math Alive at Home Ask your child to name a number between 50 and 99, and then to write that number word.

Name ____

Find Needed Information

- You can reread a problem to find information you need.

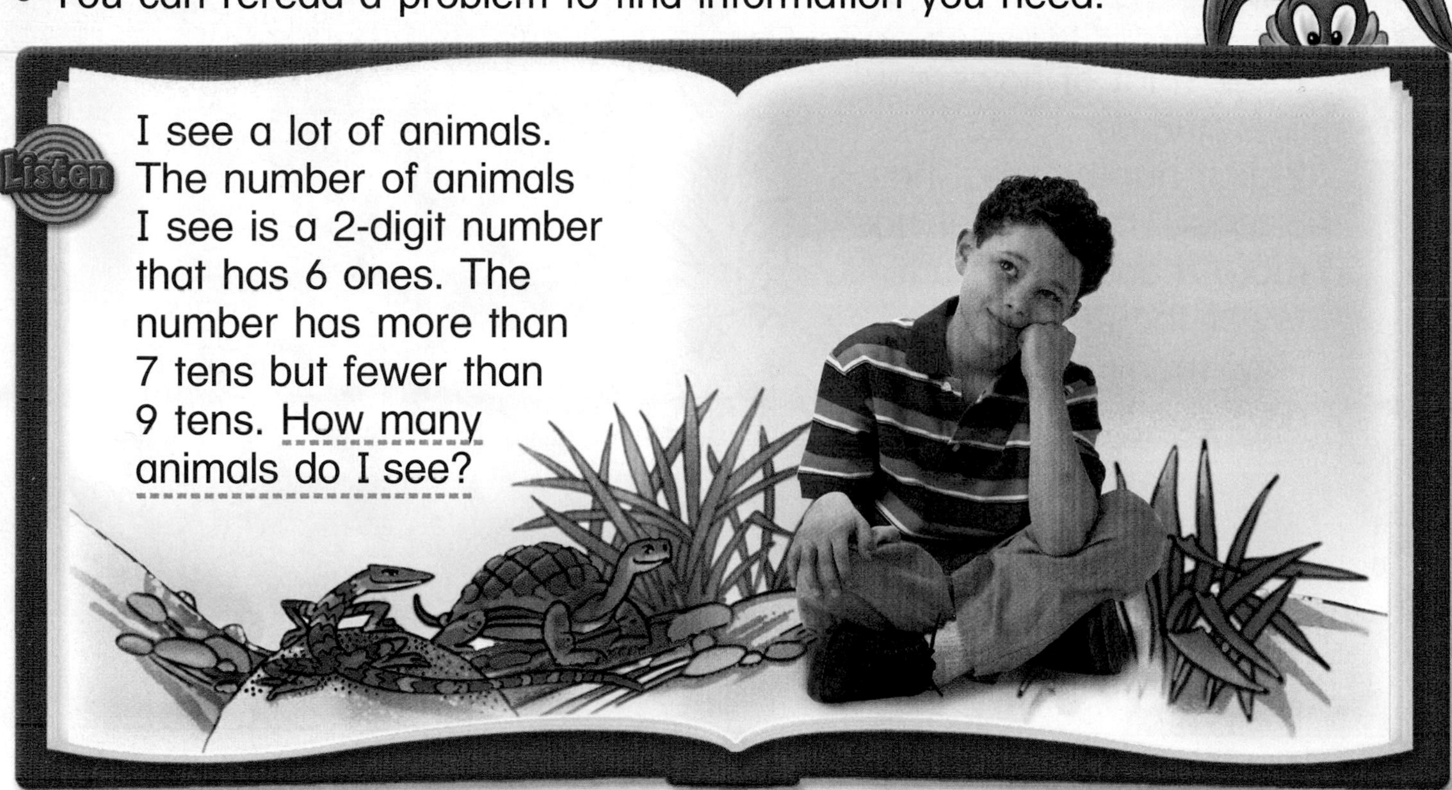

Listen
I see a lot of animals. The number of animals I see is a 2-digit number that has 6 ones. The number has more than 7 tens but fewer than 9 tens. How many animals do I see?

1. Reread the problem. Draw a line under the question you need to answer.

2. How many digits does the number have? ____ digits

3. How many ones does the number have? ____ ones

4. Reread the part of the problem that tells how many tens the number has. Then fill in the blanks.

more than ____ but fewer than ____ tens

5. How many tens does the number have? ____ tens

6. Now solve the problem. Fill in the blanks.

____ tens ____ ones

I see _____ animals.

Copyright © by William H. Sadlier, Inc. All rights reserved.

Practice

Find Needed Information

Listen
I see a lot of flowers. The number I see is a 2-digit number that has 5 tens. The number has more than 2 ones but fewer than 4 ones. How many flowers do I see?

7. Reread the problem. Draw a line under the question you need to answer.

8. How many digits does the number have?

____ digits

9. How many tens does the number have?

____ tens

10. Reread the part of the problem that tells how many ones the number has. Then fill in the blanks.

more than ____ but fewer than ____ ones

11. How many ones does the number have?

____ ones

12. Now solve the problem. Fill in the blanks.

____ ____
tens ones

I see _____ flowers.

Math Alive at Home Today your child found needed information to work through math problems.

Name ______________________________

Place Value of Two-Digit Numbers

Let's Learn!

What is the **value** of each digit in 45?

45

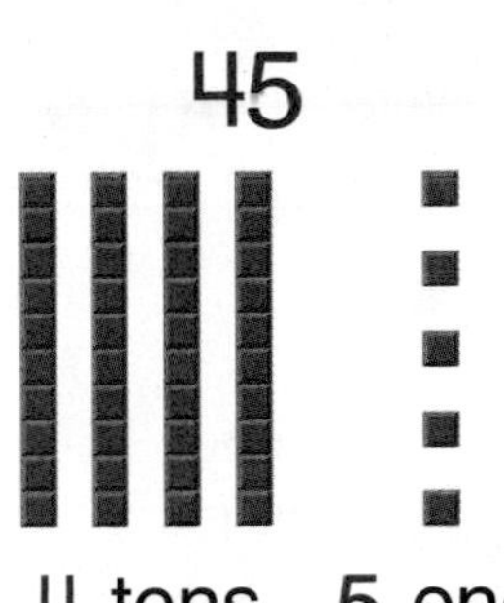

4 tens   5 ones

To tell the value of each digit, look at its place in the number.

4 tens = 40
The value of 4 in 45 is 40.

5 ones = 5
The value of 5 in 45 is 5.

Circle the value of the underlined digit.

1. $6\underline{2}$ (2) 20	**2.** $\underline{4}4$ 4 40	**3.** $\underline{1}3$ 1 10
4. $\underline{9}0$ 9 90	**5.** $3\underline{3}$ 3 30	**6.** $8\underline{0}$ 0 10
7. $5\underline{1}$ 1 10	**8.** $\underline{7}2$ 7 70	**9.** $2\underline{4}$ 4 40
10. $\underline{5}6$ 5 50	**11.** $2\underline{8}$ 8 80	**12.** $\underline{3}7$ 3 30

13. How do you find the value of a digit in a number?

Copyright © by William H. Sadlier, Inc. All rights reserved.

Practice

Look at the place
of each digit
in the number.

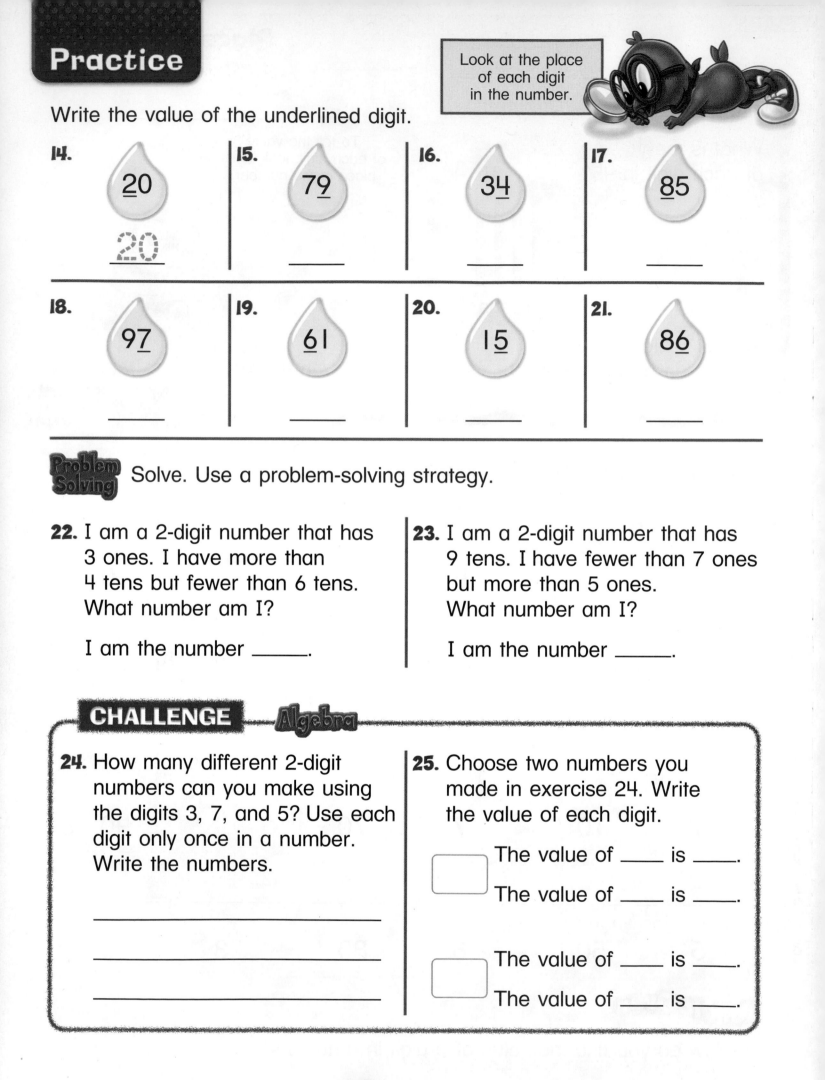

Write the value of the underlined digit.

14.  20 — 20

15.  79 ______

16.  34 ______

17.  85 ______

18.  97 ______

19.  61 ______

20.  15 ______

21.  86 ______

Solve. Use a problem-solving strategy.

22. I am a 2-digit number that has 3 ones. I have more than 4 tens but fewer than 6 tens. What number am I?

I am the number ______.

23. I am a 2-digit number that has 9 tens. I have fewer than 7 ones but more than 5 ones. What number am I?

I am the number ______.

CHALLENGE

24. How many different 2-digit numbers can you make using the digits 3, 7, and 5? Use each digit only once in a number. Write the numbers.

______

______

______

25. Choose two numbers you made in exercise 24. Write the value of each digit.

☐ The value of ____ is ____.
The value of ____ is ____.

☐ The value of ____ is ____.
The value of ____ is ____.

Math Alive at Home Ask your child to tell you the value of the digit 4 in the number 41, 9 in 29, and 6 in 76. (40, 9, 6)

Name ___________________________

Expanded Form

Let's Learn!

Write the **expanded form** of 32.

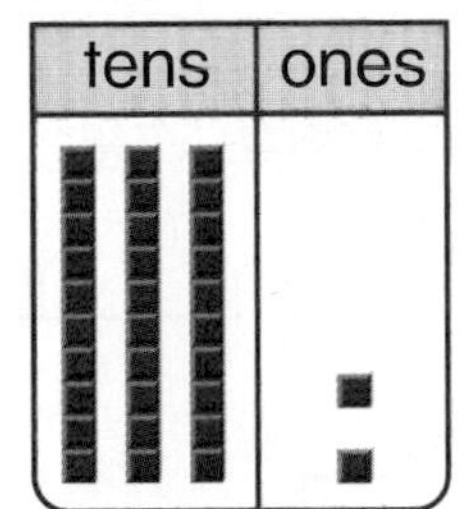

3 tens 2 ones

3 tens = 30
2 ones = 2

30 + 2 is the expanded form of 32.

Math Words
expanded form

Write how many tens and ones.
Then write the expanded form.

1. 59

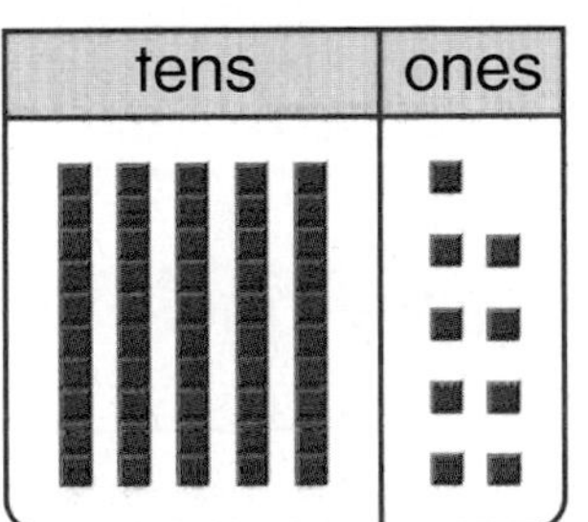

5 tens 9 ones
50 + 9

2. 44

tens	ones

___ tens ___ ones
___ + ___

3. 12

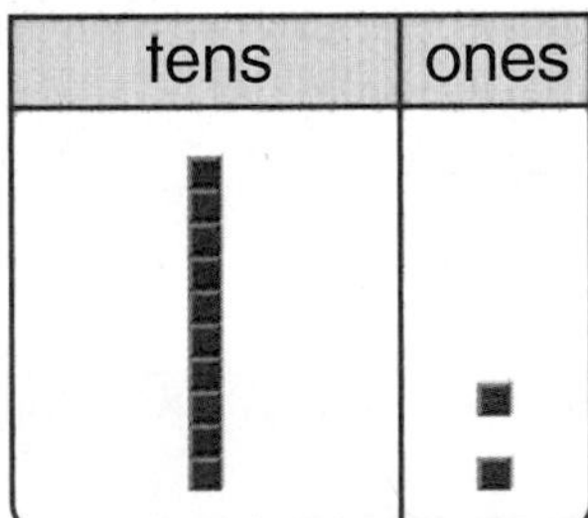

___ ten ___ ones
___ + ___

4. 66

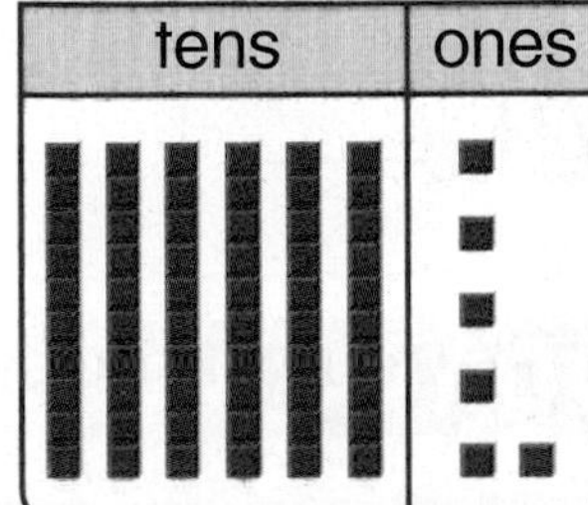

___ tens ___ ones
___ + ___

5. What is the expanded form of 70?

Copyright © by William H. Sadlier, Inc. All rights reserved.

Practice

6 tens is 60.

Complete. Write each number in expanded form.

6. 8 tens 1 one = 81
80 + 1

7. 6 tens 3 ones = ____
____ + ____

8. 9 tens 5 ones = ____
____ + ____

9. 3 tens 3 ones = ____
____ + ____

10. 7 tens 6 ones = ____
____ + ____

11. 9 tens 0 ones = ____
____ + ____

12. 5 tens 7 ones = ____
____ + ____

13. 4 tens 8 ones = ____
____ + ____

14. 2 tens 2 ones = ____
____ + ____

15. 1 ten 9 ones = ____
____ + ____

Write the number in expanded form.

16. 39 ___ + ___

17. 67 ___ + ___

18. 89 ___ + ___

19. 74 ___ + ___

20. 40 ___ + ___

21. 55 ___ + ___

DO YOU REMEMBER?

Add.

22. 4 + 3 + 7 = ____

23. 2 + 1 + 8 + 4 = ____

Subtract.

24. 18 − 9 = ____

25. 15 − 7 = ____

Math Alive at Home Ask your child to tell you the expanded form for 85, 60, and 14. (80+5, 60+0, 10+4)

Name ____________________

Check Your Progress
Lessons 1-7

TEST PREPARATION

Listen to your teacher read the directions.
Fill in the circle under the correct answer.

1.

tens	ones
3	9

39 ○ 93 ○ 40 ○ 90 ○

2. 83 ones

30 tens 8 ones ○ 8 tens 3 ones ○

8 tens 30 ones ○ 80 tens 3 ones ○

3.

tens	ones

4 tens 5 ones ○ 5 tens 5 ones ○

5 tens 0 ones ○ 0 tens 5 ones ○

4. 9 tens 6 ones

69 ○ 99 ○ 96 ○ 90 ○

5. 31

31 ○ 30 + 1 ○ 3 + 1 ○ 13 ○

6. 50

5 tens 5 ones ○ 50 tens 0 ones ○

5 tens 0 ones ○ 0 tens 5 ones ○

7.

tens	ones
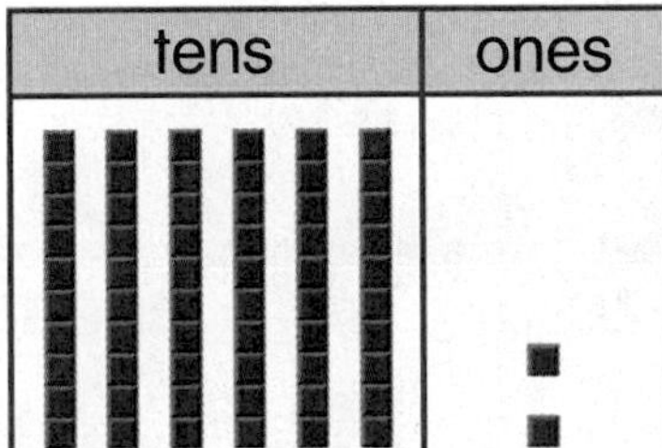	

6 tens 2 ones ○ 6 tens 6 ones ○

5 tens 2 ones ○ 2 tens 6 ones ○

8. eighty-eight

86 ○ 88 ○ 80 ○ 68 ○

Copyright © by William H. Sadlier, Inc. All rights reserved.

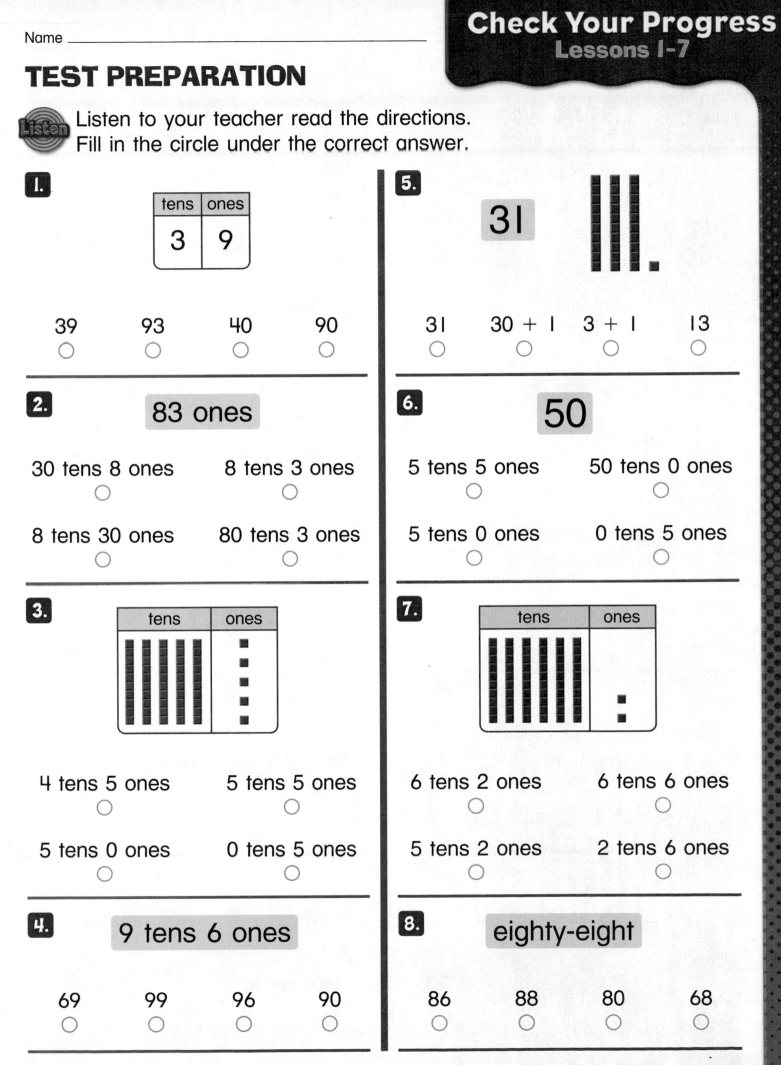

Fill in the circle under the correct answer.

9. What is the value of the underlined digit?

7<u>4</u>

40	7	4	70
○	○	○	○

10. Which number completes the expanded form of 43?

? + 3

30	44	3	40
○	○	○	○

11. What is the number word for 2 tens 0 ones?

two-zero	twenty
○	○
twenty-zero	twenty-two
○	○

12. What is the number?

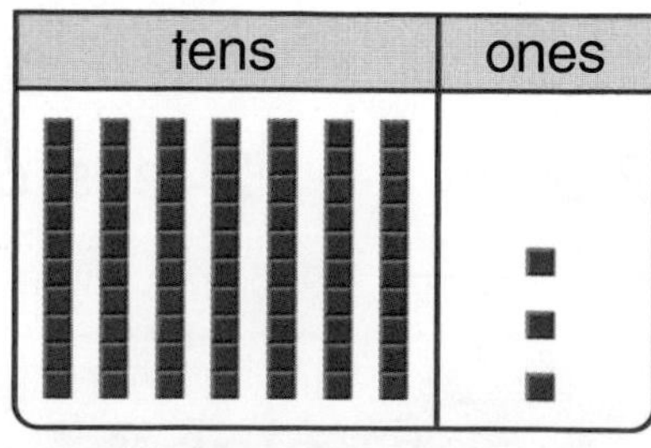

70	73	63	30
○	○	○	○

13. What is the value of the underlined digit?

<u>3</u>7

3	7	30	70
○	○	○	○

14. Choose the expanded form of 66.

60 + 1	10 + 1
○	○
60 + 6	10 + 6
○	○

15. What is the number for 8 tens 2 ones?

28	20	80	82
○	○	○	○

16. What is the number word for 47?

forty-seven	fourteen
○	○
four-seven	forty
○	○

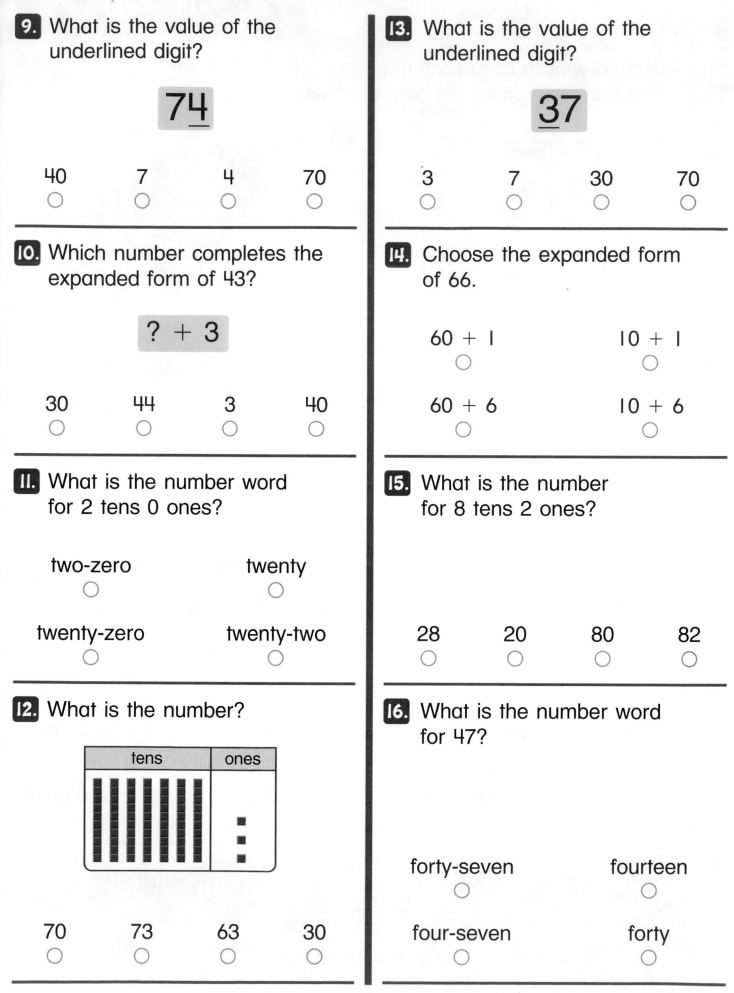

Name ______________________________

Let's Learn!

Compare 25 and 32.

Compare the tens.

Two tens is fewer than three tens.

25 **is less than** 32.

$25 < 32$

Compare 35 and 35.

The tens and ones are the same.

The numbers are equal.

35 **is equal to** 35.

$35 = 35$

Compare 57 and 54.

The tens are the same. Compare the ones.

Seven ones is more than four ones.

57 **is greater than** 54.

$57 > 54$

Math Words

is less than <
is greater than >
is equal to =

Compare. Write **is less than**, **is equal to**, or **is greater than**.
Then write <, =, or >.

1. 48 is greater than 27. 48 (>) 27	**2.** 34 ______________ 45. 34 ( ) 45
3. 16 ______________ 19. 16 ( ) 19	**4.** 91 ______________ 96. 91 ( ) 96
5. 18 ______________ 18. 18 ( ) 18	**6.** 12 ______________ 11. 12 ( ) 11
7. 91 ______________ 19. 91 ( ) 19	**8.** 67 ______________ 67. 67 ( ) 67

9. When you compare two 2-digit numbers, why is it important to compare the tens first?

Copyright © by William H. Sadlier, Inc. All rights reserved.

Practice

is less than <
is equal to =
is greater than >

Compare. Write <, =, or >.

10. 32  < 52	**11.** 75 ◯ 57	
12. 89 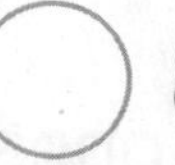 89	**13.** 82 ◯ 84	**14.** 79 ◯ 74
15. 63 ◯ 93	**16.** 40 ◯ 40	**17.** 66 ◯ 79
18. 29 ◯ 25	**19.** 17 ◯ 71	**20.** 93 ◯ 93

21. sixty-two  sixty-five	**22.** fourteen  forty
23. eighty ◯ eighteen	**24.** ninety ◯ ninety

Solve. Use a problem-solving strategy.

25. I am a number greater than 80.
I am less than 85.
What number could I be?

____

26. Todd finds sixteen flowers.
Cora finds thirty flowers.
Who finds more flowers?

____

CHALLENGE

Add or subtract. Compare. Write <, =, or >.

27. 5 + 6  7 + 4	**28.** 15 − 8 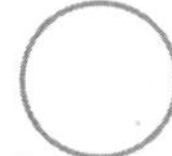 17 − 9
29. 17 − 8 ◯ 6 + 3	**30.** 9 + 8  16 − 8
31. 8 + 6 ◯ 14 − 5	**32.** 18 − 9 ◯ 7 + 8

Math Alive at Home Ask your child to use a >, <, or = sign to compare 46 and 54, 73 and 37, 62 and 62. (<, >, =)

Name ______________________________

Algebra

Order Using a Number Line

Let's Learn!

Use a number line to put numbers in counting order.

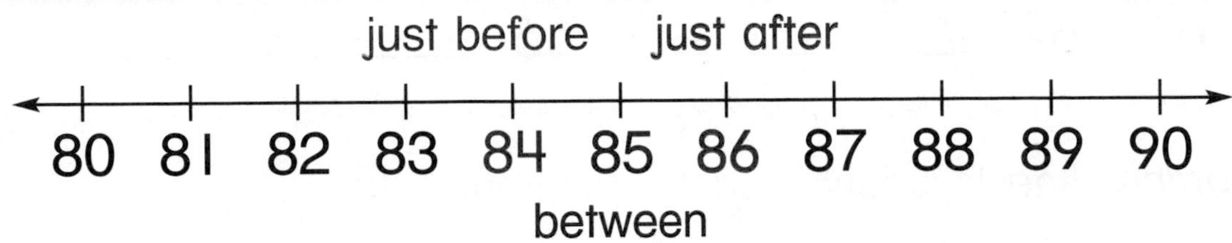

84 is just before 85.
84 is 1 less than 85.

85 is between 84 and 86.

86 is just after 85.
86 is 1 more than 85.

84, 85, 86 are in counting order from least to greatest.

Math Words
order, just before, between, just after, least to greatest

Write the missing number.

1. Just Before

37, 38
____, 50
____, 96

2. Between

57, 58, 59
19, ____, 21
98, ____, 100

3. Just After

20, 21
29, ____
65, ____

Complete the number line.

4. 32, 33, 30

30 31 ____ ____

5. 70, 67, 68

____ ____ 69 ____

6. 52, 55, 53

____ ____ 54 ____

7. 80, 78, 79

____ ____ ____ 81

Talk It Over

8. Can 53 come just before one number and just after another number? Explain.

Copyright © by William H. Sadlier, Inc. All rights reserved.

Practice

9. Complete the number line.

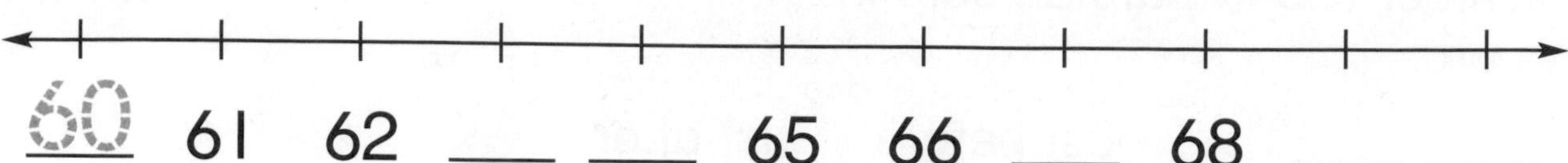

60 61 62 ___ ___ 65 66 ___ 68 ___ ___

Use the number line to answer each question.

10. Which number is the greatest? _____

11. Which number is the least? _____

12. How many numbers are between the least and the greatest? _____

What are they? ______________________________

13. What number comes just after 69? _____

14. What number comes between 60 and 62? _____

15. What number comes just before 63? _____

16. What number comes just after 65? _____

17. What number comes between 66 and 68? _____

18. What number comes just after the last number? _____

19. What number comes just before the first number? _____

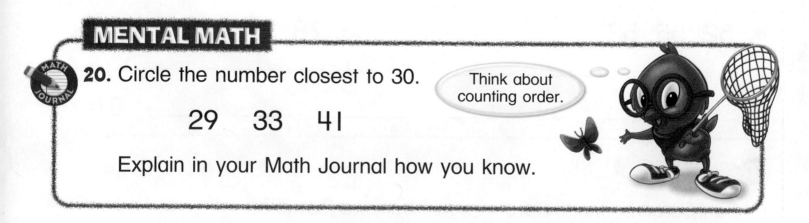

MENTAL MATH

MATH JOURNAL

20. Circle the number closest to 30.

Think about counting order.

29 33 41

Explain in your Math Journal how you know.

Math Alive at Home Give your child a two-digit number such as your age. Ask your child what numbers come just before and just after that number.

Name ______________________________

Let's Learn!

Order 25, 34, and 27 from **greatest to least**.

1. Model each number.

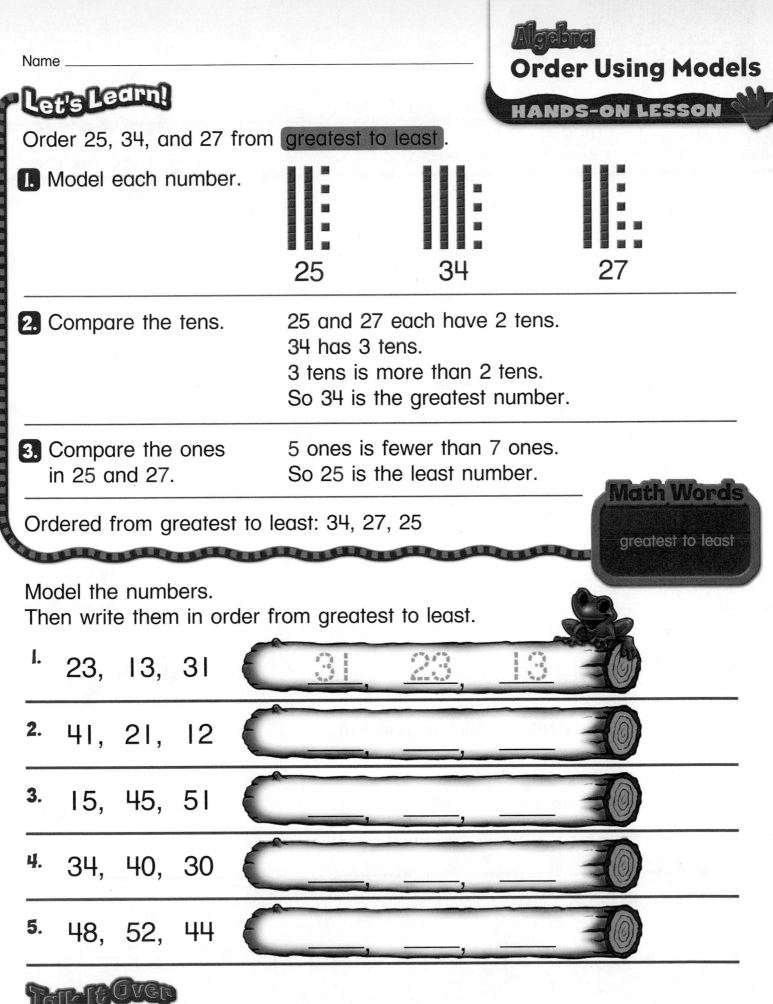

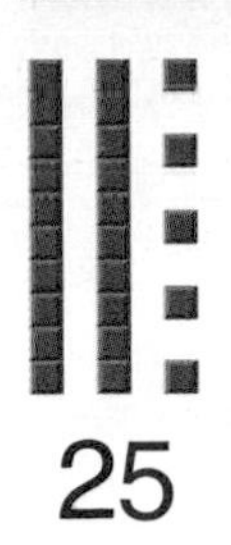
25

34

27

2. Compare the tens.

25 and 27 each have 2 tens.
34 has 3 tens.
3 tens is more than 2 tens.
So 34 is the greatest number.

3. Compare the ones in 25 and 27.

5 ones is fewer than 7 ones.
So 25 is the least number.

Ordered from greatest to least: 34, 27, 25

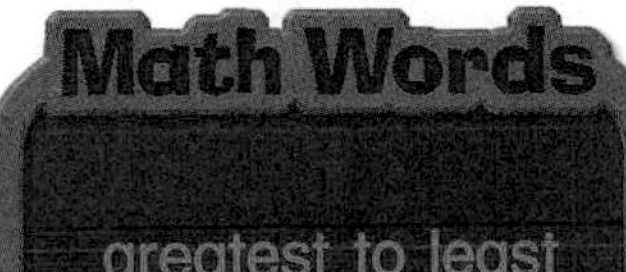

Model the numbers.
Then write them in order from greatest to least.

1. 23, 13, 31

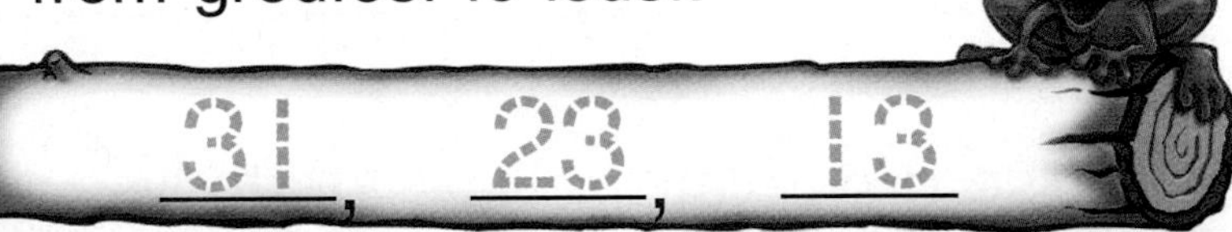

2. 41, 21, 12

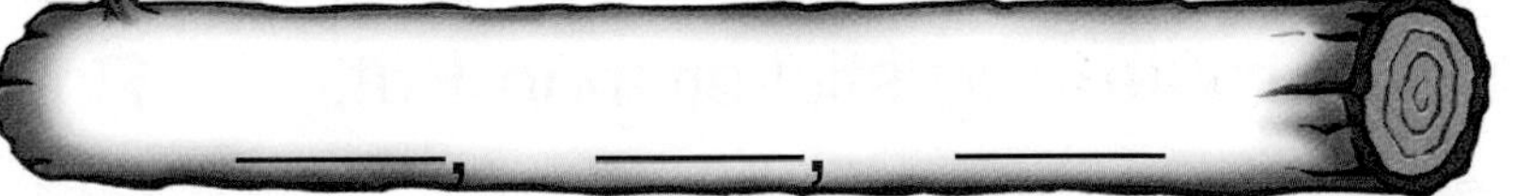

3. 15, 45, 51

4. 34, 40, 30

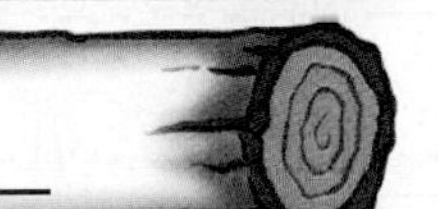

5. 48, 52, 44

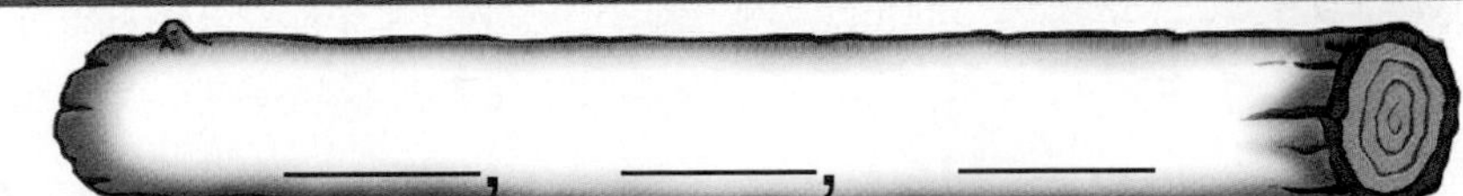

Talk It Over

6. Could you order 49, 64, 57 correctly by only comparing ones? Explain.

Copyright © by William H. Sadlier, Inc. All rights reserved.

Practice

Write the numbers in order from greatest to least.
You may use models to help you.

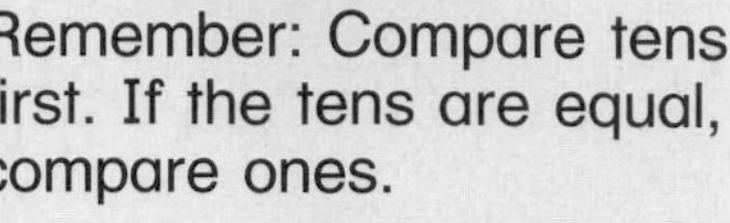

Remember: Compare tens first. If the tens are equal, compare ones.

7. 45, 25, 62  62,  45,  25

8. 72, 79, 78 ____, ____, ____

9. 78, 99, 68 ____, ____, ____

10. 11, 41, 18 ____, ____, ____

Write the numbers in order from least to greatest.

11. 47, 57, 25 ____, ____, ____

12. 39, 93, 97 ____, ____, ____

13. 85, 83, 38 ____, ____, ____

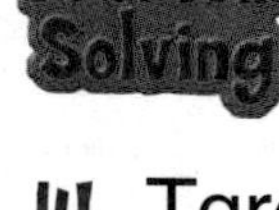

Solve. Use a problem-solving strategy.

14. Tara buys 1 more frog sticker than Pat.
Pat buys 1 fewer than Deven.
Deven buys 35 frog stickers.
Who buys the fewest stickers?

Pat buys ____.

Tara buys ____.

______ buys the fewest.

DO YOU REMEMBER?

Write the missing addend.

15. 7 + ___ = 10	16. 5 + ___ = 13	17. 8 + ___ = 15
18. 6 + ___ = 12	19. 10 + ___ = 14	20. 9 + ___ = 17

Math Alive at Home List the ages of each family member. Have your child order the ages from greatest to least, then from least to greatest.

Name ____

Estimate

Let's Learn!

Estimate about how many flowers are in the package.

You can use a small group to help you estimate, or make a good guess, about how many are in a larger group.

10 flowers

about 40 flowers

About how many of each are on the tray?
Circle your estimate.

1.

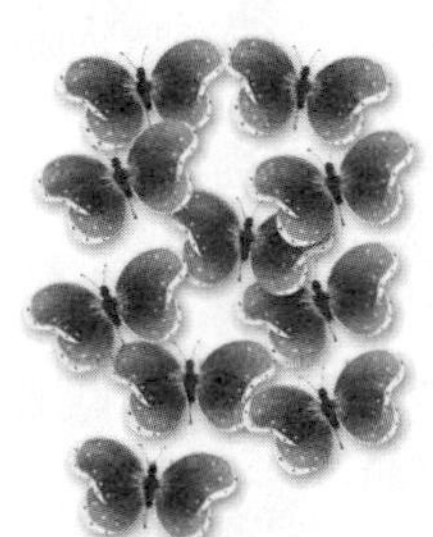
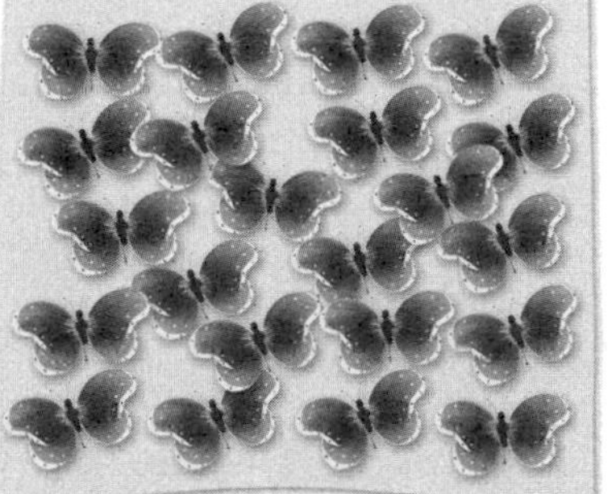

10 butterflies

(about 20) (circled)
about 40

2.

10 beetles

about 20
about 50

3.

10 flowers

about 30
about 50

4.

10 leaves

about 30
about 60

Write About It

5. How does seeing 10 objects help you estimate about how many are in a larger group?

Copyright © by William H. Sadlier, Inc. All rights reserved.

Practice

Remember: Use the group of 10 to help estimate about how many.

About how many of each are there on the tray? Circle your estimate.

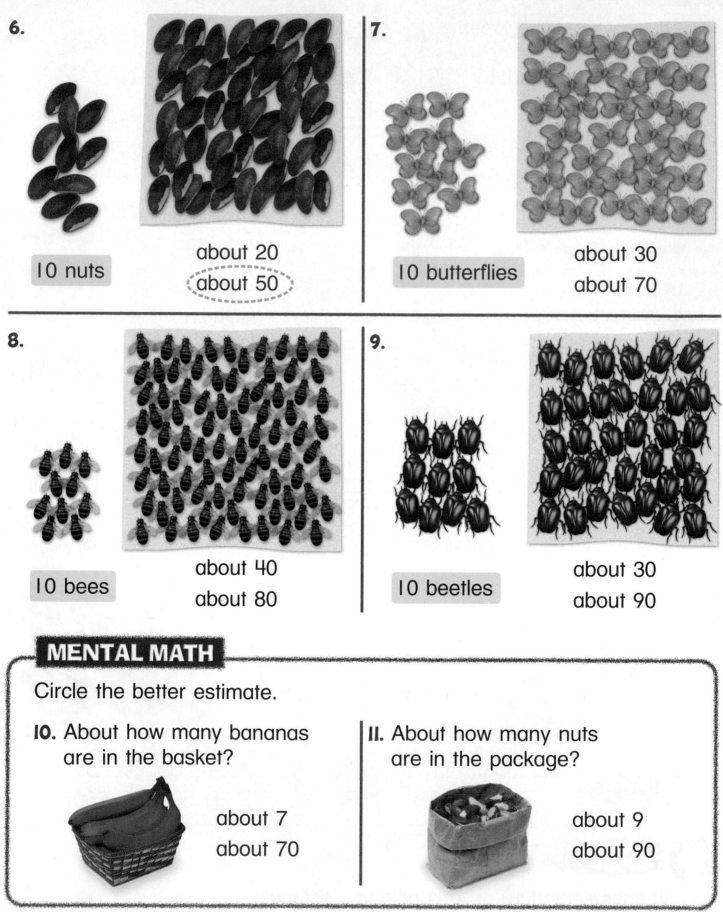

6.

10 nuts

about 20

about 50

7.

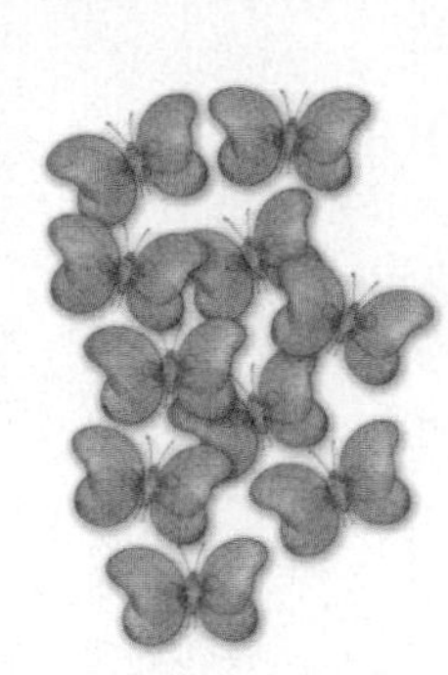

10 butterflies

about 30

about 70

8.

10 bees

about 40

about 80

9.

10 beetles

about 30

about 90

MENTAL MATH

Circle the better estimate.

10. About how many bananas are in the basket?

about 7

about 70

11. About how many nuts are in the package?

about 9

about 90

Math Alive at Home Ask your child how many bananas you should buy at the store, 10 or 50. Talk with your child about which amount makes more sense.

Name ______________________________

Round to the Nearest Ten

Let's Learn!

Round numbers to tell about how many.

Look at the ones digit.
5 ones or more, round up.
Fewer than 5 ones, round down.

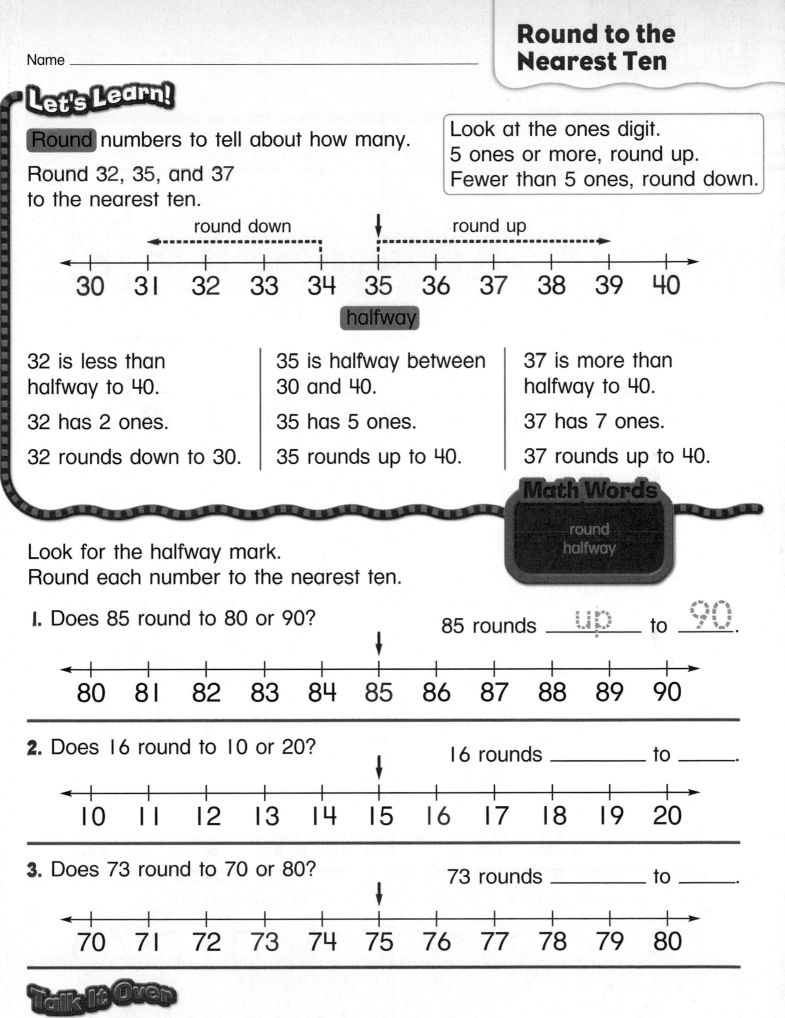

Round 32, 35, and 37
to the nearest ten.

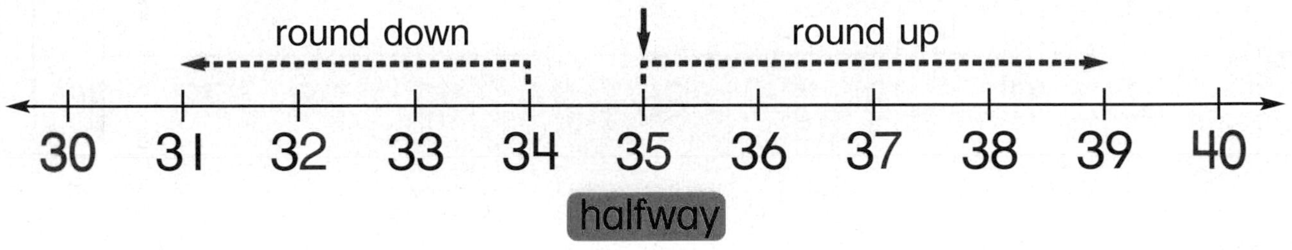

halfway

32 is less than halfway to 40.	35 is halfway between 30 and 40.	37 is more than halfway to 40.
32 has 2 ones.	35 has 5 ones.	37 has 7 ones.
32 rounds down to 30.	35 rounds up to 40.	37 rounds up to 40.

Look for the halfway mark.
Round each number to the nearest ten.

1. Does 85 round to 80 or 90? 85 rounds __up__ to __90__.

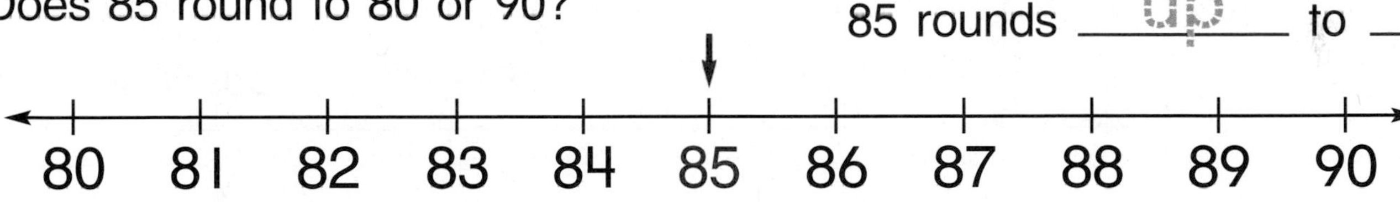

2. Does 16 round to 10 or 20? 16 rounds ________ to _____.

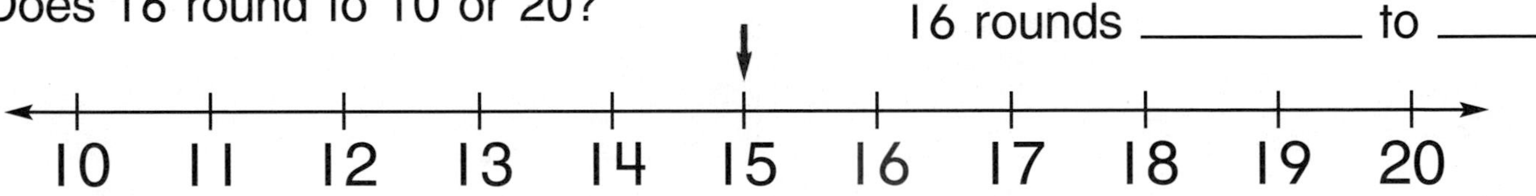

3. Does 73 round to 70 or 80? 73 rounds ________ to _____.

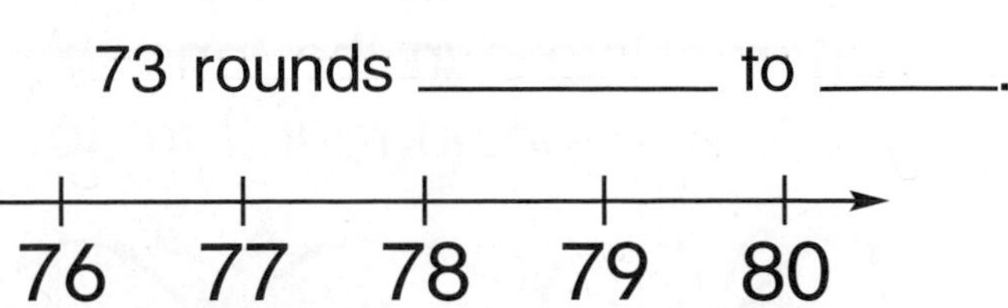

70 71 72 73 74 75 76 77 78 79 80

4. What could the digits in the ones place be to round a number down and to round a number up?

Copyright © by William H. Sadlier, Inc. All rights reserved.

Practice

Remember:
5 ones or more, round up.
Fewer than 5 ones, round down.

Round each number to the nearest ten.

5. 24

24 rounds to .

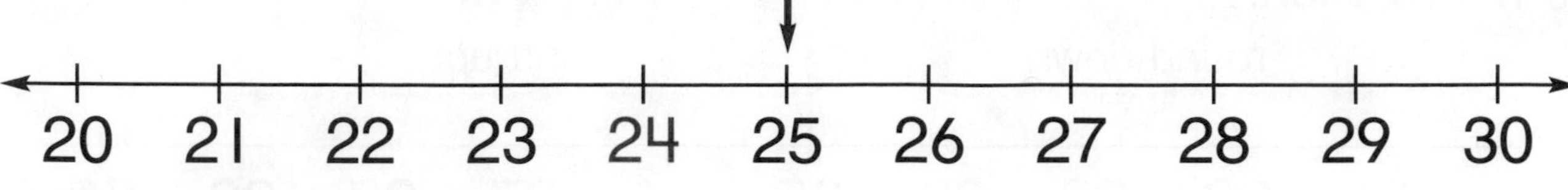

6. 88

88 rounds to _____.

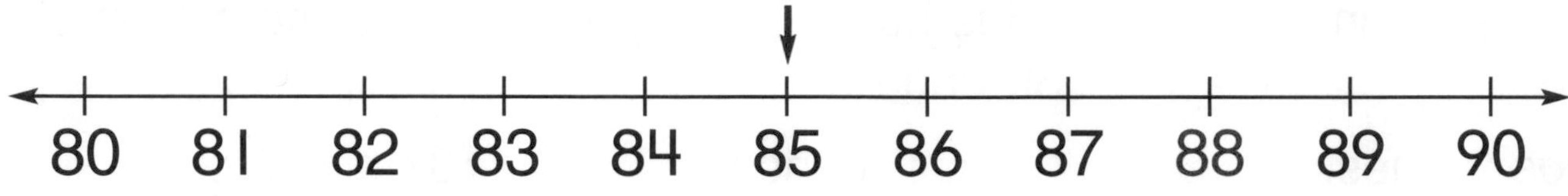

7. 95

95 rounds to _____.

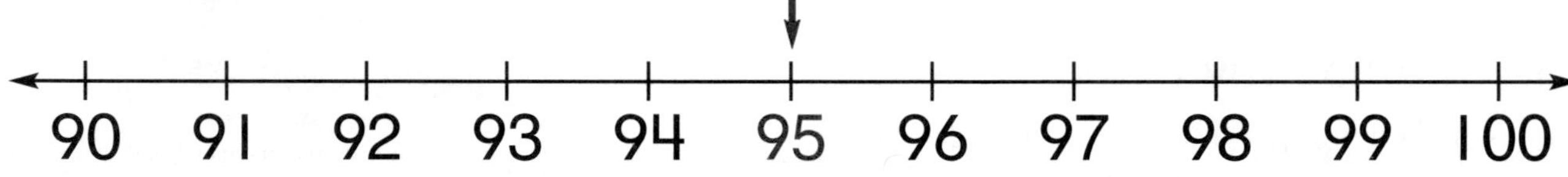

8. fifty-one

_____ rounds to _____.

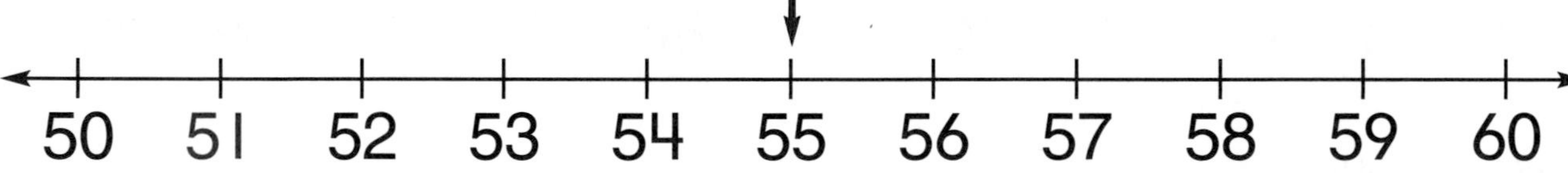

CHALLENGE

9. Name two numbers with different digits in the tens place that would round to 40.

10. Name the least number and the greatest number that would round to 50.

Math Alive at Home Ask your child to round the following numbers using the number lines above: 26, 85, 97, 53. (30, 90, 100, 50)

Name ______________________

Check Your Progress
Lessons 8-12

TEST PREPARATION

Listen to your teacher read the directions.
Fill in the circle under the correct answer.

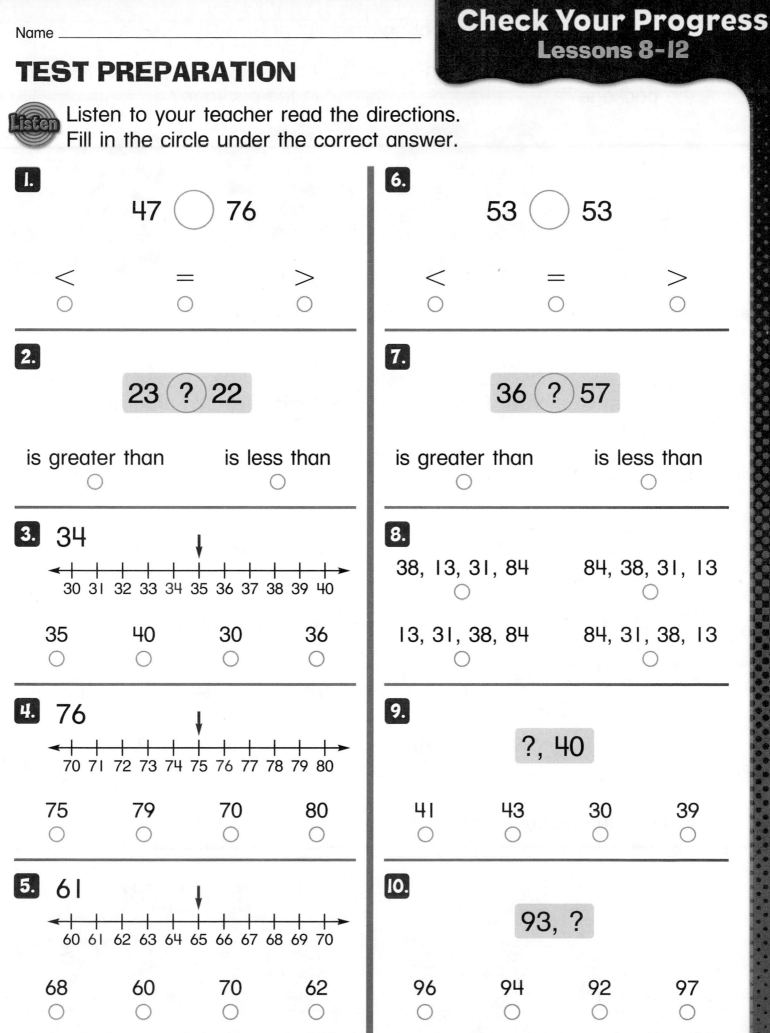

1. 47 ◯ 76

< ○ = ○ > ○

2. 23 (?) 22

is greater than ○ is less than ○

3. 34

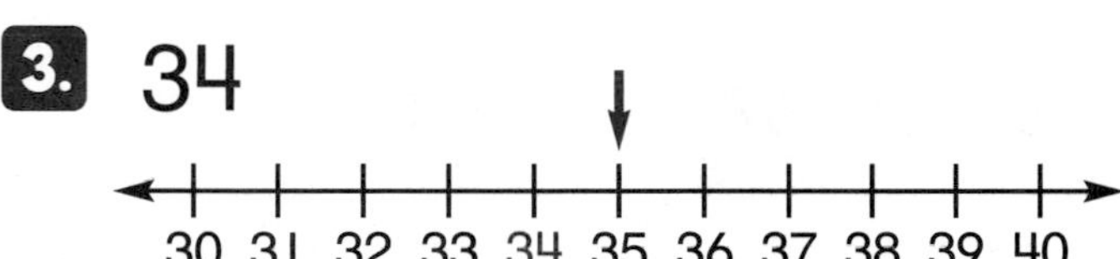

35 ○ 40 ○ 30 ○ 36 ○

4. 76

70 71 72 73 74 75 76 77 78 79 80

75 ○ 79 ○ 70 ○ 80 ○

5. 61

60 61 62 63 64 65 66 67 68 69 70

68 ○ 60 ○ 70 ○ 62 ○

6. 53 ◯ 53

< ○ = ○ > ○

7. 36 (?) 57

is greater than ○ is less than ○

8.

38, 13, 31, 84 ○ 84, 38, 31, 13 ○

13, 31, 38, 84 ○ 84, 31, 38, 13 ○

9. ?, 40

41 ○ 43 ○ 30 ○ 39 ○

10. 93, ?

96 ○ 94 ○ 92 ○ 97 ○

Copyright © by William H. Sadlier, Inc. All rights reserved.

Fill in the circle under the correct answer.

11. About how many nuts are in the package?

10 nuts

about 50 ○　　about 20 ○

12. Which list is in order from greatest to least?

82, 92, 83 ○　　92, 83, 82 ○

82, 83, 92 ○　　92, 82, 83 ○

13. Round 89 to the nearest ten.

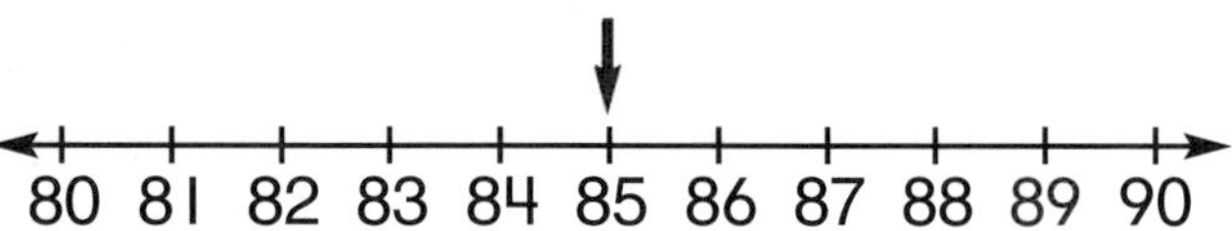

85 ○　　80 ○　　95 ○　　90 ○

14. Choose the number that comes just before.

?, 56

57 ○　　55 ○　　54 ○　　50 ○

15. About how many butterflies are in the package?

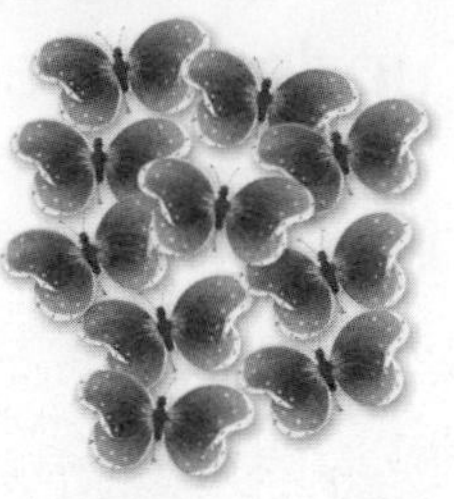

10 butterflies

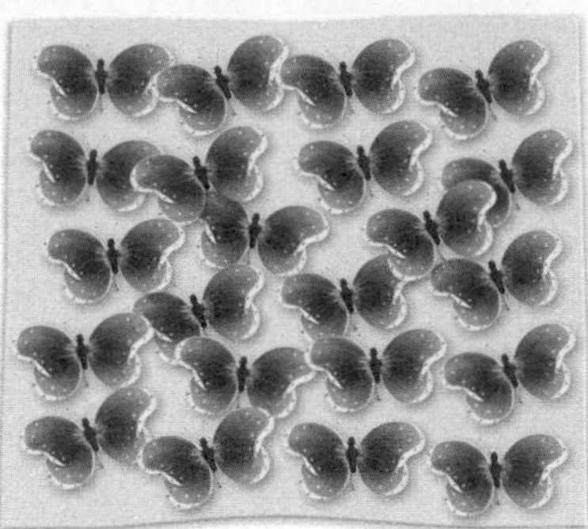

about 30 ○　　about 80 ○

16. Which list is in order from least to greatest?

67, 29, 92 ○　　29, 67, 92 ○

92, 29, 67 ○　　29, 92, 67 ○

17. Round 65 to the nearest ten.

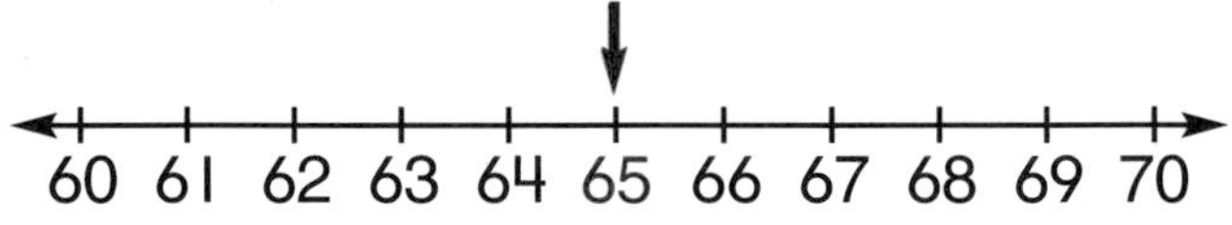

50 ○　　60 ○　　70 ○　　80 ○

18. Choose <, =, or >.

87 (?) 78

< ○　　= ○　　> ○

Name ______________________________

Even and Odd Numbers

HANDS-ON LESSON

Let's Learn!

Even Numbers

If a number is even, you can make pairs with none left.

2
4
6
8
10

Odd Numbers

If a number is odd, you can make pairs with one left over.

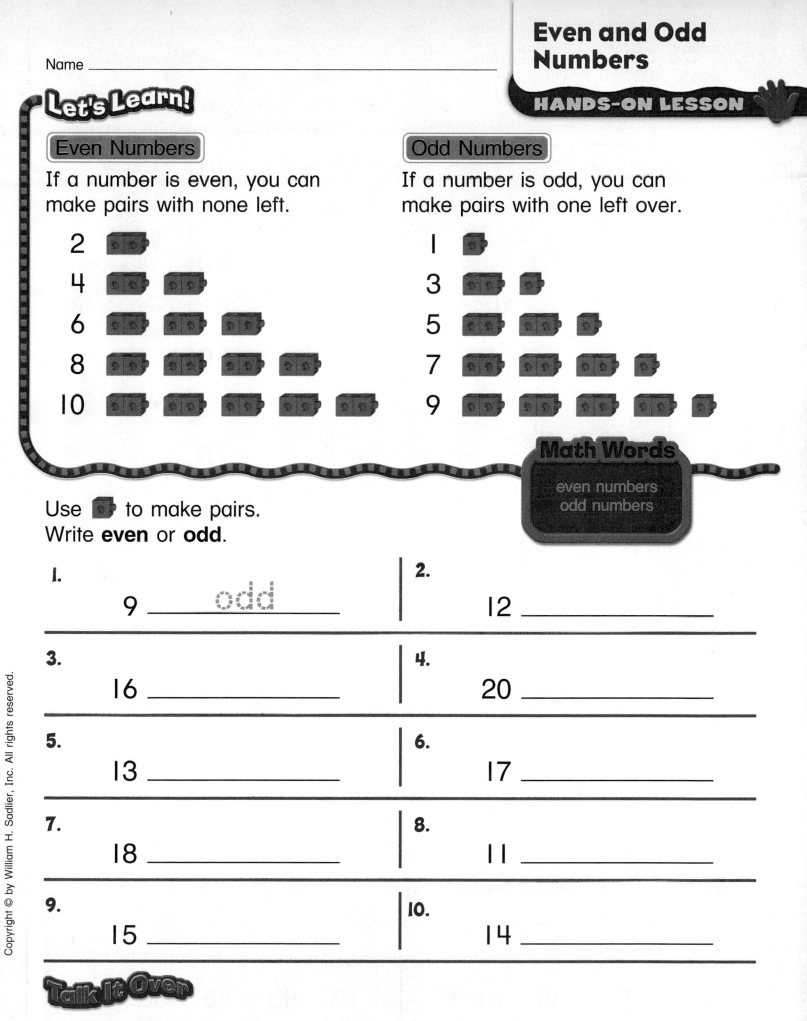

1
3
5
7
9

Use cubes to make pairs.
Write **even** or **odd**.

1. 9 odd	2. 12 ______
3. 16 ______	4. 20 ______
5. 13 ______	6. 17 ______
7. 18 ______	8. 11 ______
9. 15 ______	10. 14 ______

11. What would be the next even number after 28? How do you know?

Copyright © by William H. Sadlier, Inc. All rights reserved.

Practice

12. Write the missing numbers.

1	2	3	4	5	6	7	8	9	10
11	12	13							20
21		23	24						30
31			34						40
41				45					50
51					56				60
61						67			70
71	72	73	74	75	76	77	78	79	80
81								89	90
91									100

13. Color even numbers 

and odd numbers 

.

14. What 5 digits are in the ones place of even numbers?

____

15. What 5 digits are in the ones place of odd numbers?

____

TEST PREPARATION

Fill in the circle under the correct answer.

16. Which number is even?

67 ○ 94 ○ 35 ○ 81 ○

17. Which number is odd?

12 ○ 43 ○ 86 ○ 30 ○

Math Alive at Home Ask your child to pair pennies in order to show why 23 is an odd number and 24 is an even number.

Name ______________________

Algebra
Count by 3s and 4s

Let's Learn!

I can **count by 3s**.

I can **count by 4s**.

1	2	3	4	5	6	7	8	9	10
11	12	13	14	15	16	17	18	19	20
21	22	23	24	25	26	27	28	29	30
31	32	33	34	35	36	37	38	39	40
41	42	43	44	45	46	47	48	49	50

1	2	3	4	5	6	7	8	9	10
11	12	13	14	15	16	17	18	19	20
21	22	23	24	25	26	27	28	29	30
31	32	33	34	35	36	37	38	39	40
41	42	43	44	45	46	47	48	49	50

Math Words

count by 3s
count by 4s

1. Count by 3s.
Color the count-by-3 numbers.

51	52	53	54	55	56	57	58	59	60
61	62	63	64	65	66	67	68	69	70
71	72	73	74	75	76	77	78	79	80
81	82	83	84	85	86	87	88	89	90
91	92	93	94	95	96	97	98	99	100

2. Count by 4s.
Color the count-by-4 numbers.

51	52	53	54	55	56	57	58	59	60
61	62	63	64	65	66	67	68	69	70
71	72	73	74	75	76	77	78	79	80
81	82	83	84	85	86	87	88	89	90
91	92	93	94	95	96	97	98	99	100

3. Write the next three numbers in this pattern.

69, 72, 75, ____, ____, ____

4. Write the next three numbers in this pattern.

76, 80, 84, ____, ____, ____

Talk It Over

5. When you start at zero and count by 3s, will you say even or odd numbers? Explain.

Copyright © by William H. Sadlier, Inc. All rights reserved.

Practice

Count by 3s or 4s to find how many in all.

6. How many oranges in all? 24 oranges

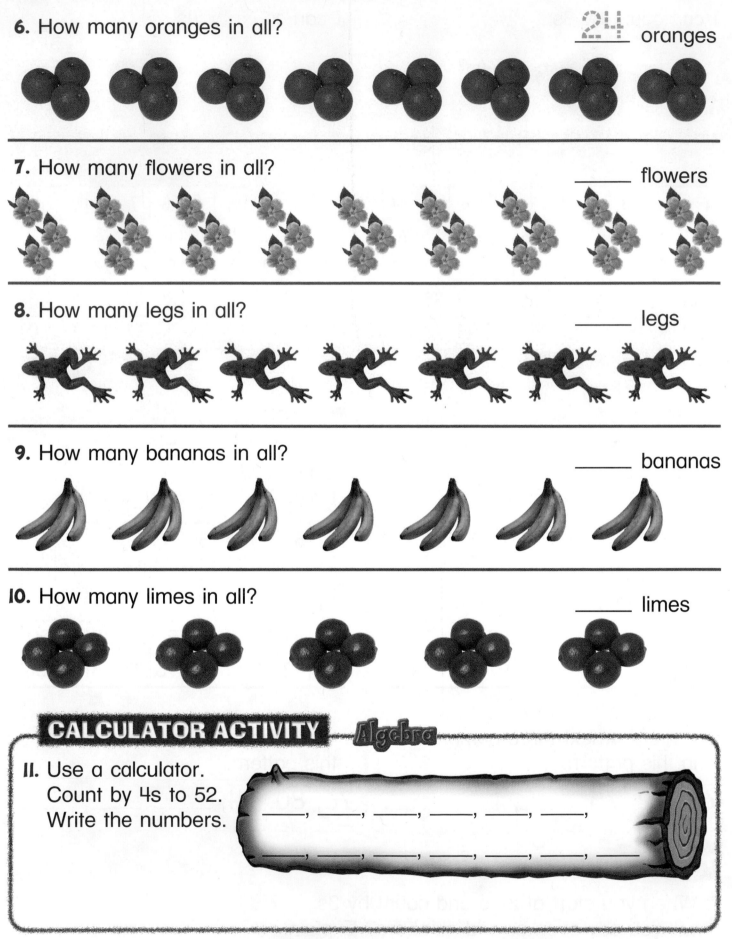

7. How many flowers in all? ____ flowers

8. How many legs in all? ____ legs

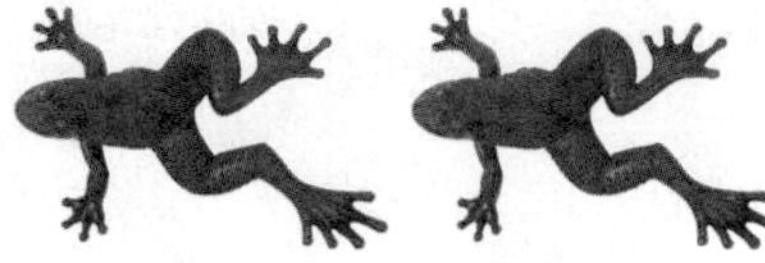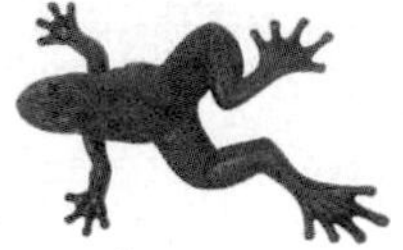

9. How many bananas in all? ____ bananas

10. How many limes in all? ____ limes

CALCULATOR ACTIVITY Algebra

11. Use a calculator.
Count by 4s to 52.
Write the numbers.

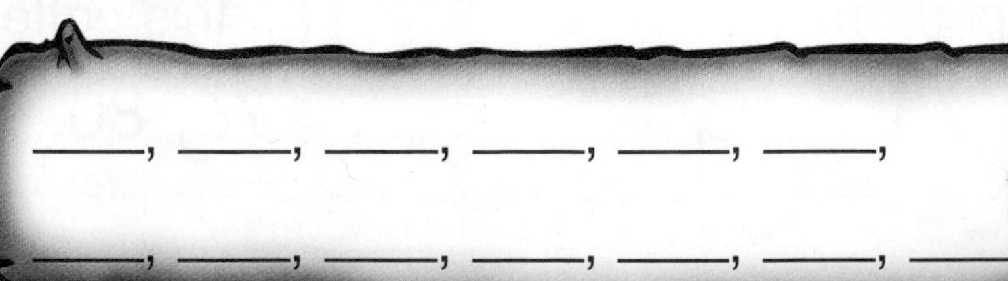

____, ____, ____, ____, ____, ____,

____, ____, ____, ____, ____, ____, ____

Math Alive at Home Draw 10 triangles. Ask your child to tell how many sides in all by counting by 3s. (30)

Name ______________________________

Algebra

Counting Patterns

Let's Learn!

Mario colors four number patterns.

He colors two patterns by counting on.

Count on by 1s: 79, 80, 81, 82

Count on by 10s: 52, 62, 72, 82

He colors two patterns by counting back.

Count back by 1s: 36, 35, 34, 33

Count back by 10s: 49, 39, 29, 19

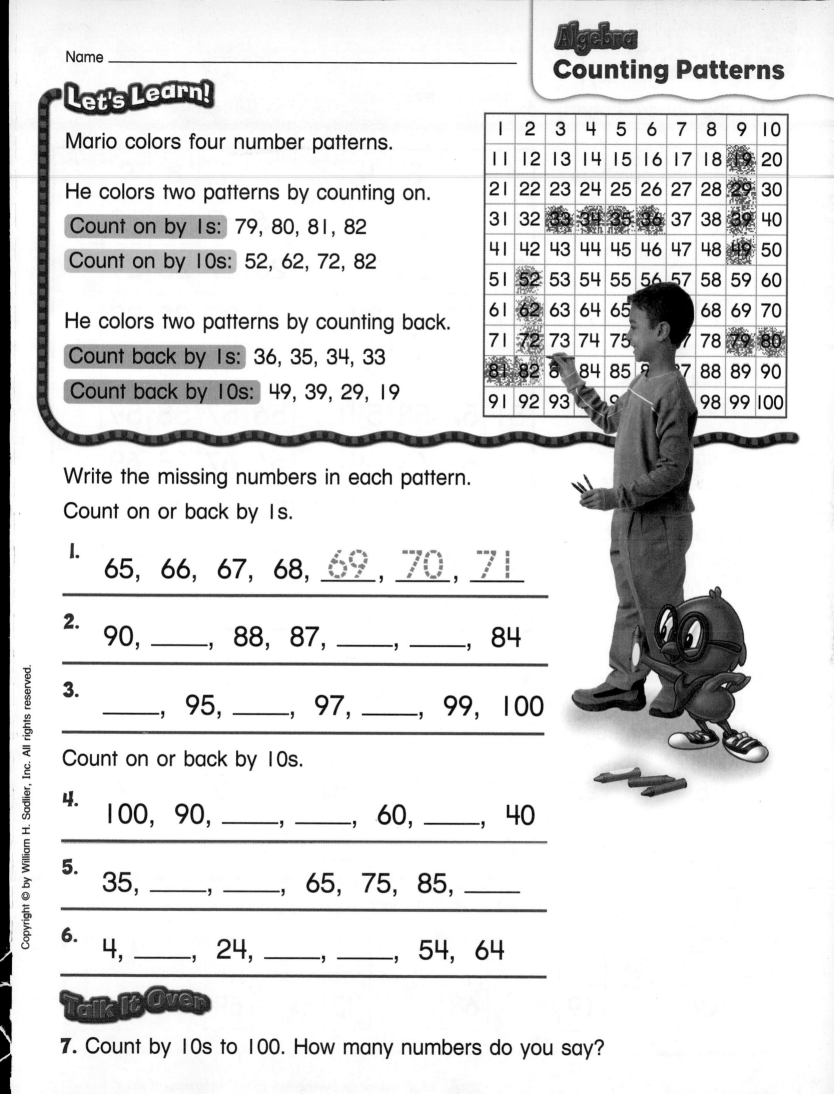

1	2	3	4	5	6	7	8	9	10
11	12	13	14	15	16	17	18	19	20
21	22	23	24	25	26	27	28	29	30
31	32	33	34	35	36	37	38	39	40
41	42	43	44	45	46	47	48	49	50
51	52	53	54	55	56	57	58	59	60
61	62	63	64	65			68	69	70
71	72	73	74	75		7	78	79	80
81	82	8	84	85	8	7	88	89	90
91	92	93		9			98	99	100

Write the missing numbers in each pattern.

Count on or back by 1s.

1. 65, 66, 67, 68, 69, 70, 71

2. 90, ____, 88, 87, ____, ____, 84

3. ____, 95, ____, 97, ____, 99, 100

Count on or back by 10s.

4. 100, 90, ____, ____, 60, ____, 40

5. 35, ____, ____, 65, 75, 85, ____

6. 4, ____, 24, ____, ____, 54, 64

7. Count by 10s to 100. How many numbers do you say?

Copyright © by William H. Sadlier, Inc. All rights reserved.

Practice

Make number patterns.

Use the hundred chart.

8. Count by 5s.
Write the numbers.

9. Count by 2s.
✘ the numbers.

10. Count by 10s.
Color the numbers.

11. Count by 25s.
Circle the numbers.

12. Count by 50s.
✓ the numbers.

13. Write the numbers that have all the marks.

______

1	2	3	4	5	6	7	8	9	10
11	12	13	14		16	17	18	19	
21	22	23	24		26	27	28	29	
31	32	33	34		36	37	38	39	
41	42	43	44		46	47	48	49	
51	52	53	54		56	57	58	59	
61	62	63	64		66	67	68	69	
71	72	73	74		76	77	78	79	
81	82	83	84		86	87	88	89	
91	92	93	94		96	97	98	99	

CHALLENGE

Use the hundred chart above.
Write the number that is 10 more than each.

14.

8	22	46	35	50	63
18					

Write the number that is 10 less than each.

15.

26					
36	19	68	40	54	85

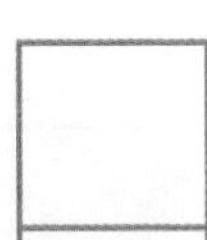

Math Alive at Home Ask your child to name the next four numbers in this pattern and to tell you by what number she/he counted. *72, 74, 76, 78. (80, 82, 84, 86; by 2s)*

Name ______________________________

Ordinals to 31st

Let's Learn!

Ordinal numbers tell position.

Rainforest Tour — Line starts here

1st first, 2nd second, 3rd third, 4th fourth, 5th fifth, 6th sixth, 7th seventh, 8th eighth, 9th ninth, 10th tenth

Math Words

ordinal numbers

Circle the correct position of each child.
Write the ordinal number.

1.  eighth / ninth / tenth  10th

2.  first / second / third

3.  sixth / seventh / eighth

4.  third / fourth / fifth

5. If the line of children above started at the other end, what would be the ordinal position of the boy in the wheelchair?

Copyright © by William H. Sadlier, Inc. All rights reserved.

Practice

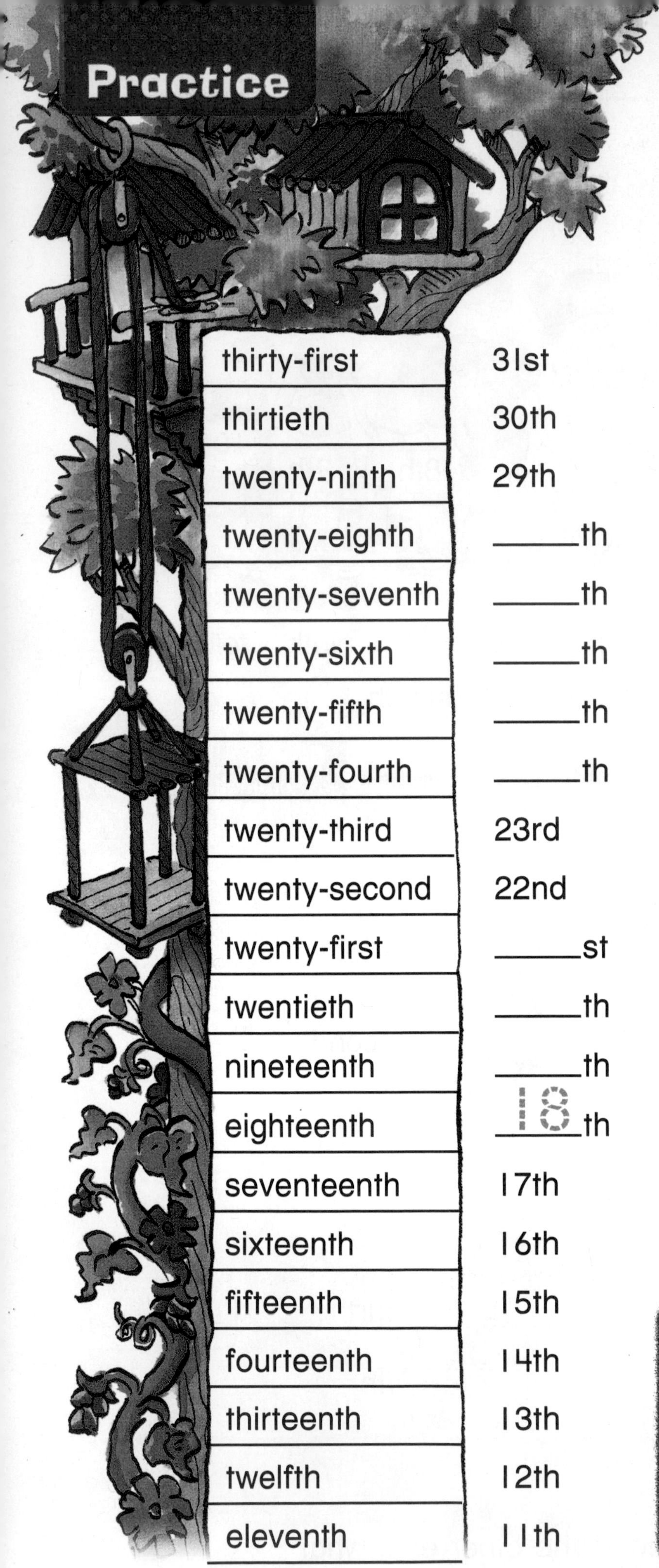

thirty-first	31st
thirtieth	30th
twenty-ninth	29th
twenty-eighth	____th
twenty-seventh	____th
twenty-sixth	____th
twenty-fifth	____th
twenty-fourth	____th
twenty-third	23rd
twenty-second	22nd
twenty-first	____st
twentieth	____th
nineteenth	____th
eighteenth	18th
seventeenth	17th
sixteenth	16th
fifteenth	15th
fourteenth	14th
thirteenth	13th
twelfth	12th
eleventh	11th

6. Look at the tree house. Write the missing ordinal numbers.

Color these steps 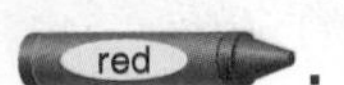

.

7. twenty-fifth　twenty-sixth
twenty-seventh　twenty-second
twenty-ninth　thirty-first

Color these steps blue.

8. 24th　20th　19th
30th　21st　16th
28th　23rd　18th

9. Color the steps between the 11th and fifteenth yellow.

10. Which step comes just before the 20th?

____

11. Which step comes just after the 29th?

____

CRITICAL THINKING

12. Three hikers are in line. Janell is in back of Nancy. Nancy is in back of Mike. Who is second in this line?

____

Math Alive at Home Ask your child to use the picture at the left to name two steps between the 19th and the 23rd steps. (any two of the 20th, 21st, or 22nd)

Name ____________________

Problem Solving
Strategy

Use Logical Reasoning

Use logical reasoning!

Read Lynn sees many frogs.
The number is between 14 and 18.
You say the number when you count by 2s from 0.
How many frogs does Lynn see?

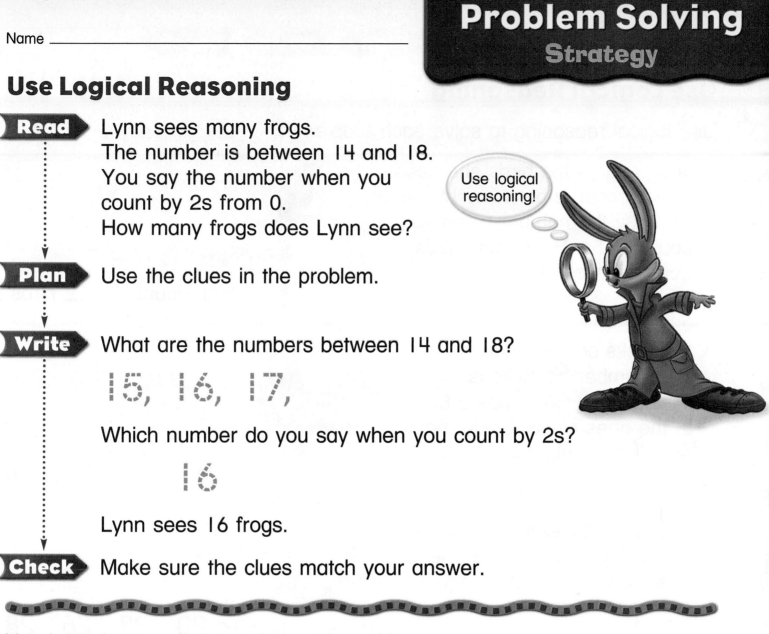

Plan Use the clues in the problem.

Write What are the numbers between 14 and 18?

15, 16, 17,

Which number do you say when you count by 2s?

16

Lynn sees 16 frogs.

Check Make sure the clues match your answer.

Use logical reasoning to solve each problem.

1. The number of monkeys is between 13 and 19. You say the number when you count by 4s. What is the number of monkeys?

The number of monkeys is ______.

2. Willie counts some leaves. The number of leaves is between 25 and 29. It is an odd number. How many leaves does he count?

Willie counts ______ leaves.

Copyright © by William H. Sadlier, Inc. All rights reserved.

Practice

Read → Plan → Write → Check

Use Logical Reasoning

Use logical reasoning to solve each problem.

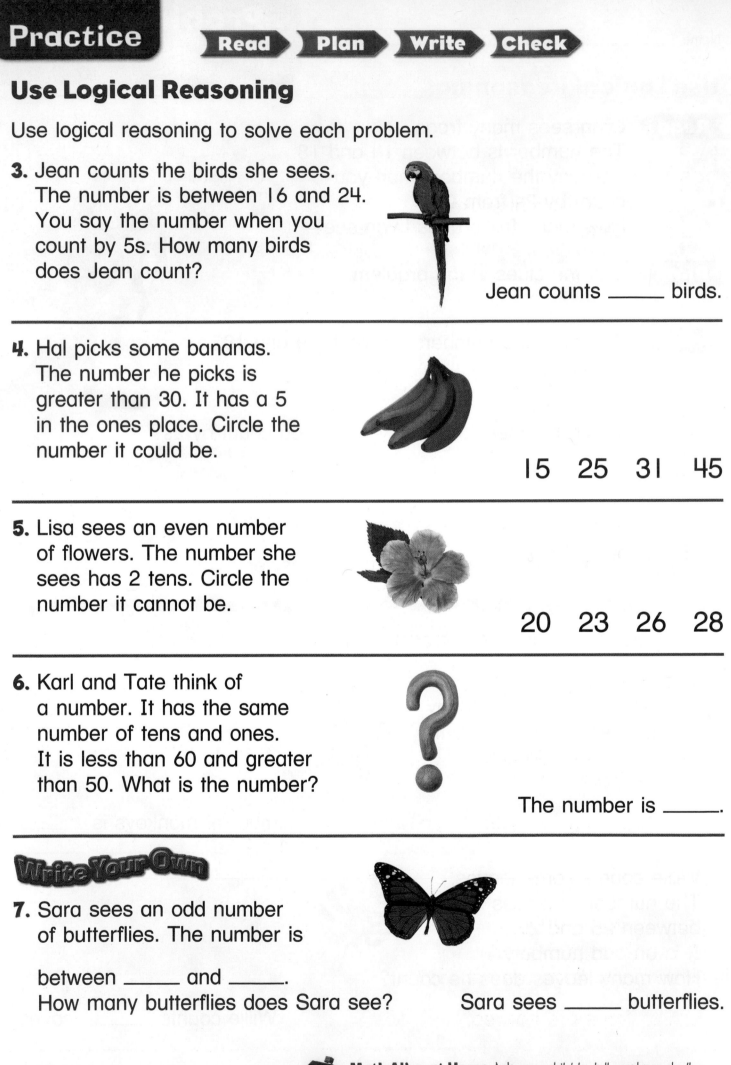

3. Jean counts the birds she sees. The number is between 16 and 24. You say the number when you count by 5s. How many birds does Jean count?

Jean counts _____ birds.

---

4. Hal picks some bananas. The number he picks is greater than 30. It has a 5 in the ones place. Circle the number it could be.

15 25 31 45

---

5. Lisa sees an even number of flowers. The number she sees has 2 tens. Circle the number it cannot be.

20 23 26 28

---

6. Karl and Tate think of a number. It has the same number of tens and ones. It is less than 60 and greater than 50. What is the number?

The number is _____.

7. Sara sees an odd number of butterflies. The number is

between _____ and _____.
How many butterflies does Sara see?

Sara sees _____ butterflies.

Math Alive at Home Ask your child to tell you how she/he used logical reasoning to solve some of the problems in this lesson.

Name ____________________

Read Plan Write Check

Mixed Strategies

Use a strategy you have learned.

1. Jess has 10 animal stickers.
   6 are tigers.
   The rest are lions.
   How many stickers are lions?

   _____ stickers are lions.

2. There are 13 lizards in the jungle.
   6 can climb trees.
   5 have stripes.
   How many do not have stripes?

   _____ do not have stripes.

3. Brian counts the plants he sees.
   The number is between 13 and
   17. You say the number when you
   count by 3s. How many plants does
   Brian count?

   Brian counts _____ plants.

4. John finishes 8 puzzles.
   Lee finishes 4 puzzles.
   What is the total number
   of puzzles they finish?

   They finish _____ puzzles.

5. Sherry sees 12 frogs.
   4 of the frogs are red.
   How many frogs are not red?

   _____ frogs are not red.

Copyright © by William H. Sadlier, Inc. All rights reserved.

Practice

Read → Plan → Write → Check

Use a strategy you have learned.

Strategy File
Act It Out
Use Logical Reasoning
Choose the Operation
Draw a Picture

6. Harry thinks of a number.
It is an even number less than 70.
It has more than 3 ones.
What is Harry's number?

62 63 68 76

Harry's number is _____.

---

7. Ty thinks of an odd number.
It has more tens than ones.
What is Ty's number?

34

28

Ty's number is _____.

---

8. Gus sees 18 butterflies.
9 fly away.
How many butterflies are left?

_____ butterflies are left.

---

9. Kate sees 7 blue birds.
Rob sees 3 red birds.
Marta sees 2 yellow birds.
How many birds do the children see?

The children see _____ birds.

---

10. A turtle walks in line.
12 turtles are in front of him.
3 turtles are behind him.
How many turtles are in line?

_____ turtles are in line.

Math Alive at Home Ask your child to tell you how she/he solved some of the problems in this lesson.

Name ____________________

TEST PREPARATION

Listen to your teacher read the directions.
Fill in the circle under the correct answer.

1. even
2 tens

18 ○ 21 ○ 24 ○ 17 ○

2. 40, ?, 50, 55, ?, 65, 70, ?

41, 56, 71 ○ 50, 60, 80 ○
45, 60, 75 ○ 45, 56, 70 ○

3. odd

16 ○ 24 ○ 21 ○ 12 ○

4.

 twenty-ninth	 thirtieth	 ?

thirtieth ○ thirty-first ○
twenty-eighth ○ twenty-seventh ○

5.     

24 ○ 20 ○ 25 ○ 5 ○

6. sixteenth, ?

thirteenth ○ nineteenth ○
twenty-sixth ○ seventeenth ○

7.   

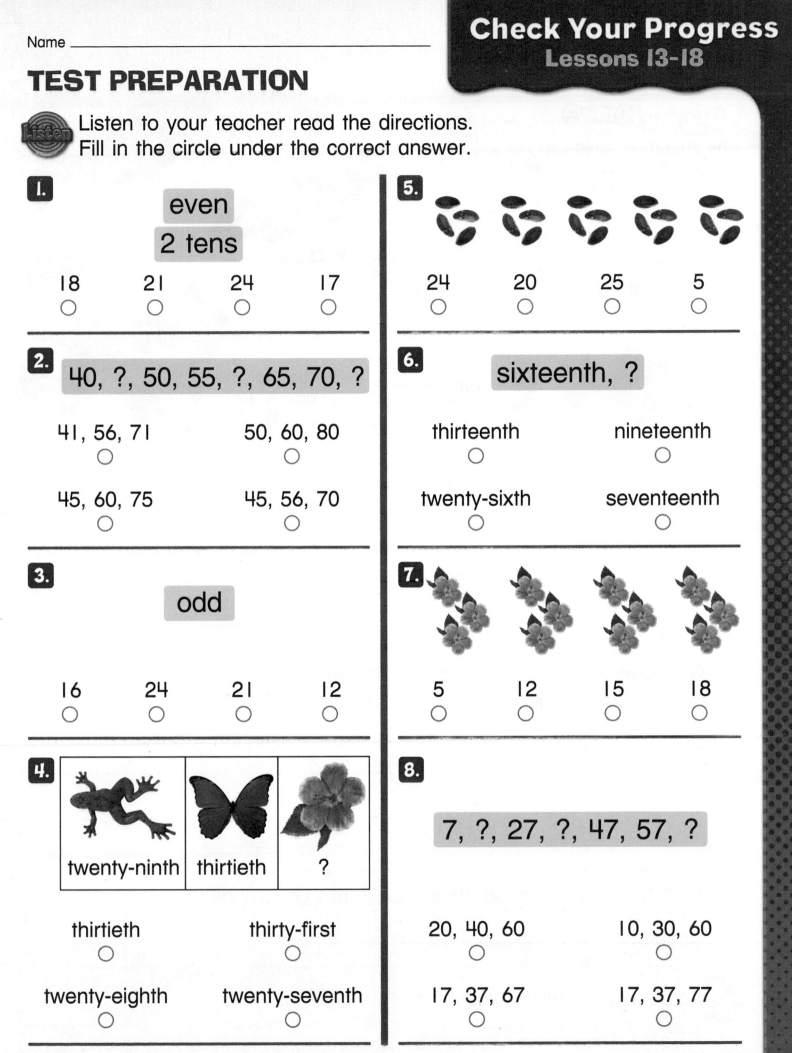

5 ○ 12 ○ 15 ○ 18 ○

8. 7, ?, 27, ?, 47, 57, ?

20, 40, 60 ○ 10, 30, 60 ○
17, 37, 67 ○ 17, 37, 77 ○

Copyright © by William H. Sadlier, Inc. All rights reserved.

Connection
Math and Science

Name ______________________________

Did You Know?
All butterflies have two pairs of wings covered with scales.

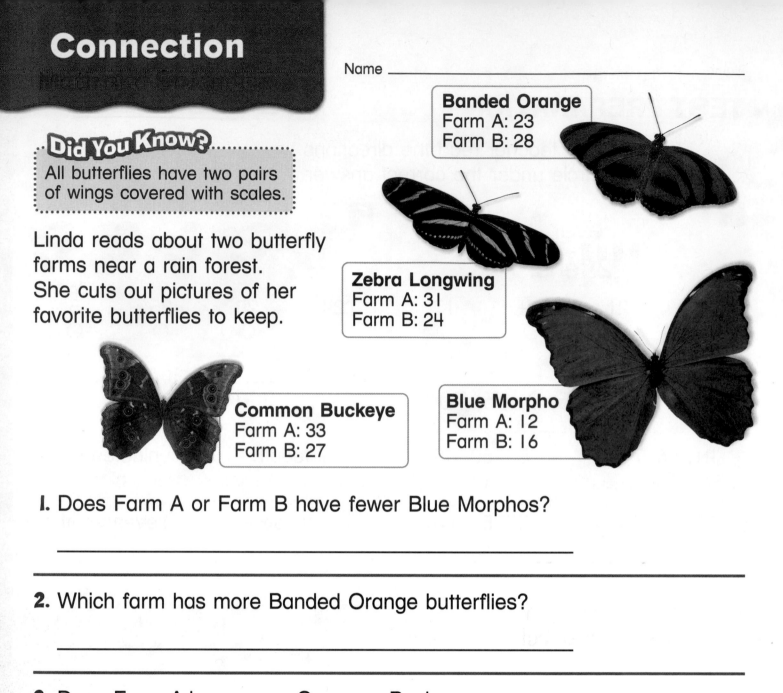

Linda reads about two butterfly farms near a rain forest. She cuts out pictures of her favorite butterflies to keep.

Common Buckeye
Farm A: 33
Farm B: 27

1. Does Farm A or Farm B have fewer Blue Morphos?

   ____

2. Which farm has more Banded Orange butterflies?

   ____

3. Does Farm A have more Common Buckeyes or Zebra Longwings?

   more ______________________________

4. Which farm has fewer Common Buckeyes?

   ____

5. Which farm has an even number of Zebra Longwings?

   ____

You can put this in your Math Portfolio.

Name ______________________________

Chapter 2 Test

1. Write the place value and the number word.

tens	ones

____

2. Count by 1s. Write the missing numbers.

____, 13, 14, 15, ____, 17, 18,

19, ____, 21, 22, 23, ____, 25,

26, 27, ____, 29, 30, 31, ____

3. Write 36 in expanded form.

____ + ____

4. What is the value of the digit 4 in 41?

____

5. Write the numbers in order from least to greatest.

____, ____, ____

6. Write **even** or **odd**.

90 ____

73 ____

7. Does 23 round to 20 or 30?

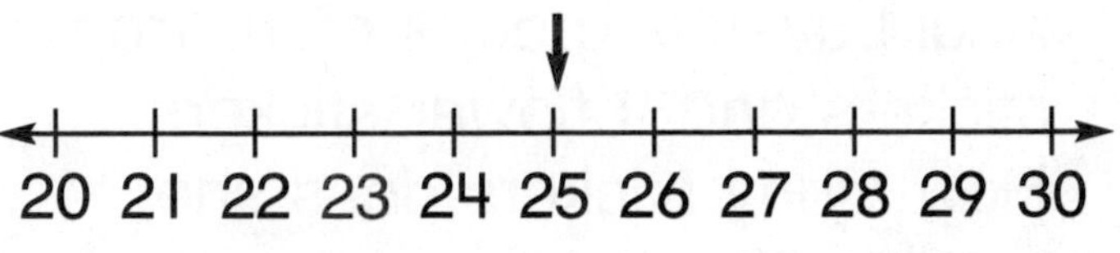

23 rounds to ____.

8. Write the number for each number word.

thirty-five ____

sixty-eight ____

Copyright © by William H. Sadlier, Inc. All rights reserved.

9. Write the numbers in order from greatest to least.

47 39 50

____, ____, ____

10. Count back by 10s. Write the missing numbers.

75, ____, 55, 45, ____

11. Are there about 20 nuts or about 40 nuts in the package?

10 nuts

about ____ nuts

12. Color numbers to count by 5s.

1	2	3	4	5	6	7	8	9	10
11	12	13	14	15	16	17	18	19	20
21	22	23	24	25	26	27	28	29	30
31	32	33	34	35	36	37	38	39	40
41	42	43	44	45	46	47	48	49	50

13. What is the value of the digit 8 in 98?

____

14. Write 60 in expanded form.

____ + ____

Solve. Use a problem-solving strategy.

15. David buys 29 snake stickers. Gloria buys 32 snake stickers. Who buys more stickers?

____

16. Clara is 24th in line. Alex is just after Clara. What place in line is Alex?

Alex is ____ in line.

17. I am a 2-digit number that has 9 ones. I have more than 6 tens but fewer than 8 tens. What number am I?

I am the number ____.

18. Arial buys six groups of 10 frog stickers and 4 flower stickers. How many stickers does she buy in all?

____ stickers

Name ____________________

1. Make 3 two-digit numbers using each digit below once.
Then write each number in expanded form.

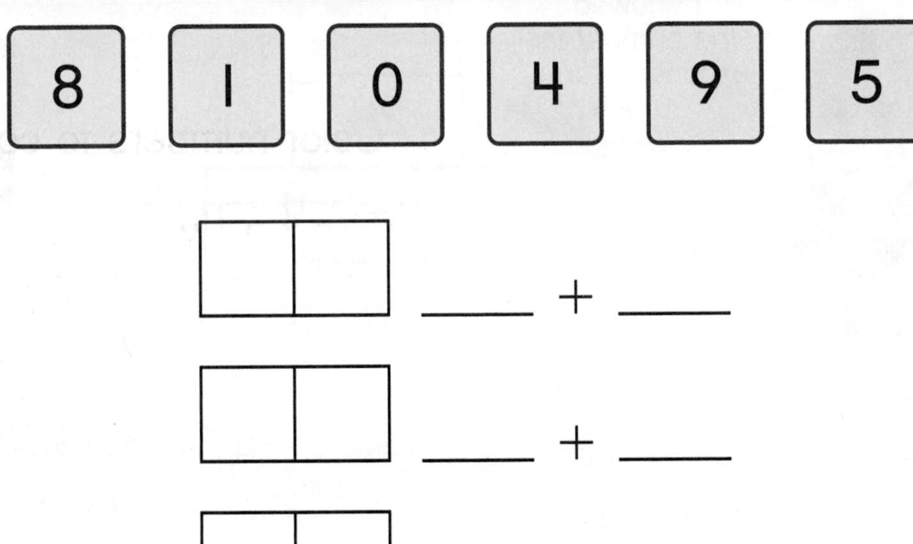

Order your numbers from least to greatest.

____, ____, ____

2. Write the missing number. Color to match the rule.

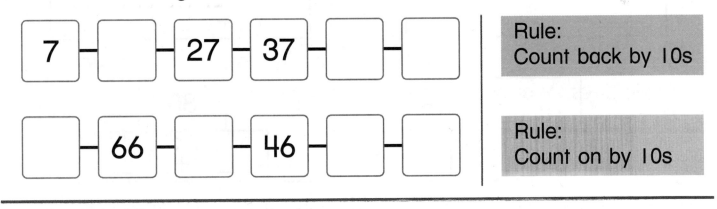

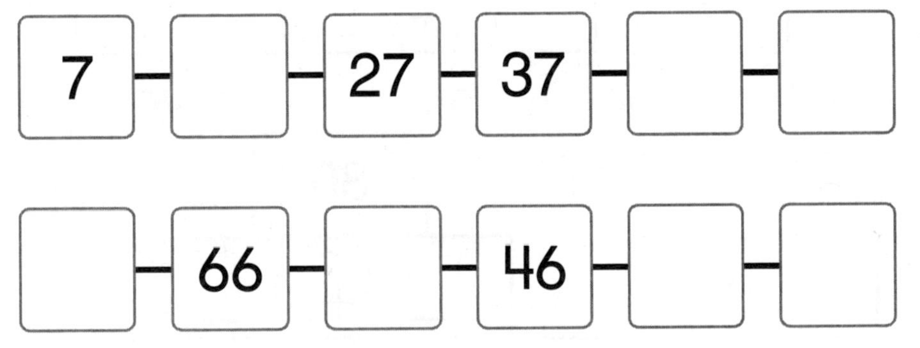

Rule:
Count back by 10s

Rule:
Count on by 10s

3. Write three even two-digit numbers.

____

4. Write three odd two-digit numbers.

____

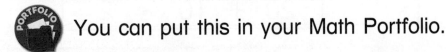

You can put this in your Math Portfolio.

Copyright © by William H. Sadlier, Inc. All rights reserved.

Enrichment

Name ______________________________

Ways to Make Larger Numbers

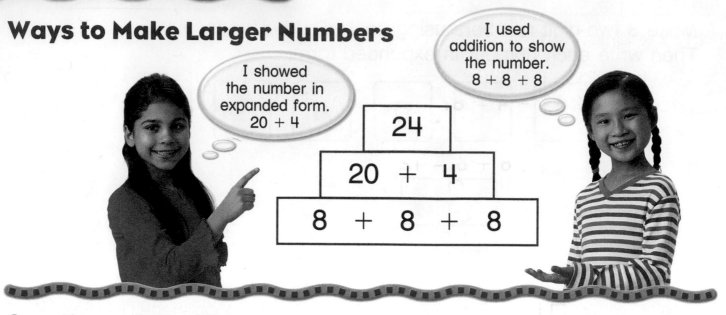

I showed the number in expanded form.
20 + 4

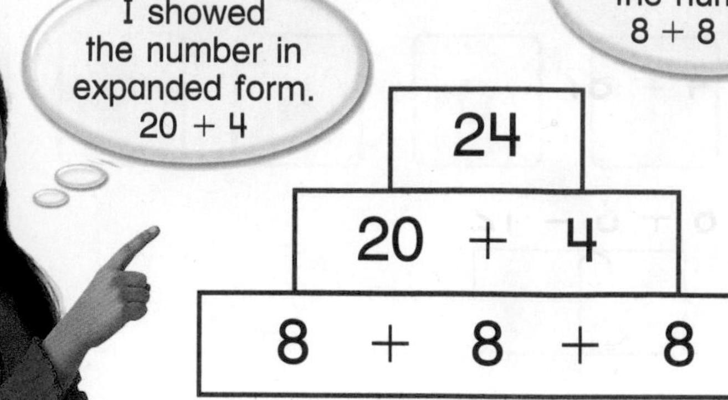

I used addition to show the number.
8 + 8 + 8
24
20 + 4
8 + 8 + 8

Complete to show different ways to make the same number. Use expanded form and addition.

1.

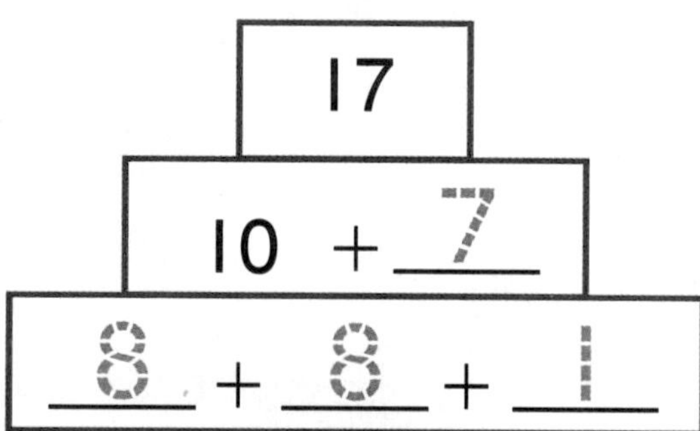

2.

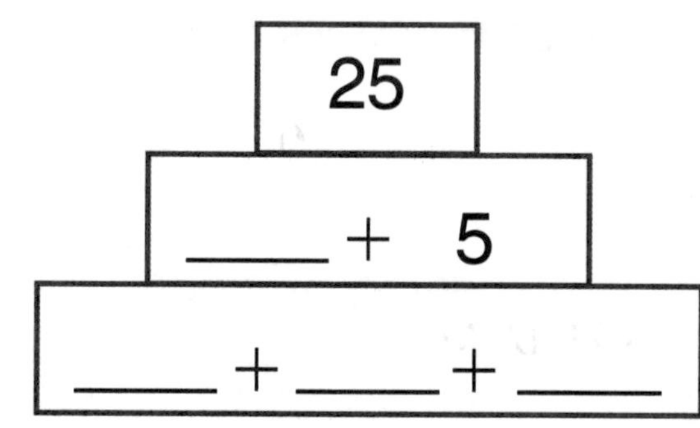

3.

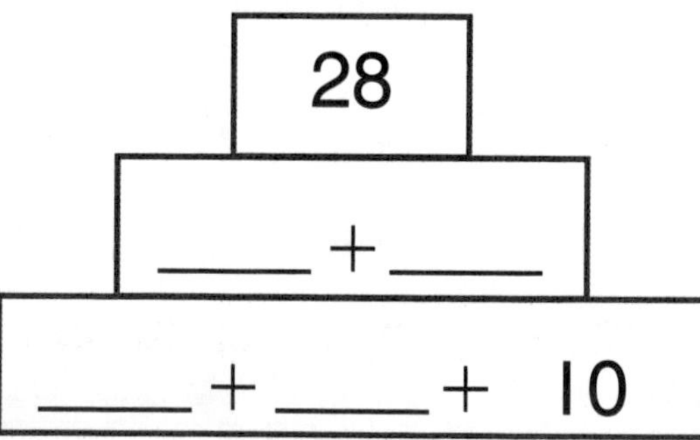

4.

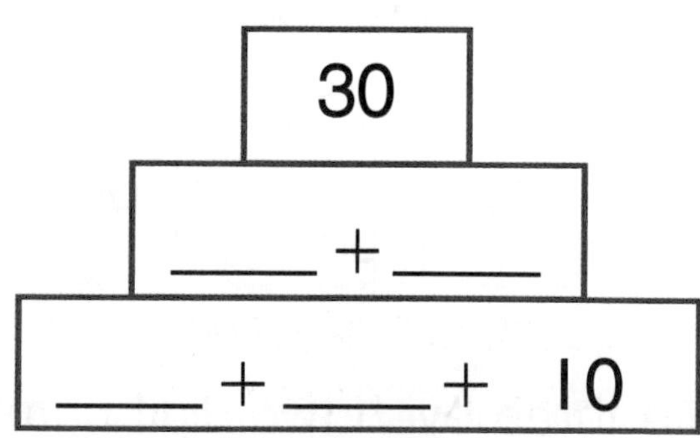

5.

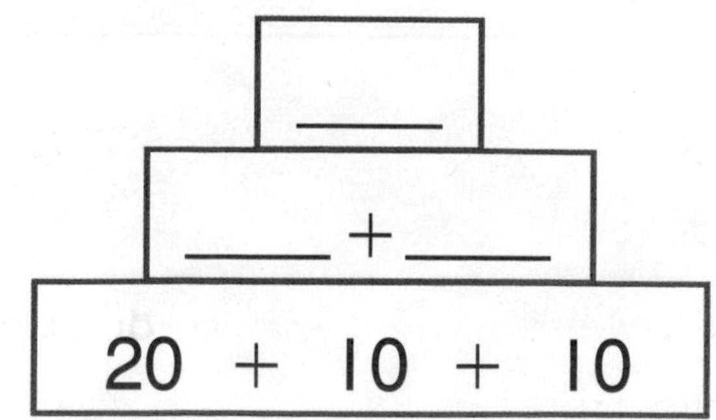

6.

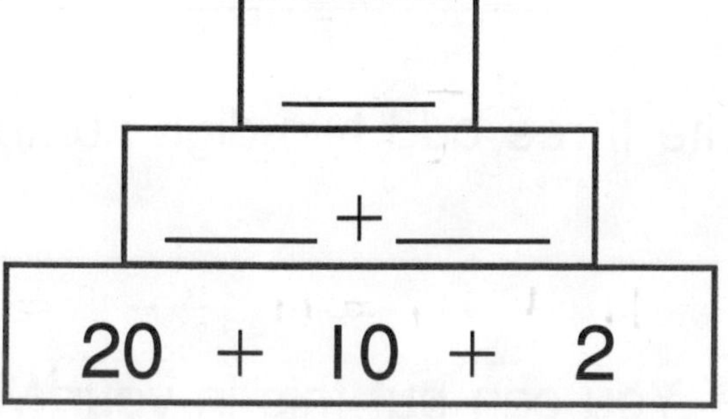

Name ______________________

Cumulative Review
Chapters 1-2

TEST PREPARATION

Fill in the circle under the correct answer.

1. Which addition fact would you use to check 12 − 4 = 8?

4 + 7 = 11	6 + 6 = 12
○	○
8 + 4 = 12	9 + 3 = 12
○	○

2. Which is the missing addend?

? + 6 = 14

8	7	6	5
○	○	○	○

3. Find the sum.

2 + 5 = ?

7	6	9	8
○	○	○	○

4. Which addition sentence is most likely to come next?

1 + 2 = 3
2 + 3 = 5
3 + 4 = 7
4 + 5 = 9

5 + 6 = 11	4 + 7 = 11	5 + 7 = 12
○	○	○

5. Which is a fact family for the numbers 3, 4, and 7?

4 + 3 = 7 4 − 3 = 1 3 + 4 = 7 7 − 4 = 3	4 + 3 = 7 7 − 3 = 4 3 + 4 = 7 7 − 4 = 3
○	○

6. Which is a doubles +1 fact for 6 + 6 = 12?

7 + 5 = 12	6 + 7 = 13
○	○
4 + 6 = 10	6 + 8 = 14
○	○

7. Find the sum.

6 + 4 + 2 + 3 = ?

15	14	12	13
○	○	○	○

8. Choose the missing numbers.

73, ?, 75, 76, ?, 78, 79, ?, 81, 82

72, 76, 80	74, 77, 81
○	○
74, 77, 80	76, 80, 84
○	○

Copyright © by William H. Sadlier, Inc. All rights reserved.

Fill in the circle under the correct answer.

9. Maria buys 10 monkey stickers. She gives 3 to her friend. How many stickers does she have left?

9	7	8	13
○	○	○	○

10. Jason colors 47 paper leaves. He puts 10 on each vine. How many complete vines can he make?

4	5	57	67
○	○	○	○

11. Ben sells 73 toy frogs on Monday, 58 on Tuesday, and 69 on Wednesday. When does he sell the most?

Monday	Tuesday	Wednesday
○	○	○

12. Michael has 1 toy bird, 9 toy frogs, and 2 toy monkeys. How many toys does Michael have in all?

192	6	11	12
○	○	○	○

13. Ray has 8 leaf stickers. Jen gives him some more. Now he has 16 stickers in all. How many stickers did Jen give Ray?

2	10	8	16
○	○	○	○

14. Erika sees 3 birds. Rhea sees 9 different birds. How many birds do they see in all?

12	13	14	6
○	○	○	○

15. Kim finds 42 leaves. Jack finds 53 leaves. Who finds more leaves?

Kim	Jack
○	○

16. Dawn buys 15 parrot stickers. Ed buys 8 parrot stickers. How many fewer stickers does Ed buy?

9	8	7	6
○	○	○	○

Data and Graphs: Using Operations

CHAPTER 3

Meet Our Members

Summer | Fall | Winter | Spring

Listen Listen to your teacher read the story.

How many more members joined the Friends Club in the fall than in the summer?

Copyright © by W... All rights reserved.

Dear Family,

Today our class began Chapter 3. We will learn about using graphs. Let's do the activity below together so I can review the skills I will need in order to understand the math in this chapter. Then you can read some of the new vocabulary I will learn in Chapter 3.

Love, ______________

Graph It!

Draw a set of boxes like those below to make a graph. Cut out different amounts (from 1 to 5) of a paper shape in three different colors. Have your child place each paper shape in the appropriate column above the name of the color. Then have your child tell which color is shown the most and which is shown the least.

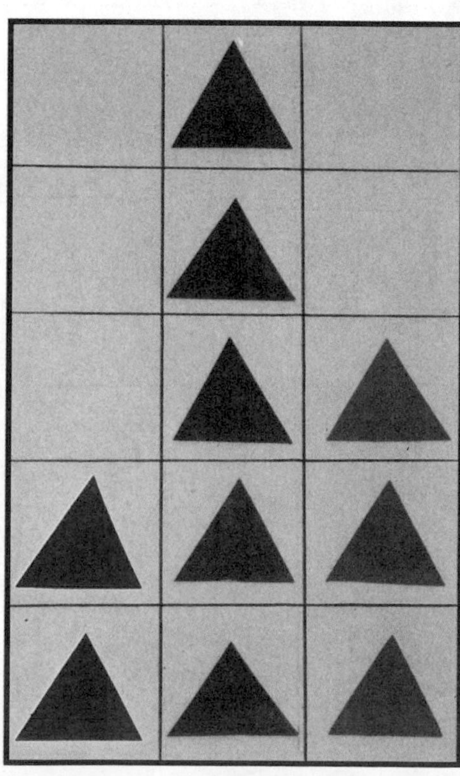

Red ▲ Green ▲ Blue ▲

Chapter 3

also on-line

Venn diagram

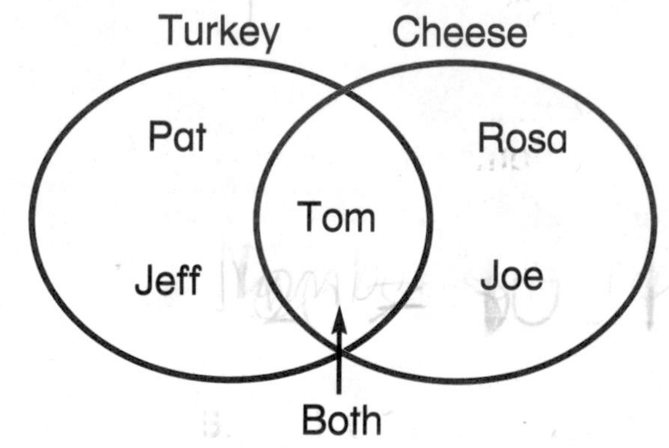

circle graph

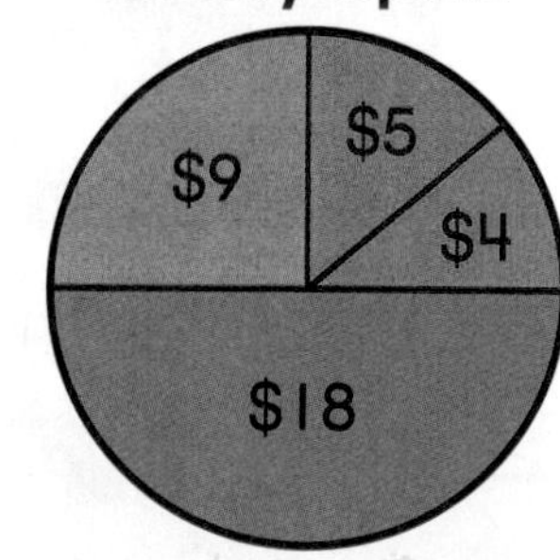

line plot

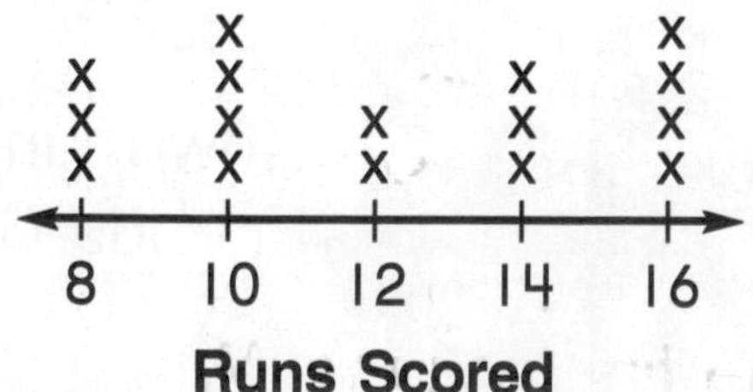

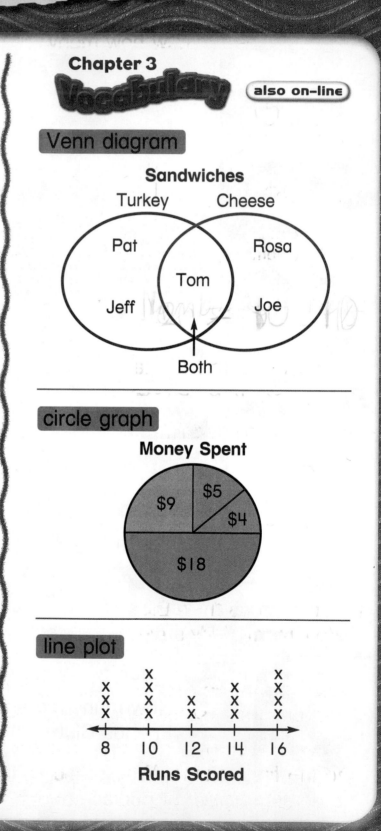

VISIT US ON-LINE www.sadlier-oxford.com

Name ______________________________

Surveys

Let's Learn!

I took a survey and asked 13 friends, "Which is your favorite pet, a cat or a dog?"

Favorite Pet	
Pet	Tally
cat	𝍸
dog	𝍸 |||

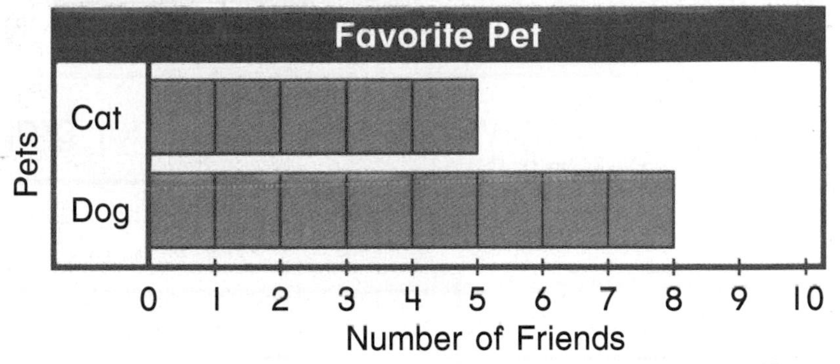

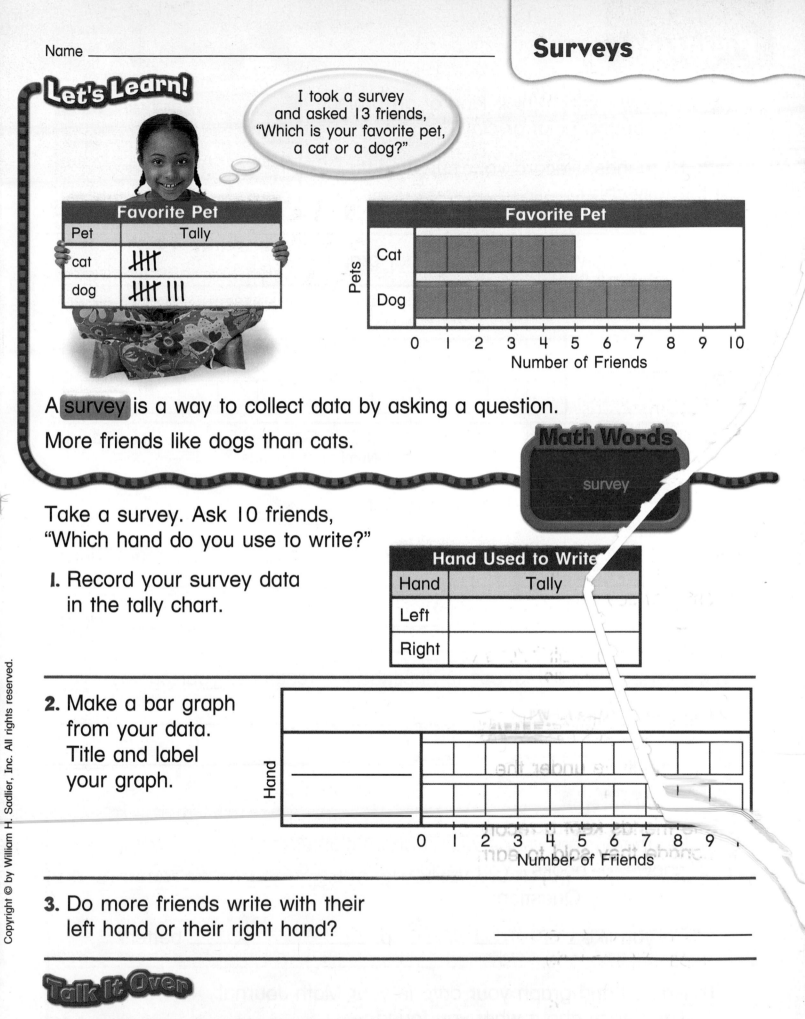

A **survey** is a way to collect data by asking a question.

More friends like dogs than cats.

Math Words
survey

Take a survey. Ask 10 friends, "Which hand do you use to write?"

1. Record your survey data in the tally chart.

Hand Used to Write	
Hand	Tally
Left	
Right	

2. Make a bar graph from your data. Title and label your graph.

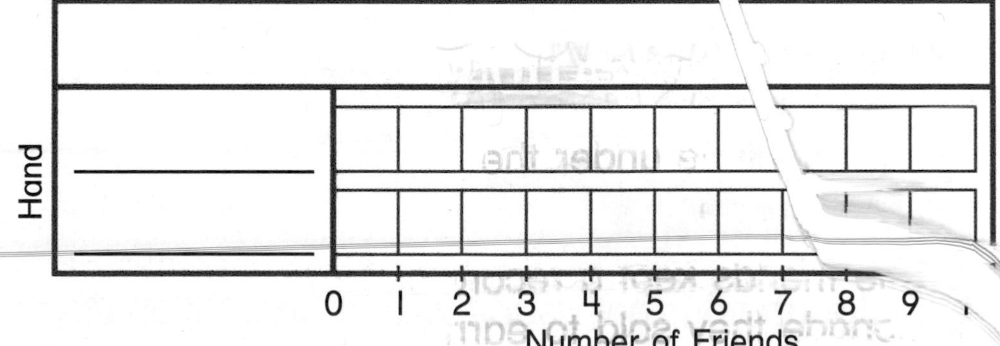

3. Do more friends write with their left hand or their right hand? ______________________

4. If you surveyed 10 more friends, do you think more would write with their left hand or right hand? Why?

Copyright © by William H. Sadlier, Inc. All rights reserved.

Practice

Take a survey. Ask, "Which kind of art project do you like better, paint or clay?"

Favorite Art Project	
Project	Tally
Paint	
Clay	

5. Ask 12 friends. Record your survey data in the tally chart.

6. Use your survey data to make a bar graph.

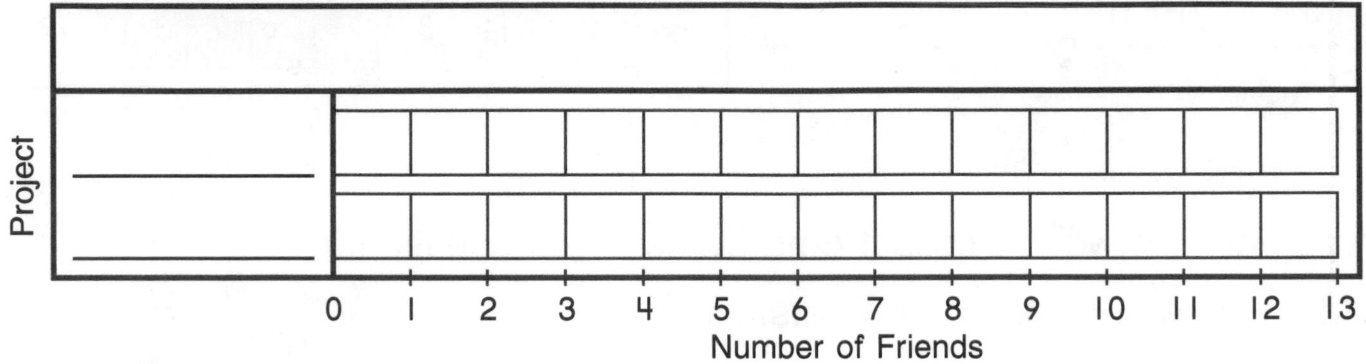

7. Which project did your friends like more? ____________

   How many more friends voted for it? ____________ more friends

8. How many friends like to paint? ____ friends

9. Write one or two sentences to describe the results of your survey.

____

____

CHALLENGE

Make up your own survey. Is it about clothes, TV shows, or books? You decide.

10. My Survey Question:

    Do you like ____________ or ____________ better?

11. Record and graph your data in your Math Journal. Then write about what you found.

Math Alive at Home Ask your child to explain how he/she organized the results of the survey above.

Name ____________________

Range, Mode, and Median

Let's Learn!

Lee graphed the ages of her five best friends.

To tell about a whole set of data, you can use the range, mode, and median.

Order the data.

6, 7, 8, 9, 9

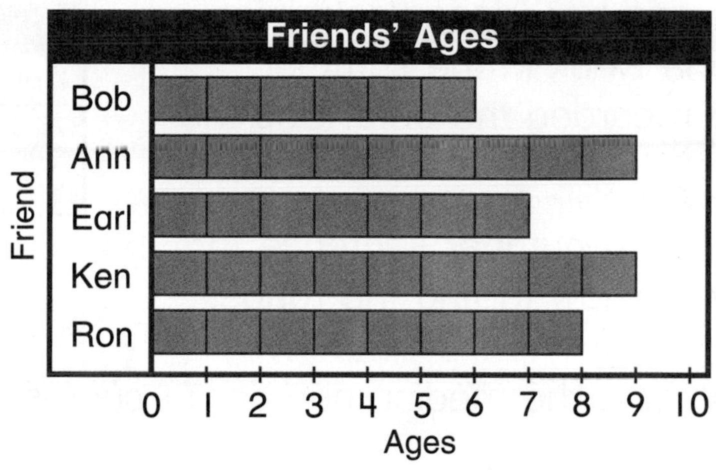

The **range** is the greatest number minus the least number.

(6), 7, 8, 9, (9)

9 − 6 = 3

The range is 3 years.

The **mode** is the number that is seen most often.

6, 7, 8, (9), (9)

The mode is 9 years.

More of Lee's friends are 9 than any other age.

The **median** is the middle number in an ordered set of data.

6, 7, (8), 9, 9

The median age is 8.

Just as many of Lee's friends are younger than 8 as are older than 8.

Math Words
range
mode
median

Tracy's baseball team played 7 games.
The baseballs show the runs scored in 7 games.

3 runs, 2 runs, 6 runs, 8 runs, 11 runs, 5 runs, 3 runs

1. What is the fewest number of runs scored in a game? 2

2. What is the range of the number of runs scored? ____

3. What is the mode of the numbers? ____

4. What is the median? ____

Talk It Over

5. What do the range, mode, and median number of runs tell you about the set of data for the baseball games?

Copyright © by William H. Sadlier, Inc. All rights reserved.

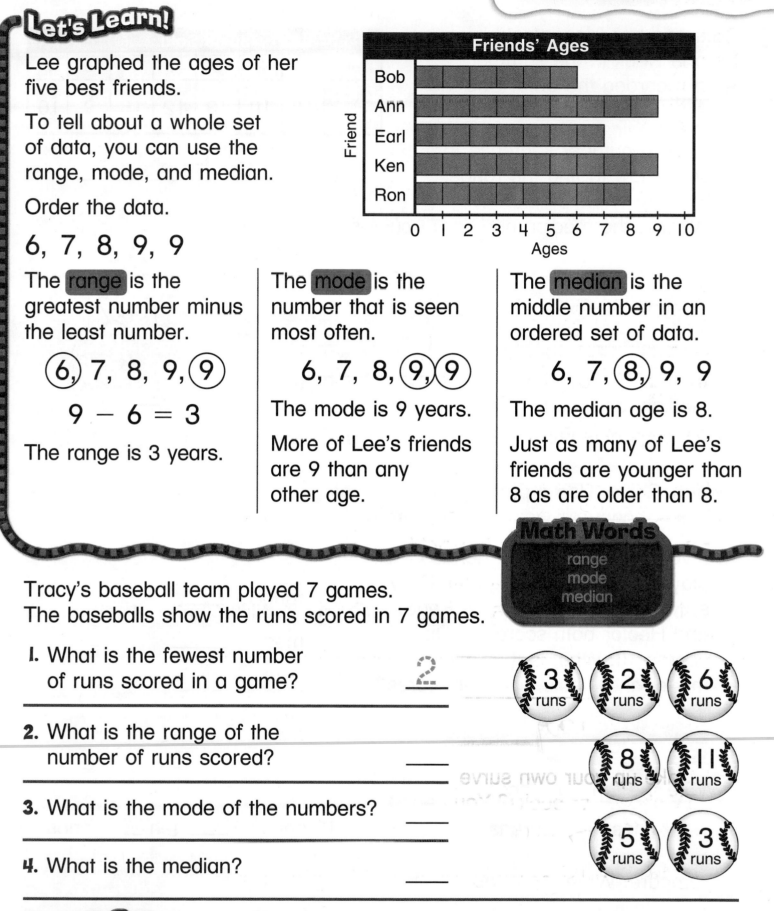

Practice

Alice and her friends sold juice for one week in the summer. Alice recorded the data. Use the table to answer the questions.

Juice Sold							
Day	1	2	3	4	5	6	7
Cups Sold	18	10	13	12	15	9	10

6. Write a number sentence to show how to find the range. 18 − 9 = 9

7. What is the median number of cups sold? ____

8. What is the mode of Alice's data? ____

9. In your Math Journal, explain what the range, median, and mode of Alice's data tell about the juice sold in a week.

Problem Solving Solve. Use a problem-solving strategy. Show your work on a separate sheet of paper.

10. Five friends from the Friends Club play a new computer game. Gary scores 17. Jean scores 9. Peggy and Hector both score 12. Diane scores 10. What is the range, mode, and median of their scores?

range ____

mode ____

median ____

DO YOU REMEMBER?

Write the tens and ones.

11. 84 ones = ____ tens ____ ones | 12. 19 ones = ____ ten ____ ones

Compare. Write <, =, or >.

13. 56 ◯ 65 | 14. 90 ◯ 79 | 15. 38 ◯ 35

Math Alive at Home On a sheet of paper, write five numbers less than 12, repeating at least one. Ask your child to identify the range, mode, and median for this set of numbers.

Name ______________________________

Understand Data

Let's Learn!

You can look for a pattern in data to **predict**, or guess, what the next data might be.

The bar graph shows sales of T-shirts.

In the fifth week, would you predict that sales would be about 10 or about 50 T-shirts?

Think

Sales got better each week. There is a pattern of increasing sales.

The number sold the fifth week is likely to be about 50.

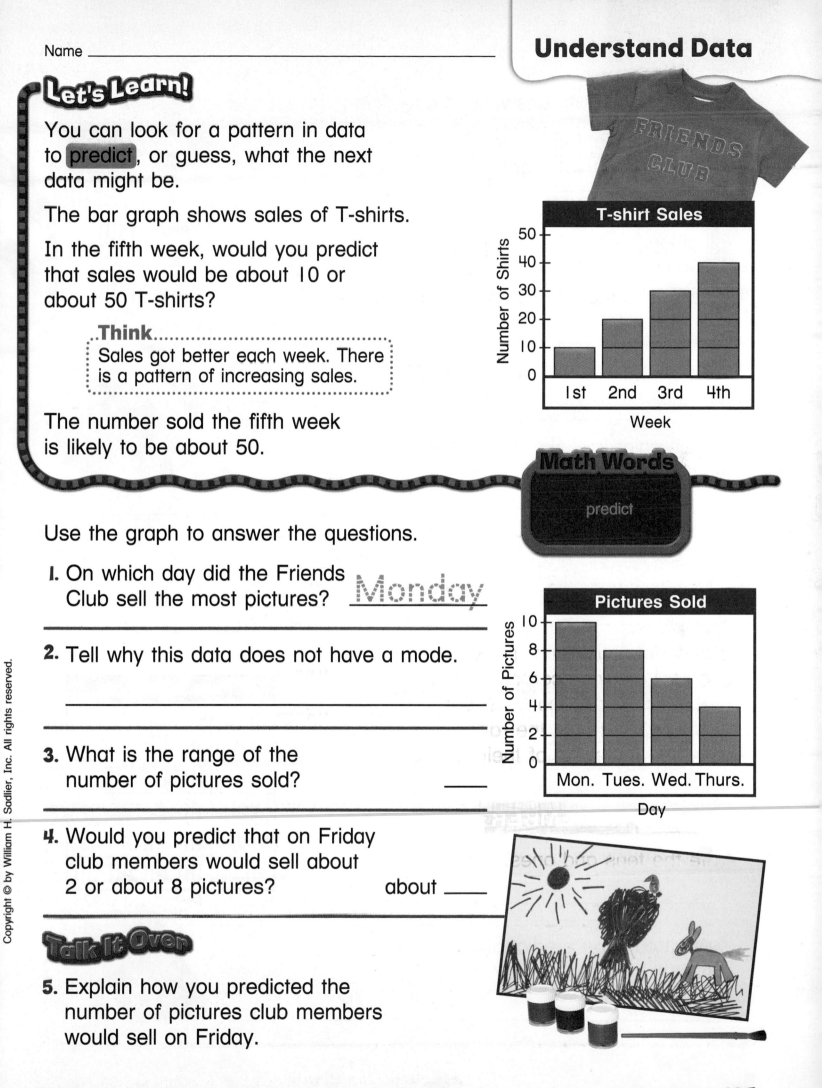

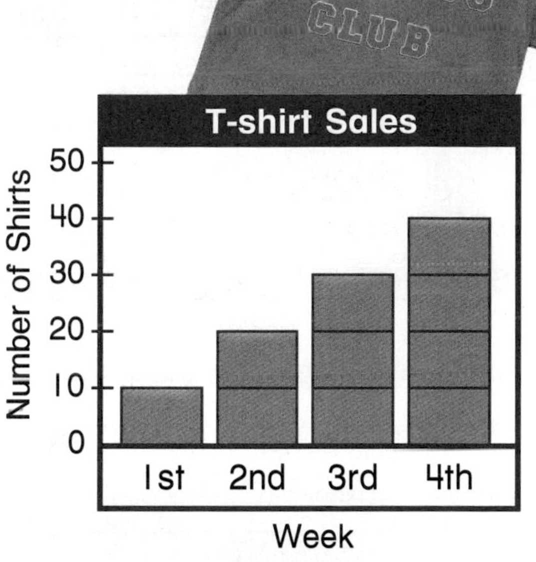

Math Words

predict

Use the graph to answer the questions.

1. On which day did the Friends Club sell the most pictures? Monday

2. Tell why this data does not have a mode.

____

____

3. What is the range of the number of pictures sold? ____

4. Would you predict that on Friday club members would sell about 2 or about 8 pictures? about ____

Pictures Sold

Number of Pictures: 0, 2, 4, 6, 8, 10

Day: Mon. Tues. Wed. Thurs.

5. Explain how you predicted the number of pictures club members would sell on Friday.

Copyright © by William H. Sadlier, Inc. All rights reserved.

Practice

Use the tally chart to answer the questions.

Club Banner	
Color	Tally
Red	卌 |||
Yellow	||||
Blue	卌
Green	||||
Orange	|||

6. What color banner did most club members vote for? red

7. What is the range of votes for all colors? ____

8. What is the mode for this data? ____

9. What is the median for this data? ____

10. Which color is likely to be picked for the club banner? ________

11. Explain how you can predict which color will be picked for the club banner.

____

CHALLENGE

12. One week the friends sold fruit ices. The weather for four days was warm and sunny. One day was rainy and cool. Which day do you think that was?

____

13. Explain why you chose that day.

____

14. What can you predict about sales of fruit ices next week?

____

Fruit Ices Sold	
Day	Tally
Mon.	卌 ||||
Tues.	卌 卌 卌
Wed.	|||
Thurs.	卌 卌 卌
Fri.	卌 卌 卌 ||||

Math Alive at Home Ask your child how he/she made a prediction in exercise 14.

Name ____________________

Check Your Progress
Lessons 1-6

TEST PREPARATION

Listen to your teacher read the directions.
Fill in the circle under the correct answer.

Flowers Picked	
Alice	✿ ✿ ✿
Lisa	✿
Jeff	✿ ✿
Erica	✿ ✿ ✿ ✿
Key: Each ✿ stands for 3 flowers.	

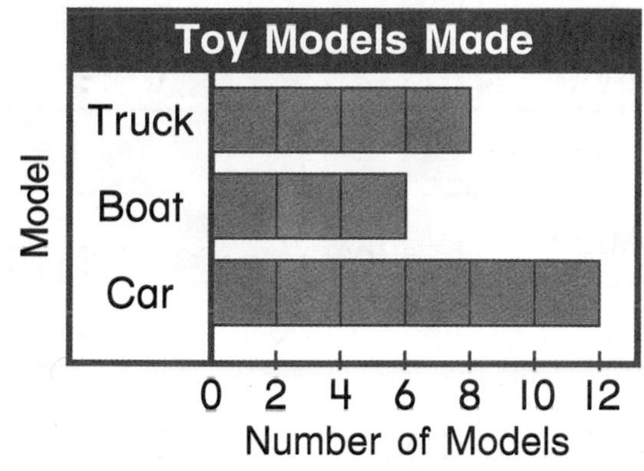

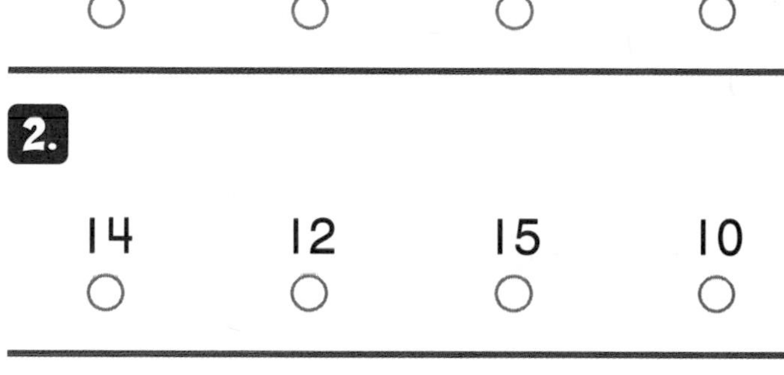

1. Lisa ○ Jeff ○ Alice ○ Erica ○

2. 14 ○ 12 ○ 15 ○ 10 ○

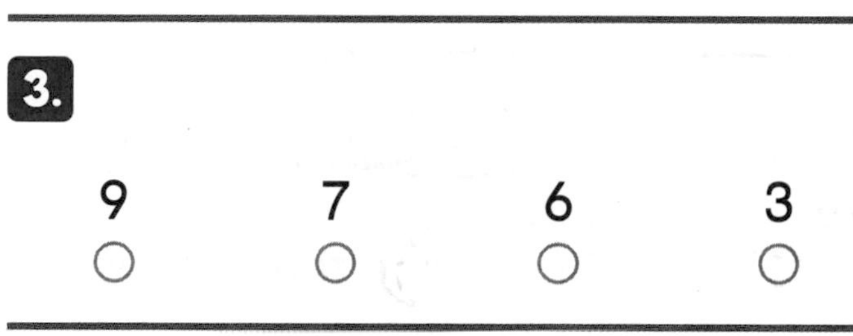

3. 9 ○ 7 ○ 6 ○ 3 ○

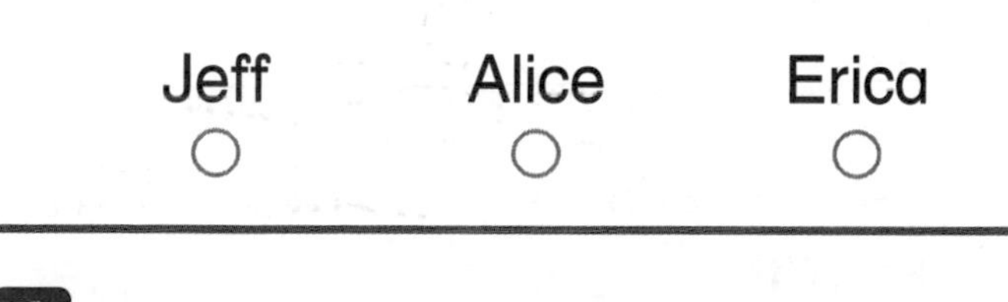

4. Jeff ○ Alice ○ Erica ○

5. Lisa ○ Jeff ○ Erica ○

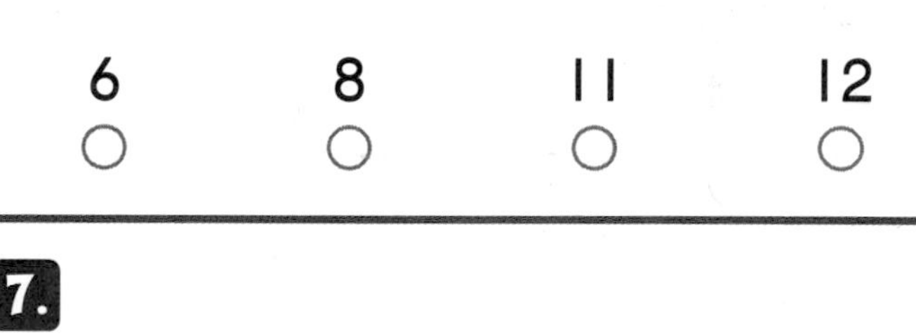

6. 6 ○ 8 ○ 11 ○ 12 ○

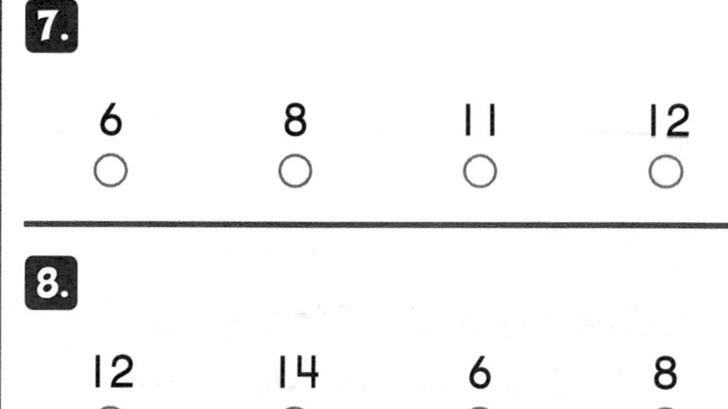

7. 6 ○ 8 ○ 11 ○ 12 ○

8. 12 ○ 14 ○ 6 ○ 8 ○

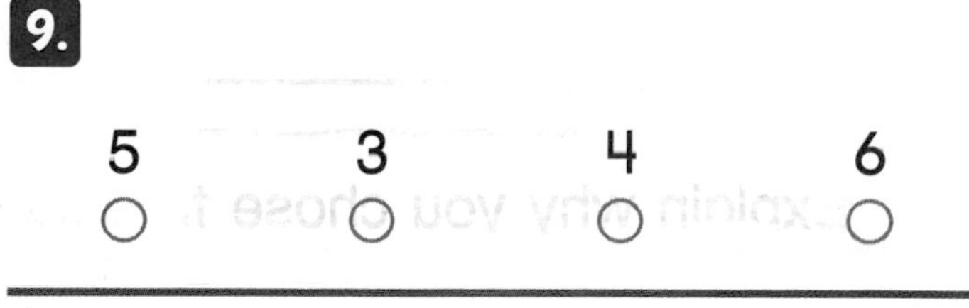

9. 5 ○ 3 ○ 4 ○ 6 ○

10. 1 ○ 2 ○ 6 ○ 8 ○

Copyright © by William H. Sadlier, Inc. All rights reserved.

Fill in the circle under the correct answer.

Use the graph for exercises 11–14.

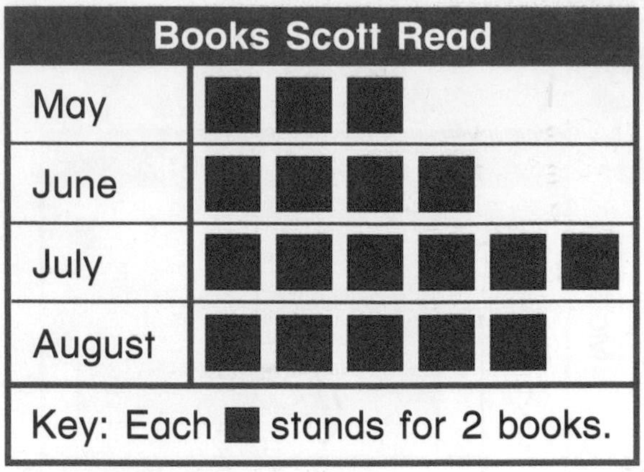

Books Scott Read	
May	■ ■ ■
June	■ ■ ■ ■
July	■ ■ ■ ■ ■ ■
August	■ ■ ■ ■ ■
Key: Each ■ stands for 2 books.	

11. In which month did Scott read the most books?

August ○ May ○ June ○ July ○

12. How many books did Scott read in May and June?

19 ○ 14 ○ 13 ○ 16 ○

13. In which month did Scott read more than 10 books?

August ○ May ○ June ○ July ○

14. In which month did Scott read fewer than 7 books?

August ○ May ○ June ○ July ○

Use the tally chart for exercises 15–18.

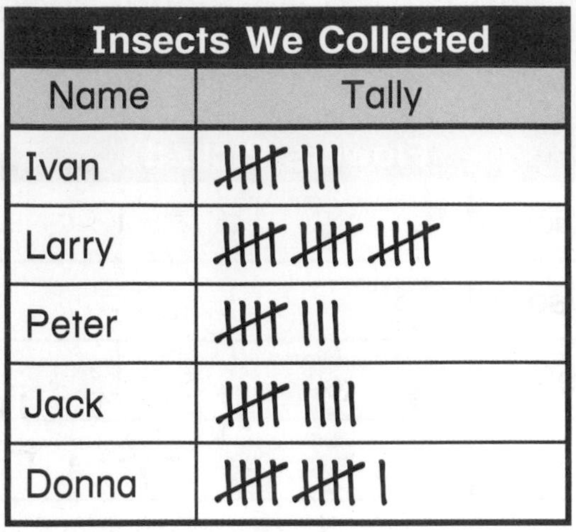

Insects We Collected

Name	Tally
Ivan	𝍸 III
Larry	𝍸 𝍸 𝍸
Peter	𝍸 III
Jack	𝍸 IIII
Donna	𝍸 𝍸 I

15. Who collected the most insects?

Ivan ○ Jack ○ Peter ○ Larry ○

16. Find the mode of the number of insects the friends collected.

15 ○ 8 ○ 9 ○ 11 ○

17. Find the range of the number of insects collected.

7 ○ 10 ○ 9 ○ 12 ○

18. Find the median of the number of insects collected.

8 ○ 11 ○ 9 ○ 15 ○

Name ______________________

Performance Assessment
Chapter 3

Chris plants flowers in the Friends Club Garden. She makes a tally chart to show how many flowers.

Friends Club Garden	
Flower	Tally
	卌 卌 II
	卌 卌 卌

1. Use the tally chart to make a pictograph.

Friends Club Garden	
Key: Each ☺ stands for 3 flowers.	

2. Use the tally chart to make a bar graph

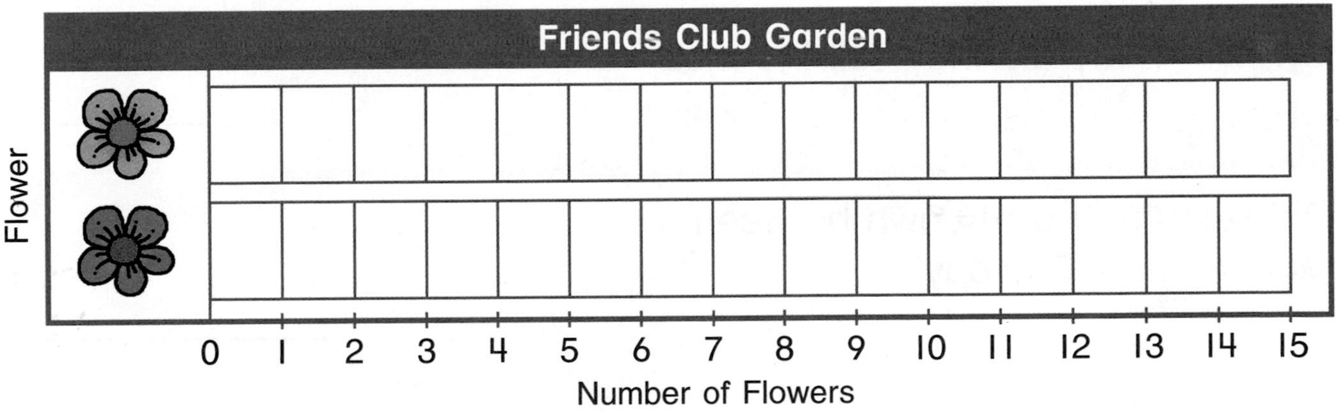

3. Write a question that can be answered by reading the bar graph. Then answer the question.

____

____

____

Copyright © by William H. Sadlier, Inc. All rights reserved.

Enrichment

Name ____________________

Line Graphs

A line graph uses a line to show data.

The line, which moves up or down, helps you see how data changes over time.

To find how many picture frames the Friends Club sold each day, look at the dot above the day. Then read across.

20 frames were sold on Monday.

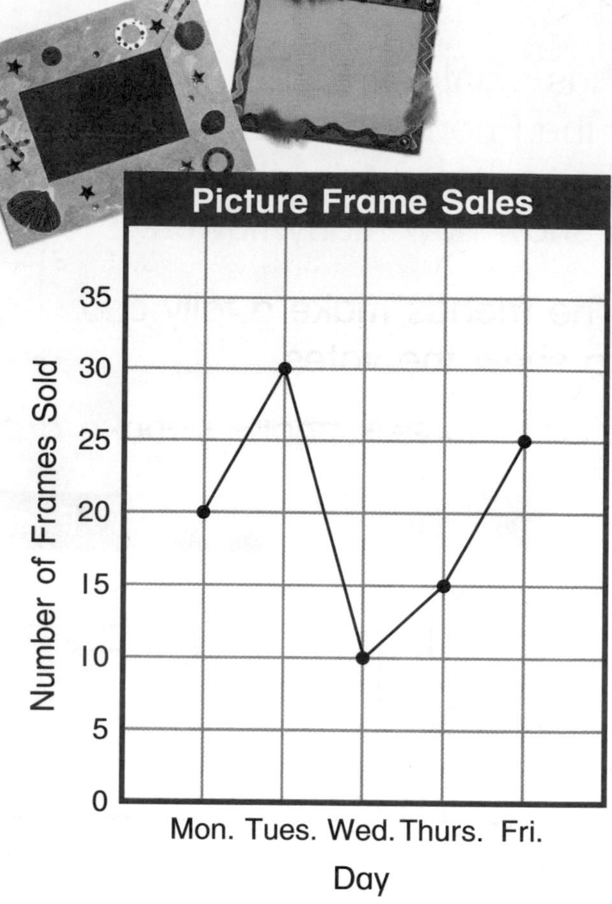

1. How many picture frames did club members sell on Wednesday? 10

2. On which day did they sell the most? ____________

3. Did sales go up or down between Monday and Tuesday? ____________

4. Did sales go up or down between Thursday and Friday? ____________

5. Between which two days did sales go down?
   between ____________ and ____________

6. On which day did the Friends Club sell the least? ____________

Read ALOUD

The New Mascot

Friday is a big day for the Friends Club. Everyone will vote for a club mascot. There are 3 mascots to choose from. The friends make a tally chart to show the votes.

Read Henry's rhyme about the first mascot.

Vote for Gary the Gecko.
He's smooth and he's green.
He's the coolest lizard
that you've ever seen!
Friends CLUB
VOTE
VOTE
Gary

Our New Mascot	
Name	Tally
Gary	𝍸 II

How many votes does Gary get?

____ votes

Copyright © by William H. Sadlier, Inc. All rights reserved.

Read Sarah's rhyme about the second mascot.

Vote for Dusty the Dog.
He's your friend.
There is no doubt!
And we all know that friendship
is what our club's all about!
VOTE
Dusty

Our New Mascot	
Name	Tally
Gary	𝍸 II
Dusty	𝍸 IIII

How many votes does Dusty get?

_____ votes

Read Ellen's rhyme about the third mascot.

Vote for Peggy the Parakeet.
She can fly, hop, and walk.
If we make her our mascot,
we can teach her to talk!
VOTE!
Peggy

Who would you vote for?

Copyright © by William H. Sadlier, Inc. All rights reserved.

Our New Mascot	
Name	Tally
Gary	𝍸 II
Dusty	𝍸 IIII
Peggy	𝍸 I

The winner is ______________!

Welcome to the new mascot!

Name ______________________________

TEST PREPARATION

Fill in the circle under the correct answer.

1. Which list is in order from least to greatest?

73, 37, 56, 94 ○ 37, 56, 73, 94 ○

94, 73, 56, 37 ○ 37, 94, 73, 56 ○

2. Which number word is most likely to come next?

twenty, thirty, forty, ?

fifty ○ sixty ○ seventy ○ eighty ○

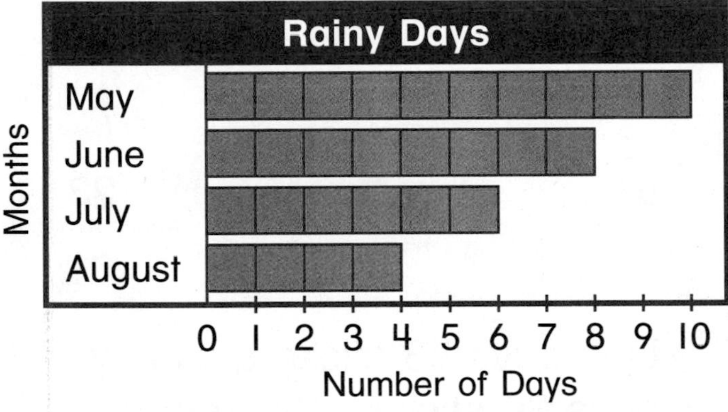

3. How many days did it rain in the months of June and August?

8 ○ 4 ○ 12 ○ 13 ○

4. Which month had between 6 and 10 rainy days?

June ○ July ○ August ○

5. Which is the related addition sentence for 11 − 4 = 7?

3 + 4 = 7 ○ 7 + 4 = 11 ○

2 + 5 = 7 ○ 11 − 7 = 4 ○

6. How many tens and ones are in 44 ones?

0 tens 40 ones ○ 40 tens 4 ones ○

40 tens 0 ones ○ 4 tens 4 ones ○

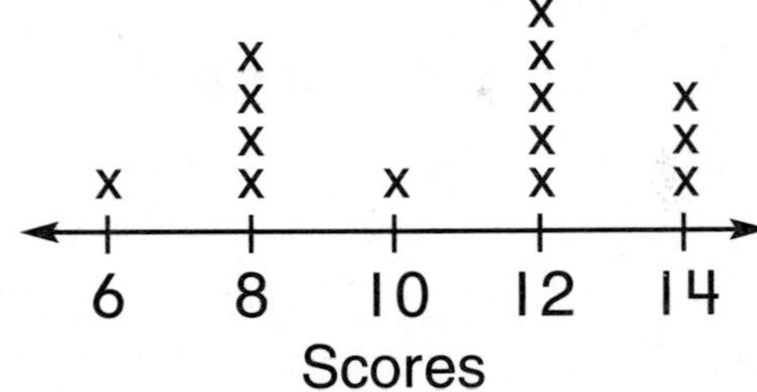

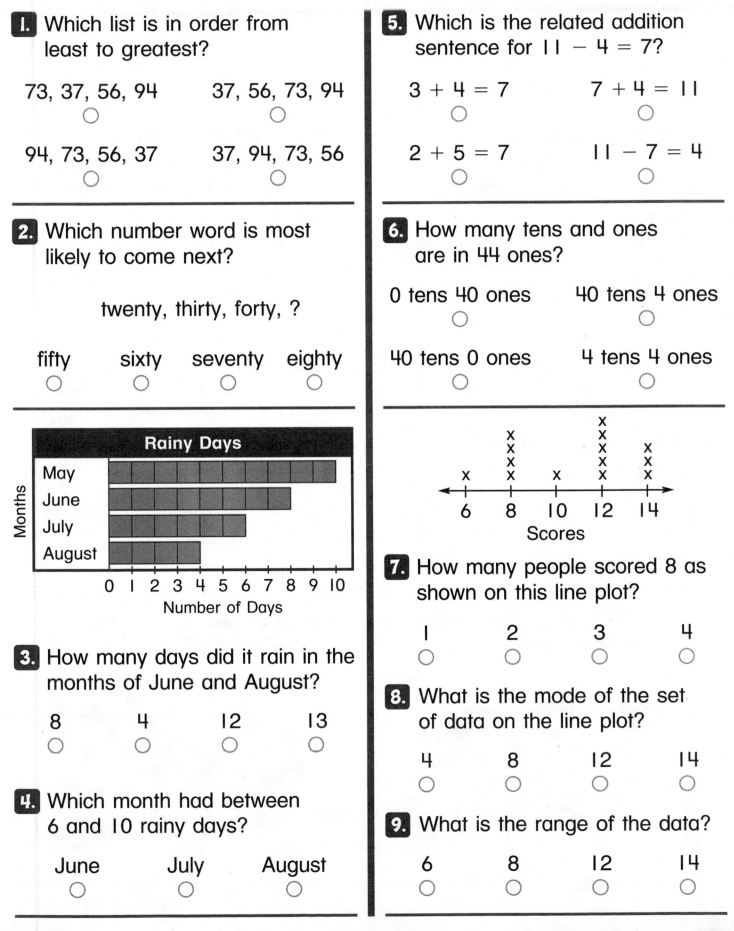

7. How many people scored 8 as shown on this line plot?

1 ○ 2 ○ 3 ○ 4 ○

8. What is the mode of the set of data on the line plot?

4 ○ 8 ○ 12 ○ 14 ○

9. What is the range of the data?

6 ○ 8 ○ 12 ○ 14 ○

Copyright © by William H. Sadlier, Inc. All rights reserved.

Fill in the circle under the correct answer.

10. Teri sees 4 pigs. Susan sees 2 pigs and 1 horse. Kate sees 3 cows. How many pigs do the girls see?

6 ○ 7 ○ 9 ○ 10 ○

11. Jerome finds 3 shells on Monday, 2 shells on Tuesday, and 9 shells on Wednesday. How many shells does he find in all?

5 ○ 12 ○ 14 ○ 15 ○

12. There are 12 horses. There are 6 horse riders. How many more horses than horse riders are there?

2 ○ 6 ○ 14 ○ 18 ○

13. Cindy has 10 flowers. She finds 9 more. How many flowers does she have now?

1 ○ 10 ○ 19 ○ 29 ○

14. Zak buys three groups of 10 monkey stickers. Then he buys 5 bird stickers. How many stickers does he buy?

13 ○ 15 ○ 30 ○ 35 ○

15. I am a 2-digit number that has 8 ones. I have more than 5 tens but fewer than 7 tens. What number am I?

85 ○ 86 ○ 58 ○ 68 ○

16. Pete has 9 stickers. His friend gives him some more. Now he has 14 stickers. How many stickers did Pete's friend give him?

5 ○ 6 ○ 10 ○ 23 ○

17. Don buys 43 stickers. Cathy buys 39 stickers. Who buys more stickers?

Don ○ Cathy ○

Addition: Two-Digit Numbers

Listen Listen to your teacher read the story.

Which two places would you like to visit?
How many points would you need to get in?

Copyright © by William H. Sadlier, Inc. All rights reserved.

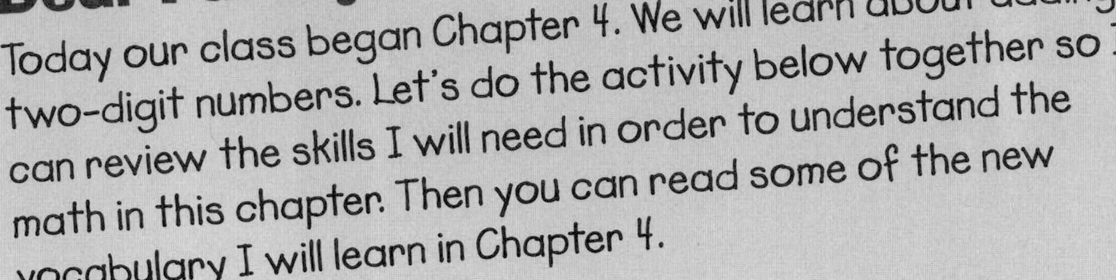

Dear Family,

Today our class began Chapter 4. We will learn about adding two-digit numbers. Let's do the activity below together so I can review the skills I will need in order to understand the math in this chapter. Then you can read some of the new vocabulary I will learn in Chapter 4.

Love, ________________

Back to Basics

Use small objects such as beans, pasta, or pennies to help your child review basic addition facts. Place two groups that contain from 1 to 9 objects on a table. Ask your child how many are in each group and how many there are in all.

7 + 6 = 13

Chapter 4 Vocabulary

also on-line

10 ones = 1 ten

regroup ones as tens

trade 10 ones for 1 ten

5 tens 14 ones =
6 tens 4 ones

To **round** to the nearest ten, look at the ones.
5 ones or more, round up.
Fewer than 5 ones, round down.

estimate about how many

Round each addend.
Add to estimate the sum.

$$\begin{array}{rcr} 63 & \longrightarrow & 60 \\ +\,18 & \longrightarrow & +20 \\ \hline & & \text{about } 80 \end{array}$$

For Additional Resources:
VISIT US ON-LINE www.sadlier-oxford.com

Name ______________________

Add Ones and Tens

Let's Learn!

The second grade takes a trip to the zoo. Forty-three children ride in Bus 1. Twenty-two children ride in Bus 2. How many children ride in all?

Model the addends.

tens	ones
6 tens	5 ones

First add the ones.

	tens	ones
	4	3
+	2	2
		5

Then add the tens.

	tens	ones
	4	3
+	2	2
	6	5

65 children ride in all.

Add. You may use models to check.

1.

	tens	ones
	3	1
+	1	8
	4	9

2.

	tens	ones
	1	2
+	6	5

3.

	tens	ones
	1	5
+	2	3

4.

	tens	ones
	2	1
+	3	4

5. 22 + 62

6. 48 + 30

7. 60 + 17

8. 36 + 52

9. 42 + 57

10. 35 + 31

11. 15 + 52

12. 76 + 13

13. 45 + 44

14. 70 + 29

15. How does knowing addition facts help you add two-digit numbers?

Copyright © by William H. Sadlier, Inc. All rights reserved.

Practice

Remember to add the ones first.

Find the sum.

16. $\begin{array}{r} 33 \\ +16 \\ \hline 49 \end{array}$

17. $\begin{array}{r} 25 \\ +40 \\ \hline \end{array}$

18. $\begin{array}{r} 22 \\ +75 \\ \hline \end{array}$

19. $\begin{array}{r} 26 \\ +13 \\ \hline \end{array}$

20. $\begin{array}{r} 72 \\ +25 \\ \hline \end{array}$

21. $\begin{array}{r} 41 \\ +36 \\ \hline \end{array}$

22. $\begin{array}{r} 63 \\ +24 \\ \hline \end{array}$

23. $\begin{array}{r} 52 \\ +46 \\ \hline \end{array}$

24. $\begin{array}{r} 87 \\ +10 \\ \hline \end{array}$

25. $\begin{array}{r} 14 \\ +71 \\ \hline \end{array}$

Solve. Use a problem-solving strategy. Show your work on a separate sheet of paper.

26. Fourteen children ride a camel at the zoo. Then 34 more children take the camel ride. How many children ride the camel?

_____ children

27. Twelve children buy tickets to see the seals. Then 47 more children buy tickets. How many children buy tickets?

_____ children

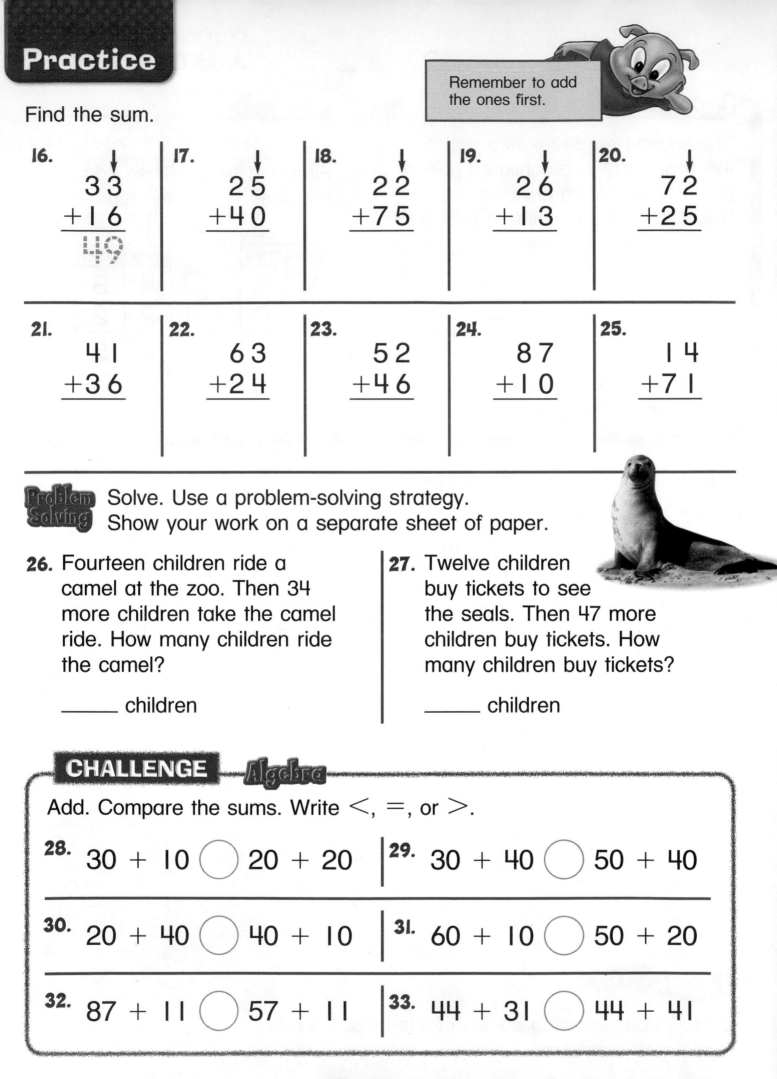

CHALLENGE Algebra

Add. Compare the sums. Write $<$, $=$, or $>$.

28. 30 + 10 ◯ 20 + 20

29. 30 + 40 ◯ 50 + 40

30. 20 + 40 ◯ 40 + 10

31. 60 + 10 ◯ 50 + 20

32. 87 + 11 ◯ 57 + 11

33. 44 + 31 ◯ 44 + 41

Math Alive at Home Ask your child to use the numbers 4, 3, 2, and 1 to make three different 2-digit addition problems and to find the sums. Have her/him use each digit only once in each problem.

Name ______________________________

Mental Math Addition

Let's Learn!

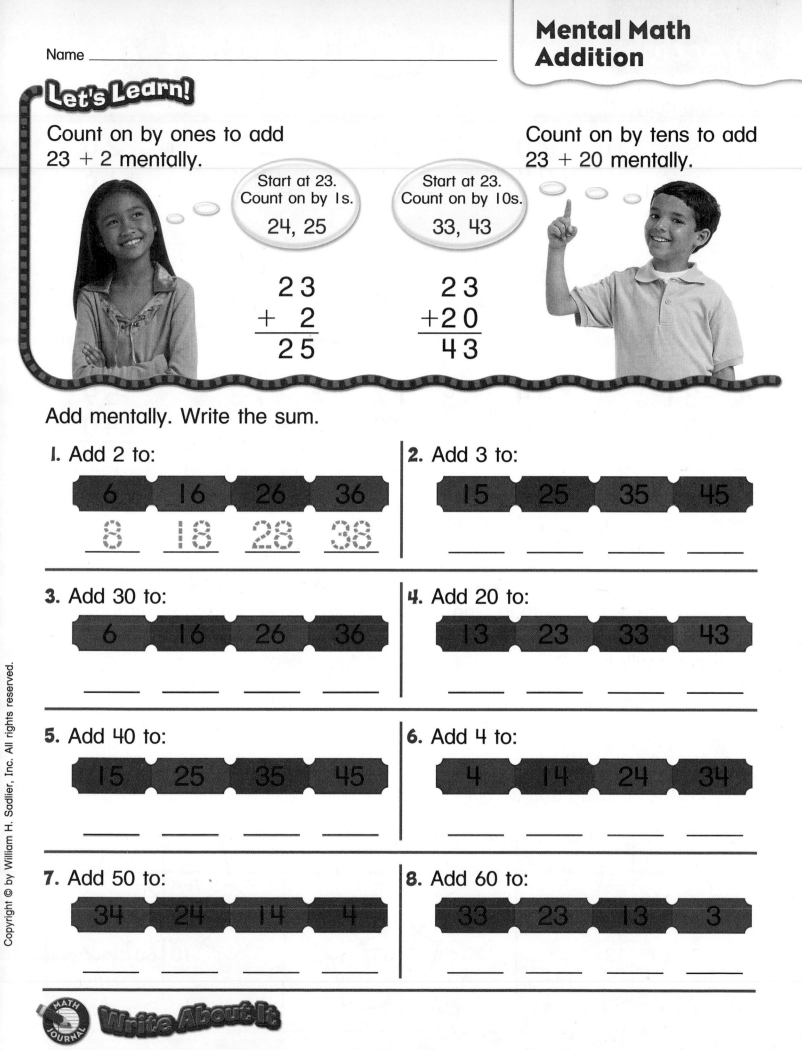

Count on by ones to add 23 + 2 mentally.

Start at 23. Count on by 1s. 24, 25

$$\begin{array}{r} 23 \\ +\ \ 2 \\ \hline 25 \end{array}$$

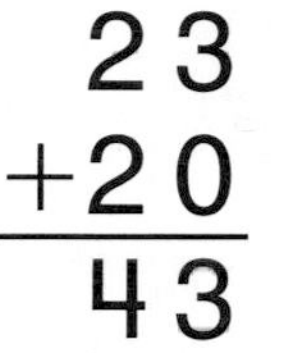

Start at 23. Count on by 10s. 33, 43

$$\begin{array}{r} 23 \\ +20 \\ \hline 43 \end{array}$$

Count on by tens to add 23 + 20 mentally.

Add mentally. Write the sum.

1. Add 2 to:

6	16	26	36
8	18	28	38

2. Add 3 to:

15	25	35	45
____	____	____	____

3. Add 30 to:

6	16	26	36
____	____	____	____

4. Add 20 to:

13	23	33	43
____	____	____	____

5. Add 40 to:

15	25	35	45
____	____	____	____

6. Add 4 to:

4	14	24	34
____	____	____	____

7. Add 50 to:

34	24	14	4
____	____	____	____

8. Add 60 to:

33	23	13	3
____	____	____	____

9. Which has a greater sum: 35 + 4 or 35 + 40? Why?

Copyright © by William H. Sadlier, Inc. All rights reserved.

Practice

Count on by ones or tens.

Add mentally.

10. $46 + 2$ = 48	11. $70 + 24$	12. $40 + 35$	13. $4 + 84$	14. $20 + 16$
15. $93 + 3$	16. $33 + 50$	17. $56 + 20$	18. $42 + 30$	19. $54 + 2$
20. $31 + 20$	21. $44 + 5$	22. $17 + 30$	23. $73 + 4$	24. $59 + 40$

Solve. Use a problem-solving strategy.
Show your work on a separate sheet of paper.

25. Dan has 35 nature stickers. Sally has 20 more than Dan. How many nature stickers does Sally have?

_____ stickers

26. José sees forty-two birds. Mary sees 3 more birds than José. How many birds does Mary see?

_____ birds

CHALLENGE

Write the missing sums.

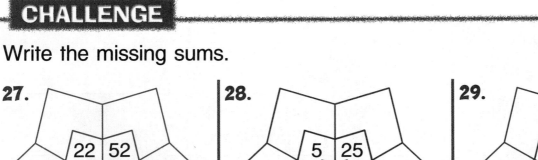

27. 3+ : 22, 52, 32, 12, 42, 62 (15)

28. 20+ : 5, 25, 45, 35, 15, 55

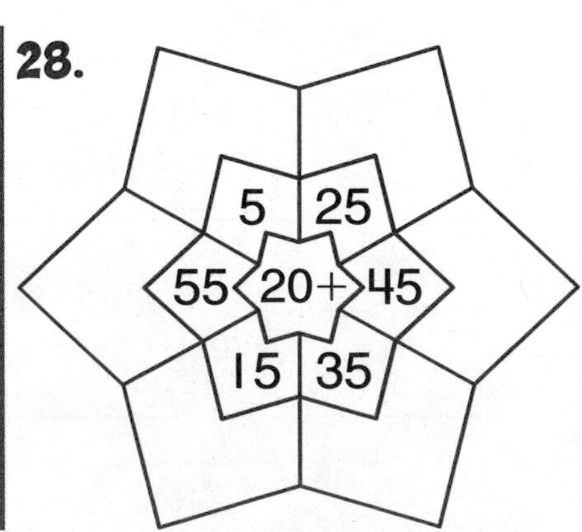

29. 34+ : 50, 20, 40, 60, 10, 30

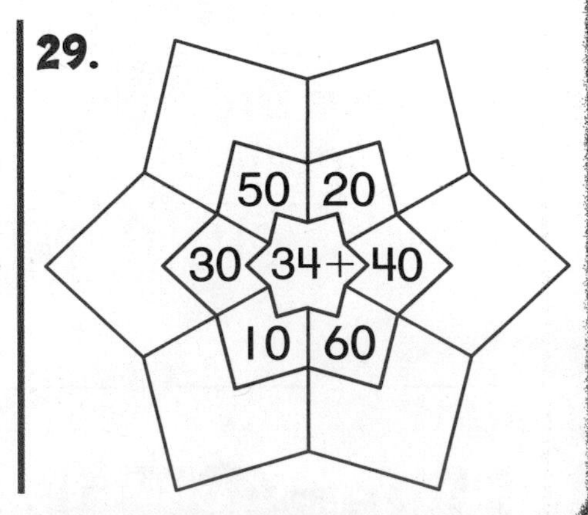

Math Alive at Home Ask your child to add 30 to the following numbers: 26, 31, 59. (56, 61, 89)

Regroup Ones as Tens: Use Models

HANDS-ON LESSON

Name ______________________________

Let's Learn!

There are more than 9 ones.
Regroup the ones.

10 ones = 1 ten
Trade 10 ones for 1 ten.

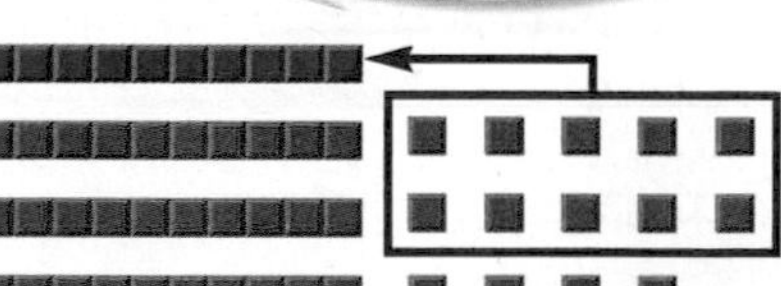

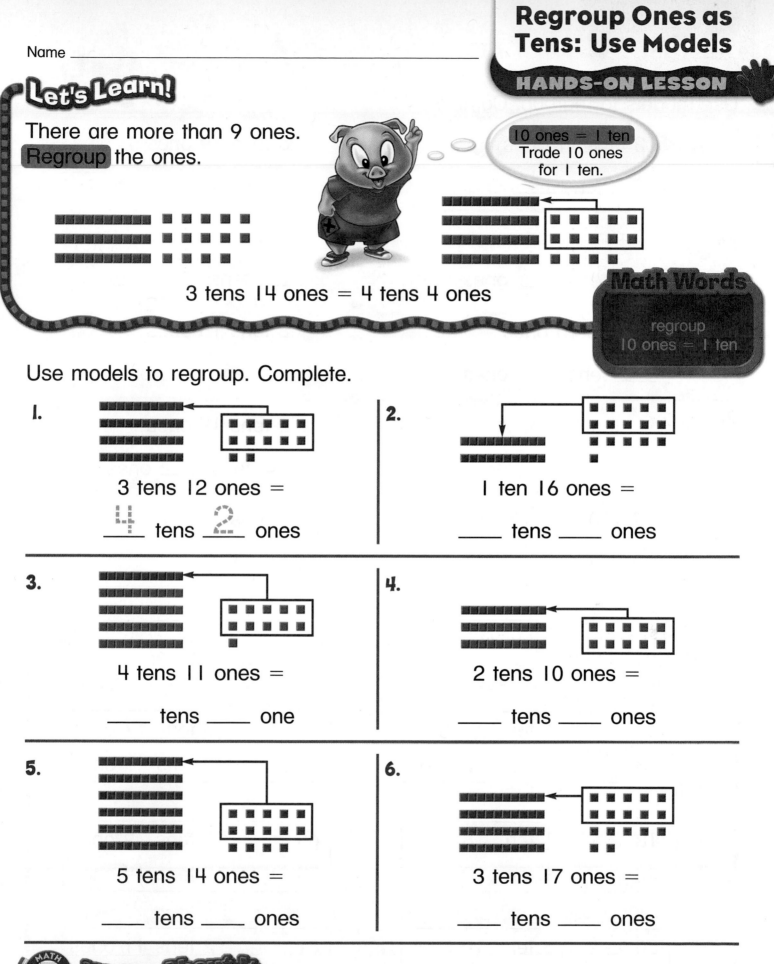

3 tens 14 ones = 4 tens 4 ones

Math Words
regroup
10 ones = 1 ten

Use models to regroup. Complete.

1.

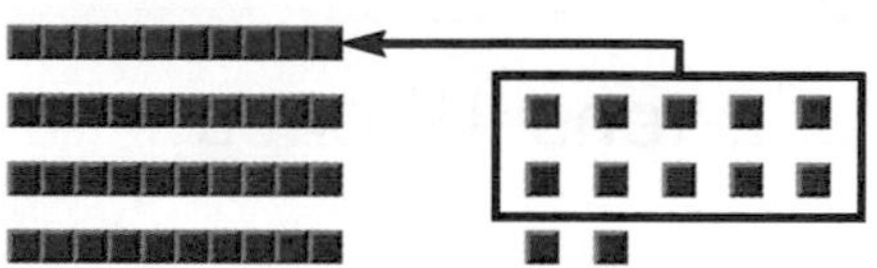

3 tens 12 ones =

4 tens 2 ones

2.

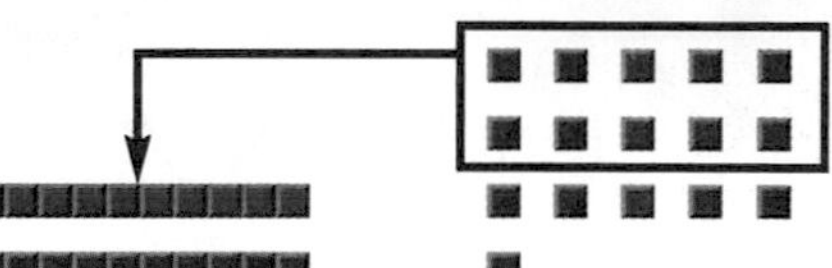

1 ten 16 ones =

____ tens ____ ones

3.

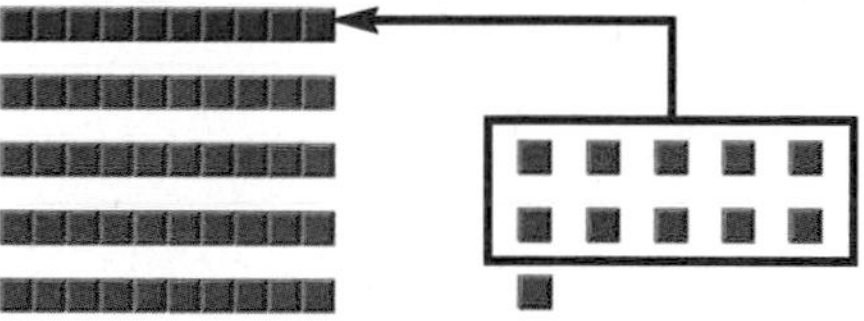

4 tens 11 ones =

____ tens ____ one

4.

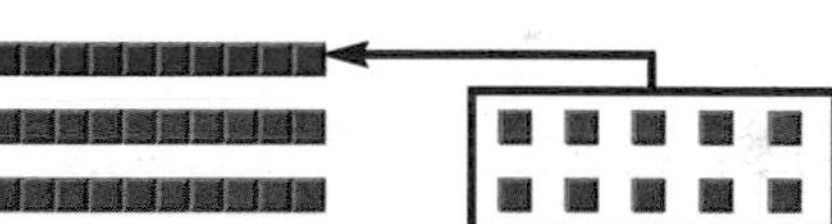

2 tens 10 ones =

____ tens ____ ones

5.

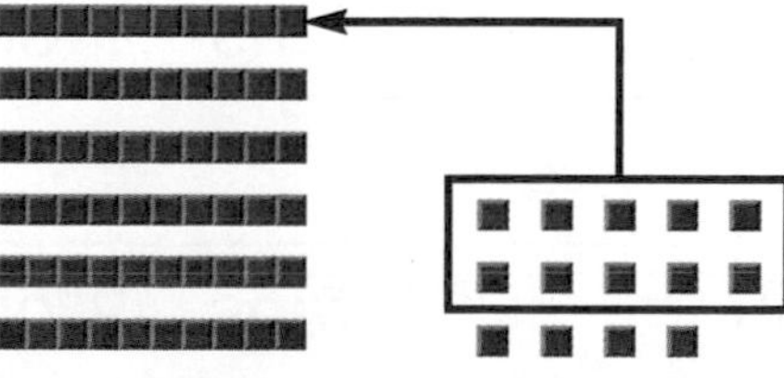

5 tens 14 ones =

____ tens ____ ones

6.

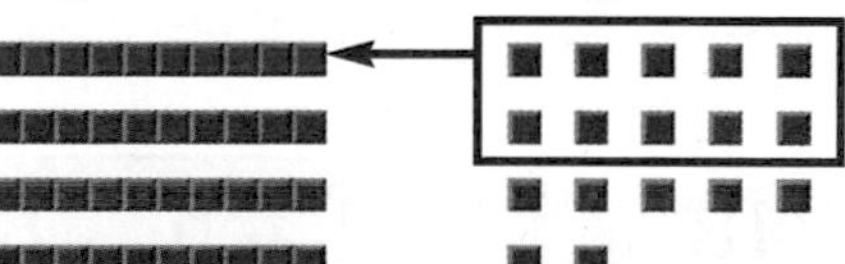

3 tens 17 ones =

____ tens ____ ones

7. What happens to the number of tens when 10 ones are regrouped as 1 ten?

Copyright © by William H. Sadlier, Inc. All rights reserved.

Practice

Use models to regroup. Complete.

8. 3 tens 11 ones = 4 tens 1 one	**9.** 6 tens 19 ones = ____ tens ____ ones
10. 7 tens 10 ones = ____ tens ____ ones	**11.** 5 tens 13 ones = ____ tens ____ ones
12. 6 tens 15 ones = ____ tens ____ ones	**13.** 8 tens 18 ones = ____ tens ____ ones
14. 1 ten 17 ones = ____ tens ____ ones	**15.** 2 tens 14 ones = ____ tens ____ ones
16. 7 tens 12 ones = ____ tens ____ ones	**17.** 4 tens 16 ones = ____ tens ____ ones

MENTAL MATH

Match.

18.

63	6 tens 13 ones
73	6 tens 3 ones

19.

37	3 tens 17 ones
47	3 tens 7 ones

20.

18	1 ten 8 ones
28	1 ten 18 ones

21.

64	5 tens 4 ones
54	5 tens 14 ones

22.

80	8 tens 10 ones
90	8 tens 0 ones

23.

31	2 tens 11 ones
21	2 tens 1 one

Math Alive at Home Ask your child to explain how to regroup 1 ten 13 ones as 2 tens 3 ones.

Name ______________________

Find Hidden Information

- Sometimes you need to find hidden information to solve a problem.

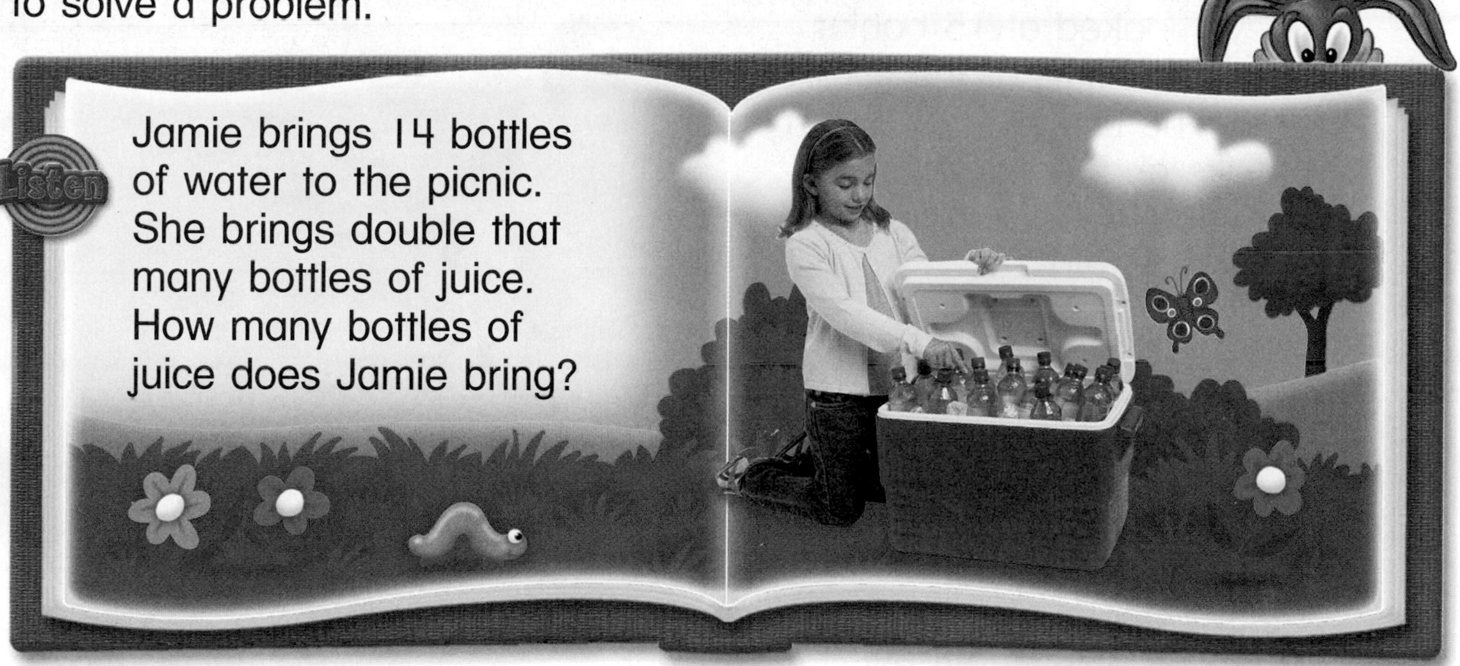

Listen
Jamie brings 14 bottles of water to the picnic. She brings double that many bottles of juice. How many bottles of juice does Jamie bring?

1. How many bottles of water does Jamie bring? Write the missing number.

Jamie brings __14__ bottles of water.

2. How many bottles of juice does Jamie bring? Write the missing word.

Jamie brings ______________ that many bottles of juice.

3. Now find the hidden information. Add to find the number you get when you double 14.

☐
+ ☐
———

Think
Double means to use the same number twice.

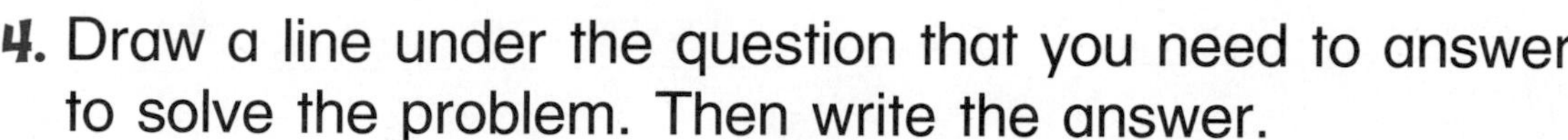

4. Draw a line under the question that you need to answer to solve the problem. Then write the answer.

Jamie brings ______________ bottles of juice.

Copyright © by William H. Sadlier, Inc. All rights reserved.

Practice

Find Hidden Information

Listen
Kevin looked at 15 books about animals at the library. Then he looked at a dozen books about airplanes. How many books did he look at in all?
ANIMALS
ANIMALS

5. How many books about animals did Kevin look at? Write the missing number.

Kevin looked at 15 books about animals.

6. How many books about airplanes did he look at? Write the missing word.

He looked at a ____________ books about airplanes.

7. Now find the hidden information. Write the missing number.

A dozen books is the same as _____ books.

8. Draw a line under the question that you need to answer to solve the problem. Then add to solve the problem.

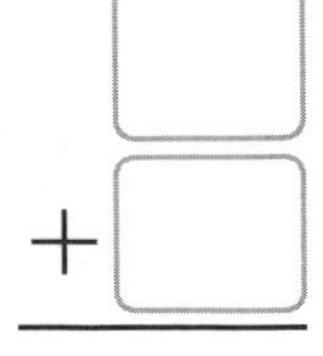

Kevin looked at _____ books in all.

Math Alive at Home Ask your child to explain the hidden information in the problem on this page.

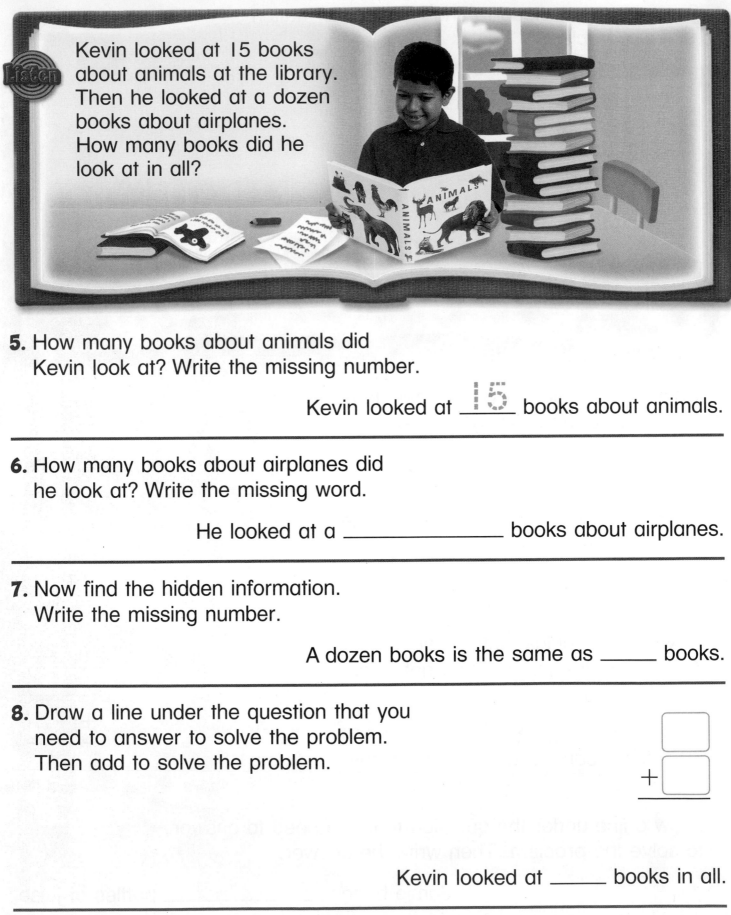

Name ______________________________

Regroup Ones as Tens: Model and Record

HANDS-ON LESSON

Let's Learn!

Al finds 27 shells at the beach. Rose finds double that number of shells. How many shells does Rose have?

Remember:
Add the regrouped ten.

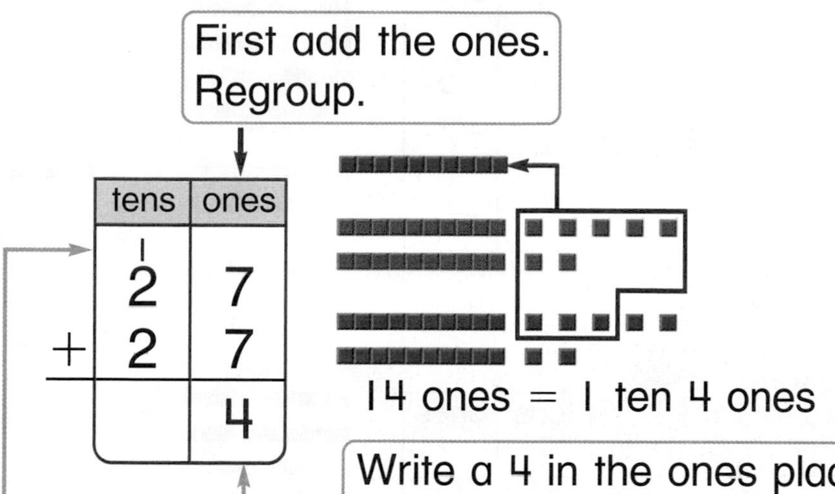

First add the ones.
Regroup.
tens
ones
1
2
7
+ 2
7
4
14 ones = 1 ten 4 ones
Write a 4 in the ones place and a small 1 in the tens place.

Then add the tens.

tens	ones
$\overset{1}{2}$	7
+ 2	7
5	4

Rose has 54 shells.

Add. Use models to regroup.

1.

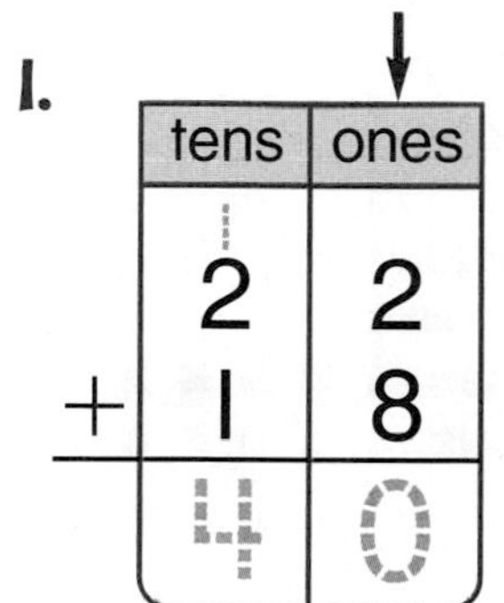

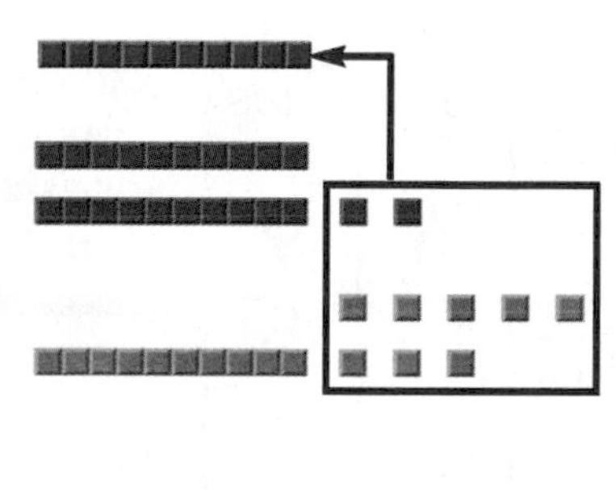

2.

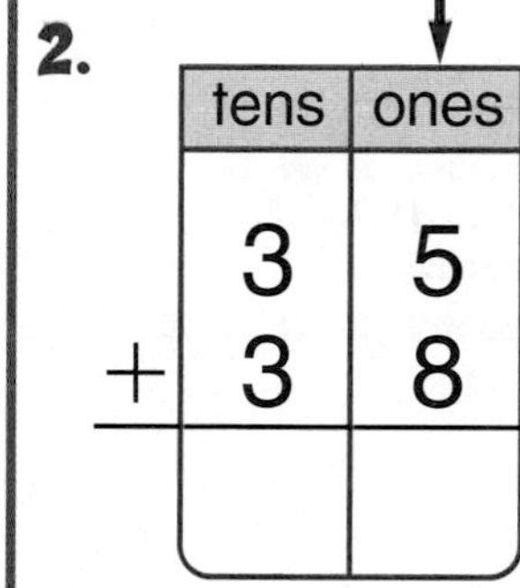

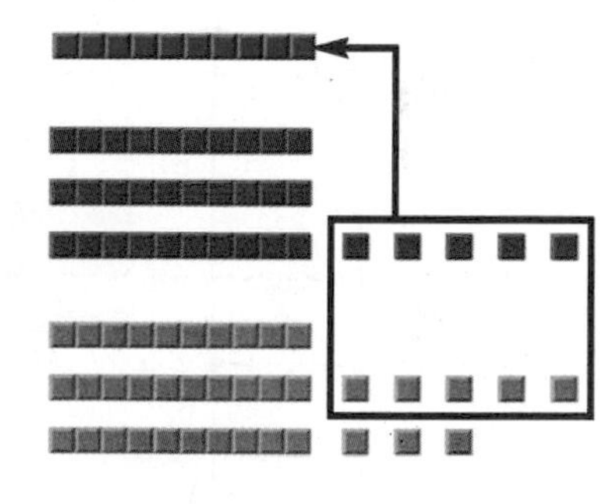

3.

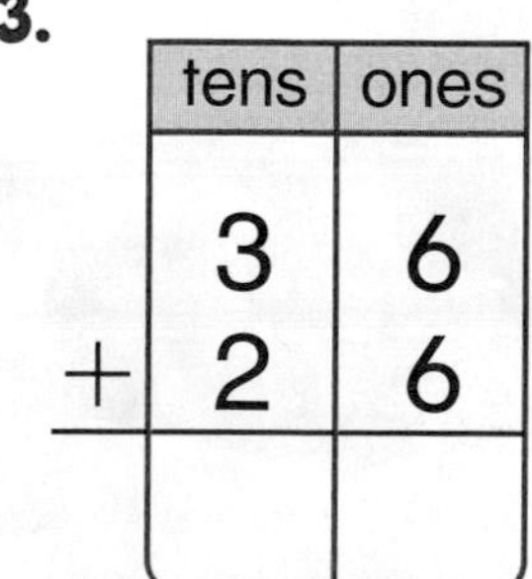

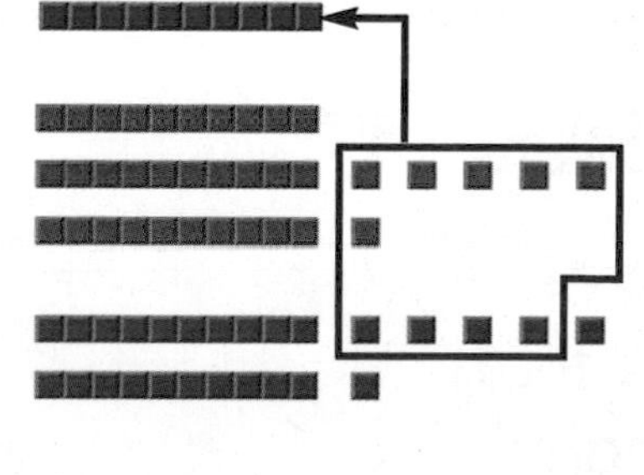

4.

tens	ones
4	4
+ 1	9

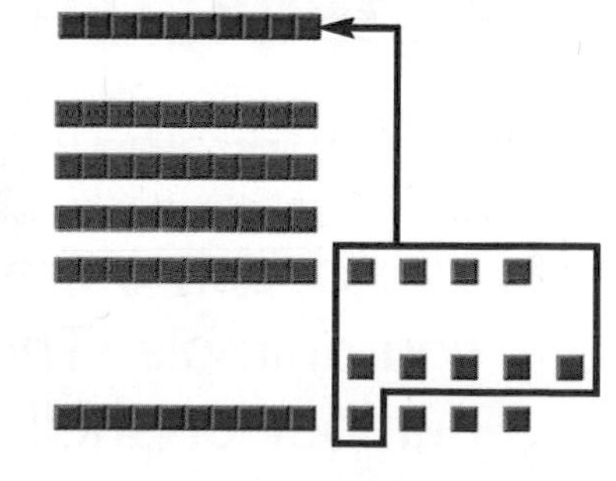

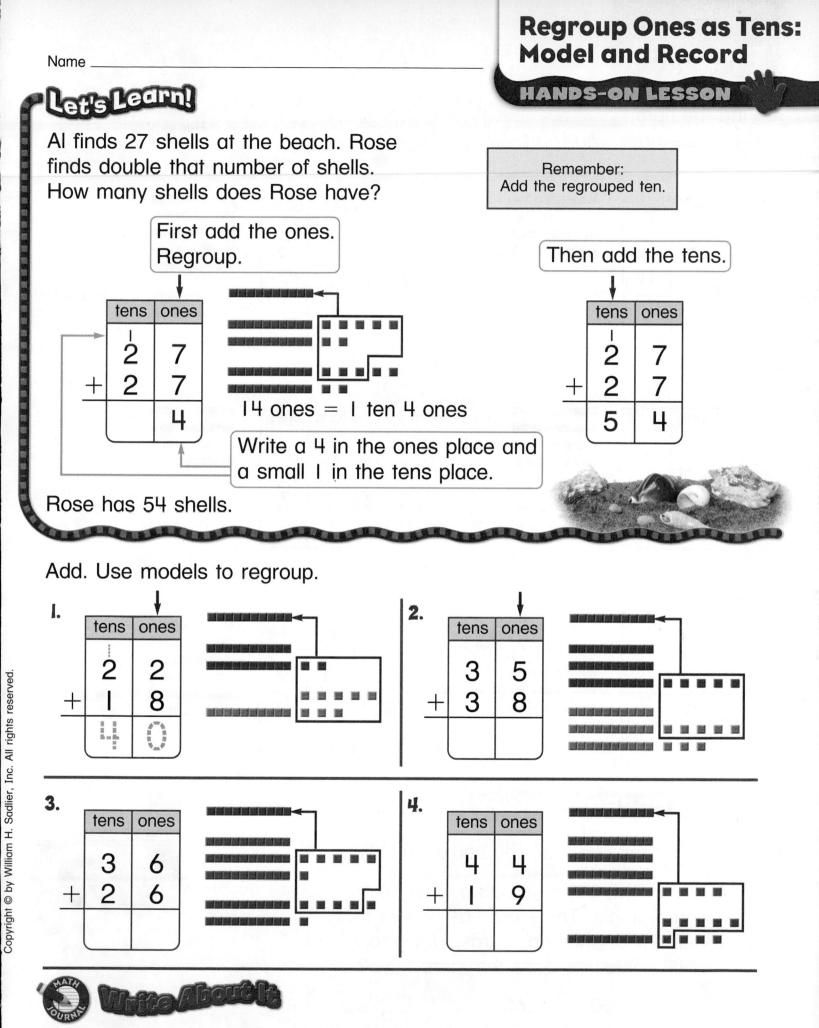

5. Explain why you write 1 in the tens place when you regroup.

Copyright © by William H. Sadlier, Inc. All rights reserved.

Practice

Find the sum.
Circle the ones you regroup.

6.

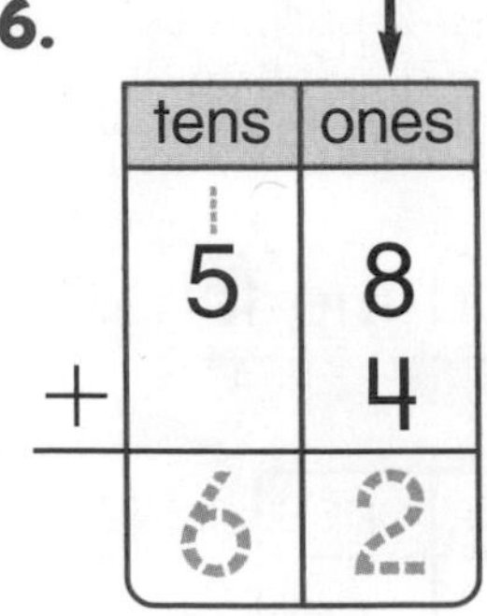

	tens	ones
	5	8
+		4
	6	2

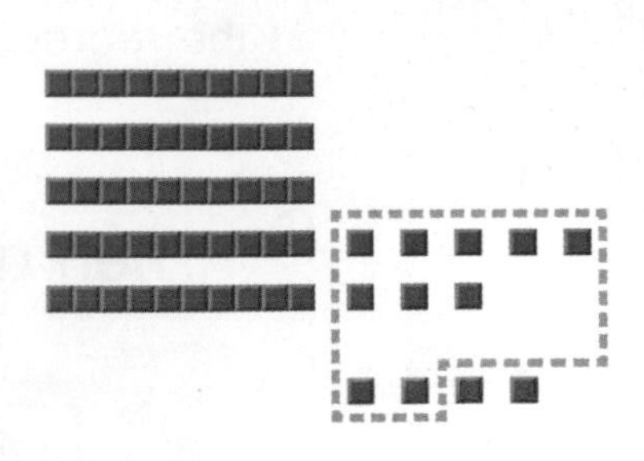

7.

	tens	ones
	5	3
+	2	7

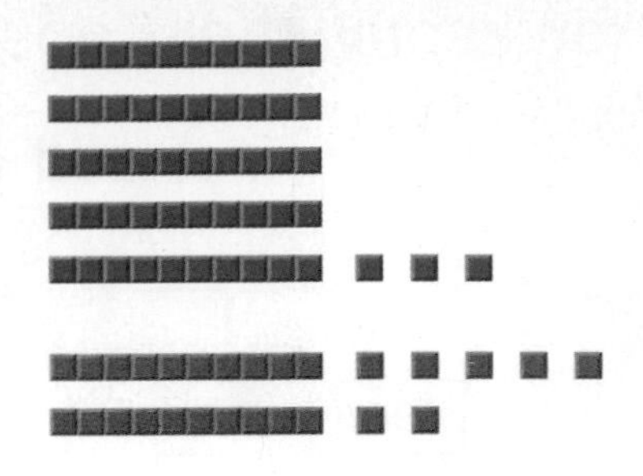

8.

	tens	ones
	4	6
+	3	3

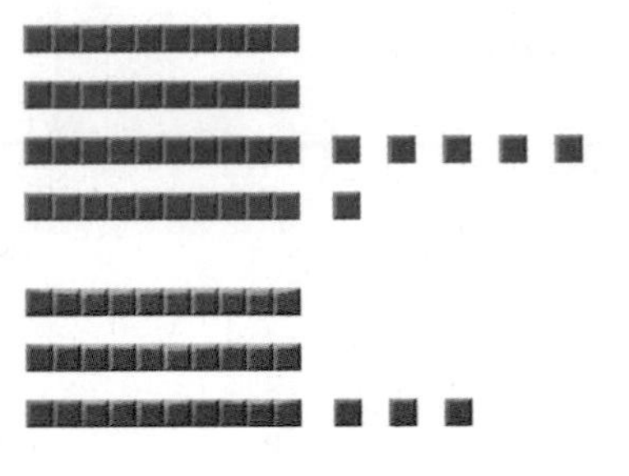

9.

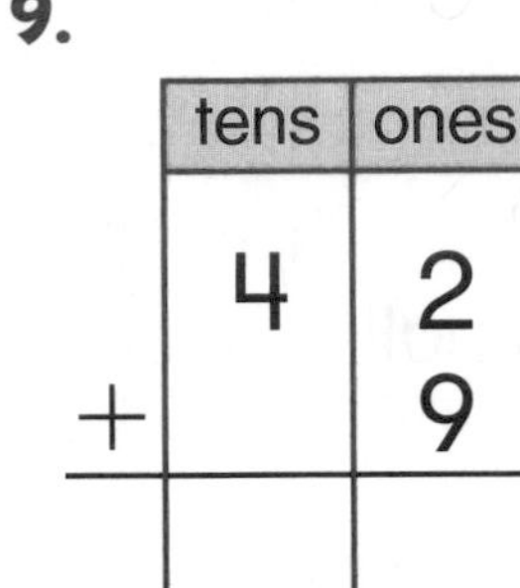

	tens	ones
	4	2
+		9

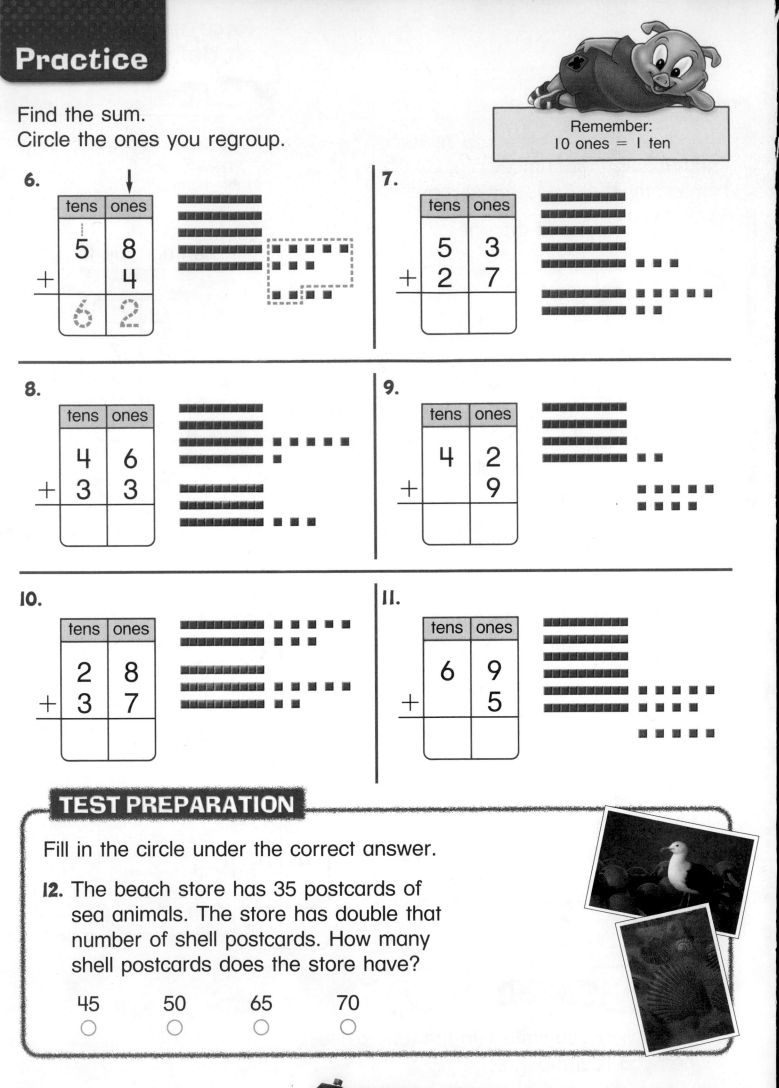

10.

	tens	ones
	2	8
+	3	7

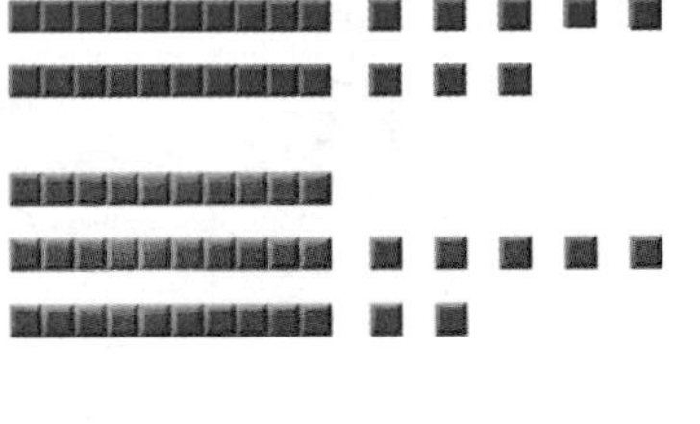

11.

	tens	ones
	6	9
+		5

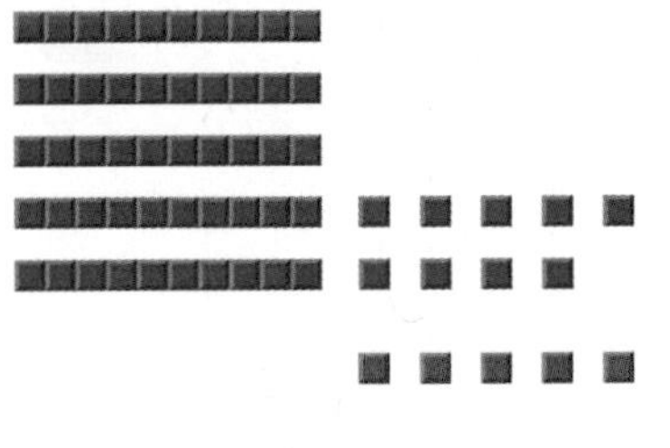

TEST PREPARATION

Fill in the circle under the correct answer.

12. The beach store has 35 postcards of sea animals. The store has double that number of shell postcards. How many shell postcards does the store have?

45	50	65	70
○	○	○	○

Math Alive at Home Ask your child to explain how to regroup to add 16 + 17. (regroup: 6 + 7 = 13 ones or 1 ten 3 ones)

Name ____________________

Regroup Ones as Tens

Let's Learn!

At the orchard, Mike picked 34 red apples, 28 green apples, and 23 yellow apples. How many green and yellow apples did Mike pick?

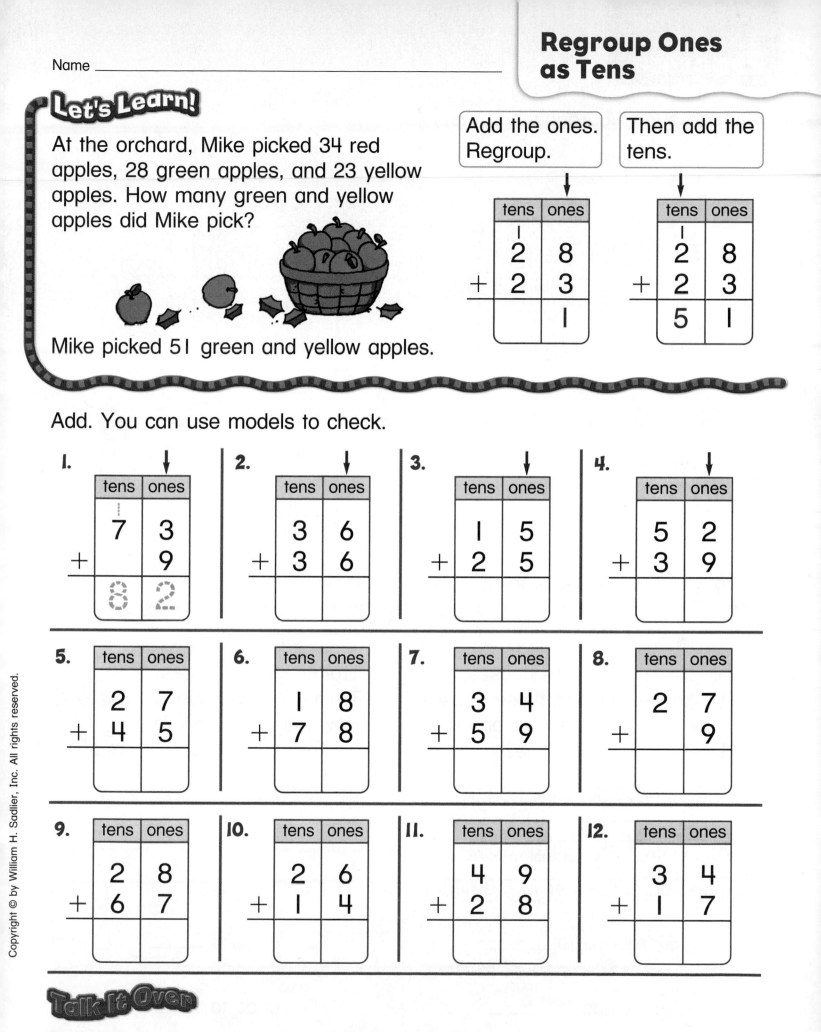

Mike picked 51 green and yellow apples.

Add the ones. Regroup.

	tens	ones
	1	
	2	8
+	2	3
		1

Then add the tens.

	tens	ones
	1	
	2	8
+	2	3
	5	1

Add. You can use models to check.

1.

	tens	ones
	7	3
+		9
	8	2

2.

	tens	ones
	3	6
+	3	6

3.

	tens	ones
	1	5
+	2	5

4.

	tens	ones
	5	2
+	3	9

5.

	tens	ones
	2	7
+	4	5

6.

	tens	ones
	1	8
+	7	8

7.

	tens	ones
	3	4
+	5	9

8.

	tens	ones
	2	7
+		9

9.

	tens	ones
	2	8
+	6	7

10.

	tens	ones
	2	6
+	1	4

11.

	tens	ones
	4	9
+	2	8

12.

	tens	ones
	3	4
+	1	7

Talk It Over

13. Why is knowing how to add three addends important when regrouping?

Copyright © by William H. Sadlier, Inc. All rights reserved.

Practice

Find the sum. Regroup where needed.

14.	15.	16.	17.	18.
15 +16 31	37 + 3	53 +26	57 + 7	37 +42

19.	20.	21.	22.	23.
69 + 9	36 +29	89 + 4	56 +17	68 +16

24.	25.	26.	27.	28.
79 +13	46 +45	19 +32	14 +68	28 +59

Solve. Use a problem-solving strategy.
Show your work on a separate sheet of paper.

29. Oak Drive has 37 houses. Maple Lane has 14 houses, with 42 people living in those houses. How many houses are on Oak Drive and Maple Lane?

_____ houses

30. Train A has 29 riders. Train B has 46 riders. Train C has 52 riders. How many people are on Trains A and C?

_____ people

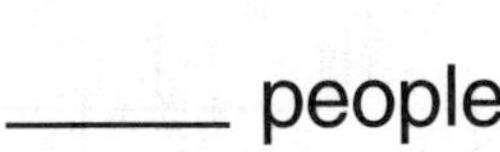

DO YOU REMEMBER?

Round each number to the nearest ten.

31. 57 rounds to _____.

32. 73 rounds to _____.

33. 44 rounds to _____.

34. 15 rounds to _____.

Math Alive at Home Ask your child to add 49 + 3 and to explain how she/he regrouped the ones. (52; 9 + 3 = 12 ones or 1 ten 2 ones)

Name ______________________________

Estimate Sums

Let's Learn!

To **estimate** means to find about how many.

To estimate the sum of 34 + 37:
- first, **round** each addend to the nearest ten
- then add the rounded numbers

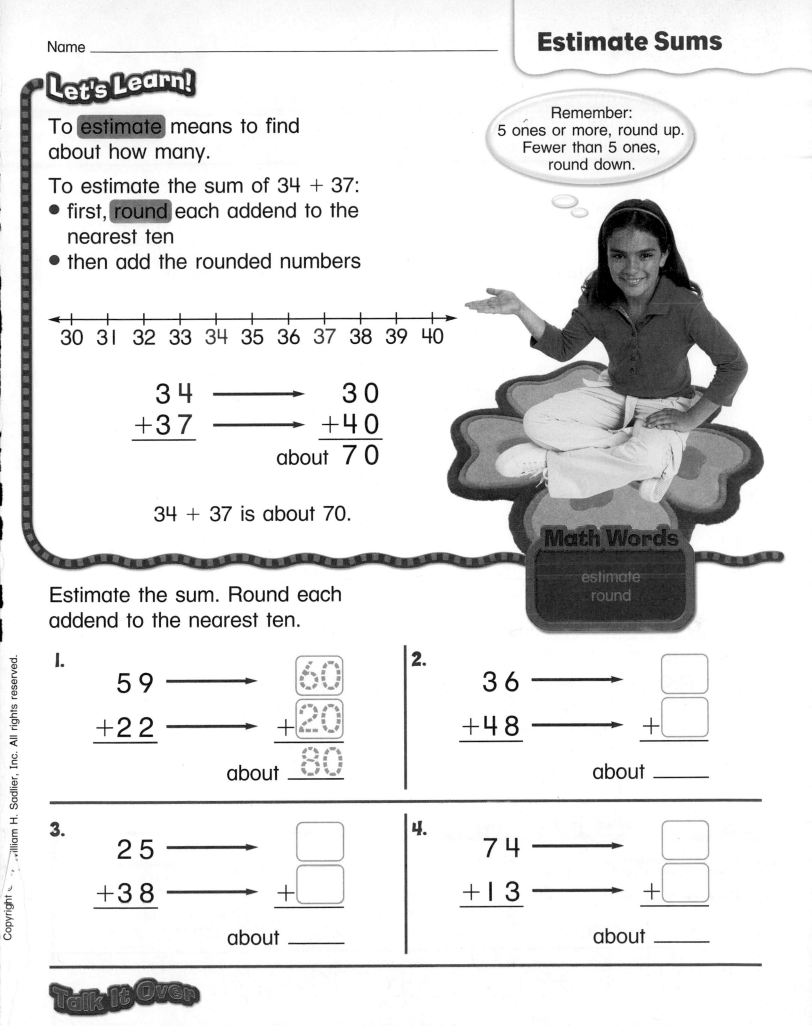

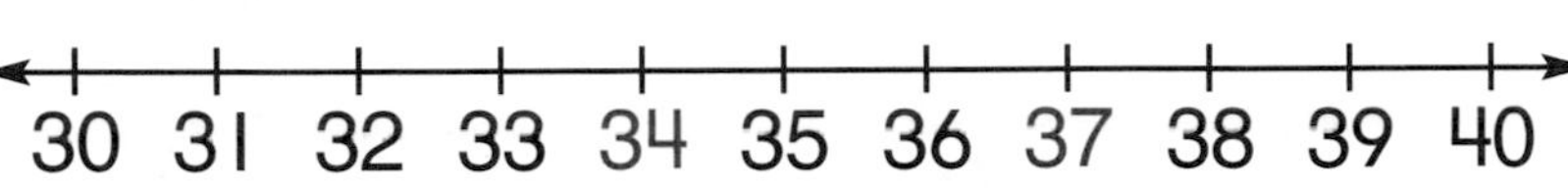

Remember:
5 ones or more, round up.
Fewer than 5 ones, round down.
Math Words
estimate
round

$$\begin{array}{r} 34 \\ +37 \\ \hline \end{array} \longrightarrow \begin{array}{r} 30 \\ +40 \\ \hline \text{about } 70 \end{array}$$

34 + 37 is about 70.

Estimate the sum. Round each addend to the nearest ten.

1. 59 → 60
+22 → +20
about 80

2. 36 → ☐
+48 → +☐
about ____

3. 25 → ☐
+38 → +☐
about ____

4. 74 → ☐
+13 → +☐
about ____

5. Explain how you would estimate the sum of 44 + 35.

Copyright © William H. Sadlier, Inc. All rights reserved.

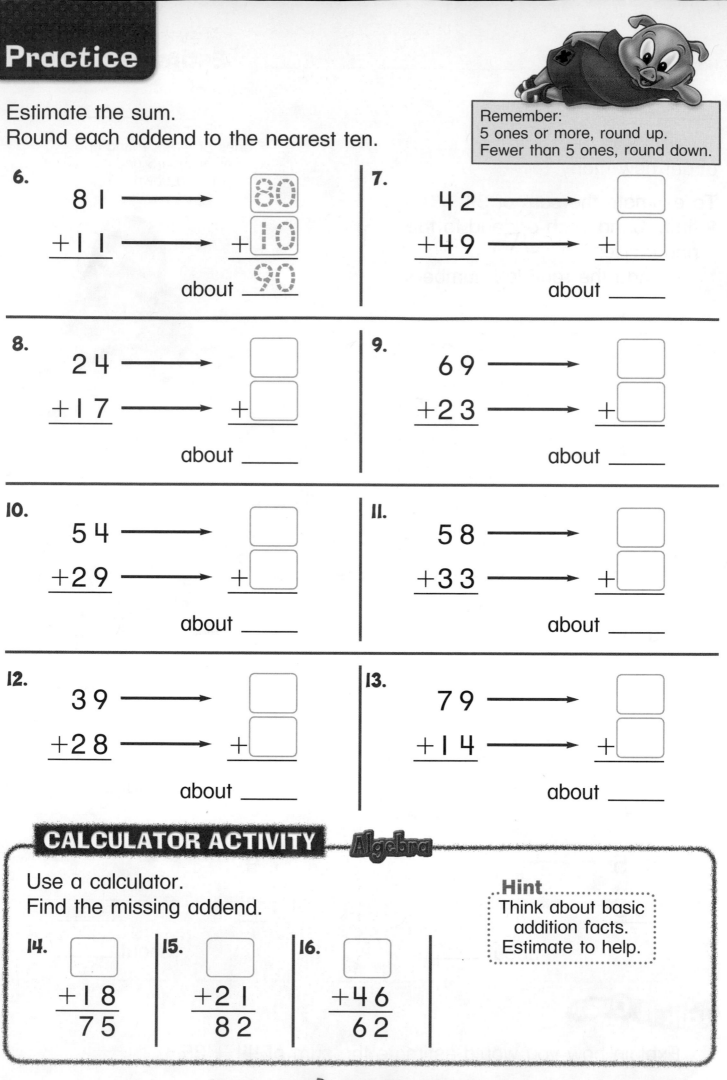

Practice

Estimate the sum.
Round each addend to the nearest ten.

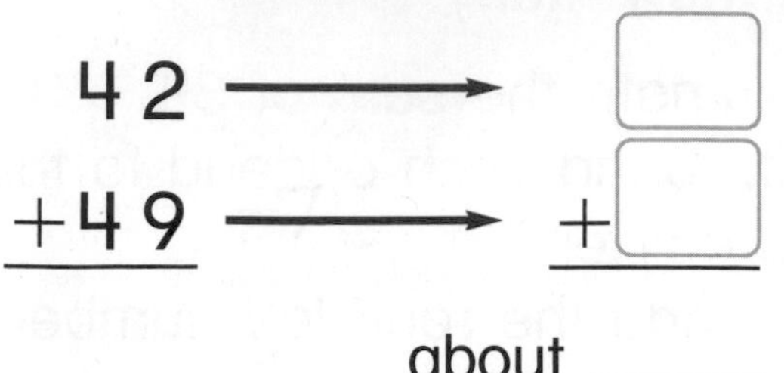

Remember:
5 ones or more, round up.
Fewer than 5 ones, round down.

6.
81 → 80
+11 → +10
about 90

7.
42 → ☐
+49 → +☐
about ____

8.
24 → ☐
+17 → +☐
about ____

9.
69 → ☐
+23 → +☐
about ____

10.
54 → ☐
+29 → +☐
about ____

11.
58 → ☐
+33 → +☐
about ____

12.
39 → ☐
+28 → +☐
about ____

13.
79 → ☐
+14 → +☐
about ____

CALCULATOR ACTIVITY

Algebra

Use a calculator.
Find the missing addend.

14. ☐ + 18 = 75

15. ☐ + 21 = 82

16. ☐ + 46 = 62

Hint Think about basic addition facts. Estimate to help.

Math Alive at Home Ask your child to estimate the sums of 48 + 25, 13 + 78, and 26 + 19. (50 + 30 = 80, about 80; 10 + 80 = 90, about 90; 30 + 20 = 50, about 50)

Name ______________________________

Rewrite Two-Digit Addition

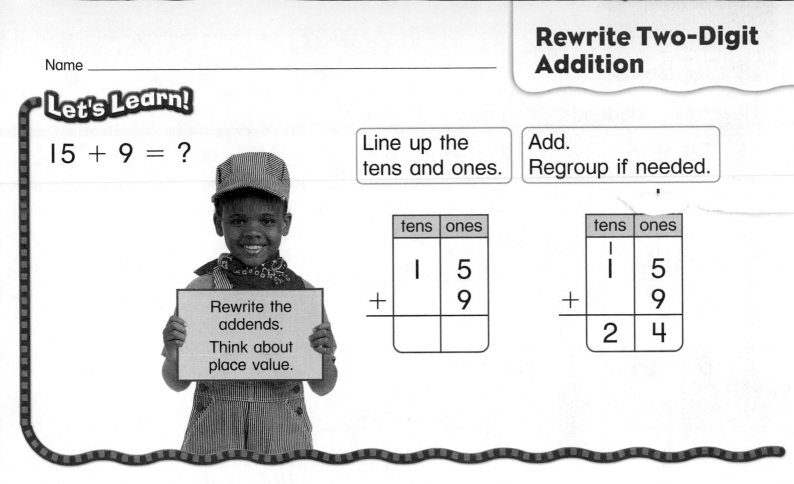

Let's Learn!

15 + 9 = ?

Line up the tens and ones.

	tens	ones
	1	5
+		9

Add. Regroup if needed.

	tens	ones
	1	
	1	5
+		9
	2	4

Rewrite the addends. Add. Regroup where needed.

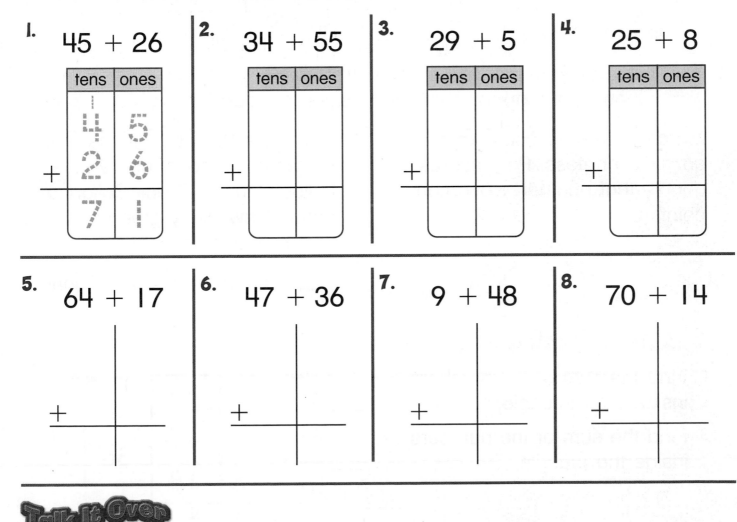

1. 45 + 26

	tens	ones
	1	
	4	5
+	2	6
	7	1

2. 34 + 55

	tens	ones
+		

3. 29 + 5

	tens	ones
+		

4. 25 + 8

	tens	ones
+		

5. 64 + 17

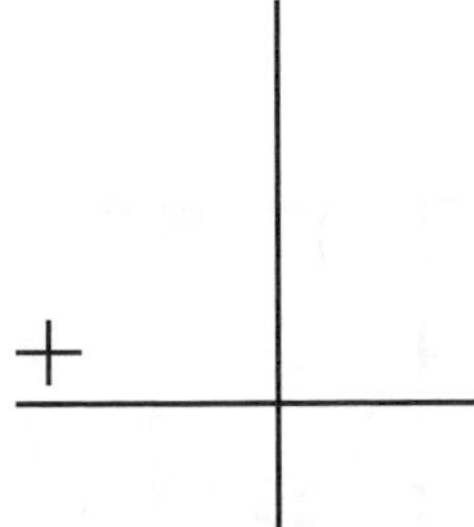

6. 47 + 36

7. 9 + 48

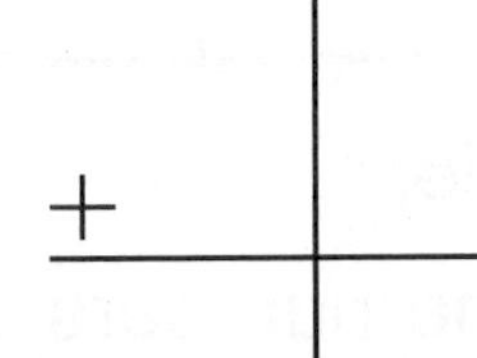

8. 70 + 14

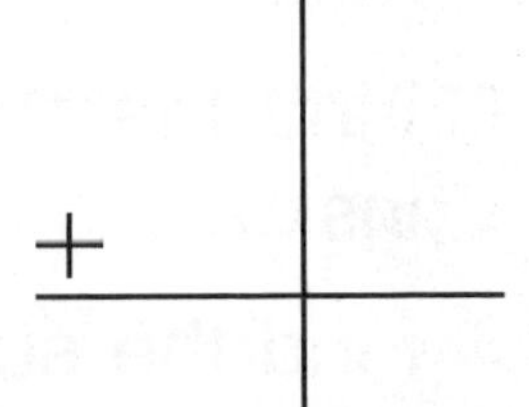

Talk It Over

9. Explain how you would line up the addends to add 57 + 8.

Copyright © by William H. Sadlier, Inc. All rights reserved.

Practice

Remember:
Line up the tens and ones.

Rewrite the addends. Then add.

10. 24 + 6

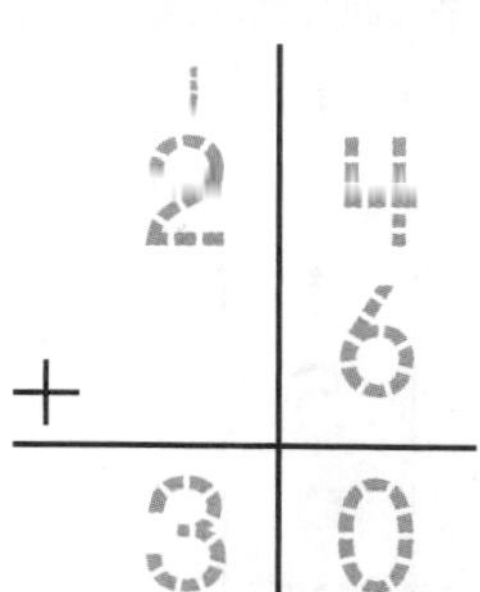

11. 39 + 6

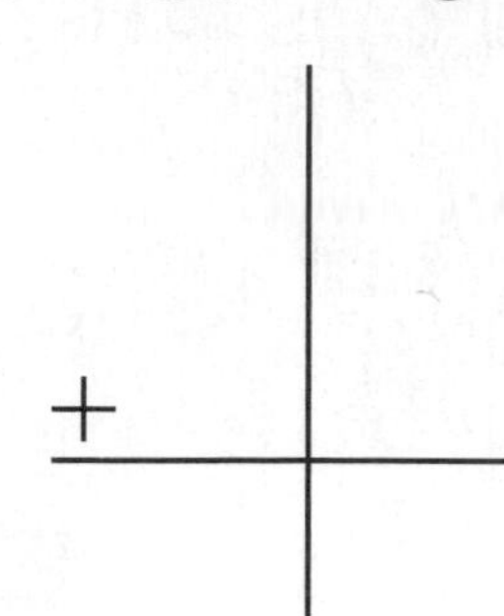

12. 59 + 21

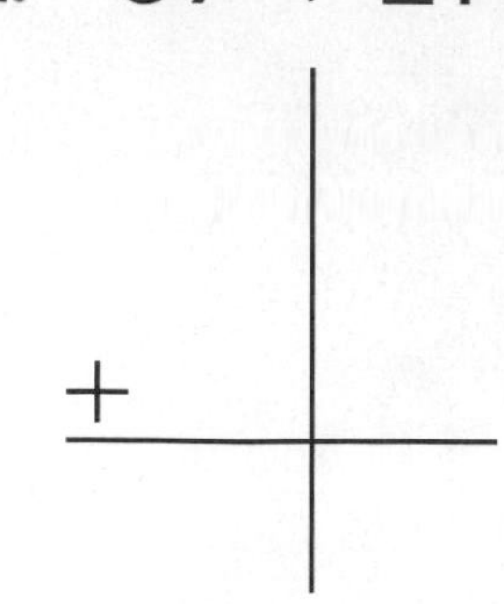

13. 25 + 45

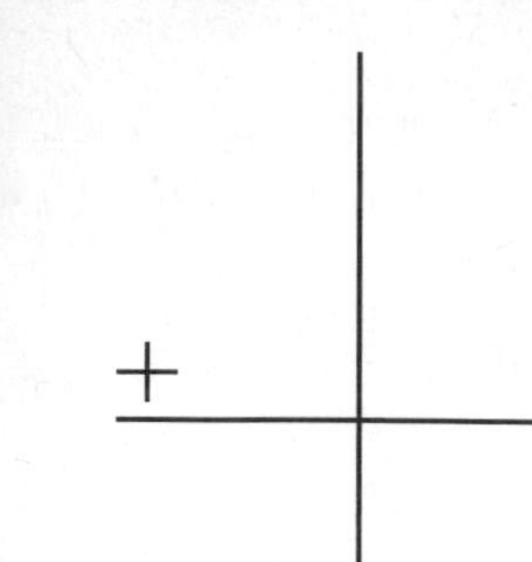

14. 5 + 87

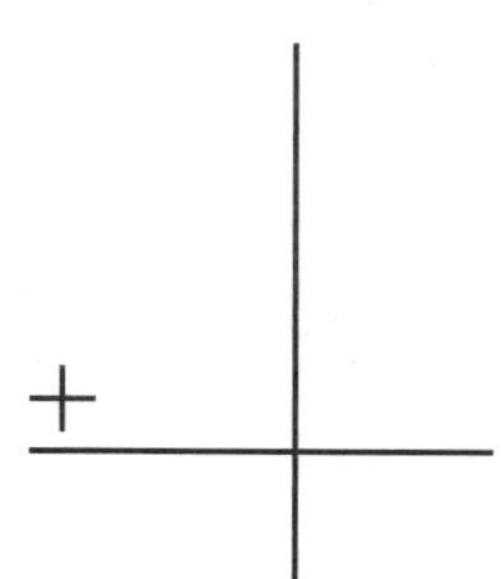

15. 43 + 40

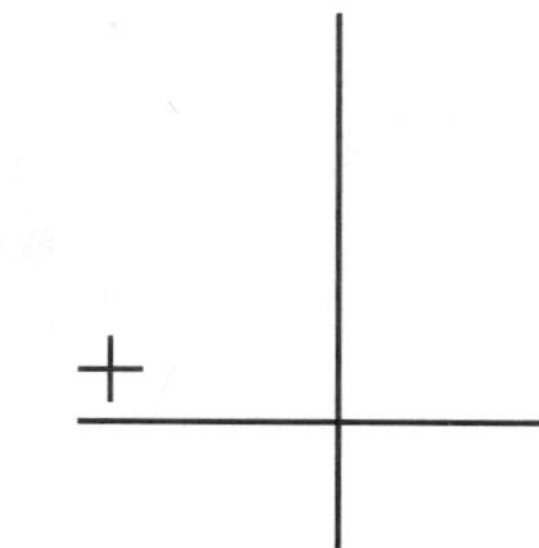

16. 38 + 35

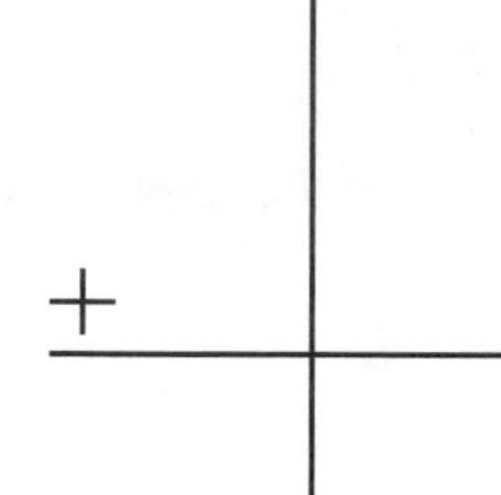

17. 14 + 46

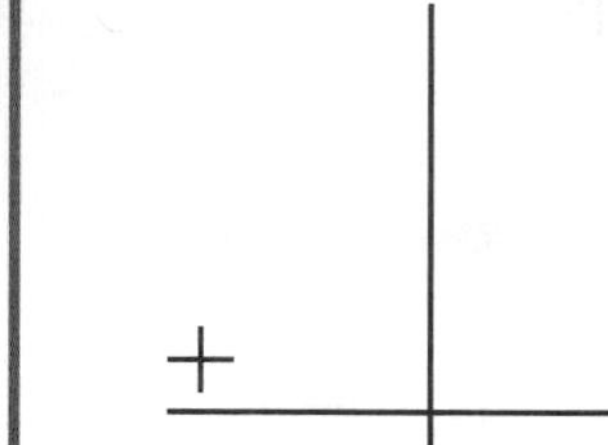

Solve. Use a problem-solving strategy.
Show your work on a separate sheet of paper.

18. Marco scores 26 points at a game of ringtoss. Pam scores double that number. How many points does Pam score?

_____ points

19. There are 27 red balloons, 48 green balloons, and 9 blue balloons in the Break Balloons game. How many green and blue balloons are there?

_____ green and blue balloons

CHALLENGE

20. Find the sum of the numbers inside the rectangle. _____

21. Find the sum of the numbers inside the triangle. _____

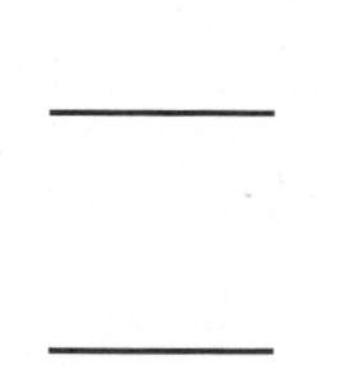

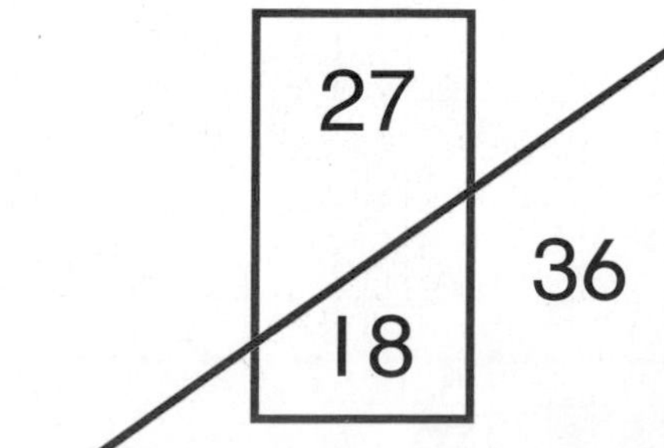

Math Alive at Home Ask your child to rewrite 48 + 36 vertically and to add the numbers. (84)

Name ______________________

Algebra

Three Addends

Let's Learn!

There were 13 people on the bus.
At the next stop, 21 people got on.
At Pine Park, 6 people got on.
How many people are on the bus?

13 + 21 + 6 = ?

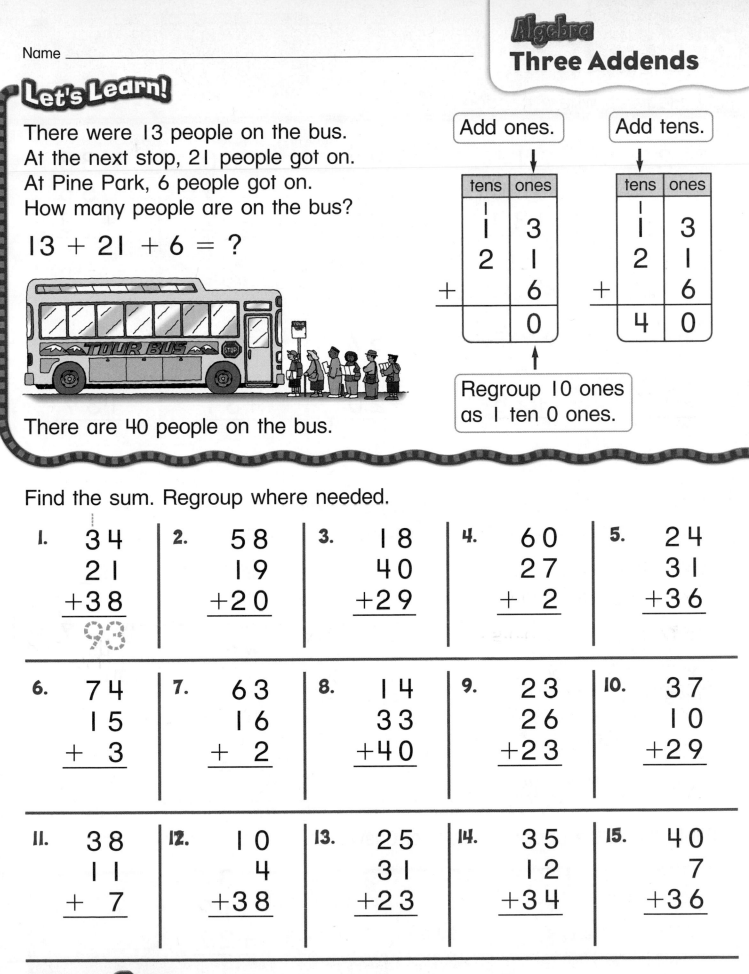

There are 40 people on the bus.

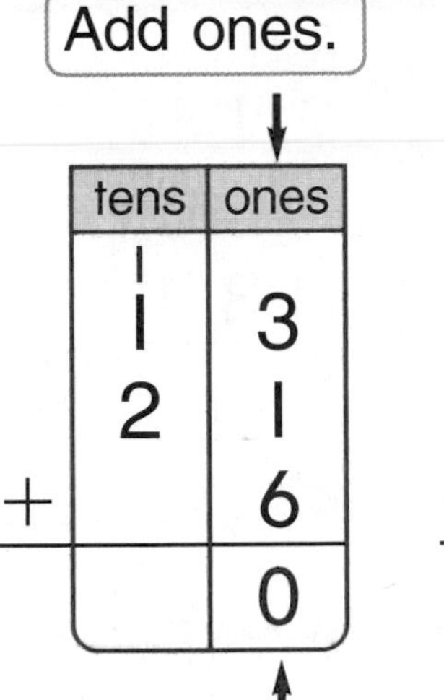

Add ones.

	tens	ones
	1	
	1	3
	2	1
+		6
		0

Regroup 10 ones as 1 ten 0 ones.

Add tens.

	tens	ones
	1	
	1	3
	2	1
+		6
	4	0

Find the sum. Regroup where needed.

1.	2.	3.	4.	5.
34	58	18	60	24
21	19	40	27	31
+38	+20	+29	+ 2	+36
93				

6.	7.	8.	9.	10.
74	63	14	23	37
15	16	33	26	10
+ 3	+ 2	+40	+23	+29

11.	12.	13.	14.	15.
38	10	25	35	40
11	4	31	12	7
+ 7	+38	+23	+34	+36

16. How is adding three 2-digit addends the same as adding two 2-digit addends?

Copyright © by William H. Sadlier, Inc. All rights reserved.

Practice

Add. Regroup where needed.

17. 24 + 14 + 8 = 46

18. 11 + 26 + 34

19. 44 + 22 + 33

20. 60 + 19 + 2

21. 33 + 56 + 3

22. 71 + 6 + 17

23. 8 + 61 + 28

24. 57 + 13 + 20

25. 37 + 22 + 31

26. 40 + 3 + 39

Solve. Use a problem-solving strategy. Show your work on a separate sheet of paper.

27. On Friday 10 people take a boat ride on the lake. 25 people take a boat ride on Saturday and 44 people take it on Sunday. How many people take a boat ride?

_____ people

28. Marta collects 22 leaves in the park. Sam and Lola collect 36 leaves each. How many leaves do the three children collect?

_____ leaves

TEST PREPARATION

Fill in the circle under the correct answer.

29. 13 + 8 + 48

○ 59 ○ 69 ○ 78 ○ 79

30. 36 + 12 + 27

○ 55 ○ 66 ○ 75 ○ 76

Math Alive at Home Ask your child to add 54 + 5 + 26, then to explain how she/he regrouped to find the sum. (85; 4 + 5 + 6 = 15 ones or 1 ten 5 ones; add the 1 regrouped ten to 5 + 2 or 7 tens)

Name ______________________________

TEST PREPARATION

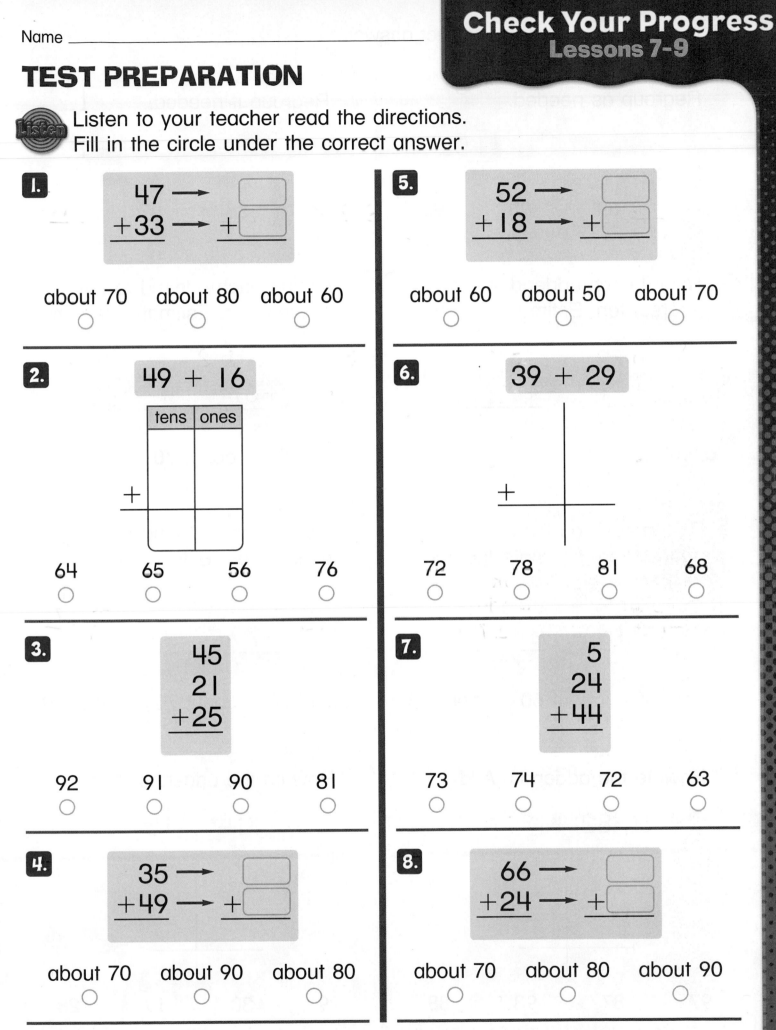

Listen to your teacher read the directions.
Fill in the circle under the correct answer.

1.

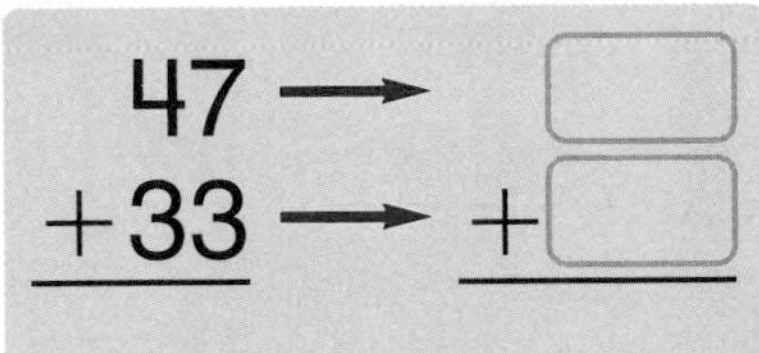

about 70 ○ about 80 ○ about 60 ○

2.

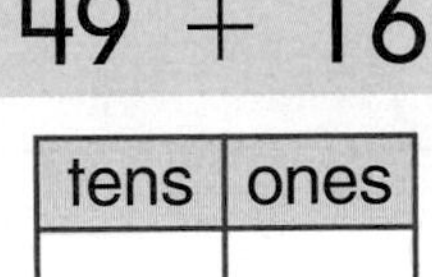

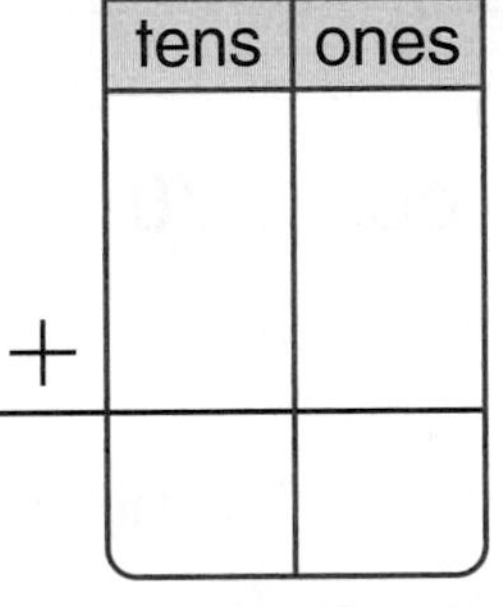

64 ○ 65 ○ 56 ○ 76 ○

3.

$$\begin{array}{r} 45 \\ 21 \\ +25 \\ \hline \end{array}$$

92 ○ 91 ○ 90 ○ 81 ○

4.

35 →
+49 → +

about 70 ○ about 90 ○ about 80 ○

5.

52 →
+18 → +

about 60 ○ about 50 ○ about 70 ○

6.

39 + 29

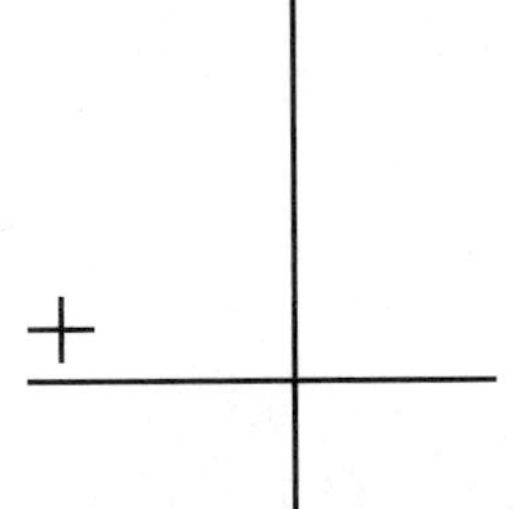

72 ○ 78 ○ 81 ○ 68 ○

7.

$$\begin{array}{r} 5 \\ 24 \\ +44 \\ \hline \end{array}$$

73 ○ 74 ○ 72 ○ 63 ○

8.

66 →
+24 → +

about 70 ○ about 80 ○ about 90 ○

Copyright © by William H. Sadlier, Inc. All rights reserved.

Fill in the circle under the correct answer.

9. Find the sum.
Regroup as needed.

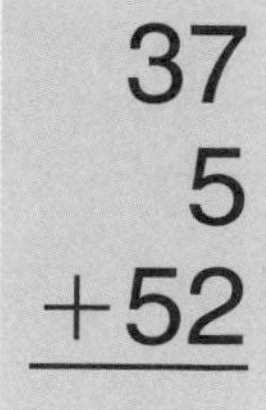

94 ○ 84 ○ 93 ○ 95 ○

10. Round each addend to the nearest ten. Estimate the sum.

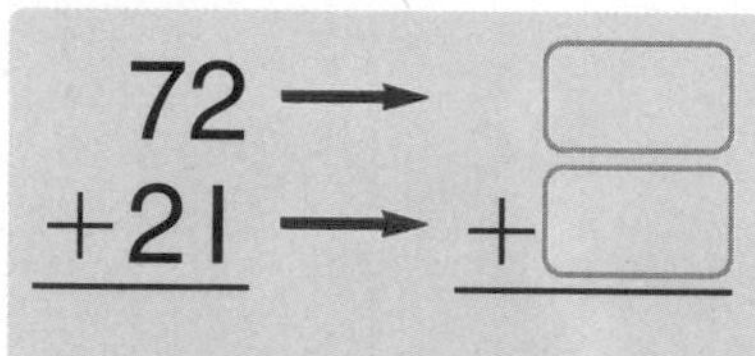

about 90 ○ about 70 ○ about 80 ○

11. Round each addend to the nearest ten. Estimate the sum.

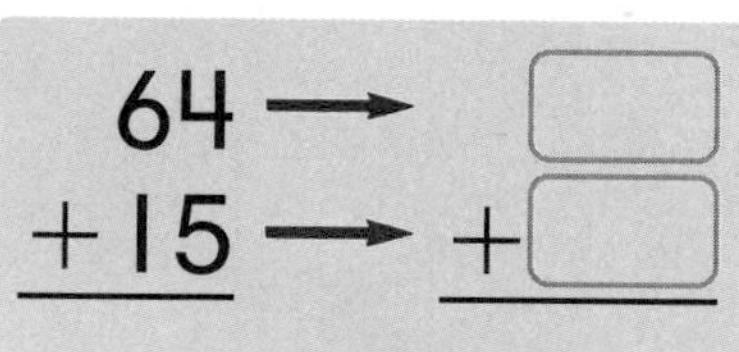

about 80 ○ about 60 ○ about 70 ○

12. Rewrite the addends. Add.

82 + 6

\+

97 ○ 87 ○ 98 ○ 88 ○

13. Find the sum.
Regroup if needed.

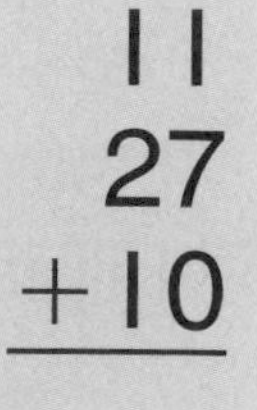

58 ○ 38 ○ 47 ○ 48 ○

14. Round each addend to the nearest ten. Estimate the sum.

19 →
+67 → +

about 90 ○ about 70 ○ about 80 ○

15. Round each addend to the nearest ten. Estimate the sum.

13 →
+79 → +

about 80 ○ about 70 ○ about 90 ○

16. Rewrite the addends. Add.

14 + 15

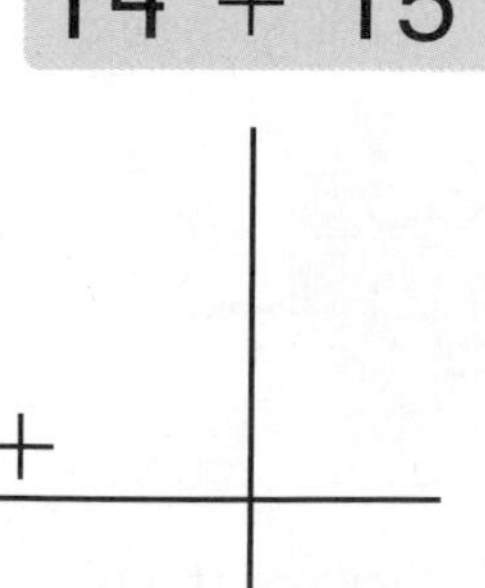

29 ○ 30 ○ 19 ○ 28 ○

Name ____________________

Add: Choose the Method

Let's Learn!

Different methods work better for different problems.
Choose the method that works better for you.

I can add mentally for this problem.

I have to regroup. I use paper and pencil for this problem.

21¢ + 2¢ + 10¢ = 33¢
I start at 21 and count on
22, 23, 33.

$$\begin{array}{r} \overset{1}{4}5 \\ 13 \\ +29 \\ \hline 87 \end{array}$$

Choose the method. ✓ (pencil) or (Mental Math). Then add.

1. $\begin{array}{r} 18 \\ 1 \\ +40 \\ \hline \end{array}$ Mental Math

2. $\begin{array}{r} 53 \\ 17 \\ +21 \\ \hline \end{array}$ 

3. $\begin{array}{r} 24 \\ 34 \\ +\ 4 \\ \hline \end{array}$ 

4. $\begin{array}{r} 24 \\ +61 \\ \hline \end{array}$ 

5. $\begin{array}{r} 33 \\ +32 \\ \hline \end{array}$ 

6. $\begin{array}{r} 26 \\ +25 \\ \hline \end{array}$ 

7. $\begin{array}{r} 48 \\ +\ 2 \\ \hline \end{array}$ 

8. $\begin{array}{r} 5 \\ +93 \\ \hline \end{array}$ 

9. $\begin{array}{r} 78 \\ +15 \\ \hline \end{array}$ 

10. Why is it easier to use mental math to add 28 + 30 and easier to use paper and pencil to add 28 + 36?

Copyright © by William H. Sadlier, Inc. All rights reserved.

Practice

Find the sum. Choose the method that works better for you.

11. 39 + 9 = 48	12. 28 + 2	13. 57 + 3	14. 86 + 6	15. 75 + 5
16. 65 + 3 + 30	17. 44 + 34 + 19	18. 13 + 43 + 29	19. 2 + 52 + 30	20. 12 + 40 + 3
21. 19 + 57	22. 30 + 38	23. 47 + 52	24. 26 + 54	25. 20 + 48

Solve. Use a problem-solving strategy.
Show your work on a separate sheet of paper.

26. In the morning 22 tickets are sold for the Monster Museum. Later, 30 more tickets are sold. How many tickets are sold for the Monster Museum?

_____ tickets

27. On Saturday 37 people take rides in the hot air balloon. On Sunday 48 people take rides in the balloon. How many people take rides?

_____ people

CRITICAL THINKING

2 4 5 6

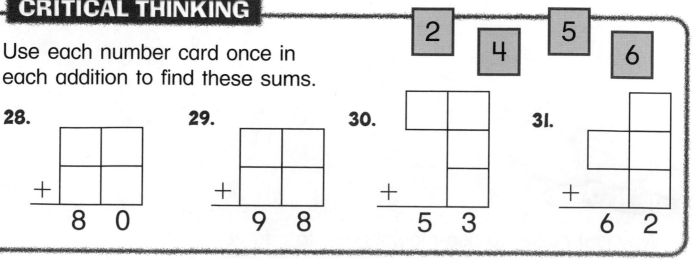

Use each number card once in each addition to find these sums.

28.
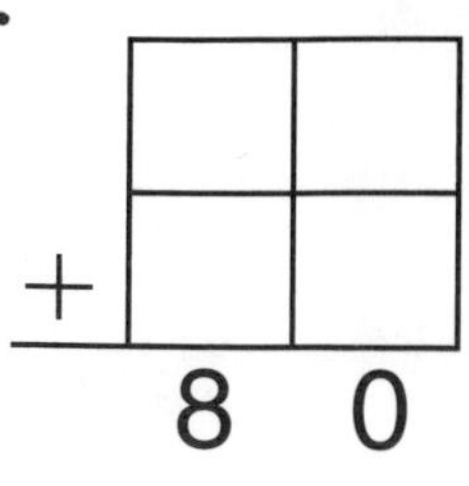
80

29.
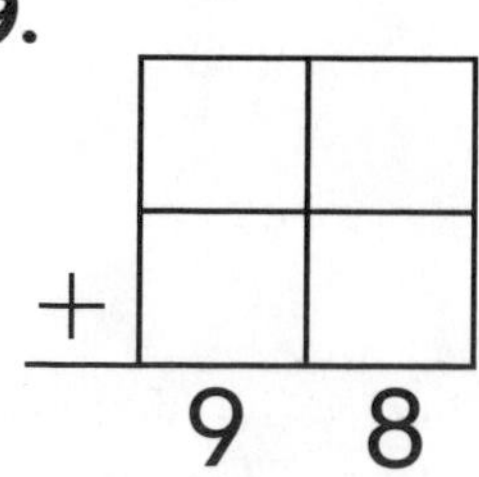
98

30.
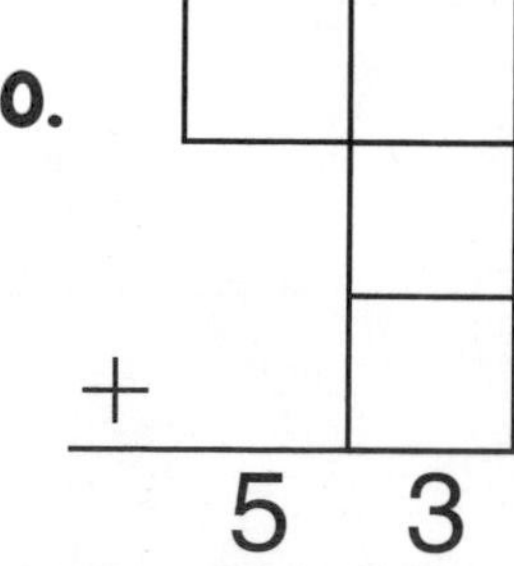
53

31.
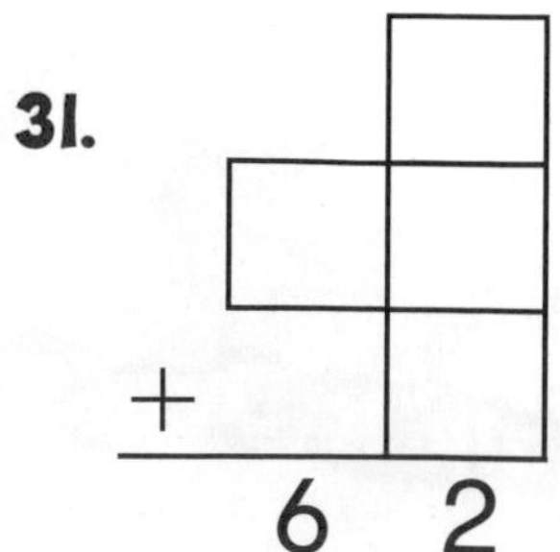
62

Math Alive at Home Tell your child the age of three people in your family, then have her/him find the sum of the ages.

Name ____________________

Addition Practice

Let's Learn!

Think carefully about when to regroup.

Regrouping is needed.	No regrouping is needed.
$\begin{array}{r} \scriptstyle 1 \\ 59 \\ +27 \\ \hline 86 \end{array}$	$\begin{array}{r} 25 \\ +63 \\ \hline 88 \end{array}$

Add. Regroup where needed.

1. $\begin{array}{r} 78 \\ +13 \\ \hline 91 \end{array}$	2. $\begin{array}{r} 57 \\ +23 \\ \hline \end{array}$	3. $\begin{array}{r} 24 \\ +62 \\ \hline \end{array}$	4. $\begin{array}{r} 37 \\ +\ 5 \\ \hline \end{array}$	5. $\begin{array}{r} 29 \\ +54 \\ \hline \end{array}$
6. $\begin{array}{r} 12 \\ +28 \\ \hline \end{array}$	7. $\begin{array}{r} 85 \\ +\ 5 \\ \hline \end{array}$	8. $\begin{array}{r} 30 \\ +20 \\ \hline \end{array}$	9. $\begin{array}{r} 53 \\ +18 \\ \hline \end{array}$	10. $\begin{array}{r} 68 \\ +28 \\ \hline \end{array}$
11. $\begin{array}{r} 44 \\ +\ 9 \\ \hline \end{array}$	12. $\begin{array}{r} 69 \\ +15 \\ \hline \end{array}$	13. $\begin{array}{r} 26 \\ +27 \\ \hline \end{array}$	14. $\begin{array}{r} 15 \\ +46 \\ \hline \end{array}$	15. $\begin{array}{r} 70 \\ +20 \\ \hline \end{array}$
16. $\begin{array}{r} 25 \\ 30 \\ +25 \\ \hline \end{array}$	17. $\begin{array}{r} 12 \\ 25 \\ +33 \\ \hline \end{array}$	18. $\begin{array}{r} 43 \\ 11 \\ +19 \\ \hline \end{array}$	19. $\begin{array}{r} 52 \\ 32 \\ +\ 7 \\ \hline \end{array}$	20. $\begin{array}{r} 74 \\ 12 \\ +13 \\ \hline \end{array}$

Talk It Over

21. Choose one exercise above for which you needed to regroup. Explain why you regrouped.

Copyright © by William H. Sadlier, Inc. All rights reserved.

Practice

Find the sum. Regroup where needed.

22.	23.	24.	25.	26.
61 14 +13	12 43 +29	76 3 +10	24 24 +24	23 34 +17

27.	28.	29.	30.	31.
21 36 +15	24 43 +29	39 40 + 9	43 14 +12	52 15 +17

Solve. Use a problem-solving strategy. Show your work on a separate sheet of paper.

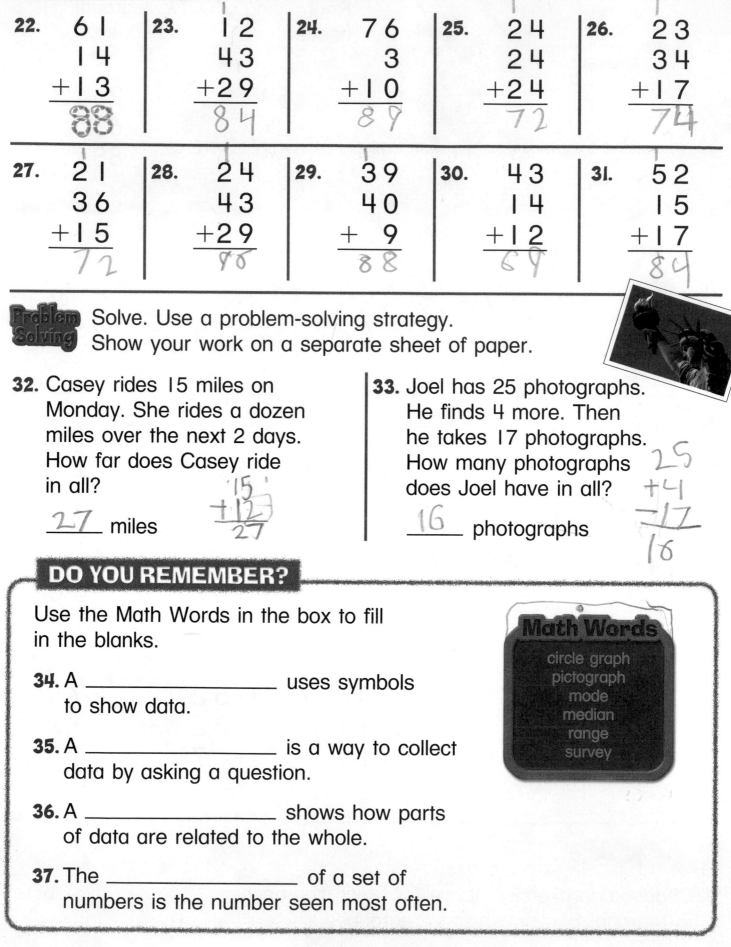

32. Casey rides 15 miles on Monday. She rides a dozen miles over the next 2 days. How far does Casey ride in all?

_____ miles

33. Joel has 25 photographs. He finds 4 more. Then he takes 17 photographs. How many photographs does Joel have in all?

_____ photographs

DO YOU REMEMBER?

Use the Math Words in the box to fill in the blanks.

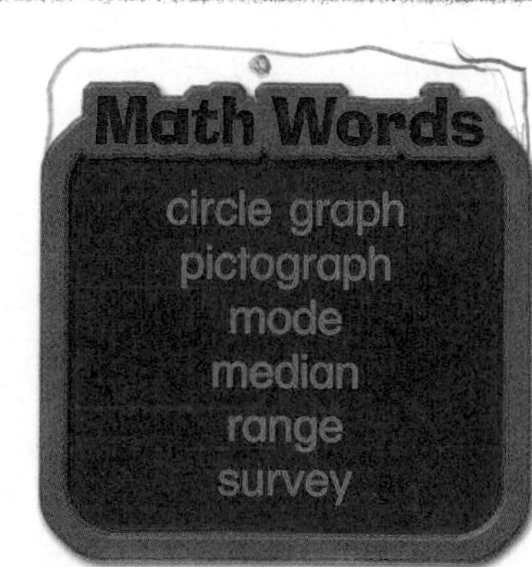

34. A _______________ uses symbols to show data.

35. A _______________ is a way to collect data by asking a question.

36. A _______________ shows how parts of data are related to the whole.

37. The _______________ of a set of numbers is the number seen most often.

Math Alive at Home Ask your child to add 46 + 39 and explain how she/he found the sum. (85; 6 + 9 = 15 ones or 1 ten 5 ones; add the regrouped ten to 4 + 3 or 7 tens)

Name ______________________________

Problem Solving
Strategy

Use More Than One Step

Read Tim finds 12 smooth stones at the beach. Andy finds 23 stones. Tim gives away 5 stones. How many stones do the boys then have in all?

Do you need to add, subtract, or compare in each step?

Plan

Step 1
Subtract to find how many Tim has.

Step 2
Add to find how many the boys have altogether.

Write

$$\begin{array}{r} 12 \\ -\ 5 \\ \hline 7 \end{array} \qquad \begin{array}{r} 23 \\ +\ 7 \\ \hline 30 \end{array}$$

The boys have 30 stones altogether.

Check Model the problem to check your answer.

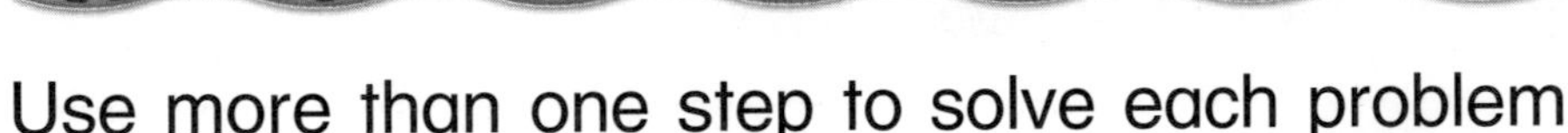

Use more than one step to solve each problem.

1. On Saturday, Joan rides 14 miles on a bike tour. On Sunday she rides 3 more miles than she did on Saturday. How many miles does she ride both days in all?

$$\begin{array}{r} 14 \\ +\ 3 \\ \hline 17 \end{array} \qquad \begin{array}{r} 17 \\ +\ 14 \\ \hline 31 \end{array}$$

_____ miles

2. Fay finds 25 shells. Beth finds 36 shells. Fay finds 5 more shells. Who has more shells?

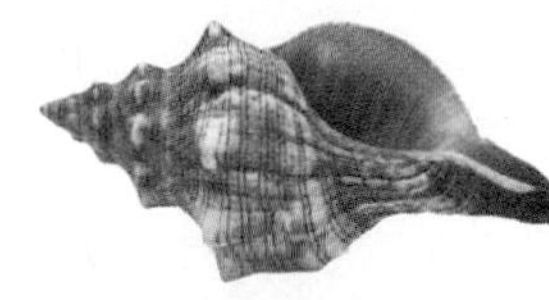

____

3. Sam has 14 stamps. He gives 6 to Joe. Then Sam buys 18 more. How many stamps does Sam have then?

_____ stamps

Copyright © by William H. Sadlier, Inc. All rights reserved.

Practice

Read › **Plan** › **Write** › **Check**

Use More Than One Step

4. 18 ducks are in the park.
9 ducks fly away.
Then 26 more ducks come.
How many ducks are in the park now?

_____ ducks

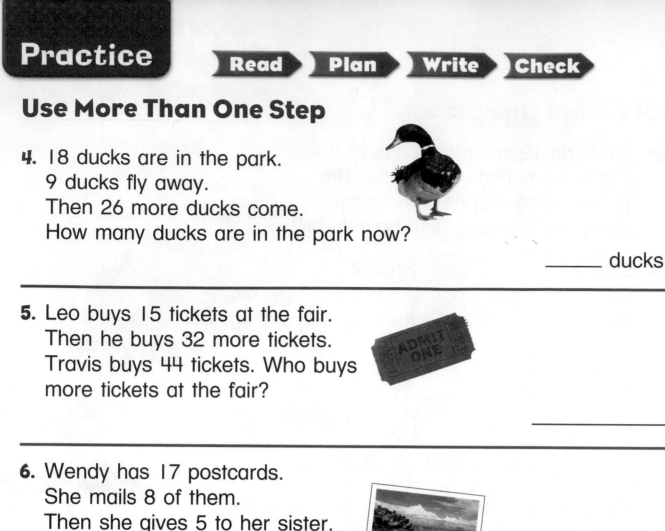

5. Leo buys 15 tickets at the fair.
Then he buys 32 more tickets.
Travis buys 44 tickets. Who buys more tickets at the fair?

____

---

6. Wendy has 17 postcards.
She mails 8 of them.
Then she gives 5 to her sister.
How many postcards does Wendy have left?

_____ postcards

---

7. Bob and Susan take a two-day canoe trip. They ride 15 miles the first day. The next day they ride 7 miles more than the first day.
How many miles is the trip?

_____ miles

8. Jake and Ella are at the pet store.

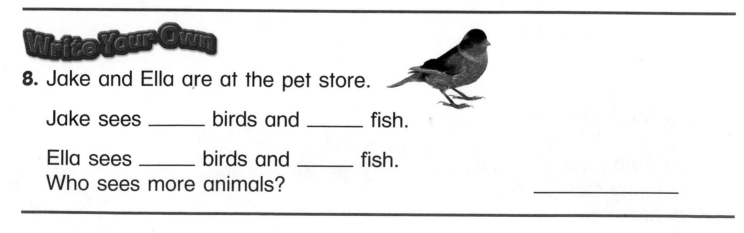

Jake sees _____ birds and _____ fish.

Ella sees _____ birds and _____ fish.
Who sees more animals?

____

Math Alive at Home Ask your child how she/he used more than one step to solve the problems in this lesson.

Name ______________________________________

Problem Solving
Applications

Read ▸ **Plan** ▸ **Write** ▸ **Check**

Mixed Strategies

Use a strategy you have learned.

1. Ray travels 15 miles.
   Holly travels 9 miles.
   How many more miles
   does Ray travel than Holly?

   _____ miles

---

2. People in a hiking club hike 14 miles
   on Monday. On Tuesday they hike
   5 more miles than they did on Monday.
   How many miles do they hike both days?

   _____ miles

3. 26 people ride the ferry on Monday.
   Two dozen people ride the ferry on
   Tuesday. How many people altogether
   ride the ferry both days?

   _____ people

4. Kerry sees 19 planes at the festival.
   8 planes do tricks. Kerry sees 12 more
   planes on the way home. How many
   planes does Kerry see?

   _____ planes

5. Gary's ticket number is less than 15.
   It is an odd number. The number doubled
   is just before 23. What is Gary's number?

   _____

Copyright © by William H. Sadlier, Inc. All rights reserved.

Practice

Read Plan Write Check

Use a strategy you have learned.

6. On Friday 32 people rode donkeys into the Grand Canyon. On Saturday 21 more people rode donkeys than on Friday. How many people rode donkeys on both days?

_____ people

---

7. Marla counts 18 people riding in one cable car in San Francisco. She counts double that number in the next cable car. How many people ride in both cable cars?

_____ people

---

8. In Florida, Abby sees 17 pelicans. She also sees 29 flamingos and 36 trees. How many birds does she see?

_____ birds

---

9. At the state fair, Ted sees 12 balloons. Tina sees 2 more balloons than Ted. Liang sees 10 more balloons than Tina. How many balloons does Liang see?

_____ balloons

---

10. A dozen people are in line for tickets at the Lobster Fest. The first, fifth, and last two people are awarded free tickets. How many people do not get free tickets?

_____ people

Math Alive at Home Ask your child to tell you how she/he solved some of the problems in this lesson.

Name ____________________

TEST PREPARATION

Listen to your teacher read the directions.
Fill in the circle under the correct answer.

1.

$$\begin{array}{r} 59 \\ 13 \\ +17 \\ \hline \end{array}$$

99 ○ 88 ○ 89 ○ 79 ○

2.

$$\begin{array}{r} 8 \\ +55 \\ \hline \end{array}$$

53 ○ 63 ○ 54 ○ 64 ○

3.

$$\begin{array}{r} 14 \\ 7 \\ +34 \\ \hline \end{array}$$

54 ○ 45 ○ 56 ○ 55 ○

4.

$$\begin{array}{r} 32 \\ 8 \\ +56 \\ \hline \end{array}$$

86 ○ 84 ○ 96 ○ 94 ○

5.

$$\begin{array}{r} 23 \\ +30 \\ \hline \end{array}$$

43 ○ 54 ○ 53 ○ 63 ○

6.

$$\begin{array}{r} 42 \\ 27 \\ +28 \\ \hline \end{array}$$

98 ○ 86 ○ 87 ○ 97 ○

7.

$$\begin{array}{r} 69 \\ +24 \\ \hline \end{array}$$

83 ○ 93 ○ 95 ○ 85 ○

8. Krista finds 23 shells at the beach. Mark finds 38 shells. Then Krista finds 17 more shells. Who has more shells?

Krista ○ Mark ○

Copyright © by William H. Sadlier, Inc. All rights reserved.

Connection

Name ______________________

Did You Know?

The Four Corners Monument is the spot where Utah, Arizona, New Mexico and Colorado meet. If you go there, you can stand in all four states at the same time. When there, you can also plan trips to Mesa Verde and Chaco Canyon. There you can see ancient towns that were built by Native Americans.

Four Corners National Monument

Mesa Verde National Park in Colorado

Chaco Canyon National Historic Park in New Mexico

Add to solve each problem.

1. A bus with 43 visitors arrives at the Four Corners Monument. Then a bus with 36 visitors arrives. Finally, a dozen more visitors arrive. How many visitors arrive in all? _____ visitors

2. Henry plans a trip to the Four Corners Monument and Mesa Verde. He needs to travel 29 miles to reach Four Corners. Then he has to travel another 63 miles to reach Mesa Verde. How far will he travel in all? _____ miles

3. Rosa gets ready to visit Chaco Canyon. She watches a video about the canyon for 26 minutes. Then she looks at a map for 18 minutes. How much time does she spend getting ready? _____ minutes

Name ______________________

Chapter 4 Test

1. Add mentally. Add 2 to:

14	24	34	44
____	____	____	____

5. Add mentally. Add 30 to:

25	35	45	55
____	____	____	____

2. Round the addends to the nearest ten. Estimate the sum.

$$\begin{array}{r} 26 \rightarrow \square \\ +55 \rightarrow +\square \\ \hline \end{array}$$

about ____

6. Regroup ones as tens.

5 tens 13 ones =

____ tens ____ ones

3. Find the sum.
Circle the ones you regroup.

	tens	ones
	4	7
+		8

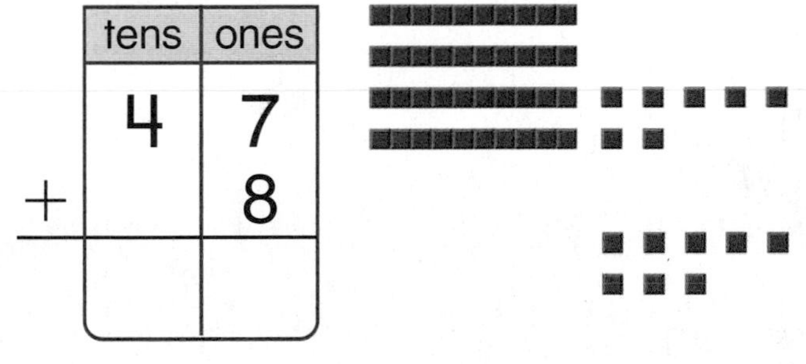

7. Rewrite the addends. Add.
Regroup if needed.

68 + 18

	tens	ones
+		

4. Rewrite the addends. Add.
Regroup if needed.

58 + 5

	tens	ones
+		

8. Regroup ones as tens.

7 tens 11 ones =

____ tens ____ one

Copyright © by William H. Sadlier, Inc. All rights reserved.

Add.

9.	10.	11.	12.	13.
57	77	82	9	51
+29	+13	+17	+83	+ 8

14.	15.	16.	17.	18.
65	27	18	46	35
4	25	9	12	52
+28	+31	+71	+32	+12

Solve. Use a problem-solving strategy.
Watch for multistep problems.

19. Todd collects 27 shells at the beach. Nora and Joe collect 26 shells each. How many shells do Todd, Nora, and Joe collect in all?

They collect _____ shells in all.

20. There were 48 children on a boat ride. A dozen more children join them. How many children are there on the boat ride then?

There are _____ children on the boat ride.

21. In the school play, Clara sees 35 singers and 36 dancers. About how many children does Clara see on stage in all?

Clara sees about _____ children on stage in all.

22. Al reads 17 stories about far away places to visit. Sandy reads 12 more stories than Al. How many stories do they read in all?

They read _____ stories in all.

Name ______________________________

1. Complete the table for each rule.
Make up 3 two-digit numbers less than 90.
Write them in the IN column.
Use the rule to find the numbers for OUT.

Rule: +3	
IN	OUT

Rule: +10	
IN	OUT

Find the sum mentally. Tell your strategy.

2. $\begin{array}{r} 32 \\ 20 \\ +20 \\ \hline \end{array}$ ______________________

3. $\begin{array}{r} 29 \\ 3 \\ +30 \\ \hline \end{array}$ ______________________

4. Choose two numbers in the box that when rounded give an estimated sum of 60. Complete the estimate.

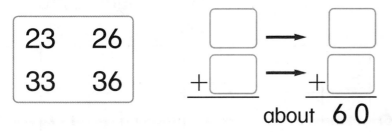

23	26
33	36

$\begin{array}{r} \square \\ +\square \\ \hline \end{array} \rightarrow \begin{array}{r} \square \\ +\square \\ \hline \text{about } 60 \end{array}$

Tell how to estimate.

____

____

You can put this in your Math Portfolio.

Copyright © by William H. Sadlier, Inc. All rights reserved.

Enrichment

Name ______________________________

Magic Squares

This is a magic square.

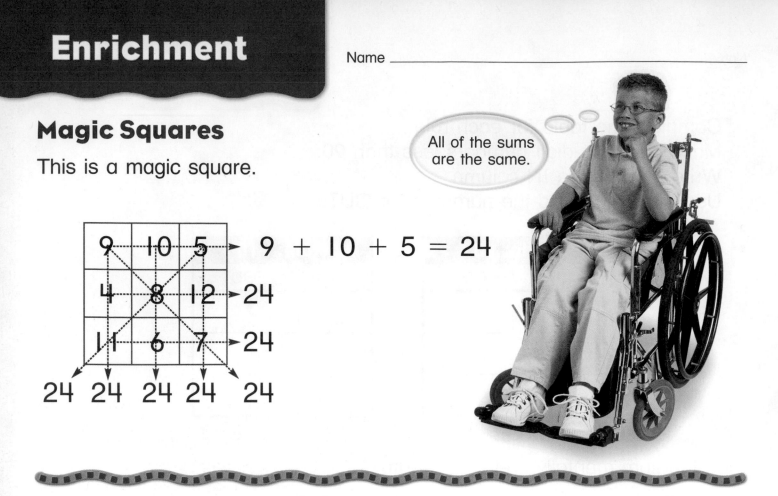

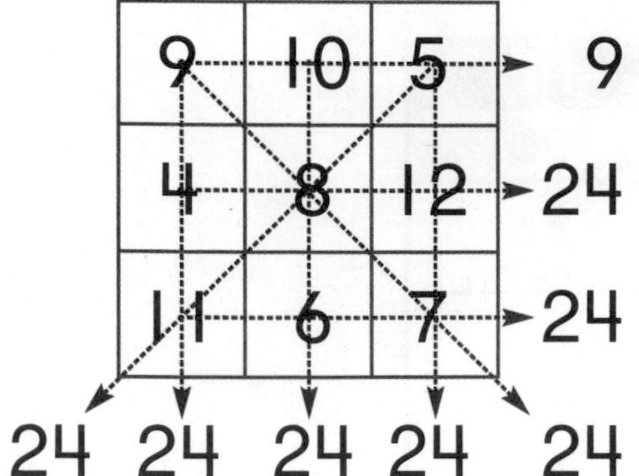

9 + 10 + 5 = 24

Write the numbers to make a magic square.
Show your work on a separate sheet of paper.

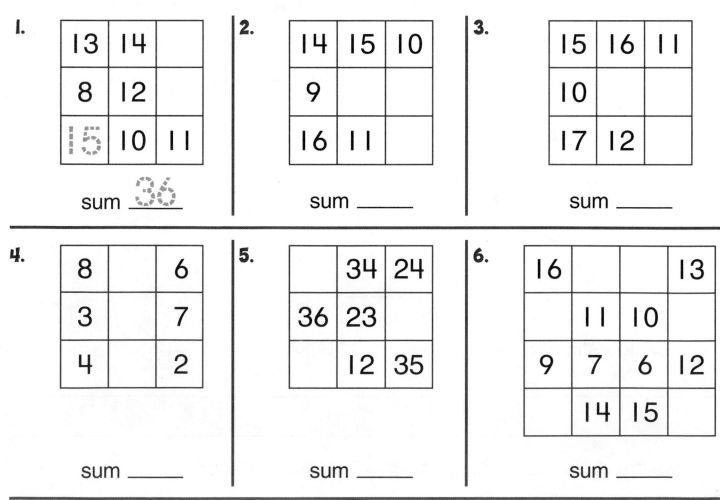

1.

13	14	
8	12	
15	10	11

sum 

2.

14	15	10
9		
16	11	

sum ______

3.

15	16	11
10		
17	12	

sum ______

4.

8		6
3		7
4		2

sum ______

5.

	34	24
36	23	
	12	35

sum ______

6.

16			13
	11	10	
9	7	6	12
	14	15	

sum ______

Name ______________________________

TEST PREPARATION

Fill in the circle under the correct answer.

1. Choose the addition fact you would use to check your answer.

14 − 8 = ?

5 + 9 = 14 ○	6 + 8 = 14 ○
4 + 6 = 10 ○	7 + 7 = 14 ○

2. Add.

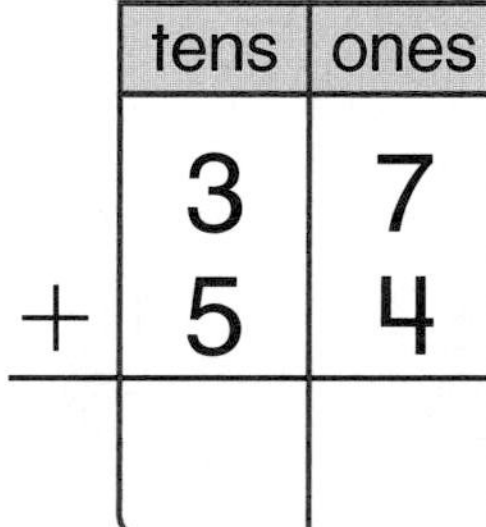

91 ○ 90 ○ 81 ○ 93 ○

3. Which number is even?

7 ○ 13 ○ 17 ○ 10 ○

4. Which ordinal number comes just after thirtieth?

thirty-first ○	twenty-ninth ○
twelfth ○	fourteenth ○

5. Which is a fact family for the numbers 8, 9, and 17?

8 + 9 = 17	17 − 9 = 8	8 + 9 = 17
9 + 8 = 17	17 − 8 = 9	9 + 8 = 17
17 − 8 = 9	8 + 8 = 16	17 − 8 = 9
17 − 9 = 8	9 + 9 = 18	9 + 1 = 10
○	○	○

6. Who collected the least bugs?

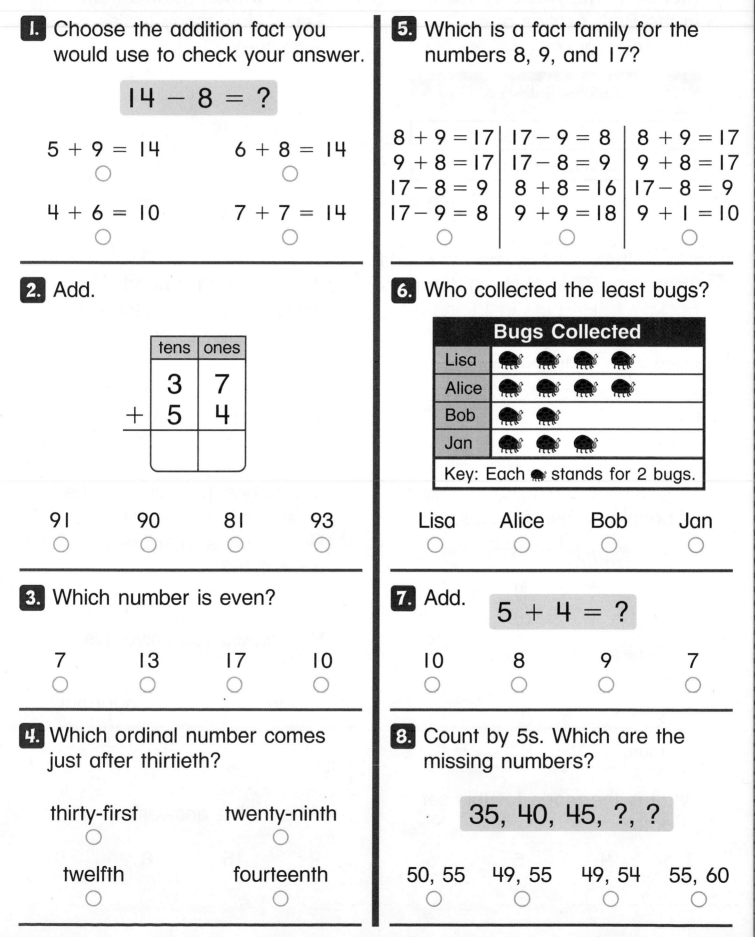

Bugs Collected	
Lisa	🐞 🐞 🐞 🐞
Alice	🐞 🐞 🐞 🐞
Bob	🐞 🐞
Jan	🐞 🐞 🐞
Key: Each 🐞 stands for 2 bugs.	

Lisa ○ Alice ○ Bob ○ Jan ○

7. Add. 5 + 4 = ?

10 ○ 8 ○ 9 ○ 7 ○

8. Count by 5s. Which are the missing numbers?

35, 40, 45, ?, ?

50, 55 ○ 49, 55 ○ 49, 54 ○ 55, 60 ○

Copyright © by William H. Sadlier, Inc. All rights reserved.

Fill in the circle under the correct answer.

9. Jack surveys his friends to find which season they like. Which friend's name would you write in the Both section of a Venn diagram?

Favorite Season	
Season	Friend
Spring	Greg, Mary, Jane, Luke
Summer	Chad, Greg, Ida

Mary ○ Greg ○ Jane ○ Luke ○

10. There are 27 marbles in John's backpack. He puts in 11 more. How many marbles does John have in his backpack?

16 ○ 17 ○ 38 ○ 37 ○

11. Five children count the number of people in their families.

Our Families	
Name	Number in Family
Pat	6
Dane	5
Tim	4
Kate	3
Clara	4

What is the mode for this set of data?

3 ○ 4 ○ 5 ○ 6 ○

12. Tim sees 13 turtles. Terry sees 12 more turtles than Tim. Julie sees 10 more turtles than Terry. How many turtles does Julie see?

25 ○ 23 ○ 35 ○ 37 ○

13. 8 frogs are in a pond. Then 3 more frogs come. How many frogs are in the pond then?

5 ○ 6 ○ 10 ○ 11 ○

14. Margo has 12 stickers. She gives 3 of them to her friend. How many stickers does Margo have then?

How would you solve this problem?

add ○ subtract ○

What is the answer?

14 ○ 15 ○ 8 ○ 9 ○

Subtraction: Two-Digit Numbers

CHAPTER 5

Copyright © by William H. Sadlier, Inc. All rights reserved.

Listen

Listen to your teacher read the poem.

How many fewer stars than rainbows are there?

Dear Family,

Today our class began Chapter 5. We will learn about subtracting two-digit numbers. Let's do the activity below together so I can review the skills I will need in order to understand the math in this chapter. Then you can read some of the new vocabulary I will learn in Chapter 5.

Love, ________________

Back to Basics

Use small objects such as beans, pasta, or pennies to help your child review basic subtraction facts. Place a group that contains from 2 to 18 objects on a table. Ask your child how many are in the group. Then take away some of the objects and ask how many are left.

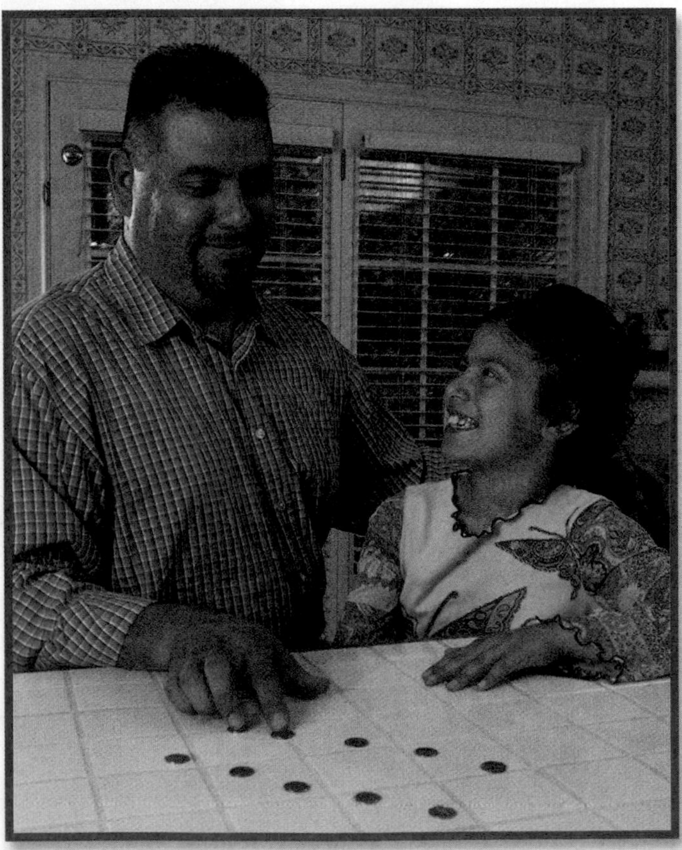

Chapter 5

also on-line

regroup tens as ones; trade 1 ten for 10 ones

1 ten = 10 ones

2 tens 5 ones = 1 ten 15 ones

To **round** to the nearest ten, look at the ones.
5 ones or more, round up.
Fewer than 5 ones, round down.

estimate about how many

Round each number.
Subtract to estimate the difference.

$$\begin{array}{r} 63 \\ -18 \\ \hline \end{array} \longrightarrow \begin{array}{r} 60 \\ -20 \\ \hline \text{about } 40 \end{array}$$

Name ______________________________

Subtract Tens and Ones

Let's Learn!

Cathy has 56 craft sticks.
She uses 24 of them on her project.
How many craft sticks does Cathy have then?

Model 56. Then take away 24.

tens	ones
5 tens (2 taken away)	6 ones (4 taken away)

First subtract the ones.

	tens	ones
	5	6
−	2	4
		2

Then subtract the tens.

	tens	ones
	5	6
−	2	4
	3	2

Cathy has 32 craft sticks left.

Subtract. You may use models to check.

1.

	tens	ones
	3	8
−	3	5
		3

2.

	tens	ones
	6	2
−	5	1

3.

	tens	ones
	5	9
−	1	4

4.

	tens	ones
	7	7
−	3	6

5. $91 - 51$

6. $75 - 53$

7. $99 - 28$

8. $48 - 47$

9. $85 - 35$

10. $49 - 31$

11. $97 - 92$

12. $44 - 20$

13. $99 - 67$

14. $86 - 13$

15. How does knowing subtraction facts help you subtract two-digit numbers?

Copyright © by William H. Sadlier, Inc. All rights reserved.

Practice

Do not write 0
when no tens
are left.

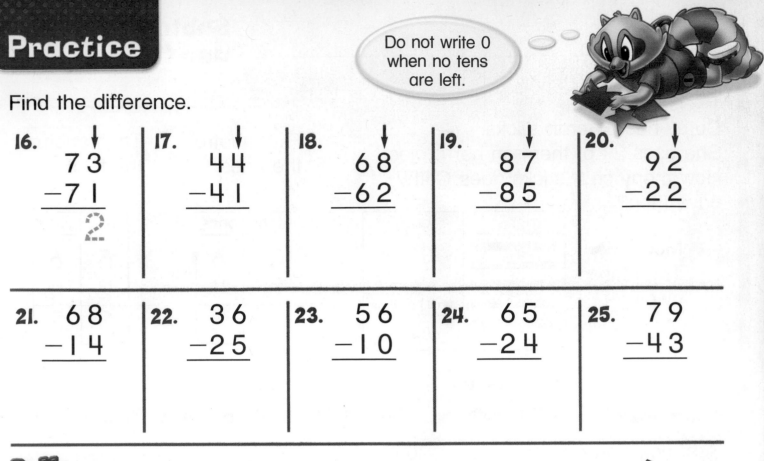

Find the difference.

16.	17.	18.	19.	20.
$73 - 71 = 2$	$44 - 41$	$68 - 62$	$87 - 85$	$92 - 22$

21.	22.	23.	24.	25.
$68 - 14$	$36 - 25$	$56 - 10$	$65 - 24$	$79 - 43$

Solve. Use a problem-solving strategy.
Show your work on a separate sheet of paper.

26. Joe uses 96 green cubes for his project. He also uses seventy-five red cubes. How many more green cubes does he use than red cubes?

_____ more green cubes

27. Alan glues 32 purple circles onto a picture. Then he glues 45 stars onto the picture. How many fewer circles does he use than stars?

_____ fewer circles

TEST PREPARATION

Fill in the circle of the correct answer.

28. $54 - 43$

○ 91
○ 97
○ 17
○ 11

29. $97 - 51$

○ 36
○ 46
○ 48
○ 68

30. $63 - 42$

○ 101
○ 25
○ 21
○ 15

31. $29 - 24$

○ 25
○ 20
○ 6
○ 5

Math Alive at Home Ask your child to use the numbers 4, 3, 2, and 1 to make three different 2-digit numbers to subtract from 85.

Name ____________________

Mental Math Subtraction

Let's Learn!

Count back by ones to subtract 23 − 2 mentally.

Start at 23.
Count back by 1s.
22, 21

$$\begin{array}{r} 23 \\ -\ 2 \\ \hline 21 \end{array}$$

Count back by tens to subtract 23 − 20 mentally.

$$\begin{array}{r} 23 \\ -20 \\ \hline 3 \end{array}$$

Start at 23.
Count back by 10s.
13, 3

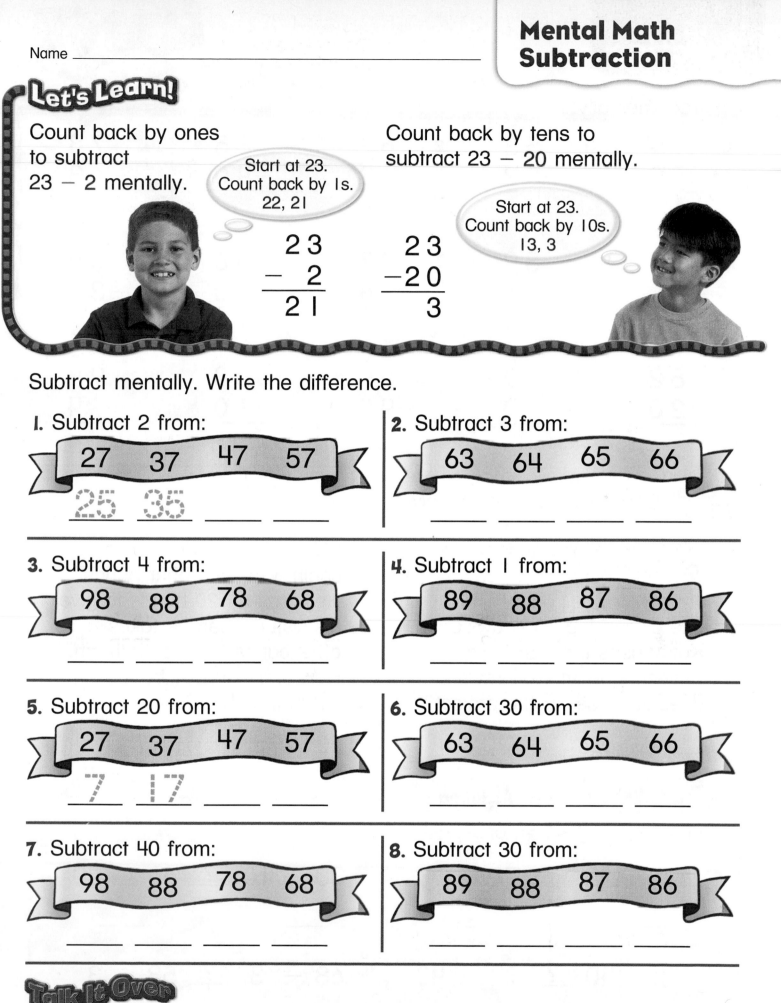

Subtract mentally. Write the difference.

1. Subtract 2 from:

27 37 47 57

25 35 ____ ____

2. Subtract 3 from:

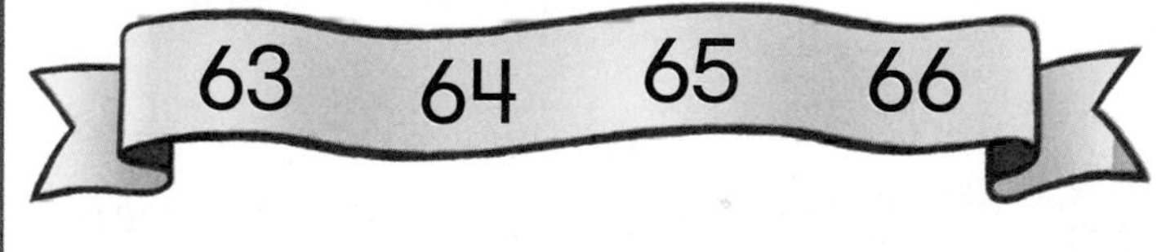

63 64 65 66

____ ____ ____ ____

3. Subtract 4 from:

98 88 78 68

____ ____ ____ ____

4. Subtract 1 from:

89 88 87 86

____ ____ ____ ____

5. Subtract 20 from:

27 37 47 57

7 17 ____ ____

6. Subtract 30 from:

63 64 65 66

____ ____ ____ ____

7. Subtract 40 from:

98 88 78 68

____ ____ ____ ____

8. Subtract 30 from:

89 88 87 86

____ ____ ____ ____

9. Without subtracting, tell which is less: 78 − 6 or 78 − 60. Explain your answer.

Copyright © by William H. Sadlier, Inc. All rights reserved.

Practice

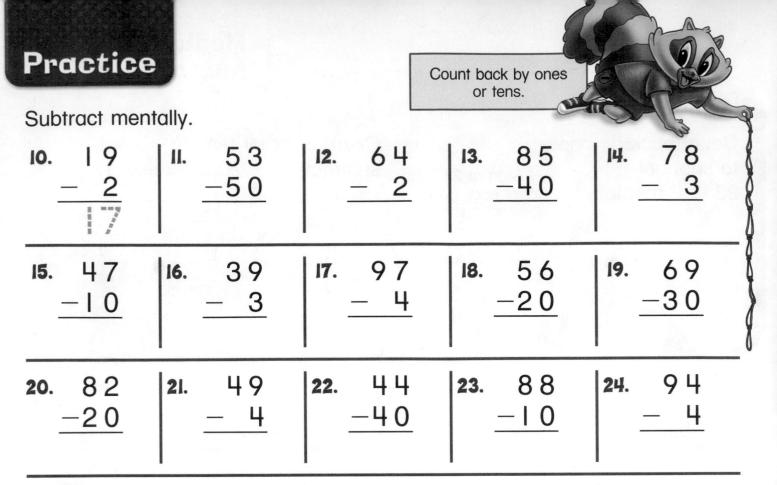

Count back by ones or tens.

Subtract mentally.

10. $19 - 2 = $ 17	11. $53 - 50$	12. $64 - 2$	13. $85 - 40$	14. $78 - 3$
15. $47 - 10$	16. $39 - 3$	17. $97 - 4$	18. $56 - 20$	19. $69 - 30$
20. $82 - 20$	21. $49 - 4$	22. $44 - 40$	23. $88 - 10$	24. $94 - 4$

Solve. Use a problem-solving strategy.

25. **Multistep** Kathy finds a box with 53 straws. She uses 1 straw for her drink. Then she gives Meg 30 straws. Kathy uses the rest for a project. How many straws does she use for the project?

_____ straws

26. **Multistep** Chris makes a chain with 75 rubber bands. He takes off 20 bands to give his sister. Then he takes off 2 bands to give his mom. How many rubber bands are left in the chain?

_____ rubber bands

CHALLENGE

Compare. Write $<$, $=$, or $>$.

27. $50 - 10$? $70 - 30$

_____ ◯ _____

28. $30 - 10$? $60 - 20$

_____ ◯ _____

29. $74 - 40$? $84 - 40$

_____ ◯ _____

30. $68 - 3$? $58 - 3$

_____ ◯ _____

Math Alive at Home Ask your child to subtract 76 – 40, 98 – 4, and 59 – 50. (36, 94, 9)

Name ________________________________

Algebra
Ways to Make Numbers

Let's Learn!

You can make numbers in different ways.

I can make 17 by adding.
10 + 7 = 17
I can make 17 by subtracting.
19 − 2 = 17

Circle the ways to make the top number.

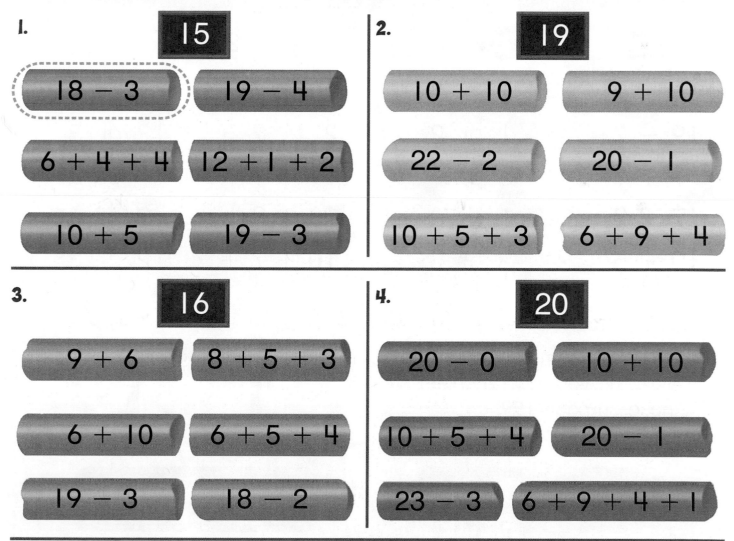

1. 15

18 − 3	19 − 4
6 + 4 + 4	12 + 1 + 2
10 + 5	19 − 3

2. 19

10 + 10	9 + 10
22 − 2	20 − 1
10 + 5 + 3	6 + 9 + 4

3. 16

9 + 6	8 + 5 + 3
6 + 10	6 + 5 + 4
19 − 3	18 − 2

4. 20

20 − 0	10 + 10
10 + 5 + 4	20 − 1
23 − 3	6 + 9 + 4 + 1

Talk It Over

5. Are there other ways to make 20 besides those you circled in exercise 4? If yes, name two other ways.

Copyright © by William H. Sadlier, Inc. All rights reserved.

Practice

Circle the number in the shaded box needed to make the top number.

6.

7 + ?	7 or 8
16 − ?	1 or 2
9 + ?	4 or 5
17 − ?	3 or 4
10 + 2 + ?	2 or 3

7.

17 + ?	2 or 3
20 − ?	1 or 2
19 + ?	0 or 1
15 + ?	4 or 5
6 + 4 + ?	8 or 9

8.

15 + ?	2 or 3
19 − ?	1 or 2
9 + ?	8 or 9
17 + ?	1 or 2
10 + 5 + ?	2 or 3

9.

18 + ?	1 or 2
22 − ?	2 or 3
19 + ?	1 or 2
20 + ?	0 or 1
10 + 7 + ?	2 or 3

CHALLENGE

10. Choose a number less than 20. Make up your own problem like those on page 199. Ask a classmate to solve it.

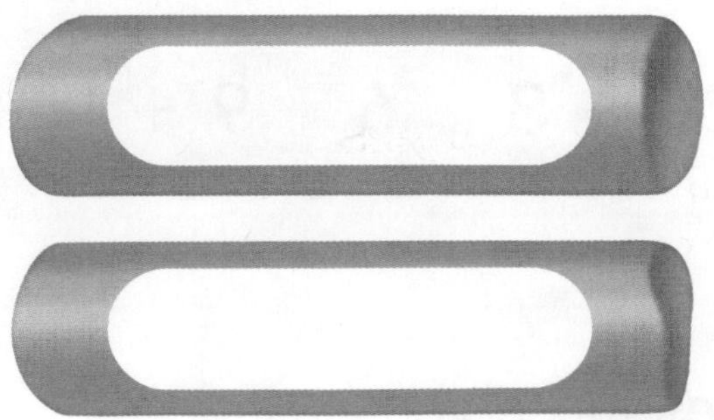

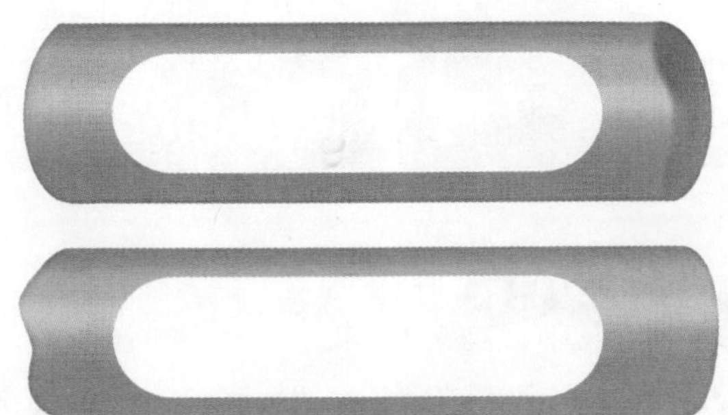

Math Alive at Home Ask your child to tell you three different ways to make the number 13. (examples: 7 + 6, 10 + 3, 16 − 3)

Name ______________________________

Regroup Tens as Ones: Use Models

HANDS-ON LESSON

Let's Learn!

Regroup tens as ones.

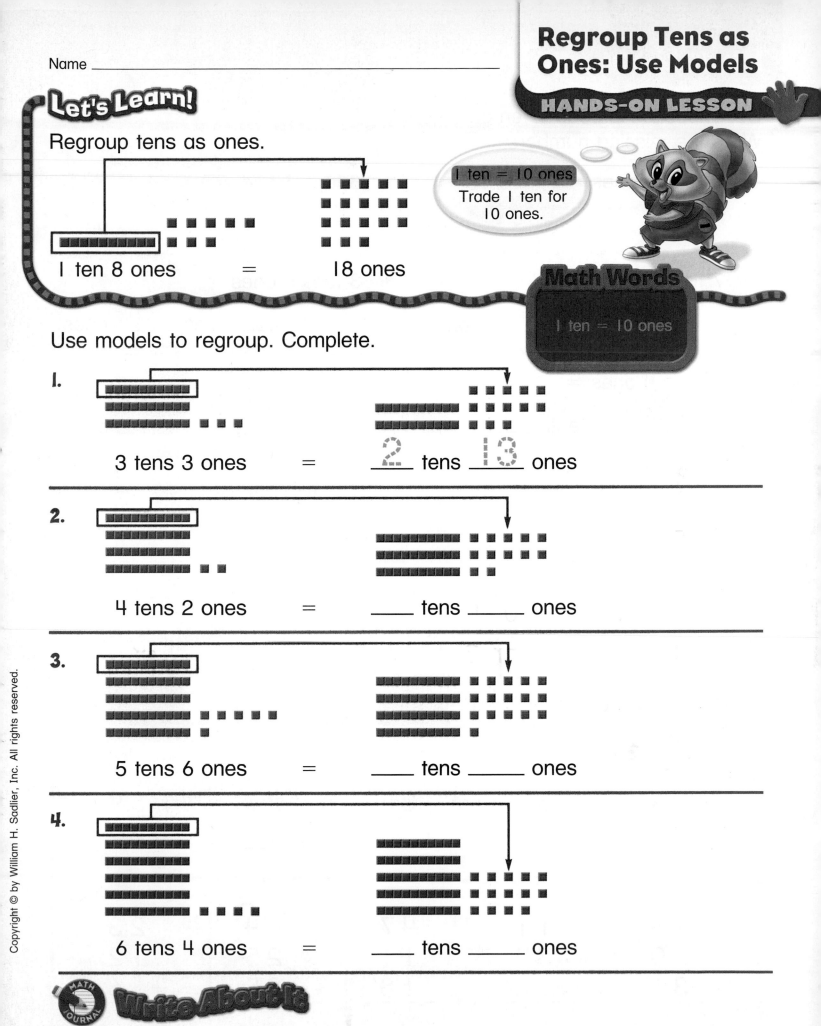

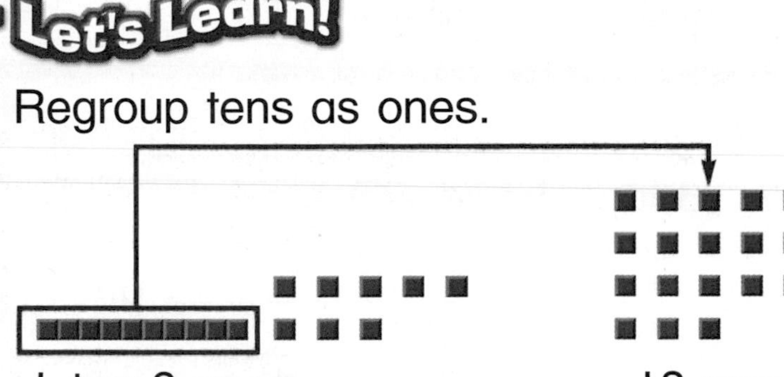

1 ten 8 ones = 18 ones

1 ten = 10 ones
Trade 1 ten for 10 ones.

Math Words

1 ten = 10 ones

Use models to regroup. Complete.

1. 3 tens 3 ones = 2 tens 13 ones

2. 4 tens 2 ones = ____ tens ____ ones

3. 5 tens 6 ones = ____ tens ____ ones

4. 6 tens 4 ones = ____ tens ____ ones

5. What happens to the number of ones when 1 ten is regrouped as 10 ones?

Copyright © by William H. Sadlier, Inc. All rights reserved.

Practice

Use models. Regroup 1 ten as 10 ones.
Write the missing numbers.

6. 9 tens 0 ones = 8 tens 10 ones

7. 8 tens 1 one = ____ tens ____ ones

8. 7 tens 8 ones = ____ tens ____ ones

9. 3 tens 5 ones = ____ tens ____ ones

10. 9 tens 4 ones = ____ tens ____ ones

11. 4 tens 9 ones = ____ tens ____ ones

12. 1 ten 2 ones = ____ tens ____ ones

13. 2 tens 6 ones = ____ ten ____ ones

14. 5 tens 7 ones = ____ tens ____ ones

15. 6 tens 3 ones = ____ tens ____ ones

DO YOU REMEMBER?

Find the sum.

16. $54 + 36$

17. $83 + 16$

18. $35 + 5$

19. $27 + 38$

20. $59 + 29$

21. $28 + 20 + 31$

22. $11 + 34 + 12$

23. $47 + 11 + 18$

24. $14 + 25 + 35$

25. $23 + 12 + 6$

Math Alive at Home Ask your child to explain how she/he would subtract 23 −7. (regroup 2 tens 3 ones as 1 ten 13 ones)

Name ______________________

Regroup Tens as Ones: Model and Record

HANDS-ON LESSON

Let's Learn!

Jean has 31 pieces of pasta.
She uses 17 to make a necklace.
How many pieces are left?

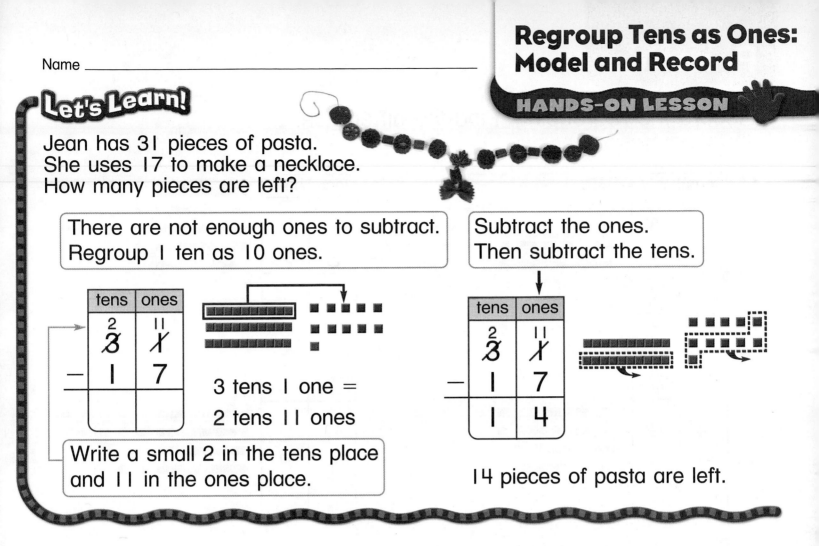

There are not enough ones to subtract.
Regroup 1 ten as 10 ones.

tens	ones
~~3~~ 2	~~1~~ 11
− 1	7

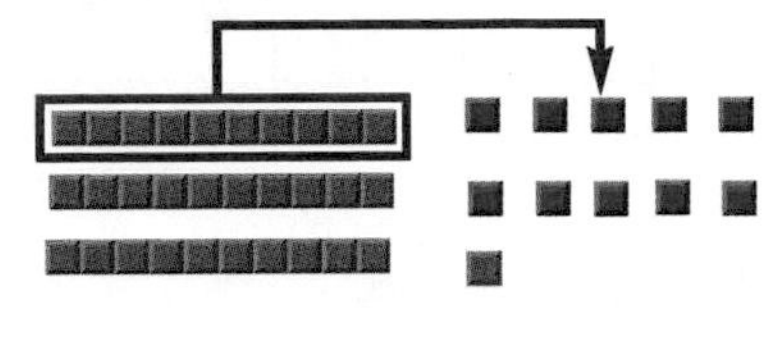

3 tens 1 one =
2 tens 11 ones

Write a small 2 in the tens place and 11 in the ones place.

Subtract the ones.
Then subtract the tens.

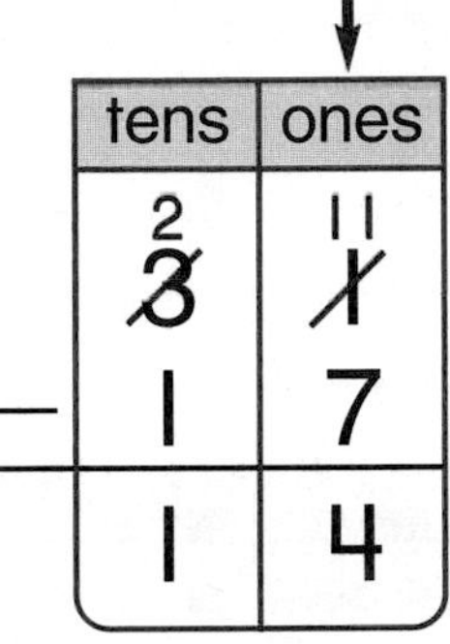

tens	ones
~~3~~ 2	~~1~~ 11
− 1	7
1	4

14 pieces of pasta are left.

Use models to regroup 1 ten as 10 ones. Subtract.

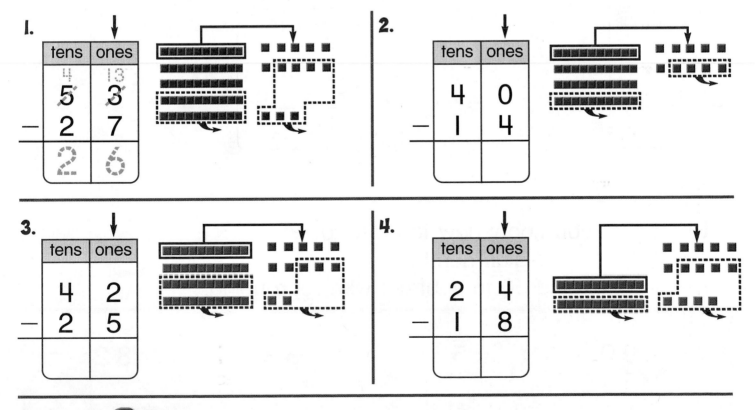

1.

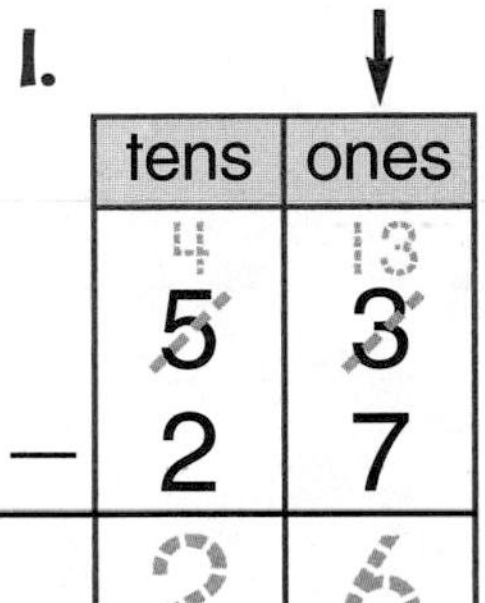

tens	ones
~~5~~ 4	~~3~~ 13
− 2	7
2	6

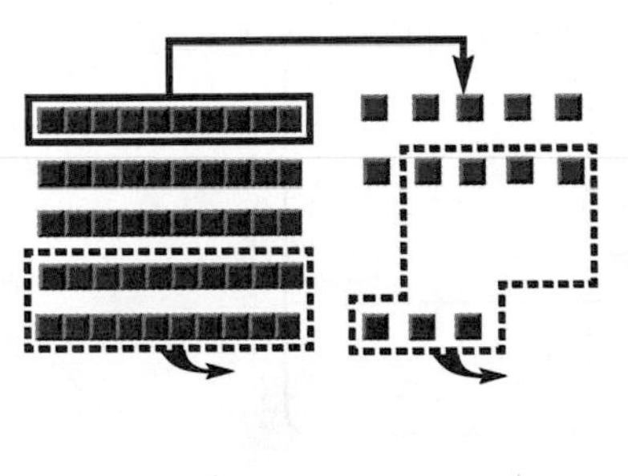

2.

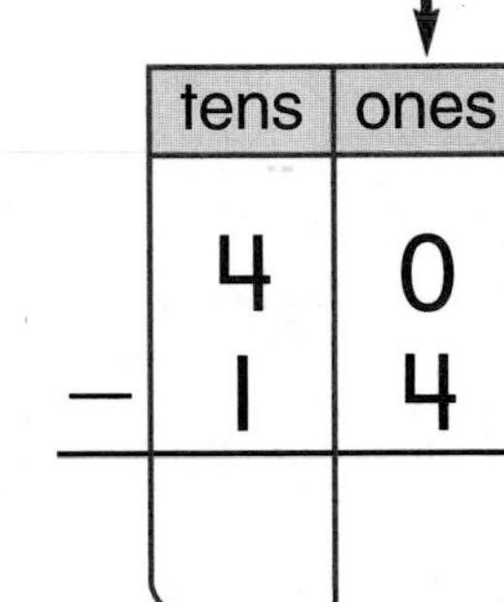

tens	ones
4	0
− 1	4

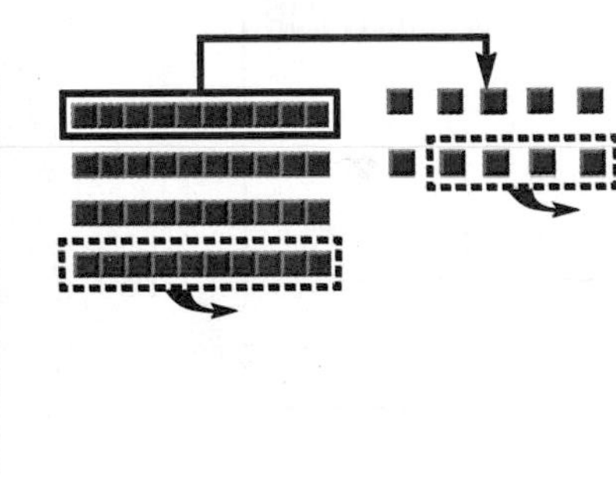

3.

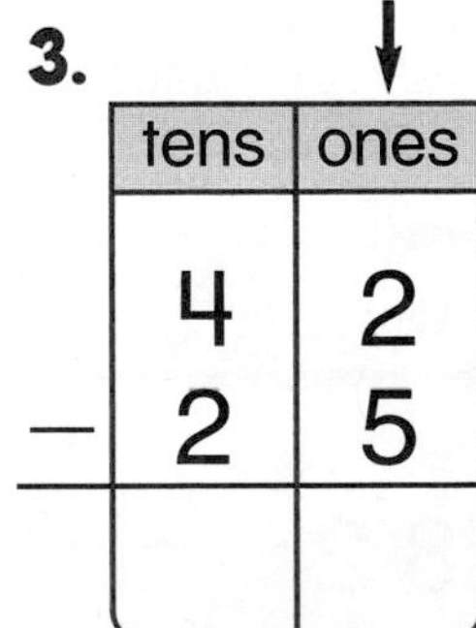

tens	ones
4	2
− 2	5

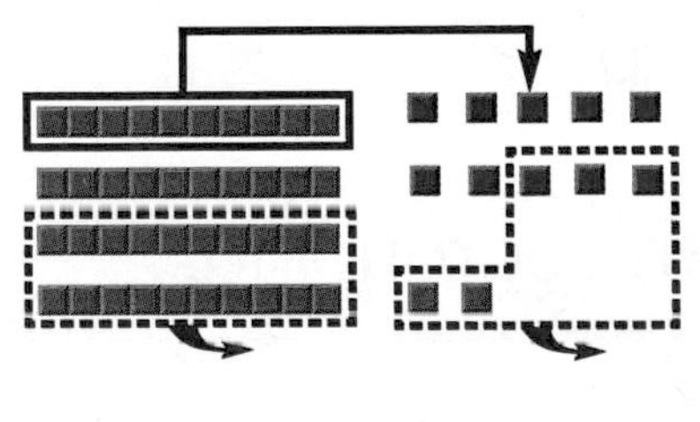

4.

tens	ones
2	4
− 1	8

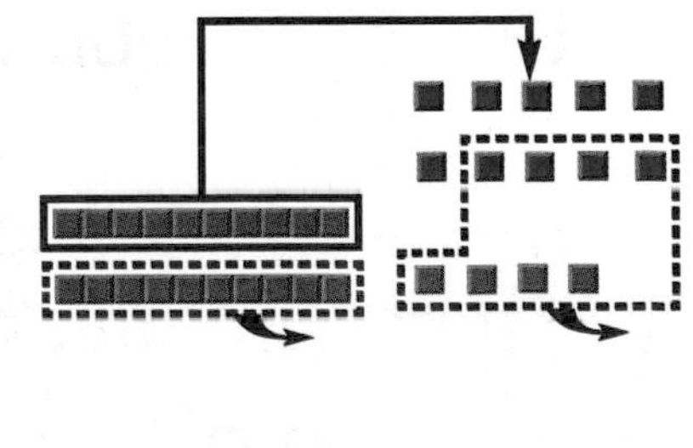

5. In the example at the top of the page, explain why 31 was regrouped as 2 tens 11 ones before subtracting.

Copyright © by William H. Sadlier, Inc. All rights reserved.

Practice

Record the regrouping. Find the difference.

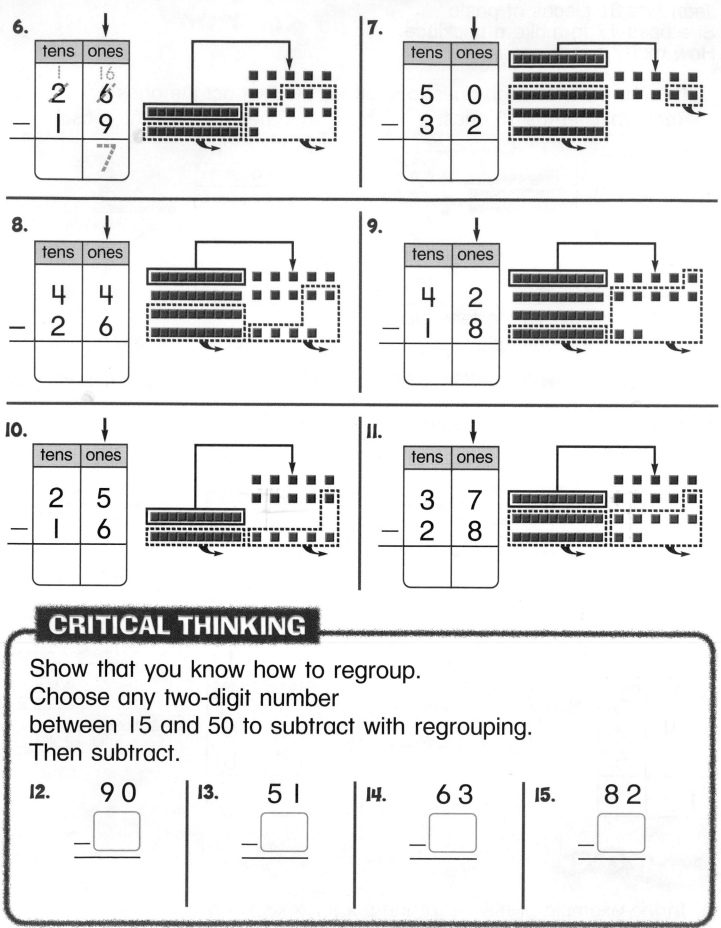

6.

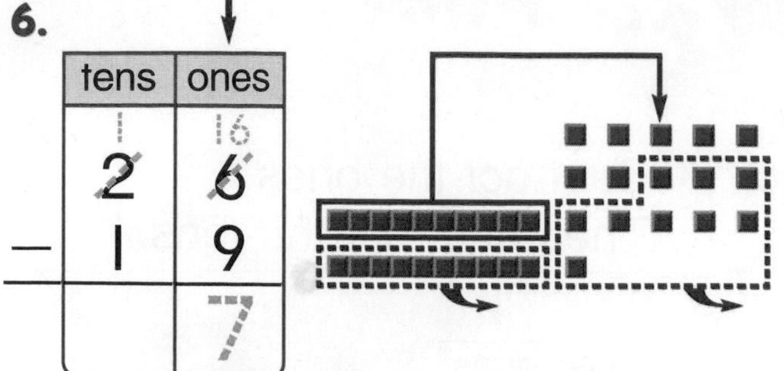

tens	ones
1	16
~~2~~	~~6~~
− 1	9
	7

7.

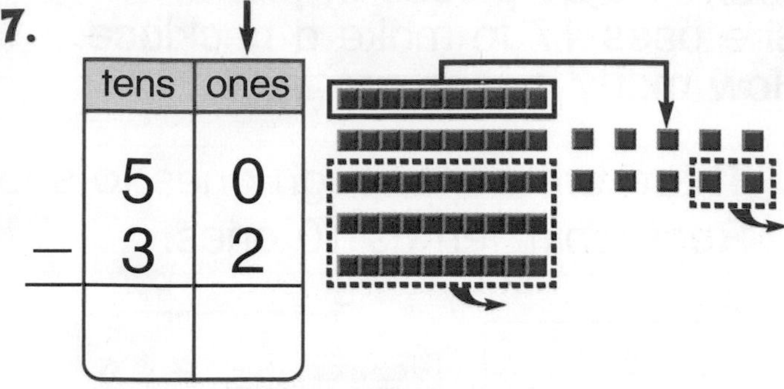

tens	ones
5	0
− 3	2

8.

tens	ones
4	4
− 2	6

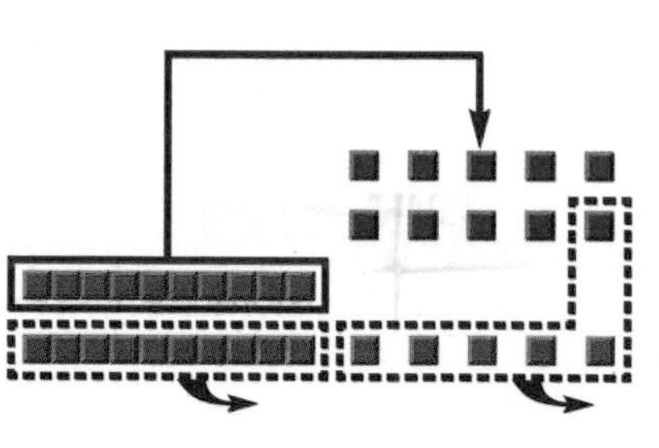

9.

tens	ones
4	2
− 1	8

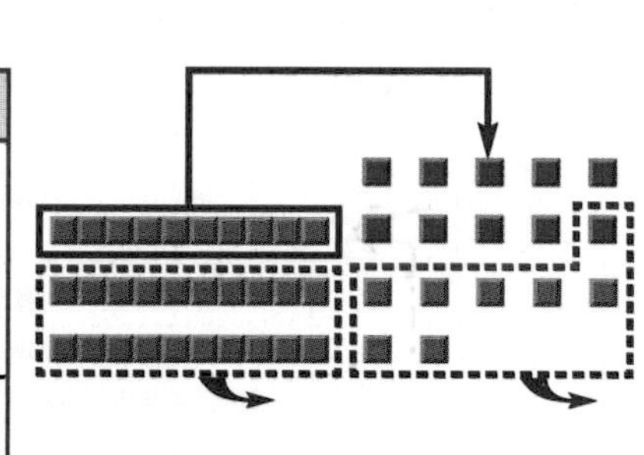

10.

tens	ones
2	5
− 1	6

11.

tens	ones
3	7
− 2	8

CRITICAL THINKING

Show that you know how to regroup.
Choose any two-digit number
between 15 and 50 to subtract with regrouping.
Then subtract.

12. 90 − ☐

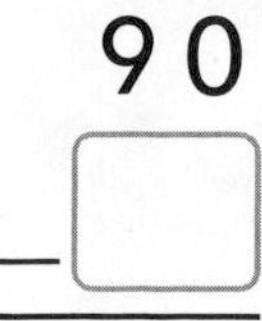

13. 51 − ☐

14. 63 − ☐

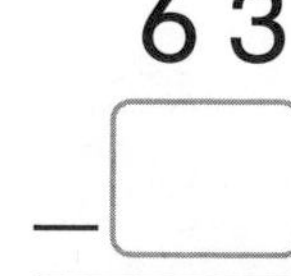

15. 82 − ☐

Math Alive at Home Ask your child to explain how to regroup to subtract 42–28. (14)

Name ____________________

Regroup Tens as Ones

Let's Learn!

Debra has 34 new crayons. She uses 6 crayons to draw a picture. How many crayons are still new?

There are not enough ones to subtract.
Regroup 1 ten as 10 ones.

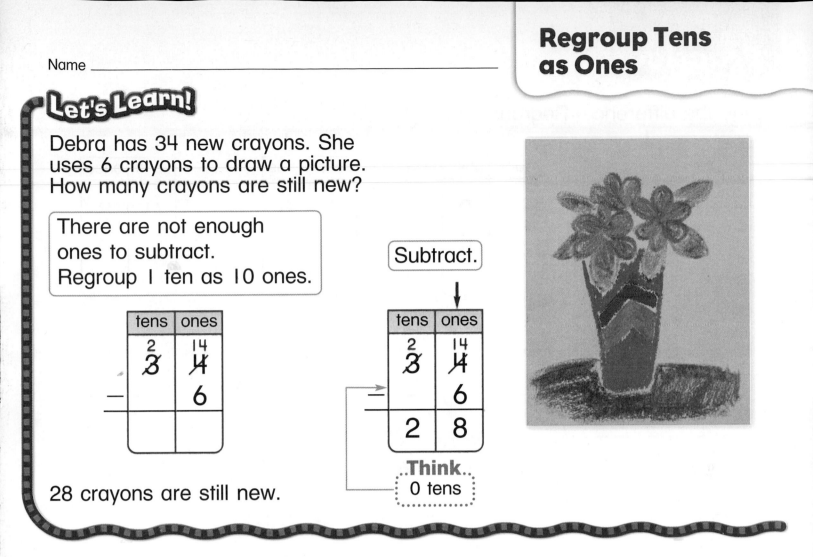

	tens	ones
	2 / ~~3~~	14 / ~~4~~
−		6

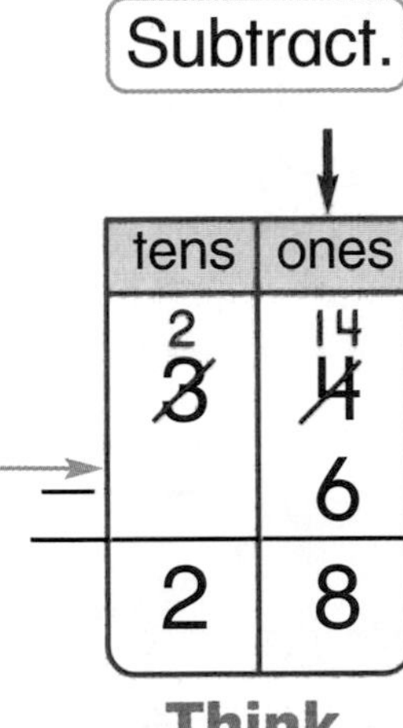

Think: 0 tens

28 crayons are still new.

Find the difference. You can use models to check.

1.

	tens	ones
	7 / ~~8~~	10 / ~~0~~
−		6
	7	4

2.

	tens	ones
	2	3
−		9

3.

	tens	ones
	7	8
−	4	9

4.

	tens	ones
	4	5
−		6

5.

	tens	ones
	3	4
−	1	5

6.

	tens	ones
	5	2
−		4

7.

	tens	ones
	8	0
−	2	3

8.

	tens	ones
	5	3
−	4	5

9. Why does the answer in exercise 8 have no tens?

Copyright © by William H. Sadlier, Inc. All rights reserved.

Practice

Find the difference. Regroup as needed.

10.

	tens	ones
	7	11
	~~8~~	~~1~~
−	7	6
		5

11.

	tens	ones
	4	0
−	1	8

12.

	tens	ones
	6	5
−	2	9

13.

	tens	ones
	3	8
−	1	8

14. $53 - 28$

15. $74 - 31$

16. $85 - 7$

17. $97 - 29$

18. $33 - 2$

19. $83 - 54$

20. $94 - 8$

21. $67 - 4$

22. $91 - 15$

23. $52 - 9$

Solve. Use a problem-solving strategy.
Show your work on a separate sheet of paper.

24. Daryl glues 27 red stars on his puppet. Then he glues on 35 blue stars. How many more blue stars does he use than red stars?

_____ more blue stars

25. Multistep Jane cuts 60 pieces of yarn for a puppet. She uses 16 pieces for the arms and 26 pieces for the legs. How many pieces of yarn does she have then?

_____ pieces of yarn

CRITICAL THINKING

26. Sean has 36 strips of paper to make a mask. Ann has 30 strips of paper. After Sean gives Ann some of his strips, they have the same number. How many strips of paper does Sean give Ann?

_____ strips of paper

Math Alive at Home Ask your child to subtract 52 − 4, 36 − 8, and 70 − 2. (48, 28, 68)

Name ______________________________

Estimate Differences

Let's Learn!

To estimate the difference of 28 − 21:

- first round each number to the nearest ten
- then subtract the rounded numbers

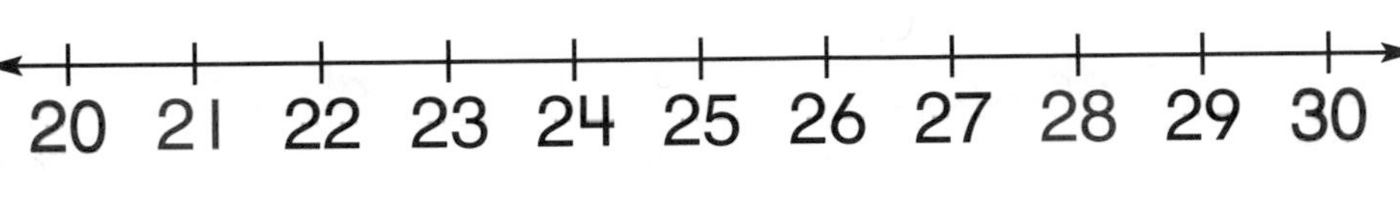
20 21 22 23 24 25 26 27 28 29 30

Remember:
5 ones or more, round up.
Fewer than 5 ones, round down.
Use the number line.

$$\begin{array}{r} 28 \\ -21 \\ \hline \end{array} \longrightarrow \begin{array}{r} 30 \\ -20 \\ \hline \text{about } 10 \end{array}$$

28 − 21 is about 10.

Estimate the difference. Round the numbers to the nearest ten.

1. 56 → 60; −35 → −40; about 20

2. 74 → ☐; −12 → −☐; about ____

3. 43 → ☐; −19 → −☐; about ____

4. 88 → ☐; −41 → −☐; about ____

MATH JOURNAL
Write About It

5. Explain how you would estimate the difference of 62 − 35.

Copyright © by William H. Sadlier, Inc. All rights reserved.

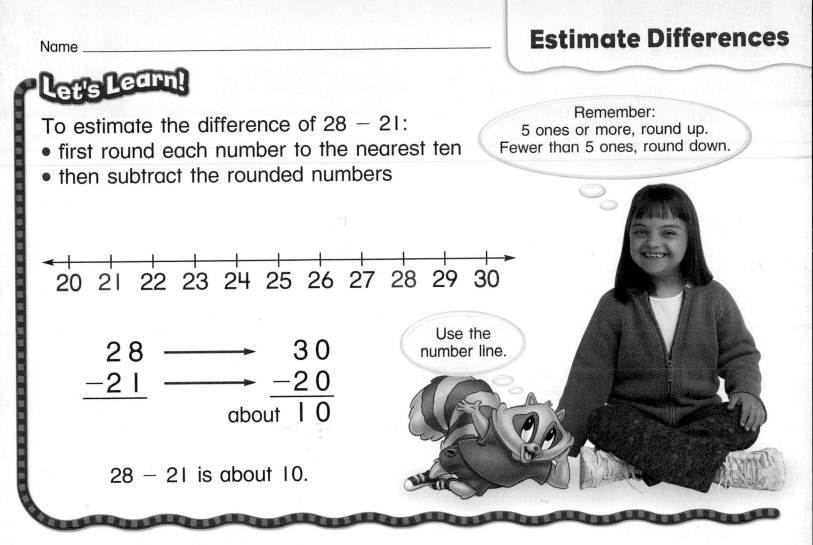

Practice

Remember:
5 ones or more, round up.
Fewer than 5 ones, round down.

Estimate the difference.
Round numbers to the nearest ten.

6. 75 → 80
−27 → −30
about 50

7. 85 → ☐
−71 → −☐
about ____

8. 53 → ☐
−38 → −☐
about ____

9. 82 → ☐
−51 → −☐
about ____

10. 68 → ☐
−39 → −☐
about ____

11. 61 → ☐
−46 → −☐
about ____

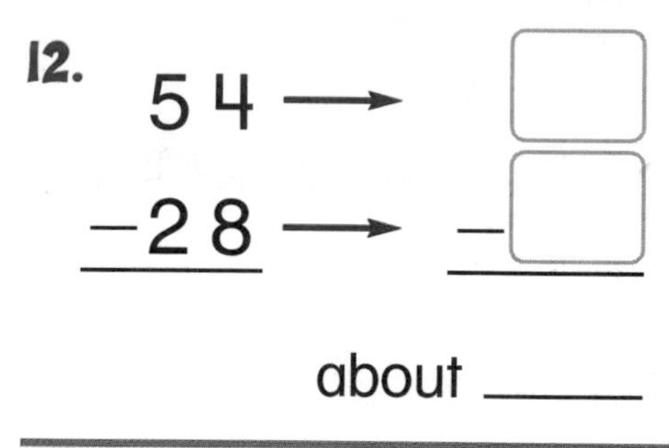

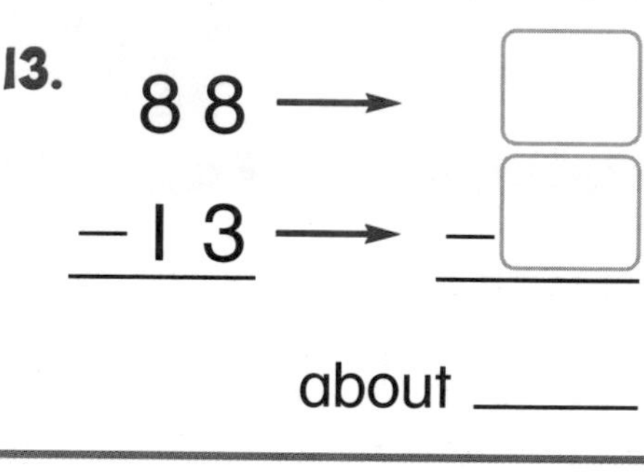

12. 54 → ☐
−28 → −☐
about ____

13. 88 → ☐
−13 → −☐
about ____

14. 56 → ☐
−29 → −☐
about ____

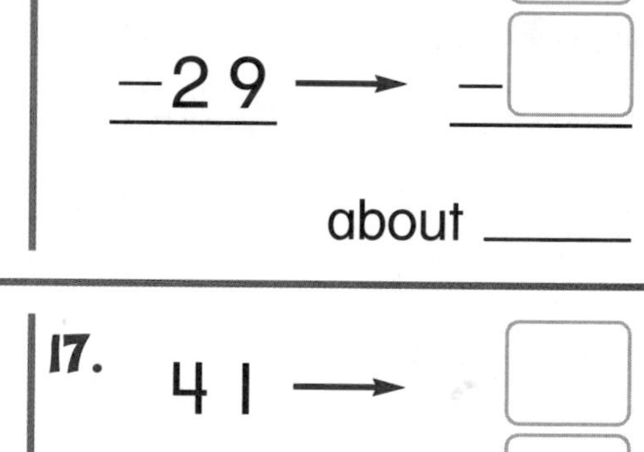

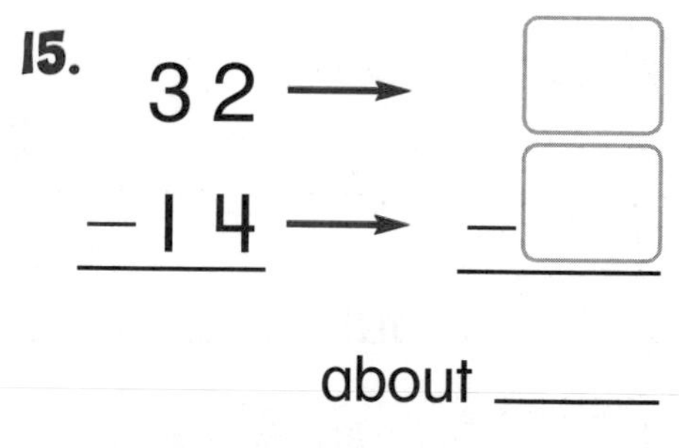

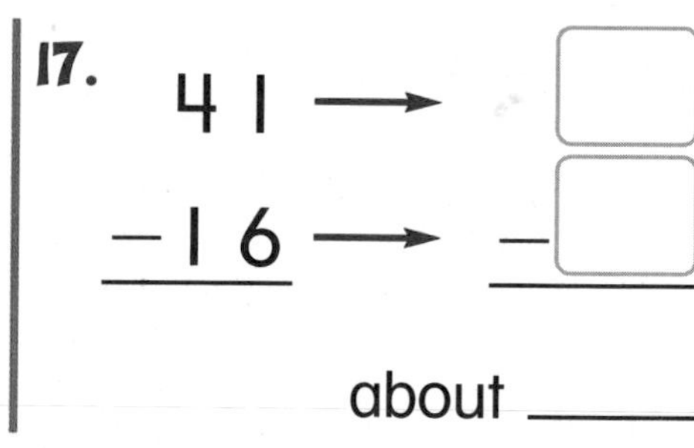

15. 32 → ☐
−14 → −☐
about ____

16. 54 → ☐
−22 → −☐
about ____

17. 41 → ☐
−16 → −☐
about ____

CALCULATOR ACTIVITY Algebra

Use estimation and a calculator to find the missing digits.

18. ☐5 − 27 = 38

19. 8☐ − 26 = 59

20. 96 − 4☐ = 48

Math Alive at Home Ask your child to explain how to estimate the difference in 48 - 13. (40)

Name ____

Rewrite Two-Digit Subtraction

Let's Learn!

There are 43 color tiles in a bag. 4 tiles are on the table. How many more tiles are in the bag?

43 − 4 = ?

Rewrite the subtraction. Think about place value.

Line up the tens and ones.

	tens	ones
	4	3
−		4
	3	9

Subtract. Regroup if needed.

	tens	ones
	3	13
	~~4~~	~~3~~
−		4
	3	9

There are 39 more tiles in the bag.

Rewrite the subtraction. Then find the difference.

1. 80 − 26

	tens	ones
	7	10
	~~8~~	~~0~~
−	2	6
	5	4

2. 78 − 29

	tens	ones
−		

3. 69 − 8

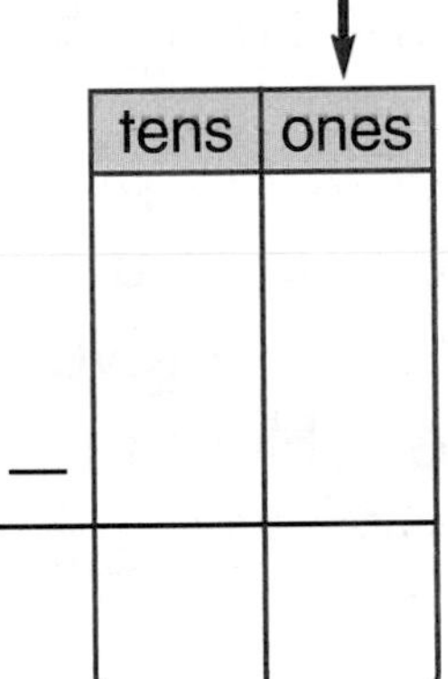

4. 83 − 5

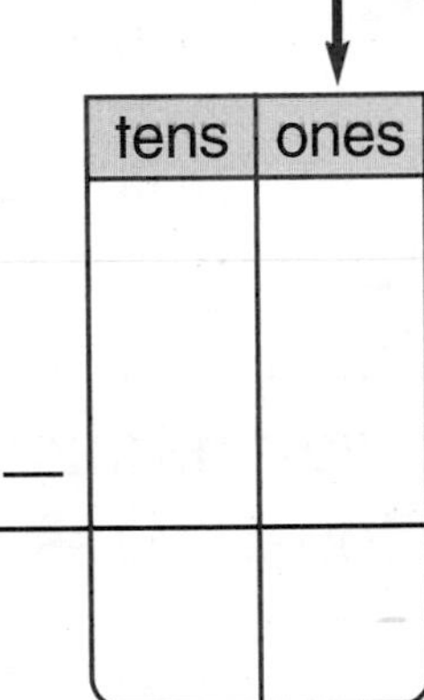

5. 27 − 9

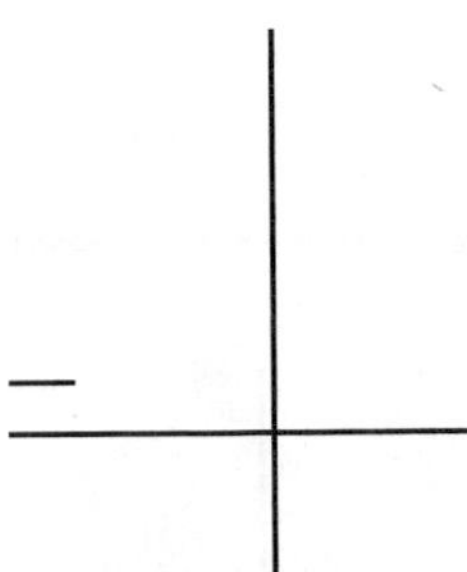

6. 95 − 27

7. 62 − 3

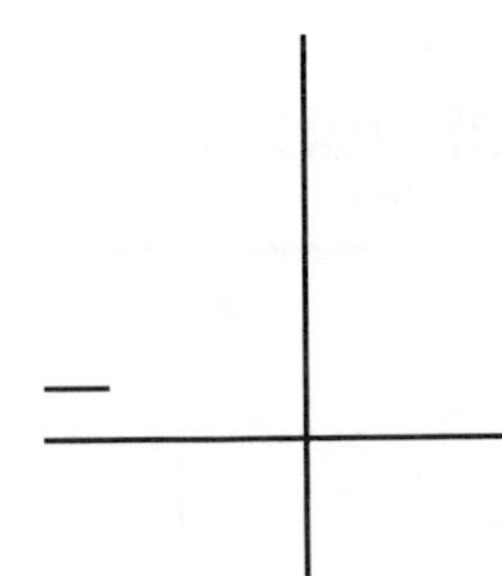

8. 98 − 57

Talk It Over

9. Explain how to rewrite the subtraction 46 − 7.

Copyright © by William H. Sadlier, Inc. All rights reserved.

Practice

Rewrite the subtraction. Then find the difference.

10. 52 − 37

	4	12
	5	2
−	3	7
	1	5

11. 43 − 7

12. 77 − 65

13. 97 − 9

14. 58 − 26

15. 67 − 8

16. 72 − 5

17. 81 − 32

Solve. Use a problem-solving strategy.
Show your work on a separate sheet of paper.

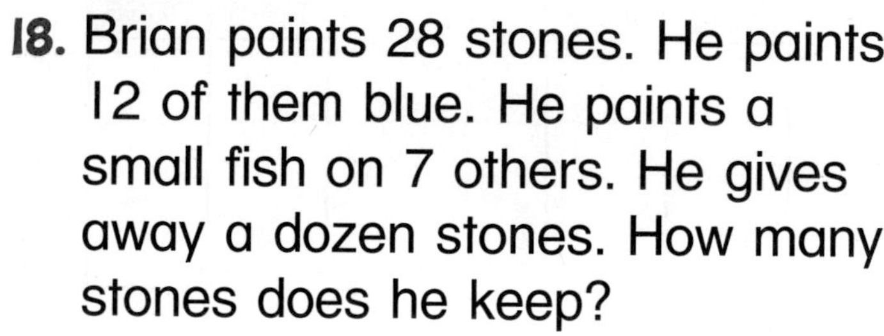

18. Brian paints 28 stones. He paints 12 of them blue. He paints a small fish on 7 others. He gives away a dozen stones. How many stones does he keep?

_____ stones

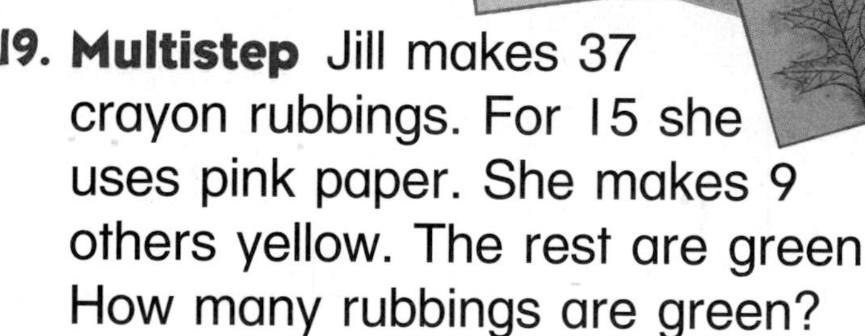

19. **Multistep** Jill makes 37 crayon rubbings. For 15 she uses pink paper. She makes 9 others yellow. The rest are green. How many rubbings are green?

_____ rubbings

CRITICAL THINKING

Show 2 ways to subtract without regrouping.

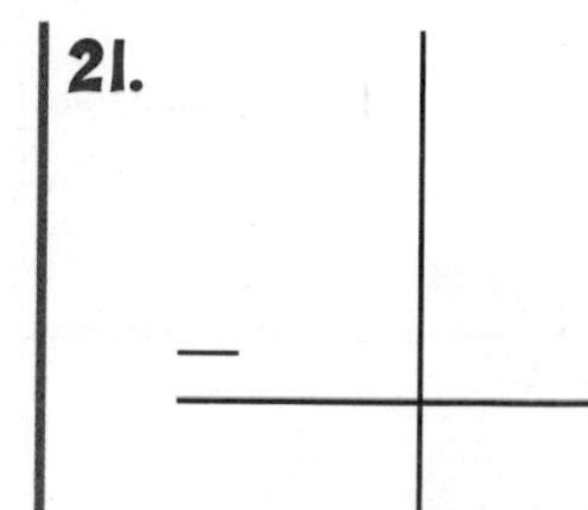

20.

21.

Show 2 ways to subtract with regrouping.

22.

23.

Math Alive at Home Ask your child to write 53 − 8 and 82 − 47 vertically and then to subtract. (45; 35)

Name ________________________________

Algebra

Add to Check

Let's Learn!

Sam glues 63 pieces of paper for his mosaic. Megan uses 37 pieces for hers. How many more pieces of paper does Sam use?

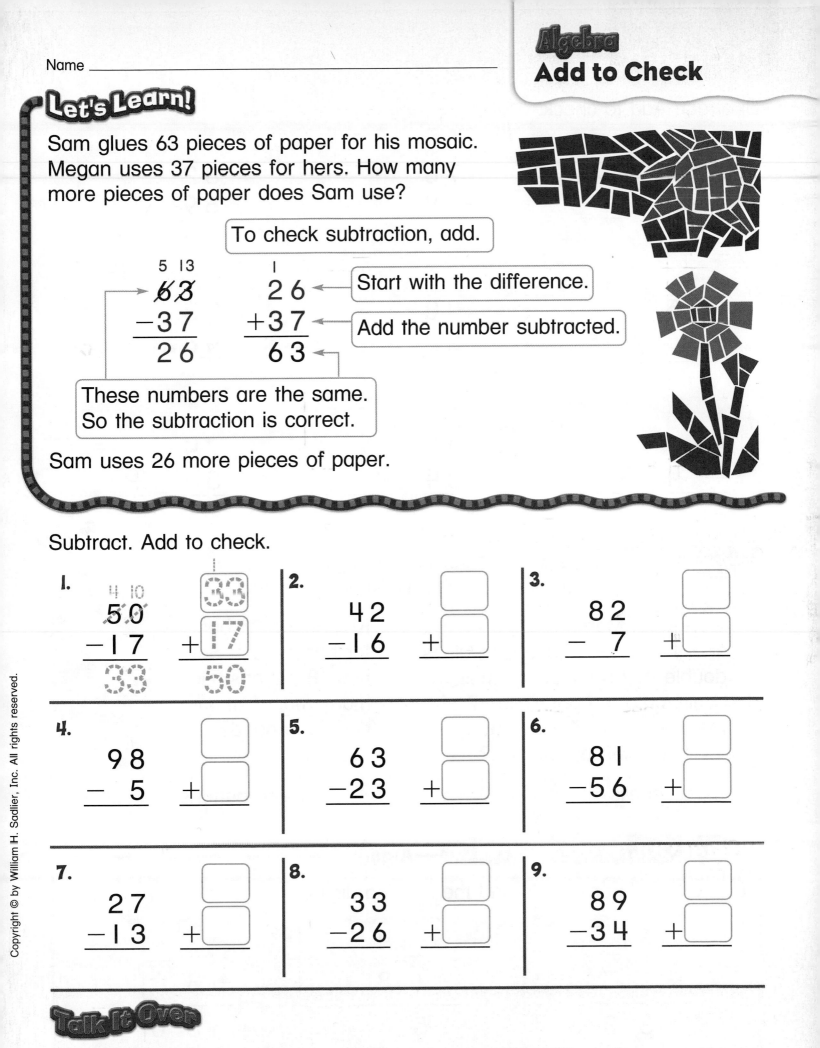

To check subtraction, add.

$$\begin{array}{r} \overset{5}{\cancel{6}}\overset{13}{\cancel{3}} \\ -37 \\ \hline 26 \end{array} \qquad \begin{array}{r} \overset{1}{2}6 \\ +37 \\ \hline 63 \end{array}$$

Start with the difference.

Add the number subtracted.

These numbers are the same. So the subtraction is correct.

Sam uses 26 more pieces of paper.

Subtract. Add to check.

1. $\begin{array}{r} \overset{4}{\cancel{5}}\overset{10}{\cancel{0}} \\ -17 \\ \hline 33 \end{array} \qquad \begin{array}{r} \overset{1}{33} \\ +17 \\ \hline 50 \end{array}$

2. $\begin{array}{r} 42 \\ -16 \\ \hline \end{array} \qquad \begin{array}{r} \square \\ +\square \\ \hline \end{array}$

3. $\begin{array}{r} 82 \\ -\ \ 7 \\ \hline \end{array} \qquad \begin{array}{r} \square \\ +\square \\ \hline \end{array}$

4. $\begin{array}{r} 98 \\ -\ \ 5 \\ \hline \end{array} \qquad \begin{array}{r} \square \\ +\square \\ \hline \end{array}$

5. $\begin{array}{r} 63 \\ -23 \\ \hline \end{array} \qquad \begin{array}{r} \square \\ +\square \\ \hline \end{array}$

6. $\begin{array}{r} 81 \\ -56 \\ \hline \end{array} \qquad \begin{array}{r} \square \\ +\square \\ \hline \end{array}$

7. $\begin{array}{r} 27 \\ -13 \\ \hline \end{array} \qquad \begin{array}{r} \square \\ +\square \\ \hline \end{array}$

8. $\begin{array}{r} 33 \\ -26 \\ \hline \end{array} \qquad \begin{array}{r} \square \\ +\square \\ \hline \end{array}$

9. $\begin{array}{r} 89 \\ -34 \\ \hline \end{array} \qquad \begin{array}{r} \square \\ +\square \\ \hline \end{array}$

10. What should you do if your answer does not check?

Copyright © by William H. Sadlier, Inc. All rights reserved.

Practice

Subtract. Add to check.

11.

$$\begin{array}{r} \overset{5}{\cancel{6}}\overset{14}{\cancel{4}} \\ -27 \\ \hline 37 \end{array} \qquad \begin{array}{r} 37 \\ +27 \\ \hline 64 \end{array}$$

12.

$$\begin{array}{r} 76 \\ -\ \ 8 \\ \hline \end{array} \qquad \begin{array}{r} \square \\ +\square \\ \hline \end{array}$$

13.

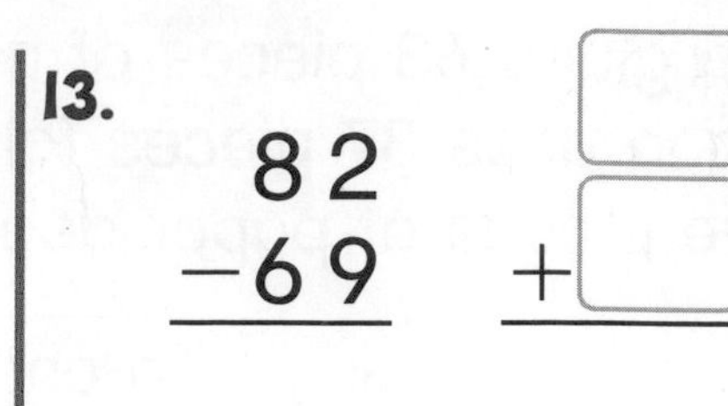

$$\begin{array}{r} 82 \\ -69 \\ \hline \end{array} \qquad \begin{array}{r} \square \\ +\square \\ \hline \end{array}$$

14.

$$\begin{array}{r} 55 \\ -26 \\ \hline \end{array} \qquad \begin{array}{r} \square \\ +\square \\ \hline \end{array}$$

15.

$$\begin{array}{r} 40 \\ -22 \\ \hline \end{array} \qquad \begin{array}{r} \square \\ +\square \\ \hline \end{array}$$

16.

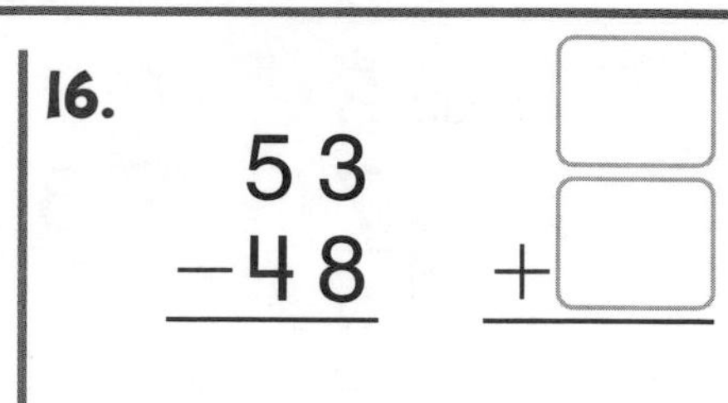

$$\begin{array}{r} 53 \\ -48 \\ \hline \end{array} \qquad \begin{array}{r} \square \\ +\square \\ \hline \end{array}$$

17.

$$\begin{array}{r} 61 \\ -\ \ 4 \\ \hline \end{array} \qquad \begin{array}{r} \square \\ +\square \\ \hline \end{array}$$

18.

$$\begin{array}{r} 93 \\ -34 \\ \hline \end{array} \qquad \begin{array}{r} \square \\ +\square \\ \hline \end{array}$$

19.

$$\begin{array}{r} 74 \\ -36 \\ \hline \end{array} \qquad \begin{array}{r} \square \\ +\square \\ \hline \end{array}$$

Solve. Use a problem-solving strategy.
Show your work on a separate sheet of paper.

20. Multistep Marco glues 14 big shells onto a box. He also glues double that number of small shells onto the box. Then 7 of the shells fall off. How many shells are left on the box?

_____ shells

21. Kim needs 25 buttons for her project. She has 18 buttons. How many more buttons does she need?

_____ more buttons

CALCULATOR ACTIVITY — Algebra

Use a calculator to help find the missing digits.

22.

$$\begin{array}{r} 8\square \\ -\square 7 \\ \hline 38 \end{array}$$

23.

$$\begin{array}{r} \square 4 \\ -18 \\ \hline 5\square \end{array}$$

24.

$$\begin{array}{r} \square 6 \\ -3\square \\ \hline 30 \end{array}$$

Math Alive at Home Ask your child to subtract 71 − 38 and then to check the answer by adding. (33)

Name ______________________________

Subtraction Practice

Let's Learn!

When you subtract, think carefully about when to regroup.

There are enough ones to subtract.
36
−12
24

There are not enough ones. I need to regroup.
2 10
30
−11
19

Subtract. Regroup where needed.

1.	2.	3.	4.	5.
36 − 24 = 12	50 − 35	17 − 3	63 − 37	90 − 10
6.	**7.**	**8.**	**9.**	**10.**
94 − 36	30 − 6	69 − 59	87 − 11	86 − 40
11.	**12.**	**13.**	**14.**	**15.**
49 − 23	63 − 18	57 − 40	71 − 13	90 − 67

Write About It

16. Do you always have to regroup if the number in all has a zero in the ones place? Explain.

Copyright © by William H. Sadlier, Inc. All rights reserved.

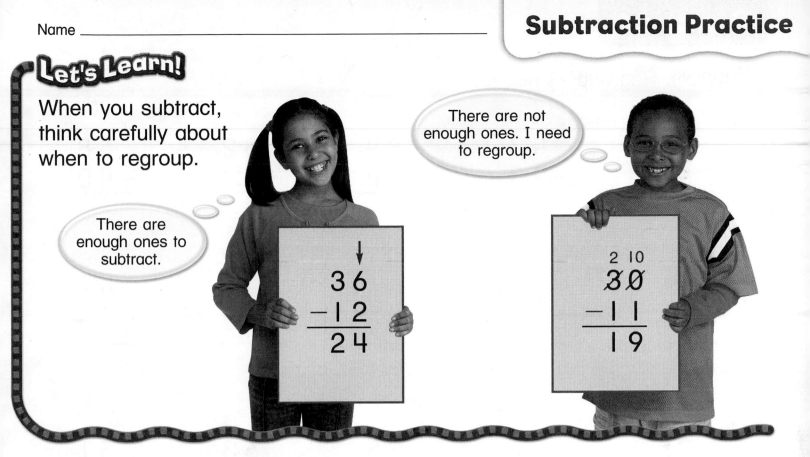

Practice

Subtract. Regroup as needed.

17. $\begin{array}{r} \overset{7}{\cancel{8}}\overset{12}{\cancel{2}} \\ -53 \\ \hline 29 \end{array}$	**18.** $\begin{array}{r} 43 \\ -28 \\ \hline \end{array}$	**19.** $\begin{array}{r} 84 \\ -76 \\ \hline \end{array}$	**20.** $\begin{array}{r} 32 \\ -17 \\ \hline \end{array}$	**21.** $\begin{array}{r} 68 \\ -40 \\ \hline \end{array}$
22. $\begin{array}{r} 87 \\ -26 \\ \hline \end{array}$	**23.** $\begin{array}{r} 91 \\ -48 \\ \hline \end{array}$	**24.** $\begin{array}{r} 30 \\ -19 \\ \hline \end{array}$	**25.** $\begin{array}{r} 78 \\ -47 \\ \hline \end{array}$	**26.** $\begin{array}{r} 45 \\ -\ 2 \\ \hline \end{array}$
27. $\begin{array}{r} 96 \\ -17 \\ \hline \end{array}$	**28.** $\begin{array}{r} 77 \\ -20 \\ \hline \end{array}$	**29.** $\begin{array}{r} 85 \\ -65 \\ \hline \end{array}$	**30.** $\begin{array}{r} 63 \\ -16 \\ \hline \end{array}$	**31.** $\begin{array}{r} 51 \\ -49 \\ \hline \end{array}$

Solve. Use a problem-solving strategy.
Show your work on a separate sheet of paper.

32. Cindy and Dave each had 63 pipe cleaners when they started their projects. Cindy has 18 left and Dave has 8 left. How many pipe cleaners did each of them use?

Cindy _____ Dave _____

33. **Multistep** Ed and Pam start with 90 beads each. After they string the beads, Ed has 43 beads and Pam has 52 beads. Altogether how many beads were strung?

_____ beads

CHALLENGE

Write a story problem for each subtraction in your Math Journal.

34. 49 − 24

35. 72 − 38

Math Alive at Home Ask your child to subtract 52 − 47 and to explain how he/she found the difference. (5)

Name ______________________________

Algebra

Chain Operations

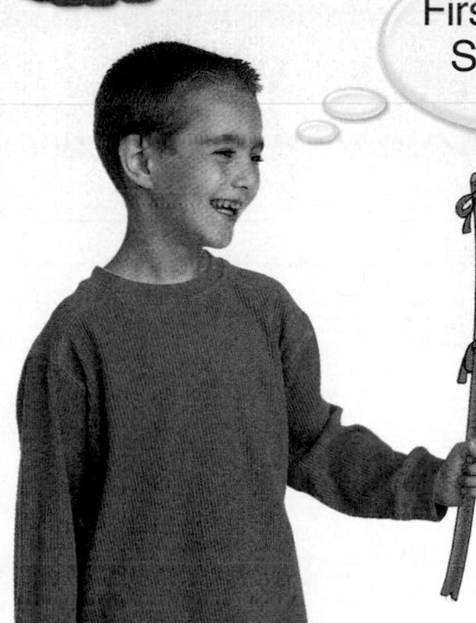

First count on.
Start at 49.
50, 51

Work from left to right.
Add or subtract.

$49 + 2 - 20$

$51 - 20 = 31$

Then count back by 10s.
41, 31

Add or subtract from left to right.

1. $68 + 10 - 3 = ?$

   $78 - 3 = 75$

2. $35 - 4 + 10 = ?$

   $31 + 10 =$ ____

3. $25 - 2 + 30 = ?$

   ____

4. $73 + 3 - 20 = ?$

   ____

5. $49 + 1 + 20 = ?$

   ____

6. $50 + 10 - 4 = ?$

   ____

7. $92 - 30 + 3 = ?$

   ____

8. $32 + 40 - 3 = ?$

   ____

9. $40 - 1 - 30 = ?$

   ____

10. $18 + 2 - 10 = ?$

   ____

11. Explain how you would solve $70 - 3 + 10$.

Copyright © by William H. Sadlier, Inc. All rights reserved.

Practice

Add or subtract from left to right.

12. 54 + 20 − 3 = ?
74 − 3 = 71
______

13. 49 − 2 − 30 = ?
______

14. 65 − 30 + 5 = ?
______

15. 20 + 5 − 25 = ?
______

16. 20 + 48 − 4 = ?
______

17. 69 + 2 + 10 = ?
______

Solve. Use a problem-solving strategy.
Show your work on a separate sheet of paper.

18. **Multistep** Kim has 48 beads. She uses a dozen to make a necklace for a friend. Then she finds 7 more beads. How many beads does she have now?

_____ beads

19. **Multistep** Peter has 40 markers. His dad buys him 28 more. He gives 8 markers to his brother. How many markers does Peter have now?

_____ markers

MENTAL MATH

Find ▲.

20. 50 + 30 − ▲ = 77
▲ = _____

21. 80 − 20 + ▲ = 65
▲ = _____

22. 90 + 3 − ▲ = 43
▲ = _____

23. 72 − 2 − ▲ = 30
▲ = _____

24. 65 + 2 − ▲ = 37
▲ = _____

25. 44 − 3 + ▲ = 51
▲ = _____

Math Alive at Home Ask your child to solve 53 + 20 − 4. (69)

Name ______________________

Check Your Progress
Lessons 7–11

TEST PREPARATION

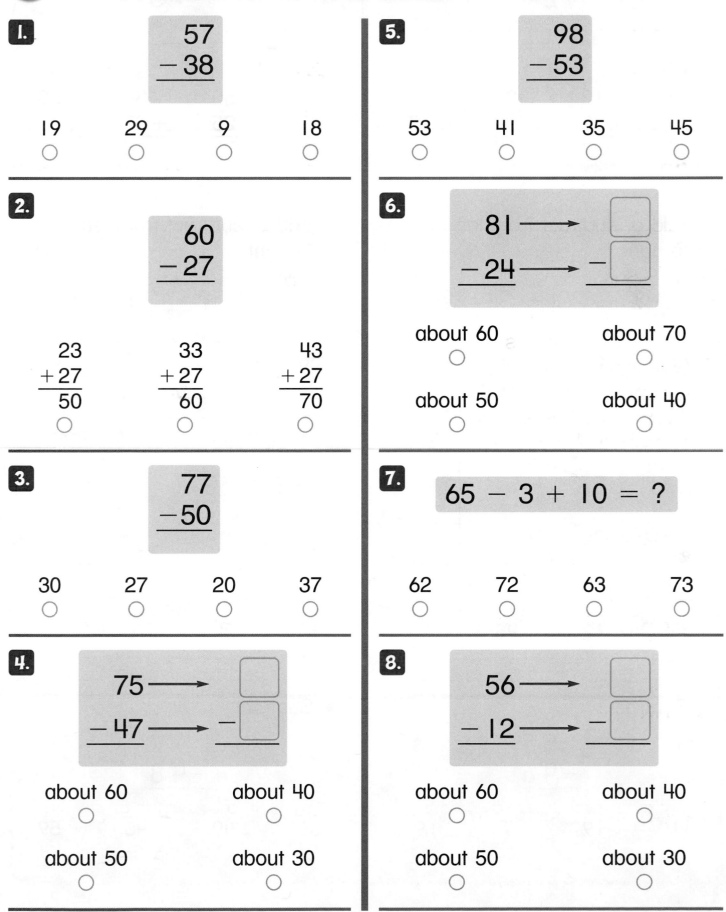

Listen to your teacher read the directions.
Fill in the circle under the correct answer.

1. 57 − 38

19 ○ 29 ○ 9 ○ 18 ○

2. 60 − 27

23 + 27 = 50 ○ 33 + 27 = 60 ○ 43 + 27 = 70 ○

3. 77 − 50

30 ○ 27 ○ 20 ○ 37 ○

4. 75 → □, − 47 → − □

about 60 ○ about 40 ○

about 50 ○ about 30 ○

5. 98 − 53

53 ○ 41 ○ 35 ○ 45 ○

6.

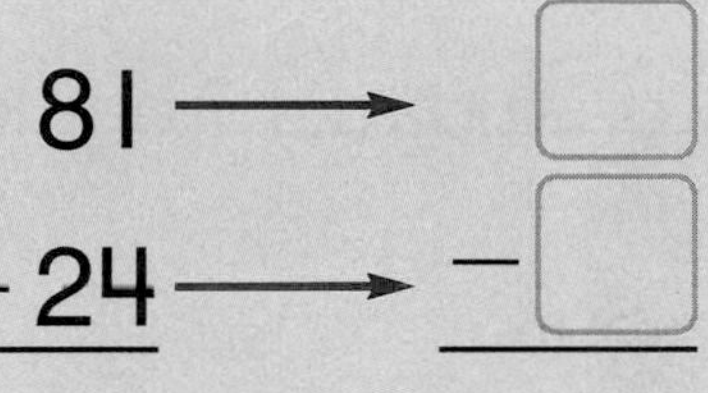

81 → □, − 24 → − □

about 60 ○ about 70 ○

about 50 ○ about 40 ○

7. 65 − 3 + 10 = ?

62 ○ 72 ○ 63 ○ 73 ○

8. 56 → □, − 12 → − □

about 60 ○ about 40 ○

about 50 ○ about 30 ○

Copyright © by William H. Sadlier, Inc. All rights reserved.

Fill in the circle under the correct answer.

9. Choose which you would use to check your subtraction.

$$\begin{array}{r} 24 \\ -\ 7 \\ \hline \end{array}$$

$\begin{array}{r} 14 \\ +10 \\ \hline 24 \end{array}$	$\begin{array}{r} 12 \\ +12 \\ \hline 24 \end{array}$	$\begin{array}{r} 20 \\ +\ 4 \\ \hline 24 \end{array}$	$\begin{array}{r} 17 \\ +\ 7 \\ \hline 24 \end{array}$
○	○	○	○

10. Add or subtract from left to right.

48 + 20 − 3 = ?

71	65	55	61
○	○	○	○

11. Rewrite the numbers. Subtract.

93 − 58

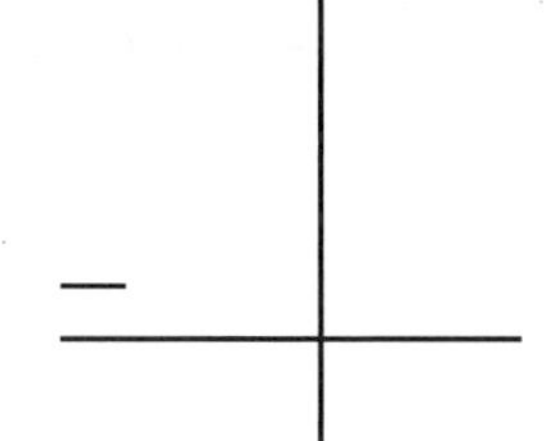

35	12	45	23
○	○	○	○

12. Subtract.

$$\begin{array}{r} 55 \\ -46 \\ \hline \end{array}$$

11	19	7	9
○	○	○	○

13. Choose which you would use to check your subtraction.

$$\begin{array}{r} 75 \\ -48 \\ \hline \end{array}$$

$\begin{array}{r} 27 \\ +48 \\ \hline 75 \end{array}$	$\begin{array}{r} 50 \\ +25 \\ \hline 75 \end{array}$	$\begin{array}{r} 38 \\ +37 \\ \hline 75 \end{array}$	$\begin{array}{r} 30 \\ +45 \\ \hline 75 \end{array}$
○	○	○	○

14. Add or subtract from left to right.

81 + 4 − 30 = ?

56	66	55	65
○	○	○	○

15. Rewrite the numbers. Subtract.

85 − 63

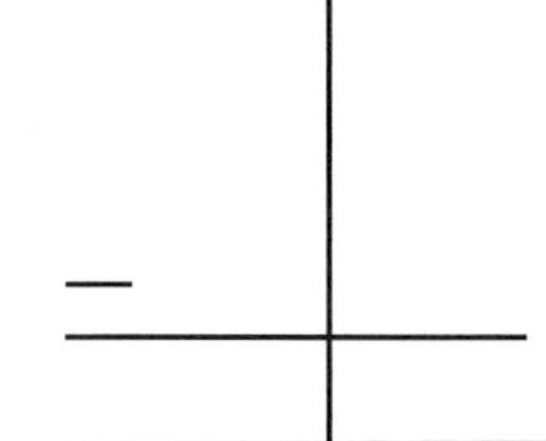

12	22	28	32
○	○	○	○

16. Subtract.

$$\begin{array}{r} 97 \\ -48 \\ \hline \end{array}$$

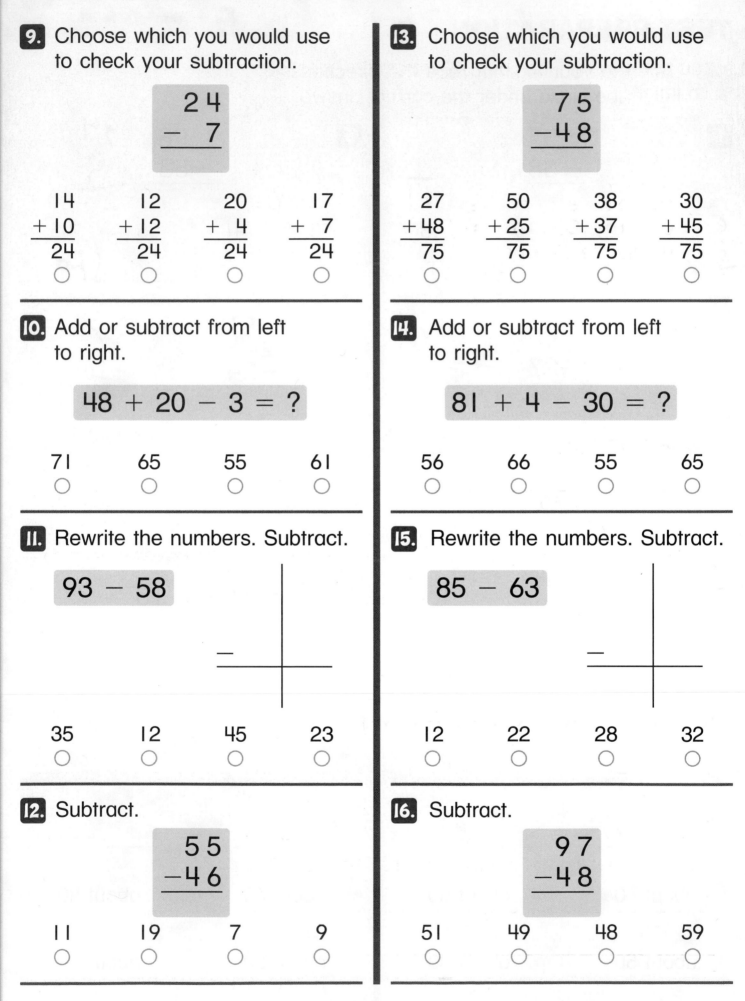

51	49	48	59
○	○	○	○

Name ______________________________

Ask a Question

- You can ask an addition or subtraction question to complete a math problem.

Listen
Robin and Derek make scrapbooks. Robin uses 34 sheets of paper. Derek uses 41 sheets of paper.
Robin's Scrapbook
READ
READING

1. Write an addition question to complete the problem above.

____

____

2. Add. Write a sentence that answers your question.

____

____

3. Write a subtraction question to complete the problem.

____

____

4. Subtract. Write a sentence that answers your question.

____

____

Copyright © by William H. Sadlier, Inc. All rights reserved.

Practice

Ask a Question

Listen
Karen has a basket she wants to fill with paper flowers. She has 29 paper tulips and 15 paper roses for her basket.

5. Write an addition question to complete the problem above.

____

____

6. Add. Write a sentence that answers your question.

____

____

7. Write a subtraction question to complete the problem.

____

____

8. Subtract. Write a sentence that answers your question.

____

____

Math Alive at Home Today your child asked questions to form and work through math problems.

Name ______________________________

Choose the Method

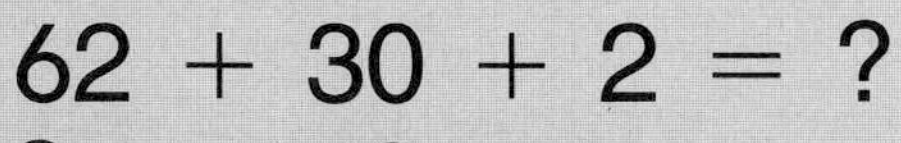

You can add or subtract using mental math or paper and pencil.

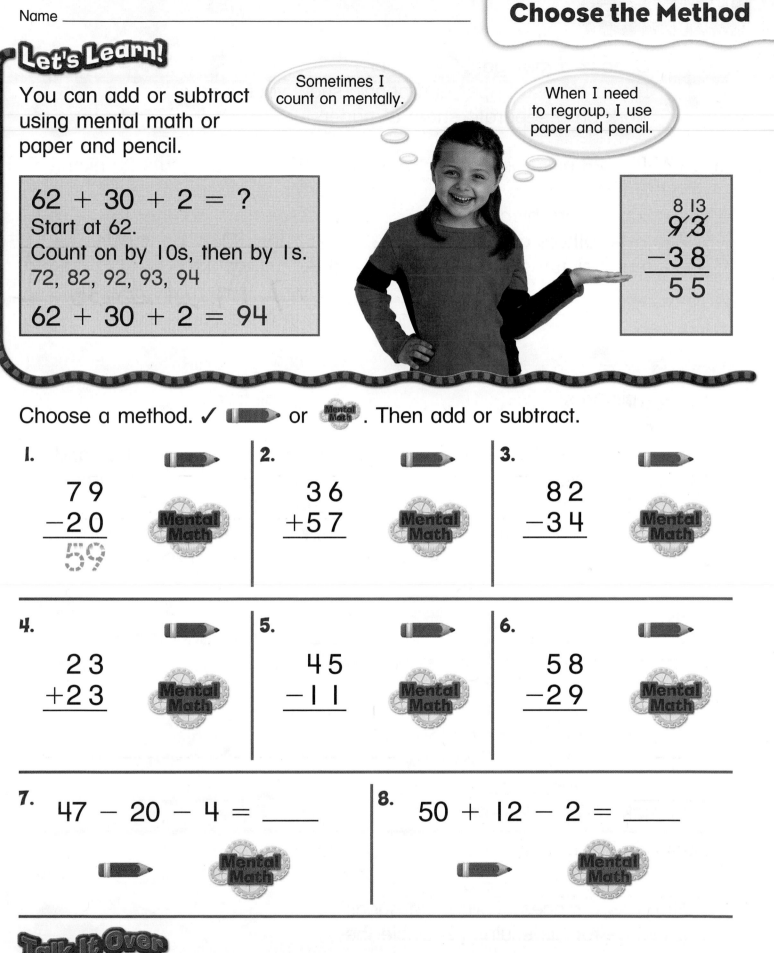

$62 + 30 + 2 = ?$
Start at 62.
Count on by 10s, then by 1s.
72, 82, 92, 93, 94

$62 + 30 + 2 = 94$

$$\begin{array}{r} \overset{8}{\cancel{9}}\overset{13}{\cancel{3}} \\ -38 \\ \hline 55 \end{array}$$

Choose a method. ✓  or Mental Math. Then add or subtract.

1. $\begin{array}{r} 79 \\ -20 \\ \hline 59 \end{array}$ 

2. $\begin{array}{r} 36 \\ +57 \\ \hline \end{array}$ 

3. $\begin{array}{r} 82 \\ -34 \\ \hline \end{array}$ 

4.  $\begin{array}{r} 23 \\ +23 \\ \hline \end{array}$ 

5. $\begin{array}{r} 45 \\ -11 \\ \hline \end{array}$ 

6. 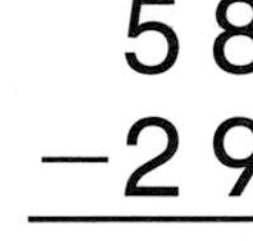 $\begin{array}{r} 58 \\ -29 \\ \hline \end{array}$ 

7. $47 - 20 - 4 =$ ____

8. $50 + 12 - 2 =$ ____

9. Which method would you use to subtract $83 - 20$? Explain why you chose that method.

Copyright © by William H. Sadlier, Inc. All rights reserved.

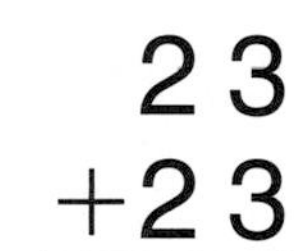

Practice

Choose a method. ✓ paper and pencil or Mental Math.
If you choose paper and pencil, show your work on a separate sheet of paper.

10. Julie cuts 28 pictures from a magazine to make a collage. Ten pictures are black-and-white. The others are in color. How many pictures are in color?

_____ pictures

11. Multistep Daryl cuts 24 pictures from one magazine and 17 pictures from another to use in a collage. Then he decides he does not want to use 9 of the pictures. How many does he use in his collage?

_____ pictures

12. Multistep Cheryl wants to use 35 different colors to paint a mural. She finds 9 colors in one box and 13 in another. How many more colors does she need?

_____ more colors

13. Raz cuts 18 blue squares and double that number of purple squares to make a border for a picture. How many purple squares does Raz cut?

_____ purple squares

CRITICAL THINKING

14. Each sculpture uses 10 pieces of wire. Nina has 46 pieces of wire. How many more does she need to make five sculptures?

_____ more pieces

15. Ron has 8 pieces of wire. He needs 25 wires for his sculpture. Circle the smallest package he should buy.

Math Alive at Home Ask your child to explain why she/he used the method chosen for problems 10–13 on this page.

Name ____________________

Mixed Practice

Let's Learn!

Look for the + or − sign.
Decide if you need to regroup.
Then add or subtract.

$$\begin{array}{r} 23 \\ +45 \\ \hline 68 \end{array} \qquad \begin{array}{r} 86 \\ -34 \\ \hline 52 \end{array} \qquad \begin{array}{r} ^{1} \\ 29 \\ +61 \\ \hline 90 \end{array} \qquad \begin{array}{r} ^{6\ 13} \\ \not{7}\not{3} \\ -56 \\ \hline 17 \end{array}$$

Find the sum.

1. $\begin{array}{r} 21 \\ +32 \\ \hline 53 \end{array}$	2. $\begin{array}{r} 18 \\ +48 \\ \hline 66 \end{array}$	3. $\begin{array}{r} 67 \\ +24 \\ \hline \end{array}$	4. $\begin{array}{r} 80 \\ +10 \\ \hline \end{array}$	5. $\begin{array}{r} 34 \\ +14 \\ \hline \end{array}$
6. $\begin{array}{r} 31 \\ +39 \\ \hline \end{array}$	7. $\begin{array}{r} 55 \\ +30 \\ \hline \end{array}$	8. $\begin{array}{r} 93 \\ +\ 6 \\ \hline \end{array}$	9. $\begin{array}{r} 27 \\ +27 \\ \hline \end{array}$	10. $\begin{array}{r} 27 \\ +53 \\ \hline \end{array}$

Find the difference.

11. $\begin{array}{r} ^{8\ 15} \\ \not{9}\not{5} \\ -27 \\ \hline 68 \end{array}$	12. $\begin{array}{r} 48 \\ -17 \\ \hline 31 \end{array}$	13. $\begin{array}{r} 20 \\ -\ 9 \\ \hline \end{array}$	14. $\begin{array}{r} 62 \\ -24 \\ \hline \end{array}$	15. $\begin{array}{r} 79 \\ -22 \\ \hline \end{array}$
16. $\begin{array}{r} 95 \\ -48 \\ \hline \end{array}$	17. $\begin{array}{r} 50 \\ -12 \\ \hline \end{array}$	18. $\begin{array}{r} 58 \\ -15 \\ \hline \end{array}$	19. $\begin{array}{r} 80 \\ -74 \\ \hline \end{array}$	20. $\begin{array}{r} 98 \\ -60 \\ \hline \end{array}$

Talk It Over

21. How is regrouping in addition the same as regrouping in subtraction? How is it different?

Copyright © by William H. Sadlier, Inc. All rights reserved.

Practice

Add or subtract. Regroup where needed.

22. $\begin{array}{r} 13 \\ +33 \\ \hline 46 \end{array}$	23. $\begin{array}{r} 78 \\ -18 \\ \hline \end{array}$	24. $\begin{array}{r} 28 \\ +\ 3 \\ \hline \end{array}$	25. $\begin{array}{r} 20 \\ +30 \\ \hline \end{array}$	26. $\begin{array}{r} 99 \\ -51 \\ \hline \end{array}$
27. $\begin{array}{r} 94 \\ -35 \\ \hline \end{array}$	28. $\begin{array}{r} 70 \\ +23 \\ \hline \end{array}$	29. $\begin{array}{r} 87 \\ -30 \\ \hline \end{array}$	30. $\begin{array}{r} 63 \\ +36 \\ \hline \end{array}$	31. $\begin{array}{r} 45 \\ +15 \\ \hline \end{array}$
32. $\begin{array}{r} 63 \\ -26 \\ \hline \end{array}$	33. $\begin{array}{r} 97 \\ -47 \\ \hline \end{array}$	34. $\begin{array}{r} 36 \\ +\ 6 \\ \hline \end{array}$	35. $\begin{array}{r} 74 \\ -29 \\ \hline \end{array}$	36. $\begin{array}{r} 25 \\ +69 \\ \hline \end{array}$

Solve. Use a problem-solving strategy.
Show your work on a separate sheet of paper.

37. Marie sees a beautiful quilt made with 22 blue stripes, 18 yellow stripes, and 30 yellow flowers. How many stripes are on the quilt?

_____ stripes

38. Multistep Bill sees a quilt made with 36 large circles and a dozen small circles. There are also 22 blue rectangles on the quilt. How many more circles than rectangles are on the quilt?

_____ more circles

DO YOU REMEMBER?

Use the Math Words in the box to fill in the blanks.

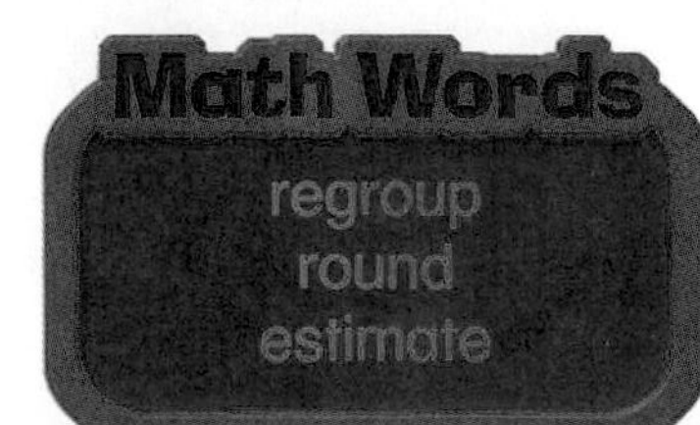

39. To find the nearest ten for a number is to ______________.

40. To find about how many is to ______________.

41. To trade 10 ones for 1 ten is to ______________.

Math Alive at Home Ask your child to add 57 + 25 and to subtract 80 − 31. (82, 49)

Name ______________________________

Estimate or Exact Answer

Cal's and Lea's friends decide to put their art supplies together. About how many crayons do Cal and Lea's friends have altogether?

To find about how many, estimate.

$$\begin{array}{r} 44 \\ +35 \\ \hline \end{array} \longrightarrow \begin{array}{r} 40 \\ +40 \\ \hline \text{about } 80 \end{array}$$

Cal and Lea's friends have about 80 crayons altogether.

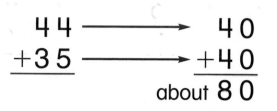

Art Supplies			
Friends	Scissors	Rulers	Crayons
Cal's friends	12	28	44
Lea's friends	23	17	35

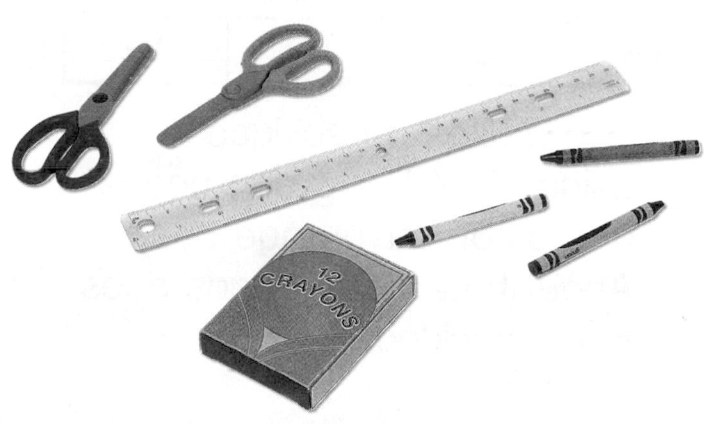

Use the table to find each answer.

1. How many more scissors do Lea's friends have than Cal's?

$$\begin{array}{r} 23 \\ -12 \\ \hline 11 \end{array}$$

11 more scissors

2. About how many rulers do both groups of friends have in all?

about ______ rulers

3. How many art supplies in all do Lea's friends have?

______ art supplies

4. Lea's friends get 14 more crayons. How many crayons do Lea's friends have then?

______ crayons

Talk It Over

5. How do you know when to estimate an answer instead of finding an exact answer?

Practice

Use the table to solve each problem.

Beads We Collected			
Name			
Lynn	48	21	56
Eve	32	38	29
Owen	65	43	19

6. Eve makes a necklace using all of her green beads and all of her orange beads. About how many beads does Eve's necklace have?

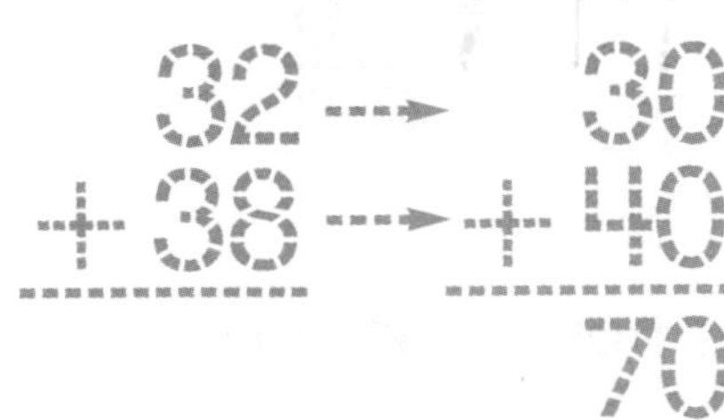

about 70 beads

7. Owen gives 5 of his purple beads to Eve. How many purple beads does Owen have left?

_____ purple beads

8. Lynn doubles her number of orange beads. About how many orange beads does Lynn have then?

about _____ orange beads

CHALLENGE 

Use each rule and starting numbers to make a pattern.

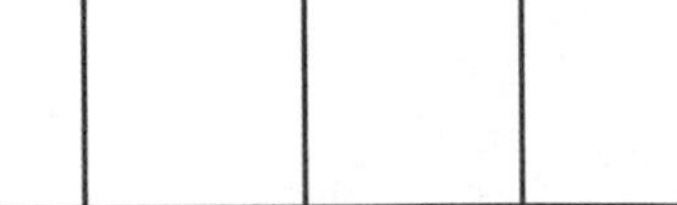

9. Rule: +1, −10

64	65	55				

10. Rule: −2, +10

6	4	14				

11. Rule: −10, +5

90	80	85				

Math Alive at Home Ask your child to tell you how he/she found the answer to exercises 6 and 7.

Name ______________________

Chapter 5 Test

1. Subtract mentally.
Subtract 4 from:

58 48 38 28

____ ____ ____ ____

2. Estimate the difference.

$$\begin{array}{r} 94 \\ -68 \\ \hline \end{array} \longrightarrow \begin{array}{r} \square \\ -\square \\ \hline \end{array}$$

about ____

3. Write the number needed to make 16.

7 + 4 + ____ = 16

4. Add or subtract from left to right.

78 − 3 + 20 = ____

5. Regroup 1 ten.

7 tens 5 ones =

____ tens ____ ones

6. Find the difference.

$$\begin{array}{r} 99 \\ -36 \\ \hline \end{array}$$

7. Record the regrouping.
Find the difference.

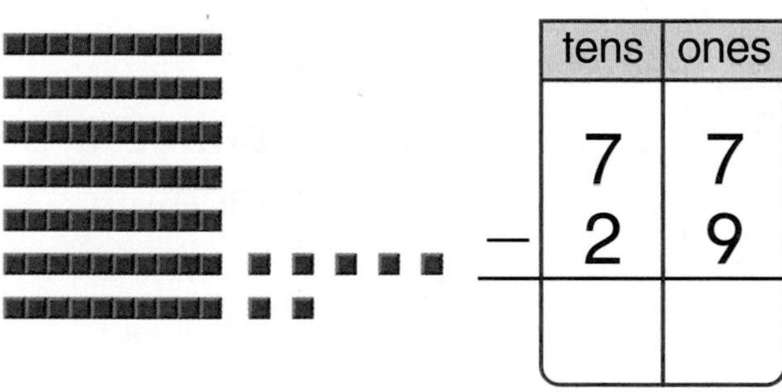

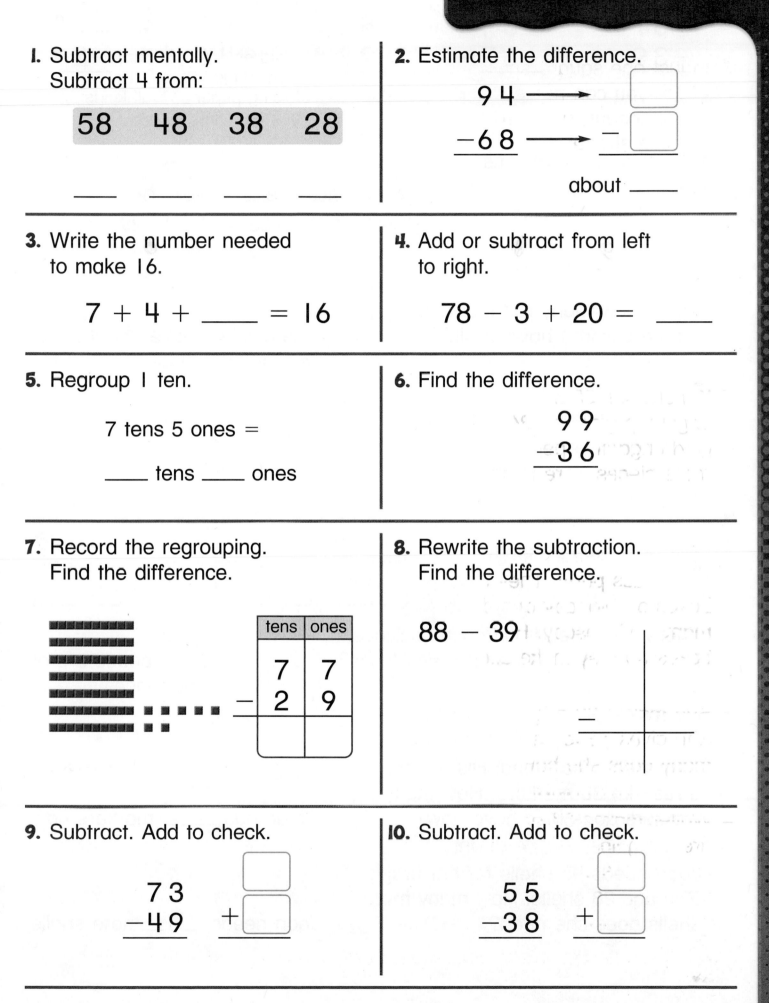

	tens	ones
	7	7
−	2	9

8. Rewrite the subtraction.
Find the difference.

88 − 39

9. Subtract. Add to check.

$$\begin{array}{r} 73 \\ -49 \\ \hline \end{array} \quad \begin{array}{r} \square \\ +\square \\ \hline \end{array}$$

10. Subtract. Add to check.

$$\begin{array}{r} 55 \\ -38 \\ \hline \end{array} \quad \begin{array}{r} \square \\ +\square \\ \hline \end{array}$$

Copyright © by William H. Sadlier, Inc. All rights reserved.

Subtract. Regroup as needed.

11.	12.	13.	14.	15.
$\begin{array}{r} 67 \\ -39 \\ \hline \end{array}$	$\begin{array}{r} 84 \\ -67 \\ \hline \end{array}$	$\begin{array}{r} 55 \\ -28 \\ \hline \end{array}$	$\begin{array}{r} 91 \\ -46 \\ \hline \end{array}$	$\begin{array}{r} 70 \\ -24 \\ \hline \end{array}$

Use the table for problems 16 and 17.

Color Markers				
Name	Red	Blue	Yellow	Green
Jane	17	23	37	29
Sam	34	39	28	42

16. About how many red markers do the children have in all?

The children have about ____ red markers in all.

17. How many more green markers does Sam have than Jane?

Sam has ____ more green markers than Jane.

Solve. Watch for multistep problems.

Necklaces						
Beads						

18. There are 5 beads on each necklace. How many beads are on 6 necklaces?

____ beads are on 6 necklaces.

19. Mac has 27 markers. He gives 7 markers to a friend. His mother gives him 38 markers. How many markers does Mac have now?

Mac has ____ markers now.

20. Joan needs 45 shells for her project. She has 28 shells. How many more shells does she need?

Joan needs ____ more shells.

Math Alive at Home This test is a formal assessment of your child's understanding of the content presented in Chapter 5.

Name ______________________

1. Use one of the numbers in the box.
Estimate the difference for each.

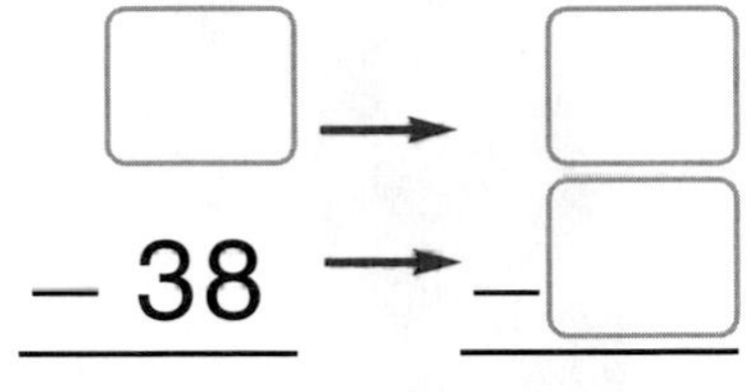

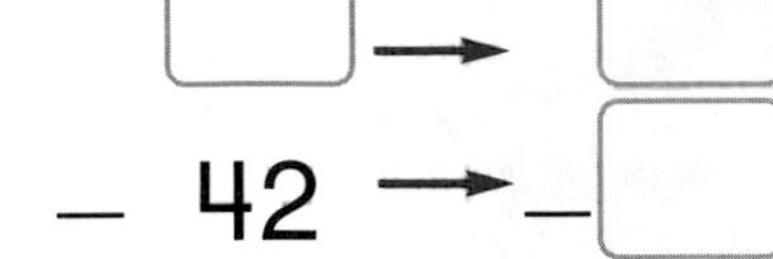

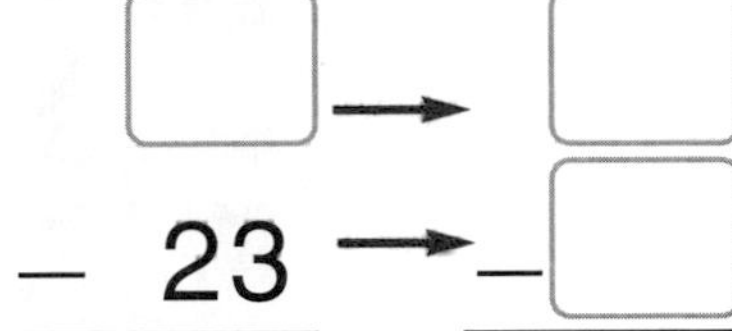

about ____ about ____ about ____

2. Explain how you estimated one of the subtractions above.

____

____

3. Write 3 different ways to make 18.

___ − ___ + ___ = 18

___ − ___ − ___ = 18

___ + ___ − ___ = 18

4. Write 3 different ways to make 24.

___ − ___ + ___ = 24

___ − ___ − ___ = 24

___ + ___ − ___ = 24

5. Choose a number to subtract.

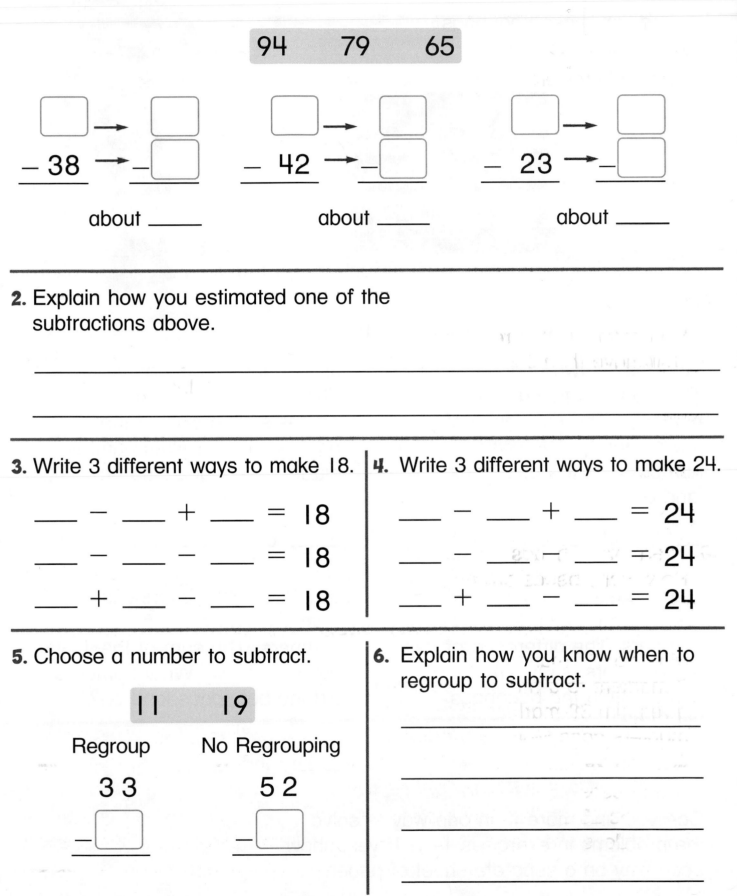

Regroup No Regrouping

33 52

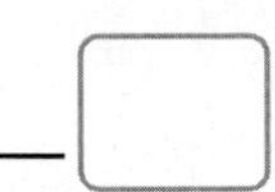

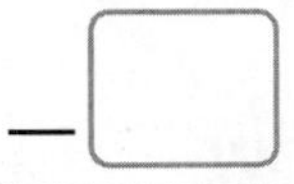

6. Explain how you know when to regroup to subtract.

____

____

____

____

Copyright © by William H. Sadlier, Inc. All rights reserved.

Enrichment

Name ____________________

More Than One Solution

Meg and Jim make beanbags to play a math game.

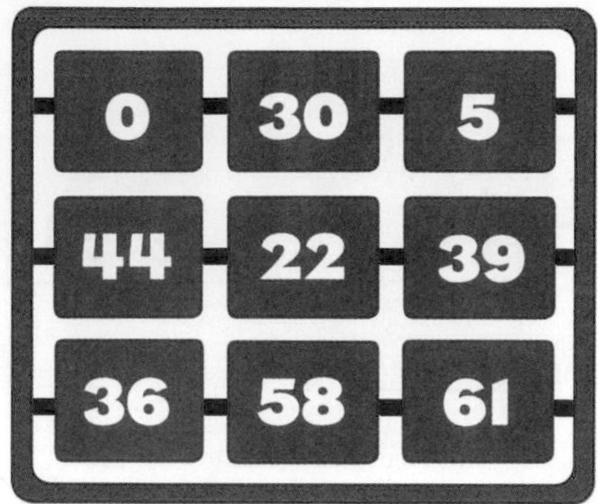

Find the two numbers that make each difference or sum. You may use a calculator to help.

1. Meg tosses two beanbags. They land on two different numbers. The difference of the numbers is 39. What numbers did the beanbags land on?

   _____ and _____

2. Jim tosses two beanbags. They land on two different numbers. The sum of the numbers is 97. What numbers did the beanbags land on?

   _____ and _____

3. Meg tosses two beanbags. They land on two different numbers. The difference of the numbers is 58. What numbers did the beanbags land on?

   _____ and _____

4. Jim tosses two beanbags. They land on two different numbers. The sum of the numbers is 66. What numbers did the beanbags land on?

   _____ and _____

5. Can you find more than one way to solve the problems in exercises 1–4? If yes, show each way on a separate sheet of paper.

The Surprise

We will make something silly.
We will use these supplies.
We will also use subtraction
to make our surprise.

We have 23 pom-poms in different colors.
We need 90 pom-poms all together.

How many more pom-poms do we need?

____ more pom-poms

Copyright © by William H. Sadlier, Inc. All rights reserved.

We have 36 beads.
Twenty-nine are small,
and the rest are large.

How many are large?

___ beads

We have 18 strips of paper.
We use 11.

How many do we have left?

___ strips of paper

Copyright © by William H. Sadlier, Inc. All rights reserved.

Surprise!

Here's what we made
using pom-poms and paper
and beads and some glue.
And don't forget subtraction–
we used that too!

Name ______________________________

TEST PREPARATION

Fill in the circle under the correct answer.

1. Add.

	tens	ones
	4	6
+	3	3

78 ○ 59 ○ 79 ○ 69 ○

2. Add.

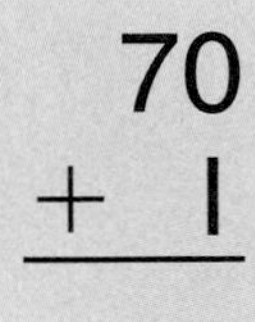

91 ○ 81 ○ 80 ○ 71 ○

3. Estimate the difference.

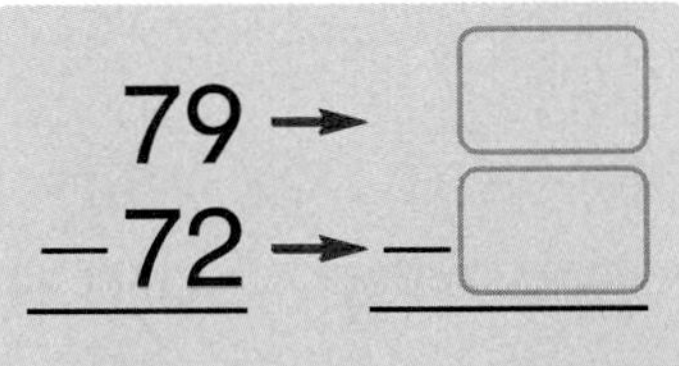

about 40 ○ about 10 ○

about 20 ○ about 30 ○

4. Which number tells how many?

73 ○ 63 ○ 54 ○ 53 ○

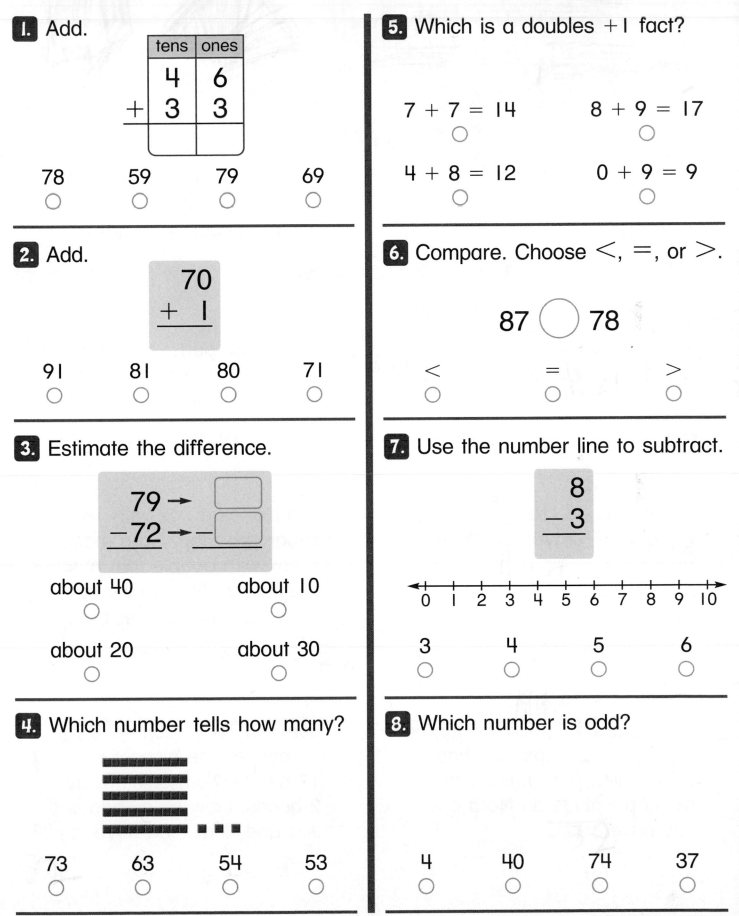

5. Which is a doubles + 1 fact?

7 + 7 = 14 ○ 8 + 9 = 17 ○

4 + 8 = 12 ○ 0 + 9 = 9 ○

6. Compare. Choose <, =, or >.

< ○ = ○ > ○

7. Use the number line to subtract.

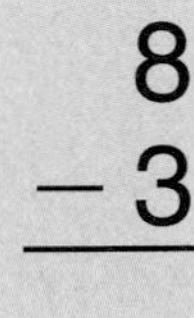

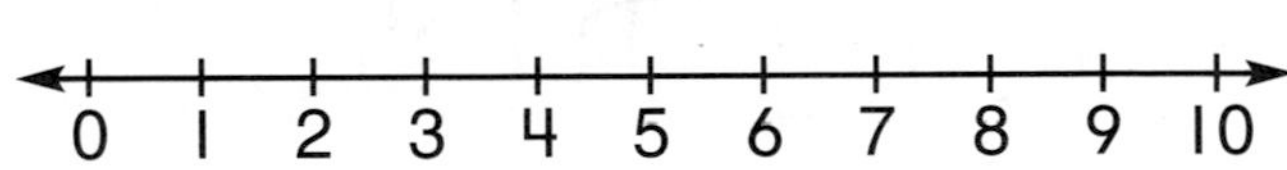

3 ○ 4 ○ 5 ○ 6 ○

8. Which number is odd?

4 ○ 40 ○ 74 ○ 37 ○

Copyright © by William H. Sadlier, Inc. All rights reserved.

Solve. Watch for multistep problems.
Use the graph for problems 9 and 10.

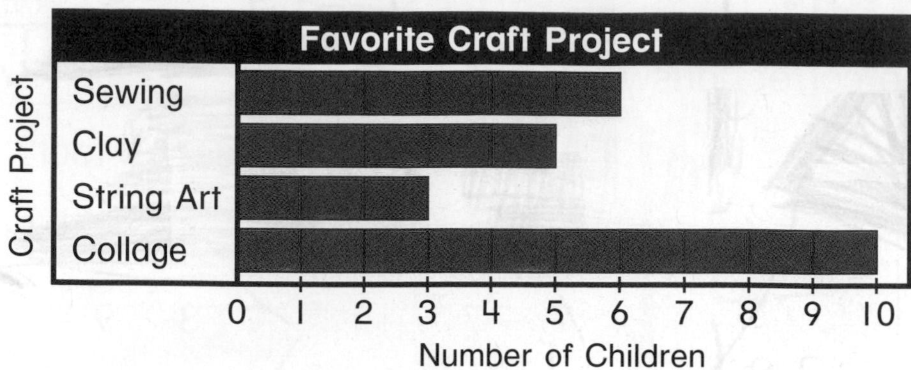

9. Three more children vote for clay. How many children like clay then?

6 ○ 5 ○ 8 ○ 9 ○

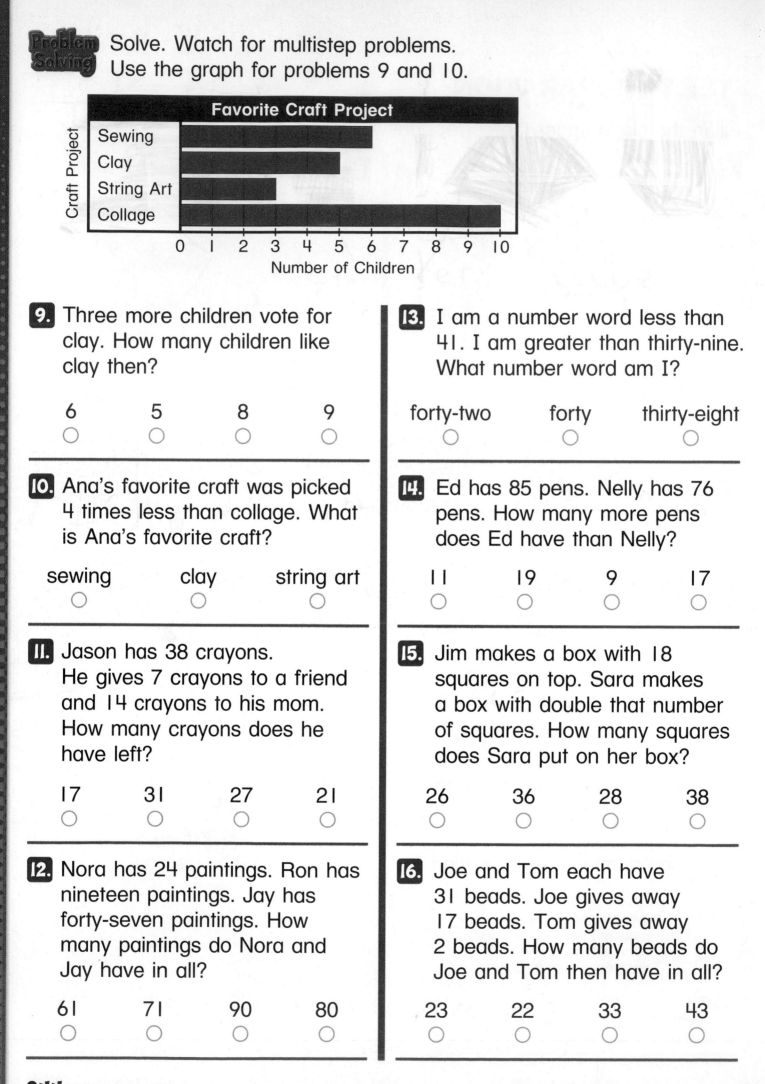

10. Ana's favorite craft was picked 4 times less than collage. What is Ana's favorite craft?

sewing ○ clay ○ string art ○

11. Jason has 38 crayons. He gives 7 crayons to a friend and 14 crayons to his mom. How many crayons does he have left?

17 ○ 31 ○ 27 ○ 21 ○

12. Nora has 24 paintings. Ron has nineteen paintings. Jay has forty-seven paintings. How many paintings do Nora and Jay have in all?

61 ○ 71 ○ 90 ○ 80 ○

13. I am a number word less than 41. I am greater than thirty-nine. What number word am I?

forty-two ○ forty ○ thirty-eight ○

14. Ed has 85 pens. Nelly has 76 pens. How many more pens does Ed have than Nelly?

11 ○ 19 ○ 9 ○ 17 ○

15. Jim makes a box with 18 squares on top. Sara makes a box with double that number of squares. How many squares does Sara put on her box?

26 ○ 36 ○ 28 ○ 38 ○

16. Joe and Tom each have 31 beads. Joe gives away 17 beads. Tom gives away 2 beads. How many beads do Joe and Tom then have in all?

23 ○ 22 ○ 33 ○ 43 ○

Geometry

CHAPTER 6

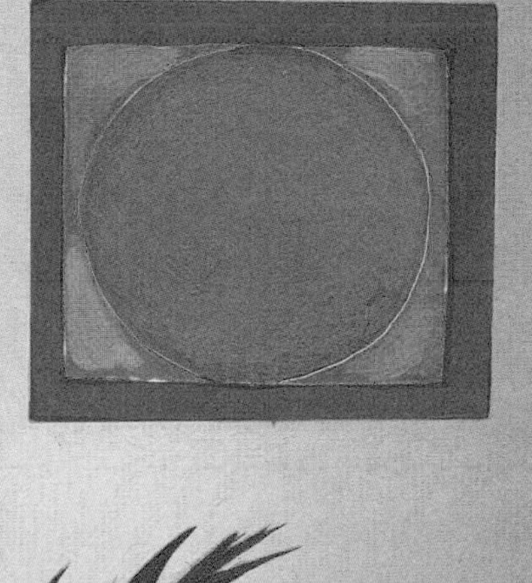

Listen to your teacher read the story.
What shapes do you see in each painting?

Copyright © by William H. Sadlier, Inc. All rights reserved.

Dear Family,

Today our class began Chapter 6. We will learn about geometry. Let's do the activity below together so I can review the skills I will need in order to understand the math in this chapter. Then you can read some of the new vocabulary I will learn in Chapter 6.

Love, ____________________

Spying Shapes

Cut out paper circles, squares, triangles, and rectangles of different sizes and colors. Spread them out on a table. Hold up a circle and ask your child to name it and then to find all the other circles. Repeat this with the squares, triangles, and rectangles.

Chapter 6

Vocabulary also on-line

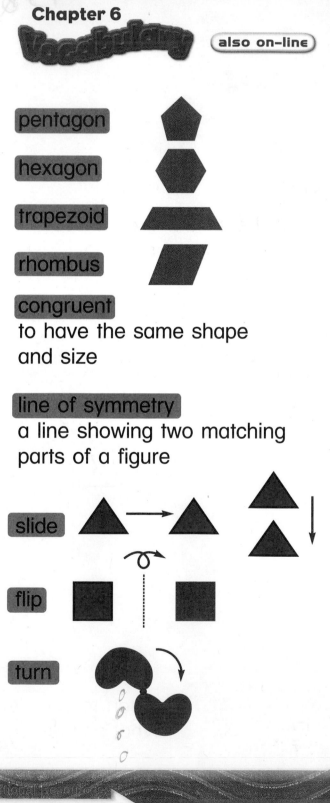

pentagon

hexagon

trapezoid

rhombus

congruent
to have the same shape and size

line of symmetry
a line showing two matching parts of a figure

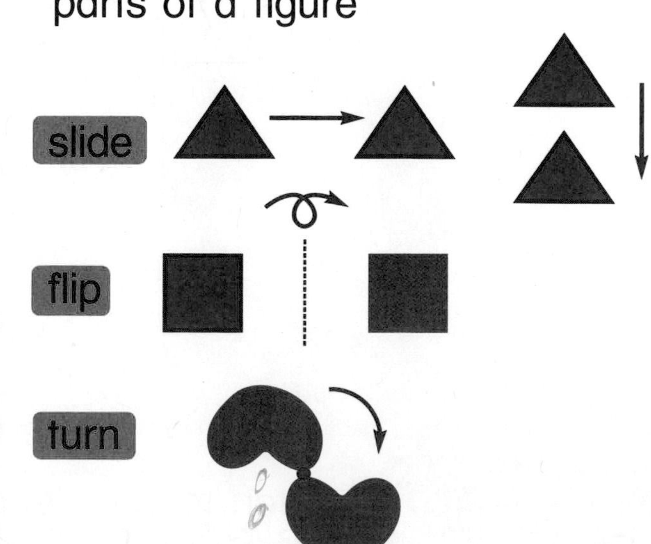

For Additional Resources
VISIT US ON-LINE www.sadlier-oxford.com

Name ______________________________

Algebra

Slides and Flips

HANDS-ON LESSON

Let's Learn!

These figures have 2 sides. Each side is a different color. Here are two ways to move the figures.

A **slide** is the movement of a figure to the right or left or up or down.

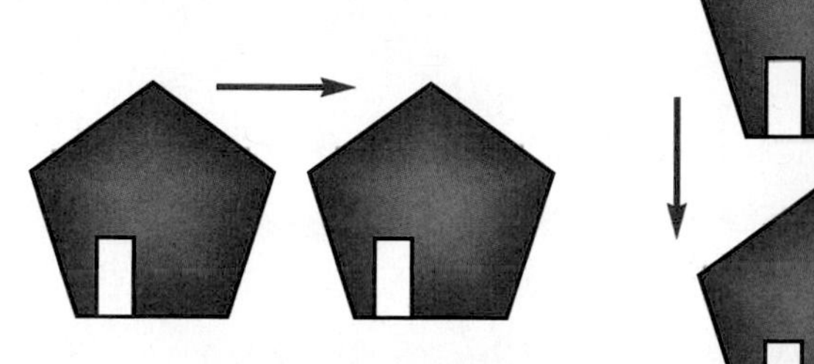

A **flip** is the movement of a figure to its other side.

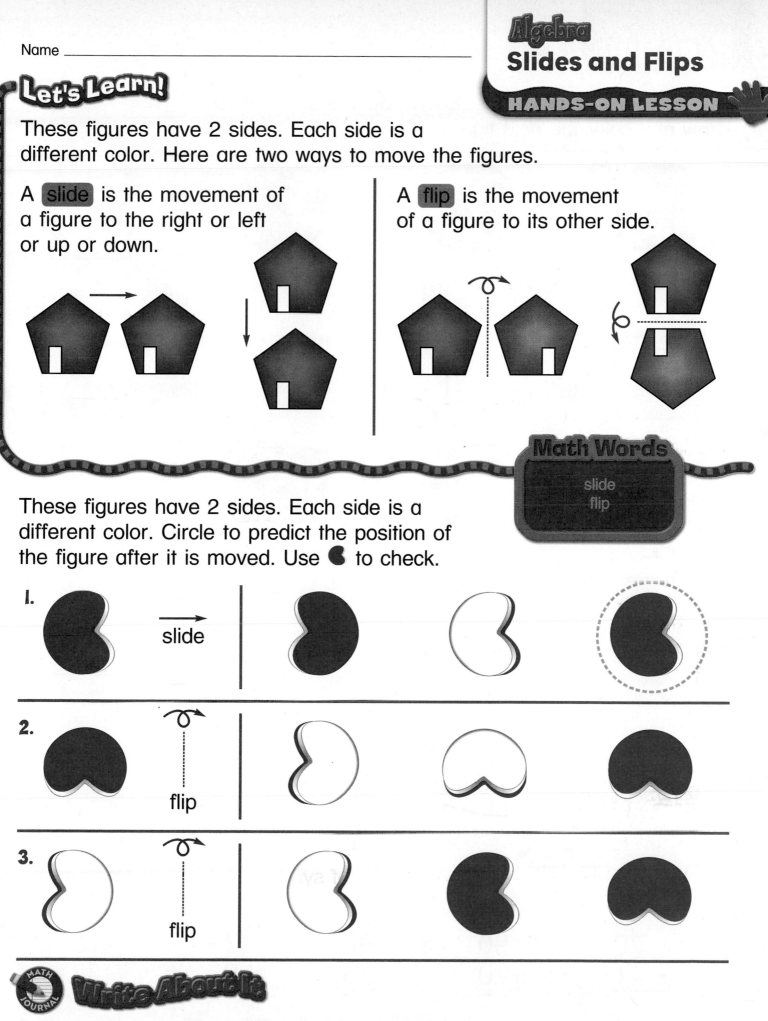

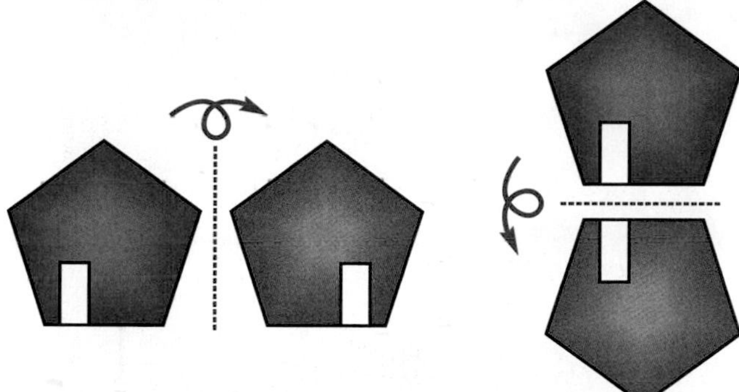

These figures have 2 sides. Each side is a different color. Circle to predict the position of the figure after it is moved. Use a bean to check.

1. 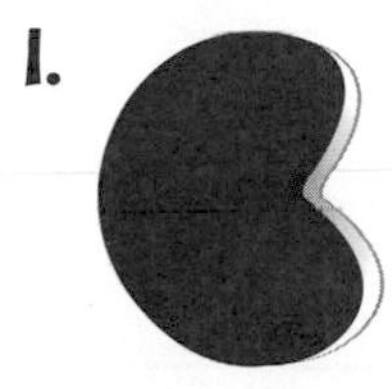 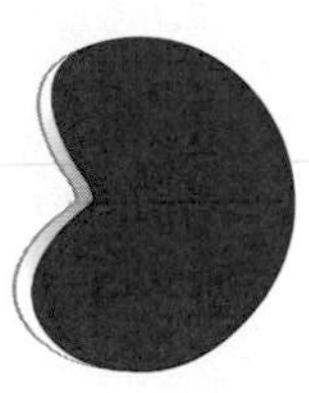

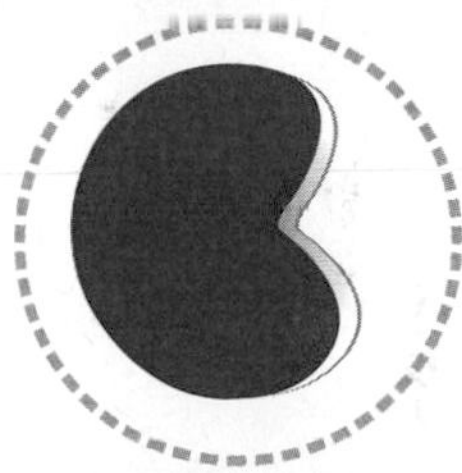

2.  

3. 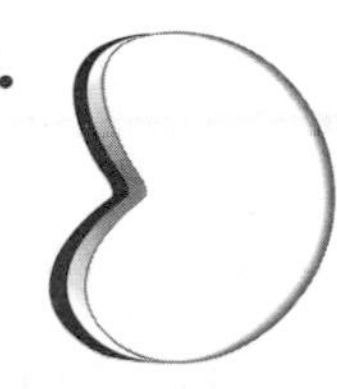 

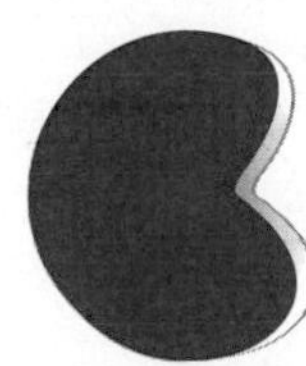 

4. Explain how a flip is different from a slide.

Copyright © by William H. Sadlier, Inc. All rights reserved.

Practice

These figures have 2 sides. Each side is a different color.
Draw and color the next figure.

5.  slide  slide  slide 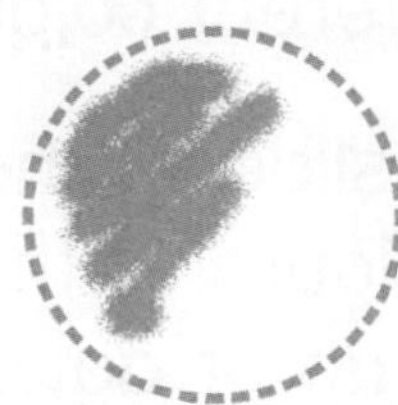 ______

6.  flip  flip  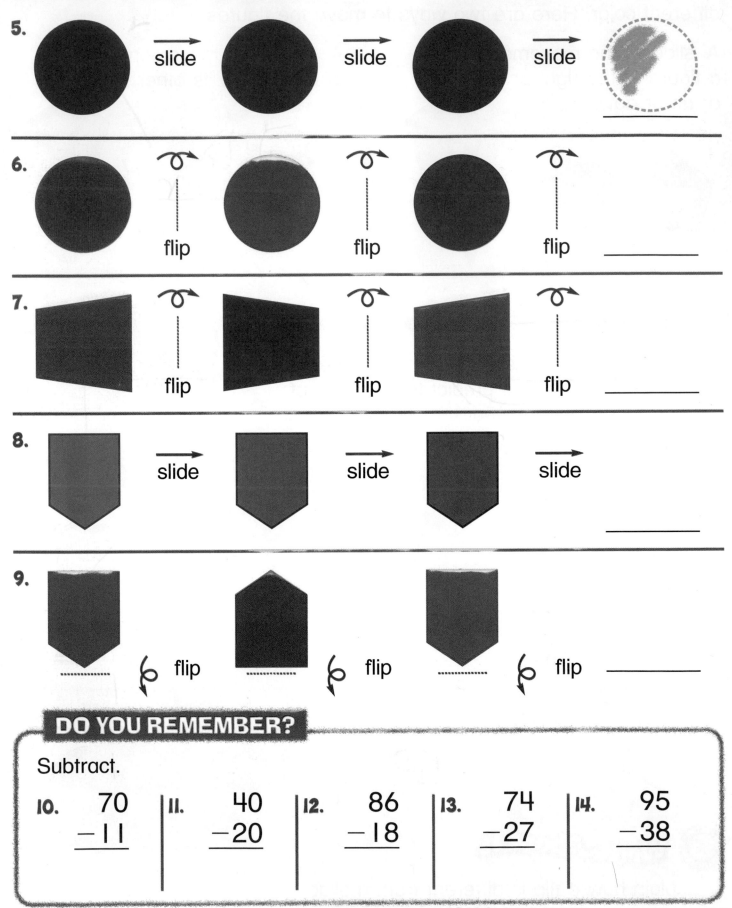 flip ______

7.  flip  flip  flip ______

8.  slide  slide  slide ______

9.  flip  flip  flip ______

DO YOU REMEMBER?

Subtract.

10. $\begin{array}{r} 70 \\ -11 \\ \hline \end{array}$

11. $\begin{array}{r} 40 \\ -20 \\ \hline \end{array}$

12. $\begin{array}{r} 86 \\ -18 \\ \hline \end{array}$

13. $\begin{array}{r} 74 \\ -27 \\ \hline \end{array}$

14. $\begin{array}{r} 95 \\ -38 \\ \hline \end{array}$

Math Alive at Home Have your child color each side of a paper circle in a different color. Then ask him/her to slide the figure and then flip the figure.

Name ___________________________________

Algebra

Turns

HANDS-ON LESSON

Let's Learn!

Diana makes a pinwheel design with a pattern block.
She turns the pattern block to make each part of the design.

This is how the figure moved when she turned it.

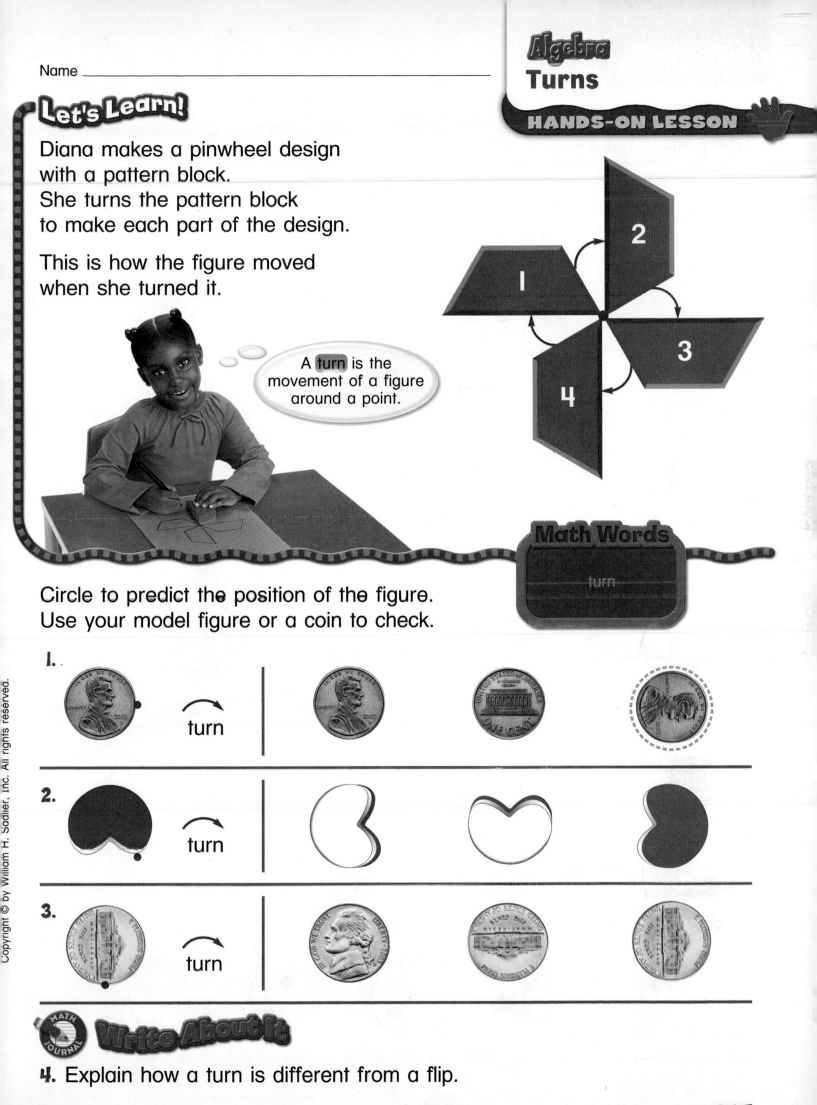

A turn is the movement of a figure around a point.

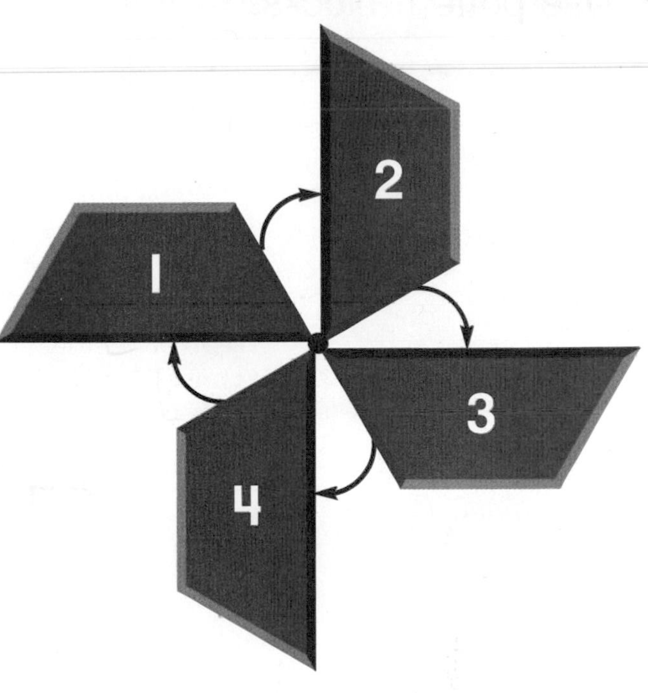

Math Words

turn

Circle to predict the position of the figure.
Use your model figure or a coin to check.

1.  turn |  

2.  turn |   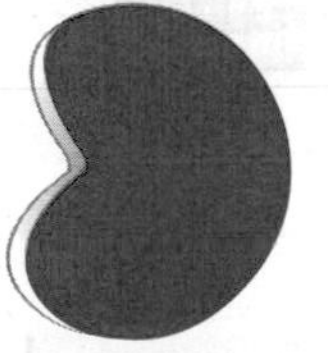

3.  turn |   

Write About It

4. Explain how a turn is different from a flip.

Copyright © by William H. Sadlier, Inc. All rights reserved.

Practice

Draw to show 4 turns for each figure.
Use pattern blocks.

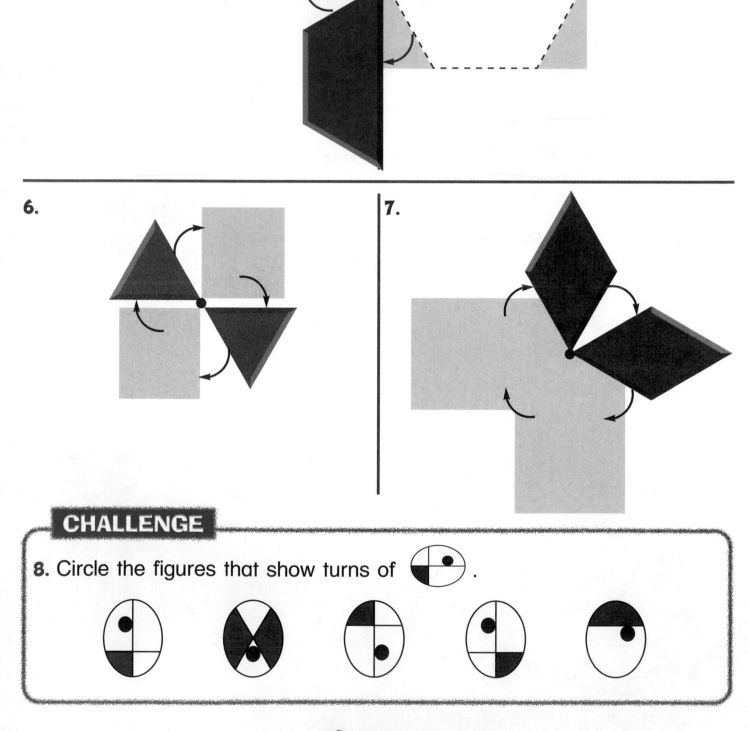

5.

6.

7.

CHALLENGE

8. Circle the figures that show turns of .

Math Alive at Home Have your child turn a dime or quarter to face 3 different directions, as shown with the figures on this page.

Name ______________________________

TEST PREPARATION

Listen to your teacher read the directions.
Fill in the circle under the correct answer.

1.

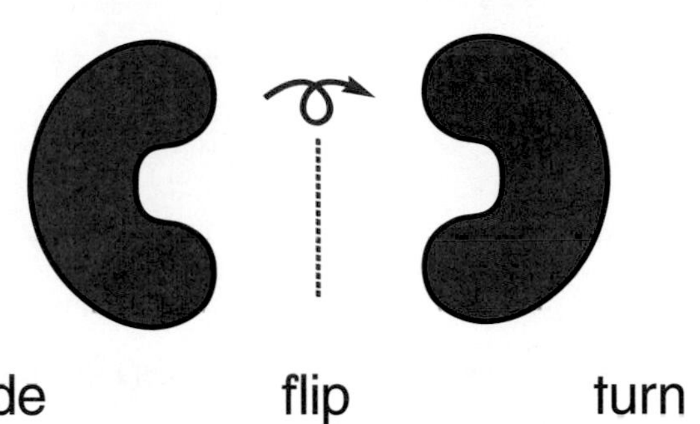

slide ○ flip ○ turn ○

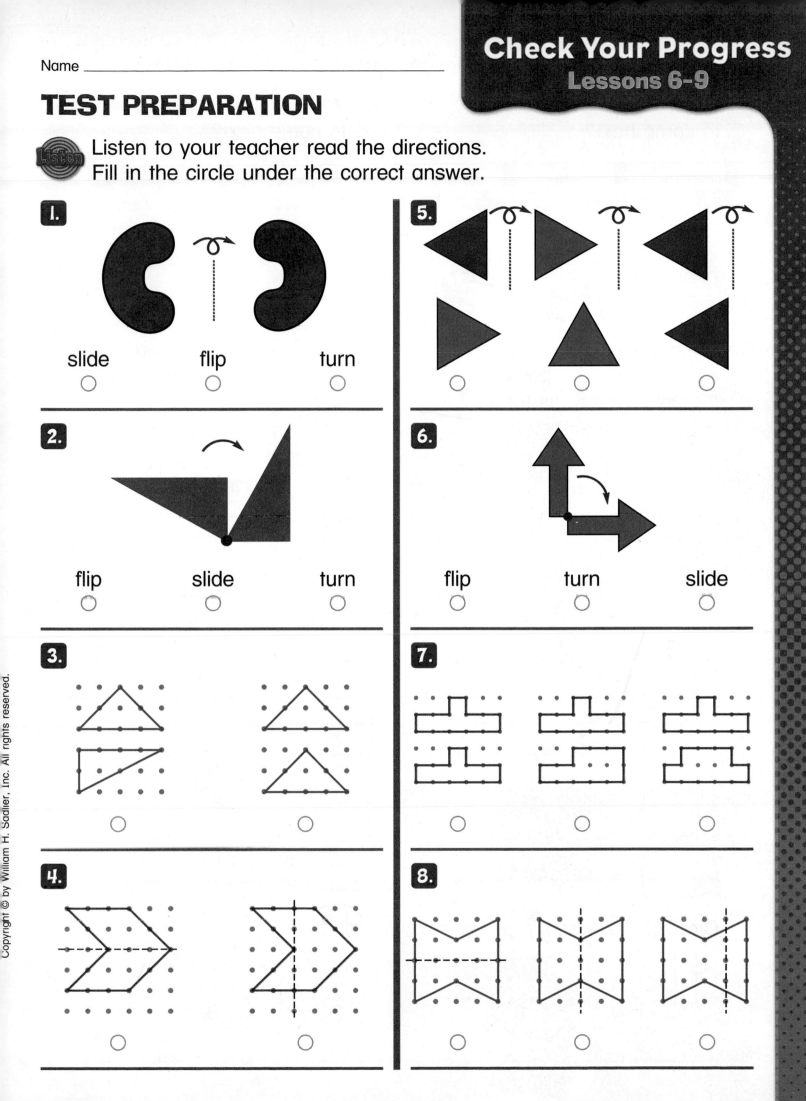

2.

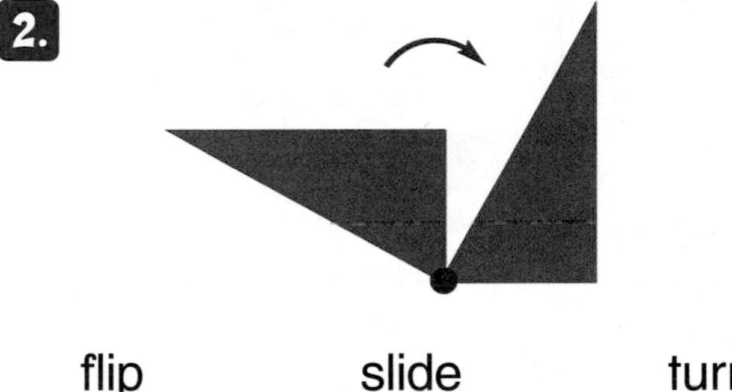

flip ○ slide ○ turn ○

3.

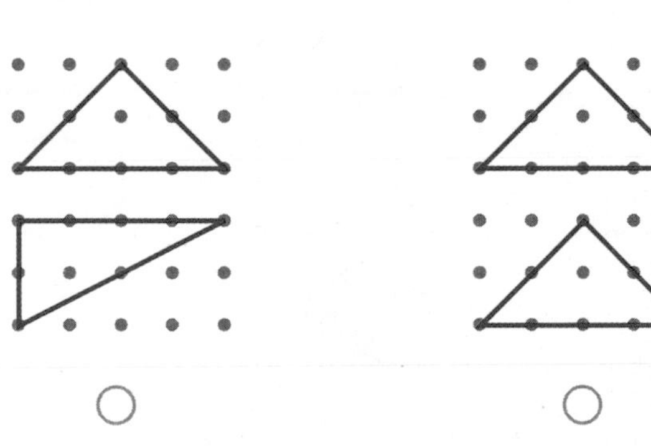

○ ○

4.

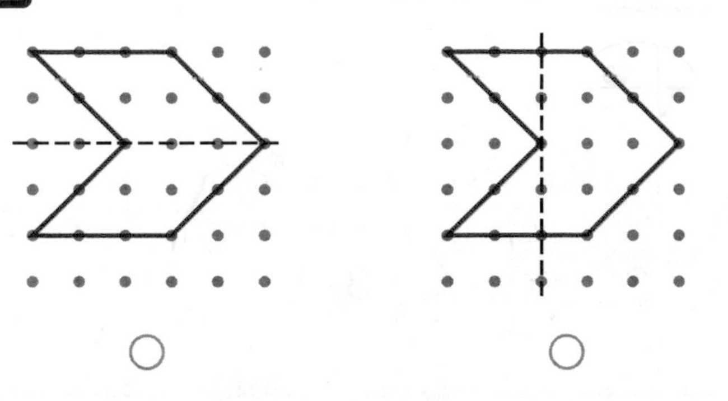

○ ○

5.

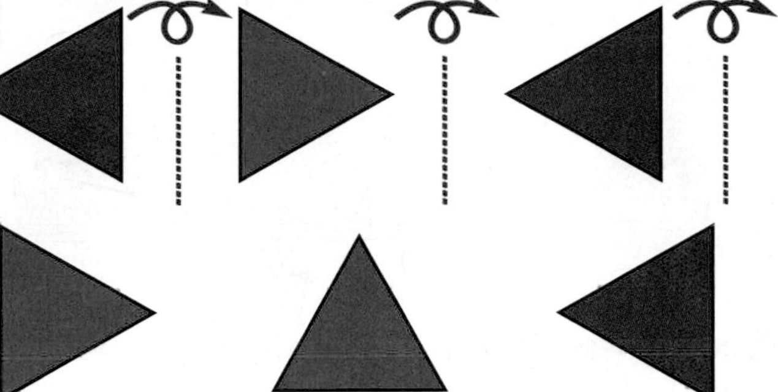

○ ○ ○

6.

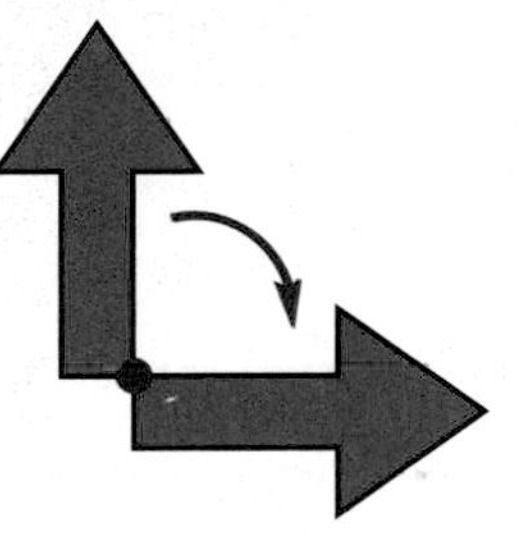

flip ○ turn ○ slide ○

7.

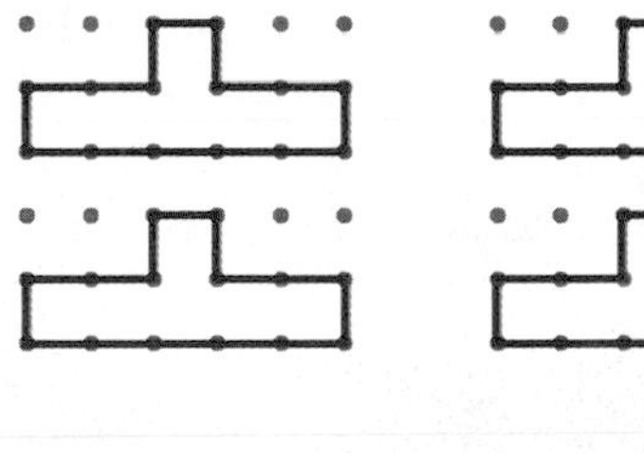

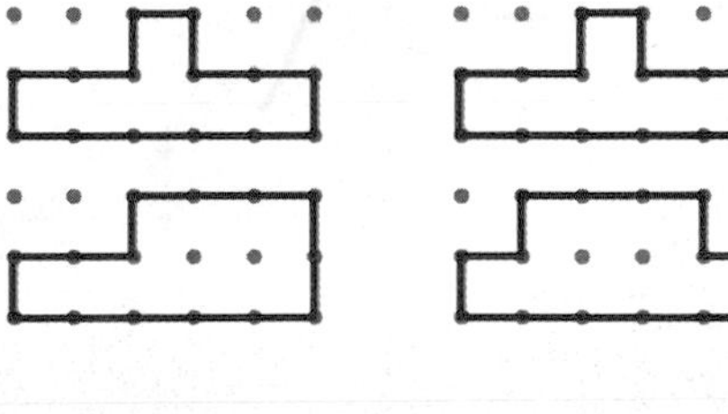

○ ○ ○

8.

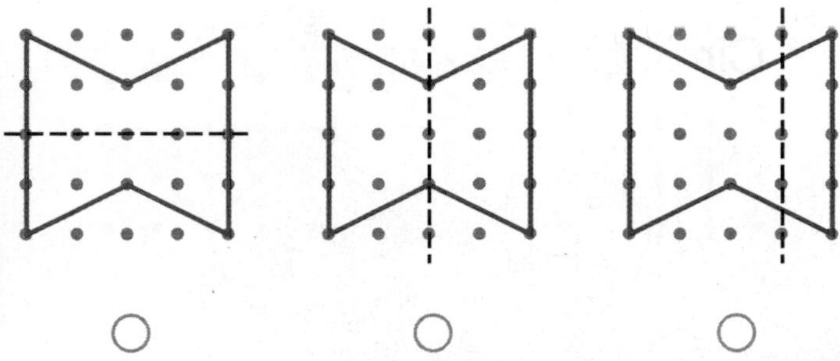

○ ○ ○

Copyright © by William H. Sadlier, Inc. All rights reserved.

Fill in the circle under the correct answer.

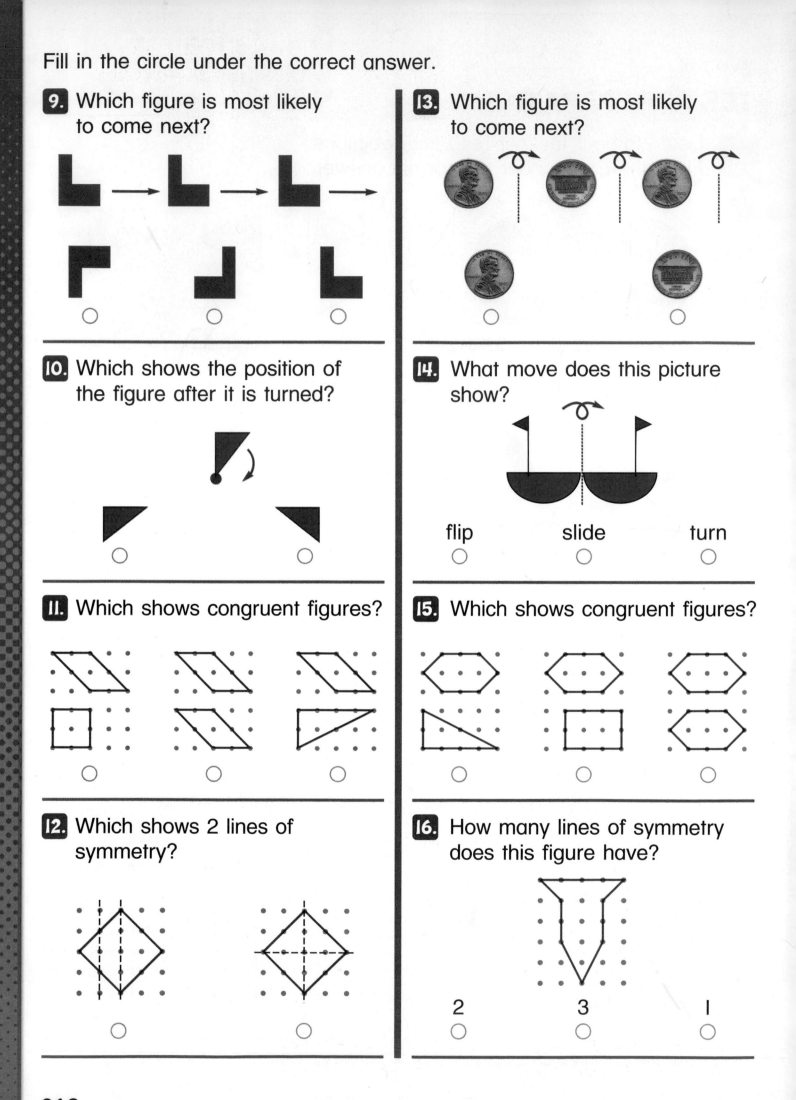

9. Which figure is most likely to come next?

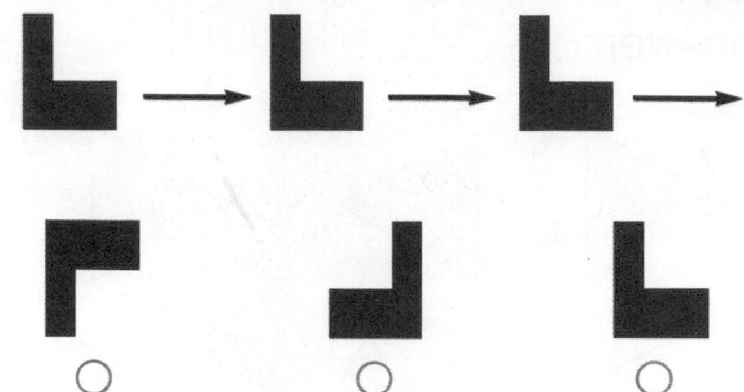

10. Which shows the position of the figure after it is turned?

11. Which shows congruent figures?

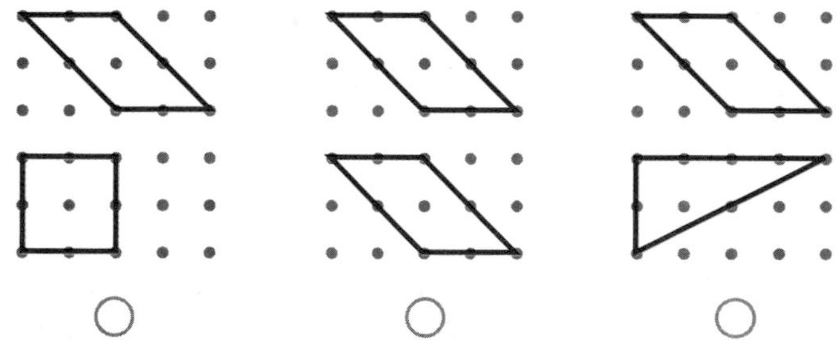

12. Which shows 2 lines of symmetry?

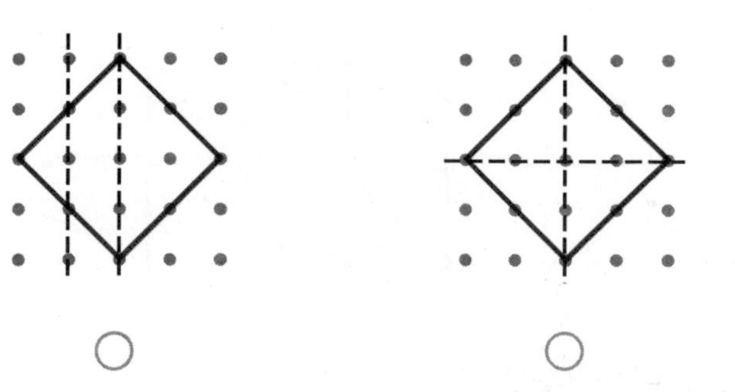

13. Which figure is most likely to come next?

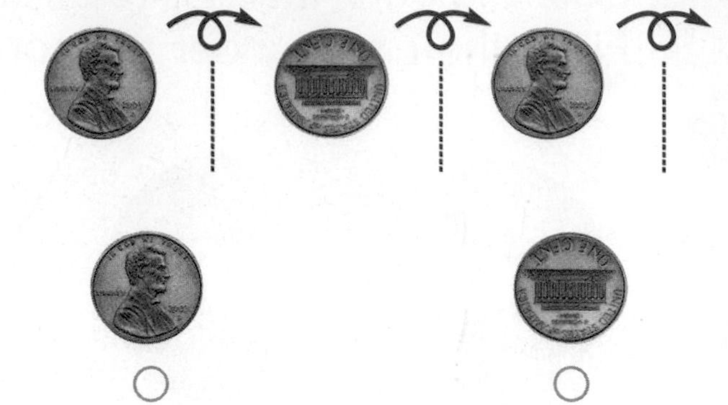

14. What move does this picture show?

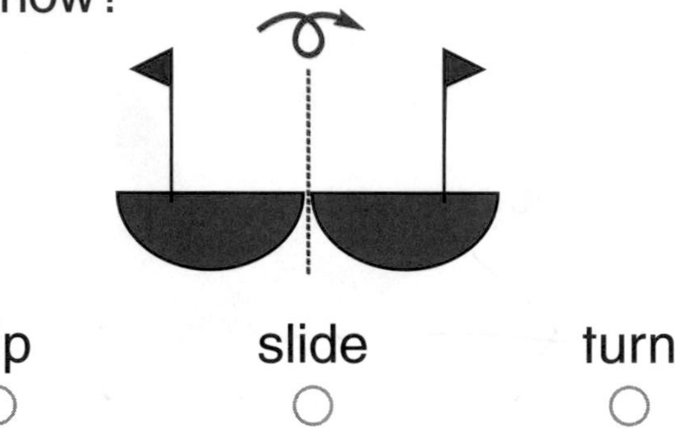

flip　　slide　　turn

15. Which shows congruent figures?

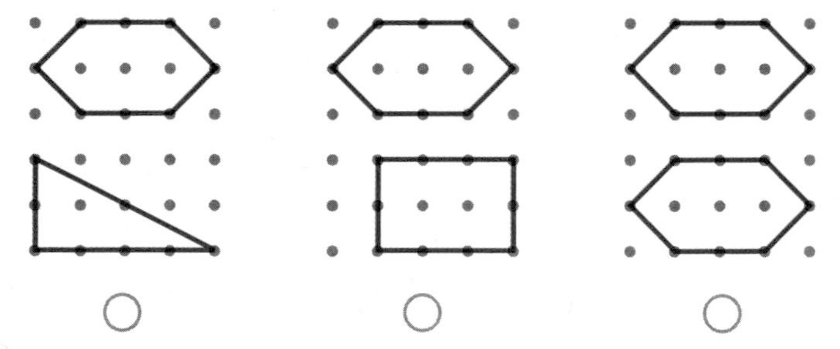

16. How many lines of symmetry does this figure have?

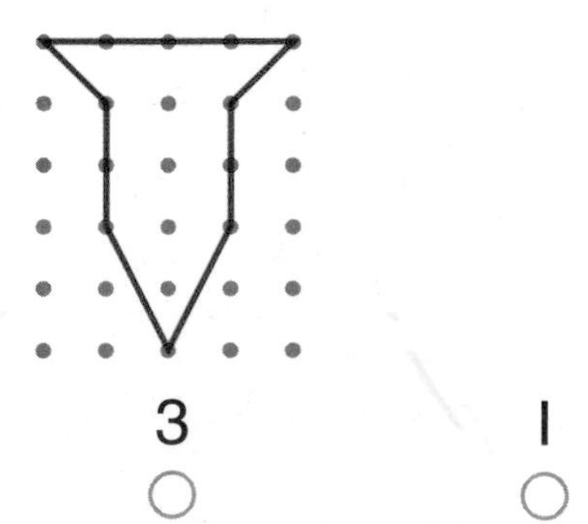

2　　3　　1

Name ______________________________

Find a Pattern

Let's Learn!

Sandra is making a **pattern** with shapes.
What shape is most likely to come next in the pattern?

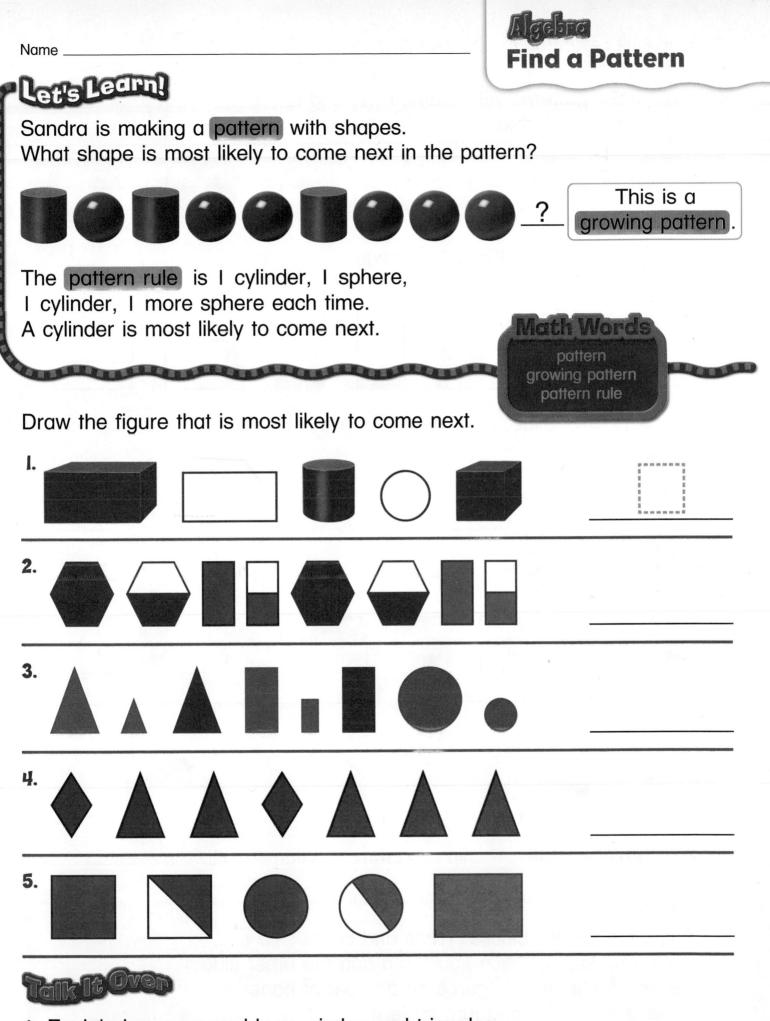

_?_

This is a **growing pattern**.

The **pattern rule** is 1 cylinder, 1 sphere, 1 cylinder, 1 more sphere each time.
A cylinder is most likely to come next.

Math Words
pattern
growing pattern
pattern rule

Draw the figure that is most likely to come next.

1. ______

2. ______

3. ______

4. ______

5. ______

6. Explain how you could use circles and triangles to make the pattern in exercise 2.

Copyright © by William H. Sadlier, Inc. All rights reserved.

Practice

You can make patterns with slides, flips, and turns.
Name and color the next move in each row.

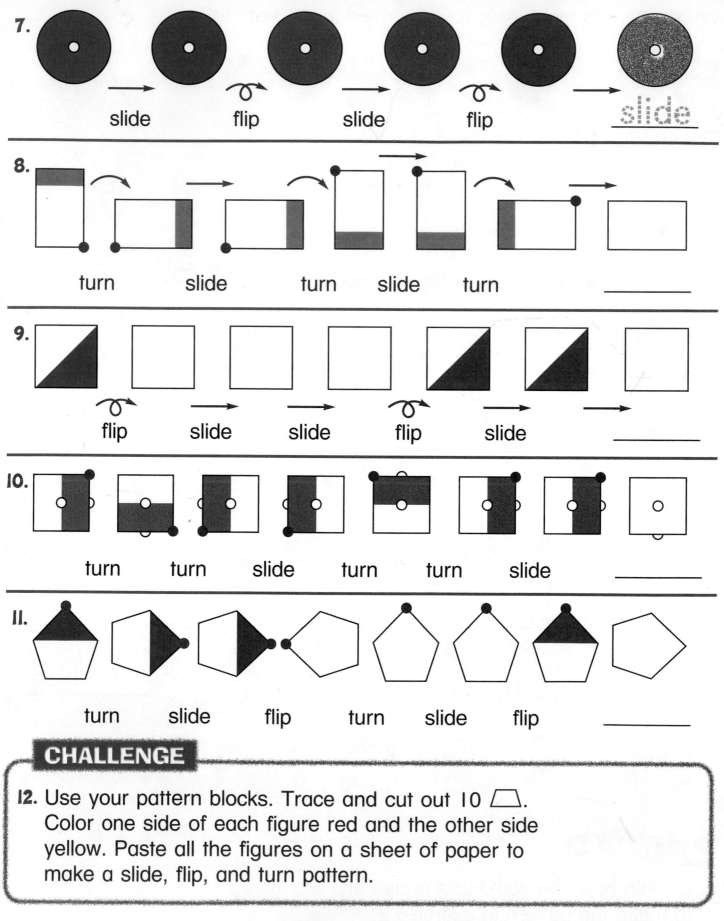

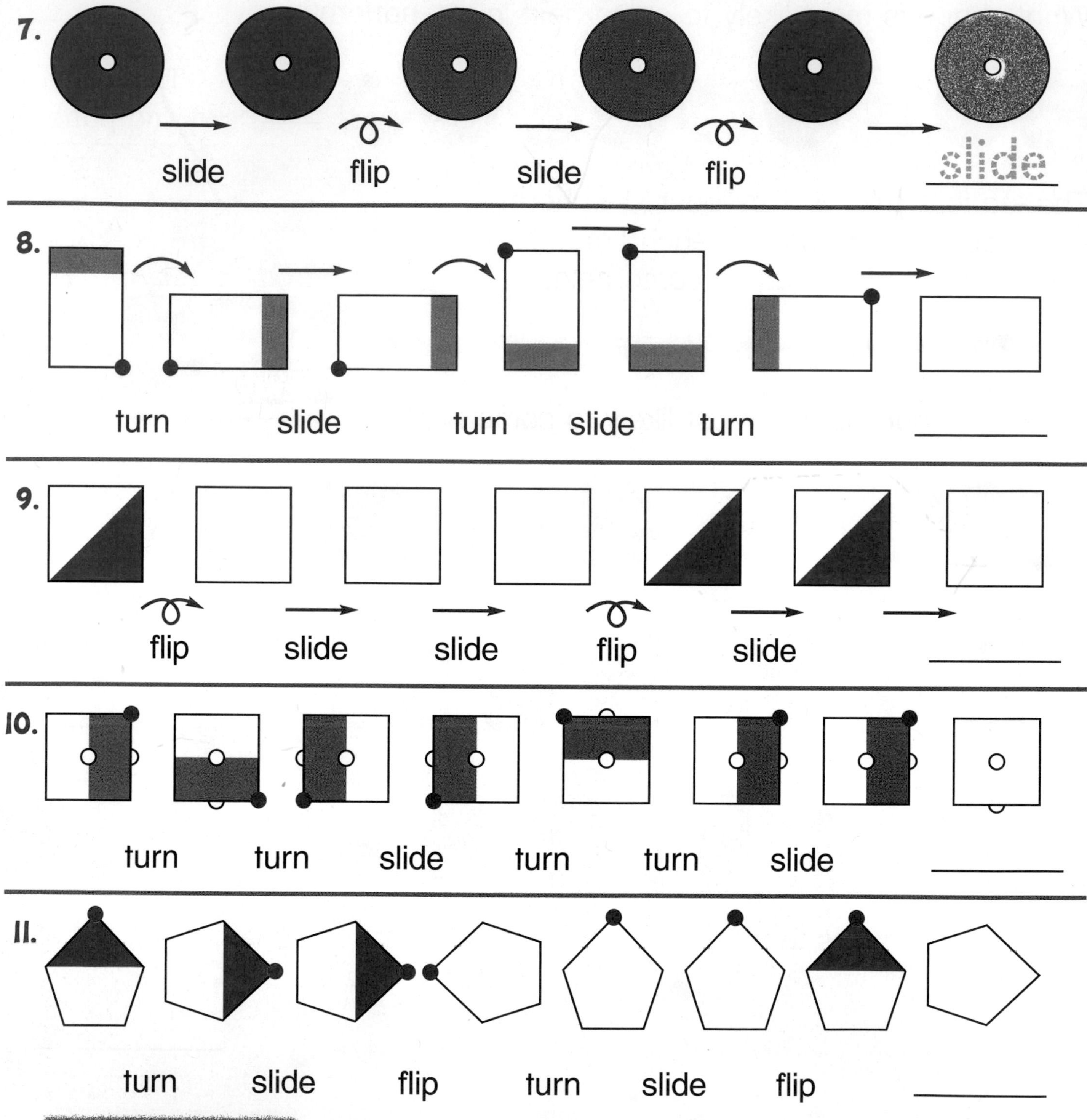

CHALLENGE

12. Use your pattern blocks. Trace and cut out 10 ⏢. Color one side of each figure red and the other side yellow. Paste all the figures on a sheet of paper to make a slide, flip, and turn pattern.

Math Alive at Home Have your child draw 5 red and 5 blue triangles and make a pattern using all 10 figures.

Name ______________________

Ways to Make Figures

HANDS-ON LESSON

Let's Learn!

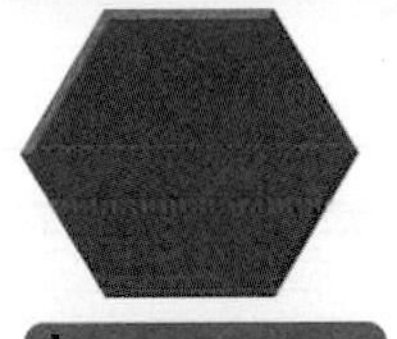

hexagon

trapezoid

rhombus

I separated a hexagon to make 2 trapezoids.

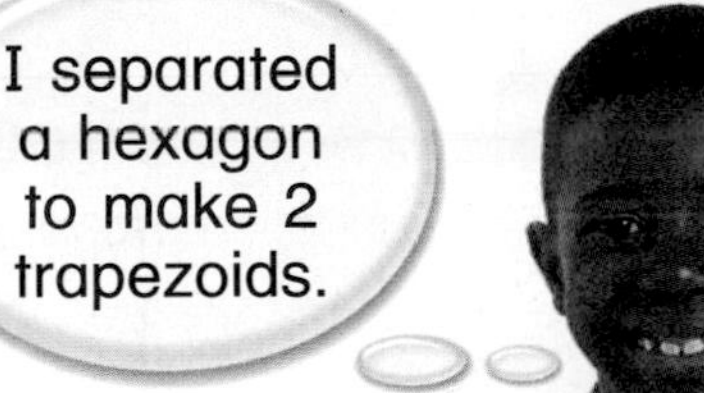

I put together a rhombus and a triangle to make 1 trapezoid.

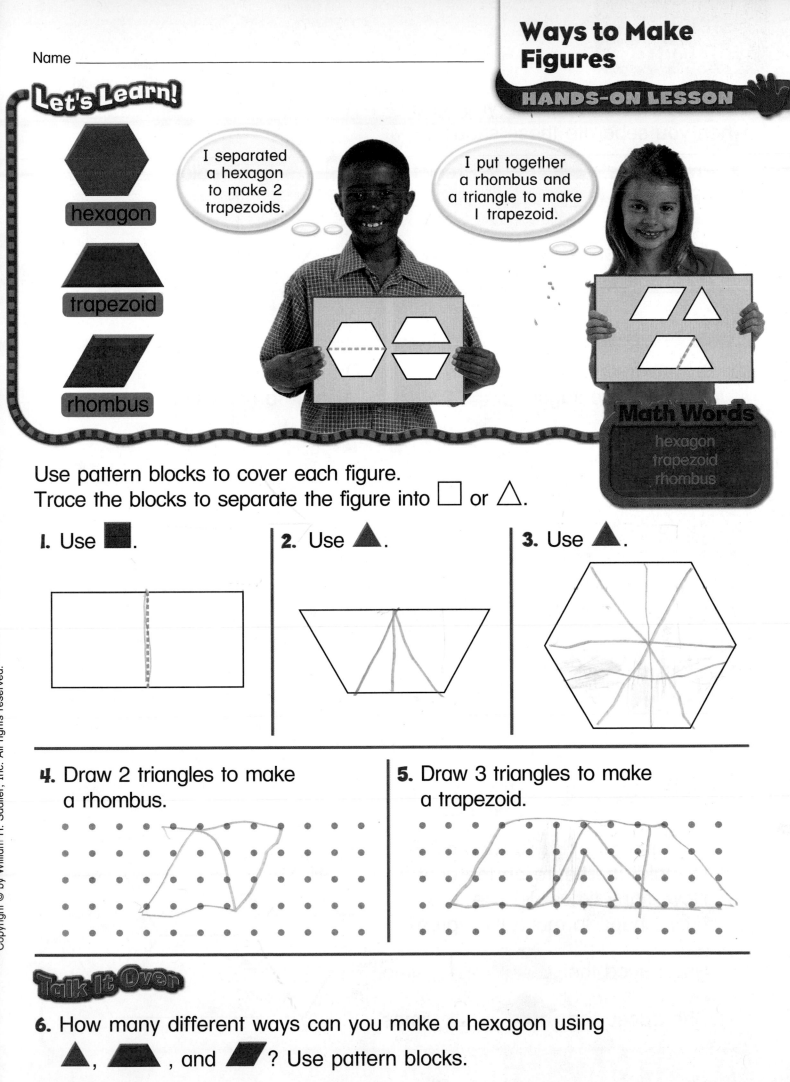

Math Words
hexagon
trapezoid
rhombus

Use pattern blocks to cover each figure.
Trace the blocks to separate the figure into □ or △.

1. Use .

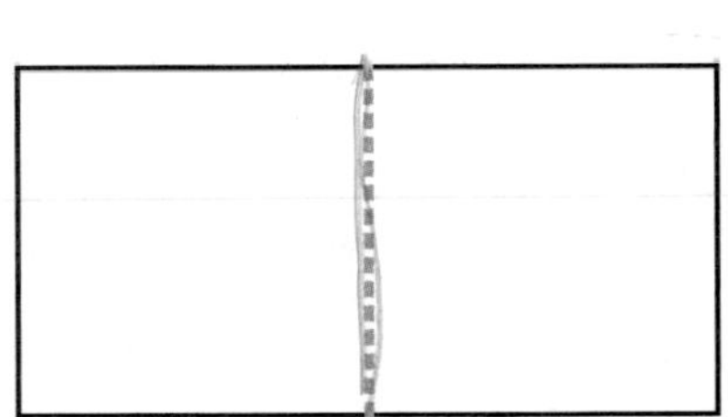

2. Use ▲.

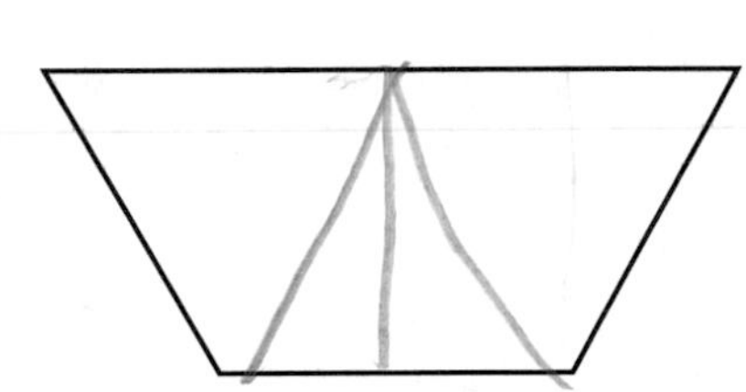

3. Use ▲.

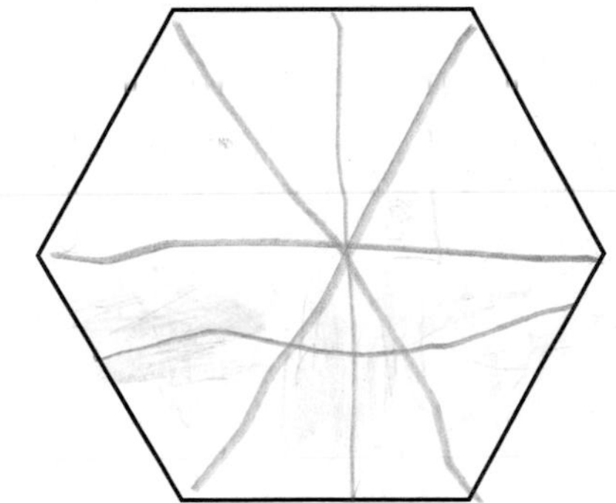

4. Draw 2 triangles to make a rhombus.

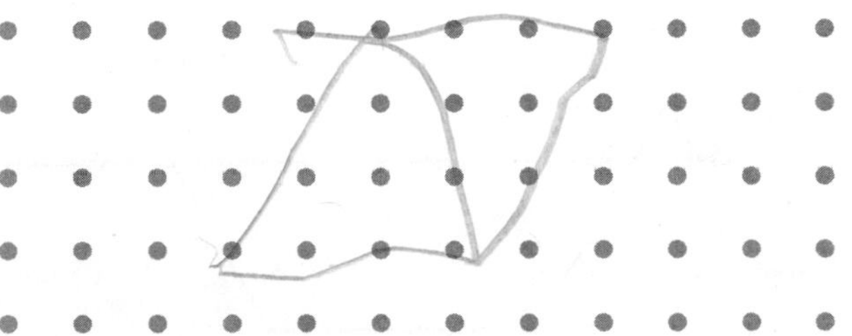

5. Draw 3 triangles to make a trapezoid.

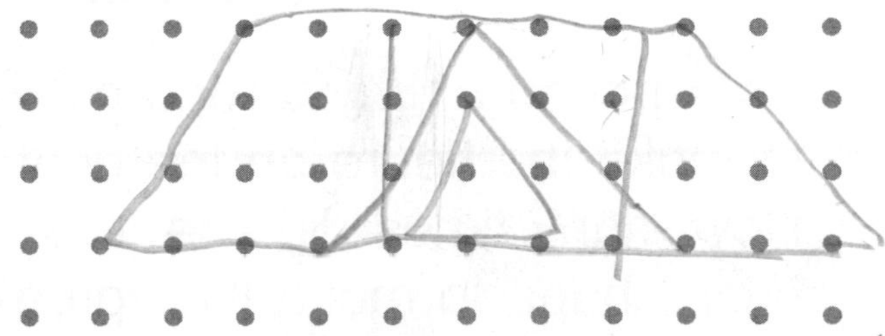

6. How many different ways can you make a hexagon using

▲, ▬, and ▰? Use pattern blocks.

Copyright © by William H. Sadlier, Inc. All rights reserved.

Practice

Use pattern blocks to check.

Predict how many figures you have when you separate these shapes.

7. Predict 2 

8. Predict 3 

9. Predict 2 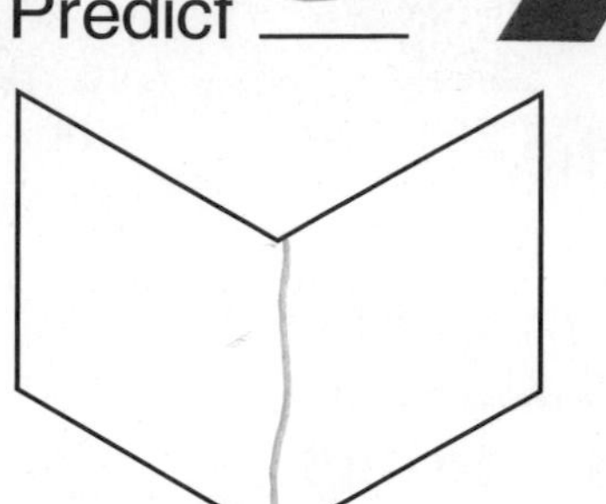

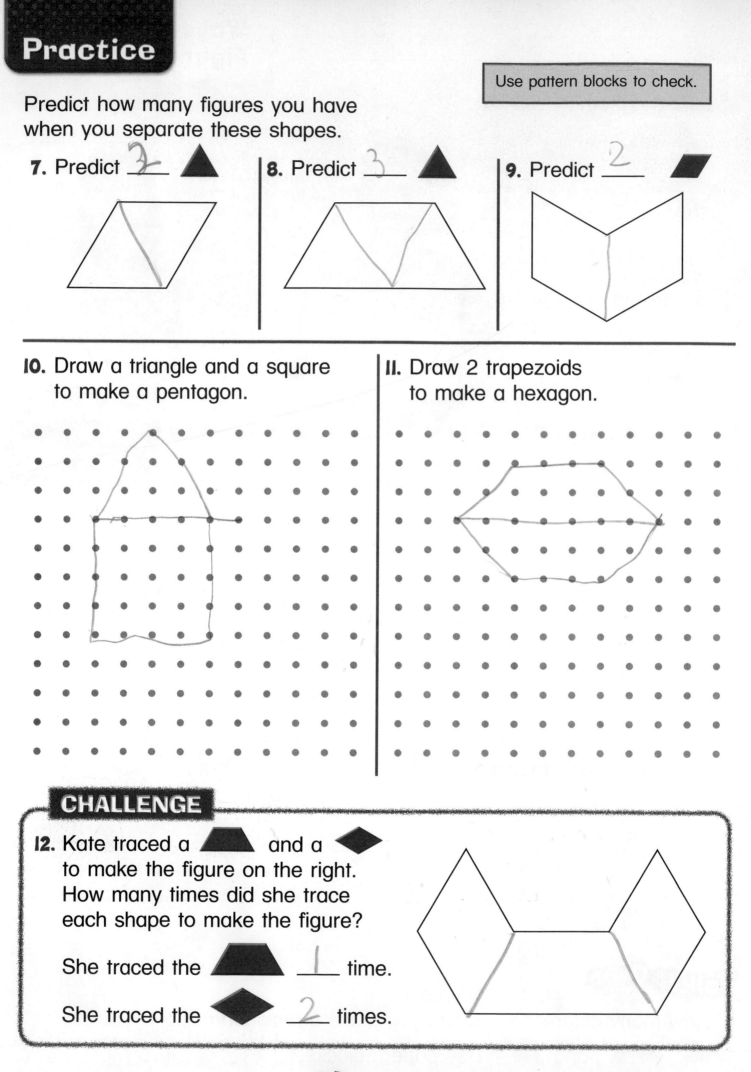

10. Draw a triangle and a square to make a pentagon.

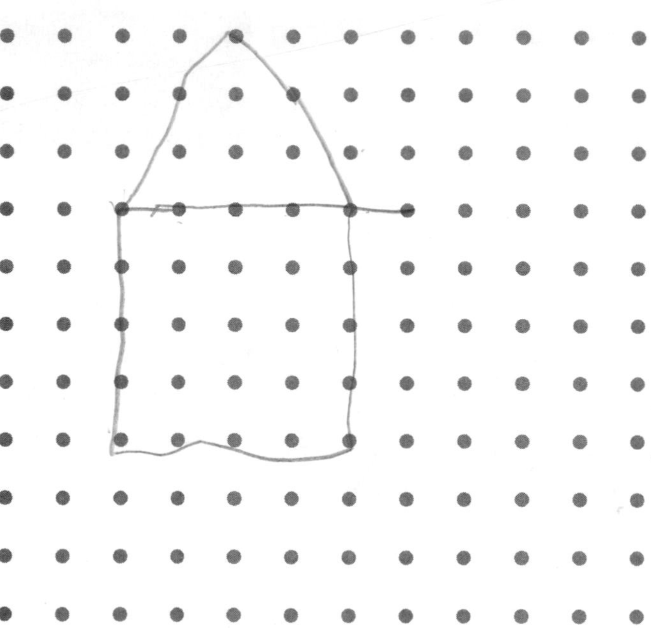

11. Draw 2 trapezoids to make a hexagon.

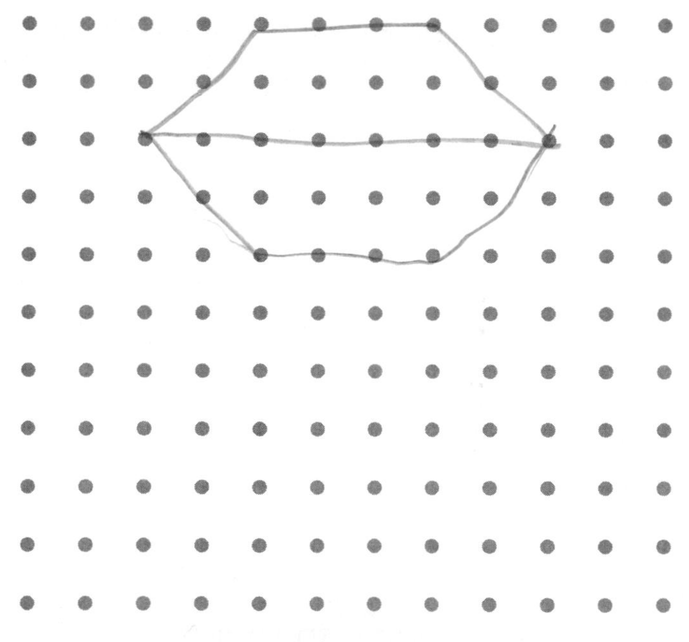

CHALLENGE

12. Kate traced a  and a  to make the figure on the right. How many times did she trace each shape to make the figure?

She traced the trapezoid 1 time.

She traced the rhombus 2 times.

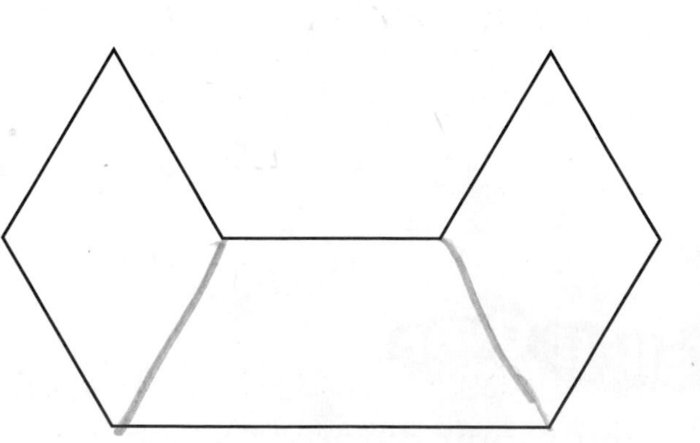

Math Alive at Home Have your child draw 2 squares together to make a new figure and name the figure.

Name ____________________

Understand Math Words

• In some problems you need to know the meaning of math words to solve the problem or answer the question.

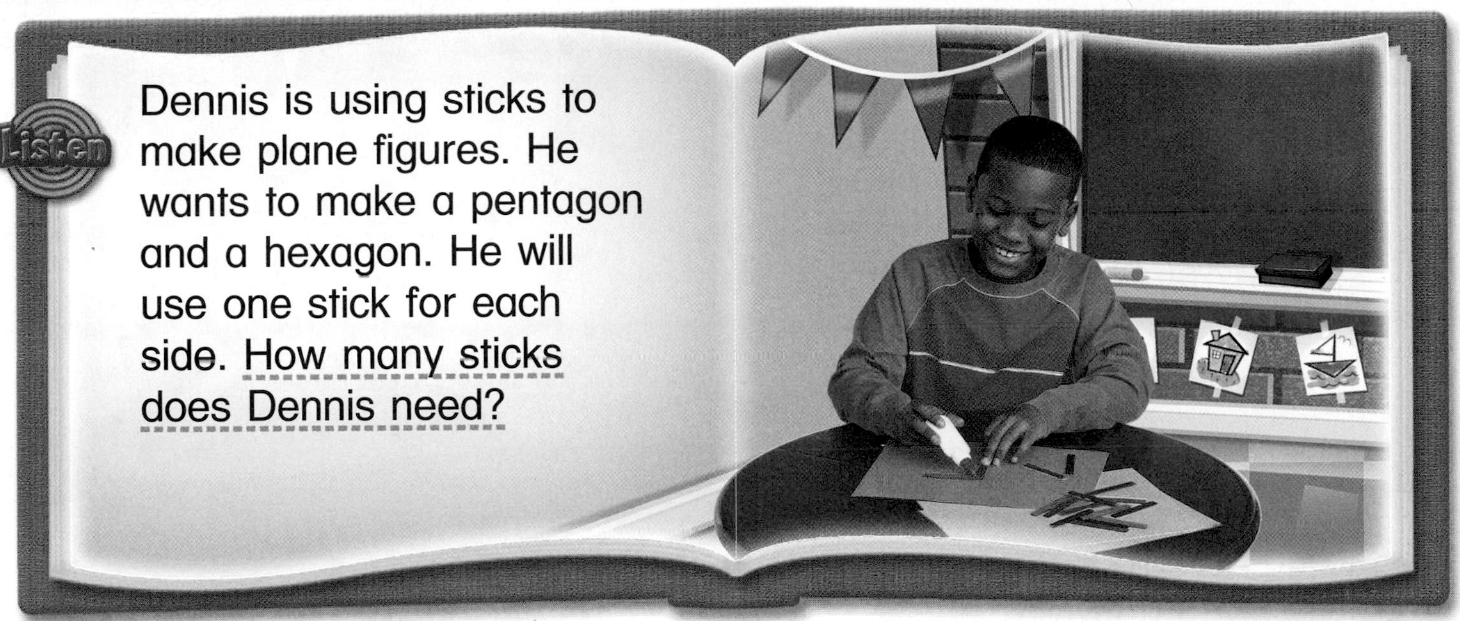

Dennis is using sticks to make plane figures. He wants to make a pentagon and a hexagon. He will use one stick for each side. How many sticks does Dennis need?

1. Reread the problem. Draw a line under the question you need to answer.

2. Make sure you understand the math words in the problem. Circle the pentagon. Trace the sides in [crayon]. Then write the number of sides a pentagon has.

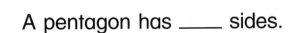

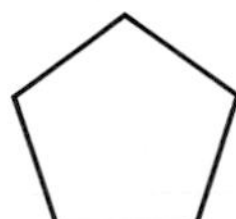

A pentagon has ____ sides.

3. Circle the hexagon. Trace the sides in [crayon]. Then write the number of sides a hexagon has.

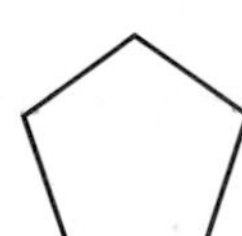
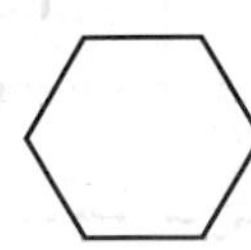

A hexagon has ____ sides.

4. Now add to solve the problem.

____ + ____ = ____

Dennis will need ____ sticks.

Copyright © by William H. Sadlier, Inc. All rights reserved.

Practice

Understand Math Words

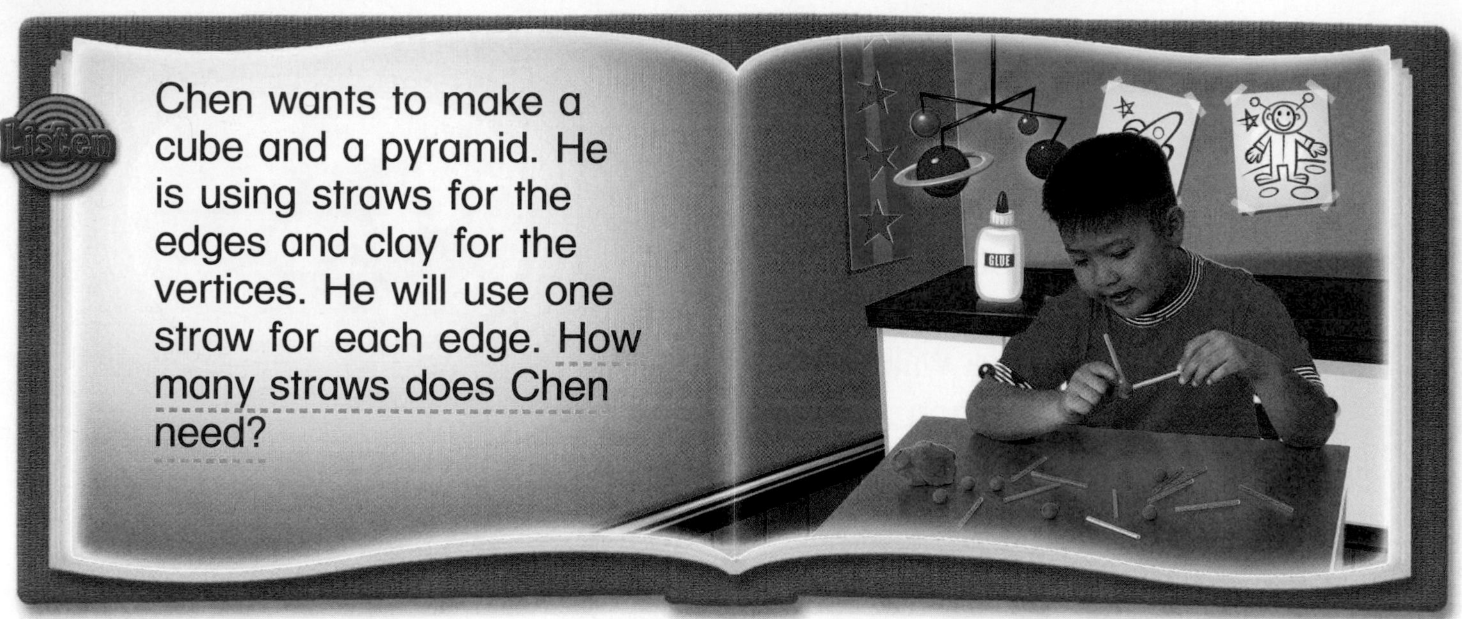

Chen wants to make a cube and a pyramid. He is using straws for the edges and clay for the vertices. He will use one straw for each edge. How many straws does Chen need?

5. Reread the problem. Draw a line under the question you need to answer.

---

6. Make sure you understand the math words in the problem. Circle the cube. Trace the edges in (crayon). Then write the number of edges a cube has.

 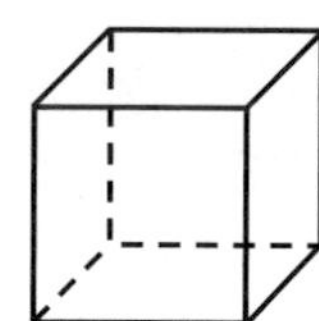  

A cube has ____ edges.

---

7. Circle the pyramid. Trace the edges in (crayon). Then write the number of edges a pyramid has.

 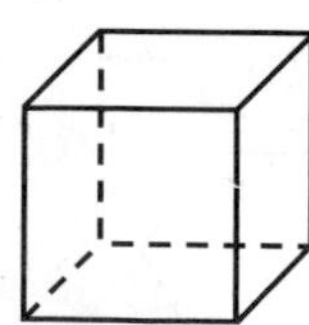 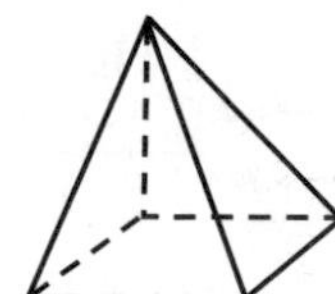 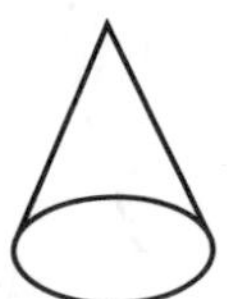

A pyramid has ____ edges.

---

8. Now add to solve the problem.

____ + ____ = ____

Chen will need ____ straws.

Math Alive at Home Today your child worked through math problems by understanding math words.

Name ________________________________

Ordered Pairs

Let's Learn!

An **ordered pair** is a set of two numbers used to locate points on a grid.

Look at the grid.
What figure is at point (6, 3)?

To find out,
1. Start at 0.
2. Move across.

The first number tells you to move 6 spaces to the right.

3. Move up.

The second number tells you to move 3 spaces up.

The ▲ is at point (6, 3).

Where is the ■?
The ■ is at point (5, 1).

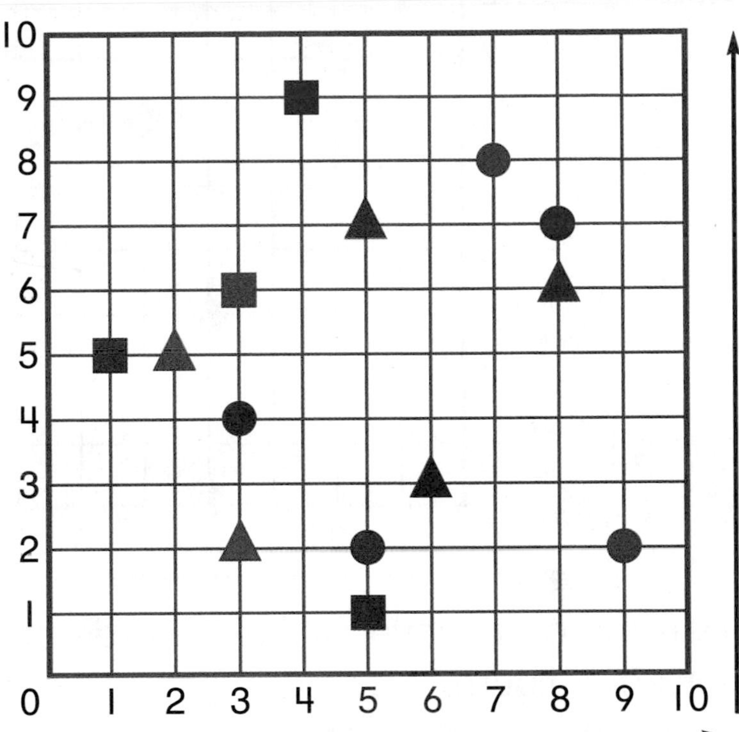

Math Words
ordered pair

Use the grid above. Write the ordered pair for each figure.

  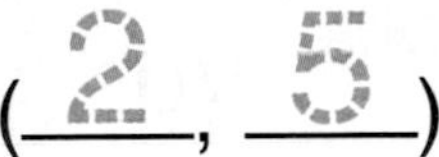

1. ▲ (2, 5)

2. ■ (___, ___)

3. ▲ (___, ___)

4. ● (___, ___)

5. ▲ (___, ___)

6. ● (___, ___)

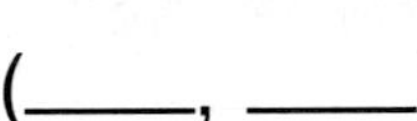

Draw the figure at each point.

7. (5, 2) 
8. (1, 5)
9. (5, 7)
10. (3, 4)
11. (8, 7)
12. (3, 6)

13. What is the difference between point (3, 8) and point (8, 3)?

Copyright © by William H. Sadlier, Inc. All rights reserved.

Practice

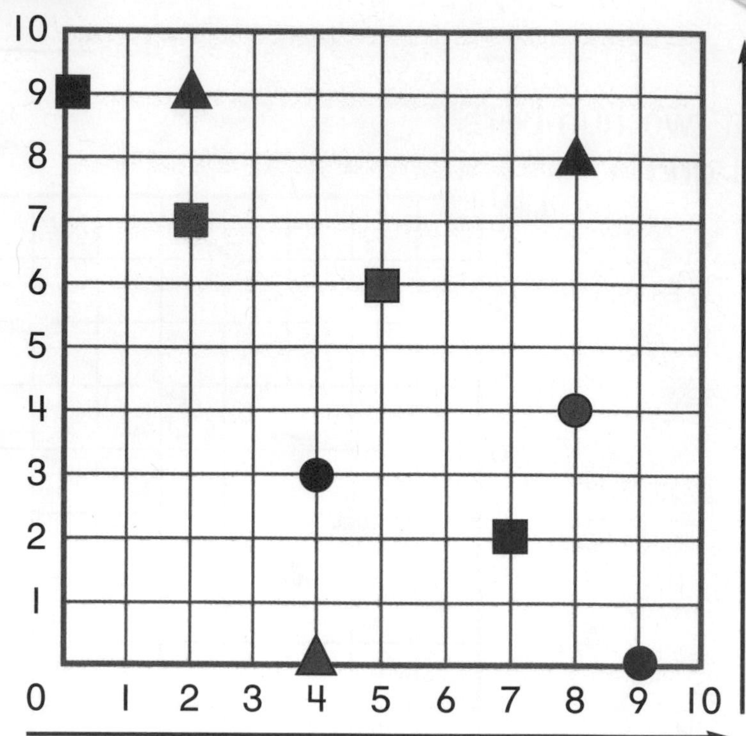

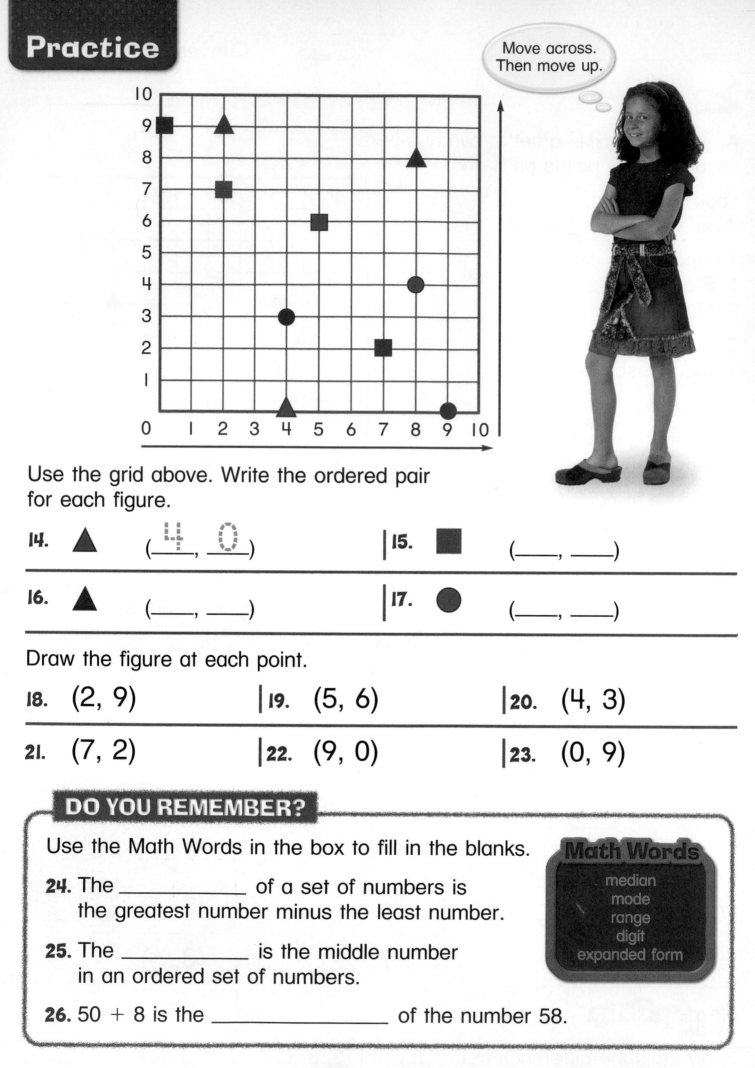

Use the grid above. Write the ordered pair for each figure.

14.  (4, 0)

15.  (____, ____)

16.  (____, ____)

17.  (____, ____)

Draw the figure at each point.

18. (2, 9)

19. (5, 6)

20. (4, 3)

21. (7, 2)

22. (9, 0)

23. (0, 9)

DO YOU REMEMBER?

Use the Math Words in the box to fill in the blanks.

24. The __________ of a set of numbers is the greatest number minus the least number.

25. The __________ is the middle number in an ordered set of numbers.

26. 50 + 8 is the ______________ of the number 58.

Math Words
median
mode
range
digit
expanded form

Math Alive at Home Have your child explain how to find an ordered pair on the grid above.

Name ________________________________

Algebra
Problem Solving Strategy

Use a Pattern

Read How can you show this pattern using letters or colors?

○ □ □ ○ □ □ ○ □ □

Plan Look for the pattern rule.
Use the same rule to make a new pattern with letters, then with colors.
The rule is 1 figure, then 2 of a different figure.

You can show
the same pattern
in different ways.

Think
Use 1 letter, then 2 of a different letter.
Use 1 color, then 2 of a different color.

Write

○	□	□	○	□	□	○	□	□
A	B	B	A	B	B	A	B	B

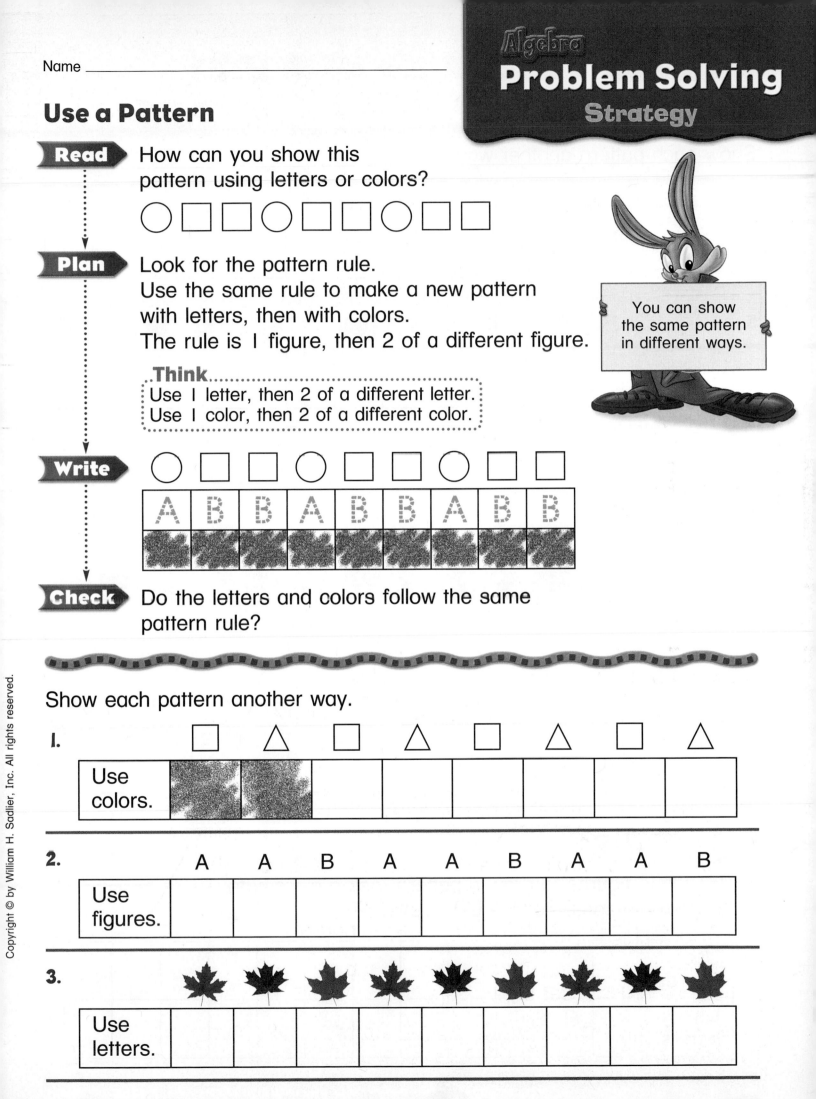

Check Do the letters and colors follow the same pattern rule?

Show each pattern another way.

1. □ △ □ △ □ △ □ △

Use colors.								

2. A A B A A B A A B

Use figures.									

3.

Use letters.									

Copyright © by William H. Sadlier, Inc. All rights reserved.

Practice

Read → Plan → Write → Check

Use a Pattern

Show each pattern another way.

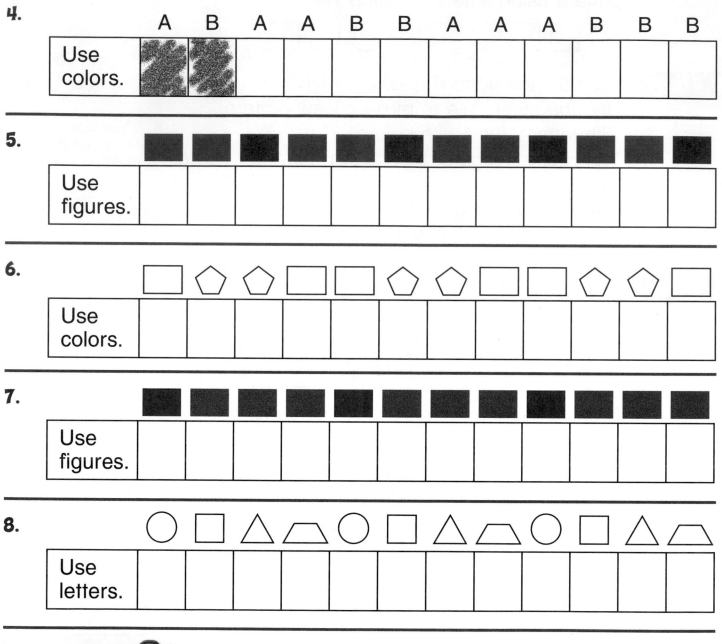

4.

	A	B	A	A	B	B	A	A	A	B	B	B
Use colors.												

5.

Use figures.												

6.

Use colors.												

7.

Use figures.												

8.

Use letters.												

9. Use plane figures to draw a pattern. Ask a classmate to show the same pattern using letters.

Use figures.												
Use letters.												

Math Alive at Home Ask your child to describe one of the patterns above using colors, shapes, and number words.

Name ______________________________

Problem Solving
Applications

Read Plan Write Check

Mixed Strategies

Use a strategy you have learned.

Strategy File
Use Logical Reasoning
Use More Than One Step
Use a Pattern

1. Sarah, Tom, and Paul each have a figure. Sarah's figure has more than 4 vertices. Tom's figure has 2 fewer sides than Sarah's. The other figure is Paul's. Color Sarah's figure green, Tom's figure orange, and Paul's figure purple.

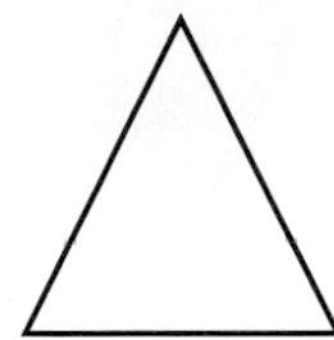 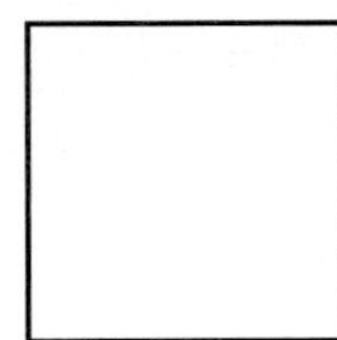 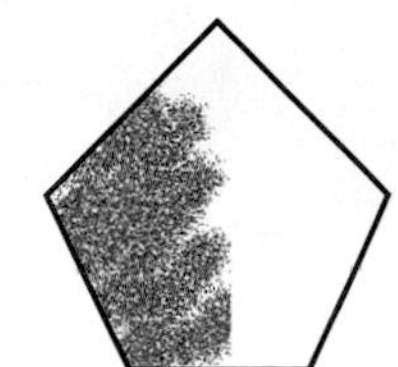

2. Ty has 26 puzzle pieces. Mia has 3 fewer than Ty. How many puzzle pieces do they have altogether?

_____ puzzle pieces

3. Sam wants to paint a cube and a pyramid. How many faces will he paint altogether?

_____ faces

 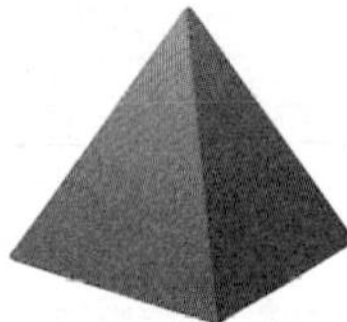

4. Show the same pattern with figures and colors.

	A	B	A	B	A	B	A	B
Use Figures								
Use Colors								

Copyright © by William H. Sadlier, Inc. All rights reserved.

Practice

Read Plan Write Check

Use a strategy you have learned.

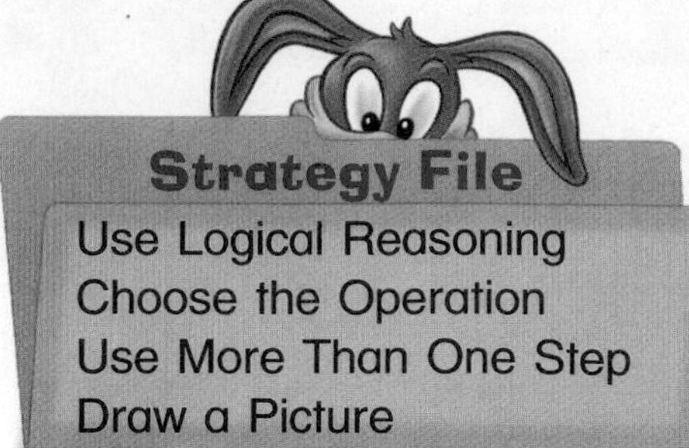

5. Hope finds a dozen buttons. Leo finds as many as Hope. How many buttons do they find altogether?

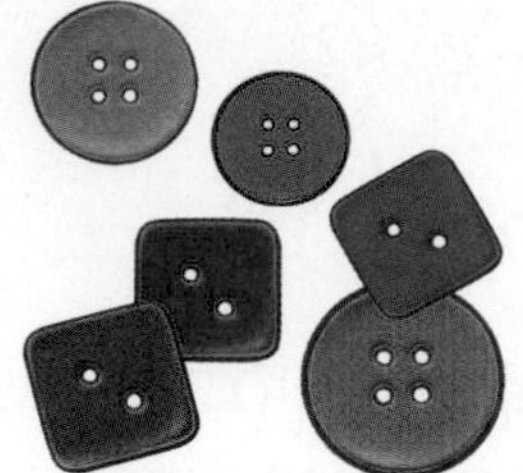

____ buttons

---

6. Matt's figure is orange. Kerri's figure has twice as many vertices as Matt's. Circle Kerri's figure.

---

7. Ben has 18 yellow cubes. He gives 5 to Heather. Then he gets 30 blue cubes. How many cubes does Ben have now?

____ cubes

---

8. Frank writes an odd number. It has more tens than ones. Circle the number that cannot be Frank's.

53 81 65 45

---

9. Melissa is doing a puzzle. All of the pieces are congruent. How many pieces are missing from the puzzle?

____ pieces

Math Alive at Home Ask your child to tell you how he/she solved some of the problems in this lesson.

Name ________________________________

TEST PREPARATION

Listen to your teacher read the directions.
Fill in the circle under the correct answer.

1.

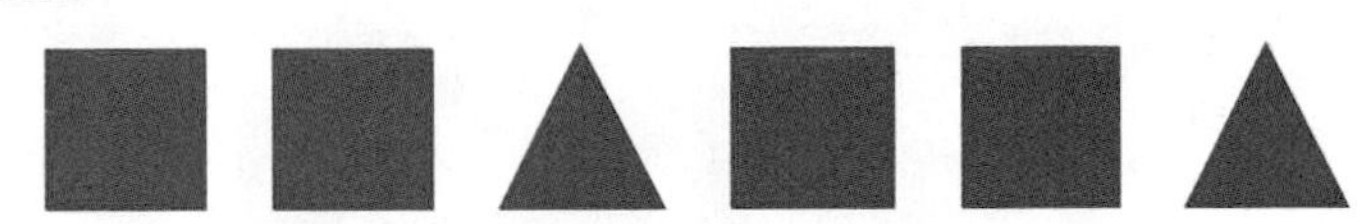

A A B B A A

○ ○

2.

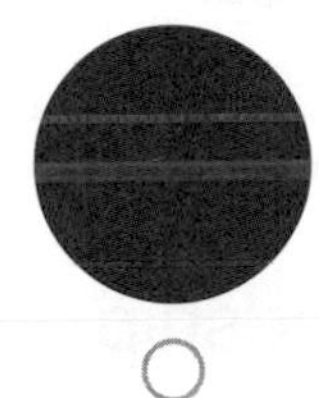

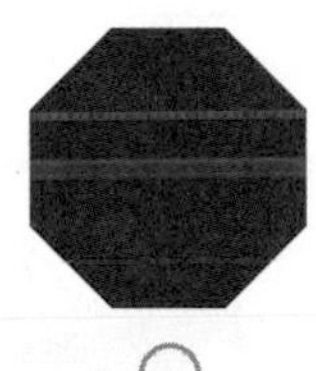

○ ○

3.

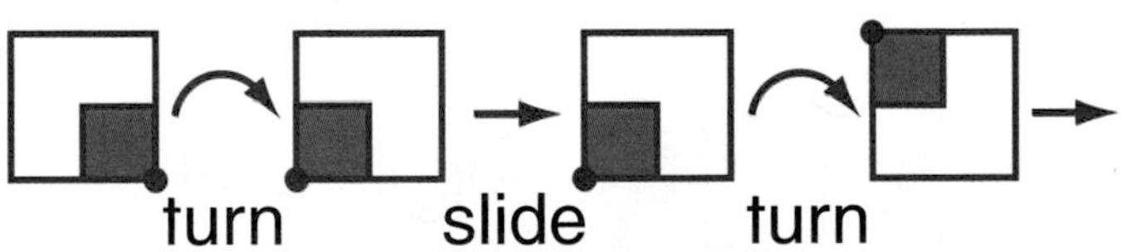

flip ○ slide ○ turn ○

4.

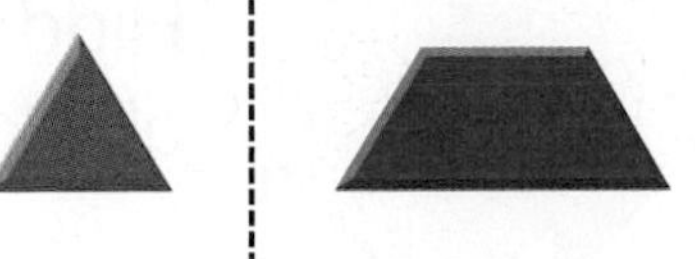

2 ○ 4 ○ 3 ○ 5 ○

5.

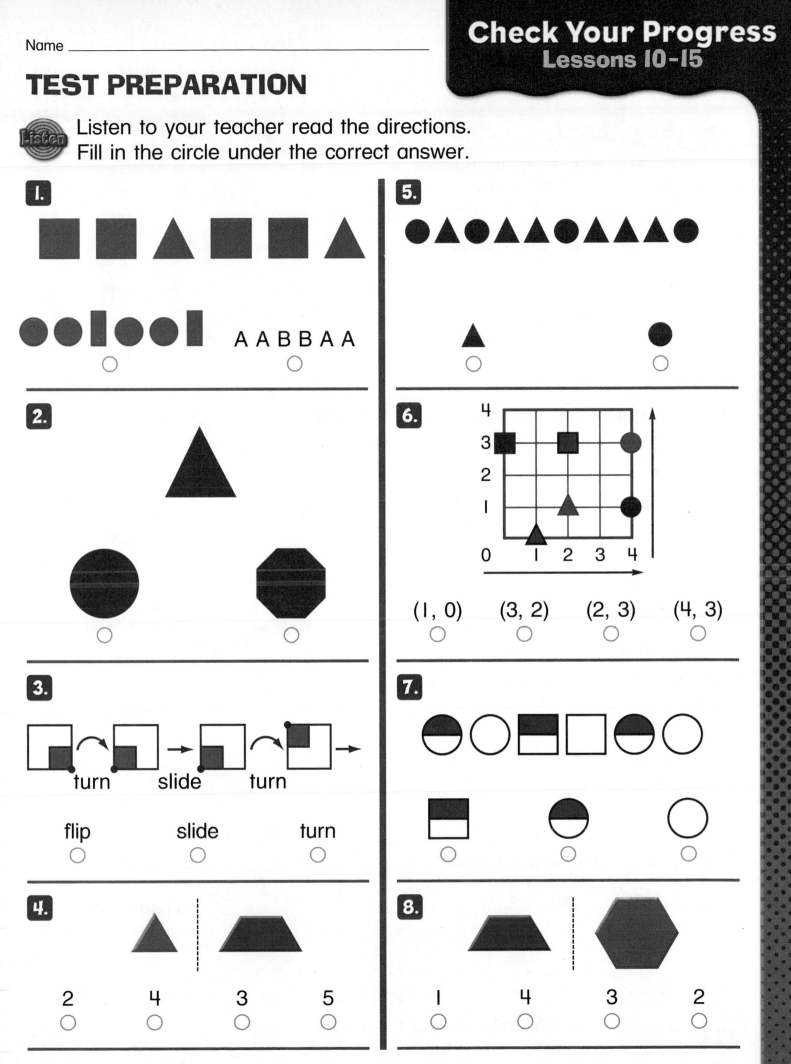

○ ○

6.

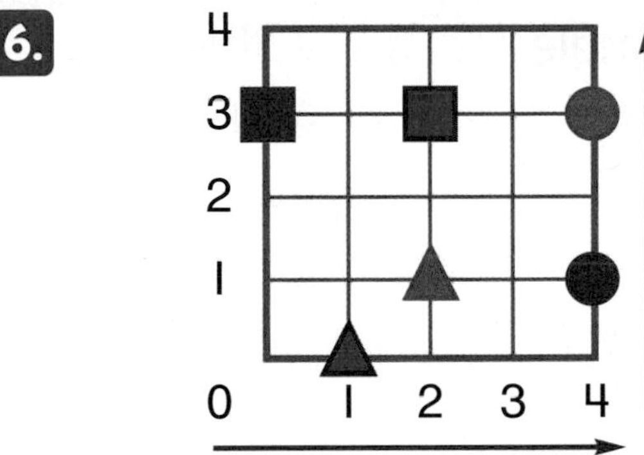

(1, 0) ○ (3, 2) ○ (2, 3) ○ (4, 3) ○

7.

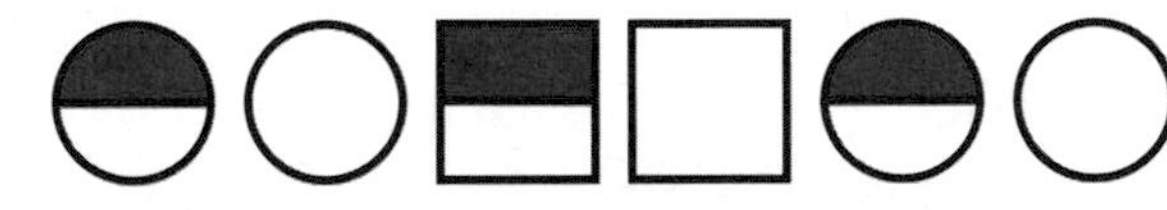

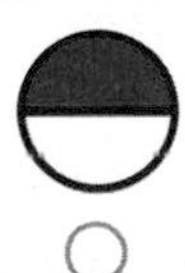

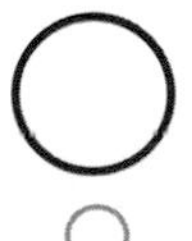

○ ○ ○

8.

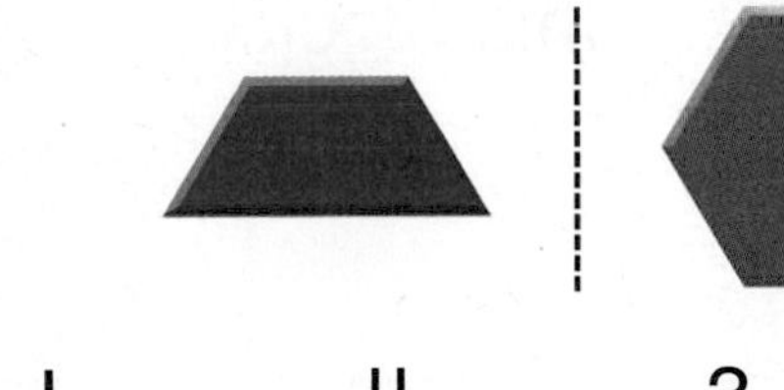

1 ○ 4 ○ 3 ○ 2 ○

Copyright © by William H. Sadlier, Inc. All rights reserved.

Connection

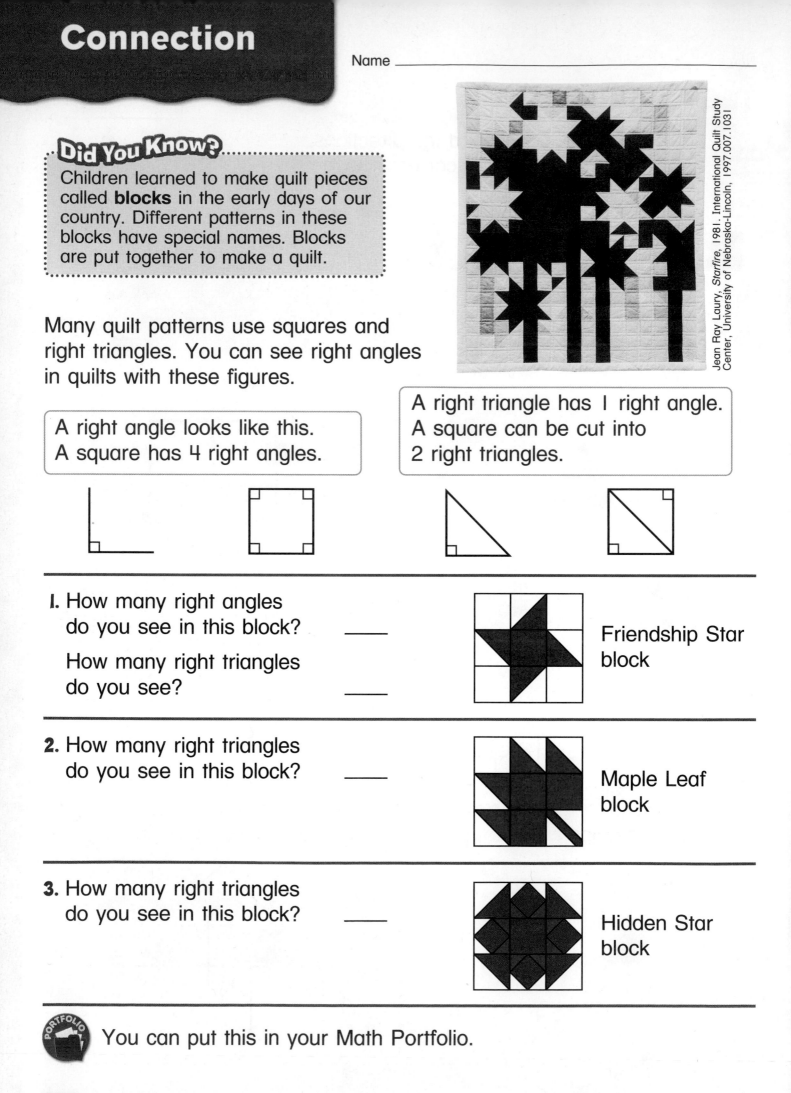

Name ______________________________

Jean Ray Laury, *Starfire,* 1981. International Quilt Study Center, University of Nebraska-Lincoln, 1997.007.1031

Did You Know?

Children learned to make quilt pieces called **blocks** in the early days of our country. Different patterns in these blocks have special names. Blocks are put together to make a quilt.

Many quilt patterns use squares and right triangles. You can see right angles in quilts with these figures.

A right angle looks like this.
A square has 4 right angles.

A right triangle has 1 right angle.
A square can be cut into 2 right triangles.

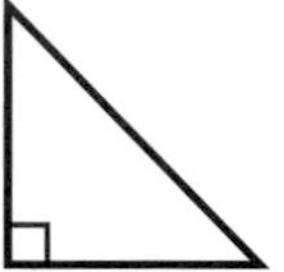

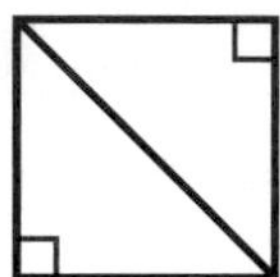

1. How many right angles do you see in this block? ____

   How many right triangles do you see? ____

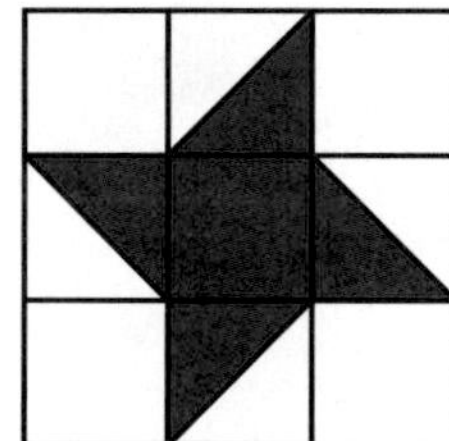

Friendship Star block

2. How many right triangles do you see in this block? ____

Maple Leaf block

3. How many right triangles do you see in this block? ____

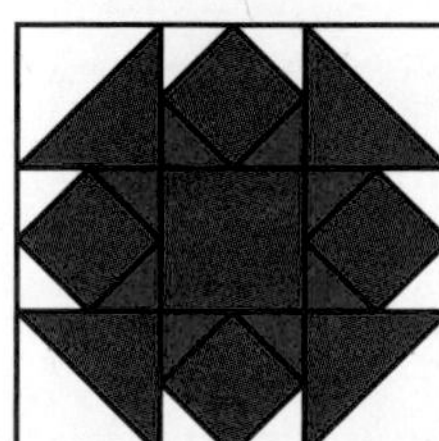

Hidden Star block

You can put this in your Math Portfolio.

Name ___________________________

Chapter 6 Test

1. Write the name of the figure.

____

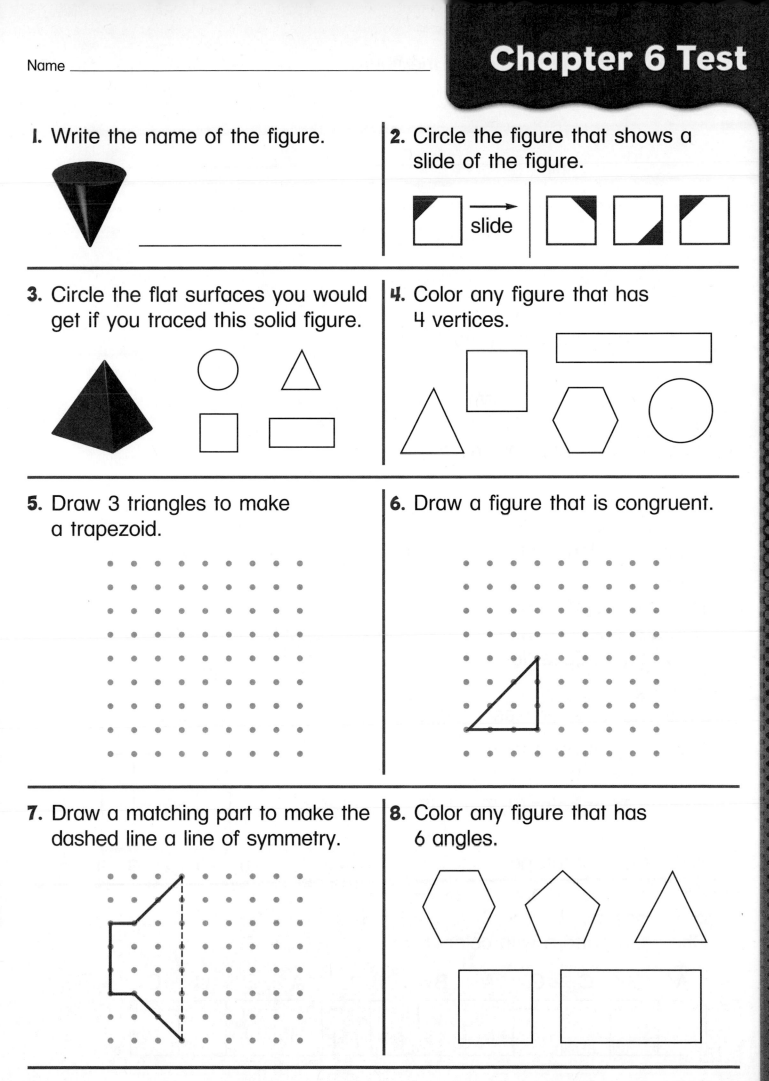

2. Circle the figure that shows a slide of the figure.

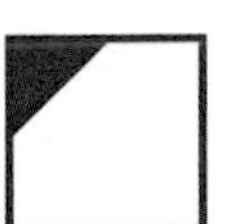

3. Circle the flat surfaces you would get if you traced this solid figure.

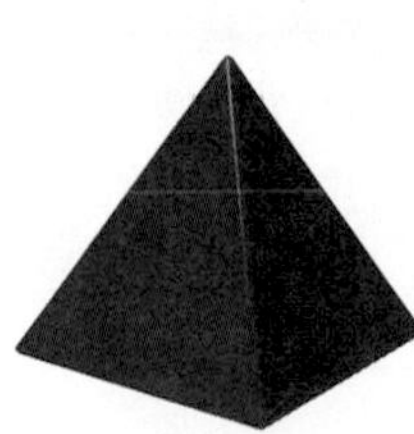

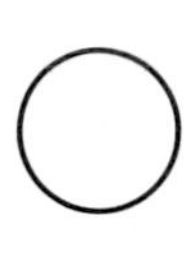

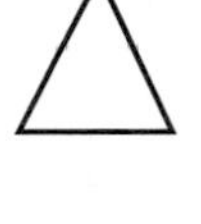

4. Color any figure that has 4 vertices.

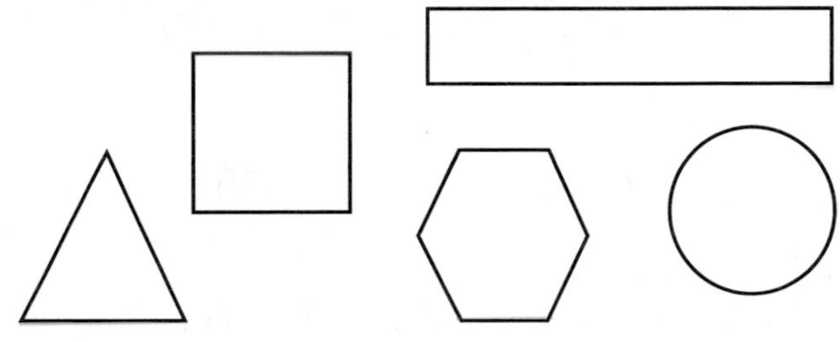

5. Draw 3 triangles to make a trapezoid.

6. Draw a figure that is congruent.

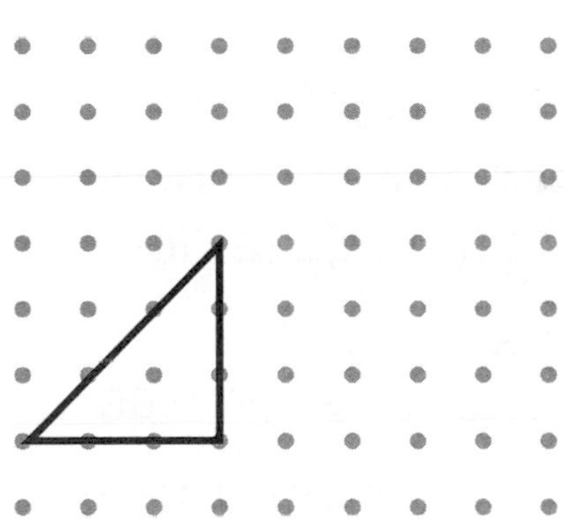

7. Draw a matching part to make the dashed line a line of symmetry.

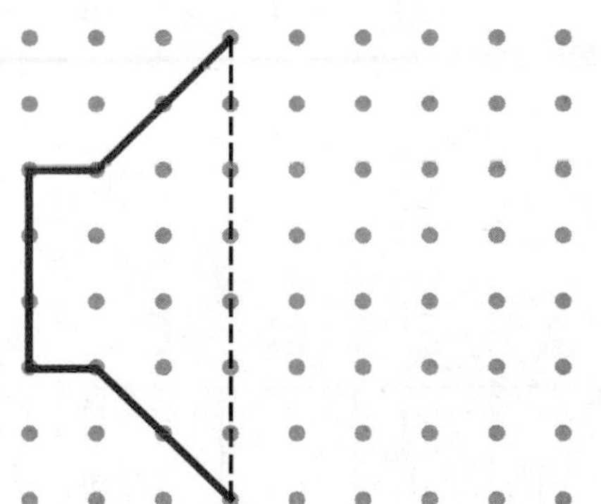

8. Color any figure that has 6 angles.

Copyright © by William H. Sadlier, Inc. All rights reserved.

Circle to predict the position of the figure after it is moved.

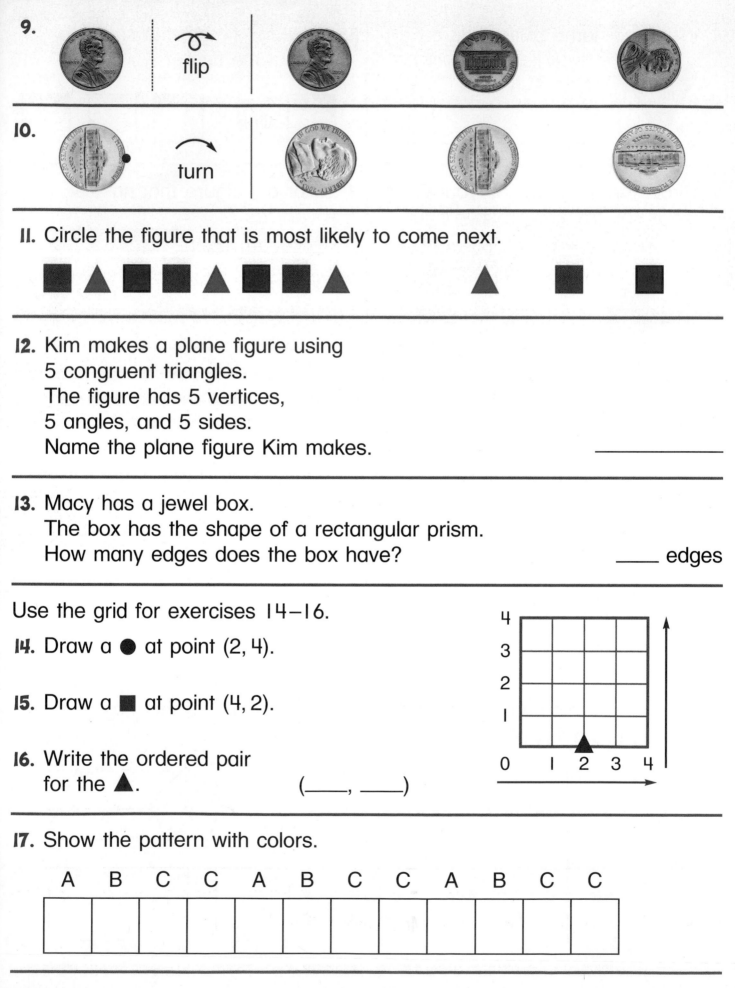

9. flip

10. turn

11. Circle the figure that is most likely to come next.

■ ▲ ■ ■ ▲ ■ ■ ▲ ▲ ■ ■

12. Kim makes a plane figure using
5 congruent triangles.
The figure has 5 vertices,
5 angles, and 5 sides.
Name the plane figure Kim makes. ________

13. Macy has a jewel box.
The box has the shape of a rectangular prism.
How many edges does the box have? ____ edges

Use the grid for exercises 14–16.

14. Draw a ● at point (2, 4).

15. Draw a ■ at point (4, 2).

16. Write the ordered pair
for the ▲. (____, ____)

4
3
2
1
0 1 2 3 4

17. Show the pattern with colors.

A	B	C	C	A	B	C	C	A	B	C	C

Name ______________________

Performance Assessment
Chapter 6

1. Draw a figure with more than one line of symmetry.

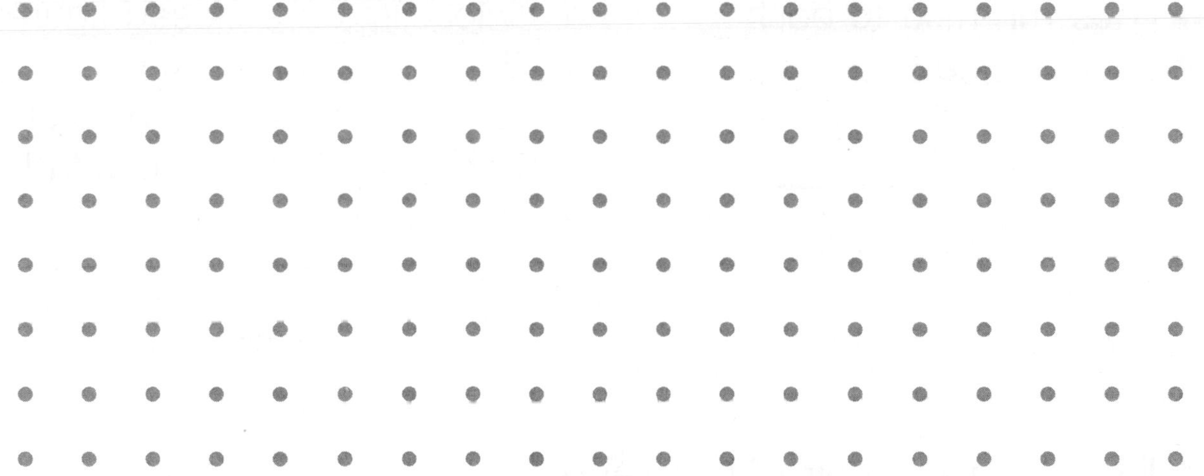

2. Now draw all of the figure's lines of symmetry.

3. Explain why the lines you drew are lines of symmetry.

____

____

____

4. Choose your own way to sort these figures.
Color the group. Tell how you sorted.

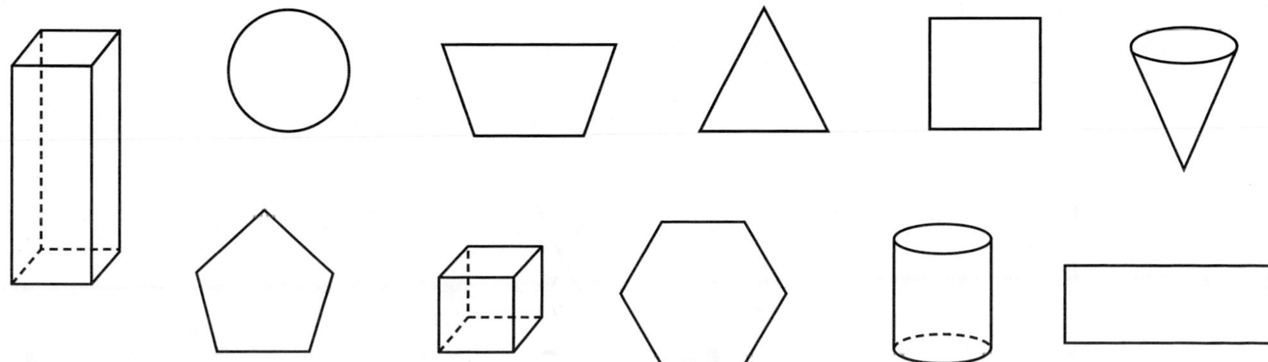

I sorted ______________________.

You can put this in your Math Portfolio.

Copyright © by William H. Sadlier, Inc. All rights reserved.

Enrichment

Name ______________________________

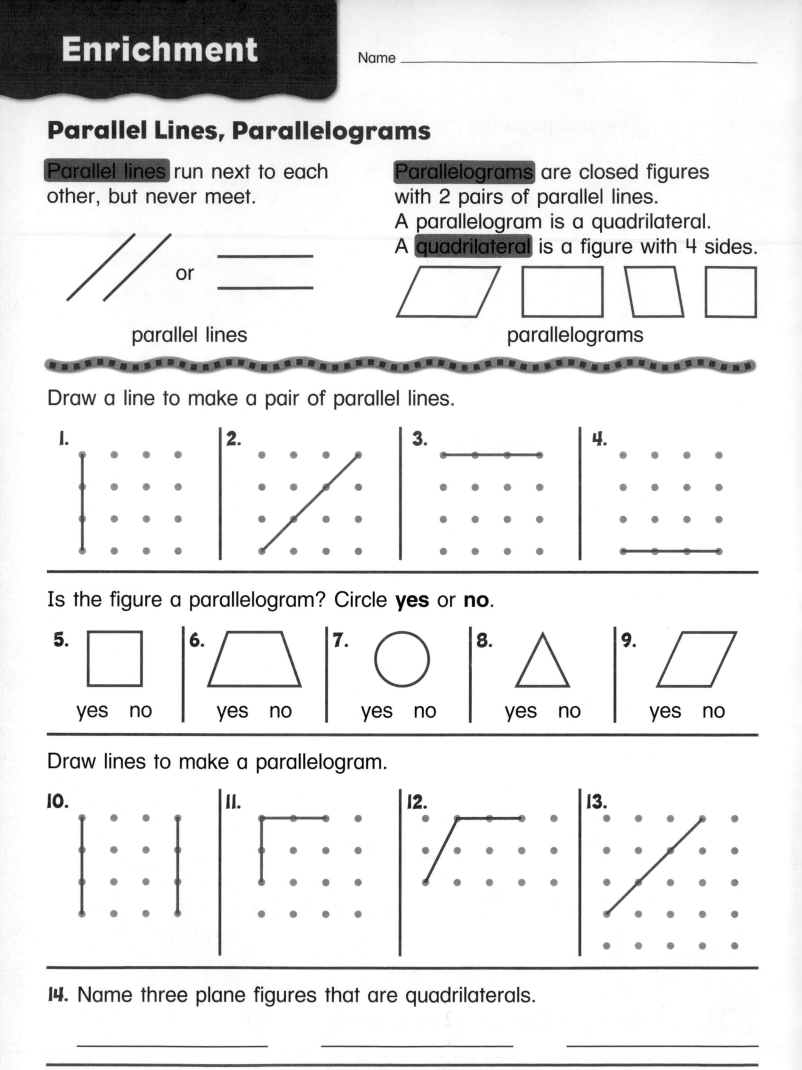

Parallel Lines, Parallelograms

Parallel lines run next to each other, but never meet.

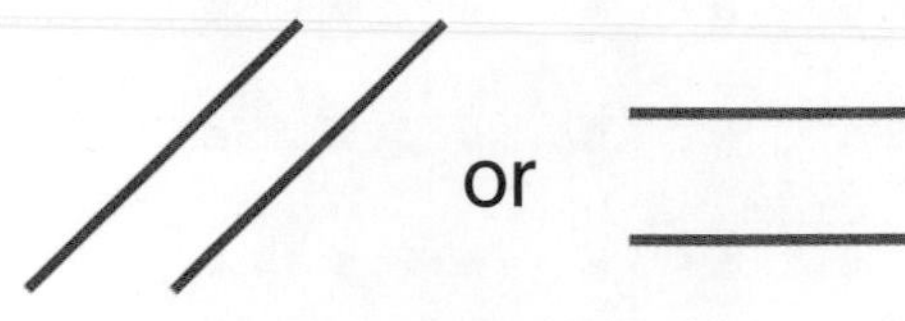

parallel lines

Parallelograms are closed figures with 2 pairs of parallel lines.
A parallelogram is a quadrilateral.
A **quadrilateral** is a figure with 4 sides.

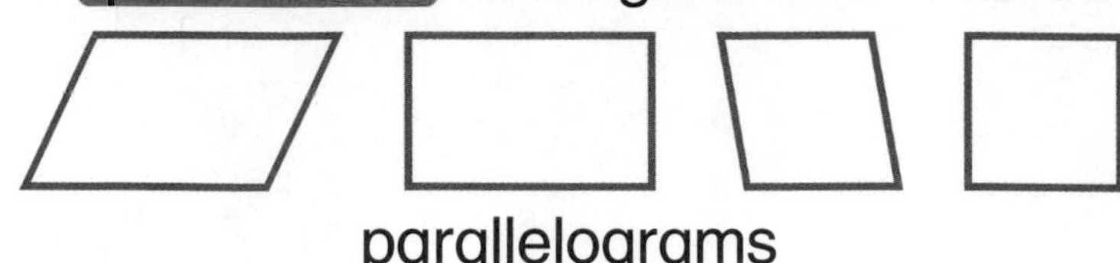

parallelograms

Draw a line to make a pair of parallel lines.

1. 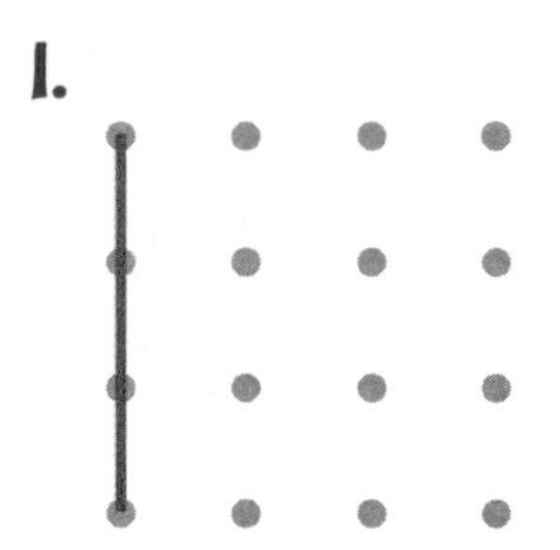

2. 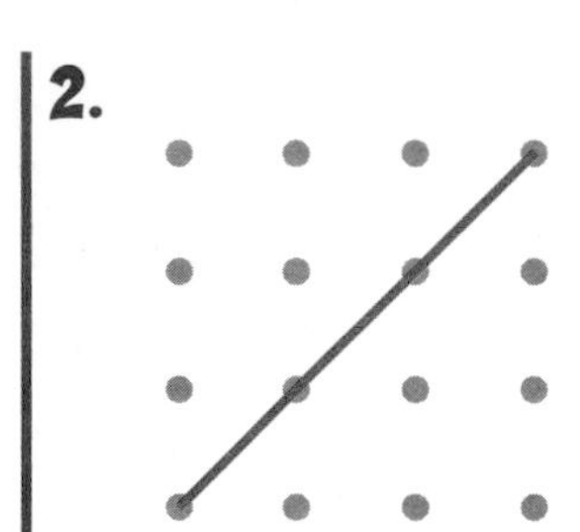

3. 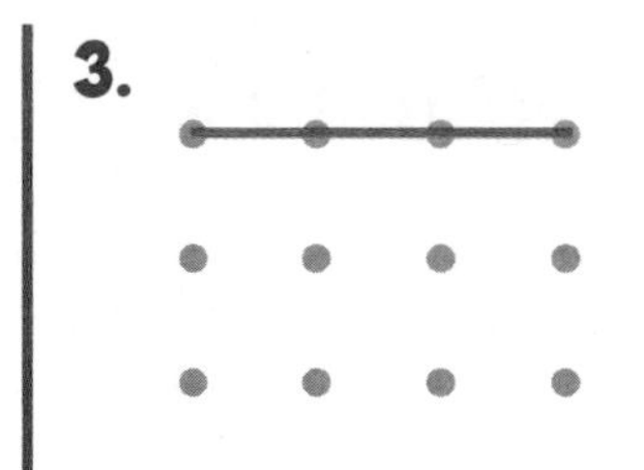

4. 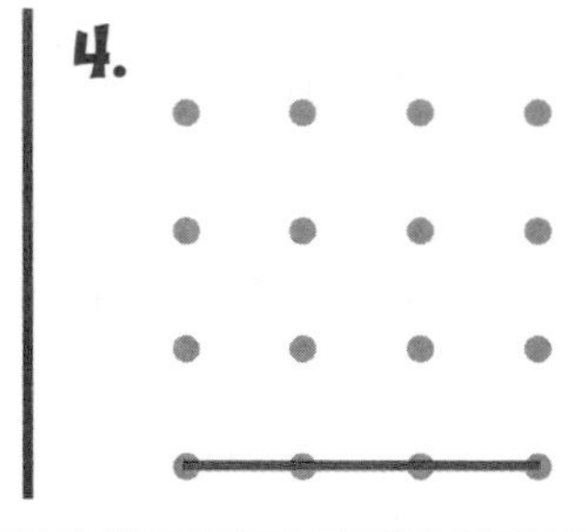

Is the figure a parallelogram? Circle **yes** or **no**.

5. yes no

6. 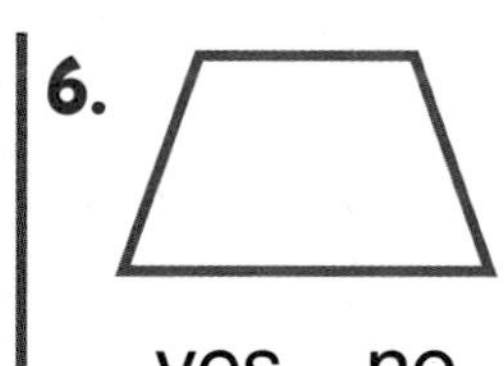 yes no

7. yes no

8. 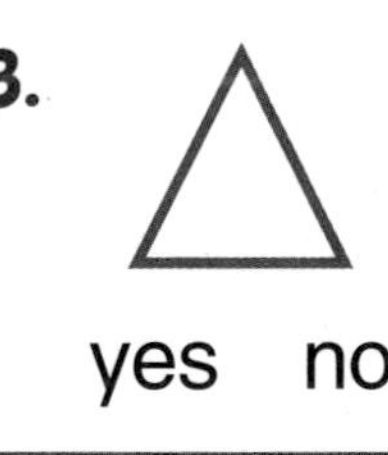 yes no

9. 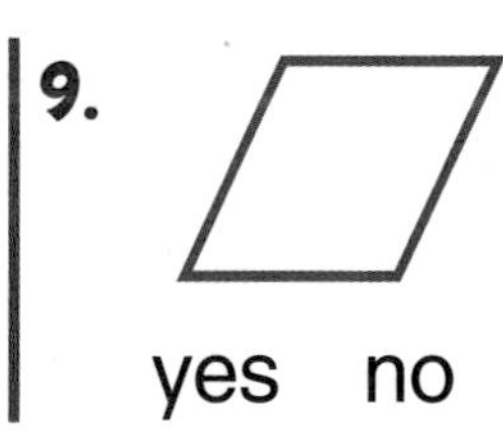 yes no

Draw lines to make a parallelogram.

10. 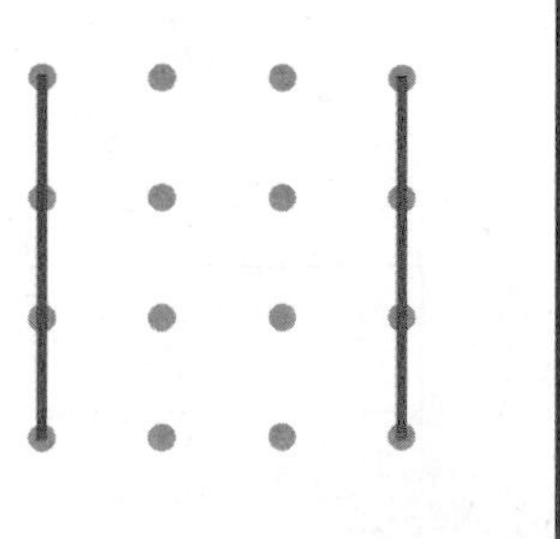

11. 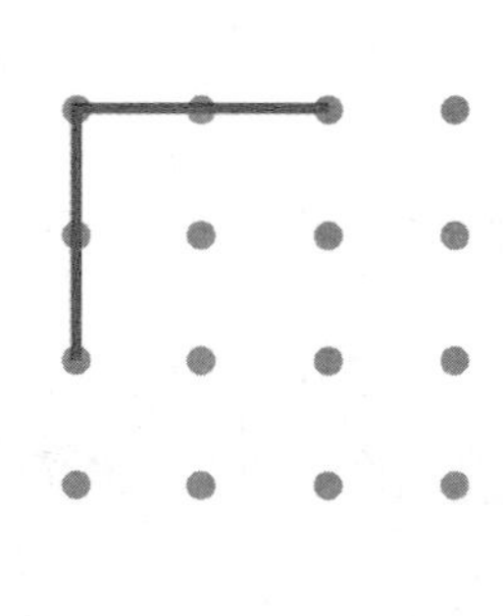

12.

13. 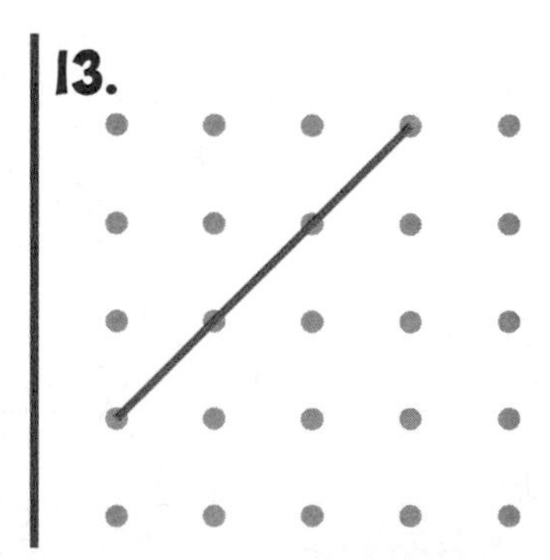

14. Name three plane figures that are quadrilaterals.

______________ ______________ ______________

Name ____________________

TEST PREPARATION

Fill in the circle under the correct answer.

1. Which shows a line of symmetry?

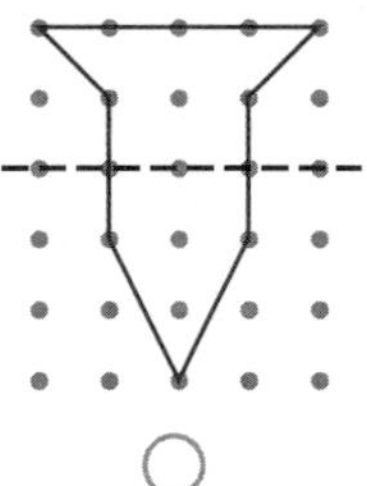 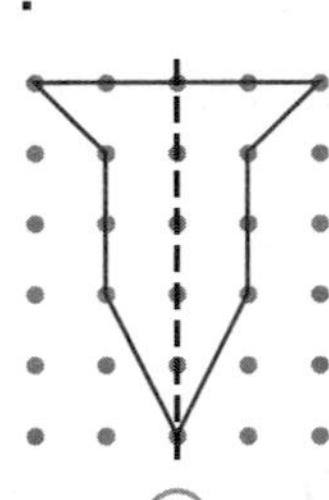 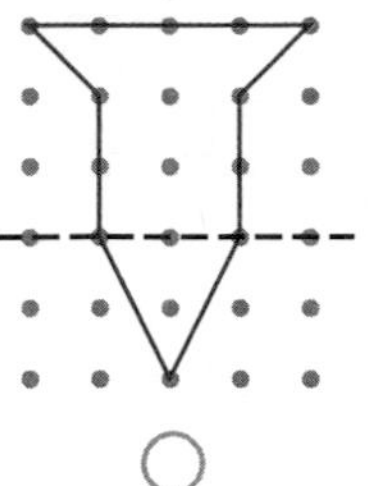

○ ○ ○

2. How was the figure moved?

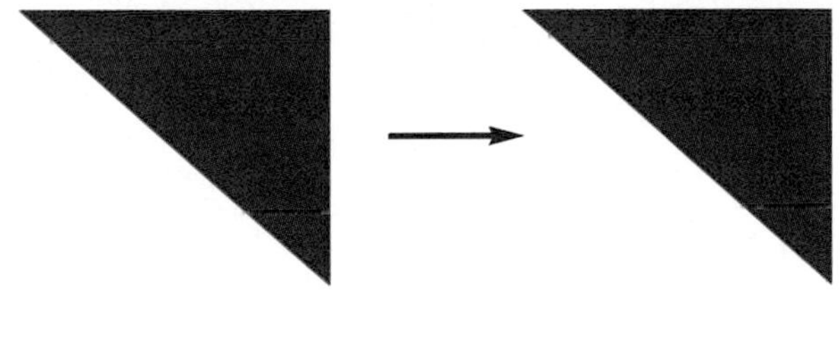

slide	flip	turn
○	○	○

3. Find the difference.

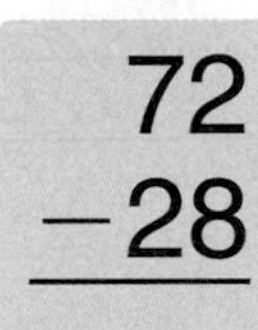

$$\begin{array}{r} 72 \\ -28 \\ \hline \end{array}$$

44	43	34	45
○	○	○	○

4. Add.

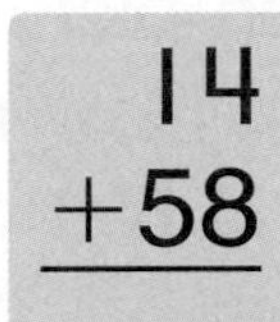

$$\begin{array}{r} 14 \\ +58 \\ \hline \end{array}$$

72	62	73	82
○	○	○	○

5. Choose the solid figure the object looks like.

cylinder	cone	sphere
○	○	○

6. Which color did most people vote for?

Favorite Color

red	yellow	green	orange
○	○	○	○

7. Which list is in order from greatest to least?

27, 45, 33	33, 45, 27
○	○
45, 33, 27	27, 33, 45
○	○

8. How many edges does this figure have?

12	10	8	9
○	○	○	○

Copyright © by William H. Sadlier, Inc. All rights reserved.

Fill in the circle under the correct answer.
Watch for multistep problems.

9. A flower shop has 25 red roses and 30 yellow roses. The number of pink roses in the shop is ten more than 22. How many roses does the shop have in all?

55	65	77	87
○	○	○	○

10. Jenny is twenty-first in line. Nick is 3 places before Jenny. What place in line is Nick?

24th	23rd	20th	18th
○	○	○	○

11. Kim has a pancake stand at the fair. She sells 28 pancakes the first day and 56 pancakes the second day. How many pancakes does Kim sell in all?

74	84	73	83
○	○	○	○

12. Tom finds 14 shells on Monday. He finds 9 shells on Tuesday. How many more shells did he find on Monday?

11	21	7	5
○	○	○	○

13. A bike tour group rides 18 miles the first day. The group rides double that number of miles the second day. How many miles do they ride both days?

36	44	54	56
○	○	○	○

14. Charlie plays a new game. His scores are 17, 31, 23, 28, and 31. What is the mode of these scores?

14	23	31	28
○	○	○	○

15. Tom buys 25 stickers. 10 of them are bug stickers. Gary buys 35 stickers. He gives 10 stickers away. How many stickers do both boys have altogether?

30	40	50	60
○	○	○	○

16. Joan has 17 pictures. Norm has a dozen pictures. Don has 24 pictures. How many pictures do Joan and Norm have in all?

29	31	41	40
○	○	○	○

CHAPTER 7

Money and Time

Listen

Listen to your teacher read the story.

Which item in the store costs the most? Which item costs the least?

Dear Family,

Today our class began Chapter 7. We will learn about money and time. Let's do the activity below together so I can review the skills I will need in order to understand the math in this chapter. Then you can read some of the new vocabulary I will learn in Chapter 7.

Love, ____________

Coin Sort

Put a set of quarters, dimes, nickels, and pennies on a table, with some heads and tails of each coin showing. Have your child identify each kind of coin, tell its value, and tell which coin has the greatest value and which has the least value. Then have your child sort the coins, putting all coins of the same value together.

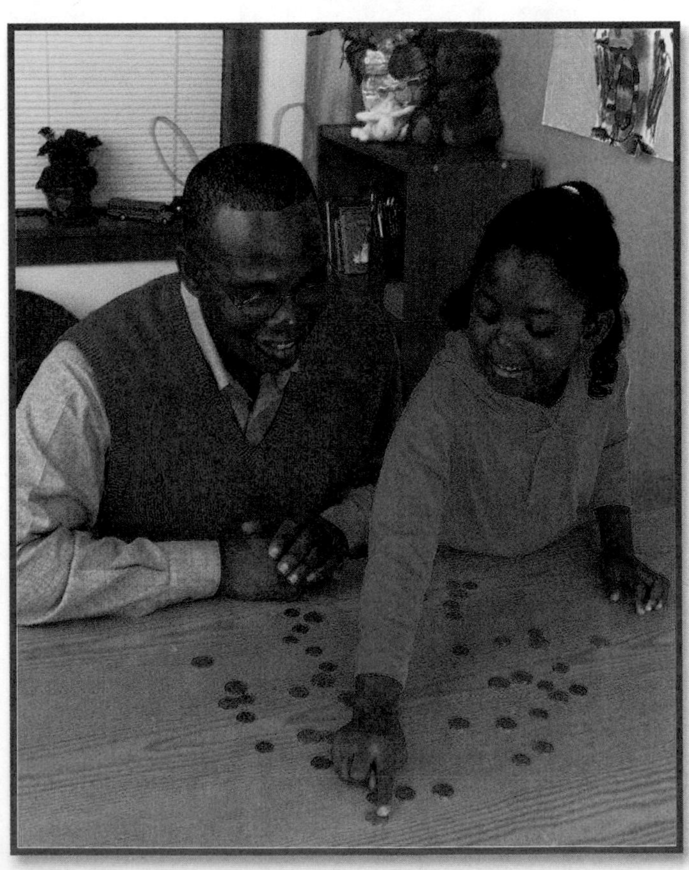

Chapter 7 Vocabulary

also on-line

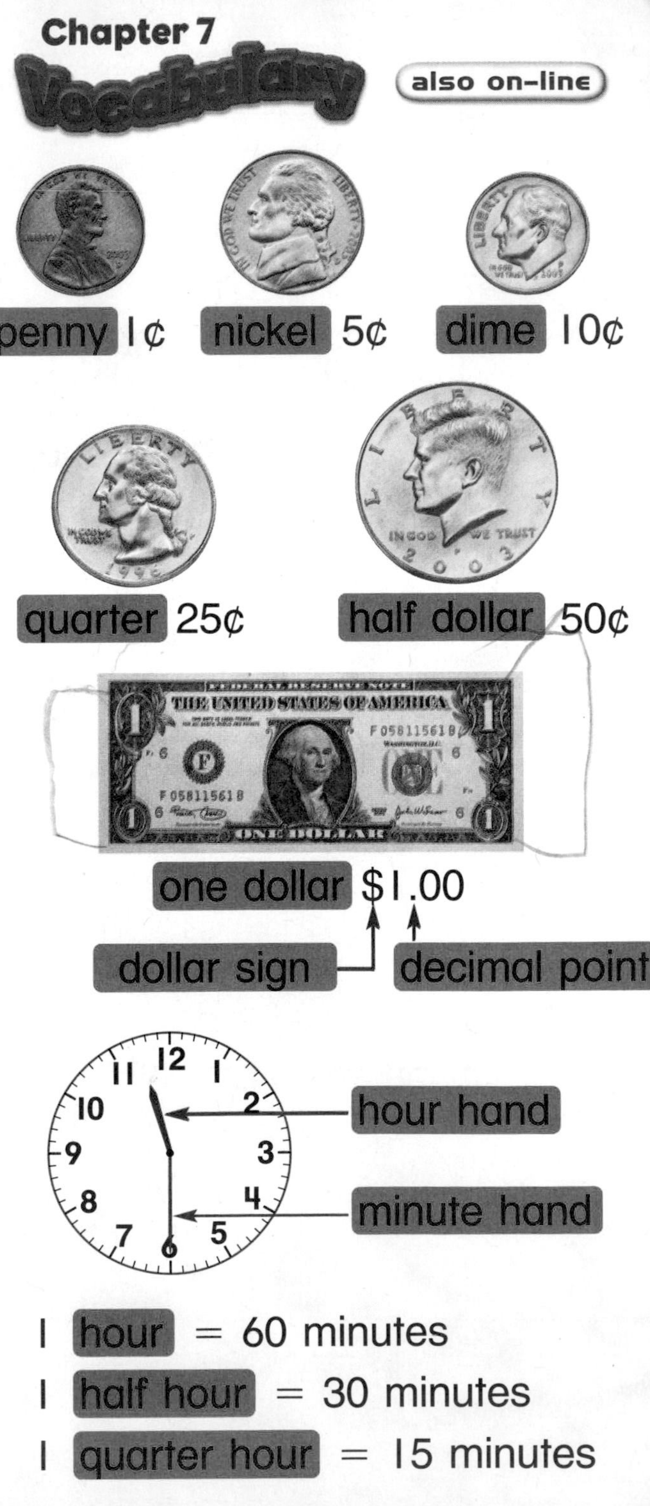

1 hour = 60 minutes

1 half hour = 30 minutes

1 quarter hour = 15 minutes

For Additional Resources: VISIT US ON-LINE www.sadlier-oxford.com

Name ______________________

Pennies, Nickels, and Dimes

Let's Learn!

What is the total amount of these coins?

Put the coins in order from greatest to least value.

Count on by 10s for dimes. Count on by 5s for nickels. Count on by 1s for pennies.

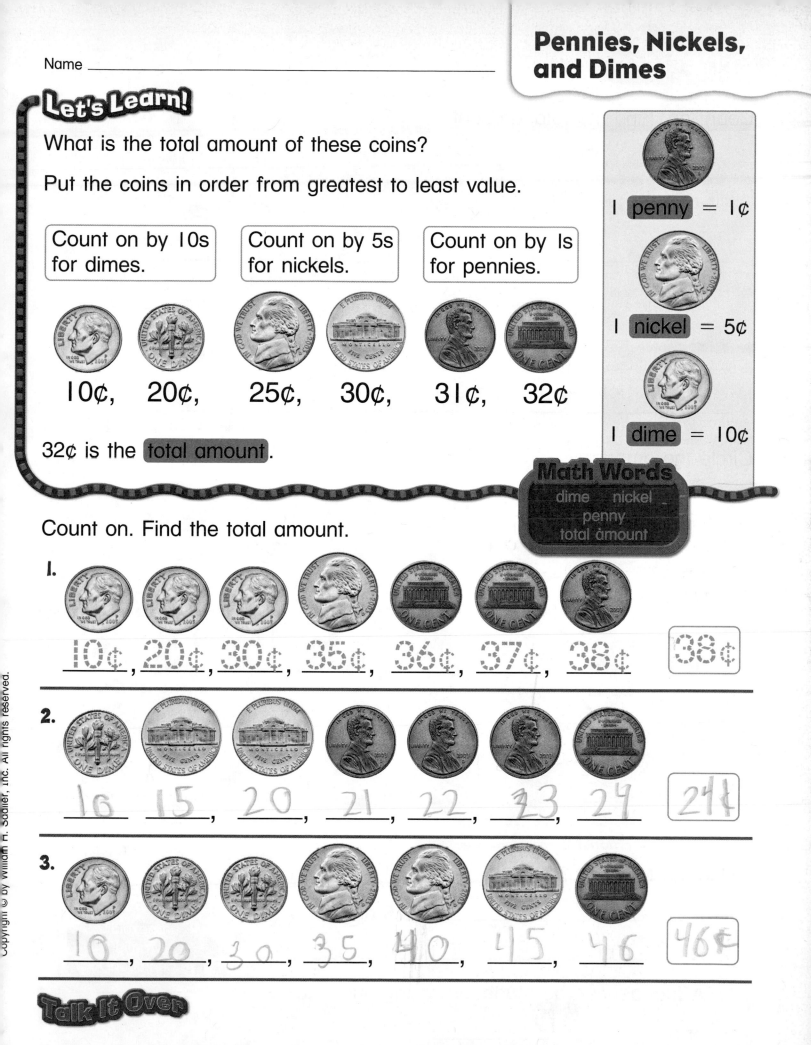

10¢, 20¢, 25¢, 30¢, 31¢, 32¢

32¢ is the **total amount**.

Math Words
dime nickel
penny
total amount

Count on. Find the total amount.

1. 

10¢, 20¢, 30¢, 35¢, 36¢, 37¢, 38¢

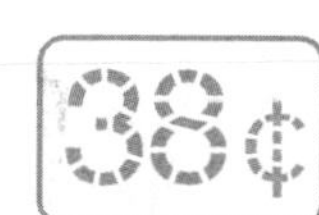

2. 

10 15, 20, 21, 22, 23, 24

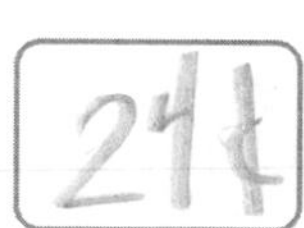

3. 

10, 20, 30, 35, 40, 45, 46

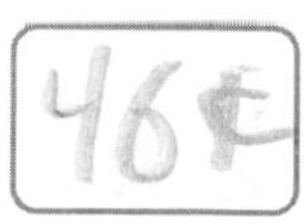

Talk It Over

4. How does sorting like coins and then ordering them from greatest to least value help you find the total amount?

Copyright © by William H. Sadlier, Inc. All rights reserved.

Practice

Count on. Find the total amount.

5.     

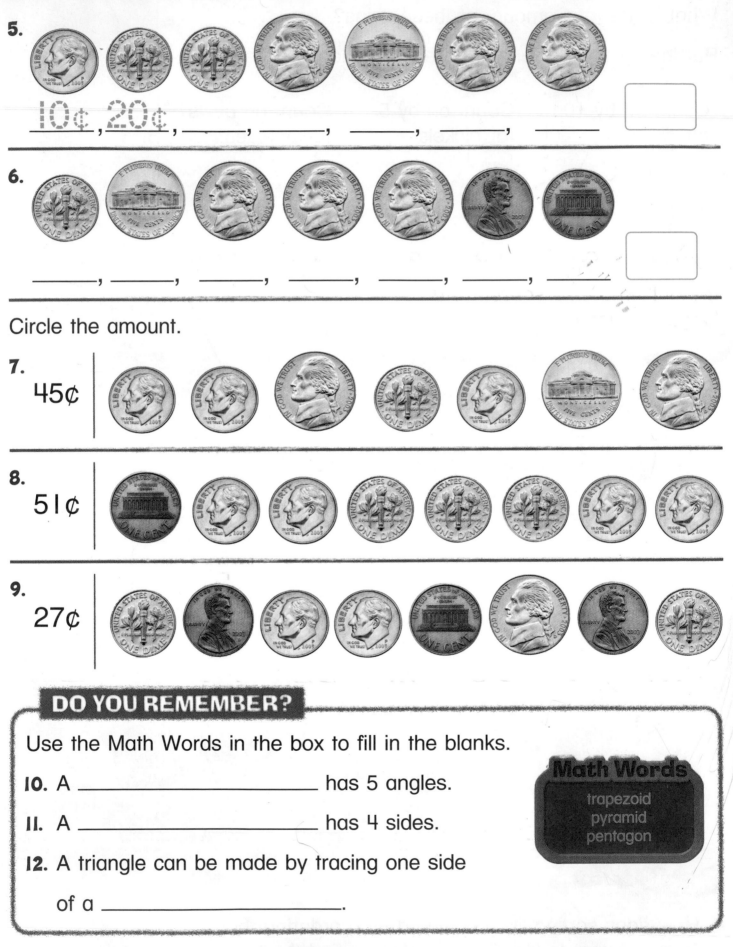

10¢, 20¢, ______, ______, ______, ______, ______ ☐

6.       

______, ______, ______, ______, ______, ______, ______ ☐

Circle the amount.

7. 45¢       

8. 51¢        

9. 27¢        

DO YOU REMEMBER?

Use the Math Words in the box to fill in the blanks.

10. A ______________________ has 5 angles.

11. A ______________________ has 4 sides.

12. A triangle can be made by tracing one side of a ______________________.

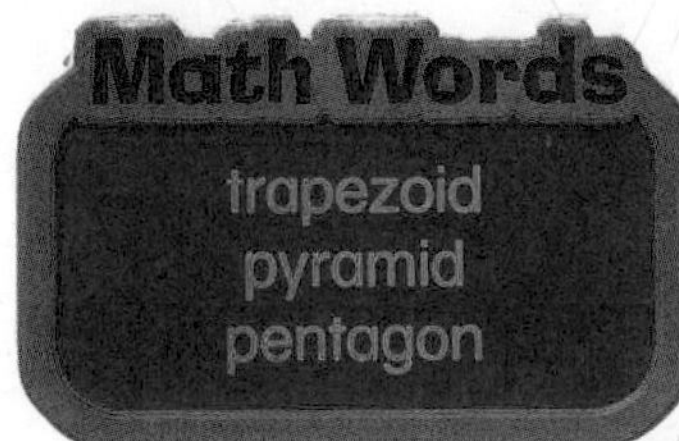

Math Alive at Home Give your child some pennies, nickels, and dimes totaling less than one dollar. Ask him/her to find the total amount.

Name ______________________________

Let's Learn!

Darlene is saving to buy a book about time travel. What is the amount she has saved so far?

1 **quarter** = 25¢

Count on by 25s for quarters.

Then count on by 10s, 5s, and 1s.

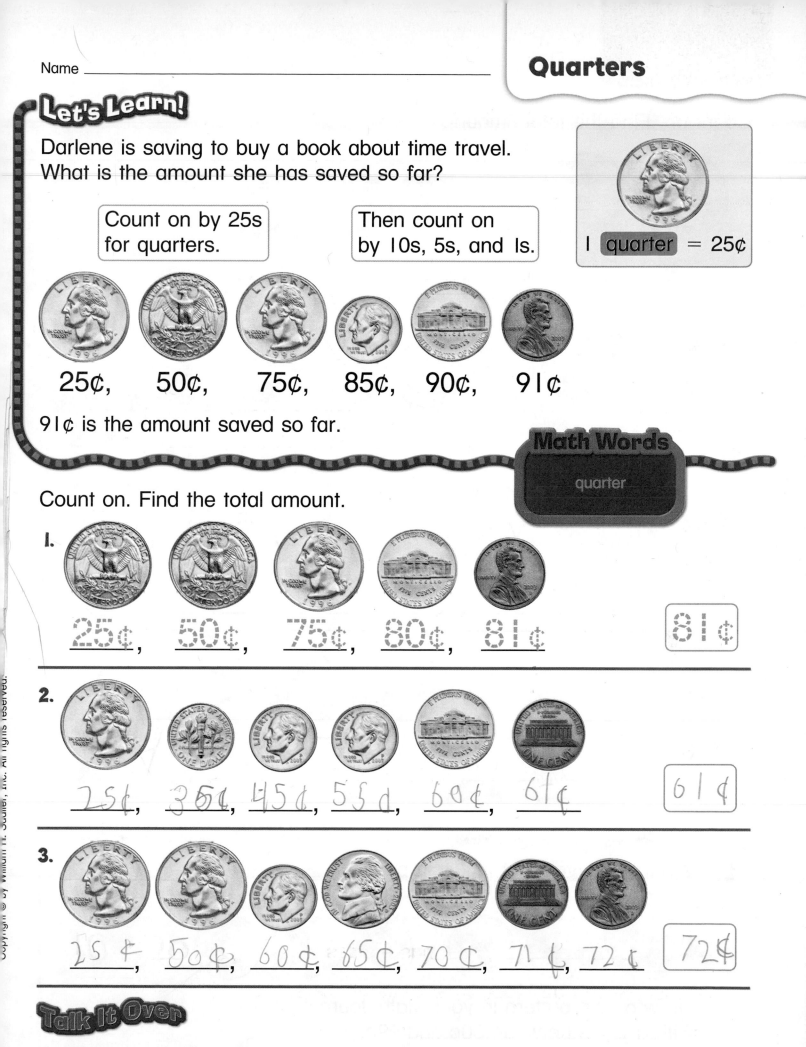

25¢, 50¢, 75¢, 85¢, 90¢, 91¢

91¢ is the amount saved so far.

Math Words

quarter

Count on. Find the total amount.

1.      

25¢, 50¢, 75¢, 80¢, 81¢ — 81¢

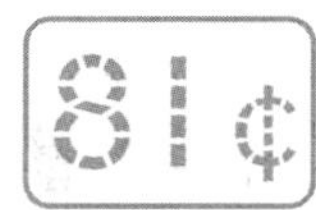

2.      

25¢, 35¢, 45¢, 55¢, 60¢, 61¢ — 61¢

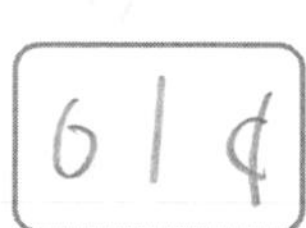

3.      

25¢, 50¢, 60¢, 65¢, 70¢, 71¢, 72¢ — 72¢

Talk It Over

4. Name three different ways to show 25¢.

Copyright © by William H. Sadlier, Inc. All rights reserved.

Practice

Count on. Find the total amount.

5.     

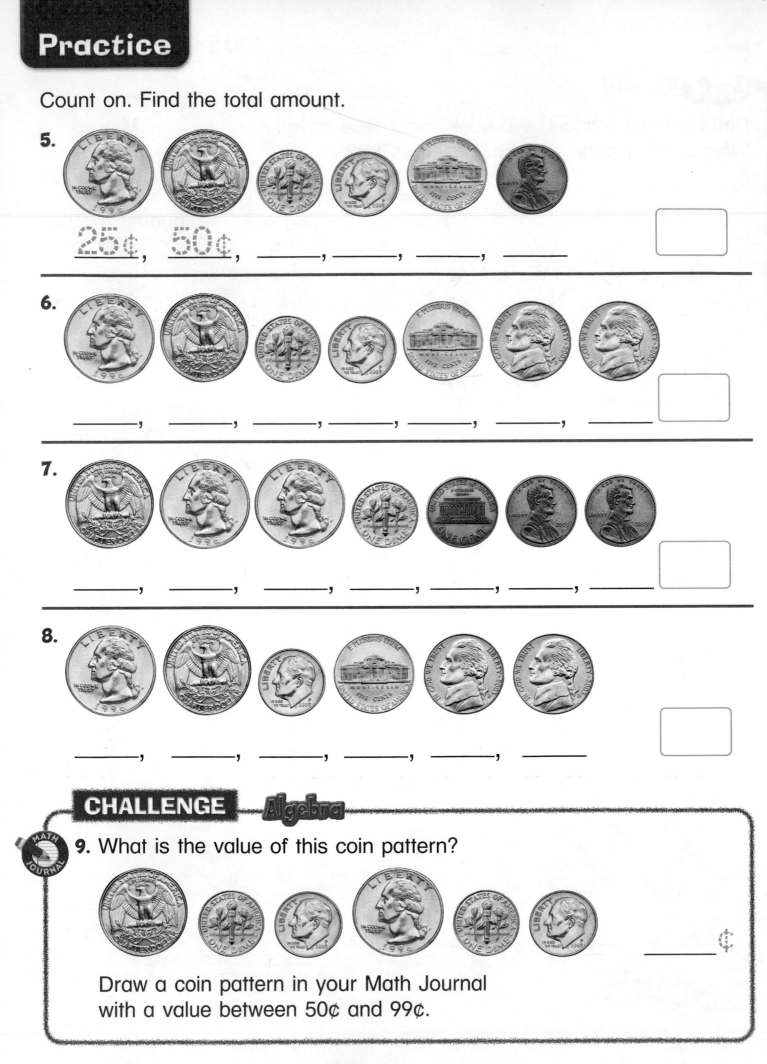

25¢, 50¢, ____, ____, ____, ____ ☐

6.      

____, ____, ____, ____, ____, ____, ____ ☐

7.       

____, ____, ____, ____, ____, ____, ____ ☐

8.      

____, ____, ____, ____, ____, ____ ☐

CHALLENGE

MATH JOURNAL

9. What is the value of this coin pattern?

____ ¢

Draw a coin pattern in your Math Journal with a value between 50¢ and 99¢.

Math Alive at Home Place 2 quarters, 2 dimes, and 2 nickels on a table. Ask your child to show 55¢ and 75¢.

Name ______________________________

Dollars and Cents

Let's Learn!

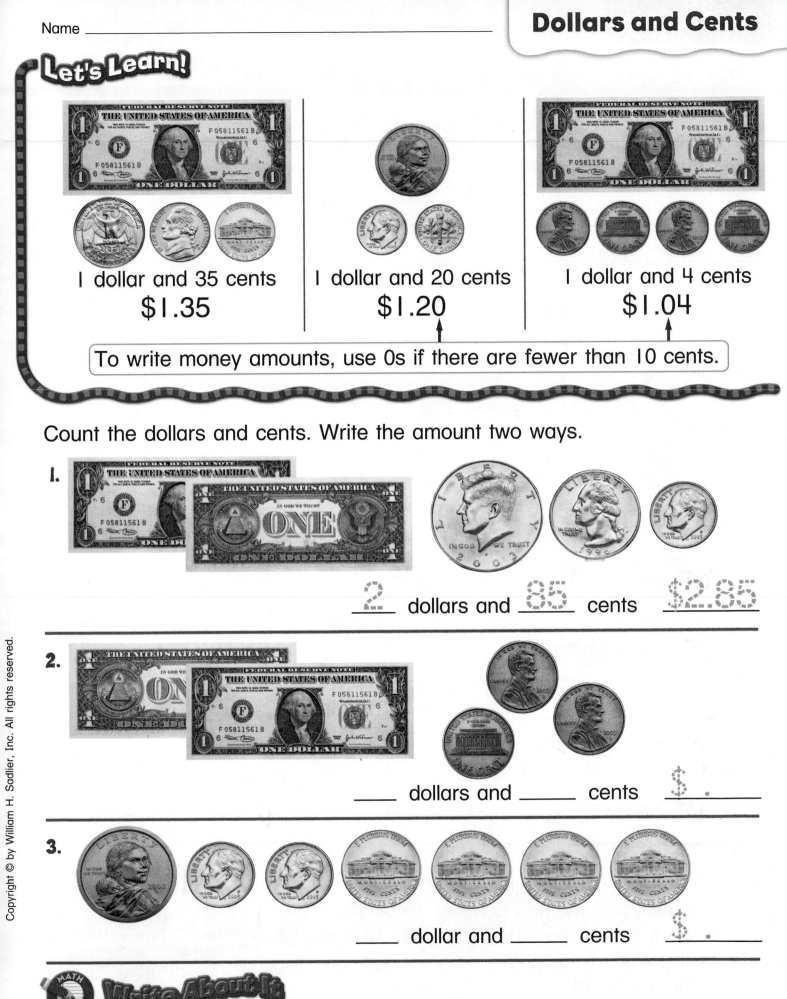

I dollar and 35 cents
$1.35

I dollar and 20 cents
$1.20

I dollar and 4 cents
$1.04

To write money amounts, use 0s if there are fewer than 10 cents.

Count the dollars and cents. Write the amount two ways.

1.    

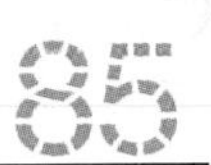 2 dollars and 85 cents  $2.85

2.  

____ dollars and ____ cents 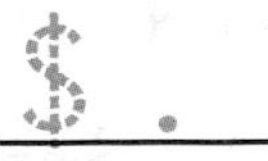 $___.___

3.       

____ dollar and ____ cents $___.___

Write About It

4. What does the 0 stand for in $1.04 and in $1.40?

Copyright © by William H. Sadlier, Inc. All rights reserved.

Practice

Remember:
Write 0s if there are no dimes or pennies.

Write the amount. Use a dollar sign and decimal point.

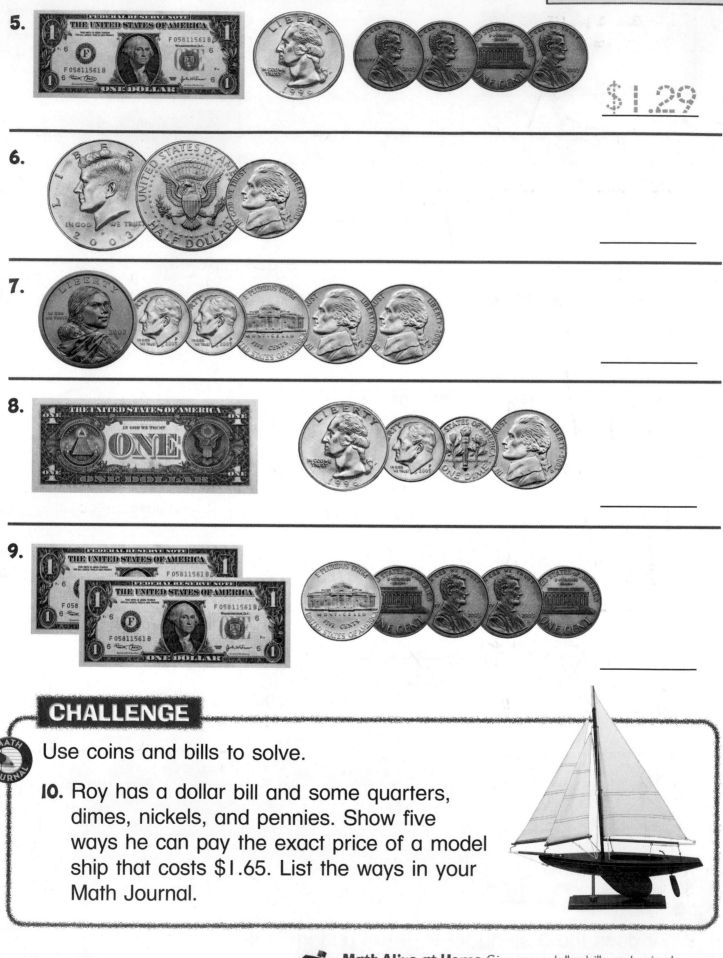

5.    $1.29

6.  ______

7.  ______

8.   ______

9.   ______

CHALLENGE

Use coins and bills to solve.

10. Roy has a dollar bill and some quarters, dimes, nickels, and pennies. Show five ways he can pay the exact price of a model ship that costs $1.65. List the ways in your Math Journal.

Math Alive at Home Give some dollar bills and coins to your child. Ask her/him to count the value of the bills and coins aloud and to write the total amount.

Name ______________________________

Check Your Progress
Lessons 4-9

TEST PREPARATION

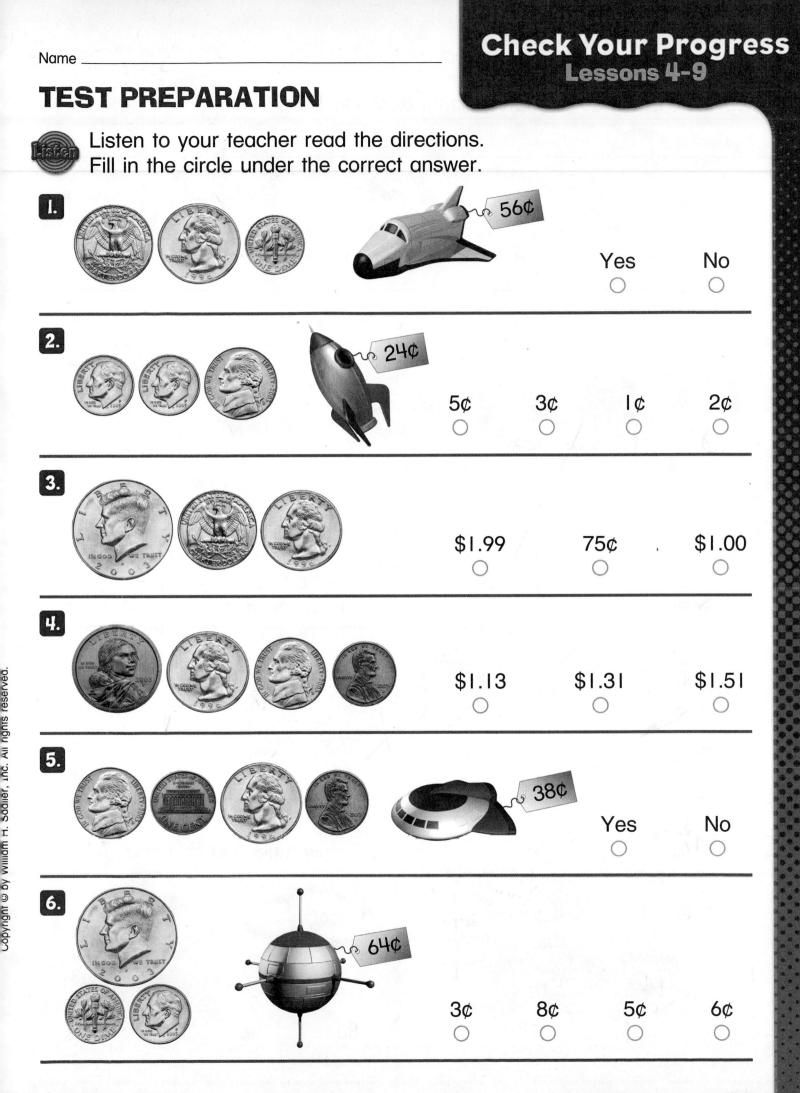

Listen to your teacher read the directions.
Fill in the circle under the correct answer.

1.

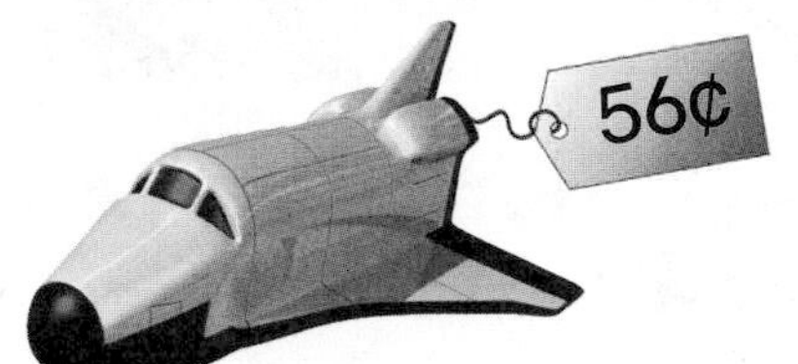

Yes ○ No ○

2.

5¢ ○ 3¢ ○ 1¢ ○ 2¢ ○

3.

$1.99 ○ 75¢ ○ $1.00 ○

4.

$1.13 ○ $1.31 ○ $1.51 ○

5.

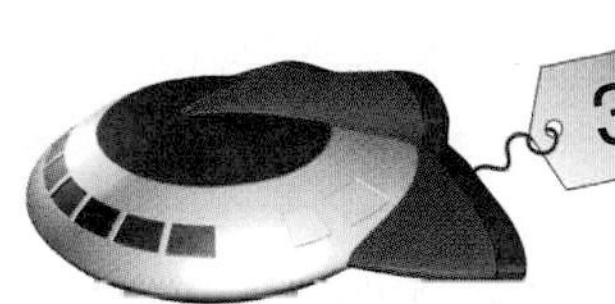

Yes ○ No ○

6.

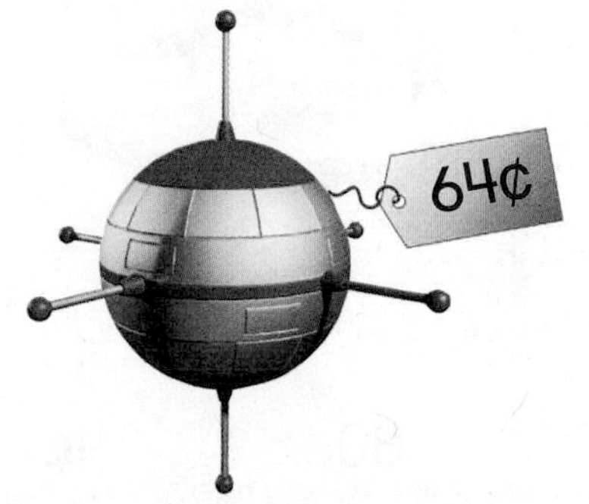

3¢ ○ 8¢ ○ 5¢ ○ 6¢ ○

Copyright © by William H. Sadlier, Inc. All rights reserved.

Fill in the circle under the correct answer.

7. Which shows the same amount as these coins?

○ ○

8. Count the dollars and cents. Which shows the total amount?

$1.06	$1.09	$1.90	$1.60
○	○	○	○

9. Find the total amount. Is the total enough money to buy the toy?

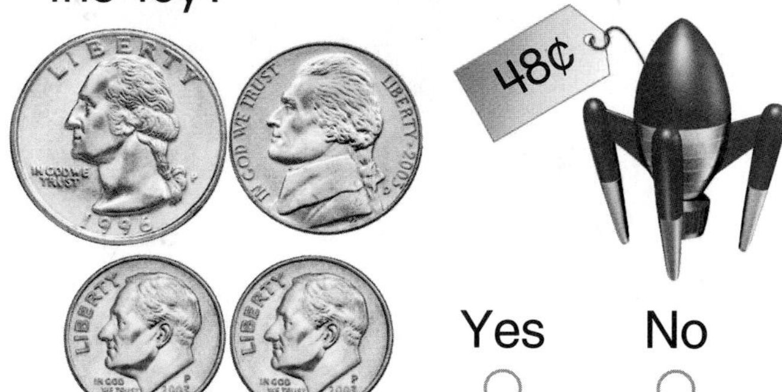

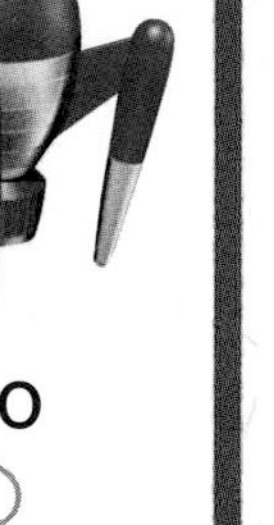

Yes	No
○	○

10. Jerry wants to buy a toy that costs 96¢. He has only 58¢. How much more money does he need?

36¢	46¢	38¢	48¢
○	○	○	○

11. Is this amount equal to $1.00?

Yes	No
○	○

12. Laura bought these two toys. How much did she spend?

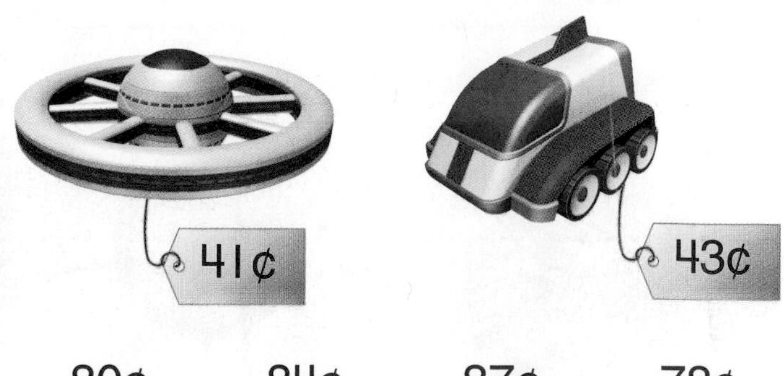

80¢	84¢	87¢	78¢
○	○	○	○

Name ____________________

Let's Learn!

The tick marks around the face of a clock stand for minutes.
There are five minutes from one number to the next.

1 **hour** = 60 minutes

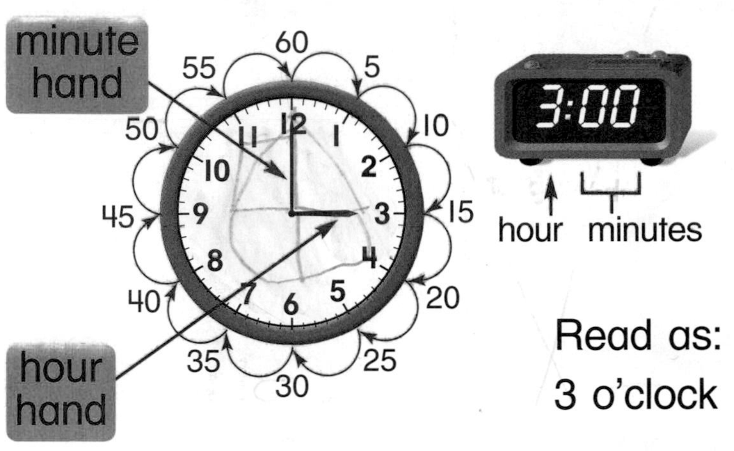

Read as:
3 o'clock

1 **half hour** = 30 minutes

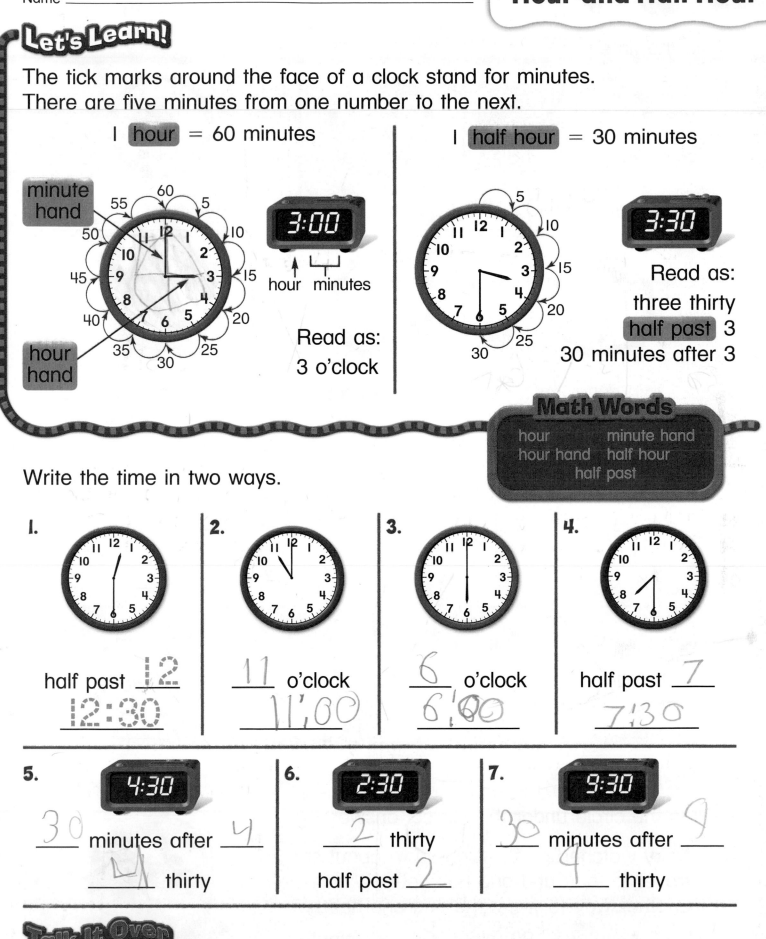

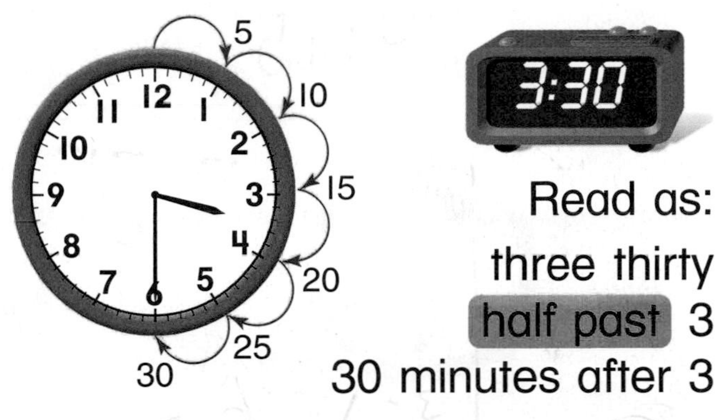

Read as:
three thirty
half past 3
30 minutes after 3

Math Words
hour — minute hand
hour hand — half hour
half past

Write the time in two ways.

1.

half past 12
12:30

2.

11 o'clock
11:00

3.

6 o'clock
6:00

4.

half past 7
7:30

5.

30 minutes after 4
4 thirty

6.

2 thirty
half past 2

7.

30 minutes after 9
9 thirty

8. What is the difference in the position of the hour and minute hands at 3:00 and 3:30?

Copyright © by William H. Sadlier, Inc. All rights reserved.

Practice

Write the time.

9. 

30 minutes after 11

10. 

7 o'clock

11. 

half past 1

12. 

30 minutes after 6

13. 

9 o'clock

14. 

30 minutes after 5

Find the same time on the clocks above. Color to match.

15. 

16. 

17. 

18. 

19. 

20. 

CHALLENGE

Fill in the circle under the correct answer.

21. Mary watched a television show about space travel for one and one half hours. What is another way to write one and one half hours?

60 minutes	90 minutes	150 minutes
○	○	○

Math Alive at Home At the hour and half hour, draw your child's attention to a clock and ask her/him to tell you the time.

Name ______________________

Five Minutes

Let's Learn!

What time is it?

To find the hour, look at the shorter hand, the hour hand.

To find the minutes, start at 12. Count by 5s until you reach the minute hand.

The hour hand moves very slowly from 2 to 3. Say 2 as the hour until the hour hand points exactly to the 3. Then say 3 for the hour.

35 minutes after 2

The time is 2:35.

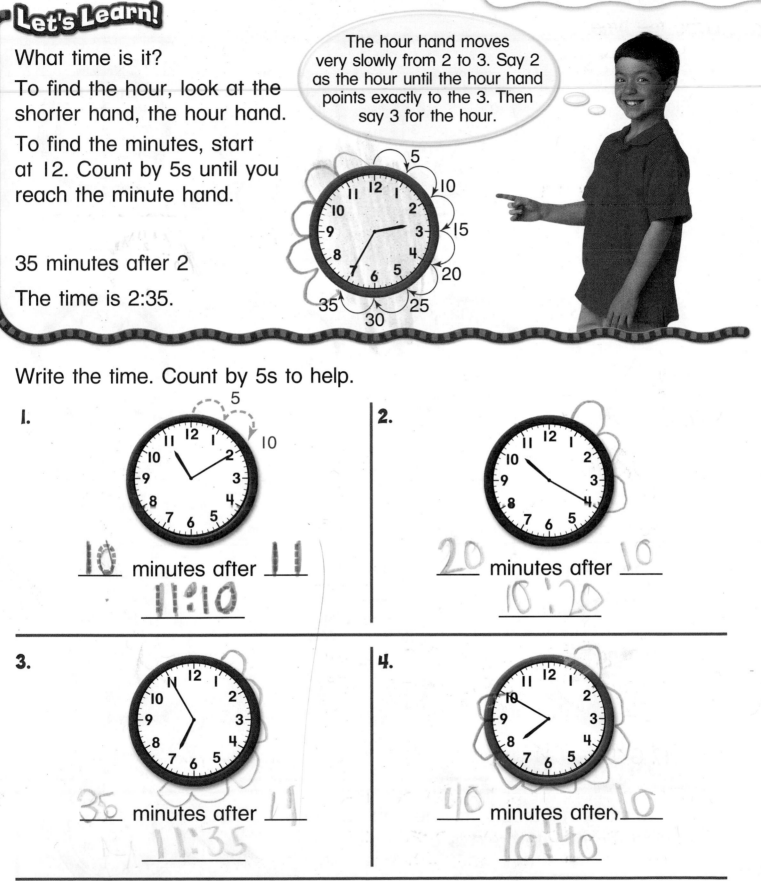

Write the time. Count by 5s to help.

1.

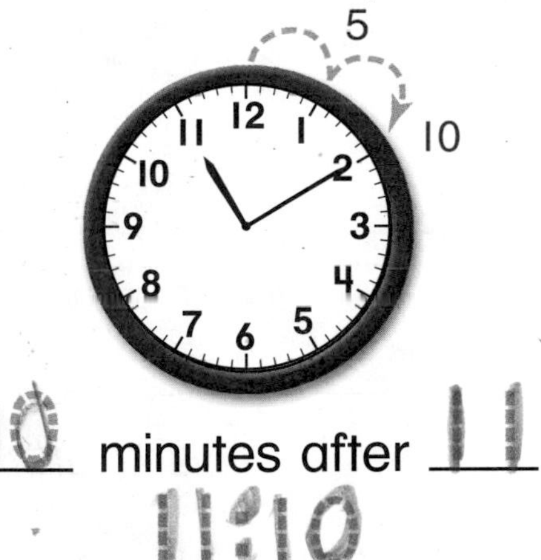

10 minutes after 11

11:10

2.

20 minutes after 10

10:20

3.

35 minutes after 11

11:35

4.

40 minutes after 10

10:40

5. What time is it when the hour hand is between 9 and 10 and the minute hand points to 8? Explain how you know.

Copyright © by William H. Sadlier, Inc. All rights reserved.

Practice

Write the time.

6.

7:05

7.

8.

9.

10.

11.

12.

13.

Draw the minute hand on the clock.

14. nine twenty

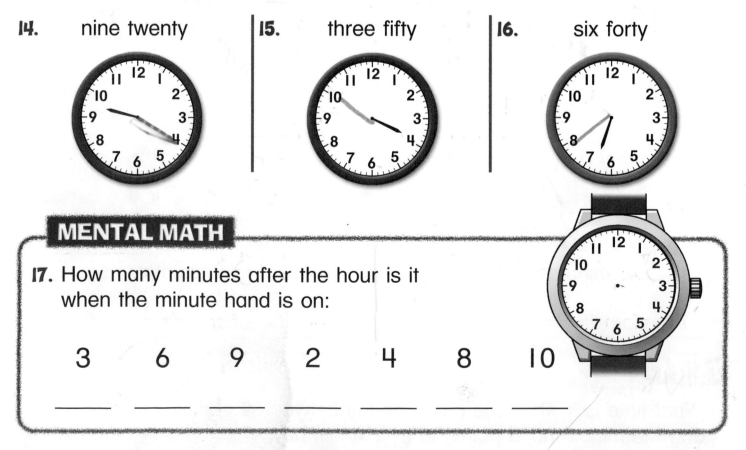

15. three fifty

16. six forty

MENTAL MATH

17. How many minutes after the hour is it when the minute hand is on:

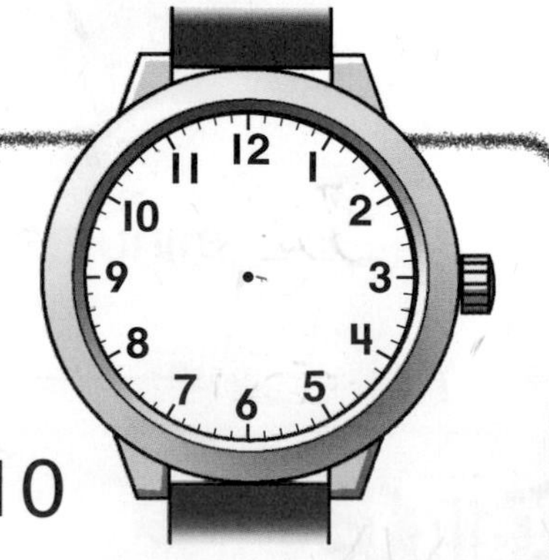

3	6	9	2	4	8	10
____	____	____	____	____	____	____

Math Alive at Home Ask your child where the minute hand would be for 20, 40, and 55 minutes after the hour. (on the 4, 8, 11)

Name ____________________

Let's Learn!

There are 15 minutes in 1 quarter hour.

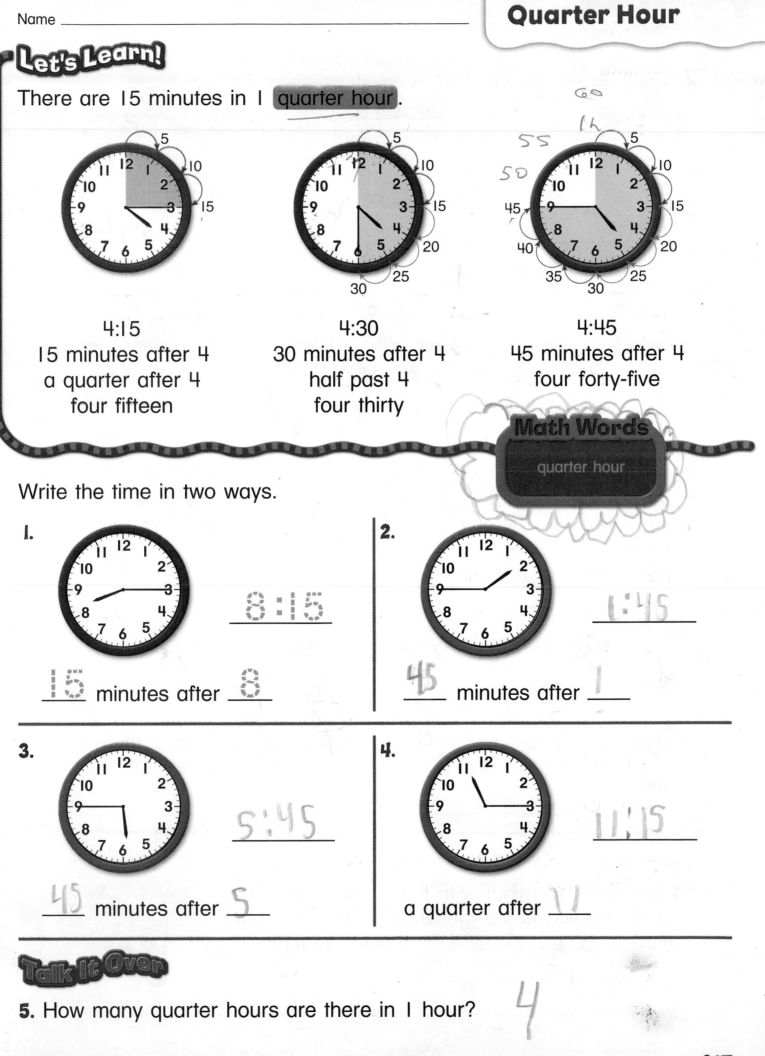

4:15
15 minutes after 4
a quarter after 4
four fifteen

4:30
30 minutes after 4
half past 4
four thirty

4:45
45 minutes after 4
four forty-five

Math Words
quarter hour

Write the time in two ways.

1.

8:15

15 minutes after 8

2.

1:45

45 minutes after 1

3.

5:45

45 minutes after 5

4.

11:15

a quarter after 11

Talk It Over

5. How many quarter hours are there in 1 hour? 4

Copyright © by William H. Sadlier, Inc. All rights reserved.

Practice

Write the time shown on the clock.

6.  9:15

7.  3:15

8.  10:30

Draw the minute hand to show each time.

9. 

10. 

11. 

12. 

13. 

14. 

Solve. Use a problem-solving strategy.

15. John's class was to meet at the space museum at 9:30. John got to the museum at 9:45. Was he early or late?

late

16. Tina was to meet a friend outside the museum at 4:30. She went outside at 4:15. Was she early or late?

early

CHALLENGE

17. A bus takes 15 minutes to travel one way from the bus station to the museum. How long in hours and minutes does it take for 5 one-way trips?

1 hour 15 minutes

Math Alive at Home At the quarter hour, draw your child's attention to a clock and ask her/him to tell you the time.

Name ______________________________

Before the Hour

What time is it?

Times after the half hour can also be read as before the next hour.

To find the time, count each number by 5s from the minute hand to 12.

The time is:
15 minutes before 11
a quarter to 11

You can also read the time as 45 minutes after 10 or 10:45.

Write the time in two ways. Count by 5s to help.

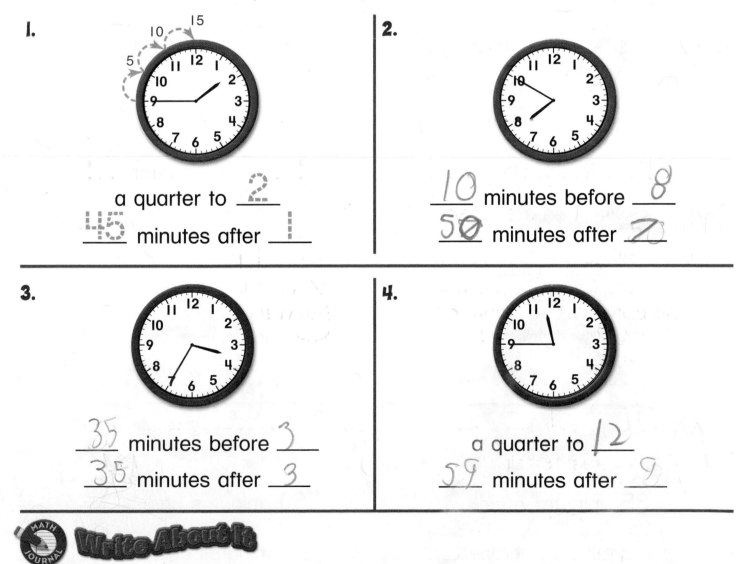

1.

a quarter to 2

45 minutes after 1

2.

10 minutes before 8

50 minutes after 7

3.

35 minutes before 3

35 minutes after 3

4.

a quarter to 12

59 minutes after 9

5. What are two ways to read the time for 2:45?

Copyright © by William H. Sadlier, Inc. All rights reserved.

Practice

Write the time in two ways.

6.

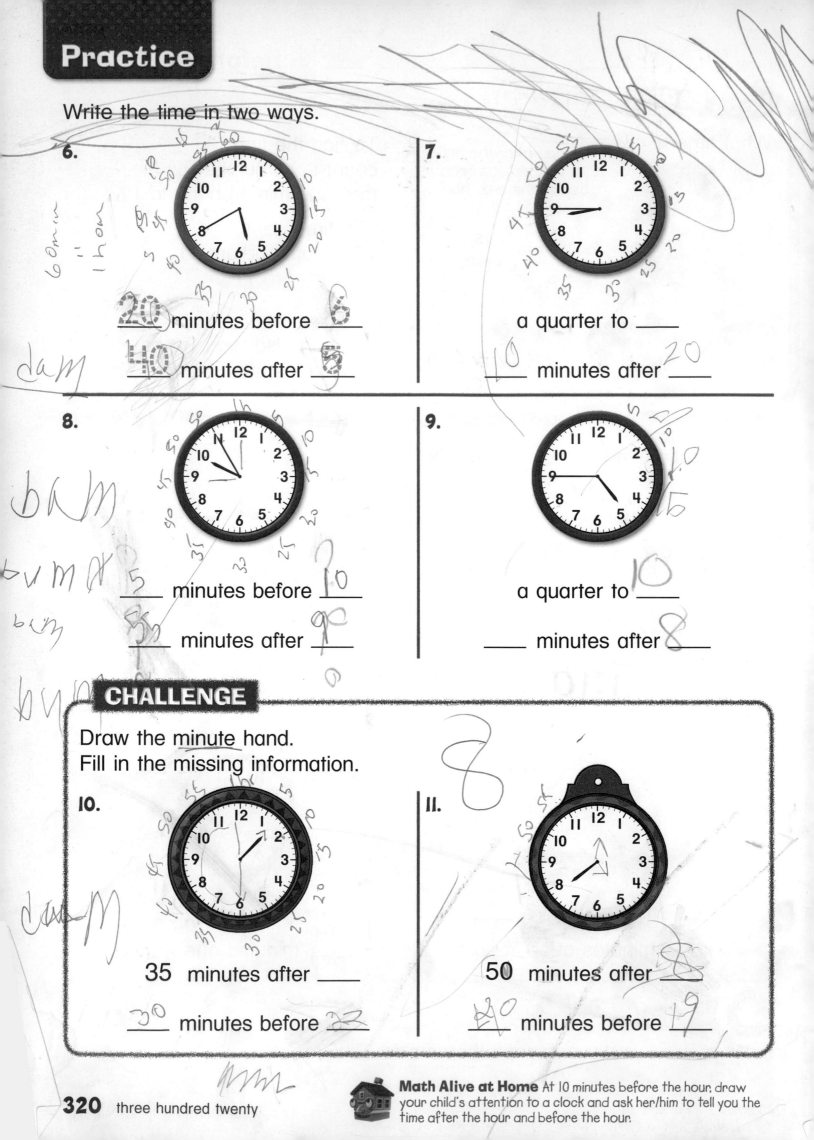

____ minutes before ____

____ minutes after ____

7.

a quarter to ____

____ minutes after ____

8.

____ minutes before ____

____ minutes after ____

9.

a quarter to ____

____ minutes after ____

CHALLENGE

Draw the minute hand.
Fill in the missing information.

10.

35 minutes after ____

____ minutes before ____

11.

50 minutes after ____

____ minutes before ____

Math Alive at Home At 10 minutes before the hour, draw your child's attention to a clock and ask her/him to tell you the time after the hour and before the hour.

Name ___________________

TEST PREPARATION

Listen to your teacher read the directions. Fill in the circle under the correct answer.

1.

10 minutes after 10 ○
30 minutes after 9 ○
30 minutes after 10 ○
30 minutes after 11 ○

2.

○ ○ ○

3.

1 o'clock ○
2 o'clock ○
12 o'clock ○
6 o'clock ○

4.

3:30 ○
6:15 ○
6:03 ○
3:32 ○

5.

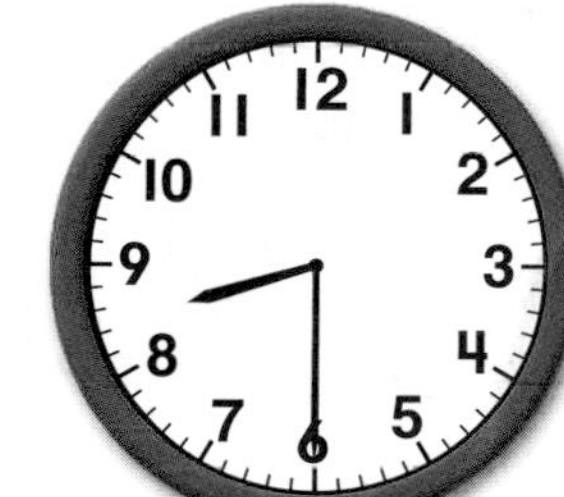

8:15 ○
9:30 ○
8:30 ○
8:45 ○

6.

10:25 ○
5:50 ○
5:40 ○
6:10 ○

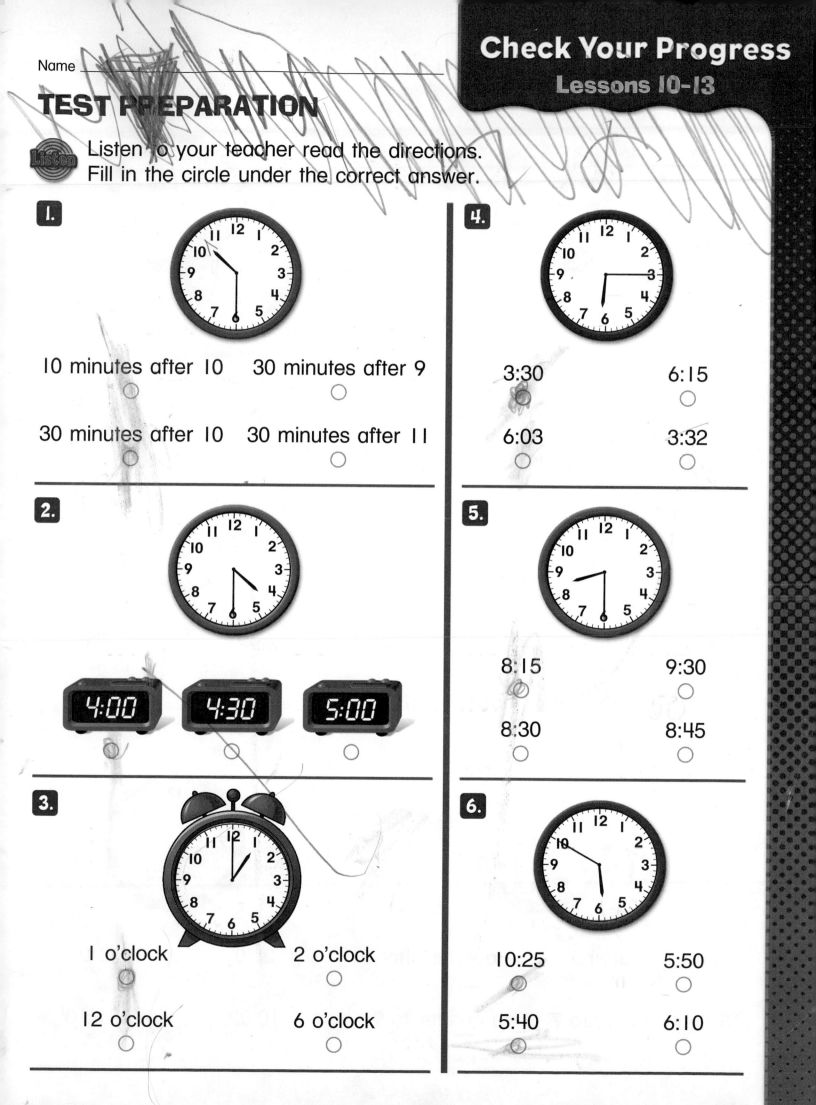

Fill in the circle under the correct answer.
What time is it?

7.

a quarter after 11 ○ a quarter after 10 ○

a quarter to 11 ○ a quarter to 12 ○

10.

12:15 ○ 3:15 ○

3:00 ○ 12:00 ○

8.

1 minute after 10 ○ 20 minutes after 2 ○

20 minutes after 1 ○ 4 minutes after 1 ○

11.

7:35 ○ 8:40 ○

7:40 ○ 8:35 ○

9.

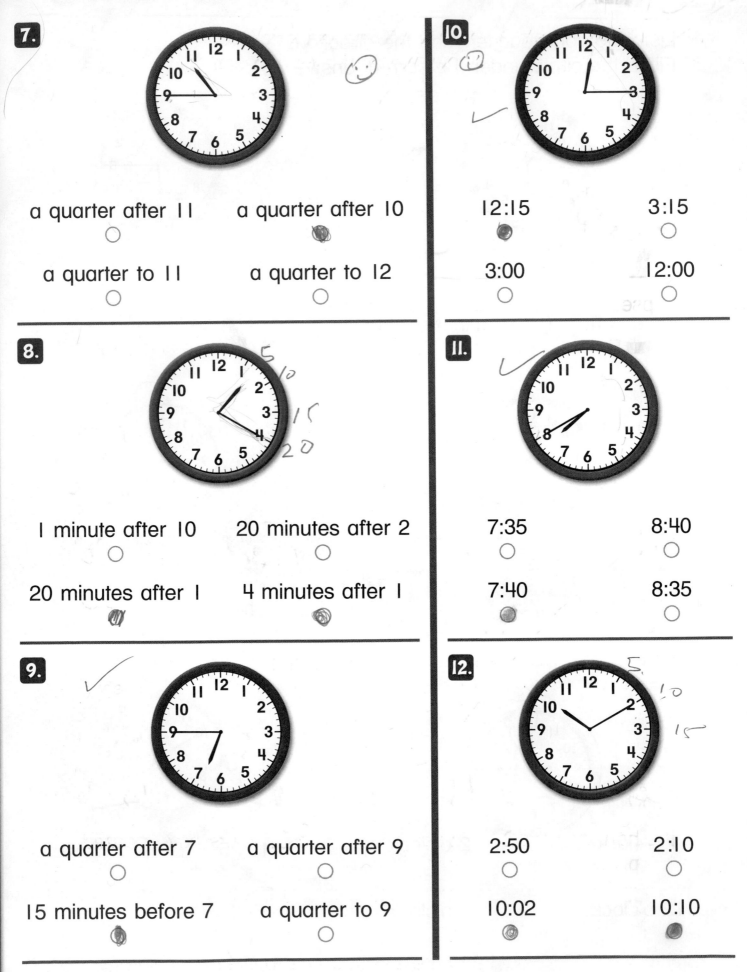

a quarter after 7 ○ a quarter after 9 ○

15 minutes before 7 ○ a quarter to 9 ○

12.

2:50 ○ 2:10 ○

10:02 ○ 10:10 ○

Name ______________________

Elapsed Time

Let's Learn!

A show about planets starts at 8:00 and ends at 9:30.
Find the **elapsed time**, or how much time has passed.

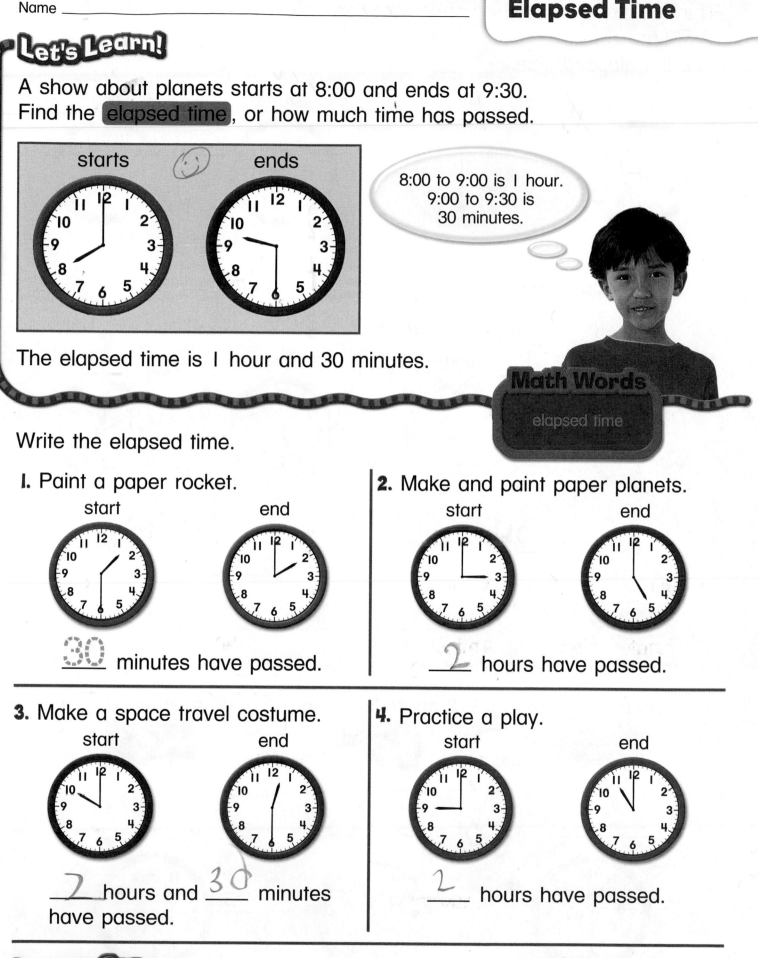

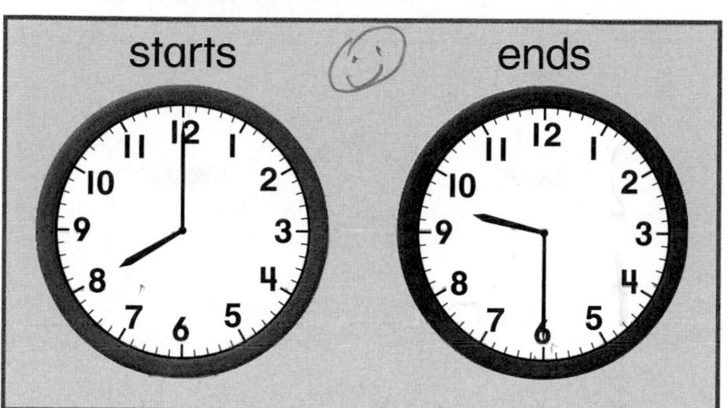

8:00 to 9:00 is 1 hour.
9:00 to 9:30 is
30 minutes.

The elapsed time is 1 hour and 30 minutes.

Write the elapsed time.

1. Paint a paper rocket.

start end

30 minutes have passed.

2. Make and paint paper planets.

start end

2 hours have passed.

3. Make a space travel costume.

start end

2 hours and 30 minutes have passed.

4. Practice a play.

start end

2 hours have passed.

Talk It Over

5. Explain how you would find the elapsed time between 11:30 and 1:00.

Copyright © by William H. Sadlier, Inc. All rights reserved.

Practice

Write the elapsed time.

6. start

end

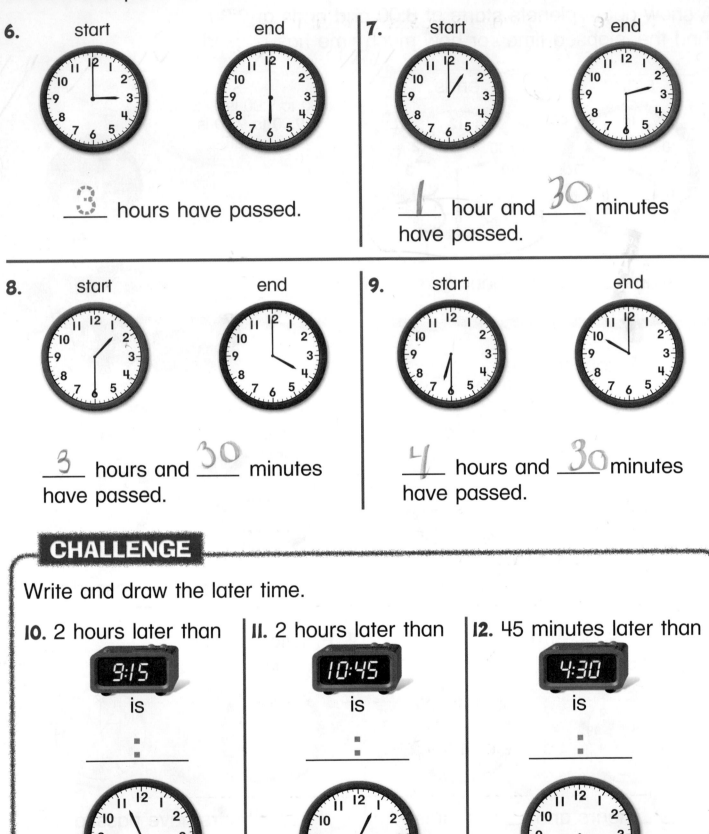

3 hours have passed.

7. start

end

1 hour and 30 minutes have passed.

8. start

end

3 hours and 30 minutes have passed.

9. start

end

4 hours and 30 minutes have passed.

CHALLENGE

Write and draw the later time.

10. 2 hours later than

is

___ : ___

11. 2 hours later than

is

___ : ___

12. 45 minutes later than

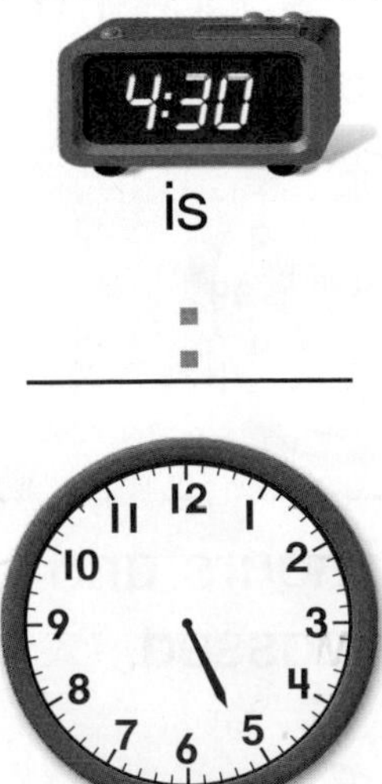

is

___ : ___

Math Alive at Home Ask your child to make up a story using elapsed time. Tell her/him to include the starting, ending, and elapsed times.

Name ______________________

Read a Schedule

- A schedule shows what happens at what time.

Today is Joe's first day at space camp. He made a schedule to show what he will do.

Time	Event
8:00 – 9:00	Breakfast
9:00 – 10:00	Exercising
10:00 – 12:00	Moon Walking Class
12:00 – 1:00	Lunch
1:00 – 2:30	Mission to Mars Class
2:30 – 3:00	Space Station Video

1. How many activities does Joe have between breakfast and lunch? two

2. At what time is lunch? ______________

3. How long is moon walking class?

____

4. How long is the space station video?

____

5. What will Joe be doing at 9:15?

____

6. Where will Joe be at 1:45?

____

Practice

Read a Schedule

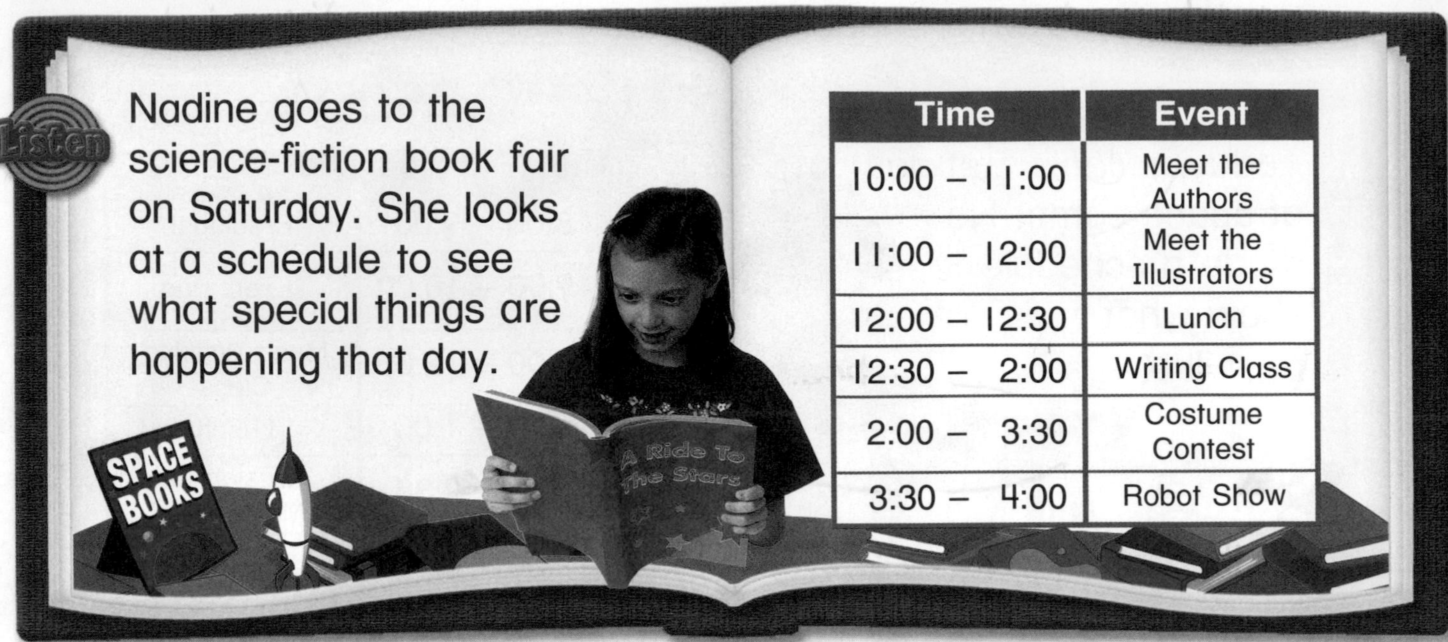

Nadine goes to the science-fiction book fair on Saturday. She looks at a schedule to see what special things are happening that day.

Time	Event
10:00 – 11:00	Meet the Authors
11:00 – 12:00	Meet the Illustrators
12:00 – 12:30	Lunch
12:30 – 2:00	Writing Class
2:00 – 3:30	Costume Contest
3:30 – 4:00	Robot Show

7. How many events are there after lunch?

three

8. At what time is the costume contest?

9. How long is the costume contest?

10. Which two events are one half hour long?

11. Which event will be taking place at 10:15?

12. Where will Nadine be at 12:45?

Math Alive at Home Today your child read a schedule to work through math problems.

Name ____________________

Estimate Time

Let's Learn!

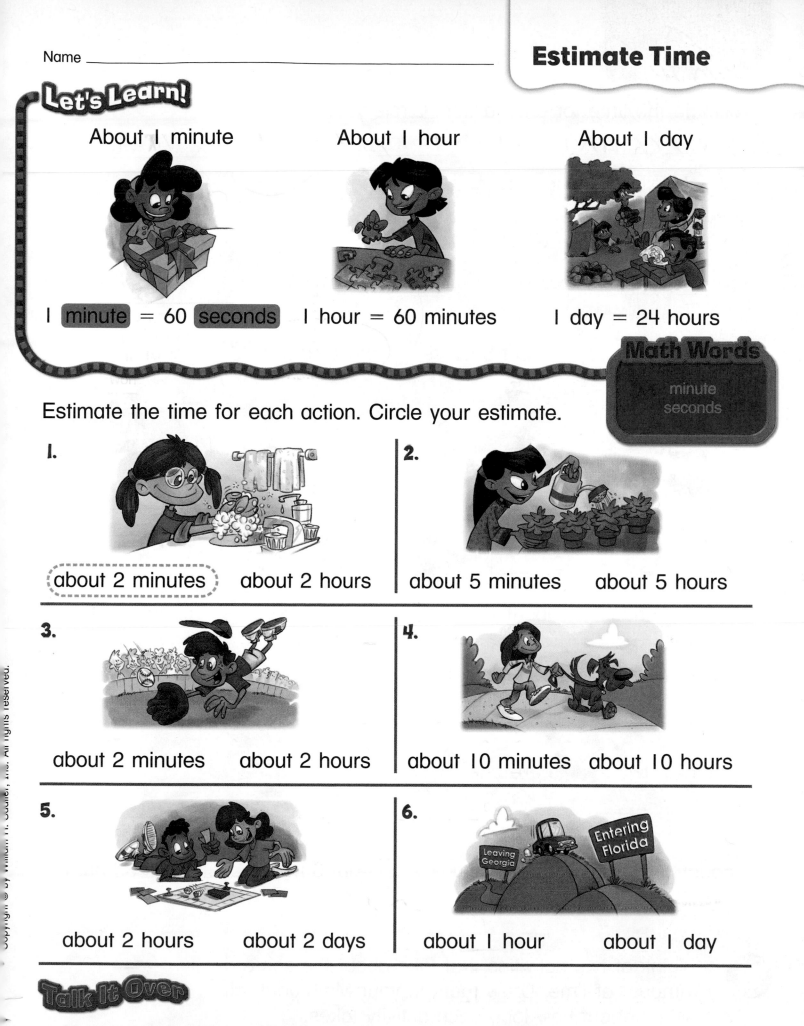

About 1 minute

1 **minute** = 60 **seconds**

About 1 hour

1 hour = 60 minutes

About 1 day

1 day = 24 hours

Math Words
minute
seconds

Estimate the time for each action. Circle your estimate.

1.

about 2 minutes   about 2 hours

2.

about 5 minutes   about 5 hours

3.

about 2 minutes   about 2 hours

4.

about 10 minutes   about 10 hours

5.

about 2 hours   about 2 days

6.

about 1 hour   about 1 day

7. Name some other actions and estimate the number of minutes, hours, or days to do them.

Copyright © by William H. Sadlier, Inc. All rights reserved.

Practice

Estimate the time for each action. Circle your estimate.

8.

about 5 minutes   about 5 hours

9.

about 10 minutes   about 10 hours

10.

about 1 hour   about 1 minute

11.

about 2 hours   about 2 days

12.

about 1 minute   about 1 day

13.

about 3 minutes   about 3 hours

CHALLENGE

MATH JOURNAL

14. Think of two activities that take about the same amount of time. Draw them in your Math Journal. Write about how long each activity takes.

Math Alive at Home Ask your child to name activities that last about 1 minute, 1 hour, or 1 day.

Name ______________________________

Calendar

Let's Learn!

A **calendar** shows days, **weeks**, and **months**.

A **date** names the month and the number of the day.

1 **year** = 12 months or 52 weeks or 365 days

January

S	M	T	W	T	F	S
		1	2	3	4	5
6	7	8	9	10	11	12
13	14	15	16	17	18	19
20	21	22	23	24	25	26
27	28	29	30	31		

February

S	M	T	W	T	F	S
					1	2
3	4	5	6	7	8	9
10	11	12	13	14	15	16
17	18	19	20	21	22	23
24	25	26	27	28		

March

S	M	T	W	T	F	S
					1	2
3	4	5	6	7	8	9
10	11	12	13	14	15	16
17	18	19	20	21	22	23
24	25	26	27	28	29	30
31						

April

S	M	T	W	T	F	S
	1	2	3	4	5	6
7	8	9	10	11	12	13
14	15	16	17	18	19	20
21	22	23	24	25	26	27
28	29	30				

May

S	M	T	W	T	F	S
			1	2	3	4
5	6	7	8	9	10	11
12	13	14	15	16	17	18
19	20	21	22	23	24	25
26	27	28	29	30	31	

June

S	M	T	W	T	F	S
						1
2	3	4	5	6	7	8
9	10	11	12	13	14	15
16	17	18	19	20	21	22
23	24	25	26	27	28	29
30						

July

S	M	T	W	T	F	S
	1	2	3	4	5	6
7	8	9	10	11	12	13
14	15	16	17	18	19	20
21	22	23	24	25	26	27
28	29	30	31			

August

S	M	T	W	T	F	S
				1	2	3
4	5	6	7	8	9	10
11	12	13	14	15	16	17
18	19	20	21	22	23	24
25	26	27	28	29	30	31

September

S	M	T	W	T	F	S
1	2	3	4	5	6	7
8	9	10	11	12	13	14
15	16	17	18	19	20	21
22	23	24	25	26	27	28
29	30					

October

S	M	T	W	T	F	S
		1	2	3	4	5
6	7	8	9	10	11	12
13	14	15	16	17	18	19
20	21	22	23	24	25	26
27	28	29	30	31		

November

S	M	T	W	T	F	S
					1	2
3	4	5	6	7	8	9
10	11	12	13	14	15	16
17	18	19	20	21	22	23
24	25	26	27	28	29	30

December

S	M	T	W	T	F	S
1	2	3	4	5	6	7
8	9	10	11	12	13	14
15	16	17	18	19	20	21
22	23	24	25	26	27	28
29	30	31				

Math Words

calendar week
month date year

Use the calendar to answer the questions.

1. What date is one week after April 8? April 15
2. The shortest month is february.
3. Which month is just before September? August
4. How many months have 30 days? 4 31 days? 7
5. How many days are in two weeks? 14 days
6. What date is two weeks before May 16? may 2

Talk It Over

7. What are the date and day just after December 31?

Copyright © by William H. Sadlier, Inc. All rights reserved.

Practice

8. Complete the calendar.

December						
Sunday	Monday	Tuesday	Wednesday	Thursday	Friday	Saturday
		1	2	3	4	5
6	7	8	9		11	12
13		15	16		18	19

Use the calendar above to answer each question.

9. On which day is the thirty-first? ______________

10. How many Mondays are in this month? ______________

11. What is the date of the fourth Friday? ______________

12. On which day and date did the last month end? ______________

CRITICAL THINKING

Estimate. Circle about how long.

13. build a house
days
months

14. go on vacation
week
hour

15. grow a tree
days
years

16. Circle the activity above that would take the shortest time.

Math Alive at Home Ask your child to use the previous page to find and circle the birthdays of members of your family.

Name ______________________________

Problem Solving
Strategy

Guess and Test

Read Brian has 4 coins totaling 55¢.
Circle the coins Brian has.

Use logical reasoning to make good guesses.

Plan Guess which 4 coins might have a sum of 55¢. Test each guess.

Think
4 dimes or 4 nickels will not be enough.
Try coin groups with 1 quarter.

Write Guess | quarter, 2 dimes, | nickel

25¢, 35¢, 45¢, 50¢ not enough

Guess 2 quarters, 2 dimes

25¢, 50¢, 60¢, 70¢ too much

Guess | quarter, 3 dimes

25¢, 35¢, 45¢, 55¢ ✓

Check Use real coins and count on to check.
Does the total amount equal 55¢?

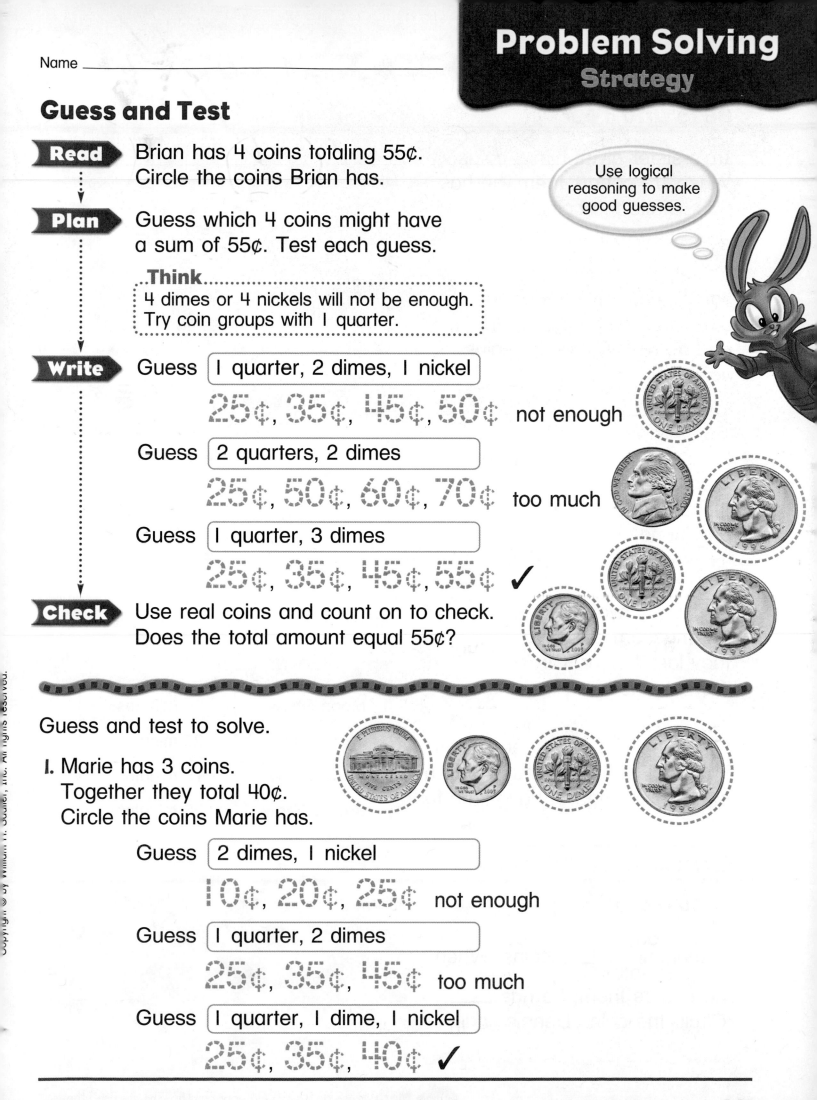

Guess and test to solve.

I. Marie has 3 coins.
Together they total 40¢.
Circle the coins Marie has.

Guess 2 dimes, | nickel

10¢, 20¢, 25¢ not enough

Guess | quarter, 2 dimes

25¢, 35¢, 45¢ too much

Guess | quarter, | dime, | nickel

25¢, 35¢, 40¢ ✓

Copyright © by William H. Sadlier, Inc. All rights reserved.

Practice

Read → Plan → Write → Check

Guess and Test

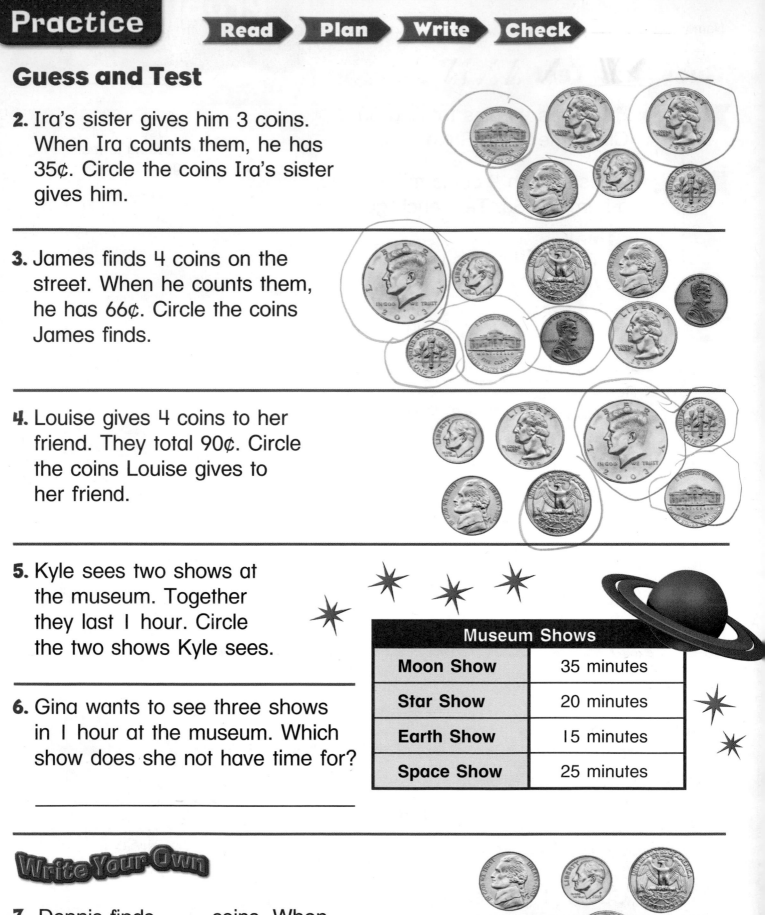

2. Ira's sister gives him 3 coins. When Ira counts them, he has 35¢. Circle the coins Ira's sister gives him.

---

3. James finds 4 coins on the street. When he counts them, he has 66¢. Circle the coins James finds.

---

4. Louise gives 4 coins to her friend. They total 90¢. Circle the coins Louise gives to her friend.

---

5. Kyle sees two shows at the museum. Together they last 1 hour. Circle the two shows Kyle sees.

---

6. Gina wants to see three shows in 1 hour at the museum. Which show does she not have time for?

____

Museum Shows	
Moon Show	35 minutes
Star Show	20 minutes
Earth Show	15 minutes
Space Show	25 minutes

7. Dennis finds ____ coins. When he counts them, he has ____. Circle the coins Dennis finds.

Math Alive at Home Ask your child how he/she used the Guess and Test strategy to solve the problems in this lesson.

Name ______________________________

Read Plan Write Check

Mixed Strategies

Use a strategy you have learned.

Strategy File

Make a Table
Use More Than One Step
Guess and Test

1. The tour of each room in a castle takes 5 minutes. How many minutes will it take for a tour of 5 rooms?

_____ minutes

---

2. Theresa has 3 quarters to spend. She buys a paper toy for 27¢ and a necklace for 35¢. How much money does she have left?

______

---

3. Carol wants to buy a doll that costs 90¢. She has 2 quarters, 2 dimes, and a nickel. How much more money does she need?

______

---

4. Ten children can ride in each car of an old train. How many children can ride in 8 cars?

_____ children

---

5. Sean buys a model space shuttle that costs 60¢. He pays with three coins and gets 15¢ in change. Circle the coins Sean used to pay.

---

6. Gina has 28¢. Troy has double that much. Circle the three coins Troy has.

Copyright © by William H. Sadlier, Inc. All rights reserved.

Practice

Read → Plan → Write → Check

Use a strategy you have learned.

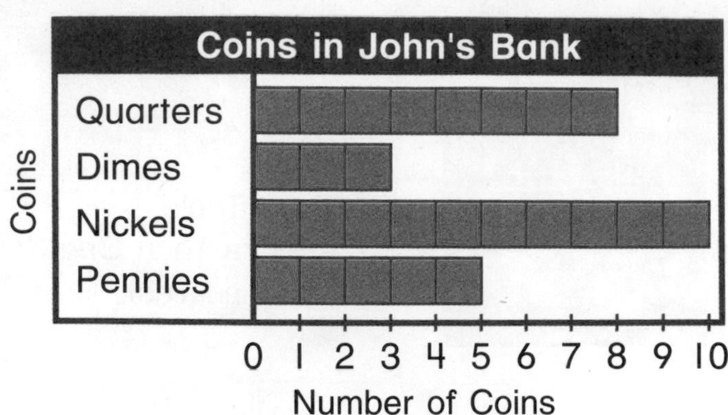

7. John wants to change the quarters in his bank for one-dollar bills. How many bills will he get?

_____ bills

8. How much money does John have in his bank in dimes, nickels, and pennies?

_____

9. Ed arrives at the museum first. Luna arrives later than Sue. Sue arrives 45 minutes after Ed. Write the name next to the time each person arrives.

_____ 10:15

_____ 9:00

_____ 9:45

10. Kelly counts dinosaurs. The number is between 45 and 55. The number has 6 ones in the ones place. How many dinosaurs does Kelly count?

____ dinosaurs

11. Alan picks two numbers from a bag. Their sum is 52. Cross out the number Alan does not pick.

29

Math Alive at Home Ask your child to tell you how he/she solved some of the problems in this lesson.

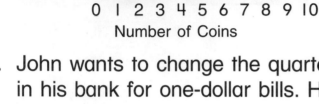

Name ______________________________

Check Your Progress
Lessons 14–19

TEST PREPARATION

Listen to your teacher read the directions.
Fill in the circle under the correct answer.

1.

start

end

15 minutes ○ 5 hours ○

3 hours ○ 25 minutes ○

2.

15 minutes ○ 15 hours ○

15 days ○ 5 hours ○

February						
Sunday	Monday	Tuesday	Wednesday	Thursday	Friday	Saturday
	1	2	3	4	5	6
7	8	9	10	11	12	13
14	15	16	17	18	19	20
21	22	23	24	25	26	27
28						

3.

February 24 ○ March 3 ○

February 17 ○ March 1 ○

4.

Wednesday ○ Thursday ○

Friday ○ Saturday ○

5. Mark has four coins. Together the coins total 65¢. Choose the coins Mark has.

○

○

○

Copyright © by William H. Sadlier, Inc. All rights reserved.

Connection

Math and Science

Name ______________________________

Did You Know?

Our planet Earth turns. Our part of Earth faces the Sun during the day and faces away from the Sun at night. It takes 24 hours for Earth to make one full turn.

The letters **a.m.** show the 12 hours from 12 midnight to 12 noon.

The letters **p.m.** show the 12 hours from 12 noon to 12 midnight.

12 a.m. midnight

12 p.m. noon

Write the end time. Then write the elapsed time.

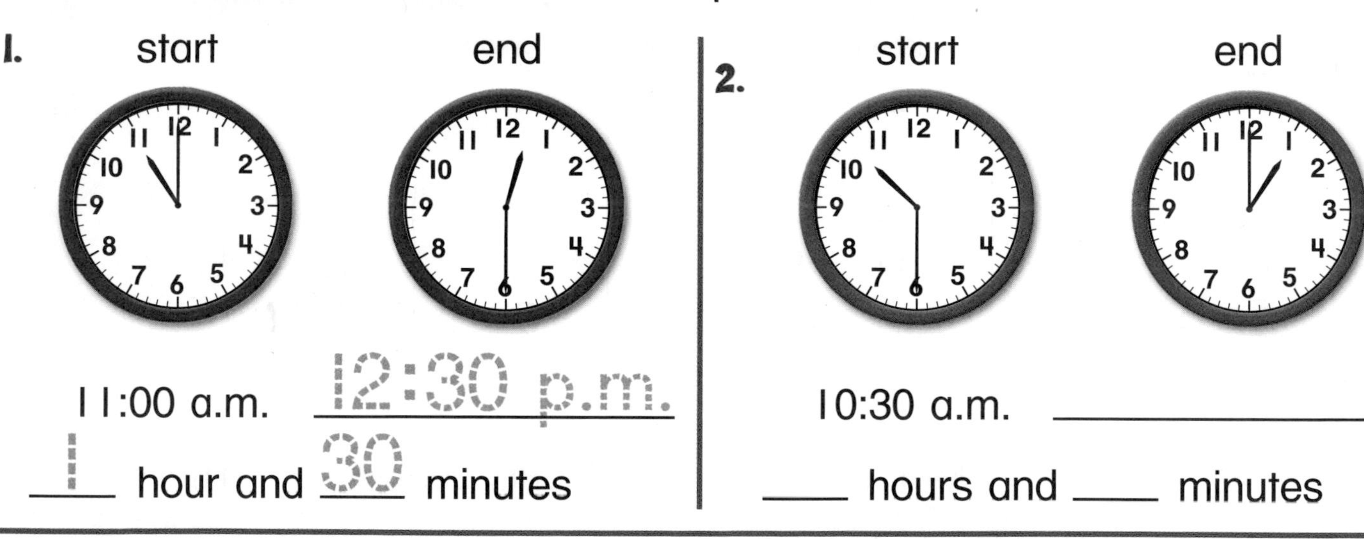

1. start end

11:00 a.m. 12:30 p.m.

1 hour and 30 minutes

2. start end

10:30 a.m. ____________

____ hours and ____ minutes

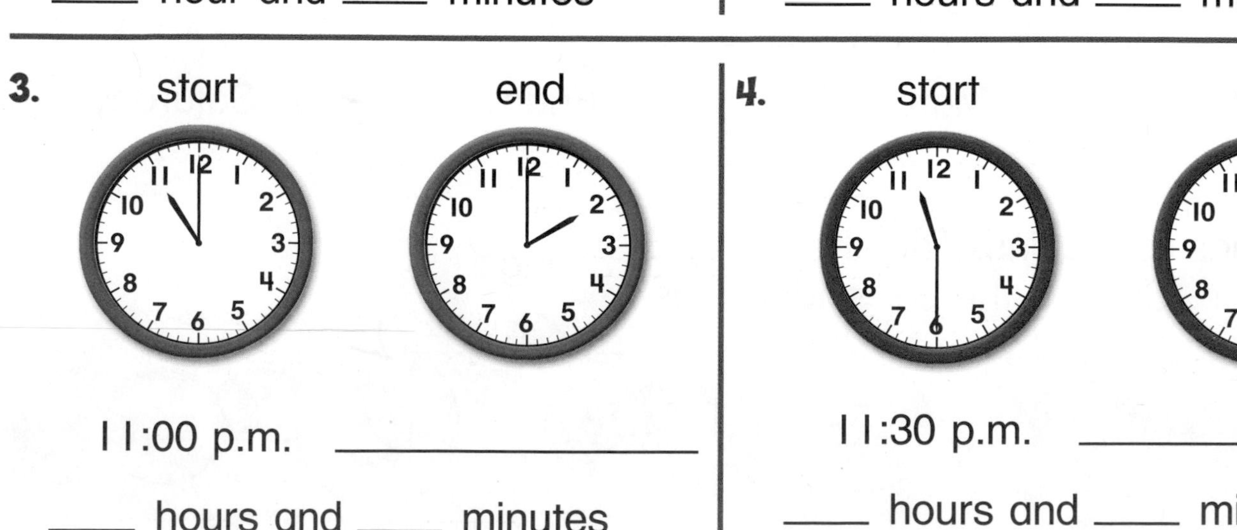

3. start end

11:00 p.m. ____________

____ hours and ____ minutes

4. start end

11:30 p.m. ____________

____ hours and ____ minutes

Name ______________________________

Chapter 7 Test

1. Circle the amount.

33¢        

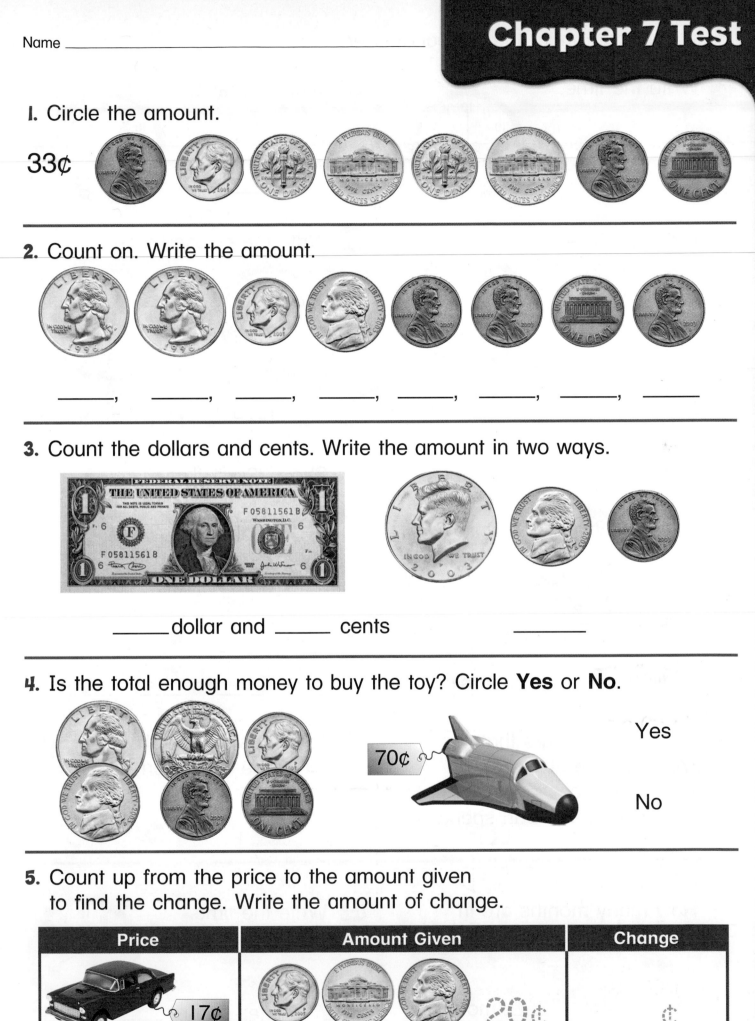

2. Count on. Write the amount.

____, ____, ____, ____, ____, ____, ____, ____

3. Count the dollars and cents. Write the amount in two ways.

____ dollar and ____ cents ____

4. Is the total enough money to buy the toy? Circle **Yes** or **No**.

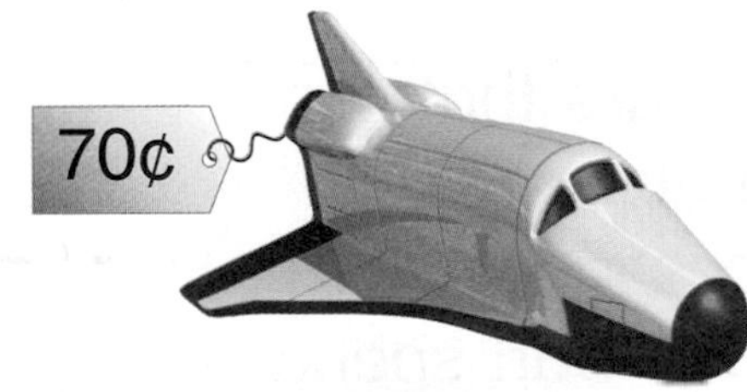

Yes

No

5. Count up from the price to the amount given to find the change. Write the amount of change.

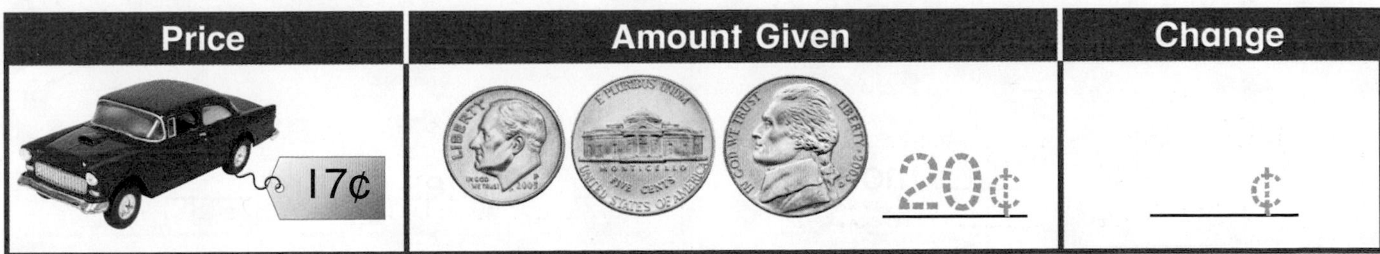

Price	Amount Given	Change
17¢	20¢	____¢

Copyright © by William H. Sadlier, Inc. All rights reserved.

Fill in the circle under the correct answer.

6. Write the time.

____ o'clock

7. Write the time.

____

8. Write the time.

a quarter to ____

9. Write the elapsed time.

____ hours and ____ minutes

10. Circle to estimate the time.

5 minutes   5 hours

11. Show 42¢ in three ways.

____	____	____	____
____	____	____	____
____	____	____	____

12. Carl buys two cars that cost 27¢ each. He also buys a plane that costs 32¢. How much does Carl spend?

____

13. Terry has 4 coins that total 50¢. Circle the coins Terry has.

14. How many months are in one year?

____ months

15. Write the time.

____ minutes before ____

Name ______________________________

A store has colored beads
with letters on them.
Each vowel bead costs 10¢.
Each consonant bead costs 5¢.

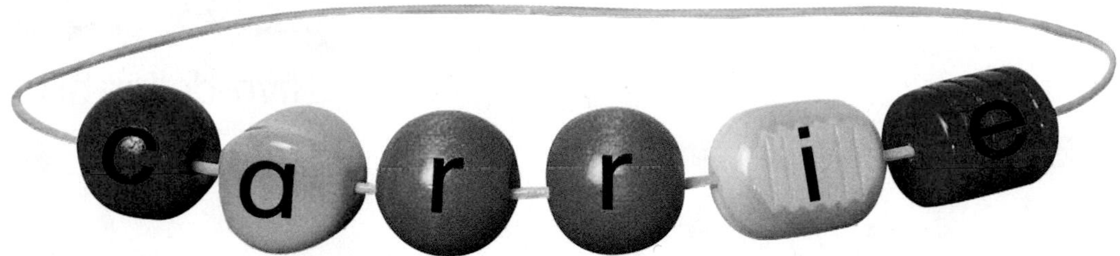

Make name bracelets for 2 people you care about.
Write one name on each line below.
Then write how much the bracelet cost.

1. ______________________________ Cost: ________

2. ______________________________ Cost: ________

3. Whose bracelet costs more? ____________________

4. Think of an activity that you like.
Write a start time and end time for the activity.

start	end
___:00	___:30

Find the elapsed time for the activity.

___ hours and ___ minutes

5. Write an action that takes about 5 minutes.

____

6. Write an action that takes about 2 hours.

____

You can put this in your Math Portfolio.

Copyright © by William H. Sadlier, Inc. All rights reserved.

Enrichment

Name ____________________

five-dollar bill

Five-Dollar Bill

Tony has 1 five-dollar bill, 1 one-dollar bill, 2 dimes, and 2 nickels. How much money does Tony have?

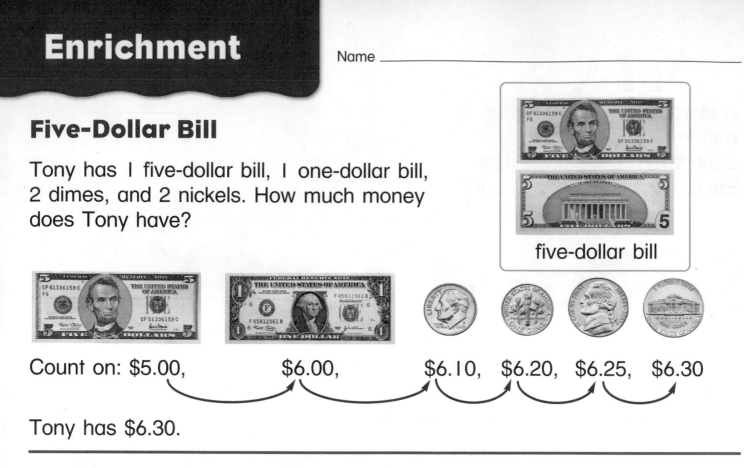

Count on: $5.00, $6.00, $6.10, $6.20, $6.25, $6.30

Tony has $6.30.

Write the amount. Use a dollar sign and decimal point.

1.   ________

2.   ________

3.   ________

4.  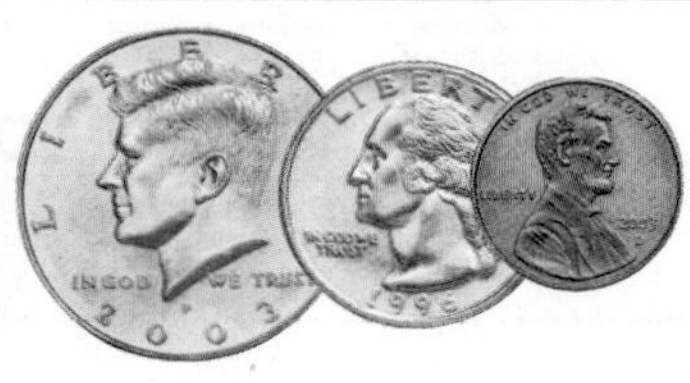 ________

The Time Machine

Read ALOUD

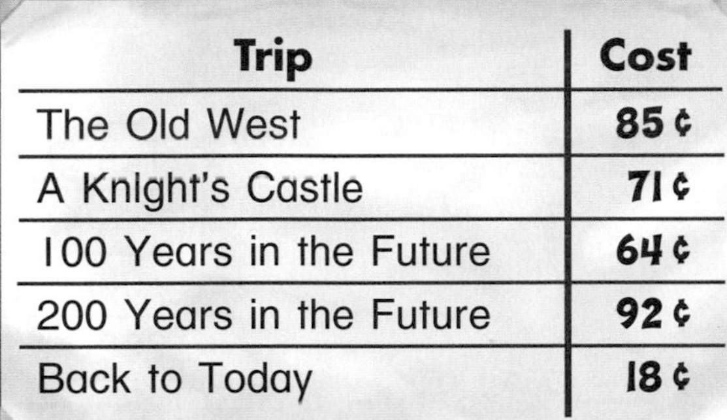

Trip	Cost
The Old West	85¢
A Knight's Castle	71¢
100 Years in the Future	64¢
200 Years in the Future	92¢
Back to Today	18¢

Jack and Jeanine built a big machine.
It was the oddest thing you've ever seen.
If you put in quarters, nickels, pennies, and dimes,
you could travel back or forward in time.

Jeanine put in some coins and said, "Let's try a test.
Let's see if we can travel back to the Old West."

Which coins did Jeanine put in?

Copyright © by William H. Sadlier, Inc. All rights reserved.

Trip	Cost
The Old West	85¢
A Knight's Castle	71¢
100 Years in the Future	64¢
200 Years in the Future	92¢
Back to Today	18¢

"Well, here we are! It works!" said Jeanine. "This is a pretty good time machine."

Jack put in some coins and said, "Yes, you're right. Now let's visit a castle that belongs to a knight."

Which coins did Jack put in?

"I can hardly believe it. We're here!" shouted Jack. "But it's almost dinnertime. We have to get back!"

Jeanine put in some coins and said,
"Yes, this was great.
But we should hurry back.
We do not want to be late."

Which coins did Jeanine put in?

Copyright © by William H. Sadlier, Inc. All rights reserved.

It was exactly 6 o'clock. The clock started to chime,
as Jack and Jeanine came home right on time!

Name ______________________________

TEST PREPARATION

Fill in the circle under the correct answer.

1. Count on. Which shows the amount in dollars and cents?

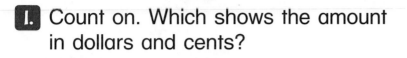

$1.20	$1.12	$1.22
○	○	○

2. Add.

$$\begin{array}{r} 60 \\ +\ 39 \\ \hline \end{array}$$

98	99	89	88
○	○	○	○

3. How many lines of symmetry does the figure have?

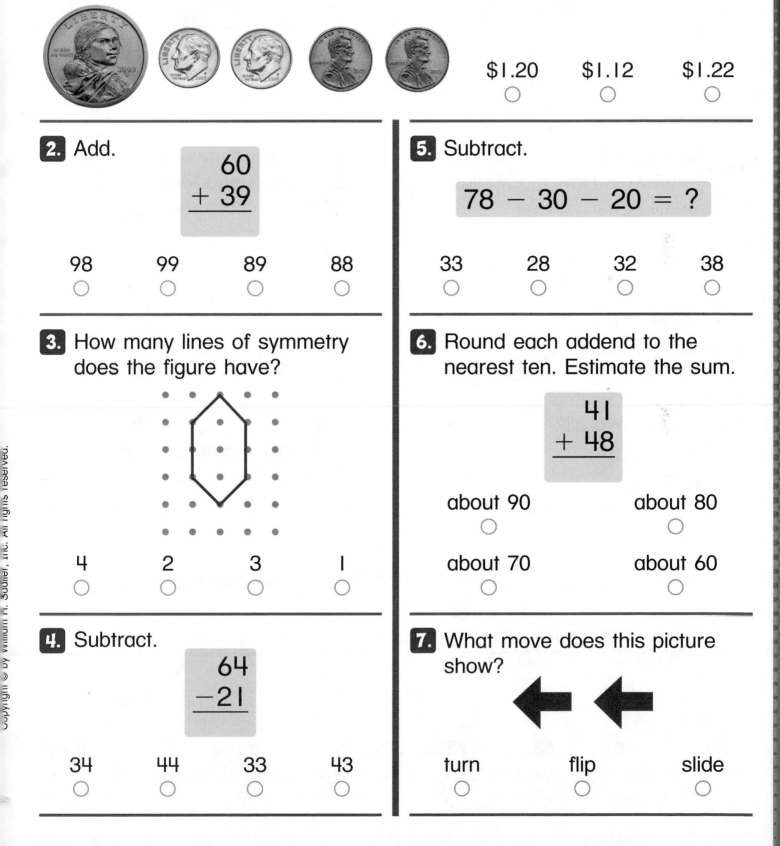

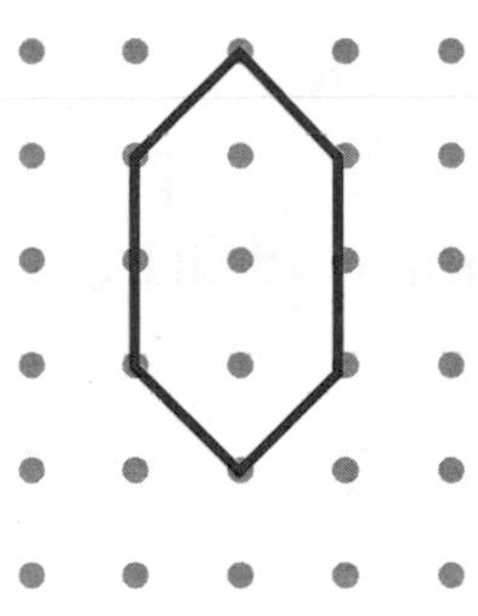

4	2	3	1
○	○	○	○

4. Subtract.

$$\begin{array}{r} 64 \\ -21 \\ \hline \end{array}$$

34	44	33	43
○	○	○	○

5. Subtract.

$78 - 30 - 20 = ?$

33	28	32	38
○	○	○	○

6. Round each addend to the nearest ten. Estimate the sum.

$$\begin{array}{r} 41 \\ +\ 48 \\ \hline \end{array}$$

about 90	about 80
○	○
about 70	about 60
○	○

7. What move does this picture show?

turn	flip	slide
○	○	○

Copyright © by William H. Sadlier, Inc. All rights reserved.

Fill in the circle under the correct answer.
Watch for multistep problems.

8. Curt buys a toy for 87¢. He gives the cashier 3 quarters, 1 dime, and 1 nickel. What is the amount of change Curt gets from the cashier?

1¢	2¢	3¢	4¢
○	○	○	○

9. Ana sees 48 birds in her yard. 19 fly away. How many birds are still in her yard?

39	37	29	27
○	○	○	○

10. There were 35 dancers and 57 singers in the school. How many singers and dancers were there in all?

82	83	92	93
○	○	○	○

11. Joan buys two silver hearts for 28¢ each. She also buys a roll of stickers for 17¢. How much does Joan spend?

35¢	4¢	63¢	73¢
○	○	○	○

12. Find the sum. Regroup.

$$\begin{array}{r} 25 \\ 2 \\ +35 \\ \hline \end{array}$$

52	63	62	54
○	○	○	○

13. Tim has 3 dimes and 1 nickel. Zoe has 2 quarters. Who has more money?

Tim	Zoe
○	○

14. At the bus stop, 26 children wait for a ride to school. The first bus reaches the stop at 8:00. It picks up 13 children. How many children must take the next bus?

13	19	39	49
○	○	○	○

15. How many angles does this figure have?

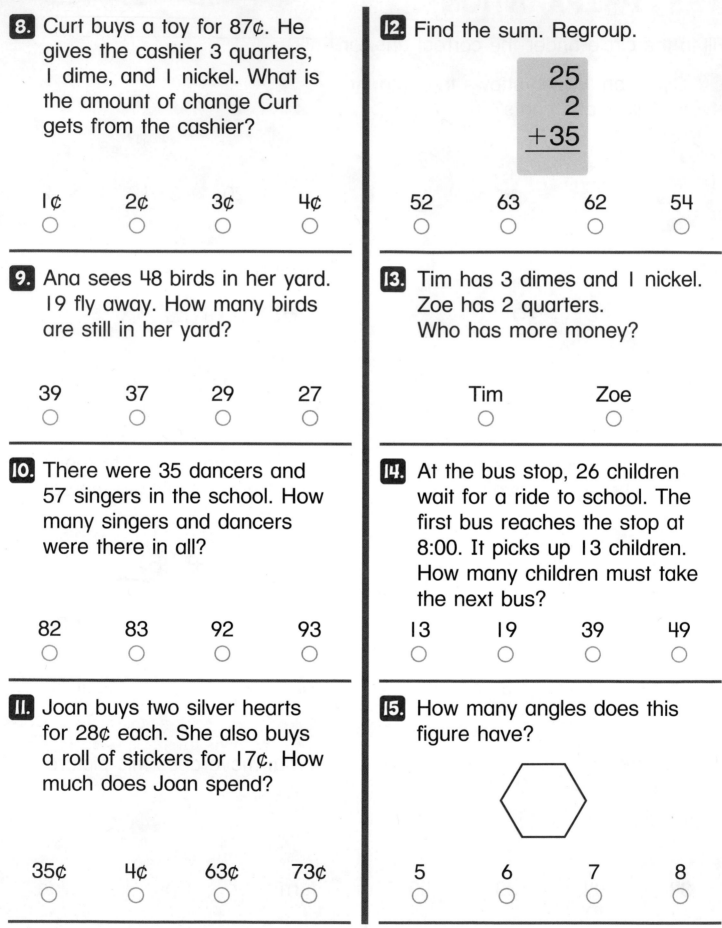

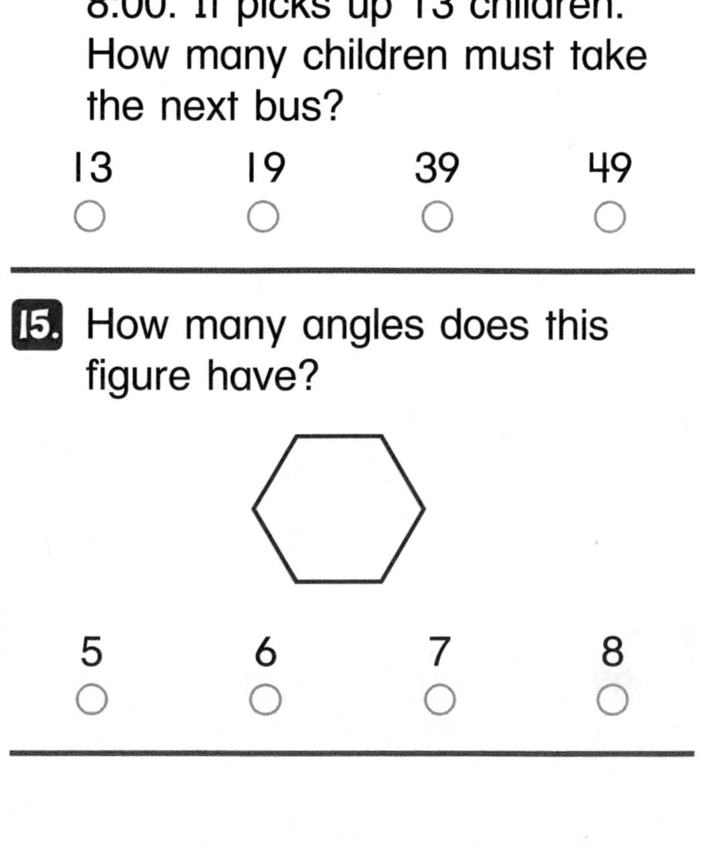

5	6	7	8
○	○	○	○

Place Value to 1000

CHAPTER 8

Listen

Listen to your teacher read the poem.

How many items have come out of the Ten-o-matic?

Dear Family,

Today our class began Chapter 8. We will learn about place value to 1000. Let's do the activity below together so I can review the skills I will need in order to understand the math in this chapter. Then you can read some of the new vocabulary I will learn in Chapter 8.

Love, ____________

What Is My Number?

Draw the ten rods and ones units shown below. Ask your child to write how many tens and ones and the number shown by the models drawn. Continue the activity by drawing different numbers of ten rods and ones units, then having your child write the number. Do this for several numbers to 99. You might also ask her/him to order the numbers from greatest to least or from least to greatest.

Chapter 8 Vocabulary

also on-line

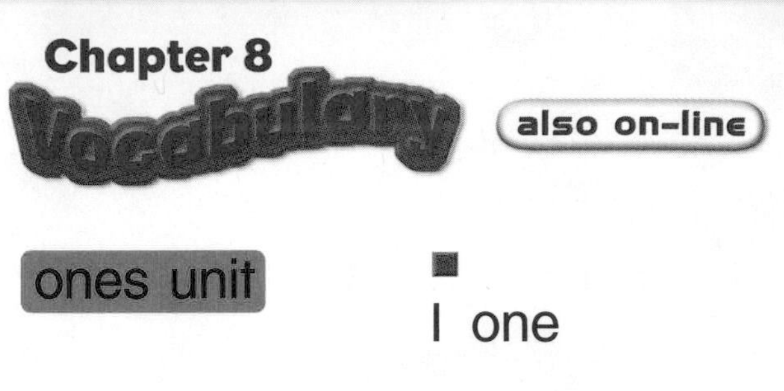

ones unit — 1 one

ten rod

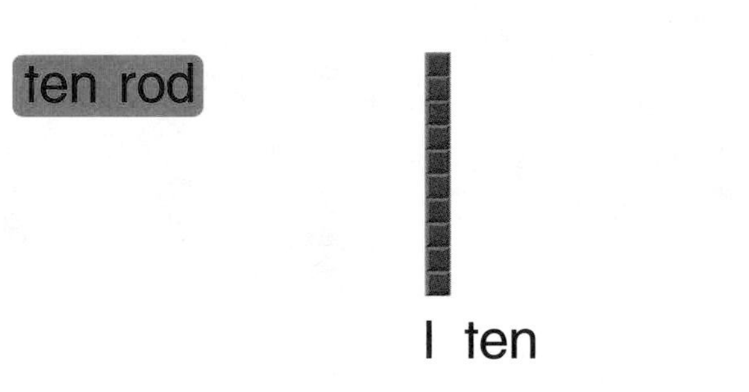

1 ten

hundred flat

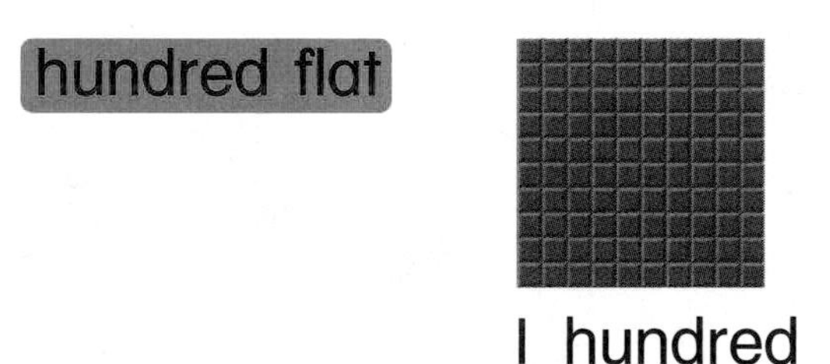

1 hundred

one hundred — 100

3-digit number — 423

place-value chart

hundreds	tens	ones
4	2	3

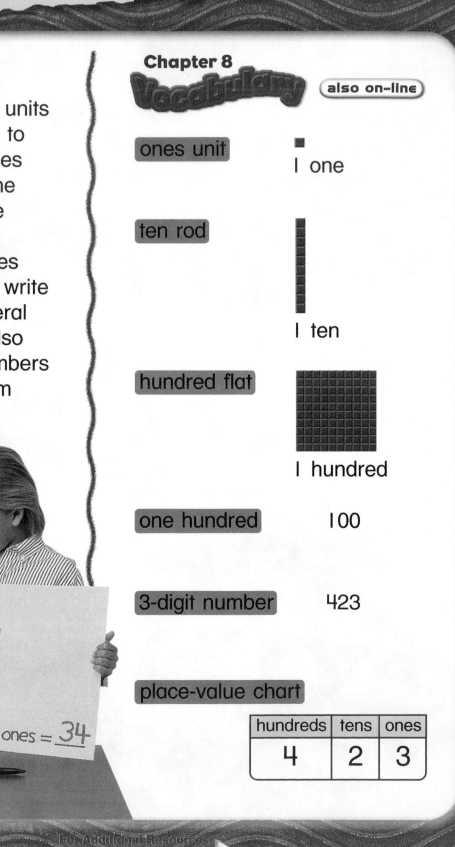

For Additional Resources
VISIT US ON-LINE www.sadlier-oxford.com

Name ______________________________

Hundreds

HANDS-ON LESSON

Let's Learn!

You can show the same numbers using different place-value models. Group 10 tens to make 100.

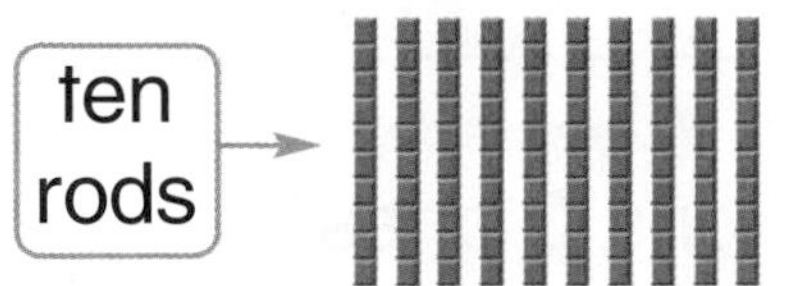

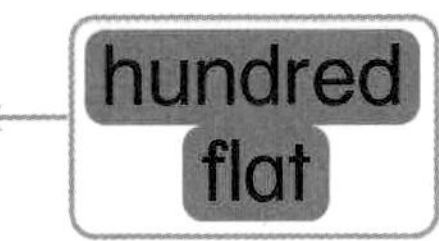

hundreds	tens	ones
1	0	0

10 tens = 100
one hundred

Math Words
hundred flat
one hundred

Model each. Group 10 tens to make hundreds. Circle the groups. Write how many hundreds.

1.

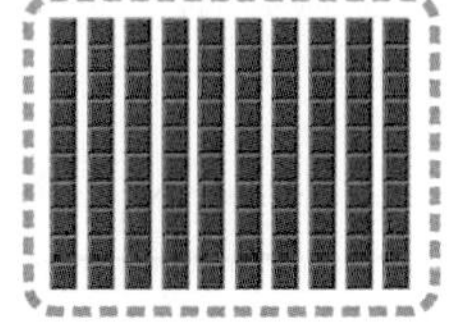

hundreds	tens	ones
2	0	0

200

two hundred

2.

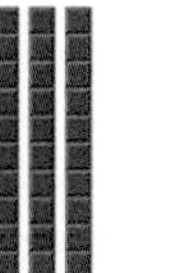

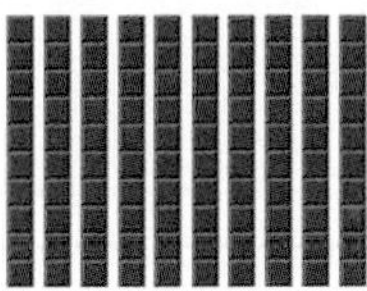

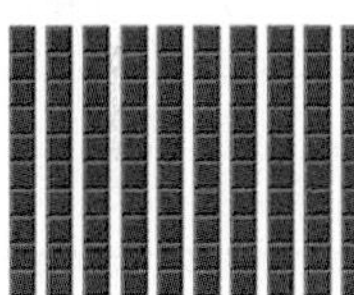

hundreds	tens	ones

______

______ hundred

3.

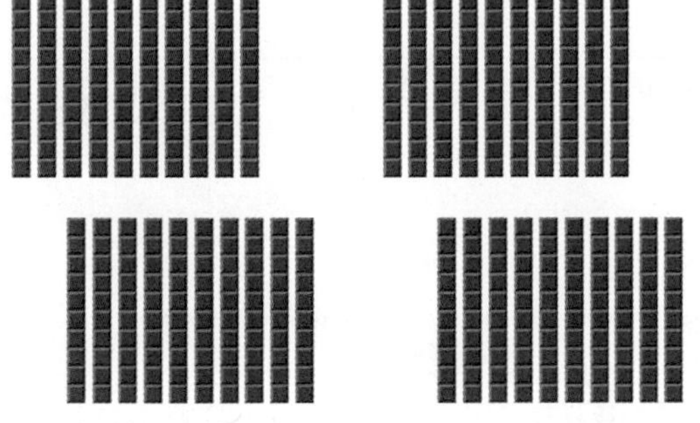

hundreds	tens	ones

______

______ hundred

4.

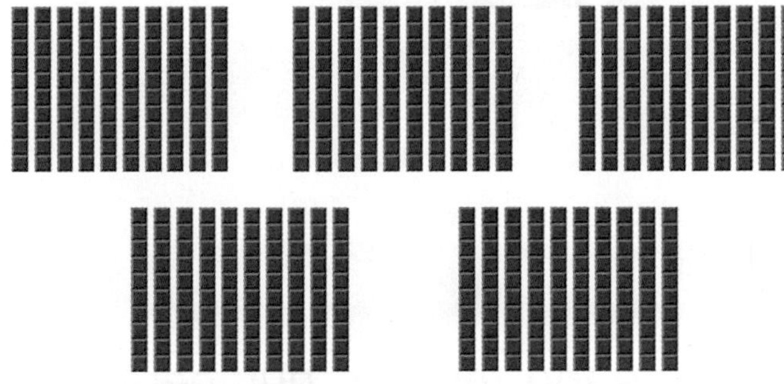

hundreds	tens	ones

______

______ hundred

5. Explain how to model hundreds as you count from 100 to 900 and from 900 to 100.

Copyright © by William H. Sadlier, Inc. All rights reserved.

Practice

Write the number and the number word.

6. 7 hundreds 0 tens 0 ones
700 seven hundred

7. 2 hundreds 0 tens 0 ones
_____ _______________

8. 9 hundreds 0 tens 0 ones
_____ _______________

9. 6 hundreds 0 tens 0 ones
_____ _______________

10. 3 hundreds 0 tens 0 ones
_____ _______________

11. 8 hundreds 0 tens 0 ones
_____ _______________

12. 5 hundreds 0 tens 0 ones
_____ _______________

13. 4 hundreds 0 tens 0 ones
_____ _______________

Color to match.

14. 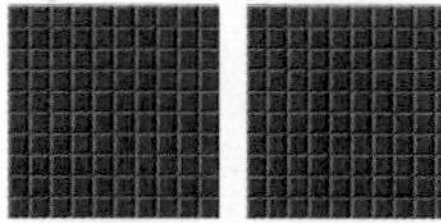

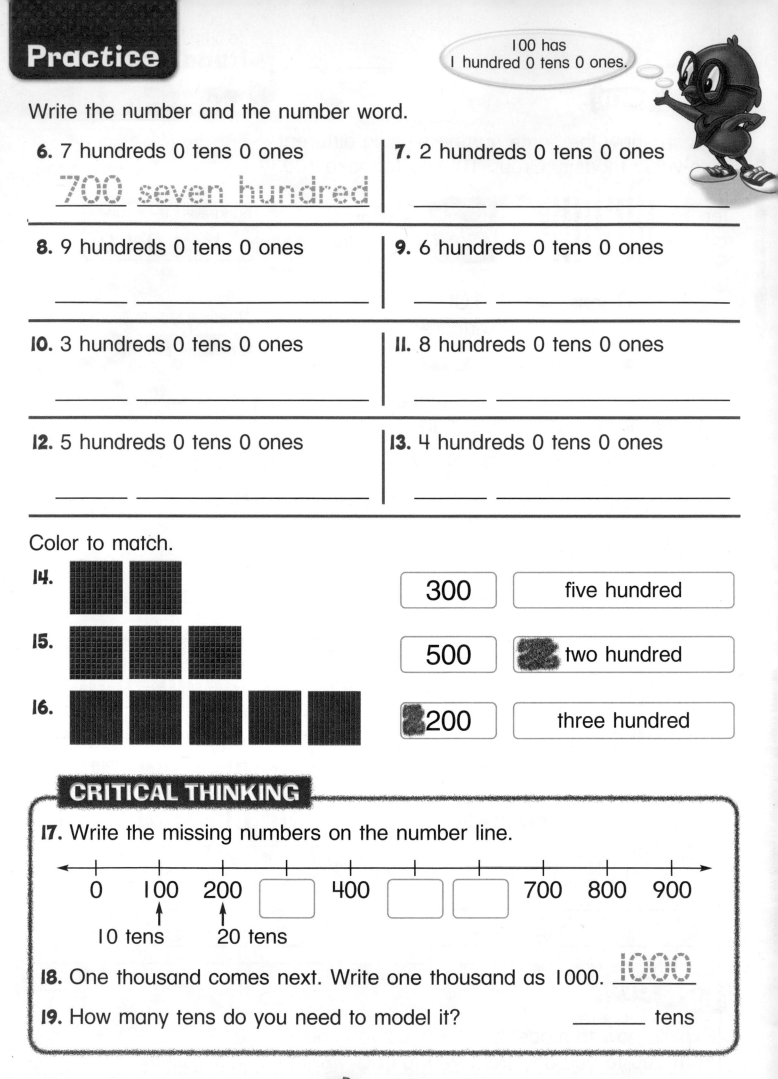

15. 

16. 

300	five hundred
500	 two hundred
 200	three hundred

CRITICAL THINKING

17. Write the missing numbers on the number line.

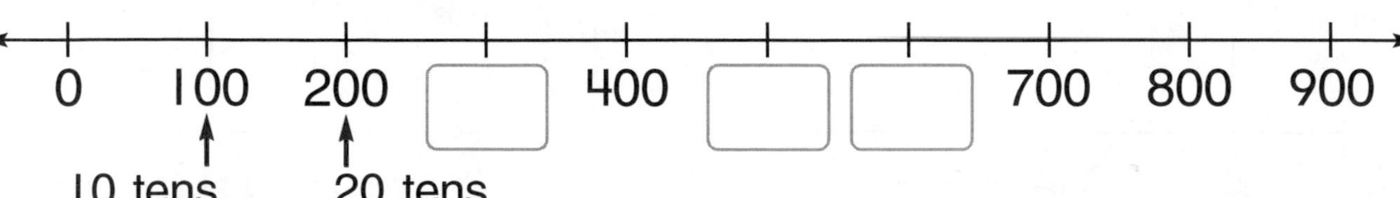

18. One thousand comes next. Write one thousand as 1000. 1000

19. How many tens do you need to model it? _____ tens

Math Alive at Home Ask your child to count by 100s from 100 to 900.

Hundreds, Tens, and Ones

HANDS-ON LESSON

Name ______________________________

Let's Learn!

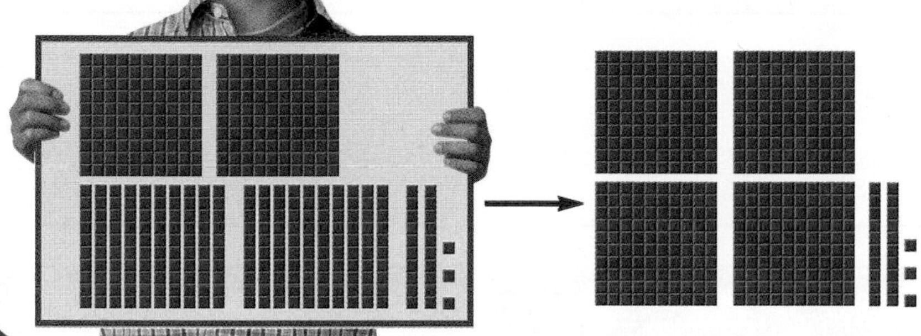

A **3-digit number** has hundreds, tens, and ones.

hundreds	tens	ones
4	2	3

423

four hundred twenty-three

Math Words

3-digit number

Model each. Group 10 tens to make hundreds. Circle the groups. Write how many hundreds, tens, and ones.

1.

hundreds	tens	ones
5	0	6

506

five hundred six

2.

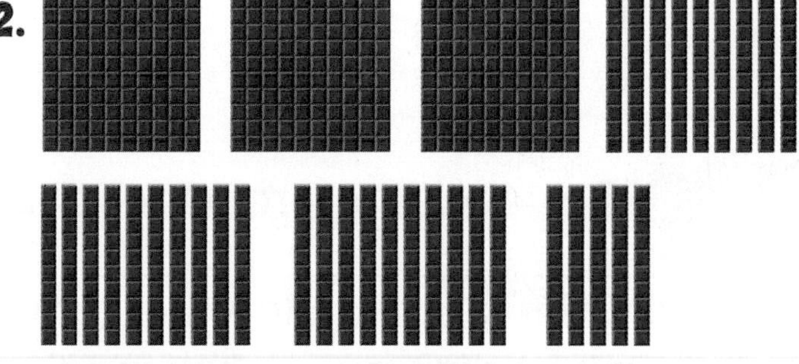

hundreds	tens	ones

______

____

3.

hundreds	tens	ones

______

____

4.

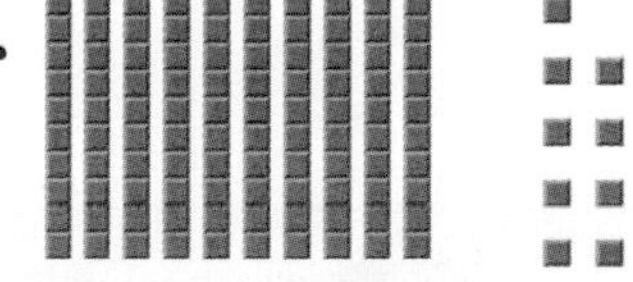

hundreds	tens	ones

______

____

5. Explain the different value of the 4s in 490, 504, and 648.

Copyright © by William H. Sadlier, Inc. All rights reserved.

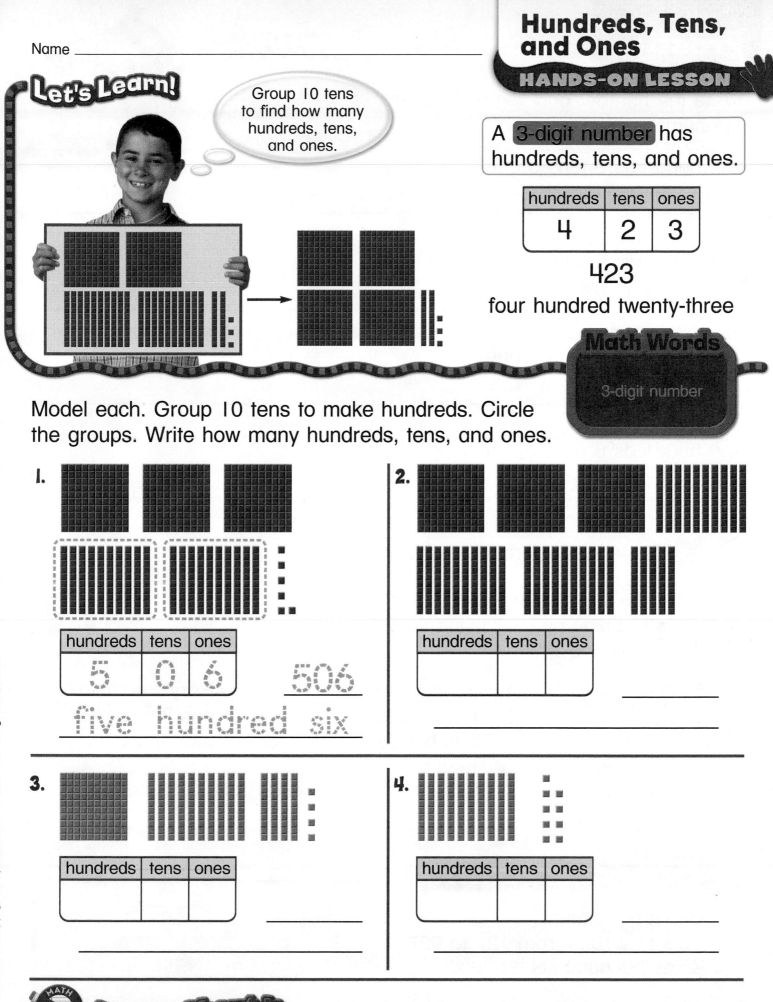

Practice

Remember to write 0
as a place holder.

Write the number and the number word.

6. 7 hundreds 0 tens 5 ones

705 seven hundred five

7. 8 hundreds 3 tens 0 ones

______ ______________________________

8. 9 hundreds 6 tens 4 ones

______ ______________________________

9. 4 hundreds 8 tens 7 ones

______ ______________________________

Problem Solving

Solve. Use a problem-solving strategy.

3
4
2

10. Marta, Jenna, and Rory each make a different 3-digit number using these cards. Write each one's number.

Marta's number has the most hundreds and fewest ones.	Jenna's number has an odd number as the tens digit.	Rory's number has 2 more ones than tens.
______	______	______

CALCULATOR ACTIVITY

11. Use a calculator.
Count by 100s from 127 to 927.
Write the numbers.

127, ____, ____, ____, ____, ____, ____, ____, 927

Math Alive at Home Have your child use the cards in exercise 10 and tell you what number would have the fewest hundreds and the most ones. (234)

Name ____________________

Place Value of Three-Digit Numbers

Let's Learn!

What is the value of each digit in 568?

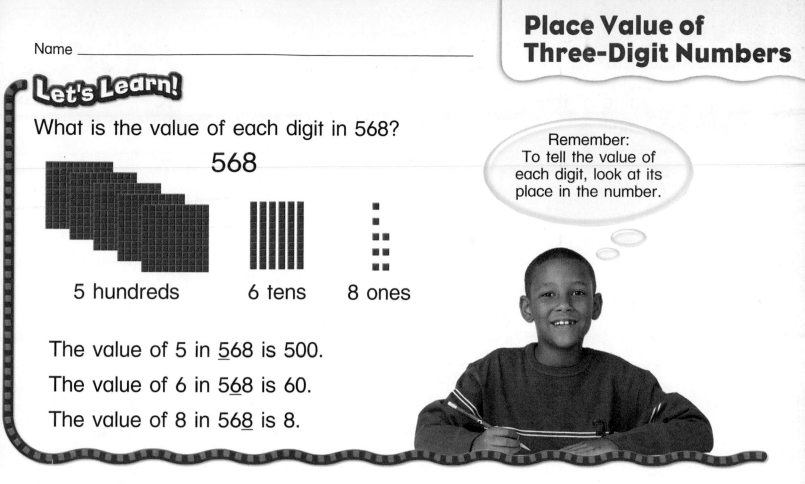

568

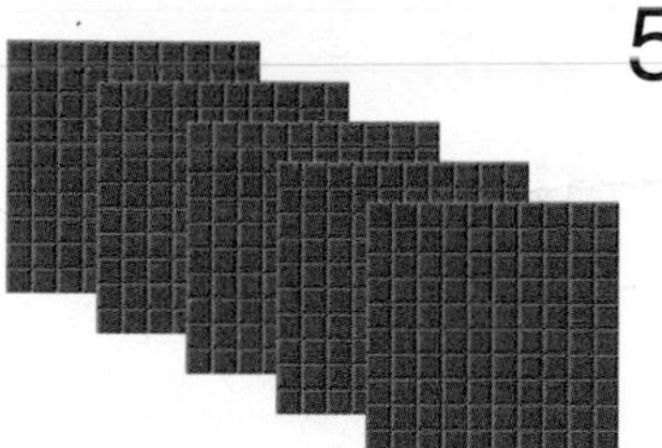

5 hundreds 6 tens 8 ones

Remember:
To tell the value of each digit, look at its place in the number.

The value of 5 in $\underline{5}68$ is 500.

The value of 6 in $5\underline{6}8$ is 60.

The value of 8 in $56\underline{8}$ is 8.

Circle the value of the underlined digit.

1. $3\underline{7}2$			**2.** $\underline{9}54$			**3.** $51\underline{6}$		
7	70	700	9	90	900	6	60	600
4. $75\underline{8}$			**5.** $6\underline{2}3$			**6.** $\underline{1}90$		
8	80	800	2	20	200	1	10	100
7. $\underline{4}87$			**8.** $2\underline{1}9$			**9.** $\underline{3}46$		
4	40	400	1	10	100	3	30	300
10. $\underline{8}09$			**11.** $7\underline{5}5$			**12.** $36\underline{3}$		
8	80	800	5	50	500	3	30	300

13. Explain why the 2 in 259 does not have the least value of the three digits.

Practice

Remember:
To tell the value of each digit, look at its place in the number.

Write the value of the underlined digit.

14. 754 700	**15.** 738 ______	**16.** 592 ______	**17.** 477 ______
18. 896 ______	**19.** 923 ______	**20.** 461 ______	**21.** 849 ______
22. 224 ______	**23.** 673 ______	**24.** 495 ______	**25.** 882 ______

Solve. Use a problem-solving strategy.
Circle your answer.

26. For our class picnic, our teacher had some sandwiches in a cooler. How many sandwiches do you think she had?

3 30 300

27. My uncle bought some fruit bars for my brothers and me. How many fruit bars do you think he bought?

4 40 400

DO YOU REMEMBER?

28. Write the amount.

______

29. Write the times.

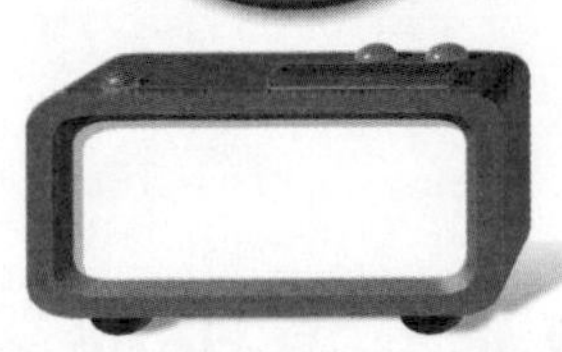

Math Alive at Home Ask your child to tell you the value of each digit in the number 247. (2 = 200, 4 = 40, 7 = 7)

Name ______________________________

Expanded Form with Hundreds, Tens, and Ones

HANDS-ON LESSON

Let's Learn!

A place-value chart can help you write 3-digit numbers in expanded form.

Show the value of each digit in a number to write its expanded form.

325

hundreds	tens	ones
3	2	5

300 + 20 + 5
expanded form

Model each number. Complete the place-value chart. Then write the number in expanded form.

1. 873

hundreds	tens	ones
8	7	3

800 + 70 + 3

2. 456

hundreds	tens	ones

____

3. 198

hundreds	tens	ones

____

4. 281

hundreds	tens	ones

____

5. 604

hundreds	tens	ones

____

6. 930

hundreds	tens	ones

____

7. Explain how you would write the expanded form of 808.

Practice

Write each number in expanded form.
Then write the number.

8. 4 hundreds 0 tens 2 ones 400 + 0 + 2 402

9. 8 hundreds 3 tens 0 ones _____ + _____ + _____ _____

10. 9 hundreds 8 tens 1 one _____ + _____ + _____ _____

11. 6 hundreds 2 tens 7 ones _____ + _____ + _____ _____

12. 3 hundreds 0 tens 9 ones _____ + _____ + _____ _____

13. 7 hundreds 9 tens 6 ones _____ + _____ + _____ _____

14. 5 hundreds 4 tens 4 ones _____ + _____ + _____ _____

15. 6 hundreds 6 tens 5 ones _____ + _____ + _____ _____

16. 2 hundreds 0 tens 3 ones _____ + _____ + _____ _____

Solve. Use a problem-solving strategy.

17. Taylor modeled 2 hundred flats, 2 ten rods, and 4 ones units. Raul added another hundred flat. Rita took away 2 ten rods. What is Taylor's number now?

Taylor's number is _____ now.

MENTAL MATH

Write the number.

18. 300 + 40 + 3 = _____	19. 100 + 50 + 5 = _____
20. _____ = 700 + 70 + 9	21. _____ = 200 + 30 + 8
22. _____ = 600 + 1	23. _____ = 400 + 2

Math Alive at Home Provide number cards 0 through 9 for your child to make 3-digit numbers and have her/him tell the expanded form of each number.

Name ______________________________

Algebra

Counting Patterns with 3-Digit Numbers

Let's Learn!

Jane made this chart to show counting by 25s.

Then she used the chart to show other number patterns that help her count.

She circled numbers to count by 50s.

She colored numbers to count by 100s from 25.

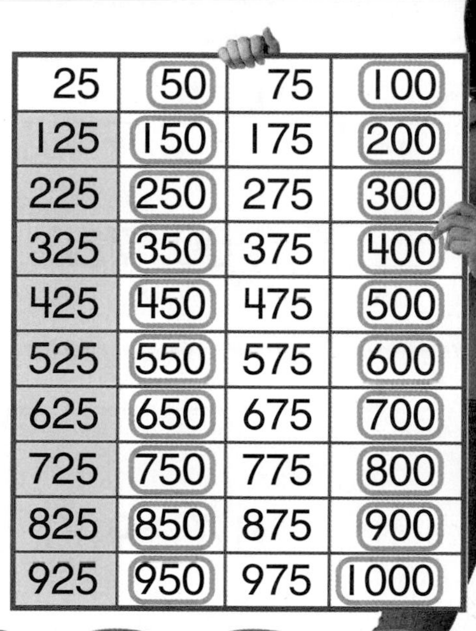

25	(50)	75	(100)
125	(150)	175	(200)
225	(250)	275	(300)
325	(350)	375	(400)
425	(450)	475	(500)
525	(550)	575	(600)
625	(650)	675	(700)
725	(750)	775	(800)
825	(850)	875	(900)
925	(950)	975	(1000)

Look for a pattern when counting.

Write the missing numbers.
Then circle the counting pattern.

1. 218, 318, 418, 518, 618, 718 — Count by: 10s 50s (100s)

2. 137, 147, ____, 167, ____, 187 — Count by: 10s 25s 100s

3. 263, 264, ____, ____, 267, 268 — Count by: 1s 10s 50s

4. 500, ____, 600, 650, ____, 750 — Count by: 10s 50s 100s

5. 700, 725, ____, 775, ____, 825 — Count by: 25s 50s 100s

6. ____, 153, ____, 173, 183, ____ — Count by: 1s 10s 50s

Math Journal — Write About It

7. Tell the two numbers that are most likely to come next in the pattern 500, 600, 700, 800. Explain how you know.

Copyright © by William H. Sadlier, Inc. All rights reserved.

Practice

Count by 10s, 25s, 50s, or 100s. Write the missing numbers.

8. 90, 100, 110, 120, _____, 140, 150, _____

9. 203, _____, 403, _____, 603, _____, 803, _____

10. 600, _____, 700, 750, _____, 850, _____, _____

11. 110, 210, _____, _____, 510, _____, 710, _____

12. 825, _____, 875, 900, _____, 950, _____, 1000

13. 746, 756, _____, _____, 786, _____, _____

Write the number 10 more than each.

14. 718 _____ | 15. 407 _____ | 16. 990 _____ | 17. 689 _____

Solve. Use a problem-solving strategy.

18. Jay's number is 2 tens more than 700.
Dee's number is 2 hundreds more than Jay's.
Brad's number is 2 ones more than Dee's.
What number do they each have?

Jay _____

Dee _____

Brad _____

TEST PREPARATION

19. Fill in the circle under the correct answer.

Look at the numbers in the box.
What number goes in the blank?

650, 675, _____, 725, 750

625	685	700	775
○	○	○	○

Math Alive at Home Ask your child to tell you the number 10 more than 432, 25 more than 525, 50 more than 650, and 100 more than 673. (442, 550, 700, 773)

Name ______________________________

Check Your Progress
Lessons 1-5

TEST PREPARATION

Listen to your teacher read the directions.
Fill in the circle under the correct answer.

1.

400 ○ 200 ○ 300 ○ 100 ○

5. 481 (the 1 is underlined)

10 ○ 1 ○ 100 ○

2. 9 hundreds 0 tens 0 ones

900 ○ 99 ○ 90 ○ 9 ○

6. nine hundred twenty-five

952 ○ 925 ○ 921 ○ 912 ○

3. 7 hundreds 5 tens 2 ones

- seven hundred twenty-five ○
- two hundred fifty-seven ○
- five hundred seventy-two ○
- seven hundred fifty-two ○

7. 677

- six hundred seventy-six ○
- seven hundred sixty-seven ○
- six hundred seventy ○
- six hundred seventy-seven ○

4.

three hundred ○ two hundred ○

four hundred ○ one hundred ○

8.

hundreds	tens	ones
8	3	6

$800 + 30 + 6$ ○ $8 + 3 + 6$ ○

$860 + 3$ ○ $800 + 3 + 60$ ○

Fill in the circle under the correct answer.

9. Which is the expanded form for the number 114?

1 + 1 + 4 ○ 100 + 10 + 4 ○

110 + 40 ○ 100 + 1 + 4 ○

10. Which is the expanded form for 5 hundreds 4 tens 9 ones?

5 + 4 + 9 ○ 540 + 90 ○

5 + 40 + 9 ○ 500 + 40 + 9 ○

11. What is the value of the underlined digit?

398

90 ○ 900 ○ 9 ○

12. Choose the missing numbers.

250, 300, ?, 400, ?, 500, 550

350, 450 ○ 325, 425 ○

310, 410 ○ 200, 300 ○

13. What is the value of the underlined digit?

763

7 ○ 70 ○ 700 ○

14. Which number is 10 more than 433?

440 ○ 445 ○ 443 ○ 444 ○

15. What number has 4 hundreds 6 tens 3 ones?

436 ○ 364 ○ 463 ○ 634 ○

16. Choose the missing numbers.

100, 200, ?, 400, 500, 600, ?

250, 650 ○ 350, 750 ○

200, 600 ○ 300, 700 ○

Name ______________________________

Algebra

Compare Numbers to 1000

Let's Learn!

Compare 132 and 214.

Compare the hundreds.

One hundred is fewer than two hundreds.

132 is less than 214.

$132 < 214$

Compare 269 and 269.

The hundreds, tens, and ones are the same.

The numbers are equal.

269 is equal to 269.

$269 = 269$

Compare 235 and 213.

The hundreds are the same. Compare the tens.

Three tens are more than one ten.

235 is greater than 213.

$235 > 213$

Compare. Write **is less than**, **is equal to**, or **is greater than**. Then write $<$, $=$, or $>$.

If hundreds and tens are the same, compare ones.

1. 472 __is less than__ 478. 472 ($<$) 478
2. 531 ______________ 571. 531 ( ) 571
3. 746 ______________ 746. 746 ( ) 746
4. 835 ______________ 829. 835 ( ) 829
5. 327 ______________ 427. 327 ( ) 427
6. 256 ______________ 254. 256 ( ) 254
7. 230 ______________ 46. 230 ( ) 46

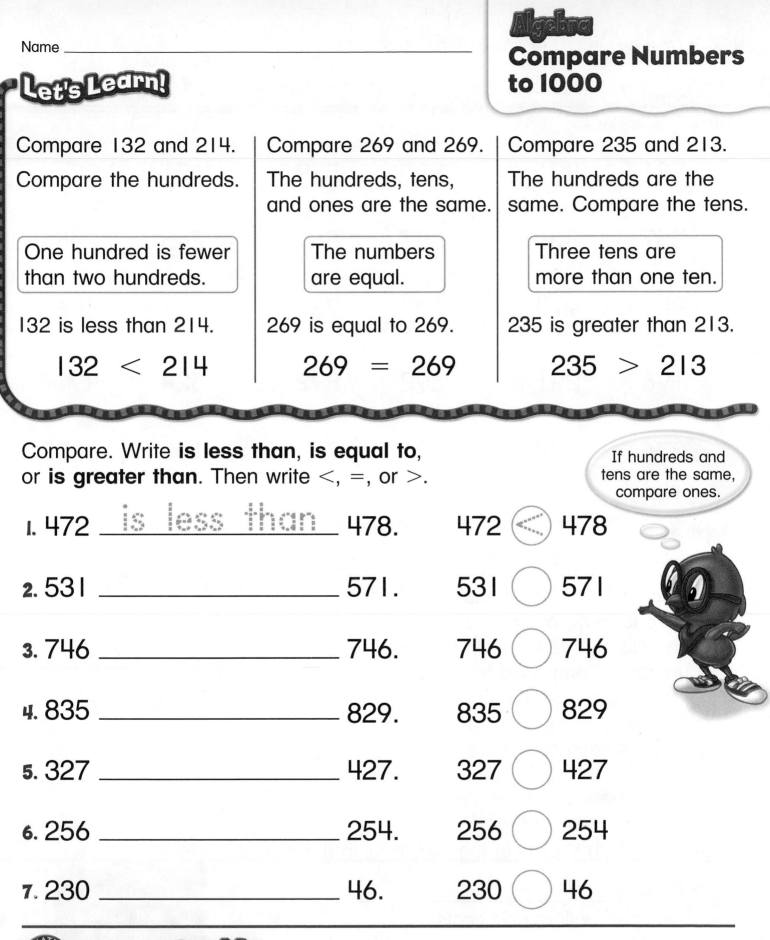

Write About It

8. Explain why you should compare hundreds before tens when comparing two 3-digit numbers.

Copyright © by William H. Sadlier, Inc. All rights reserved.

Practice

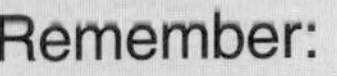

Remember:
< is less than
= is equal to
> is greater than

Compare.
Write <, =, or >.

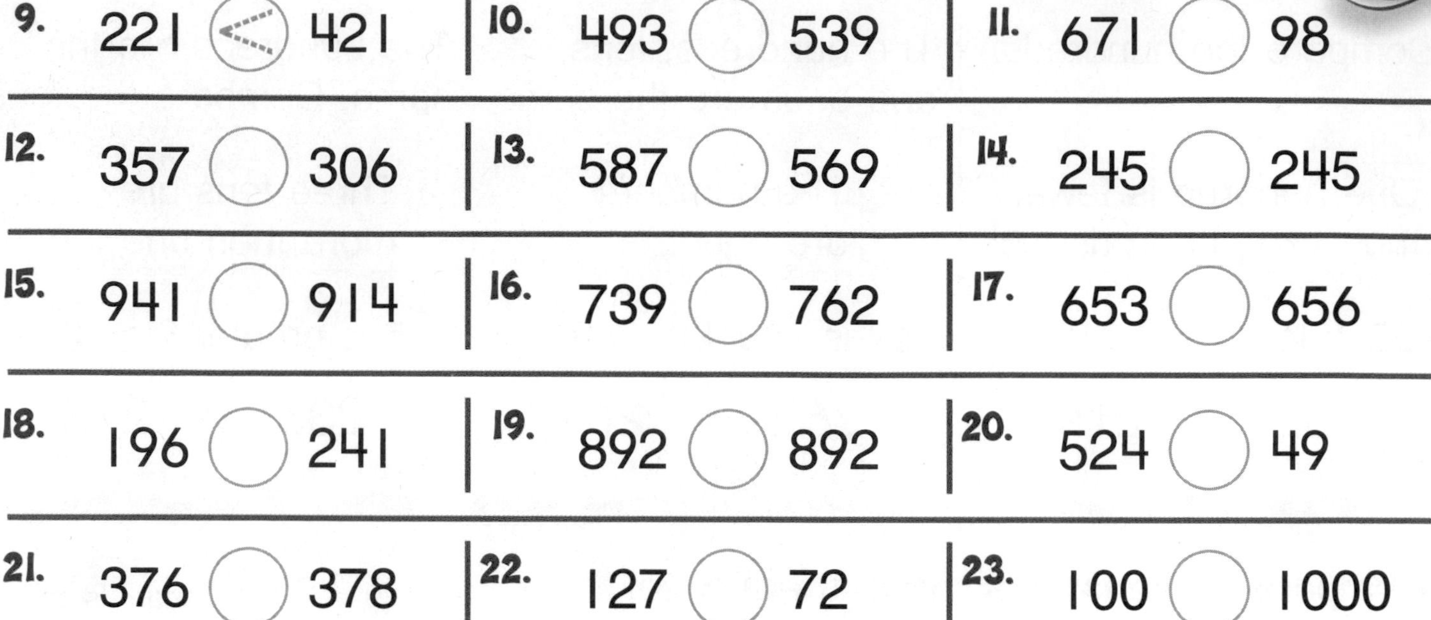

9. 221 (<) 421	10. 493 ◯ 539	11. 671 ◯ 98
12. 357 ◯ 306	13. 587 ◯ 569	14. 245 ◯ 245
15. 941 ◯ 914	16. 739 ◯ 762	17. 653 ◯ 656
18. 196 ◯ 241	19. 892 ◯ 892	20. 524 ◯ 49
21. 376 ◯ 378	22. 127 ◯ 72	23. 100 ◯ 1000

Solve. Use a problem-solving strategy.

24. P.J., Sue, and Feng each compared different numbers. Sue and Feng compared numbers with fewer than 4 hundreds. Feng used the tens place to compare his numbers. Write each name with the numbers each compares.

_______ 347 (?) 374

_______ 561 (?) 570

_______ 216 (?) 219

DO YOU REMEMBER?

Use the Math Words in the box to fill in the blanks.

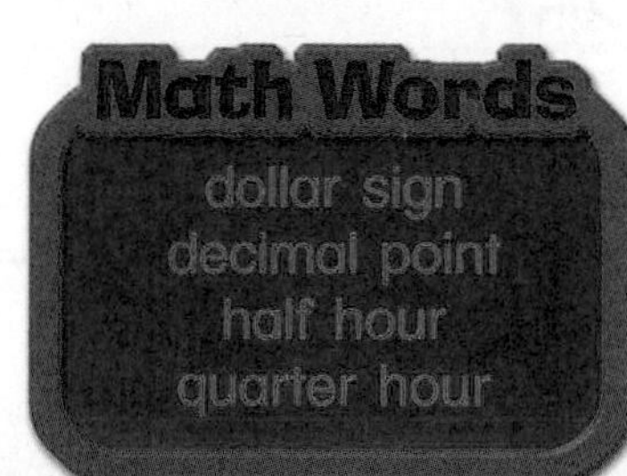

25. Write a ______________________ between dollars and cents.

26. Fifteen minutes is a ______________________.

27. Write a ______________ to the left of the dollar amount.

Math Alive at Home Write two 3-digit numbers and ask your child to tell which number is greater.

Name ____________________

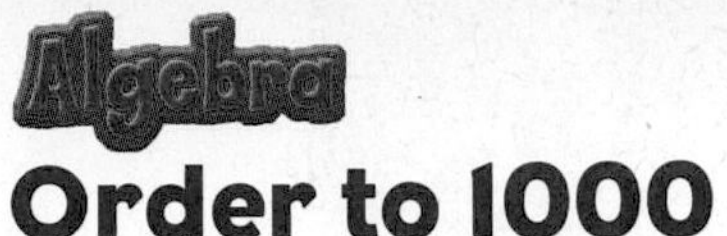

Order to 1000

Let's Learn!

To order numbers, compare hundreds, then tens, then ones.

408 280 618 448

2 hundreds is fewer than 4 hundreds and 6 hundreds.

280 least — 408 — 448 — 618 greatest

0 tens is fewer than 4 tens.

So the numbers from least to greatest are 280, 408, 448, 618.
The numbers from greatest to least are 618, 448, 408, 280.

Write the numbers in order from least to greatest.

1. 138 

138, 243, ______, ______

2. 177 

______, ______, ______, ______

3. 502 

______, ______, ______, ______

Write the numbers in order from greatest to least.

4. 

884, 785, ______, ______

5. 

______, ______, ______, ______

6. 169 

156 

______, ______, ______, ______

Talk It Over

7. Tell which of the numbers you ordered in exercise 3 are just before and just after 500.

Copyright © by William H. Sadlier, Inc. All rights reserved.

Practice

Write the numbers in order from least to greatest.

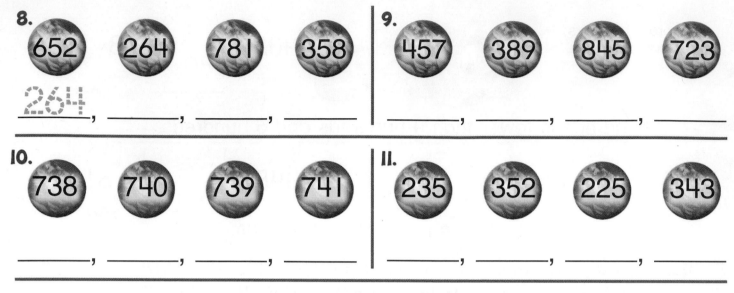

8.  652 264 781 358

264, ______, ______, ______

9. 457 389 845 723

______, ______, ______, ______

10.  738 740 739 741

______, ______, ______, ______

11. 235 352 225 343

______, ______, ______, ______

Write the numbers in order from greatest to least.

12.  583 748 973 657

______, ______, ______, ______

13.  476 798 485 713

______, ______, ______, ______

Problem Solving Solve. Use a problem-solving strategy.

14. On which night did the most people watch fireworks at the amusement park?

____

15. On which night did the fewest people watch the fireworks?

____

Thursday	Friday
707	607
Saturday	**Sunday**
670	770

CRITICAL THINKING 

Write the rule for each number pattern.

16. 407, 507, 607, 707, 807, 907 Rule: ______________

17. 100, 150, 250, 300, 400, 450 Rule: ______________

Math Alive at Home Write four different 3-digit numbers that all begin with 7 and have your child put the numbers in order from greatest to least.

Name ______________________

Use a Table

- You can use a table to compare data.

Listen

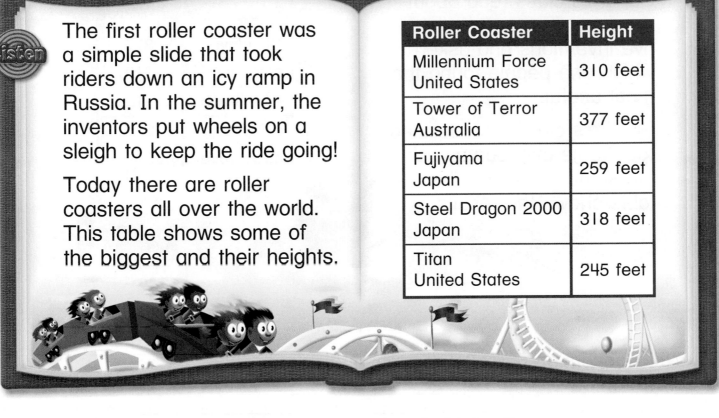

The first roller coaster was a simple slide that took riders down an icy ramp in Russia. In the summer, the inventors put wheels on a sleigh to keep the ride going!

Today there are roller coasters all over the world. This table shows some of the biggest and their heights.

Roller Coaster	Height
Millennium Force United States	310 feet
Tower of Terror Australia	377 feet
Fujiyama Japan	259 feet
Steel Dragon 2000 Japan	318 feet
Titan United States	245 feet

1. Which of the two roller coasters in Japan is higher?

2. Which of the two roller coasters in the United States is higher?

____

3. Which is higher, the Fujiyama or the Titan?

____

4. Which is higher, the Steel Dragon 2000 or the Millennium Force?

____

5. Which is the highest roller coaster of all listed in the table?

____

Copyright © by William H. Sadlier, Inc. All rights reserved.

Practice

Use a Table

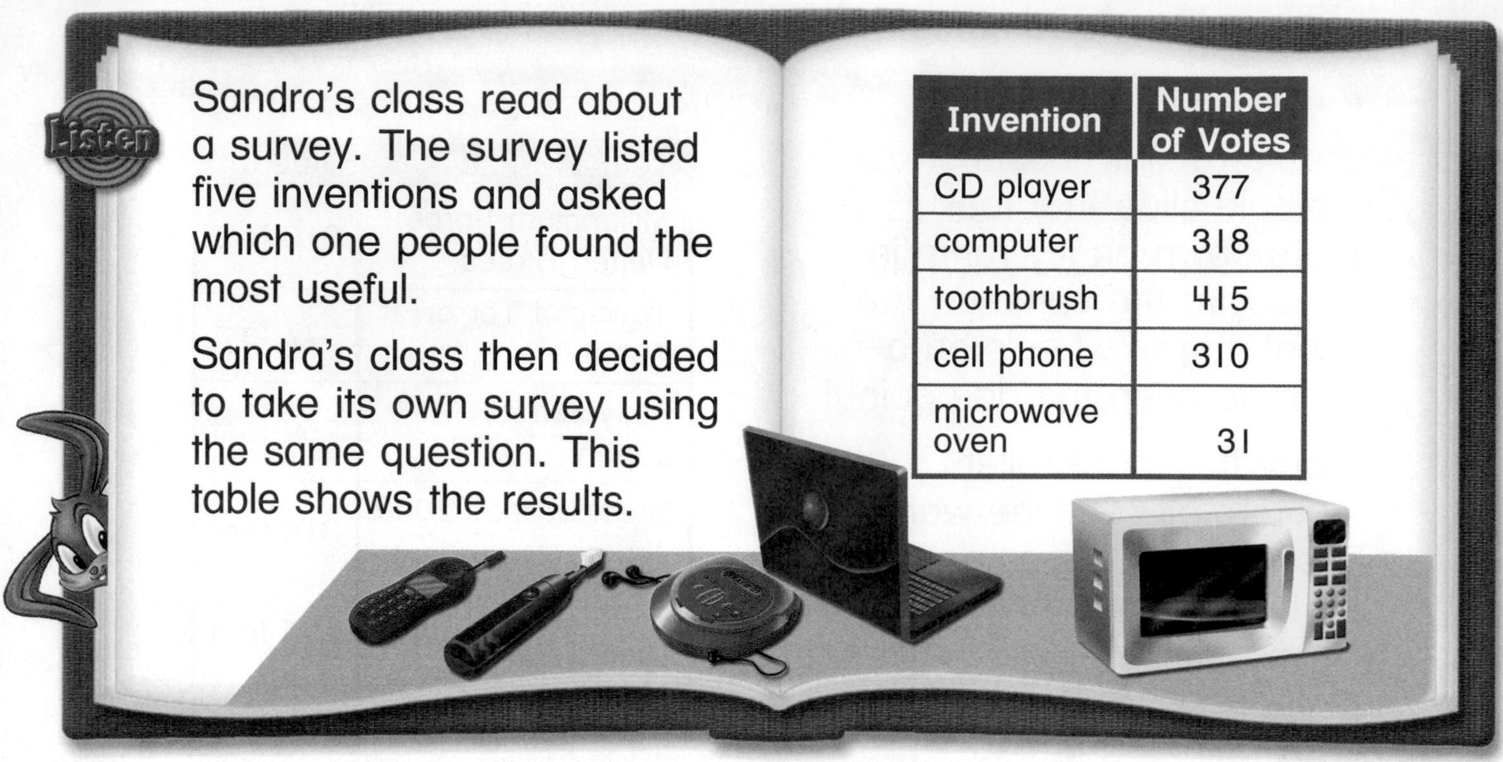

Sandra's class read about a survey. The survey listed five inventions and asked which one people found the most useful.

Sandra's class then decided to take its own survey using the same question. This table shows the results.

Invention	Number of Votes
CD player	377
computer	318
toothbrush	415
cell phone	310
microwave oven	31

6. Which invention received the most votes?

toothbrush

7. Which invention received the fewest votes?

8. Which received more votes, the computer or the cell phone?

9. Which received more votes, the CD player or the cell phone?

10. Suppose Sandra's class listed the inventions in order from most to fewest votes. Which invention would the class list in fourth place?

Math Alive at Home Today your child used a table to work through math problems. Have him/her explain how he/she solved the problems in this lesson.

Round to the Nearest Hundred

Name ______________________________

Let's Learn!

Round each number to the nearest hundred. Use the number line.

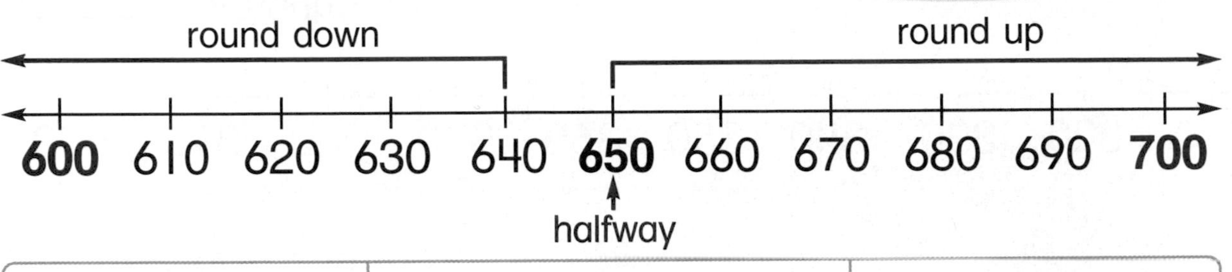

630	650	660
630 is less than halfway to 700. 630 has 3 tens. 630 rounds down to 600.	650 is halfway between 600 and 700. 650 has 5 tens. 650 rounds up to 700.	660 is more than halfway to 700. 660 has 6 tens. 660 rounds up to 700.

Look for the halfway mark.
Round each number to the nearest hundred.

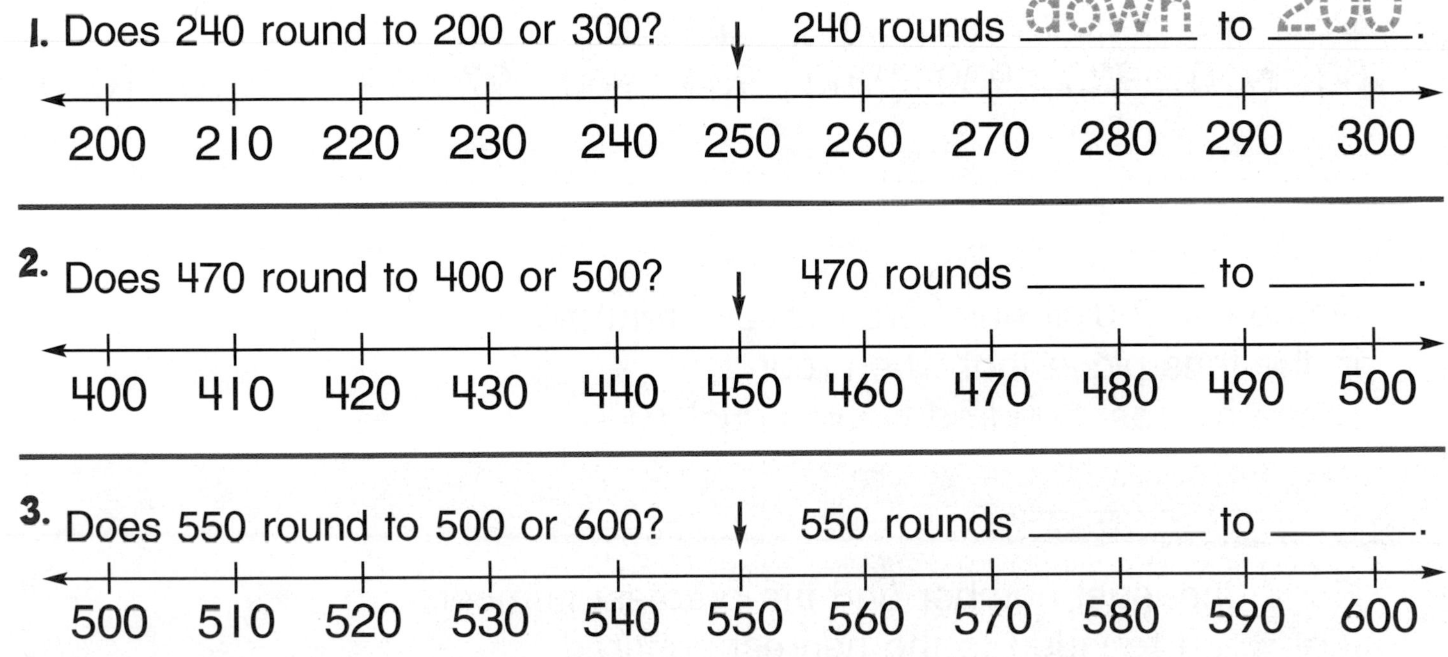

1. Does 240 round to 200 or 300? 240 rounds down to 200.

2. Does 470 round to 400 or 500? 470 rounds ________ to ______.

3. Does 550 round to 500 or 600? 550 rounds ________ to ______.

Talk It Over

4. Name two 3-digit numbers. Name one that would round down to the nearest hundred and one that would round up to the nearest hundred.

Copyright © by William H. Sadlier, Inc. All rights reserved.

Practice

Round each number to the nearest hundred.

5. 330

330 rounds to 300.

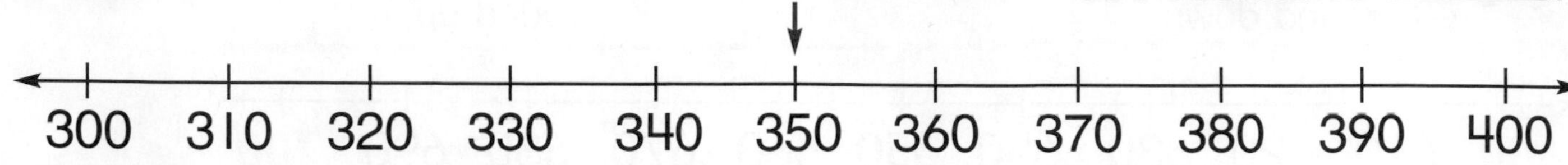

6. 760

760 rounds to ______.

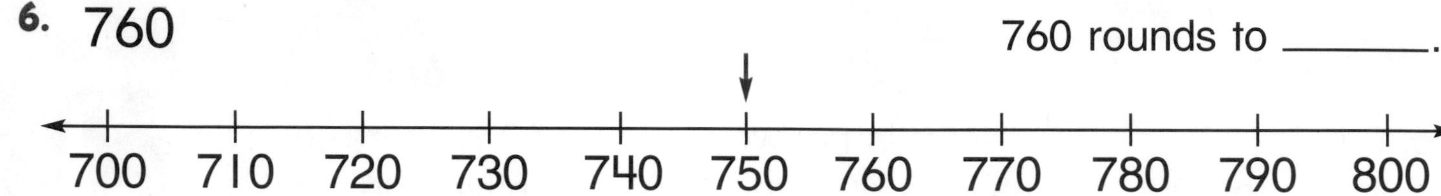

7. 878

878 rounds to ______.

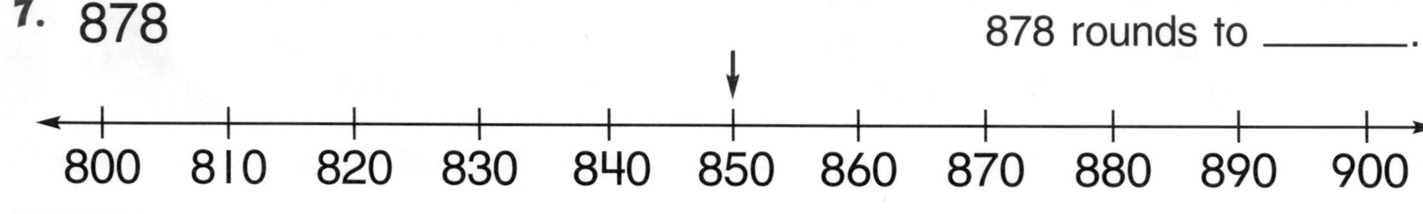

8. 950

950 rounds to ______.

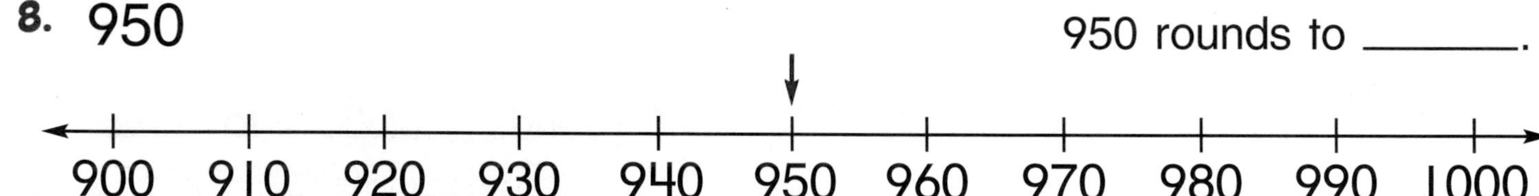

CHALLENGE

9. Name two 3-digit numbers with different digits in the tens place that when rounded to the nearest hundred would equal 1000.

______, ______

10. Name the least number and the greatest number that when rounded to the nearest hundred would equal 500.

______, ______

Math Alive at Home Ask your child to use the number lines above to round these numbers: 310, 750, 880. (300, 800, 900)

Name ______

Make an Organized List

Read How many numbers between 100 and 200 have 3 tens in the tens place?

Plan Make a list of numbers between 100 and 200 that have 3 tens. Then count the numbers.

Think

3 tens = 30

Write 130, 131, 132, 133, 134, 135, 136, 137, 138, 139

10 numbers between 100 and 200 have 3 tens.

Check Are the numbers you wrote between 100 and 200? Do they all have 3 tens?

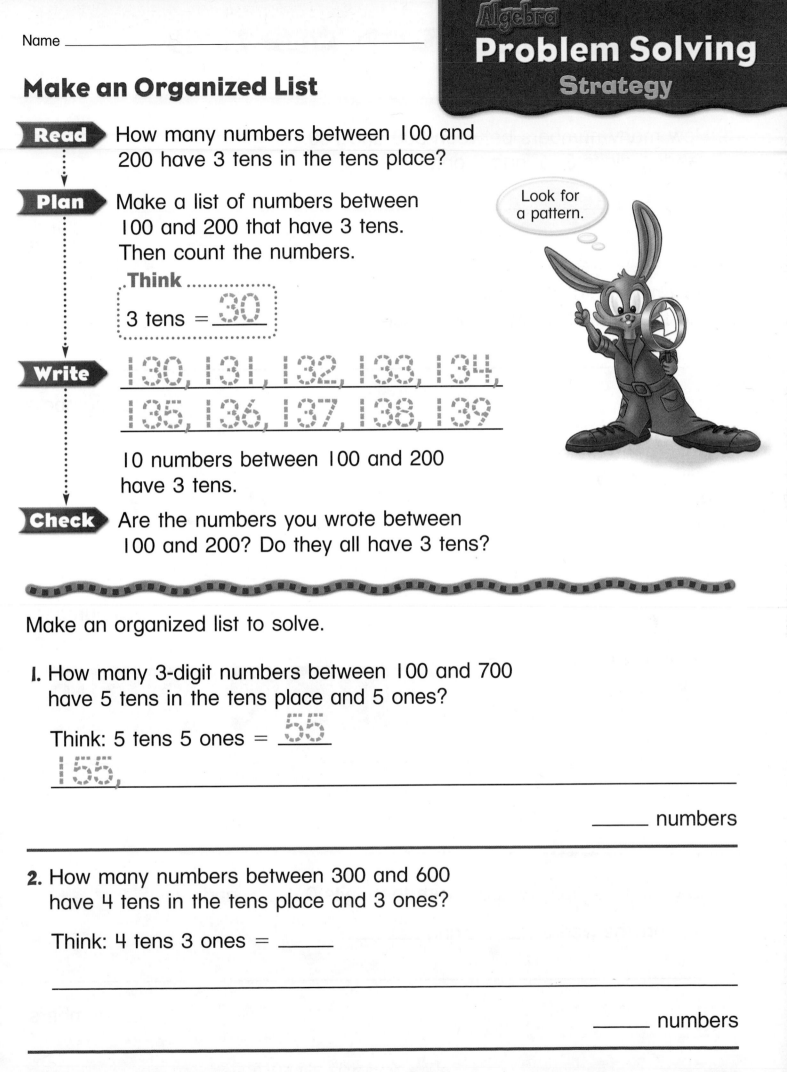

Make an organized list to solve.

1. How many 3-digit numbers between 100 and 700 have 5 tens in the tens place and 5 ones?

   Think: 5 tens 5 ones = 55

   155, ______

   ______ numbers

2. How many numbers between 300 and 600 have 4 tens in the tens place and 3 ones?

   Think: 4 tens 3 ones = ______

   ______

   ______ numbers

Copyright © by William H. Sadlier, Inc. All rights reserved.

Practice

Read Plan Write Check

Make an Organized List

3. How many numbers between 300 and 700 use the digits 3, 6, and 9 only once?

369,

_____ numbers

4. How many 3-digit numbers greater than 200 use the digits 1, 2 and 5 only once?

_____ numbers

5. How many 3-digit numbers less than 400 can Ashley make? She uses each of these 4 cards only once in each number.

_____ numbers

6. Daryl has these 6 cards. How many 3-digit numbers can he make?

_____ numbers

7. How many 3-digit numbers with the digits 0, ____, and ____ are between ______ and ______?

_____ numbers

Math Alive at Home Ask your child how she/he made an organized list to solve the problems in this lesson.

Name ____

Problem Solving
Applications

Read ▶ Plan ▶ Write ▶ Check

Mixed Strategies

Use a strategy you have learned.

Strategy File
Draw a Picture
Use Logical Reasoning
Make an Organized List
Use More Than One Step
Make a Table

1. Tammy writes all the numbers less than 100 that have 5 ones in the ones place. How many numbers does Tammy write?

_____ numbers

---

2. Jack has 22 magnets. He puts 10 in each row. How many complete rows can Jack make?

_____ complete rows

---

3. The red and blue cubes are Darla's. The other cubes are Kyle's. Whose cubes have a greater sum?

____________'s cubes

---

4. Each car on a Ferris wheel holds 5 people. How many people can ride in 6 cars?

_____ people

---

5. Tim thinks of a 2-digit number. It has fewer than 8 ones. When Tim rounds it to the nearest ten, he gets 60. Circle Tim's number.

58

Copyright © by William H. Sadlier, Inc. All rights reserved.

Practice

Read Plan Write Check

Use a strategy you have learned.

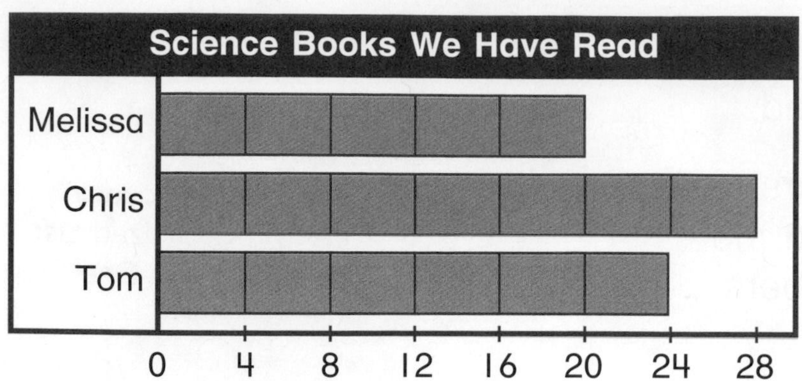

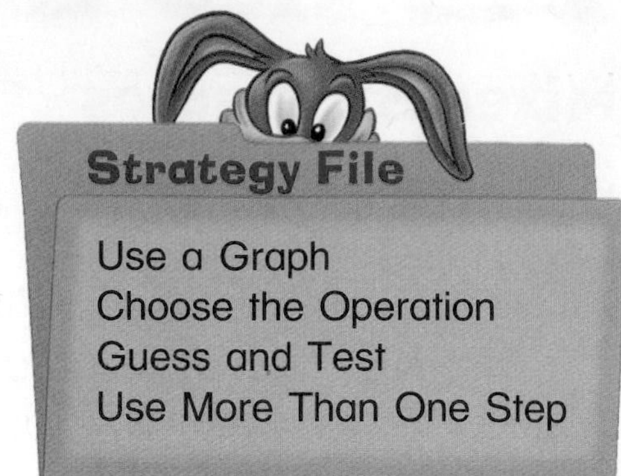

Strategy File
Use a Graph
Choose the Operation
Guess and Test
Use More Than One Step

6. If Tom reads 10 more books, how many books will he have read in all?

_____ books

---

7. How many more books does Melissa have to read to total the number read by Chris and Tom together?

_____ books

---

8. A scientist tags 95 hornbills. 70 of them are green. She also tags 85 toucans. How many birds does the scientist tag?

_____ birds

---

9. Keith adds the contents of two of his science beakers together. The total is 89 ounces. Circle the beakers whose contents Keith adds.

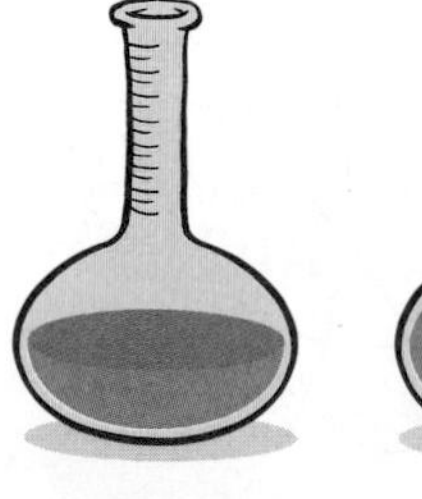

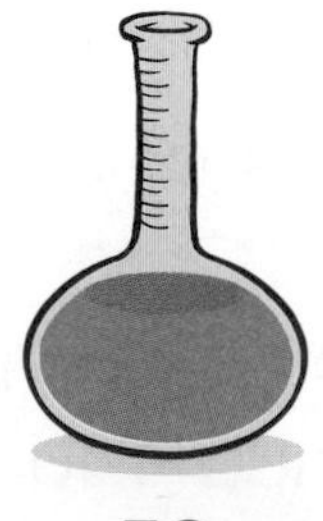

36 ounces | 43 ounces | 52 ounces | 37 ounces

Math Alive at Home Ask your child to tell you how she/he solved some of the problems in this lesson.

Name ______________________

TEST PREPARATION

Listen to your teacher read the directions.
Fill in the circle under the correct answer.

1. 485 ___?___ 328

○ is less than
○ is equal to
○ is greater than

2.

220, 200, 202 ○

200, 202, 220 ○

220, 202, 200 ○

202, 200, 220 ○

3. 576 ○ 647

< ○   = ○   > ○

4. 851 ___?___ 851

○ is less than
○ is equal to
○ is greater than

5. How many 3-digit numbers less than 300 can Carol make? She uses each of these cards only once in each number.

6 ○   3 ○   4 ○   5 ○

6.

258, 418, 613, 838 ○

838, 418, 613, 258 ○

838, 613, 418, 258 ○

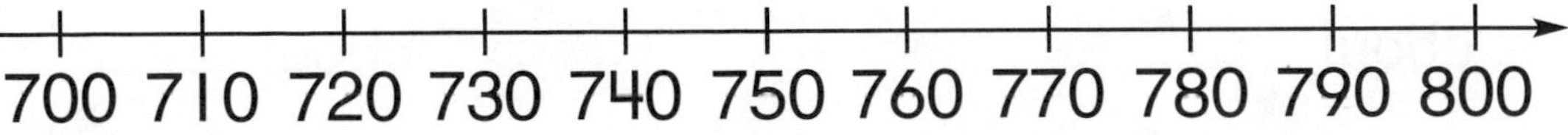

7. 740

730 ○   700 ○   750 ○   800 ○

8. 760

750 ○   770 ○   800 ○   700 ○

Copyright © by William H. Sadlier, Inc. All rights reserved.

Connection

Name ____________________

Round money amounts the same way you round whole numbers.

Did You Know?
Paper money was invented in China more than 1000 years ago. Before there was paper money, people used coins made from gold and other metals.

is about

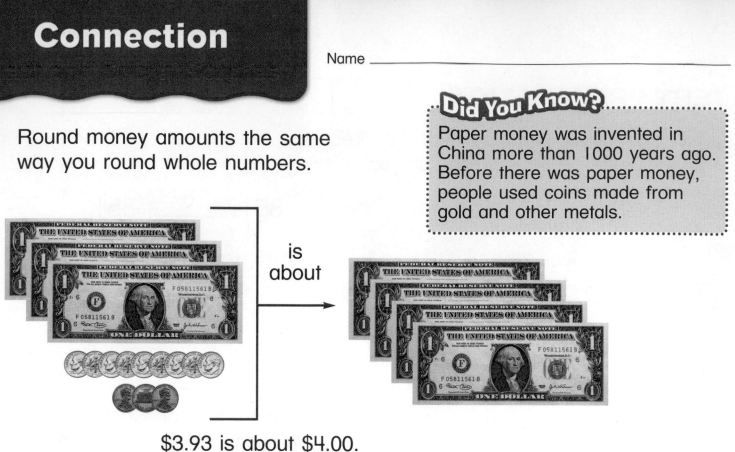

$3.93 is about $4.00.
$3.93 rounds up to $4.00.

Look at the prices. Then round each to the nearest dollar. Write about how much.

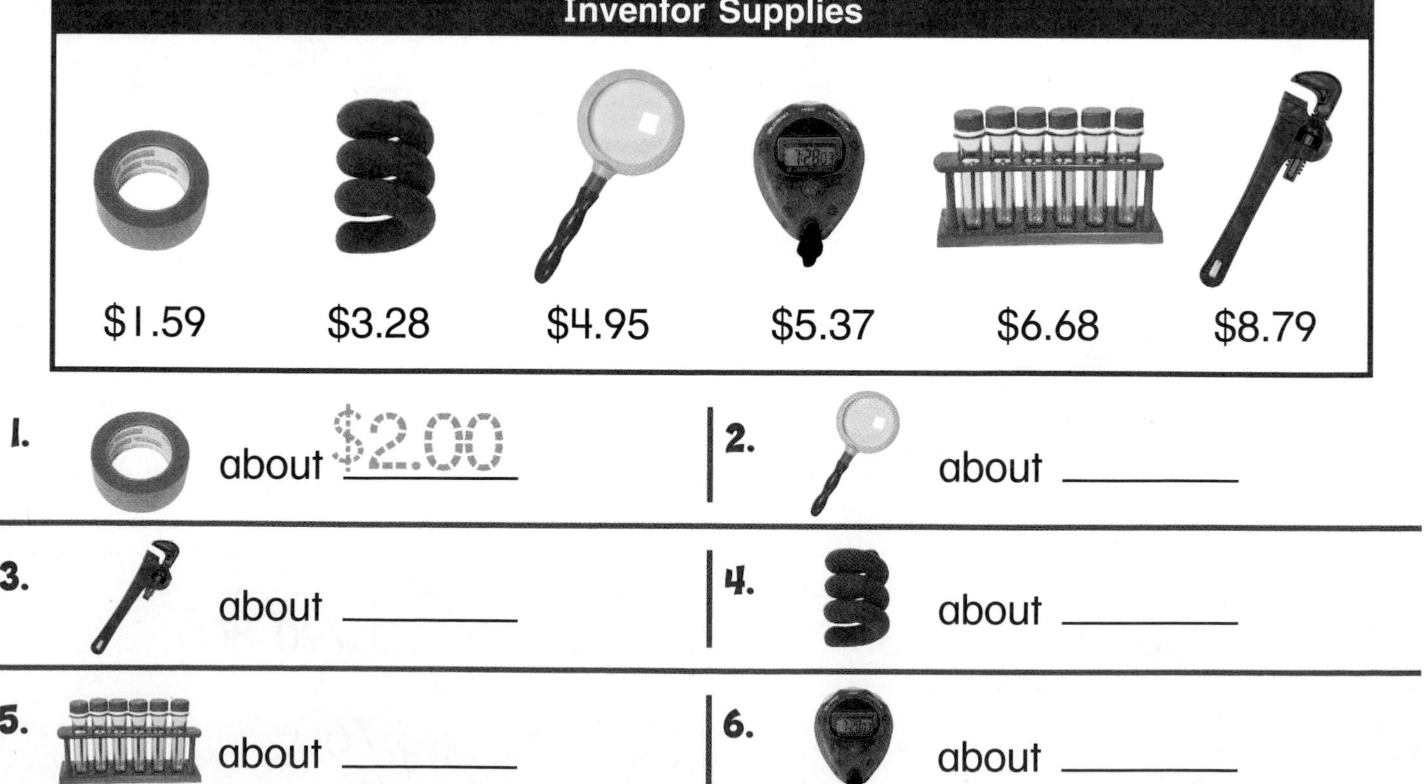

1. about $2.00
2. about ______
3. about ______
4. about ______
5. about ______
6. about ______

You can put this in your Math Portfolio.

Name ______________________

Chapter 8 Test

1. Write the number and the number word.

4 hundreds 0 tens 0 ones ______ ______________________

2. Round 430 to the nearest hundred.

430 rounds to ______.

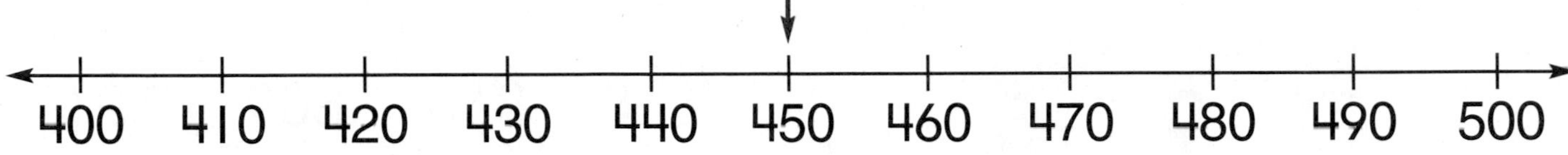

3. Write the number and the number word.

hundreds	tens	ones
5	2	5

______

____

4. Write the expanded form of 231.

______ + ______ + ______

5. Write the value of the underlined digit.

<u>7</u>31

______

6. Write the numbers in order from least to greatest.

743 374 437 347

______, ______, ______, ______

7. Write the missing numbers.

200, 225, ______, 275, ______

8. Compare. Write <, =, or >.

213 ◯ 213

9. Write the value of the underlined digit.

6<u>5</u>4

______

Copyright © by William H. Sadlier, Inc. All rights reserved.

10. Write the missing numbers.

300, ______, 400, 450, ______

11. Write the expanded form of 939.

______ + ______ + ______

12. What numbers made from the digits on these cards have the fewest hundreds?

The numbers ______ and ______.

13. Write the numbers in order from greatest to least.

860 868 809 821

______, ______, ______, ______

14. John modeled this number. Mary added 2 hundred flats. Bob took away 3 ten rods. What is John's number now?

John's number is ______ now.

15. Margaret has these six cards. How many 3-digit numbers can she make?

______ numbers

16. Jill's number is 3 ones more than 500. Ann's number is 3 tens more than Jill's. What is Ann's number?

Ann's number is ______.

17. Compare. Write <, =, or >.

686 ◯ 668

18. Write the value of the underlined digit.

90<u>4</u>

______

19. Write the missing numbers.

437, 447, ______, 467, ______

Name ______________________________

Make 3-digit numbers using any three digits below.

   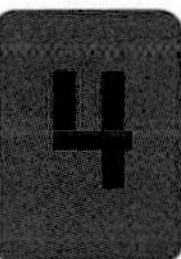  

Complete a table for each number.

1.

Number	
Expanded form	
Rounded to the nearest hundred	

2.

Number	
Expanded form	
Rounded to the nearest hundred	

3.

Number	
Expanded form	
Rounded to the nearest hundred	

4.

Number	
Expanded form	
Rounded to the nearest hundred	

5. Order the numbers in the four exercises above from greatest to least.

______, ______, ______, ______

Copyright © by William H. Sadlier, Inc. All rights reserved.

Enrichment

Name ______________________

Explore Thousands

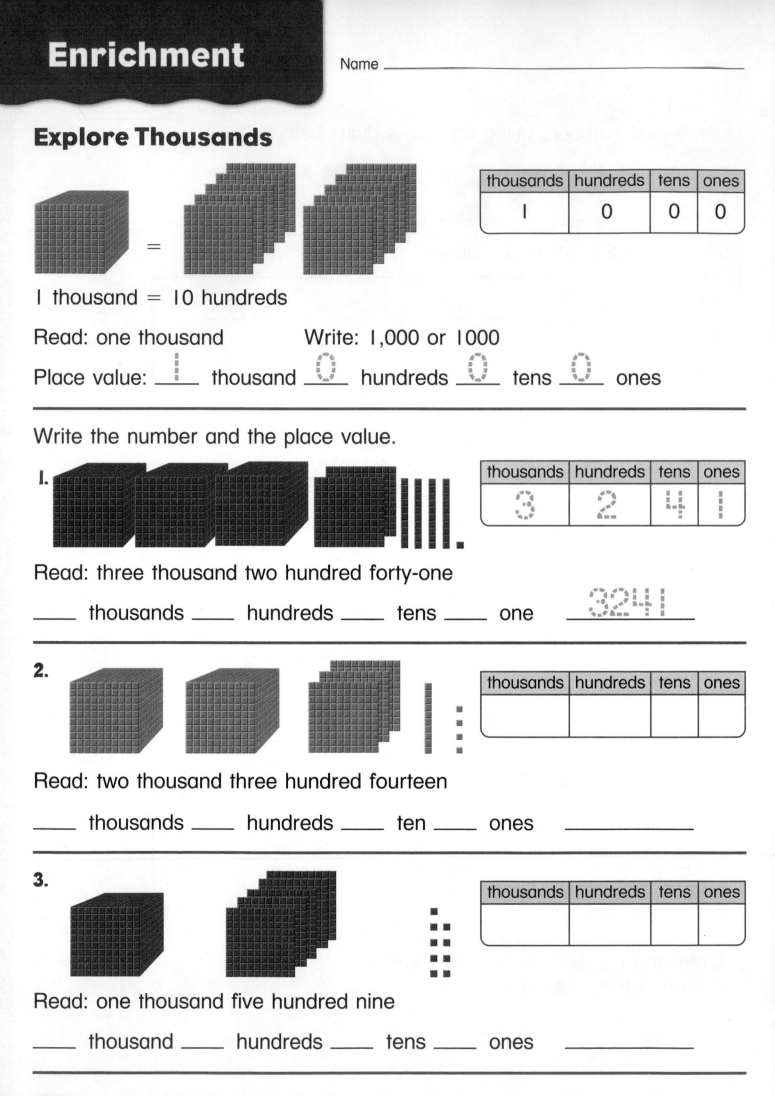

thousands	hundreds	tens	ones
1	0	0	0

1 thousand = 10 hundreds

Read: one thousand Write: 1,000 or 1000

Place value: 1 thousand 0 hundreds 0 tens 0 ones

Write the number and the place value.

1. 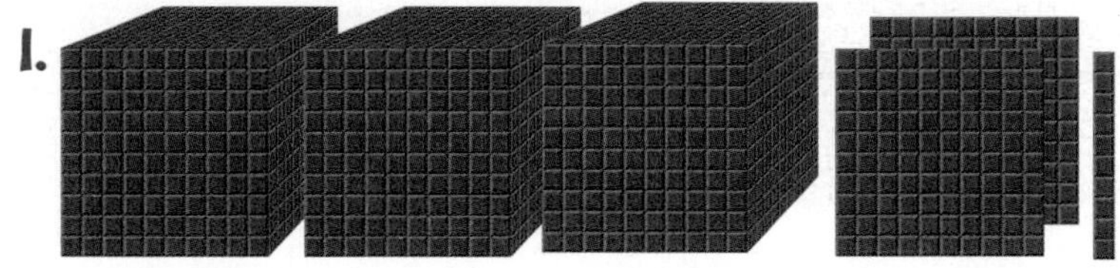

thousands	hundreds	tens	ones
3	2	4	1

Read: three thousand two hundred forty-one

____ thousands ____ hundreds ____ tens ____ one 3241

2. 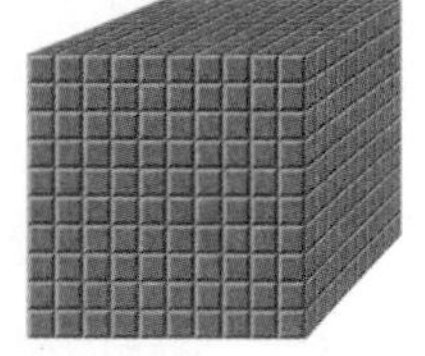 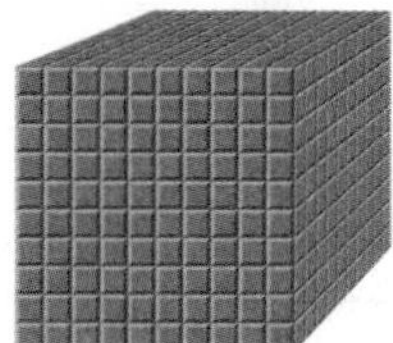 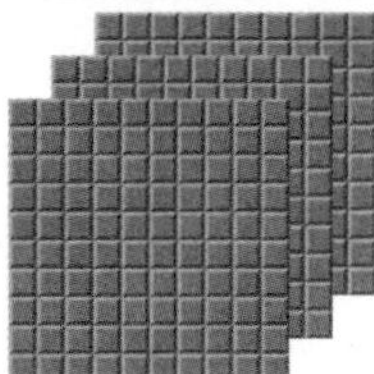 

thousands	hundreds	tens	ones

Read: two thousand three hundred fourteen

____ thousands ____ hundreds ____ ten ____ ones ____________

3.   

thousands	hundreds	tens	ones

Read: one thousand five hundred nine

____ thousand ____ hundreds ____ tens ____ ones ____________

Name ______________________________

TEST PREPARATION

Fill in the circle next to the correct answer.

1. Round 570 to the nearest hundred.

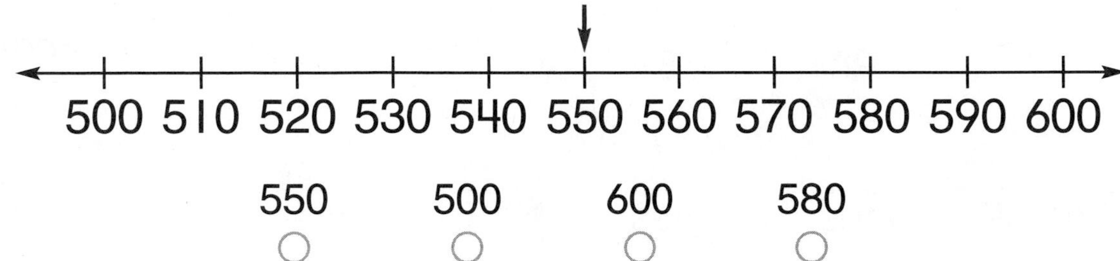

○ 550 ○ 500 ○ 600 ○ 580

2. Choose the missing numbers. 110, 120, ?, 140, ?, 160, ?

○ 140, 160, 180 ○ 130, 150, 170 ○ 150, 160, 170 ○ 120, 140, 160

3. Which list is in order from greatest to least?

○ 263, 326, 623, 632
○ 263, 632, 623, 326
○ 263, 623, 632, 326
○ 632, 623, 326, 263

4. What time is it?

○ half past 5 ○ half past 3 ○ half past 2

5. Which is another way to write 700 + 60 + 1?

○ 761 ○ 760 ○ 671 ○ 176

6. How did the figure move?

○ flip ○ slide ○ turn

7. Find the difference.

$$\begin{array}{r} 86 \\ -58 \\ \hline \end{array}$$

○ 39 ○ 36 ○ 28 ○ 38

8. Find the missing addend.

? + 9 = 17

○ 6 ○ 8 ○ 7 ○ 9

Copyright © by William H. Sadlier, Inc. All rights reserved.

Watch for multistep problems.

9. Add.

$$\begin{array}{r} 39 \\ +47 \\ \hline \end{array}$$

○ 76 ○ 86 ○ 98 ○ 78

10. Mike has 54 crayons. He gives 33 crayons to his sister. His mother buys him 22 more. How many crayons does he have then?

○ 21 ○ 31 ○ 33 ○ 43

11. Jerry lives 26 blocks from a park. Sam lives 40 blocks from the same park. How many blocks farther is Sam from the park than Jerry?

○ 14 ○ 24 ○ 26 ○ 66

12. What is the elapsed time?

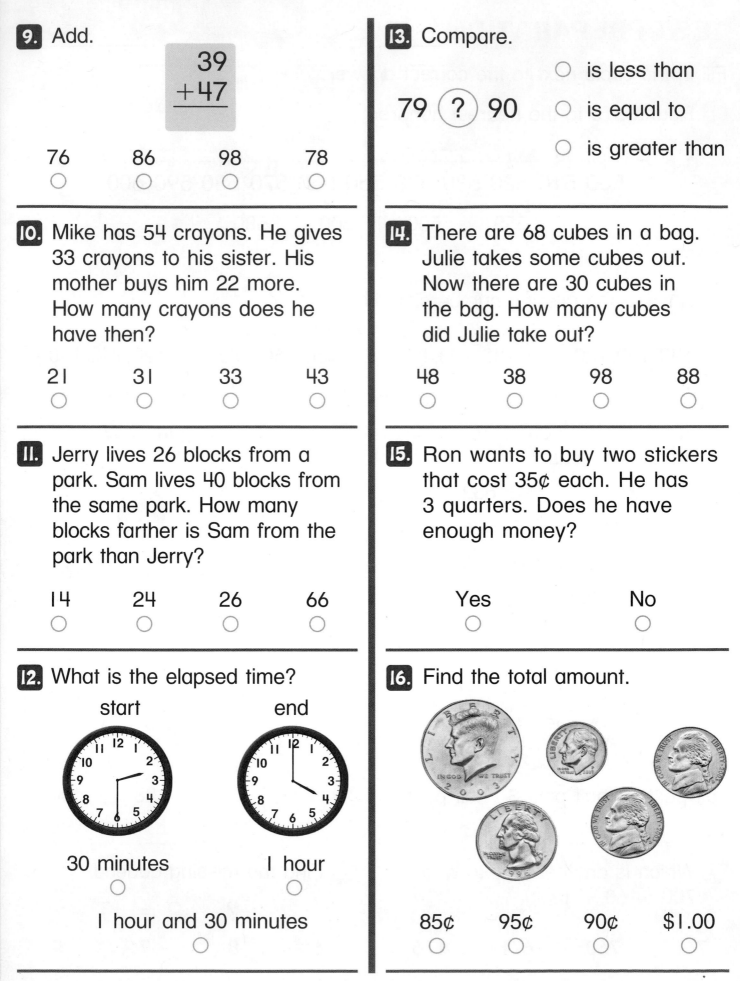

start

end

○ 30 minutes ○ 1 hour

○ 1 hour and 30 minutes

13. Compare.

79 (?) 90

○ is less than

○ is equal to

○ is greater than

14. There are 68 cubes in a bag. Julie takes some cubes out. Now there are 30 cubes in the bag. How many cubes did Julie take out?

○ 48 ○ 38 ○ 98 ○ 88

15. Ron wants to buy two stickers that cost 35¢ each. He has 3 quarters. Does he have enough money?

○ Yes ○ No

16. Find the total amount.

○ 85¢ ○ 95¢ ○ 90¢ ○ $1.00

CHAPTER
9
Addition and Subtraction: Three-Digit Numbers
SECTION
STARS
S
1
Listen
Listen to your teacher read the poem.
How many fans got headbands and pennants as prizes?

Dear Family,

Today our class began Chapter 9. We will learn about adding and subtracting three-digit numbers. Let's do the activity below together so I can review the skills I will need in order to understand the math in this chapter. Then you can read some of the new vocabulary I will learn in Chapter 9.

Love, ____________

Regrouping Reminders

Write the addition and subtraction problems below on a sheet of paper for your child to solve. Ask your child to tell whether he/she needs to regroup to add or subtract and to explain the regrouping for each problem. Understanding how to regroup ones as tens for addition and tens as ones for subtraction will help your child understand the regrouping in three-digit addition and subtraction.

Chapter 9 Vocabulary

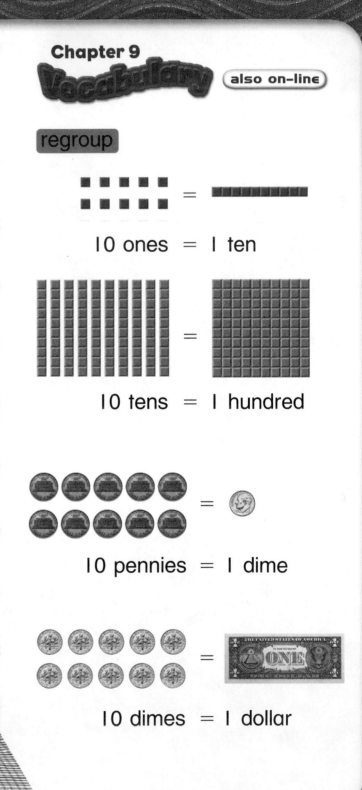

also on-line

regroup

10 ones = 1 ten

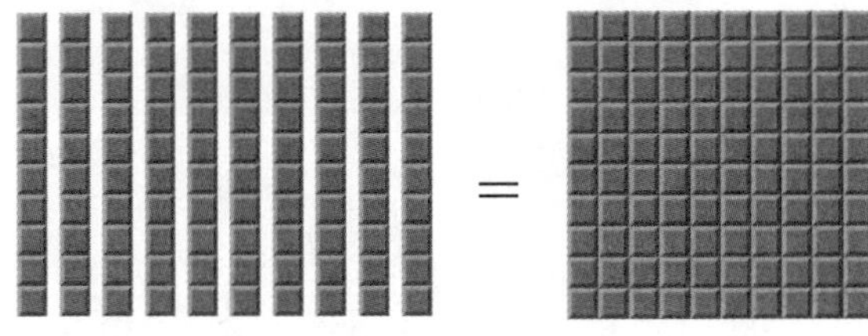

10 tens = 1 hundred

10 pennies = 1 dime

10 dimes = 1 dollar

For Additional Resources VISIT US ON-LINE www.sadlier-oxford.com

Name ____________________

Add Hundreds, Tens, and Ones

Let's Learn!

123 + 12 = ?

To find the sum, line up the addends by place value.

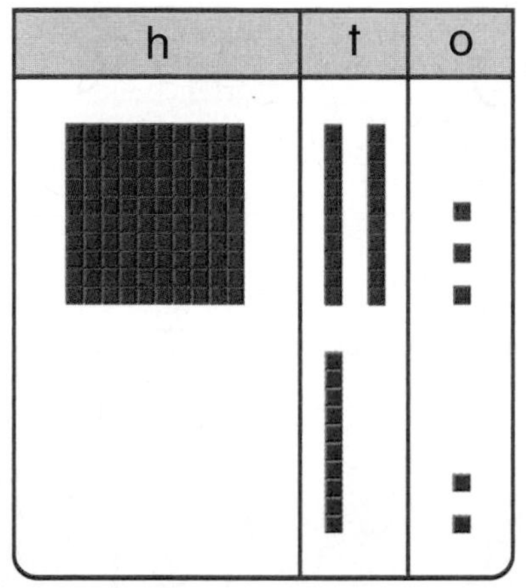

First add the ones.

	h	t	o
	1	2	3
+		1	2
			5

Next add the tens.

	h	t	o
	1	2	3
+		1	2
		3	5

Then add the hundreds.

	h	t	o
	1	2	3
+		1	2
	1	3	5

Find the sum.

1.

	h	t	o
	4	6	4
+	1	2	1
	5	8	5

2.

	h	t	o
	7	2	4
+	2	5	3

3.

	h	t	o
	8	6	3
+		1	0

4. 603 + 304

5. 310 + 350

6. 102 + 84

7. 274 + 602

8. 215 + 83

9. 240 + 342

10. 331 + 167

11. 600 + 93

12. 175 + 414

13. 935 + 50

Talk It Over

14. Without adding, tell which sum is greater: 215 + 200 or 215 + 20. Explain why.

Practice

Add ones, then tens, then hundreds.

Add.

15.	16.	17.	18.	19.
100	908	213	527	674
+200	+ 60	+764	+ 41	+225
300				

20.	21.	22.	23.	24.
752	314	425	635	624
+ 40	+ 80	+163	+ 11	+124

25.	26.	27.	28.	29.
610	705	203	348	131
+ 35	+ 42	+673	+ 31	+465

Use a problem-solving strategy to solve.
Show your work on a separate sheet of paper.

30. Leroy reads two books about soccer. One book has 120 pages and the other book has 76 pages. How many pages does Leroy read?

_______ pages

31. Peggy counts 148 fans for her team at a soccer game and 111 fans for the other team. How many fans are at the game?

_______ fans

MENTAL MATH

Add. Write the sums.

32.

	634	319	123	857	442	565	902
Add 30 to:							

33.

	856	429	541	730	915	605	322
Add 40 to:							

Math Alive at Home Ask your child to show how to add 247 + 120 and 247 + 12. (367, 259)

Name ____________________

Count On 1, 10, and 100

Let's Learn!

You can count on to add mentally.

460 + 1 = ?	460 + 10 = ?	460 + 100 = ?
Count on 1. 460, 461	Count on 10. 460, 470	Count on 100. 460, 560
460 + 1 = 461	460 + 10 = 470	460 + 100 = 560

Write the number 1 more than each.

1. 629, 630
2. 457, ______
3. 136, ______
4. 819, ______

Write the number 10 more than each.

5. 701, ______
6. 528, ______
7. 890, ______
8. 450, ______

Write the number 100 more than each.

9. 267, ______
10. 485, ______
11. 833, ______
12. 608, ______

Add.

13. 940 + 1 = ______
14. 736 + 10 = ______
15. 179 + 1 = ______
16. 219 + 10 = ______
17. 565 + 10 = ______
18. 613 + 100 = ______
19. 858 + 100 = ______
20. 745 + 100 = ______

Talk It Over

21. Without adding, tell whether 834 + 10 or 834 + 100 is more.

Copyright © by William H. Sadlier, Inc. All rights reserved.

Practice

Write +1, +10, or +100 to explain the pattern.

Continue the pattern.
Then explain the pattern.

22. 435, 535, 635, 735 Pattern: +100

23. 618, 619, 620, ______ Pattern: ______

24. 319, 329, 339, ______ Pattern: ______

25. 933, 943, 953, ______ Pattern: ______

26. 298, 398, 498, ______ Pattern: ______

27. 527, 528, 529, ______ Pattern: ______

Solve. Use a problem-solving strategy.

28. **Multistep** In her computer game Bean Ball, Jean's score is 215. Norm's score is 10 points more than Jean's. Margo's score is 100 points more than Norm's. What is Margo's score?

______

29. **Multistep** In the Blue Star game, Jean's score is 385. Margo's score is 100 points more than Jean's. Norm's score is 10 points more than Margo's. What is Norm's score?

______

DO YOU REMEMBER?

Use the Math Words in the box to fill in the blanks.

30. You can trade 10 ones units for

1 ______________.

31. You can trade 10 ten rods for

1 ______________.

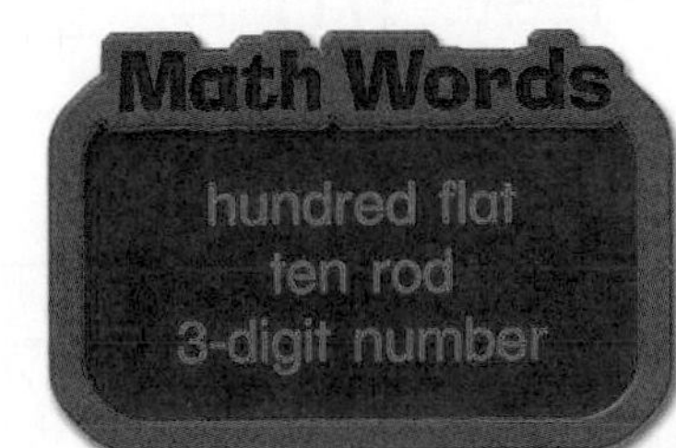

Math Words
hundred flat
ten rod
3-digit number

Math Alive at Home Write two 3-digit numbers between 100 and 889. Have your child write the number 10 more than and 100 more than each of the 3-digit numbers.

Name ______________________________

Regroup Tens as Hundreds Using Models

HANDS-ON LESSON

Let's Learn!

There are more than 9 tens.
Regroup tens as hundreds.

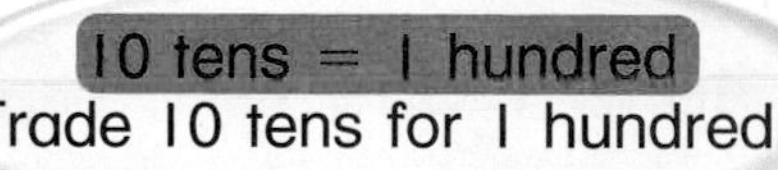

10 tens = 1 hundred
Trade 10 tens for 1 hundred.

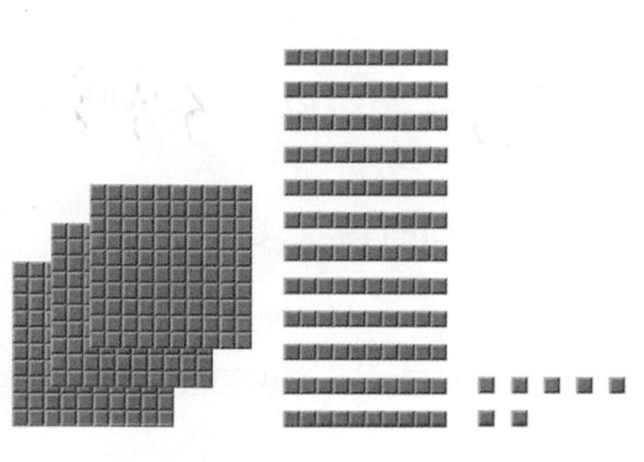

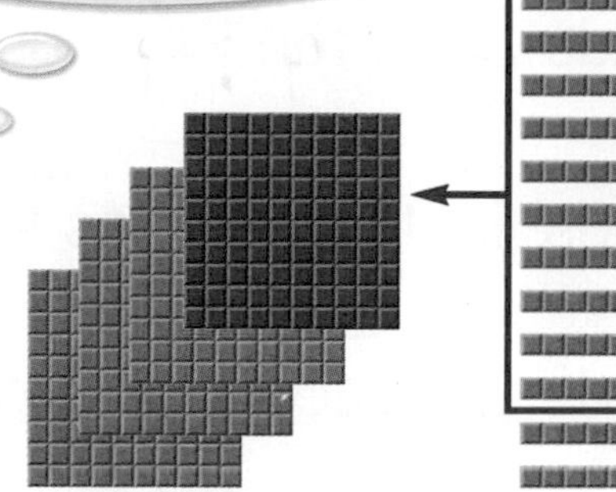

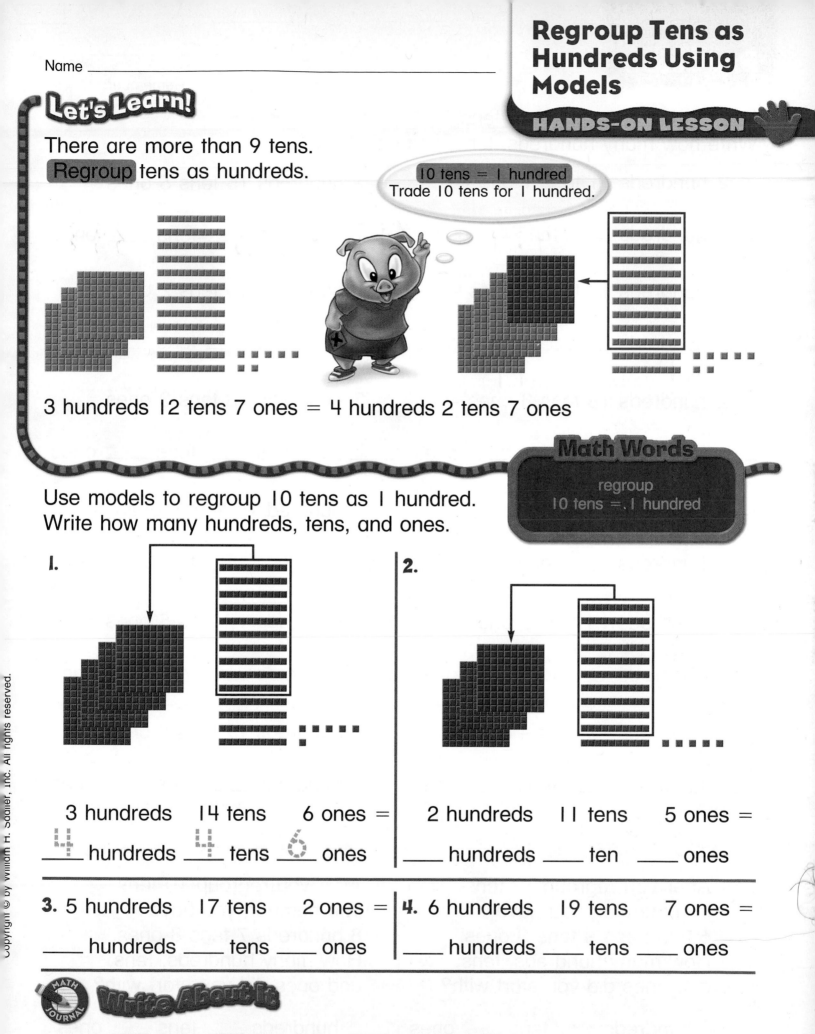

3 hundreds 12 tens 7 ones = 4 hundreds 2 tens 7 ones

Math Words

regroup
10 tens = 1 hundred

Use models to regroup 10 tens as 1 hundred.
Write how many hundreds, tens, and ones.

1.

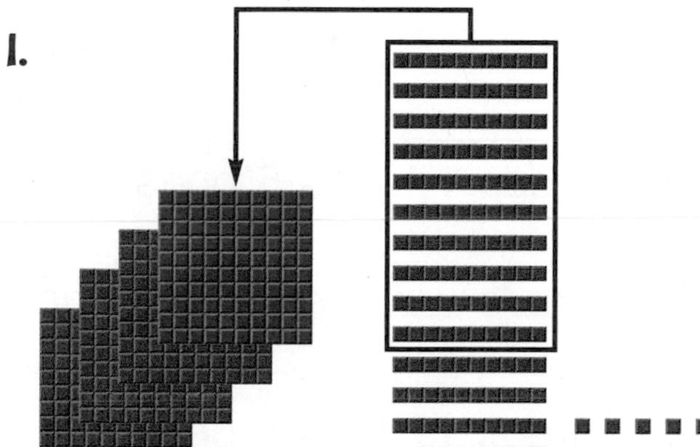

3 hundreds 14 tens 6 ones =
4 hundreds 4 tens 6 ones

2.

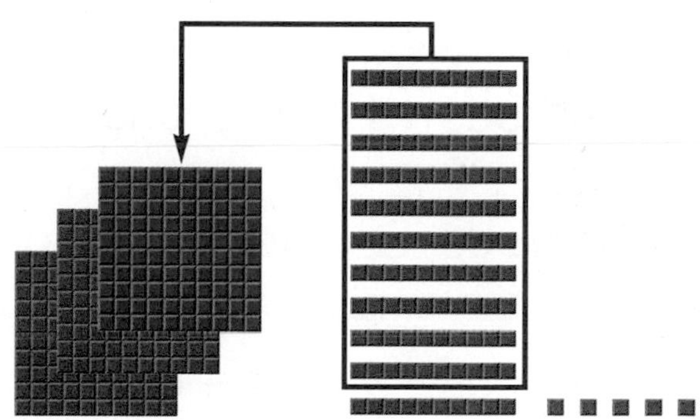

2 hundreds 11 tens 5 ones =
____ hundreds ____ ten ____ ones

3. 5 hundreds 17 tens 2 ones =
____ hundreds ____ tens ____ ones

4. 6 hundreds 19 tens 7 ones =
____ hundreds ____ tens ____ ones

MATH JOURNAL
Write About It

5. Explain what happens to the number of hundreds and tens when 10 tens are regrouped as 1 hundred.

Copyright © by William H. Sadlier, Inc. All rights reserved.

Practice

Remember:
10 tens = 1 hundred

Use models to regroup 10 tens.
Write how many hundreds, tens, and ones.

6. 2 hundreds 11 tens 1 one =

3 hundreds 1 ten 1 one

7. 8 hundreds 15 tens 6 ones =

____ hundreds ____ tens ____ ones

8. 7 hundreds 12 tens 9 ones =

____ hundreds ____ tens ____ ones

9. 4 hundreds 16 tens 2 ones =

____ hundreds ____ tens ____ ones

10. 2 hundreds 18 tens 8 ones =

____ hundreds ____ tens ____ ones

11. 3 hundreds 13 tens 3 ones =

____ hundreds ____ tens ____ ones

12. 6 hundreds 19 tens 4 ones =

____ hundreds ____ tens ____ ones

13. 1 hundred 15 tens 6 ones =

____ hundreds ____ tens ____ ones

14. 7 hundreds 14 tens 7 ones =

____ hundreds ____ tens ____ ones

15. 4 hundreds 17 tens 5 ones =

____ hundreds ____ tens ____ ones

16. 8 hundreds 13 tens 4 ones =

____ hundreds ____ tens ____ ones

17. 5 hundreds 19 tens 8 ones =

____ hundreds ____ tens ____ ones

CRITICAL THINKING

18. After you regroup 10 tens in a number, you have 6 hundreds 4 tens 3 ones. How many hundreds, tens, and ones did you start with?

____ hundreds ____ tens ____ ones

19. After you regroup 10 tens in a number, you have 8 hundreds 7 tens 8 ones. How many hundreds, tens, and ones did you start with?

____ hundreds ____ tens ____ ones

Math Alive at Home Ask your child how many tens are in 1 hundred. (10)

Name ______________________________

Add: Regroup Tens as Hundreds

Let's Learn!

156 girls and 252 boys take ice-skating classes. How many students take ice-skating classes?

156 + 252 = ?

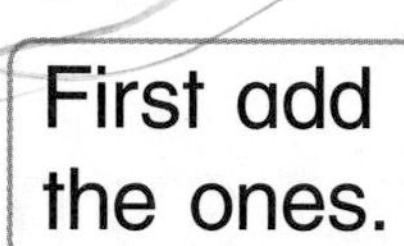

First add the ones.

	h	t	o
	1	5	6
+	2	5	2
			8

Next add the tens. More than 9 tens. Regroup.

	h	t	o
	1		
	1	5	6
+	2	5	2
		0	8

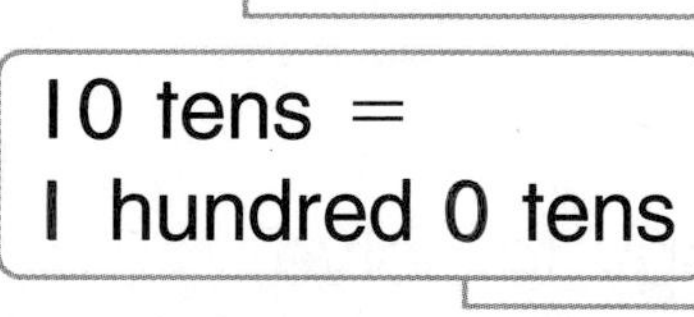

10 tens = 1 hundred 0 tens

Then add the hundreds.

	h	t	o
	1		
	1	5	6
+	2	5	2
	4	0	8

408 students take ice-skating classes.

Find the sum. Regroup tens as hundreds as needed.

1.

	h	t	o
	1		
	3	7	4
+		9	4
	4	6	8

2.

	h	t	o
	4	5	6
+	2	9	1

3.

	h	t	o
	6	4	5
+		7	4

4. 795 + 42

5. 211 + 197

6. 381 + 426

7. 551 + 81

8. 183 + 393

Talk It Over

9. Explain when you need to regroup tens to add.

Copyright © by William H. Sadlier, Inc. All rights reserved.

Practice

Add. Regroup as needed.

10.	11.	12.	13.	14.
592 + 127	345 + 73	482 + 363	236 + 42	791 + 195

15.	16.	17.	18.	19.
485 + 134	263 + 456	542 + 65	142 + 86	390 + 237

20.	21.	22.	23.	24.
672 + 62	384 + 545	168 + 460	476 + 83	158 + 251

Use a problem-solving strategy to solve.
Show your work on a separate sheet of paper.

25. Multistep The boys score 153 points in a school game. The girls score 20 points more than the boys. How many points do the players score altogether?

______ points

26. Team A gets 164 points in a Toss-the-Ball game. Team B gets the same number of points. How many points do Teams A and B get in all?

______ points

CRITICAL THINKING

Without adding, color the numbers with the greatest sum (blue) and the least sum (yellow).

27. 262 + 216 / 216 + 26 / 262 + 262

28. 358 + 574 / 358 + 358 / 358 + 99

Math Alive at Home Ask your child to add 132 + 128 and 123 + 182 (260; 305)

Name ____________________

TEST PREPARATION

Listen to your teacher read the directions.
Fill in the circle under the correct answer.

1.

$$\begin{array}{r} 345 \\ +323 \\ \hline \end{array}$$

665	668	656	566
○	○	○	○

2.

$$\begin{array}{r} 210 \\ +507 \\ \hline \end{array}$$

177	716	717	771
○	○	○	○

3.

$653 + 10 = ?$

654	664	663	753
○	○	○	○

4. 2 hundreds 13 tens 7 ones

3 hundreds 3 tens 7 ones ○

3 hundreds 7 tens 7 ones ○

2 hundreds 7 tens 7 ones ○

2 hundreds 3 tens 7 ones ○

5.

$$\begin{array}{r} 547 \\ +\ \ 38 \\ \hline \end{array}$$

855	575	585	558
○	○	○	○

6.

$$\begin{array}{r} 208 \\ +363 \\ \hline \end{array}$$

571	175	751	715
○	○	○	○

7.

$$\begin{array}{r} 344 \\ +116 \\ \hline \end{array}$$

644	464	640	460
○	○	○	○

8. 4 hundreds 11 tens 8 ones

5 hundreds 8 tens 1 one ○

4 hundreds 1 ten 8 ones ○

5 hundreds 1 ten 8 ones ○

4 hundreds 1 ten 7 ones ○

Copyright © by William H. Sadlier, Inc. All rights reserved.

Fill in the circle under the correct answer.

9. Add. Regroup when needed.

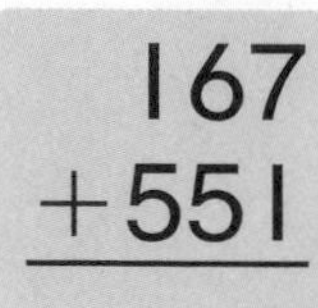

$$\begin{array}{r} 167 \\ +551 \\ \hline \end{array}$$

187 ○ 718 ○ 781 ○ 618 ●

10.

$$\begin{array}{r} 571 \\ +268 \\ \hline \end{array}$$

839 ● 859 ○ 739 ○ 749 ○

11.

$$\begin{array}{r} 280 \\ +694 \\ \hline \end{array}$$

784 ○ 874 ● 970 ○ 974 ○

12.

$$\begin{array}{r} 350 \\ +570 \\ \hline \end{array}$$

820 ○ 920 ○ 910 ○ 810 ○

13. What number is most likely to come next in the pattern?

572, 672, 772, ?

782 ○ 882 ○ 872 ○ 972 ○

14. Add. Regroup twice if needed.

$$\begin{array}{r} 427 \\ +\ 83 \\ \hline \end{array}$$

510 ○ 490 ○ 590 ○ 410 ○

15.

$$\begin{array}{r} 357 \\ +465 \\ \hline \end{array}$$

812 ○ 712 ○ 822 ○ 722 ○

16.

$$\begin{array}{r} 289 \\ +485 \\ \hline \end{array}$$

764 ○ 774 ○ 664 ○ 674 ○

17. Regroup the tens.

5 hundreds 15 tens 9 ones

6 hundreds 9 tens 5 ones ○

5 hundreds 5 tens 9 ones ○

6 hundreds 5 tens 9 ones ○

Name ______________________

Add Money: No Regrouping

Let's Learn!

Marta spent $1.55 yesterday and $1.24 today at the ball game. How much did Marta spend?

Yesterday	Today

Marta spent $2.79.

Add dollars and cents the same way you add hundreds, tens, and ones.

Start at the right. Add.

$$\begin{array}{r} \$1.55 \\ +\ 1.24 \\ \hline 2\ 79 \end{array}$$

Then write the $ and ..

$$\begin{array}{r} \$1.55 \\ +\ 1.24 \\ \hline \$2.79 \end{array}$$

Find the sum. Model to check.

1. $3.23 + 1.24 = $4.47
2. $4.51 + 3.17 = $7.68
3. $1.70 + 3.15 = $4.85
4. $1.03 + 2.13 = $3.16
5. $0.24 + 4.02 = $4.26
6. $7.20 + 0.46 = $7.66
7. $1.22 + 0.63 = $1.65
8. $2.41 + 1.45 = $3.86
9. $1.70 + 4.27 = $5.97
10. $1.45 + 6.03 = $7.48
11. $2.36 + 5.63 = $7.99
12. $4.80 + 1.09 = $5.89
13. $1.63 + 8.10 = $9.73
14. $6.45 + 2.20 = $8.65
15. $0.32 + 3.57 = $3.89
16. $3.48 + 2.51 = $5.99

17. Explain how adding $1.55 and $1.24 is like adding 155 and 124 and how it is different.

Copyright © by William H. Sadlier, Inc. All rights reserved.

Practice

Remember: Write the $ and . in the sum.

Find the sum.

18. $\begin{array}{r} \$5.46 \\ +\ 3.22 \\ \hline \$8.68 \end{array}$

19. $\begin{array}{r} \$2.85 \\ +\ 2.04 \\ \hline \end{array}$

20. $\begin{array}{r} \$2.03 \\ +\ 7.34 \\ \hline \end{array}$

21. $\begin{array}{r} \$5.43 \\ +\ 1.16 \\ \hline \end{array}$

22. $\begin{array}{r} \$1.65 \\ +\ 4.12 \\ \hline \end{array}$

23. $\begin{array}{r} \$7.54 \\ +\ 2.05 \\ \hline \end{array}$

24. $\begin{array}{r} \$3.70 \\ +\ 3.15 \\ \hline \end{array}$

25. $\begin{array}{r} \$4.62 \\ +\ 3.01 \\ \hline \end{array}$

26. $\begin{array}{r} \$1.12 \\ +\ 5.80 \\ \hline \end{array}$

27. $\begin{array}{r} \$1.32 \\ +\ 2.05 \\ \hline \end{array}$

28. $\begin{array}{r} \$3.43 \\ +\ 1.45 \\ \hline \end{array}$

29. $\begin{array}{r} \$6.48 \\ +\ 3.01 \\ \hline \end{array}$

Solve. Use a problem-solving strategy.
Show your work on a separate sheet of paper.

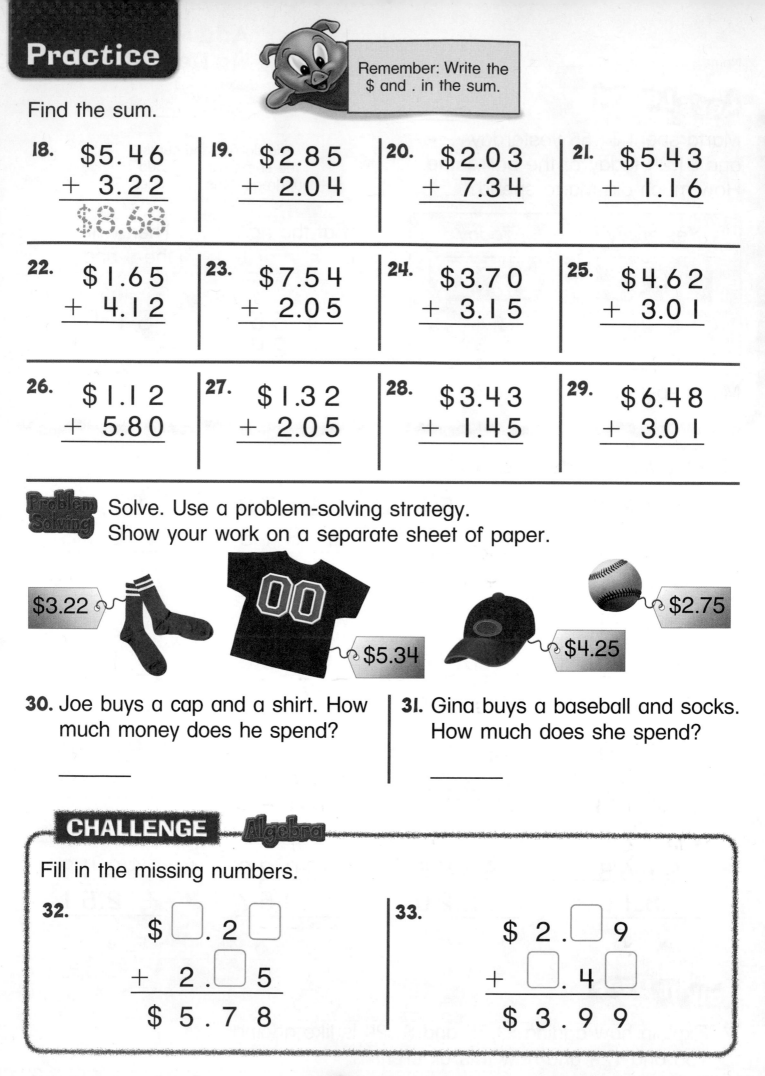

30. Joe buys a cap and a shirt. How much money does he spend?

_____

31. Gina buys a baseball and socks. How much does she spend?

_____

CHALLENGE

Fill in the missing numbers.

32. $\begin{array}{r} \$\ \square\,.\,2\ \square \\ +\ \ 2\,.\,\square\ 5 \\ \hline \$\ 5\,.\,7\ 8 \end{array}$

33. $\begin{array}{r} \$\ 2\,.\,\square\ 9 \\ +\ \ \square\,.\,4\ \square \\ \hline \$\ 3\,.\,9\ 9 \end{array}$

Math Alive at Home Ask your child to add \$4.50 + \$5.40 and to add \$4.05 + \$5.40. (\$9.90, \$9.45)

Name ______________________________

Find Needed Information

- You can reread a problem to find the information you need.

Listen
Sam and Jackie get ready for a day at the pool. Sam buys goggles for $2.63 and sandals for $5.25. Jackie buys sunglasses for $4.56 and a hat for $3.10. Who spends more money?
LIFEGUARD ON DUTY

1. Reread the problem. Draw a line under the question you need to answer.

2. How much does Sam spend?

   Sam spends ______ on goggles and ______ on sandals.

3. How much does Jackie spend?

   Jackie spends ______ on sunglasses and ______ on a hat.

4. Add to find the total amount that each child spends.

   Sam $ ☐ + ☐ = $ ____ **Jackie** $ ☐ + ☐ = $ ____

5. Now compare the sums to solve the problem.

   ______________ spends more money.

Copyright © by William H. Sadlier, Inc. All rights reserved.

Practice

Find Needed Information

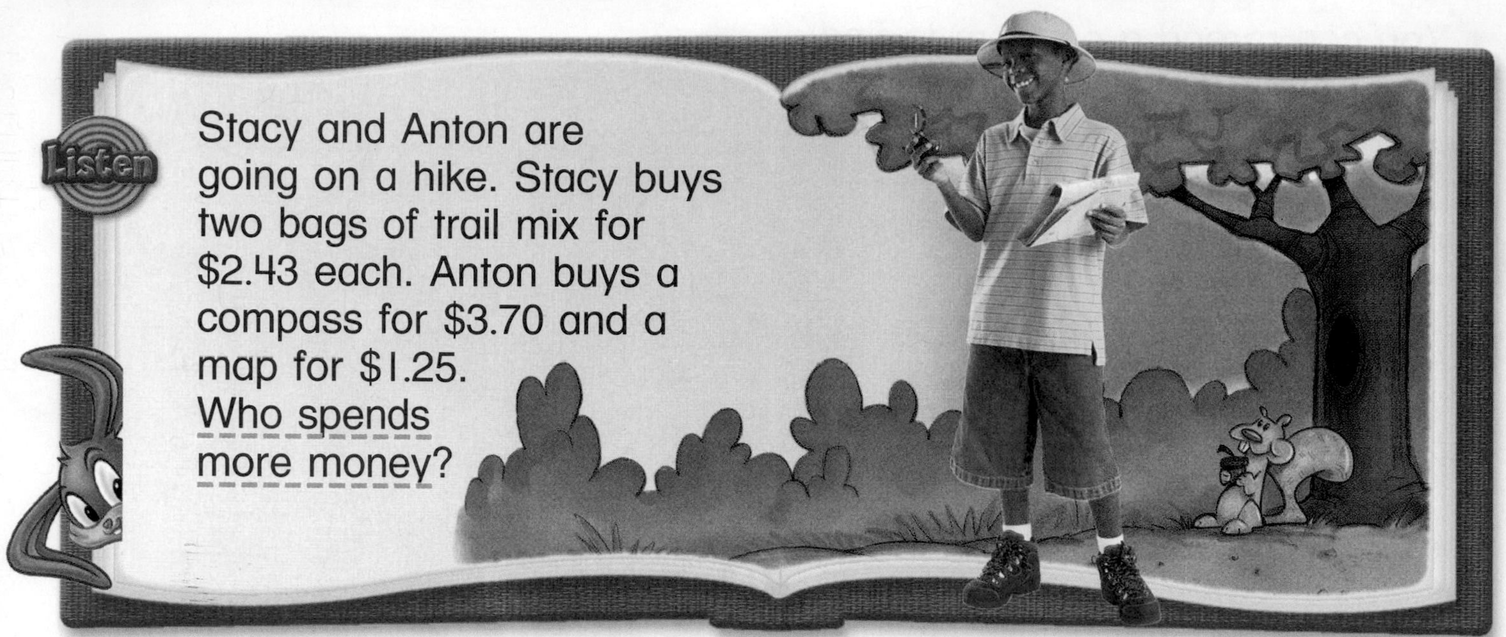

Listen
Stacy and Anton are going on a hike. Stacy buys two bags of trail mix for $2.43 each. Anton buys a compass for $3.70 and a map for $1.25.
Who spends more money?

6. Reread the problem. Draw a line under the question you need to answer.

7. How much does Stacy spend?

   Stacy spends _______ each on two bags of trail mix.

8. How much does Anton spend?

   Anton spends _______ on a compass and _______ on a map.

9. Add to find the total amount that each child spends.

   Stacy
   $ ☐
   + ☐
   $

   Anton
   $ ☐
   + ☐
   $

10. Now compare the sums to solve the problem.

    _______________ spends more money.

Math Alive at Home Today your child found needed information to work through math problems. Have him/her explain how he/she solved the problems in this lesson.

Name ____________________

Add Money: Regroup Dimes or Pennies

Let's Learn!

I need to regroup dimes to add $1.54 and $0.85.
10 dimes = 1 dollar
$1
13 dimes = 1 dollar 3 dimes
1
$1.54
+ 0.85
$2.39

Find the sum. Regroup pennies or dimes.

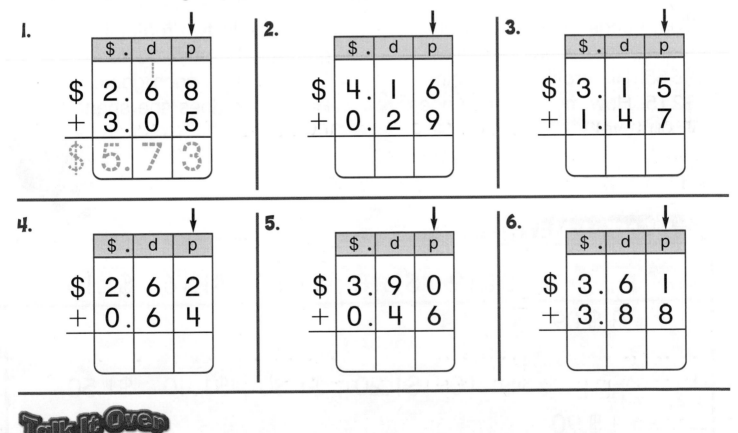

1.

	$.	d	p
$	2.	6	8
+	3.	0	5
$	5.	7	3

2.

	$.	d	p
$	4.	1	6
+	0.	2	9

3.

	$.	d	p
$	3.	1	5
+	1.	4	7

4.

	$.	d	p
$	2.	6	2
+	0.	6	4

5.

	$.	d	p
$	3.	9	0
+	0.	4	6

6.

	$.	d	p
$	3.	6	1
+	3.	8	8

Talk It Over

7. Explain how regrouping pennies is like regrouping ones and how regrouping dimes is like regrouping tens.

Copyright © by William H. Sadlier, Inc. All rights reserved.

Practice

Remember: Write the $ and . in the sum.

Add. Regroup when needed.

8. \$5.07 + 4.34 = \$9.41	9. \$4.53 + 2.18	10. \$1.29 + 0.21	11. \$3.07 + 5.05	12. \$6.06 + 0.84
13. \$6.51 + 1.78	14. \$3.13 + 3.94	15. \$8.70 + 0.65	16. \$2.80 + 4.80	17. \$3.44 + 1.81
18. \$5.71 + 2.81	19. \$2.38 + 1.24	20. \$4.94 + 0.73	21. \$1.42 + 3.48	22. \$7.36 + 0.92

Solve. Use a problem-solving strategy. Show your work on a separate sheet of paper.

23. Tom needs \$9.80 to buy his team soccer shirt. He saves \$6.55. His brother gives him \$2.15. How much money does Tom have?

______

24. Gia goes to two football games. She pays \$3.70 for a ticket to each game. How much does she spend?

______

MENTAL MATH

25.

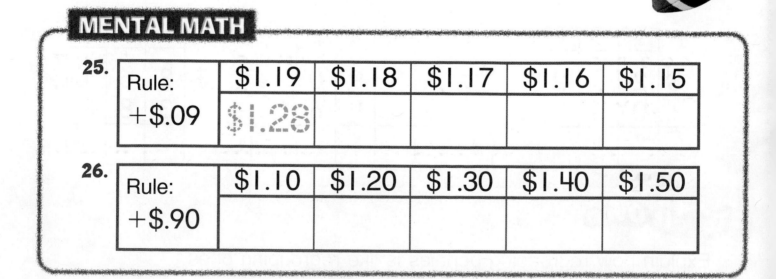

Rule: +\$.09	\$1.19	\$1.18	\$1.17	\$1.16	\$1.15
	\$1.28				

26.

Rule: +\$.90	\$1.10	\$1.20	\$1.30	\$1.40	\$1.50

Math Alive at Home Ask your child to add \$1.75 + \$1.16 and to explain the regrouping. (\$2.91; 5 pennies + 6 pennies = 11 pennies = 1 dime 1 penny)

Add Money: Regroup Twice

Name ______________________________

Let's Learn!

$1.65 + $1.45 = ?

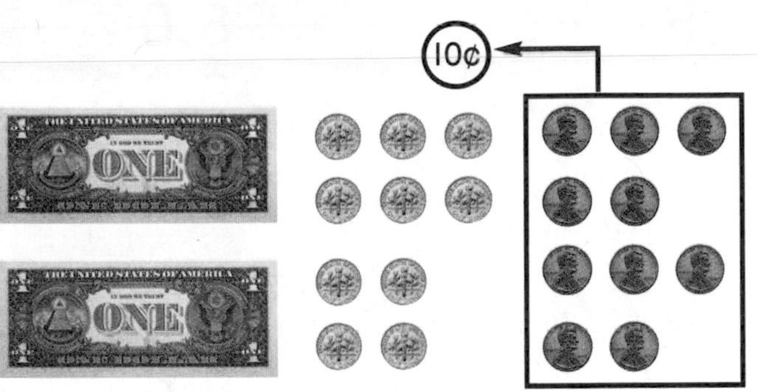

10¢

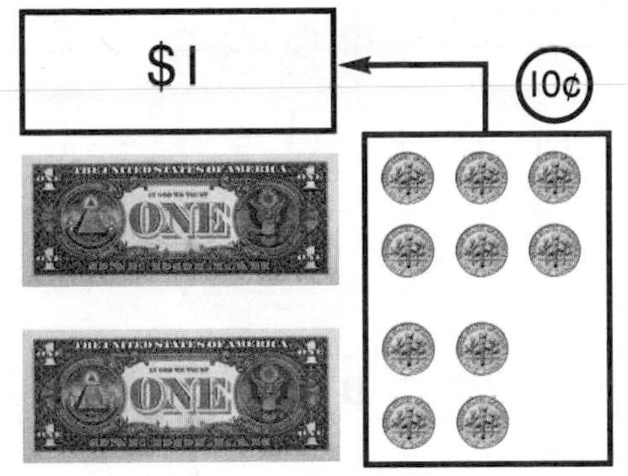

$1
10¢

Regroup twice.
10 pennies = 1 dime
10 dimes = 1 dollar

First add the pennies. Regroup.

	$.	d	p
		1	
$	1 .	6	5
+	1 .	4	5
			0

Next add the dimes. Regroup.

	$.	d	p
	1	1	
$	1 .	6	5
+	1 .	4	5
		1	0

Then add the dollars.

	$.	d	p
	1	1	
$	1 .	6	5
+	1 .	4	5
$	3 .	1	0

Find the sum. Regroup twice.

1.

	$.	d	p
	1	1	
$	2 .	5	3
+	1 .	4	8
$	4 .	0	1

2.

	$.	d	p
$	1 .	9	6
+	0 .	4	7

3.

	$.	d	p
$	1 .	8	6
+	0 .	6	9

4. $3.57 + 1.66

5. $2.83 + 2.69

6. $5.99 + 0.89

7. $3.47 + 0.57

Talk It Over

8. Which sum is the greater amount? Explain.

$3.87 + $0.33 $3.87 + $3.30

Copyright © by William H. Sadlier, Inc. All rights reserved.

Practice

Remember: Write the $ and . in the sum.

Find the sum. Regroup when needed.

9. $6.82 + 0.28 = $7.10	10. $2.39 + 3.91	11. $4.16 + 2.87	12. $8.07 + 0.98
13. $1.98 + 2.09	14. $2.25 + 2.96	15. $7.61 + 0.99	16. $2.64 + 4.69
17. $1.76 + 4.73	18. $3.24 + 1.56	19. $3.89 + 2.78	20. $5.54 + 1.84
21. $5.48 + 3.88	22. $7.99 + 1.25	23. $3.45 + 5.77	24. $5.53 + 0.57

Solve. Use a problem-solving strategy.
Show your work on a separate sheet of paper.

25. A book about ice-skating stars costs $4.96. That is the same as the cost of a book about bike racing. How much do both books cost? ______

26. **Multistep** Sara buys socks for $2.75 and shorts for $5.25. Amy buys a shirt for $3.65 and shorts for $3.79. Who spends more money? ______

DO YOU REMEMBER?

27. Write the number that is 10 more: 143, ______ 279, ______

28. Write the number that is 100 more: 781, ______ 432, ______

Math Alive at Home Ask your child to add $2.95 + $1.45 and to explain the regrouping. ($4.40; 5 ones + 5 ones = 10 ones = 1 ten 0 ones; 9 tens + 4 tens + 1 ten = 14 tens = 1 hundred 4 tens)

Name ______________________

TEST PREPARATION

Listen to your teacher read the directions.
Fill in the circle under the correct answer.

1.

$$\begin{array}{r} \$6.35 \\ +\ \ 3.42 \\ \hline \end{array}$$

$9.77	$8.77	$7.87	$7.97
○	○	○	○

2.

$$\begin{array}{r} \$4.04 \\ +\ \ 4.35 \\ \hline \end{array}$$

$8.39	$7.39	$8.44	$4.39
○	○	○	○

3.

$$\begin{array}{r} \$1.21 \\ +\ \ 6.21 \\ \hline \end{array}$$

$7.44	$7.42	$6.42	$7.24
○	○	○	○

4.

$$\begin{array}{r} \$2.60 \\ +\ \ 3.25 \\ \hline \end{array}$$

$5.58	$8.55	$5.75	$5.85
○	○	○	○

5.

$$\begin{array}{r} \$2.83 \\ +\ \ 4.13 \\ \hline \end{array}$$

$5.76	$6.93	$6.96	$5.96
○	○	○	○

6.

$$\begin{array}{r} \$1.67 \\ +\ \ 2.01 \\ \hline \end{array}$$

$3.66	$2.68	$3.68	$3.86
○	○	○	○

7.

$$\begin{array}{r} \$1.60 \\ +\ \ 4.68 \\ \hline \end{array}$$

$6.38	$6.28	$5.82	$5.28
○	○	○	○

8.

$$\begin{array}{r} \$6.19 \\ +\ \ 1.74 \\ \hline \end{array}$$

$7.93	$7.39	$7.83	$6.93
○	○	○	○

9.

$$\begin{array}{r} \$3.12 \\ +\ \ 2.91 \\ \hline \end{array}$$

$6.90	$5.03	$6.03	$5.93
○	○	○	○

10.

$$\begin{array}{r} \$3.94 \\ +\ \ 1.37 \\ \hline \end{array}$$

$4.31	$5.31	$5.21	$4.21
○	○	○	○

Copyright © by William H. Sadlier, Inc. All rights reserved.

Fill in the circle under the correct answer.
Find the sum. Regroup when needed.

11.

$$\begin{array}{r} \$5.50 \\ +\ \ 0.96 \\ \hline \end{array}$$

$5.46 ○ $6.46 ○ $6.36 ○ $5.56 ○

12.

$$\begin{array}{r} \$3.48 \\ +\ \ 5.37 \\ \hline \end{array}$$

$7.75 ○ $8.75 ○ $9.85 ○ $8.85 ○

13.

$$\begin{array}{r} \$2.45 \\ +\ \ 5.88 \\ \hline \end{array}$$

$7.33 ○ $8.33 ○ $7.23 ○ $8.23 ○

14.

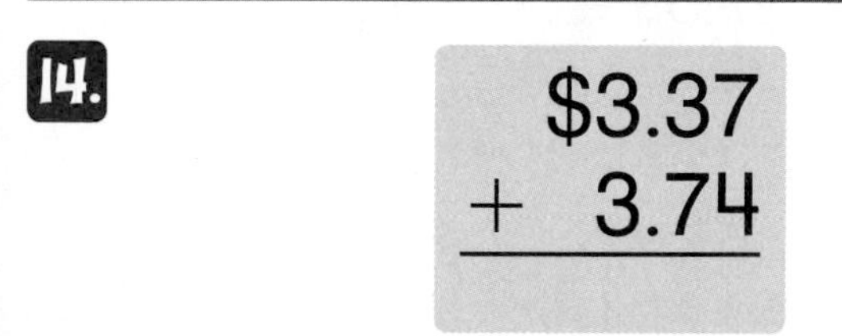

$$\begin{array}{r} \$3.37 \\ +\ \ 3.74 \\ \hline \end{array}$$

$7.01 ○ $6.11 ○ $6.01 ○ $7.11 ○

15.

$$\begin{array}{r} \$2.73 \\ +\ \ 6.30 \\ \hline \end{array}$$

$8.00 ○ $8.43 ○ $8.03 ○ $9.03 ○

16.

$$\begin{array}{r} \$7.98 \\ +\ \ 0.65 \\ \hline \end{array}$$

$8.63 ○ $7.63 ○ $8.53 ○ $7.53 ○

17.

$$\begin{array}{r} \$1.87 \\ +\ \ 1.89 \\ \hline \end{array}$$

$2.66 ○ $3.66 ○ $3.76 ○ $2.76 ○

18.

$$\begin{array}{r} \$5.59 \\ +\ \ 1.65 \\ \hline \end{array}$$

$6.14 ○ $7.24 ○ $7.14 ○ $6.24 ○

19.

$$\begin{array}{r} \$4.53 \\ +\ \ 2.78 \\ \hline \end{array}$$

$7.11 ○ $7.41 ○ $7.14 ○ $7.31 ○

20.

$$\begin{array}{r} \$6.54 \\ +\ \ 2.39 \\ \hline \end{array}$$

$8.93 ○ $9.93 ○ $8.85 ○ $9.95 ○

Name ____________________

Subtract Hundreds, Tens, and Ones

Let's Learn!

Find the difference. 354 − 251 = ?
Line up the numbers by place value.

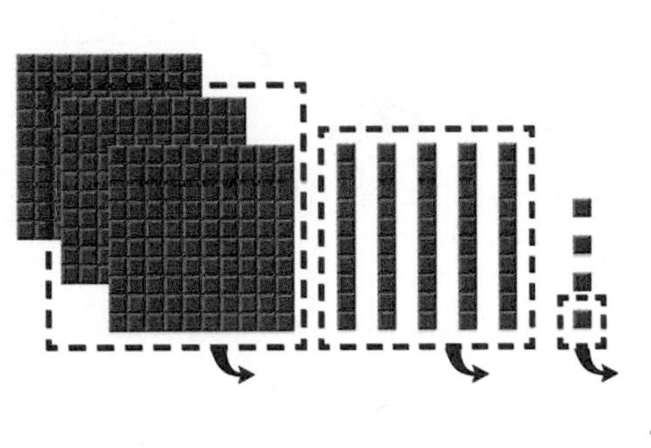

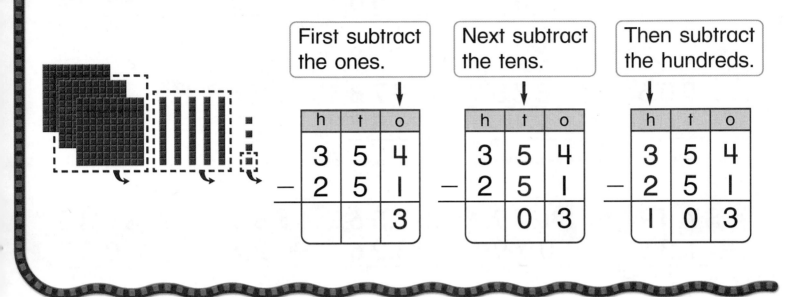

First subtract the ones.

	h	t	o
	3	5	4
−	2	5	1
			3

Next subtract the tens.

	h	t	o
	3	5	4
−	2	5	1
		0	3

Then subtract the hundreds.

	h	t	o
	3	5	4
−	2	5	1
	1	0	3

Find the difference. Use models to check.

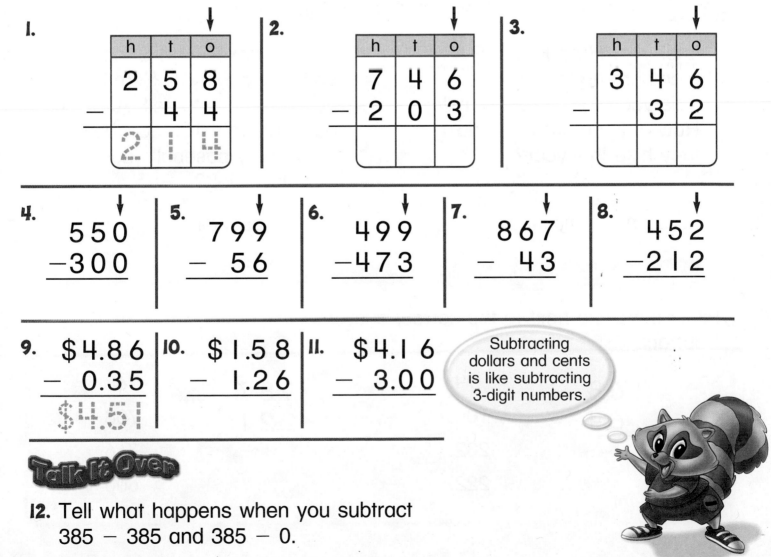

1.

	h	t	o
	2	5	8
−		4	4
	2	1	4

2.

	h	t	o
	7	4	6
−	2	0	3

3.

	h	t	o
	3	4	6
−		3	2

4. 550 − 300

5. 799 − 56

6. 499 − 473

7. 867 − 43

8. 452 − 212

9. \$4.86 − 0.35 = \$4.51

10. \$1.58 − 1.26

11. \$4.16 − 3.00

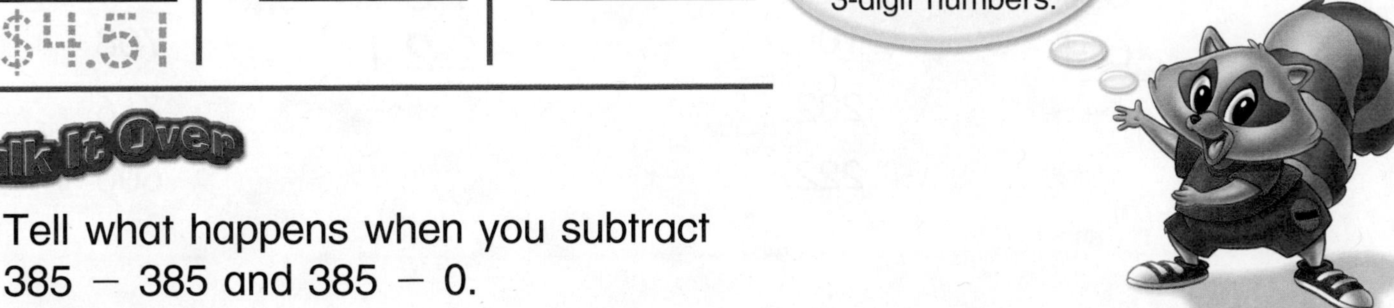

Subtracting dollars and cents is like subtracting 3-digit numbers.

12. Tell what happens when you subtract 385 − 385 and 385 − 0.

Copyright © by William H. Sadlier, Inc. All rights reserved.

Practice

Subtract.

Subtract ones, then tens, then hundreds.

13.	14.	15.	16.	17.
732 − 21 711	585 − 53	867 − 46	348 − 22	998 − 37

18.	19.	20.	21.	22.
906 −405	875 −245	478 −158	789 −245	482 − 60

23.	24.	25.	26.	27.
\$7.49 − 1.36	\$1.79 − 0.79	\$7.56 − 3.26	\$6.19 − 2.17	\$9.35 − 0.34

Solve. Use a problem-solving strategy.

28. Last year Hal's Hiking Club members hiked 105 miles. This year they hike 217 miles. How many more miles do they hike this year?

_____ more miles

29. When Sam's Sport Shop opened on May 1, Sam had 265 baseballs to sell. After 60 days, he sold 153 baseballs. How many baseballs does Sam have left?

_____ baseballs

TEST PREPARATION

Fill in the circle next to the correct answer.
Subtract.

30.
168
− 64

○ 94
○ 104
○ 232
○ 222

31.
987
−221

○ 768
○ 708
○ 766
○ 606

Math Alive at Home Ask your child to subtract 566 − 333 and 566 − 303 and to subtract the same amounts using dollars and cents. (233, 263; \$2.33, \$2.63)

Name ______________________________

Count Back 1, 10, and 100

You can count back to subtract mentally.

480 − 1 = ?	480 − 10 = ?	480 − 100 = ?
Count back 1. 480, 479	Count back 10. 480, 470	Count back 100. 480, 380
480 − 1 = 479	480 − 10 = 470	480 − 100 = 380

Write the number 1 less than each.

1. 325, 326, | 2. ______, 452 | 3. ______, 613 | 4. ______, 807

Write the number 10 less than each.

5. 177, 187 | 6. ______, 566 | 7. ______, 319 | 8. ______, 790

Write the number 100 less than each.

9. 576, 676 | 10. ______, 505 | 11. ______, 400 | 12. ______, 967

Subtract.

13. 910 − 1 = ______ | 14. 547 − 10 = ______

15. 234 − 1 = ______ | 16. 457 − 10 = ______

17. 575 − 10 = ______ | 18. 736 − 100 = ______

19. 889 − 100 = ______ | 20. 229 − 100 = ______

21. Without subtracting, tell whether 348 − 10 or 348 − 100 is less.

Practice

Write −1, −10, or −100 to explain the pattern.

Continue the pattern. Then explain the pattern.

22. 627, 626, 625, 624 Pattern: −1

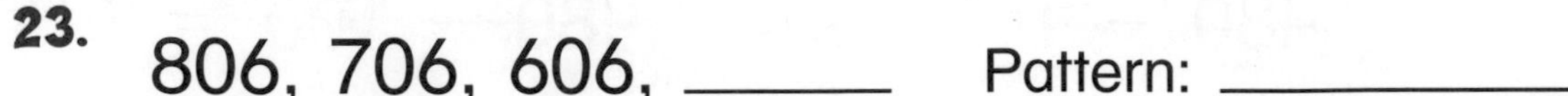

23. 806, 706, 606, ______ Pattern: ____________

24. 754, 744, 734, ______ Pattern: ____________

25. 462, 362, 262, ______ Pattern: ____________

26. 530, 529, 528, ______ Pattern: ____________

27. 398, 388, 378, ______ Pattern: ____________

Solve. Use a problem-solving strategy.

28. Multistep In a computer game, Ron's score is 315. Terry's score is 10 points less than Ron's. Joan's score is 100 points less than Terry's. What is Joan's score? ______

29. Multistep Ed's score is 225. Marie's score is 100 points less than Ed's. Dave's score is 10 points less than Marie's. What is Dave's score? ______

CHALLENGE

Use information in the table to solve.

30. Whose score in the computer game was 300 points lower than Tony's? ________

31. Whose score was 30 points lower than Rita's? ________

Name	Score
Rita	485
Mike	185
Dawn	285
Jesse	455
Tony	585

Math Alive at Home Write two 3-digit numbers. Have your child write the numbers 10 less than and 100 less than each of the 3-digit numbers.

Name ______________________________

Subtract: Regroup Tens as Ones

Let's Learn!

246 tickets were sold for the first boat race and 138 for the second race. How many more tickets were sold for the first race?

$$246 - 138 = ?$$

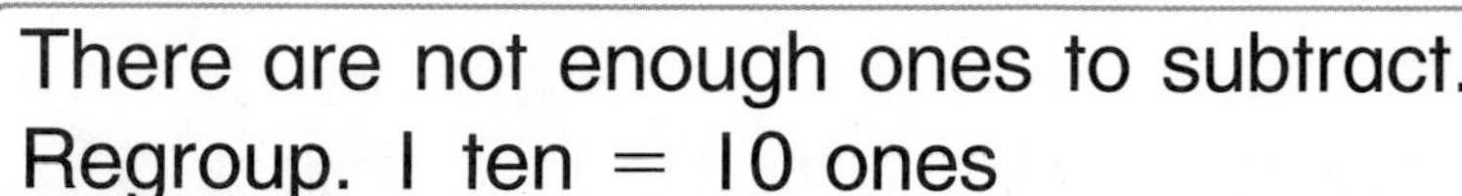

There are not enough ones to subtract.
Regroup. 1 ten = 10 ones

Subtract.

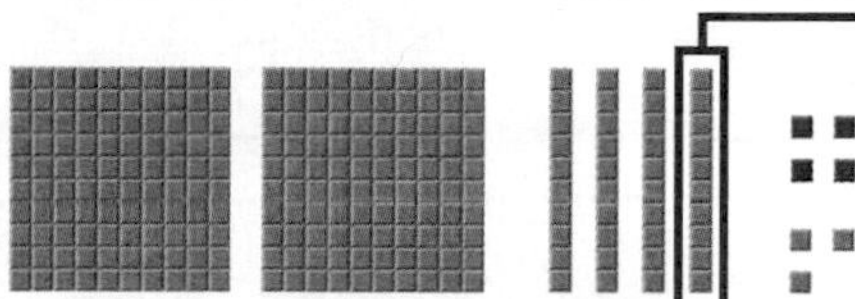

	h	t	o
		3	16
	2	~~4~~	~~6~~
−	1	3	8

4 tens 6 ones = 3 tens 16 ones

	h	t	o
		3	16
	2	~~4~~	~~6~~
−	1	3	8
	1	0	8

108 more tickets were sold for the first race.

Subtract. Regroup tens as ones.

1.

	h	t	o
	4	8	0
−	4	3	2

2.

	h	t	o
	6	4	7
−	2	1	9

3.

	h	t	o
	1	8	0
−		4	4

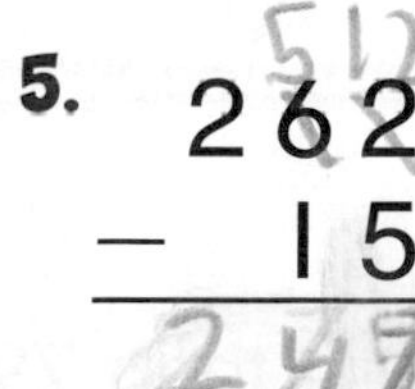

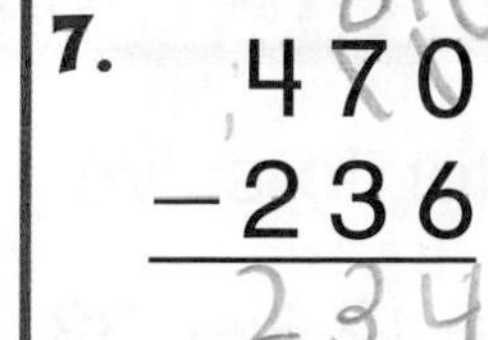

4. $\begin{array}{r} 712 \\ -106 \\ \hline \end{array}$

5. $\begin{array}{r} 262 \\ -\ 15 \\ \hline \end{array}$

6. $\begin{array}{r} 361 \\ -228 \\ \hline \end{array}$

7. $\begin{array}{r} 470 \\ -236 \\ \hline \end{array}$

8. $\begin{array}{r} 193 \\ -176 \\ \hline \end{array}$

Talk It Over

9. Check your answer to exercise 4 by adding. Do you need to regroup when you check?

Practice

Subtract. Regroup as needed.

10. $\begin{array}{r} 432 \\ -\ 29 \\ \hline 403 \end{array}$	**11.** $\begin{array}{r} 263 \\ -\ 14 \\ \hline \end{array}$	**12.** $\begin{array}{r} 781 \\ -645 \\ \hline \end{array}$	**13.** $\begin{array}{r} 810 \\ -305 \\ \hline \end{array}$	**14.** $\begin{array}{r} 758 \\ -347 \\ \hline \end{array}$
15. $\begin{array}{r} 820 \\ -608 \\ \hline \end{array}$	**16.** $\begin{array}{r} 562 \\ -\ 43 \\ \hline \end{array}$	**17.** $\begin{array}{r} 575 \\ -337 \\ \hline \end{array}$	**18.** $\begin{array}{r} 481 \\ -108 \\ \hline \end{array}$	**19.** $\begin{array}{r} 679 \\ -\ 56 \\ \hline \end{array}$
20. $\begin{array}{r} 992 \\ -517 \\ \hline \end{array}$	**21.** $\begin{array}{r} 783 \\ -526 \\ \hline \end{array}$	**22.** $\begin{array}{r} 977 \\ -847 \\ \hline \end{array}$	**23.** $\begin{array}{r} 851 \\ -534 \\ \hline \end{array}$	**24.** $\begin{array}{r} 690 \\ -122 \\ \hline \end{array}$

Solve. Use a problem-solving strategy.
Show your work on a separate sheet of paper.

25. Super Store has 280 football jerseys to sell. School teams call in orders this week for 168 jerseys. How many football jerseys will the store have left after these orders are filled?

______ jerseys

26. Multistep The store orders 175 football helmets one month and the same number the next month. After two months, it sold 114 helmets. How many helmets are left to sell?

______ helmets

CALCULATOR ACTIVITY

Use your calculator to solve.

27. I am less than 465 − 337.
I am more than 343 − 217.
I am __________.

28. I am more than 790 − 473.
I am less than 587 − 268.
I am __________.

Math Alive at Home Write 362 − 143 vertically. Then ask your child to subtract the numbers and to explain the regrouping. (219; regroup 6 tens 2 ones as 5 tens 12 ones in order to subtract.)

Name ______________________________

Regroup Hundreds as Tens Using Models

HANDS-ON LESSON

Let's Learn!

Regroup hundreds as tens.

1 hundred = 10 tens
Trade 1 hundred for 10 tens.

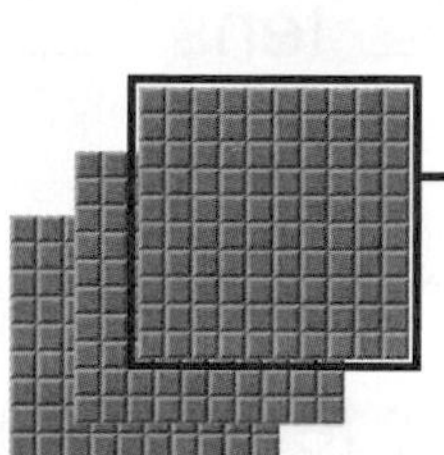

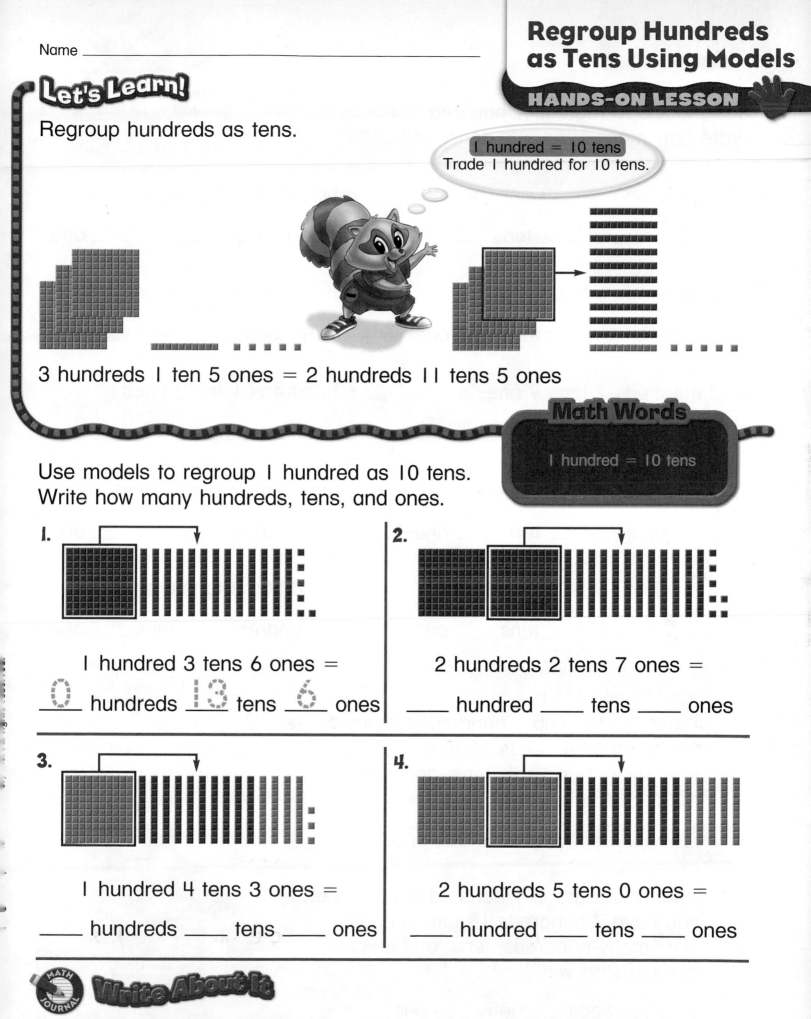

3 hundreds 1 ten 5 ones = 2 hundreds 11 tens 5 ones

Math Words

1 hundred = 10 tens

Use models to regroup 1 hundred as 10 tens.
Write how many hundreds, tens, and ones.

1.

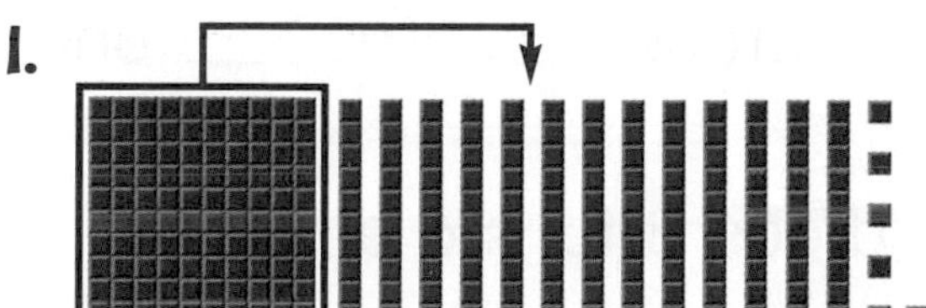

1 hundred 3 tens 6 ones =

0 hundreds 13 tens 6 ones

2.

2 hundreds 2 tens 7 ones =

____ hundred ____ tens ____ ones

3.

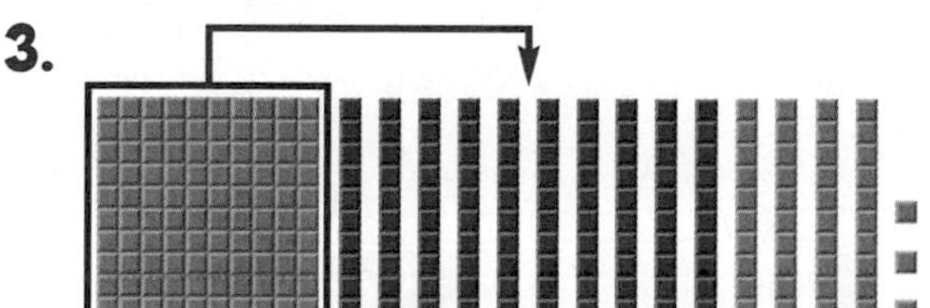

1 hundred 4 tens 3 ones =

____ hundreds ____ tens ____ ones

4.

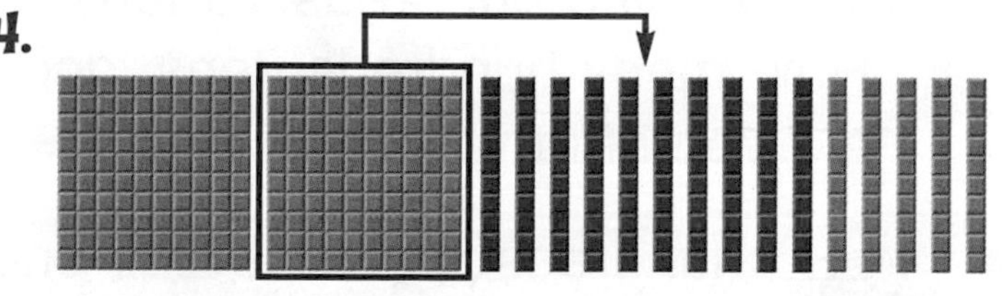

2 hundreds 5 tens 0 ones =

____ hundred ____ tens ____ ones

MATH JOURNAL
Write About It

5. Explain what happens to the number of hundreds and tens when 1 hundred is regrouped as 10 tens.

Practice

Remember:
1 hundred = 10 tens

Use models to regroup 1 hundred.
Write how many hundreds, tens, and ones.

6. 1 hundred 0 tens 4 ones =
0 hundreds 10 tens 4 ones

7. 8 hundreds 7 tens 6 ones =
___ hundreds ___ tens ___ ones

8. 3 hundreds 6 tens 5 ones =
___ hundreds ___ tens ___ ones

9. 5 hundreds 2 tens 1 one =
___ hundreds ___ tens ___ one

10. 2 hundreds 7 tens 9 ones =
___ hundred ___ tens ___ ones

11. 6 hundreds 1 ten 2 ones =
___ hundreds ___ tens ___ ones

12. 8 hundreds 4 tens 3 ones =
___ hundreds ___ tens ___ ones

13. 9 hundreds 3 tens 7 ones =
___ hundreds ___ tens ___ ones

14. 7 hundreds 5 tens 8 ones =
___ hundreds ___ tens ___ ones

15. 4 hundreds 8 tens 6 ones =
___ hundreds ___ tens ___ ones

CRITICAL THINKING

16. After you regroup 1 hundred in a number, you have 6 hundreds 15 tens 3 ones. How many hundreds, tens, and ones did you start with?

___ hundreds ___ tens ___ ones

17. After you regroup 1 hundred in a number, you have 7 hundreds 18 tens 8 ones. How many hundreds, tens, and ones did you start with?

___ hundreds ___ tens ___ ones

1 hundred = 10 tens

Math Alive at Home Ask your child how she/he regrouped hundreds as tens for one of the exercises from number 7 to 14 on this page.

Name ______________________________

Subtract: Regroup Hundreds as Tens

Let's Learn!

104 − 41 = ?

Subtract the ones.

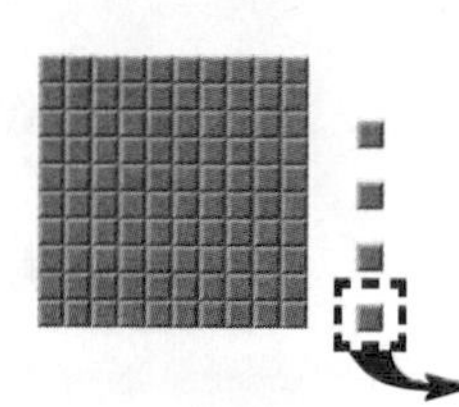

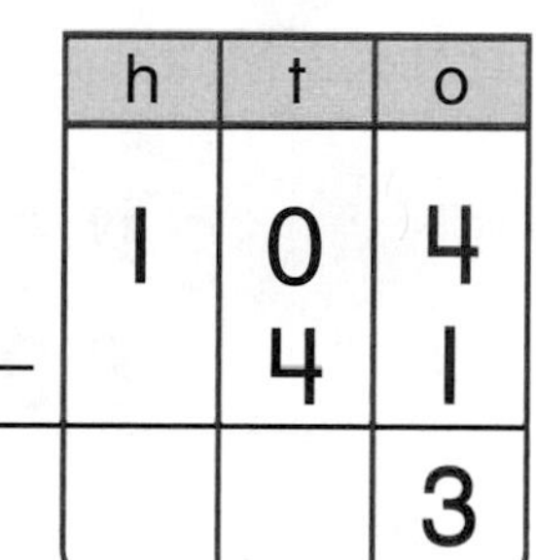

	h	t	o
	1	0	4
−		4	1
			3

Not enough tens.
Regroup hundreds as tens.
Then subtract the tens.

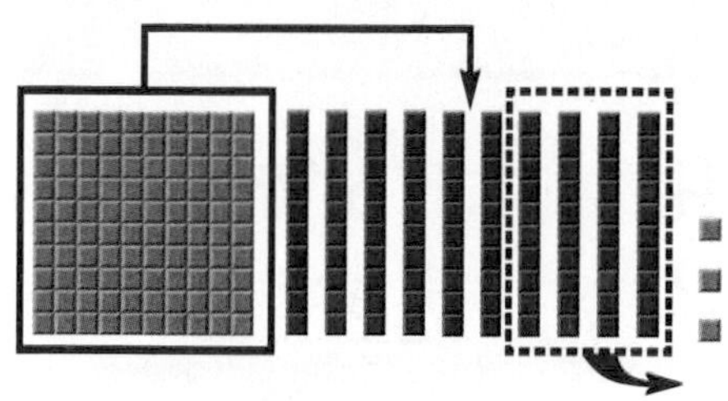

	h	t	o
	0 ~~1~~	10 ~~0~~	4
−		4	1
		6	3

1 hundred 0 tens = 0 hundreds 10 tens

Subtract the hundreds.

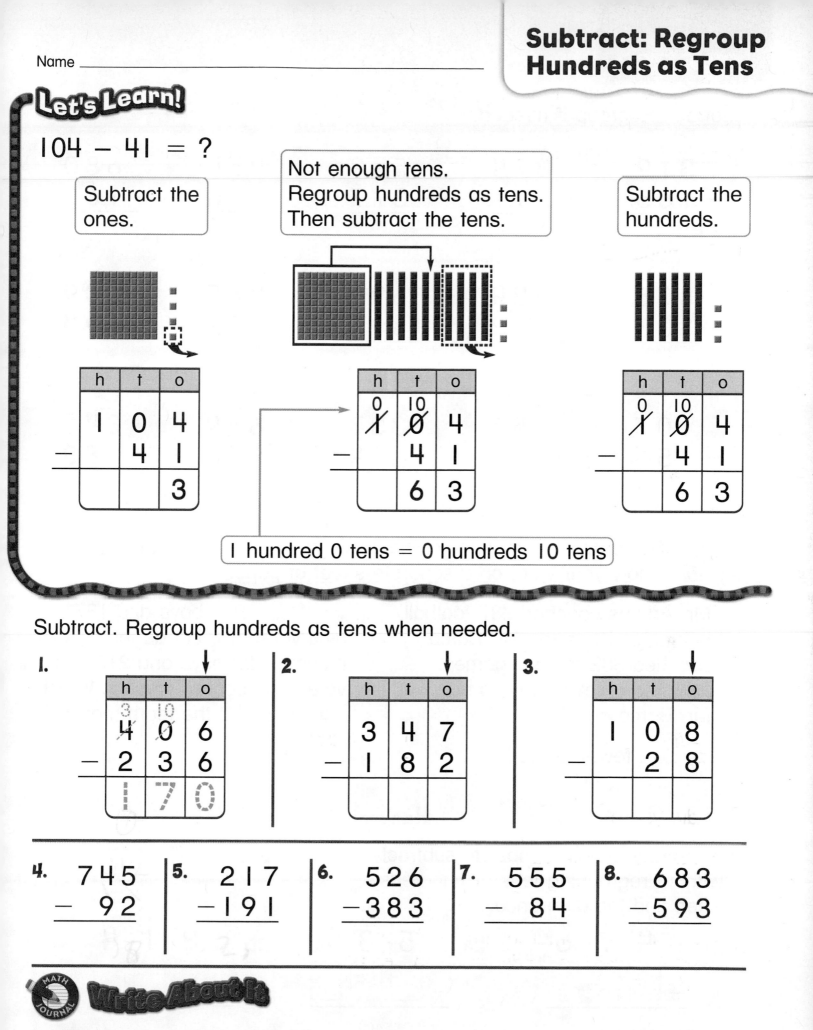

	h	t	o
	0 ~~1~~	10 ~~0~~	4
−		4	1
		6	3

Subtract. Regroup hundreds as tens when needed.

1.

	h	t	o
	3 ~~4~~	10 ~~0~~	6
−	2	3	6
	1	7	0

2.

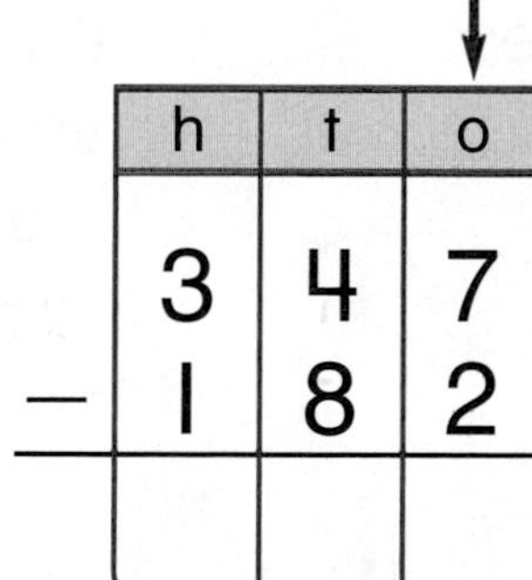

	h	t	o
	3	4	7
−	1	8	2

3.

	h	t	o
	1	0	8
−		2	8

4. 745 − 92

5. 217 − 191

6. 526 − 383

7. 555 − 84

8. 683 − 593

9. How is regrouping hundreds as tens like regrouping tens as ones?

Practice

Subtract. Regroup if needed.

10. $\begin{array}{r} \overset{2}{\cancel{3}}\overset{11}{\cancel{1}}9 \\ -165 \\ \hline 154 \end{array}$	**11.** $\begin{array}{r} 874 \\ -291 \\ \hline \end{array}$	**12.** $\begin{array}{r} 549 \\ -377 \\ \hline \end{array}$	**13.** $\begin{array}{r} 454 \\ -170 \\ \hline \end{array}$	**14.** $\begin{array}{r} 680 \\ -160 \\ \hline \end{array}$
15. $\begin{array}{r} 808 \\ -333 \\ \hline \end{array}$	**16.** $\begin{array}{r} 924 \\ -172 \\ \hline \end{array}$	**17.** $\begin{array}{r} 699 \\ -391 \\ \hline \end{array}$	**18.** $\begin{array}{r} 465 \\ -292 \\ \hline \end{array}$	**19.** $\begin{array}{r} 609 \\ -194 \\ \hline \end{array}$
20. $\begin{array}{r} 107 \\ -\ \ 55 \\ \hline \end{array}$	**21.** $\begin{array}{r} 656 \\ -\ \ 76 \\ \hline \end{array}$	**22.** $\begin{array}{r} 337 \\ -\ \ 94 \\ \hline \end{array}$	**23.** $\begin{array}{r} 669 \\ -\ \ 28 \\ \hline \end{array}$	**24.** $\begin{array}{r} 843 \\ -\ \ 83 \\ \hline \end{array}$

Solve. Use a problem-solving strategy.
Show your work on a separate sheet of paper.

25. Mr. Adams coached 437 football games in 18 years. Mr. Barco coached 382 football games. How many fewer games did Mr. Barco coach?

55 fewer games

26. **Multistep** 212 boys and 137 girls vote for a cat as team mascot. 122 boys and 218 girls vote for a dog as mascot. Which animal will be the team mascot?

______

CRITICAL THINKING

Write any 3-digit number to subtract without regrouping tens or hundreds. Then find the difference.

27. 4 7 5
− ☐☐☐

28. 5 3 2
− ☐☐☐

29. 3 1 4
− ☐☐☐

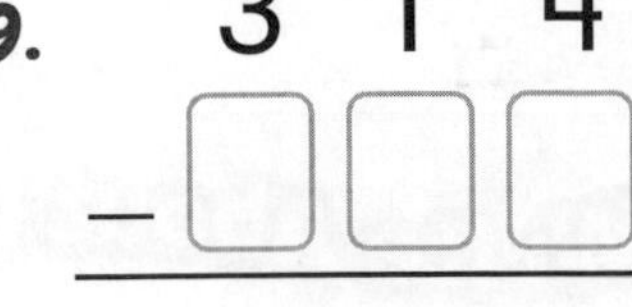

Math Alive at Home Ask your child to subtract 624 − 353 and to explain the regrouping. (271; 6 hundreds 2 tens equals 5 hundreds 12 tens.)

Name ______________________________

Subtract: Regroup Twice

Let's Learn!

The Bolts scored 124 points. The Stars scored 186 points. The team that scores 345 wins. How many more points do the Stars need to win?

Subtract 186 from 345.

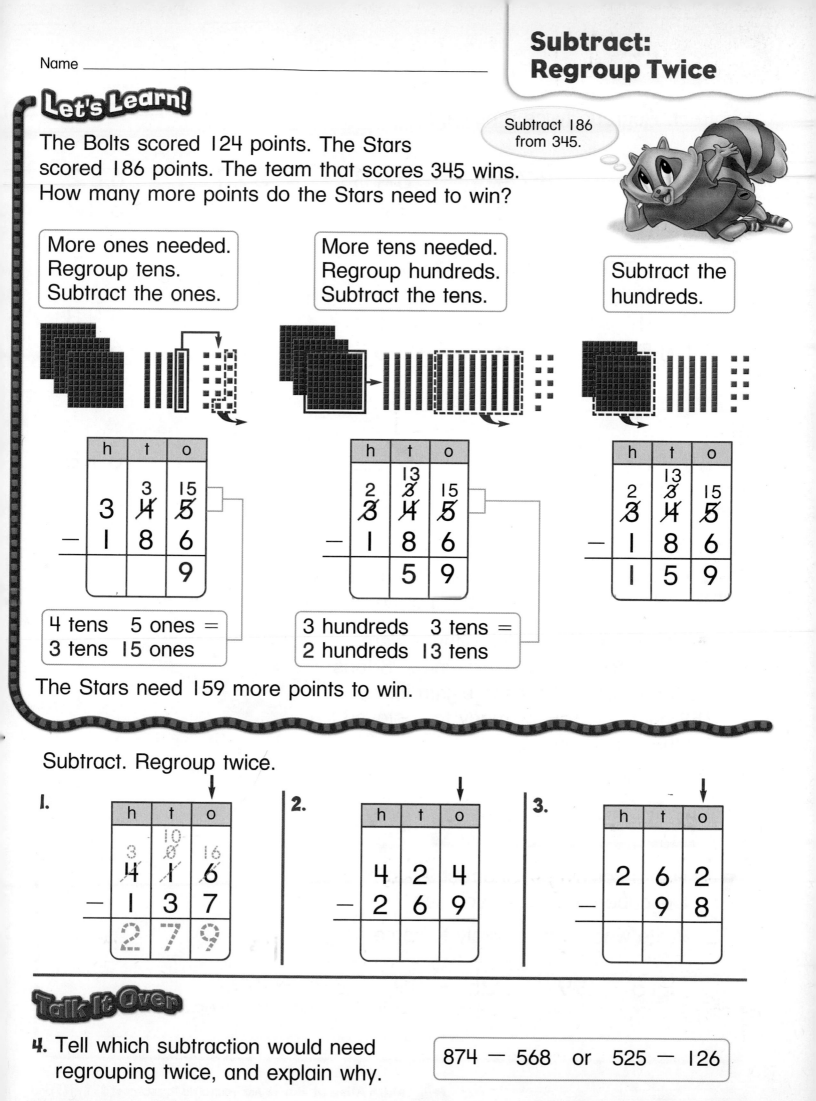

More ones needed.
Regroup tens.
Subtract the ones.

More tens needed.
Regroup hundreds.
Subtract the tens.

Subtract the hundreds.

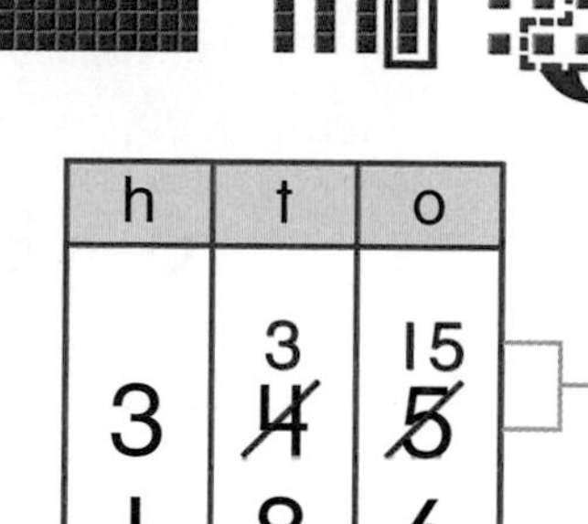

	h	t	o
		3	15
	3	~~4~~	~~5~~
−	1	8	6
			9

4 tens 5 ones =
3 tens 15 ones

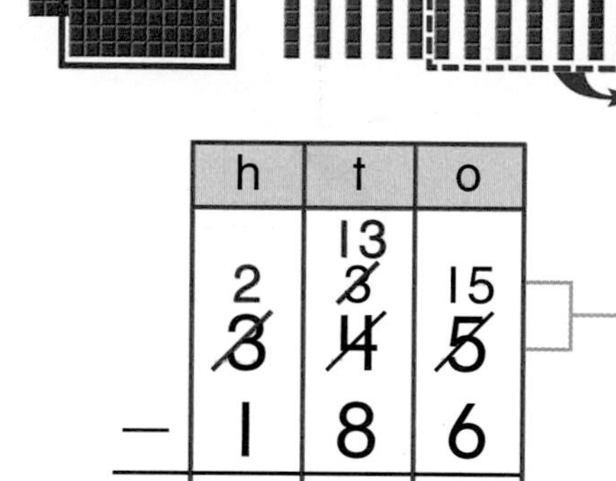

	h	t	o
		13	
	2	~~3~~	15
	~~3~~	~~4~~	~~5~~
−	1	8	6
		5	9

3 hundreds 3 tens =
2 hundreds 13 tens

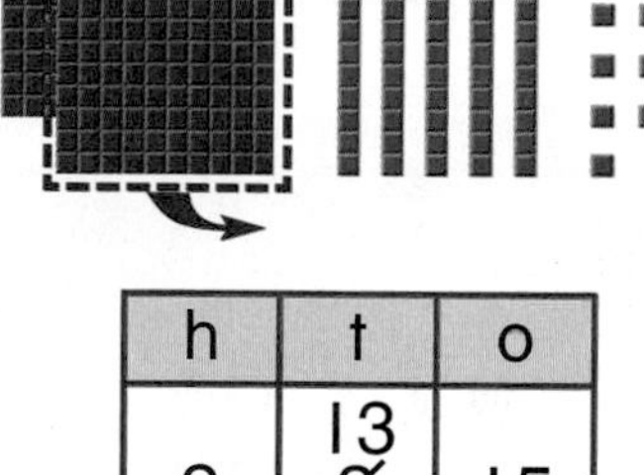

	h	t	o
		13	
	2	~~3~~	15
	~~3~~	~~4~~	~~5~~
−	1	8	6
	1	5	9

The Stars need 159 more points to win.

Subtract. Regroup twice.

1.

	h	t	o
		10	
	3	~~0~~	16
	~~4~~	~~1~~	~~6~~
−	1	3	7
	2	7	9

2.

	h	t	o
	4	2	4
−	2	6	9

3.

	h	t	o
	2	6	2
−		9	8

Talk It Over

4. Tell which subtraction would need regrouping twice, and explain why.

874 − 568 or 525 − 126

Practice

Subtract. Regroup twice if needed.

5.	6.	7.	8.	9.
16 8 6 15 975 − 398 577	874 − 178	843 − 367	527 − 149	682 − 382

10.	11.	12.	13.	14.
474 − 185	523 − 234	715 − 36	798 − 565	843 − 698

15.	16.	17.	18.	19.
978 − 377	924 − 79	952 − 265	465 − 297	618 − 49

Solve. Use a problem-solving strategy.
Show your work on a separate sheet of paper.

20. Multistep At the stadium, there were 314 fans for the Speeders and 228 fans for the Racers. After the eighth inning, 158 people left. How many fans stayed for the end of the game?

_______ fans

CALCULATOR ACTIVITY Algebra

21. Use a calculator. Subtract 99 from each. Describe the pattern you see.

Write what is most likely to come next.

215 − 99	225 − 99	235 − 99	

Math Alive at Home Ask your child to subtract 353 − 175 and to explain the regrouping. (178; regroup 5 tens 3 ones as 4 tens 13 ones, then regroup 3 hundreds 4 tens as 2 hundreds 14 tens.)

Name ______________________________

Check Your Progress
Lessons 11–16

TEST PREPARATION

Listen to your teacher read the directions.
Fill in the circle under the correct answer.

1.

$$\begin{array}{r} 398 \\ -\ 215 \\ \hline \end{array}$$

183 ○ 381 ○ 283 ○ 238 ○

2.

$$\begin{array}{r} 467 \\ -\ 236 \\ \hline \end{array}$$

213 ○ 312 ○ 331 ○ 231 ○

3.

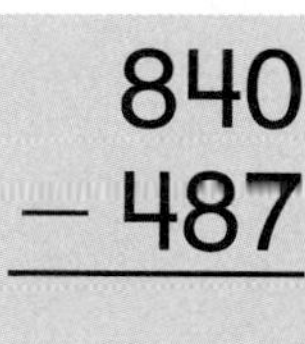

$$\begin{array}{r} 840 \\ -\ 487 \\ \hline \end{array}$$

453 ○ 353 ○ 463 ○ 363 ○

4.

5 hundreds 3 tens 6 ones

5 hundreds 13 tens 6 ones ○

4 hundreds 10 tens 6 ones ○

4 hundreds 3 tens 6 ones ○

4 hundreds 13 tens 6 ones ○

5.

10 less than 647

646 ○ 547 ○ 637 ○ 636 ○

6.

$$\begin{array}{r} 592 \\ -\ 265 \\ \hline \end{array}$$

237 ○ 327 ○ 437 ○ 326 ○

7.

$$\begin{array}{r} 274 \\ -\ 247 \\ \hline \end{array}$$

27 ○ 72 ○ 0 ○ 127 ○

8.

7 hundreds 5 tens 2 ones

6 hundreds 10 tens 2 ones ○

7 hundreds 15 tens 2 ones ○

6 hundreds 15 tens 2 ones ○

6 hundreds 9 tens 3 ones ○

Fill in the circle under the correct answer.

9. Regroup 1 hundred.

8 hundreds 1 ten 0 ones

- ○ 8 hundreds 10 tens 0 ones
- ○ 7 hundreds 11 tens 0 ones
- ○ 8 hundreds 11 tens 0 ones
- ○ 7 hundreds 10 tens 0 ones

10. 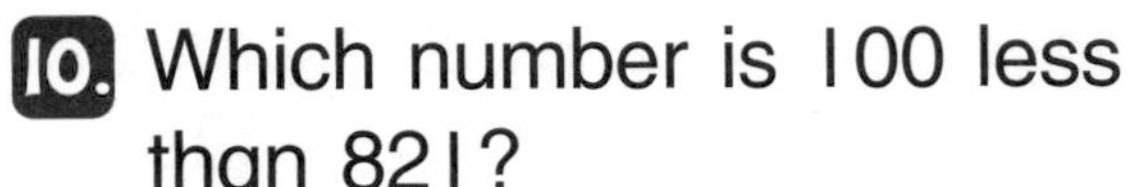
Which number is 100 less than 821?

721	921	811	820
○	○	○	○

11. Subtract.

$$\begin{array}{r} 975 \\ -\ \ 93 \\ \hline \end{array}$$

982	882	992	892
○	○	○	○

12. Subtract.

$$\begin{array}{r} 617 \\ -452 \\ \hline \end{array}$$

156	165	265	155
○	○	○	○

13. Regroup 1 hundred.

6 hundreds 4 tens 7 ones

- ○ 6 hundreds 10 tens 7 ones
- ○ 5 hundreds 14 tens 7 ones
- ○ 6 hundreds 14 tens 7 ones
- ○ 5 hundreds 10 tens 7 ones

14. Subtract.

$$\begin{array}{r} 665 \\ -\ \ 78 \\ \hline \end{array}$$

687	633	523	587
○	○	○	○

15. Subtract.

$$\begin{array}{r} 713 \\ -616 \\ \hline \end{array}$$

98	197	97	179
○	○	○	○

16. Subtract.

$$\begin{array}{r} 828 \\ -179 \\ \hline \end{array}$$

649	749	771	966
○	○	○	○

Name ______________________________

Subtract Money: Regroup Dollars or Dimes

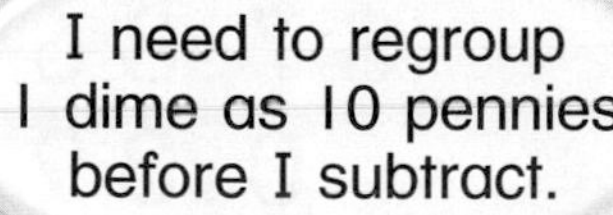

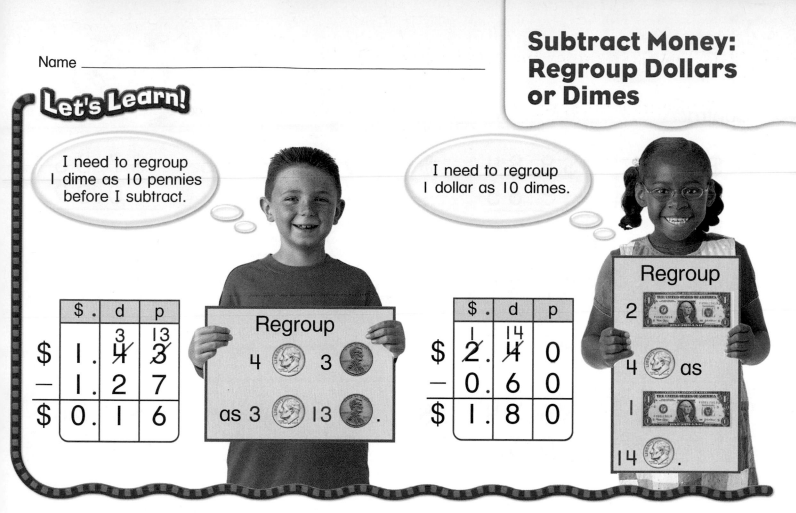

I need to regroup I dime as 10 pennies before I subtract.

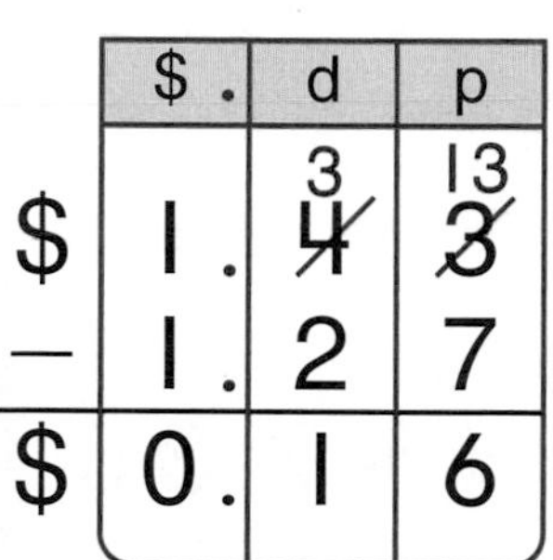

	$.	d	p
		3	13
$	1 .	~~4~~	~~3~~
−	1 .	2	7
$	0 .	1	6

I need to regroup I dollar as 10 dimes.

	$.	d	p
	1	14	
$	~~2~~ .	~~4~~	0
−	0 .	6	0
$	1 .	8	0

Subtract. Regroup dimes as pennies.

1.

	$.	d	p
		6	11
$	4 .	~~7~~	~~1~~
−	0 .	2	8
$	4 .	4	3

2.

	$.	d	p
$	5 .	5	8
−	3 .	4	9
$	.		

3.

	$.	d	p
$	3 .	9	2
−	1 .	4	7
$	.		

Find the difference. Regroup dollars as dimes.

4.

	$.	d	p
	8	15	
$	~~9~~ .	~~5~~	5
−	5 .	6	4
$	3 .	9	1

5.

	$.	d	p
$	4 .	6	6
−	0 .	7	3
$	.		

6.

	$.	d	p
$	5 .	2	7
−	3 .	5	0
$	.		

Talk It Over

7. Explain how regrouping dollars and dimes to subtract is like regrouping hundreds and tens.

Practice

Remember: Write
$ and . in the difference.

Subtract.

8. \$4.36 − 1.56 \$2.80	9. \$8.84 − 3.65	10. \$5.29 − 2.39	11. \$6.78 − 4.12	12. \$7.86 − 0.39
13. \$8.78 − 4.97	14. \$7.52 − 5.37	15. \$4.50 − 2.90	16. \$5.64 − 1.38	17. \$3.99 − 0.65
18. \$9.57 − 4.18	19. \$6.74 − 0.59	20. \$7.25 − 2.45	21. \$6.95 − 1.72	22. \$9.36 − 1.93

Problem Solving

Solve. Use a problem-solving strategy.
Show your work on a separate sheet of paper.

23. Multistep Tai has \$9.55 to spend at the sports fair. Rhonda has \$5.64. After Tai gives Rhonda \$1.50, how much more money does Tai have than Rhonda?

_______ more

MENTAL MATH

Subtract mentally.

24.

Rule: −\$0.05	\$2.26	\$2.25	\$2.24	\$2.23	\$2.22

25.

Rule: −\$0.50	\$3.60	\$3.50	\$3.40	\$3.30	\$3.20

Math Alive at Home Ask your child to subtract \$7.53 – \$4.91 and to explain the regrouping. (\$2.62; regroup 7 dollars 5 dimes as 6 dollars 15 dimes.)

Name ______________________________

Subtract Money: Regroup Twice

Let's Learn!

Joan had $3.23. She spent $1.75 on a Field Day hat. How much does Joan have left?

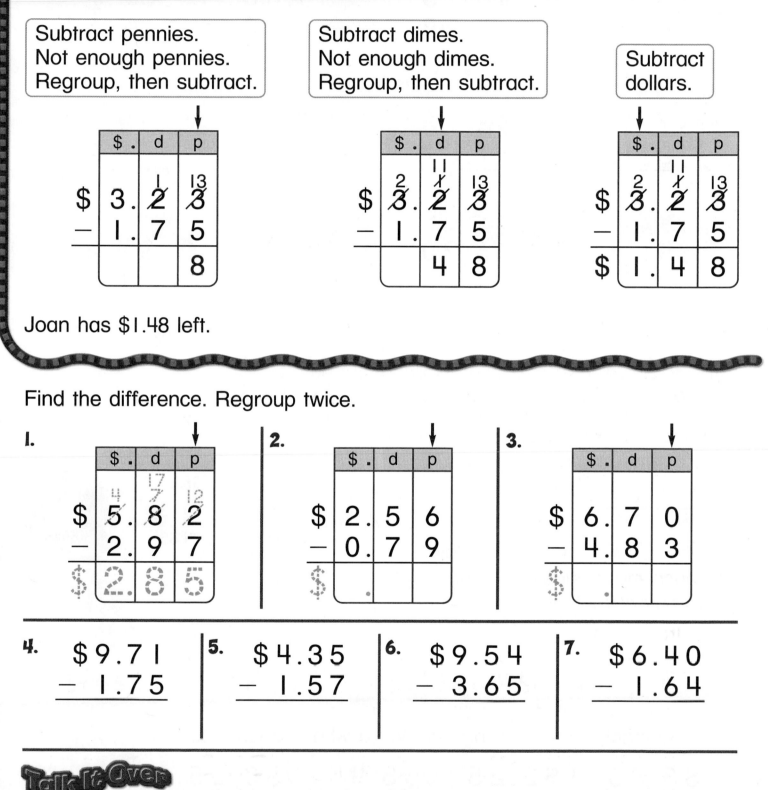

Subtract pennies. Not enough pennies. Regroup, then subtract.

	$.	d	p
		1	13
$	3.	~~2~~	~~3~~
−	1.	7	5
			8

Subtract dimes. Not enough dimes. Regroup, then subtract.

	$.	d	p
	2	11 ~~1~~	13
$	~~3~~.	~~2~~	~~3~~
−	1.	7	5
		4	8

Subtract dollars.

	$.	d	p
	2	11 ~~1~~	13
$	~~3~~.	~~2~~	~~3~~
−	1.	7	5
$	1.	4	8

Joan has $1.48 left.

Find the difference. Regroup twice.

1.

	$.	d	p
	4	17 ~~7~~	12
$	~~5~~.	~~8~~	~~2~~
−	2.	9	7
$	2.	8	5

2.

	$.	d	p
$	2.	5	6
−	0.	7	9
$	.		

3.

	$.	d	p
$	6.	7	0
−	4.	8	3
$	.		

4. $9.71 − 1.75

5. $4.35 − 1.57

6. $9.54 − 3.65

7. $6.40 − 1.64

Talk It Over

8. Tell whether you would use paper and pencil or mental math to find each difference. Explain why.

$6.87 − $4.80 $3.15 − $1.66

Practice

Remember: Write $ and . in the difference.

Find the difference. Regroup as needed.

9. \$5.16 − 0.47 = \$4.69	10. \$8.75 − 2.38	11. \$4.60 − 1.52	12. \$6.77 − 2.67
13. \$7.30 − 2.45	14. \$3.18 − 1.87	15. \$7.51 − 4.64	16. \$9.19 − 5.24
17. \$4.36 − 1.75	18. \$6.20 − 4.65	19. \$2.32 − 0.59	20. \$7.24 − 1.76

Solve. Use a problem-solving strategy.
Show your work on a separate sheet of paper.

21. How much more does the plaque cost than the ribbon?

____

Field Day Supplies	
trophy	\$7.49
ribbon	\$0.98
plaque	\$4.85

22. Mrs. Connor has \$5.50. How much more does she need to buy a trophy?

____

CRITICAL THINKING

23. Subtract. Look for a pattern. Write what comes next.

\$3.05	\$3.25	\$3.45	\$3.65	\$ ☐
− 0.95	− 0.90	− 0.85	− 0.80	− ☐

Math Alive at Home Ask your child to explain when regrouping twice is needed to subtract 3-digit money amounts. (when there are not enough pennies and not enough dimes to subtract)

Name ____________________

Estimate to Add or Subtract

Let's Learn!

You can estimate sums and differences.

Round each number to the nearest hundred. Then add or subtract.

Remember:
5 tens or more, round up.
Fewer than 5 tens, round down.

480	nearest hundred →	500	
+230	nearest hundred →	+200	
		about 700	

620	nearest hundred →	600
−390	nearest hundred →	−400
		about 200

Round to the nearest hundred. Add or subtract.

1. 310 → 300
+450 → + 500
about 800

2. 560 → ☐
+270 → + ☐
about

3. 730 → ☐
−440 → − ☐
about

4. 880 → ☐
−290 → − ☐
about

5. 240 → ☐
+660 → + ☐
about

6. 530 → ☐
+350 → + ☐
about

7. 510 → ☐
−280 → − ☐
about

8. 370 → ☐
−220 → − ☐
about

9. Explain how to estimate 430 + 480 and 690 − 420.

Copyright © by William H. Sadlier, Inc. All rights reserved.

Practice

Remember:
5 tens or more, round up.
Fewer than 5 tens, round down.

Round to the nearest hundred. Add or subtract.

10. 210 → 200
+430 → + 400
about 600

11. 190 → ☐
+570 → + ☐
about ☐

12. 650 → ☐
+240 → + ☐
about ☐

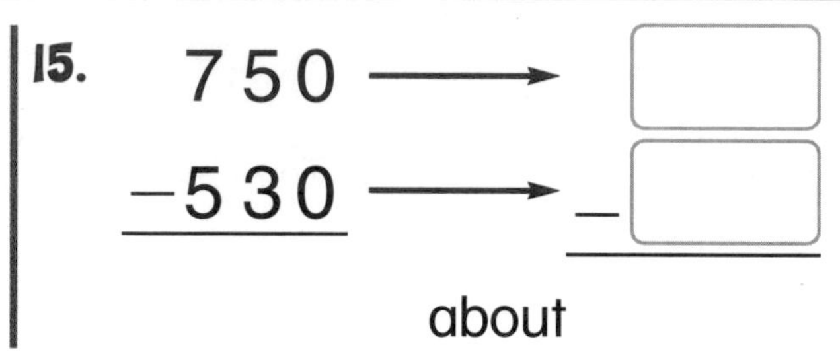

13. 630 → ☐
−420 → − ☐
about ☐

14. 810 → ☐
−640 → − ☐
about ☐

15. 750 → ☐
−530 → − ☐
about ☐

Solve. Use a problem-solving strategy.
Show your work on a separate sheet of paper.

16. Barry's Bookstore sold 290 books about sports in the first 24 weeks of the year. It sold 360 sports books in the next 16 weeks. About how many sports books has Barry's Bookstore sold?

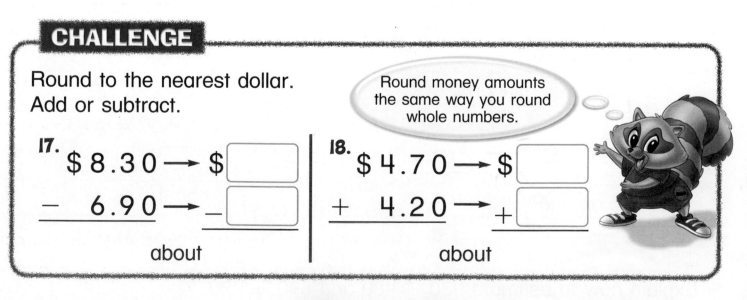

about ______

CHALLENGE

Round to the nearest dollar.
Add or subtract.

Round money amounts the same way you round whole numbers.

17. \$8.30 → \$ ☐
− 6.90 → − ☐
about ☐

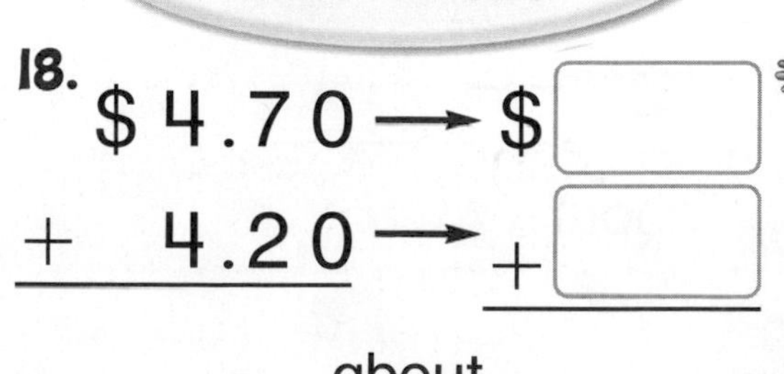

18. \$4.70 → \$ ☐
+ 4.20 → + ☐
about ☐

Math Alive at Home Ask your child how he/she would estimate 229 + 386 and 922 − 587. (200 + 400 = 600; 900 − 600 = 300)

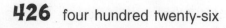

Name ______________________________

Use Logical Reasoning

Read What is the difference of the numbers inside the circle?

Plan Find the numbers inside the circle. Subtract the lesser number from the greater number.

Write

The difference is 26.

Check Add to check your subtraction.

Use logical reasoning.

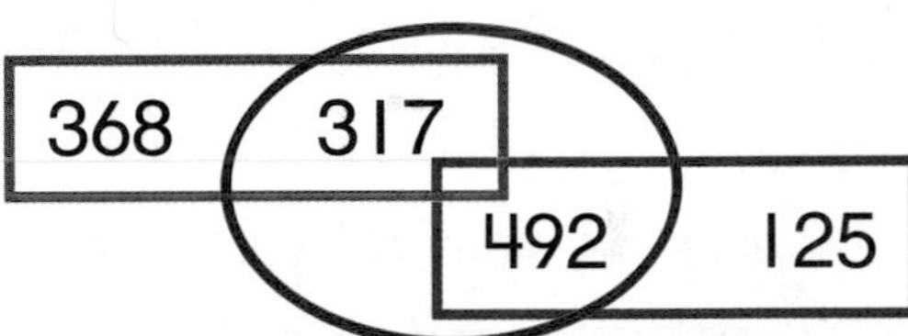

1. Which numbers have the lesser sum, the numbers inside the yellow shape or the numbers inside the red shape?

Hint
317 is in both shapes.
368 is less than 492.

The numbers inside the yellow shape have the lesser sum.

2. What is the sum of the numbers **not** inside the red shape?

The sum is ______.

3. What is the sum of the numbers inside the blue shape?

The sum is ______.

Copyright © by William H. Sadlier, Inc. All rights reserved.

Practice

Read · Plan · Write · Check

Use Logical Reasoning

4. What is the sum of the numbers inside the circle?

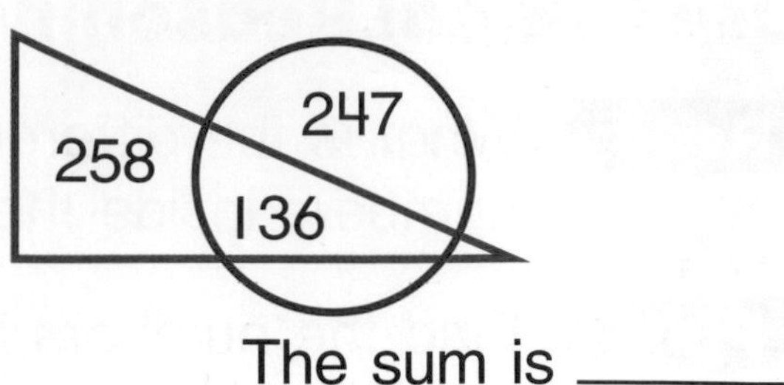

The sum is ______.

5. Which numbers have the lesser sum, the numbers inside the rectangle or the numbers inside the triangle?

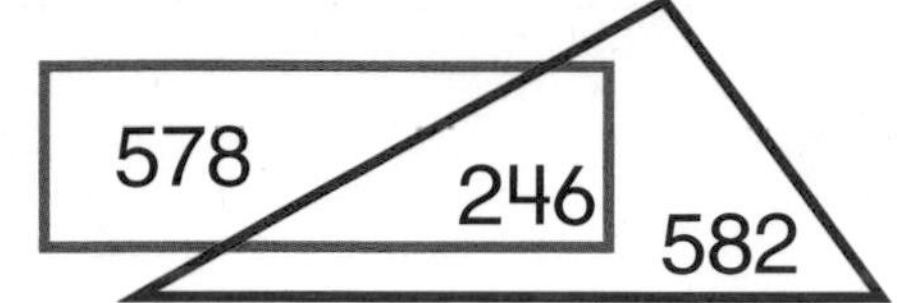

The numbers inside the ______ have the lesser sum.

6. Which numbers have the greater difference, the numbers **not** inside the circle or the numbers **not** inside the triangle?

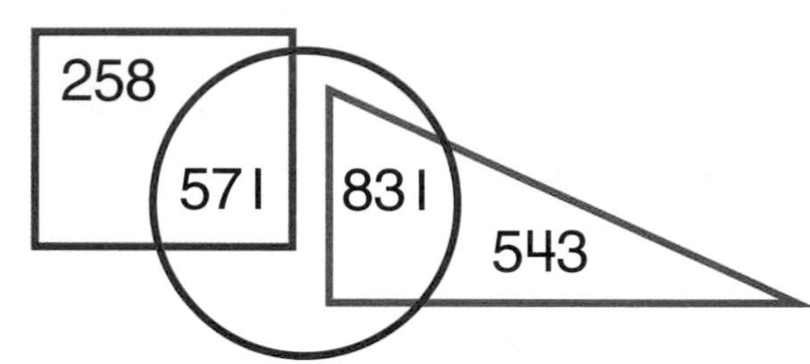

The numbers **not** inside the ______ have the greater difference.

7. What is the difference of the numbers outside the square?

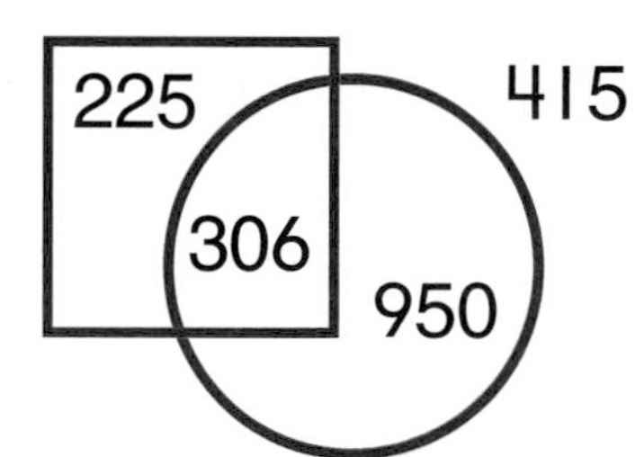

The difference is ______.

Write one 3-digit number inside the ◺ and one 3-digit number inside the ⬡.

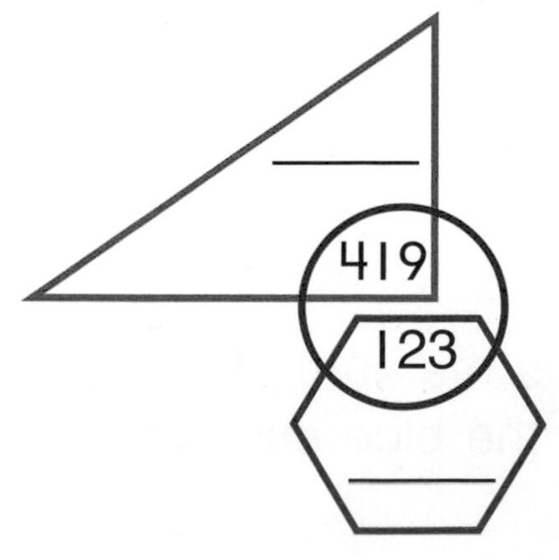

8. Which numbers have the greater difference, the numbers inside the ◺ or inside the ⬡?

The numbers inside the ______ have the greater difference.

Math Alive at Home Ask your child how he/she used logical reasoning to solve the problems in this lesson.

Name ______________________________

Problem Solving
Applications

Read → Plan → Write → Check

Mixed Strategies

Use a strategy you have learned.

Strategy File
- Use More Than One Step
- Choose the Operation
- Use a Pattern

Sale			
T-shirt	$6.89	Baseball	$5.95
Sun Visor	$3.79	Apple	$0.85
Juice	$2.00	Game	$6.19

1. Before the sale, a T-shirt cost $8.39. How much less does it cost on sale?

A T-shirt costs ______ less.

2. Drew wants to buy 2 juices and an apple. How much money does he need?

Drew needs ______.

---

3. Aram buys a sun visor and a juice. Sandy buys a game. How much more does Sandy spend than Aram?

Sandy spends ______ more.

---

4. Kate's team scores 346 points one year and 219 points the next. How many points does the team score in both years?

The team scores ______ points.

---

5. Show this pattern with letters.

Copyright © by William H. Sadlier, Inc. All rights reserved.

Practice

Read Plan Write Check

Use a strategy you have learned.

Strategy File
Use Logical Reasoning
Use More Than One Step
Make a List
Choose the Operation

6. Tasha has $2.84. She spends some money. Then she has 3 quarters left. How much does Tasha spend?

   Tasha spends ______.

---

7. Terri makes 3-digit numbers using these cards. How many 3-digit numbers less than 500 can she make?

   Terri can make ______ numbers.

---

8. Alice had $0.90. She spends $0.55 for an apple and $0.20 for a sticker. How much money does she have left?

   Alice has ______ left.

---

9. What is the sum of the numbers **not** inside the green circle?

   ______

10. What is the difference of the numbers **inside** the purple circle?

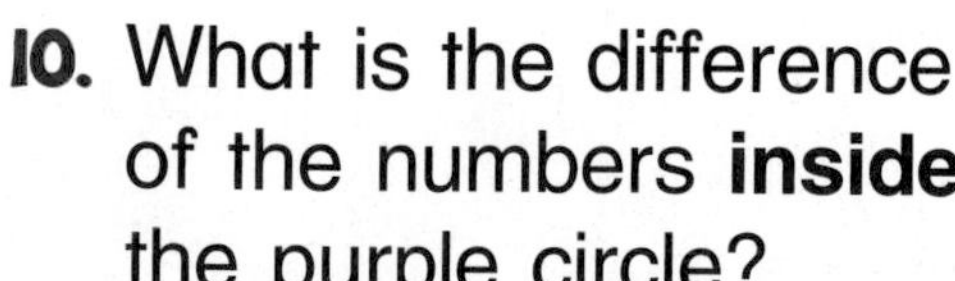

   ______

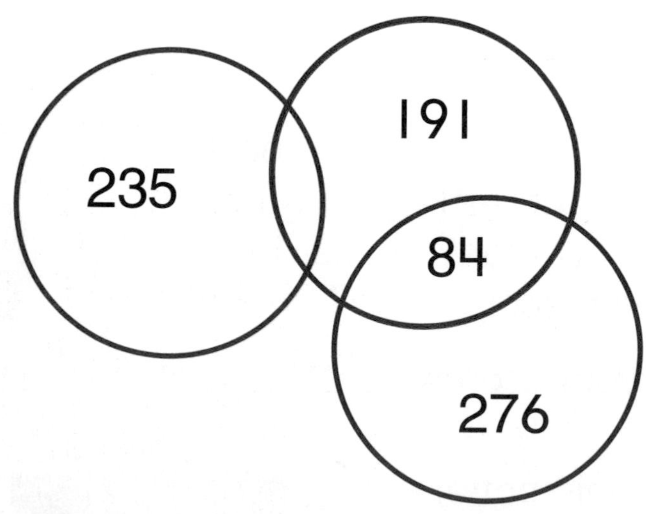

11. What is the difference of the numbers **not** inside the green circle?

   ______

Math Alive at Home Ask your child to tell you how he/she solved some of the problems in this lesson.

Name ____________________

Check Your Progress
Lessons 17–21

TEST PREPARATION

Listen to your teacher read the directions.
Fill in the circle under the correct answer.

1. $\begin{array}{r} \$9.27 \\ -\ 3.41 \\ \hline \end{array}$

$6.66 ○ $6.88 ○ $6.76 ○ $5.86 ○

2. $\begin{array}{r} \$4.83 \\ -\ 3.59 \\ \hline \end{array}$

$1.24 ○ $2.24 ○ $1.34 ○ $8.42 ○

3. $\begin{array}{r} \$6.80 \\ -\ 2.78 \\ \hline \end{array}$

$4.12 ○ $4.02 ○ $4.18 ○ $3.02 ○

4.

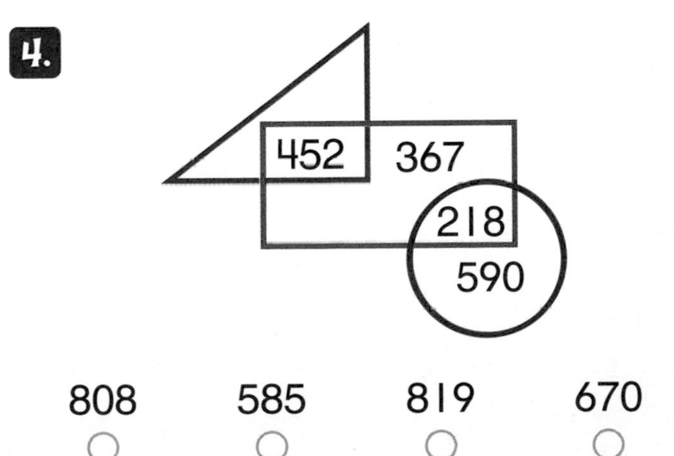

808 ○ 585 ○ 819 ○ 670 ○

5. $\begin{array}{r} \$6.24 \\ -\ 5.66 \\ \hline \end{array}$

$1.58 ○ $0.58 ○ $0.48 ○ $1.68 ○

6. $\begin{array}{r} \$4.31 \\ -\ 1.72 \\ \hline \end{array}$

$3.59 ○ $2.69 ○ $2.59 ○ $6.03 ○

7.

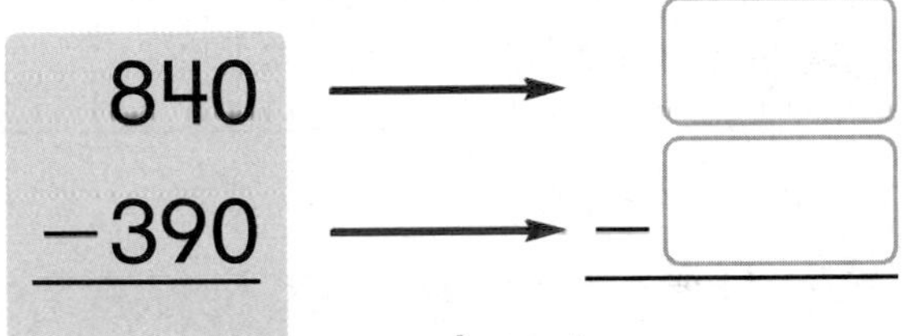

about

400 ○ 600 ○ 500 ○ 300 ○

8.

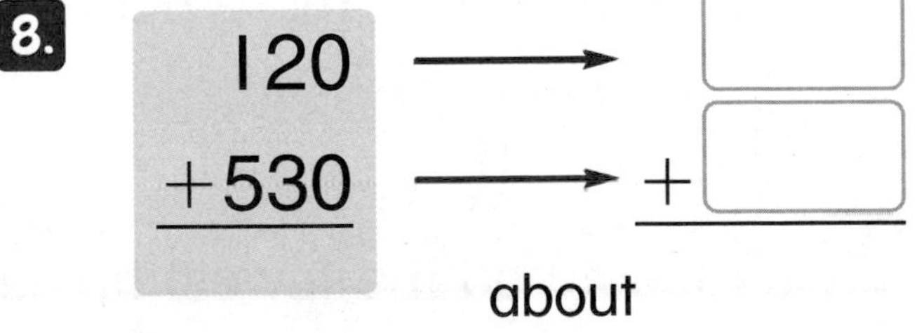

about

300 ○ 400 ○ 600 ○ 500 ○

Copyright © by William H. Sadlier, Inc. All rights reserved.

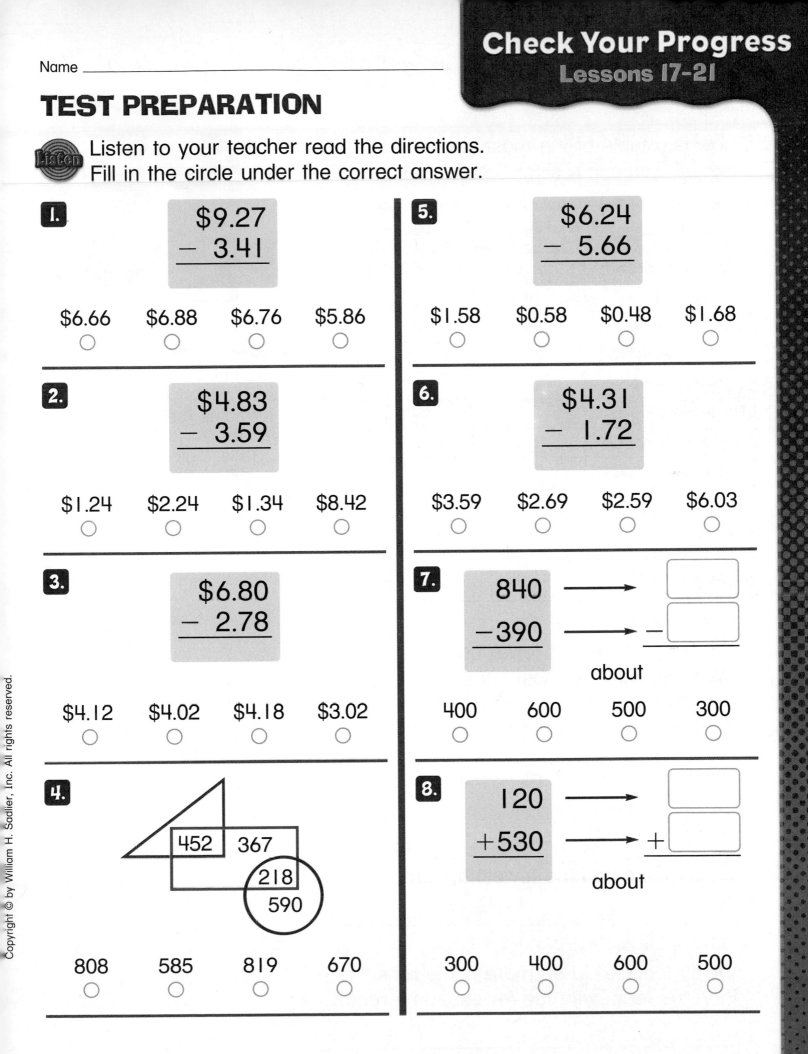

Connection

Math and Real World

Name ______________________________

"Hammerin' Hank"

Below is a table of the most home runs hit by eight baseball teams in a single season, as of May, 2004.

Team	Number of Home Runs	Year
Milwaukee Brewers	216	1982
Florida Marlins	166	2001
Texas Rangers	246	2001
Oakland Athletics	243	1996
Seattle Mariners	264	1997
Baltimore Orioles	257	1996
Chicago White Sox	216	2000
Pittsburgh Pirates	171	1999

Did You Know?

Hank Aaron hit 755 home runs in his 23-year career. He held the record for home runs until 2004. He played for Milwaukee and Atlanta. He was elected to the Baseball Hall of Fame in 1982.

Use the table to answer the questions.

1. Which team had the most home runs?

   Seattle Mariners

2. Which team had 93 fewer home runs than the team with the most home runs?

   ____

3. Which team had 30 more home runs than the Chicago White Sox?

   ____

4. Which team had the fewest home runs?

   ____

5. Which teams had 50 more home runs than the team with the fewest home runs?

   ____

Name ______________________

Chapter 9 Test

1. Write the number that is most likely to come next in the pattern. Then explain the pattern.

656, 655, 654, ______

Pattern: ______

2. Round to the nearest hundred. Subtract.

$$\begin{array}{r} 860 \\ -240 \\ \hline \end{array} \longrightarrow \begin{array}{r} \square \\ -\square \\ \hline \end{array}$$

about

3. Add. Regroup if needed.

$$\begin{array}{r} 437 \\ +125 \\ \hline \end{array}$$

4. Subtract.

$$\begin{array}{r} 698 \\ -469 \\ \hline \end{array}$$

5. Subtract. Regroup if needed.

$$\begin{array}{r} 738 \\ -548 \\ \hline \end{array}$$

6. Add.

$$\begin{array}{r} 513 \\ +\ 86 \\ \hline \end{array}$$

7. Subtract. Regroup if needed.

$$\begin{array}{r} 762 \\ -297 \\ \hline \end{array}$$

8. Subtract.

$$\begin{array}{r} \$7.77 \\ -\ 0.84 \\ \hline \end{array}$$

9. Add.

$$\begin{array}{r} 279 \\ +585 \\ \hline \end{array}$$

10. Round to the nearest hundred. Add.

$$\begin{array}{r} 450 \\ +370 \\ \hline \end{array} \longrightarrow \begin{array}{r} \square \\ +\square \\ \hline \end{array}$$

about

Copyright © by William H. Sadlier, Inc. All rights reserved.

11. Add.

$$\begin{array}{r} \$7.26 \\ +\ 2.52 \\ \hline \end{array}$$

12. Find the difference.

$$\begin{array}{r} \$8.43 \\ -\ 6.95 \\ \hline \end{array}$$

13. Subtract.

$$\begin{array}{r} 967 \\ -\ 541 \\ \hline \end{array}$$

14. Write the number that is most likely to come next in the pattern.

634, 644, 654, ______

15. Subtract.

$$\begin{array}{r} \$9.75 \\ -\ 4.29 \\ \hline \end{array}$$

16. Add.

$$\begin{array}{r} \$6.29 \\ +\ 1.76 \\ \hline \end{array}$$

Solve. Use a problem-solving strategy. Watch for multistep problems.

17. Clare sells 498 raffle tickets on Saturday and 396 tickets on Sunday. How many tickets does Clare sell in all?

______ tickets

18. 146 children were in a hiking club. Then 27 children dropped out of the club. This year 168 more children join the club. How many children are now in the club?

______ children

19. Which numbers have the lesser sum, the numbers inside the rectangle or the numbers inside the triangle?

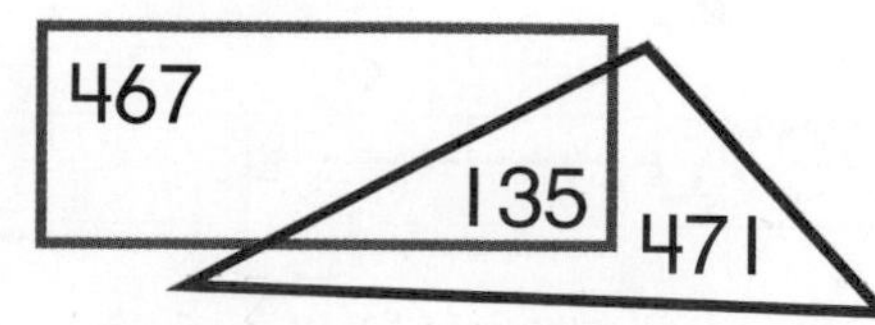

the numbers inside the ______

20. Which numbers have the greater difference, the numbers not inside the circle or the numbers not inside the triangle?

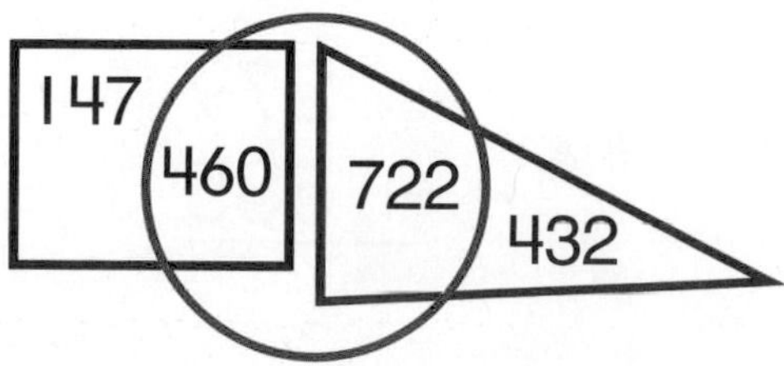

the numbers not inside the ______

Name ____________________

1. Pick a number between 150 and 500.
Make up a +1, +10, or +100 pattern.
Write the rule. Write the pattern.

My number is ______.

My rule is ______.

My pattern is: ______, ______, ______, ______

2. Pick a number between 450 and 950.
Make up a −1, −10, or −100 pattern.
Write the rule. Write the pattern.

My number is ______.

My rule is ______.

My pattern is: ______, ______, ______, ______

Write a 3-digit number in each ☐ to show no regrouping, regrouping ones, and regrouping tens. Complete the addition and subtraction.

No regrouping	Regroup ones	Regroup tens
3. 435 + ☐	5. 435 + ☐	7. 435 + ☐
4. 564 − ☐	6. 564 − ☐	8. 564 − ☐

Copyright © by William H. Sadlier, Inc. All rights reserved.

You can put this in your Math Portfolio.

Enrichment

Name ____________________

Add Three 3-Digit Addends

Sunnydale School and Halmouth School will play their seventh football game on Saturday. Below is a table showing how many fans came to the first 6 games.

Game	Sunnydale Fans	Halmouth Fans
1	153	403
2	205	316
3	297	280
4	310	265
5	335	224
6	339	203

1. How many Sunnydale fans came to the first, second, and third games?

    fans

   $$\begin{array}{r} 153 \\ 205 \\ +\ 297 \\ \hline 655 \end{array}$$

2. How many Halmouth fans came to the first, second, and third games?

   ______ fans

3. How many Sunnydale fans came to the fourth, fifth, and sixth games?

   ______ fans

4. How many Halmouth fans came to the fourth, fifth, and sixth games?

   ______ fans

5. Is the number of each team's fans that comes to the games increasing, decreasing, or staying about the same?

   ____

   ____

6. Which team is likely to have more fans at the seventh game? Explain why.

   ____

   ____

The Great Race

Read ALOUD

Nome
FINISH
Koyuk
Ruby
McGrath
Finger Lake
The Iditarod
START
Anchorage

Hi, my name is Scooter the sled dog. This year I'm going to pull a sled in the Iditarod, one of the most famous races in the world. The race is over 1,000 miles long and stretches across Alaska.

Copyright © by William H. Sadlier, Inc. All rights reserved.

The race starts in a city called Anchorage. After about two days and 194 miles, we will pass through a town called Finger Lake. After about two more days and 219 miles we will pass through a town called McGrath.

How many miles will we run from Anchorage to McGrath?

$$\begin{array}{r} 194 \text{ miles} \\ +219 \text{ miles} \\ \hline \text{miles} \end{array}$$

Copyright © by William H. Sadlier, Inc. All rights reserved.

From McGrath, we will race 233 miles to a town called Ruby. Then, we will race 334 more miles to Koyuk. When we finally reach Koyuk, it will be the eighth day of the race—if we go really fast, that is!

How many miles will we run from McGrath to Koyuk?

$$\begin{array}{r} 233 \text{ miles} \\ +\ 334 \text{ miles} \\ \hline \text{miles} \end{array}$$

Look back at your sums. Now add them to see how far we will travel by the end of the eighth day.

$$\begin{array}{r l} & \square \text{ miles} \\ + & \square \text{ miles} \\ \hline & \square \text{ miles} \end{array}$$

Can you believe it? I will have run almost 1,000 miles in eight days!

I'm almost at the finish line. Wish me luck!

Name ______________________________

Cumulative Review
Chapters 1-9

TEST PREPARATION

Fill in the circle next to the correct answer.

1. Add.

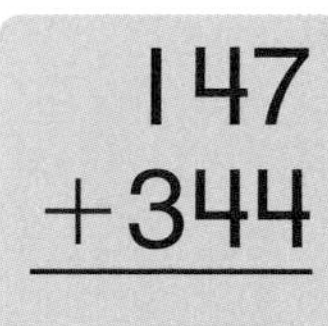

$$\begin{array}{r} 147 \\ +344 \\ \hline \end{array}$$

491 ○ 482 ○ 492 ○ 481 ○

2. How many edges does a pyramid have?

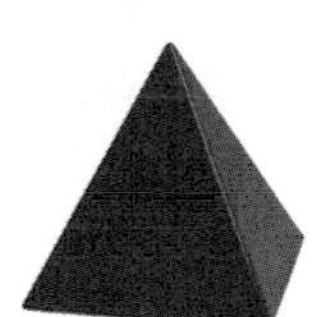

7 ○ 8 ○ 6 ○ 5 ○

3. What time is it?

a quarter past 3 ○

a quarter to 3 ○

ten past 9 ○

4. How many days are in a week?

6 ○ 7 ○ 30 ○ 5 ○

5. Round to the nearest hundred. Add.

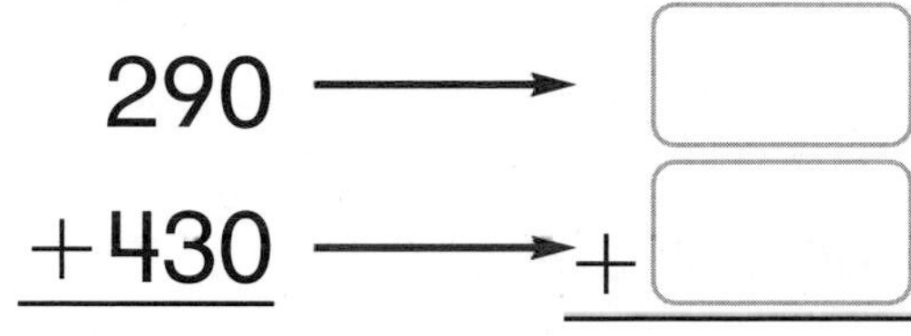

290 → ☐

+430 → + ☐

about

600 ○ 500 ○ 700 ○ 800 ○

6. Which is the number word for 9 hundreds 4 tens 7 ones?

○ nine hundred forty-seven
○ four hundred ninety-seven
○ nine hundred seventy-four
○ nine hundred fifty-seven

7. Six of which pattern block would cover the plane figure completely?

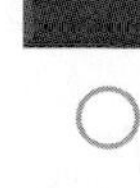

○

○

8. Which is another way to write 400 + 30 + 4?

434 ○ 344 ○ 443 ○ 334 ○

Fill in the circle under the correct answer.
Watch for multistep problems.

9. What is the missing addend?

$9 + ? = 19$

8	9	10	7
○	○	○	○

10. Find the sum.

$$\begin{array}{r} 79 \\ +15 \\ \hline \end{array}$$

84	85	94	95
○	○	○	○

11. Jack drew a pattern using only a ◆ and a ●.
Which figure is most likely to come next in his pattern?

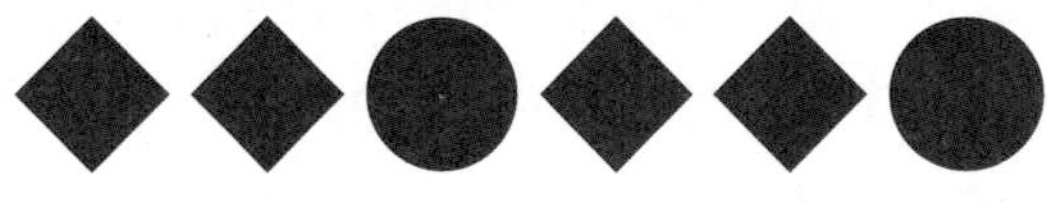

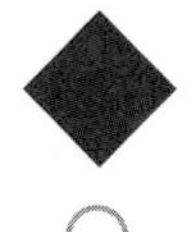 ○

 ○

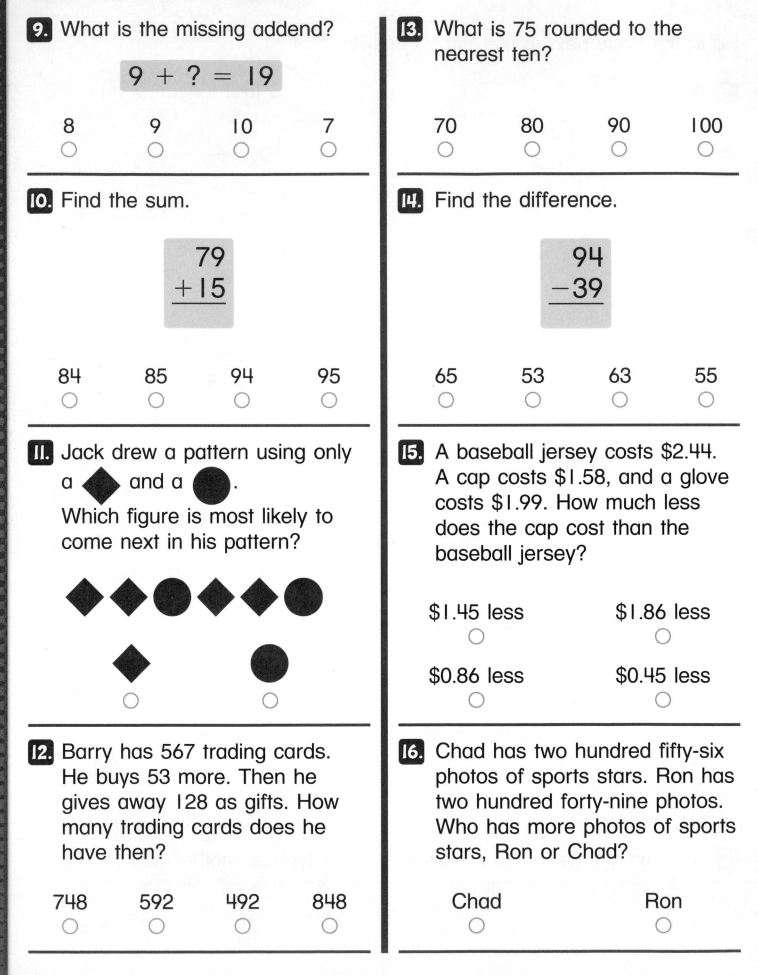

12. Barry has 567 trading cards. He buys 53 more. Then he gives away 128 as gifts. How many trading cards does he have then?

748	592	492	848
○	○	○	○

13. What is 75 rounded to the nearest ten?

70	80	90	100
○	○	○	○

14. Find the difference.

$$\begin{array}{r} 94 \\ -39 \\ \hline \end{array}$$

65	53	63	55
○	○	○	○

15. A baseball jersey costs \$2.44. A cap costs \$1.58, and a glove costs \$1.99. How much less does the cap cost than the baseball jersey?

\$1.45 less	\$1.86 less
○	○
\$0.86 less	\$0.45 less
○	○

16. Chad has two hundred fifty-six photos of sports stars. Ron has two hundred forty-nine photos. Who has more photos of sports stars, Ron or Chad?

Chad	Ron
○	○

Listen

Listen to your teacher read the poem.
Which fruits are cut into equal parts?

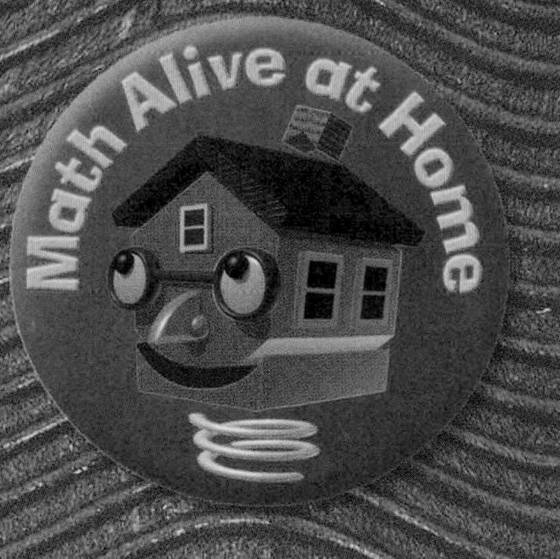

Dear Family,

Today our class began Chapter 10. We will learn about fractions and probability. Let's do the activity below together so I can review the skills I will need in order to understand the math in this chapter. Then you can read some of the new vocabulary I will learn in Chapter 10.

Love, ______________

Biggest Part, Smallest Part

Draw a circle graph like the graph below on a sheet of paper. Ask your child which colors are used for the biggest part of the circle and for the smallest part of the circle. Then ask your child how to find the greatest number and the least number on the graph. Understanding that the biggest part of the circle shows the greatest number and the smallest part of the circle shows the least number will help your child think about more likely and less likely outcomes on spinners in this chapter.

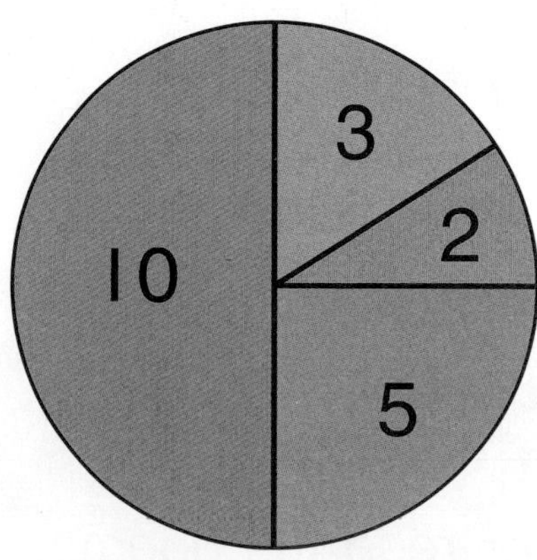

Chapter 10

also on-line

fraction part of a set or part of a whole

equal fractions fractions that name the same part of a whole or a set

$$\frac{1}{2} = \frac{2}{4}$$

outcome result

more likely (red)

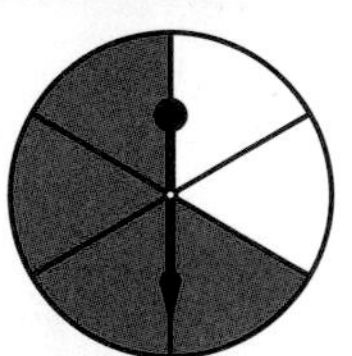

less likely (red)

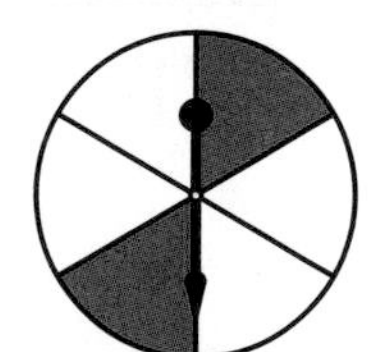

equally likely

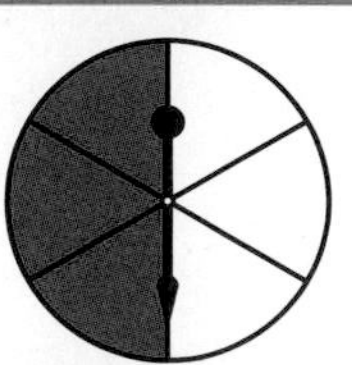

certain (red)

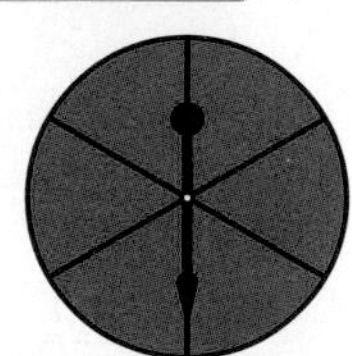

possible (red)

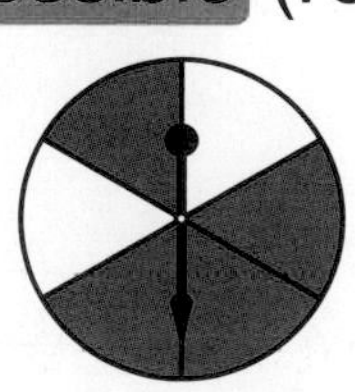

impossible (red)

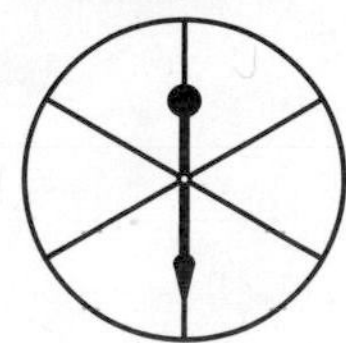

For Additional Resources: VISIT US ON-LINE www.sadlier-oxford.com

Name ____________________

Let's Learn!

You can write a **fraction** for a part of a whole.

The top number tells how many parts are colored.
The bottom number tells how many parts are in the whole.

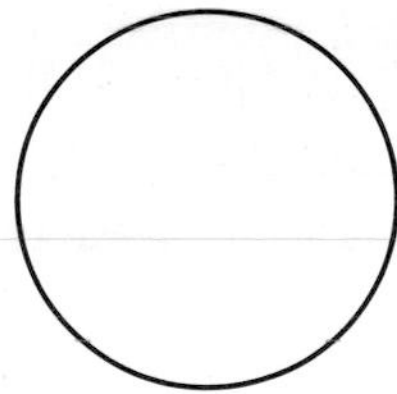

I whole

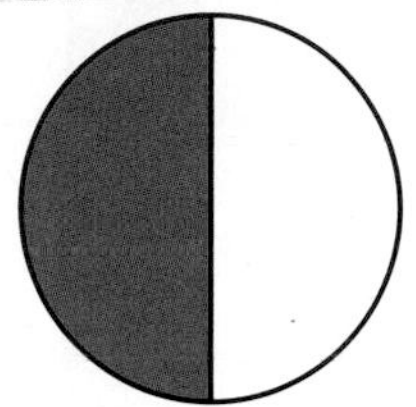

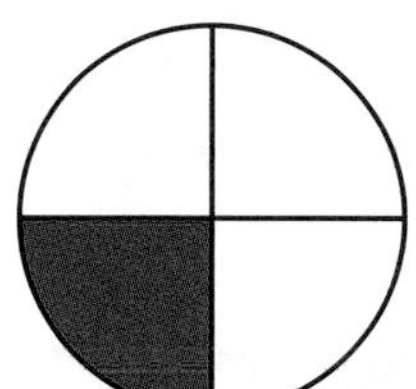

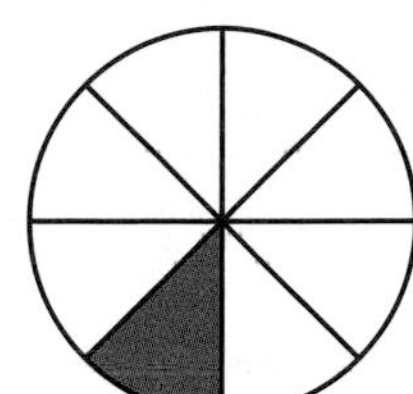

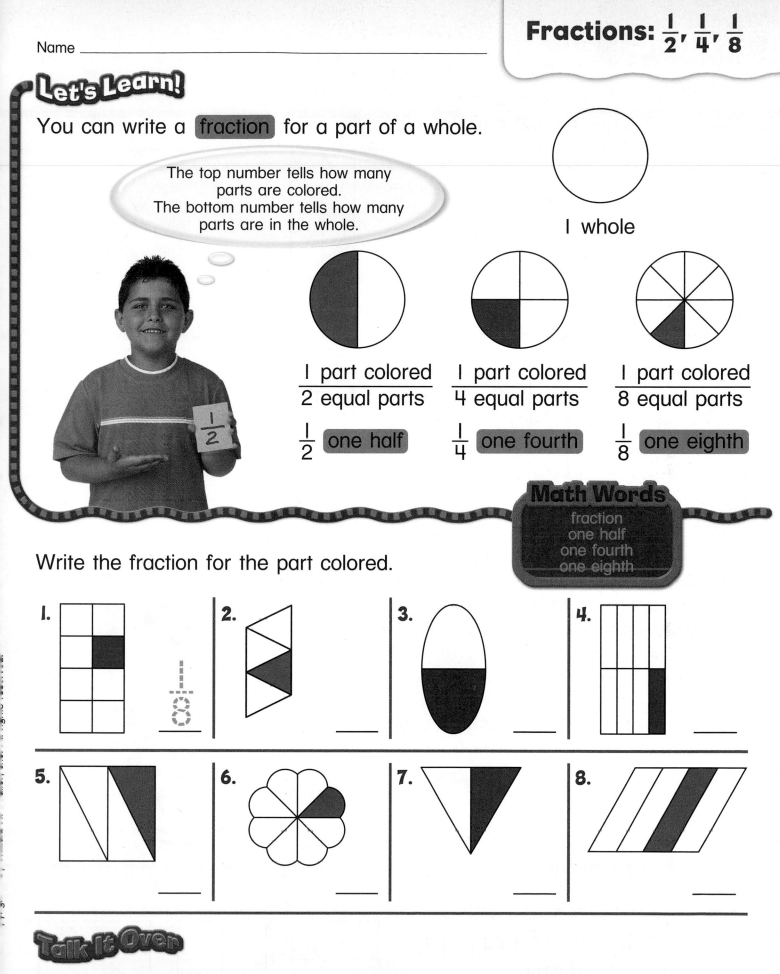

$\frac{\text{1 part colored}}{\text{2 equal parts}}$	$\frac{\text{1 part colored}}{\text{4 equal parts}}$	$\frac{\text{1 part colored}}{\text{8 equal parts}}$
$\frac{1}{2}$ **one half**	$\frac{1}{4}$ **one fourth**	$\frac{1}{8}$ **one eighth**

Math Words
fraction
one half
one fourth
one eighth

Write the fraction for the part colored.

1.  $\frac{1}{8}$

2. 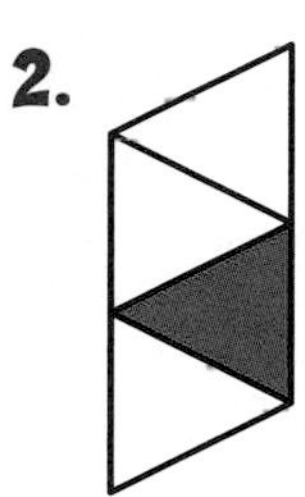 ____

3. 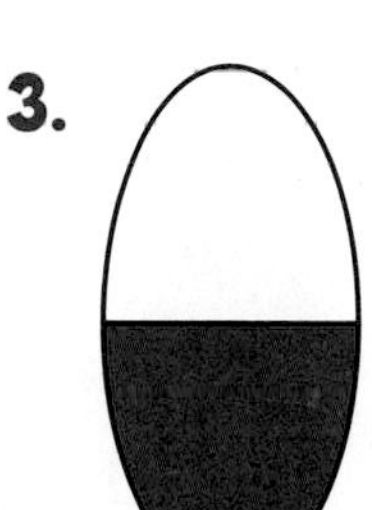 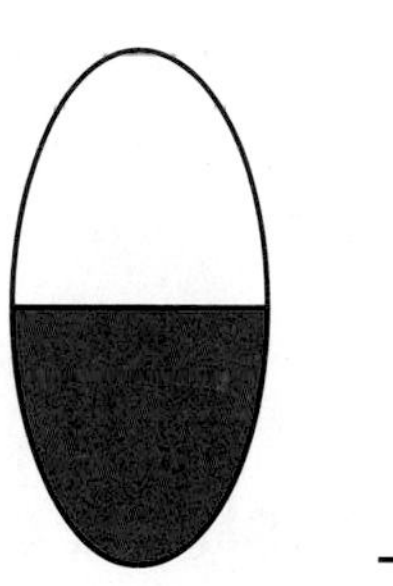 ____

4. 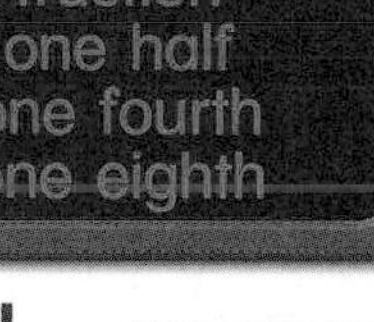 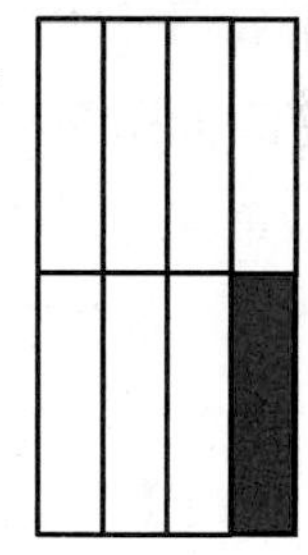 ____

5. 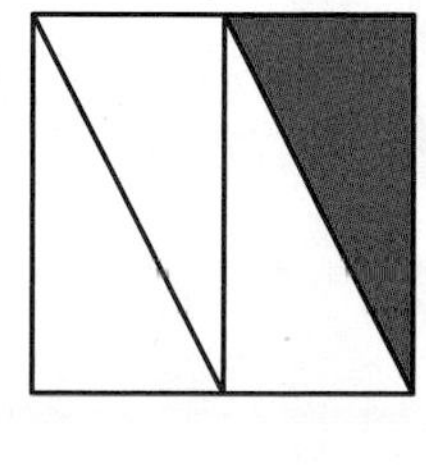 ____

6. 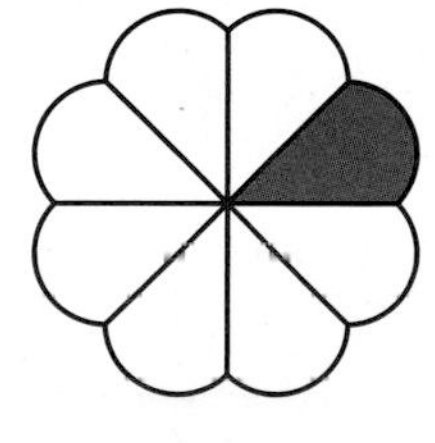 ____

7. 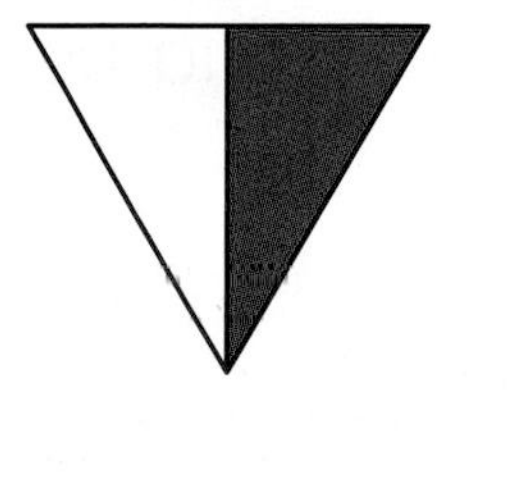 ____

8. 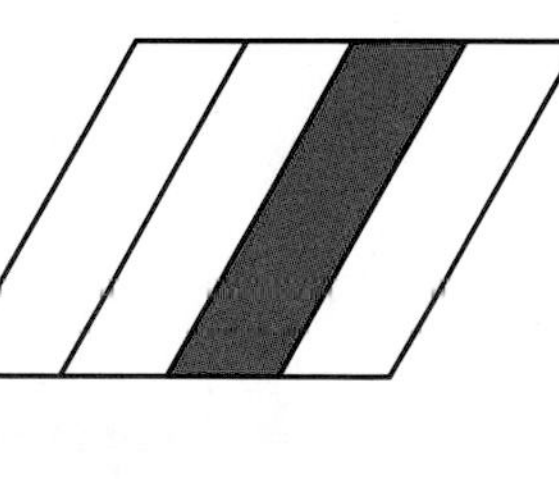 ____

Talk It Over

9. What pattern do you see in 2 equal parts making halves, 4 equal parts making fourths, and 8 equal parts making eighths?

Practice

Color 1 part of each whole.
Write the fraction for the part you colored.

10. 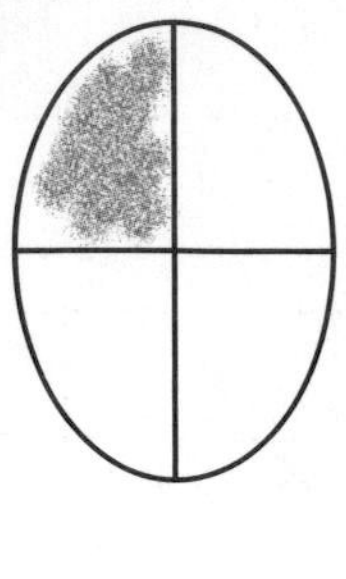 $\frac{1}{4}$

11. 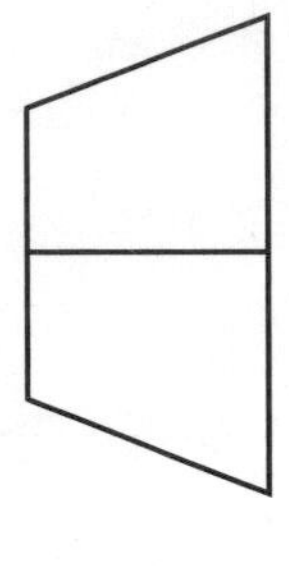 ____

12. 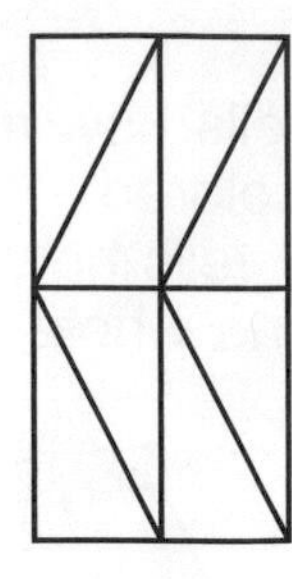 ____

13.  ____

14. 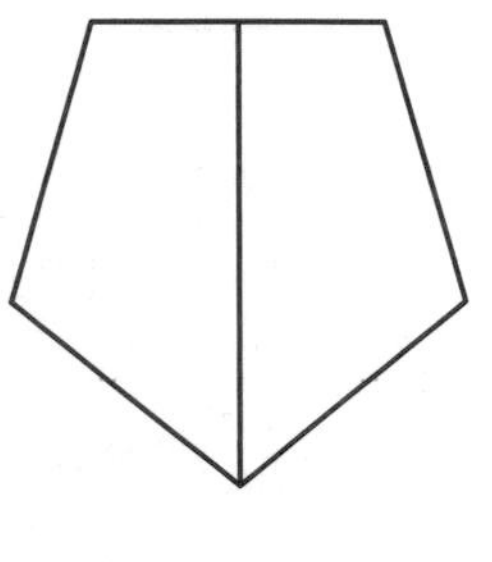 ____

15. 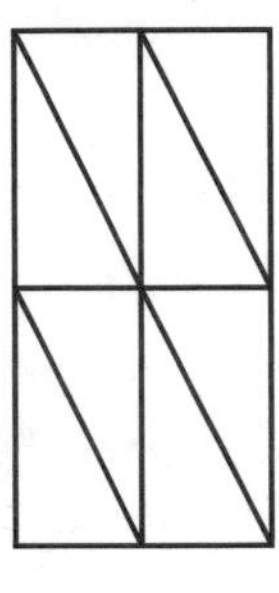 ____

16. 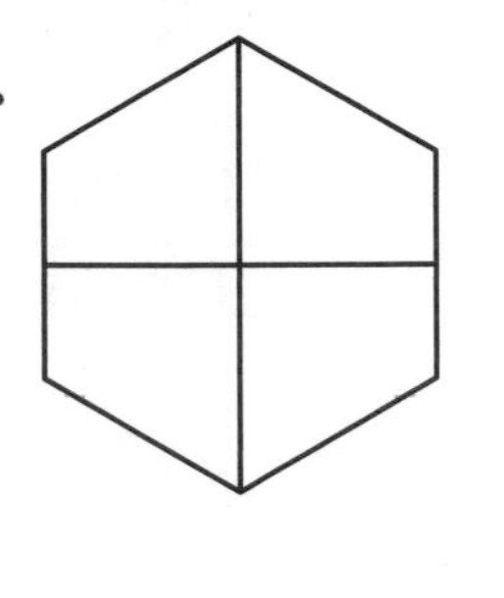 ____

17. 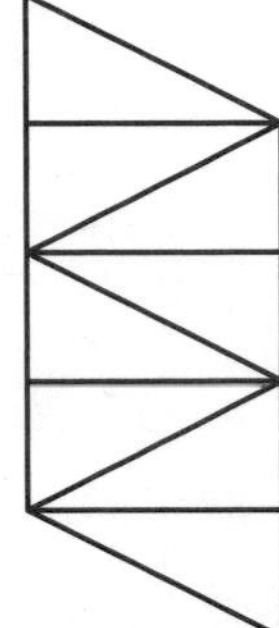 ____

Solve. Use a problem-solving strategy.

18. Daria's dad puts up a banner for her birthday party. What fractional part of the banner is green?

____

19. Daria and her 7 friends share a pizza equally at the party. What fractional part of the pizza does Daria eat?

____

CHALLENGE

20. Draw lines to finish cutting each square into 4 equal parts in a different way.
Color $\frac{1}{4}$ of each square.

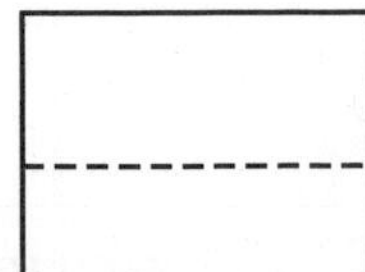 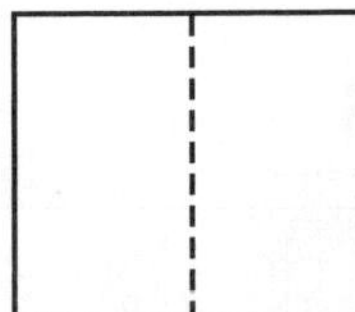 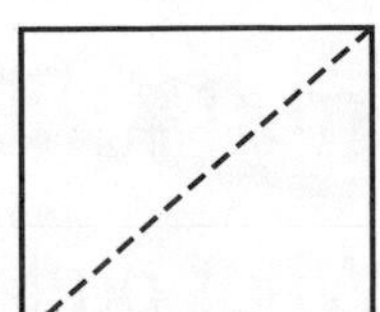

Math Alive at Home Draw squares and divide them into 2, 4, or 8 equal parts. Ask your child to color one part of each square and to tell you the fraction for the part colored.

Name ______________________________

one third $\frac{1}{3}$

one fifth $\frac{1}{5}$

one sixth $\frac{1}{6}$

one seventh $\frac{1}{7}$

one ninth $\frac{1}{9}$

one tenth $\frac{1}{10}$

one twelfth $\frac{1}{12}$

one eleventh $\frac{1}{11}$

Math Words

one third	one fifth
one sixth	one seventh
one ninth	one tenth
one eleventh	one twelfth

Write the fraction for the part colored.

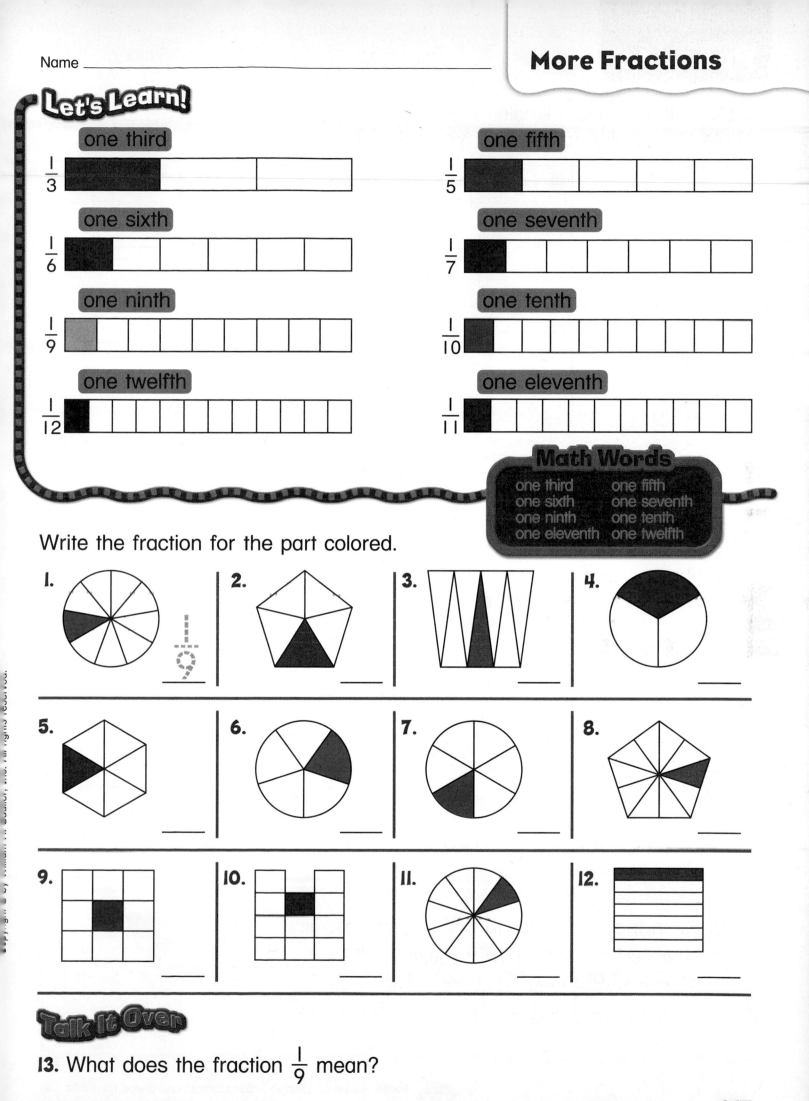

1. 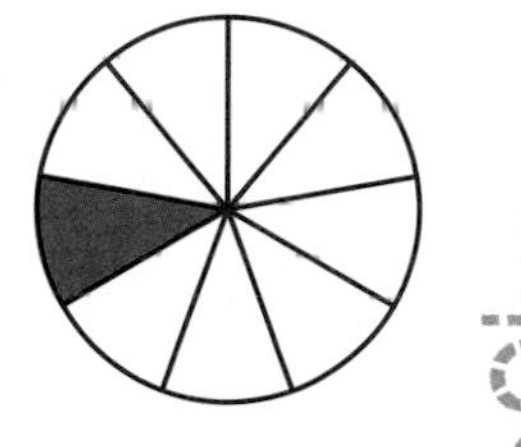

______

2. 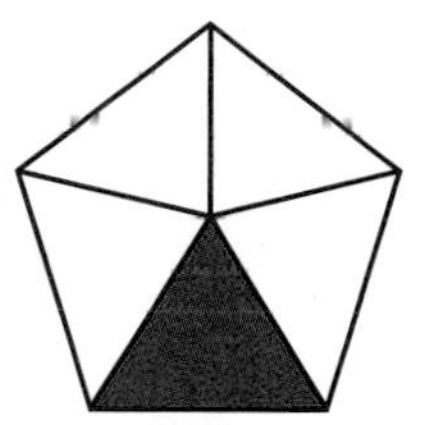 ______

3. 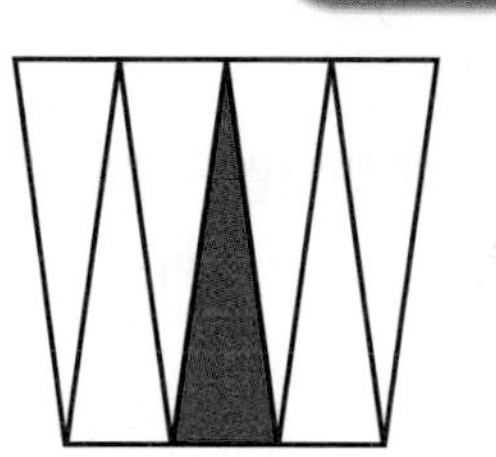 ______

4. 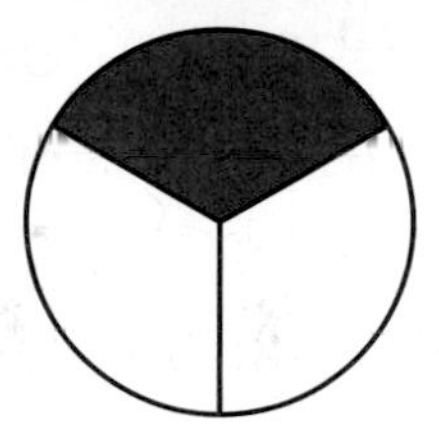 ______

5. 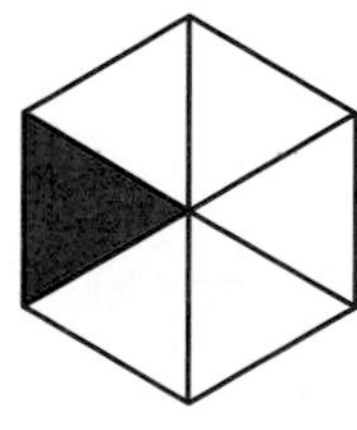 ______

6. 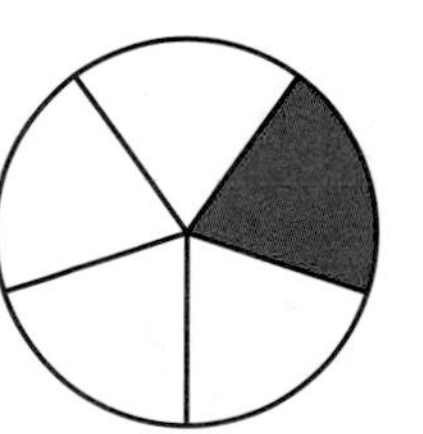 ______

7. 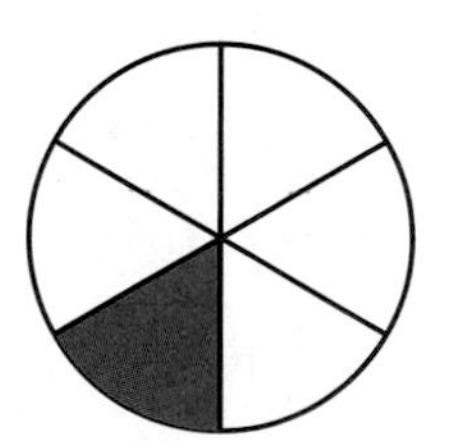 ______

8. 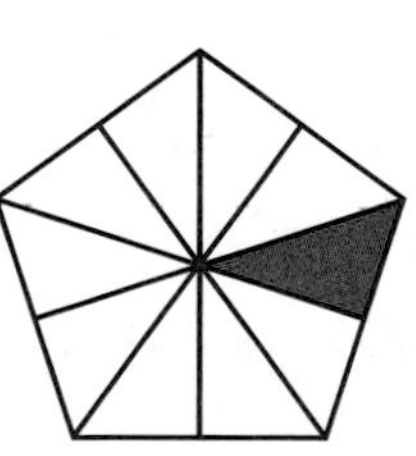 ______

9. 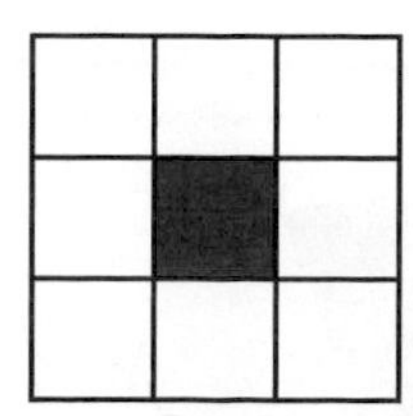 ______

10. 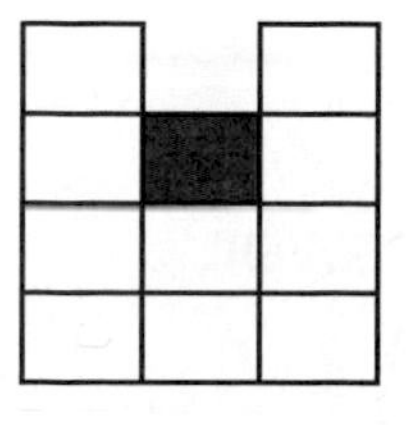 ______

11. 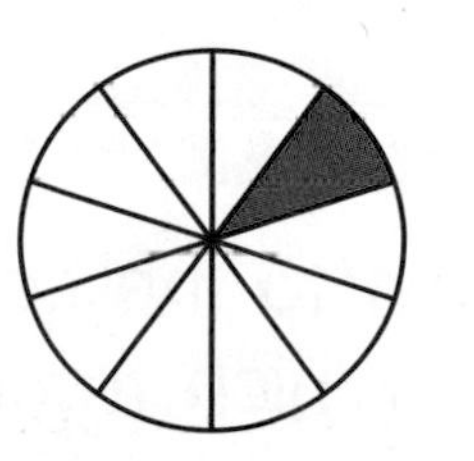 ______

12. 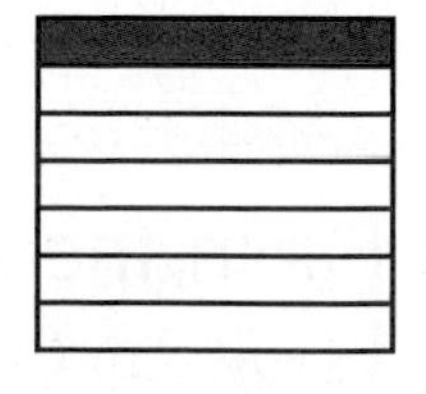 ______

13. What does the fraction $\frac{1}{9}$ mean?

Practice

Color 1 part of each whole.
Write the fraction for the part you colored.

14. 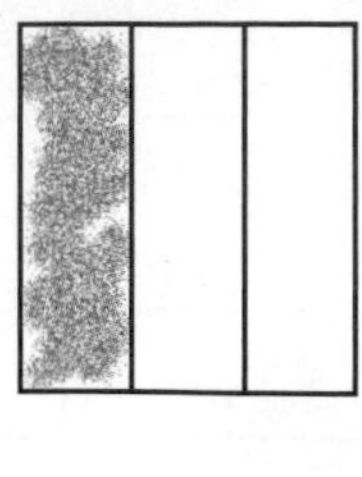 $\frac{1}{3}$

15. 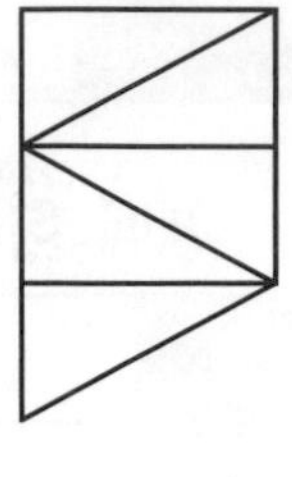 ____

16. 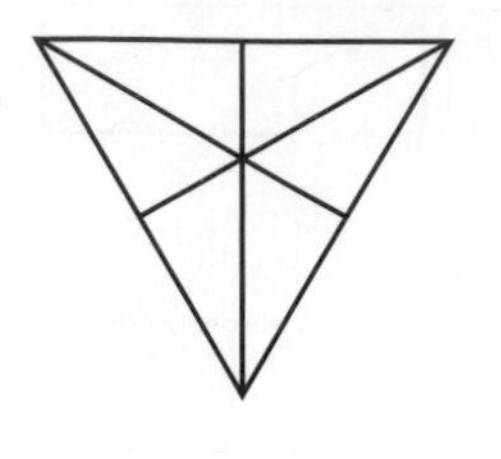 ____

17. 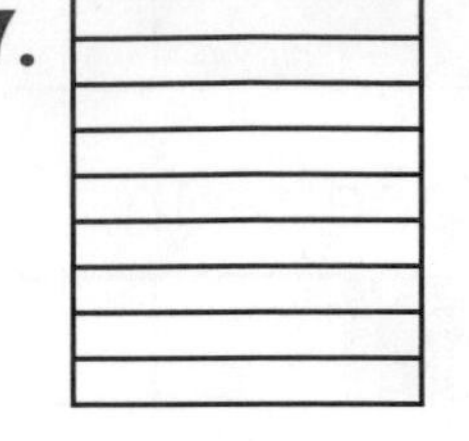 ____

18. 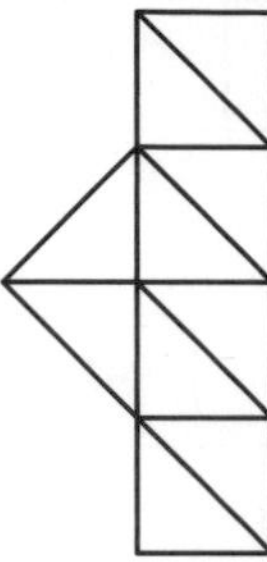 ____

19. 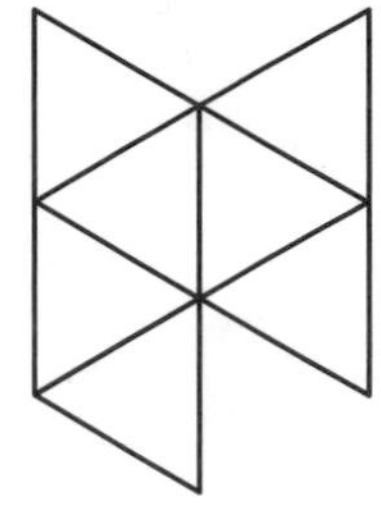 ____

20. 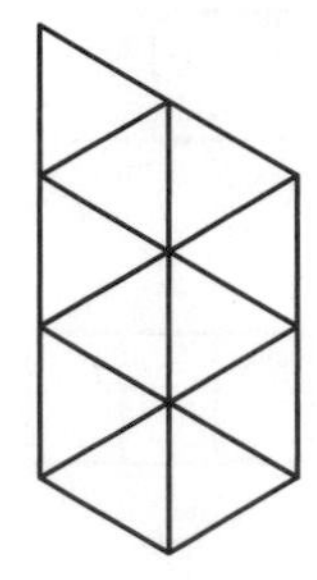 ____

21. 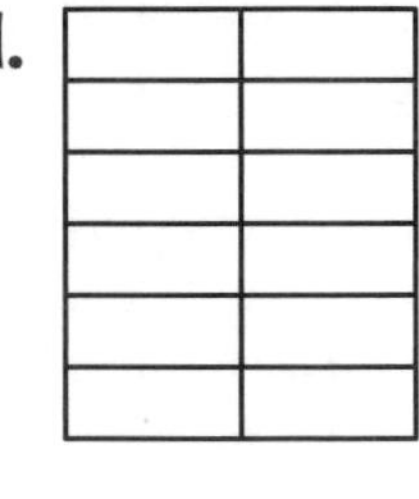 ____

Solve. Use a problem-solving strategy.

22. Debra's friends play a game with this spinner. The spinner has five equal parts. Two parts are red, two are yellow, and the rest is blue. What fractional part of the spinner is blue?

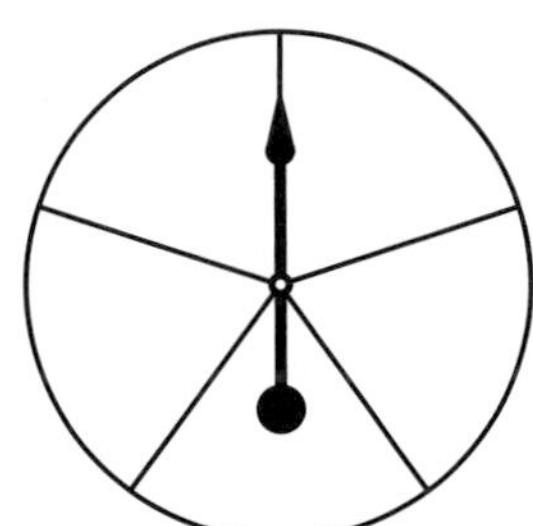

____

23. Leon gives Debra a shirt with this design. It has 9 red squares and 1 white square. What fractional part of the design is not red?

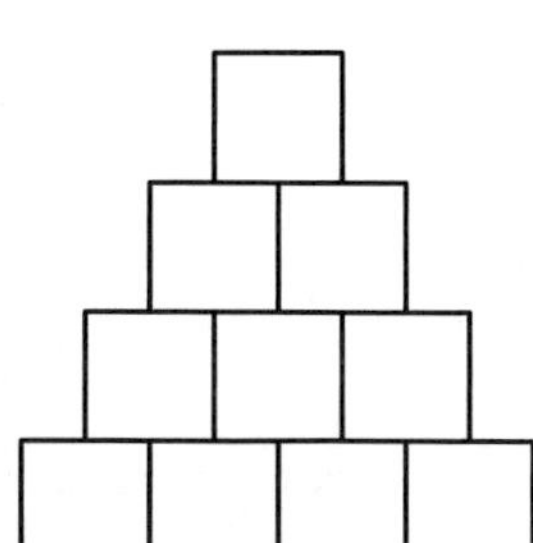

____

TEST PREPARATION

24. Fill in the circle next to the correct answer. Look at the circle. Which fraction tells what part of the circle is colored?

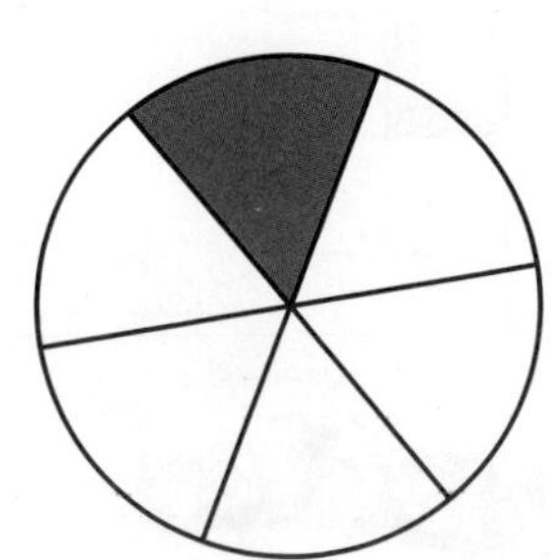

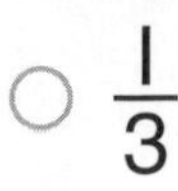 ○ $\frac{1}{3}$ 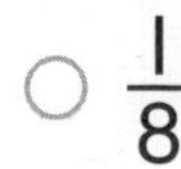 ○ $\frac{1}{8}$ 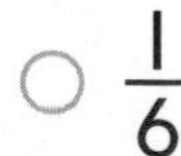 ○ $\frac{1}{6}$ ○ $\frac{1}{4}$

Math Alive at Home Draw squares and divide them into 3, 6, 9, 10, or 12 equal parts. Ask your child to color one part of each and to tell the fraction for the part colored.

Name ______________________________

Compare Fractions

Let's Learn!

Pat folds a sheet of paper into 3 equal parts. Jack folds a sheet of paper the same size as Pat's into 2 equal parts. They each color 1 equal part. Who colors the larger part?

The figure with fewer parts has larger parts.

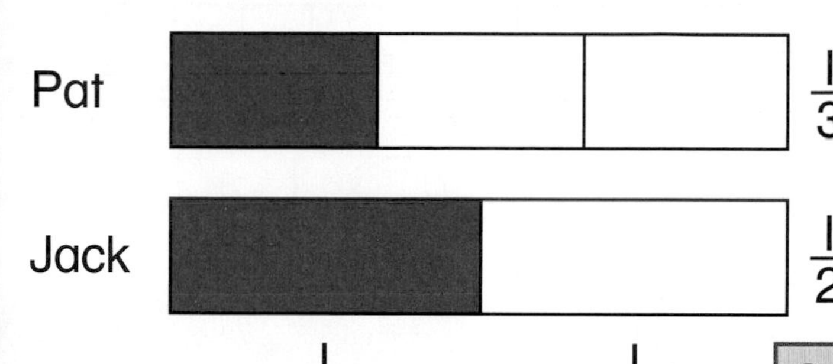

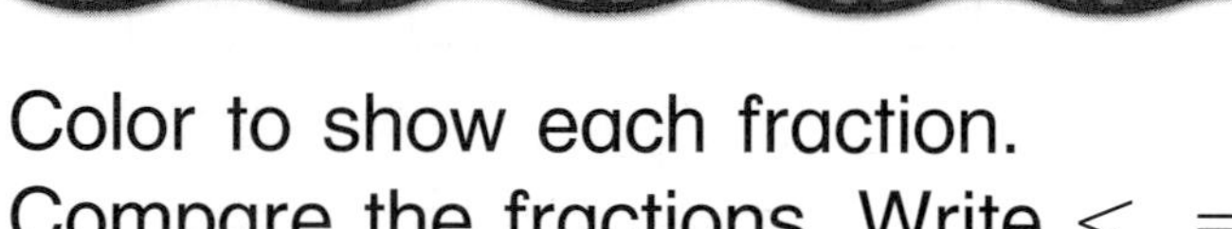

One half is greater than one third.

Jack colors the larger part.

Color to show each fraction.
Compare the fractions. Write <, =, or >.

1.

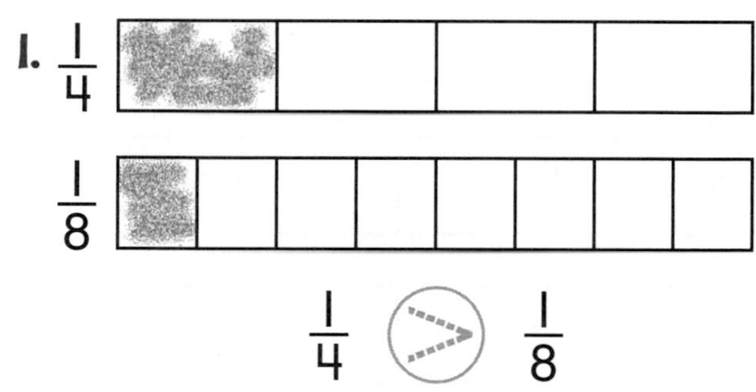

2.

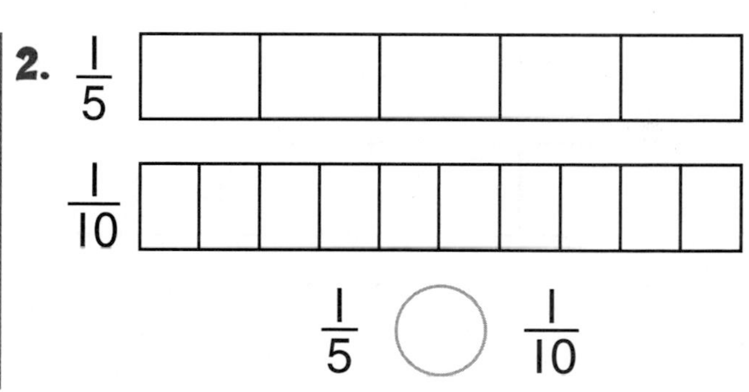

3.

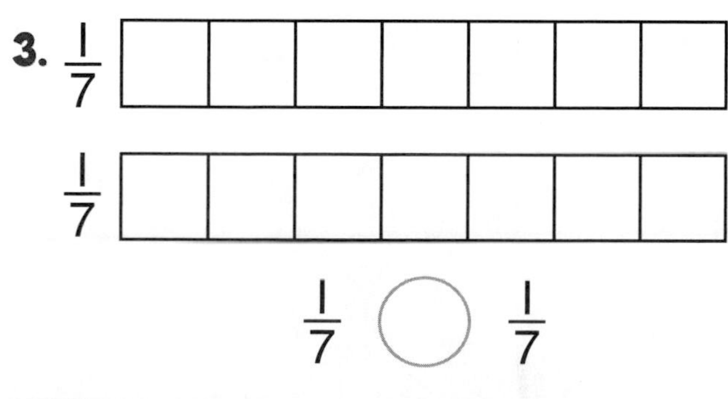

4.

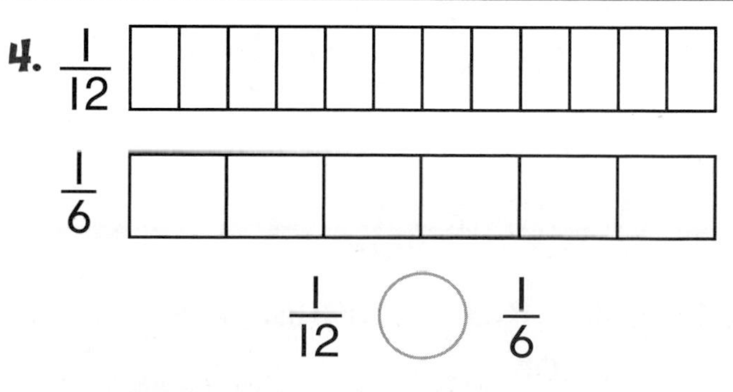

Write About It!

5. Explain why $\frac{1}{3}$ of a sheet of paper is greater than $\frac{1}{6}$ of a sheet of paper that is the same size.

Practice

Color to show each fraction.
Compare the fractions.
Write <, =, or >.

6. $\frac{1}{3}$ 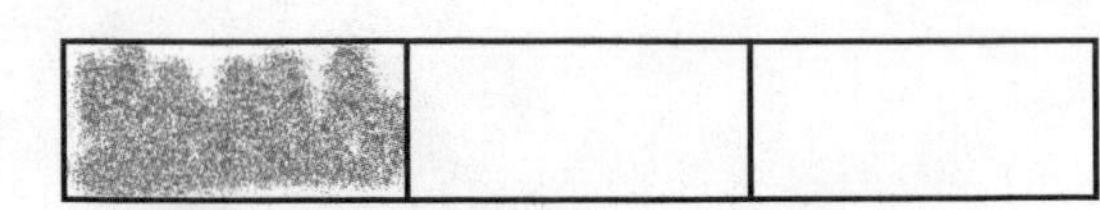

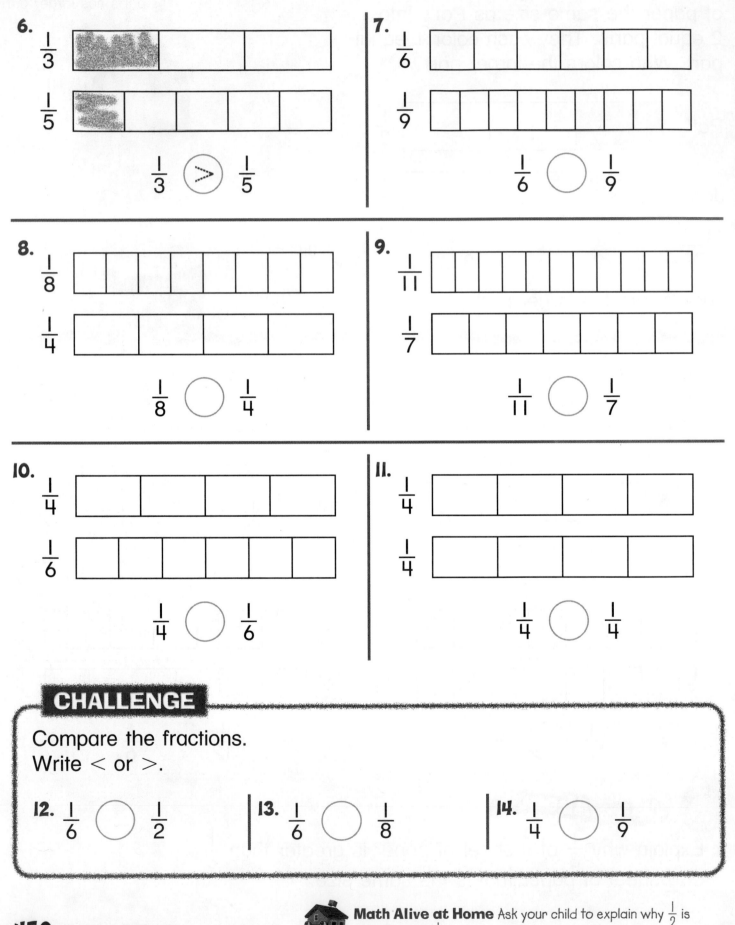

$\frac{1}{5}$ 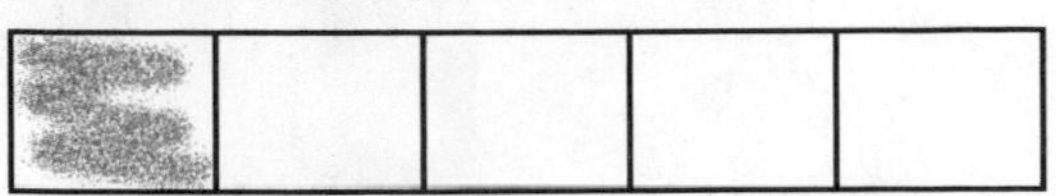

$\frac{1}{3}$ (>) $\frac{1}{5}$

7. $\frac{1}{6}$ 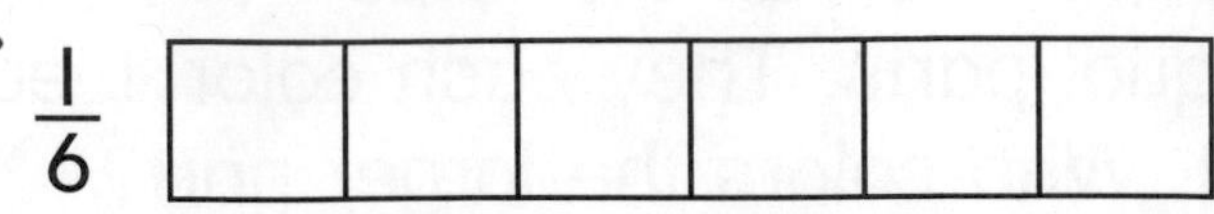

$\frac{1}{9}$ 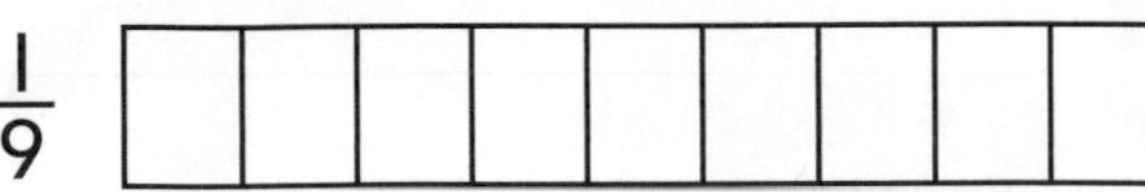

$\frac{1}{6}$ ◯ $\frac{1}{9}$

8. $\frac{1}{8}$

$\frac{1}{4}$

$\frac{1}{8}$ ◯ $\frac{1}{4}$

9. $\frac{1}{11}$ 

$\frac{1}{7}$

$\frac{1}{11}$  $\frac{1}{7}$

10. $\frac{1}{4}$

$\frac{1}{6}$ 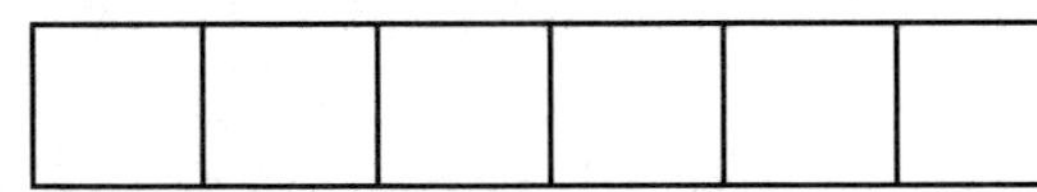

$\frac{1}{4}$ ◯ $\frac{1}{6}$

11. $\frac{1}{4}$ 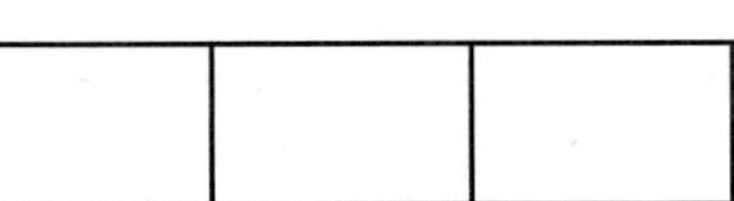

$\frac{1}{4}$

$\frac{1}{4}$  $\frac{1}{4}$

CHALLENGE

Compare the fractions.
Write < or >.

12. 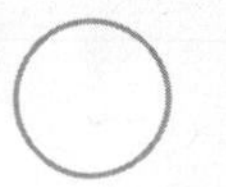 $\frac{1}{6}$ ◯ $\frac{1}{2}$

13. $\frac{1}{6}$ ◯ $\frac{1}{8}$

14. $\frac{1}{4}$ ◯ $\frac{1}{9}$

Math Alive at Home Ask your child to explain why $\frac{1}{2}$ is greater than $\frac{1}{8}$.

Name ______________________________

Let's Learn!

Order the fractions $\frac{1}{2}$, $\frac{1}{4}$, and $\frac{1}{3}$ from least to greatest.
First compare the fractions, then order them.

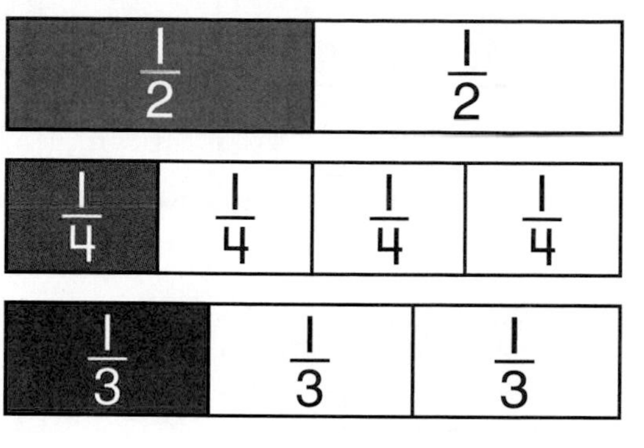

$\frac{1}{4}$, $\frac{1}{3}$, $\frac{1}{2}$
least to greatest

You can use fraction bars to model each fraction.

Model each with fraction bars.
Then color to show each fraction.
Write the fractions in order from least to greatest.

1. $\frac{1}{6}$ | $\frac{1}{6}$ | $\frac{1}{6}$ | $\frac{1}{6}$ | $\frac{1}{6}$ | $\frac{1}{6}$ | $\frac{1}{6}$ |

$\frac{1}{12}$ | $\frac{1}{12}$ | $\frac{1}{12}$ | $\frac{1}{12}$ | $\frac{1}{12}$ | $\frac{1}{12}$ | $\frac{1}{12}$ | $\frac{1}{12}$ | $\frac{1}{12}$ | $\frac{1}{12}$ | $\frac{1}{12}$ | $\frac{1}{12}$ | $\frac{1}{12}$ |

$\frac{1}{4}$ | $\frac{1}{4}$ | $\frac{1}{4}$ | $\frac{1}{4}$ | $\frac{1}{4}$ |

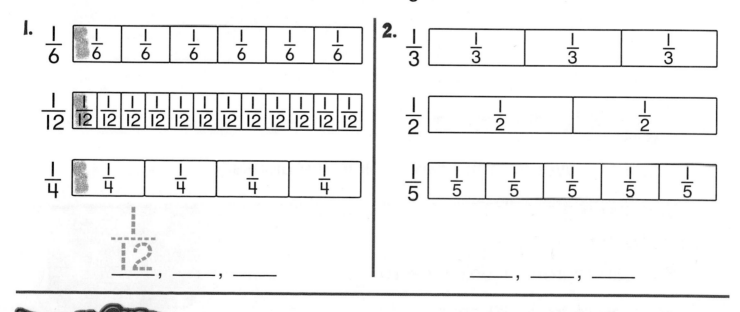

$\frac{1}{12}$, ____, ____

2. $\frac{1}{3}$ | $\frac{1}{3}$ | $\frac{1}{3}$ | $\frac{1}{3}$ |

$\frac{1}{2}$ | $\frac{1}{2}$ | $\frac{1}{2}$ |

$\frac{1}{5}$ | $\frac{1}{5}$ | $\frac{1}{5}$ | $\frac{1}{5}$ | $\frac{1}{5}$ | $\frac{1}{5}$ |

____, ____, ____

Talk It Over

3. Explain how you can order fractions mentally without coloring fraction bars.

Practice

Model each with fraction bars.
Then color to show each fraction.
Write the fractions in order from greatest to least.

4.

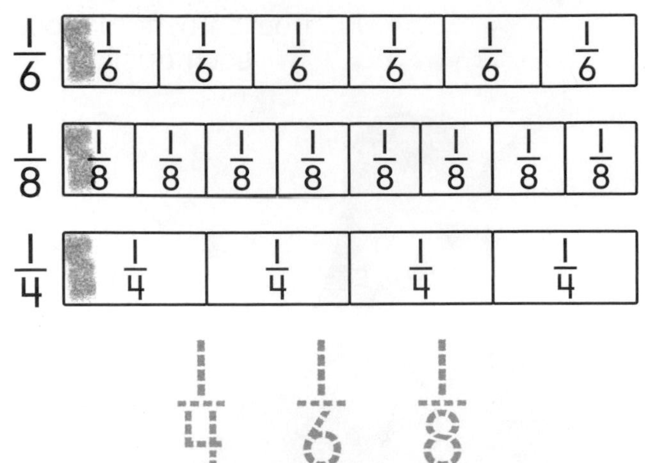

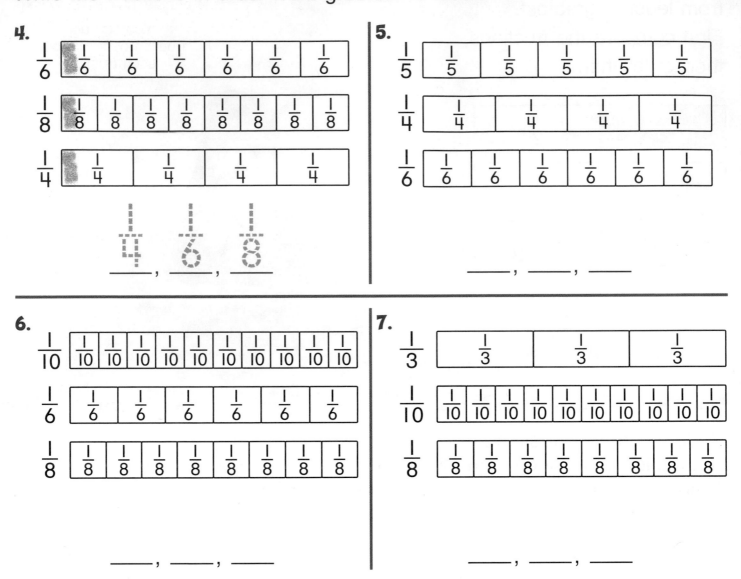

$\frac{1}{4}$, $\frac{1}{6}$, $\frac{1}{8}$

5.

$\frac{1}{5}$	$\frac{1}{5}$	$\frac{1}{5}$	$\frac{1}{5}$	$\frac{1}{5}$	$\frac{1}{5}$

$\frac{1}{4}$	$\frac{1}{4}$	$\frac{1}{4}$	$\frac{1}{4}$	$\frac{1}{4}$

$\frac{1}{6}$	$\frac{1}{6}$	$\frac{1}{6}$	$\frac{1}{6}$	$\frac{1}{6}$	$\frac{1}{6}$	$\frac{1}{6}$

____, ____, ____

6.

$\frac{1}{10}$	$\frac{1}{10}$	$\frac{1}{10}$	$\frac{1}{10}$	$\frac{1}{10}$	$\frac{1}{10}$	$\frac{1}{10}$	$\frac{1}{10}$	$\frac{1}{10}$	$\frac{1}{10}$	$\frac{1}{10}$

$\frac{1}{6}$	$\frac{1}{6}$	$\frac{1}{6}$	$\frac{1}{6}$	$\frac{1}{6}$	$\frac{1}{6}$	$\frac{1}{6}$

$\frac{1}{8}$	$\frac{1}{8}$	$\frac{1}{8}$	$\frac{1}{8}$	$\frac{1}{8}$	$\frac{1}{8}$	$\frac{1}{8}$	$\frac{1}{8}$	$\frac{1}{8}$

____, ____, ____

7.

$\frac{1}{3}$	$\frac{1}{3}$	$\frac{1}{3}$	$\frac{1}{3}$

$\frac{1}{10}$	$\frac{1}{10}$	$\frac{1}{10}$	$\frac{1}{10}$	$\frac{1}{10}$	$\frac{1}{10}$	$\frac{1}{10}$	$\frac{1}{10}$	$\frac{1}{10}$	$\frac{1}{10}$	$\frac{1}{10}$

$\frac{1}{8}$	$\frac{1}{8}$	$\frac{1}{8}$	$\frac{1}{8}$	$\frac{1}{8}$	$\frac{1}{8}$	$\frac{1}{8}$	$\frac{1}{8}$	$\frac{1}{8}$

____, ____, ____

DO YOU REMEMBER?

Use the Math Words in the box to fill in the blanks.

8. You can regroup 1 __________ as 10 tens.

9. You can regroup 1 dollar as 10 __________.

10. You can regroup 10 ones as 1 __________.

11. One hundred cents equals one __________.

Math Alive at Home Ask your child to explain how he/she decided the order of the fractions in one of the exercises on this page.

Name ____________________

Other Fractions

Let's Learn!

Fractions can name more than one equal part.

Remember:
The top number tells how many equal parts are colored.
The bottom number tells how many equal parts are in the whole.

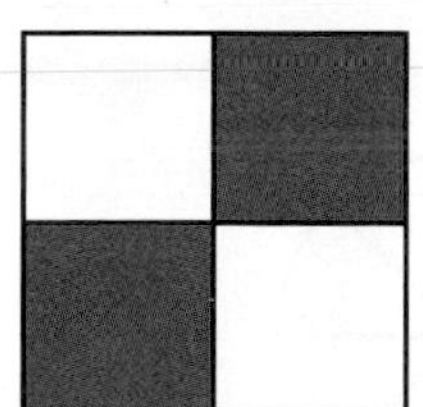

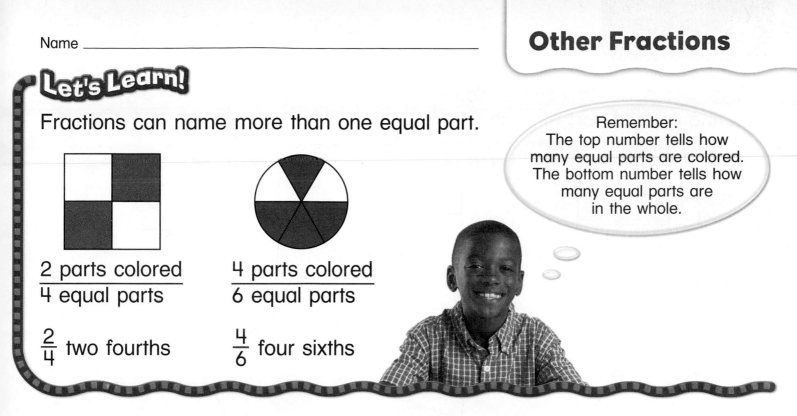

$\frac{\text{2 parts colored}}{\text{4 equal parts}}$

$\frac{2}{4}$ two fourths

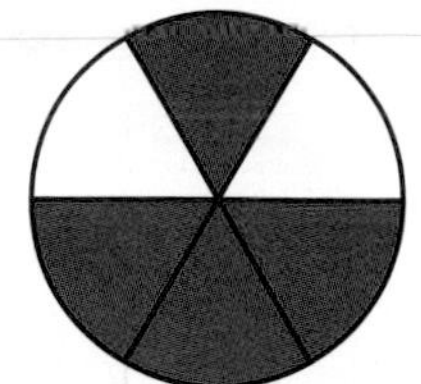

$\frac{\text{4 parts colored}}{\text{6 equal parts}}$

$\frac{4}{6}$ four sixths

Write the fraction for the colored part of each whole.

1. 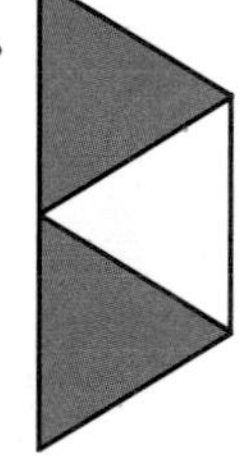 $\frac{2}{3}$

2. 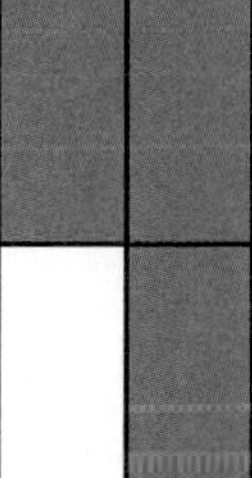 ____

3. 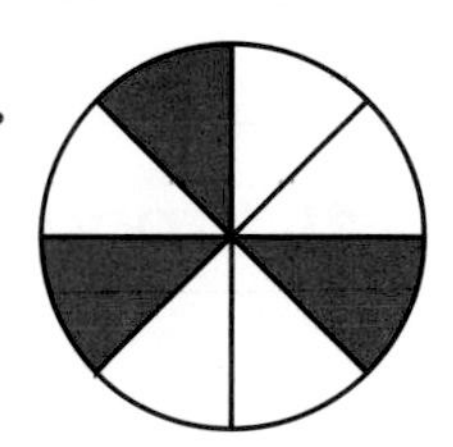 ____

4. 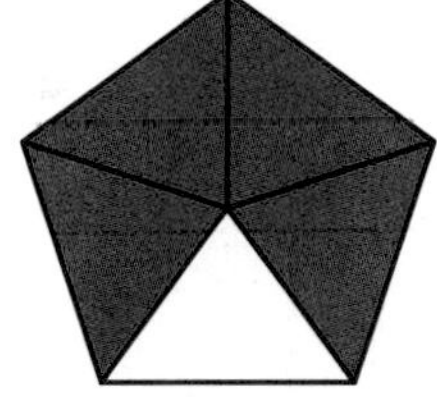 ____

5. 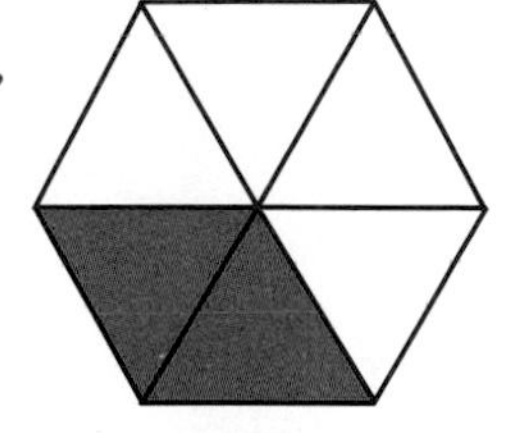 ____

6. 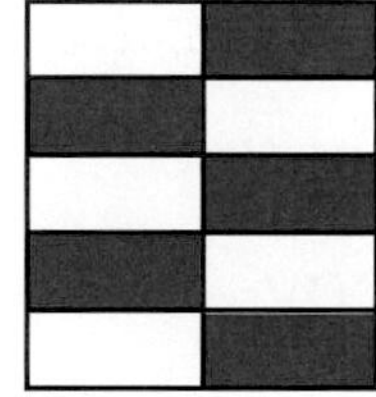 ____

7. 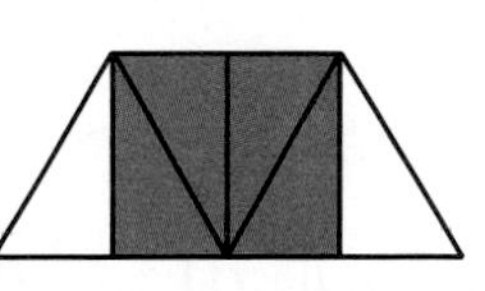 ____

8. 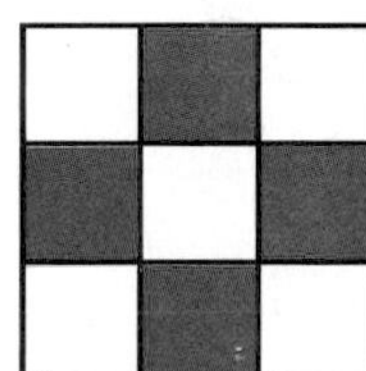 ____

9.  ____

10.  ____

11. 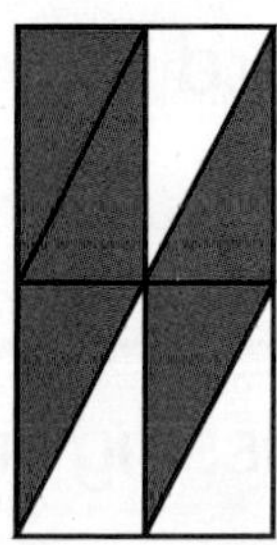 ____

12.  ____

13. Explain how you would show $\frac{7}{8}$ of a rectangle.

Practice

Color the parts. Write the fraction for the colored part of each whole.

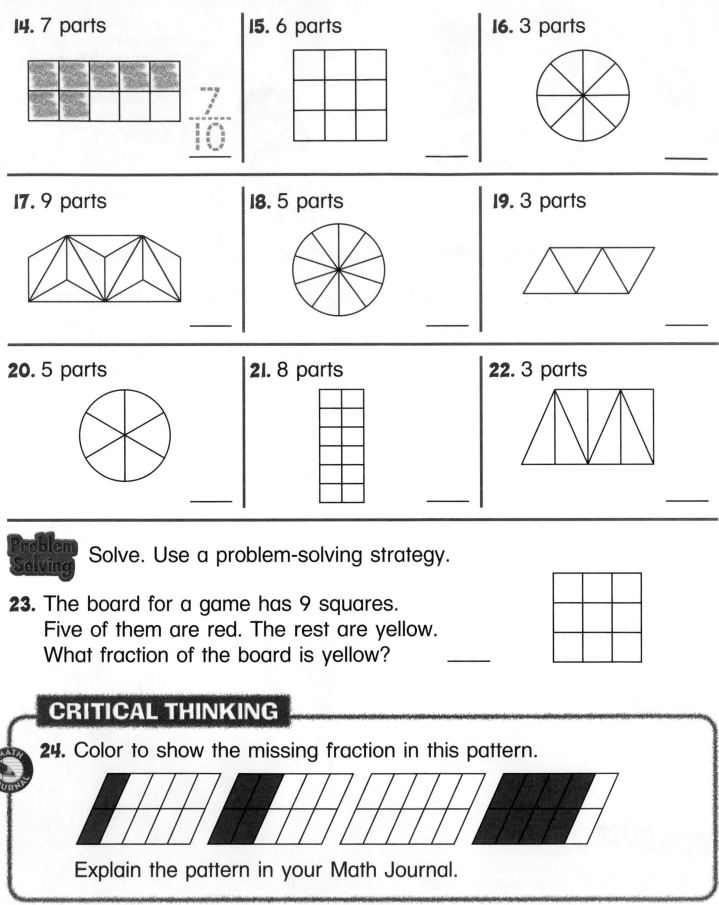

14. 7 parts

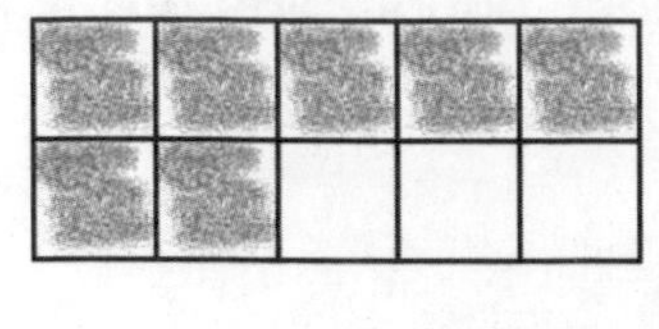

$\frac{7}{10}$

15. 6 parts

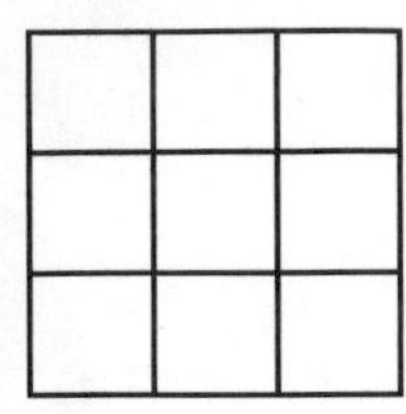

___

16. 3 parts

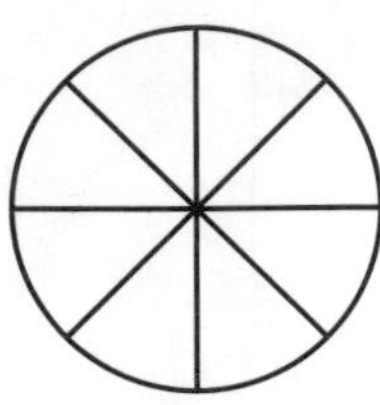

___

17. 9 parts

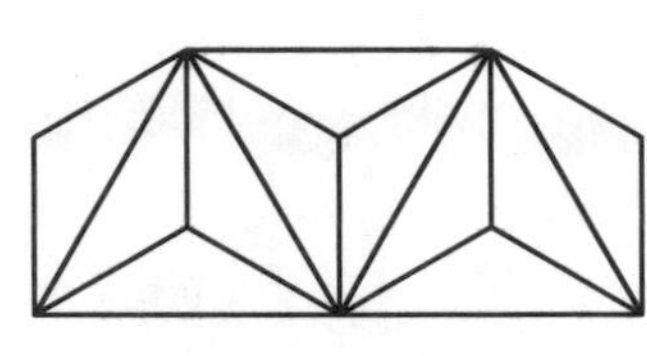

___

18. 5 parts

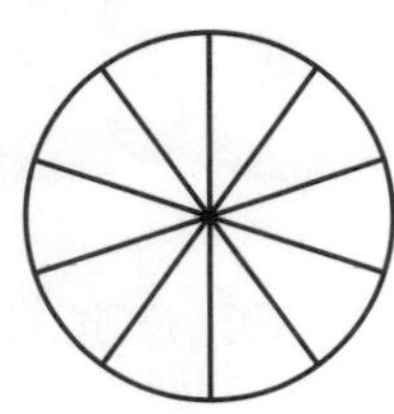

___

19. 3 parts

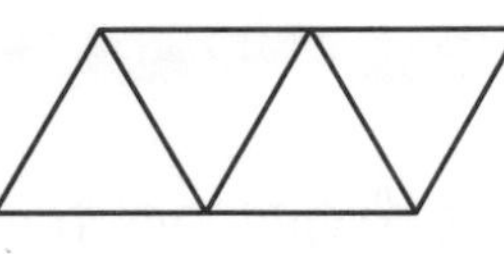

___

20. 5 parts

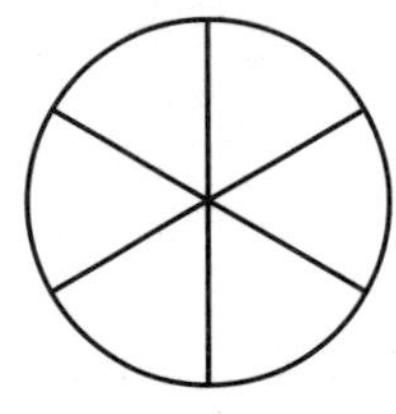

___

21. 8 parts

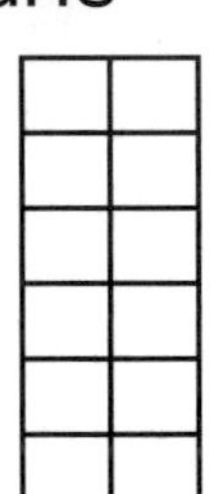

___

22. 3 parts

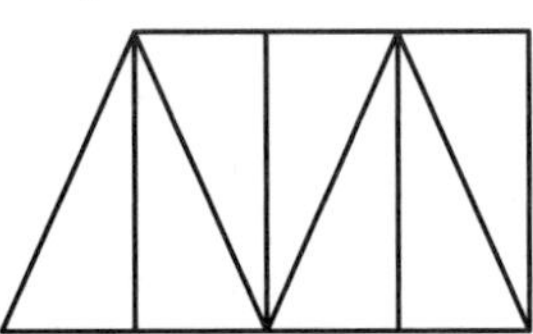

___

Solve. Use a problem-solving strategy.

23. The board for a game has 9 squares. Five of them are red. The rest are yellow. What fraction of the board is yellow? ___

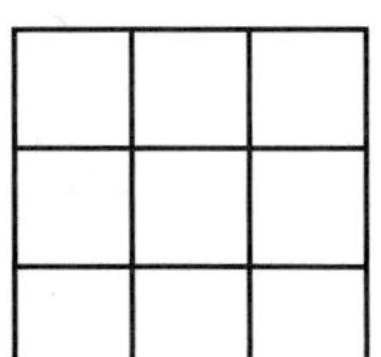

CRITICAL THINKING

24. Color to show the missing fraction in this pattern.

Explain the pattern in your Math Journal.

Math Alive at Home Choose several exercises above and ask your child to tell you the fraction for the parts that are not colored.

Name ____________________

Check Your Progress
Lessons 1-5

TEST PREPARATION

Listen to your teacher read the directions.
Fill in the circle under the correct answer.

1.

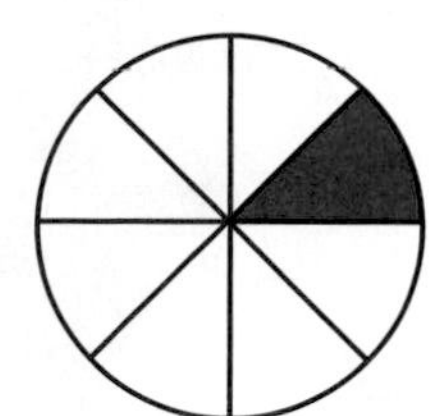

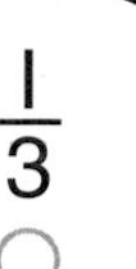

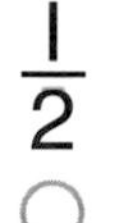

$\frac{1}{4}$ ○ $\frac{1}{3}$ ○ $\frac{1}{8}$ ○ $\frac{1}{2}$ ○

2.

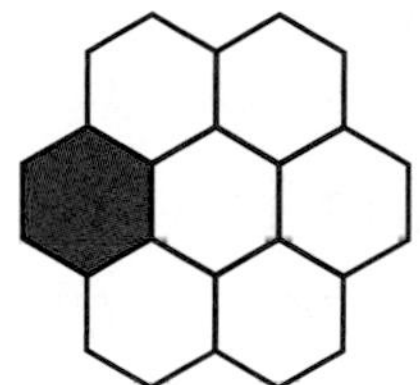

$\frac{1}{6}$ ○ $\frac{1}{9}$ ○ $\frac{1}{8}$ ○ $\frac{1}{7}$ ○

3.

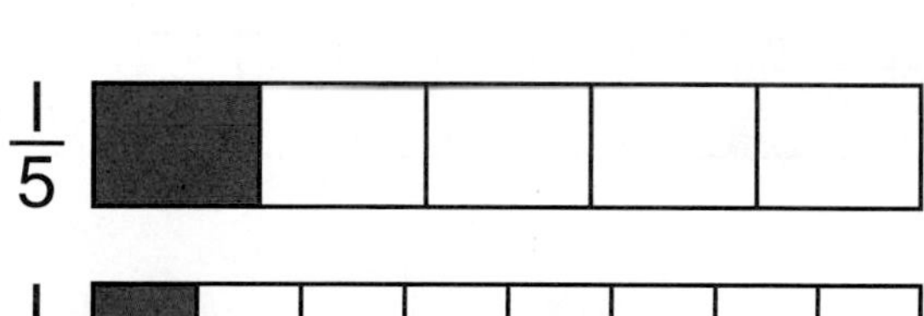

$\frac{1}{5}$

$\frac{1}{8}$

$\frac{1}{5}$ ○ $\frac{1}{8}$

$<$ ○ $=$ ○ $>$ ○

4.

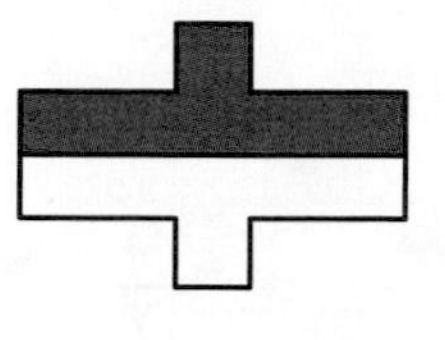

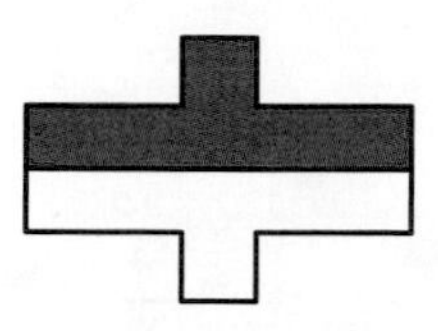

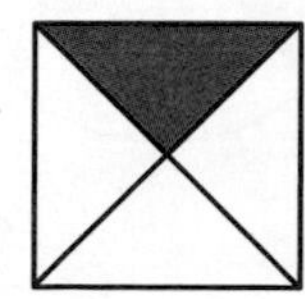

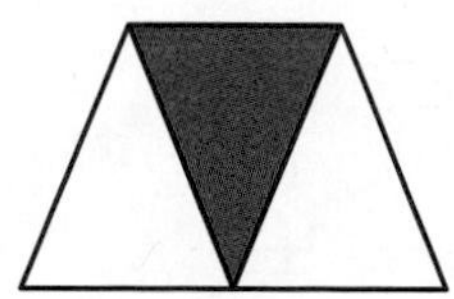

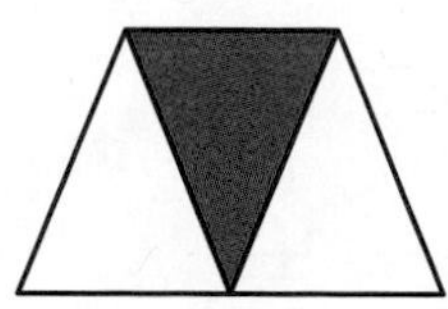

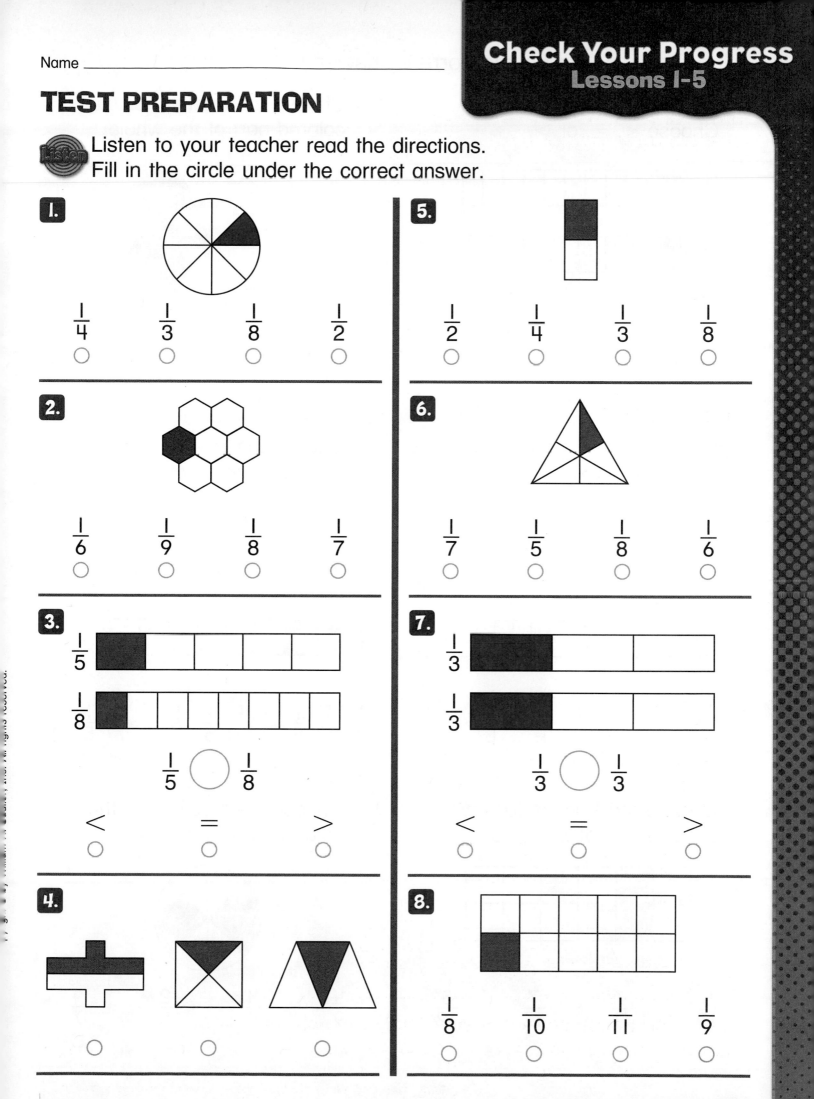

○ ○ ○

5.

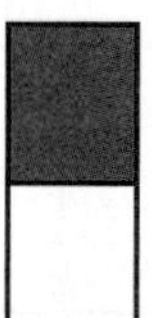

$\frac{1}{2}$ ○ $\frac{1}{4}$ ○ $\frac{1}{3}$ ○ $\frac{1}{8}$ ○

6.

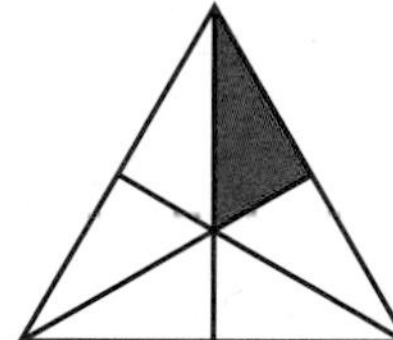

$\frac{1}{7}$ ○ $\frac{1}{5}$ ○ $\frac{1}{8}$ ○ $\frac{1}{6}$ ○

7.

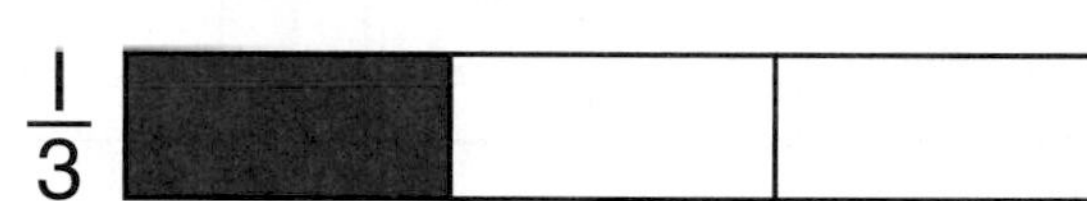

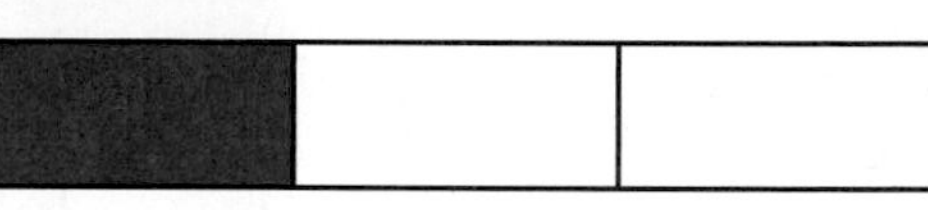

$\frac{1}{3}$

$\frac{1}{3}$

$\frac{1}{3}$ ○ $\frac{1}{3}$

$<$ ○ $=$ ○ $>$ ○

8.

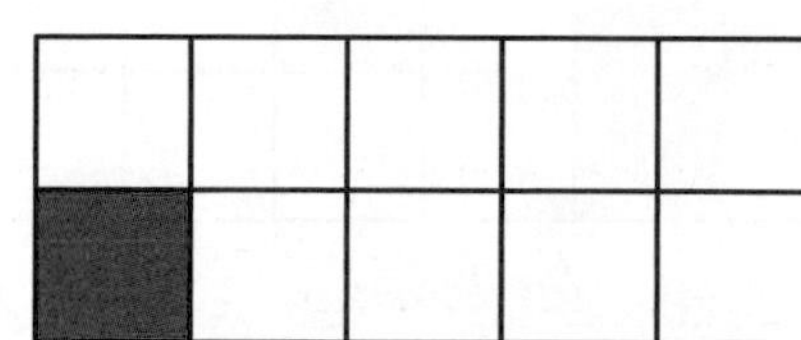

$\frac{1}{8}$ ○ $\frac{1}{10}$ ○ $\frac{1}{11}$ ○ $\frac{1}{9}$ ○

Fill in the circle under the correct answer.

9. Compare the fractions.
Choose <, =, or >.

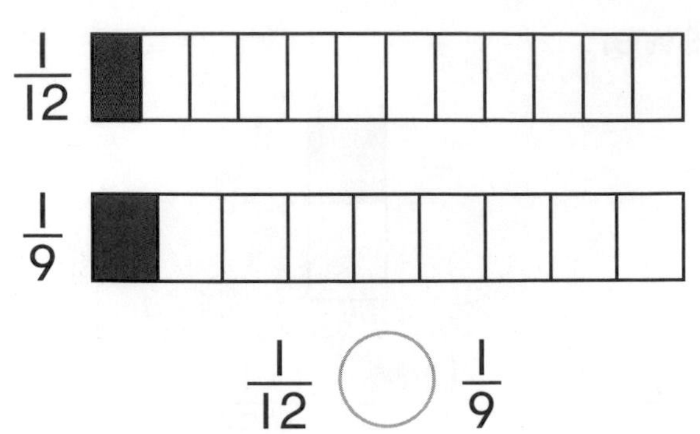

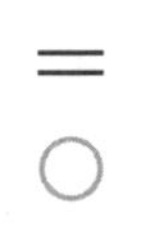

10. Choose the fractions in order from greatest to least.

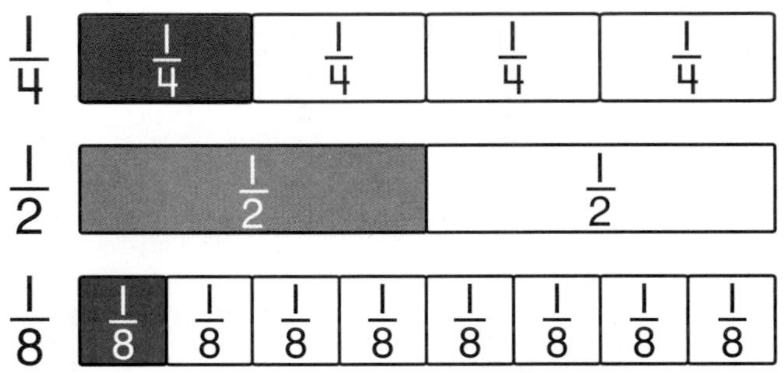

$\frac{1}{2}, \frac{1}{4}, \frac{1}{8}$ ○ $\frac{1}{8}, \frac{1}{2}, \frac{1}{4}$ ○ $\frac{1}{8}, \frac{1}{4}, \frac{1}{2}$ ○

11. Choose the fraction for the colored part of the whole.

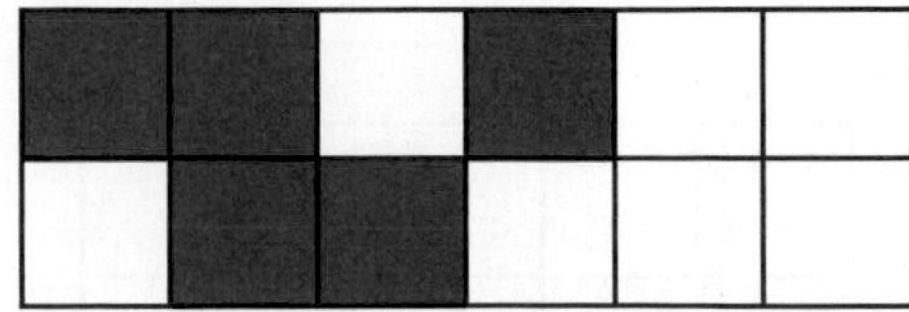

$\frac{5}{10}$ ○ $\frac{7}{11}$ ○ $\frac{7}{12}$ ○ $\frac{5}{12}$ ○

12. Choose the fraction for the colored part of the whole.

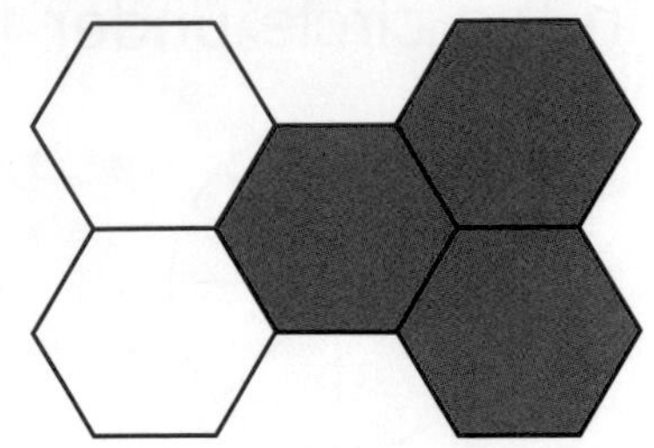

$\frac{4}{5}$ ○ $\frac{2}{5}$ ○ $\frac{3}{5}$ ○ $\frac{3}{7}$ ○

13. Choose the fractions in order from least to greatest.

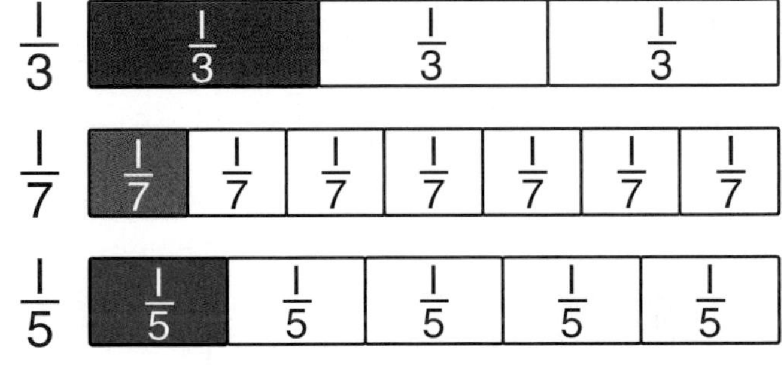

$\frac{1}{3}, \frac{1}{7}, \frac{1}{5}$ ○ $\frac{1}{3}, \frac{1}{5}, \frac{1}{7}$ ○ $\frac{1}{7}, \frac{1}{5}, \frac{1}{3}$ ○

14. Choose the fraction for the colored part of the whole.

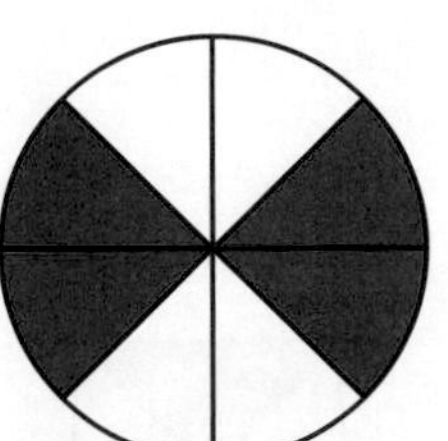

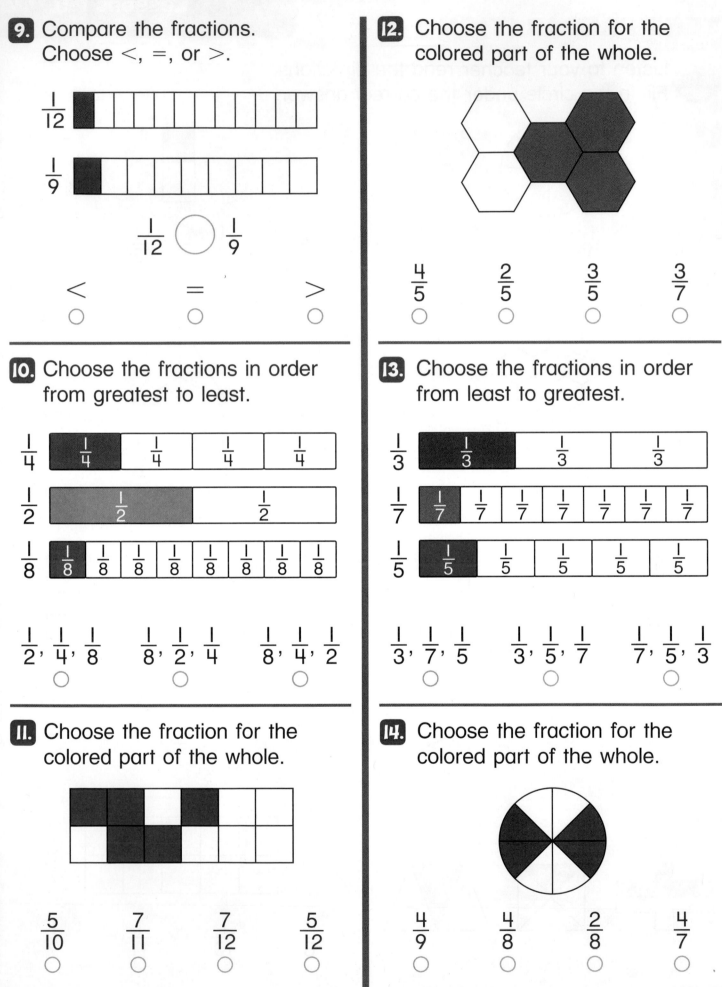

$\frac{4}{9}$ ○ $\frac{4}{8}$ ○ $\frac{2}{8}$ ○ $\frac{4}{7}$ ○

Name ______________________________

Algebra
Fractions Equal to 1

Let's Learn!

When you count all the equal parts, you make 1.

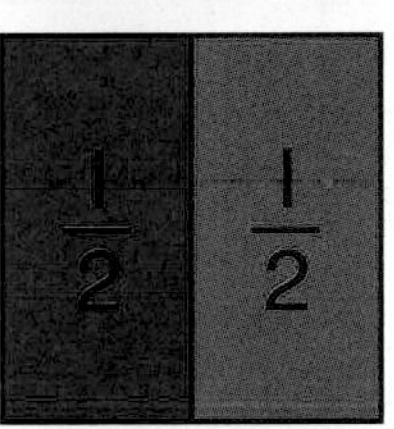

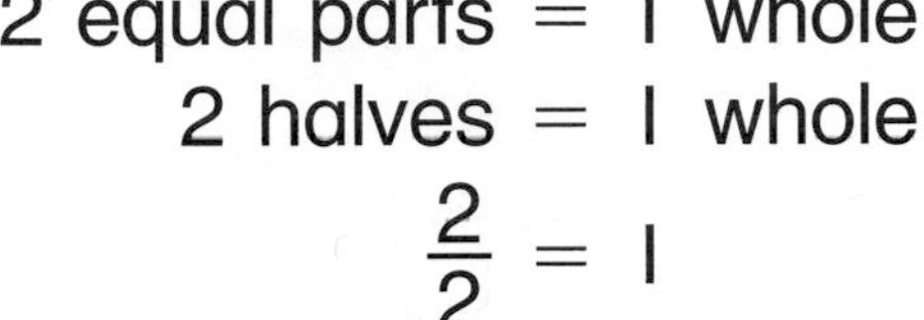

$\frac{2}{2} = 1$

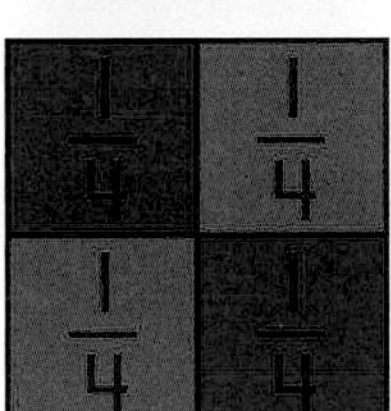

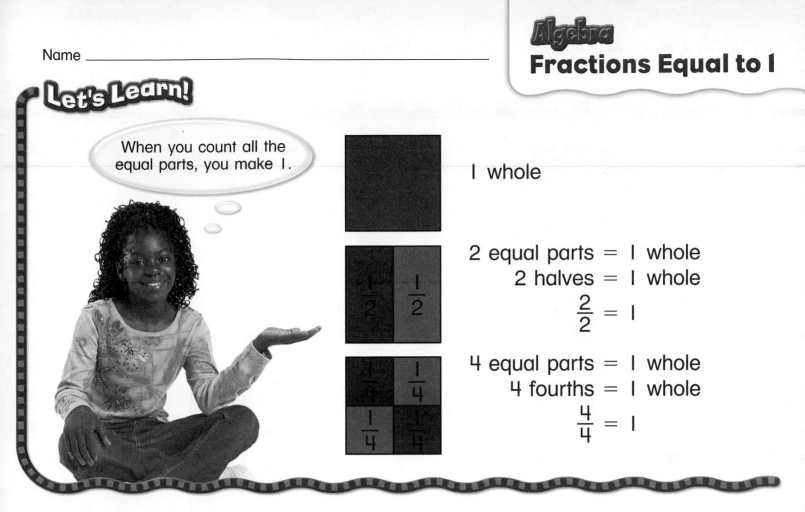

4 equal parts = 1 whole
4 fourths = 1 whole
$\frac{4}{4} = 1$

Count the parts colored.
Write a fraction for each whole.

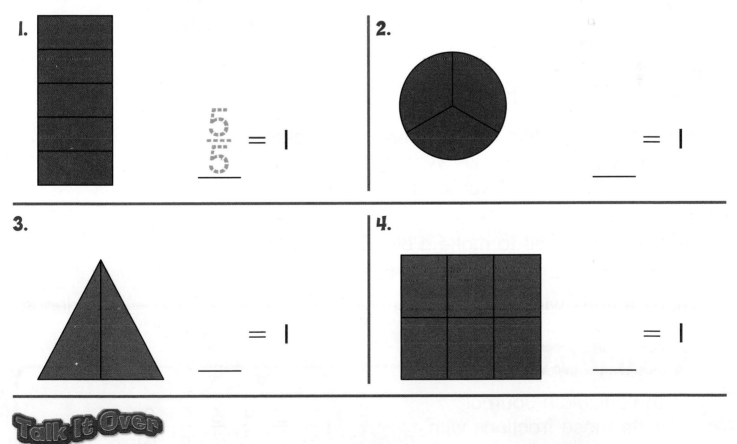

1. 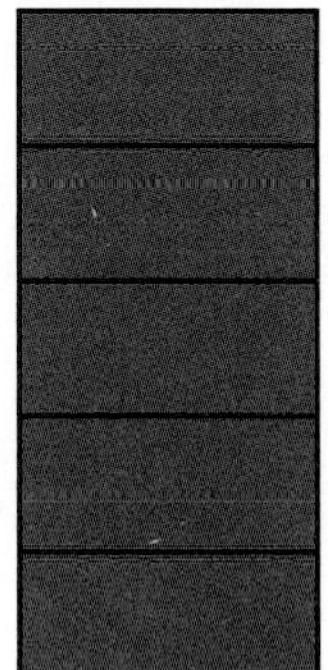

$\frac{5}{5} = 1$

2. 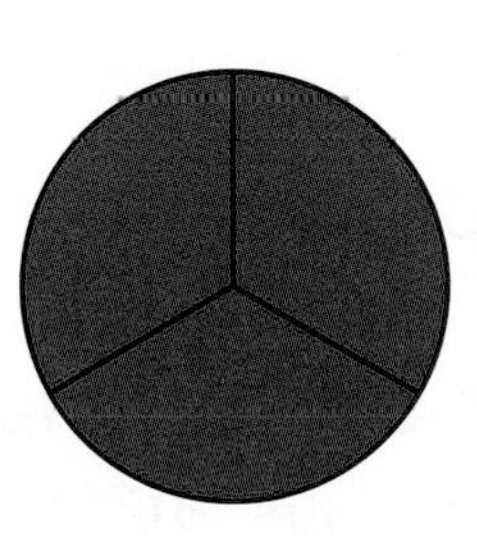

$\frac{\_\_}{\_\_} = 1$

3. 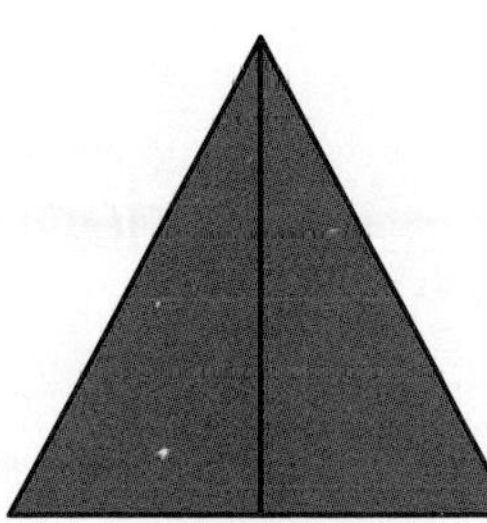

$\frac{\_\_}{\_\_} = 1$

4. 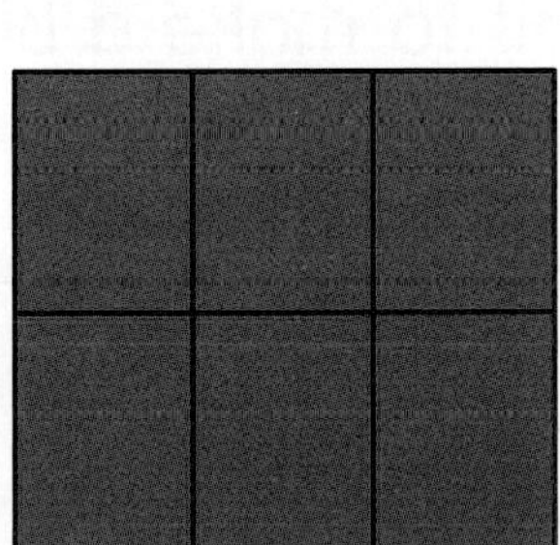

$\frac{\_\_}{\_\_} = 1$

Talk It Over

5. Tell which figure does not show $\frac{3}{3}$ and explain why.

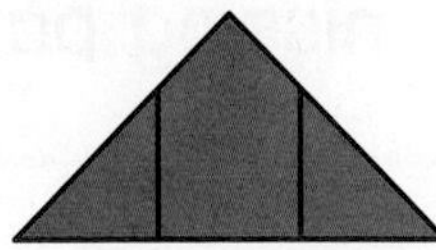

Copyright © by William H. Sadlier, Inc. All rights reserved.

Practice

Color and write the fraction to show one whole.

6.

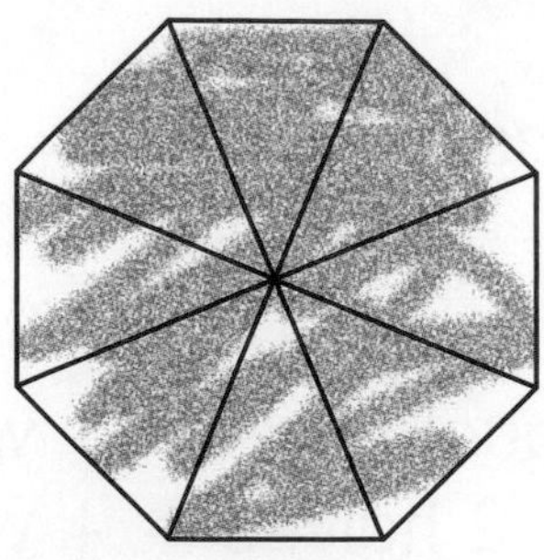

$\frac{8}{8}$

How many eighths are in one whole? 8

7.

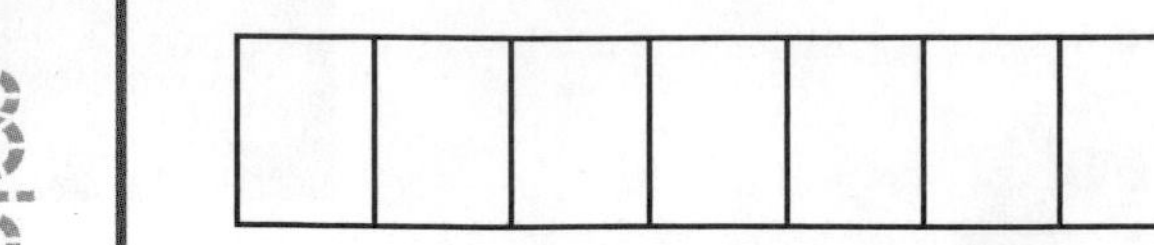

____

How many sevenths are in one whole? ____

8.

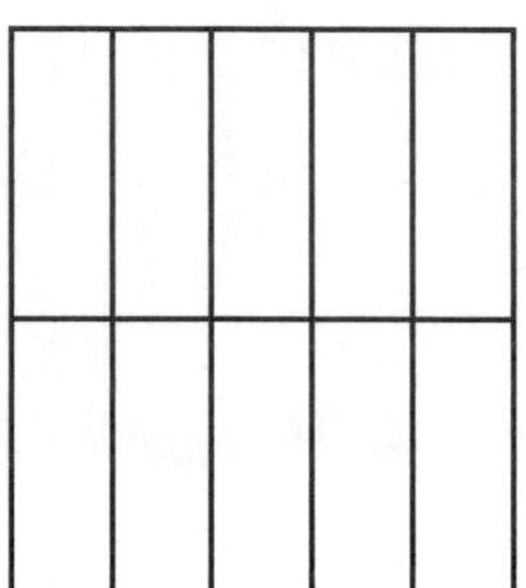

____

How many tenths are in one whole? ____

9.

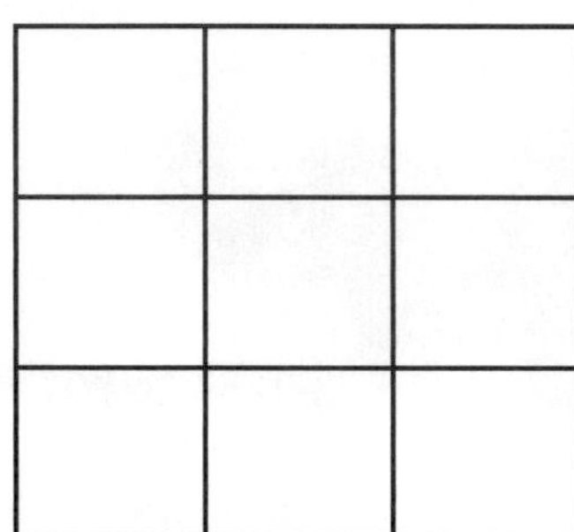

____

How many ninths are in one whole? ____

Solve. Use a problem-solving strategy.

10. Eight children make a quilt. They each make an equal part of the quilt. What fractional part of the quilt does each child make? ____

11. Jay's friends want to make a birthday banner. Each friend will make $\frac{1}{4}$ of the banner. How many friends will make the banner? ____ friends

MATH JOURNAL

12. In your Math Journal, write these fractions with their missing parts.

$1 = \frac{2}{2}, \frac{4}{?}, \frac{6}{?}, \frac{?}{8}, \frac{?}{10}$

Math Alive at Home Cut a sandwich into 2 equal pieces and ask your child to name the fraction for the whole sandwich. ($\frac{2}{2}$)

Name ______________________________

Estimate Fractions

Let's Learn!

You can use fractions to estimate about how much.

About how much of each package is blue?

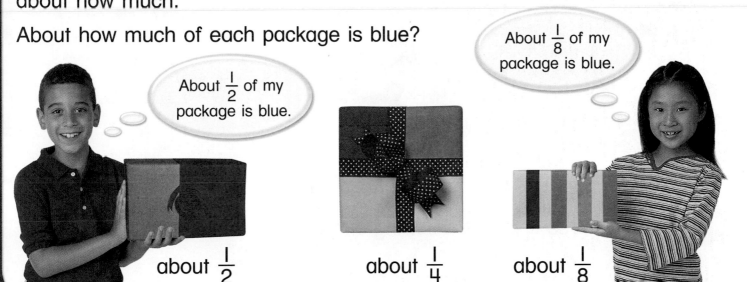

about $\frac{1}{2}$

about $\frac{1}{4}$

about $\frac{1}{8}$

Write **about $\frac{1}{2}$**, **about $\frac{1}{4}$**, or **about $\frac{1}{8}$** to estimate the colored part of the whole.

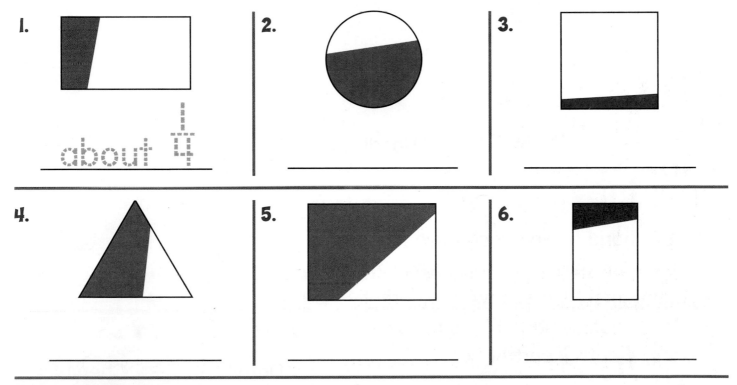

1. 

about $\frac{1}{4}$

2. 

____

3. 

____

4. 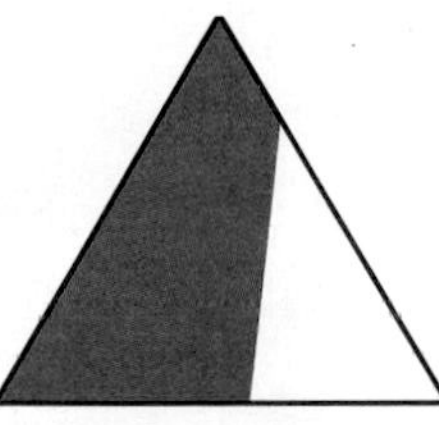

____

5. 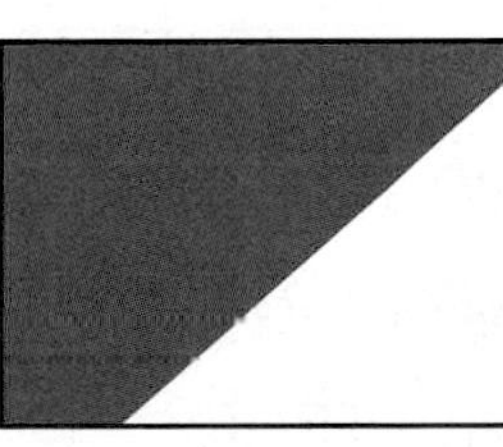

____

6. 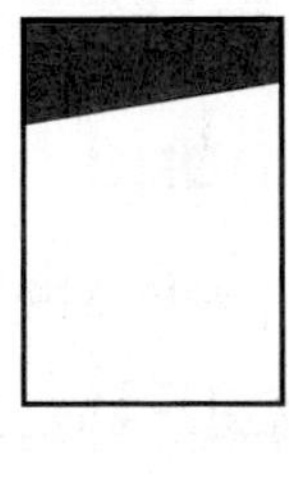

____

Talk It Over

7. Suppose about one half of a floor is blue and about one fourth of the floor is white. Is the floor more blue or more white? Explain.

Copyright © by William H. Sadlier, Inc. All rights reserved.

Practice

Write **about** $\frac{1}{2}$, **about** $\frac{1}{4}$, or **about** $\frac{1}{8}$ to estimate the colored part of the whole.

8. 
about $\frac{1}{4}$

9. 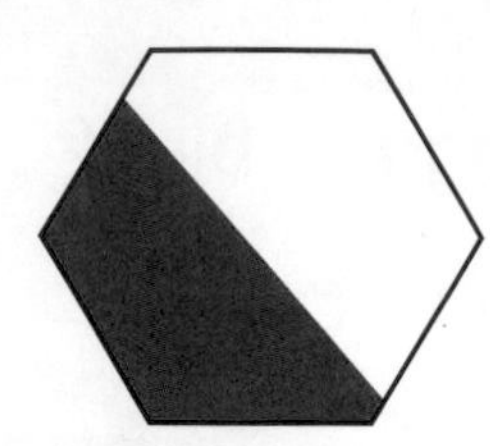
____

10. 
____

Solve. Use a problem-solving strategy.

11. Sarah pours about $\frac{1}{2}$ glass of juice, Terry pours about $\frac{1}{4}$ glass, and Randi pours about $\frac{1}{8}$ glass. Label each glass with a fraction. Draw lines to match the girls with their glasses of juice.

Sarah Randi Terry

CRITICAL THINKING

12. Darryl and Cheryl each have a sandwich about the same size. Their Mom cuts each sandwich differently. Darryl eats 2 parts of his sandwich. Cheryl eats 1 part of hers.

They each have about $\frac{1}{2}$ of their sandwich left.

Draw to show how each sandwich was cut.

Darryl

Cheryl

Math Alive at Home Pour a glass one fourth full of water and ask your child about how full the glass is. Repeat, filling the glass to one half full.

Name ______________________________

Algebra

Equal Fractions of a Whole

Let's Learn!

Fractions that name the same part of a whole are called **equal fractions**.

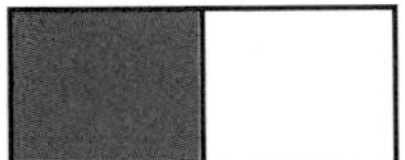 1 of 2 equal parts equals $\frac{1}{2}$.

 2 of 4 equal parts equals $\frac{2}{4}$.

$$\frac{1}{2} = \frac{2}{4}$$

$\frac{1}{2}$ and $\frac{2}{4}$ are equal fractions.

Count the number of parts in each whole. Then count how many parts are colored. Write the equal fractions.

1. 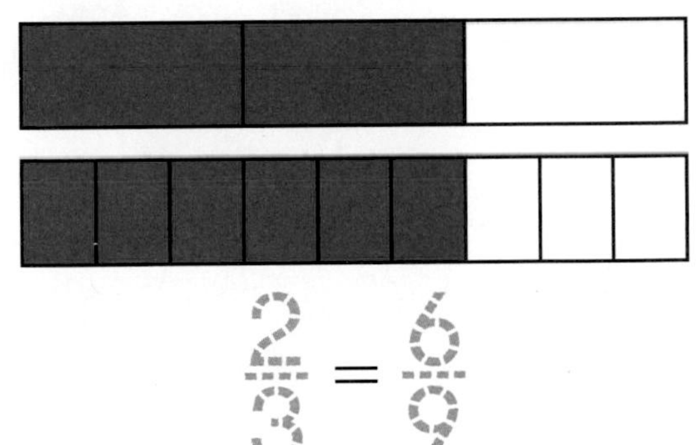

$\frac{2}{3} = \frac{6}{9}$

2. 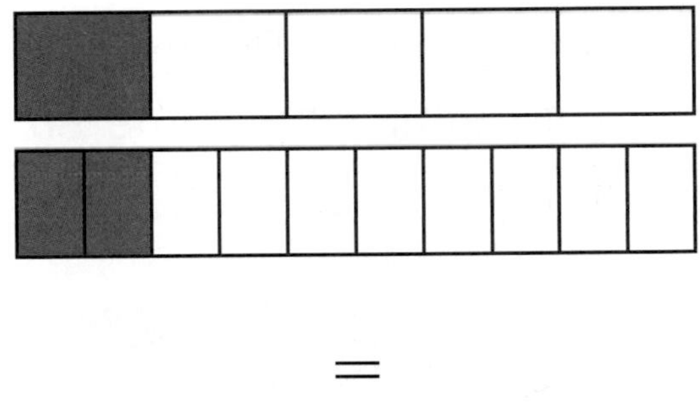

___ = ___

3. 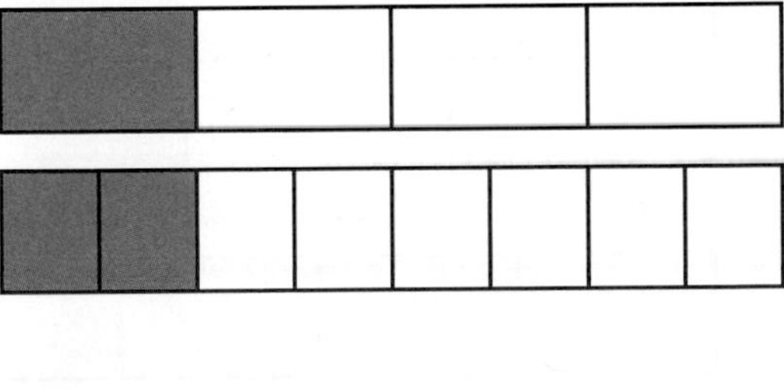

___ = ___

4. 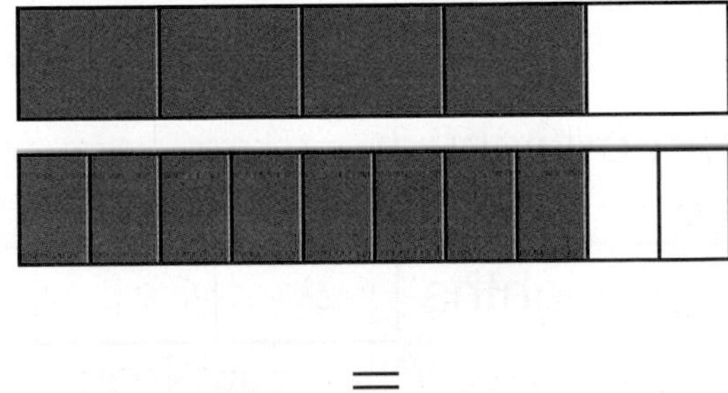

___ = ___

Talk It Over

5. Explain what equal fractions are.

Copyright © by William H. Sadlier, Inc. All rights reserved.

Practice

Write the equal fractions.

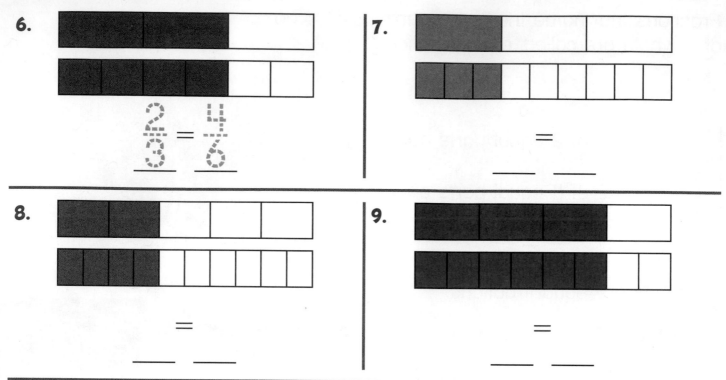

6. $\frac{2}{3} = \frac{4}{6}$

7. ___ = ___

8. ___ = ___

9. ___ = ___

Problem Solving Solve. Use a problem-solving strategy.

10. Joan cut a pan of gelatin into thirds. Pat cut a pan of gelatin the same size into sixths. How many sixths equal $\frac{1}{3}$? ___

CRITICAL THINKING

Color each strip.

11. two fourths

12. three sixths

13. four eighths

14. Did you color less than one half, one half, or more than one half of each strip? ___

15. What fraction would most likely come next if the pattern above continues? ___

Math Alive at Home Draw 2 rectangles of equal size. Divide one rectangle into 5 equal parts and the other into 10 equal parts. Have your child color the figures to show any 2 equal fractions.

Name ______________________

Part of a Set

Let's Learn!

Fractions can name equal parts of a set or a group.

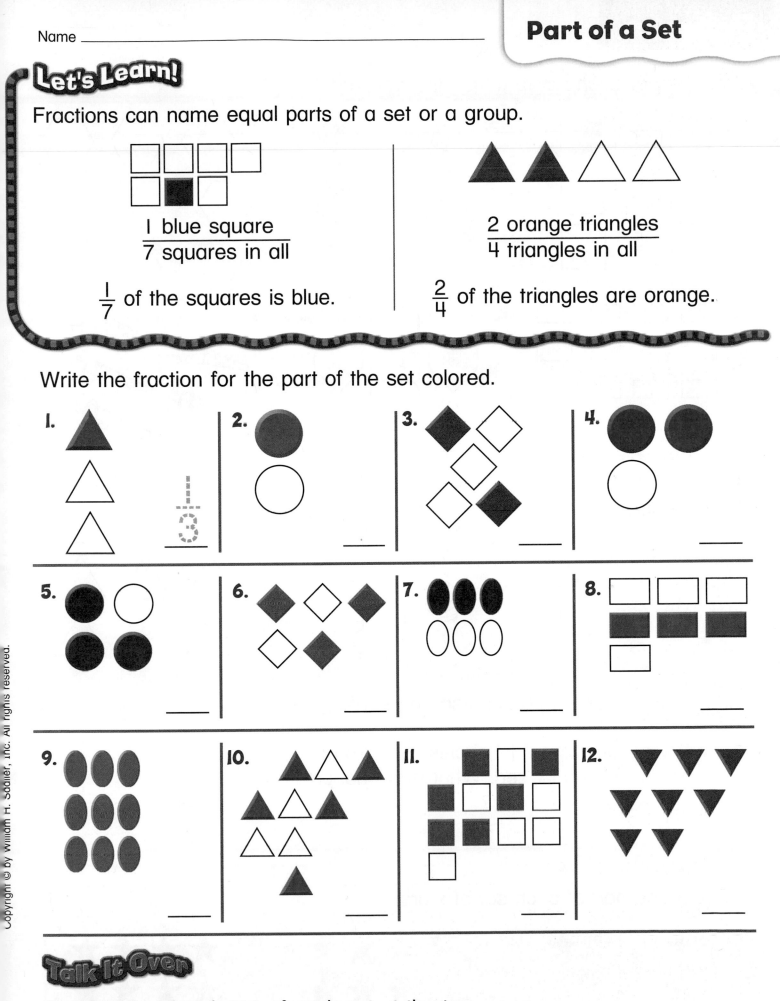

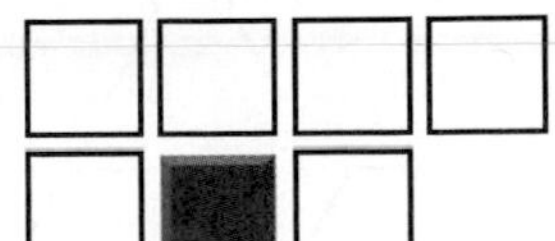

$\frac{\text{1 blue square}}{\text{7 squares in all}}$

$\frac{1}{7}$ of the squares is blue.

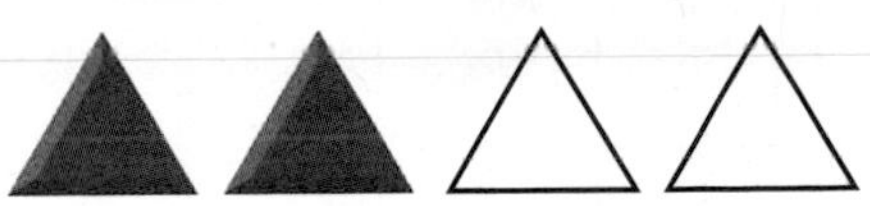

$\frac{\text{2 orange triangles}}{\text{4 triangles in all}}$

$\frac{2}{4}$ of the triangles are orange.

Write the fraction for the part of the set colored.

1. 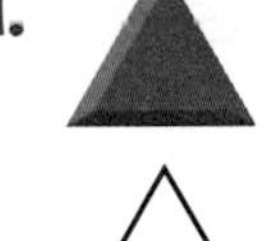  $\frac{1}{3}$

2.  ____

3. 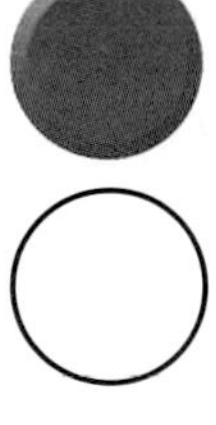 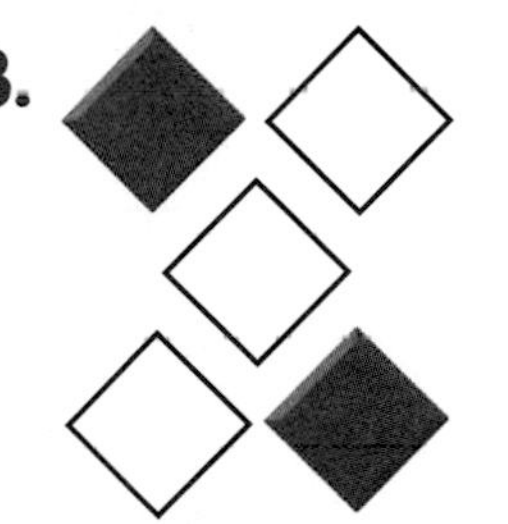 ____

4. 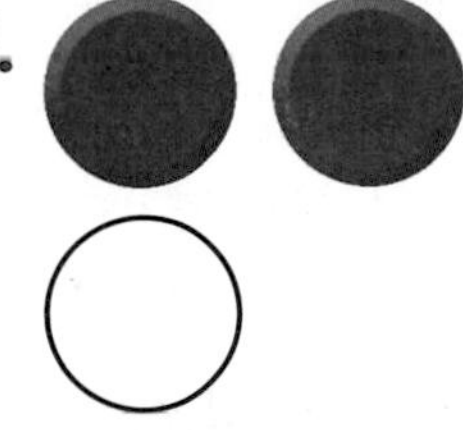 ____

5. 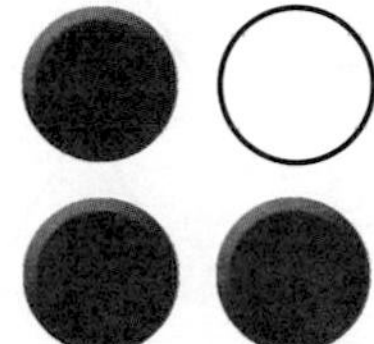 ____

6. 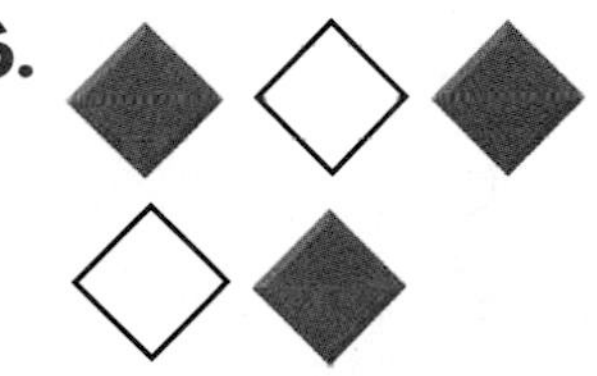 ____

7. 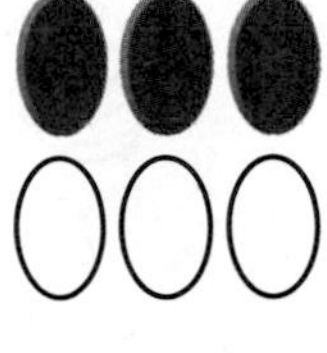 ____

8. 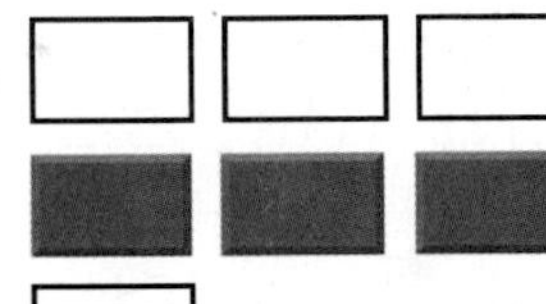 ____

9.  ____

10.  ____

11.  ____

12.  ____

13. What fractional part of each set at the top of the page is not colored?

Copyright © by William H. Sadlier, Inc. All rights reserved.

Practice

Color part of each set to match the fraction.

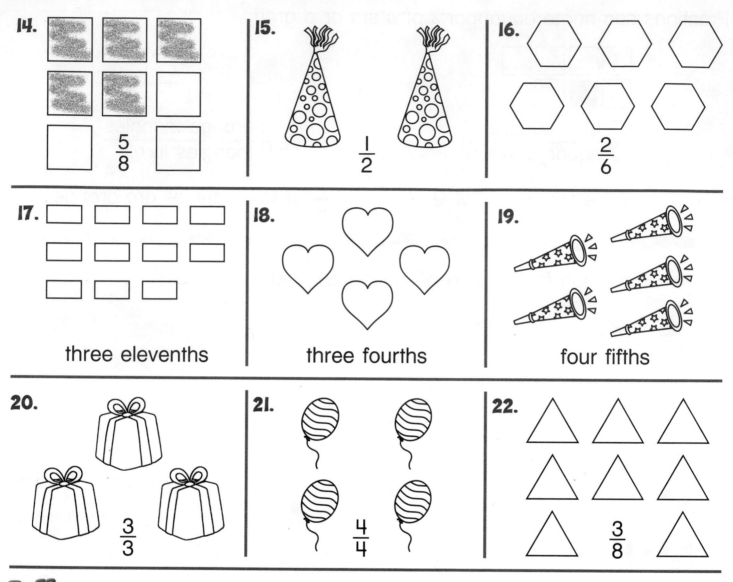

14. $\frac{5}{8}$

15. $\frac{1}{2}$

16. $\frac{2}{6}$

17. three elevenths

18.

three fourths

19.

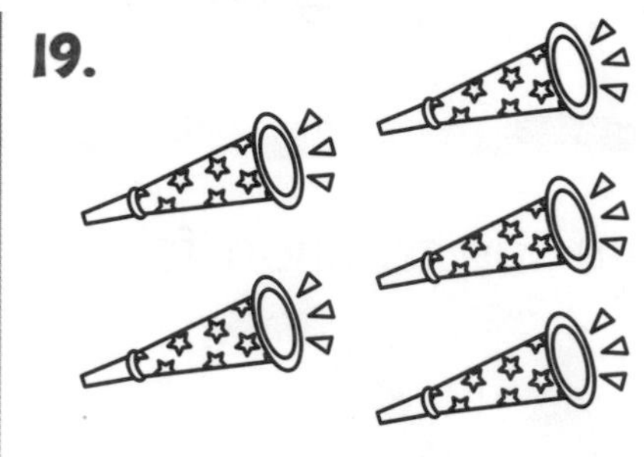

four fifths

20. $\frac{3}{3}$

21. $\frac{4}{4}$

22. $\frac{3}{8}$

Solve. Use a problem-solving strategy.

23. Multistep Joel drew 12 circles. He colored 2 circles blue and 7 red. What fractional part of the set is left to color?

_____ are left to color.

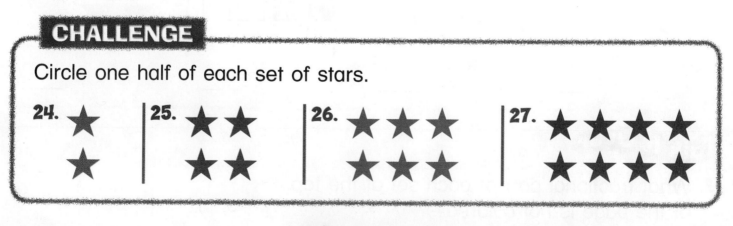

CHALLENGE

Circle one half of each set of stars.

24. ★ ★

25. ★★ ★★

26. ★★★ ★★★

27. ★★★★ ★★★★

Math Alive at Home Draw a set of 6 circles. Have your child color some of the circles and write a fraction for the part of the set colored.

Name ____________________

Algebra

Equal Fractions of a Set

Let's Learn!

Larry and Pam each have 6 stickers.

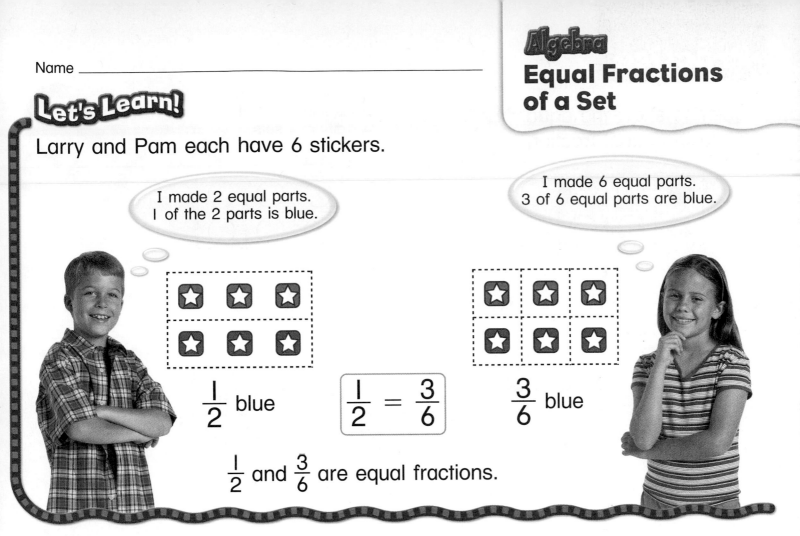

I made 2 equal parts.
1 of the 2 parts is blue.

I made 6 equal parts.
3 of 6 equal parts are blue.

$\frac{1}{2}$ blue

$\frac{1}{2} = \frac{3}{6}$

$\frac{3}{6}$ blue

$\frac{1}{2}$ and $\frac{3}{6}$ are equal fractions.

Color to show the equal fraction.
Write the equal fraction.

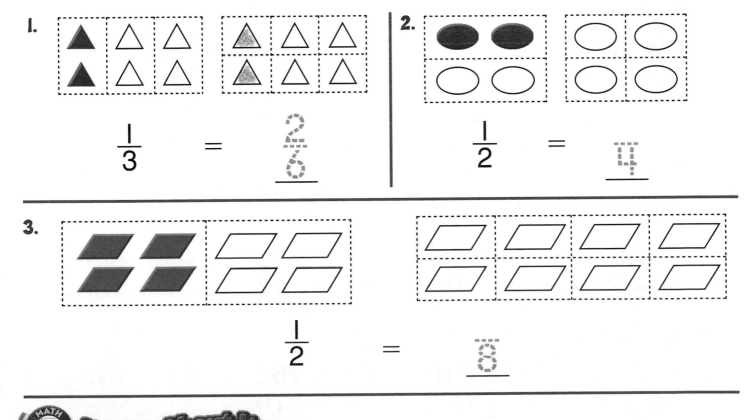

1.  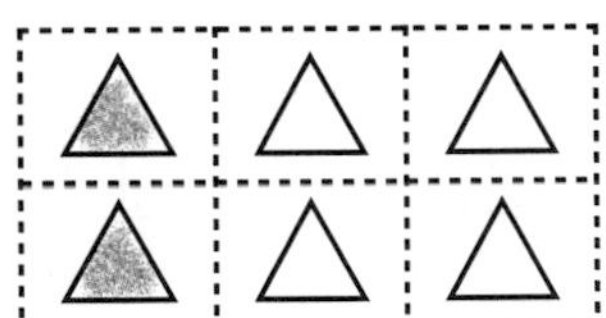

$\frac{1}{3} = \frac{2}{6}$

2.  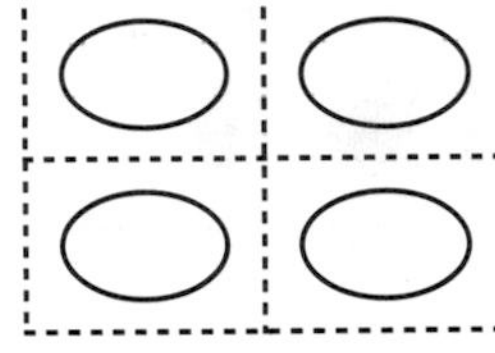

$\frac{1}{2} = \frac{}{4}$

3. 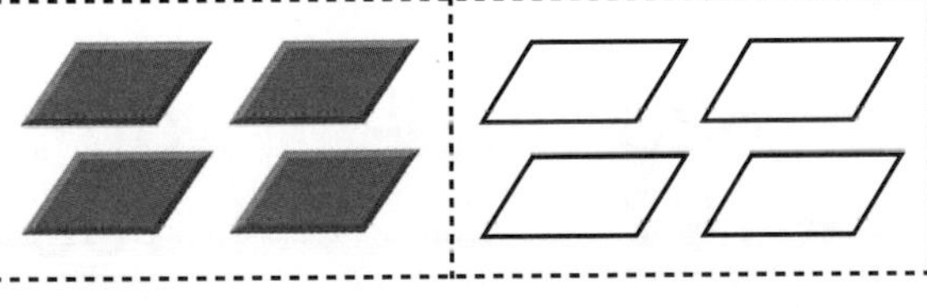

$\frac{1}{2}$ 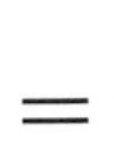 

4. Explain how you know $\frac{1}{5}$ and $\frac{2}{10}$ are equal fractions.

Copyright © by William H. Sadlier, Inc. All rights reserved.

Practice

Color to show the equal fraction.
Write the equal fraction.

Equal fractions name the same part of different sets.

5.

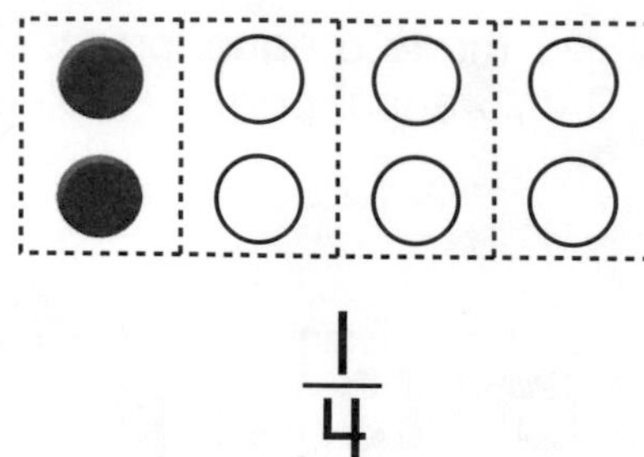

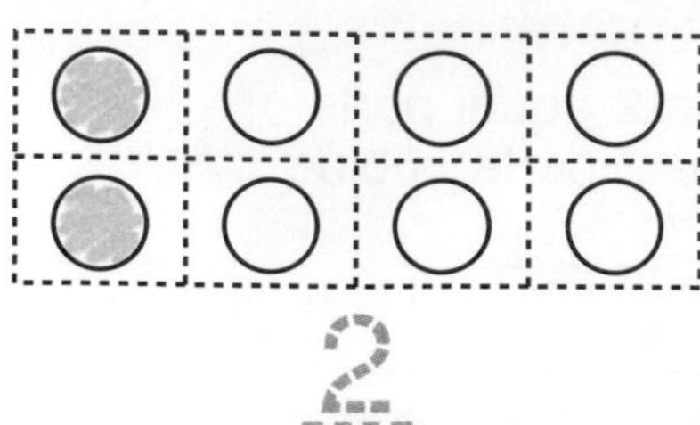

$\frac{1}{4} = \frac{2}{8}$

6.

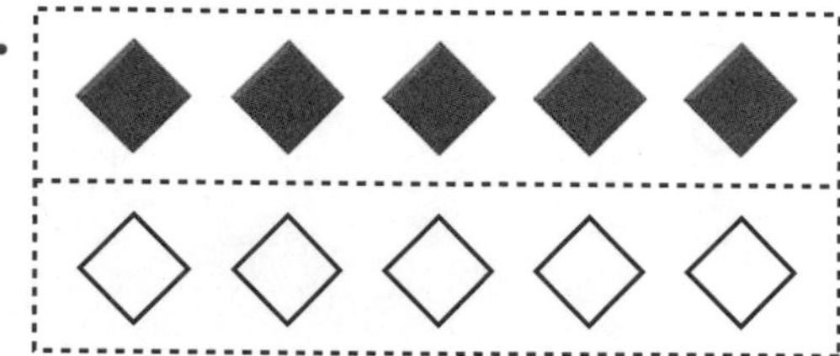

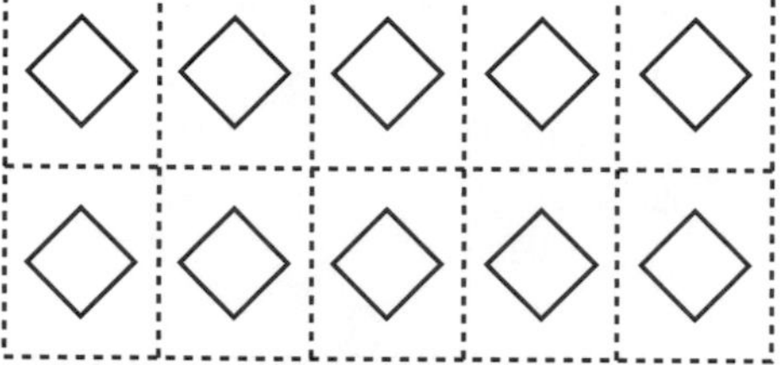

$\frac{1}{2} = \frac{}{10}$

7.

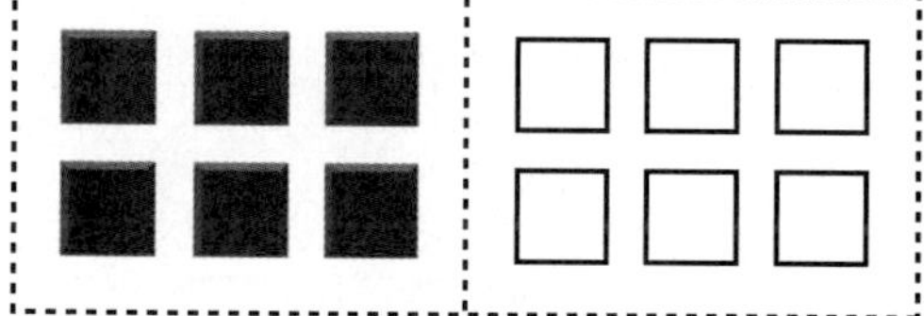

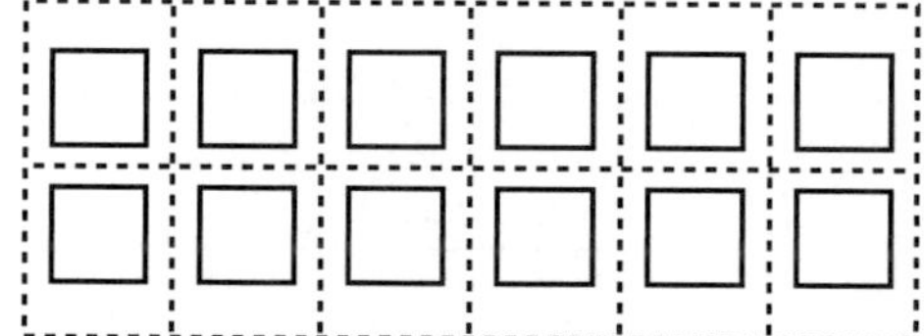

$\frac{1}{2} = \frac{}{12}$

DO YOU REMEMBER?

Add or subtract.

8.	9.	10.	11.
239 + 462	718 + 92	623 + 197	564 + 106

12.	13.	14.	15.
975 − 638	841 − 128	752 − 314	693 − 489

Math Alive at Home Put two sets of 6 spoons (3 large and 3 small) on a table. Ask your child to name 2 equal fractions for the number of small spoons in each set. ($\frac{3}{6} = \frac{1}{2}$)

Name ______________________

TEST PREPARATION

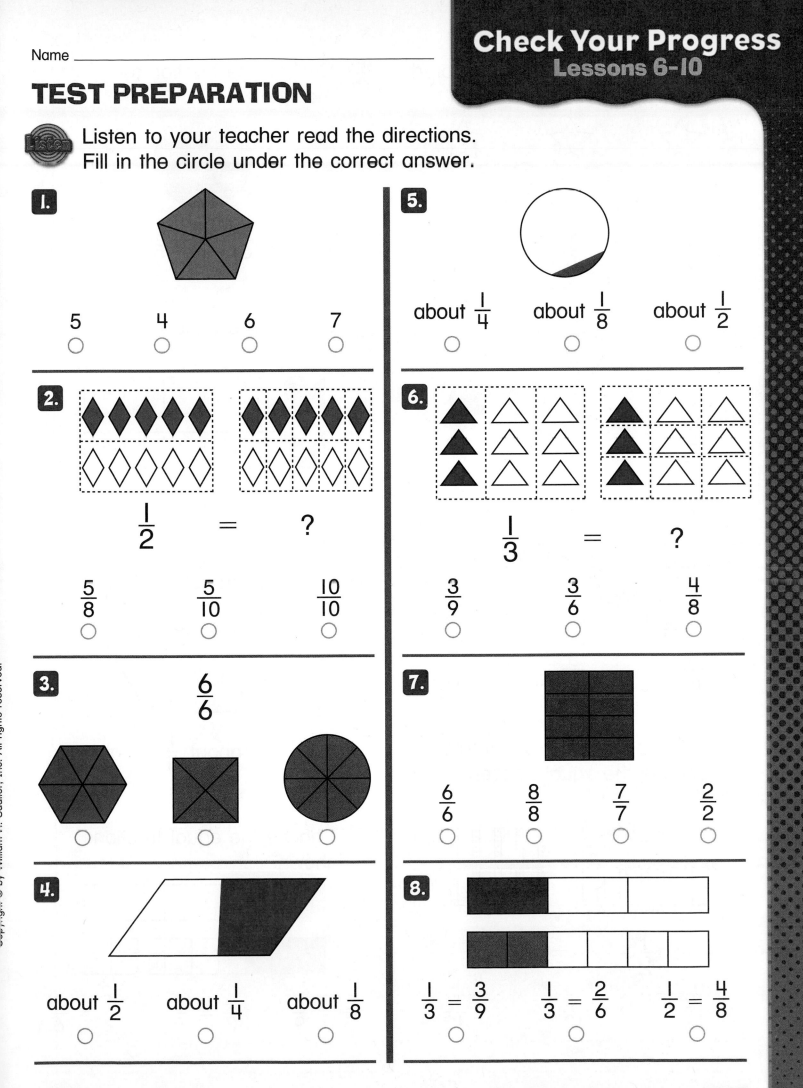

Listen to your teacher read the directions.
Fill in the circle under the correct answer.

1.

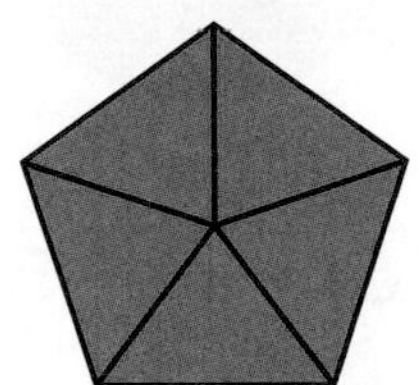

5 ○ 4 ○ 6 ○ 7 ○

2.

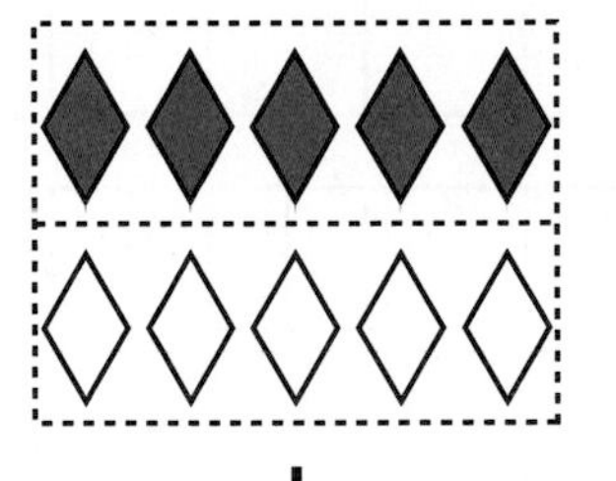

$\frac{1}{2} = ?$

$\frac{5}{8}$ ○ $\frac{5}{10}$ ○ $\frac{10}{10}$ ○

3.

$\frac{6}{6}$

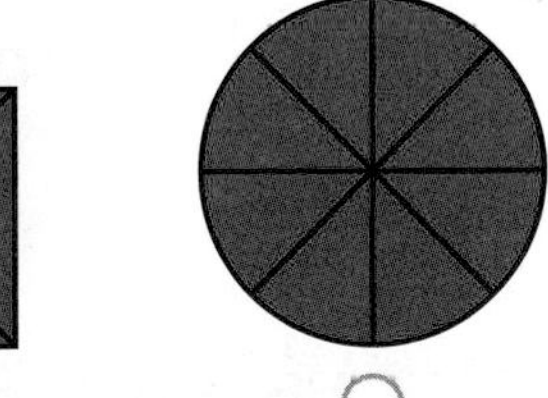

○ ○ ○

4.

about $\frac{1}{2}$ ○ about $\frac{1}{4}$ ○ about $\frac{1}{8}$ ○

5.

about $\frac{1}{4}$ ○ about $\frac{1}{8}$ ○ about $\frac{1}{2}$ ○

6.

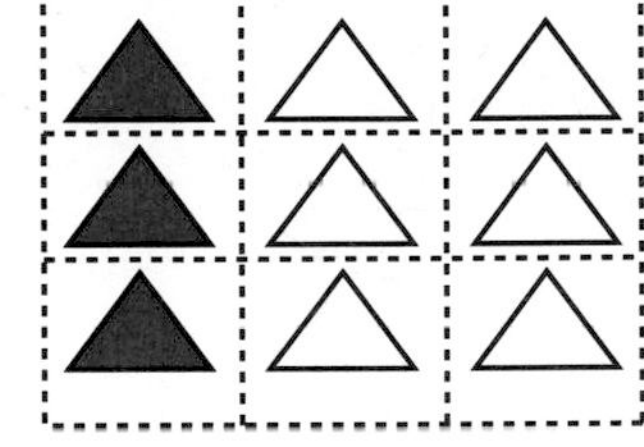

$\frac{1}{3} = ?$

$\frac{3}{9}$ ○ $\frac{3}{6}$ ○ $\frac{4}{8}$ ○

7.

$\frac{6}{6}$ ○ $\frac{8}{8}$ ○ $\frac{7}{7}$ ○ $\frac{2}{2}$ ○

8.

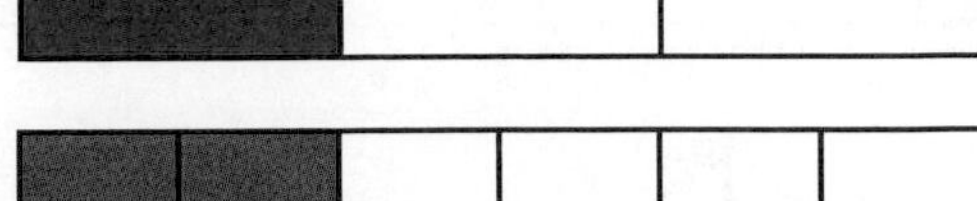

$\frac{1}{3} = \frac{3}{9}$ ○ $\frac{1}{3} = \frac{2}{6}$ ○ $\frac{1}{2} = \frac{4}{8}$ ○

Choose the fraction for the colored part of the set in exercises 9–11.

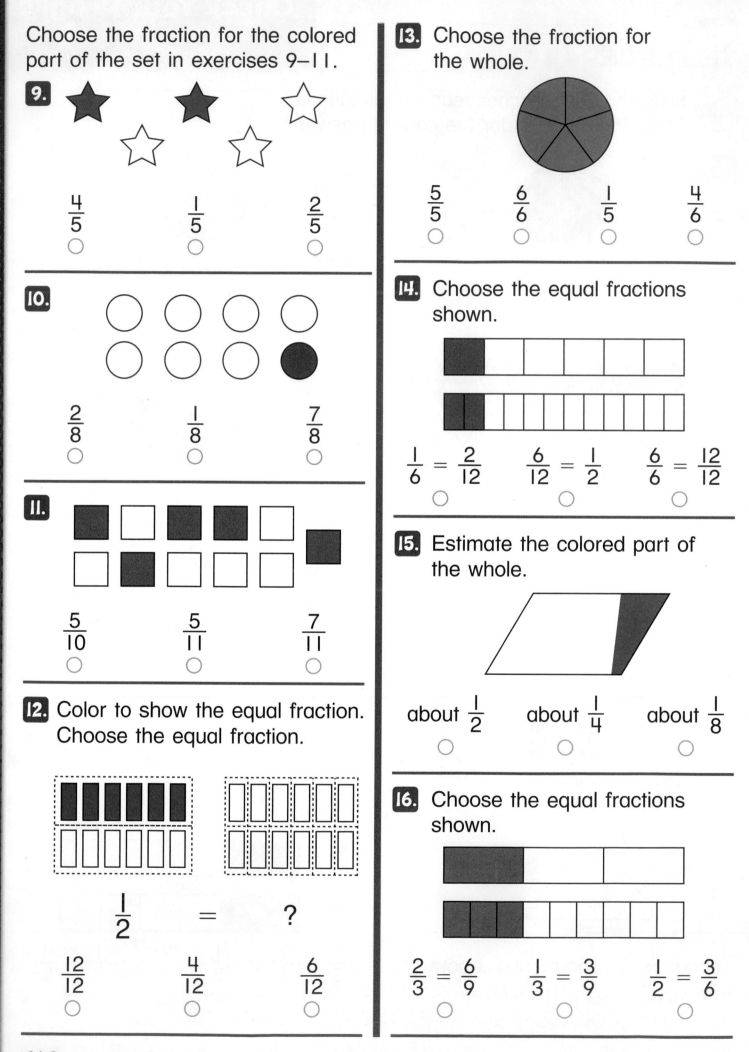

$\frac{4}{5}$ ○ $\frac{1}{5}$ ○ $\frac{2}{5}$ ○

10.

$\frac{2}{8}$ ○ $\frac{1}{8}$ ○ $\frac{7}{8}$ ○

11.

$\frac{5}{10}$ ○ $\frac{5}{11}$ ○ $\frac{7}{11}$ ○

12. Color to show the equal fraction. Choose the equal fraction.

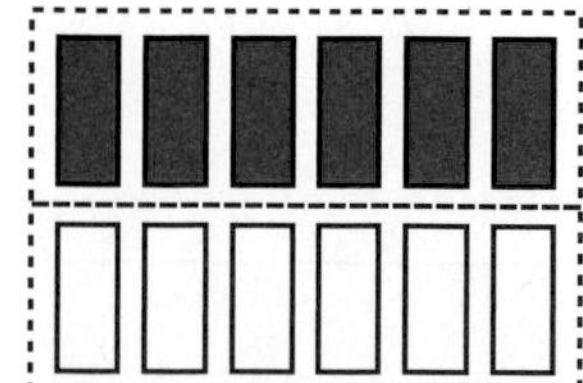 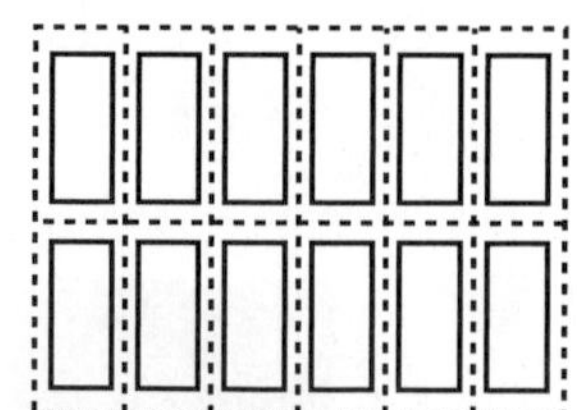

$\frac{1}{2} = ?$

$\frac{12}{12}$ ○ $\frac{4}{12}$ ○ $\frac{6}{12}$ ○

13. Choose the fraction for the whole.

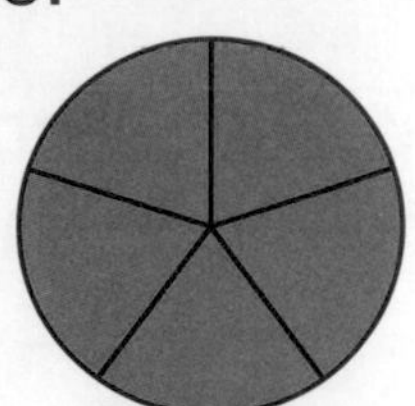

$\frac{5}{5}$ ○ $\frac{6}{6}$ ○ $\frac{1}{5}$ ○ $\frac{4}{6}$ ○

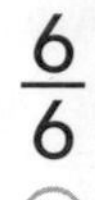

14. Choose the equal fractions shown.

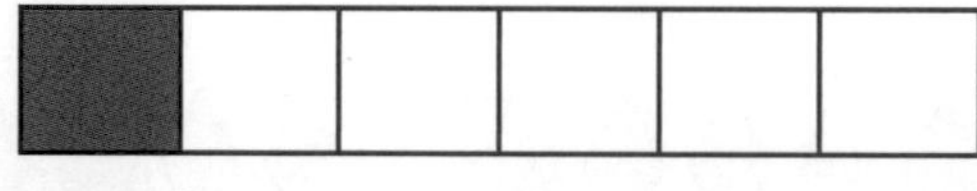

$\frac{1}{6} = \frac{2}{12}$ ○ $\frac{6}{12} = \frac{1}{2}$ ○ $\frac{6}{6} = \frac{12}{12}$ ○

15. Estimate the colored part of the whole.

about $\frac{1}{2}$ ○ about $\frac{1}{4}$ ○ about $\frac{1}{8}$ ○

16. Choose the equal fractions shown.

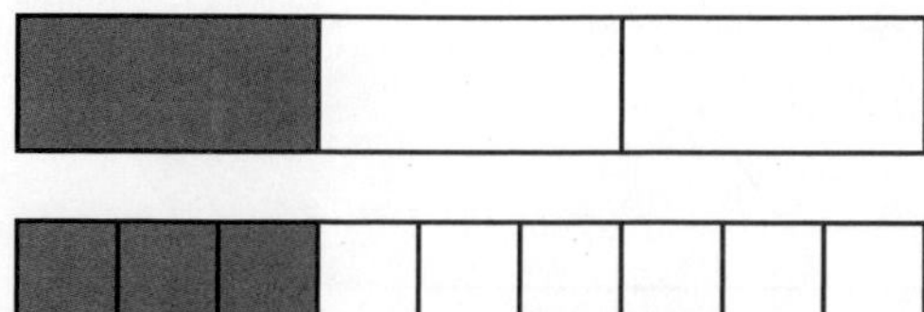

$\frac{2}{3} = \frac{6}{9}$ ○ $\frac{1}{3} = \frac{3}{9}$ ○ $\frac{1}{2} = \frac{3}{6}$ ○

Name ____________________

Predict Outcomes

HANDS-ON LESSON

Let's Learn!

The spinner has 3 **outcomes**: yellow, green, and red. Which outcome, or result, do you think will occur the most?

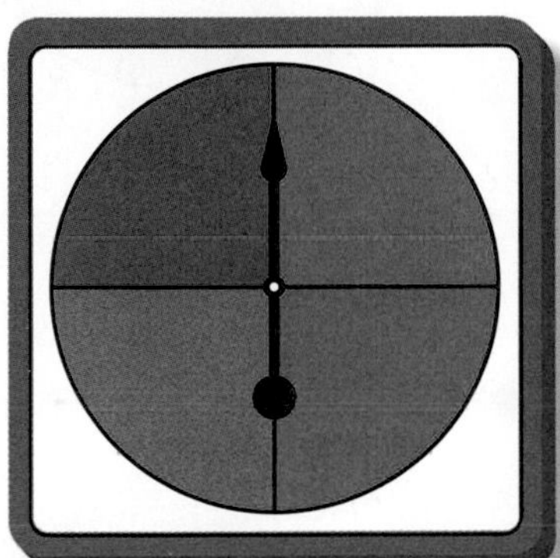

Yellow takes up more space. I predict the spinner will land on yellow more than green or red.
Math Words
outcome

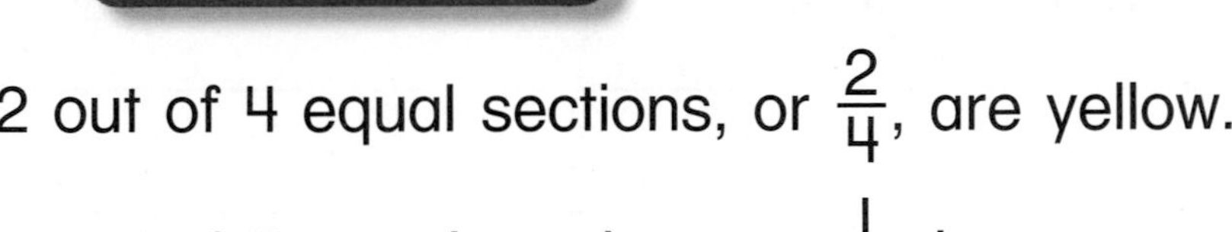

2 out of 4 equal sections, or $\frac{2}{4}$, are yellow.

1 out of 4 equal sections, or $\frac{1}{4}$, is green.

1 out of 4 equal sections, or $\frac{1}{4}$, is red.

1. Use the spinner above. Use a pencil and a paper clip. Spin 12 times. Tally to record each outcome.

Color	Tally
yellow	
green	
red	

Write the outcome for each color.

2. ____ out of 12 times the spinner landed on yellow.

3. ____ out of 12 times the spinner landed on green.

4. ____ out of 12 times the spinner landed on red.

Talk It Over

5. Look at the results above. Was the girl's prediction right? If you spin the spinner 12 more times, which color would you predict landing on the most? Explain your reasoning.

Copyright © by William H. Sadlier, Inc. All rights reserved.

Practice

Complete. Then write a fraction for each color.

6. 1 out of 6 sections is yellow. $\frac{1}{6}$ is yellow.

7. ____ out of ____ sections are red. $\frac{\_\_}{6}$ are red.

8. ____ out of ____ sections are green. $\frac{\_\_}{6}$ are green.

9. Predict which color the spinner would land on the most. Explain your reasoning. ______

10. Use the spinner above.
Use a pencil and a paper clip.
Spin 12 times.
Tally to record each outcome.

Color	Tally
yellow	
green	
red	

Write the outcome for each color.

11. ____ out of 12 times the spinner landed on yellow.

12. ____ out of 12 times the spinner landed on green.

13. ____ out of 12 times the spinner landed on red.

14. Was your prediction right? ______

CRITICAL THINKING

15. If you were to spin the spinner above 12 more times, would you make the same prediction? Explain your reasoning.

Math Alive at Home Have your child make a spinner with four equal parts and color the spinner to make blue the color the spinner would land on the most.

Name ______________________________

How Likely?

Let's Learn!

How likely is each spinner to land on blue?

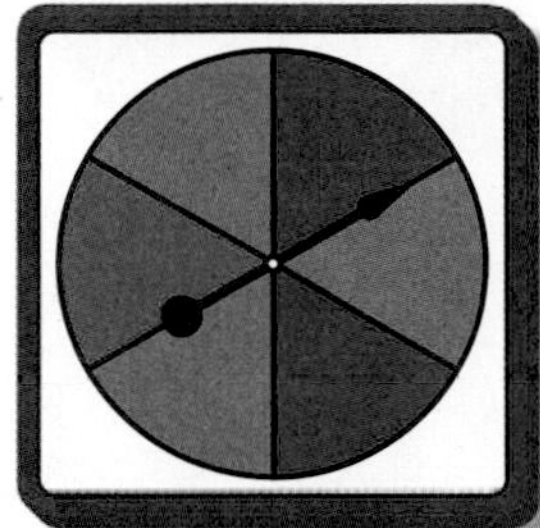

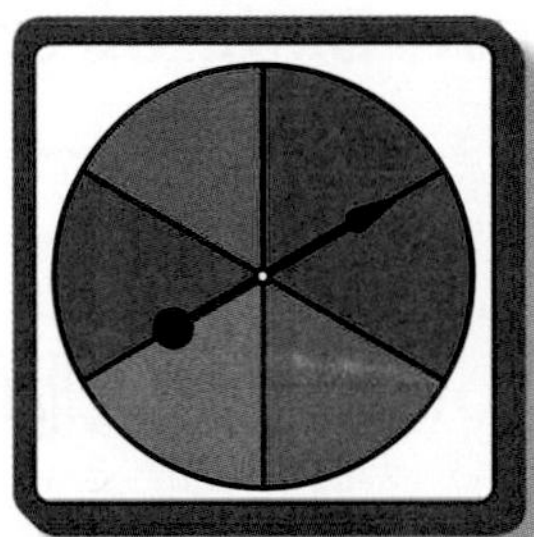

Each spinner has 3 possible outcomes: yellow, blue, or red.

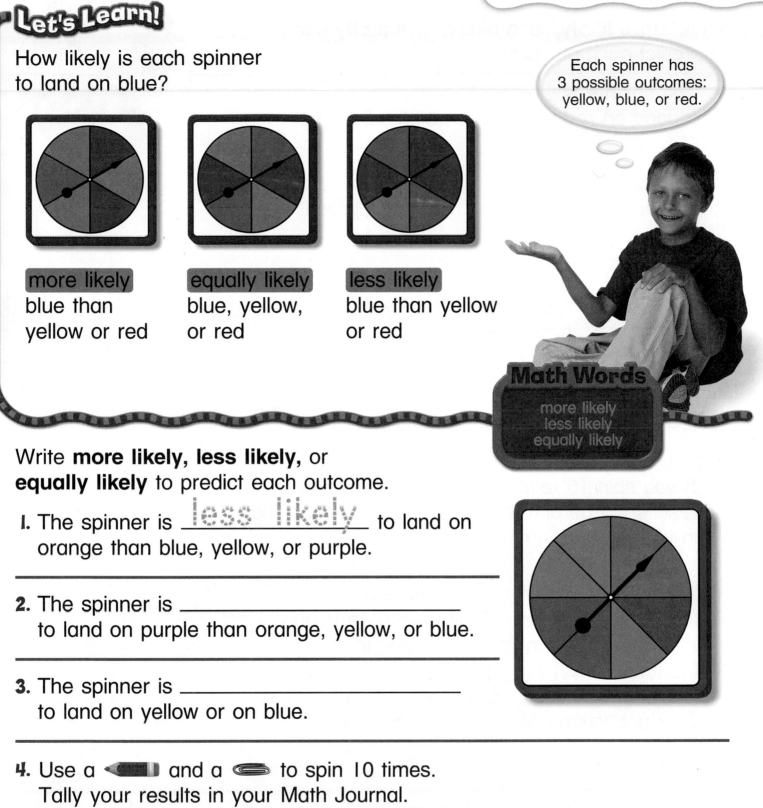

more likely blue than yellow or red

equally likely blue, yellow, or red

less likely blue than yellow or red

Math Words
more likely
less likely
equally likely

Write **more likely, less likely,** or **equally likely** to predict each outcome.

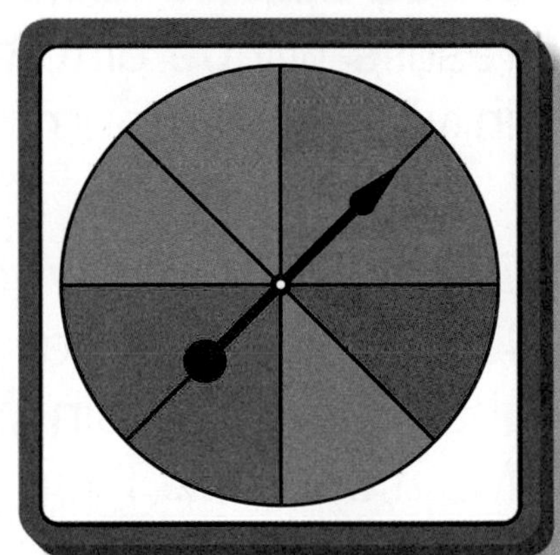

1. The spinner is less likely to land on orange than blue, yellow, or purple.

2. The spinner is ______________ to land on purple than orange, yellow, or blue.

3. The spinner is ______________ to land on yellow or on blue.

4. Use a pencil and a paper clip to spin 10 times. Tally your results in your Math Journal. Then compare your predictions with your results. What do you notice?

MATH JOURNAL
Write About It

5. Explain how you can tell when a spinner is more likely, less likely, or equally likely to land on a color.

Practice

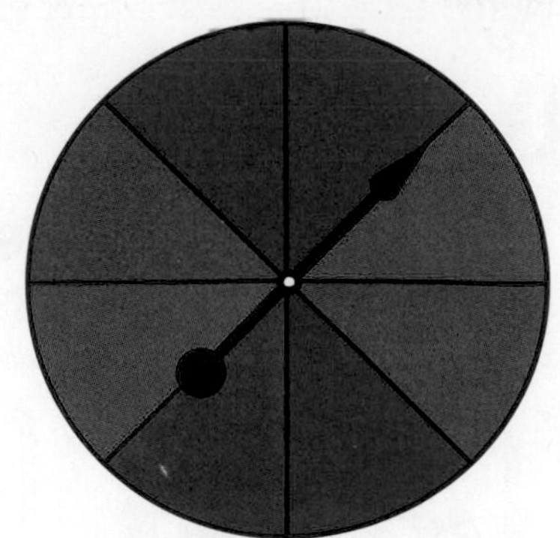

Write **more likely, less likely,** or **equally likely** to predict each outcome.

6. The spinner is more likely ______ to land on red than yellow, blue, or green.

7. The spinner is ______ to land on blue than yellow, red, or green.

8. The spinner is ______ to land on green or on yellow.

9. Use a pencil and a paper clip to spin 10 times. Tally your results in your Math Journal. Then compare your predictions with your results. What do you notice?

10. If you spin 10 more times, do you think your results will be different? Explain your reasoning in your Math Journal.

11. If you flip a penny, are you more likely, less likely, or equally likely to land on heads than tails? Explain your reasoning in your Math Journal. Then flip a penny 10 times. Record your results. Compare them with your predictions. What do you notice?

CHALLENGE

12. Nick puts marbles in each bowl. There is an equal chance to pick blue, red, or yellow from each bowl. Color to show the marbles Nick put in each bowl.

Math Alive at Home Help your child make a spinner with 10 equal parts. Have your child color the spinner so that it is equally likely to land on any of 5 different colors.

Name ______________________________

Certain, Possible, Impossible

Let's Learn!

Without looking, is it certain, possible, or impossible to pick a ● from each bowl?

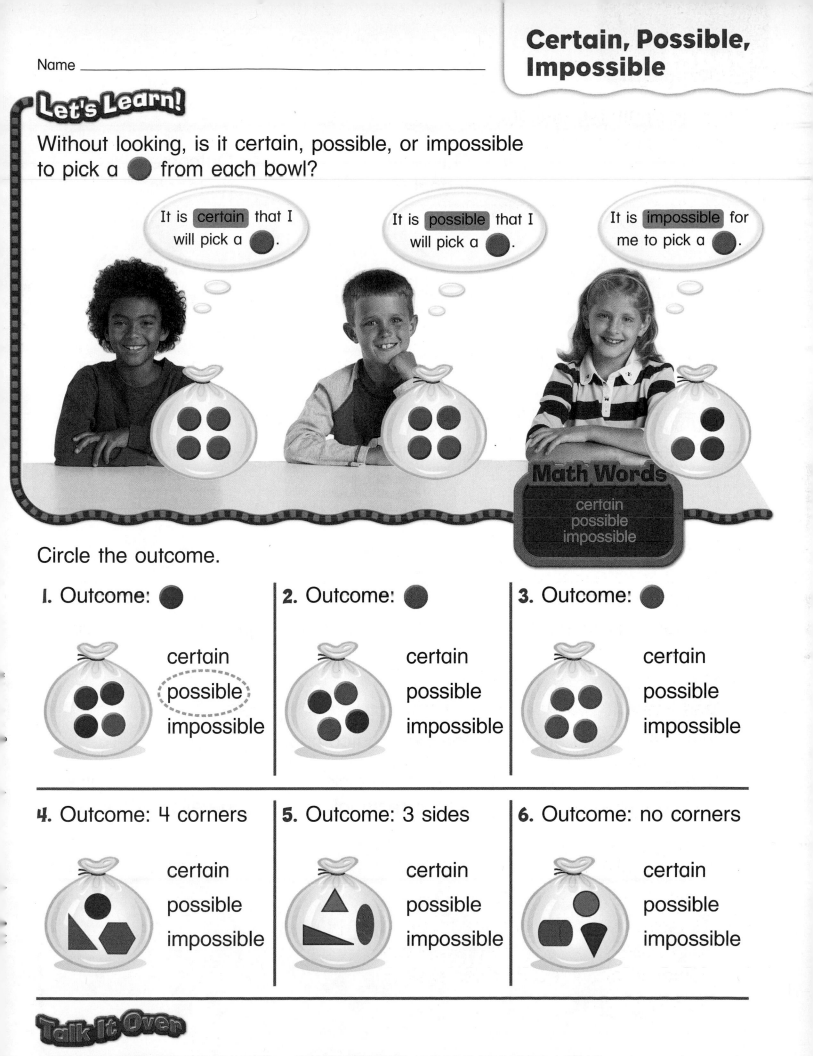

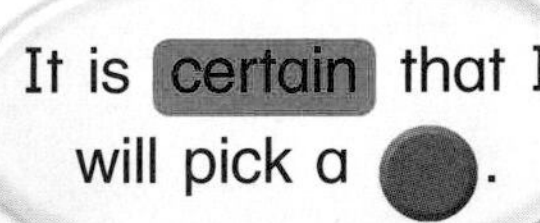
It is certain that I will pick a ●.

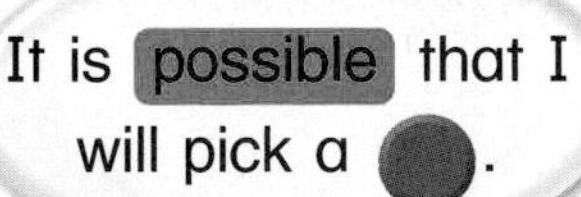
It is possible that I will pick a ●.

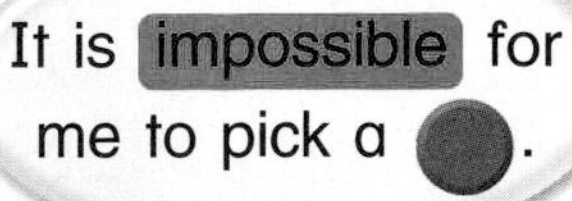
It is impossible for me to pick a ●.

Math Words
certain
possible
impossible

Circle the outcome.

1. Outcome: ●

certain
possible
impossible

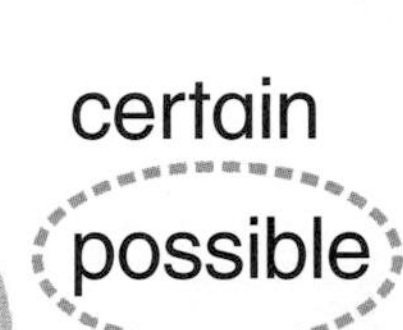

2. Outcome: ●

certain
possible
impossible

3. Outcome: ●

certain
possible
impossible

4. Outcome: 4 corners

certain
possible
impossible

5. Outcome: 3 sides

certain
possible
impossible

6. Outcome: no corners

certain
possible
impossible

Talk It Over

7. What would be an impossible outcome for exercise 1?

Practice

Circle to show the outcome.

8. Outcome: 4 sides

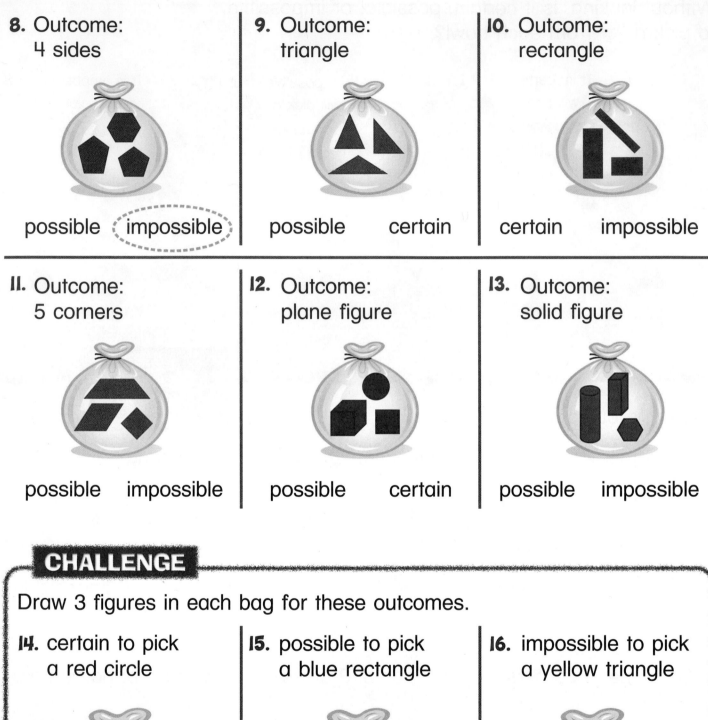

possible impossible

9. Outcome: triangle

possible certain

10. Outcome: rectangle

certain impossible

11. Outcome: 5 corners

possible impossible

12. Outcome: plane figure

possible certain

13. Outcome: solid figure

possible impossible

CHALLENGE

Draw 3 figures in each bag for these outcomes.

14. certain to pick a red circle

15. possible to pick a blue rectangle

16. impossible to pick a yellow triangle

Math Alive at Home Put 3 pennies and 1 nickel in a clear jar and ask your child to predict the outcome of picking a penny from the jar. (possible)

Name ________________________________

Understand Math Words

- In some problems you need to know the meaning of math words to solve the problem.

Listen
Mike is picking a prize at a party. He closes his eyes. Is it certain, possible, or impossible that he will pick a toy truck?
Happy Birthday

1. Reread the problem. Draw a line under the question you need to answer.

2. Make sure you understand the math words in the question. Circle the correct word in each sentence.

If something is certain, it will always sometimes happen.

If something is possible, it will never sometimes happen.

If something is impossible, it will sometimes never happen.

3. Now look at the picture. How many of each kind of prize do you see? Write the numbers.

______ ball ______ robot ______ toy trucks

4. Solve the problem. Write the missing math word.

It is __________________ that Mike will pick a toy truck.

Practice

Understand Math Words

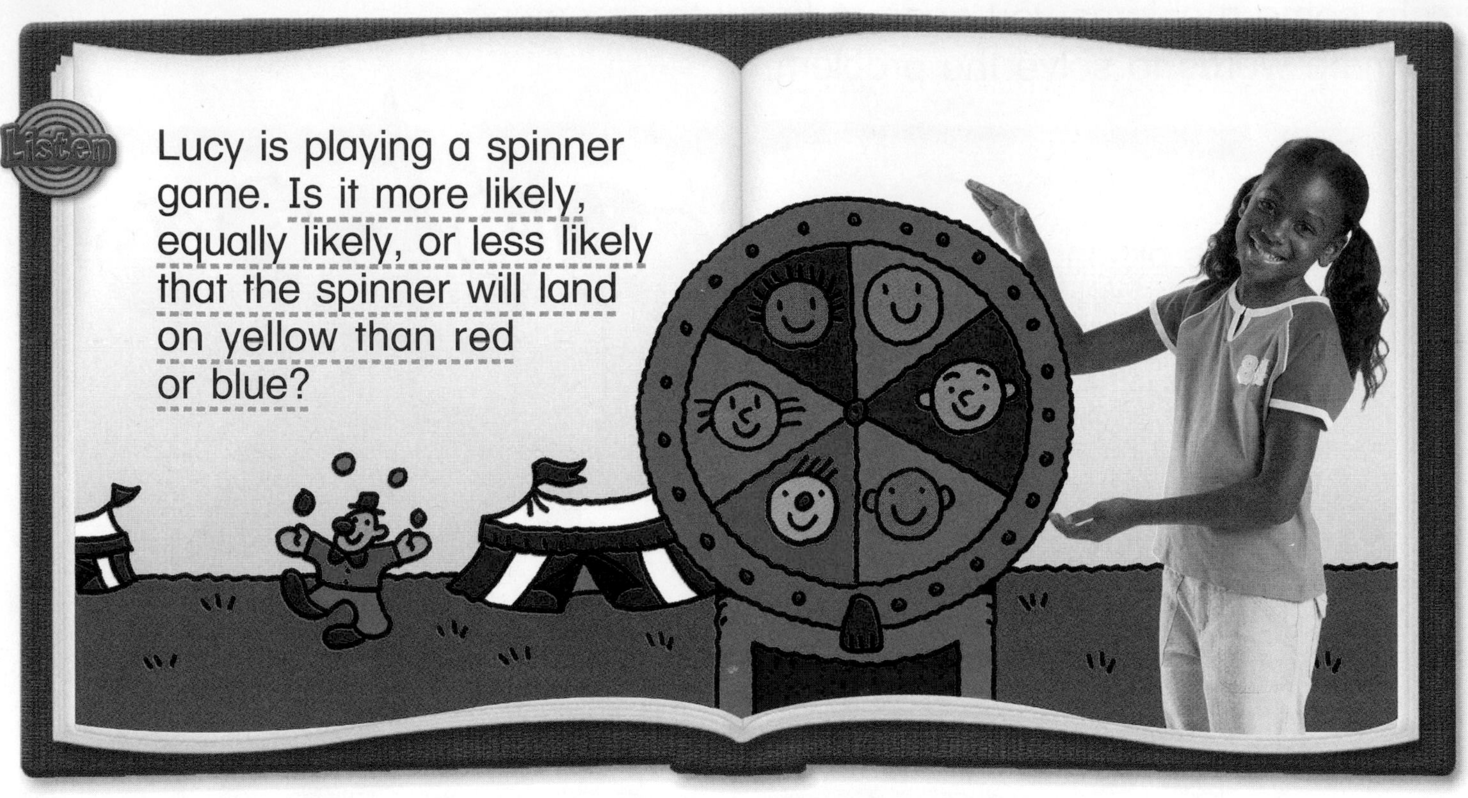

Listen
Lucy is playing a spinner game. Is it more likely, equally likely, or less likely that the spinner will land on yellow than red or blue?

5. Reread the problem. Draw a line under the question you need to answer.

6. Make sure you understand the math words in the question. Circle the correct word in each sentence.

   If something is more likely, it will happen more less often.

   If something is equally likely, it will happen as more often.

   If something is less likely, it will happen as less often.

7. Now look at the picture. How many of each color do you see? Write the numbers.

   _____ red _____ blue _____ yellow

8. Solve the problem. Write the missing math words.

   It is ____________________ that the spinner will land on yellow than red or blue.

Math Alive at Home Today your child worked through math problems by understanding math words.

Name ______________________

Problem Solving
Strategy

Draw a Picture

Read Alex and Kay share 4 muffins equally. Each of them gets one half of the muffins. How many muffins does each get?

Plan Draw to show the number of muffins in all.

$\frac{1}{2}$ means 1 of 2 equal parts of a set.

Circle to show two equal parts. Count how many are in each part.

Write

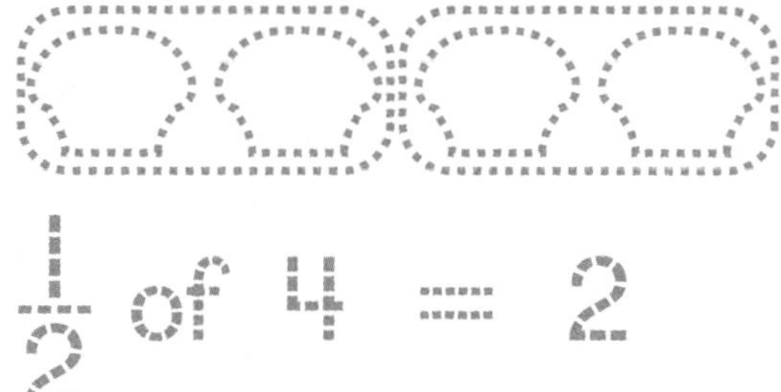

$\frac{1}{2}$ of 4 = 2

Each gets 2 muffins.

Check Use counters to act out the problem.

Draw a picture to solve each problem.

1. Trisha serves 12 berry tarts at the party. One half is eaten. How many are left?

$\frac{1}{2}$ of 12 = 6

____ tarts are left.

---

2. Sheila has 9 party favors. She gives $\frac{1}{3}$ of them to Tom. How many party favors does Tom get?

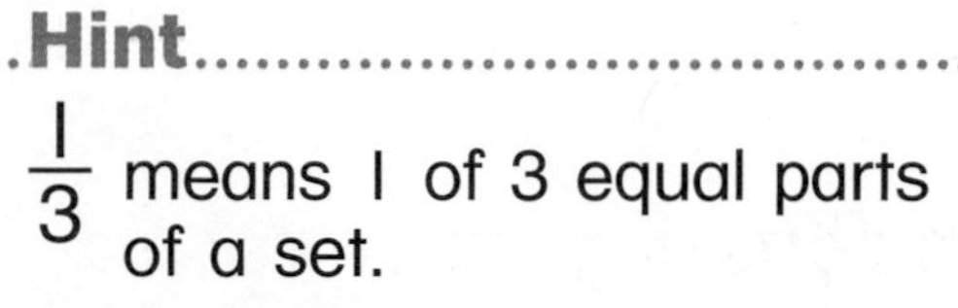

Hint $\frac{1}{3}$ means 1 of 3 equal parts of a set.

$\frac{1}{3}$ of ____ = ____

Tom gets ____ party favors.

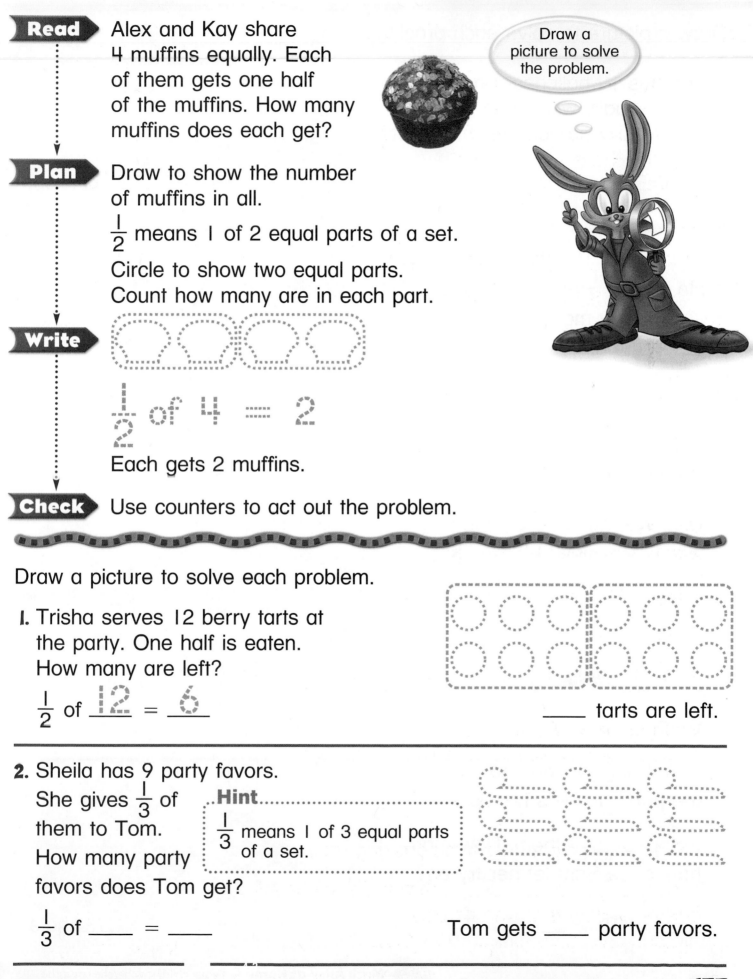

Practice

Read Plan Write Check

Draw a Picture

Draw a picture to solve each problem.

3. Lori has 14 balloons. She shares them equally with Anna. How many balloons does each girl get?

$\frac{1}{2}$ of 14 = ____   ____ balloons

4. Jacob gets 15 gifts at the party. He opens $\frac{1}{3}$ of them before lunch. How many gifts does he open before lunch?

$\frac{1}{3}$ of ____ = ____   ____ gifts

5. Mindy makes 12 bows. She shares them equally with two friends. How many bows does each person get?

$\frac{1}{3}$ of ____ = ____   ____ bows

6. Write $\frac{1}{2}$ or $\frac{1}{3}$. Solve.

Sam brings 18 hats to the party. He lets his sister

try on ____ of them. How many hats does Sam let her try on?

____ of 18 = ____   ____ hats

Math Alive at Home Ask your child how he/she used the Draw a Picture strategy to solve the problems in this lesson.

Name ______________________________

Problem Solving
Applications

Read › Plan › Write › Check

Mixed Strategies

Use a strategy you have learned.

1. Zack and Lara play a game. The game's board has 24 squares. $\frac{1}{2}$ of the set of squares is blue. How many squares are **not** blue?

_____ squares are **not** blue.

---

2. A card game has 16 cards. Mack wins $\frac{1}{4}$ of the cards. Linda wins the same number as Mack. Pete wins the rest of the cards. How many cards does Linda win?

Linda wins _____ cards.

---

3. Paul moves 23 spaces. Barry moves 10 less than Paul. Tate moves 2 more than Barry. Who moves the least spaces?

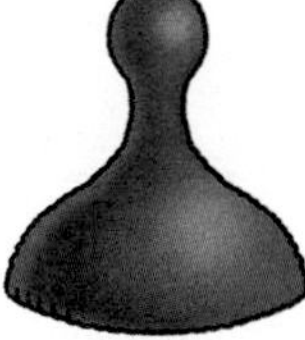

________ moves the least spaces.

---

4. Lee buys two packs of party favors. Each pack has 25 favors. He gives out 32 favors at his party. How many favors are left?

_____ favors are left.

Practice

Read → Plan → Write → Check

Strategy File
- Draw a Picture
- Use a Graph
- Use Logical Reasoning

Use a strategy you have learned.

5. Missy's quilt has 4 squares. Each square has 4 congruent triangles. 8 of the triangles are red. The rest are blue. How many triangles are blue?

_____ triangles are blue.

---

6. Jason places his game pieces in a row. The tallest is fifteenth in the row. There are 5 more after it. How many game pieces are in the row?

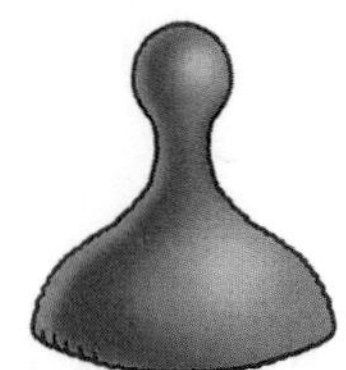

_____ game pieces are in the row.

---

7. Joel makes a pattern using a dozen cylinders. The third, sixth, ninth, and last are yellow. How many are not yellow?

_____ are not yellow.

---

8. Two boys left Tony's party early. What fractional part of the group of boys left early?

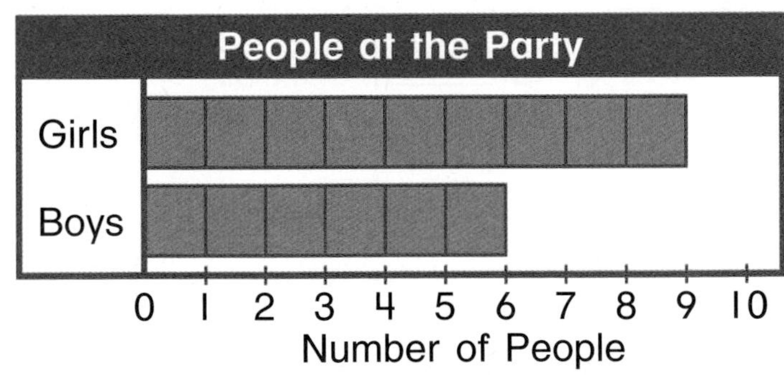

_____ of the boys left early.

---

9. Joy, Tom, and Ray each choose one card. Ray chooses the card with the least number. Joy's card has an even number of ones. What number card did Tom choose?

723 **273** **372**

Tom chose _____.

Math Alive at Home Ask your child to tell you how she/he solved some of the problems in this lesson.

Name ______________________________

Check Your Progress
Lessons 11–16

TEST PREPARATION

Listen to your teacher read the directions. Fill in the circle by the correct answer.

1.

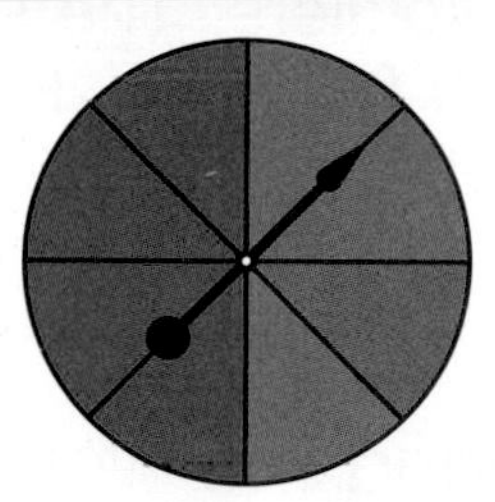
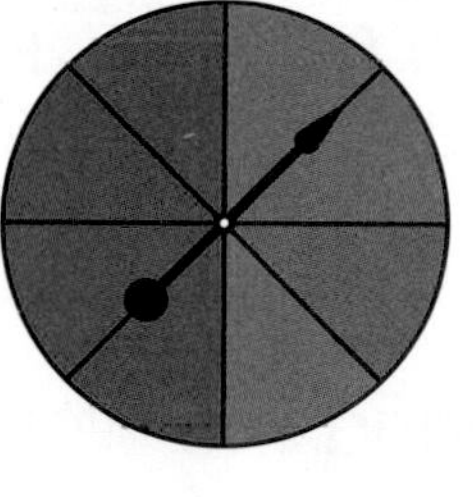

○ red ○ blue ○ green

2.

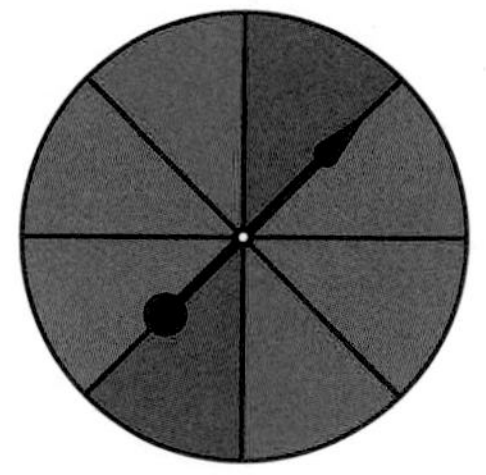

○ red ○ yellow ○ green

3.

$\frac{1}{2}$ of $10 = ?$

○ 3 ○ 4 ○ 5 ○ 6

4.

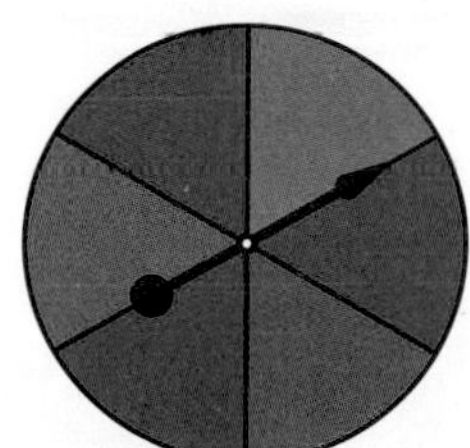

○ more likely
○ less likely
○ equally likely

5. Outcome: solid figure

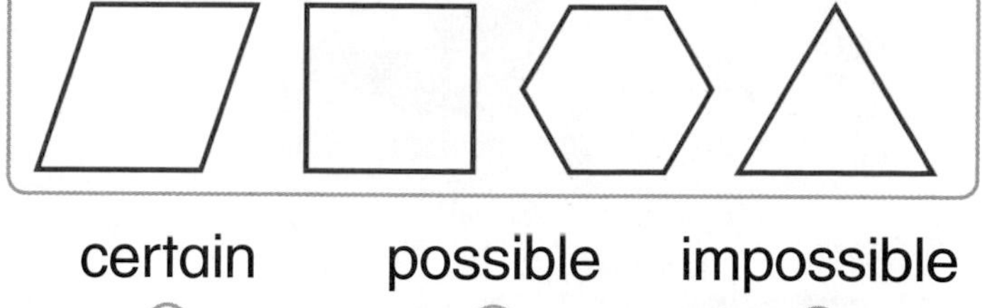

○ certain ○ possible ○ impossible

6. Outcome: 4 sides

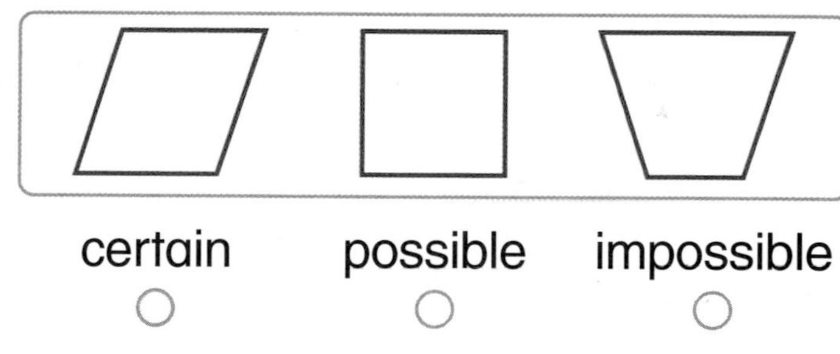

○ certain ○ possible ○ impossible

7.

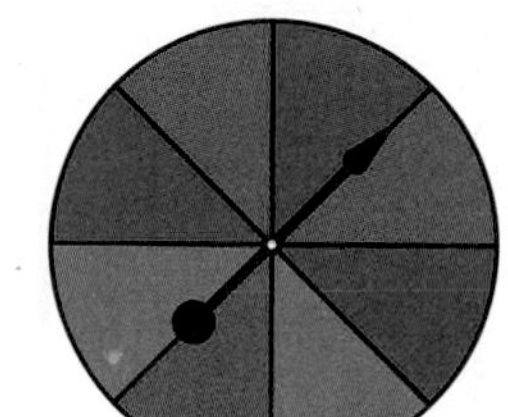

○ more likely
○ less likely
○ equally likely

8.

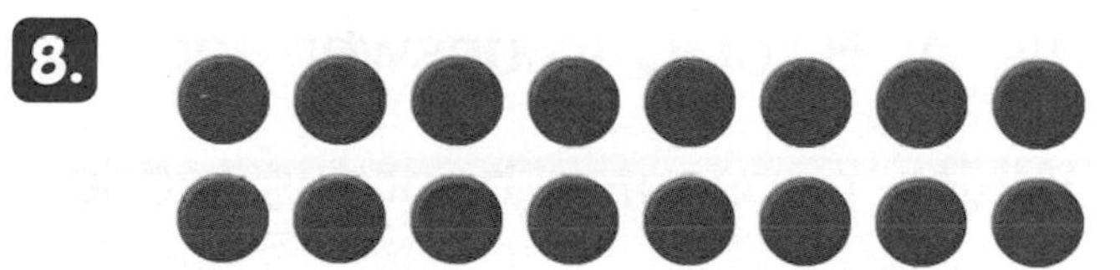

$\frac{1}{2}$ of $16 = ?$

○ 4 ○ 6 ○ 8 ○ 2

Connection

Name ____________________

Did You Know?

Hopscotch started long ago as a training exercise for Roman soldiers. The soldiers used boards over 100 feet long. Roman children later played the game on smaller boards, just for fun.

Today, children around the world play hopscotch. They use many different kinds of boards.

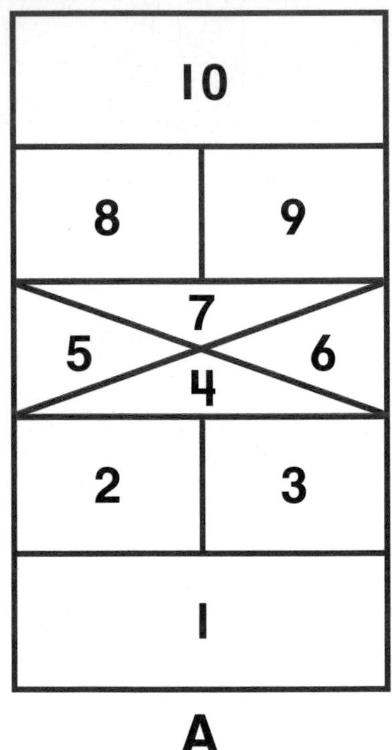

A

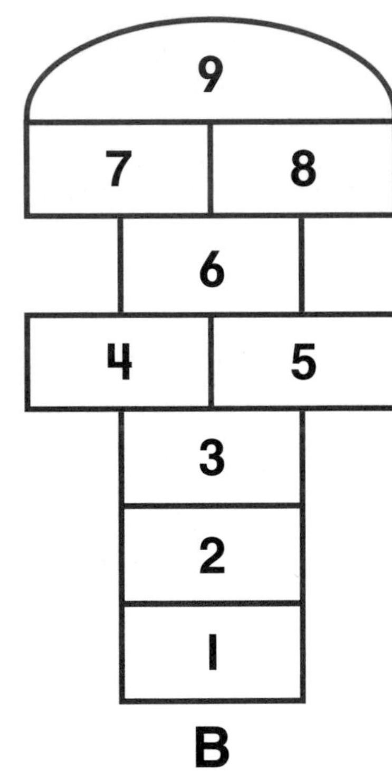

B

9
8
7
6
5
4
3
2
1

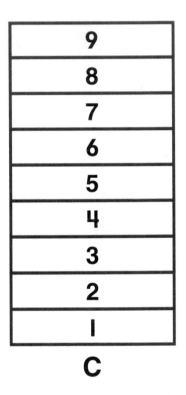

C

Write **A**, **B**, or **C** to answer each question.

1. Which hopscotch board is made up of all equal parts? ____
2. On which hopscotch board is it impossible to hop on a green line? ____
3. Which hopscotch board has the most parts? ____

You can put this in your Math Portfolio.

Name ______________________

Chapter 10 Test

1. Count the parts colored. Write a fraction for the whole.

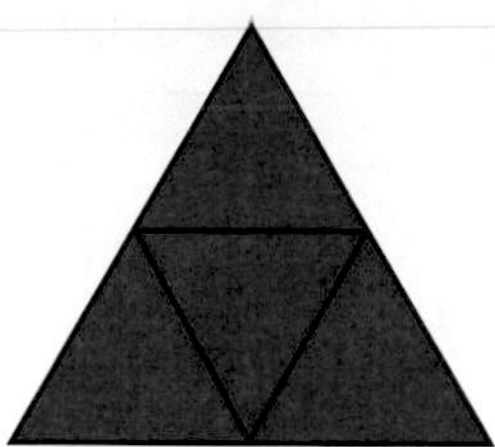

______

2. Circle the outcome.

outcome: corners

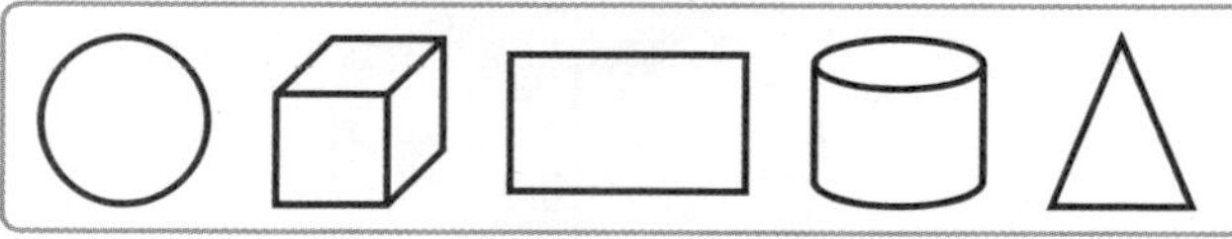

possible impossible

3. Color to show each fraction. Order from least to greatest.

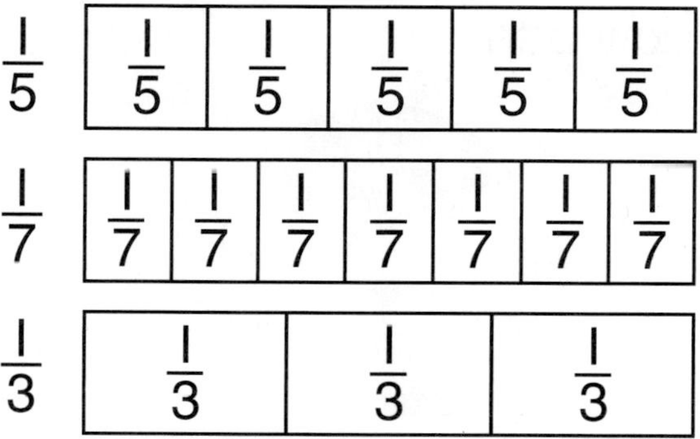

____, ____, ____

4. Write the equal fractions shown.

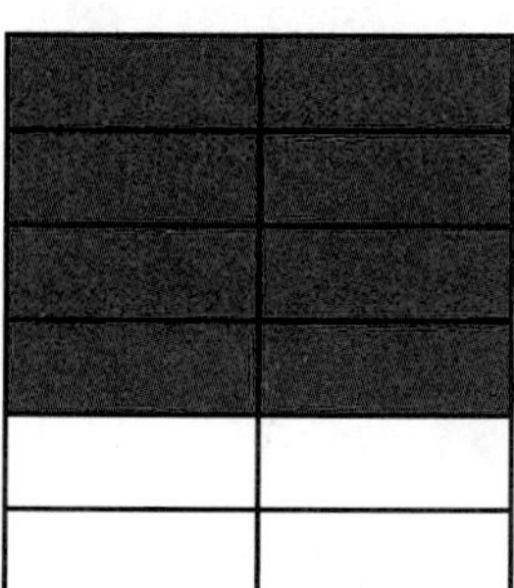

____ = ____

5. Write the fraction for the colored part of the whole.

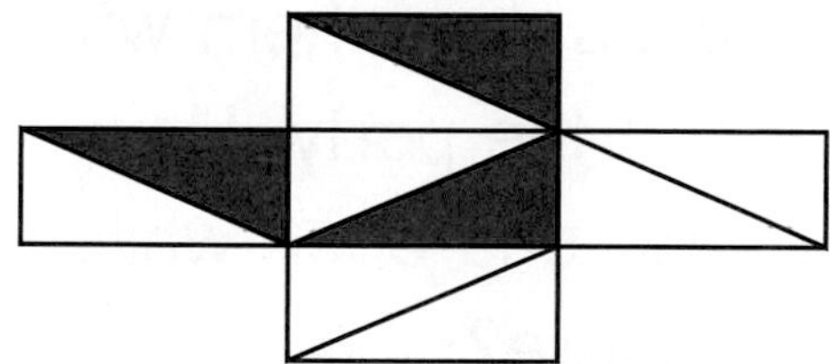

____

6. Color part of the set to match the fraction.

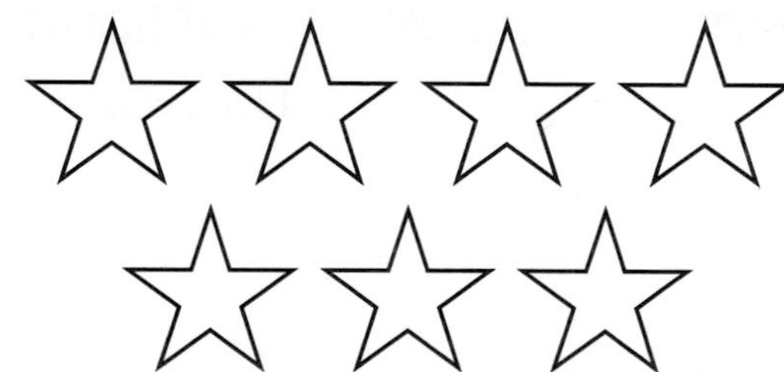

five sevenths

7. Write **about $\frac{1}{2}$**, **about $\frac{1}{4}$**, or **about $\frac{1}{8}$** to estimate the colored part of the whole.

____

8. Is the spinner more likely, equally likely, or less likely to land on green than red or blue?

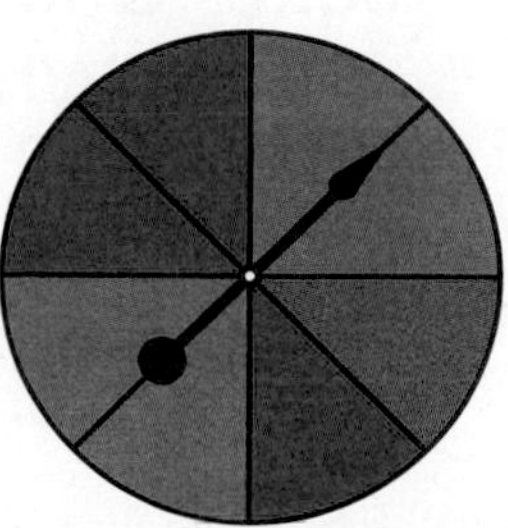

____

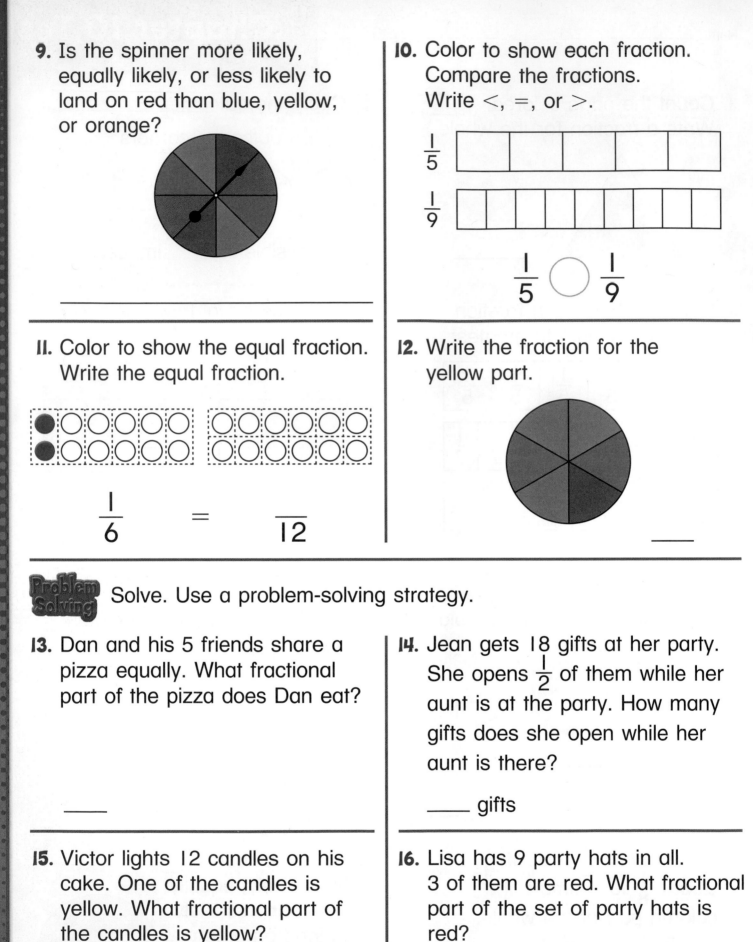

9. Is the spinner more likely, equally likely, or less likely to land on red than blue, yellow, or orange?

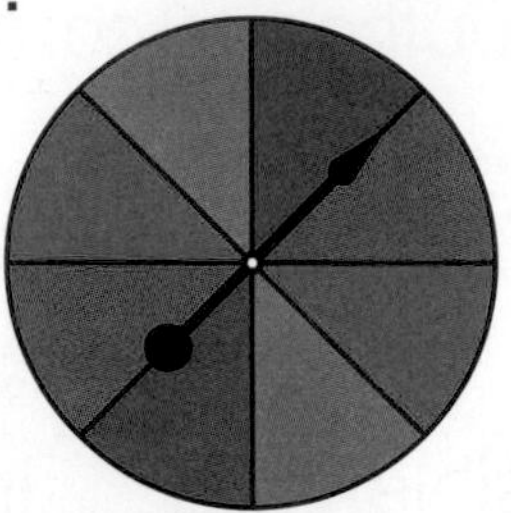

______

10. Color to show each fraction. Compare the fractions. Write <, =, or >.

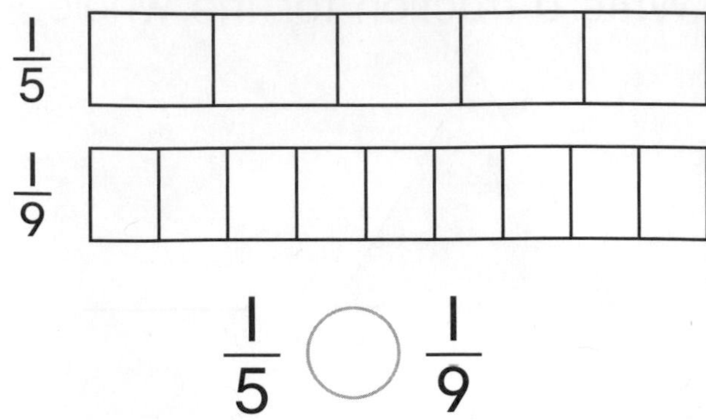

$\frac{1}{5}$ ◯ $\frac{1}{9}$

11. Color to show the equal fraction. Write the equal fraction.

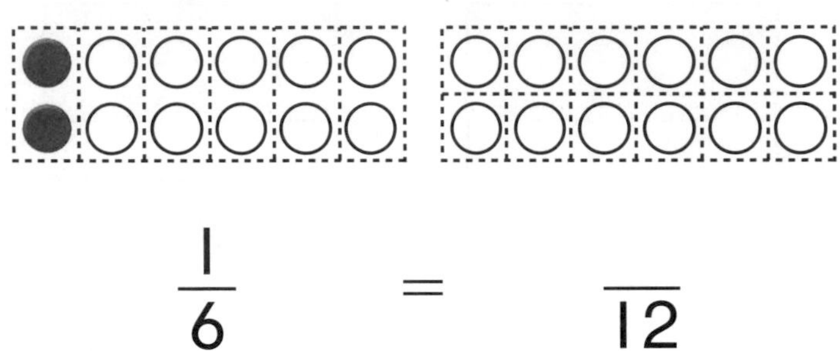

$\frac{1}{6} = \frac{\quad}{12}$

12. Write the fraction for the yellow part.

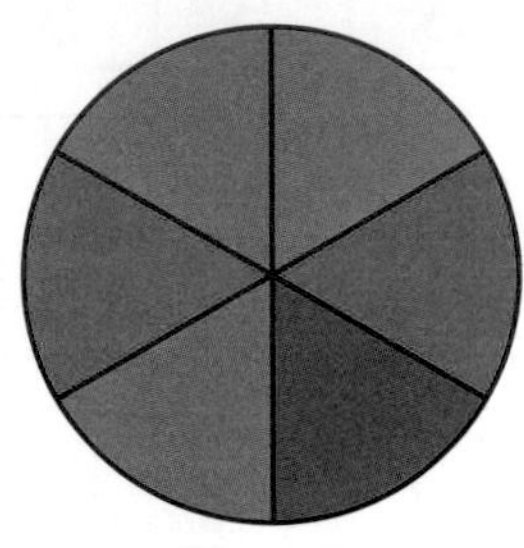

______

Problem Solving Solve. Use a problem-solving strategy.

13. Dan and his 5 friends share a pizza equally. What fractional part of the pizza does Dan eat?

______

14. Jean gets 18 gifts at her party. She opens $\frac{1}{2}$ of them while her aunt is at the party. How many gifts does she open while her aunt is there?

______ gifts

15. Victor lights 12 candles on his cake. One of the candles is yellow. What fractional part of the candles is yellow?

______

16. Lisa has 9 party hats in all. 3 of them are red. What fractional part of the set of party hats is red?

______

Name ______________________________

1. Color to show two equal fractions. Write the fractions.

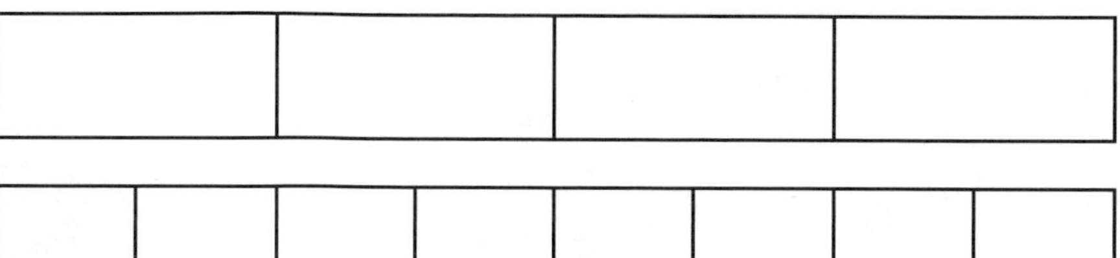

___

___

2. Color some sections red and some blue.

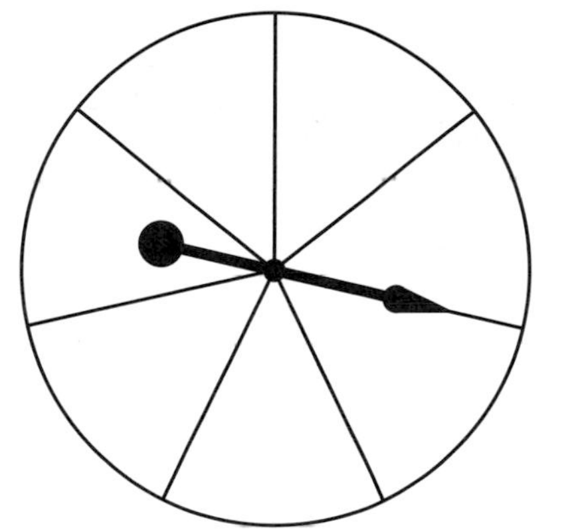

Use the spinner in exercise 2 to complete exercises 3 and 4.

3. Complete. Then write a fraction for each colored part.

____ out of ____ equal sections are red. ____ are red.

____ out of ____ equal sections are blue. ____ are blue.

4. Explain which color the spinner is more likely to land on.

____

____

____

You can put this in your Math Portfolio.

Enrichment

Name ______________________

You can
estimate how full
a container is.

Estimate Volume

This container is half full. 

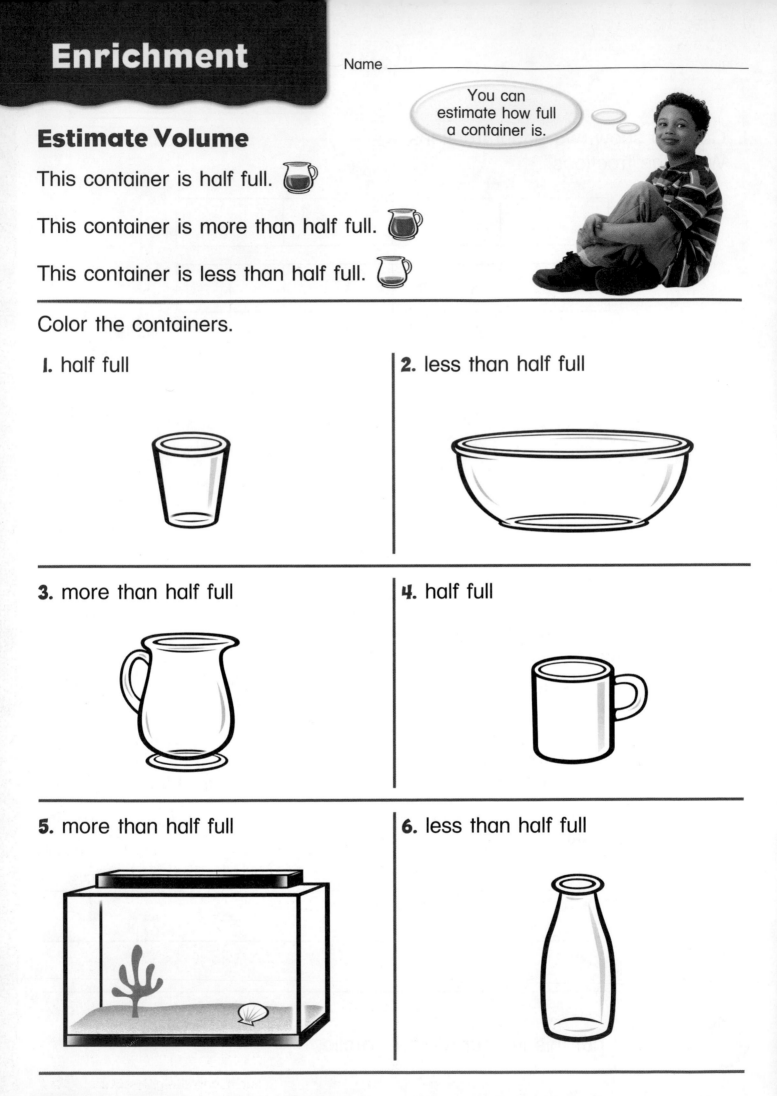

This container is more than half full. 

This container is less than half full. 

Color the containers.

1. half full

2. less than half full

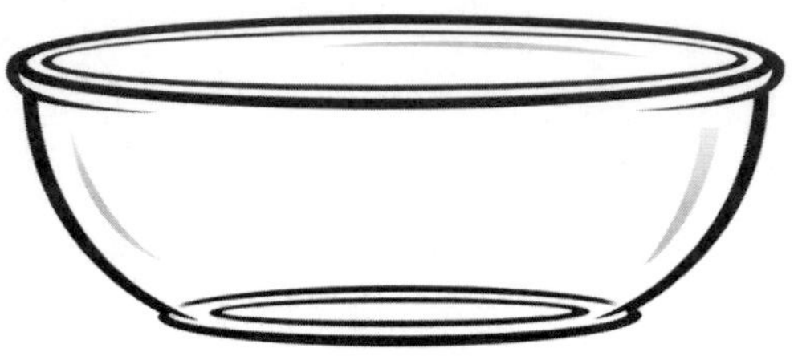

3. more than half full

4. half full

5. more than half full

6. less than half full

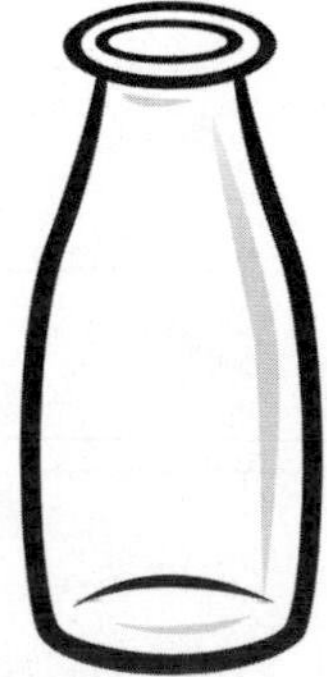

Name ________________________________

TEST PREPARATION

Fill in the circle under the correct answer.

1. Order from greatest to least.

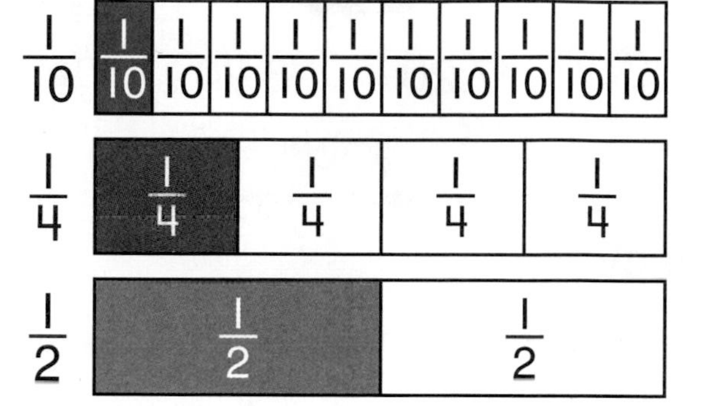

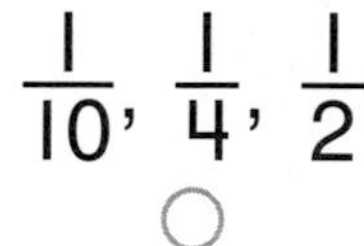
$\frac{1}{10}, \frac{1}{4}, \frac{1}{2}$ ○

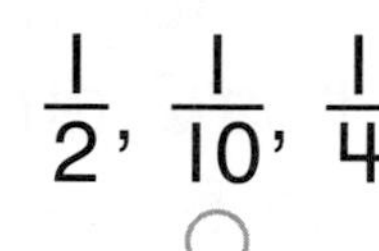
$\frac{1}{2}, \frac{1}{10}, \frac{1}{4}$ ○

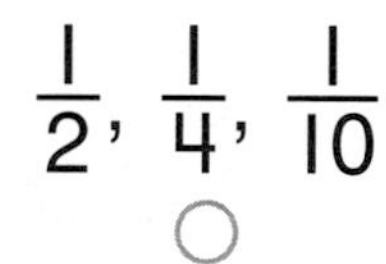
$\frac{1}{2}, \frac{1}{4}, \frac{1}{10}$ ○

2. Find the sum.

$$\begin{array}{r} \$1.67 \\ +\ 0.74 \\ \hline \end{array}$$

$1.41	$2.31	$1.31	$2.41
○	○	○	○

3. Which shows the total amount?

57¢	47¢	50¢	37¢
○	○	○	○

4. Which two colors is it equally likely to spin on this spinner?

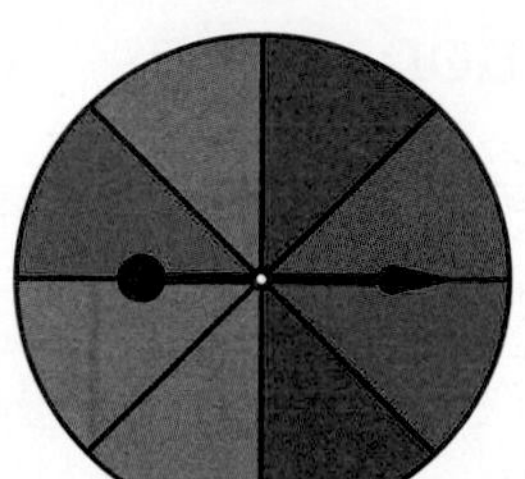

○ red and blue
○ red and yellow
○ blue and green

5. Which is the expanded form for this number?

hundreds	tens	ones
3	5	9

500 + 90 + 3	300 + 50 + 9
○	○
3 + 5 + 9	300 + 90 + 5
○	○

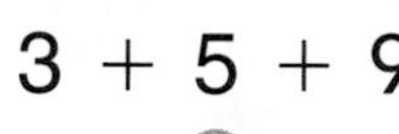

6. Add.

$$\begin{array}{r} 173 \\ +232 \\ \hline \end{array}$$

405	504	450	540
○	○	○	○

7. Compare. Choose <, =, or >.

308  803

<	=	>
○	○	○

8. Which numbers complete the pattern?

232, __?__, 252, 262, __?__

242, 272	233, 263	242, 282
○	○	○

9. How many fourths are in a whole?

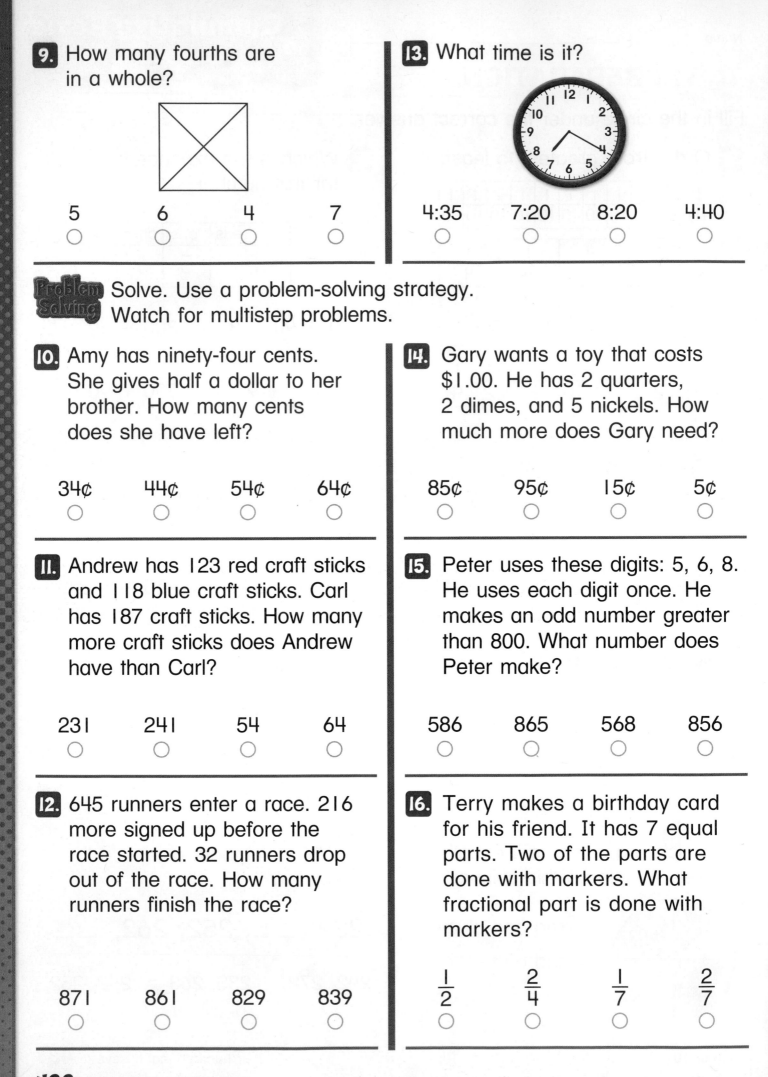

5 ○ 6 ○ 4 ○ 7 ○

13. What time is it?

4:35 ○ 7:20 ○ 8:20 ○ 4:40 ○

Problem Solving Solve. Use a problem-solving strategy. Watch for multistep problems.

10. Amy has ninety-four cents. She gives half a dollar to her brother. How many cents does she have left?

34¢ ○ 44¢ ○ 54¢ ○ 64¢ ○

11. Andrew has 123 red craft sticks and 118 blue craft sticks. Carl has 187 craft sticks. How many more craft sticks does Andrew have than Carl?

231 ○ 241 ○ 54 ○ 64 ○

12. 645 runners enter a race. 216 more signed up before the race started. 32 runners drop out of the race. How many runners finish the race?

871 ○ 861 ○ 829 ○ 839 ○

14. Gary wants a toy that costs $1.00. He has 2 quarters, 2 dimes, and 5 nickels. How much more does Gary need?

85¢ ○ 95¢ ○ 15¢ ○ 5¢ ○

15. Peter uses these digits: 5, 6, 8. He uses each digit once. He makes an odd number greater than 800. What number does Peter make?

586 ○ 865 ○ 568 ○ 856 ○

16. Terry makes a birthday card for his friend. It has 7 equal parts. Two of the parts are done with markers. What fractional part is done with markers?

$\frac{1}{2}$ ○ $\frac{2}{4}$ ○ $\frac{1}{7}$ ○ $\frac{2}{7}$ ○

Measurement

CHAPTER 11

Listen

Listen to your teacher read the poem.

Which shadow is the longest?
Which shadow is the shortest?

Copyright © by William H. Sadlier, Inc. All rights reserved.

Dear Family,

Today our class began Chapter 11. We will learn about measurement. Let's do the activity below together so I can review the skills I will need in order to understand the math in this chapter. Then you can read some of the new vocabulary I will learn in Chapter 11.

Love, ________________

Before and After

Draw a number line like the one below. Have your child point to each number as he/she counts from 1 to 12 on the number line. Then have your child find the number 3 on the number line. Ask which number comes just before 3 and which number comes just after 3. Continue with other numbers. Reviewing the order of numbers on a number line will help your child use a ruler to measure.

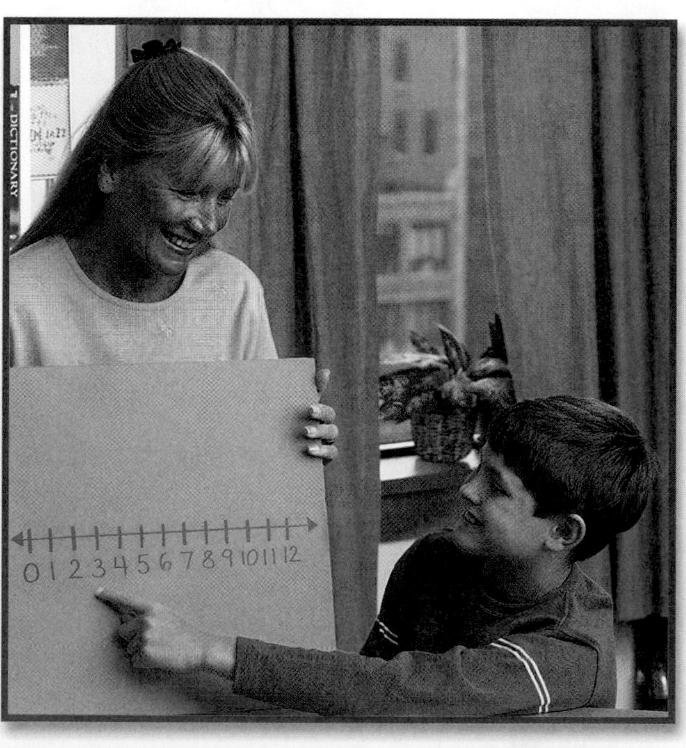

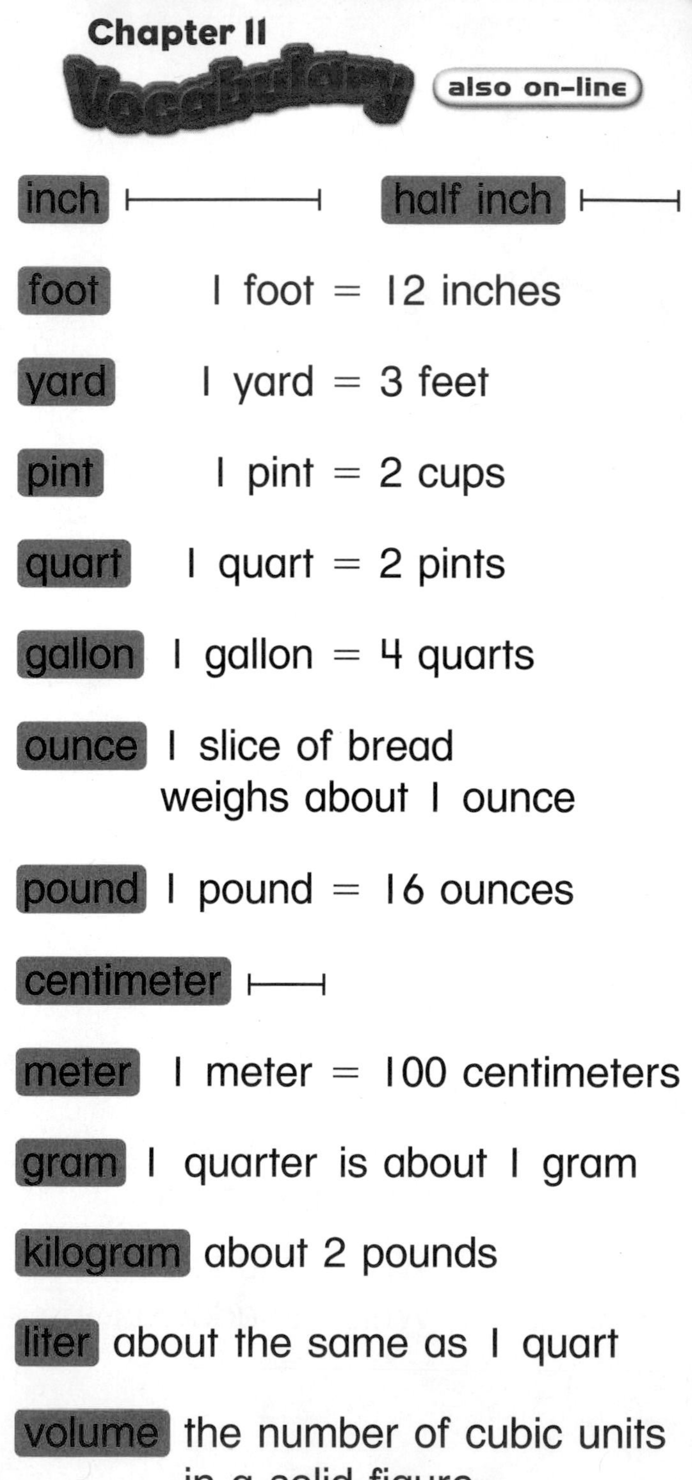

Chapter 11 **Vocabulary** (also on-line)

- **inch** ├──┤ **half inch** ├─┤
- **foot** 1 foot = 12 inches
- **yard** 1 yard = 3 feet
- **pint** 1 pint = 2 cups
- **quart** 1 quart = 2 pints
- **gallon** 1 gallon = 4 quarts
- **ounce** 1 slice of bread weighs about 1 ounce
- **pound** 1 pound = 16 ounces
- **centimeter** ├┤
- **meter** 1 meter = 100 centimeters
- **gram** 1 quarter is about 1 gram
- **kilogram** about 2 pounds
- **liter** about the same as 1 quart
- **volume** the number of cubic units in a solid figure

VISIT US ON-LINE www.sadlier-oxford.com

Name ______________________________

Nonstandard Units

HANDS-ON LESSON

Let's Learn!

An **estimate** of **length** tells about how long.

I estimate that this pencil is about 2 (paper clips) long.

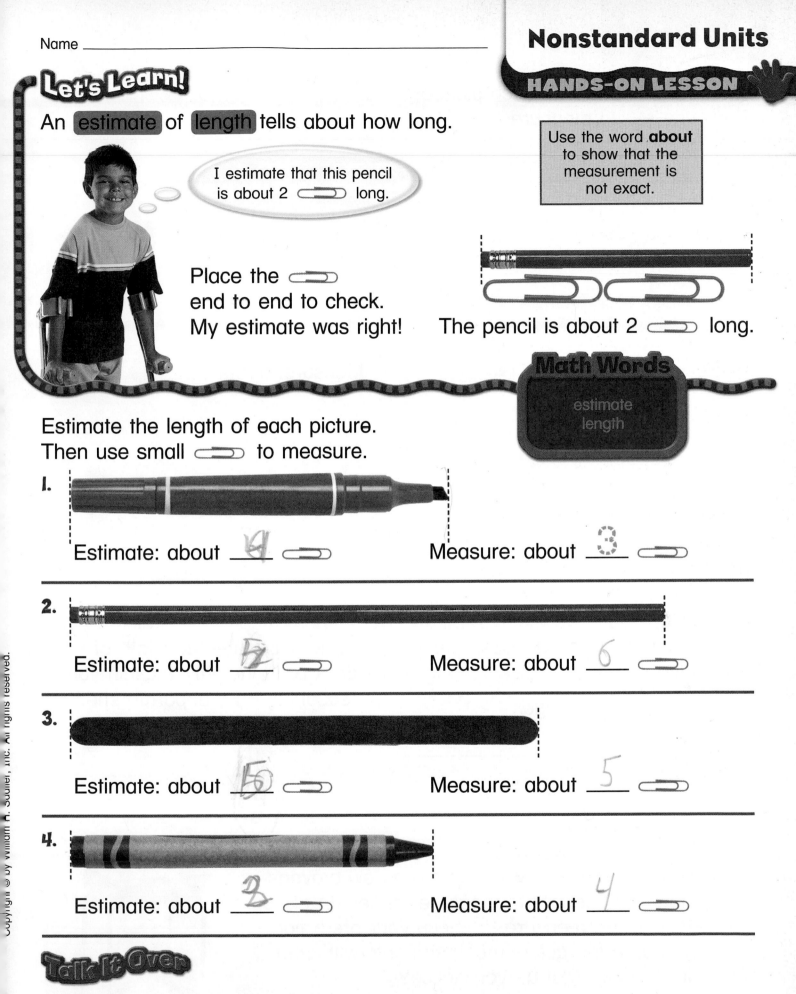

Use the word **about** to show that the measurement is not exact.

Place the (paper clips) end to end to check. My estimate was right!

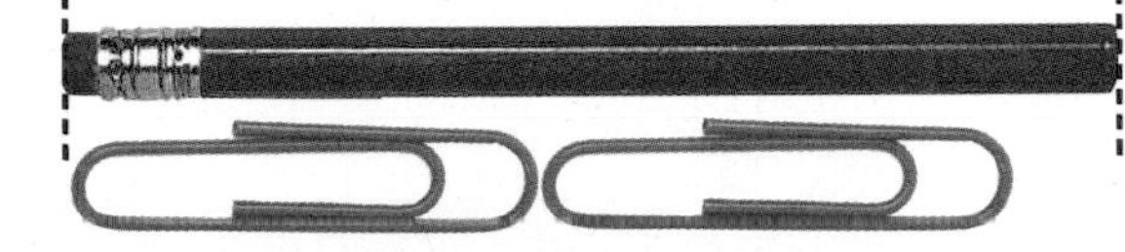

The pencil is about 2 (paper clips) long.

Math Words
estimate
length

Estimate the length of each picture. Then use small (paper clips) to measure.

1.

Estimate: about __4__ (paper clips) Measure: about __3__ (paper clips)

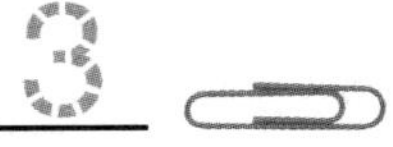

2.

Estimate: about __5__ (paper clips) Measure: about __6__ (paper clips)

3.

Estimate: about __5__ (paper clips) Measure: about __5__ (paper clips)

4.

Estimate: about __3__ (paper clips) Measure: about __4__ (paper clips)

5. Explain how you would order the objects above from shortest to longest.

Copyright © by William H. Sadlier, Inc. All rights reserved.

Practice

Estimate the length of each picture.
Then use [cube] to measure.

6.

Estimate: about ____ [cube] Measure: about 7 [cube]

7.

Estimate: about ____ [cube] Measure: about ____ [cube]

8.

Estimate: about ____ [cube] Measure: about ____ [cube]

Problem Solving Solve. Use a problem-solving strategy.

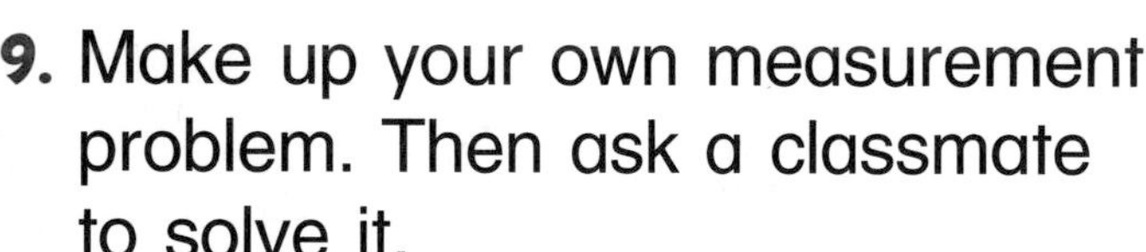

9. Make up your own measurement problem. Then ask a classmate to solve it.

Predict which is longer.

____________ or ____________

Use [cube] to check.

10. Without measuring, which do you think is longer—the width of your desk or its height? Explain your reasoning on a separate sheet of paper. Measure to check.

CRITICAL THINKING

MATH JOURNAL

11. Predict whether it will take more new crayons or more new pencils to measure the length of your desk. Then measure to check your prediction. Compare the actual measurements with your prediction. What do you notice?

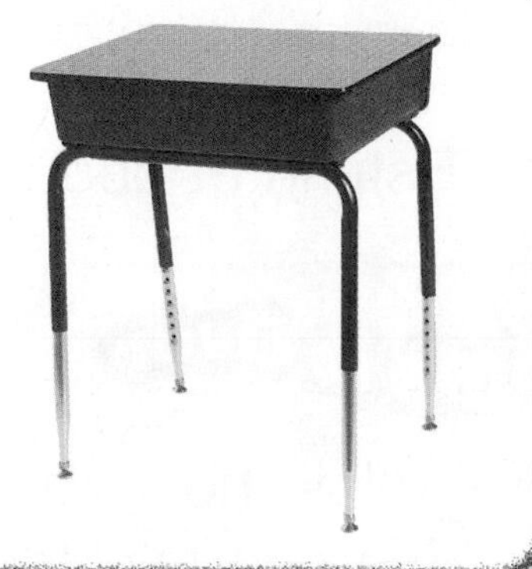

Math Alive at Home Have your child measure three long, thin objects with pennies. Then ask your child to order the objects from shortest to longest.

Name ______________________________

Inches

HANDS-ON LESSON

Let's Learn!

You can measure length or height in inches.
An **inch** is a **unit of measure**.

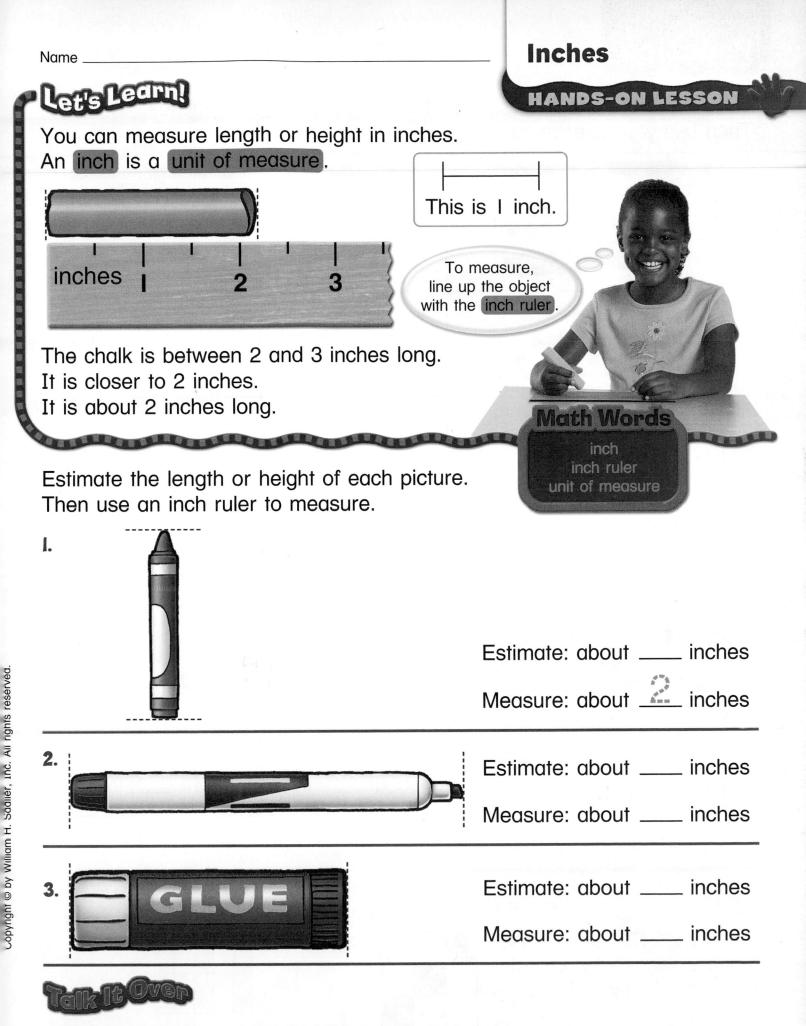

This is 1 inch.

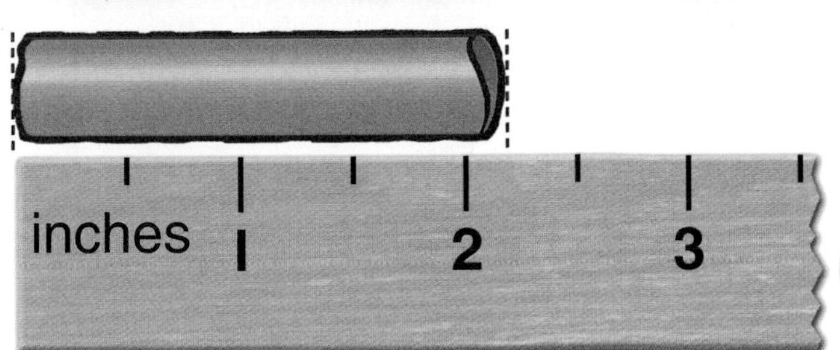

To measure, line up the object with the **inch ruler**.

The chalk is between 2 and 3 inches long.
It is closer to 2 inches.
It is about 2 inches long.

Math Words
inch
inch ruler
unit of measure

Estimate the length or height of each picture.
Then use an inch ruler to measure.

1. 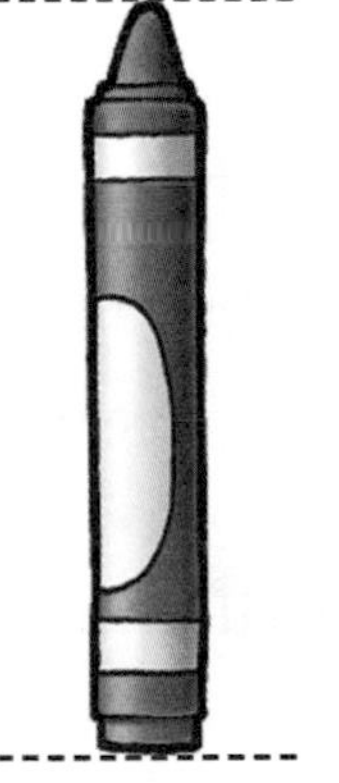

Estimate: about ____ inches

Measure: about __2__ inches

2. 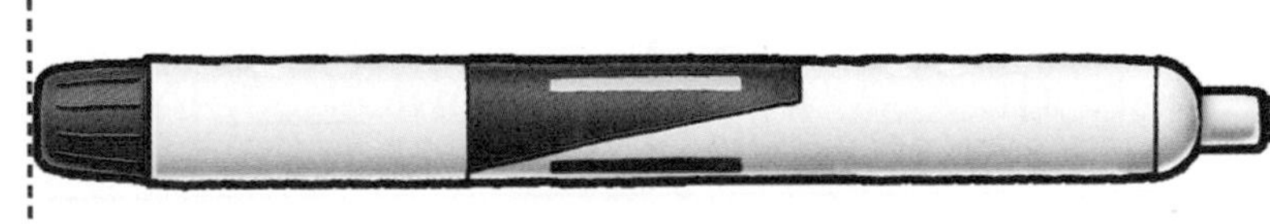

Estimate: about ____ inches

Measure: about ____ inches

3. 

Estimate: about ____ inches

Measure: about ____ inches

4. Explain how you estimated the length or height in each exercise above.

Copyright © by William H. Sadlier, Inc. All rights reserved.

Practice

in. means inch.

Find these real objects. Estimate their length or height in inches. Then use your ruler to measure.

	Object	Estimate	Measure
5.		about ____ in.	about ____ in.
6.	ERASER	about ____ in.	about ____ in.
7.		about ____ in.	about ____ in.
8.		about ____ in.	about ____ in.
9.		about ____ in.	about ____ in.
10.		about ____ in.	about ____ in.

DO YOU REMEMBER?

Write the fraction for the part colored.

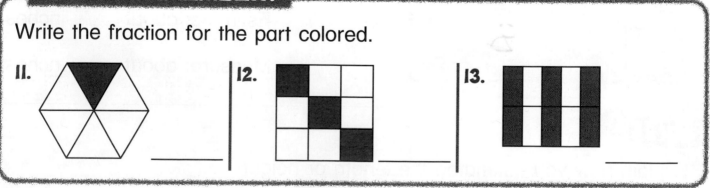

11. 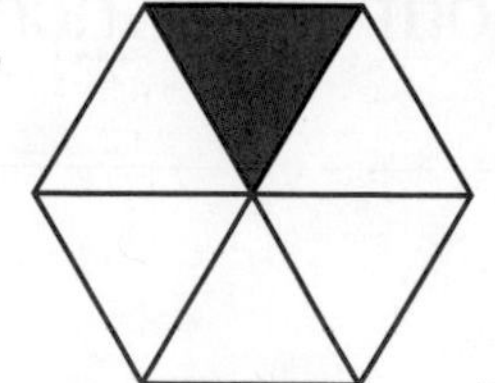 ______

12.  ______

13. 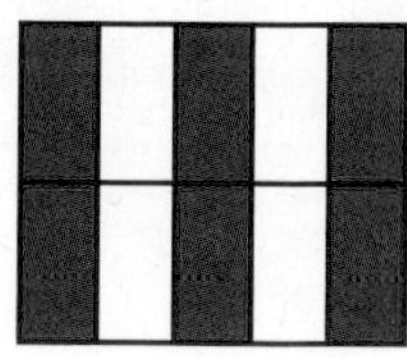 ______

Math Alive at Home *Say a measurement such as 2 inches or 5 inches. Have your child use an inch ruler to find objects of that length.*

Name ______________________

Half Inch

HANDS-ON LESSON

Let's Learn!

When the length of an object falls closer to a half-inch mark than to an inch mark, you can measure to the nearest **half inch**.

A half inch is halfway to an inch.

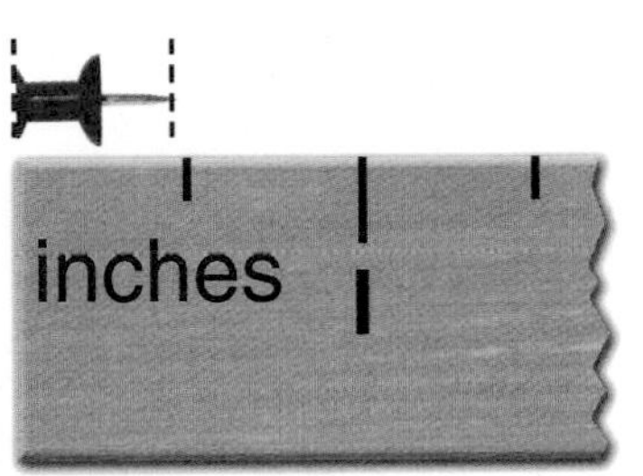

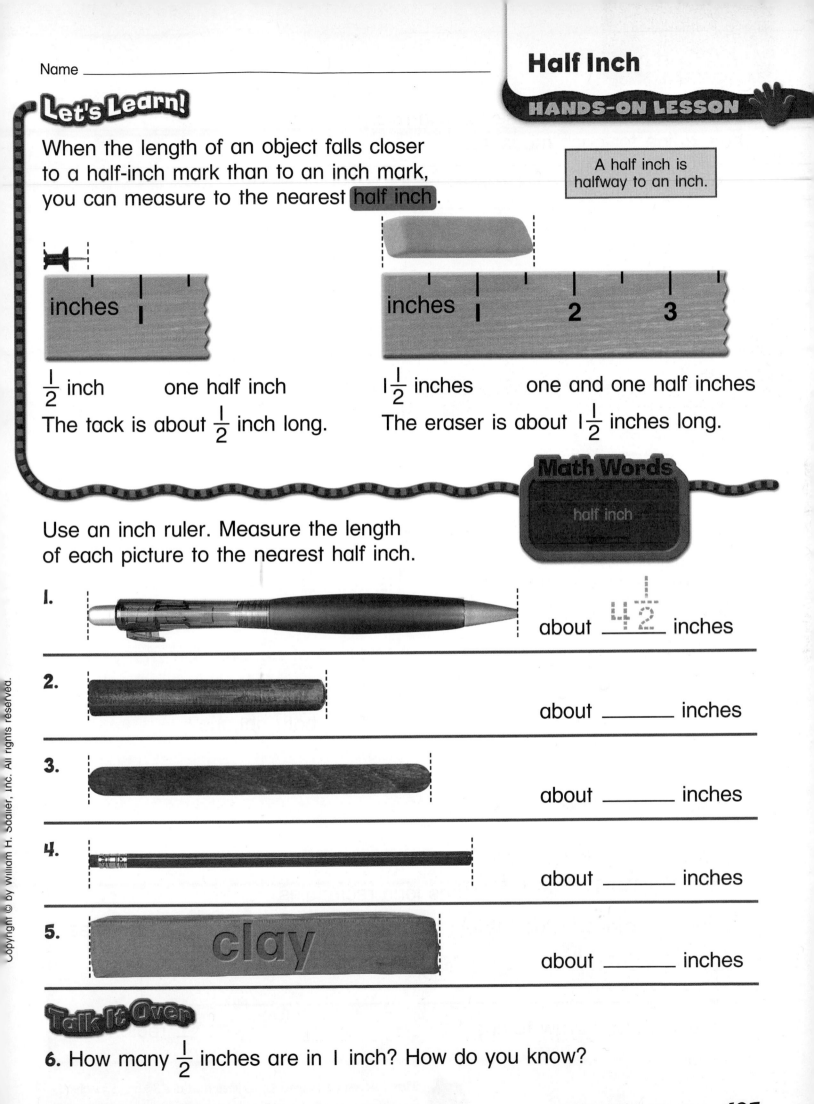

$\frac{1}{2}$ inch one half inch

The tack is about $\frac{1}{2}$ inch long.

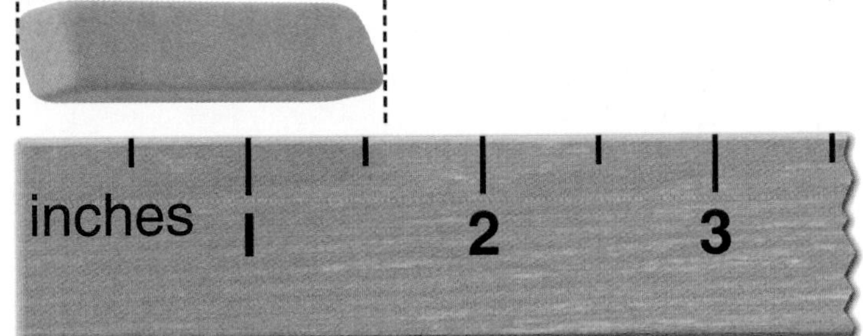

$1\frac{1}{2}$ inches one and one half inches

The eraser is about $1\frac{1}{2}$ inches long.

Use an inch ruler. Measure the length of each picture to the nearest half inch.

1.  about $4\frac{1}{2}$ inches

2. about ______ inches

3. about ______ inches

4. about ______ inches

5. 

about ______ inches

6. How many $\frac{1}{2}$ inches are in 1 inch? How do you know?

Copyright © by William H. Sadlier, Inc. All rights reserved.

Practice

Start at the blue mark. Use an inch ruler.
Draw a line for each measure.

7. $2\frac{1}{2}$ inches

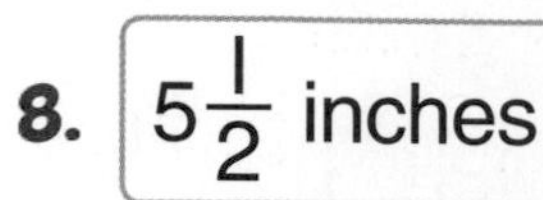

8. $5\frac{1}{2}$ inches

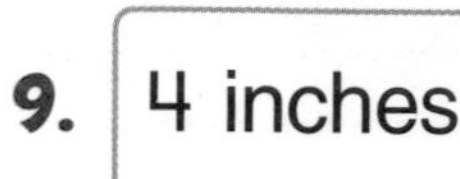

9. 4 inches

10. $3\frac{1}{2}$ inches

Solve. Use a problem-solving strategy.

11. Len has $8\frac{1}{2}$ inches of tape. How many half-inch pieces can he cut from the tape?

____ half-inch pieces

12. **Multistep** Sue has a 7-inch piece of ribbon and a 3-inch piece of ribbon. How many half-inch pieces can she cut from both ribbons?

____ half-inch pieces

CHALLENGE

13. Measure the length of the rectangle. Estimate how many $1\frac{1}{2}$ inches long rectangles you can make inside the big rectangle. ____ rectangles

Measure and draw to check. ____ rectangles

Math Alive at Home Draw lines that are $3\frac{1}{2}$ and $5\frac{1}{2}$ inches long. Have your child use an inch ruler to measure each line and tell its length.

Name ______________________________

Feet and Yards

Let's Learn!

A foot and a yard are units of measure.

I **foot** = 12 inches

A ruler shows I foot.

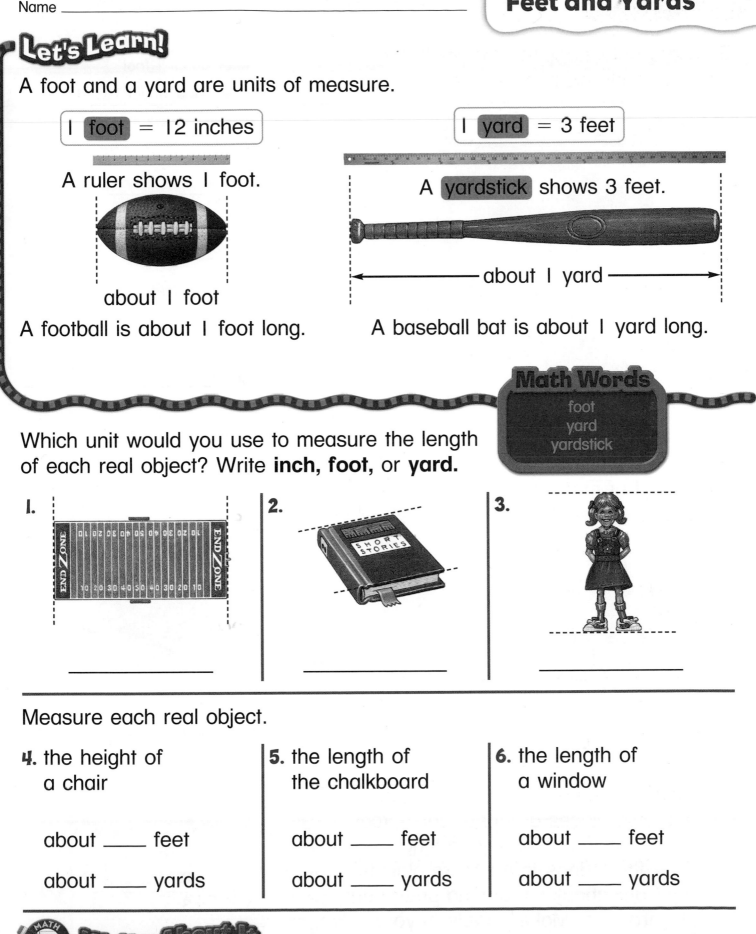

about I foot

A football is about I foot long.

I **yard** = 3 feet

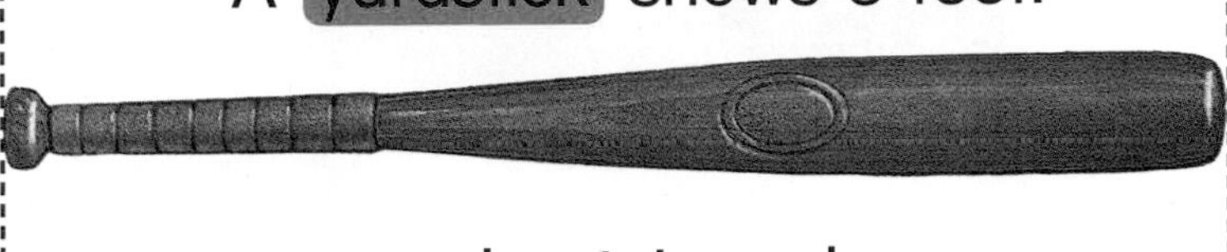

A **yardstick** shows 3 feet.

about I yard

A baseball bat is about I yard long.

Which unit would you use to measure the length of each real object? Write **inch, foot,** or **yard.**

1.

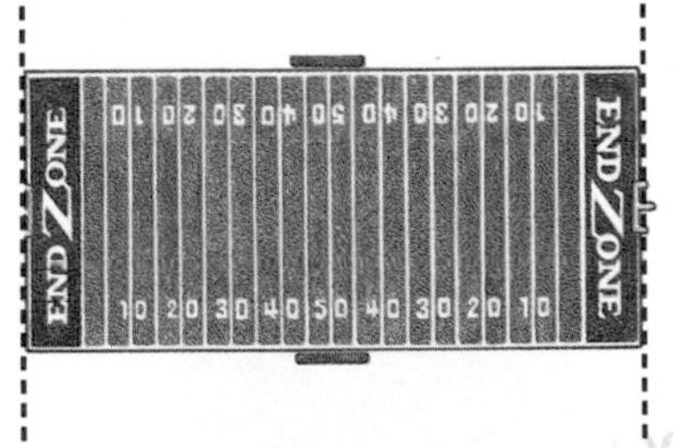

____

2.

____

3.

____

Measure each real object.

4. the height of a chair

about ____ feet

about ____ yards

5. the length of the chalkboard

about ____ feet

about ____ yards

6. the length of a window

about ____ feet

about ____ yards

7. Explain whether the measure of the objects above would be a greater number or a lesser number if measured in inches.

Copyright © by William H. Sadlier, Inc. All rights reserved.

Practice

To estimate, remember:
about 1 foot
about 1 yard

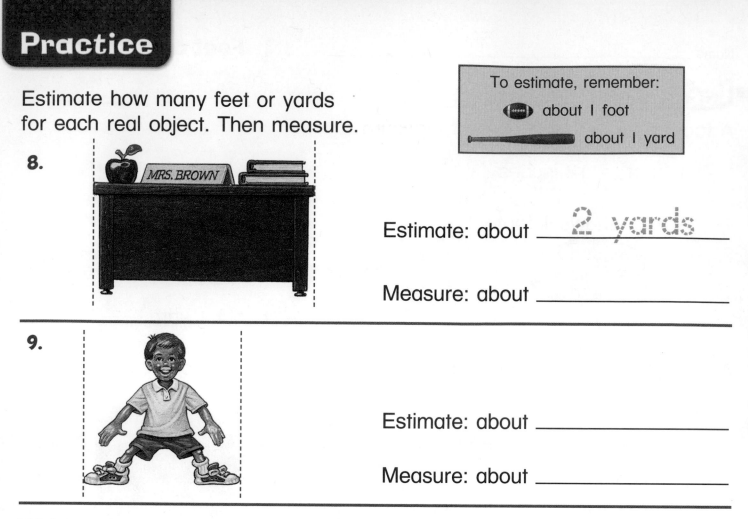

Estimate how many feet or yards for each real object. Then measure.

8.

Estimate: about 2 yards

Measure: about ________

9.

Estimate: about ________

Measure: about ________

Which unit of measure would you use to measure each real object? Write **inches, feet,** or **yards.**

10.

4 ________

11.

7 ________

12.

8 ________

CHALLENGE

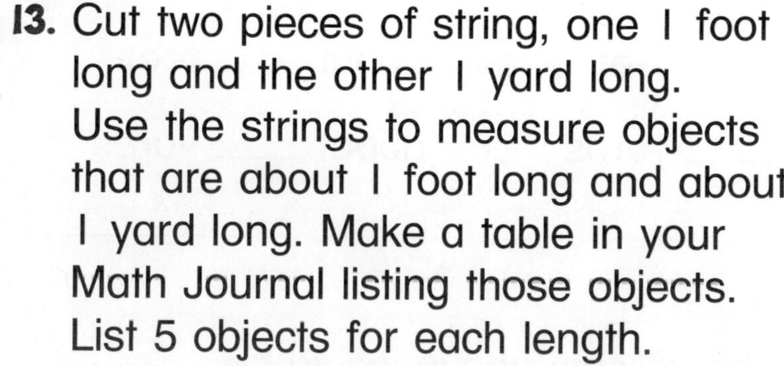

13. Cut two pieces of string, one 1 foot long and the other 1 yard long. Use the strings to measure objects that are about 1 foot long and about 1 yard long. Make a table in your Math Journal listing those objects. List 5 objects for each length.

About 1 foot	About 1 yard
1.	1.
2.	2.
3.	3.
4.	4.
5.	5.

Math Alive at Home Have your child find an object that he/she thinks is about 1 foot long and another about 1 yard long. Then have your child measure to check.

Check Your Progress
Lessons 1-4

Name ______________________

TEST PREPARATION

Listen to your teacher read the directions.
Fill in the circle under the correct answer.

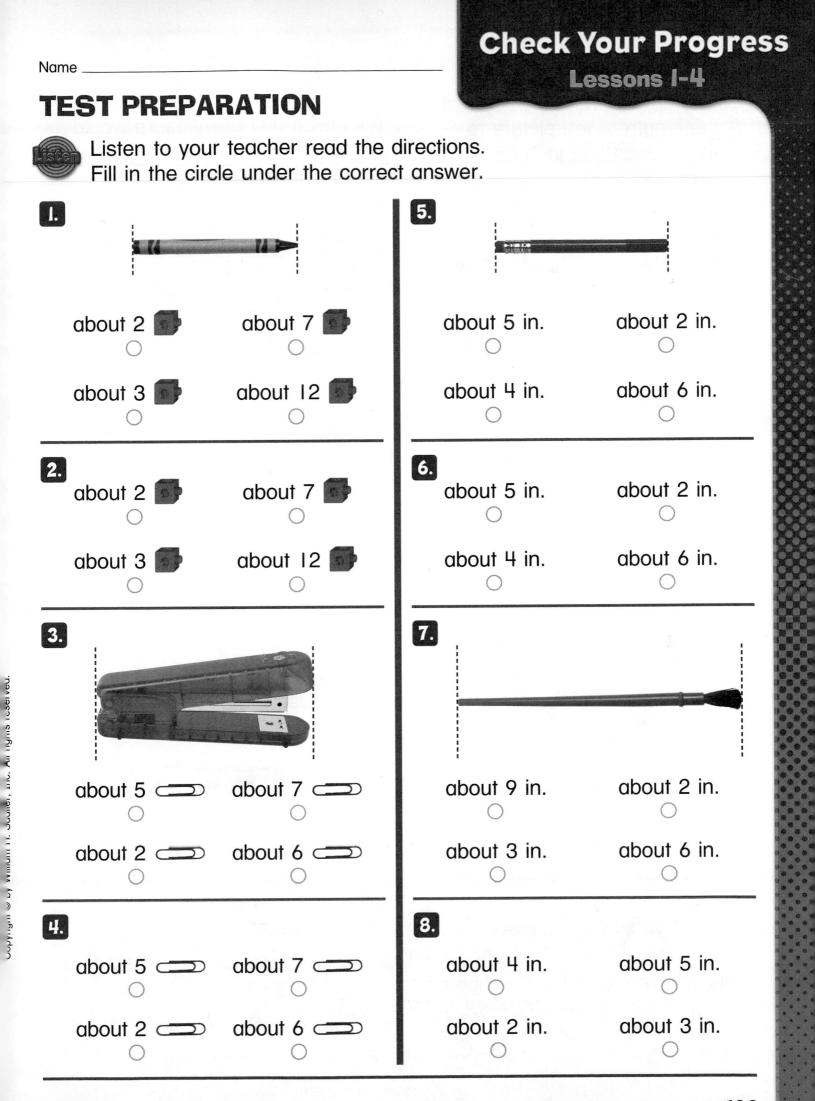

1.

about 2 ○ | about 7 ○
about 3 ○ | about 12 ○

2.

about 2 ○ | about 7 ○
about 3 ○ | about 12 ○

3.

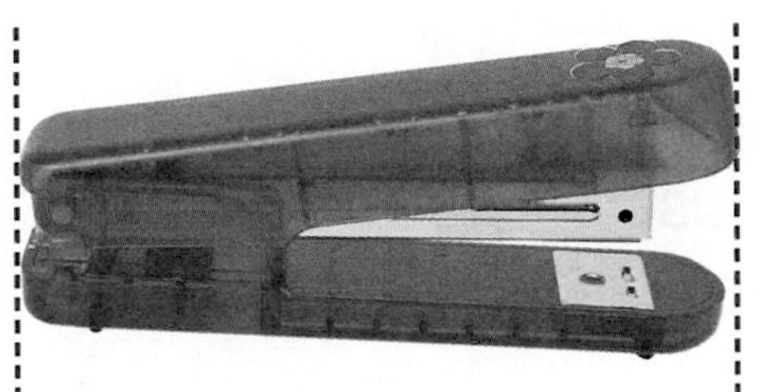

about 5  ○ | about 7 ○
about 2   ○ | about 6 ○

4.

about 5  ○ | about 7 ○
about 2  ○ | about 6 ○

5.

about 5 in.  ○ | about 2 in. ○
about 4 in.  ○ | about 6 in. ○

6.

about 5 in.  ○ | about 2 in. ○
about 4 in.  ○ | about 6 in. ○

7.

about 9 in.  ○ | about 2 in. ○
about 3 in.  ○ | about 6 in. ○

8.

about 4 in.  ○ | about 5 in. ○
about 2 in.  ○ | about 3 in. ○

Copyright © by William H. Sadlier, Inc. All rights reserved.

Fill in the circle under the correct answer.

Use an inch ruler to measure the length of the picture to the nearest half inch for exercises 9–12.

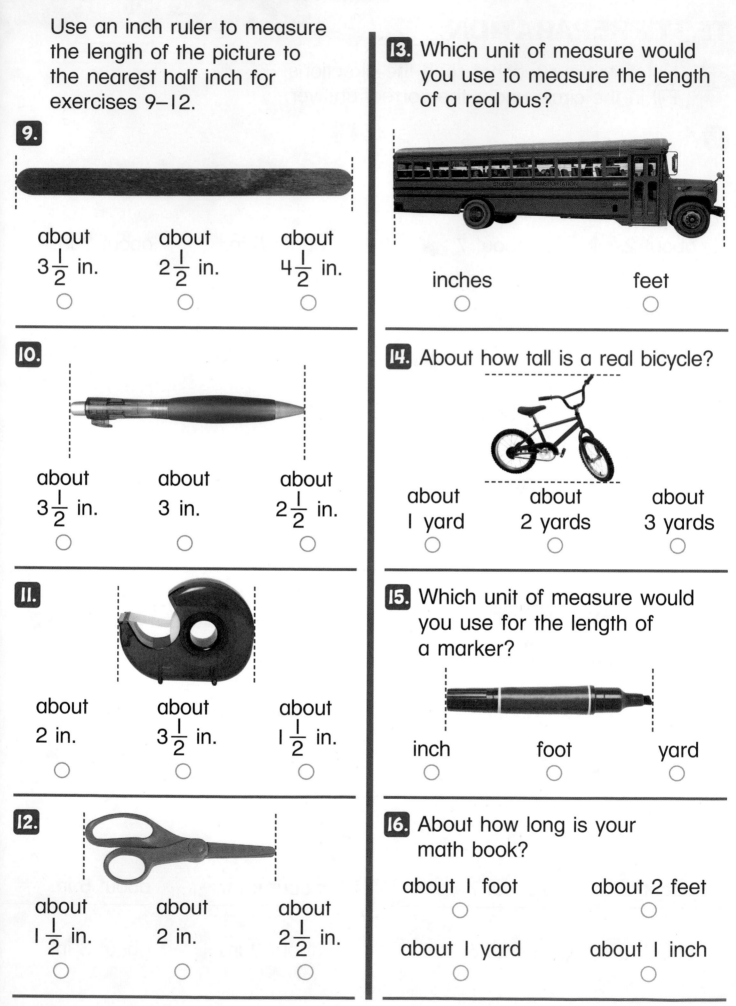

9.

about $3\frac{1}{2}$ in.	about $2\frac{1}{2}$ in.	about $4\frac{1}{2}$ in.
○	○	○

10.

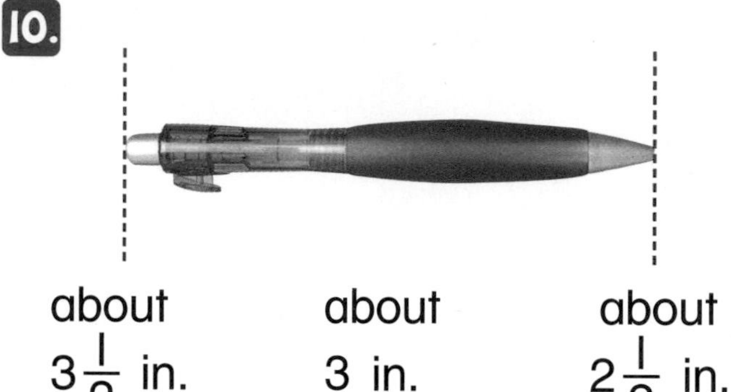

about $3\frac{1}{2}$ in.	about 3 in.	about $2\frac{1}{2}$ in.
○	○	○

11.

about 2 in.	about $3\frac{1}{2}$ in.	about $1\frac{1}{2}$ in.
○	○	○

12.

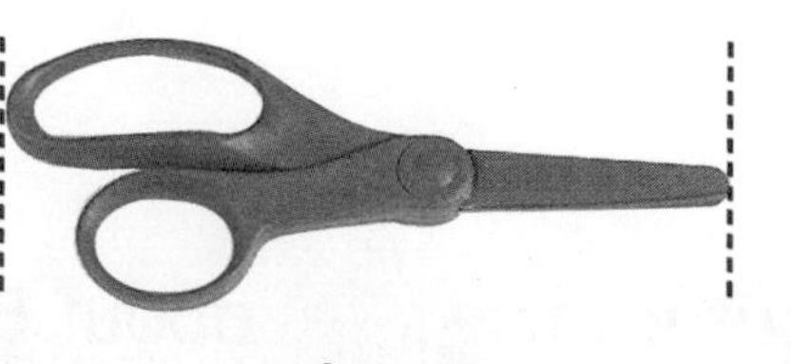

about $1\frac{1}{2}$ in.	about 2 in.	about $2\frac{1}{2}$ in.
○	○	○

13. Which unit of measure would you use to measure the length of a real bus?

inches	feet
○	○

14. About how tall is a real bicycle?

about 1 yard	about 2 yards	about 3 yards
○	○	○

15. Which unit of measure would you use for the length of a marker?

inch	foot	yard
○	○	○

16. About how long is your math book?

about 1 foot	about 2 feet
○	○
about 1 yard	about 1 inch
○	○

Name ______________________________

Cups, Pints, and Quarts

Let's Learn!

You can measure liquids or how much a container holds in cups, pints, or quarts.

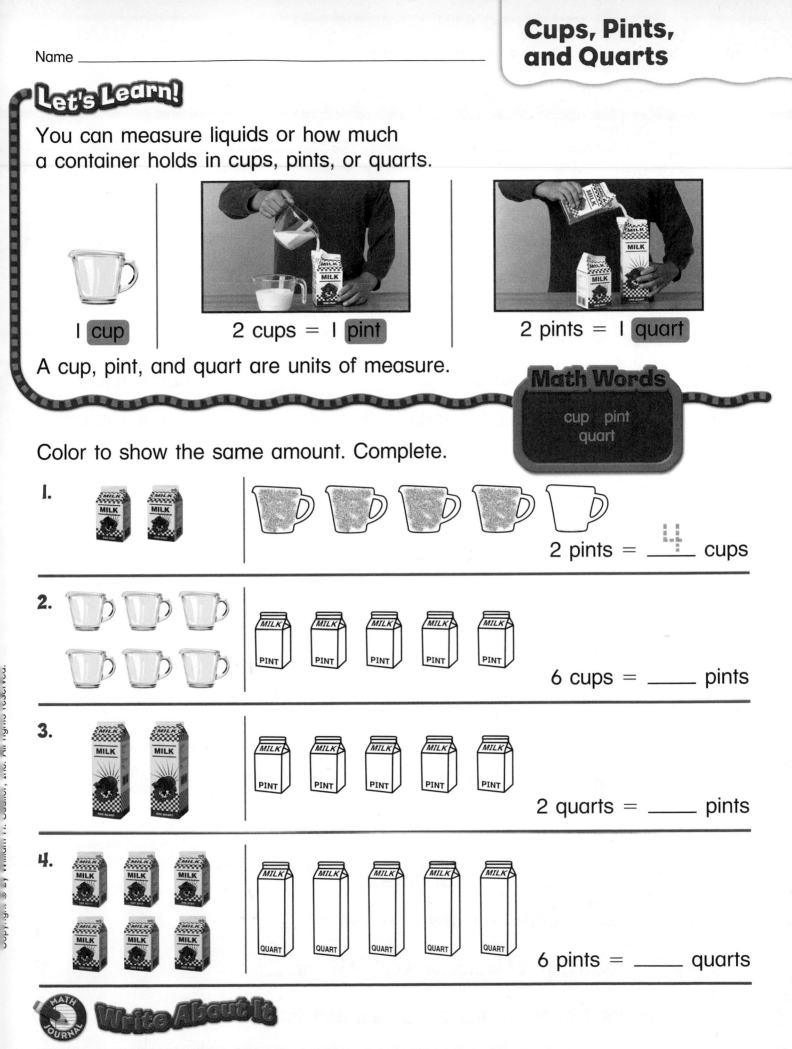

1 cup

2 cups = 1 pint

2 pints = 1 quart

A cup, pint, and quart are units of measure.

Color to show the same amount. Complete.

1.  

2 pints = 4 cups

2. 

6 cups = _____ pints

3. 

2 quarts = _____ pints

4.  

 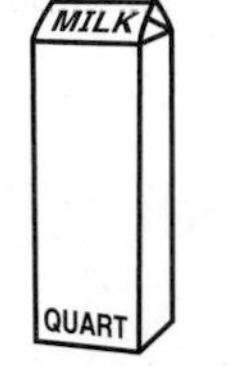 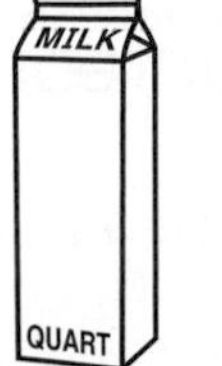 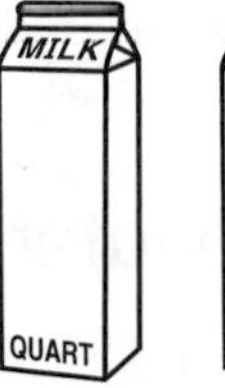 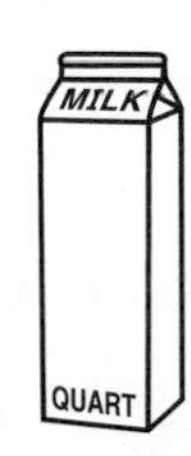

6 pints = _____ quarts

5. Is 1 quart equal to 4 cups? Explain how you know.

Copyright © by William H. Sadlier, Inc. All rights reserved.

Practice

About how much does each real container hold?
Circle the better estimate.

6.

about 1 cup

about 1 pint

7.

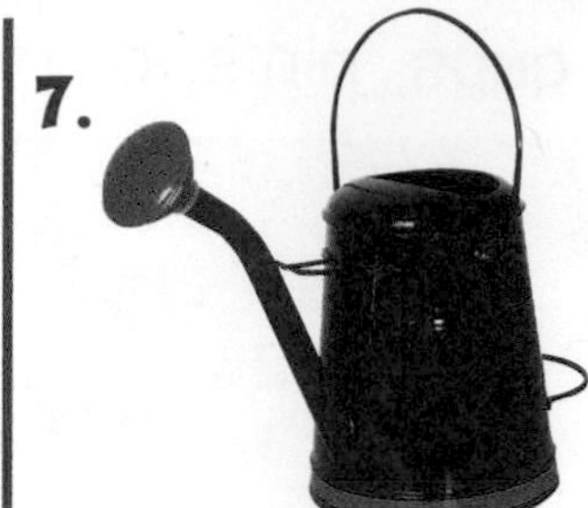

about 2 cups

about 2 quarts

8.

about 3 cups

about 3 quarts

9.

about 1 pint

about 1 quart

Solve. Use a problem-solving strategy.
Show your work on a separate sheet of paper.

10. Mia's jar holds 1 pint. Kerry's jar holds 1 cup. Julie's jar holds the most. Write the letter to show which jar belongs to each girl.

Mia ____ Kerry ____ Julie ____

11. Lee needs 1 pint of grape juice to make punch. How many cups of grape juice does he need?

____ cups

CRITICAL THINKING

Write R for reasonable or U for unreasonable.

12. Sara drinks 5 quarts of water at dinner. ____

13. Martin uses 1 pint of water to wash the car. ____

14. Kate pours 1 quart of milk into 2 pint bottles. ____

Math Alive at Home Have your child use a measuring cup to find containers that hold about 1 cup, about 1 pint, and about 1 quart.

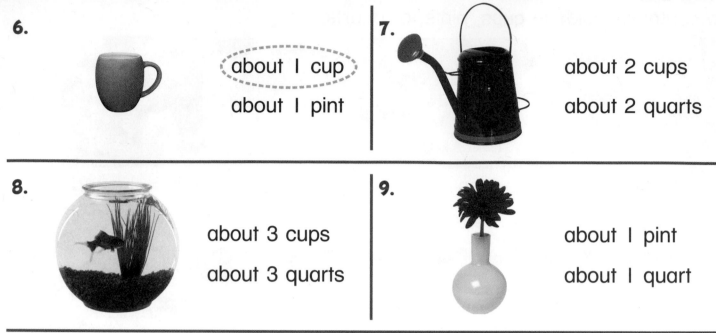

Name ______________________________

Find Hidden Information

- Sometimes you need to find hidden information to solve a problem.

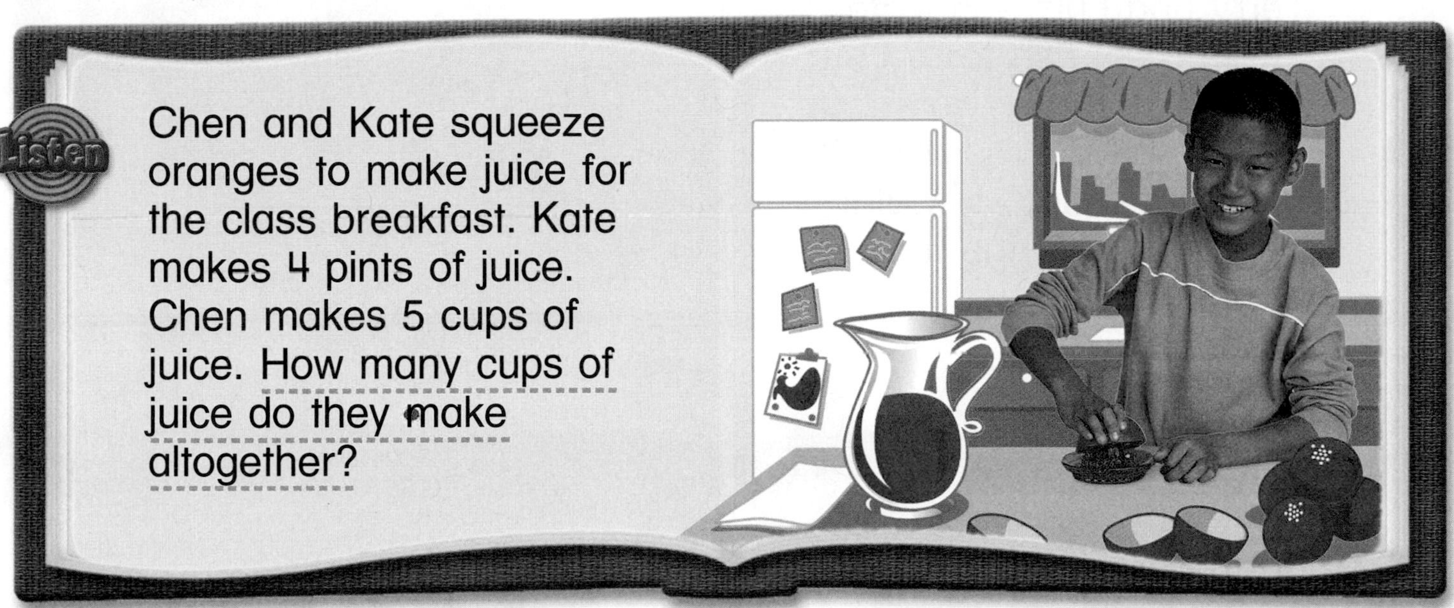

Chen and Kate squeeze oranges to make juice for the class breakfast. Kate makes 4 pints of juice. Chen makes 5 cups of juice. How many cups of juice do they make altogether?

1. Reread the problem. Draw a line under the question you need to answer.

---

2. How much juice does each child make? Finish each sentence.

   Kate makes ______________ of juice.

   Chen makes ______________ of juice.

---

3. To compare the different amounts, you need to use the same unit of measure. Now find the hidden information.
   1 pint = _____ cups

   Rewrite the amounts as cups.

   Kate makes _____ cups of juice.

   Chen makes _____ cups of juice.

---

4. Solve the problem.

   The children make _____ cups of juice altogether.

Practice

Find Hidden Information

Listen
Terry and Luis add water to the class fish tank. Luis adds 3 quarts of water. Terry adds 5 pints of water. How many pints of water do they add to the tank in all?

5. Reread the problem. Draw a line under the question you need to answer.

---

6. How much water does each child add? Finish each sentence.

Luis adds ________________ of water.

Terry adds ________________ of water.

---

7. To compare the different amounts, you need to use the same unit of measure. Now find the hidden information.
1 quart = ______ pints

Rewrite the amounts as pints.

Luis adds ______ pints of water.

Terry adds ______ pints of water.

---

8. Solve the problem.

The children add ______ pints of water in all.

Math Alive at Home Today your child used hidden information to work through math problems.

Name ______________________________

Gallons

Let's Learn!

A gallon is a unit of measure.

You can also measure liquids or how much a container holds in gallons.

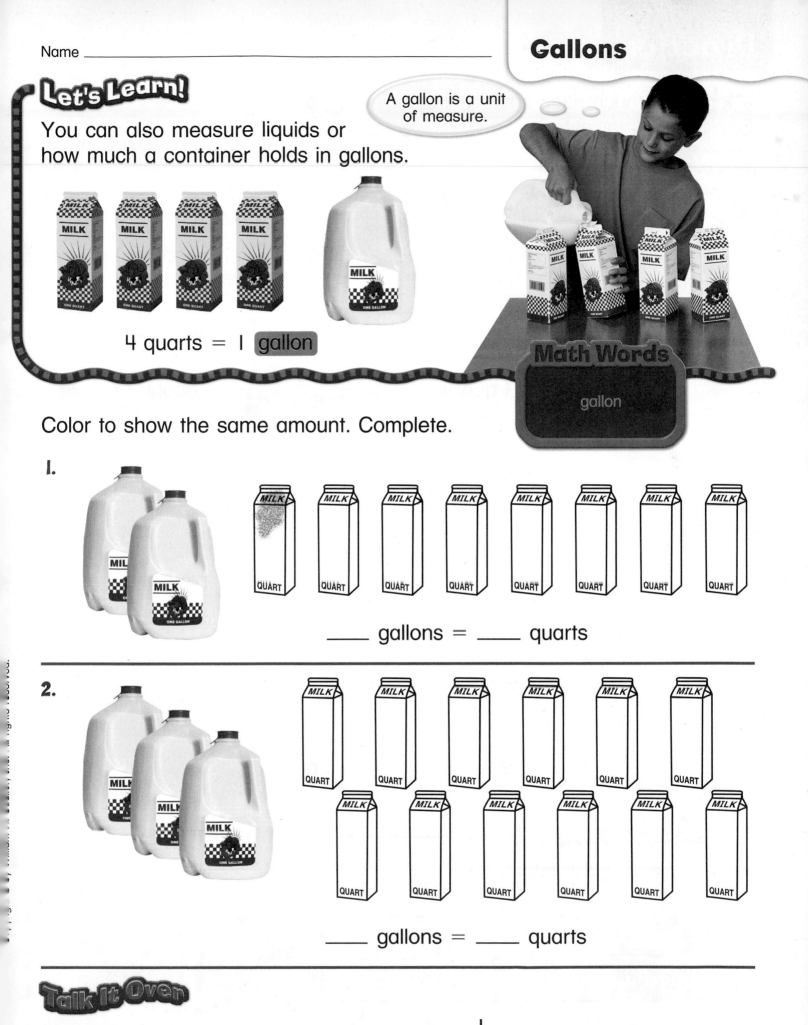

4 quarts = 1 gallon

Math Words

gallon

Color to show the same amount. Complete.

1.

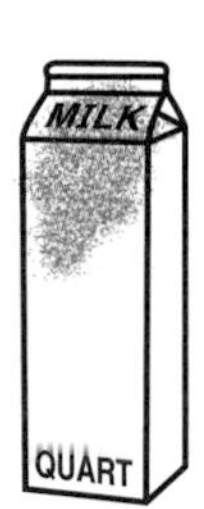
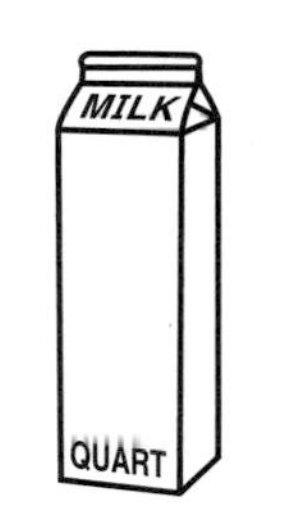
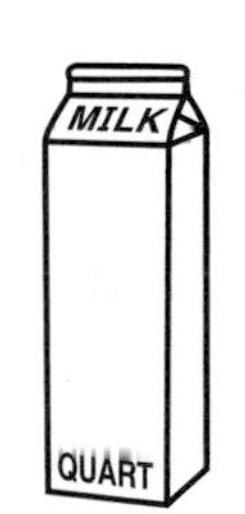
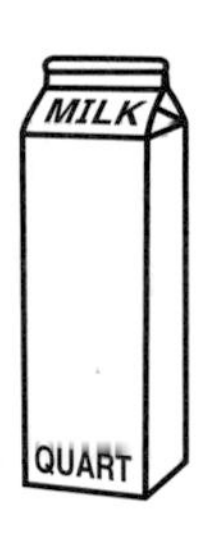
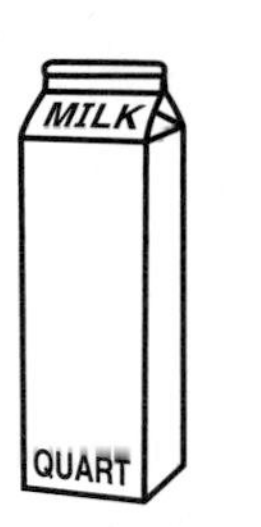
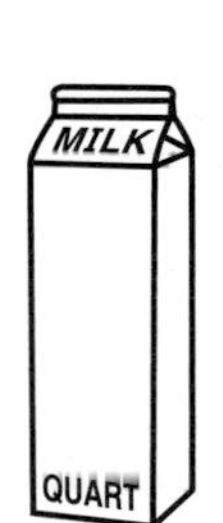
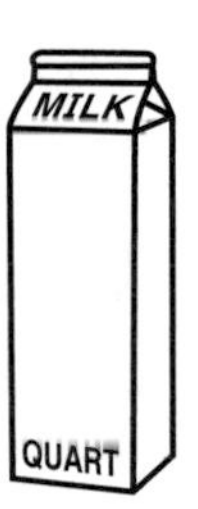
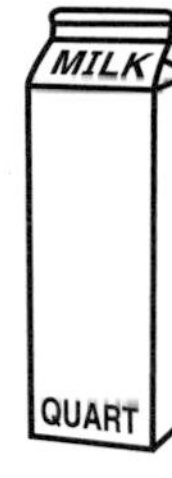

____ gallons = ____ quarts

2.

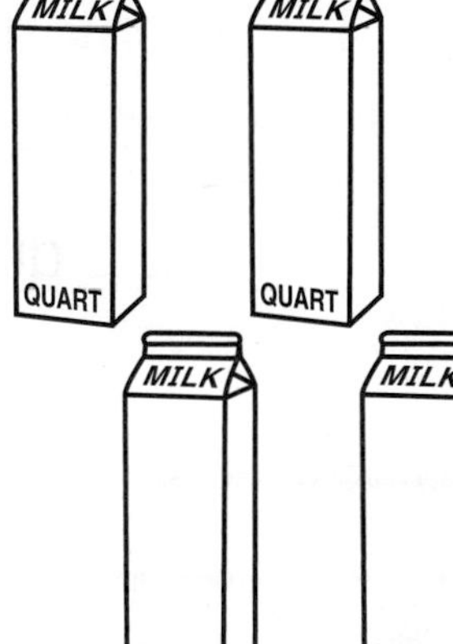
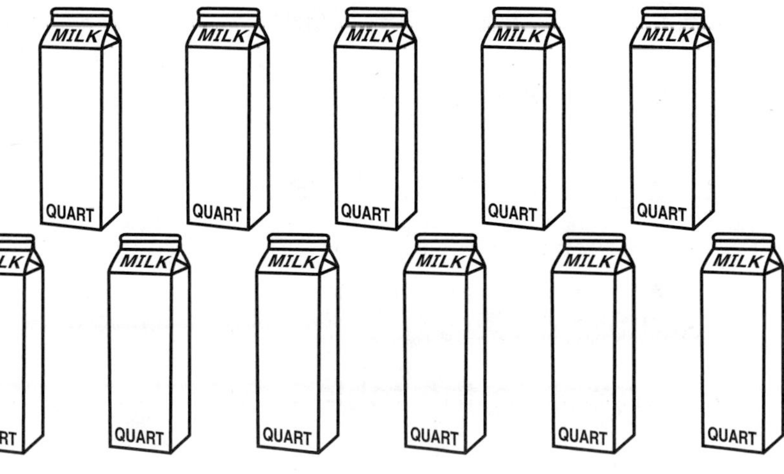

____ gallons = ____ quarts

3. Explain how you know how many quarts a $\frac{1}{2}$-gallon container holds.

Practice

About how much does each real container hold? Circle the better estimate.

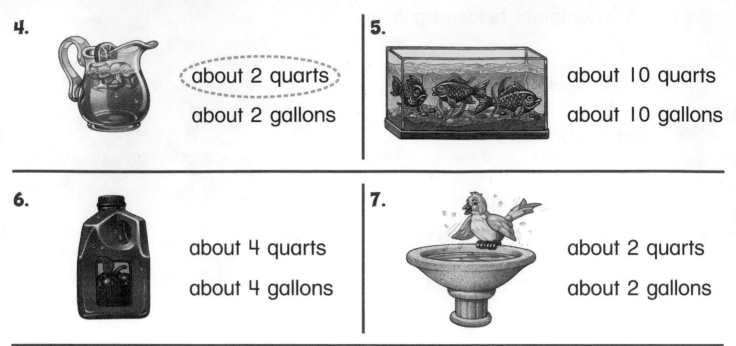

4.

about 2 quarts

about 2 gallons

5.

about 10 quarts

about 10 gallons

6.

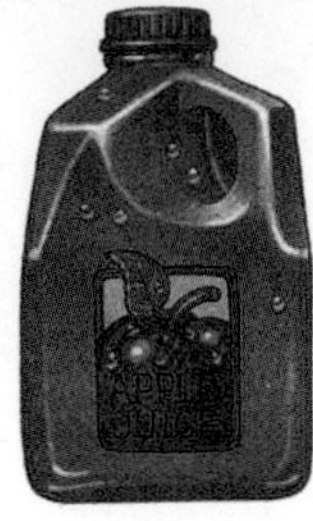

about 4 quarts

about 4 gallons

7.

about 2 quarts

about 2 gallons

Solve. Use a problem-solving strategy. Show your work on a separate sheet of paper.

8. Multistep Tanya buys 2 gallons of milk. Kim buys 3 quarts of milk. Sam buys 1 gallon and 2 quarts. Who buys the most milk? Who buys the least?

________ buys the most.

________ buys the least.

9. Multistep Lisa's teacher makes $2\frac{1}{2}$ gallons of lemonade for a class party. Jared's dad brings 6 quarts of lemonade. How many quarts of lemonade does Lisa's teacher have now?

____ quarts

MENTAL MATH

10. Complete the table.

Gallons	1	2	3	4	5
Quarts	4				

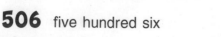

Math Alive at Home Have your child use an empty quart container to fill a gallon container. Then ask your child how many quarts there are in one gallon. (4)

Name ___________________________

Ounces and Pounds

HANDS-ON LESSON

Let's Learn!

You can use a **balance** to weigh objects.
Measure weight in ounces or pounds.
An **ounce** and a **pound** are units of measure.

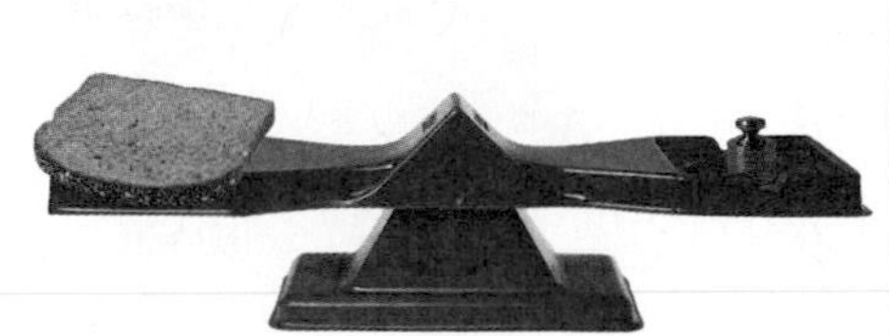

1 slice of bread weighs about 1 ounce.

3 bananas weigh about 1 pound.

1 pound = 16 ounces

Math Words
balance
ounce
pound

About how much does each real object weigh?
Circle the better estimate.
Then use a balance and weights to check.

1. 

about 2 ounces

about 2 pounds

2. 

about 1 ounce

about 1 pound

3. 

about 10 ounces

about 10 pounds

4. 

about 2 ounces

about 2 pounds

5. 

about 3 ounces

about 3 pounds

6. 

about 7 ounces

about 7 pounds

7. Order the objects in exercises 4–6 above from lightest to heaviest.

Practice

About how much does each real object weigh?
Circle the better estimate.

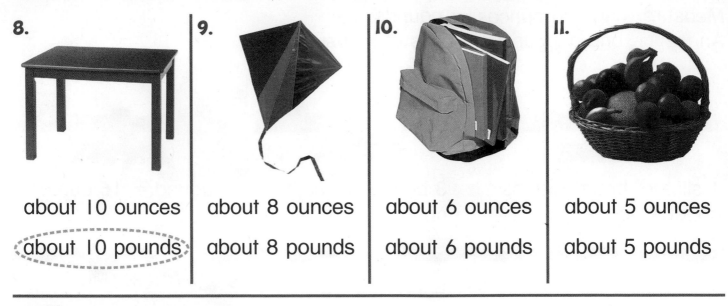

8.	9.	10.	11.

about 10 ounces	about 8 ounces	about 6 ounces	about 5 ounces
about 10 pounds	about 8 pounds	about 6 pounds	about 5 pounds

Solve. Use a problem-solving strategy.

12. Al can carry up to 3 pounds in his backpack. He packs it with a $1\frac{1}{2}$ pound lunch box and an extra pair of shoes that weighs $1\frac{1}{2}$ pounds. Can Al carry all his things in his backpack?

____

13. Gen wants to know the weight of her books. Her math book weighs about $1\frac{1}{2}$ pounds, her reading book weighs about 2 pounds, and her lunch box weighs about $\frac{1}{2}$ pound. How much do her books weigh?

about ____ pounds

CRITICAL THINKING Algebra

14. Ted weighs objects **A, B,** and **C.** Which object weighs the most?

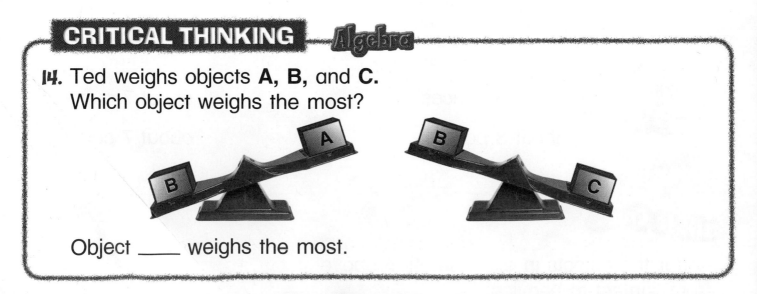

Object ____ weighs the most.

Math Alive at Home Ask your child to show you something that weighs about an ounce and something that weighs about a pound. Have your child weigh the objects to check.

Name ______________________________

Check Your Progress

Lessons 5-8

TEST PREPARATION

Listen to your teacher read the directions.
Fill in the circle under the correct answer.

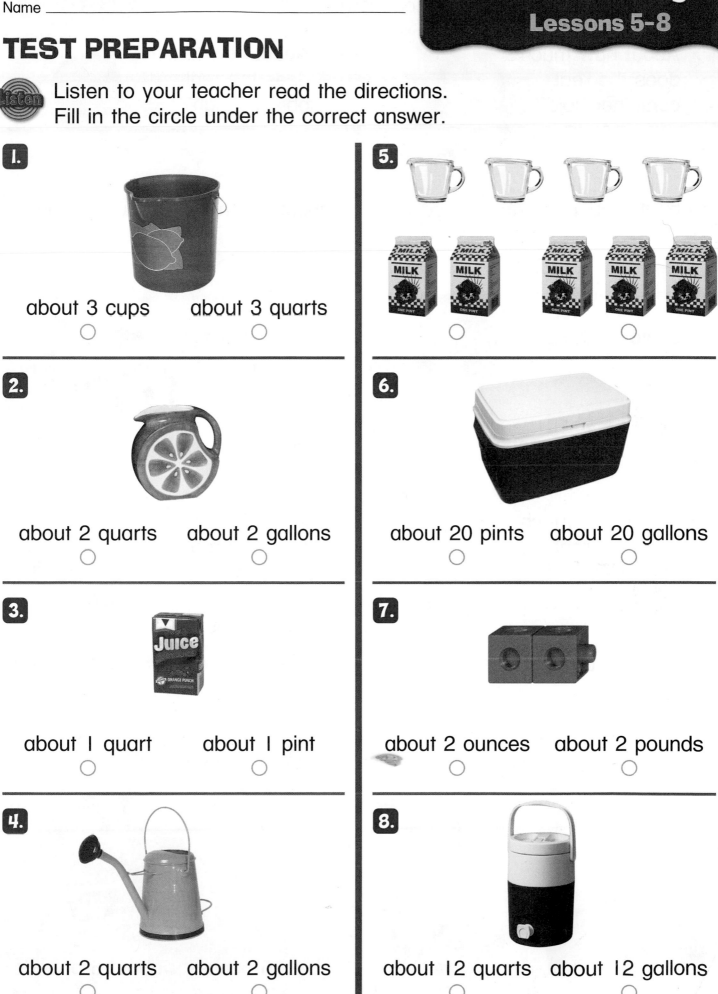

1.

about 3 cups ○ about 3 quarts ○

2.

about 2 quarts ○ about 2 gallons ○

3.

about 1 quart ○ about 1 pint ○

4.

about 2 quarts ○ about 2 gallons ○

5.

○ ○

6.

about 20 pints ○ about 20 gallons ○

7.

about 2 ounces ○ about 2 pounds ○

8.

about 12 quarts ○ about 12 gallons ○

Fill in the circle under the correct answer.

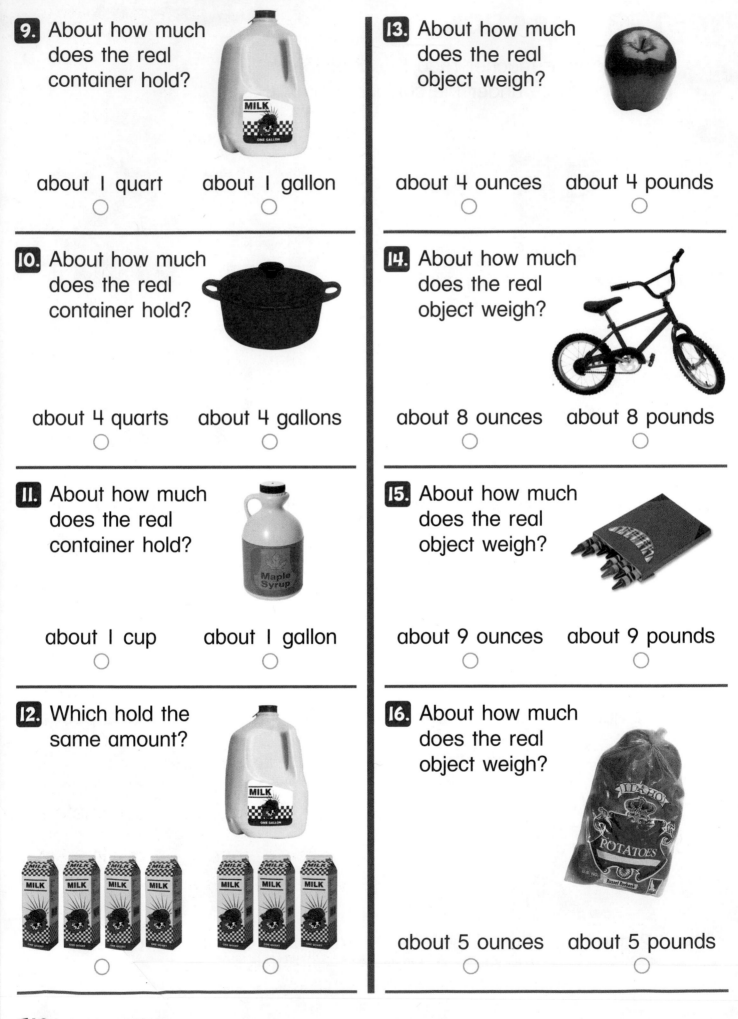

9. About how much does the real container hold?

about 1 quart ○ about 1 gallon ○

10. About how much does the real container hold?

about 4 quarts ○ about 4 gallons ○

11. About how much does the real container hold?

about 1 cup ○ about 1 gallon ○

12. Which hold the same amount?

○

○

13. About how much does the real object weigh?

about 4 ounces ○ about 4 pounds ○

14. About how much does the real object weigh?

about 8 ounces ○ about 8 pounds ○

15. About how much does the real object weigh?

about 9 ounces ○ about 9 pounds ○

16. About how much does the real object weigh?

about 5 ounces ○ about 5 pounds ○

Name ________________________________

Centimeters

HANDS-ON LESSON

Let's Learn!

You can measure length or height in centimeters. A **centimeter** is a unit of measure.

My pinky is about 1 centimeter wide. I estimate the length of the chalk is about 5 centimeters. Measure with a **centimeter ruler** to check.

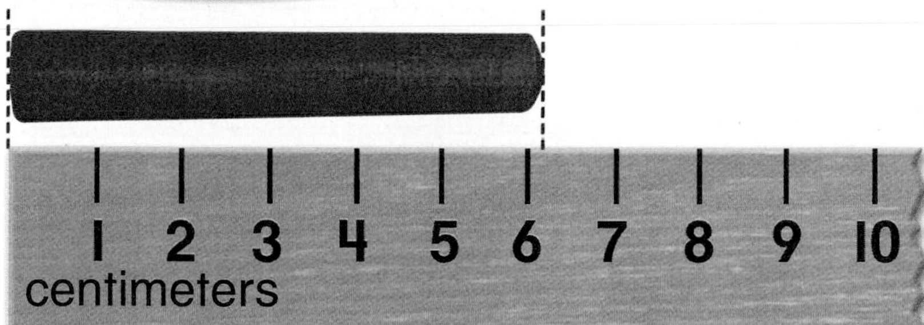

The chalk is closer to 6 centimeters. It is about 6 centimeters long.

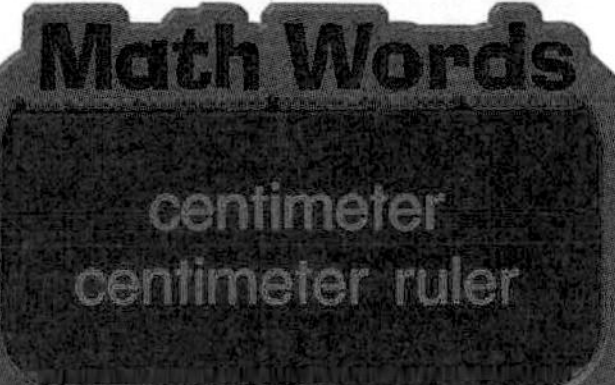

First estimate the length or height of each picture. Then use a centimeter ruler to measure.

1. Estimate: about ____ centimeters
   Measure: about 7 centimeters

2. Estimate: about ____ centimeters Measure: about ____ centimeters

3. 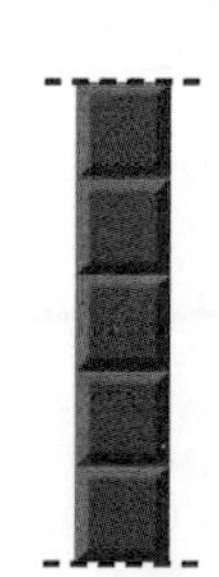
   Estimate: about ____ centimeters
   Measure: about ____ centimeters

4. Explain how the measures of objects on this page would change if you used an inch ruler to measure.

Practice

cm means centimeter

Find these real objects. Estimate their length or height in centimeters. Then use a centimeter ruler to measure.

	Object	Estimate	Measure
5.	ERASER	about ____ cm	about ____ cm
6.		about ____ cm	about ____ cm
7.		about ____ cm	about ____ cm
8.	blue	about ____ cm	about ____ cm

Solve. Use a problem-solving strategy.
Show your work on a separate sheet of paper.

9. Jake is 125 centimeters tall. Ann is 15 centimeters shorter than Jake. How tall is Ann?

Ann is ____ centimeters tall.

TEST PREPARATION

Fill in the circle under the correct answer.

10. Look at the figures below. Which figure is about as tall as it is long?

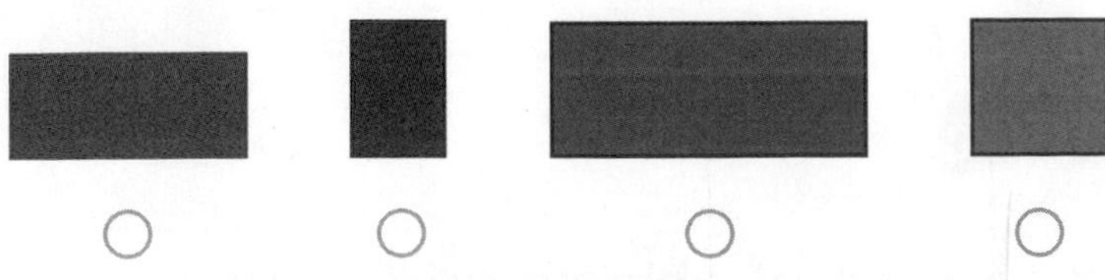

○ ○ ○ ○

Math Alive at Home *Say a measurement such as 10 or 15 centimeters. Have your child use a centimeter ruler to draw a line that length.*

Name ______________________________

Meters

HANDS-ON LESSON

Let's Learn!

You can measure long or tall objects in **meters**. A meter is a unit of measure.

I can spread my arms about 1 meter wide.

A meter is 100 centimeters. You can measure meters with a **meterstick**.

Math Words
meter
meterstick

Estimate about how many meters for each real object. Then use a meterstick to measure.

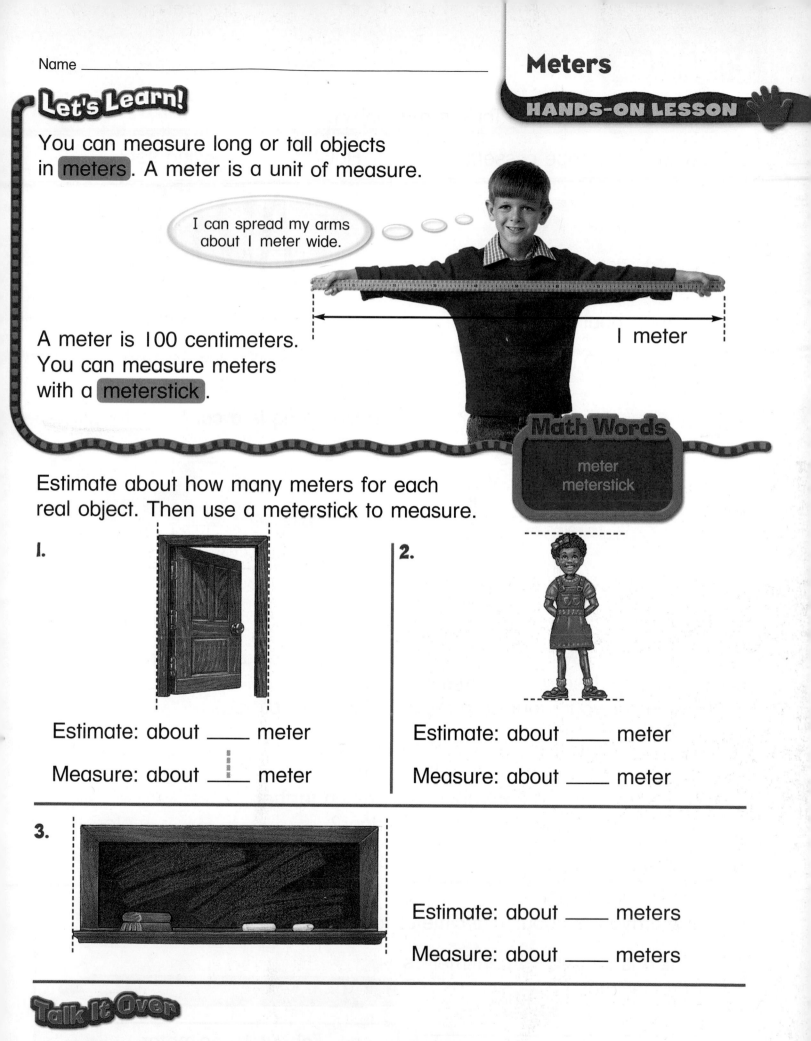

1.

Estimate: about ____ meter

Measure: about 1 meter

2.

Estimate: about ____ meter

Measure: about ____ meter

3.

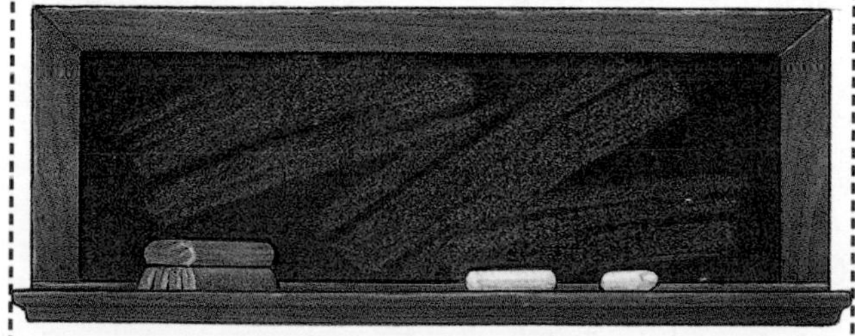

Estimate: about ____ meters

Measure: about ____ meters

Talk It Over

4. Explain how you measure an object that is longer than one meterstick.

Practice

Remember:
1 meter = 100 centimeters

Circle the better estimate for the real object.

5. How long is a tape cassette?

about 1 meter

about 10 centimeters

6. How tall is the swing set?

about 3 meters

about 3 centimeters

7. How wide is an open book?

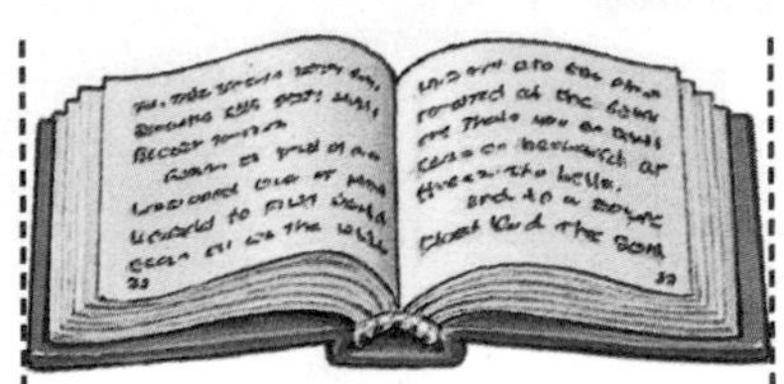

about 30 meters

about 30 centimeters

8. How long is a car?

about 5 meters

about 50 centimeters

Solve. Use a problem-solving strategy.
Show your work on a separate sheet of paper.

9. Peter's classroom is 28 meters from the front door of the school. Janet's classroom is 42 meters from the front door. How much farther is Janet's classroom from the front door? ____ meters

CHALLENGE

A new crayon is about 1 decimeter long.

1 decimeter = 10 centimeters

10. Which is longer, 15 centimeters or 1 decimeter?

____

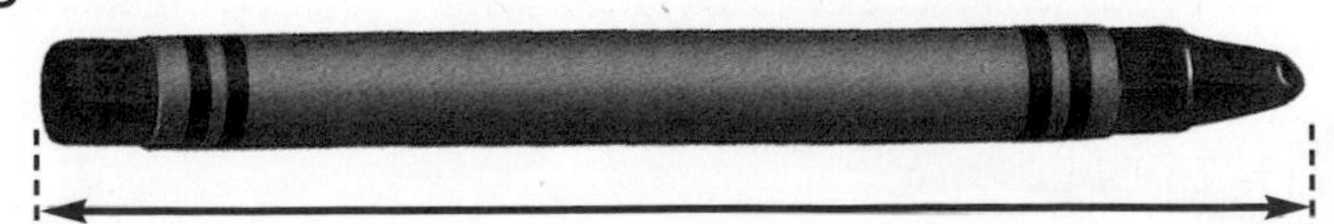

about 1 decimeter

Math Alive at Home Have your child find an object about one meter long.

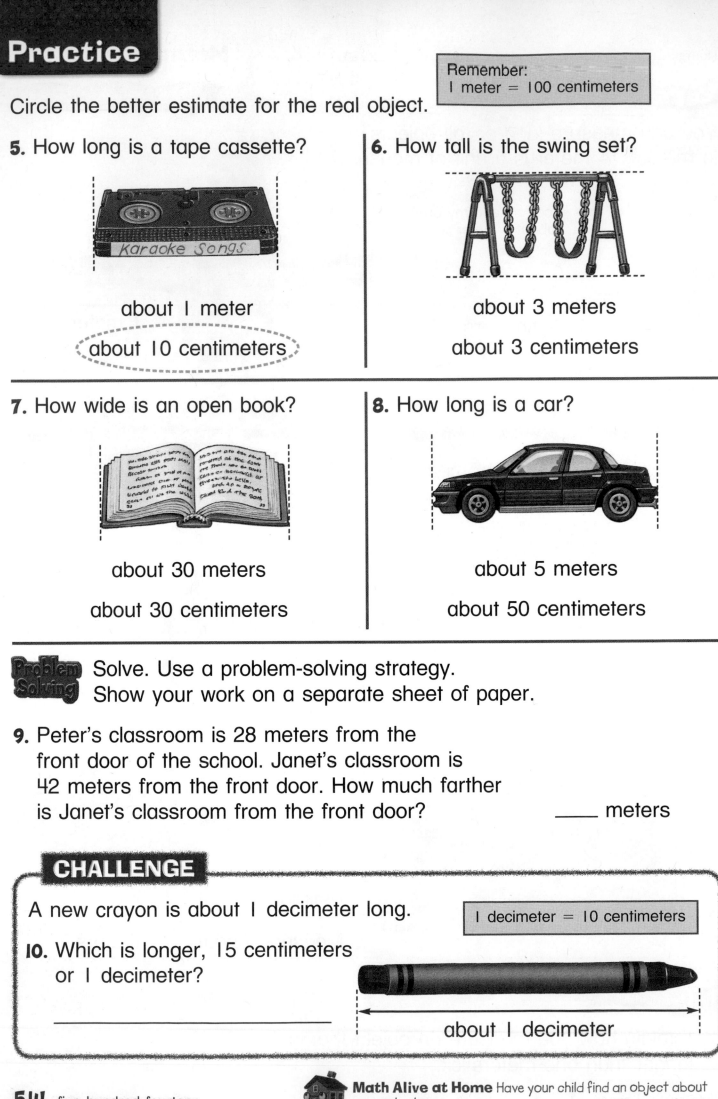

Name ______________________

Perimeter

HANDS-ON LESSON

Let's Learn!

How much ribbon does Lee need to put a border around her picture?

The distance around a plane figure is the **perimeter**.

2 in.

1 in.  1 in.

2 in.

To find the perimeter, measure the length of each side. Then add the measures.

Lee needs 6 in. of ribbon.

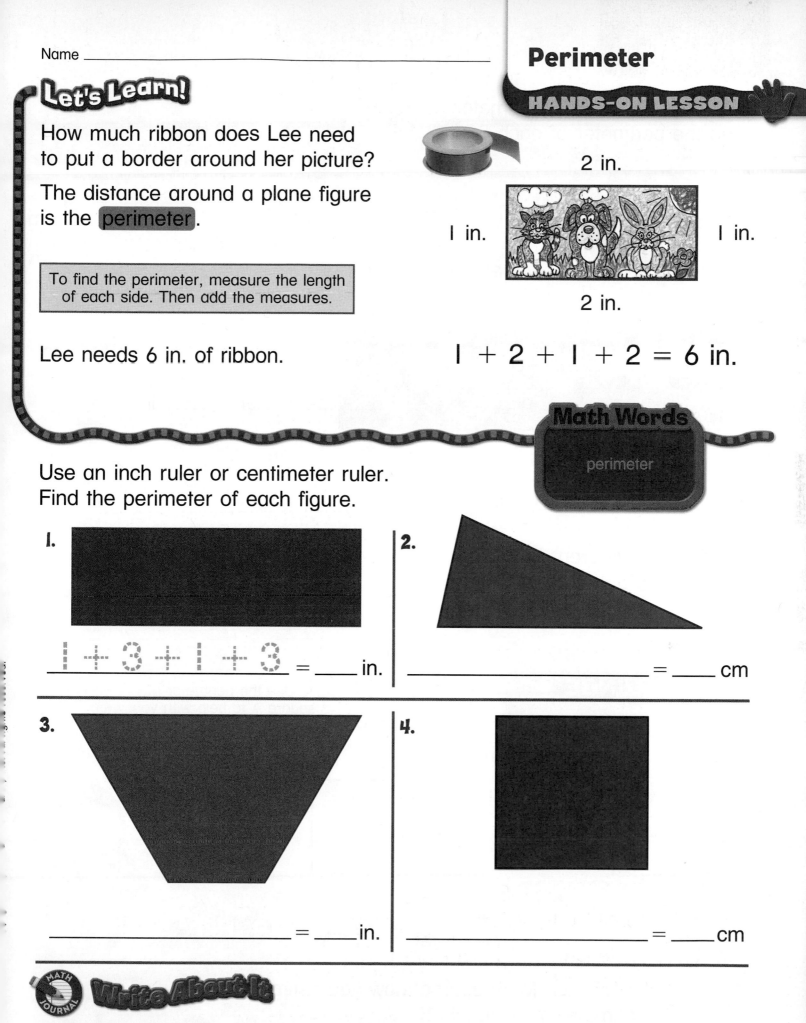

1 + 2 + 1 + 2 = 6 in.

Math Words

perimeter

Use an inch ruler or centimeter ruler.
Find the perimeter of each figure.

1.

1 + 3 + 1 + 3 = ____ in.

2.

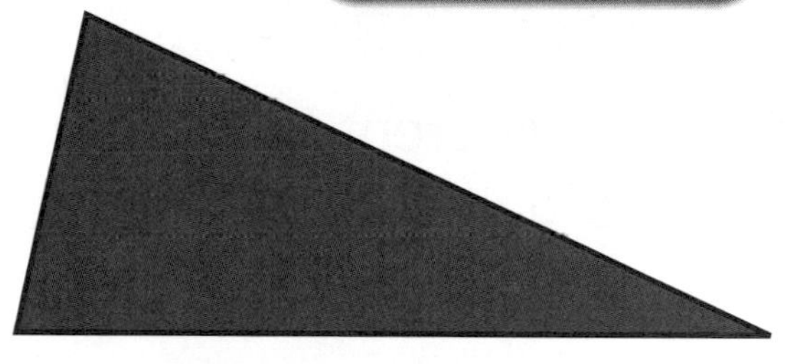

______________________ = ____ cm

3.

______________________ = ____ in.

4.

______________________ = ____ cm

5. Explain why you only have to measure one side of a square to find its perimeter.

Practice

Use an inch ruler or centimeter ruler.
Find the perimeter of each figure.

6. 

2 + 2 + 2 + 2 + 2 + 2 = ____ cm

perimeter = ____ cm

7. 

________________ = ____ in.

perimeter = ____ in.

Solve.
Use a problem-solving strategy.

8. Draw two different figures, each with a perimeter of 12 •—•.

CHALLENGE

Use the perimeter of square A to help with your estimate.

9. Estimate the perimeter of rectangle B in inches. Then measure to check.

A

perimeter = 4 in.

B

estimate = ____ in.

perimeter = ____ in.

10. Explain in your Math Journal how you estimated the perimeter of rectangle B.

Math Alive at Home Have your child measure the perimeter of an object such as a sheet of paper or a picture.

Name ____________________

Area

Let's Learn!

Area is the amount of space taken up by a plane figure.

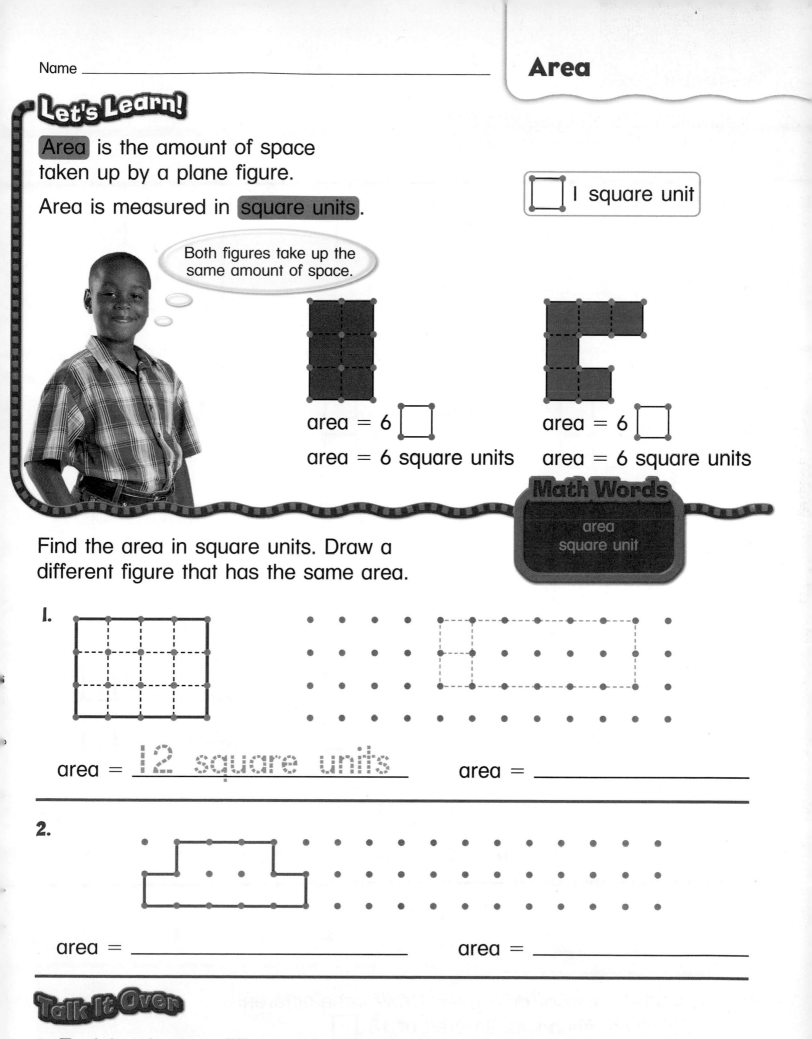

Area is measured in **square units**.

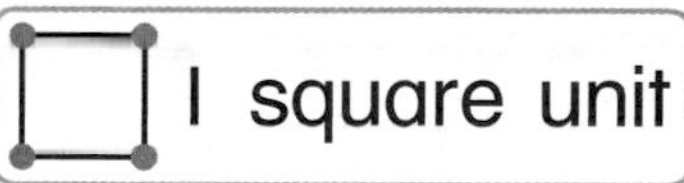

I square unit

Both figures take up the same amount of space.

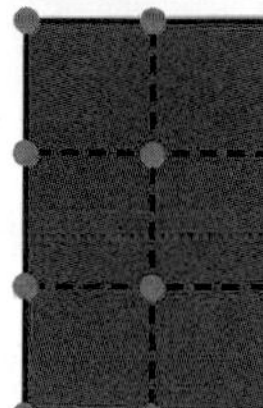

area = 6 □

area = 6 square units

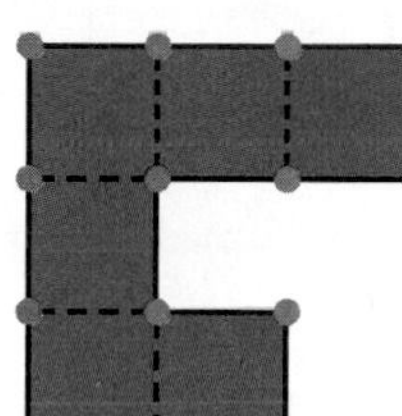

area = 6 □

area = 6 square units

Math Words
area
square unit

Find the area in square units. Draw a different figure that has the same area.

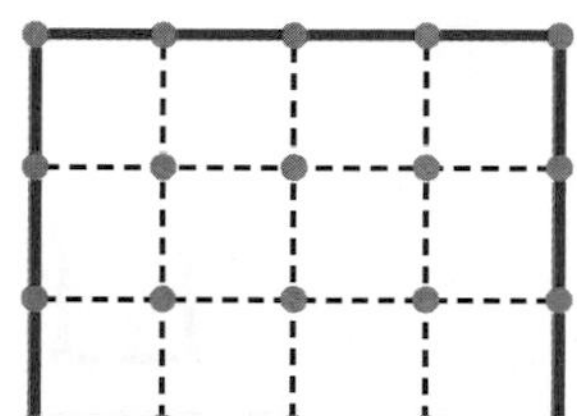

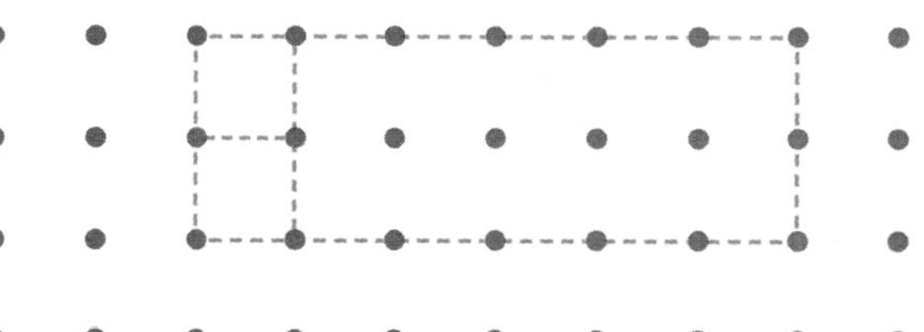

area = 12 square units   area = ____________

2.

area = ____________   area = ____________

Talk It Over

3. Explain why two different shapes may have the same area but a different perimeter. Draw pictures to show your reasoning.

Practice

□ 1 square unit

Estimate the area in square units.
Then draw □ to find the area.

4.

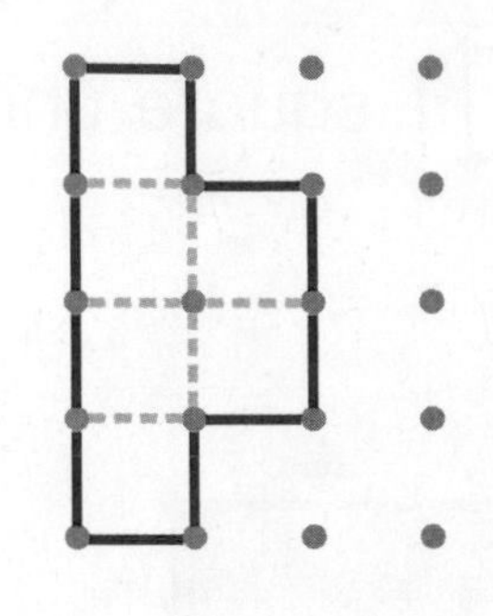

about ____ □

area = 6 □

5.

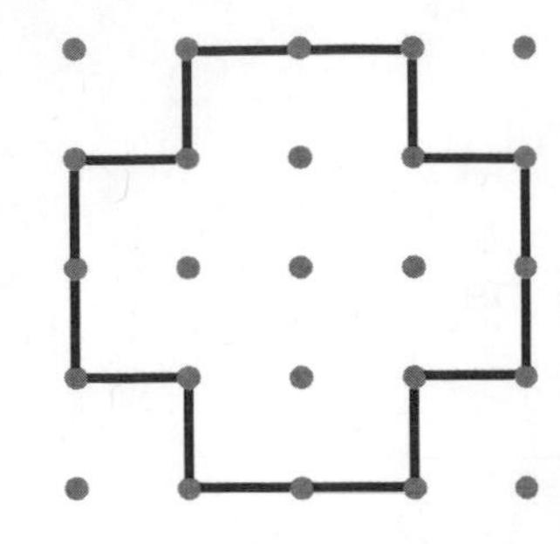

about ____ □

area = ____ □

6.

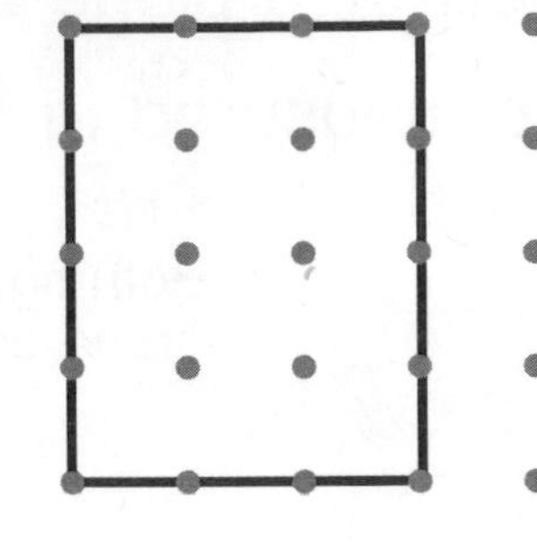

about ____ □

area = ____ □

7.

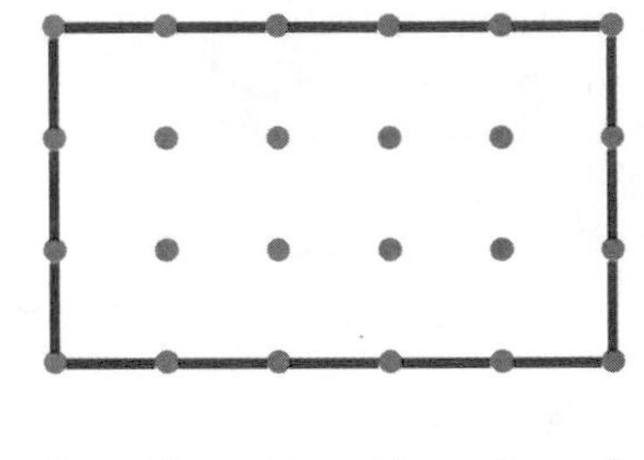

about ____ □

area = ____ □

8.

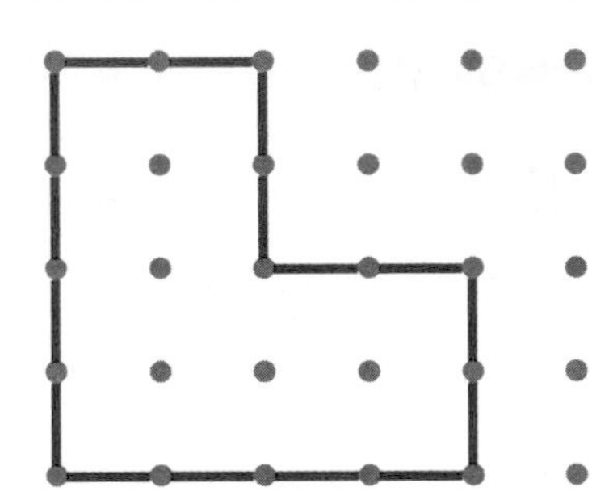

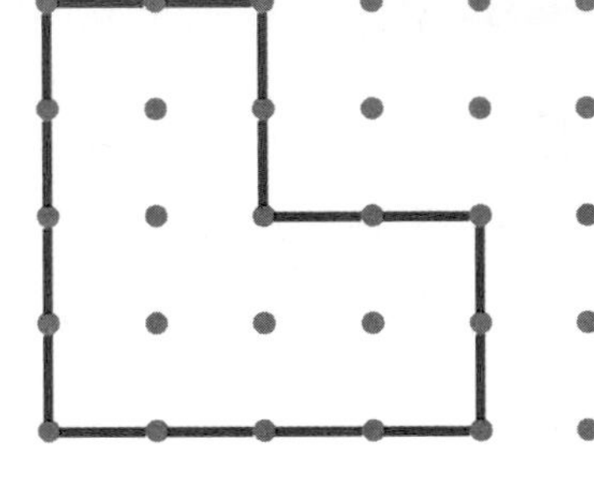

about ____ □

area = ____ □

9.

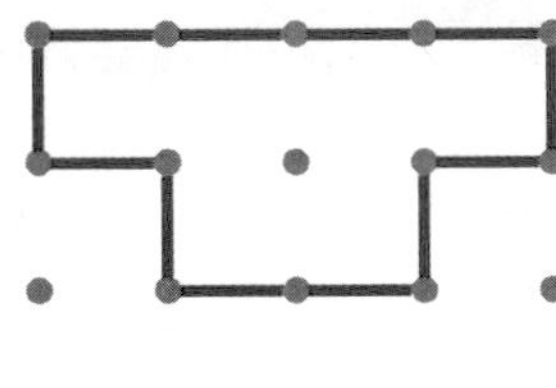

about ____ □

area = ____ □

Problem Solving Solve. Use a problem-solving strategy.

10. Draw a figure with an area of 5 □
and a perimeter of 10 ——.

CHALLENGE

11. Use grid paper or dot paper. Draw three different rectangles, each with an area of 18 □.

Math Alive at Home Ask your child how he/she would use 1-inch paper squares to find the area of a rectangular placemat or napkin.

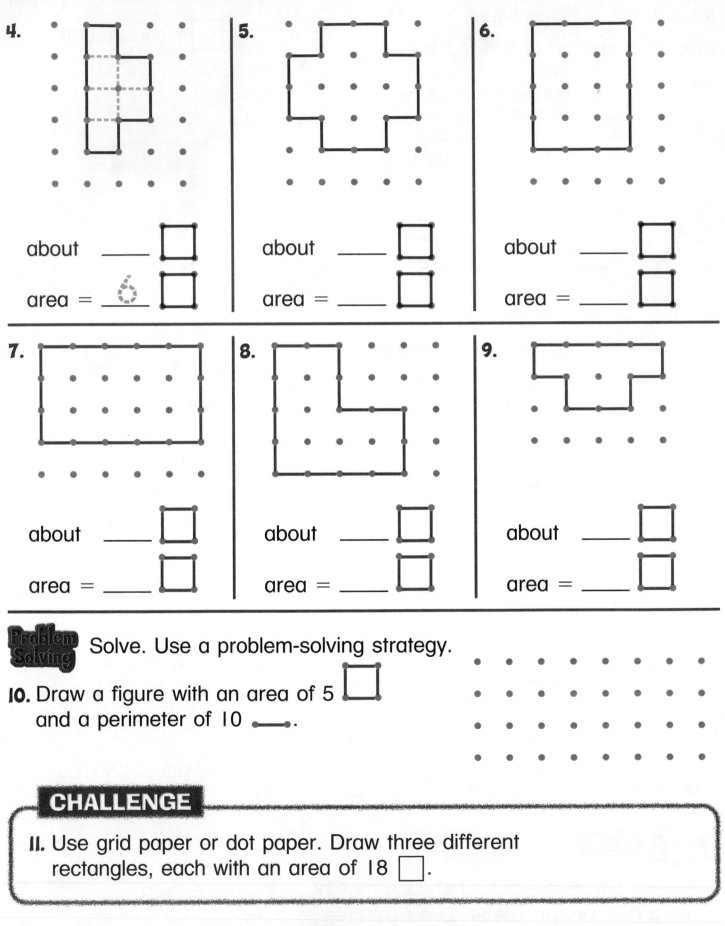

Name ______________________

Grams and Kilograms

Let's Learn!

You can measure how heavy an object is in **grams** and **kilograms**. A gram and a kilogram are units of measure.

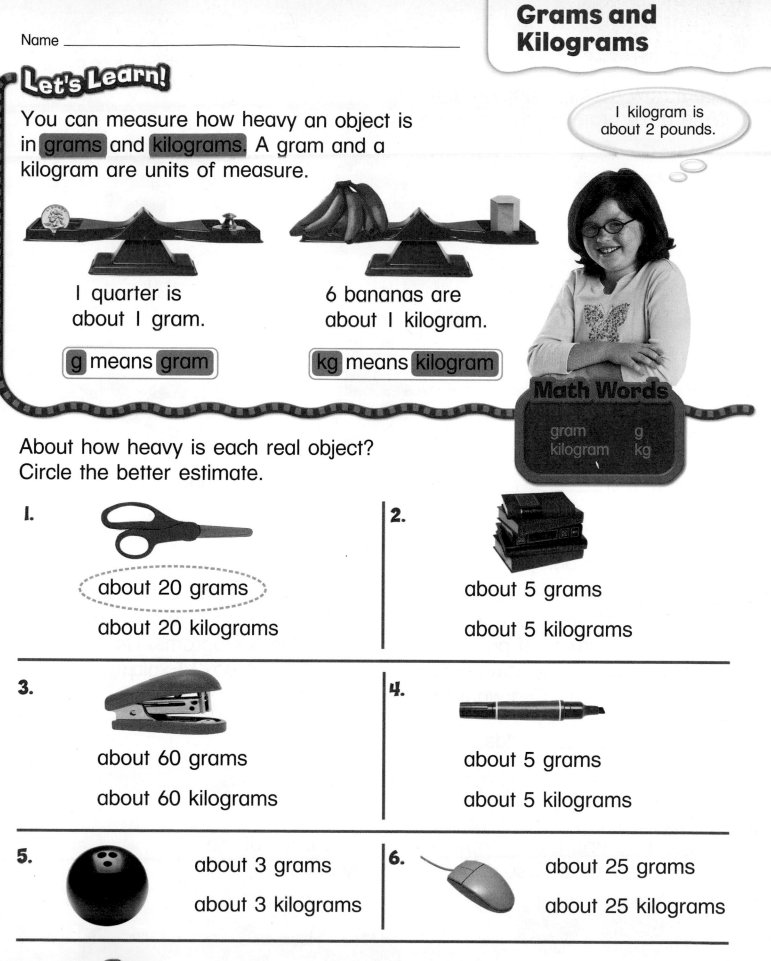

I quarter is about I gram.

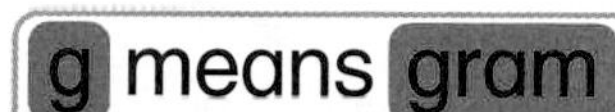

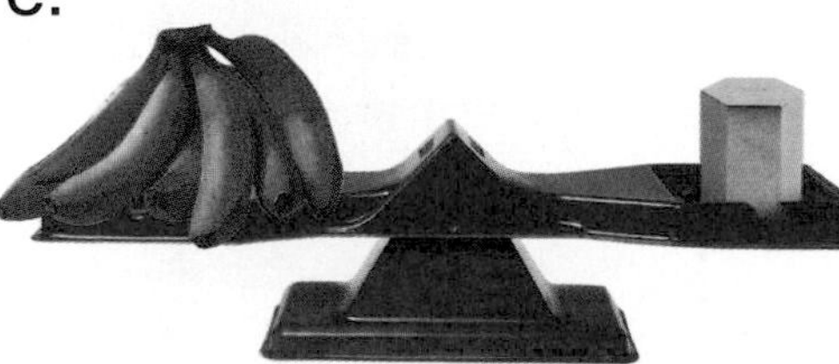

6 bananas are about I kilogram.

kg means kilogram

I kilogram is about 2 pounds.

Math Words

gram g
kilogram kg

About how heavy is each real object? Circle the better estimate.

1.

about 20 grams

about 20 kilograms

2.

about 5 grams

about 5 kilograms

3.

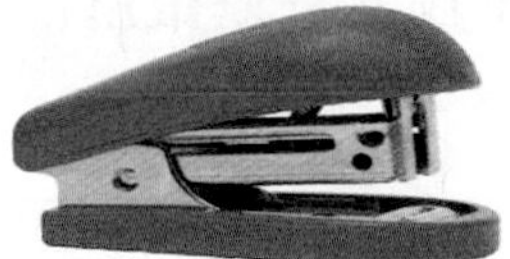

about 60 grams

about 60 kilograms

4.

about 5 grams

about 5 kilograms

5.

about 3 grams

about 3 kilograms

6.

about 25 grams

about 25 kilograms

Talk It Over

7. Order the objects in exercises 4–6 from lightest to heaviest. Explain how you know.

Practice

Remember:
1 quarter is about 1 gram.
6 bananas are about 1 kilogram.

About how heavy is each real object?
Write **g** for grams or **kg** for kilograms.

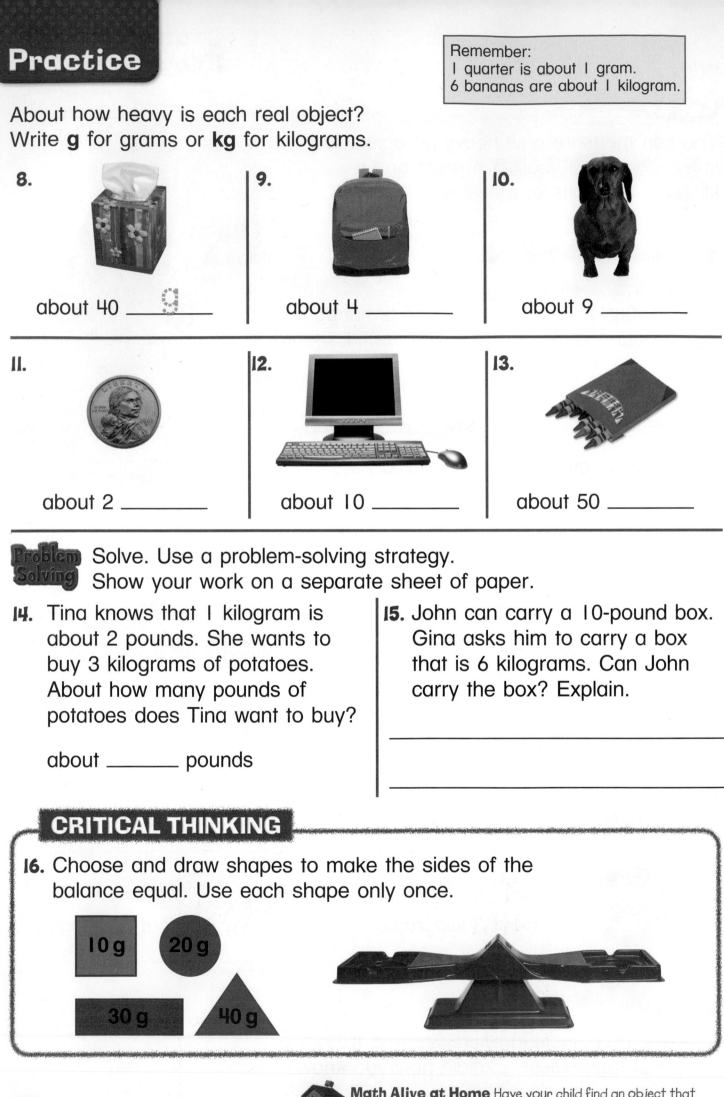

8. 

about 40 g

9. 

about 4 ______

10. 

about 9 ______

11. 

about 2 ______

12. 

about 10 ______

13. 

about 50 ______

Solve. Use a problem-solving strategy.
Show your work on a separate sheet of paper.

14. Tina knows that 1 kilogram is about 2 pounds. She wants to buy 3 kilograms of potatoes. About how many pounds of potatoes does Tina want to buy?

about ______ pounds

15. John can carry a 10-pound box. Gina asks him to carry a box that is 6 kilograms. Can John carry the box? Explain.

______

______

CRITICAL THINKING

16. Choose and draw shapes to make the sides of the balance equal. Use each shape only once.

10 g   20 g   30 g   40 g

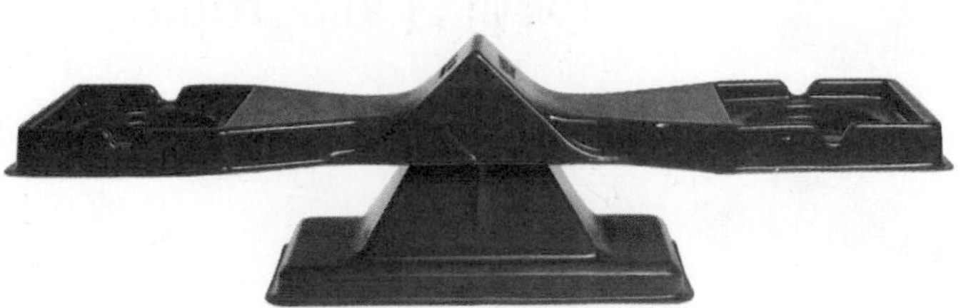

Math Alive at Home Have your child find an object that he/she estimates is about 1 gram and another that he/she estimates is about 1 kilogram.

Name ____________________

Liters

Let's Learn!

You can measure how much liquid a container holds in **liters**. A liter is a unit of measure.

One liter of liquid holds about the same as 1 quart.

less than 1 liter

1 liter

more than 1 liter

Math Words

liter

About how much does each real object hold? Circle the best estimate.

1. 

less than 1 liter
about 1 liter
more than 1 liter

2. 

less than 1 liter
about 1 liter
more than 1 liter

3. 

less than 1 liter
about 1 liter
more than 1 liter

4. 

less than 1 liter
about 1 liter
more than 1 liter

5. 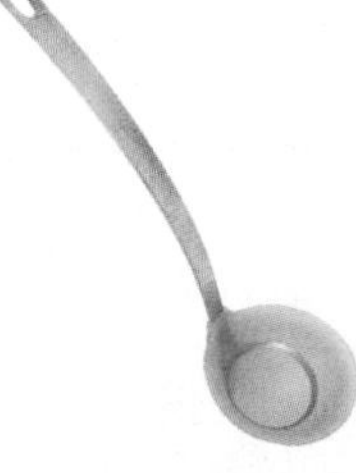

less than 1 liter
about 1 liter
more than 1 liter

6. 

less than 1 liter
about 1 liter
more than 1 liter

7. Would a large fish tank hold about 4 liters or about 40 liters of water? Explain how you know.

Copyright © by William H. Sadlier, Inc. All rights reserved.

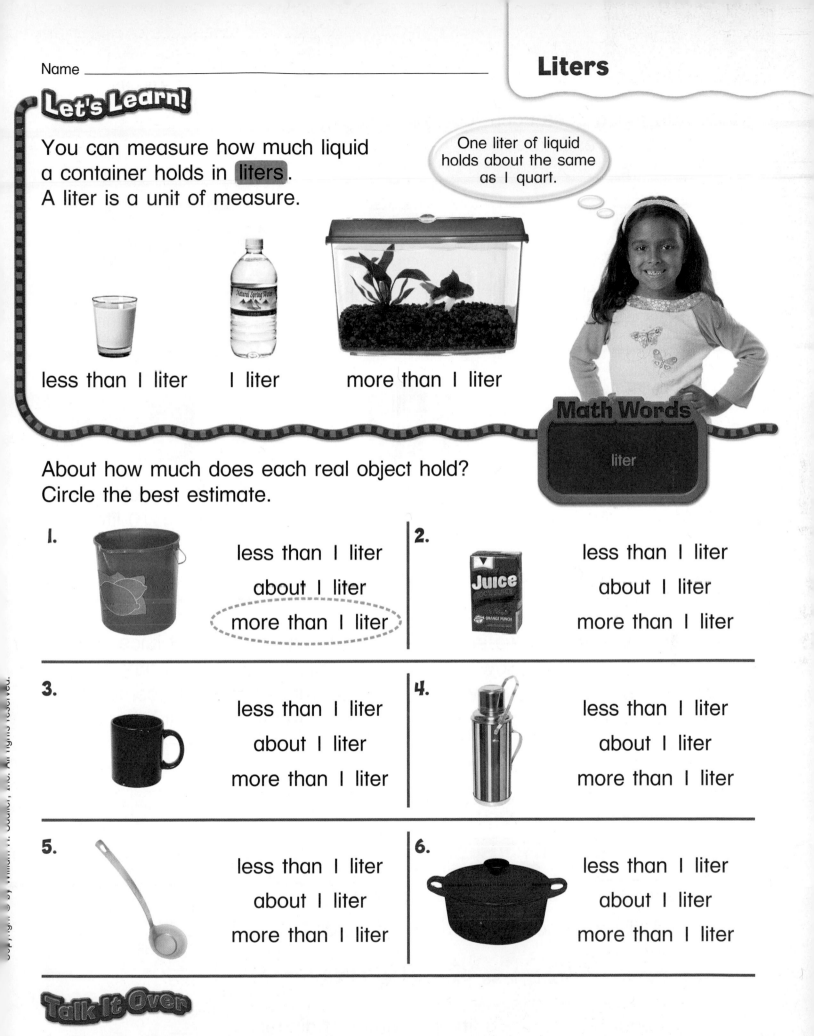

Practice

Remember:
1 liter is about 1 quart.

About how much does each real object hold?
Circle the better estimate.

8. 

about 1 liter (circled) | about 10 liters

9. 

about 4 liters | about 40 liters

10. 

about 2 liters | about 20 liters

11. 

about 5 liters | about 50 liters

12. 

about 3 liters | about 30 liters

13. 

about 1 liter | about 10 liters

Solve. Use a problem-solving strategy.
Show your work on a separate sheet of paper.

14. Marie uses 8 liters of water to fill a bucket half way. How many more liters of water will she need to fill the bucket to the top?

____ more liters

15. Tim has 12 liters of juice. He wants to pour equal amounts of juice into 6 different containers. How many liters will he pour into each container?

____ liters

CRITICAL THINKING

Write R for reasonable, U for unreasonable.

16. Jackie fills a teapot with 10 liters of water. ____

17. A coffee mug holds less than 1 liter. ____

18. Petra and Matt drink 60 liters of water at dinner. ____

Math Alive at Home Have your child find containers that hold less than one liter and more than one liter. Have him/her use a liter bottle to fill each container with water to check.

Name ____________________

Check Your Progress

Lessons 9-14

TEST PREPARATION

Listen to your teacher read the directions.
Fill in the circle next to the correct answer.

1.

- ○ about 7 centimeters
- ○ about 7 meters

2.

- ○ about 8 cm
- ○ about 2 cm
- ○ about 6 cm
- ○ about 4 cm

3.

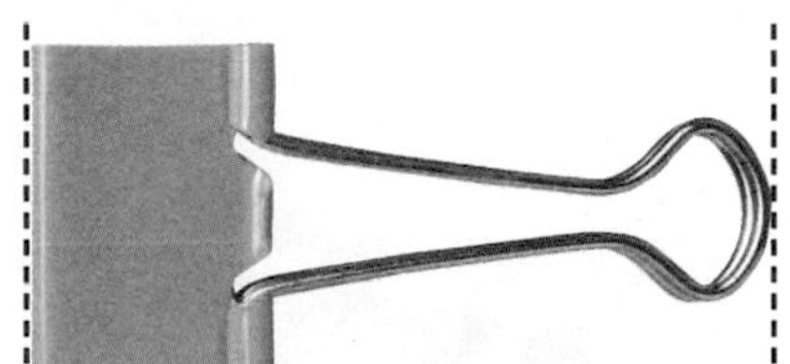

- ○ about 5 cm
- ○ about 4 cm
- ○ about 7 cm
- ○ about 2 cm

4.

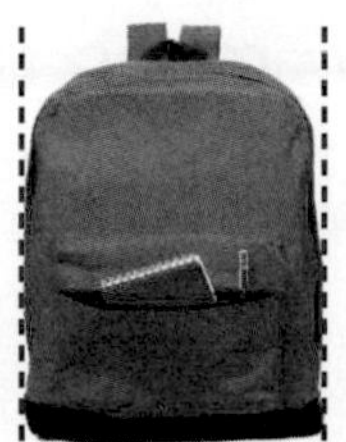

- ○ about 20 centimeters
- ○ about 2 meters

5.

- ○ about 1 centimeter
- ○ about 1 meter

6.

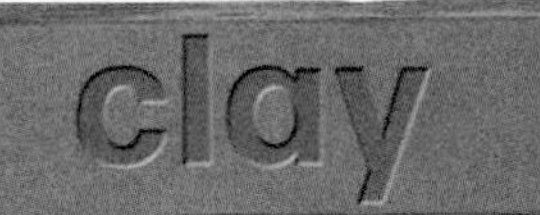

- ○ about 8 cm
- ○ about 20 cm
- ○ about 2 cm
- ○ about 15 cm

7.

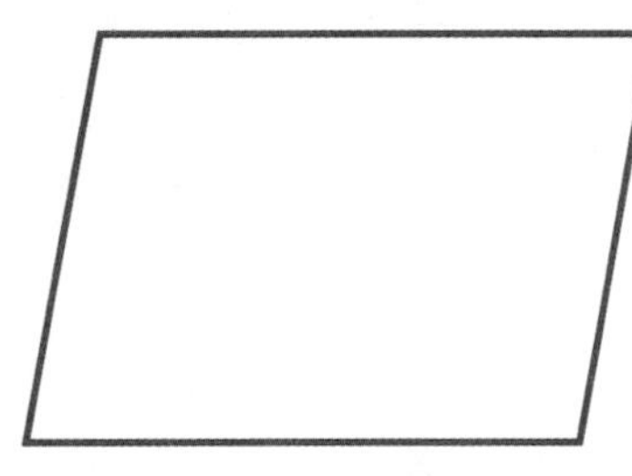

- ○ 18 cm
- ○ 14 cm
- ○ 15 cm
- ○ 16 cm

8.

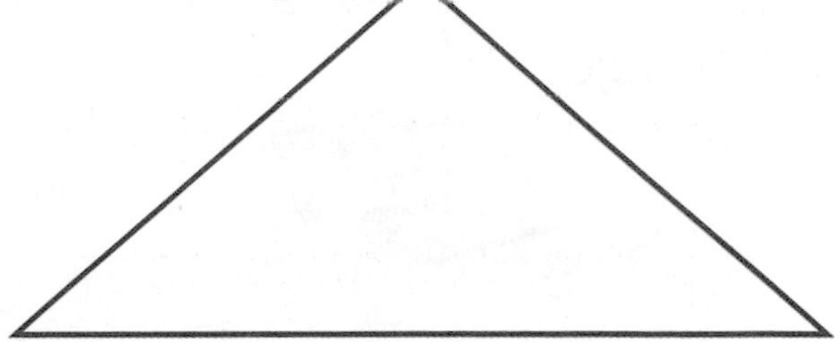

- ○ 7 in.
- ○ 8 in.
- ○ 9 in.
- ○ 4 in.

Fill in the circle under the correct answer.
Find the area in square units for exercises 9–11.

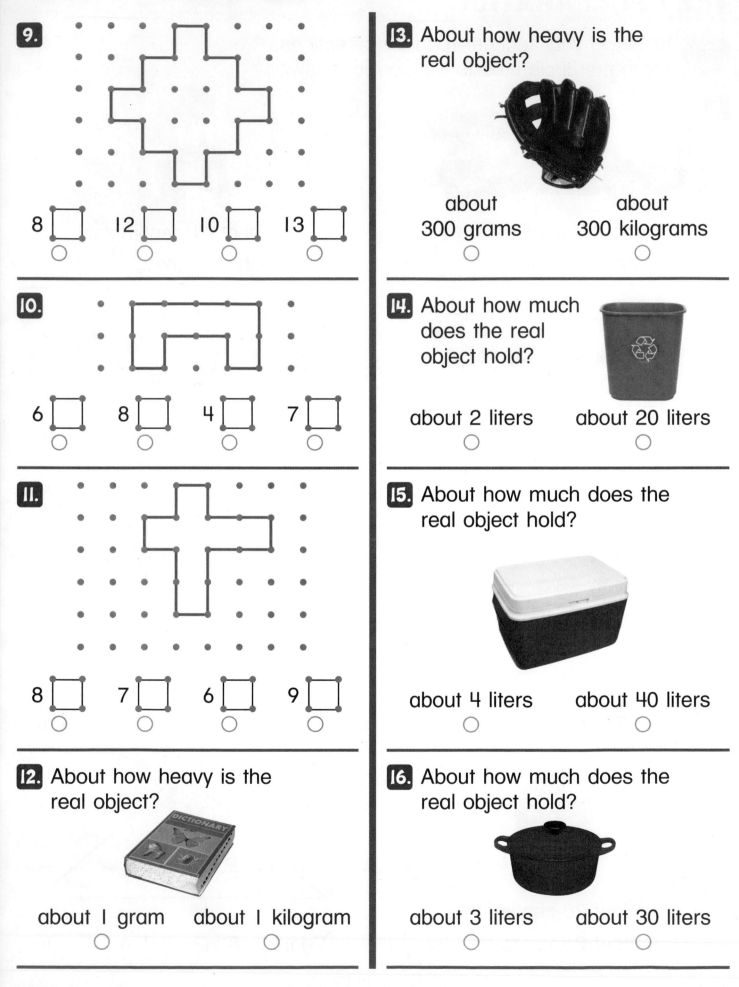

9.

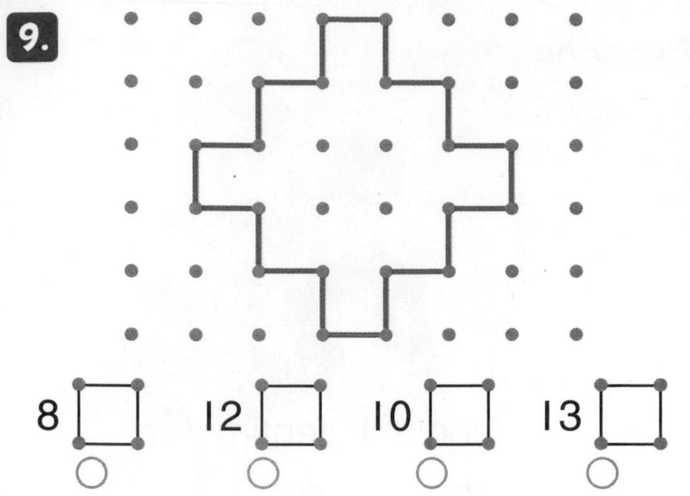

8 ◯ 12 ◯ 10 ◯ 13 ◯

10.

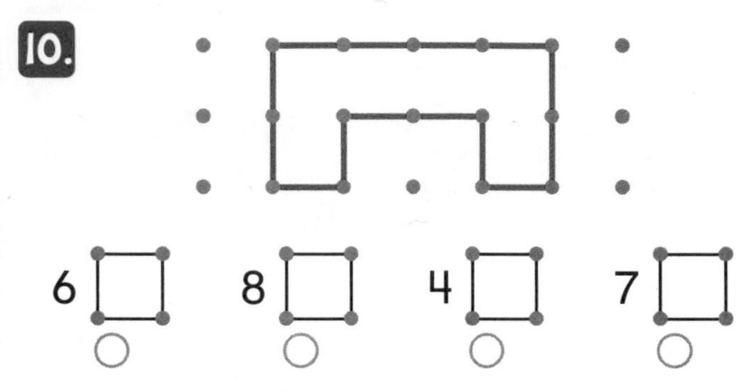

6 ◯ 8 ◯ 4 ◯ 7 ◯

11.

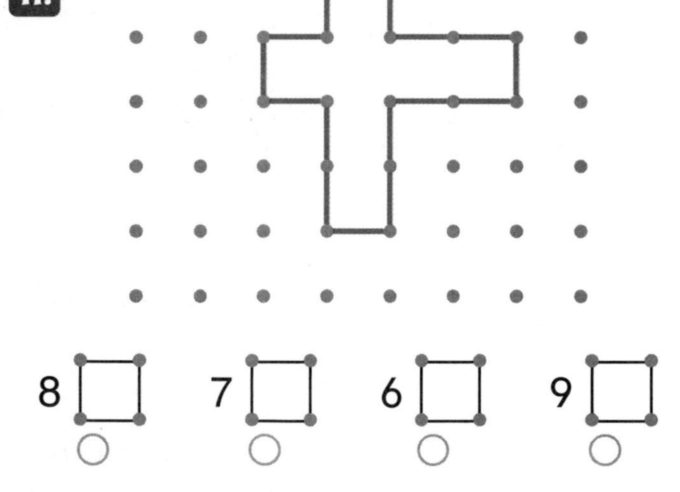

8 ◯ 7 ◯ 6 ◯ 9 ◯

12. About how heavy is the real object?

about 1 gram ◯ about 1 kilogram ◯

13. About how heavy is the real object?

about 300 grams ◯ about 300 kilograms ◯

14. About how much does the real object hold?

about 2 liters ◯ about 20 liters ◯

15. About how much does the real object hold?

about 4 liters ◯ about 40 liters ◯

16. About how much does the real object hold?

about 3 liters ◯ about 30 liters ◯

Name ______________________________

Volume

HANDS-ON LESSON

Let's Learn!

The **volume** of a solid figure is the number of cubic units in the figure.

This is 1 **cubic unit**. 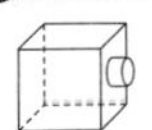

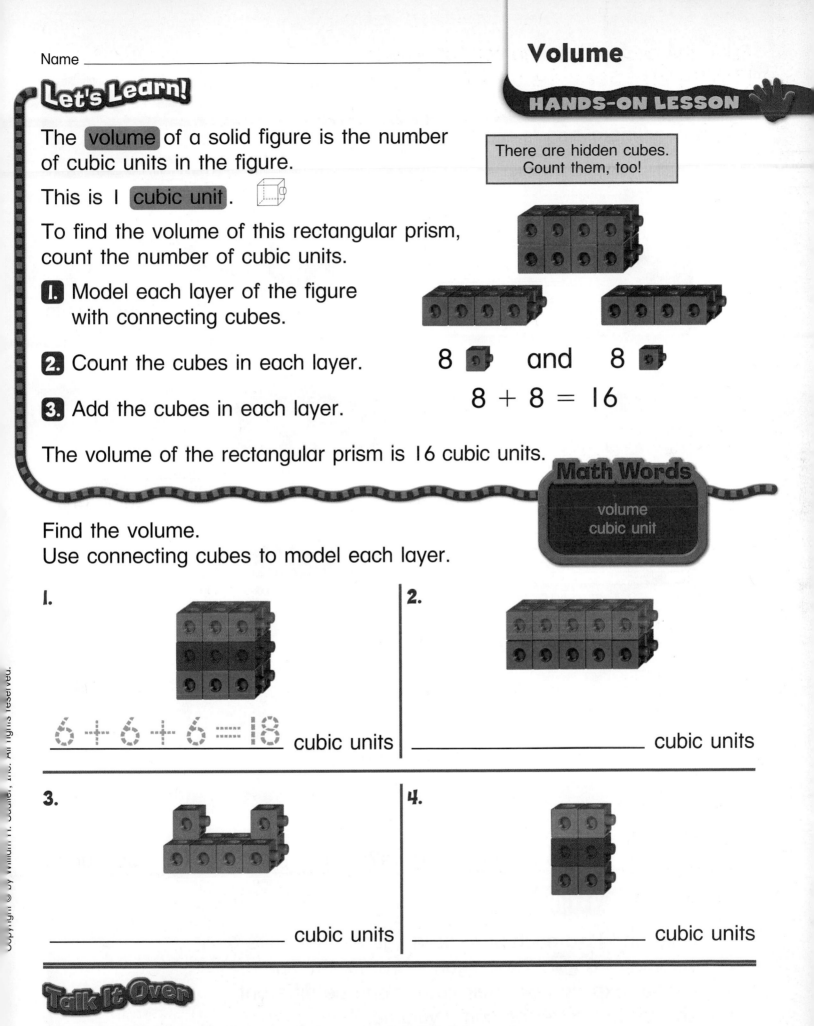

To find the volume of this rectangular prism, count the number of cubic units.

There are hidden cubes. Count them, too!

1. Model each layer of the figure with connecting cubes.

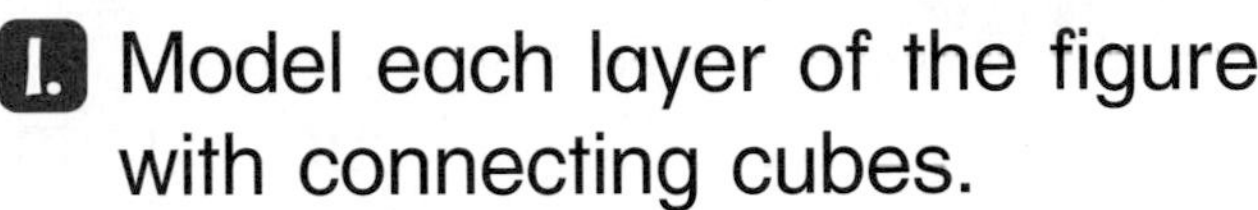

2. Count the cubes in each layer. 8 and 8

3. Add the cubes in each layer. $8 + 8 = 16$

The volume of the rectangular prism is 16 cubic units.

Math Words
volume
cubic unit

Find the volume.
Use connecting cubes to model each layer.

1.

$6 + 6 + 6 = 18$ cubic units

2.

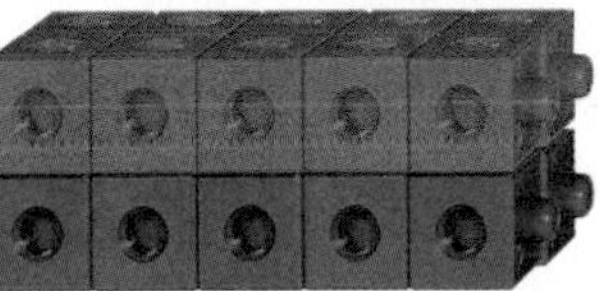

______________ cubic units

3.

______________ cubic units

4.

______________ cubic units

Talk It Over

5. How can you find the volume of a solid figure when not all the cubes can be seen?

Copyright © by William H. Sadlier, Inc. All rights reserved.

Practice

Remember to count the hidden cubes.

Find the volume.
Use connecting cubes to model each layer.

6.

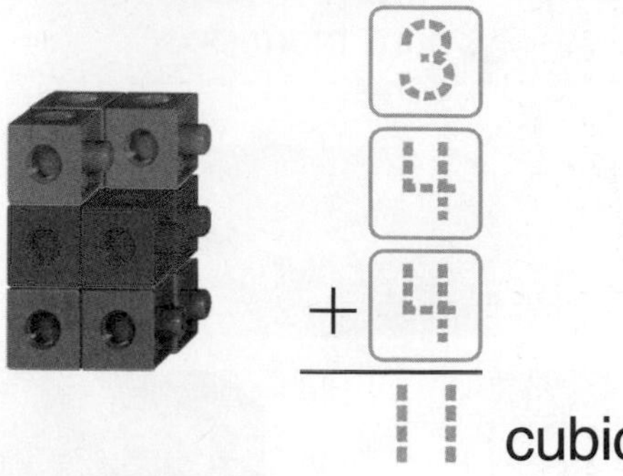

3
4
+ 4
11 cubic units

7.

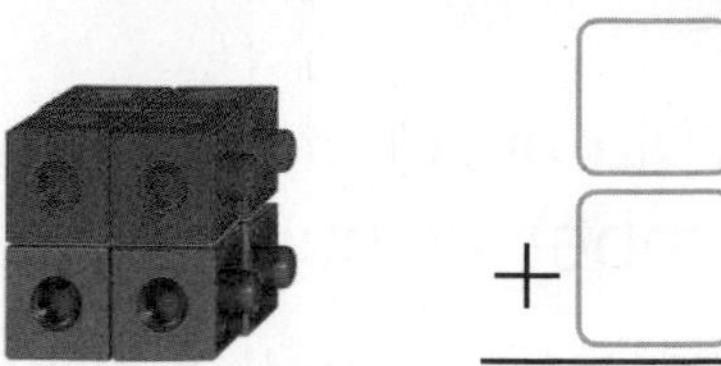

☐
+ ☐
cubic units

8.

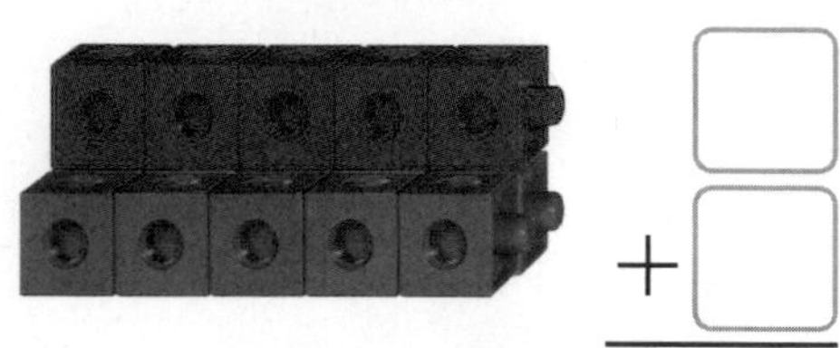

☐
+ ☐
cubic units

9.

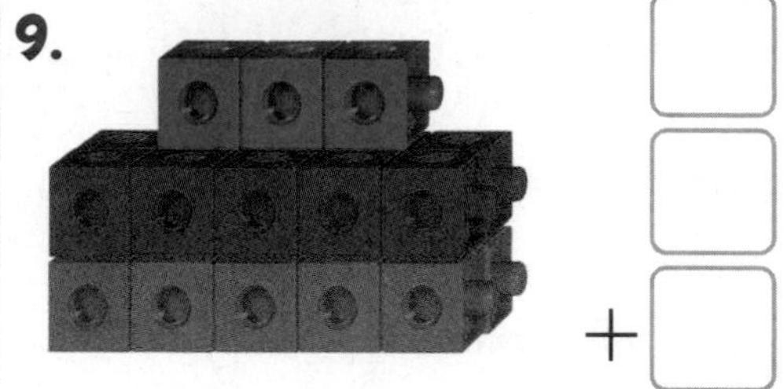

☐
☐
+ ☐
cubic units

10.

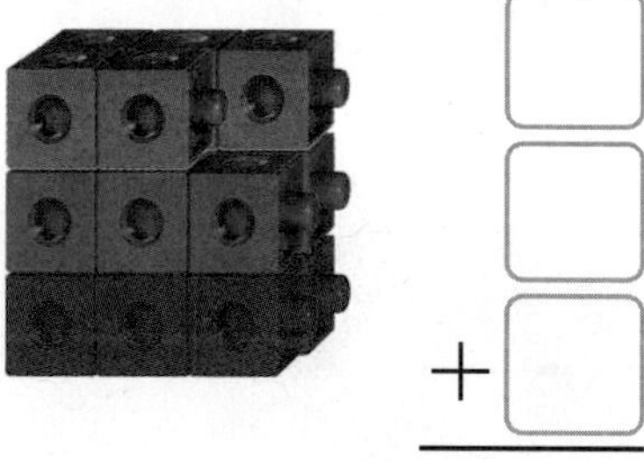

☐
☐
+ ☐
cubic units

11.

☐
☐
+ ☐
cubic units

Solve. Use a problem-solving strategy.

12. Chuck makes a solid figure that is 3 cubes long, 2 cubes wide, and 2 cubes high.
What is the volume of Chuck's figure? The volume is ____ cubic units.

MATH JOURNAL

13. Jake and Lisa each build solid figures that have a volume of 8 cubes. Their figures are not the same shape. Explain how their figures can be different shapes but have the same volume.

Math Alive at Home Have your child explain how he/she found the volume of the figure in exercise 11 above. (Add 8 + 8 + 8 = 24.)

Name ______________________________

Temperature

Let's Learn!

You can measure temperature in **degrees Fahrenheit (°F)** or **degrees Celsius (°C)**.

These thermometers measure the same temperature using a different **scale**.

Each line on these thermometers stands for 2 degrees.

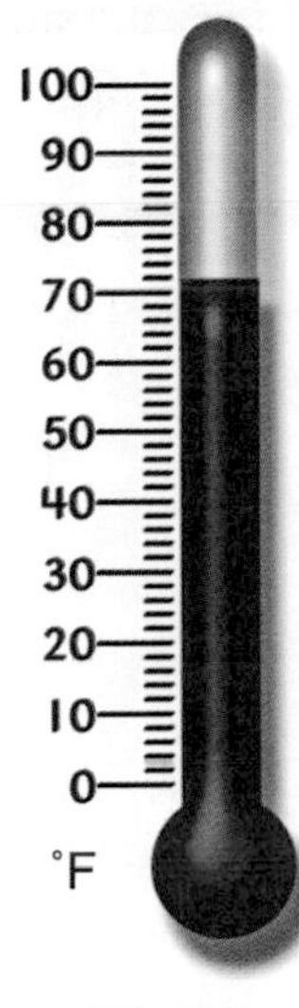

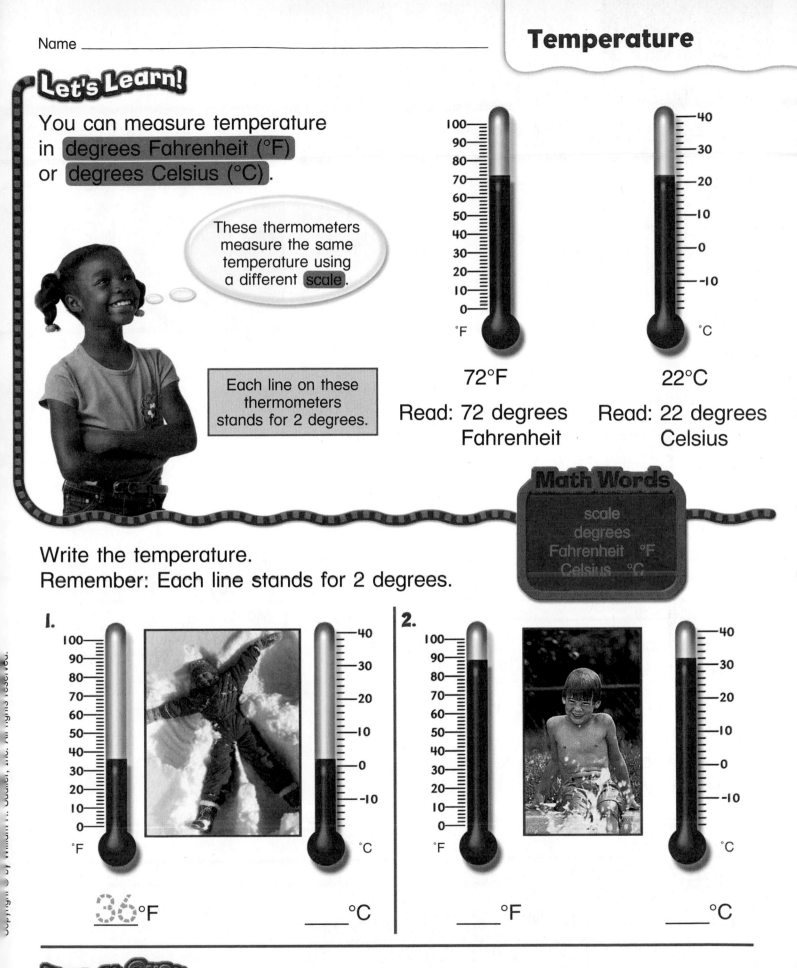

72°F

Read: 72 degrees Fahrenheit

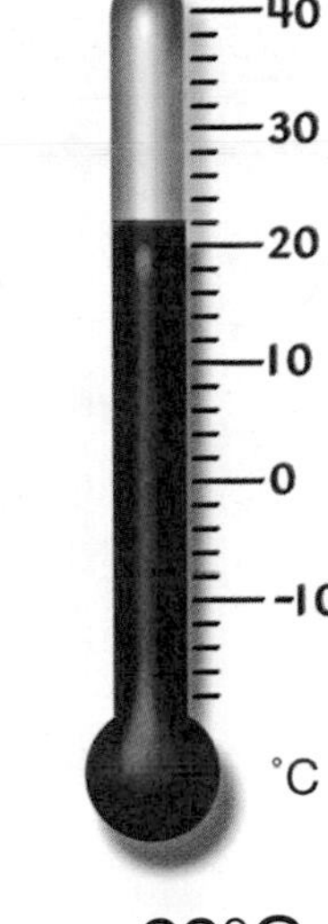

22°C

Read: 22 degrees Celsius

Math Words

scale
degrees
Fahrenheit °F
Celsius °C

Write the temperature.
Remember: Each line stands for 2 degrees.

1.

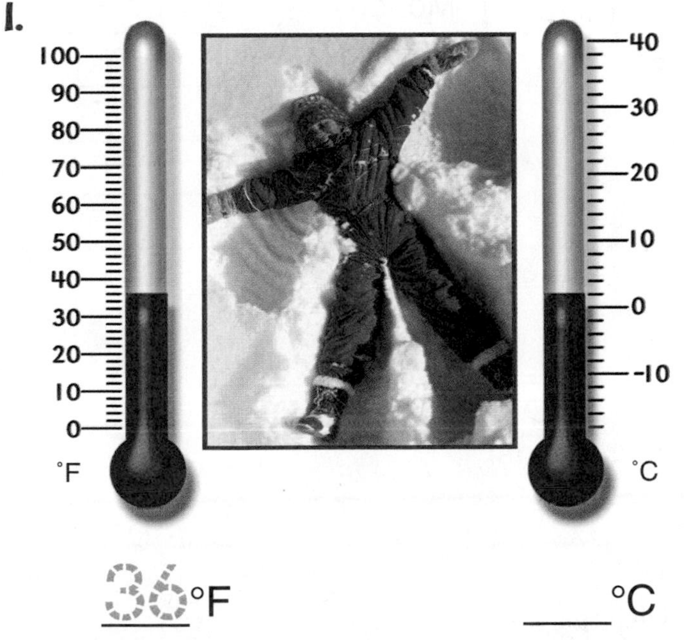

36 °F ____ °C

2.

100
90
80
70
60
50
40
30
20
10
0
°F

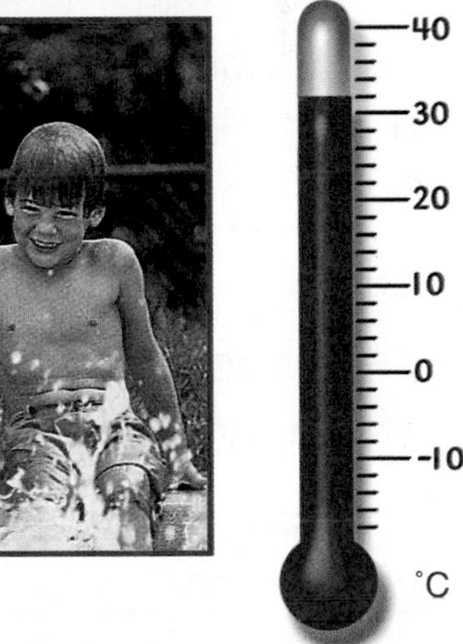

____ °F ____ °C

Talk It Over

3. What do you notice about the difference in the number scales for Fahrenheit and Celsius thermometers?

Copyright © by William H. Sadlier, Inc. All rights reserved.

Practice

Write the temperatures.

Remember: Each line stands for 2 degrees.

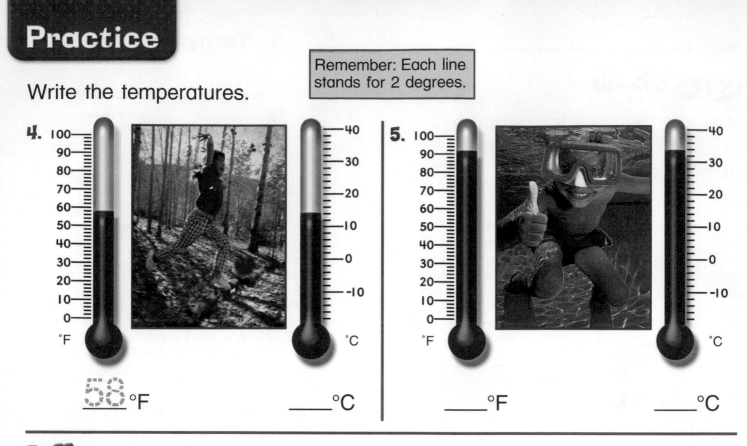

4. 

58 °F ____ °C

5. 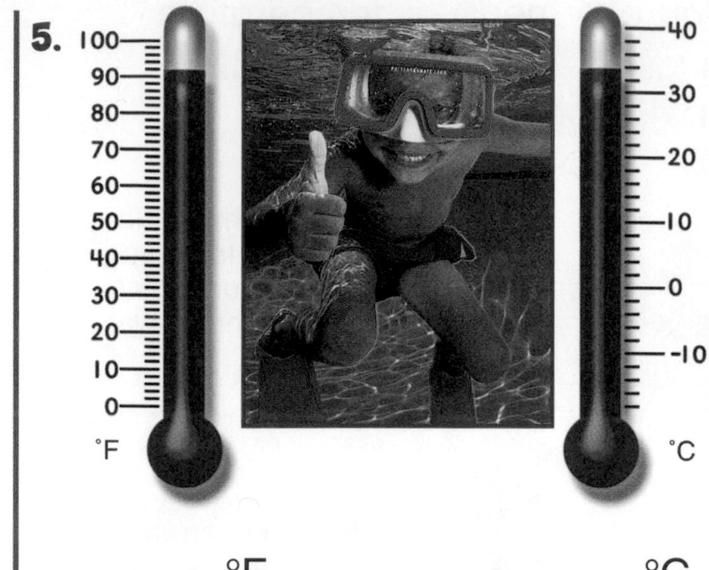

____ °F ____ °C

Solve. Use a problem-solving strategy.
Show your work on a separate sheet of paper.

Our Weather Week	
Day	**Temperature**
Monday	57°F
Tuesday	48°F
Wednesday	51°F
Thursday	62°F
Friday	58°F

6. Which was the hottest day of this week?

____

7. How much cooler was the temperature on Tuesday than Friday?

____ cooler

8. What was the range in temperatures for the five days?

____ degrees

CHALLENGE

9. Record in your Math Journal the high temperature of the day for one week.

10. Compare the temperatures.
On which day was the highest temperature? ____________________

Math Alive at Home Help your child use a thermometer to tell the current temperature in degrees Fahrenheit and Celsius.

Name ______________________________

Choose Tools and Units of Measure

Let's Learn!

I can use an **inch ruler** to measure how **tall** the carton is.

I can use a **measuring cup** to measure how much the carton **holds.**

An inch ruler and a measuring cup are measuring tools.

An inch and a quart are units of measure.

Math Words
measuring tools

Think of these real objects.
Circle the unit of measure you would use.

1. How long is it?

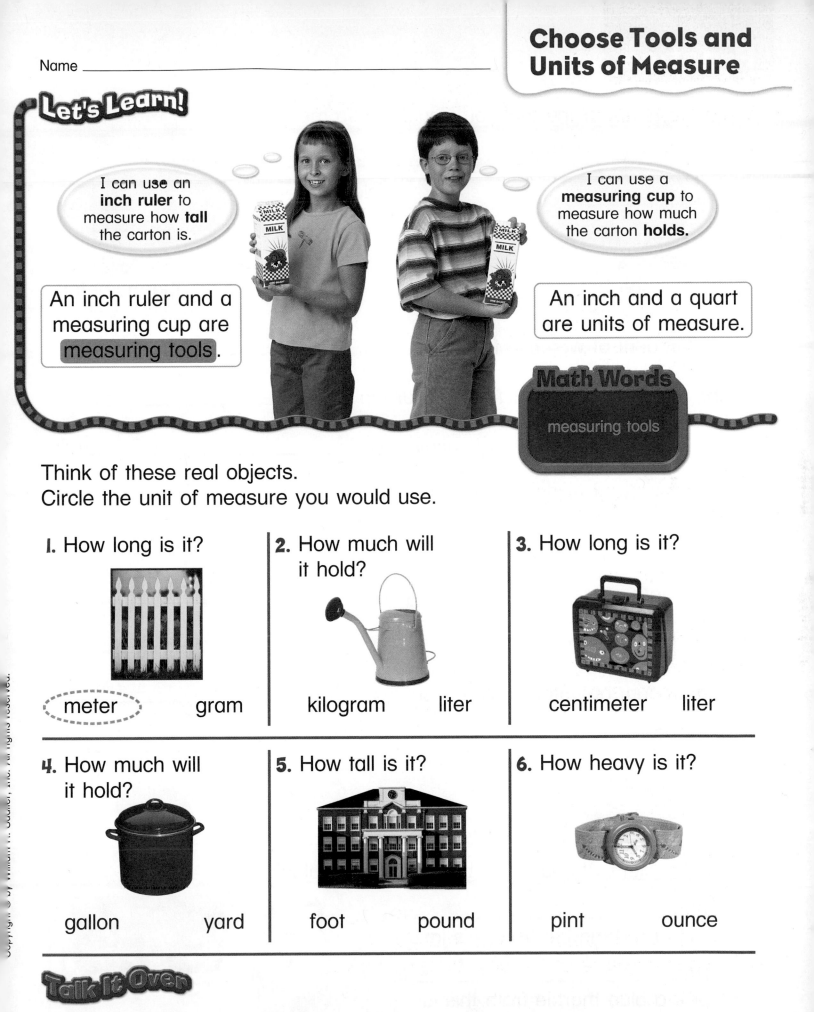

meter gram

2. How much will it hold?

kilogram liter

3. How long is it?

centimeter liter

4. How much will it hold?

gallon yard

5. How tall is it?

foot pound

6. How heavy is it?

pint ounce

7. Would you use a centimeter ruler or a meterstick to measure the height of a fence? Explain why.

Copyright © by William H. Sadlier, Inc. All rights reserved.

Practice

Write the name of the tool you would use to measure.

yardstick			
balance	ruler	cup	thermometer

8. the amount of water to fill a pot cup

9. the distance from your foot to your hip ______

10. the temperature on a very sunny day ______

11. the amount of milk in a pitcher ______

12. the weight of a bag of apples ______

13. the length of a book ______

14. the length of a hall ______

15. the amount of water to fill a vase ______

16. the weight of a rock ______

DO YOU REMEMBER?

Use the Math Words in the box to fill in the blanks.

17. It is ______ to pick a red marble from this jar.

18. It is ______ to pick a blue marble from this jar.

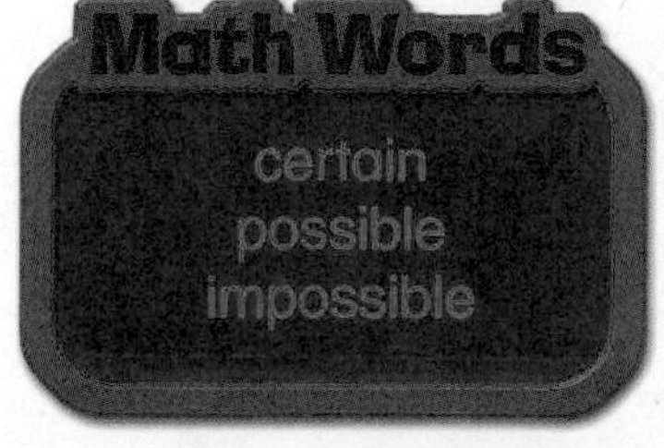

Math Alive at Home Have your child name household items that could be measured with an inch ruler, with a cup, and with a balance.

Name ______________________

Problem Solving
Strategy

Use a Map

Read Fran walks from the music room to the cafeteria. Then she walks to the library. How far does she walk in all?

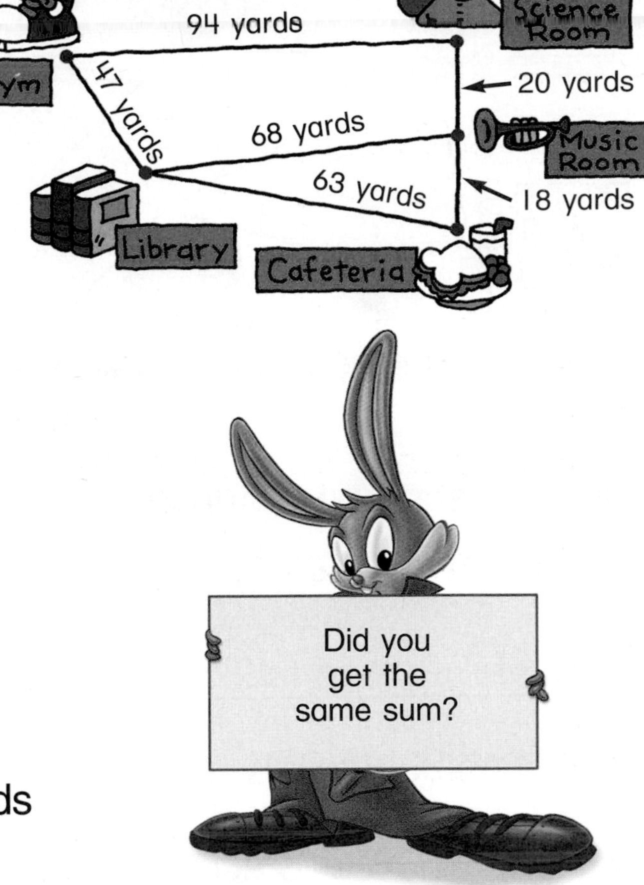

Plan Find the numbers you need on the map. Then add.

Write

$$\begin{array}{r} 18 \\ +\ 63 \\ \hline 81 \end{array}$$

Fran walks 81 yards in all.

Check Change the order of the addends to solve the problem again.

Use the map above to solve.

1. April walks from the library to the gym. Then she walks to the science room. How much farther does April walk to the science room than to the gym?

$$\begin{array}{r} \overset{8}{\cancel{9}}\overset{14}{\cancel{4}} \\ -\ 47 \\ \hline 47 \end{array}$$

47 yards farther

2. José walks from the science room to the music room. Then he walks to the library along the shortest path. How many yards does José walk altogether?

_____ yards altogether

Practice

Read Plan Write Check

Use a Map

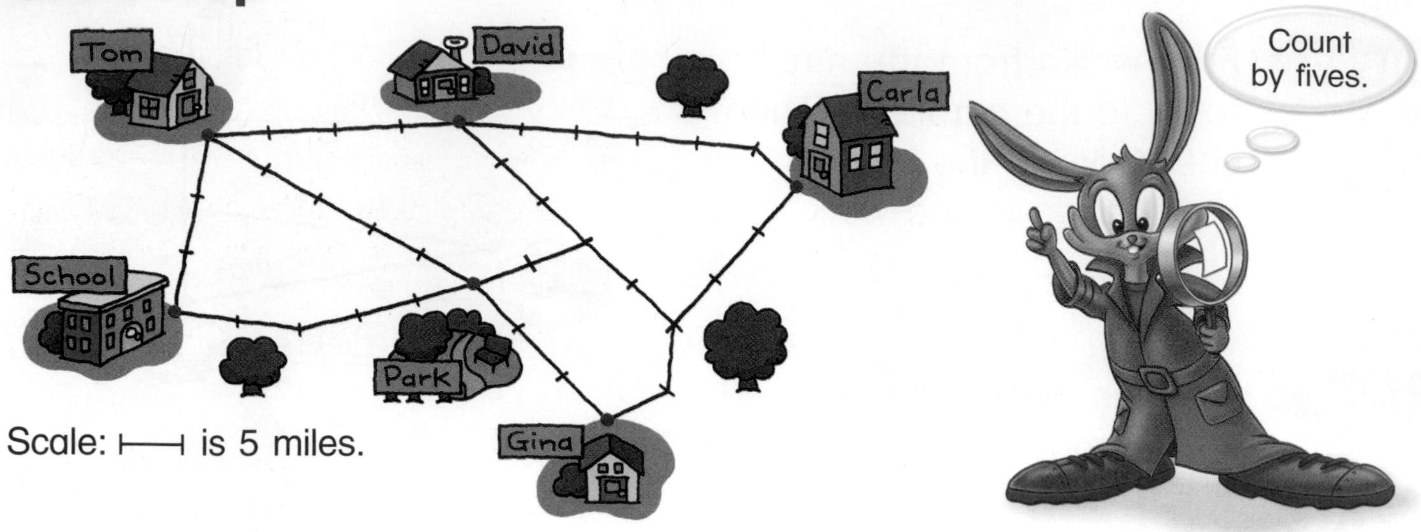

Scale: ⊢⊣ is 5 miles.

Find the shortest distance.

3. David's house to Gina's house 35 miles

4. Carla's house to Tom's house ______ miles

5. School to David's house ______ miles

6. Gina's house to school ______ miles

7. Carla rides to the park from her house. How far will she go if she stops to visit David first? ______ miles

8. Tom wants to visit David, Gina and Carla. What is the shortest distance he can travel to visit all three? ______ miles

Use the map above. In your Math Journal, write a problem for each question.

9. How far did you ride in all?

10. How much farther did you ride?

Math Alive at Home Ask your child how he/she used a map to solve the problems in this lesson.

Name ____________________

Problem Solving
Applications

Read → Plan → Write → Check

Mixed Strategies

Strategy File
Draw a Picture
Use More Than One Step
Use a Map

Use a strategy you have learned.

1. Tami has a paper clip that is $\frac{1}{2}$ inch long. Her book is 16 paper clips long. How many inches long is Tami's book?

____ inches long

---

2. Mae collects 19 baseball cards. Her sister collects a dozen baseball cards. Then her sister gives 5 of her cards away. How many cards do Mae and her sister have then?

____ baseball cards

---

3. Beth is at the park. She wants to go to the theater and then to the zoo. How much farther will she travel if she goes to the zoo first and then the theater?

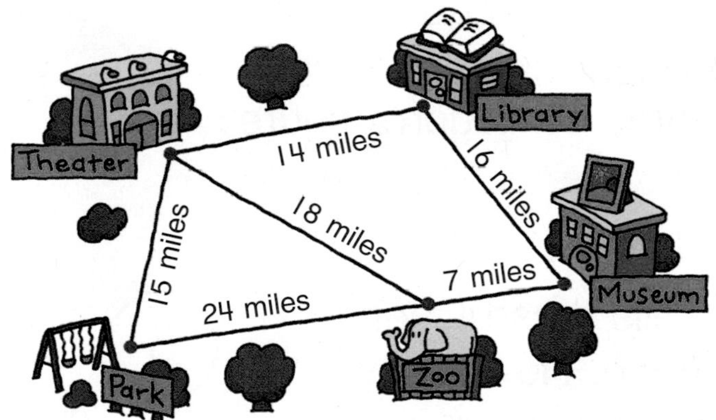

____ miles farther

4. Callie needs to go from the museum to the theater. What is the shortest distance she can go?

____ miles

Practice

Read → Plan → Write → Check

Use a strategy you have learned.

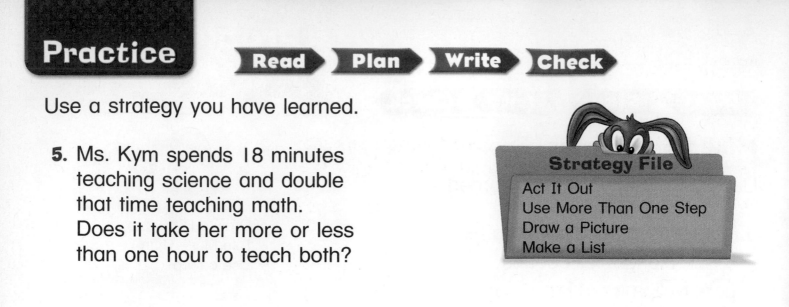

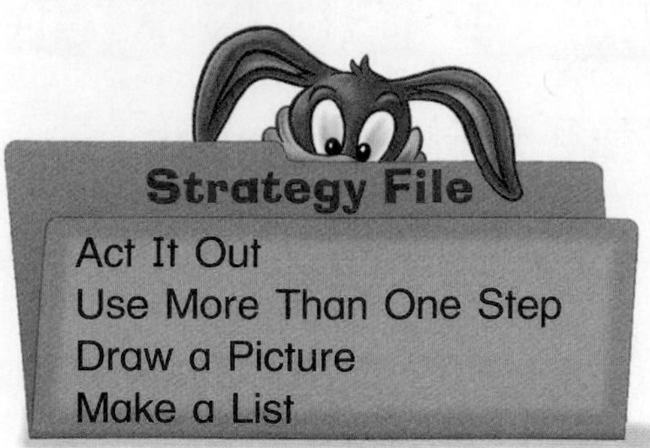

5. Ms. Kym spends 18 minutes teaching science and double that time teaching math. Does it take her more or less than one hour to teach both?

It takes her ________ than one hour.

---

6. One liter of juice costs 45¢. Josh gives the cashier 3 quarters and 2 dimes for 2 liters. What is Josh's change?

______

---

7. Hogan makes a figure out of cubes. The figure is 4 cubes long, 2 cubes wide, and 3 cubes high. What is the volume of Hogan's figure?

____ cubes

---

8. Daria pulls these tokens from a bag. How many three-digit numbers can she make with the tokens?

____ three-digit numbers

---

9. Gus passes 15 houses on the way to school. $\frac{1}{3}$ of the houses are blue. How many houses are blue?

____ houses

Math Alive at Home Ask your child to tell you how he/she solved some of the problems in this lesson.

Name ________________________________

TEST PREPARATION

Listen to your teacher read the directions.
Fill in the circle by the correct answer.

1.

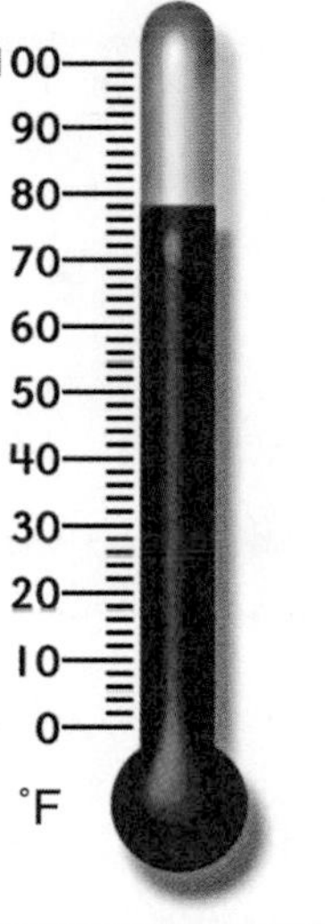

- ○ 88°F
- ○ 78°F
- ○ 70°F
- ○ 38°F

2.

   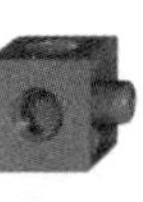   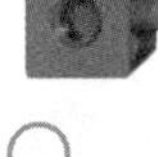

20 ○ 18 ○ 25 ○ 27 ○

3. Bob walks from his house to John's house. Then he walks to Sue's house. How far does Bob walk?

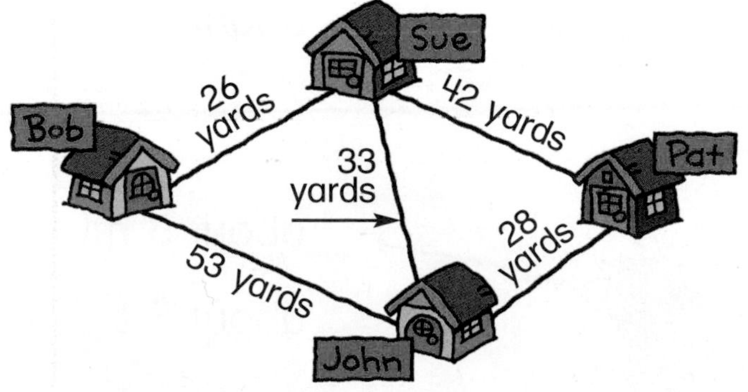

53 yards ○ 81 yards ○ 86 yards ○

4.

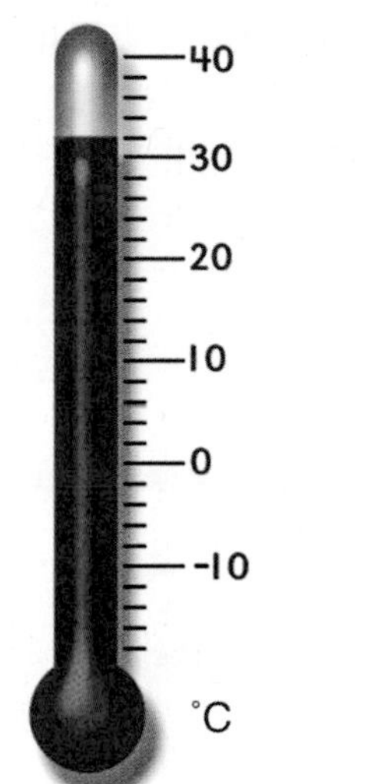

- ○ 34°C
- ○ 31°C
- ○ 35°C
- ○ 32°C

5.

quart ○ ounce ○ cup ○ inch ○

6.

 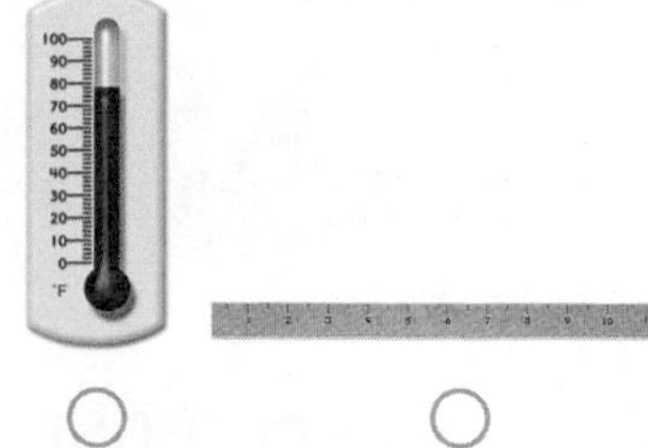

○ ○ ○

Connection

Name ______________________________

Did You Know?

Scientists use milliliters to measure small amounts of liquid. There are 20 drops of water in 1 milliliter. mL means milliliters.

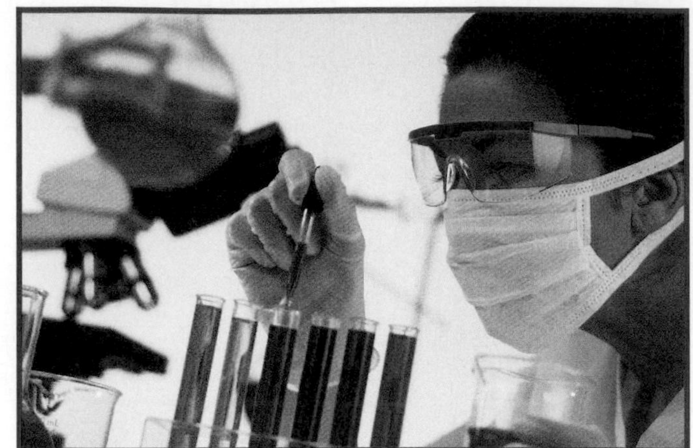

There are one thousand milliliters in 1 liter.

1000 mL = 1 L

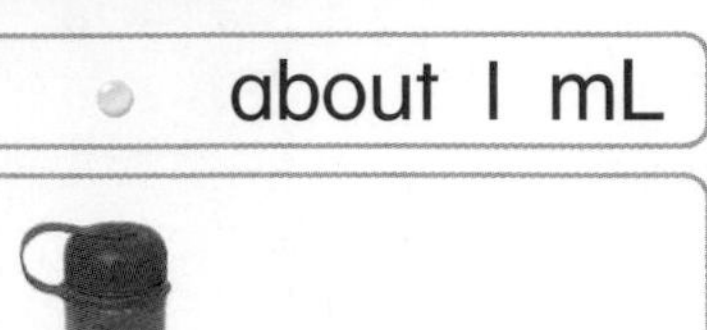

about 1 mL

about 1 L

Circle the better estimate.

1. 

about 8 mL

about 8 L

2. 

about 1 mL

about 1 L

3. 

about 3 mL

about 3 L

4. 

about 3 mL

about 3 L

5. 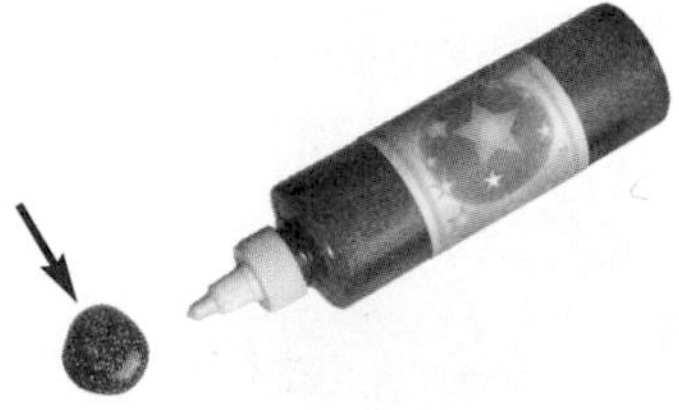

about 3 mL

about 3 L

6. 

about 4 mL

about 4 L

7. 

about 1 mL

about 1 L

8. 

about 5 mL

about 5 L

You can put this in your Math Portfolio.

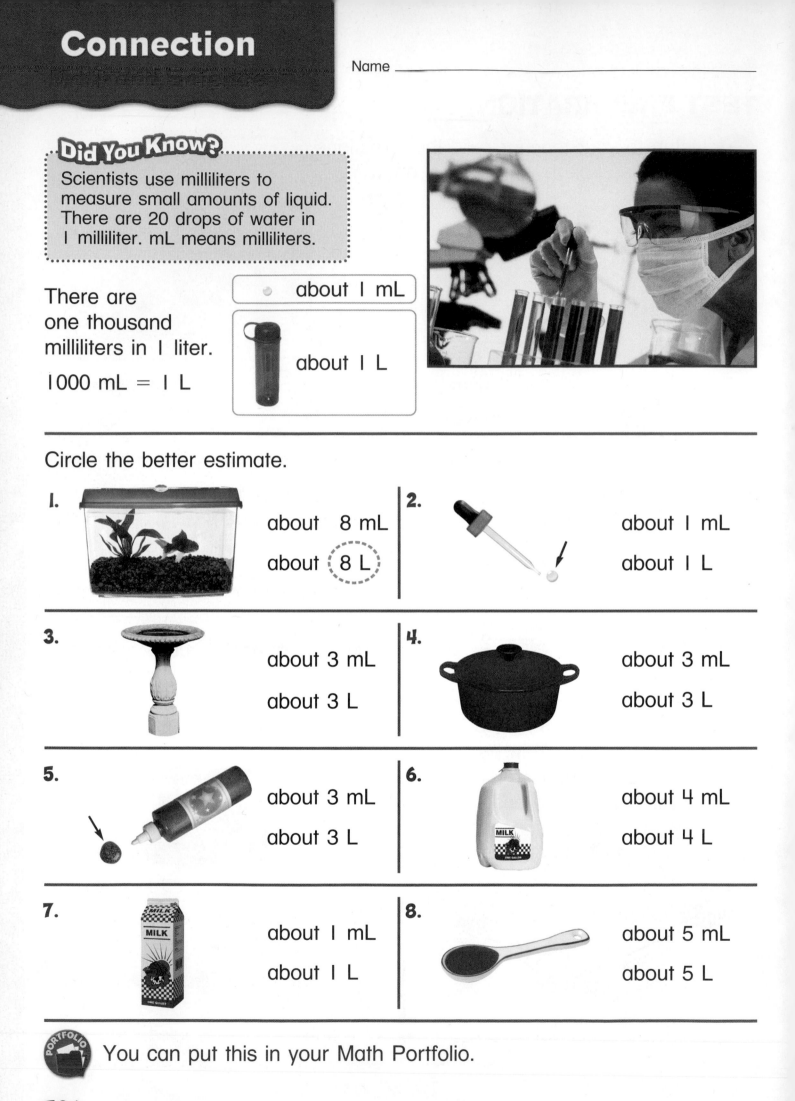

Name ________________________________

Chapter 11 Test

1. Estimate about how long. Then use [cube] to measure.

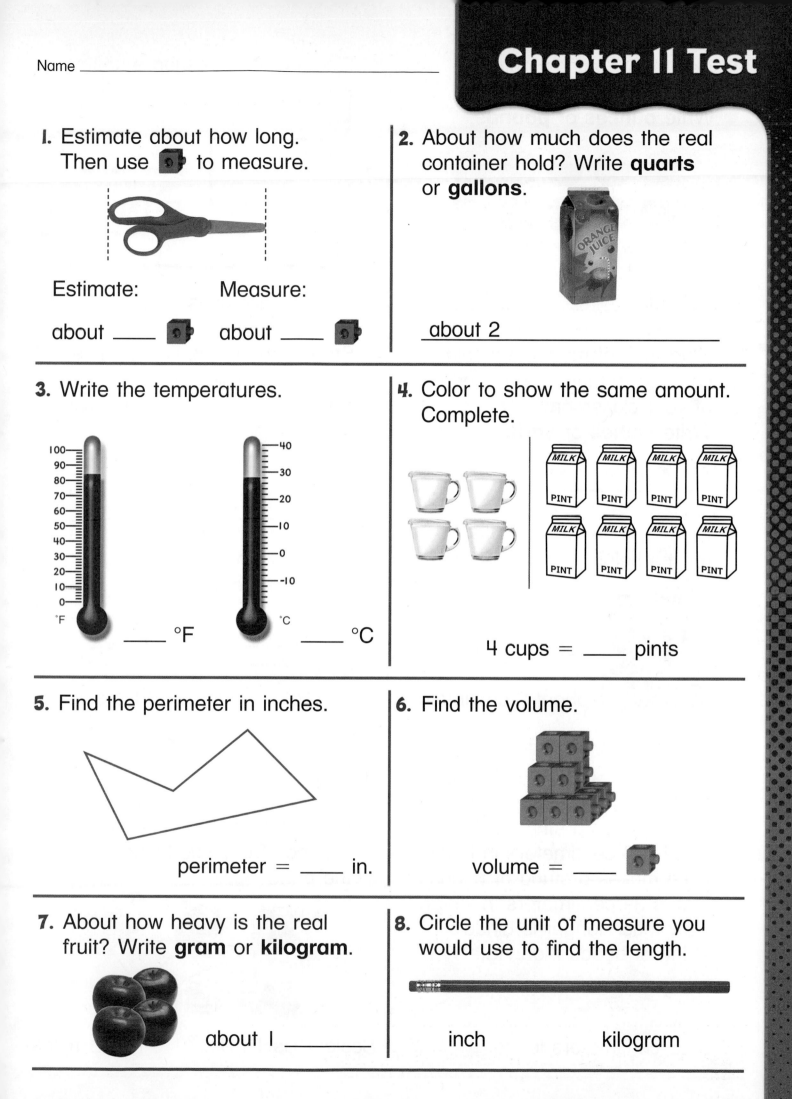

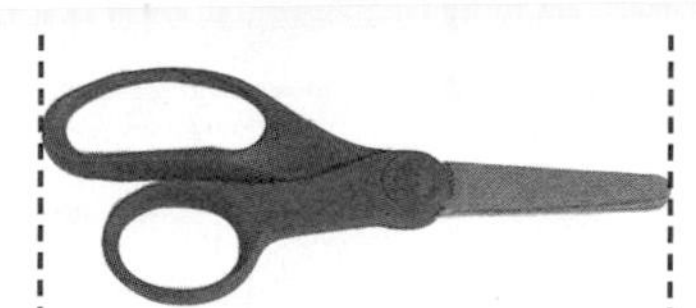

Estimate: about ____ [cube]

Measure: about ____ [cube]

2. About how much does the real container hold? Write **quarts** or **gallons**.

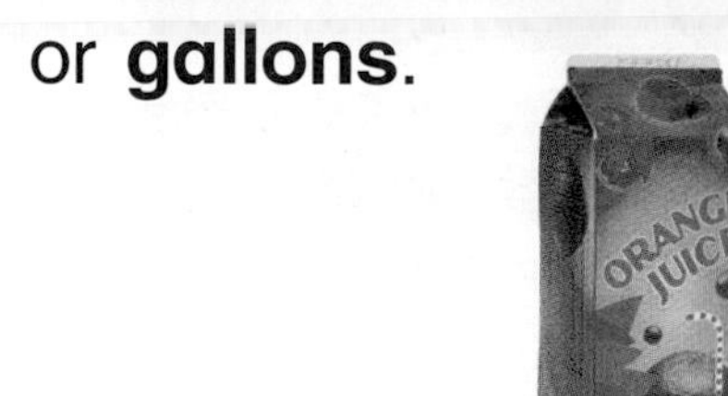

about 2 ________________

3. Write the temperatures.

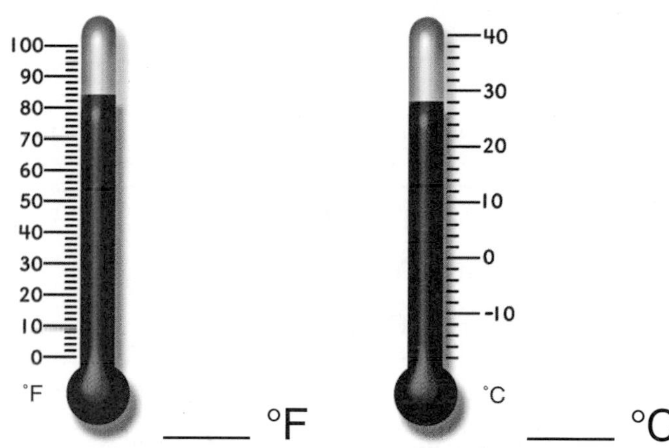

____ °F ____ °C

4. Color to show the same amount. Complete.

4 cups = ____ pints

5. Find the perimeter in inches.

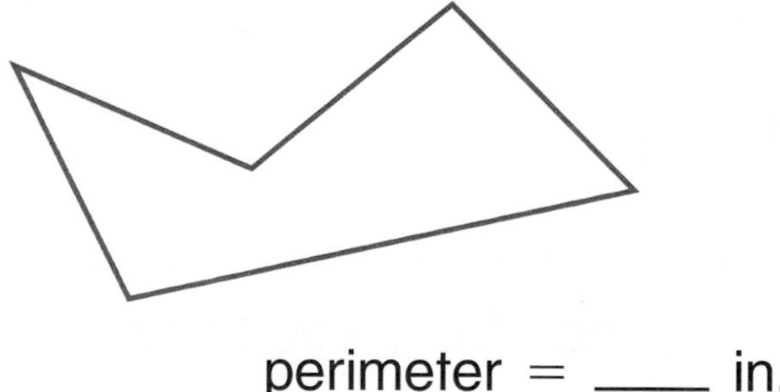

perimeter = ____ in.

6. Find the volume.

volume = ____ [cube]

7. About how heavy is the real fruit? Write **gram** or **kilogram**.

about 1 ________

8. Circle the unit of measure you would use to find the length.

inch kilogram

9. About how much would 10 oranges weigh?
Write **ounces** or **pounds**.

about 5 ____________________

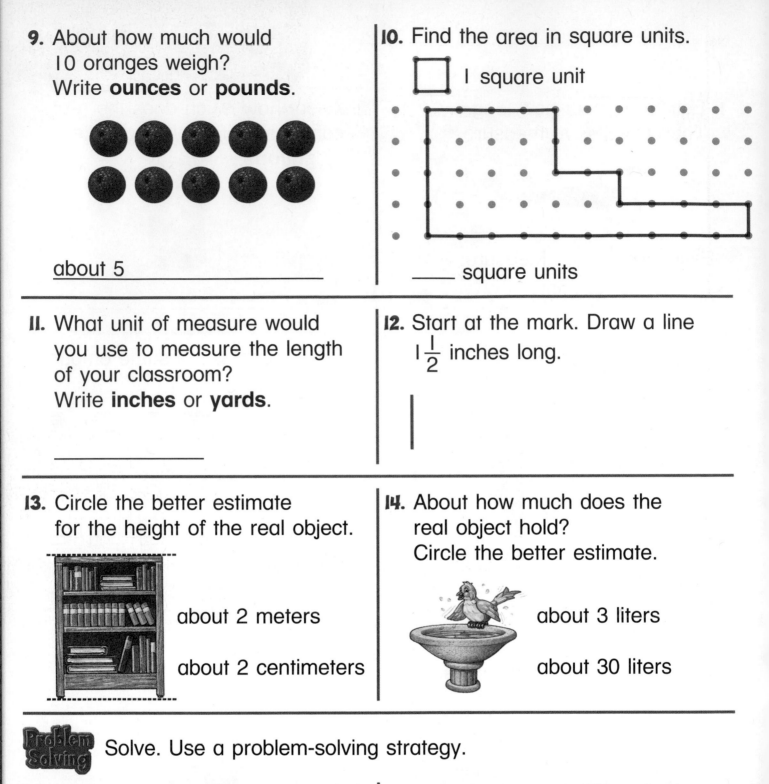

10. Find the area in square units.

1 square unit

____ square units

11. What unit of measure would you use to measure the length of your classroom?
Write **inches** or **yards**.

____

12. Start at the mark. Draw a line $1\frac{1}{2}$ inches long.

13. Circle the better estimate for the height of the real object.

about 2 meters

about 2 centimeters

14. About how much does the real object hold?
Circle the better estimate.

about 3 liters

about 30 liters

Solve. Use a problem-solving strategy.

15. Linda makes a string of beads that is 50 centimeters in length. Ruth makes a string of beads that is 34 centimeters in length. How much longer is Linda's string of beads than Ruth's?

____ centimeters longer

16. Use the map. Find the shortest distance from Pearl's house to the park.

Scale: ⊢⊣ is 1 mile.

____ miles

Name ______________________________

1. Use an inch ruler. Start at the dot. Draw a rectangle that is 4, 5, or 6 inches long and 2 inches high.

•

2. Find the perimeter of the rectangle you drew in inches and in centimeters.

_______ in.

_______ cm

3. Find the area in square units. Draw a different figure that has the same area.

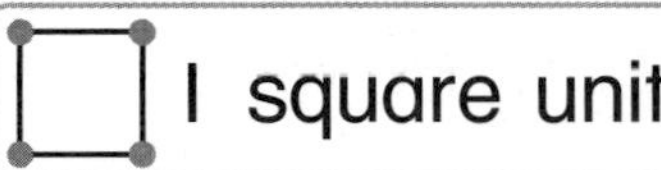

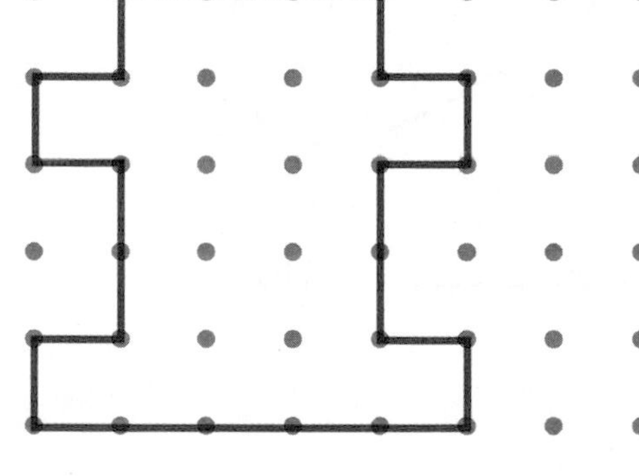

area = _______ square units

area = _______ square units

4. Explain how you made a different figure that has the same area.

____

____

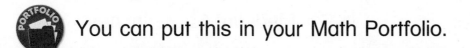

You can put this in your Math Portfolio.

Enrichment

Name ______________________________

Perimeter of Curved Objects

You can measure around a **curved** object or path.

Use a string on the object to estimate the length. Then place the string along an inch ruler to measure.

Estimate. Then measure.

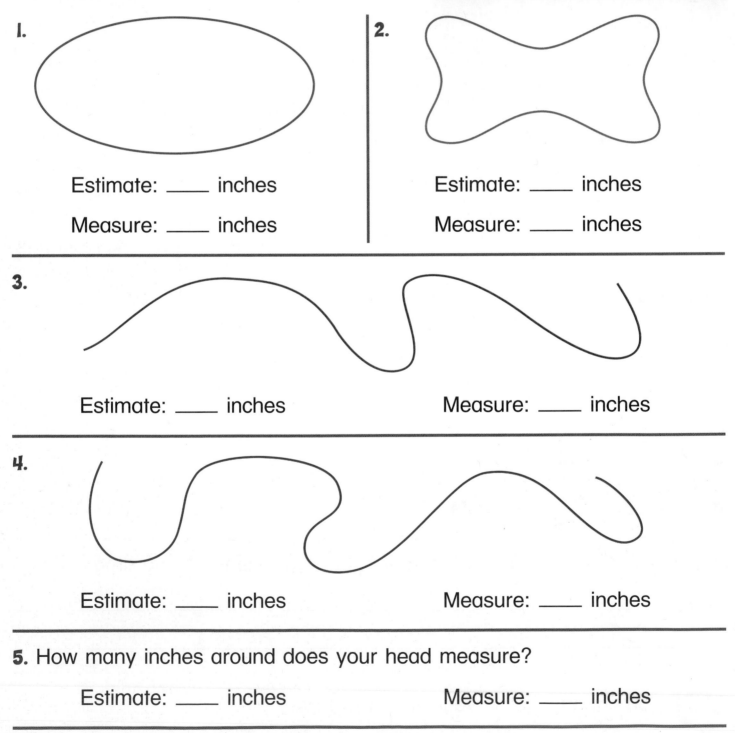

1.

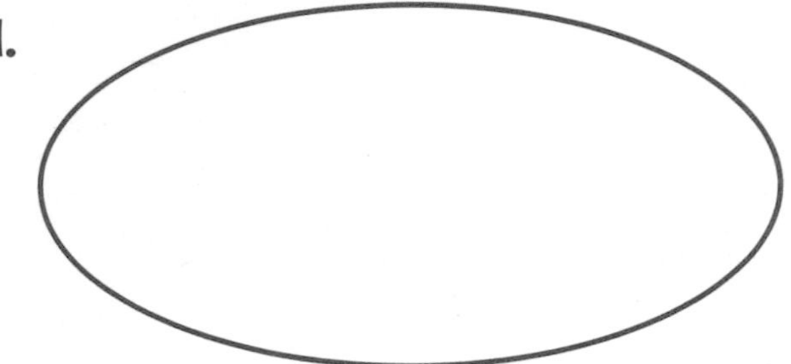

Estimate: ____ inches

Measure: ____ inches

2.

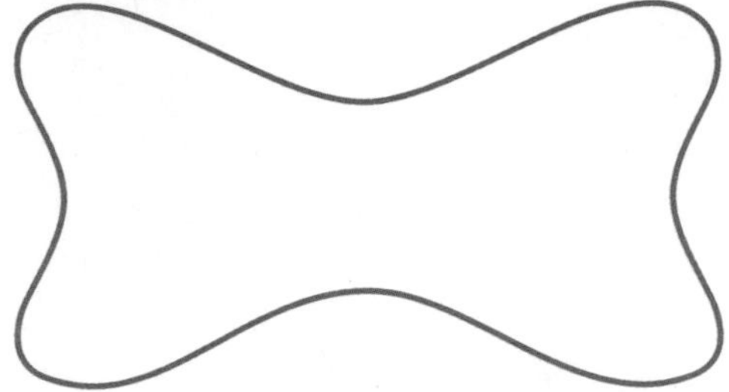

Estimate: ____ inches

Measure: ____ inches

3.

Estimate: ____ inches   Measure: ____ inches

4.

Estimate: ____ inches   Measure: ____ inches

5. How many inches around does your head measure?

Estimate: ____ inches   Measure: ____ inches

Read ALOUD

The History Lesson

It is the first day of Inchworm school. Ms. Green greets her students.

“Good morning, class. Today we are going to learn about the history of measurement. Tomorrow we will begin to measure things in inches.”

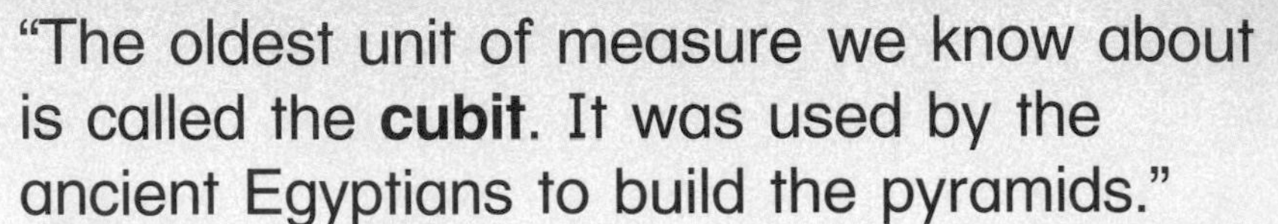

"The oldest unit of measure we know about is called the **cubit**. It was used by the ancient Egyptians to build the pyramids."

"A cubit was about equal to the distance from a person's elbow to the middle finger."

ANCIENT EGYPT

Pyramids

What unit would you use to measure the height of a pyramid today?

gallons pounds meters

"The ancient Greeks used a container called an **amphora** to measure honey and other liquids. We will see some of these containers when we visit the history museum next week."

What unit would we use to measure honey and other liquids today?

yards pints centimeters

"During the Middle Ages, doctors weighed herbs and other medicines on balances. They used **grains of wheat** as a unit of measure."

"Well, that's our lesson for today, class. I'll see you at the same time tomorow. So long until then!"

What unit of measure would we use to weigh herbs and other light things today?

ounces gallons liters

Name ______________________

Cumulative Review
Chapters 1-11

TEST PREPARATION

Fill in the circle next to the correct answer.

1. Use a centimeter ruler. Find the perimeter of the figure.

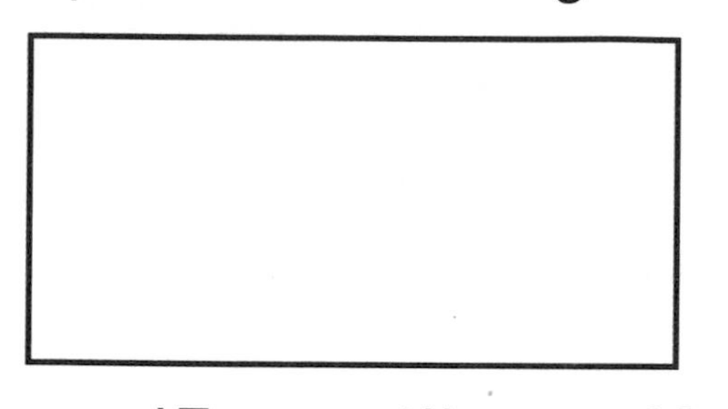

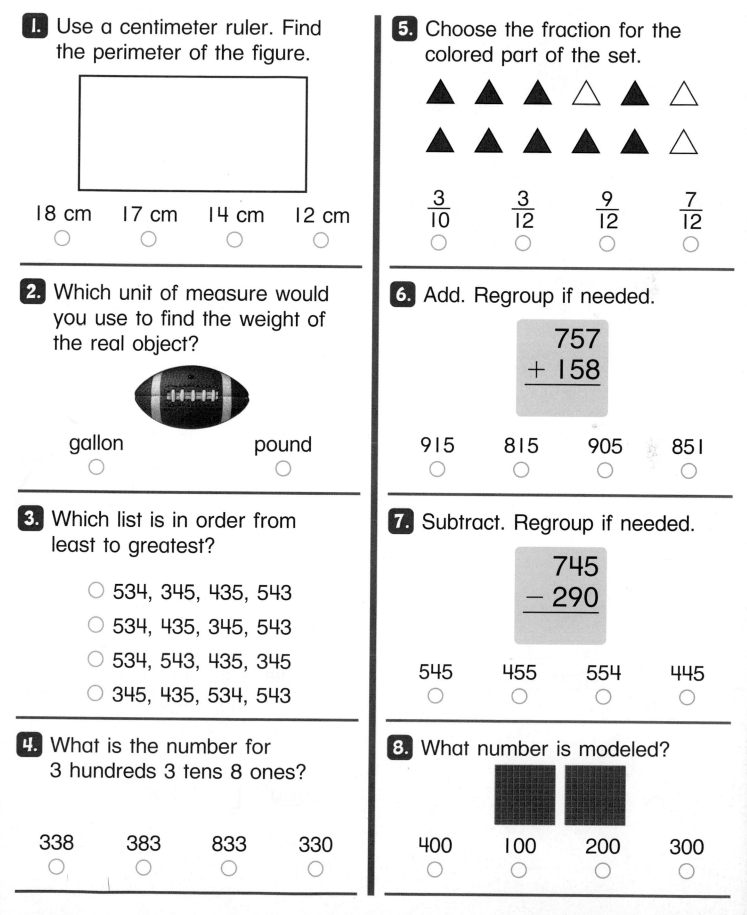

○ 18 cm ○ 17 cm ○ 14 cm ○ 12 cm

2. Which unit of measure would you use to find the weight of the real object?

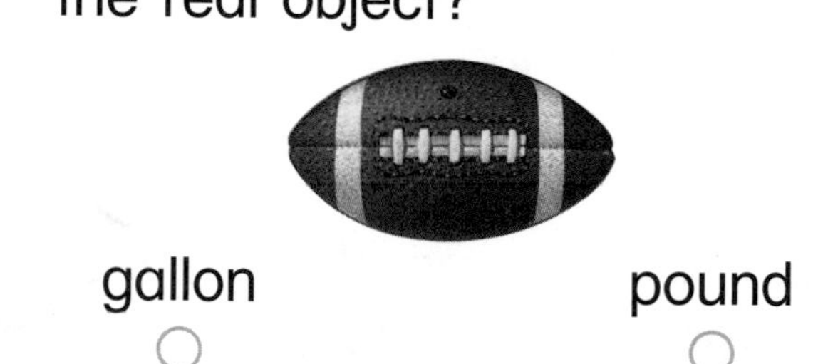

○ gallon ○ pound

3. Which list is in order from least to greatest?

○ 534, 345, 435, 543
○ 534, 435, 345, 543
○ 534, 543, 435, 345
○ 345, 435, 534, 543

4. What is the number for 3 hundreds 3 tens 8 ones?

○ 338 ○ 383 ○ 833 ○ 330

5. Choose the fraction for the colored part of the set.

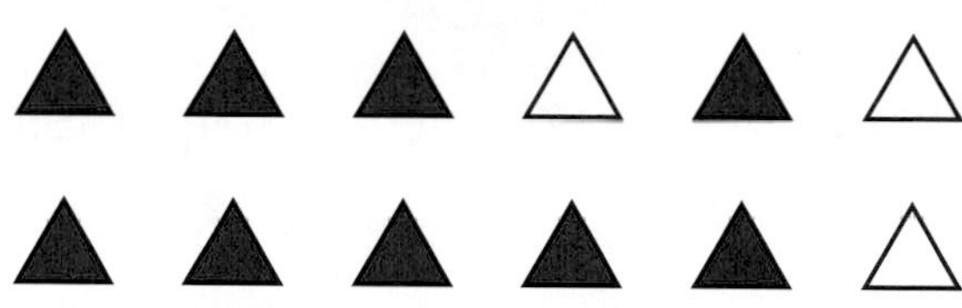

○ $\frac{3}{10}$ ○ $\frac{3}{12}$ ○ $\frac{9}{12}$ ○ $\frac{7}{12}$

6. Add. Regroup if needed.

$$\begin{array}{r} 757 \\ +\ 158 \\ \hline \end{array}$$

○ 915 ○ 815 ○ 905 ○ 851

7. Subtract. Regroup if needed.

$$\begin{array}{r} 745 \\ -\ 290 \\ \hline \end{array}$$

○ 545 ○ 455 ○ 554 ○ 445

8. What number is modeled?

○ 400 ○ 100 ○ 200 ○ 300

Fill in the circle by the correct answer.

9. Is it certain, possible, or impossible to pick a blue marble out of this bag?

○ certain ○ possible ○ impossible

13. About how heavy is the real fruit?

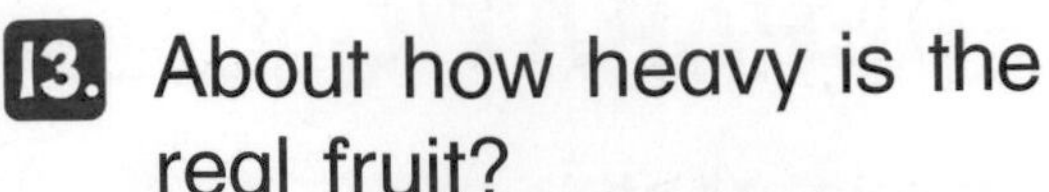

○ about 1 gram

○ about 1 kilogram

Solve. Use a problem-solving strategy. Watch for multistep problems.

10. One book costs $3.99. Ella buys two books. How much does she spend?

○ $6.88 ○ $6.98 ○ $7.88 ○ $7.98

14. Ben has 97¢. He buys one toy for 53¢ and another toy for 39¢. How much change does he get?

○ 82¢ ○ 92¢ ○ 5¢ ○ 84¢

11. Adam, Mary, Sam, and Neil share one pitcher of juice equally. What fractional part of the juice does each child get?

○ $\frac{4}{4}$ ○ $\frac{1}{2}$ ○ $\frac{3}{4}$ ○ $\frac{1}{4}$

15. Amy's father needs 2 pints of water to make soup. How many cups of water does he need?

12. Lily has 4 coins. Together they total 65¢. Which coins does Lily have?

○

○

16. Which numbers have the greater sum, the numbers inside the rectangle or the numbers inside the triangle?

379 286 397

○ inside rectangle ○ inside triangle

CHAPTER 12

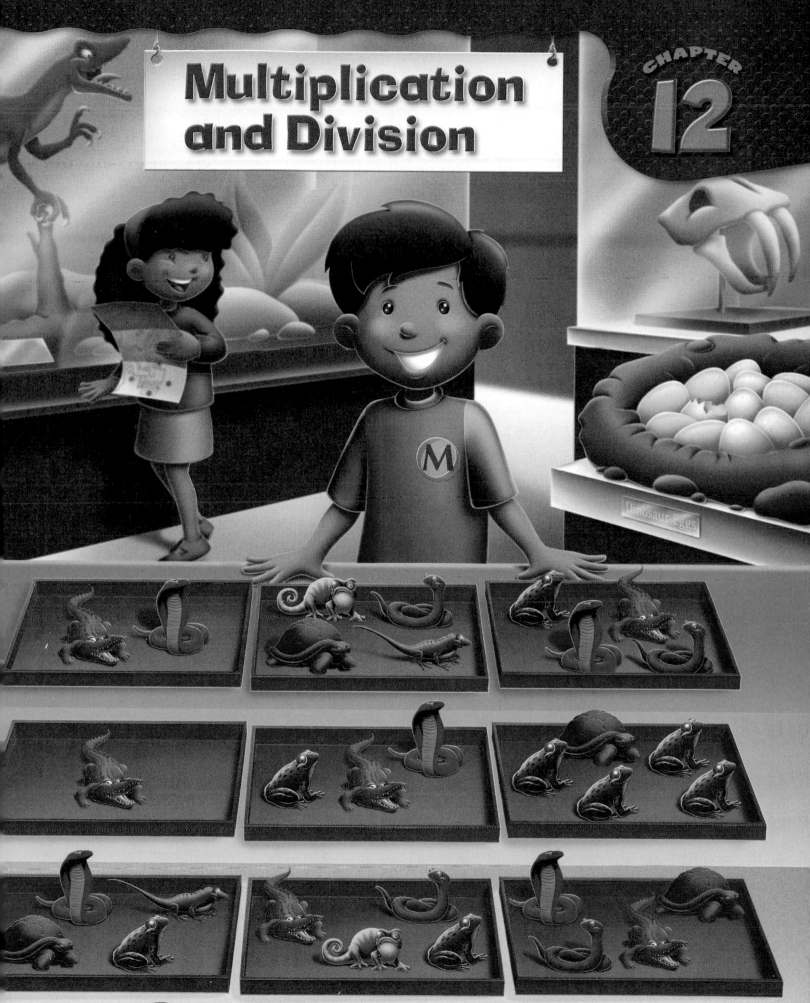

Multiplication and Division

Dinosaur Eggs

Listen to your teacher read the story.
Which row of figures should Danny buy?

Dear Family,

Today our class began Chapter 12. We will learn about multiplication and division. Let's do the activity below together so I can review the skills I will need in order to understand the math in this chapter. Then you can read some of the new vocabulary I will learn in Chapter 12.

Love, ______________

Doubles and More

Have your child solve the additions below. These additions serve as a review of adding doubles and adding more than two addends. Practice with repeated addition will help your child learn the concepts of multiplication in Chapter 12.

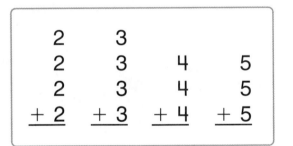

2	3		
2	3	4	5
2	3	4	5
+ 2	+ 3	+ 4	+ 5

Chapter 12

also on-line

multiply to join equal groups

multiplication sentence

$7 \times 3 = 21$

multiplication sign (points to ×)   **product** (points to 21)

factors $(7) \times (3) = 21$

divide to separate into equal groups or share

division sentence

$10 \div 2 = 5$

division sign (points to ÷)   **quotient** (points to 5)

How many groups of 3 in 20?

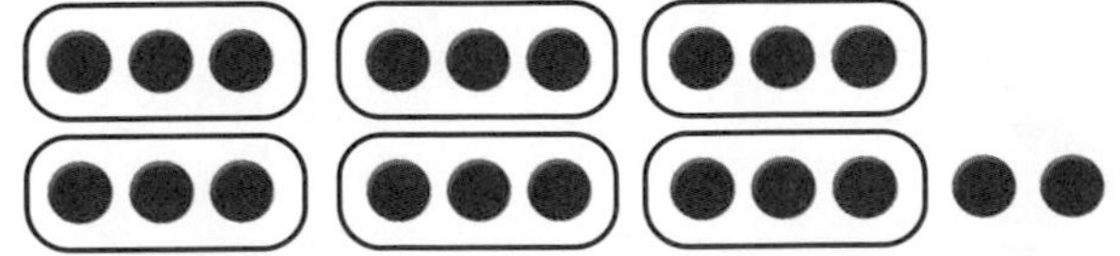

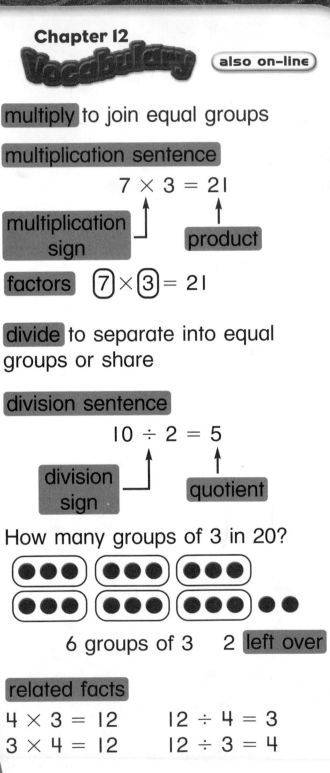

6 groups of 3   2 **left over**

related facts

$4 \times 3 = 12$ $12 \div 4 = 3$

$3 \times 4 = 12$ $12 \div 3 = 4$

For Additional Resources VISIT US ON-LINE www.sadlier-oxford.com

Name ____________________

Multiplication as Repeated Addition

HANDS-ON LESSON

Let's Learn!

How many blocks are there?

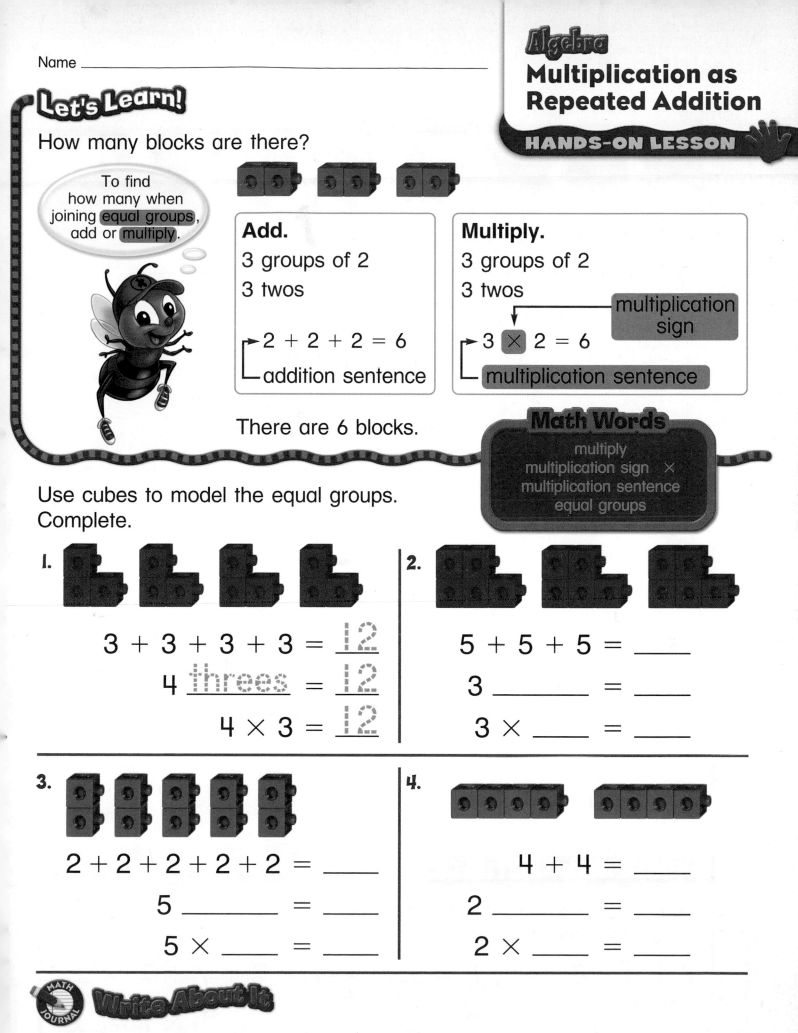

To find
how many when
joining equal groups,
add or multiply.

Add.
3 groups of 2
3 twos

2 + 2 + 2 = 6
addition sentence

Multiply.
3 groups of 2
3 twos

3 × 2 = 6
multiplication sign
multiplication sentence

There are 6 blocks.

Math Words
multiply
multiplication sign ×
multiplication sentence
equal groups

Use cubes to model the equal groups.
Complete.

1.    

3 + 3 + 3 + 3 = 12

4 threes = 12

4 × 3 = 12

2.   

5 + 5 + 5 = ____

3 ________ = ____

3 × ____ = ____

3. 

2 + 2 + 2 + 2 + 2 = ____

5 ________ = ____

5 × ____ = ____

4.  

4 + 4 = ____

2 ________ = ____

2 × ____ = ____

MATH JOURNAL
Write About It

5. How are addition and multiplication alike?
How are they different?

Practice

Complete.

6. 

4 + 4 + 4 + 4 = 16

4 fours = 16

4 × 4 = 16

7. 

2 + ___ + ___ + ___ = ___

4 ______ = ___

4 × ___ = ___

8. 

5 + ___ = ___

2 ______ = ___

2 × ___ = ___

9. 

3 + ___ + ___ = ___

3 ______ = ___

3 × ___ = ___

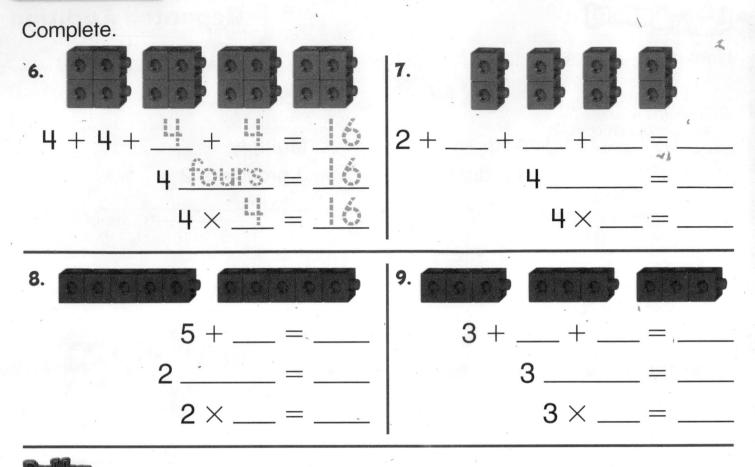

Solve. Use a problem-solving strategy.

10. For party favors, Ed puts 3 marbles in each bag. How many marbles will be in 4 bags?

___ marbles

11. Tim has 3 bags of 4 marbles. Ana has 2 bags of 5 marbles. Who has more marbles?

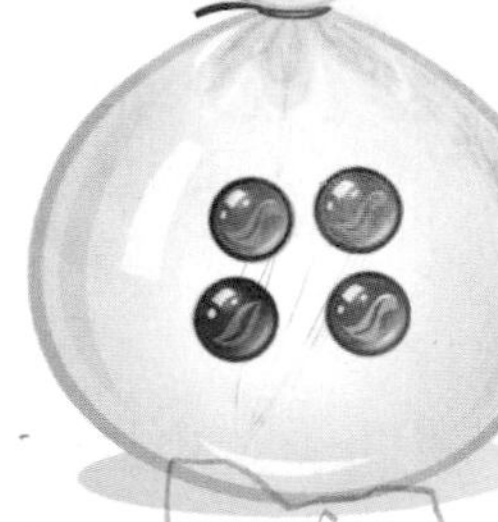

______

CALCULATOR ACTIVITY

Use a calculator to do the repeated addition. Then complete the multiplication sentence.

12. 8 + 8 + 8 + 8 + 8 = ___

5 × 8 = ___

13. 7 + 7 + 7 + 7 = ___

4 × 7 = ___

Math Alive at Home Ask your child to draw 3 groups of 4 objects and to write the addition and multiplication sentences for the drawing. (4 + 4 + 4 = 12; 3 x 4 = 12)

Name ____________________

Algebra
Multiply Groups of 2

Let's Learn!

Jerry collects stamps. The stamps come in packages of two. He buys 6 packages. How many stamps does Jerry buy?

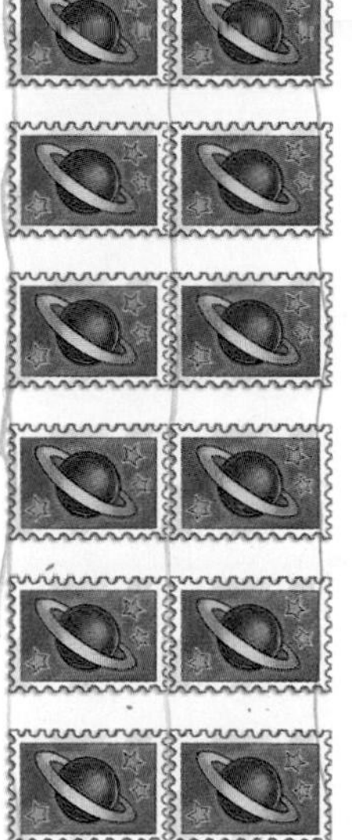

To find how many, multiply 2 by 6.

Think
How many are 6 twos?
2 + 2 + 2 + 2 + 2 + 2

You can write multiplication two ways.

6 × 2 = 12

number of groups — number in each group — in all

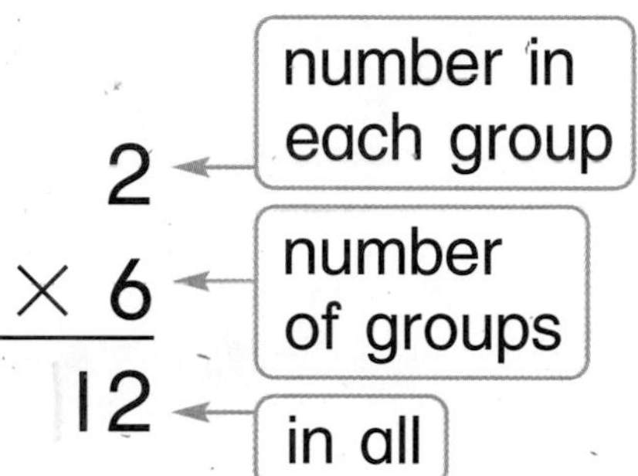

Jerry buys 12 stamps.

Find how many in all. Multiply.

1. 3 twos

3 × 2 = 6

$$\begin{array}{r} 2 \\ \times\ 3 \\ \hline 6 \end{array}$$

2. 4 twos

4 × 2 = 8

$$\begin{array}{r} 2 \\ \times\ 4 \\ \hline 8 \end{array}$$

3.

8 twos

8 × 2 = 16

$$\begin{array}{r} 2 \\ \times\ 8 \\ \hline 16 \end{array}$$

4.

7 twos

7 × 2 = 14

$$\begin{array}{r} 2 \\ \times\ 7 \\ \hline 14 \end{array}$$

Talk It Over

5. Explain why 2 + 2 + 3 does not mean the same as 3 × 2.

Practice

Find how many in all. Multiply.

6. 

$$\begin{array}{r} 2 \\ \times\ 2 \\ \hline 4 \end{array}$$

7. 

$$\begin{array}{r} 2 \\ \times\ 6 \\ \hline \end{array}$$

8. 

$$\begin{array}{r} 2 \\ \times\ 1 \\ \hline \end{array}$$

9.

$0 \times 2 =$ ____

10. 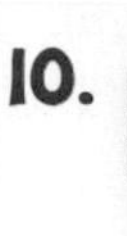   

$9 \times 2 =$ ____

11.  

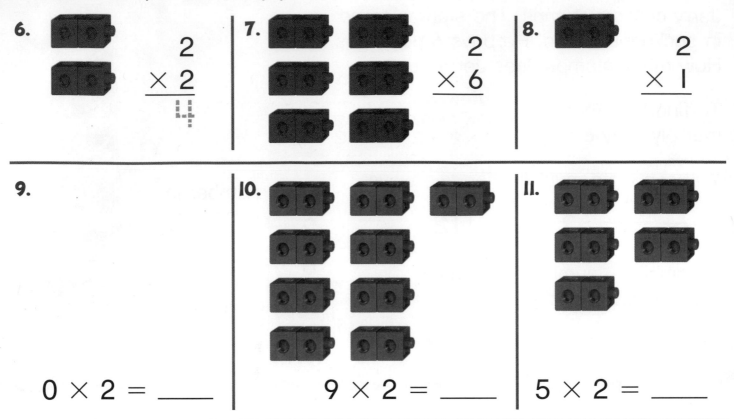

$5 \times 2 =$ ____

Multiply. Write the missing numbers.
Look for a pattern.

12.

											Number:
	2	2	2	2	2	2	2	2	2	2	← in each group
×	0	1	2	3	4	5	6	7	8	9	← of groups
	0	2	4								← in all

CRITICAL THINKING

13. Write the addition sentence and the multiplication sentence that this number line shows.

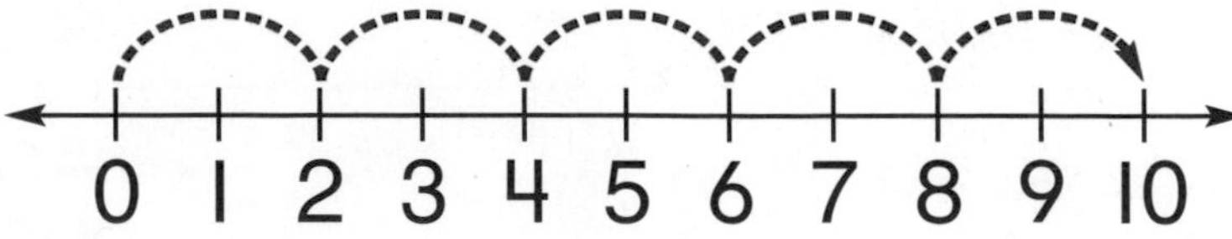

____

____

Math Alive at Home Ask your child to show you two ways to write 5 times 2. (5×2; $\begin{array}{r} 2 \\ \times\ 5 \\ \hline \end{array}$)

Name ______________________________

Algebra

Multiply Groups of 3

Let's Learn!

Pat has 2 boxes. She puts 3 marbles in each box. How many marbles are in the boxes altogether?

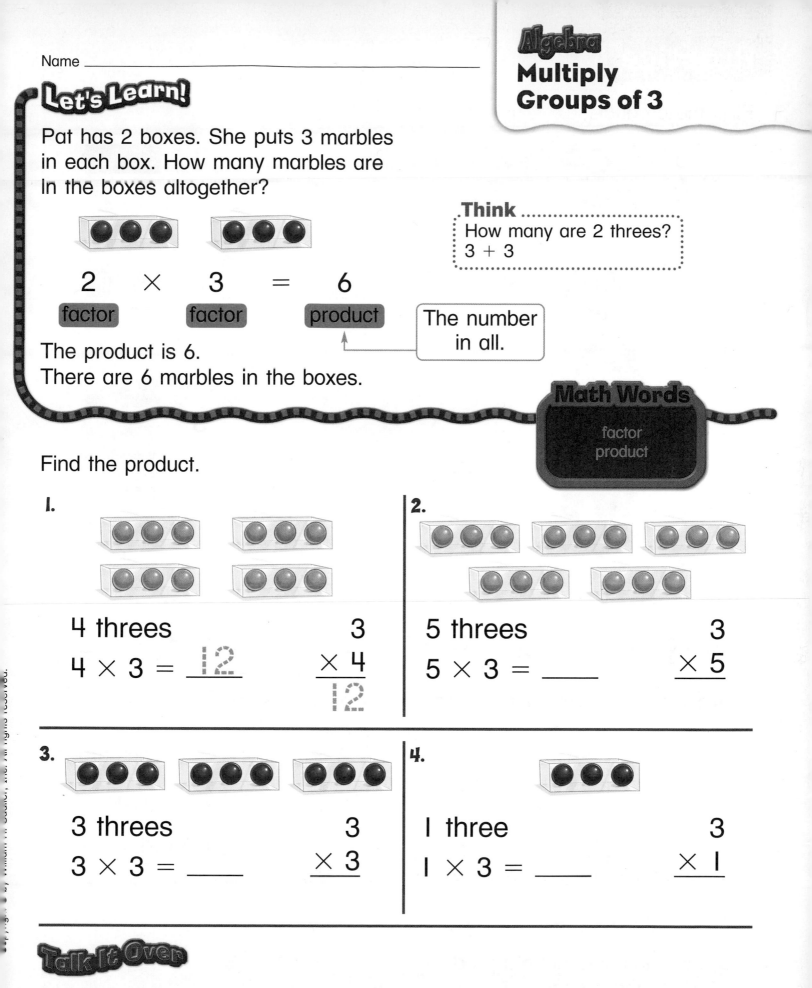

Think
How many are 2 threes?
3 + 3

$2 \times 3 = 6$

factor factor product

The number in all.

The product is 6.
There are 6 marbles in the boxes.

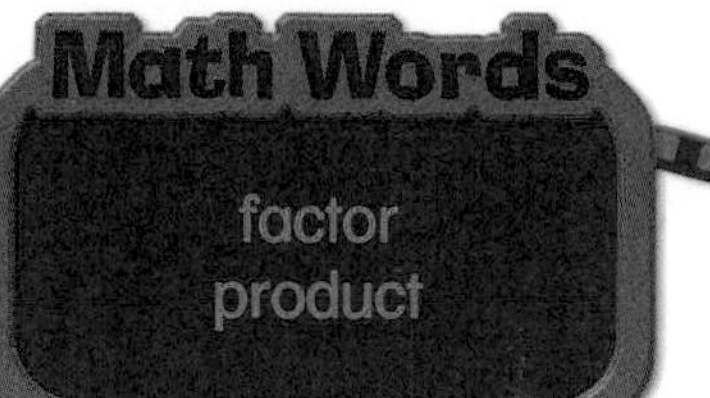

Find the product.

1.

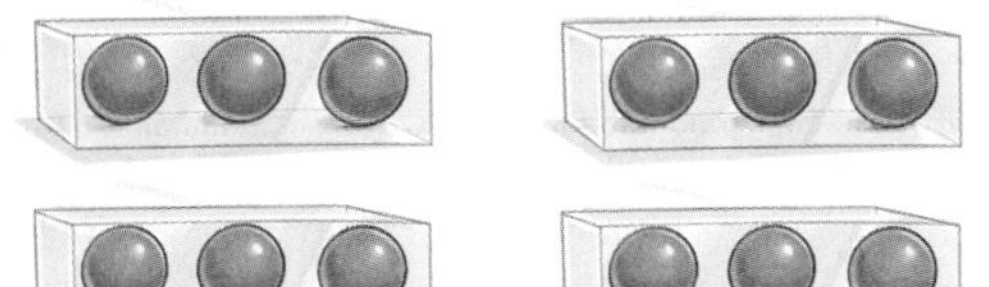

4 threes

$4 \times 3 = $ 12

$$\begin{array}{r} 3 \\ \times\ 4 \\ \hline 12 \end{array}$$

2.

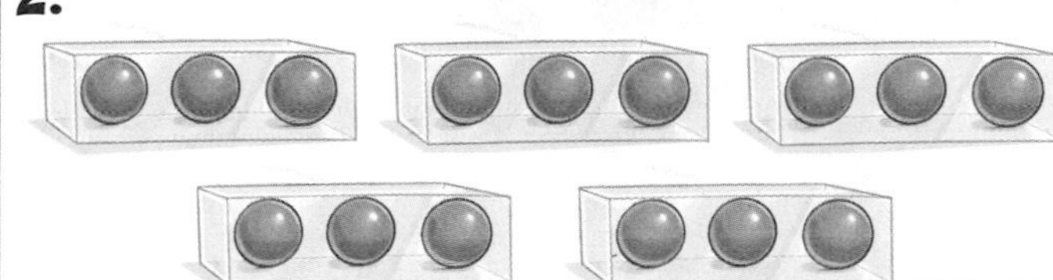

5 threes

$5 \times 3 = $ ____

$$\begin{array}{r} 3 \\ \times\ 5 \\ \hline \end{array}$$

3.

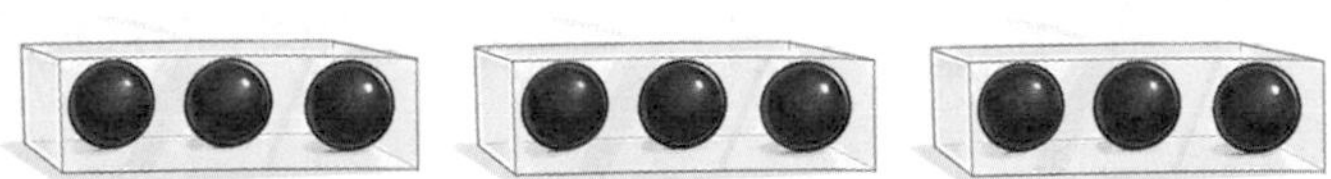

3 threes

$3 \times 3 = $ ____

$$\begin{array}{r} 3 \\ \times\ 3 \\ \hline \end{array}$$

4.

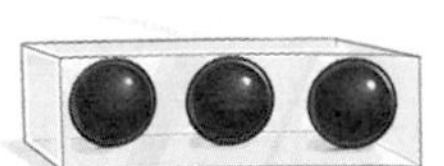

1 three

$1 \times 3 = $ ____

$$\begin{array}{r} 3 \\ \times\ 1 \\ \hline \end{array}$$

5. In 5×3, how many groups do you have? How many are in each group?

Practice

Find the product.

6. $\begin{array}{r} 3 \\ \times\ 6 \\ \hline 18 \end{array}$

7. $\begin{array}{r} 3 \\ \times\ 1 \\ \hline \end{array}$

8. $\begin{array}{r} 3 \\ \times\ 8 \\ \hline \end{array}$

9. $\begin{array}{r} 3 \\ \times\ 7 \\ \hline \end{array}$

10. $\begin{array}{r} 3 \\ \times\ 9 \\ \hline \end{array}$

11. $3 \times 3 =$ ____

12. $0 \times 3 =$ ____

13. $5 \times 3 =$ ____

Multiply. Write the missing numbers. Look for a pattern.

14.

											Number:
	3	3	3	3	3	3	3	3	3	3	← in each group
×	0	1	2	3	4	5	6	7	8	9	← of groups
	0	3	6								← in all

CRITICAL THINKING

15. Two numbers have a product of 12 and a sum of 7. What are the two numbers?

____ and ____

Math Alive at Home Ask your child to model the multiplication sentence for exercise 10.

Name ____________________

Visualize

- Sometimes it helps to visualize information when you read a problem. One way to visualize information is to draw a picture.

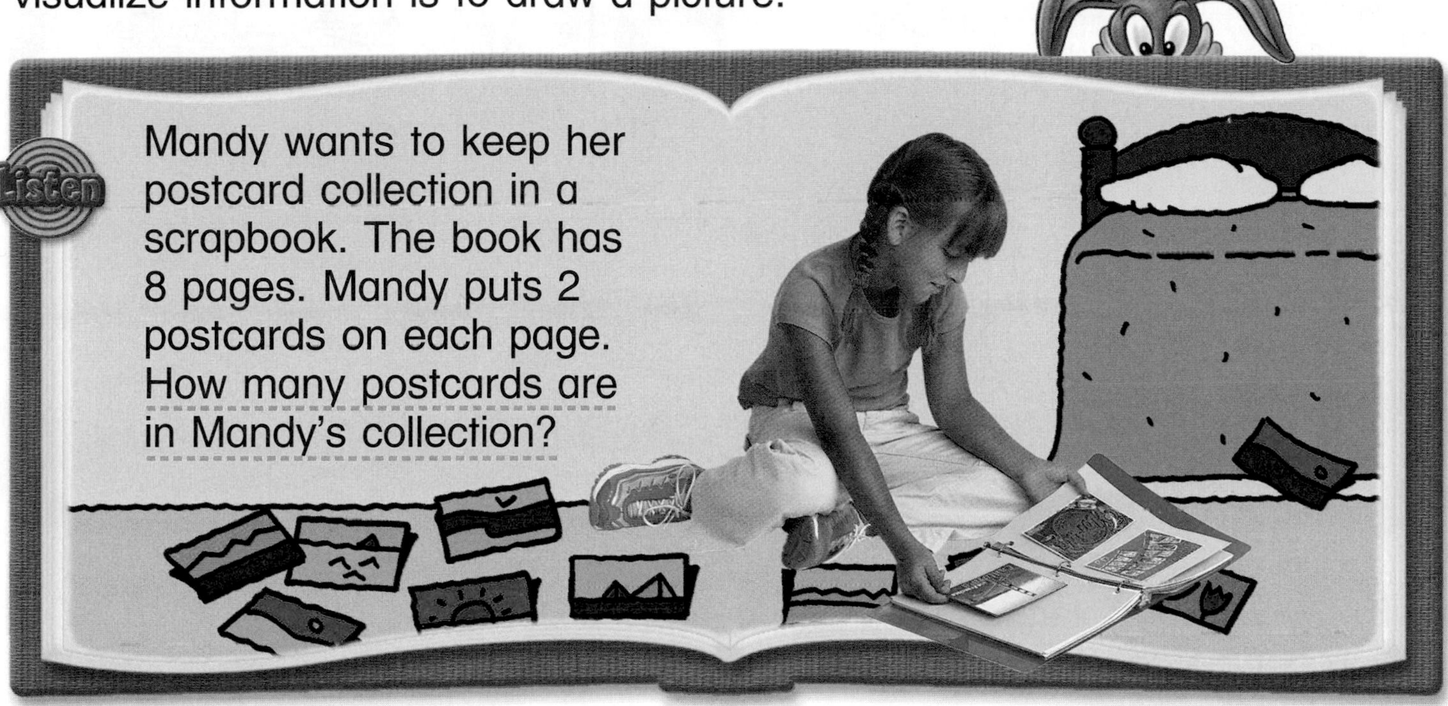

Listen
Mandy wants to keep her postcard collection in a scrapbook. The book has 8 pages. Mandy puts 2 postcards on each page. How many postcards are in Mandy's collection?

1. Reread the problem. Draw a line under the question you need to answer.

2. How many pages are in Mandy's scrapbook? ____ pages

   How many cards does Mandy put on each page? ____ cards

3. To visualize the problem, draw 8 pages with 2 postcards on each page.

4. Now solve the problem. Multiply to find how many postcards are in Mandy's collection. $8 \times 2 =$ ____

   There are ____ postcards in Mandy's collection.

Copyright © by William H. Sadlier, Inc. All rights reserved.

Practice

Visualize

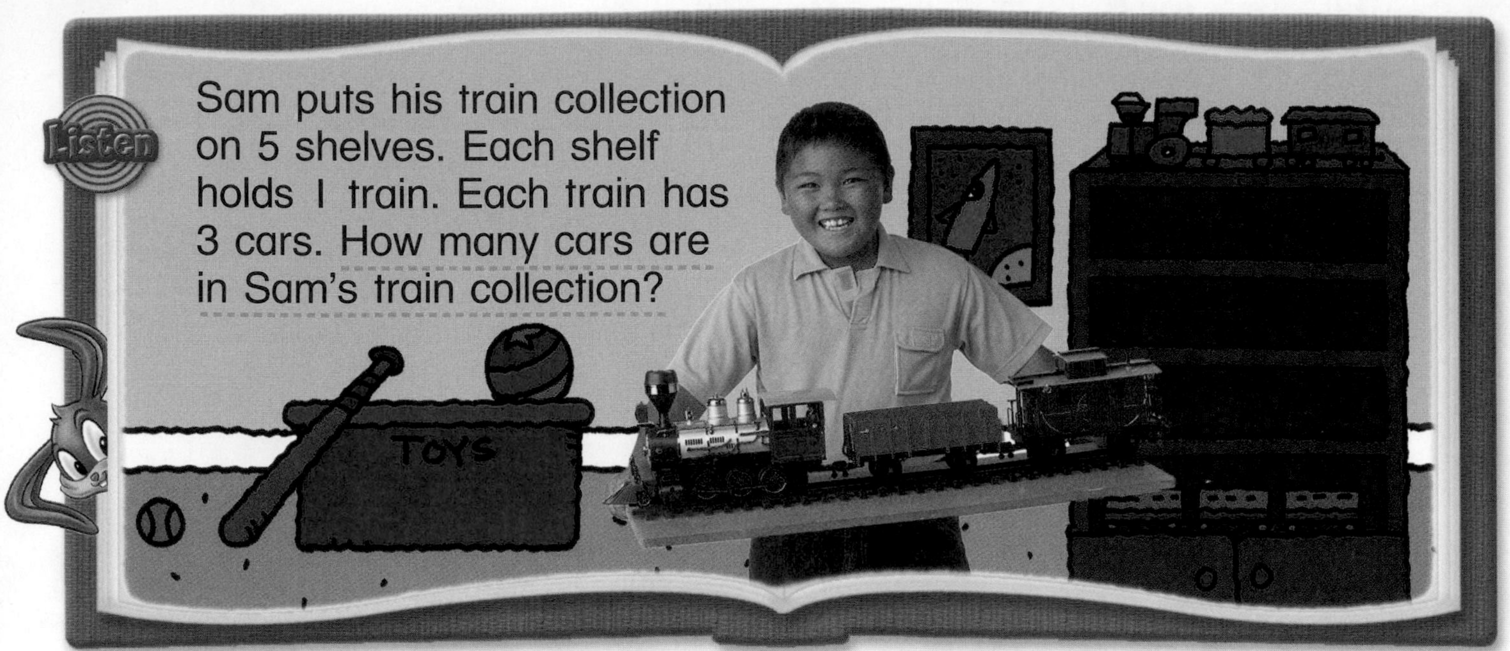

Listen
Sam puts his train collection on 5 shelves. Each shelf holds 1 train. Each train has 3 cars. How many cars are in Sam's train collection?
TOYS

5. Reread the problem. Draw a line under the question you need to answer.

---

6. How many shelves hold the train collection? ____ shelves

How many cars are on each train? ____ cars

---

7. To visualize the problem, draw 5 shelves with 3 train cars on each shelf.

---

8. Now solve the problem. Multiply to find how many cars are in Sam's train collection. $5 \times 3 =$ ____

There are ____ cars in Sam's train collection.

Math Alive at Home Today your child used the skill of Visualizing to work through math problems.

Name ______________________________

Algebra

Multiply Groups of 4

Let's Learn!

Kim strings beads on 3 strings.
She puts 4 beads on each string.
How many beads does Kim string?

Think
How many are 3 fours?
4 + 4 + 4

$3 \times 4 = 12$

3 ↑ number of groups; 4 ↑ number in each group; 12 ↑ in all

$$\begin{array}{rl} 4 & \text{factor} \\ \times\ 3 & \text{factor} \\ \hline 12 & \text{product} \end{array}$$

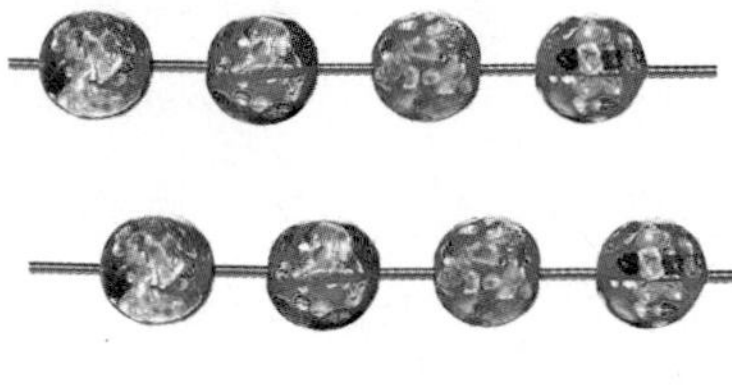

The product is 12.
Kim strings 12 beads.

Find the product.

1.

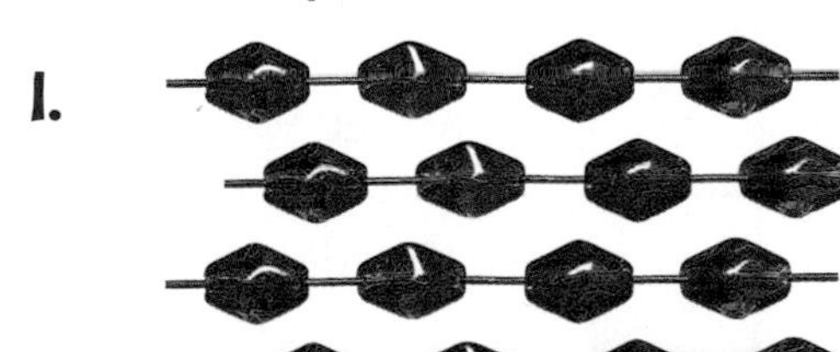

$5 \times 4 =$ 20

$$\begin{array}{r} 4 \\ \times\ 5 \\ \hline 20 \end{array}$$

2.

$7 \times 4 =$ ____

$$\begin{array}{r} 4 \\ \times\ 7 \\ \hline \end{array}$$

3.

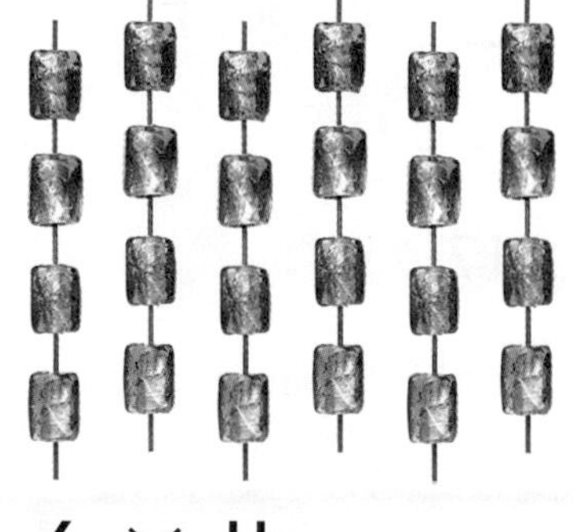

$6 \times 4 =$ ____

$$\begin{array}{r} 4 \\ \times\ 6 \\ \hline \end{array}$$

4.

$4 \times 4 =$ ____

$$\begin{array}{r} 4 \\ \times\ 4 \\ \hline \end{array}$$

5. $0 \times 4 =$ ____

6. $8 \times 4 =$ ____

7. $9 \times 4 =$ ____

8. How is counting by 4s the same as multiplying by 4?

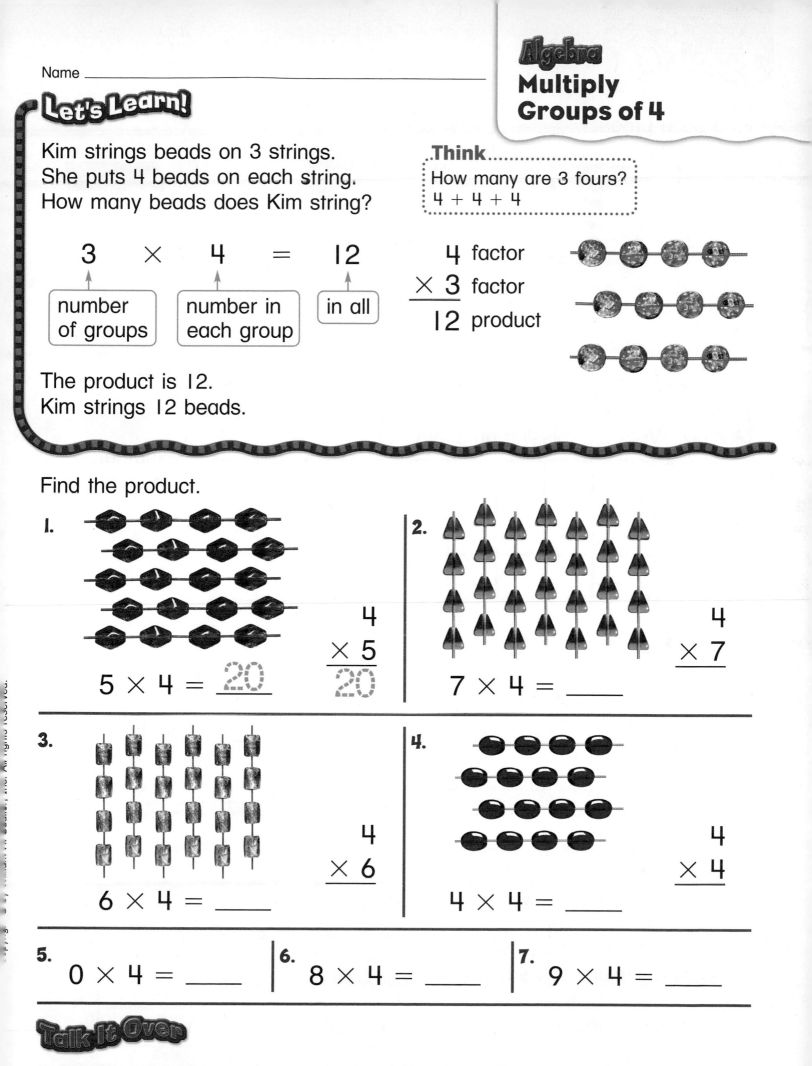

Practice

Find each product.

9. $\begin{array}{r} 4 \\ \times\ 3 \\ \hline 12 \end{array}$

10. $\begin{array}{r} 4 \\ \times\ 5 \\ \hline \end{array}$

11. $\begin{array}{r} 4 \\ \times\ 1 \\ \hline \end{array}$

12. $9 \times 4 =$ ____

13. $8 \times 4 =$ ____

14. $2 \times 4 =$ ____

Multiply. Write the missing numbers.

15.

											Number:
	4	4	4	4	4	4	4	4	4	4	← in each group
×	0	1	2	3	4	5	6	7	8	9	← of groups
	0	4	8								← in all

Find each product.

16. $1 \times 4 =$ ____ $1 \times 3 =$ ____ $1 \times 2 =$ ____ $1 \times 1 =$ ____

17. $0 \times 4 =$ ____ $0 \times 3 =$ ____ $0 \times 2 =$ ____ $0 \times 1 =$ ____

18. In your Math Journal, write a rule for the facts in exercise 16 and a rule for the facts in exercise 17.

CRITICAL THINKING

19. How many bottles were recycled each day? On a separate sheet of paper, explain how you could use multiplication to find the answer.

Bottles Recycled	
Monday	🍶 🍶 🍶 🍶 🍶 🍶
Tuesday	🍶 🍶 🍶 🍶
Key: Each 🍶 = 4 bottles.	

Math Alive at Home Ask your child to model the multiplication sentences for the table in exercise 15.

Name ____________________

Algebra

Multiply Groups of 5

Let's Learn!

An **array** is an arrangement of objects in rows and columns.

I use an array to model multiplication on grid paper.

array

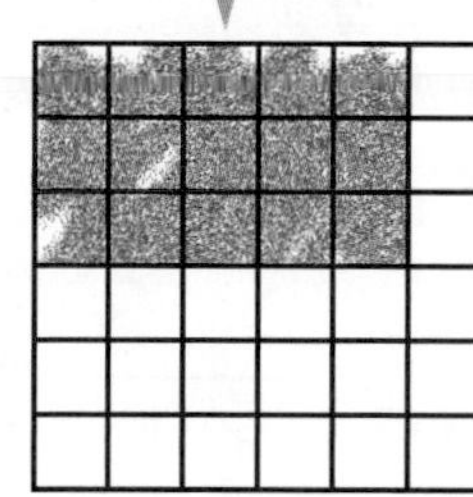

3 equal rows
5 in each row

3 fives = 15

$3 \times 5 = 15$

$$\begin{array}{r} 5 \\ \times\ 3 \\ \hline 15 \end{array}$$

Math Words

array

Look at these arrays. Multiply.

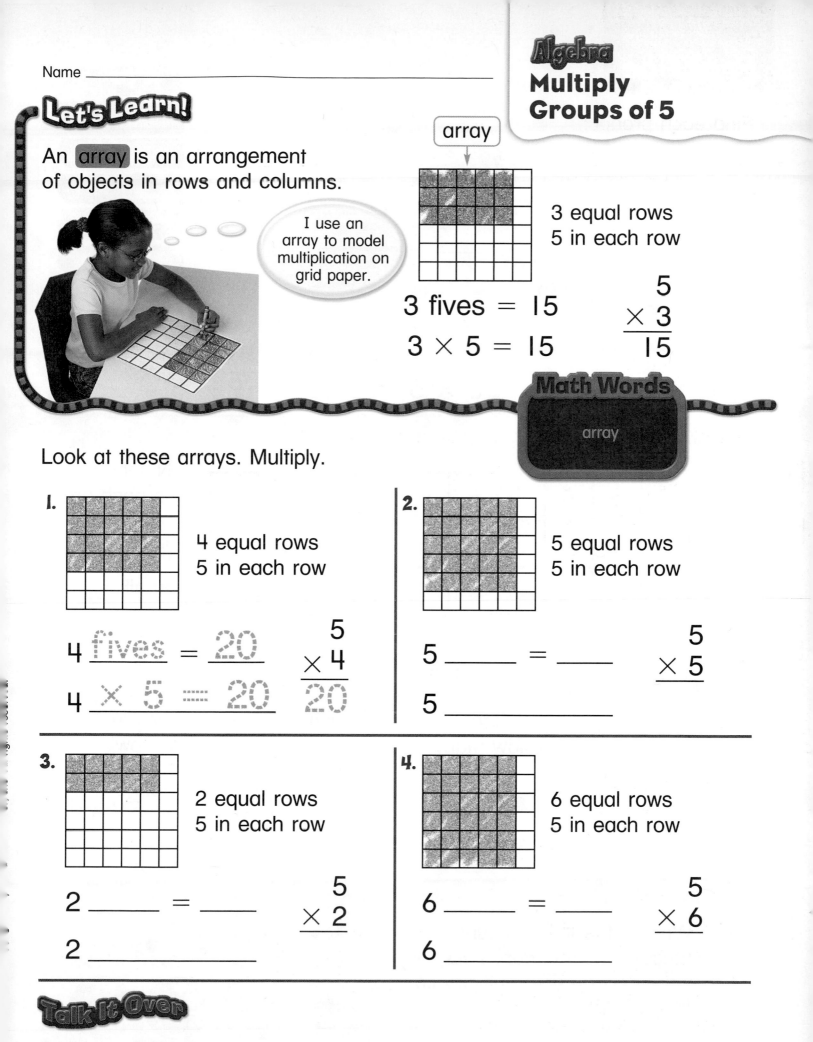

1.

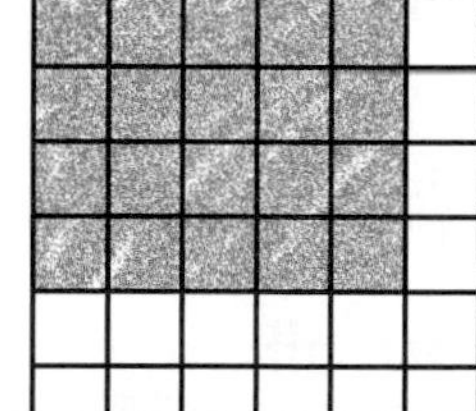

4 equal rows
5 in each row

4 fives = 20

4 × 5 = 20

$$\begin{array}{r} 5 \\ \times\ 4 \\ \hline 20 \end{array}$$

2.

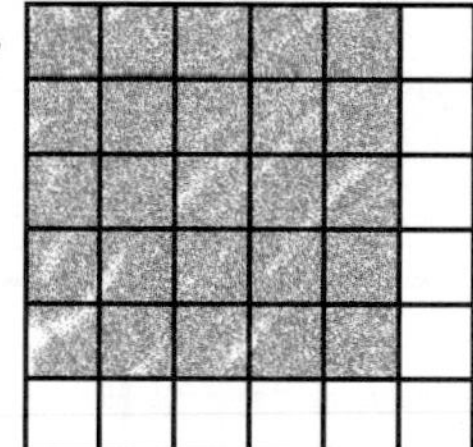

5 equal rows
5 in each row

5 ______ = ______

5 ______________

$$\begin{array}{r} 5 \\ \times\ 5 \\ \hline \end{array}$$

3.

2 equal rows
5 in each row

2 ______ = ______

2 ______________

$$\begin{array}{r} 5 \\ \times\ 2 \\ \hline \end{array}$$

4.

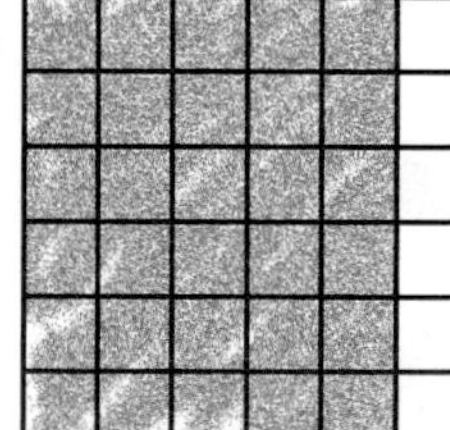

6 equal rows
5 in each row

6 ______ = ______

6 ______________

$$\begin{array}{r} 5 \\ \times\ 6 \\ \hline \end{array}$$

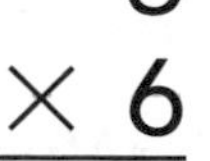

Talk It Over

5. What addition sentences can you write for exercises 1 and 2?

Practice

Find each product.

6.

$$\begin{array}{r} 5 \\ \times\ 1 \\ \hline 5 \end{array}$$

7.

$$\begin{array}{r} 5 \\ \times\ 3 \\ \hline \end{array}$$

8.

$$\begin{array}{r} 5 \\ \times\ 7 \\ \hline \end{array}$$

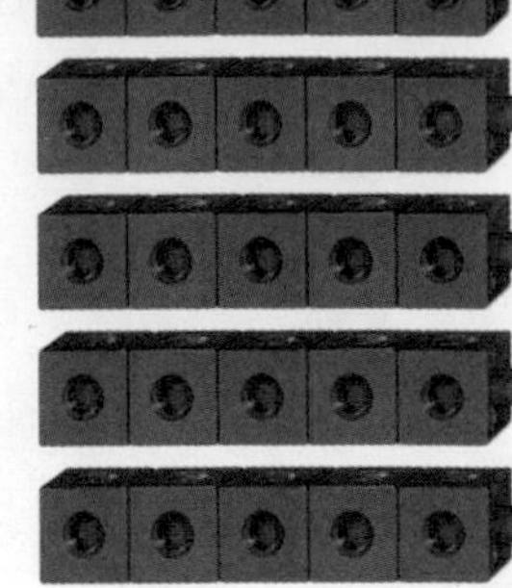

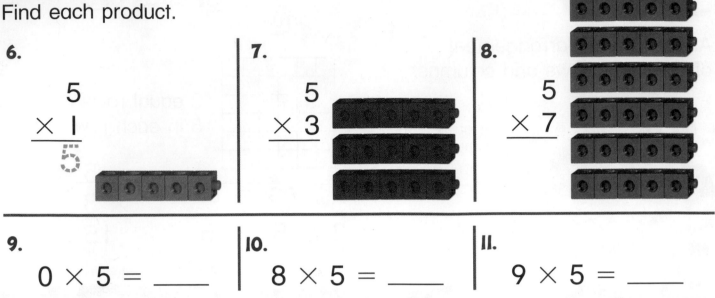

9. $0 \times 5 =$ ____

10. $8 \times 5 =$ ____

11. $9 \times 5 =$ ____

Multiply. Write the missing numbers.

12.

	5	5	5	5	5	5	5	5	5	5	← Number: in each group
×	0	1	2	3	4	5	6	7	8	9	← of groups
	0	5	10								← in all

Solve. Use a problem-solving strategy.

13. Each of the toy trains Jerome collects has 5 cars. How many cars are on 6 trains?

____ cars

14. Each pack of coins Sherri collects has 5 coins. How many coins are in 8 packs?

____ coins

CHALLENGE

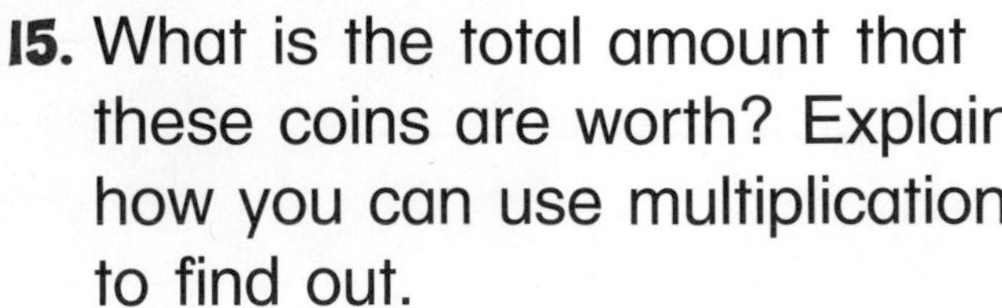

15. What is the total amount that these coins are worth? Explain how you can use multiplication to find out.

Math Alive at Home Ask your child to use small objects to model 3 rows of 5 and to write the multiplication sentence to show how many. (3x5=15)

Name ______________________________

Related Multiplication Facts

The product stays the same when you change the **order** of the factors.

2 equal rows
5 in each row

$2 \times 5 = 10$

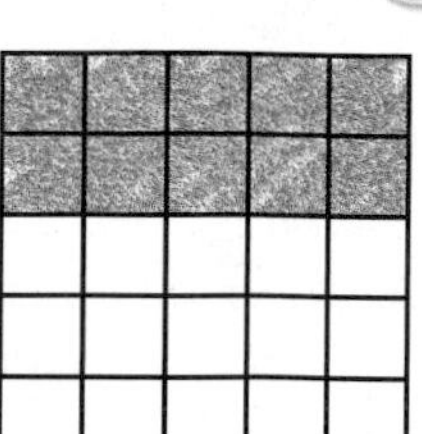

5 equal rows
2 in each row

$5 \times 2 = 10$

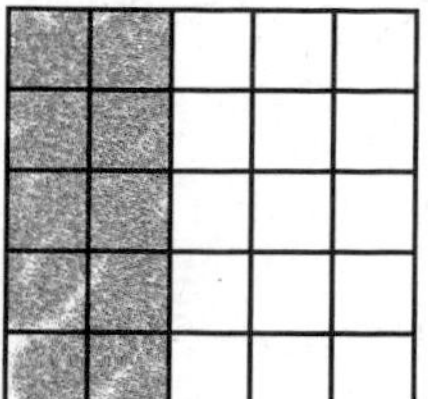

Math Words
order

Color each grid. Multiply.
Use grid paper for exercises 5 and 6.

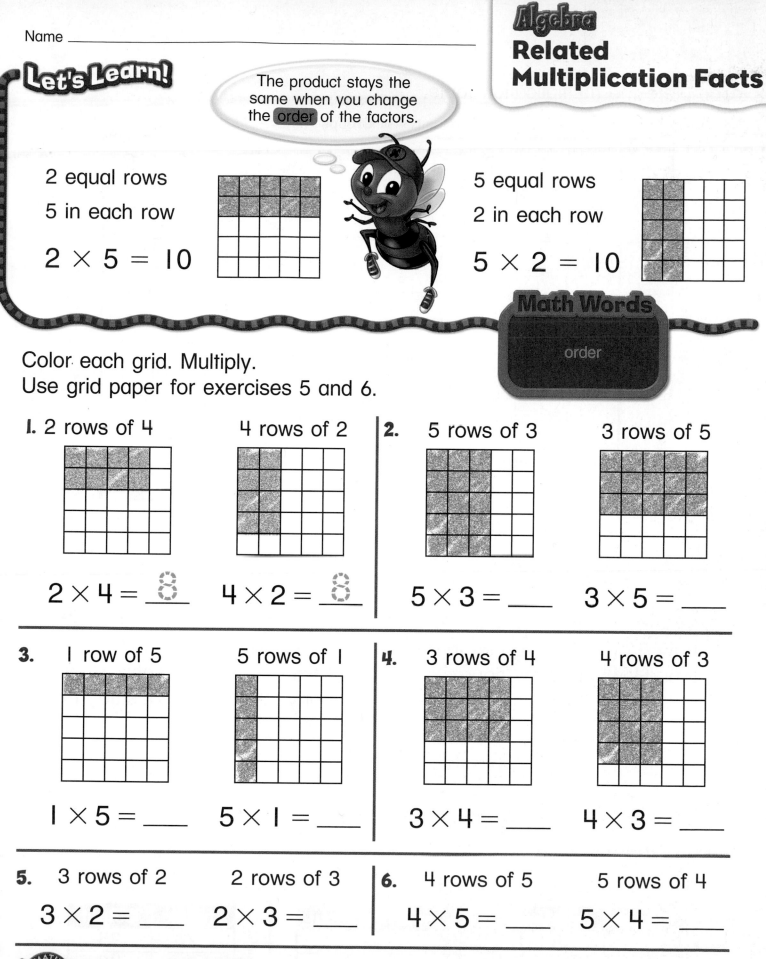

1. 2 rows of 4 — 4 rows of 2

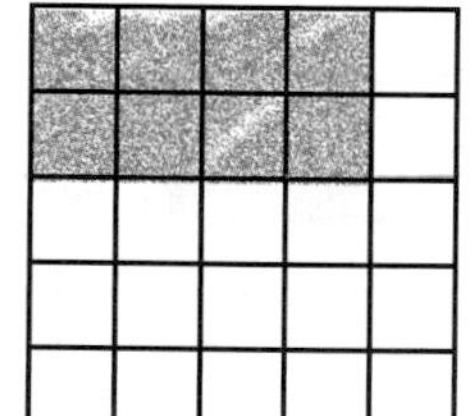

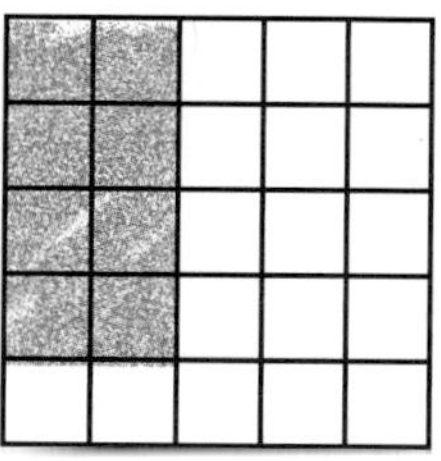

$2 \times 4 =$ 8 — $4 \times 2 =$ 8

2. 5 rows of 3 — 3 rows of 5

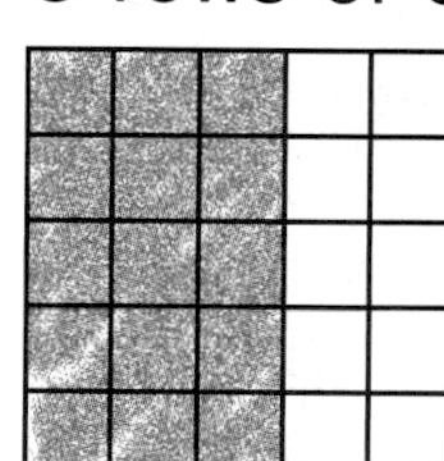

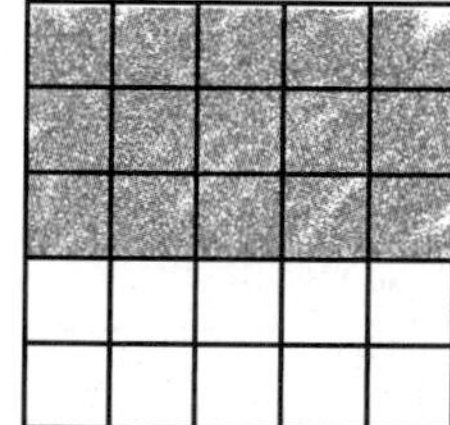

$5 \times 3 =$ ____ — $3 \times 5 =$ ____

3. 1 row of 5 — 5 rows of 1

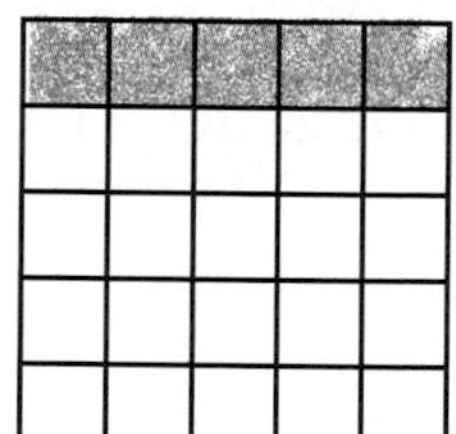

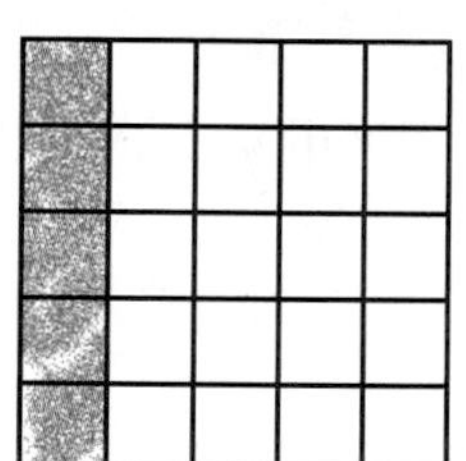

$1 \times 5 =$ ____ — $5 \times 1 =$ ____

4. 3 rows of 4 — 4 rows of 3

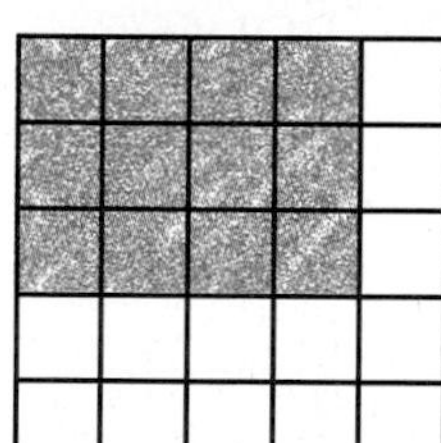

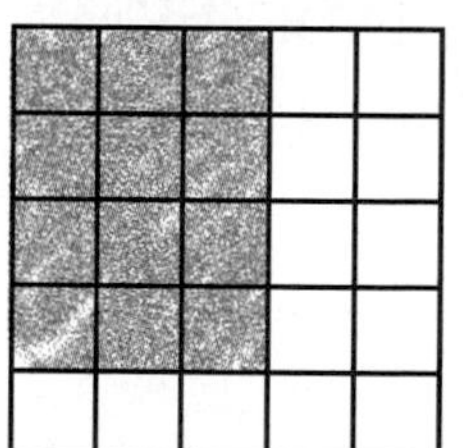

$3 \times 4 =$ ____ — $4 \times 3 =$ ____

5. 3 rows of 2 — 2 rows of 3

$3 \times 2 =$ ____ — $2 \times 3 =$ ____

6. 4 rows of 5 — 5 rows of 4

$4 \times 5 =$ ____ — $5 \times 4 =$ ____

7. How does knowing that 9 rows of 4 equals 36 help you know what 4 rows of 9 equals?

Practice

Complete the multiplication table.

8.

Number of Groups (across) / Number in Each Group (down)

×	0	1	2	3	4	5	6	7	8	9
0	0			0						
1		1	2	3						
2	0	2	4	6						
3			6			15				
4			8							
5					20					

Solve. Use a problem-solving strategy.
Show your work on a separate sheet of paper.

9. Mark has 4 clear boxes. He puts 5 of his toy figures in each box. How many toy figures does Mark have?

_____ toy figures

10. Jean has her toy figures on 5 shelves. She puts 4 figures on each shelf. How many toy figures does Jean have?

_____ toy figures

CRITICAL THINKING

Write the rule.

11. Rule: × _____

Input	Output
2	8
3	12
4	16

12. Rule: × _____

Input	Output
5	15
6	18
7	21

13. Rule: × _____

Input	Output
7	35
8	40
9	45

Math Alive at Home Ask your child to use small objects to show 2 rows of 8 and 8 rows of 2. Then ask her/him to write the multiplication sentences for these. (2x8, 8x2)

Name ____________________

Check Your Progress
Lessons 1-7

TEST PREPARATION

Listen to your teacher read the directions.
Fill in the circle by the correct answer.

1. $6 \times 3 = ?$

- ○ $3 + 3 + 3 + 3 + 3$
- ○ $4 + 4 + 4 + 4 + 4$
- ○ $3 + 3 + 3 + 3 + 3 + 3$

2.

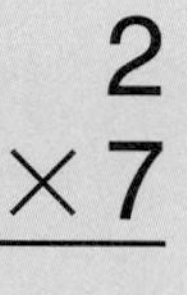

2×7

- ○ 16
- ○ 9
- ○ 14
- ○ 12

3. $6 \times 2 = ?$

- ○ 12
- ○ 14
- ○ 10
- ○ 8

4.

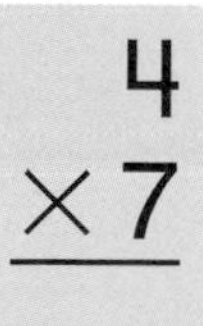

4×7

- ○ 21
- ○ 11
- ○ 27
- ○ 28

5. $2 \times 2 = ?$

- ○ $2 + 2 + 2 + 2$
- ○ $2 + 2$
- ○ $2 + 2 + 2$

6.

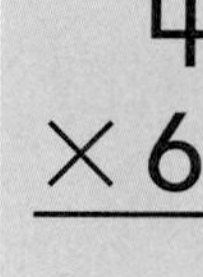

4×6

- ○ 24
- ○ 18
- ○ 36
- ○ 32

7. $4 \times 5 = ?$

- ○ 30
- ○ 25
- ○ 35
- ○ 20

8. $5 \times 0 = ?$

1	5	0	10
○	○	○	○

Fill in the circle by the correct answer.

9. Find the product.

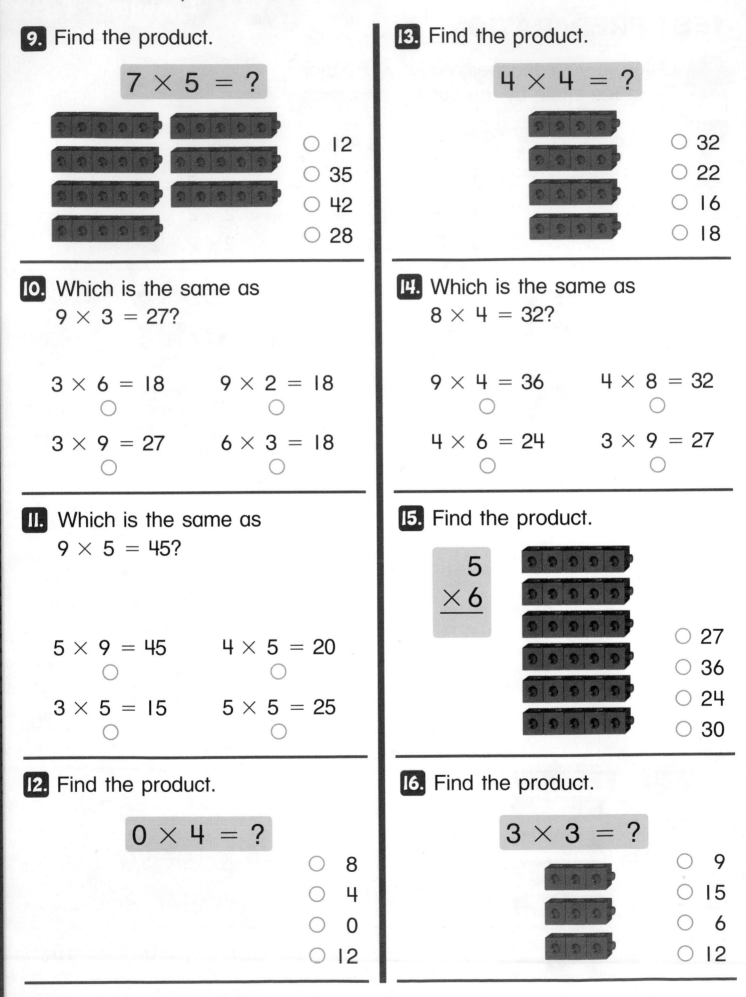

$7 \times 5 = ?$

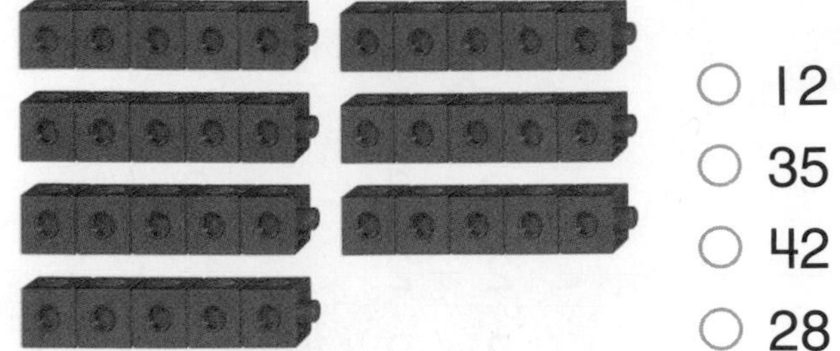

○ 12
○ 35
○ 42
○ 28

10. Which is the same as $9 \times 3 = 27$?

○ $3 \times 6 = 18$
○ $9 \times 2 = 18$
○ $3 \times 9 = 27$
○ $6 \times 3 = 18$

11. Which is the same as $9 \times 5 = 45$?

○ $5 \times 9 = 45$
○ $4 \times 5 = 20$
○ $3 \times 5 = 15$
○ $5 \times 5 = 25$

12. Find the product.

$0 \times 4 = ?$

○ 8
○ 4
○ 0
○ 12

13. Find the product.

$4 \times 4 = ?$

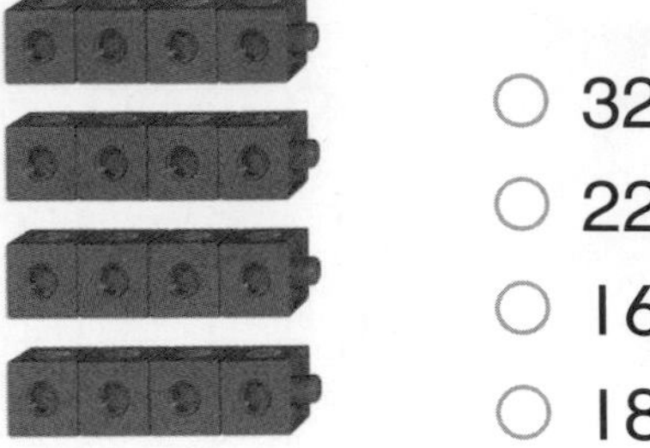

○ 32
○ 22
○ 16
○ 18

14. Which is the same as $8 \times 4 = 32$?

○ $9 \times 4 = 36$
○ $4 \times 8 = 32$
○ $4 \times 6 = 24$
○ $3 \times 9 = 27$

15. Find the product.

$$\begin{array}{r} 5 \\ \times 6 \\ \hline \end{array}$$

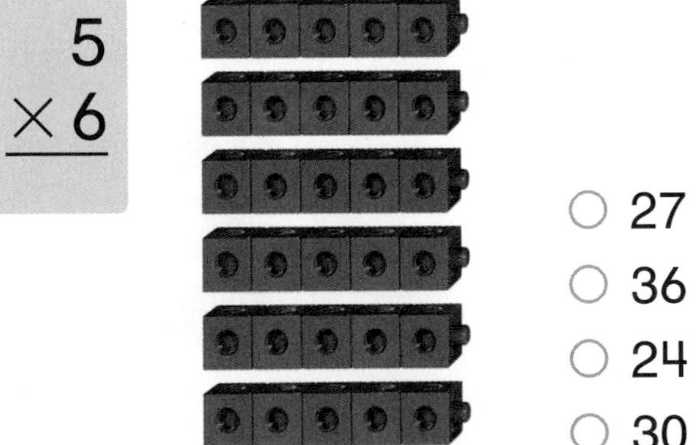

○ 27
○ 36
○ 24
○ 30

16. Find the product.

$3 \times 3 = ?$

○ 9
○ 15
○ 6
○ 12

Division as Repeated Subtraction

HANDS-ON LESSON

Name ________________________________

Let's Learn!

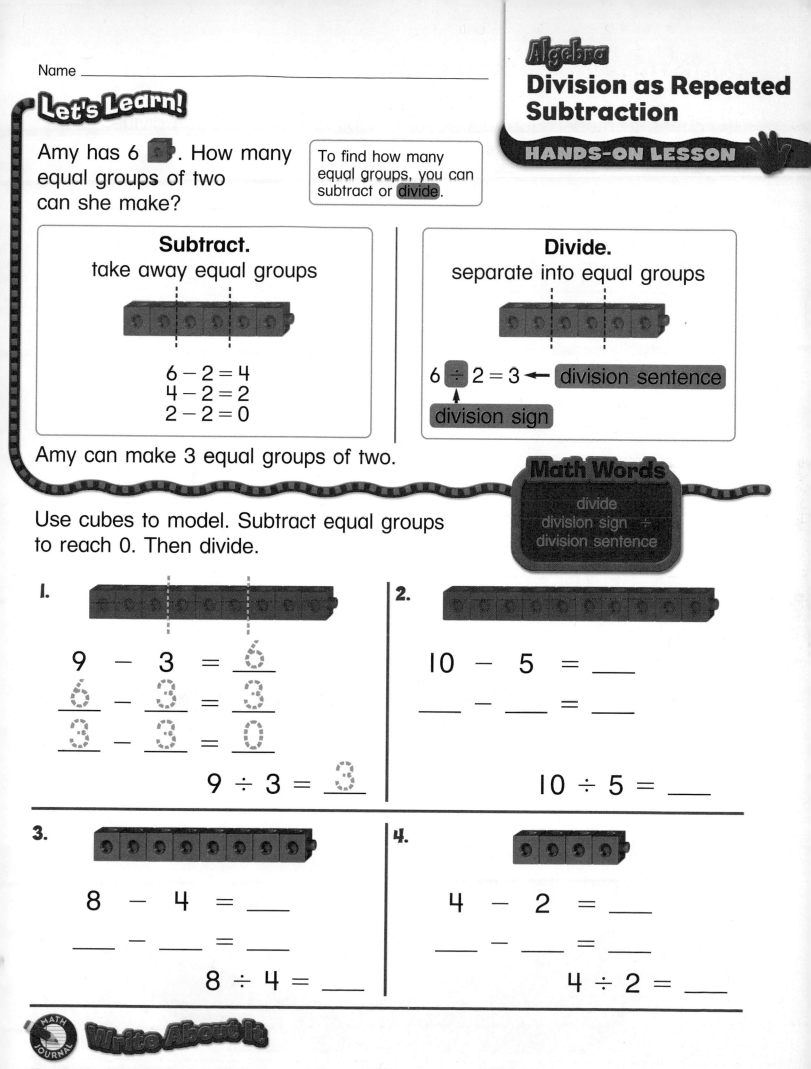

Amy has 6 cubes. How many equal groups of two can she make?

To find how many equal groups, you can subtract or **divide**.

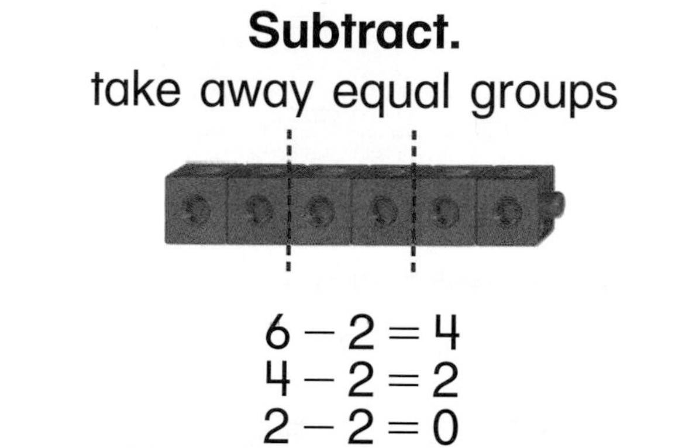

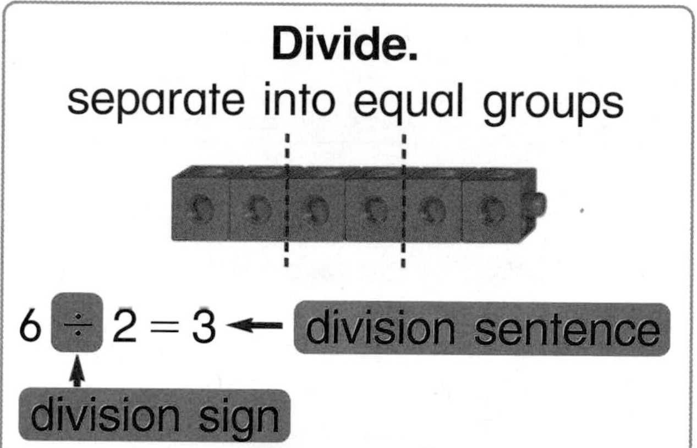

Divide.
separate into equal groups
6 ÷ 2 = 3 ← division sentence
division sign

Amy can make 3 equal groups of two.

Math Words
divide
division sign ÷
division sentence

Use cubes to model. Subtract equal groups to reach 0. Then divide.

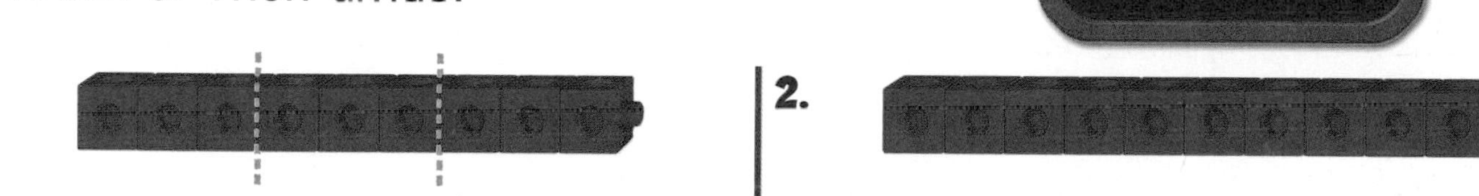

1.

$9 - 3 = \underline{6}$

$\underline{6} - \underline{3} = \underline{3}$

$\underline{3} - \underline{3} = \underline{0}$

$9 \div 3 = \underline{3}$

2.

$10 - 5 = \_\_\_$

$\_\_\_ - \_\_\_ = \_\_\_$

$10 \div 5 = \_\_\_$

3.

$8 - 4 = \_\_\_$

$\_\_\_ - \_\_\_ = \_\_\_$

$8 \div 4 = \_\_\_$

4.

$4 - 2 = \_\_\_$

$\_\_\_ - \_\_\_ = \_\_\_$

$4 \div 2 = \_\_\_$

5. How does subtracting equal groups help you divide?

Practice

Use cubes to model. Subtract equal groups to reach 0. Then divide.

6. 20 − 5 = 15
15 − 5 = 10
10 − 5 = 5
5 − 5 = 0
20 ÷ 5 = 4

7. 16 − 4 = ____
____ − ____ = ____
____ − ____ = ____
____ − ____ = ____
16 ÷ 4 = ____

8. 15 − 3 = ____
____ − ____ = ____
____ − ____ = ____
____ − ____ = ____
____ − ____ = ____
15 ÷ 3 = ____

9. 10 − 2 = ____
____ − ____ = ____
____ − ____ = ____
____ − ____ = ____
____ − ____ = ____
10 ÷ 2 = ____

Solve. Use a problem-solving strategy.
Show your work on a separate sheet of paper.

10. Joel puts 14 figures into boxes. Two figures fit in each box. How many boxes does Joel need?

____ boxes

11. Pam saves 18 box tops. She needs 3 box tops for each prize. How many prizes will she get?

____ prizes

DO YOU REMEMBER?

12. Find the perimeter in inches.

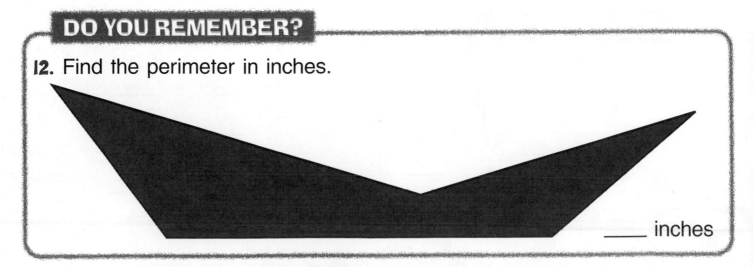

____ inches

Math Alive at Home Ask your child to use small objects to show how to divide 8 by 2, using repeated subtraction.

Name ______________________________

Algebra

Separate Groups of 2

Let's Learn!

Linda wants to separate the 8 shells she collected into equal groups of 2. How many equal groups of 2 can she make?

To separate into equal groups, divide.

8	÷	2	=	4
number in all		number in each group		number of groups

The answer in division is the **quotient**.

Linda can make 4 equal groups of 2 shells each.

Separate each group into equal groups of 2. Then complete the division sentence.

1. How many twos are in 10?

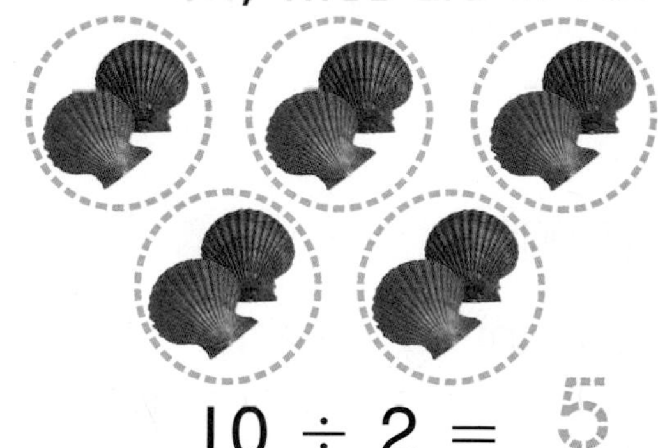

$10 \div 2 =$ 5

2. How many twos are in 4?

$4 \div 2 =$ ____

3. How many twos are in 2?

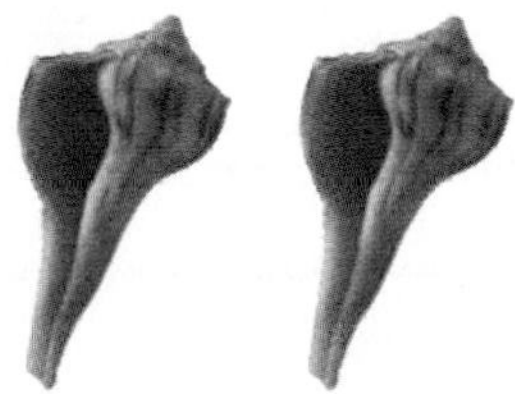

$2 \div 2 =$ ____

4. How many twos are in 12?

$12 \div 2 =$ ____

Talk It Over

5. How is counting back by 2 the same as dividing?

Practice

Separate each group into equal groups of 2.
Then write the division sentence.

6. How many twos are in 18?

18 ÷ 2 = 9

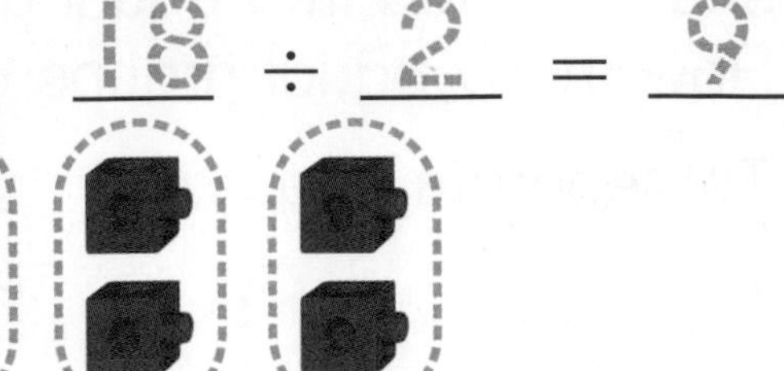

7. How many twos are in 14?

____ ÷ ____ = ____

8. How many twos are in 16?

____ ÷ ____ = ____

Problem Solving Solve. Use a problem-solving strategy.
Show your work on a separate sheet of paper.

9. Mike saves $2 a week to buy shells for his collection. How many weeks will it take him to save $12?

____ weeks

10. Ray is painting 6 shells. He wants to give pairs of shells as gifts. How many gifts can he give?

____ gifts

CHALLENGE

11. Multistep Anna has 6 boxes of shells.
There are 3 shells in each box.
She wants to give each friend 2 shells.
How many friends can Anna give shells to? ____ friends

Math Alive at Home Ask your child to divide 10 small objects into equal groups of 2 and to tell how many twos are in 10. (5)

Name ______________________

Algebra

Separate Groups of 3

Let's Learn!

Sam wants to put the cars he collects on shelves. He puts 3 cars on each shelf. How many shelves does Sam need for 12 cars?

Think
How many threes in 12?

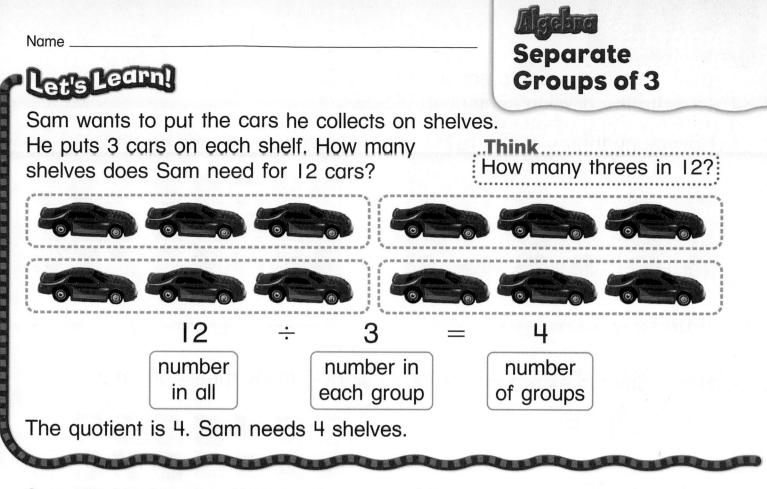

12	÷	3	=	4
number in all		number in each group		number of groups

The quotient is 4. Sam needs 4 shelves.

Separate each group into equal groups of 3.
Then complete the division sentence.

1. How many threes are in 9?

$9 \div 3 =$ 3

2. How many threes are in 6?

$6 \div 3 =$ ___

3. How many threes are in 3?

$3 \div 3 =$ ___

4. Explain how you would divide 27 by 3.

Practice

Separate each group into equal groups of 3.
Then write the division sentence.

5. How many threes are in 18?

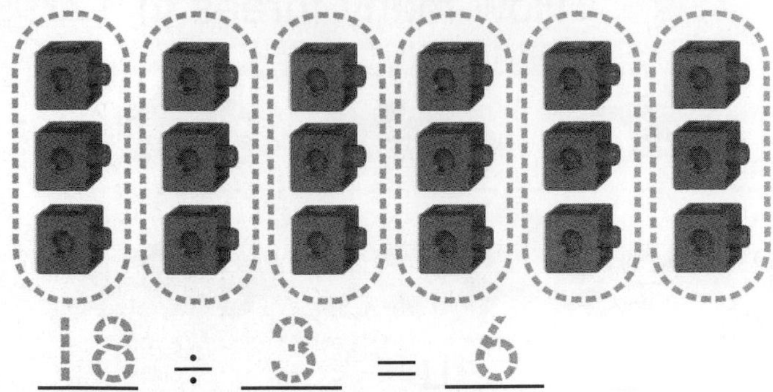

18 ÷ 3 = 6

6. How many threes are in 24?

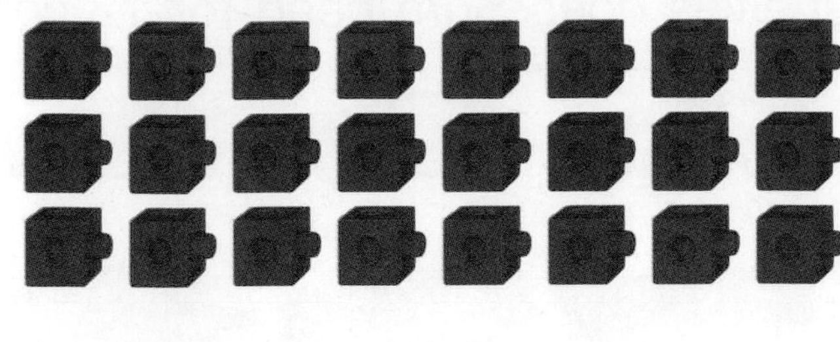

___ ÷ ___ = ___

7. How many threes are in 27?

___ ÷ ___ = ___

8. How many threes are in 21?

___ ÷ ___ = ___

Solve. Use a problem-solving strategy.
Show your work on a separate sheet of paper.

9. Jean has 9 cars. She wants to put 3 cars in each box. How many boxes does she need?

___ boxes

10. Ben has 15 cars. He puts 3 on each shelf. On how many shelves does Ben have cars?

___ shelves

DO YOU REMEMBER?

Circle the unit of measure you would use.

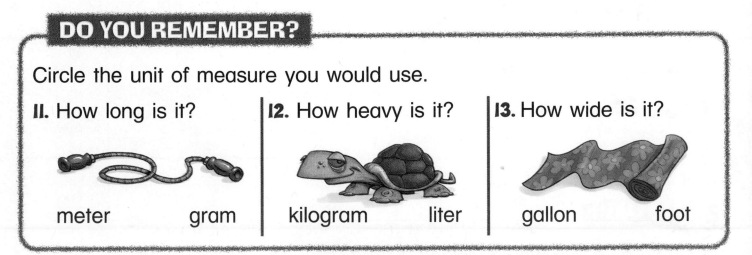

11. How long is it?

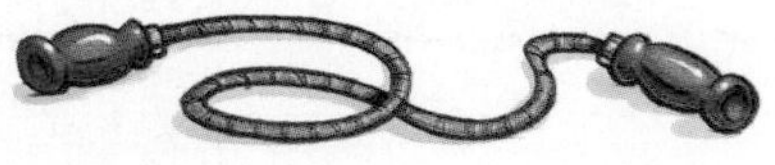

meter gram

12. How heavy is it?

kilogram liter

13. How wide is it?

gallon foot

Math Alive at Home Ask your child to divide 12 small objects into equal groups of 3 and to tell how many threes are in 12. (4)

Name ______________________

Algebra

Separate Groups of 4

Let's Learn!

Leo has 8 pennants. He wants to put them into equal groups of 4. How many equal groups of 4 can Leo make?

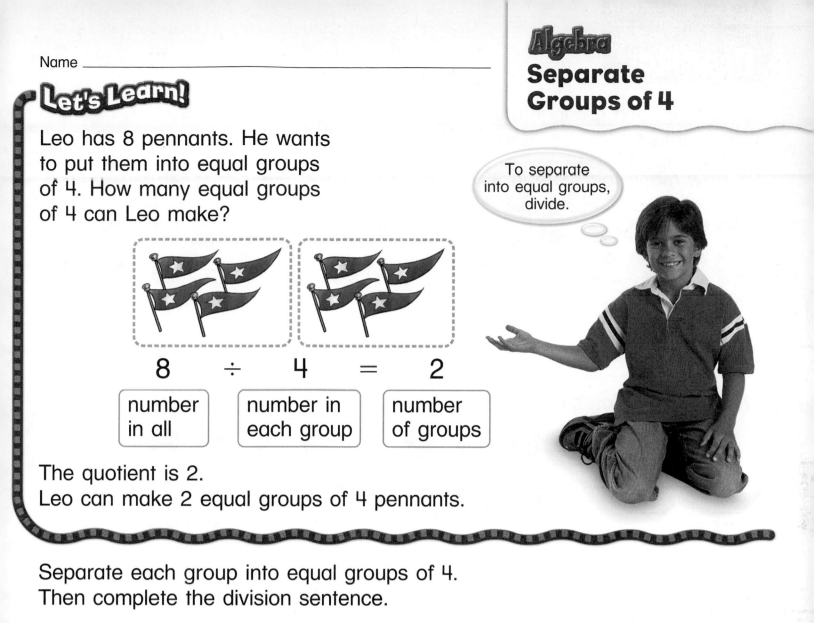

$8 \div 4 = 2$

number in all	number in each group	number of groups

The quotient is 2.
Leo can make 2 equal groups of 4 pennants.

To separate into equal groups, divide.

Separate each group into equal groups of 4.
Then complete the division sentence.

1. How many fours are in 12?

$12 \div 4 =$ 3

2. How many fours are in 16?

$16 \div 4 =$ ____

3. How many fours are in 4?

$4 \div 4 =$ ____

4. How many fours are in 20?

$20 \div 4 =$ ____

Talk It Over

5. You have 16 ▲ in all. Can you make more equal groups of 2 or more equal groups of 4? Explain.

Practice

Separate each group into equal groups of 4.
Then write the division sentence.

6. How many fours are in 32?

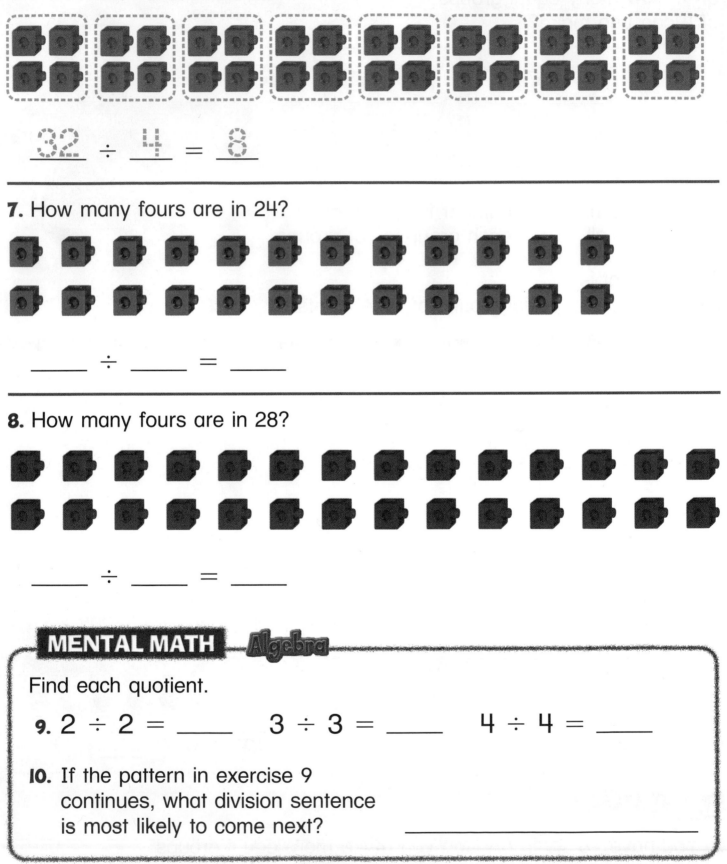

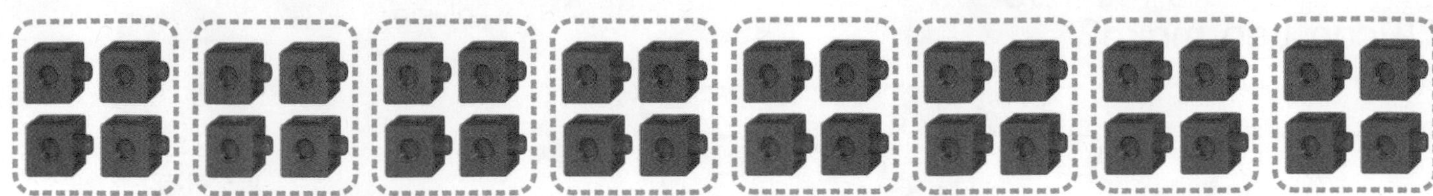

32 ÷ 4 = 8

7. How many fours are in 24?

____ ÷ ____ = ____

8. How many fours are in 28?

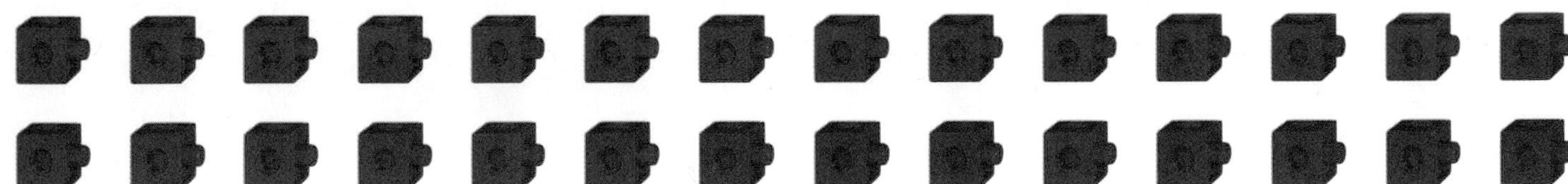

____ ÷ ____ = ____

MENTAL MATH Algebra

Find each quotient.

9. 2 ÷ 2 = ____ 3 ÷ 3 = ____ 4 ÷ 4 = ____

10. If the pattern in exercise 9 continues, what division sentence is most likely to come next? ________

Math Alive at Home Ask your child to divide 12 small objects into equal groups of 4 and to tell how many fours are in 12. (3)

Name ______________________________

Algebra

Separate Groups of 5

Let's Learn!

Sara has 10 rocks in her collection.
She wants to put them in equal groups of 5.
How many equal groups of 5 can Sara make?

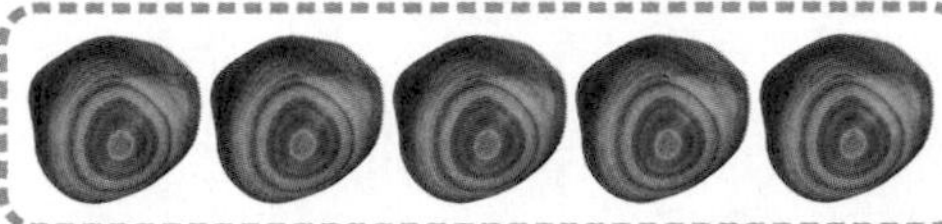

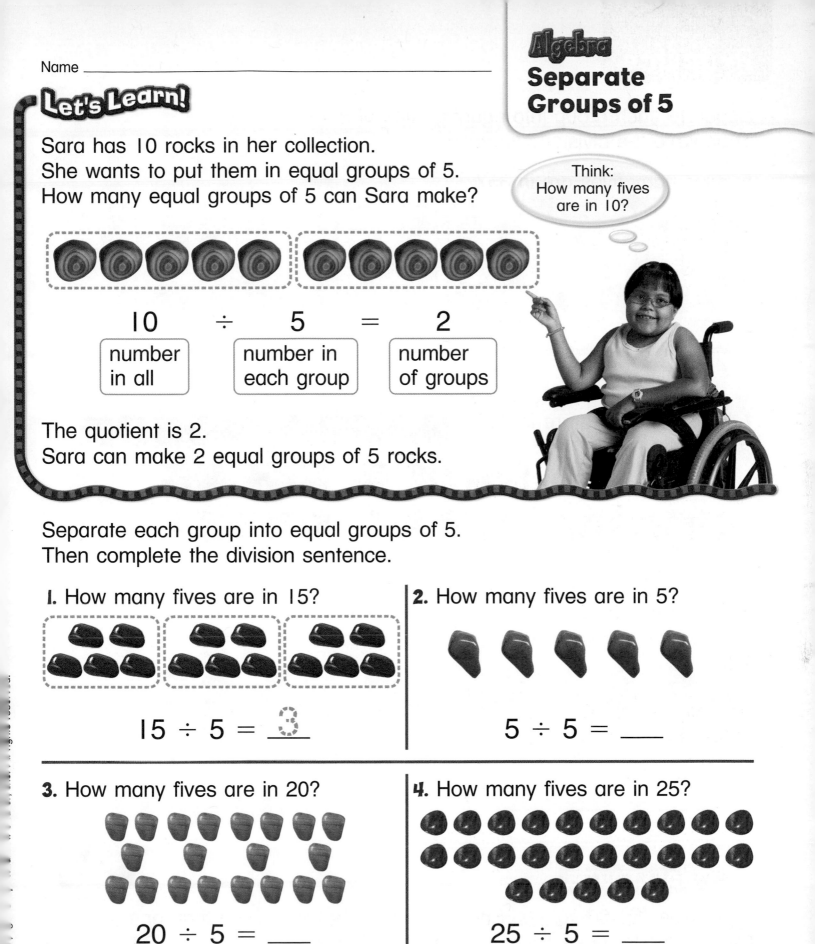

10	÷	5	=	2
number in all		number in each group		number of groups

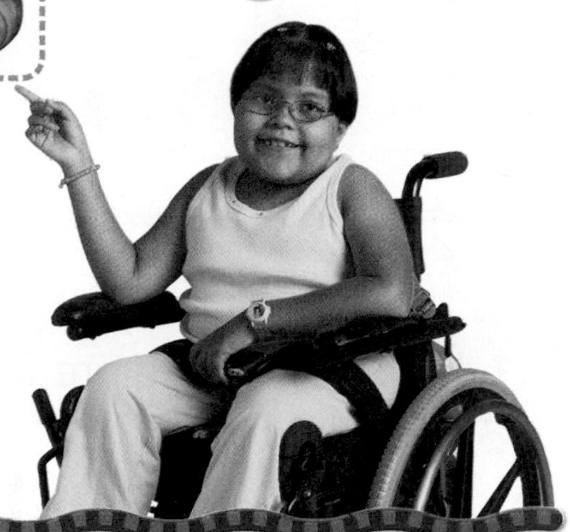
Think:
How many fives are in 10?

The quotient is 2.
Sara can make 2 equal groups of 5 rocks.

Separate each group into equal groups of 5.
Then complete the division sentence.

1. How many fives are in 15?

15 ÷ 5 = 3

2. How many fives are in 5?

5 ÷ 5 = ___

3. How many fives are in 20?

20 ÷ 5 = ___

4. How many fives are in 25?

25 ÷ 5 = ___

Talk It Over

5. Without finding the quotients for 20 ÷ 5 and 20 ÷ 4, tell which quotient would be greater. Explain your reasoning.

Practice

Separate each group into equal groups of 5.
Then write the division sentence.

6. How many fives are in 35?

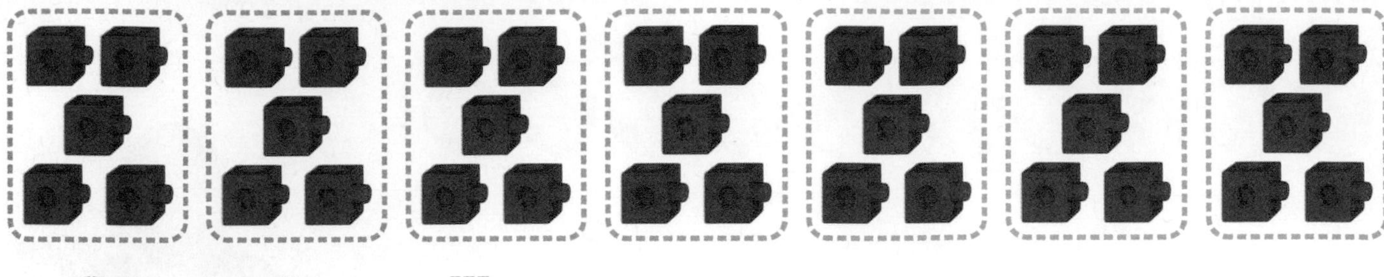

35 ÷ 5 = 7

7. How many fives are in 40?

_____ ÷ _____ = _____

8. How many fives are in 30?

_____ ÷ _____ = _____

CHALLENGE

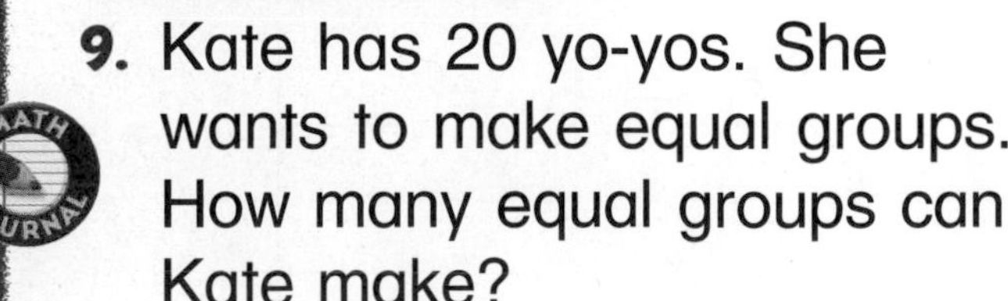

9. Kate has 20 yo-yos. She wants to make equal groups. How many equal groups can Kate make?

_____ equal groups

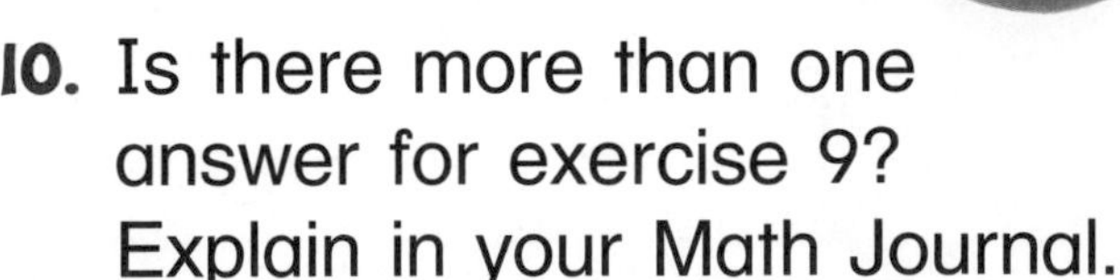

10. Is there more than one answer for exercise 9? Explain in your Math Journal.

Math Alive at Home Ask your child to divide 15 small objects into equal groups of 5 and to tell how many fives are in 15. (3)

Name ______________________

Separate with Leftovers

Sometimes when you separate objects into equal groups, you can have some left over.

Put 10 pennies in groups of 5.
How many groups did you make?

2 groups of 5
0 left over

Put 13 pennies in groups of 5.
How many groups did you make?

2 groups of 5
3 left over

Circle equal groups.
Then complete.

1. How many groups of 3 in 12?

4 groups of 3 0 left over

2. How many groups of 2 in 13?

____ groups of 2 ____ left over

3. How many groups of 5 in 16?

____ groups of 5 ____ left over

4. How many groups of 4 in 18?

____ groups of 4 ____ left over

Talk It Over

5. If you divide a group of pennies into equal groups of 5, could you have 6 pennies left over? Explain.

Practice

Find how many groups and how many left over.
Use models or draw a picture to help with exercises 8–11.

6. How many groups of 3 in 10?

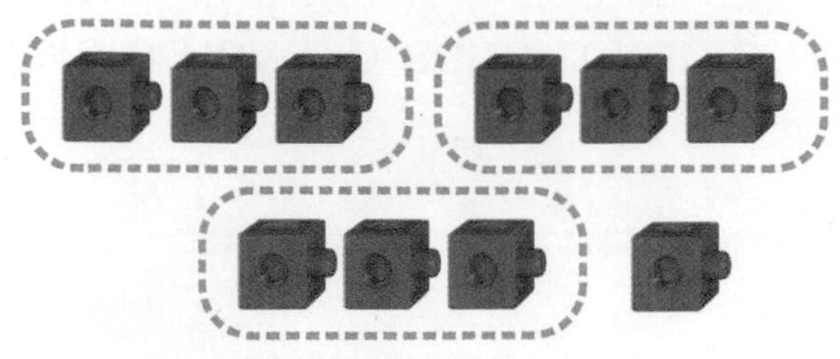

3 threes 1 left over

7. How many groups of 4 in 14?

____ fours ____ left over

8. How many groups of 2 in 12?

____ twos ____ left over

9. How many groups of 5 in 23?

____ fives ____ left over

10. How many groups of 4 in 21?

____ fours ____ left over

11. How many groups of 5 in 19?

____ fives ____ left over

Solve. Use a problem-solving strategy.
Show your work on a separate sheet of paper.

12. Fran has 26 pictures. She puts 5 pictures on each page of an album.
How many pages can she fill?
How many pictures are left over for the next page?

____ pages filled

____ picture left over

CRITICAL THINKING

MATH JOURNAL

13. Judy divides a group of 12 pennies into equal groups and has no leftovers. Charles divides 12 pennies into equal groups and has 2 left over. Explain in your Math Journal how this might happen.

Math Alive at Home Ask your child to divide a group of 11 pennies into equal groups of 3 and to tell how many pennies are left over. (2)

Name ______________________________

Share with Leftovers

Let's Learn!

Thirteen marbles are shared equally among four friends. How many does each friend receive?

Tally to solve.

When you **share equally**, you can have some left over.

||| ||| ||| |||

Each receives 3 marbles. There is 1 left over.

Math Words

share equally

Share equally. Tally to solve.

1. Share 20 beads equally among 5 friends.

|||| |||| |||| |||| ||||

Each receives 4.

There are 0 left over.

2. Share 22 shells equally among 4 friends.

Each receives ____.

There are ____ left over.

3. Share 8 pennies equally between 2 friends.

Each receives ____.

There are ____ left over.

4. Share 19 trading cards equally among 3 friends.

Each receives ____.

There is ____ left over.

5. Explain why there are leftovers in exercises 2 and 4.

Copyright © by William H. Sadlier, Inc. All rights reserved.

Practice

Share equally. Tally to solve.

6. Share 18 pictures equally among 5 friends.

Each receives 3.

There are 3 left over.

7. Share 17 stamps equally among 4 friends.

Each receives ____.

There is ____ left over.

8. Share 11 marbles equally between 2 friends.

Each receives ____.

There is ____ left over.

9. Share 13 bottle caps equally among 3 friends.

Each receives ____.

There is ____ left over.

Solve. Use a problem-solving strategy. Show your work on a separate sheet of paper.

10. Ron gives 20 pens to Pat and 3 of his friends. How many pens does each person get? ____ pens

DO YOU REMEMBER?

Use the Math Words in the box to fill in the blanks.

11. The number of cubic units in a solid figure is the ______________________.

12. The distance around a plane figure is the ______________.

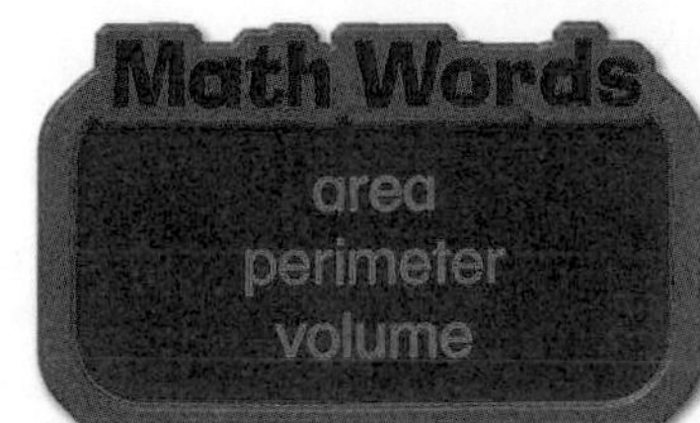

Math Alive at Home Ask your child to show how to share 17 pennies with 5 friends and to tell the number left over. ($17 \div 5 = 3$ groups of 5 with 2 left over)

Name ______________________________

Algebra

Relate Multiplication and Division

Let's Learn!

I show 3 groups of 4. How many are there in all?

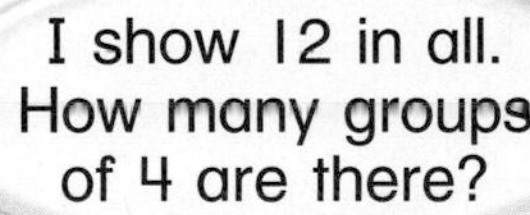

I show 12 in all. How many groups of 4 are there?

12 ÷ 4 = 3

These are **related facts**. They use the same numbers.

12 in all

3 groups of 4

Math Words

related facts

Write the related facts.

How many in all?

1. 2 groups of 5 ■

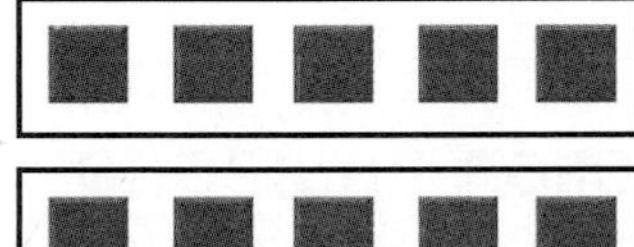

How many groups?

Put 10 ■ in groups of 5.

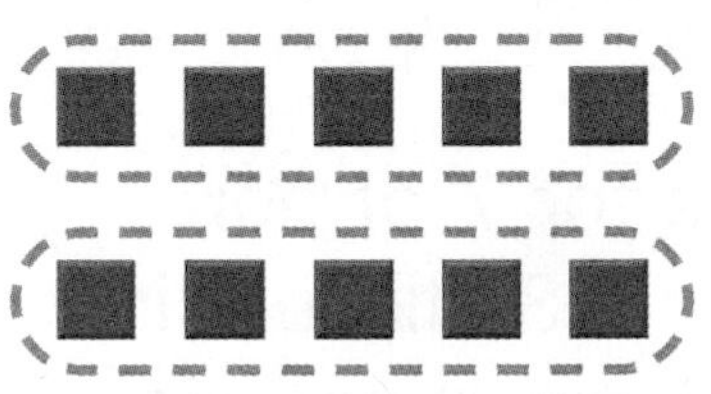

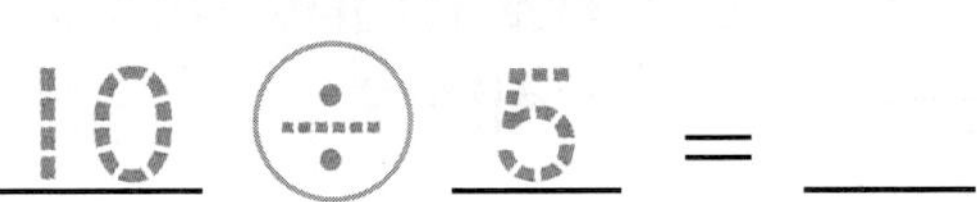

2. 6 groups of 3 ■

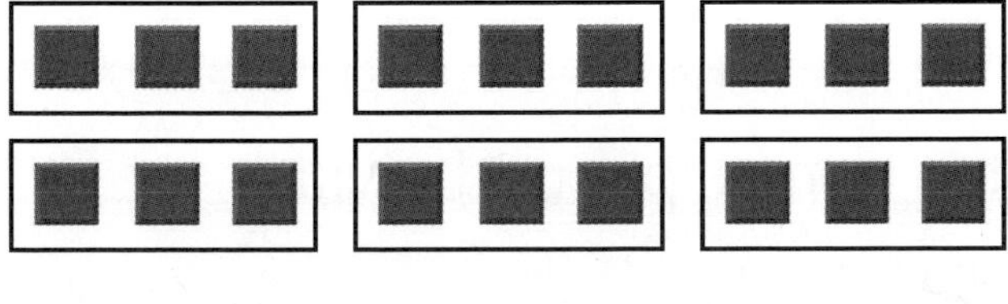

Put 18 ■ in groups of 3.

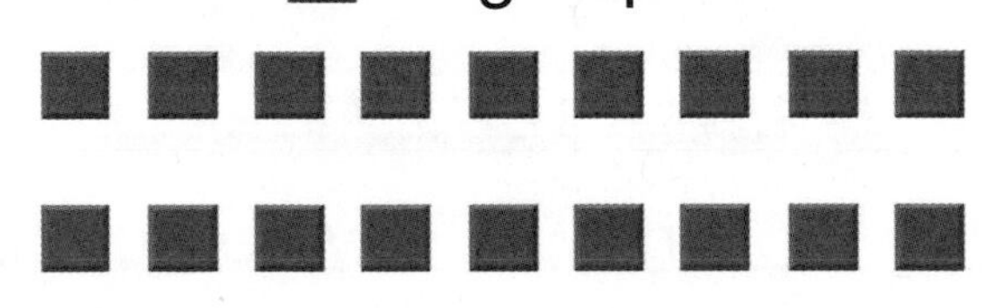

___ ◯ ___ = ___

Write About It!

3. How are the number sentences in each exercise alike? How are they different?

Copyright © by William H. Sadlier, Inc. All rights reserved.

Practice

Write the related facts.

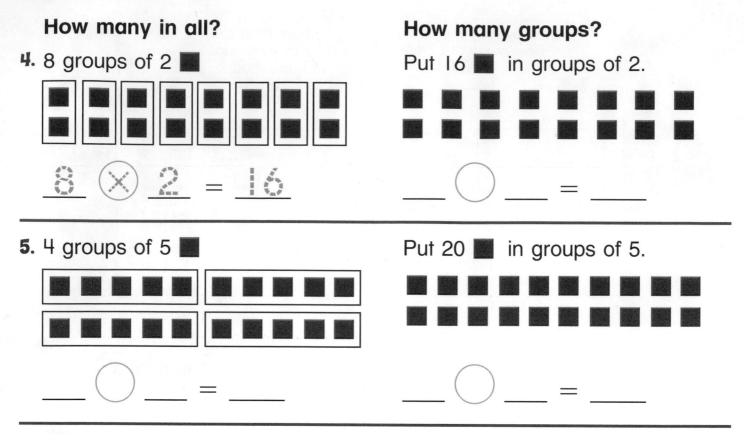

How many in all?

4. 8 groups of 2 ■

8 ⊗ 2 = 16

How many groups?

Put 16 ■ in groups of 2.

___ ◯ ___ = ___

5. 4 groups of 5 ■

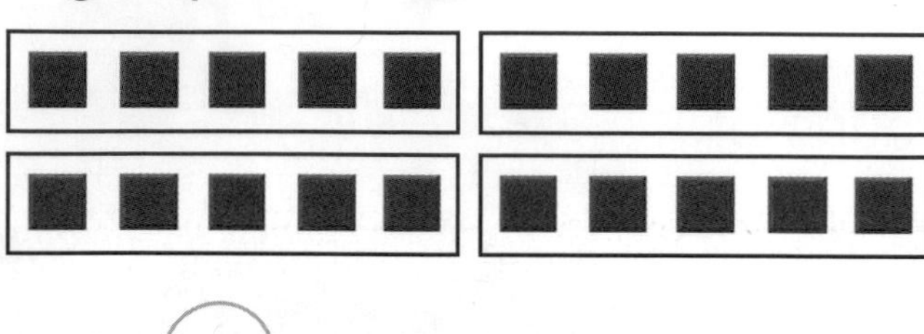

___ ◯ ___ = ___

Put 20 ■ in groups of 5.

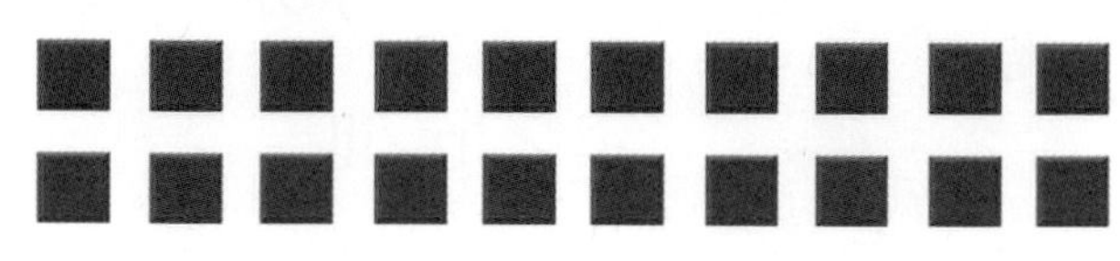

___ ◯ ___ = ___

Solve. Use a problem-solving strategy.
Show your work on a separate sheet of paper.

6. Lin makes gifts for 7 of her friends. She puts 3 stickers in each gift box. How many stickers does Lin give as gifts?

   ___ stickers

7. Paul gives 21 action figures to friends. Each friend gets 3 action figures. How many friends does Paul give action figures to?

   ___ friends

CALCULATOR ACTIVITY

Use the × and ÷ keys on a calculator to multiply and divide.

8. $6 \times 4 =$ ___ $\qquad 24 \div 4 =$ ___
9. $5 \times 3 =$ ___ $\qquad 15 \div 3 =$ ___
10. $8 \times 5 =$ ___ $\qquad 40 \div 5 =$ ___
11. $9 \times 2 =$ ___ $\qquad 18 \div 2 =$ ___

Math Alive at Home Ask your child to show how 2 x 4 and 8 ÷ 4 are related facts. (2 x 4 = 8 and 8 ÷ 4 = 2)

Name ______________________________

TEST PREPARATION

Listen to your teacher read the directions.
Fill in the circle under the correct answer.

1.

16 − 4 = 12
12 − 4 = 8
8 − 4 = 4
4 − 4 = 0

5 ○ 4 ○ 6 ○ 3 ○

2.

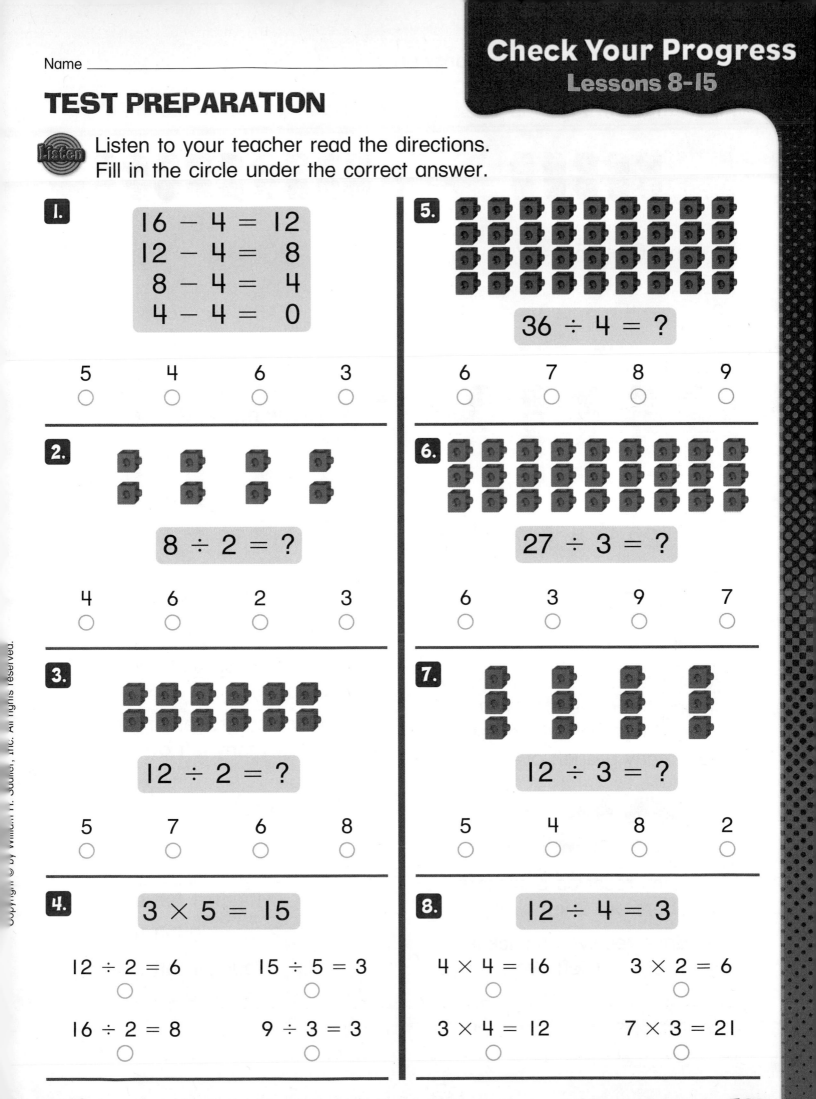

8 ÷ 2 = ?

4 ○ 6 ○ 2 ○ 3 ○

3.

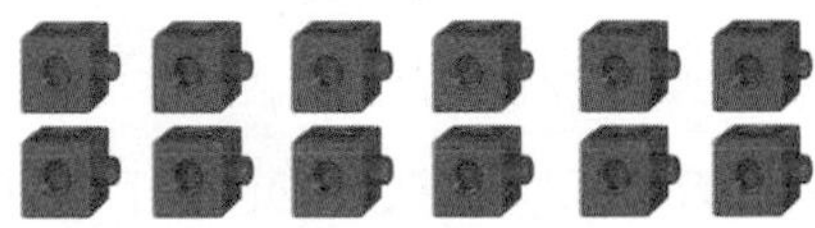

12 ÷ 2 = ?

5 ○ 7 ○ 6 ○ 8 ○

4.

3 × 5 = 15

12 ÷ 2 = 6 ○ 15 ÷ 5 = 3 ○

16 ÷ 2 = 8 ○ 9 ÷ 3 = 3 ○

5.

36 ÷ 4 = ?

6 ○ 7 ○ 8 ○ 9 ○

6.

27 ÷ 3 = ?

6 ○ 3 ○ 9 ○ 7 ○

7.

12 ÷ 3 = ?

5 ○ 4 ○ 8 ○ 2 ○

8.

12 ÷ 4 = 3

4 × 4 = 16 ○ 3 × 2 = 6 ○

3 × 4 = 12 ○ 7 × 3 = 21 ○

Copyright © by William H. Sadlier, Inc. All rights reserved.

Fill in the circle by the correct answer.

9. How many fives are in 10?

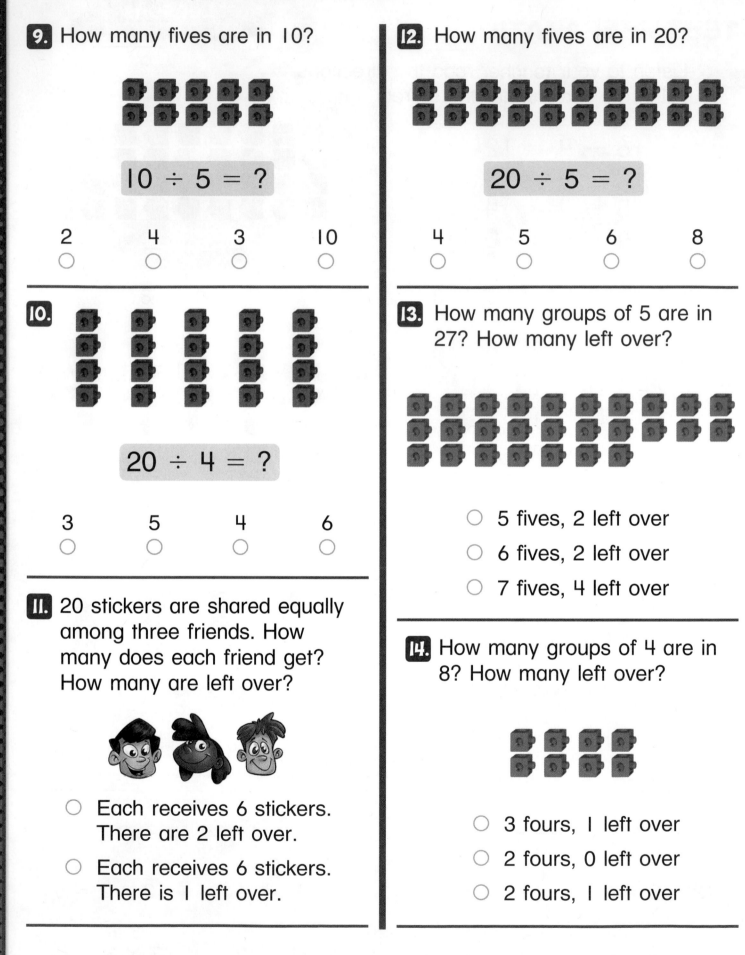

$10 \div 5 = ?$

○ 2 ○ 4 ○ 3 ○ 10

10.

$20 \div 4 = ?$

○ 3 ○ 5 ○ 4 ○ 6

11. 20 stickers are shared equally among three friends. How many does each friend get? How many are left over?

○ Each receives 6 stickers. There are 2 left over.

○ Each receives 6 stickers. There is 1 left over.

12. How many fives are in 20?

$20 \div 5 = ?$

○ 4 ○ 5 ○ 6 ○ 8

13. How many groups of 5 are in 27? How many left over?

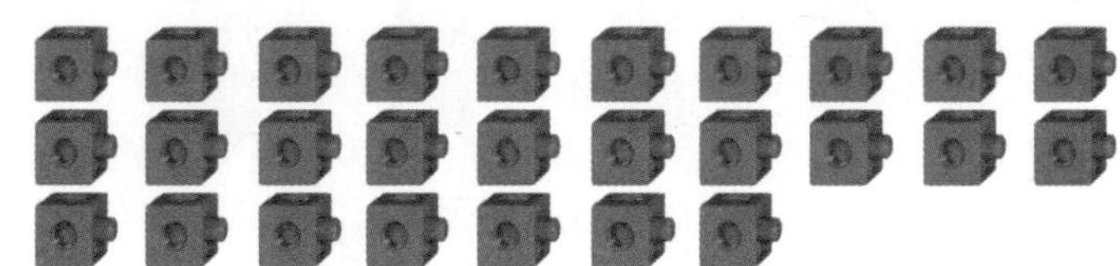

○ 5 fives, 2 left over

○ 6 fives, 2 left over

○ 7 fives, 4 left over

14. How many groups of 4 are in 8? How many left over?

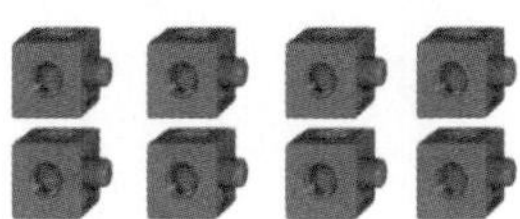

○ 3 fours, 1 left over

○ 2 fours, 0 left over

○ 2 fours, 1 left over

Name ____________________

Algebra

Symbols for Numbers

Let's Learn!

Daria wrote a number sentence.
She used a symbol for some numbers.
Does the symbol equal 10?

Replace each ● with 10.
Then solve both sides
of the number sentence.

$$476 + ● = 596 - ●$$

Does $476 + 10 = 596 - 10$?

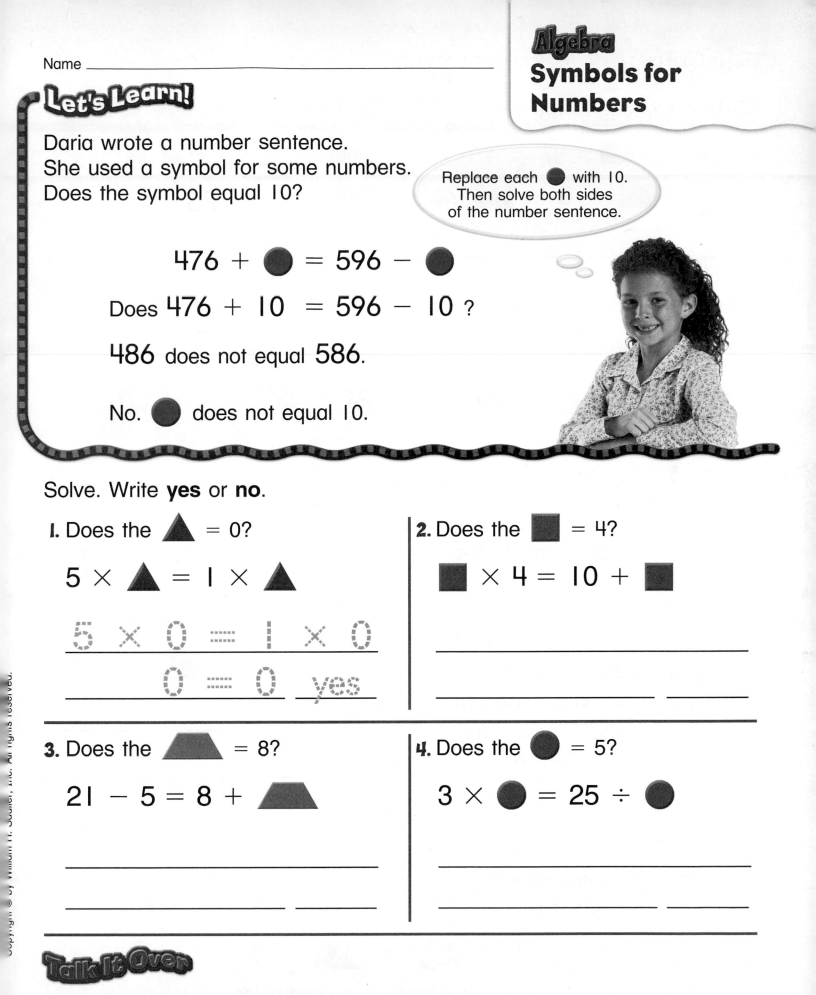

486 does not equal 586.

No. ● does not equal 10.

Solve. Write **yes** or **no**.

1. Does the ▲ = 0?

$5 \times ▲ = 1 \times ▲$

$5 \times 0 = 1 \times 0$

$0 = 0$ yes

2. Does the ■ = 4?

$■ \times 4 = 10 + ■$

____

______________ ______

3. Does the ⏢ = 8?

$21 - 5 = 8 + ⏢$

____

______________ ______

4. Does the ● = 5?

$3 \times ● = 25 \div ●$

____

______________ ______

Talk It Over

5. Explain how you know when the value of a symbol makes a number sentence true.

Copyright © by William H. Sadlier, Inc. All rights reserved.

Practice

Solve. Write **yes** or **no**.

6. Does the ■ = 4?

16 ÷ ■ = 8 − ■ ?

16 ÷ 4 = 8 − 4

4 = 4 yes

7. Does the ▲ = 9?

▲ + ▲ = 23 − 4

8. Does the ● = 5?

17 − ● = ● + 10

9. Does the ■ = 3?

21 ÷ ■ = 10 − ■

Solve. Use a problem-solving strategy. Show your work on a separate sheet of paper.

10. Nelson writes a number sentence. He uses ⏢ for numbers. Which of the numbers shown makes Nelson's number sentence true? Circle that number.

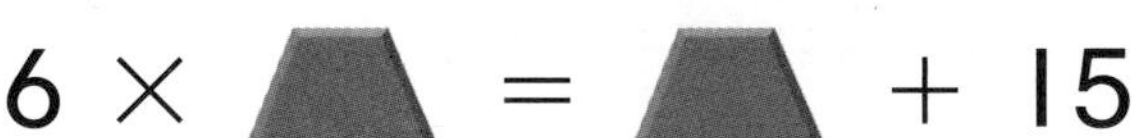

CHALLENGE

11. Can you write more than one answer for this number sentence?

1 × ⏢ = ⏢ − 0

Explain your reasoning and write some examples.

Math Alive at Home Have your child choose an exercise from this lesson and explain how she/he solved it.

Name ____________________________________

Algebra
Solve Number Sentences

Let's Learn!

Todd hid one number from each number sentence. What are the hidden numbers?

To find the hidden number, divide the product by the factor.

$3 \times ■ = 18$

$18 \div 3 = 6$

$■ = 6$

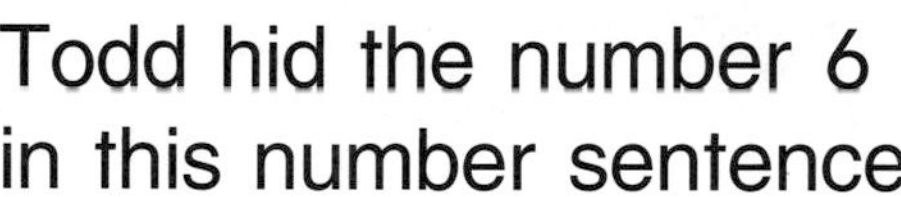

Todd hid the number 6 in this number sentence.

$4 \times ■ = 28$

$28 \div 4 = 7$

$■ = 7$

Todd hid the number 7 in this number sentence.

Find the hidden number in each number sentence.

1. $▲ \times 5 = 30$

   $30 \div 5 = 6$

   $▲ = 6$

2. $3 \times ◆ = 21$

   ____

   $◆ =$ ___

3. $2 \times ● = 16$

   ____

   $● =$ ___

4. $5 \times ■ = 35$

   ____

   $■ =$ ___

Talk It Over

5. How can you check that the hidden numbers you found in exercises 1–4 are correct?

Copyright © by William H. Sadlier, Inc. All rights reserved.

Practice

Remember:
Divide the product by the factor.

Find the hidden number in each number sentence.

6. 2 × ● = 18

18 ÷ 2 = 9

● = 9

7. 3 × ■ = 27

______

■ = ___

8. ▲ × 5 = 45

______

▲ = ___

9. 4 × ◆ = 24

______

◆ = ___

Problem Solving Solve. Use a problem-solving strategy.
Show your work on a separate sheet of paper.

10. Jack has a collection of 40 coins. He has them in 5 equal groups. How many coins are in each group?

___ coins in each group

11. Lara has 4 stamps on each page of her stamp book. She has a total of 36 stamps. On how many pages does Lara have stamps?

___ pages

TEST PREPARATION

Fill in the circle under the correct answer.

12. Gary collects 4 rocks every day. In how many days will Gary collect 16 rocks?

16	4	20	12
○	○	○	○

Math Alive at Home Have your child model the steps to find the hidden number in 3 x ▲ = 24. (▲ = 8)

Name ______________________________

Problem Solving
Strategy

Choose the Operation

Read Tracy has 3 groups of jacks. There are 5 jacks in each group. How many jacks does Tracy have?

Multiply
to join equal groups.

Plan Decide to multiply or divide. To find how many in all when groups are equal, (multiply) or divide.

Write a number sentence.

Write

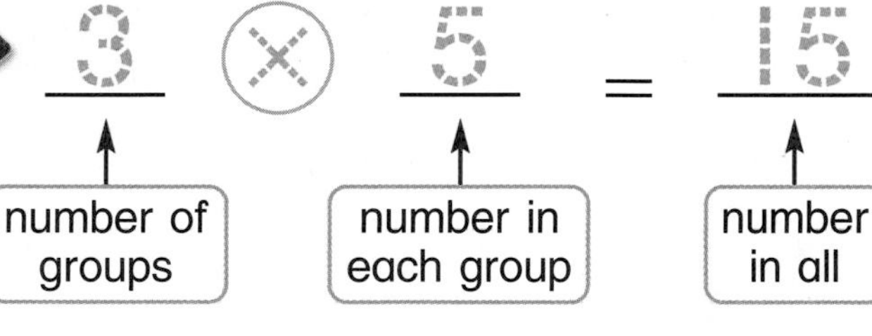

3 × 5 = 15

number of groups — number in each group — number in all

Tracy has 15 jacks.

Divide
to separate or share.

Check Draw a picture to check your answer.

Circle **multiply** or **divide**.
Solve the problem.

1. Lily has 12 beads. She puts an equal number in 3 bags. How many beads are in each bag?

multiply (divide)

____ ÷ ____ = ____

number in all — number of groups — number in each group

____ beads

2. Each of Toby's two brothers gives him 4 stamps. How many stamps do they give Toby in all?

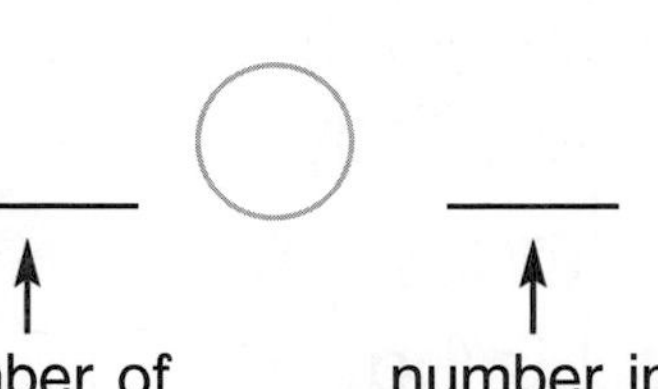

multiply divide

____ ◯ ____ = ____

number of groups — number in each group — number in all

____ stamps

Copyright © by William H. Sadlier, Inc. All rights reserved.

Practice

Read Plan Write Check

Choose the Operation

Circle **multiply** or **divide**.
Solve the problem.

Multiply to join equal groups. **Divide** to separate or share.

3. Wendy buys 8 cards. She shares them equally among 4 friends. How many cards does each friend get?

multiply divide

____ cards

---

4. Mandy has 20 toy robots. She gives them to 5 friends. Each friend gets an equal number of robots. How many robots does each friend get?

multiply divide

____ robots

---

5. Kate has 4 baskets. One is empty. The rest have 3 flowers each. How many flowers does Kate have?

multiply divide

____ flowers

Fill in numbers 2, 3, 4, or 5. Solve.

6. Liz has ____ shelves. Each shelf has ____ toy dinosaurs. How many toy dinosaurs does Liz have?

multiply divide

____ toy dinosaurs

Math Alive at Home Ask your child how he/she chose the operation to solve the problems in this lesson.

Name ________________________________

Problem Solving
Applications

Read Plan Write Check

Mixed Strategies

Use a strategy you have learned.

1. Cyndi uses 30 inches of ribbon to make 5 bows. She uses the same amount for each ribbon. How much ribbon does she use for each bow?

____ inches of ribbon

2. Iris writes a number. It is less than 50. It is an even number with fewer ones than tens. Circle the number it could be.

48 54 32 43

3. Mo draws 15 pictures. He draws the sun in 2 of the pictures. He gives an equal number of pictures to 3 teachers. How many pictures does each teacher get?

____ pictures

4. Use figures to show the pattern another way.

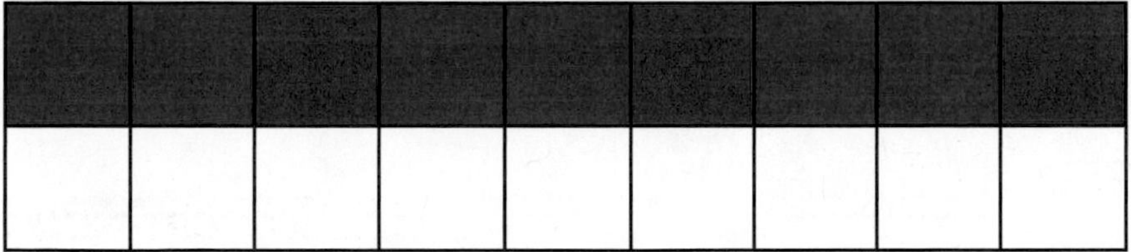

Practice

Read → Plan → Write → Check

Use a strategy you have learned.

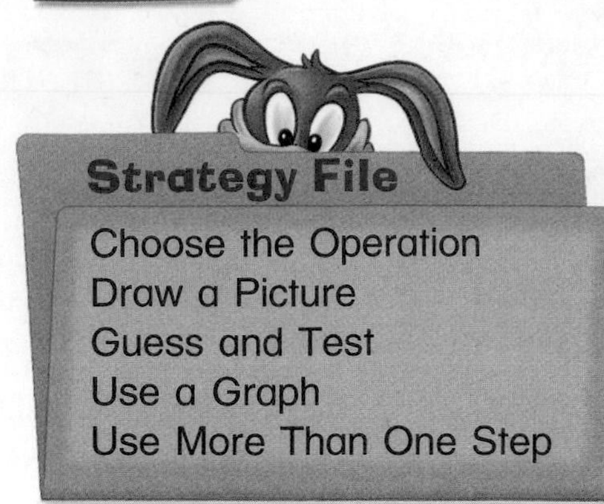

5. Cami has 18 pictures. She shares them equally among 4 of her friends. How many pictures does Cami have left over?

_____ pictures left over

6. Taylor has 50¢. He gets 3 more coins from his dad. Now he has 71¢. Circle the coins Taylor gets from his dad.

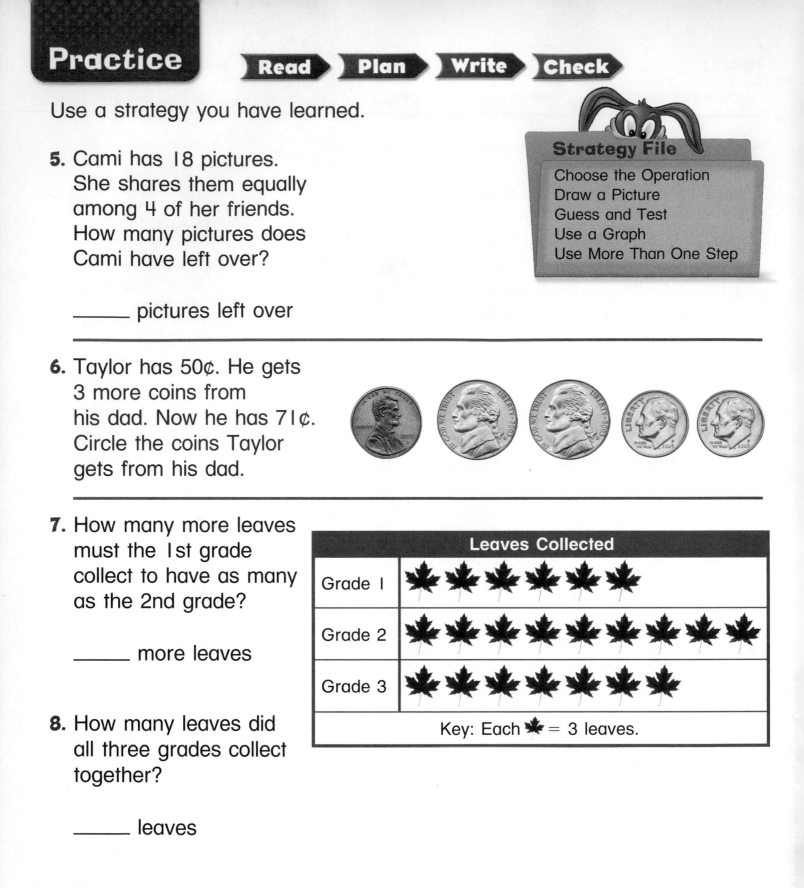

7. How many more leaves must the 1st grade collect to have as many as the 2nd grade?

_____ more leaves

Leaves Collected	
Grade 1	🍁🍁🍁🍁🍁🍁
Grade 2	🍁🍁🍁🍁🍁🍁🍁🍁🍁
Grade 3	🍁🍁🍁🍁🍁🍁🍁
Key: Each 🍁 = 3 leaves.	

8. How many leaves did all three grades collect together?

_____ leaves

9. How many more leaves must these grades collect to have a total of 90 leaves?

_____ more leaves

Math Alive at Home Ask your child to tell you how she/he solved some of the problems in this lesson.

Name ______________________________

TEST PREPARATION

Listen to your teacher read the directions.
Fill in the circle under the correct answer.

1. 8 ÷ ● = 9 × ●

yes ○   no ○

2. 25 ÷ ■ = 10 + ■

yes ○   no ○

3. 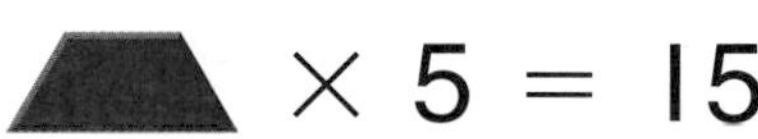 × 5 = 15

 = ?

6 ○   4 ○   5 ○   3 ○

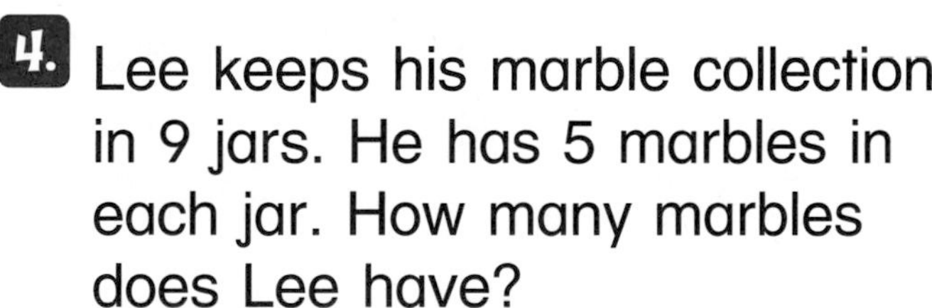

4. Lee keeps his marble collection in 9 jars. He has 5 marbles in each jar. How many marbles does Lee have?

multiply   divide

35 ○   40 ○   45 ○   50 ○

5. 4 × ■ = 32

■ = ?

3 ○   9 ○   8 ○   5 ○

6. 7 × ▲ = ▲ + 24

yes ○   no ○

7. ▬ × 4 = 24

▬ = ?

6 ○   5 ○   3 ○   4 ○

8. Sharon has 24 stickers. She shares them equally among 3 friends. How many stickers does each friend get?

multiply   divide

7 ○   8 ○   9 ○   5 ○

Copyright © by William H. Sadlier, Inc. All rights reserved.

Connection

Math and Language Arts

Name ______________________________

Did You Know?

An **analogy** is made up of two pairs of words, pictures, or numbers. The second pair has the same relationship as the first pair.

Up is to **down** as **big** is to **small**.

Apple is to **fruit** as **blue** is to **color**.

Look at the first pair. Think about how the pictures or numbers relate to each other. Then circle the picture or number to complete the second pair.

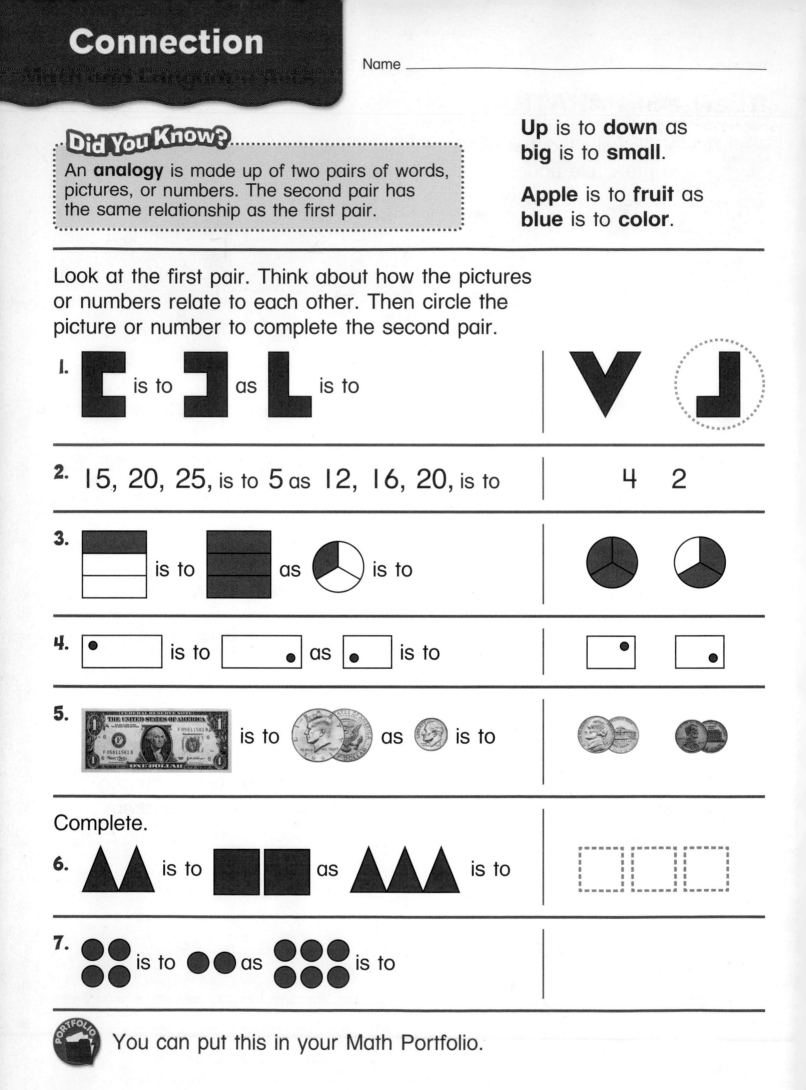

1. is to  as is to |  

2. 15, 20, 25, is to 5 as 12, 16, 20, is to | 4 2

3.  is to 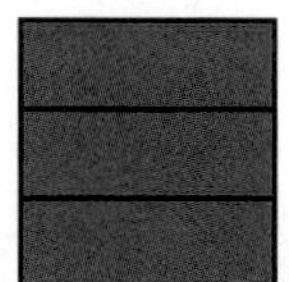 as 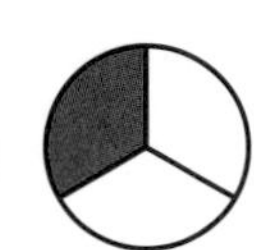 is to | 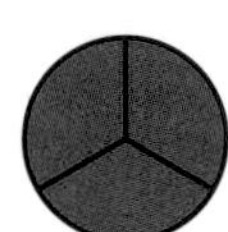 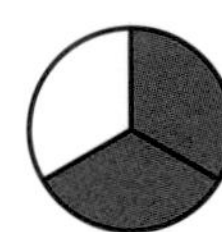

4.  is to  as  is to |  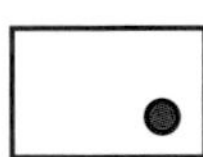

5. 

is to  as is to |  

Complete.

6. 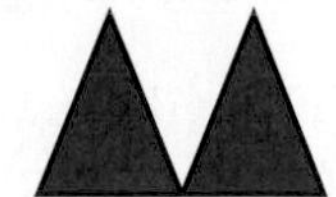 is to  as  is to | 

7.  is to  as 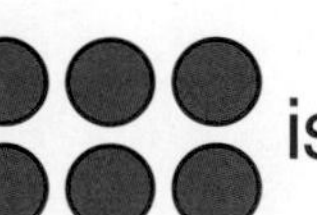 is to |

You can put this in your Math Portfolio.

Name ______________________________

Chapter 12 Test

1. Color each grid. Multiply.

2 rows of 5

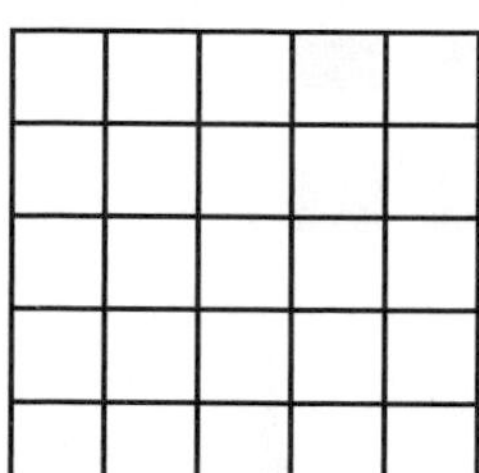

5 rows of 2

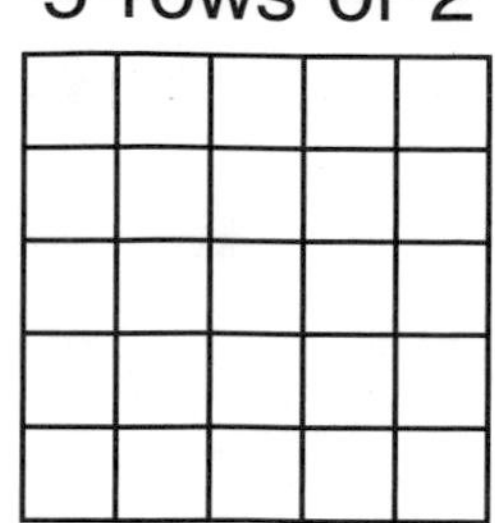

$2 \times 5 =$ ____ $5 \times 2 =$ ____

2. Put 18 in groups of 3.
Write the division sentence.

____ ◯ ____ = ____

3. Does the ★ = 0?
Write **yes** or **no**.

6 × ★ = ★ × 8

____

4. How many twos are in 16?

$16 \div 2 =$ ____

5. 23 marbles are shared equally among five friends. How many does each friend have? How many are left over?

Each has ____ marbles.

There are ____ left over.

6. How many fours are in 28?

$28 \div 4 =$ ____

7. Multiply.

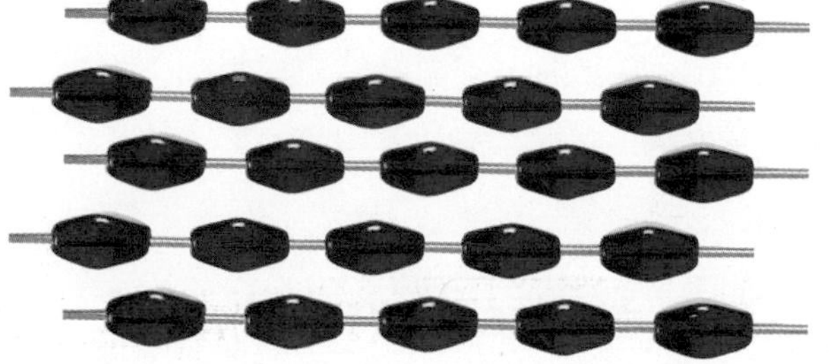

$5 \times 5 =$ ____

8. How many groups of 3 are in 16?
How many are left over?

____ threes ____ left over

Write the related facts.

How many in all?

9. 3 groups of 5

___ ◯ ___ = ___

How many groups?

Put 15 in groups of 5.

___ ◯ ___ = ___

Problem Solving Solve. Use a problem-solving strategy. Watch for multistep problems.

10. Leo reads 2 books every day. How many books will he read in one week?

_____ books

11. Bob has 5 flowerpots. He plants the same number of seeds in each pot. He plants 40 seeds in all. How many seeds are in each flowerpot?

____ seeds

12. There are 4 children in a room. Each child has 4 toys. How many toys are there in all?

____

13. Nora has 4 baskets. She puts 3 apples in each basket. How many apples are there in all?

_____ apples

14. Marie has 45 toy figures. She gives 24 to her sister. She wants to share the rest of the figures among 3 friends. How many toy figures will each friend get?

_____ toy figures

15. Ben has 6 bags. Each bag has 4 books. Ben gives 4 of his bags to Dave. How many books does Ben have now?

_____ books

Name ______________________________

1. Ben predicts that the product of two even numbers is even. Give three examples to check his prediction.

____

____

____

2. Is Ben right?

____

Fill in a number from 15 to 30. Share equally. Tally to solve.

3. Share _____ beads equally among 4 friends.

Each receives _____ beads.

There are _____ left over.

---

4. Share _____ shells equally among 5 friends.

Each receives _____ shells.

There are _____ left over.

You can put this in your Math Portfolio.

Algebra

Enrichment

Name ________________

Function Tables

Each of these tables follows a different rule.
The rules use +, −, ×, or ÷.

Write the rule and 1 more example.

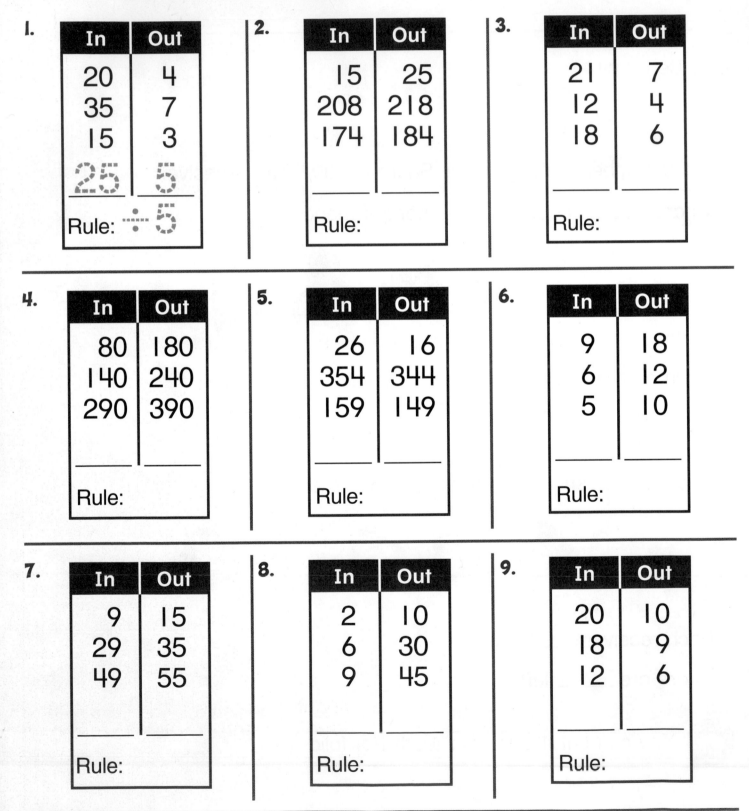

1.

In	Out
20	4
35	7
15	3
25	5

Rule: ÷ 5

2.

In	Out
15	25
208	218
174	184
___	___

Rule:

3.

In	Out
21	7
12	4
18	6
___	___

Rule:

4.

In	Out
80	180
140	240
290	390
___	___

Rule:

5.

In	Out
26	16
354	344
159	149
___	___

Rule:

6.

In	Out
9	18
6	12
5	10
___	___

Rule:

7.

In	Out
9	15
29	35
49	55
___	___

Rule:

8.

In	Out
2	10
6	30
9	45
___	___

Rule:

9.

In	Out
20	10
18	9
12	6
___	___

Rule:

Name ____________________

TEST PREPARATION

Fill in the circle under the correct answer.

1. Which color are you most likely to land on?

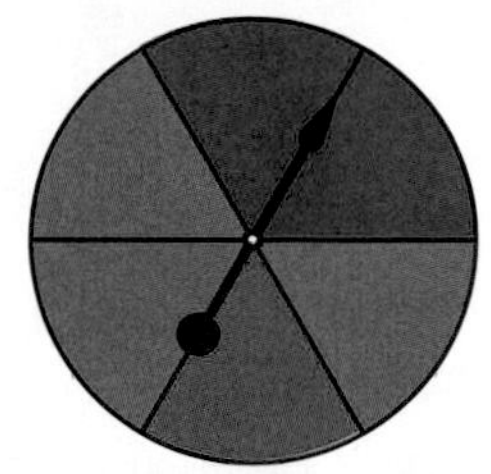

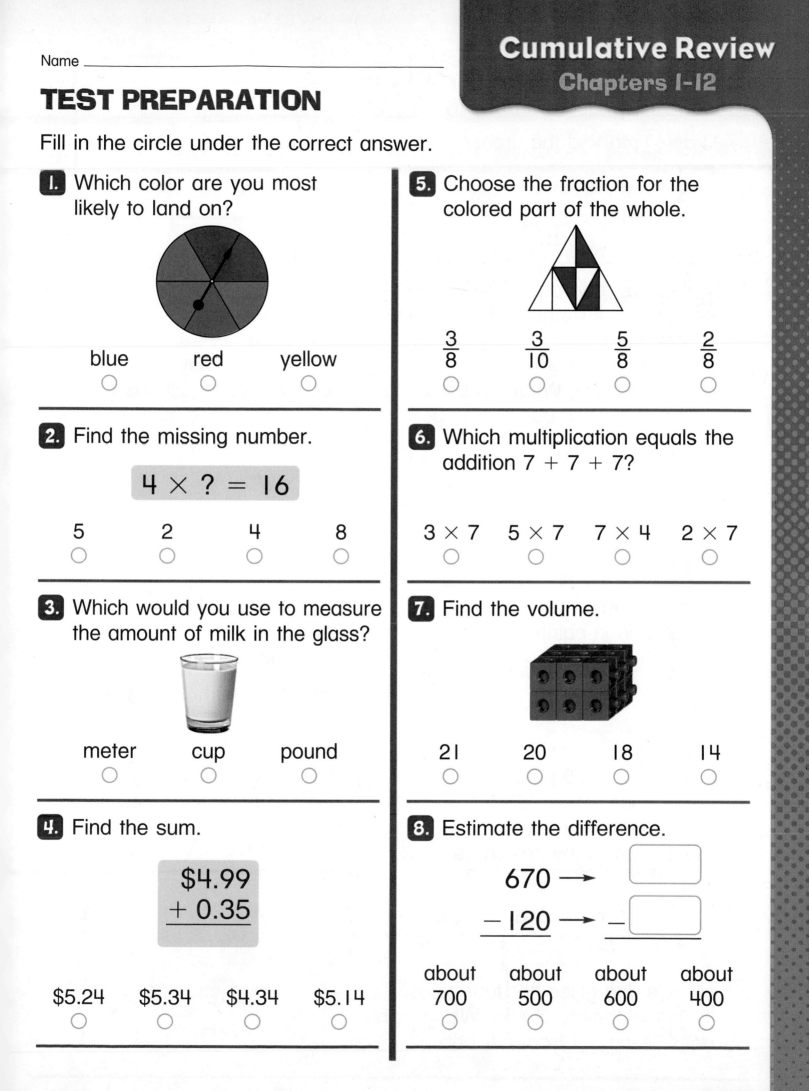

blue ○ red ○ yellow ○

2. Find the missing number.

4 × ? = 16

5 ○ 2 ○ 4 ○ 8 ○

3. Which would you use to measure the amount of milk in the glass?

meter ○ cup ○ pound ○

4. Find the sum.

$$\begin{array}{r} \$4.99 \\ +\ 0.35 \\ \hline \end{array}$$

\$5.24 ○ \$5.34 ○ \$4.34 ○ \$5.14 ○

5. Choose the fraction for the colored part of the whole.

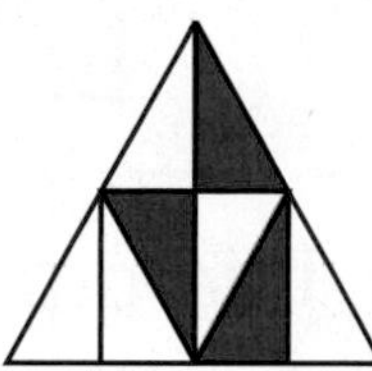

$\frac{3}{8}$ ○ $\frac{3}{10}$ ○ $\frac{5}{8}$ ○ $\frac{2}{8}$ ○

6. Which multiplication equals the addition 7 + 7 + 7?

3 × 7 ○ 5 × 7 ○ 7 × 4 ○ 2 × 7 ○

7. Find the volume.

21 ○ 20 ○ 18 ○ 14 ○

8. Estimate the difference.

670 → ☐
− 120 → − ☐

about 700 ○ about 500 ○ about 600 ○ about 400 ○

9. Look at the floor of Sam's tree house. How many square units is it?

Draw ☐ to find the area.

☐ 1 square unit.

○ 26 ☐ ○ 23 ☐

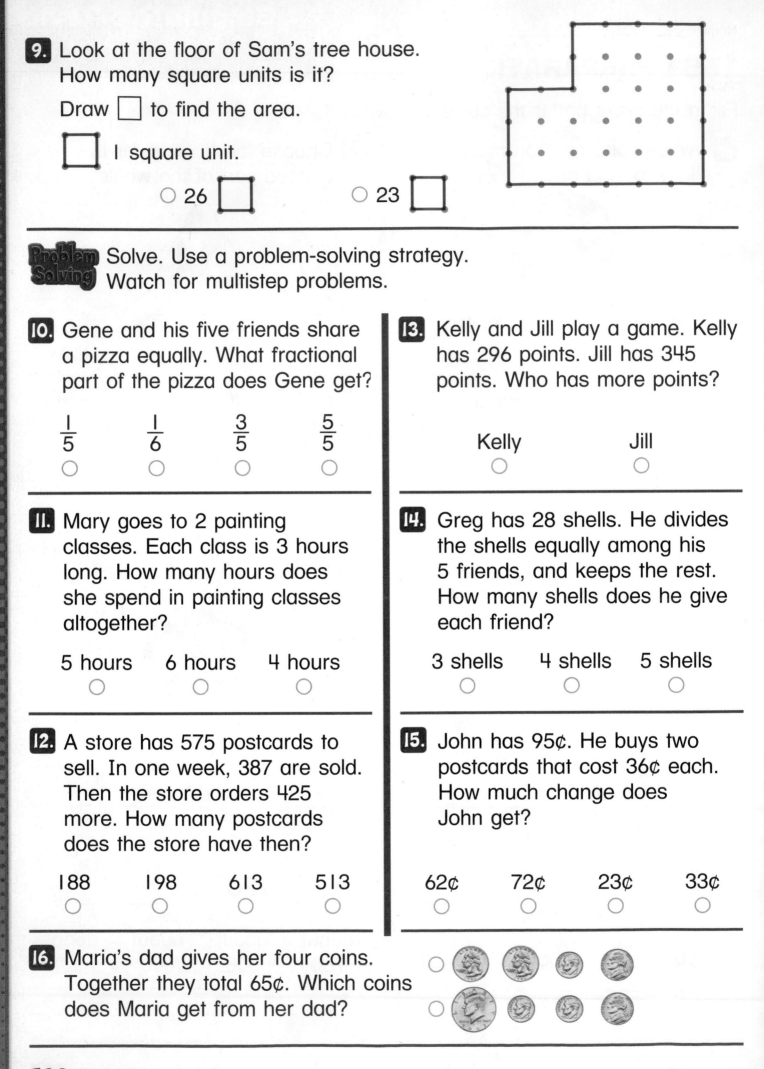

Problem Solving Solve. Use a problem-solving strategy. Watch for multistep problems.

10. Gene and his five friends share a pizza equally. What fractional part of the pizza does Gene get?

$\frac{1}{5}$ ○ $\frac{1}{6}$ ○ $\frac{3}{5}$ ○ $\frac{5}{5}$ ○

11. Mary goes to 2 painting classes. Each class is 3 hours long. How many hours does she spend in painting classes altogether?

5 hours ○ 6 hours ○ 4 hours ○

12. A store has 575 postcards to sell. In one week, 387 are sold. Then the store orders 425 more. How many postcards does the store have then?

188 ○ 198 ○ 613 ○ 513 ○

13. Kelly and Jill play a game. Kelly has 296 points. Jill has 345 points. Who has more points?

Kelly ○ Jill ○

14. Greg has 28 shells. He divides the shells equally among his 5 friends, and keeps the rest. How many shells does he give each friend?

3 shells ○ 4 shells ○ 5 shells ○

15. John has 95¢. He buys two postcards that cost 36¢ each. How much change does John get?

62¢ ○ 72¢ ○ 23¢ ○ 33¢ ○

16. Maria's dad gives her four coins. Together they total 65¢. Which coins does Maria get from her dad?

○

○

Name ______________________

Still More Practice
Chapter 1

Add.

1.	2.	3.	4.	5.
8 + 2	5 + 7	6 + 6	7 + 8	9 + 0

6. 3 + 9 = ___
7. 5 + 8 = ___
8. 9 + 7 = ___

Add. Count on, group doubles, or group to make 10.

9.	10.	11.	12.	13.	14.
4 2 + 7	5 5 + 8	7 5 + 3	4 1 + 8	7 2 + 7	8 4 + 2

Find the difference.

15. 12 − 7 = ___
16. 8 − 5 = ___
17. 10 − 4 = ___

Solve. Use a problem-solving strategy.
Count up or back. You can use a ←+++→.

18. Daryl has 12 panda stickers. Joy has 9. How many more stickers does Daryl have?

    ___ more stickers

19. Sena has 15 pages to fill with animal stickers. She fills 8. How many more pages can she fill?

    ___ more pages

Find the missing addend.

20. 6 + ☐ = 14
21. 7 + ☐ = 9
22. 8 + ☐ = 17

Write the fact family.

23. 15 6 9

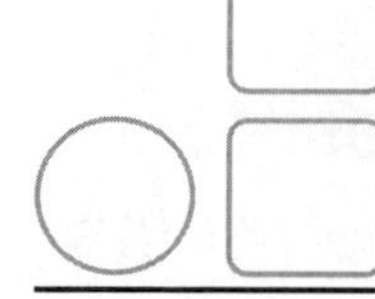
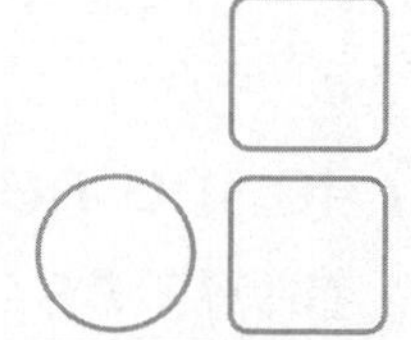
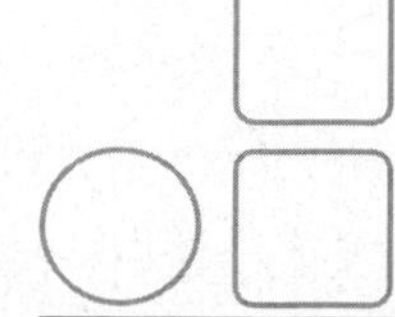

REINFORCEMENT

Still More Practice
Chapter 2

Name ______________________

Write how many tens and ones.
Then write the number, number word, or expanded form.

1. 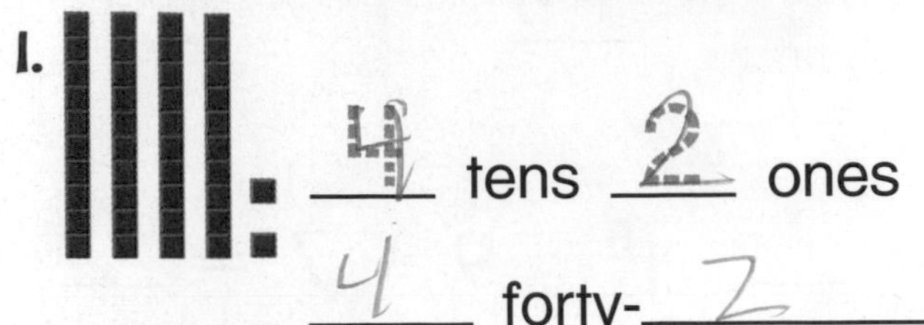

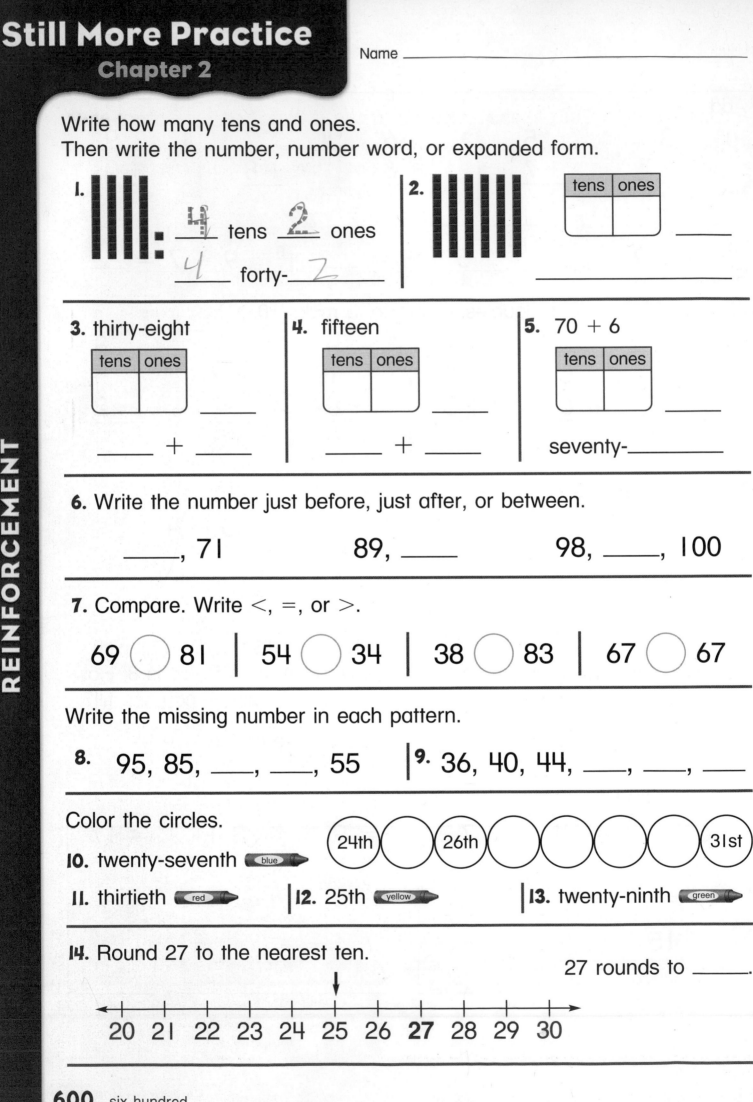

4 tens 2 ones

4 forty-2

2. 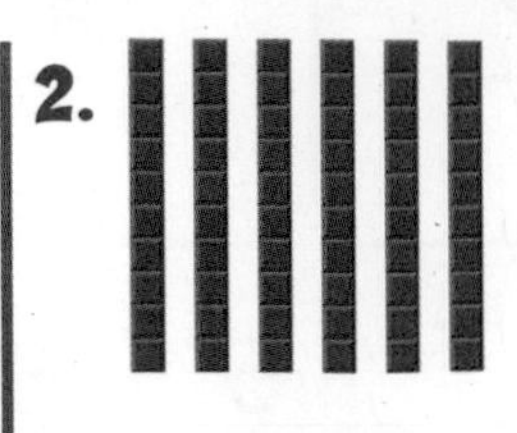

tens	ones

______

______

3. thirty-eight

tens	ones

______

______ + ______

4. fifteen

tens	ones

______

______ + ______

5. 70 + 6

tens	ones

______

seventy-______

6. Write the number just before, just after, or between.

______, 71   89, ______   98, ______, 100

7. Compare. Write <, =, or >.

69 ◯ 81 | 54 ◯ 34 | 38 ◯ 83 | 67 ◯ 67

Write the missing number in each pattern.

8. 95, 85, ____, ____, 55

9. 36, 40, 44, ____, ____, ____

Color the circles.

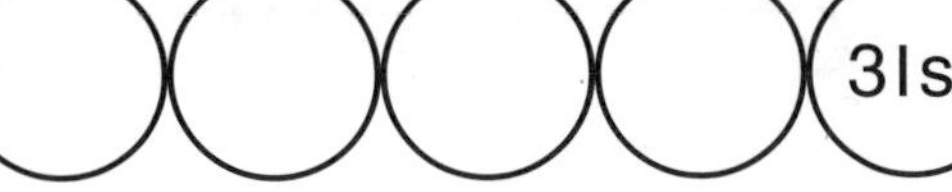

10. twenty-seventh 

11. thirtieth (red)

12. 25th 

13. twenty-ninth (green)

14. Round 27 to the nearest ten.

27 rounds to ______.

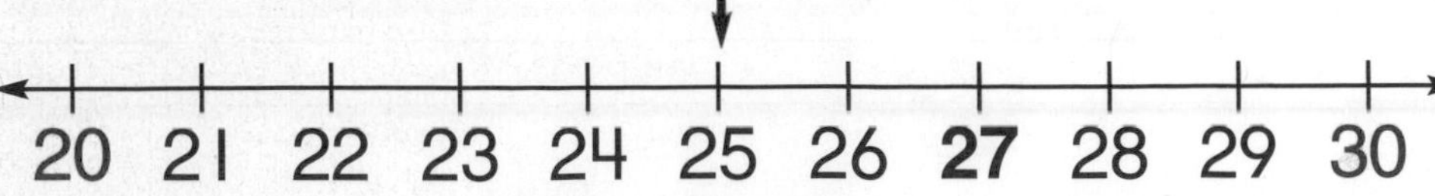

REINFORCEMENT

Name ______________________________

1. Use the data from the tally chart to make a pictograph.

Weekend Fun with Friends	
Activity	Tally
Video games	IIII
Sports	~~IIII~~ ~~IIII~~
Movies	~~IIII~~ I

Weekend Fun with Friends	
Video games	☺ ☺
Sports	○ ○ ○ ○
Movies	○ ○ ○
Key: Each ☺ stands for 2 friends.	

2. How many more friends like to play sports than go to the movies? 4 more

3. Use the data from the tally chart to make a bar graph.

Video Games with Friends	
Week	Tally
1	~~IIII~~ ~~IIII~~
2	~~IIII~~
3	~~IIII~~ ~~IIII~~ ~~IIII~~

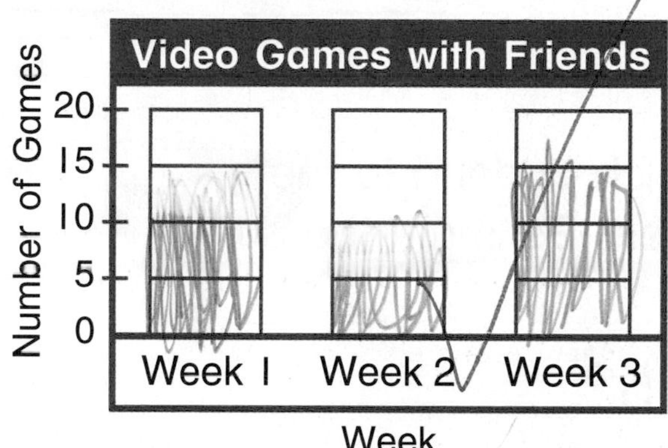

4. During which week did the friends play the most video games? week 3

5. What is the range of these friends' scores for one game?

125 = 50 = 4

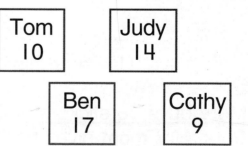

Tom 10	Judy 14
Ben 17	Cathy 9

6. Which friends like both video games?

Joe Al

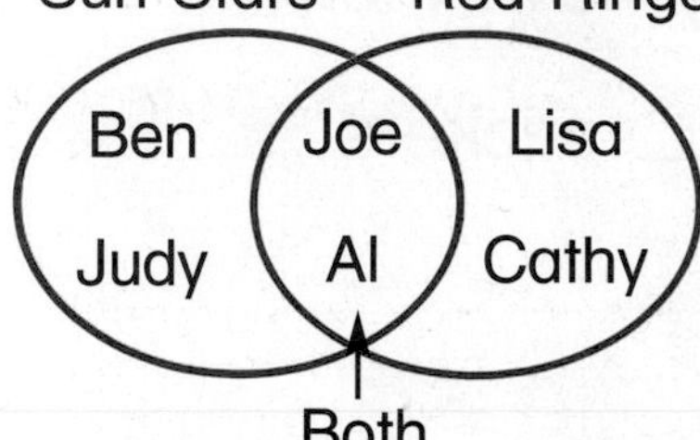

Still More Practice
Chapter 4

Name ______________________________

Add. Regroup as needed.

1.	2.	3.	4.	5.	6.
78 +13	57 +23	24 +60	37 + 2	23 +54	26 +27

7.	8.	9.	10.	11.	12.
12 +28	69 +14	85 + 3	53 +18	68 +28	12 +46

13.	14.	15.	16.	17.
61 14 +13	12 43 +29	24 24 +24	76 3 +10	23 34 +17

Round each addend to the nearest ten. Estimate the sum.

18.
52 → ☐
+35 → + ☐

about ____

Rewrite the addends. Add.

19. 73 + 9

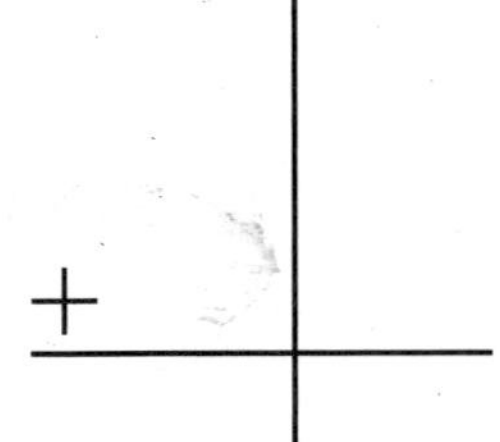

20. 64 + 28

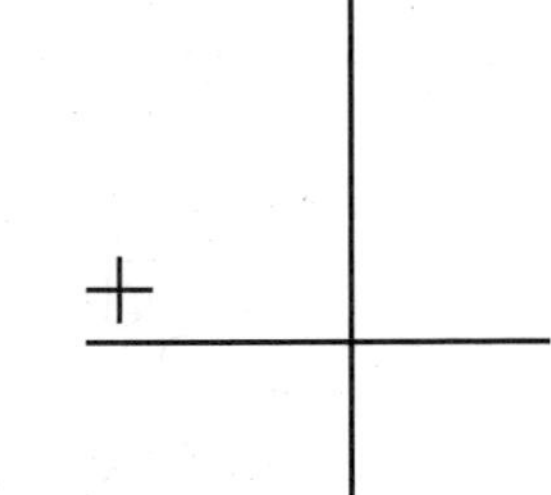

Solve. Use a problem-solving strategy.

21. Mary buys 66 stickers at Sea Park. Her mom gives her 20 more. How many stickers does Mary have then?

____ stickers

22. **Multistep** Raj takes 36 photos at Sea Park. Don takes a dozen more than Raj. How many photos do both boys take?

____ photos

REINFORCEMENT

Name ______________________________

Subtract. Regroup as needed.

1. $76 - 30$	**2.** $34 - 4$	**3.** $49 - 42$	**4.** $62 - 38$	**5.** $44 - 5$	**6.** $91 - 48$
7. $84 - 38$	**8.** $93 - 85$	**9.** $56 - 27$	**10.** $91 - 44$	**11.** $63 - 57$	**12.** $84 - 77$

Rewrite the subtraction. Then find the difference.

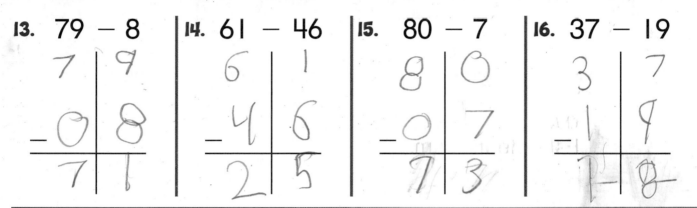

13. 79 − 8 **14.** 61 − 46 **15.** 80 − 7 **16.** 37 − 19

17. Subtract. Add to check.

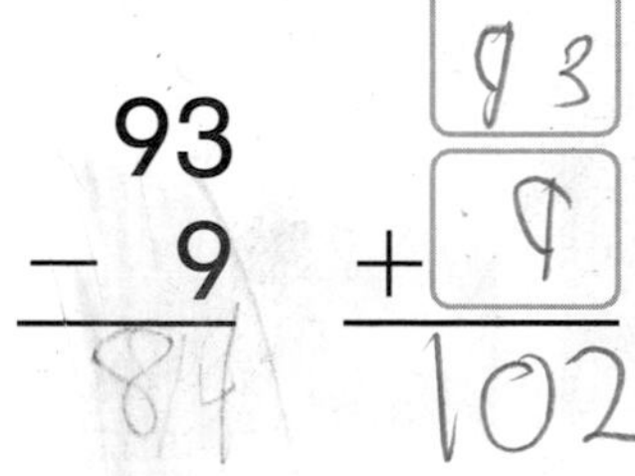

18. Round each number to the nearest ten. Estimate the difference.

58 ⟶ ☐

− 12 ⟶ − ☐

about ____

Solve. Use a problem-solving strategy.

19. Reggie wants to put 4 stickers on each page of a book. How many stickers will he need for 5 pages?

____ stickers

Pages					
Stickers					

Still More Practice
Chapter 6

Name ______________________

1. Match the figure with its name. Write the letter.

F ___ ___ ___ ___ ___

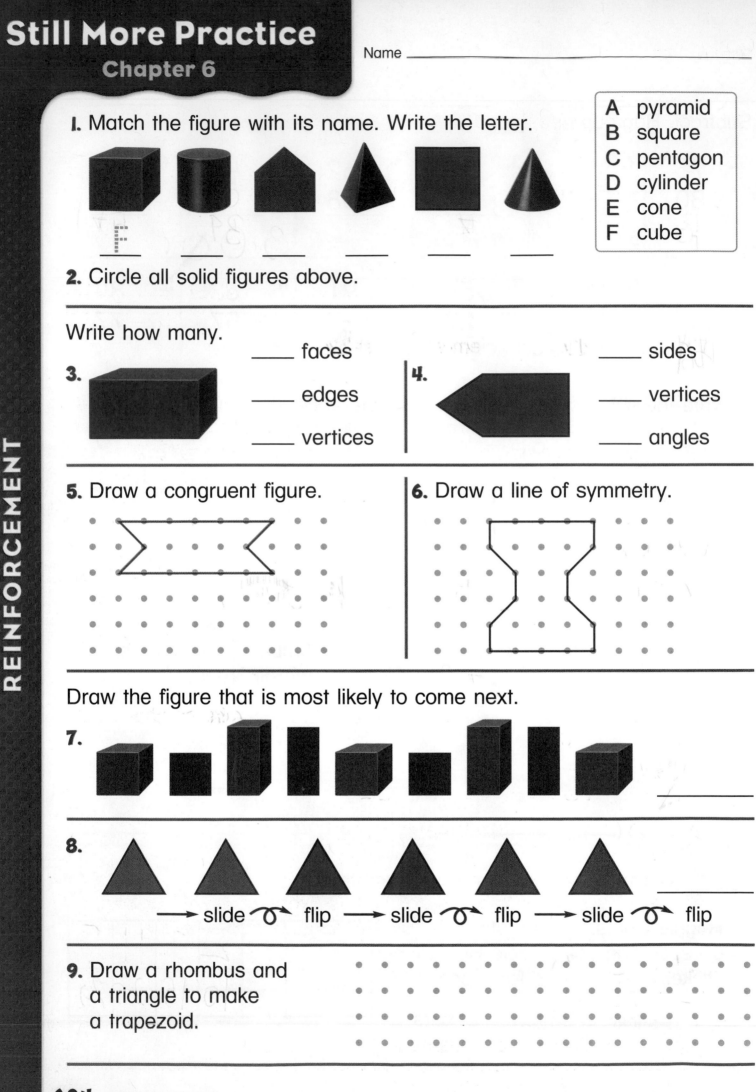

A pyramid
B square
C pentagon
D cylinder
E cone
F cube

2. Circle all solid figures above.

Write how many.

3. 

___ faces
___ edges
___ vertices

4. 

___ sides
___ vertices
___ angles

5. Draw a congruent figure.

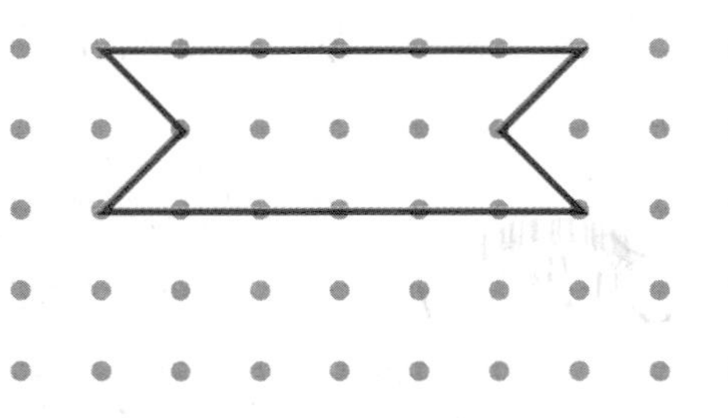

6. Draw a line of symmetry.

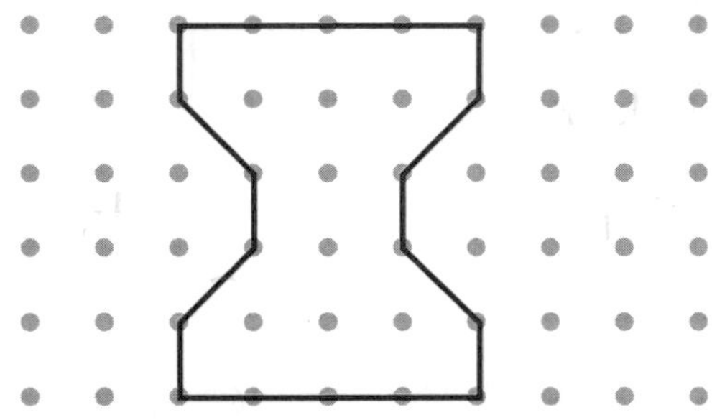

Draw the figure that is most likely to come next.

7.       

8. 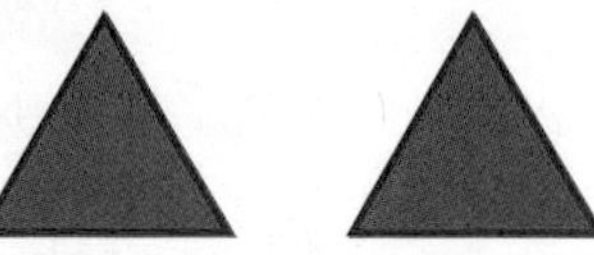    

→ slide ↷ flip → slide ↷ flip → slide ↷ flip

9. Draw a rhombus and a triangle to make a trapezoid.

REINFORCEMENT

Still More Practice
Chapter 7

Name ______________________________

Write the total amount.

1.  56¢

2.  ______

3.  ______

Solve. Use a problem-solving strategy.

4. The price is 33¢. Tom pays with 1 quarter and 2 nickels. How much change does he get?

______

5. Louise buys a star decal for 38¢ and a planet decal for 58¢. How much does she spend?

______

Write the time.

6.  3:15

7.  ______

8.  ______ minutes after ______

9.  ______ minutes after ______

______ minutes before ______

10. Write how much time has passed.

start 

end 

____ hours have passed.

11. Crayons cost 95¢. Is this enough money to buy them?

______

REINFORCEMENT

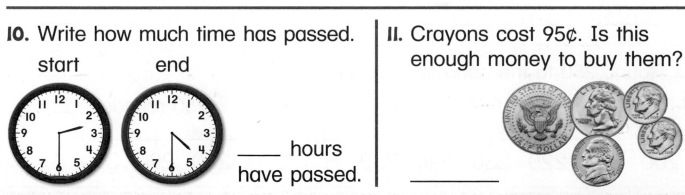

Copyright © by William H. Sadlier, Inc. All rights reserved.

Still More Practice
Chapter 8

Name ____________________

Write the number and the number word.

1. 3 hundreds 0 tens 0 ones  300 ____________________

2. 6 hundreds 3 tens 9 ones ______ ____________________

Write the number in expanded form.

3. 5 hundreds 0 tens 8 ones ____ + ____ + ____

Write the value of the underlined digit.

4. <u>3</u>27	5. 6<u>3</u>5	6. 8<u>6</u>4	7. 19<u>6</u>
____	____	____	____

Count by 10s, 25s, 50s, or 100s. Write the missing numbers.

8. 625, ____, 675, 700, ____, ____, ____, 800

9. 412, ____, 432, ____, 452, 462, ____, ____

Compare. Write $<$, $=$, or $>$.

10. 435  512 | 11. 352 ◯ 348 | 12. 131  98

Write the numbers in order from least to greatest.

13. 457 392 718 609

____, ____, ____, ____

14. 537 573 592 579

____, ____, ____, ____

15. Round 250 to the nearest hundred.

250 rounds to ____.

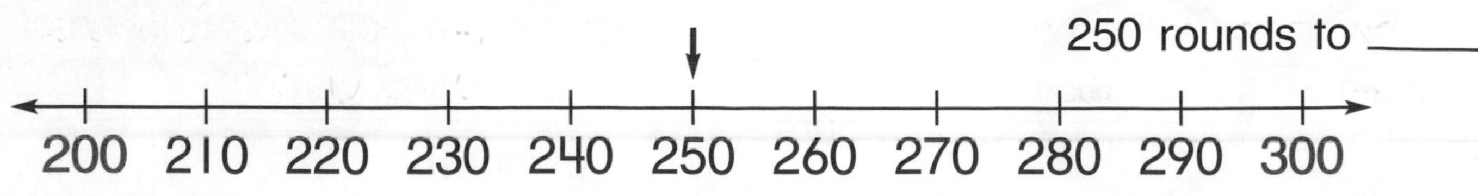

REINFORCEMENT

Name ____________________

Still More Practice
Chapter 9

Find the sum.

1.	2.	3.	4.	5.
800 + 167 = 967	363 + 28	486 + 306	192 + 693	527 + 277

6.	7.	8.	9.	10.
\$1.10 + 0.26	\$2.22 + 1.23	\$3.38 + 3.07	\$4.38 + 1.92	\$5.80 + 1.45

Subtract.

11.	12.	13.	14.	15.
749 − 28	418 − 135	586 − 139	\$6.58 − 1.64	\$9.50 − 0.35

16.	17.	18.	19.	20.
361 − 207	205 − 81	824 − 168	\$4.19 − 0.89	\$9.35 − 2.79

Round to the nearest hundred. Add or subtract.

21. 863 → ☐
− 217 → − ☐
about ____

22. 688 → ☐
+ 136 → + ☐
about ____

Solve. Use a problem-solving strategy.

23. 362 people watched the Friday game and 475 people watched the Sunday game. How many more people watched on Sunday?

____ more people

24. The score was 184 points for the first game and 227 points for the second game. How many more points were scored in the second game?

____ more points

REINFORCEMENT

Copyright © by William H. Sadlier, Inc. All rights reserved.

Still More Practice
Chapter 10

Name ______________________

REINFORCEMENT

Write the fraction for the part colored.

1. 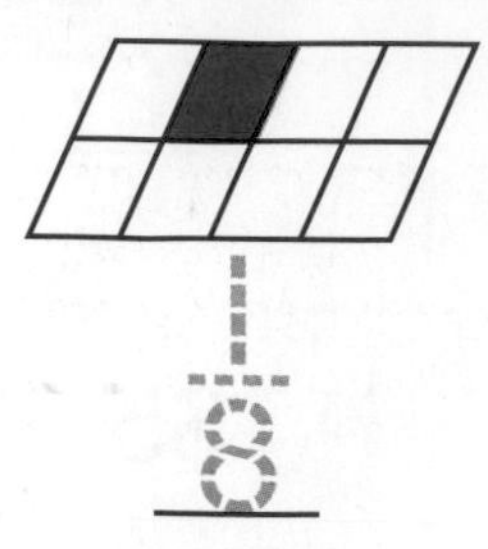

2.  ___

3. 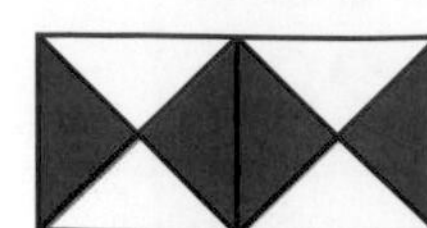 ___

4.  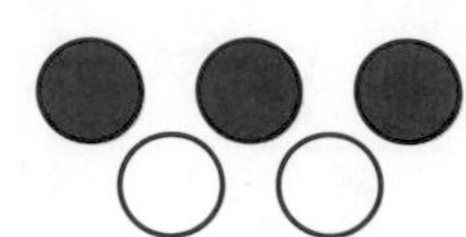 ___

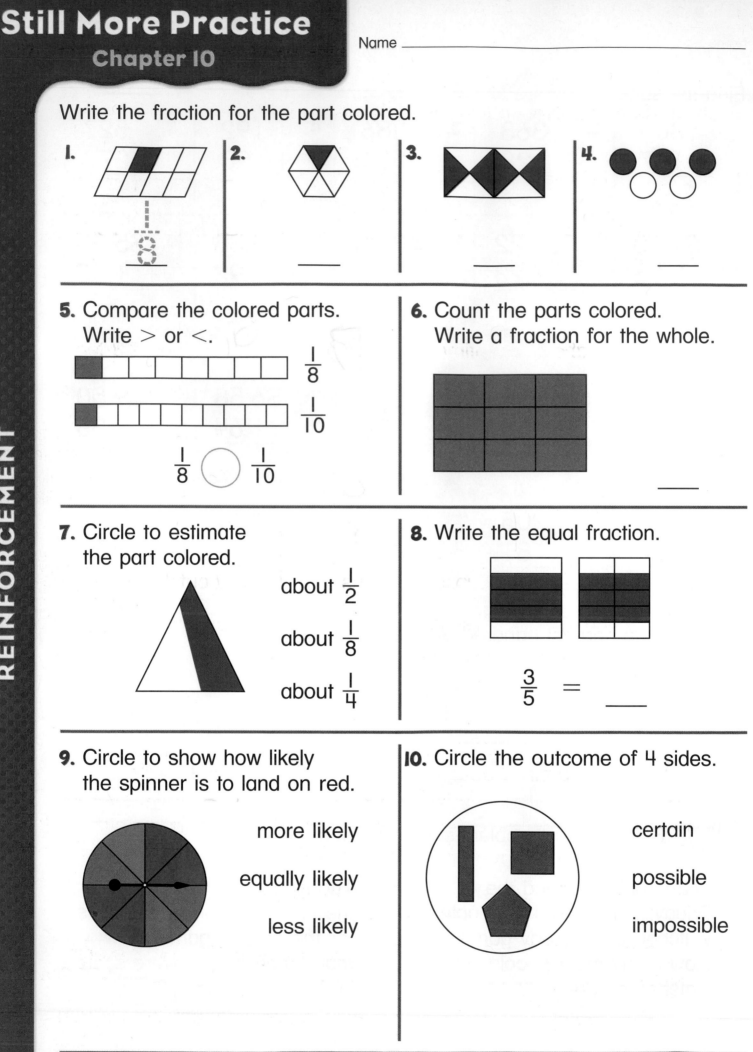

5. Compare the colored parts. Write > or <.

 $\frac{1}{8}$

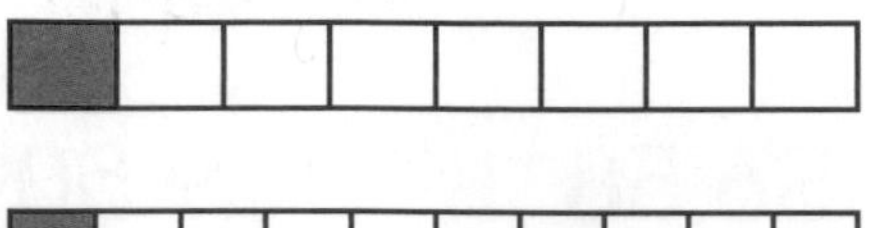 $\frac{1}{10}$

$\frac{1}{8}$ ◯ $\frac{1}{10}$

6. Count the parts colored. Write a fraction for the whole.

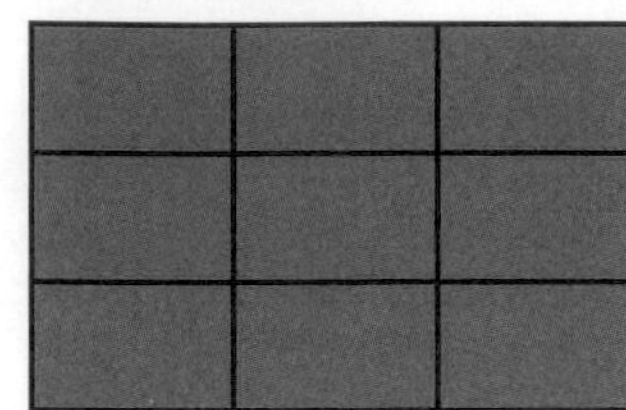 ___

7. Circle to estimate the part colored.

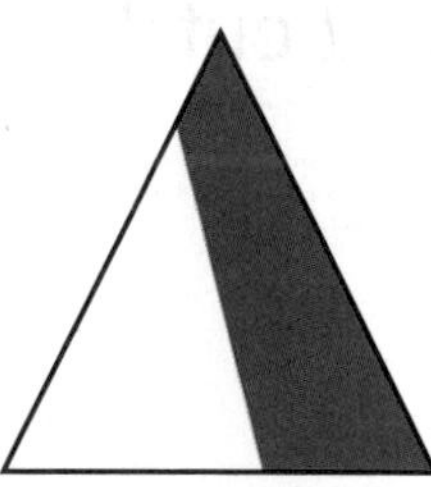

about $\frac{1}{2}$

about $\frac{1}{8}$

about $\frac{1}{4}$

8. Write the equal fraction.

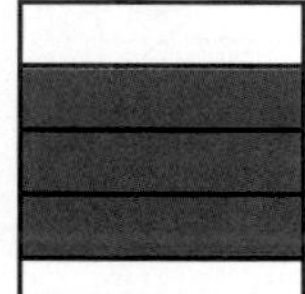 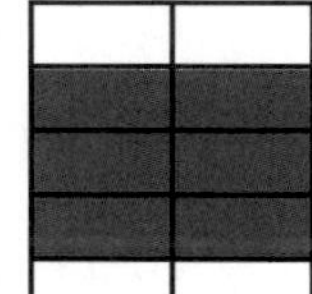

$\frac{3}{5}$ = ___

9. Circle to show how likely the spinner is to land on red.

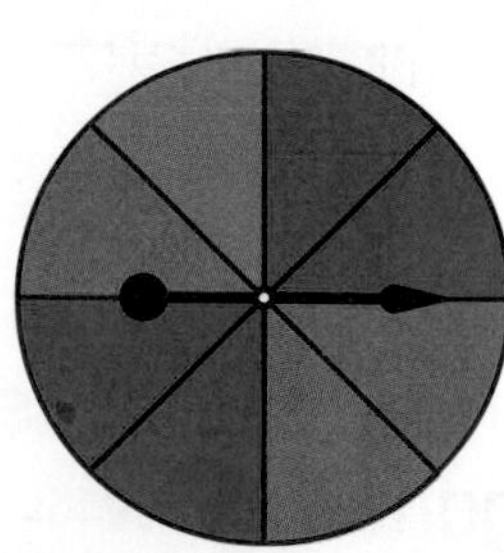

more likely

equally likely

less likely

10. Circle the outcome of 4 sides.

certain

possible

impossible

Name ______________________

Still More Practice
Chapter 11

Start at the mark. Draw a line for each measure.

1. $4\frac{1}{2}$ in. |

2. 11 cm |

Circle the better estimate.

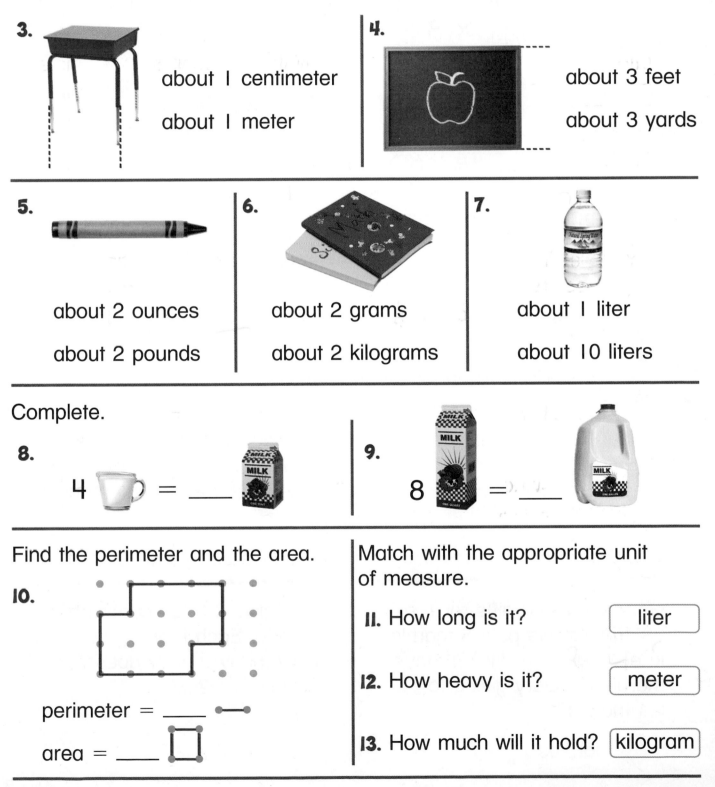

3. 

about 1 centimeter

about 1 meter

4. 

about 3 feet

about 3 yards

5. 

about 2 ounces

about 2 pounds

6. 

about 2 grams

about 2 kilograms

7. 

about 1 liter

about 10 liters

Complete.

8. 4 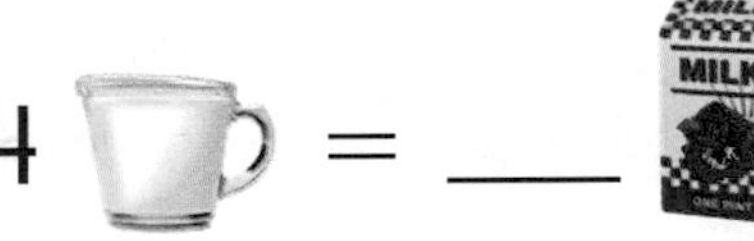 = ___

9. 8  = ___ 

Find the perimeter and the area.

10. 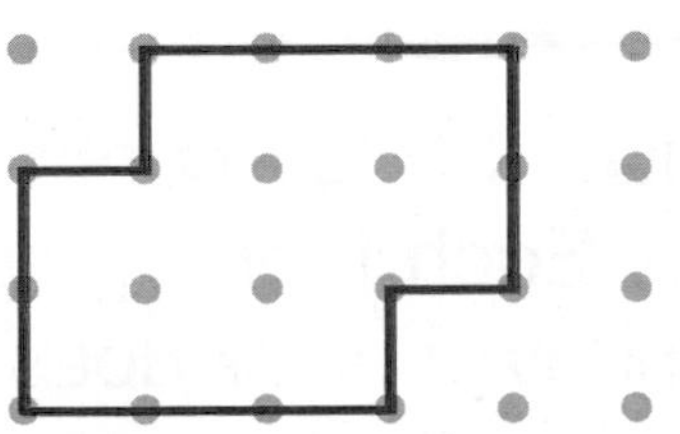

perimeter = ___

area = ___

Match with the appropriate unit of measure.

11. How long is it? liter

12. How heavy is it? meter

13. How much will it hold? kilogram

REINFORCEMENT

Copyright © by William H. Sadlier, Inc. All rights reserved.

Still More Practice
Chapter 12

Name ____________________

Find the product. You can draw or model to help.

1. $3 \times 2 = 6$
2. 2×0
3. 3×9
4. 4×2
5. 3×3
6. 5×5
7. 2×9
8. 5×1
9. 2×2
10. 5×8
11. 4×5
12. 2×6
13. 5×2
14. 4×3

Multiply.

15. $7 \times 2 =$ ___
16. $6 \times 3 =$ ___
17. $6 \times 5 =$ ___

Write how many. You can use models.

18. How many fours are in 16?

16 ÷ ___ = ___

19. How many threes are in 12?

___ ÷ ___ = ___

20. How many fives are in 20?

___ ÷ ___ = ___

Solve. Use a problem-solving strategy.

21. Ed put 4 stickers on each of 6 pages. How many stickers are there in all?

___ stickers

22. Three friends share 8 toys equally. How many toys does each friend get? How many toys are left over?

___ toys each and ___ left over

23. Gary is making gifts for 6 of his friends. He puts 5 marbles in each gift box. How many marbles is Gary giving to his friends?

___ marbles

24. Sue gives 30 toy cars to her friends. Each friend gets 5 cars. How many friends does Sue give cars to?

___ friends

Listen to your teacher read the directions.

Mental Math

Set 1

1 to 10	ten to one
5 to 14	six to fifteen
8 to 17	nine to twenty
11 to 20	four to twelve
12 to 3	eleven to zero
16 to 10	thirteen to two
20 to 8	nineteen to ten
18 to 7	sixteen to six

Set 2

___, 2, 3	7, ___, 9
___, 6, 7	9, ___, 11
___, 9, 10	0, ___, 2
___, 14, 15	12, ___, 14
9, 10, ___	15, ___, 17
0, 1, ___	11, ___, 13
14, 15, ___	18, ___, 20

Set 3

1	0, 2, 4, 6, 8, 10, 12
1	1, 3, 5, 7, 9, 11, 13
2	2, 3, 4, 5, 6, 7, 8, 9, 10
3	2, 3, 4, 5, 6, 7, 8, 9, 10
4	1, 2, 3, 4, 5, 6, 7, 8, 10
5	0, 1, 2, 3, 4, 5, 6, 7, 10
6	0, 1, 2, 3, 4, 5, 6, 10

Set 4

1	12, 10, 8, 6, 4, 2
1	11, 9, 7, 5, 3, 1
2	11, 10, 9, 8, 7, 6, 5
3	12, 11, 10, 9, 8, 7, 6
4	12, 11, 10, 9, 8, 7, 6
5	12, 11, 10, 9, 8, 7, 6
6	12, 11, 10, 9, 8, 7, 6

Set 5

7 +	3, 4, 5, 6, 7, 8, 9
8 +	3, 4, 5, 6, 7, 8, 9
9 +	3, 4, 5, 6, 7, 8, 9
17 −	9, 8
16 −	9, 8, 7
15 −	9, 8, 7, 6
14 −	9, 8, 7, 6, 5

Set 6

3, 6, 9	3, 8, 11
4, 3, 7	6, 9, 15
3, 5, 8	14, 6, 20
2, 3, 5	8, 5, 13
2, 7, 9	7, 9, 16
2, 4, 6	9, 8, 17
4, 5, 9	12, 7, 19

Set 7

4	3	6
8	5	9
11	17	12
19	14	10

twelve, ______, fourteen

nine, ______, eleven

ten, ______, twelve

eighteen, ______, twenty

Set 8

tens	ones
8	5
2	4
1	9
6	0

70 + 1

20 + 7

30 + 8

50 + 9

26	93	14
37	82	56
41	70	98

Set 9

4	8	11	20
7	5	16	6
10	1	18	15
12	14	13	19
3	13	7	12
0	10	14	16
20	2	17	8
15	14	9	1

Copyright © by William H. Sadlier, Inc. All rights reserved.

Mental Math

You do not need paper and pencil!

MAINTENANCE

Set 10

Count by	from	to
1	73	81
2	42	60
5	20	70
10	50	100
3	3	24
4	4	24
5	5	40

Set 11

Compare.

58	___	85
96	___	51
66	___	38
32	___	43
17	___	29
72	___	43
46	___	64

Set 12

Add ___ to:

3	9, 8, 7, 6, 5, 4
4	4, 5, 6, 7, 8, 9
5	9, 8, 7, 6, 5, 4
6	4, 5, 6, 7, 8, 9
7	9, 8, 7, 6, 5, 4
8	4, 5, 6, 7, 8, 9
9	9, 8, 7, 6, 5, 4

Set 13

Subtract ___ from:

9	19, 18, 17, 16, 15, 14, ...
8	18, 17, 16, 15, 14, 13, ...
7	17, 16, 15, 14, 13, 12, ...
6	16, 15, 14, 13, 12, 11, ...
5	15, 14, 13, 12, 11, 10, ...
4	14, 13, 12, 11, 10, 9, ...
3	13, 12, 11, 10, 9, 8, ...

Set 14

Fact Families

8, 12, 4	8, 15, 7
3, 11, 8	9, 7, 16
7, 3, 4	6, 3
5, 10	3, 5, 8
9, 17, 8	13, 9, 4
18, 9	14, 7

Set 15

13, 9 fly away

8, 5 more

13, 6 swim away

14, 7 fly away

5, 9 more

9, 4 more

16, lose 7

Set 16

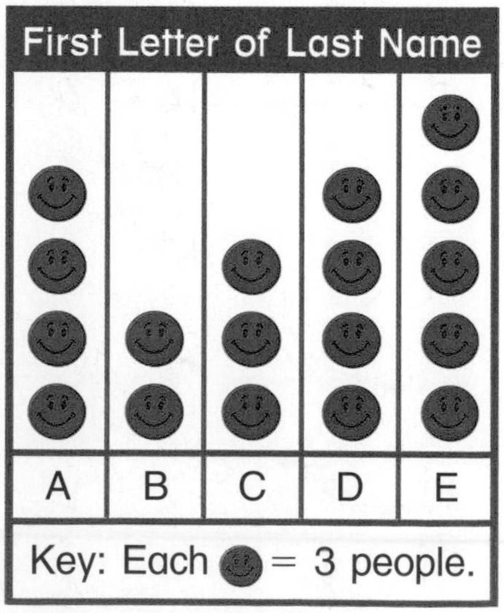
First Letter of Last Name
A
B
C
D
E
Key: Each = 3 people.

Set 17

Favorite Numbers

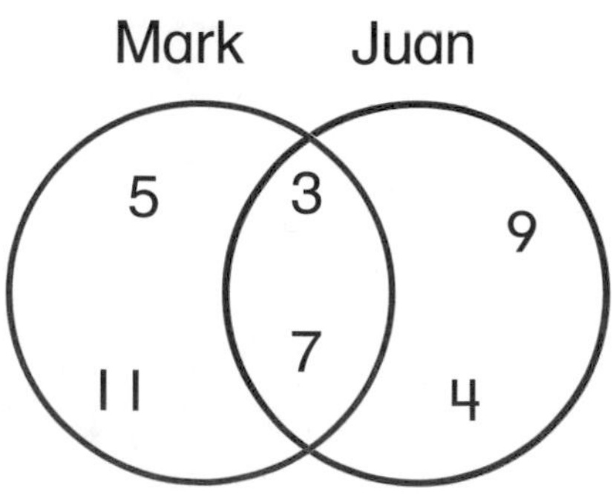
Mark
Juan
5
11
3
7
9
4

Set 18

10 + 60	40 + 40	20 + 70
10 + 80	30 + 50	60 + 20

1, 11, 21, 31, ...
3, 13, 23, 33, ...
7, 17, 27, 37, ...
9, 19, 29, 39, ...
5, 15, 25, 35, ...

Mental Math

Set 19

Add ___ to:

3	93, 83, 73, 63, 53, 43
4	4, 14, 24, 34, 44, 54
5	85, 75, 65, 55, 45, 35
6	6, 16, 26, 36, 46, 56
7	87, 77, 67, 57, 47, 37
8	8, 18, 28, 38, 48, 58
9	89, 79, 69, 59, 49, 39

Set 20

7 + 3 + 15

12 + 6 + 4

1 + 9 + 32

27 + 2 + 2

5 + 49 + 5

3 + 85 + 7

9 + 41 + 1

Set 21

$70 - 20$ $80 - 50$ $90 - 80$

$50 - 20$ $90 - 40$ $60 - 30$

98, 88, 78, 68, ...

92, 82, 72, 62, ...

96, 86, 76, 66, ...

94, 84, 74, 64, ...

Set 22

Subtract ___ from:

3	99, 88, 77, 66, 55
4	64, 65, 66, 67, 68
5	37, 47, 57, 67, 77
6	76, 77, 78, 79, 80
7	59, 48, 37, 29, 18, 7
8	88, 89, 90, 78, 79, 80
9	99, 88, 77, 66, 55

Set 23

37 − 7	35 − 11
51 − 1	88 − 11
45 − 5	79 − 11
89 − 9	46 − 11
97 − 7	91 − 11
62 − 2	62 − 11
74 − 4	53 − 11

Set 24

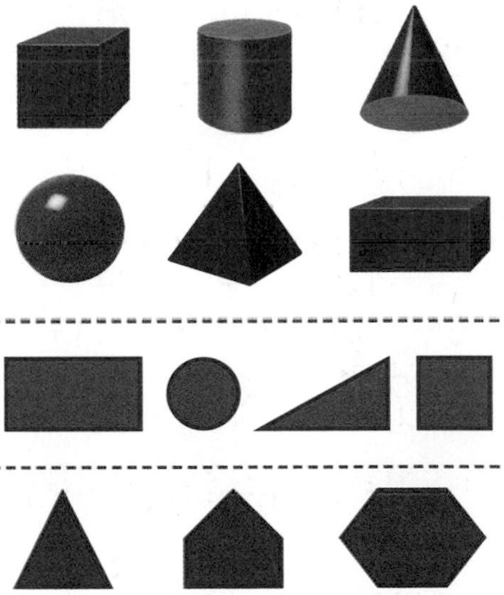

Set 25

nickels: 4, 6, 5, 10

dimes: 3, 5, 7, 9

quarters: 2, 4, 1, 3

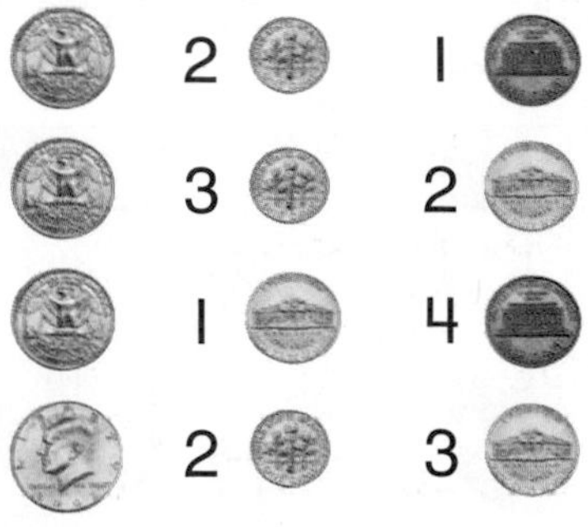

1	2	1
2	3	2
1	1	4
1	2	3

Set 26

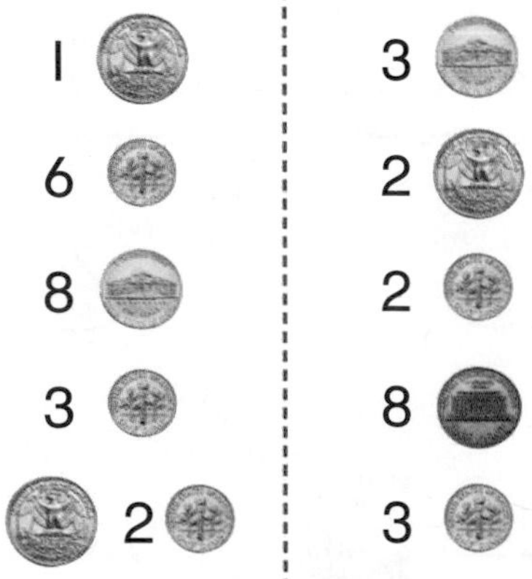

Have	Spend
1	3
6	2
8	2
3	8
1 2	3

Set 27

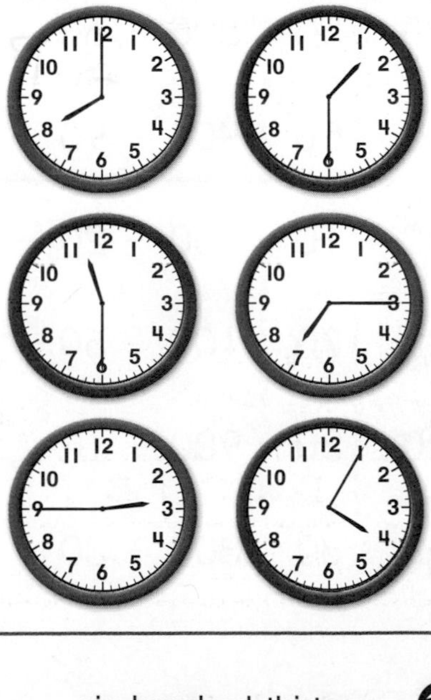

Copyright © by William H. Sadlier, Inc. All rights reserved.

Mental Math

MAINTENANCE

Set 28

1:30	2:30	3:30
9:15	8:15	7:15
10:45	11:45	12:45
9:00	9:10	9:20

Sun.	Mon.	Tues.	Wed.
	1	2	?
7	?	?	10
?	15	16	?
21	?	?	24

Set 29

hundreds	tens	ones
1	3	2
2	8	7
4	5	0

283	436	271
592	742	853
411	329	647

Set 30

Compare.

132 ___ 321

254 ___ 146

456 ___ 478

952 ___ 925

367 ___ 309

187 ___ 245

Set 31

805	508
533	335
423	432
124	214

787	687	778
634	643	534
108	808	118

Set 32

Round to the nearest hundred.

456	392
187	724
839	270
546	419
275	948
660	563
904	357

Set 33

100 + 80	300 + 40 + 8
200 + 60	400 + 50 + 1
500 + 30	600 + 70 + 5
700 + 20	800 + 90 + 6
900 + 10	200 + 50 + 2
600 + 40	400 + 80 + 7

Set 34

100 − 40	500 − 60 − 4
200 − 50	400 − 90 − 7
300 − 10	700 − 20 − 5
900 − 70	100 − 50 − 9
600 − 30	900 − 10 − 1
800 − 80	300 − 30 − 3

Set 35

Set 36

Compare.

___

___

___

___

Mental Math

Set 37

▲ △
▲ ▲
▲ △

○ ●
○ ●
○ ●
○ ●

1 1 2 1 2 1

Set 38

1 inch	1 foot
1 inch	$\frac{1}{2}$ inch
1 foot	1 yard
1 cup	1 quart
1 quart	1 pint
1 centimeter	1 meter
1 pound	1 gallon
1 kilogram	1 liter
10° F	80° F

Set 39

scale
ruler
measuring cup
balance
thermometer

inches	pounds
liters	meters
degrees	gallons

Set 40

1 centimeter   1 meter

Perimeter	Area
8 cm	6 m, 1 m
15 cm, 1 cm	2 cm
6 cm, 8 cm	4 m, 2 m

Set 41

▲ = 1¢   ■ = 10¢   ● = $1.00

85¢ + ▲	● + 16¢
■ + 16¢	● + 25¢
75¢ − ▲	$8.00 − ●
18¢ − ■	$2.11 + ●

$3.00 − ● + ■
$5.50 + ● − ▲
$1.25 − ● + ▲

Set 42

Groups of

3	2, 3, 4, 5, 10
5	10, 5, 4, 3, 2
4	2, 3, 4, 5, 10
2	10, 5, 4, 3, 2
6	2, 3, 4, 5, 10
7	2, 3, 4, 5, 10
8	2, 3, 4, 5, 10

Set 43

Multiply.

2, 3, 5, 1, 7, 8, 9, 6, 4	2
4, 9, 8, 2, 5, 3, 6, 1, 7	3
6, 1, 8, 3, 7, 5, 9, 2, 4	4
8, 2, 5, 7, 3, 1, 4, 6, 9	5

Set 44

2 + 6 = 18 − ☐
35 − 10 = 5 × ☐
2 × 5 = ☐ − 110
125 − 100 = 25 + ☐
400 − 300 = ☐ + 90
30 + 20 = 250 − ☐
95 − 20 = 85 − ☐

Set 45

How many in each?

twos in:	8, 2, 4, 10, 12, 6, 18, 14
threes in:	3, 12, 21, 9, 15, 6, 27, 18
fours in:	8, 16, 20, 32, 4, 12, 24, 36
fives in:	30, 25, 20, 15, 10, 5, 35

MAINTENANCE

Copyright © by William H. Sadlier, Inc. All rights reserved.

Glossary

also on-line

GLOSSARY OF MATH WORDS

add page 3
find how many altogether

addend page 9
a number that you add
addend + addend = sum

addition sentence page 11
a number sentence that shows addition with the symbols + and =

$$4 + 3 = 7$$

angle page 253
the space between two sides that meet

angle

area page 517
the amount of space taken up by a plane figure. Area is measured in square units.

array page 559
an arrangement of symbols in rows and columns

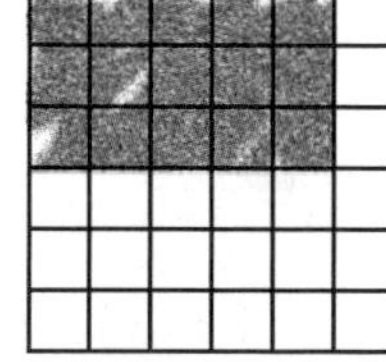

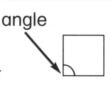

balance page 507
a device used to compare weights

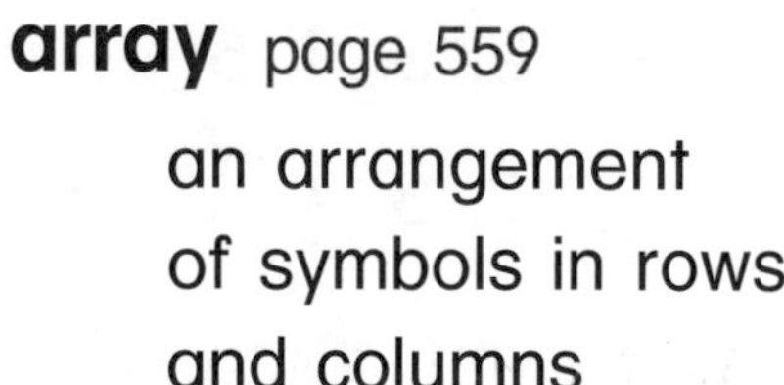

bar graph page 119
a graph that uses bars to show how many

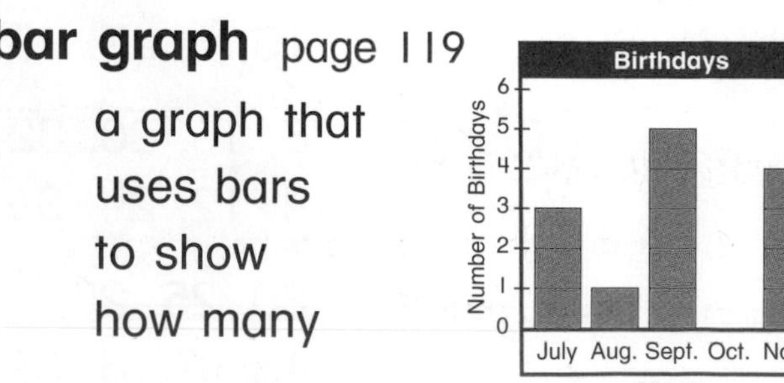

between page 83

45, 46, 47

46 is between 45 and 47.

calendar page 329
shows days, weeks, and months

Celsius (C) page 527
a temperature measurement scale

centimeter page 511
a unit of measure for length

centimeter ruler page 511
a tool used to measure length in centimeters

certain page 473
an outcome that will always happen

change page 303
the amount of money you get back when you buy something

circle graph page 131
a graph that shows how parts of data are related to the whole

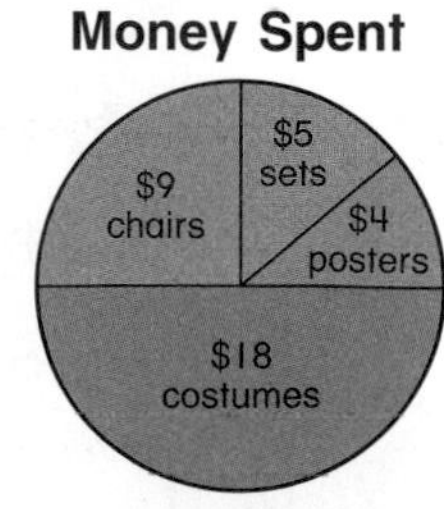

closed figure page 253
a figure that has no openings

congruent page 259
the same shape and the same size

count back page 29

to name numbers in decreasing order

count on page 9

to name numbers in increasing order

count up page 39

count from a smaller number up to a greater number to find the difference

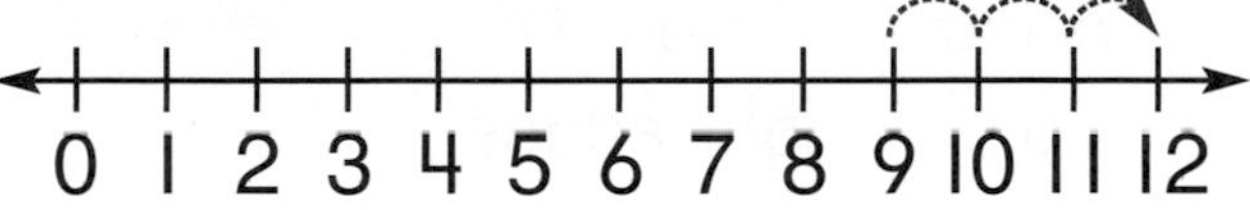

12 − 9 = 3

cubic unit page 525

a unit of measurement for volume

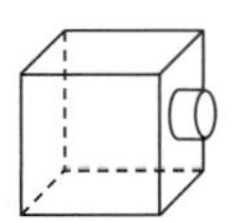

cup (c) page 501

a unit that measures how much a container holds

2 cups = 1 pint

curved line page 253

a line around a figure that is not straight

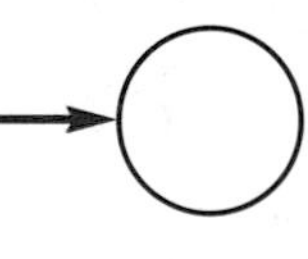

curved surface page 247

a surface of a solid figure on which that figure can be rolled

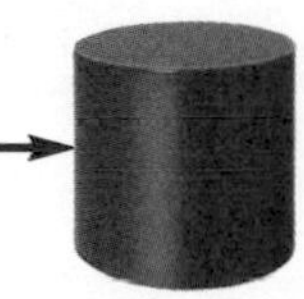

data page 117

a set of information

decimal point page 307

the point between dollars and cents

$3.50

degree (°) page 527

a unit for measuring temperature

difference page 29

the answer in subtraction

5 − 3 = ②

digit page 67

0, 1, 2, 3, 4, 5, 6, 7, 8, or 9

dime page 291

a coin that is worth 10 cents (10¢)

divide page 565

to share or separate into equal parts

division sentence page 565

a number sentence that shows division with the symbols ÷ and =

6 ÷ 3 = 2

division sign page 565 

dollar sign page 307 $

doubles fact page 17

a fact with two addends that are the same

6 + 6 = 12

Copyright © by William H. Sadlier, Inc. All rights reserved.

Glossary

also on-line

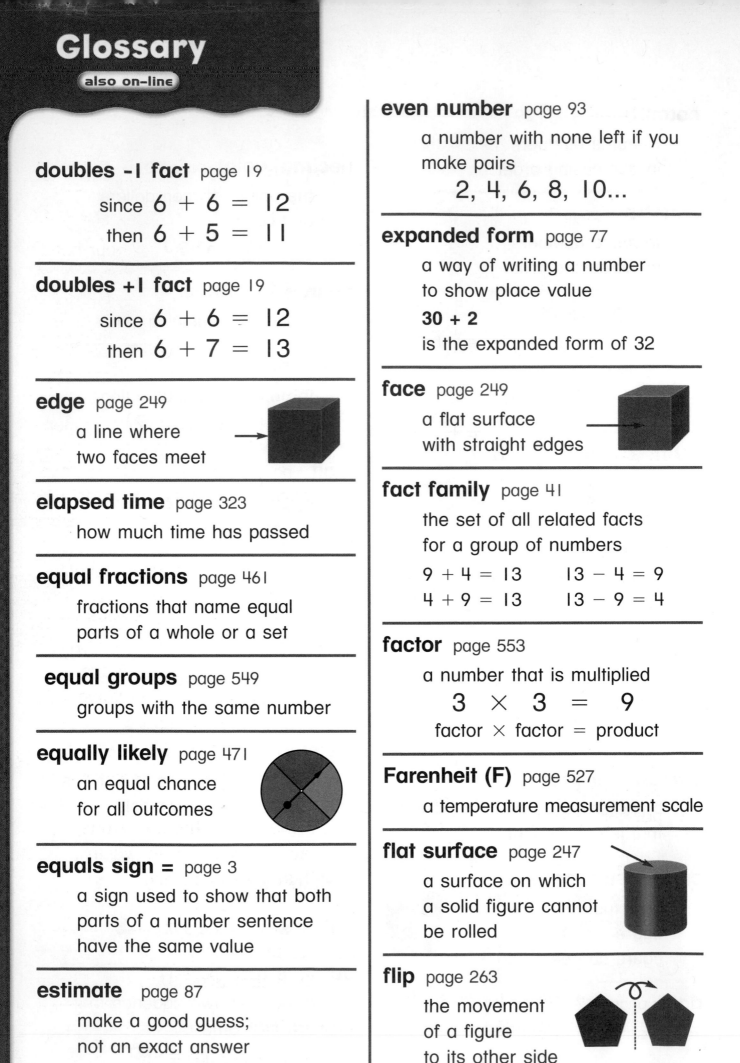

GLOSSARY OF MATH WORDS

doubles -1 fact page 19

since 6 + 6 = 12
then 6 + 5 = 11

doubles +1 fact page 19

since 6 + 6 = 12
then 6 + 7 = 13

edge page 249

a line where two faces meet

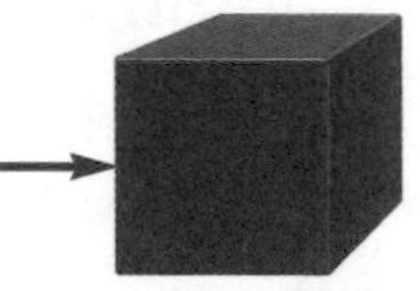

elapsed time page 323

how much time has passed

equal fractions page 461

fractions that name equal parts of a whole or a set

equal groups page 549

groups with the same number

equally likely page 471

an equal chance for all outcomes

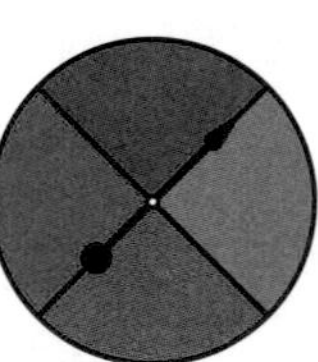

equals sign = page 3

a sign used to show that both parts of a number sentence have the same value

estimate page 87

make a good guess; not an exact answer

even number page 93

a number with none left if you make pairs

2, 4, 6, 8, 10...

expanded form page 77

a way of writing a number to show place value

30 + 2

is the expanded form of 32

face page 249

a flat surface with straight edges

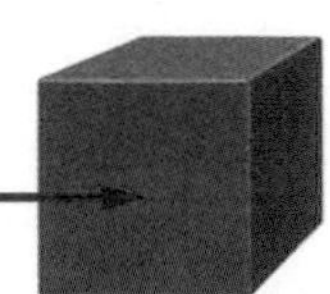

fact family page 41

the set of all related facts for a group of numbers

9 + 4 = 13	13 − 4 = 9
4 + 9 = 13	13 − 9 = 4

factor page 553

a number that is multiplied

3 × 3 = 9
factor × factor = product

Farenheit (F) page 527

a temperature measurement scale

flat surface page 247

a surface on which a solid figure cannot be rolled

flip page 263

the movement of a figure to its other side

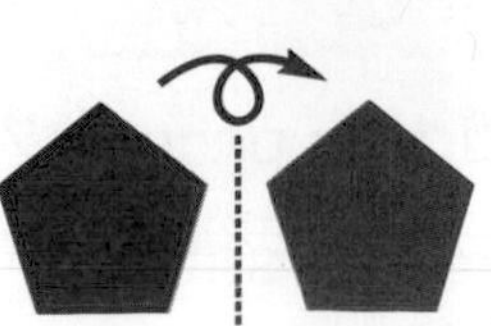

foot (ft) page 497

a unit of measure for length

1 foot = 12 inches

fraction page 445

a part of a whole or a set

$\frac{1}{2}$

gallon (gal) page 505

a unit that measures how much something holds

1 gallon=4 quarts

gram (g) page 519

a unit used to measure how heavy an object is

half dollar page 295

a coin that is worth 50 cents (50¢)

half hour page 313

30 minutes

half past page 313

30 minutes past the hour

hexagon page 271

a plane figure with six sides

hour page 313

a unit of measure for time

1 hour = 60 minutes

hour hand page 313

the hand on the clock that tells the hour

hour hand

hundred flat page 349

a square divided into 100 equal parts

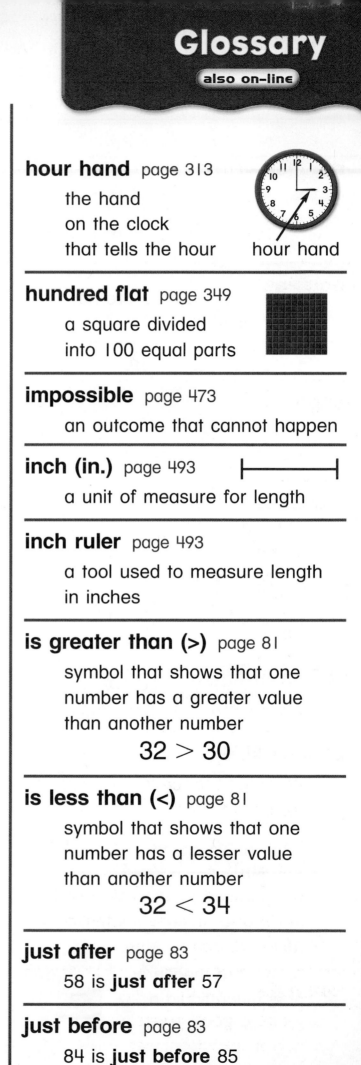

impossible page 473

an outcome that cannot happen

inch (in.) page 493

a unit of measure for length

inch ruler page 493

a tool used to measure length in inches

is greater than (>) page 81

symbol that shows that one number has a greater value than another number

$32 > 30$

is less than (<) page 81

symbol that shows that one number has a lesser value than another number

$32 < 34$

just after page 83

58 is **just after** 57

just before page 83

84 is **just before** 85

Copyright © by William H. Sadlier, Inc. All rights reserved.

key page 117

tells what each symbol in a pictograph stands for

kilogram page 519

a unit used to measure how heavy something is

6 bananas are about 1 kilogram

length page 491

the measure of a distance between two points

less likely page 471

not a good chance

line of symmetry page 261

a line on which a figure can fold so that the two halves match

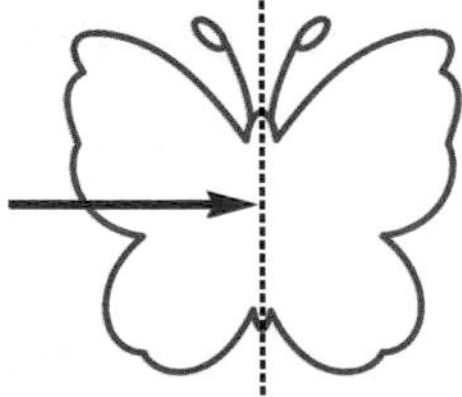

line plot page 133

a set of Xs on a number line to show data

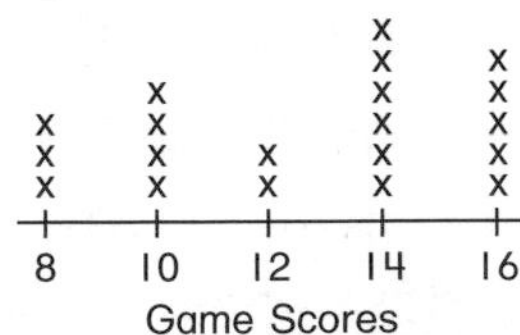

liter (L) page 521

a unit that measures how much liquid a container can hold

median page 123

the middle number in an ordered set of numbers

6, 7, 8, 9, 9 Median: 8

meter (m) page 513

a unit of measure for length

1 meter = 100 centimeters

meter stick page 513

a tool used to measure length in meters

minus sign (–) page 27

the sign used to show subtraction

minute page 313

a unit of measure for time

1 minute = 60 seconds

minute hand page 313

the hand on a clock that tells the minutes

missing addend page 43

an addend not given in an addition sentence

9 + ___ = 12

mode page 123

the number that is seen most often in an ordered set of numbers

6, 7, 8, 9, 9 Mode: 9

month page 329

a unit of measure for time

12 months = 1 year

more likely page 471

a good chance

multiply page 549

to add a number to itself
a number of times

multiplication sentence page 549

a number sentence that shows multiplication with the symbols × and =

$3 \times 2 = 6$

multiplication sign page 549

×

nickel page 291

a coin that is
worth 5 cents (5¢)

odd number page 93

a number with one left over if you make pairs

1, 3, 5, 7, 9...

one dollar page 307

one hundred cents
make a dollar

100¢ = $1.00

ordered pair page 275

a pair of numbers used to locate points on a grid

The blue triangle is at (6, 3).

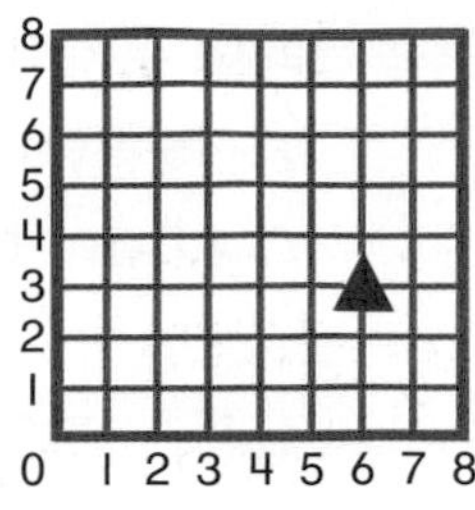

ordinal number page 99

shows place
or position

1st 2nd 3rd

ounce page 507

a unit of measure for weight

16 ounces = 1 pound

outcome page 469

the result of a probability experiment

pattern rules pages 45, 269

a pattern among a group
of numbers or figures

penny page 291

a coin that is
worth 1 cent (1¢)

pentagon page 253

a plane figure
with 5 sides

perimeter page 515

the distance around
a plane figure

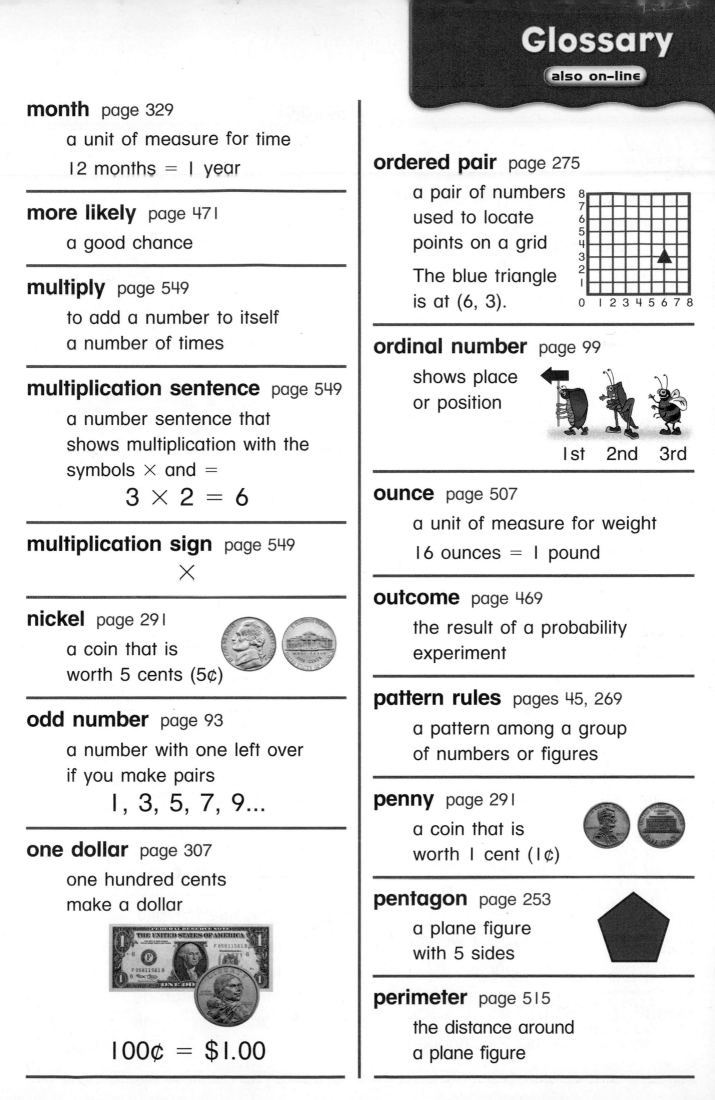

GLOSSARY OF MATH WORDS

Copyright © by William H. Sadlier, Inc. All rights reserved.

Glossary

also on-line

GLOSSARY OF MATH WORDS

pictograph page 117

a graph that uses symbols to show data

Rainy Days	
July	💧💧💧💧💧💧
August	💧💧💧
Key: Each 💧 stands for 2 days.	

pint (pt) page 501

a unit that measures how much something holds

1 pint = 2 cups

place value page 75

the value of a digit depending upon its place in a number

place-value chart page 67

a chart showing the value of a digit depending on its place in the number

tens	ones
4	2

plane figure page 251

a closed flat figure

circle

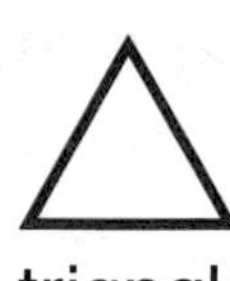
triangle

rectangle

square

plus sign (+) page 3

a sign used to show addition

pound (lb) page 507

a unit of measure for weight

1 pound = 16 ounces

possible page 473

an outcome that can happen

predict page 125

to make a guess about what might come next

product page 553

the answer in multiplication

$3 \times 3 = \textcircled{9}$

quart (qt) page 501

a unit used to measure how much something holds

1 quart = 2 pints

quarter page 293

a coin that is worth 25 cents (25¢)

quarter hour page 317

fifteen minutes

quotient page 567

the answer in division

$6 \div 3 = \textcircled{2}$

range page 123

the greatest number minus the least number in a set

6, 7, 8, 9, 9

Range: 9 − 6 = 3

regroup pages 159, 389

to rename ones as tens or tens as ones or tens as hundreds or hundreds as tens

related addition facts page 7

addition facts that use the same numbers

$2 + 6 = 8 \qquad 6 + 2 = 8$

related addition and subtraction facts page 33

addition and subtraction facts that use the same numbers

$14 - 5 = 9 \qquad 9 + 5 = 14$

related multiplication and division facts page 579

multiplication and division facts that use the same numbers

$3 \times 4 = 12 \qquad 12 \div 3 = 4$

related subtraction facts page 31

subtraction facts that use the same numbers

$13 - 4 = 9 \qquad 13 - 9 = 4$

rhombus page 271

a plane figure with four equal sides

round page 89

to change a number to a value with zero at the end

35 rounds to 40

side page 253

a straight line on a plane figure

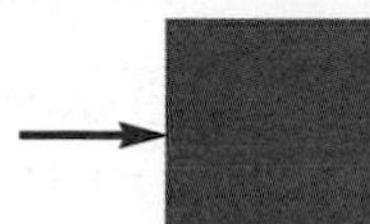

slide page 263

the movement of a figure to the right or left or up or down

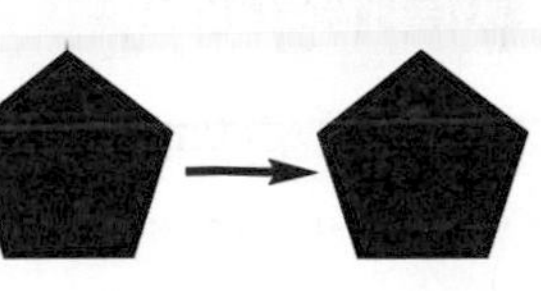

solid figures page 247

figures that are not flat

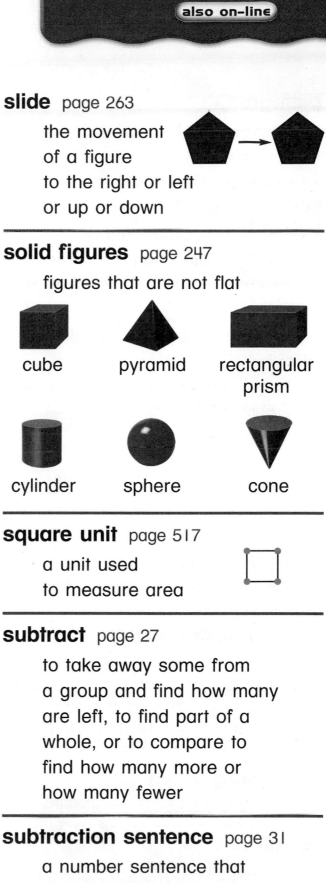

cube

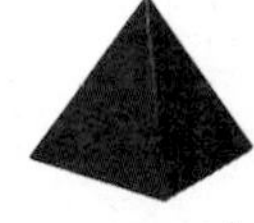

pyramid

rectangular prism

cylinder

sphere

cone

square unit page 517

a unit used to measure area

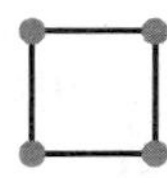

subtract page 27

to take away some from a group and find how many are left, to find part of a whole, or to compare to find how many more or how many fewer

subtraction sentence page 31

a number sentence that shows subtraction with the symbols − and =

$7 - 4 = 3$

Copyright © by William H. Sadlier, Inc. All rights reserved.

Glossary

also on-line

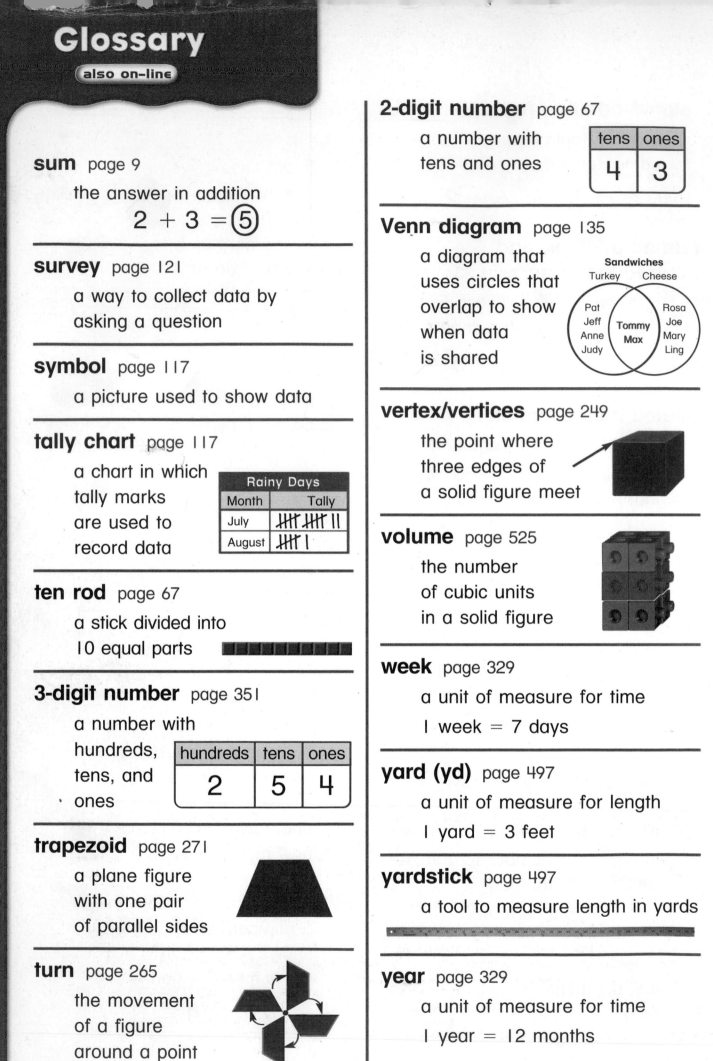

sum page 9

the answer in addition

$2 + 3 = ⑤$

survey page 121

a way to collect data by asking a question

symbol page 117

a picture used to show data

tally chart page 117

a chart in which tally marks are used to record data

Rainy Days	
Month	Tally
July	𝍸𝍸 II
August	𝍸 I

ten rod page 67

a stick divided into 10 equal parts

3-digit number page 351

a number with hundreds, tens, and ones

hundreds	tens	ones
2	5	4

trapezoid page 271

a plane figure with one pair of parallel sides

turn page 265

the movement of a figure around a point

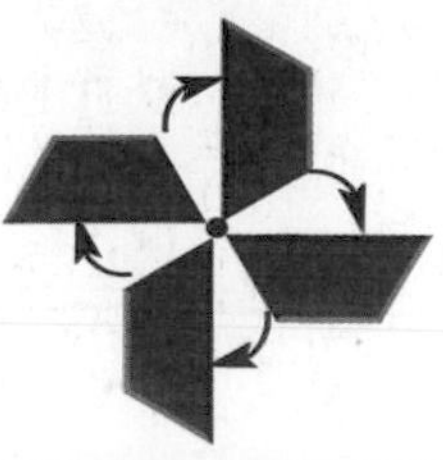

2-digit number page 67

a number with tens and ones

tens	ones
4	3

Venn diagram page 135

a diagram that uses circles that overlap to show when data is shared

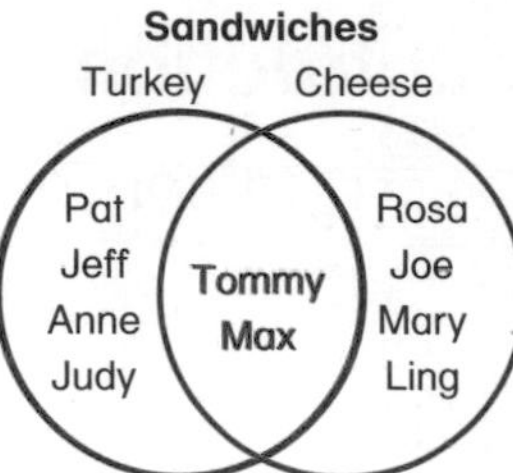

vertex/vertices page 249

the point where three edges of a solid figure meet

volume page 525

the number of cubic units in a solid figure

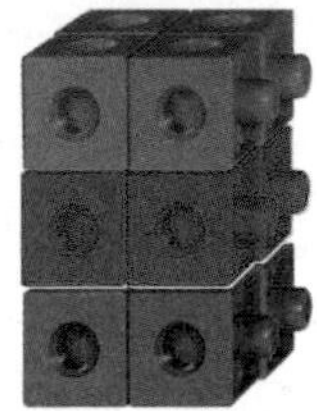

week page 329

a unit of measure for time

1 week = 7 days

yard (yd) page 497

a unit of measure for length

1 yard = 3 feet

yardstick page 497

a tool to measure length in yards

year page 329

a unit of measure for time

1 year = 12 months